The Monastic Order in England

GLASTONBURY FROM THE AIR

Dunstanus Glastoniae abbatiam composuit qualis nusquam in Anglia sit fueritve WILLIAM OF MALMESBURY *de Gestis Pontificum*

The view shows the precinct from the south-west, with the ruined Lady Chapel half hidden by foliage. The Saxon Church, completed by Dunstan, lay a little to the east of this, and his monastery was presumably adjacent to the south. The remains of the later medieval refectory can be seen immediately above the lantern of the abbot's kitchen; the cloisters lay between it and the church.

The Monastic Order in England

A HISTORY OF ITS DEVELOPMENT
FROM THE TIMES OF ST DUNSTAN TO THE
FOURTH LATERAN COUNCIL
943–1216

BY

DOM DAVID KNOWLES

Cambridge
AT THE UNIVERSITY PRESS
1950

PUBLISHED BY
THE SYNDICS OF THE CAMBRIDGE UNIVERSITY PRESS

London Office: Bentley House, N.W. 1
American Branch: New York

Agents for Canada, India, and Pakistan: Macmillan

First Edition 1940
Reprinted with corrections 1949
Reprinted 1950

First printed in Great Britain at the University Press, Cambridge
Reprinted by offset-litho by Percy Lund Humphries & Co. Ltd.

CONTENTS

𝔓art 𝔒ne. 𝔥istorical

§I. Introductory

CHAPTERS I–II

§II. 943–1066

CHAPTERS III–IV

§ III.   1066–1100

CHAPTERS V–IX

§ IV.   1100–1135

CHAPTER X

§V. 1135–1175

CHAPTERS XI–XVI

§VI. 1175–1216

CHAPTERS XVII–XXII

Part Two. Institutional

§ I. The Interior Polity of the Black Monks

CHAPTERS XXIII–XXV

§ II. The Work and Influence of the Monks

CHAPTERS XXVI–XXXI

§ III. The External Relations of the Monastery

Appendices

𝕿𝖆𝖇𝖑𝖊𝖘

PREFACE

The monastic antiquities of medieval England have, since the days of Camden, if not since those of Leland, received an attention from scholars and antiquaries such as has been given to few other branches of national history. From the end of the reign of Elizabeth, and throughout the century which has with some justice been called "the greatest age of English medieval scholarship",[1] a succession of men of eminent talents and unwearying industry collected, transcribed and edited all that they could find of the wealth of monastic records that had been in part destroyed and in part scattered at the Dissolution. Sir Thomas Bodley, Sir Robert Cotton, Camden himself, Augustine Baker, Clement Reyner, Sir Roger Twysden, Roger Dodsworth and (most illustrious of all) Sir William Dugdale—these are only a few from among the names that become familiar to every student of monastic history. They were followed by others scarcely less notable—by Tanner, by Gale, by Hearne, by Wanley and by Sparke—and these, in their turn, after an interval, by the historians and antiquarians who, in the first half of the nineteenth century, embarked on the task of publishing the whole corpus of medieval literature and records in the great collections of the Camden, Surtees and other national and regional learned societies, many of which continue, after a century of life, to put out each year new additions to their familiar series. When, half way through the century, private initiative was supplemented by the magnificent and comprehensive enterprise undertaken by the Master of the Rolls, monastic annals, chronicles and registers formed a large part of the matter selected for publication at the hands of the leading medievalists of the day; to Stubbs, above all others, is due the gratitude of those who use the sound texts which he established and the introductory matter which has lost little of its value since it first appeared. Finally, within the last fifty years monastic literature has been published or discussed by almost every medievalist of note, and has formed the chief interest of a number of scholars, among whom the names of Professor A. Hamilton Thompson and of Dr Rose Graham take a leading place.

Yet although so much learning and industry has been spent upon publishing and commenting upon the memorials of monasticism, and upon discussing in learned studies and monographs particular points of its history, no modern work is available for the general reader which may give him in adequate detail an account of the various phases of monastic life in England, together with a view of the activities of the monks within the cloister and in their manifold relations with the society of their times.

[1] Prof. David Douglas in *History*, xx (December 1935), 193.

Individual religious families and isolated periods have indeed received treatment in articles and biographies, and there are in existence not a few excellent outlines of English monastic history, but between the outline and the monograph the gap has remained unfilled, and while constitutional, economic, military and ecclesiastical histories of England exist in abundance, great and small, nothing that can truly be called a history of English monasticism has appeared since Fosbroke's *British Monachism* passed through a number of editions in the early decades of the last century. As one whose knowledge of the subject is unrivalled had recently occasion to write: "no attempt has yet been made to supply from original sources any synthetic account of English monastic life during the five crucial centuries preceding the Reformation."[1]

It is the aim of the present work to supply this want for the first half of the period, almost exactly six centuries in length, during which the regular life was lived without interruption in the monasteries of England, and to give an account, historical rather than antiquarian in character, and based entirely on contemporary sources, of the development of the monastic order in this country between the years 943 and 1216.

These limiting dates, chosen originally, perhaps, without full realization of their significance in order to put some bounds to the work of research, seem to the present writer after several years of deepening knowledge to mark moments of real division in English religious history. As the evidence on a later page will show, regular life was, and had for many decades already been, extinct in England before the revival under Dunstan in 943, and that revival, when it came, though peculiarly national in character, did not repose directly upon anything inherited from the monastic past in this country. No such absolute significance attaches to the other date, that of the Fourth Lateran Council of 1215, which so nearly coincided with the deaths of Innocent III and King John, but certainly no other year between the Norman Conquest and the reign of Henry VIII so clearly marks a division in the history of the Church in England. Here, more perhaps than in other lands of western Europe, the monastic and general legislation of the Council, the new spheres of activity claimed by the papacy, the coming of the friars, the growth of the universities, and the emergence of a new type of diocesan bishop in the long reign of the new king—all these factors gave to the monastic order in the thirteenth century a position and a character very different from those which had distinguished the body in 1100, in 1150 and even at the time of the Interdict under John.

To this period, subsequent to the Council, and to the centuries which followed till the Dissolution, it may be possible to pass in another volume at some future time. The close of the Middle Ages, no less than the epoch covered by these chapters, stands in need of full and clear examination. With the age before the times of Dunstan the case is somewhat different.

[1] Dr G. G. Coulton in *Five Centuries of Religion*, i, 441.

Certain moments, such as those of the flowering of Northumbrian monasticism, at first under Aidan and Cuthbert, and later under Wilfrid, Benet Biscop and Bede, and of the maturity of another type in the south in the days of Boniface and Aldhelm, are so familiar from the pictures given in a few wholly reliable documents that their oft-repeated story hardly needs retelling. On the other hand, the records of the times and places of which the Venerable Bede does not treat are in general so imperfect and of such questionable authenticity that an intensive critical and diplomatic investigation by specialists must precede any fresh attempt to understand the conditions under which the monks lived.

As for the period covered by this volume, no one with any knowledge of the religious history of England can be unaware of its importance and interest. It includes the times of Dunstan and Ethelwold, of Wulfstan and Lanfranc and Anselm, of Ailred of Rievaulx, Samson of Bury and Hugh of Lincoln; within its limits the Norman monasticism rose through all the stages of its growth, and the Cistercians swept over Europe like a flood; before it ended all save a dozen of the monastic houses of medieval England had been founded; in it arose the masterpieces of Romanesque architecture and of the new style of the white monks, so beautiful in itself and so important in the history of the art; in it, perhaps more than at any other time in English history, the monastic life met and satisfied the deepest spiritual needs of the age, and discharged a function most essential to the higher life of society and to the well-being and development of the nation.

This book, as will be seen, is divided into two parts, the first dealing with the historical development of the monastic body, and with the outstanding personalities among the monks, and the second describing the internal economy and external activities of the monasteries. Such a division formed no part of the original scheme; it was, however, soon found to be unavoidable; in default of some such arrangement, it would have been necessary to pause again and again in the narrative in order to note the small characteristics and changes of the various institutions in every generation, thus depriving of all unity a subject already sufficiently formless and cutting the only recognizable thread of continuity and progress. Moreover, the very real but gradual developments on every point of observance and in every sphere of activity can only be properly grasped when each department is isolated and passed in review. It is precisely because so many writers have failed to distinguish between century and century and between order and order that almost all the general descriptions of medieval monastic life lack definition, and often also historical accuracy and perspective. This division has inevitably resulted in a certain amount of repetition; some of the general conclusions arrived at in the second part have been anticipated in the earlier narrative, while it has been occasionally necessary to recapitulate a series of historical events when discussing points of institutional development. Such repetitions have been avoided wherever possible, but as it is hoped that the later chapters may be consulted by those who wish for information on individual points without reading or re-reading the whole, the sections of the second part have been made as self-contained as possible.

For somewhat similar reasons, quotations from the sources have been made as full as space allowed. All students of history are well aware that bare page references, especially when scattered over a wide range of learned literature, are of little or no direct assistance to the reader. Few will find themselves in a library where there is immediate access to all the volumes concerned; the footnotes, in consequence, can do no more than serve as a distant and sometimes very dubious guarantee of accuracy. In the following pages, therefore, relevant passages from the sources are cited wherever possible not only that the reader may have a means of checking, and even of taking exception to, statements and judgments in the text, but also that those who are primarily interested in other branches of history, but who wish for information on some aspects of monasticism, may gain some idea of the principal authorities that lie behind the chapters in question.

A single glance at the footnotes, or at the list of books to which references are given—a list which is far from being a bibliography of English monasticism—will be sufficient to show how much these pages owe to the work of others. In no department of English history, perhaps, do students owe so much, not only to the celebrated scholars of the remote and recent past, but also to that multitude of laborious workers, whether antiquarians or local historians, who have transcribed and annotated the voluminous records of the medieval world. From among all these it will not, I hope, seem invidious to name four scholars of yesterday and to-day whose work has given a wholly new precision to our knowledge of certain chapters of English monastic history: the late Dr Armitage Robinson, Dean in turn of Westminster and Wells, who studied to such good effect the early history of those churches and in particular threw such a flood of light upon the dark places of the tenth century; Professor F. M. Powicke, who has made Ailred of Rievaulx and his contemporaries live and move again before our eyes; Dr R. R. Darlington, who has reconstructed so fully the background of the lives of Wulfstan of Worcester and Aethelwig of Evesham; and Dom André Wilmart, *ce Mauriste de nos jours*, whose vast erudition, borne so lightly and displayed so gracefully, alternately stimulates and shames those who profit by its achievements.

To these scholars of the past and present all who work upon medieval history are indebted. I have beyond this the pleasant duty of acknowledging a personal debt to those who have given me direct assistance: to my friend Mr W. A. Pantin, of Oriel College, Oxford, who has been good enough to read through this volume in proof and to help me with numerous suggestions and corrections; to Professor Powicke, who kindly read the chapters on the Cistercians of the north; to Dr Rose Graham, who read the pages on the Cluniacs; to Dr Friedrich Saxl, of the Warburg Institute, and Mr Francis Wormald, of the British Museum, who gave me their expert advice on the subject of manuscript illumination; to Dom Gregory Murray, O.S.B., who read the sections on the Chant, and to Mr J. C. Dickinson, of Leeds University, who read those on the Augustinian canons: to all these I am indebted for valuable information, as also to Professor A. Hamilton Thompson, Dom Justin McCann, O.S.B., and Mr R. A. B. Mynors for help on various points, and to Dr Z. N. Brooke for his early and constant interest in this book.

For most generous help of another kind in the expenses incidental to the preparation of these pages I am indebted to my father, H. H. Knowles, to the Rev. Mother Prioress and Community of St Augustine's Priory, Ealing, and to my friend, Mr Austin Coghlan. Finally, I may be permitted to express my abiding sense of gratitude to those who built up two great collections of books: to Dom Raymund Webster, O.S.B., whose discerning foresight was largely responsible for assembling the library in which this work was begun, and to Sir Charles Hagberg Wright, LL.D., who, in the many years in which he has presided over the London Library, has done so much to anticipate all the requirements of students and connoisseurs in every branch of learning and of art. Rarely indeed does even a specialist seek in vain in that magnificent collection for the book or article that he needs; never does he fail to meet with an assistance in his search that is as courteous as it is untiring.

DAVID KNOWLES

25 March 1939

The photographic reprinting of this book has given an opportunity of correcting a number of small errors and misprints pointed out by readers and reviewers, but it has not been possible to take account in the text and footnotes of all the relevant literature that has appeared during the past ten years.

DAVID KNOWLES

PETERHOUSE
15 July 1948

List of Abbreviations

The following abbreviations are used throughout:

Acta SS *Acta Sanctorum*, ed. Bollandiana

Acta SS. OSB *Acta Sanctorum Ordinis S. Benedicti*, ed. Mabillon

CS Camden Society

Chronicle The Anglo-Saxon Chronicle, as in *Two Saxon Chronicles*, ed. Earle and Plummer

DAC *Dictionnaire d'Archéologie chrétienne et de Liturgie*, ed. Cabrol

DDC *Dictionnaire de Droit Canonique*, ed. Naz

DHG *Dictionnaire d'Histoire et de Géographie ecclésiastiques*, ed. Baudrillart

DNB *Dictionary of National Biography*

DR *Downside Review*

DS *Dictionnaire de Spiritualité*, ed. Viller

DTC *Dictionnaire de Théologie catholique*, ed. Vacant and others

EETS Early English Text Society

EHR *English Historical Review*

Epp. Cant. Epistolae Cantuarienses, ed. W. Stubbs (RS 38, vol. II)

Flor. Wig. Florence of Worcester, ed. B. Thorpe (Eng. Hist. Soc.)

GASA *Gesta Abbatum Sancti Albani*, ed. Riley (RS 28, vol. v)

HBS Henry Bradshaw Society

JE, JL *Regesta Pontificum Romanorum*, {ed. Jaffé-Ewald / ed. Jaffé-Loewenfeld}, 1885–8

JTS *Journal of Theological Studies*

Mem. Fount. Memorials of the Abbey of...Fountains, ed. Walbran (SS XXXVIII, vol. I)

MGH SS, LL and *Epp.* *Monumenta Germaniae Historica, Scriptores, Leges* and *Epistolae*

N.C. Walter Map, *de Nugis Curialium*, ed. Camden Society (1850)

OV Ordericus Vitalis, quoted by volume and page of the edition of the Société de l'Histoire de France

PL Migne, *Patrologiae series Latina*, quoted by volume and column

RB *Revue Bénédictine*

RS Rolls Series

s.a. *sub anno* or *annis*, used when quoting annals by the year's entry

SS Surtees Society

Symeon *Symeonis Dunelmensis Opera*, ed. T. Arnold (RS 75)

Ungedruckte Quellen *Ungedruckte anglo-normannische Geschichtsquellen*, ed. F. Liebermann, 1879

VCH *Victoria County History*

Will. Malmesb., *GP* William of Malmesbury, *de Gestis Pontificum* (RS 52)

Will. Malmesb., *GR* William of Malmesbury, *de Gestis Regum* (RS 90, vol. II)

Will. Malmesb., *Hist. Nov.* William of Malmesbury, *Historiae Novellae* (RS 50, vol. II)

Will. Malmesb., *de ant. Glast.* William of Malmesbury, *de antiquitate ecclesiae Glastoniensis* (ed. Gale, Scriptores XV)

Part One. Historical

CHAPTER I

THE RULE OF SAINT BENEDICT

I

The period of monastic history with which these chapters are concerned opens some two hundred years before the close of what has been called the era of the Benedictine Centuries. This name, convenient in itself and correct enough if it is recognized as being nothing more than a very loose title, may be taken to imply that for some six hundred years (*c.* 550–*c.*1150) in Italy and the countries of Europe north and west of Italy (with the important exception of the Celtic civilization) monastic life based on the Rule of St Benedict was everywhere the norm and exercised from time to time a paramount influence on the spiritual, intellectual, liturgical and apostolical life of the Western Church. In other words, during these centuries the only type of religious life available in the countries concerned was monastic, and the only monastic code was the Rule of St Benedict. This period may be said to have begun with the great expansion of Benedictine monasticism under St Gregory the Great and to have ended, in essentials, with the rise of the new orders of monks and canons *c.* 1100, but monastic influence of one kind or another continued to be dominant in the Church until the emergence of the Universities in the second half of the twelfth century, followed shortly afterwards by the foundation of the orders of Friars. As, therefore, the first part of our period is dominated by the religious ideal of the black monks, and the later part still greatly influenced by it, it is necessary to have some understanding of the nature and scope of the document on which the monastic life of the West was based.

The Rule is a relatively short piece of writing. About a quarter of its pages are occupied with detailed liturgical and penal provisions; the remainder consists of legislation covering every department of the life of the monastery, and passing almost imperceptibly from formal enactment to deep spiritual instruction. A few chapters, but those the longest and most celebrated, such as the Prologue and the chapters on the Abbot and on Humility, are wholly on this lofty level; a number of others, composed largely of formal precepts, contain a wealth of practical advice, conveyed in the most pregnant form, for all the members and officials of a monastic family.[1]

---

1 The most useful critical edition of the text of the Rule is that of Dom Butler, *S. Benedicti Regula* (Freiburg-im-Breisgau, 1912; 2 ed. 1927). I quote from this throughout by chapter and line. A text, philologically more exact and with fuller apparatus, has been edited by Dom Benno Linderbauer. For a general view of Benedictine history, polity and life Abbot Butler's *Benedictine Monachism* (1919; 2 ed. 1927) stands in a class by itself. The best commentary on the Rule is that of Dom Delatte, *Commentaire sur la Règle de*

Although some details of the Rule have given rise to controversies among both monks and scholars, it is not difficult to grasp the broad lines of the monastic life for which it was written, and which, therefore, it always tended of itself to reproduce. The monastery which it describes is a unit, completely self-contained and self-sufficient, both economically and constitutionally.[1] A community, ruled by an abbot elected by the monks for life, is supported by the produce of its fields and garden and has within the wall of its enclosure all that is necessary to convert the produce into food and to make and repair clothing and other articles of common use. It has no function in the life of the Church save to provide an ordered way of life based on the teaching of the gospel, according to which its inmates may serve God and sanctify their souls apart from the life of the world. No work done within it, whether manual, intellectual or charitable, is directed to an end outside its walls. It is the home of a spiritual family whose life and work begins and ends in the family circle; like other families it may on occasion support dependents, give hospitality and relieve the spiritual and bodily necessities of those who dwell in its neighbourhood or who seek from it such relief, but its primary concern is with itself, not with others, and the evils of corporate selfishness are excluded by its *raison d'être*, which is the service of God in simplicity of life and without contact with the world.

The life within the monastery is a common life of absolute regularity, of strict discipline, of unvarying routine. The whole ordering of the day is concerned with furthering the spiritual welfare of those who form the family, and falls into three clear divisions of not unequal length. If an average is struck over the whole year, the monk is found to be engaged for some four hours (or a little less) in the liturgical prayer of the oratory, for some four in meditative reading or prayer, and for some six (or more) in work which is either domestic, or strictly manual, or the pursuit of some simple craft.[2] The whole day, and the whole year, is spent in an atmo-

---

Saint Benoît (Paris, 1913; frequently reprinted; there is an English translation by Dom Justin McCann); it is the work of a scholar who was also for long abbot of Solesmes. Excellent short works by competent specialists on the spirit and history of the black monks abound; among them may be mentioned especially the two books by Dom Ursmer Berlière, *L'Ordre Monastique* (Paris, 1912; 3rd ed. 1924) and *L'Ascèse Bénédictine* (Paris, 1927), both covering the period from St Benedict to the end of the twelfth century, and that of Dom Henri Leclercq, *L'Ordre Bénédictin* (Paris, 1930). Dom Chapman's *St Benedict and the Sixth Century* (1929), along with much that is valuable and ingenious, contains many judgments which should be received with caution. To these may be added the articles on St Benedict and Benedictine history in the *Dictionnaire de Spiritualité* (Paris, 1935), by Dom de Puniet, Dom Schmitz and Dom Mähler, which contain very full bibliographies.

1 *Regula*, lxvi, 12: "Monasterium...ita debet constitui, ut omnia necessaria, id est, aqua, molendinum, hortus, vel artes diversae intra monasterium exerceantur."

2 St Benedict's horarium, as deducible from the Rule, has been worked out with care by Butler, *Benedictine Monachism*, 275–88, by Berlière, *L'Ascèse Bénédictine*, 51–2, and by Dom Philibert Schmitz, *Dictionnaire de Spiritualité*, art. Benoît, S.—La Règle. The silences of the Rule, together with absence of clock-times and the variations introduced for seasonal or liturgical reasons, make complete accuracy unattainable. It must also be remembered that while the time allowed for public prayer could never be broken into, that allotted to work doubtless covered the performance of numberless small and necessary duties.

sphere of silence and abstraction from the world which, while not rigidly absolute, are not broken by any specific opportunities for conversation or for departure from the monastic enclosure. For his spiritual nourishment the monk has the teaching and counsel of the abbot and elders, the treasures of earlier monastic and patristic literature, and the prayers of the psalter and the liturgy. For almost all the practical contingencies of such a life something is laid down in broad principle in the Rule.

Such, in briefest outline, is the framework which St Benedict adopted and established. Three points in it, familiar to all students of monasticism but not so familiar to the reader acquainted only with the later Middle Ages, seem to call for some remark.

The first is the liturgical service of the monks of the early sixth century. For more than a thousand years the elaborate celebration, with chant and ceremony, of the Divine Office and other liturgical functions has been considered a principal monastic duty to be accomplished by the monks of St Benedict in a manner different from that of other religious bodies, such as the Friars, who are also bound to the choral recitation of the Office; and at the present day this is often regarded as the task *par excellence* and as the peculiar province of the Benedictines. We shall see in the course of a few pages how rapidly and how naturally the Divine Office came to hold such a position, but as a matter of historical perspective we must remember that it was a development from the idea of St Benedict. In the Rule—as in other earlier and contemporary rules—the liturgical service is a simple, regular form of reading, prayer and praise, chanted in the oratory with simple modulation and without ceremonial. St Benedict does indeed say, in words which are among the most familiar of all in his Rule, that nothing shall take precedence of the Work of God, but this, as a glance at the context and sources of the words shows, is simply an assertion that of the various employments of the monk the public prayer, the direct worship of God, must take pride of place.[1] The *Opus Dei* is thus only a part, though in itself the most noble part, of the monk's daily employment; it is not the *raison d'être* of the institute.

The second point concerns the second chief employment, *lectio divina* or spiritual reading. The Rule allows a very long period daily for reading, but this reading is directed solely to the spiritual good of the individual, and the books to be read were, as St Benedict's explicit recommendations and tacit quotations show, exclusively the Scriptures, the early monastic literature and the writings of the Fathers of the Church. So much is clear from the text of the Rule, though almost every careful reader will have found difficulty when endeavouring to reconstruct in imagination St Benedict's community, made up as it was of men of the most varied mental capacity and education, and to picture it devoting between three or four

---

1 *Regula*, xliii, 5: "Ergo nihil Operi Dei praeponatur." Butler, *ad loc.*, gives as a source the Rule of St Macarius: "nihil orationi [*sc.* publicae] praeponendum est."

hours daily and even more on Sundays and feast days, year in year out, to spiritual or theological reading. Doubtless, of all the allocations of time in the Rule, this is the most summary; much of the time would be spent by many in prayer and in necessary individual occupations; the Rule itself makes provision that the slothful and the illiterate shall have some manual employment given them.[1] But the large space of time for *lectio divina* remains, and it was a spiritual and not at all an intellectual occupation. There is a considerable difference between the Monte Cassino of Benedict and the Vivarium of Cassiodorus, though in time there was something of a fusion between the types. Yet even at Monte Cassino there must have been a number of corollaries to the *lectio divina* which do not appear in the Rule. There must have been in the monastery, for instance, a certain amount of copying of manuscripts for this and for liturgical purposes; there must also have been some literary education given to the children dedicated in early years to the monastic life. And continual familiarity with the writings of the greatest of the fathers and ascetical writers could not but have exercised a considerable influence of a purely intellectual kind upon minds in any degree receptive and speculative.[2] In brief, there were already present in germ in the monastery of the Rule some of the pursuits that were in course of time to be regarded as being wholly monastic; but it is not with them that the Rule is concerned.

Thirdly, there is the question of the *opus manuum*, the manual work of the monks. The casual reader, especially if he is at all familiar with the history of the Cistercians, inevitably takes the work (*labor, opera manuum*) of the Rule to denote field and farm work. Yet here, as elsewhere, the hints and silences of the Rule and of St Gregory's *Life* of Benedict become the more tantalizing in proportion as they are more carefully noted, and there is room for a considerable difference of opinion on the point, for while St Benedict consistently supposes the field and the garden to be among the scenes of a monk's toil, it is equally clear that the harvesting of various kinds was normally done by others. Lay brothers are of course unknown to the Rule, nor is there any place in it for domestic servants; there would therefore be employment for many in every kind of domestic work, and in the domestic arts and crafts; very few of the members of the primitive Monte Cassino were clerics or in orders. Certainly, to imagine the whole community each day going out in a body to field work would be incorrect, but it would perhaps be nearer the truth than to picture the majority as occupied in quasi-intellectual or artistic work. That on

1 *Regula*, xlviii, 53: "Si quis ita neglegens et desidiosus fuerit, ut non velit aut non possit meditare aut legere, iniungatur ei opus quod faciat."

2 It is, however, worth remarking that St Benedict, for all his wide acquaintance with ecclesiastical literature, shows far fewer traces in his style and methods of thought of any training than do many of his contemporaries in the Church, thus fully bearing out the words of Gregory (*Dialog.* II, i) that he was *scienter nescius, et sapienter indoctus.*

occasion the whole body would go out to the fields is clear from the Rule and from St Gregory; that individuals had charge of scattered fields and plots is equally clear from the Rule. But the heavy normal work of the fields was done by *coloni*, and the majority of the community probably found its normal employment within the sheds and offices of the monastery building.[1]

II

The history of monasticism before St Benedict, and the estimating of his debt to the past and his influence upon succeeding ages, has occupied the attention of a number of able scholars in the past fifty years, and their findings have become a commonplace of textbooks.[2] It is universally agreed that while St Benedict was undoubtedly more familiar with earlier forms of monastic life than was at one time supposed, he nevertheless shows himself as a legislator of great originality and creative genius. It is accepted that he gave, first to central Italy, and then by transmission to the rest of Europe, a form of religious life peculiarly suited to Western temperaments and needs, and that he did this by turning away both from the eremitical ideal as it existed in Italy in his day, with its extreme physical austerity, and from the conception of the monastic life as a search for perfection now in this monastery and now in that, and by firmly basing his system on a Rule to which absolute obedience was vowed, applied by an abbot to whom that obedience was paid, in a monastery from whose family circle only death could separate the monk who had once joined himself to it. The great and permanent influence of St Benedict upon the spiritual life of the Church has thus been fully recognized; less attention has been paid to those characteristics and limitations in his teaching which were due to the age and country in which he was born, and to the natural temper of his mind. A brief consideration of some of these will help to an understanding both of the unique influence which the Rule had upon European life in the early Middle Ages, and of the waning of this influence into that of one amongst many at the renaissance of the eleventh and twelfth centuries.

The series of profound changes in every department of human life, racial, political, social, economic and intellectual, which we call the passing of the ancient civilization and the birth of the medieval world took place over a number of centuries. The transition which was beginning at the

---

1 The question of the *opus manuum* of the Rule has been debated since early times, often by disputants *de parti pris*. The only sources of evidence are the Rule and Book II of St Gregory's *Dialogues*; their evidence is well summed up in Butler, *Benedictine Monachism*, 285–6, and the attempt of Dom Chapman, *St Benedict and the Sixth Century*, 169–72, to modify his conclusions is successfully rebutted by Abbot Butler in the article *St Benedict and the Sixth Century* in the *Downside Review*, XLVIII (1930), 179–97.

2 See especially Butler, *The Lausiac History of Palladius* (Cambridge, 1898, 1904), the works quoted above in the first note, and C. Heussi, *Der Ursprung des Mönchtums* (1936).

death of Marcus Aurelius was complete shortly before the crowning of Charlemagne. But if we consider, not the whole of western Europe but its heart, Italy and southern Gaul, and look for the moment when the new rather than the old is in possession—the moment in the dawn when it is day and not night, even if it be not fully day—many will tell us that this is to be found in the reign of Theodoric in Italy.[1] Theodoric reigned from 493 till 526; Benedict's life in central Italy fell between the years 480 and 550; his lifetime, therefore, coincided exactly with the crisis of change, and a careful reader will perceive that, short and simple as the Rule is, it yet contains an extremely subtle blend of old and new. Benedict, like those other two, Augustine and Gregory, who were to influence European thought so deeply for six or seven centuries, while he anticipated so exactly the modes of feeling and ways of life of the future, had himself a grasp of the past which future generations were to lack.

Recent intensive study of pre-Benedictine monachism and of the sources of the Rule has revealed the richness of the legacy of the past which was at the disposal of Benedict;[2] in a well-known passage he specifically refers his monks to the threefold inheritance from the Fathers of Rule, of doctrine and of spiritual instruction.[3] He uses these three sources amply himself, and though he was not, like Augustine or even like Gregory, possessed of a share of the wide and poised culture of the ancient world, he had nevertheless a selective and critical faculty and a self-possession of mind which could only come to the child of a great civilization and which few show signs of possessing in the centuries after his death. Nor is it fanciful to see in his character and Rule, with its gravity and its constant reference to justice and to measure, the stamp of antique Rome.[4] Moreover, though Western culture and political life were rapidly declining, the life of the Church in Rome and central Italy attained a summit of order and legal and disciplinary control in the age of Leo the Great (440–61), Gelasius (492–6) and Hormisdas (514–23) which was not abandoned till after the days of Gregory the Great. Justice has been somewhat tardily done to this age of greatness in Rome, but within recent years the legal and administrative achievements of Gelasius, Hormisdas and their circle have been fully recognized, as also the power of Romans of the fifth and sixth centuries to think and to speak with precision, depth

1 This is the date taken for the beginning of the Middle Ages and final separation of East and West by H. St L. B. Moss, *The Birth of the Middle Ages* (1935).

2 Butler, in his edition, notes some thirty authors quoted, apart from Scripture; about twenty of these are quoted with some frequency. Chapman and others have made additions to the list.

3 *Regula*, lxxiii, 8 *seqq.*: "Quae enim pagina...Veteris ac Novi Testamenti...aut quis liber sanctorum Catholicorum Patrum...nec non et Collationes Patrum, et Instituta et Vitas eorum, sed et Regula sancti patris nostri Basilii, quid aliud sunt nisi...monachorum instrumenta virtutum?"

4 *Gravitas* occurs as a moral quality some five times in the Rule; *mensura* and its derivatives ten times.

and eloquence.[1] It would seem beyond question that Benedict derived from the firm constitution of the Roman Church, as expressed in synods and decretals, the simple, strong outline of government handed down the ages by the Rule.

But if the Rule holds within it so much of the wisdom and experience of the past, its anticipation of the needs of the future is even more striking. The ancient world, with its city life, its great seats of culture, its graded society and its wide and rapid means of communication, was rapidly disappearing. In the Empire, as in the countries of the modern world, it had been possible for men to travel far to satisfy mental or spiritual needs. In the new world that was coming into being the estate, the village, the district were the units; Europe, from being a single complex organism, was becoming an aggregate of cells, bound to one another by the loosest of ties. St Benedict lived in a society where the scope and opportunities of education, secular and theological, were yearly narrowing, and in which the numbers of the educated were yearly lessening; a society in which the family, the farm, the estate was strong and all collective organization weak; a society made up of self-contained and self-supporting units rather than of interdependent trades, industries and professions; a society continually threatened with extinction in this part or that by invasion or chaos, and which therefore needed above all some clear, simple, basic principles to which it might hold and rally.

This need was met, at every level of life, by the monastery of the Rule. Economically and materially it contained within its walls and fields all the necessaries of life and the means of converting them to man's use; living upon its own fields and exercising its own crafts, it was perfectly adapted to exist through and survive all the changes of the invasions; economically and administratively a unit, it escaped all the dangers of dismemberment short of total destruction.

Still more perfect was this suitability to the needs of the time on the moral and spiritual levels. St Benedict's monastery is a microcosm. It holds all types, all classes and all ages. Children, brought almost in infancy by their parents, ex-serfs, sons of the poor and noble, clerics and priests, the highly intelligent as well as the Goth *pauper spiritu* and those who will not or cannot read—all are there, and among them there is no distinction whatever save in the service of the altar. Only in the early centuries or backward countries of medieval times could such a community continue to be the norm, and it did not in fact endure long in its

---

1 Thus G. Le Bras, *Histoire des Collections Canoniques en Occident* (Paris, 1931), I, 22, notes the middle of the fifth century as a culminating point of legal, conciliar and theological development, and writes (p. 7) of " ce temps de brillante activité qu'inaugure le pape Gélase et que s'achève par le pontificat d'Hormisdas". Dom Chapman, *St Benedict and the Sixth Century*, 51, refers to "the superb letters of St Leo" with their "sympathetic charity and wisdom" and "their exquisite wording, unsurpassed in Latin [ecclesiastical] literature except by Cyprian".

original comprehensiveness.[1] The growing identification of monks with clerics, and the many disabilities of the serf class, made of later monasteries less of a perfect microcosm. But as long as the chaotic, transitional period lasted in Europe—that is, till the emergence of the perfect feudal state in the eleventh century—the conception of a monastery as a little world, into which souls were dedicated in infancy, continued to endure, and it need not be said that such an idea was most powerful in the centuries which saw the new nations of Europe struggling from infancy to adolescence.

III

For such a little world the legislation of the Rule is exquisitely adapted. Its proverbial discretion, shown in the careful allotment of common measures and of a due place to every element in the life, its insistence on the external, visible, audible voice and action of authority, its elementary, germinal, pregnant teaching—all this, intrinsically valuable at any time, was indispensable in a code that was to be the alphabet of the religious life to a civilization in travail. St Benedict in more than one passage, but in particular in the last chapter of the Rule, insists that his work is a code for beginners.[2] The phrase has caused some uneasiness to commentators, and those who have felt it necessary to free the legislator from a charge of false humility have often pointed to the more severe asceticism of the Eastern monks from which Benedict was consciously retreating. The explanation does not wholly satisfy, for it would logically involve the saint in a more subtle form of insincerity, in which while setting up a truer and more interior standard of perfection he would pay lip service to that which he was supplanting. The truth would rather seem to be that St Benedict intended the preceptive portions of the Rule to be, as it were, the minimum standard of an evangelical life, which could be demanded of all, but which proficients could transcend while yet fulfilling, as a skilled musician transcends without transgressing the laws of harmony. But it is also true that in the Rule the legislator addresses himself of set purpose to the beginner in a way peculiar to himself. Large sections are directly and explicitly devoted to one who is entering upon its observance,[3] or deal with penal regulations concerning those who have certainly not advanced far towards

---

1 That all these various elements were present, at least in some proportion, in the monasteries for which the Rule was written, is clear from its text and from St Gregory's *Dialogues*. Chapman, *St Benedict and the Sixth Century*, c. x, *The Social Condition of Monks*, argues with much learning that the ex-serf was very rare in the monastery, the ex-domestic slave also rare, though less so, and that the majority of recruits would have come from lower and middle class free families.

2 *Regula*, lxxiii, 21–2: "Hanc minimam inchoationis Regulam."

3 Cf. *Regula*, Prol., 6 *seqq.*: "Ad te ergo nunc mihi sermo dirigitur, quisquis...Domino Christo vero Regi militaturus, oboedientiae...arma sumis." Cf. *ibid.* 122 *seqq.*: "non illico...refugias viam salutis, quae non est nisi angusto initio incipienda."

perfection. The possibility of grave failure is everywhere allowed for;[1] not only in the monks, but in the priests, the deans, the prior and even the abbot himself;[2] and at every stage, and when dealing with every function, St Benedict sets himself to advise the one who is entering upon it. His method, which is always to indicate the practical, external steps leading towards an unseen goal, is in strong contrast to the method of the abbots in Cassian's conferences who attract the reader to the perfect life by describing its essence and interior qualities. St Benedict, as we know from his own statement, intended that his monks should supplement his teaching with the other; in the event, the wisdom of the past was in large part lost to the new Europe here as in other fields, and only the teaching of Benedict remained. We may note and deplore the loss, but there is no doubt that of the two, the Rule and Cassian's writings, the former was far better suited to be a formative influence for the many.

A full acknowledgment of the unique excellence of the Rule does not imply that it has no limitations. Some such are inevitable in every code that bears the stamp of time and place, and are in a sense merely negative. We have just mentioned one; the loss to the majority of monks in the centuries to come of the body of earlier spiritual teaching which the Rule presupposed. Another, inevitable at the time and perhaps as much a benefit as a limitation, is the absence of any machinery of organization or control for a group of monasteries. Deeper than this is a characteristic of the Rule that comes from the temper of mind and soul of its author. Just as, in its discretion and wide wisdom, the Rule, considered as a code of life, has a value beyond the teaching of the monks of the desert, so their teaching, considered as a guide for the individual soul in its interior life, surpasses that of the Rule in clarity and depth. In the monuments of the desert, and above all in the Conferences recorded by Cassian, there is a depth, a penetration, an exactness of expression, a purity of insight, a clear vision of the heights which is not found in the Rule. The degrees of the spiritual life, the divisions of active and contemplative, of natural and supernatural, of ascetic and mystic, the stages of prayer, the provinces of the virtues, are all set out there with a simplicity, directness and certainty of touch never again equalled before the thirteenth century and surpassed, perhaps, only by the Spanish saints of the Renaissance. The Egyptian and Syrian monks of the early fifth century reached, indeed, a summit of excellence in spiritual doctrine, and were still possessed of the cultural resources and habits of thought of Greek civilization which made it possible for them to express their thoughts with luminous precision. St Benedict, as is well known, was intimately familiar with Cassian, whom he

1 Cf. *Regula*, ii, 33: "duris corde"; 78: "inprobos autem et duros ac superbos, vel inoboedientes"; and the many references to the slothful.

2 *Regula*, xxi, 10 (of the deans): "si ex eis...quis inflatus superbia"; lxii, 17 (of the priests): "non sacerdos sed rebellio judicetur"; lxv, 42 (of the prior): "si repertus fuerit vitiosus aut elatione deceptus"; lxiv, 10 (of the abbot).

cites explicitly or implicitly some ninety times, a figure far outnumbering his citations or reminiscences of any other author. As if not content with this, he recommends his favourite to all his disciples as a pure source of doctrine, and even prescribes that a few pages of his writings should be read in public every day.[1] Yet between Benedict and the great abbots of Cassian—Moses, Paphnutius, Serenus, Isaac[2]—there is a difference of spiritual aim, and even of spiritual outlook. It is not chance which leads him to the pages of Proverbs rather than to the Song of Songs, to Romans and Corinthians rather than to Ephesians, Philippians and Colossians, to Matthew rather than to John.[3] The abbots of Cassian sought to lead the few to the life of contemplation; Benedict is concerned with giving to all who come the fundamental virtues of a follower of Christ. His Rule did not exclude the ideal of Cassian; rather by many of its enactments it tended towards it and pointed the way; but legislating for a microcosm it allowed for the growth of more than one type within its walls. In many of its enactments, its suggestions and its recommendations it points towards the contemplative, and even to the solitary life.[4] In other passages, and above all in its acceptance without reserve of the institution of oblation of children, a far wider scope is given. Yet if the Rule and (so far as we can ascertain it) the practice of the founder allowed great latitude of employment and left the way open to all legitimate development in more than one direction, on the essentials of the fully monastic life—simplicity,[5] and community[6] of life, enclosure,[7] silence,[8] stability,[9] regularity, the obedience of disciples to master and of all to the Rule[10]—in all this the Rule and its author are rigid and absolute.

During the centuries in which the Rule held its ground in the West,

---

1 *Regula*, xlii, 6, 13, and note 3, *supra*, p. 8. Despite these recommendations, Cassian was never a *vade-mecum* of the black monks of north-western Europe, and references to his works are rare in English writings and library lists before *c.* 1150. In the later Middle Ages the *Conferences* became one of the most widely known of spiritual classics, familiar to St Dominic and St Thomas as they had been earlier to Lanfranc.

2 Cf. *Cassiani Collationes*, 1, 3, 7, 9, 10.

3 St Benedict quotes St Matthew twenty-nine times; only two passages of St John are quoted, and in each case a strong "ascetic" sense is given to the words. There are over thirty quotations from Romans and Corinthians, only one direct and two indirect from the group Ephesians-Philippians-Colossians.

4 Cf. *Regula*, vi, vii, lxxiii, and especially i, 4–13. The last passage is an almost literal reproduction of Cassian; but it is a remarkable fact that a number of the passages in the Rule which most literally reproduce Cassian are also amongst the most enigmatic (e.g. xx, 5–10, and the re-ordering of the degrees of humility in vii).

5 *Regula*, lv, 22 (after enumerating articles of clothing): "quod supra fuerit, superfluum est, amputari debet"; xxxix, 22 (of food): "servata in omnibus parcitate."

6 *Regula*, xxxiii, 11: "omnia omnibus sint communia"; xxxiii, 1: "hoc vitium [i.e. of private possession] radicitus amputandum est de monasterio." Cf. lv, 37.

7 *Regula*, lxvi, 15: "ut non sit necessitas monachis vagandi foris, quia omnino non expedit animabus eorum."

8 *Regula*, vi, 10: "propter taciturnitatis gravitatem rara loquendi concedatur licentia."

9 *Regula*, Prol., 128: "usque ad mortem in monasterio perseverantes."

10 *Regula*, iii, 16 *seqq.*: "in omnibus omnes magistram sequantur Regulam...ipse abbas cum observatione Regulae omnia faciat."

saints of more than one vocation found a place within its four corners, and the loss of the literature of the monastic past and the needs of the unsettled times resulted in most countries in the dedication of monachism to the service of the gospel, of the liturgy and of learning. When, in the eleventh and twelfth centuries, the widespread spiritual renaissance led to a search for a life more exclusively contemplative and a conscious return to the primitive past, the Rule still for long held its place as the only norm. Only with the springing up of a more complex society, and the appearance of a new social order, did the monastic body split, as it were, horizontally into the divisions of choir monks and lay brethren and vertically into groups which were semi-eremitical, or at least purely contemplative, and groups which in greater or less degree touched the outside world with their activities.

IV

Throughout all the centuries from its composition to the rise of the new orders two circumstances, the one in a sense external and affecting the monastic institute, the other internal and affecting the individual monk, were in operation to maintain the Rule in its position of unique authority.

The first was the fact that, during all these centuries, the Rule, detached or at least detachable from all else, was the one and only warranted norm of monastic life. Though it is possible to trace a very real continuity of tradition throughout the history of black monachism, a tradition at once real and elusive, and though a body of customs, essentially the same throughout Europe, crystallized around the Rule almost at once, yet this body of customs, concerned as it was almost entirely with external, quasi-ceremonial actions, was never regarded as sacrosanct in all its parts, and the continuity of tradition was safeguarded and interpreted by no governing and legislative body of any kind. Thus there is no comparison possible between the position of the Rule in Western monachism between 550 and 1100 and that of the Carthusian customs, or the Rule of St Dominic or the Constitutions of St Ignatius in the institutes governed by those documents. With all the latter there has been from the beginning till the present day a definite body of men alongside of the document concerned with its enforcement, its interpretation and its augmentation; whatever moral or material catastrophes may have overtaken this part or that, the heart has never ceased to beat and the records of the past and its decrees have always been available to control the present and inspire the future.[1] But in the monastic order this was not the case; in all the catastrophes and

---

1 An interesting contrast could be drawn between the suppression of the Society of Jesus at the end of the eighteenth century and its restoration, when, like a machine that has been stopped for a while, it began to function in exactly the same way as before, and the various collapses of monasticism in Europe in the Dark and early Middle Ages, followed by new beginnings almost *ab ovo*.

rejuvenations of six hundred years the only constant, visible norm of monastic life was the unchanging text of the Rule.

The second circumstance was the counterpart of the first in the life of the individual. Since the Rule and the Rule alone, supplemented by no official body of spiritual doctrine, was the unique constant in all phases of monastic life, and since by universal and perhaps primitive custom a portion of its text was read in public every day of the year, its teaching and spirit sank into and coloured the minds of all monks from age to age. No other writings, save the psalms and gospels, had a position in any way comparable to it.[1] Even at the present day, when the volume of theological and spiritual literature is so enormous, and when every individual makes something of a selection for himself from the riches to hand, all those who have heard the Rule read each day over a period of years know that fragments and phrases lie in their memories and pass before their minds at moments of deliberation or crisis; they can therefore in some measure appreciate what must have been the influence of the Rule on minds more simple and memories less jaded, in centuries when the full riches of doctrine were rarely available, and when the Rule, to which obedience had been solemnly vowed, must often have been the only book with which the hearer was familiar.

V

The spirit of the Rule, that is, the peculiar shade of colour which the gospel teaching assumes as it comes to us from St Benedict, has often been described. It is above all a spirit of order and of the forming of nature to receive grace by way of gentle, steady growth. No reader can fail to remark how often the natural foundation, whether of the human family or of the purest inclinations of human nature, is taken as a basis for the higher order of things,[2] and how often St Benedict uses, not the language of high spirituality, but that of everyday intercourse, describing the simplest, smallest actions; nor can he fail to notice the gentleness, the humanity, the equilibrium of his teaching, which passes so naturally from the discipline of manners to the discipline of soul. It is a spirit alien alike to an austerity which is merely material and to a barbarism which falls below the level of human dignity. It was a spirit eminently fitted to

---

1 In the later Middle Ages, when cells and small houses had multiplied, visitations sometimes revealed an astonishing absence of the material text of the Rule and corresponding ignorance of its prescriptions, and such a state of things doubtless often obtained in the *monasteriola* of the early Middle Ages and at epochs of wholesale decadence. We may compare the analogous absence of the essential service books from parish churches. But a large and flourishing community without a knowledge of the Rule would be unthinkable, and "hidden" quotations from it abound in all monastic chronicles, letters and sermons.

2 Perhaps the most striking case is *Regula*, xxxvii, 1: "Licet ipsa natura humana trahatur ad misericordiam in his aetatibus, senum videlicet et infantum, tamen et Regulae auctoritas eis prospiciat."

humanize and Christianize the new peoples; unlike almost all codes that had preceded or were to follow it, it assumed no previous ascetic preparation, no strongly marked vocation to this or that form of life,[1] and it entirely lacked nice methods, cramping forms or anything that could lead to extravagance.[2] The character which it impressed was one of order, of peace and of benignity, and it became a force of incalculable power not only for sanctification, but also for the lower but indispensable tasks of civilizing and refining. As with all else that attains the truth of supreme simplicity by reconciling and rising above extremes that seem opposed one to another, the Rule has in the course of history often been misunderstood and its teaching debased. St Benedict's humanity and gentleness, as Christ's love and the Apostle's charity, have often been degraded to something merely human and commonplace by leaving out of the reckoning the complete self-sacrifice without which they cannot be attained. Often, and especially in the more sophisticated later centuries, words and phrases of the Rule were used by individuals and institutes to justify ways of conduct far from evangelical. But in the Rule itself the message of the gospel is never degraded. Imprecisions there are, and silences which later ages found it necessary to fill with words, but St Benedict never confuses charity with mere good nature, filial respect and obedience with human affection, peace and order with comfort and ease, measure and discretion with faintheartedness and mediocrity, and through all vicissitudes the Rule has remained one of the great formative influences in the life of the Church, outlining in majestic simplicity the broad principles of monastic life and government.[3]

1 Hence the primary disposition to be sought in a novice is: "si revera Deum quaerit" (*Regula*, lviii, 14). Dom Chapman (*St Benedict and the Sixth Century*, 25, note 2) therefore wrote: "A Benedictine novice ought to be able to say vaguely he wishes to give himself to God, and to be unable to explain any further"—a statement qualified by Abbot Butler (*DR*, xlviii, 197) as "good sound Benedictine doctrine". The publisher's proof-reader, however, perhaps misled by the otiose "vaguely", inserted a "not" after "ought" and the sentence appeared in this emended form.

2 A palmary instance of this simplicity may be seen in St Benedict's "instruction" on prayer, *Regula*, lii, 6: "si [quis] vult sibi forte secretius orare, simpliciter intret [*sc.* oratorium] et oret."

3 The wide practical wisdom of the Rule has often been acknowledged by those living in the current of the world's affairs. The present writer, while engaged in preparing these pages, met by chance an eminent public official in one of the capital cities of Europe who, though not a member of the Catholic Church or of any religious body, made a practice of reading each day in his office, before beginning work, the portion of the Rule assigned for reading in Chapter.

Since the foregoing pages were written a number of important articles on early monastic history have appeared in recently published *fascicules* of the French theological and historical *Dictionnaires*. Attention may be called in particular to a richly documented account of the Rule and polity of St Benedict in the *Dictionnaire de Droit Canonique* by Dom Philibert Schmitz, of Maredsous, who has inherited the mantle and editorial chair, and multiplied the *fiches*, of the lamented Dom Berlière. Dom Justin McCann's *St Benedict* (1937) is a well balanced and attractive introduction to the subject.

CHAPTER II

THE MONASTIC ORDER BETWEEN THE DEATH OF SAINT BENEDICT AND THE TIMES OF SAINT DUNSTAN

I

In order to have any appreciation of the English monasticism of the tenth and later centuries, of its ideals, its development and its problems, it is necessary to know something of the external history and the internal evolution of the monastic institute between the death of St Benedict (*c.* 547) and the refoundation of Glastonbury by Dunstan almost four centuries later (*c.* 943).[1] And at the outset it is essential to bear in mind the great difference that exists between the history of the monastic order previous to the rise of the Cistercians, and the history of all religious orders, monastic and others, founded since that date. In the case of the latter there have been both a single detailed code of legislation, in which changes and insertions were made at definite moments, and a clearly distinguishable body of men to whom it was applied, together with a smaller body charged with its maintenance. But in the history of the monastic order between the times of St Benedict and the times of St Bernard, and above all between the death of St Gregory the Great and the Capitularies of Aachen in 817, there is nothing of the kind. Monasticism of the most varying types existed in almost all the Christian countries of Europe before the Rule was composed, and, on the other hand, the monastery or group of monasteries for which the Rule was composed lost its corporate existence in less than half a century after the death of the Legislator. The Rule, therefore, gradually made its way and became the unique code not as a single tree might become a forest, by propagation,

---

1 No adequate general history of monasticism in these centuries has been written; Montalembert's celebrated volumes were the work of a publicist and a "romantic", and though they may be used to supplement critical history they cannot take its place. Mabillon's monumental *Acta SS. Ordinis S. Benedicti* and *Annales OSB* remain of enduring value, but as the raw material for historians rather than as food for the general reader. Of short narratives the best known to me is that of Dom Stephanus Hilpisch, *Geschichte des Benediktinischen Mönchtums* (Freiburg-im-Breisgau, 1929); though brief, it is based on a wide reading of the sources and gives clear and sane judgments on men and movements. Dom U. Berlière's *L'Ordre Monastique*, though slight in format, is the mature fruit of a lifetime of study, and contains very full bibliographies, which may be supplemented for books up to *c.* 1932 from the article *Bénédictins* by Dom M. Mähler in the *Dictionnaire de Spiritualité.* Dom Berlière's *L'Ascèse Bénédictine*, though less easily digestible than his other book, is equally a mine of documented information, and a search through the *Revue Bénédictine* will disclose numerous articles of value by Berlière, Morin, Wilmart and others. There is a good, if slightly tendencious, sketch of early monastic "constitutional history" in the introduction (known to have been largely the work of Edmund Bishop) to the English translation of Montalembert, *The Monks of the West* (1896).

but as a powerful chemical ingredient might gradually colour and give its character to a liquid into which it was infused. Western monasticism thus came gradually to look to St Benedict as its only patriarch, save in lands of purely Celtic population, but it became also a monasticism with characteristics and needs for which the Rule did not legislate, and a monasticism existing under conditions which St Benedict had never contemplated.

II

Alongside of the monastic life described in the Rule and in the *Dialogues* of St Gregory, there were in existence in Italy in the sixth century two other important varieties of the institute. The one was the type associated with the name of Cassiodorus, which, though fundamentally in harmony with the Rule, was a life less simple in its organization and less exclusively spiritual and monastic in its aims, into which intellectual and utilitarian work of all kinds entered as an essential part of its programme.[1] The other, which existed only in the great cities and above all in Rome, was the purely liturgical type, in which a body of monks acted as the choir and sometimes even as the clergy of one of the many basilicas of the City— among them were St Peter's, the Lateran, and St Paul's—and thus more nearly resembled a community of what were later called regular canons than the monks of Monte Cassino or Vivarium. Such monasteries were in existence in Rome in St Benedict's day and their number grew steadily till it reached sixty.[2] Both these types, in various circumstances, came to adopt the Rule of St Benedict, and from both Western monasticism drew some of its abiding characteristics, but it is clear that both (and in particular the basilican type) would of necessity treat the Rule from the beginning rather as a general, spiritual guide than as a precise and rigid code.

Monte Cassino, the monastery of St Benedict's later years in which he wrote his Rule and in which he died, was despoiled by the Lombards *c.* 577, and the monks were dispersed; that they migrated to Rome and settled at the Lateran is no more than a venerable tradition.[3] Cassino was

1 For Cassiodorus, *v.* Dom J. Chapman, *St Benedict and the Sixth Century*, 88–110, where it is held that Cassiodorus knew and used the Rule, and F. H. Dudden, *Gregory the Great*, II, 169–73. The *Institutes* of Cassiodorus are now within the reach of all in the excellent edition of R. A. B. Mynors; a careful reading of them gives the impression that the differences between the systems of Cassiodorus and St Benedict are less important than has sometimes been maintained.

2 For the basilical monasteries *v.* Dom G. Morin, *Les monastères bénédictins de Rome au Moyen Age (Messager des fidèles*, IV (1887), 262 *et al.*) and Dom I. Schuster (now Cardinal Archbishop of Milan), *L'Opera del monachismo nella vita liturgica a Roma*, a long excursus to his *Liber Sacramentorum* (Turin, 1923), V, 12–73 (English translation, III, 14–73). The basilicas, at least in the early period, had priests and clerics distinct from the monks for the service of the altar.

3 *V.* the important article by Dom Suso Brechter, *Monte Cassinos erste Zerstörung*, in *Studien und Mitteilungen zur Geschichte des Benediktiner-Ordens*, LVI (1938), 109–150.

restored in 717 by Petronax of Brescia, and directed by the Anglo-Saxon Willibald, who had had experience of the flourishing English monasteries. The Customs, therefore, of Monte Cassino, so far as they are known, and *a fortiori* the earliest commentary on the Rule, that of Paul Warnefrid (which in all probability was not written at Cassino), *c.* 770, though they afford precious evidence of monastic practice before the Carolingian reforms, are not the unbroken evolution of St Benedict's teaching. An unbroken tradition did indeed in all probability exist, but the thread of direct continuity cannot be traced, save by conjecture, and must therefore be said to be, if not actually broken, at least wholly lost to sight in the wide web of the monastic world.

When the fugitives from Monte Cassino and other southern monasteries arrived in Rome, the future Gregory the Great was already a monk and deacon of the Roman Church.[1] His own monastery on the Coelian, whether or not originally based on the Rule alone, certainly came to adopt it as a norm of life; at the same time, the numerous basilican monasteries in the neighbourhood and Gregory's wide plans for the Church had also their effect in moulding his conception of the monastic vocation. His writings, and above all the *Dialogues*, show that he was saturated with traditions of the life of St Benedict; he himself gives us the sources whence he drew them, and it is most probable that members of more than one monastery founded by St Benedict had found their way to Gregory's house on the Coelian and to his other monasteries in Sicily. In any case, Gregory when pope exercised a preponderant influence in determining the future character of Western monasticism, both by taking the Rule as his guide in the many actions, constitutions and decretals by which he wove the monastic body into the life of the Church and into canon law, and by his initiative, so pregnant with consequences, in sending monks to convert the heathen in England. With Gregory the Great the Rule, which, as has been seen, was itself inspired so deeply with the principles of the Church's law, became in turn the source *par excellence* for all subsequent ecclesiastical legislation on monasticism.

It is wholly impossible to attempt here even a sketch of monastic history between the death of St Gregory and the age of Charlemagne. With the monks, as with every department of the Church's organization, the epoch succeeding that of Gregory was one in which the legislation of the Roman world and its corporate bodies tended to melt into disorder, from which individual houses emerged by long and laborious growth. Monasteries of every type, following the most various Rules—Eastern, Gallic, Celtic, Benedictine, private—waxed and waned, but throughout the whole of Europe a knowledge of the Rule of St Benedict became gradually common, at first through the channels of papal legislation and Italian tradition, and later through Anglo-Saxon influence of all kinds,

---

1 For Gregory the Great, *v.* Dudden, *op. cit.*, esp. Book 2, ch. ix, *Gregory and Monasticism*.

and especially that exercised by Boniface and his followers in German lands. And, speaking very generally, throughout Europe north and west of the Alps, with the exception of the Celtic lands, a type of monastery gradually became normal which united a number of characteristics which in St Benedict's lifetime were only to be found in separation; while drawing the main outlines of its government and spiritual life from the Rule, it had the complexity and intellectual colour of a Vivarium or a Bobbio and the highly elaborate liturgical life of a basilican monastery. In addition, the most important houses grew to be vast institutions, the centres of widespread economic and territorial organizations.[1]

This development had, among others, two important consequences which all students of monastic history have noted as profoundly modifying the conception of St Benedict. One was the gradual introduction of the custom that monks should normally proceed to holy orders; the other was the disappearance of manual, and above all of agricultural, work as a normal employment of monks. The practice of monks proceeding to orders varied greatly with country and circumstances. In St Benedict's day and for some time after, a monastery had as a rule but one or two priests, presented for ordination to the bishop for the service of the house; this was the common state of things at the time of St Gregory, and is upheld in much of his legislation, but at the same time there were already exceptions. Gregory's own monastery on the Coelian, for example, sent out the band of missionaries to England most of whom were, or subsequently became, priests, and the missionary activities of monks in England in the seventh and in Germany and elsewhere in the eighth centuries made for a steady growth, at least in those countries, of the numbers raised to the priesthood. Similarly, the employment of monks in the service of a basilica in Rome and other cities and shrines of Italy and Gaul worked gradually towards the same result. Such figures as are available show a steady, though slow, increase in the proportion of priests and deacons in the monasteries, and by the tenth century it was becoming normal for all who entered the monastery when young to proceed, by slow stages, through the *cursus ordinum*, though it remained exceptional for those who entered in later life to be ordained.[2] But it may be said that by the time of Charlemagne monks had come to be classed among the lettered, and to be set on a level with all clerics. Earlier still had manual work, and above all agricultural work, ceased to be universal or even normal. Even in St Benedict's day, and under the most favourable circumstances, we have seen that the heaviest work in the fields was done by *coloni*. Many monasteries, in cities and elsewhere, had no fields in their neighbourhood; the social and economic conditions in French and

---

1 Cf. Berlière, *L'Ordre Monastique*, 105–20 and the literature cited; also Hilpisch, *Geschichte*, 113–16.
2 Some statistics are given by Berlière, *L'Ascèse Bénédictine*, 39–40.

German lands gave the work of the fields to the serfs, and the cleavage between monks and labourers was increased by the monks entering more and more frequently into orders. The important monasteries received many gifts of land, and save in the most favoured districts of intensive cultivation, such as Campania and the river valleys of southern France, this implied that the property soon became very widely scattered, and could only be exploited by large bodies of serfs. At the same time, the growth of the monastery itself, and the influx of guests, pilgrims and poor called into being a large and mixed multitude of dependents, some of them attached by a semi-religious tie, others purely servants.[1] Thus the typical large monastery of the Carolingian age, abstracting altogether from the degree of its fervour or decadence, was something very different from the monastery of the Rule. It cannot be too often repeated that in St Benedict's conception a monastery existed for the service of God and the spiritual welfare of its inmates, and for no other reason. It was to be spiritually and actually a family living for God apart from the world as truly, though less remotely, than the monks of Egypt or the hermits of Enfide. Those who attribute to the legislator farsighted designs of re-generating a crumbling society or of reasserting the nobility of work and communal service not only fail to see St Benedict and the Rule in true historical perspective, but fail also to see that he was concerned solely with the monastic life as a spiritual discipline for the service of God, and not at all with works, however necessary, of religion and charity undertaken for the world outside the walls of the monastery.[2] But the conception of a monastery as a reservoir of learning, as a centre of order and beneficence, or as the home of a class of men who made continual and as it were official intercession for the rest of society—all this, though not present in the mind of St Benedict so far as we can ascertain it, came gradually to be substituted for the original idea throughout Europe; it was an almost necessary way of thinking in a primitive society, nominally Christian in its institutions, which lacked all the manifold gradings and organizations and specializations of the ancient civilization and of the later medieval and modern world. And thus monasticism, which had begun as a flight to the desert from the civilized world, became in the Western Empire between Gregory the Great and Gregory VII an integral part of society.[3] The new monasticism of the eleventh and twelfth centuries was to be largely a reaction from this state of things.

1 Berlière, *L'Ascèse Bénédictine*, 250–2.

2 Even careful scholars such as Dom Berlière are occasionally carried away in this direction; cf. *L'Ordre Monastique*, 41. The occasional works of charity to those around Cassino noted in the *Dialogues* of St Gregory do not contradict the Rule; on the other hand, it is not suggested that St Benedict, because he did not contemplate them, would therefore have condemned all the developments that took place. Simply, they were not part of his scheme.

3 The division of the population into the fighting, working and praying classes, familiar to us from its adoption by Alfred the Great, was a commonplace of the age.

III

Monastic life of the type familiar in Italy in the sixth century, together with a knowledge of the Rule of St Benedict, came first to England with the Roman mission of the monk Augustine and his companions in 597. The band was drawn from Gregory's monastery on the Coelian; their conception of the monastic life was therefore probably something between that of the Rule and that of the basilical monasteries of the City. The first and only monastery which is known with certainty to have been founded by them was that of SS. Peter and Paul (later St Augustine's) at Canterbury, resembling in situation and functions the urban, non-basilical monasteries of Rome, such as St Andrew's itself.[1] No precise statement exists that the Rule was the code of the Canterbury house, but with our knowledge of Gregory we may assume confidently that it was so, though we may also assume that it was regarded as a rule to be used within a given frame-work of life, rather than as a code upon which every detail of that life was to be built.

Whatever expansion of monastic life took place in Kent must have been modelled on Canterbury, but within a few decades another form of monasticism, the Celtic from Iona, took a firm hold upon Northumbria;[2] between north and south, also, in Lincolnshire and the fens, monasteries were founded by the middle of the seventh century, some of which, at least, appear to have been modelled on originals in western Gaul, whither many individuals from England had proceeded early in the century.[3] Thus England soon began to show as great a diversity of types and rules as the Continent, and the Rule of St Benedict had found a foothold only in the south-east of the island.

A change came with the appearance in England of a succession of men destined to be leaders of the Church, all of whom had in one way or another become well acquainted with the monastic life familiar to Rome.[4] The first of these in point of time was Wilfrid, originally a monk of Lindisfarne, who was abroad for a number of years and visited Rome as a young man; on his return to Britain in 658 shortly before the synod of

---

1 Bede, *Hist. Ecclesiastica* I, 33, in *Opera Historica*, ed. Plummer, I, 70.

2 For Celtic monasticism, *v.* J. Ryan, S.J., *Irish Monasticism* (Dublin, 1931), and *Celtic Christianity*, by Dom L. Gougaud (1932). By far the best short account of the two currents in Northumbrian monasticism, and their fusion, is the contribution of the editor (Prof. A. Hamilton Thompson) to the volume *Bede: his Life, Times and Writings* (1935).

3 Cf. Bede, *Hist. Eccl.* III, 8 (Plummer, I, 142): "Multi de Brittania monachicae conversationis gratia Francorum uel Galliarum monasteria adire solebant."

4 For the outlines of Anglo-Saxon monasticism *v.*, besides the *Hist. Eccl.* and *Hist. Abbatum* of Bede, together with Plummer's invaluable introduction and notes, the works of Alcuin and Boniface; also the volume of essays on Bede referred to above (note 2) and the excellent précis given by S. J. Crawford, *Anglo-Saxon influence on Western Christianity, 600–800* (1933).

Whitby he brought with him, together with many other Roman traditions, the Rule of St Benedict, and probably gave it to Ripon and Hexham, though with no intention of changing all existing monastic customs there. Of far greater significance, however, was his friend and fellow-traveller the Northumbrian Biscop, who had accompanied him to Rome, and who, after a stay of two years at Lérins, a monastery which had adopted the Rule and where he probably took the name Benedict, returned to Rome again before finding his way back to England at the command of Pope Vitalian in company with the newly appointed archbishop of Canterbury, Theodore of Tarsus. On arriving at Canterbury he became for two years (669–71) abbot of the monastery of SS. Peter and Paul, till relieved of his office by the Neapolitan abbot Hadrian, sent by Vitalian to assist Theodore. Canterbury thus once more received a strong impact of Roman monasticism, and this time there was added to the liturgical tradition and the acceptance of the Rule that keen impulse towards learning, which under Theodore and Hadrian was to have such lasting results in the south, and under Biscop was to flourish so strongly in the north.

From the monastery at Canterbury and its school went forth a stream of influence whose currents we can trace directly in Aldhelm and his friends and surmise in many other monastic centres of Wessex during the next half-century. It was a period when the monastic life spread widely over the south-west of England; Glastonbury, a colony of Celtic monks, probably received the Anglo-Roman model with the conquest of Somerset by Ine,[1] and the various houses came into being which appear in the *Life* and correspondence of Boniface. It is hard to say how fully these monasteries were in origin based wholly on the Rule; probably it was known everywhere, but the English houses had a character of their own; most of them, even when celebrated for their learning—an example is Nursling in Hampshire—were small in size, and the number of *monasteriola* which were private property, owned and maintained by landowners, no doubt exceeded that of the larger houses.[2]

Meanwhile Benedict Biscop, after another visit to Rome, had returned to the north and founded Wearmouth (674) and Jarrow (685). These monasteries have become celebrated and familiar to all through the life and writings of Bede, who entered Biscop's monastery as a child. They were new foundations, receiving the Rule from the start, and Bede's description of the life, with its regular but simple liturgical psalmody alternating with reading, domestic work of all kinds, crafts such as that of the smithy and even heavy agricultural labour, is nearer in spirit to the life at Monte Cassino in St Benedict's day than is any continental

---

1 So J. Armitage Robinson, *Somerset Historical Essays*, 28, and his opinion has won general acceptance.
2 For these, *v.* F. M. Stenton, *The Early History of the abbey of Abingdon*, 51 *et al.*

example of which anything is known.[1] Yet even here we have clear evidence that the Rule, though treated with the greatest reverence, was not the only guide of the life. Biscop, when dying, exhorted the monks to observe, not the Rule, but the rule of life which he had given them, and which had been compiled from the observances of seventeen different monasteries which he had visited in the course of his travels.[2] In the same address, he alluded to the Rule of St Benedict in somewhat the same way as St Benedict himself referred to that of St Basil, as a document of great authority rather than as the one binding code.[3] In a similar spirit the liturgy of the northern houses was organized on purely Roman lines by John, archcantor of St Peter's and abbot of the basilical monastery of St Martin at Rome.

The first half of the eighth century saw the Anglo-Saxon monasticism at the highest point of its development and influence. To the learning and art of the north, and the less massive but very real culture of the south, was joined a missionary spirit common to individuals from north and south alike, which led to the evangelization of northern Europe under Boniface and his followers, and to the introduction in the new lands of a monastic life inspired by them. It was towards the end of the century that an Anglo-Saxon, Willibald, assisted in reviving monastic life at Monte Cassino.[4] Indeed, during the greater part of the eighth century the monasteries of England possessed a life, and exercised an influence, more powerful than those of any other monastic *bloc* in Europe.[5]

At the same time, in north and south alike, the tendency, common in every country and century of the early Middle Ages, for the monastic life to lose its regular character, and for houses to become merely clerical establishments or to fall wholly under lay control, was making itself felt more and more strongly. The severe charges of Bede in the letter to Ecgbert written in his last years are well known;[6] throughout the eighth century and in the early years of the ninth canons of synods and deeds of

---

1 *Hist. Abb.* § 8 (Plummer, I, 371–2). The noble recruit Eosterwine was accustomed: "ventilare [thresh] cum eis [*sc.* monachis] et triturare, oves vitulasque mulgere, in pistrino, in orto, in coquina [the words are taken from the Rule]...exerceri." When abbot: "ubi operantes invenit fratres, solebat eis confestim in opere conjungi; vel aratri gressum stiva regendo, vel ferrum malleo domando, etc."

2 *Hist. Abb.* § 11 (Plummer, I, 374–5). When dying, Benedict exhorted the brethren *de custodienda, quam statuerat, regula,* which, as he expressly told them: "Ex decem et septem monasteriis quae...optima conperi...didici et vobis salubriter obseruanda contradidi."

3 *Hist. Abb.* § 11 (Plummer, I, 374–5): "Juxta quod regula magni quondam abbatis Benedicti...continet decreta."

4 *Vita Willibaldi,* c. 3; in *MGH, SS,* xv, 102.

5 The judgment of Abbot Butler, *Benedictine Monachism,* 356: "During the later half of the seventh century and the eighth, a predominant place in the Benedictine world was held by the monks of England" is substantially correct, if by the phrase "Benedictine world" we understand the monasteries of Europe as seen by the historian of to-day; for no self-conscious "Benedictine world" was then in existence.

6 Plummer, I, 414–18.

immunity and gift show the same processes at work.[1] A very careful examination of all the documents available would be necessary before the stages and degrees of decline could be described even tentatively; here there can be no question of any such examination. It is sufficient to note that the history of monasticism in the country was soon influenced from without by the Scandinavian invasions. Lindisfarne and Jarrow were sacked for the first time in 793–4, and although monastic life survived this castrophe, it was ultimately extinguished north of the Humber by the great Danish invasion of 867–70. The fenland monasteries and Beadoricsworth (the future Bury St Edmund's) went at the same time, and, as will be seen in the following chapter, all available evidence goes to show that between c. 830 and 880 all the monasteries of Wessex and south Mercia either had become extinct during the wars or had become houses where a number of priests or clerics lived together without any full regular life. In other words, Anglo-Saxon monasticism, whether considered as an institution or as a body of tradition with a local habitation, had ceased to live by the time of Alfred.

But although direct continuity of regular life ceased, and although the break with the past was in a sense absolute, the monasticism of the early centuries exerted an influence on the revival under Dunstan that was great and permanent, and which cannot be explained merely as the re-emergence of national characteristics. There remained, first of all, the old sites, not all forgotten or obliterated; to these clung traditions, and sometimes even muniments remained which helped to mould the lives of the generations which came after. There remained also the memory that the conversion of England and the establishment of the Church had been due at every stage to monks—to Gregory, to Augustine, to Paulinus, to Aidan, to Cuthbert, to Wilfrid, to Theodore—that all the greatest and most saintly of the bishops of the past had been monks, and that from the monasteries of England had been drawn the apostles of Germany. Above all, there remained the writings of Bede, the only teacher of the first rank whom the West knew between Gregory the Great and the eleventh century. Wherever in England Latin was read, Bede's *Ecclesiastical History* was read, and it would be hard to exaggerate the strength of its influence. Bede's pages moulded the minds of Alfred, of Dunstan; of Aldwin, the restorer of monastic life in the north, and of William of St Carilef, bishop of Durham, who received him; and we can trace the same influence at work on William of Malmesbury, Symeon of Durham and many other later monastic writers. From Bede all English readers became familiar with the golden age of monasticism in the north, familiar also with the idea that monks should co-operate most closely with bishops and temporal rulers for the good of the Church and the country.

1 Cf. the canons of the council of Cloveshoe (747) on the monastic life: §§ 4, 5, 7, 19 22 in Haddan and Stubbs, *Councils*, III, 364–70.

This conception was destined in the twelfth century to give place to others, when in a more highly organized and legalized Church learning and the care of discipline passed from the monastic order to the bishops, the canonists and the schools, but until that development took place monasticism in England looked back to the past and drew its inspiration from the records of the seventh century.

IV

The years which saw the first Scandinavian invasions in the north of England saw also the development of a monastic revival in southern France and, a little later, in the Empire so important in its consequences as to mark an epoch in the history of the monastic order in the West.

Charlemagne, in the course of his surveillance of all the departments of the life of the Church, gave much attention to the spread and maintenance of regular discipline in the monasteries of his dominions. In this, as in other matters, he aimed at securing conformity to a single norm, and that the one consecrated by tradition. As in the general discipline of the Church he repeated the canons of Gelasius and Gregory, and in the chant sought out a single Roman exemplar, so in the monastic life all was to be ordered by the Rule, and all copies of the Rule were to be based on the transcript of the codex at Monte Cassino believed to be an autograph; of this Charles caused an exact reproduction to be made, which he deposited at Aachen. The paramount position already held by the Rule at the time is well shown by the familiar anecdote, according to which Charles enquired whether any other monastic code existed, and in the legislation of the eighth and ninth centuries it was commonly equated with the "sacred canons" by synods and councils. But the diversity of customs interpreting, modifying, mitigating or supplementing the Rule was very great. With these Charlemagne did not directly concern himself; his aim was to remedy abuses by using the Rule as a standard code, not to give the monastic body a new unity or uniformity, still less to change or innovate in any way. His work here, as in other fields, would have been gradually undone without having permanently affected monastic history had it not been supplemented by a strictly monastic movement that was the work of Benedict of Aniane.

The life of Benedict in his early years is one of the first and most striking examples of a type of story that was often to be repeated in the three following centuries.[1] Of noble birth, after a few years of manhood

---

1 For Benedict of Aniane, *v.* above all the *Vita* of his disciple Ardo, *PL*, CIII, 353–84. Among recent studies, there are some excellent pages in Hilpisch, *Geschichte*, 117–26, and a useful article, *St Benedict of Aniane*, by W. Williams in *DR*, LIV (July 1936), 357–74; there is a valuable sketch by E. Bishop in *Liturgica Historica*, 212–13; *v.* also arts. in *DHG* and *DDC*.

in the profession of arms under Charlemagne, he became a monk and devoted himself to the most severe physical austerities, ultimately retiring to his own lands near Montpellier, where he gathered followers and lived a life of extreme simplicity and austerity. At this period of his life, indeed, it was his declared opinion that the Rule of St Benedict was for beginners only, and he turned rather to the earlier monasticism of the desert.[1] Very soon, however, he became converted to the traditional way of life, and the monastery of Aniane became a centre distinguished from others only by its fervour of spirit. His fame spread, he was called to found and reform other houses, and he became the friend and adviser of Louis of Aquitaine. When, after the death of Charlemagne, Louis "the Pious" was in power, he summoned Benedict to the Rhineland and built for him the abbey of Inde, later Cornelimünster, which was to serve as a model for the whole Empire. Benedict himself became a kind of arch-abbot; he could visit all the monasteries of the Empire and issue what orders he thought fit. Finally, at a general meeting of abbots at Aachen in 817, a series of regulations was promulgated and became law for the Empire by which the Rule, with the interpretations, modifications and additions of Benedict, became binding on all monks; officials were appointed by the imperial authority in the various monasteries to promulgate these *capitula* and supervise their observance.[2]

The *capitula* of Aachen have in them nothing creative or of direct spiritual value.[3] Like canons and capitularies in general, they are brief enunciations or reiterations of laws and customs; to seek of them genial and pregnant teaching and deep spiritual wisdom would be as unreasonable as to demand it of all the numberless Customaries, Directories, Rules and Constitutions of the medieval and modern world. The Rule of St Benedict shares with very few others the dual character of a constitutional and spiritual guide. But the *capitula* were the outcome, not only of long practical experience, but of a careful gathering of tradition, ancient and modern, written and lived, such as had not been made since St Benedict himself composed his Rule.[4] The *Codex Regularum* and the *Concordia Regularum* remain as witness of the wide sweep of knowledge possessed by Benedict of Aniane; they were intended as *pièces justificatives* not only

1 *Vita*, 357: "Regulam quoque beati Benedicti tironibus seu infirmis positam fore contestans, ad beati Basilii dicta nec non Pachomii regulam scandere nitens, jugiter impossibiliora [!] rimabat."

2 *Vita*, 377 *seqq.*: "Perfectum itaque propagatumque est opus...et una cunctis generaliter posita observatur Regula, cunctaque monasteria ita ad formam unitatis redacta sunt, ac si ab uno magistro et in uno imbuerentur loco."

3 The best edition is that of Dom B. Albers, *Constitutiones Monasticae* (Monte Cassino, 1907), III, 115 *seqq.*

4 *Vita*, 380: "Omne quippe desiderium suum in observationem Regulae converterat, suumque hoc permaxime erat studium ut nihil intellectui ejus excederet: quam ob causam, quos peritos esse compererat, attente sciscitabatur circa longeque positos, eos etiam qui istis in partibus ad montem Casinum accederent, veluti qui non audita solummodo, sed visa perciperent, etc."

of his own legislation, but of that of St Benedict also.[1] The legislation of Aachen had therefore a twofold aim. It was directed towards establishing the authority of the Rule not only as a standard or norm, but as the one *Regula sancta, magistra Regula* with which every monk had a personal, spiritual bond; it also aimed at giving a brief directory which should supplement the Rule so as to cover the monk's whole day and total activity. Direct changes were very few, and in matters of physical austerity the tendency was to mitigate rather than to accentuate in more than one detail. In three important respects, however, Benedict of Aniane, rather by giving expression to what was already in existence than by direct innovation, influenced deeply the future history of the monastic order. Agricultural work was explicitly recognized as extraordinary for monks, as opposed to the work of the house and workshop; the teaching by monks of all except oblates was forbidden; and a considerable addition was made to the liturgical prayer of the Rule, in particular the daily office of the dead and the so-called *trina oratio* of special psalms and prayers thrice a day, together with three ceremonial visits to the various altars of the church. The first of these enactments was merely an acknowledgment of a state of things that had long existed in all parts of Europe where the social life was fully organized; the second was a natural consequence of the legislation of Charlemagne which put education as a duty upon the secular clergy; the third, in which it is more possible to see the direct action of Benedict, was partly a natural consequence of the two former, and partly aimed at providing a common mean between indiscreet prolixity of prayer and idleness. It was, in the event, to receive great and undesirable development.[2]

What may be called the constitutional machinery established by Louis the Pious and Benedict fell to pieces with the death of the saint and the gradual disintegration of the Empire, and with it went all hope of exact and controlled uniformity.[3] Here, as in all other things, there was something factitious about the measures of Charlemagne and Louis; Europe was not yet capable of evolving or maintaining a scientific constitution of any kind. But though the framework of government disappeared, the work of Benedict of Aniane had a great and permanent influence, for in the centuries which followed every new revival looked back for precedents

---

1 *Vita*, 380. The *Codex* and *Concordia* are printed in *PL*, CIII.

2 *Vita*, 379. Cf. Berlière, *L'Ascèse Bénédictine*, 48–9.

3 Some decades ago, movements towards centralization and uniformity among black monks of to-day caused contemporary historians of the order to scrutinize and criticize the career of Benedict of Aniane with one eye upon the world around them. This serves to explain the warmth of tone which is noticeable in their judgments. E.g. Berlière, *L'Ordre Monastique* (1 ed.), 115: "Le mouvement provoqué par S. Benoît d'Aniane...ne modifia point les conceptions des grands centres religieux de l'Empire, et ce fut un bonheur pour l'Eglise." (The last eight words do not appear in the third edition, p. 129.) Cf. [E. Bishop], introduction to Montalembert's *Monks of the West*, XXVI: "His scheme of rigid uniformity ...met with the fate it deserved", and Abbot Butler, *Benedictine Monachism*, 357: "The famous Capitula of Aachen...prove on examination a disappointing document."

and documents to the past, and found them in the meeting and *capitula* of Aachen. The monasticism of Cluny, Gorze and Brogne, and later that of the Dunstanic revival in England, was based upon the Customs of Benedict of Aniane.

The age of Charlemagne therefore marks an epoch in monastic history. It would not be an exaggeration to say that between 800 and 820 the monastic way of life, the *ordo monasticus*, became officially, at least within the Empire, the *ordo sancti Benedicti*,[1] and that the monks felt for the first time an *esprit de corps*, together with a persuasion, shared by all, that they had in St Benedict a common father and protector. The Rule, which had originally been written and applied as the sole and binding code for a particular kind of monastic life, and which had subsequently become a norm and standard for monasteries of the most varied observance and occupation, now became once more the *magistra Regula* for every monk, but with its scope in a sense narrowed to a particular form of life which was not that of Monte Cassino in the sixth century, nor that of Jarrow and Wearmouth in the eighth, but of Frankland in the ninth. Henceforward, in the Empire and in all lands to which the new influence went out, the Rule, together with a list of customs based to a great extent upon the *capitula* of Aachen, formed a single *bloc* of legislation and were treated as such by all. Thus, by a natural, but in a sense paradoxical development, the monastic life of the West, while becoming more explicitly "Benedictine" than before, became also identified with a way of life which was a Carolingian modification of the scheme of the original legislator. The individual who had the greatest share in this transformation was Benedict of Aniane, and it is this that gives him his unique position in monastic history.[2]

V

The work of Benedict of Aniane, as has been said, was to all appearances undone within a few years of his death in the very decades during which Anglo-Saxon monasticism was disappearing before the Danes. The second half of the ninth century was a period of growing darkness for Europe, and the monastic order shared in the general decline; secularization and relaxation of all kinds were widespread.

The new dawn had its beginnings with the foundation of Cluny in 910.[3] There was nothing novel in the aims of this revival. Full observance of

1 It need scarcely be said that *ordo*, as used in the above phrases in the early Middle Ages, does not mean "a religious Order", but "a regular way of life".

2 Cf. the judgment of E. Bishop, *Liturgica Historica*, 213: "The decrees of this meeting of Aachen...were a turning point in the history of the Benedictines, forming the basis of later legislation and practice. After the great founder himself, Benedict of Nursia, no man has more widely affected Western monachism than did the second Benedict, he of Aniane." This is put strongly, perhaps too strongly, for the two influences differed in kind as well as in degree; Benedict of Aniane has never been a spiritual guide for monks.

3 For the origins of Cluny, Gorze and Brogne, *v.* Sackur, *Die Cluniacenser*, vol. i.

the Rule—that is, the Rule as interpreted and supplemented by recent tradition—and complete independence of lay control were all that was desired. To gain the latter end, Cluny was put directly under the protection of the Apostolic See, and the freedom of action thus secured, together with her unparalleled good fortune in having for almost two centuries a succession of eminent, holy and long-lived abbots, brought the place gradually to the unique position which it held for so long. Berno, the first abbot, already received invitations or commands to reform other houses, and under his successor, Odo (abbot 924–42), the number rapidly grew, though as yet there was no machinery of central control such as afterwards came into being. Among the houses so reformed was the ancient and celebrated Fleury on the Loire, reputed to hold the body of St Benedict himself. Fleury fell under the control of Cluny *c.* 930, and was destined to have great influence upon England, at first by attracting individuals from across the Channel, and later by supplying a model for one of the centres of the revival.

Simultaneously with the rise of Cluny two other revivals on similar lines were taking place, the one in Upper, the other in Lower Lorraine. The first had as its cradle the refounded abbey of Gorze near Metz (*c.* 933) and as its inspiring genius the second abbot, John of Gorze. The second, started by Gerard of Brogne, near Namur, had as its centre the abbey founded by Gerard on his patrimony (*c.* 920). The monasticism of Gorze, which in origin at least was more physically severe than Cluny, spread throughout the district between Cologne, Metz, Verdun and Toul; that of Brogne passed into Flanders and reached, among others, the old abbeys of Ghent and St Omer. Here again near neighbourhood and dynastic connections brought it about that the monasteries of Flanders had a share in moulding English institutions.

Alike at Cluny, Gorze and Brogne the main lines of the life were based upon the work of Benedict of Aniane.[1] In all three centres the *capitula* of Aachen were known, and in all the additional psalmody and ceremonial usages were received and indeed considerably increased. At Cluny, also, even in the early years, there began to develop something of that elaboration and splendour of ceremonial that afterwards became so characteristic of the place. This, then, was the monastic life of the moment, new and fervent, when Dunstan as a boy and young man lived among the travelled bishops and foreign visitors of the "court" of King Athelstan. It was a life, especially in the centres of France and Flanders, running almost wholly upon the lines laid down by Benedict of Aniane; a life of large, well-established communities devoting a very great part of the waking hours to liturgical prayer and praise in common, accompanied by elaborate

---

1 Thus Berlière, *L'Ordre Monastique* (1 ed.), 168; (3 ed.), 198: "[Les] coutumes cluni-siennes...se basent sur les traditions de Baume [the monastery of Berno] empruntés par la voie de Saint-Savin à S. Benoît d'Aniane."

chant and ceremonial; what remained over of the day was given to domestic administration and meditative reading. Though now recognized throughout western Europe as the one and only monastic life according to the Rule of St Benedict, it had lost a number of the characteristics both of the life of Monte Cassino and of the life in other monastic centres in subsequent centuries. It had, as a body, none of the quasi-eremitical, purely contemplative elements of earlier monasticism, little of the simple, patriarchal family life of Monte Cassino, and still less of the apostolic and other activities that had in the past been characteristic of the English monks and their derivatives. It was, in its essence, a liturgical life.

Such, in briefest outline, was the development of the monastic order in Europe at the epoch when life began to return to the deserted or decaying *monasteria* of England.

CHAPTER III

THE MONASTIC REVIVAL UNDER DUNSTAN AND KING EDGAR: THE *REGULARIS CONCORDIA*

I

The beginning of the monastic revival in England, which set in being a life that was destined to endure till the Dissolution of the monasteries six hundred years later, may be dated from the year *c.* 943, when King Edmund, after his narrow escape from death on the cliffs of Cheddar, set Dunstan, still a young man, as "abbot" in the church of Glastonbury. From that moment till the final suppression in 1539 an unbroken series of generations lived the regular life and formed a sequence of tradition which, while accepting elements from without, remained in its essentials one and the same. That moment, therefore, has been chosen as the starting-point of the narrative of these pages.[1]

In order to understand the significance of Dunstan's life at Glastonbury and its consequences it is necessary to know how far, if at all, monastic

[1] The principal sources for the narrative of events are: the Lives of St Dunstan and other documents printed by Stubbs in *Memorials of St Dunstan* (1874), especially the earliest *Vita auctore B*; the *Vita S. Aethelwoldi auctore Aelfrico*, printed by J. Stevenson as Appendix I to the *Chronicon de Abingdon*, vol. II (1858); the *Vita S. Oswaldi auctore anonymo* [most probably Byrhtferth], printed by J. Raine in *Historians of the Church of York*, I, 399 *seqq.*; the account of the foundation and building of New Minster, written by a monk of the house *c.* 990, and printed by W. de G. Birch in the *Hyde Liber Vitae* (Hampshire Record Society, 1892), 3 *seqq.*; Aelfric's *Letter* to the monks of Eynsham, edited by Mary Bateson in Dean Kitchin's *Obedientiary Rolls of St Swithun's* (Hampshire Record Society, 1892), 173 *seqq.*; and finally, the *Regularis Concordia*. The last-named document, first printed by Dom Clement Reyner as one of the *pièces justificatives* of his *Apostolatus Benedictinorum in Anglia* (Douai, 1626), Appendix, 77 *seqq.*, was reprinted thence at the beginning of vol. I of the *Monasticon Anglicanum* (ed. Caley, Ellis and Bandinel), and in Migne, *PL*, CXXXVII. It was critically edited by W. S. Logeman from B.M. Cott. Tib. A 3 in *Anglia*, Neue Folge, I, together with the interlinear Old English text, but no editor has made use of the only other manuscript known to exist, B.M. Cott. Faustina, B 3. Dom Thomas Symons has long had in preparation a complete edition; in default of this, references are given to the Proem and chapters and pages as in Reyner. Almost the only recent work of value on the religious history of the period is the series of studies which were a happy consequence of Dr J. Armitage Robinson's residence at Wells as Dean. Those used most often in these pages are: *The Saxon Bishops of Wells* (Brit. Acad. Supplementary Papers, no. 4, 1919); *St Oswald and the Church of Worcester* (*ibid.* no. 5, 1919); *Somerset Historical Essays* (printed at Oxford for the Brit. Acad., 1921), nos. I, *William of Malmesbury "On the Antiquity of Glastonbury"* and II, *The Saxon Abbots of Glastonbury*; and finally, *The Times of St Dunstan* (Oxford, 1923). All these, except portions of the last, consist entirely of intricate critical disquisitions with little attempt at clarity of arrangement, and make difficult reading even for specialists; those who knew the Dean in his later years will remember how he pursued problem after problem with little taste for gathering up the threads into a connected whole; readers, however, who have the patience to turn the pages again and again will find their understanding of the period immensely deepened by the findings of his clear mind and sober judgment. It may be added that Stubbs' introduction to the *Memorials of St Dunstan* retains almost all its original value after sixty years.

life was in existence at that time there or elsewhere in England.[1] Historians of the last century were commonly agreed that at the epoch of Dunstan's boyhood and the reign of Athelstan monasticism was wholly extinct in England and that the renaissance under King Edgar was modelled wholly upon lines borrowed from abroad. More recently there has been a tendency among those who have done so much to increase our knowledge of the later Saxon period to question or modify both these general judgments. In the case of the second, we may with certain reserves accept such a revision; the sources of our knowledge, when carefully considered, make it clear that the revival had run a fruitful course for a number of years before men or ideas from overseas exercised a direct influence upon it. As regards the first, however, it seems desirable, before pronouncing any opinion, to pass in review all the evidence that is available.

We may begin by limiting the scope of our enquiry. In the century that passed between the death of St Wilfrid and the first Scandinavian invasions the number of monastic houses in almost every habitable part of England was very considerable. Besides the large and celebrated monasteries of Northumbria, of Kent, of Mercia and of Wessex the land, especially in the north and in the Thames valley, was covered with small *monasteriola* in which at one time or another the regular life had been at least nominally introduced. But by the beginning of the tenth century the invasions and settlements of the Danes, and the general collapse of civilization, had caused the disappearance of many of these. Those north of the fenland had disappeared entirely; only in the case of Lindisfarne, whose community migrated first to Chester-le-Street and then to Durham, was there any later claim to a continuity of life, and whatever elements of truth there may have been in the claim it does not concern us here, for Durham never fell within the sphere of the revival of the tenth century. There remain therefore to be accounted for the monasteries of southern Mercia, the very numerous houses, large and small, of Wessex, including those of the Thames valley, and the Kentish group. What was their condition in the reign of Alfred?

Our knowledge of the general state of England and of similar periods on the Continent would suggest that many or all of the smaller houses had disappeared, and that of the larger many had fallen into secular hands while in others the level of regular life had fallen so low as to be scarcely recognizable any longer as monastic. Such an assumption is borne out by what records have survived. In a well-known passage King Alfred states that he cannot call to mind a single man south of the Thames who, in the year 871, was able to follow the Mass in Latin or translate a letter from that language into English. This alone would go far to show that any monastic life that might still exist was only a shadow of what had been;

---

1 For the evidence on which the conclusions of the following paragraphs are based, see Appendix I, *Evidence for the disappearance of the monastic life in England before 943.*

we have more precise information from Alfred's biographer, Asser, who tells us that when Alfred decided to add to his good works by founding two monasteries, one of men and the other of women, he was forced to seek both abbot and community from abroad. Asser adds that he did this because the regular life had utterly died out in England, and none of noble or free birth would embark upon it; Alfred therefore not only collected a community from abroad under John the Old Saxon, but even brought children from overseas to be trained for the succession, and it is noteworthy that he made the settlement, not on the site of any previous monastery or near one of the chief centres of Wessex life, but on the island of Athelney. With such a beginning, and with the internal dissensions of which Asser gives us a glimpse, it is perhaps not surprising that Athelney did not flourish when its founder was no more. Whether it continued in existence as a corporate body till the days of Edgar is not clear; in any case it had no formative influence over Dunstan and his companions. A second foundation contemplated by Alfred was carried out by his son Edward in the New Minster at Winchester and, like Athelney, was ruled by one of the foreign scholars whom Alfred had summoned to his side, Grimbald of St Bertin, but it is not altogether clear that this foundation was fully monastic, and in any case it had ceased to have any monastic character many years before the revival.[1] Thus all available evidence from the reign of Alfred points to a complete collapse of monasticism by the end of the ninth century.

The statements of those who wrote a century later are still more explicit. All assert the complete material ruin of the monasteries and the disappearance of the regular life, and point to Glastonbury and Abingdon as the first houses of the revival. The reader will find their evidence set out in full on another page; its cumulative force is very great. It has indeed been argued that these writers share the enthusiasm of all who write after a reform and exaggerate in every way the evils that preceded it.[2] This is certainly true of the later Anglo-Norman historians who describe the conditions before the Conquest, but they are the spokesmen of an alien tradition which had been deliberately superimposed upon the old;

---

1 Grimbald was certainly *sacerdos et monachus* (Asser, *De Rebus Gestis Aelfredi*, § 78), but the Lotharingian reform had not yet reached St Bertin, and it is probable that even there the life was that of regular clerks rather than monks. At the New Minster he presumably organized a regular, liturgical life—he was *cantator optimus*—with nothing specifically monastic in it. Cf. the words of the *Liber Vitae* of Hyde (p. 5): "Grimbaldum... huic loco asciuit [rex Eaduuardus] ex monasterio quod nuncupatur Taruuanense.... Qui... clericorum hujus [loci] prelatus congregationi sancte conversationis indesinenter dans operam verbis operibusque eximiam vitam agebat monasticam." As W. H. Stevenson noted (*Asser*, ed. Stevenson, 310), Grimbald is described as a "Mass priest" in his obit in the *Chronicle*, *s.a.* 903 [A], though his name is immediately preceded by that of an Irish abbot, and he does not appear among the abbots in the *Liber Vitae* of Hyde. Will. Malmesb., *GP*, 173, records the tradition that Grimbald's community was one of canons [i.e. secular clerks].

2 So, e.g., Robinson, *Times of St Dunstan*, 116.

the writers of the generation that followed Dunstan have no animus against the past in England, and in any case no such charge can be made against the prologue to the *Regularis Concordia*.

It remains to check the statements of writers by the facts concerning individual houses so far as they can be ascertained. As is well known, the first half of the tenth century is one of the darkest of all periods of English history; the *Chronicle* is almost silent and there are no contemporary historians or biographers; the charters, in many cases clearly untrustworthy as they stand, have not as yet been subjected to adequate criticism as a whole. Any conclusions are therefore somewhat tentative, but when examined one by one, the number of houses concerned is smaller than might have been supposed, for there is clearly no need to investigate the history of those known to have existed in the past which had no revival under Dunstan. There remain those refounded on old monastic sites, or which in after years claimed an unbroken life. Of many of these we have precise information. The case of Glastonbury itself will be considered shortly; almost certainly it was a church of clerks in the possession of the king. Worcester, as has recently been shown, was not a monastic church at all before the days of St Oswald;[1] at Evesham the domestic tradition was that monks had been replaced by clerks under King Edmund, but probably monastic life had ceased considerably before that date.[2] Abingdon was in the king's hands with its buildings in ruins;[3] so was Bath, for it was given either by Athelstan or his successor to an exiled body from abroad.[4] Of the state of Malmesbury under Athelstan there is apparently no trustworthy record, but the great historian of the house states as a matter admitting of no dispute that Dunstan refounded it by ejecting the clerics set there by King Edwig.[5] This, in default of any other account, may be accepted as true, with the modification that the clerks had probably been there for many decades before Edwig. As for the Winchester monasteries, they were certainly held by clerks, as were Milton, Chertsey and Cerne;[6] St Albans is given by the biographer of St Oswald as one of the houses from which clerics were expelled,[7] and they were certainly in possession of Christ Church, Canterbury, whatever may have been the previous history of that establishment. Indeed, the only important monastery of

---

1 This is the conclusion of Robinson, *St Oswald and the Church of Worcester*, and it has been fully endorsed, after further examination, by Sir Ivor Atkins in his article *The Church of Worcester from the Eighth to the Twelfth Century* in *The Antiquaries Journal*, XVII, 4 (Oct. 1937), 371–91.

2 *Chron. Evesh.* 77.

3 *Vita S. Aethelwoldi*, 257. Cf. F. M. Stenton, *The Early History of the Abbey of Abingdon*, 7: "It is evident that there was no real continuity between the abbey of the eighth century and the house over which Ethelwold presided as abbot." *Ibid.* 38: "At Abingdon, in Aethelstan's reign...there was no monastery."

4 *Folcwini Gesta Abbatum S. Bertini*, ap. Pertz, *MGH, SS*, XIII, 629.

5 Will. Malmesb., *Vita S. Dunstani*, in *Memorials*, 301–2.

6 For Winchester, Chertsey and Milton, *v. Chronicle*, s.a. 964 [A].

7 So at least Eadmer, *Vita S. Oswaldi* (*Hist. York*), II, 21–2. In any case, we know from the early anonymous *Life* that St Albans was in the king's hands *en disponibilité* (*ibid.* I, 427).

which we have no information is St Augustine's, Canterbury. It is known to have existed as a corporate body at the time, and to have received a gift from Athelstan on the very day of his coronation;[1] how far it was monastic cannot be said, but it would seem that there, and there alone, is it possible that some form of the regular life still persisted. To this positive evidence may be added the absence of any reference to a monk of any existing body as either opposing or assisting the revival.

Against this supposition of a total cessation of regular life there are a few considerations which might seem to tell the other way. Asser himself in the passage quoted above vouches for the existence of many monasteries, though indeed without the full regular life, and Alfred, so he informs us, gave a fourth of his receipts in taxes to monasteries other than those of Athelney and Shaftesbury.[2] The names of many abbots, both of the houses mentioned above and others, survive as signatories to charters and can be shown to be historical personages who attended King Athelstan at home and abroad; moreover, charters of gifts to various monasteries in the early tenth century are not uncommon. When looked at more closely, however, this evidence is less significant than might seem at first glance. It is hard to point to a single charter of gift of the early tenth century which contains references to monks and is at the same time wholly trustworthy; as for the words "abbot" and "monastery", they had already had such a strange history both in England and western Europe in general for more than two centuries that it is unsafe to build any argument upon them for the existence of monastic life.[3]

Of more significance is the mention of a number of bishops who were monks in Dunstan's early manhood, and who helped to guide him and his friends. Among Dunstan's own relatives were Athelm of Wells and Canterbury and Aelfheah of Winchester, and a similar place in Oswald's history is taken by his uncle Oda of Canterbury. Oda need not detain us, for the same source that tells us that he was a monk informs us that he became one at Fleury when already archbishop;[4] clearly, therefore, whatever may have been the obligations privately undertaken by Oda, he was not a monk, still less an English monk, in the full sense of the word. The other two (and other earlier and less definite figures) cause more difficulty; it was assumed by later writers such as William of Malmesbury that they were monks of Glastonbury and the assumption has been repeated by

1 See the interesting discussions in Robinson, *Saxon Bishops of Wells*, 31–2, and *Times of St Dunstan*, 66.

2 Asser, § 102: "Quartam [partem] circum finitimis in omni Saxonia et Mercia monasteriis."

3 From Carolingian times to the present day the title of abbot has been constantly secularized or used purely by "courtesy", as in the French Church in modern times. In origin this was due to the system of *Eigenkirchen*, by which the words *abbas, abbatia* were transferred from the spiritual office to the material property and its owner.

4 *Vita S. Oswaldi (Hist. York)*, I, 413. Oda was bishop of Ramsbury in 927 at latest, and Fleury was not reformed till c. 930.

historians of our day.[1] We cannot say that it is impossible; if so, then presumably these men were individuals who endeavoured to realize throughout life ideals that others neglected. But it would seem far more probable that the monastic profession in early tenth-century England had come to be regarded as an act of private devotion, comparable to the undertaking of consecrated virginity in the early Church.

It would appear, therefore, that we are justified in regarding England in the reign of Athelstan as being wholly without any organized monastic life. The majority of the old houses were either in ruins, or occupied by clerks who performed the liturgy and instructed children who were to succeed them. A glimpse of one such semi-monastic community is given us in Athelstan's undoubtedly genuine charter to the "monastery" of Crediton in 930. The house is spoken of as a monastery (*ergasterium*) and the brethren (*fratres*), who are also the *familia* of the bishop, have common inalienable possessions and a common board-fund (*mensa*), but the place is clearly not a regular monastery.[2] The abbots who appear as signatories of charters were ecclesiastics to whom the "monasteries" had been given by the king; in some cases they may even have been laymen, though there are few clear instances of this.[3] The monastic profession and consecration survived mainly as a personal vow of celibacy and devotion, though without a doubt news of the revivals in Lorraine and Burgundy was brought to the English court in Athelstan's later years by foreigners and English travellers, and had its influence as well on older men as on the young Dunstan and others of his circle.

II

The change from this condition of things was due in origin to a single individual. Few great Englishmen have been more harshly treated at the hands of later generations than Dunstan; it is only within recent years that he has been hailed, perhaps without due discrimination, as a great statesman and one of the first welders of national unity, and his recognition as a saint and as a spiritual leader of his countrymen has been still more tardy. The character of this eminent man, in whom were combined so many varied gifts of mind and spirit, has not seldom in the past been the object of travesty, and not all recent attempts to redress the balance have been entirely felicitous.[4] Perhaps it is best to acquiesce in the judgment of

1 Will. Malmesb., *Vita S. Dunstani* (*Memorials*, 258); Robinson, *Times of St Dunstan*, 83.

2 *Crawford Charters*, ed. A. S. Napier and W. H. Stevenson (*Anecdota Oxoniensia*, Med. and Mod. Series, VII, 1895), no. IV. The date is 29 April 930, and the charter states that it was signed in the presence of many "abbots". None of the witnesses, however, use this style.

3 For a possible example see Robinson, *Saxon Bishops of Wells*, 43. The *Concordia* specifically alludes to the practice as common in England: Proem, 78: "Saecularium vero Prioratuum [*sc.* monasteriorum], ne ad magni ruinam detrimenti, uti olim acciderat, etc."

4 The fantastic pronouncements of Milman may be read in Stubbs' introduction to *Memorials*, cxviii, but as recently as 1906 Dunstan was described as "throughout life a man

one of the greatest of those who have written of him, and renounce all attempt at detailed characterization.[1] Intimate materials for such a description are indeed almost wholly wanting; from the sources we can obtain a glimpse, and a glimpse only, of a many-sided nature of great flexibility and power, inspiring others, and admired, loved, venerated— hated also, and opposed—by them; in it, so far as we can see it, there is a strong family resemblance, alike in the strength and the sweetness, to Alfred, but we have no words of Dunstan to mirror his mind for us, however fitfully, as do Alfred's writings. We can only note that throughout his life from early manhood his ability made him an outstanding figure in the life of the kingdom, and that throughout life, side by side with this, went a reputation for learning which the most learned man of his day, Abbo of Fleury, endorsed,[2] and a name for creative genius of a high order in an age when masterpieces of art were being produced in England; that as friend of the ladies Aethelfleda and Aethelwin, his seniors, as teacher at Glastonbury, as an active archbishop of Canterbury and as an old man he had always the power of winning others and of inspiring them. To his ability as statesman something like justice has been done, but it was not this, but a sense of contact with a sanctity at once admirable and lovable, that gave Dunstan his unique position in the eyes of those who knew him, and it was this that enabled him to initiate, to inspire and to organize the new monachism of England.

Dunstan was born near Glastonbury about the year 909.[3] He was connected with the royal family and had among his near relations men who filled the sees of Wells, Winchester and Canterbury. He received at Glastonbury itself the elements of his very considerable and varied culture. That venerable shrine, then a collection of small and irregular buildings in its island valley surrounded by slow streams and meres, attracted many pilgrims, especially from Ireland, who came to visit the tombs reputed to contain relics of St Patrick and St Bridget. It had been a monastery, first Celtic and then Saxon, but it would appear that monastic life had by now ceased to exist and that some kind of clerical family served the church; there were no monastic buildings, but a considerable library remained from earlier times, and doubtless many traditions of the past.[4] Here the young Dunstan studied and was tonsured, receiving also books and in-

---

of nervous, perhaps even of hysterical temperament. . .a man who saw visions and dreamed dreams" (T. Hodgkin, *Political History of England to 1066*, p. 366), and even Robinson refers to him as "this dreamy youth" (*Times of St Dunstan*, 84).

1 Stubbs, *op. cit.* introd., cxvii.

2 *V.* the letter and poems of Abbo to Dunstan in *Memorials*, 378, 410.

3 This date, instead of the traditional 925, was suggested by L. A. St L. Toke in *The Bosworth Psalter* (appendix), and established by Robinson, *Saxon Bishops of Wells*, 28 *seqq.*

4 His biographer "B" speaks of the *multa voluminum prata* in which Dunstan found pasturage at Glastonbury, as also the books of the Irish (*Memorials*, 10–11). William of Malmesbury, who knew the place well, speaks of *librorum pulchritudo et antiquitas* there (*Gesta Pontificum*, 196).

struction from the Irish whom we know from other sources to have visited the court of Athelstan. To this court he was commended soon after 925 by his uncle Athelm, whom he had followed to Canterbury, and while there fell under the influence of another kinsman, Aelfheah "the monk", who became c. 934 bishop of Winchester. Unfortunately it is impossible to be certain as to his movements in these early years, still less do we know the influences and motives that worked upon him, and the causes of the hostility with which he met. Aelfheah urged him to become a monk, but Dunstan had thoughts of marriage, and it was only a severe illness that decided him to send for the bishop and receive the monastic consecration.[1] After this, we find him as a chaplain of the bishop at Winchester, where he was ordained priest on the same day as his friend Ethelwold, but he seems also to have lived at Glastonbury, teaching those who came to him, ministering to the Lady Aethelfleda, and himself following something of the monastic way of life.[2] On Athelstan's death in 939 Dunstan became counsellor in attendance on King Edmund; he had enemies, and the king had decided to exile him. It was at this crisis that the incident occurred on the summit of Cheddar gorge. The king, faced with death when pursuing a stag, repented of his action; returning in safety, he sent for Dunstan, took him to Glastonbury, set him in the abbot's chair and promised to endow the house as a regular monastery. Clearly some such proposal must have been long debated, but we know nothing of what led up to it. From that day, however, in 943 or 944, dates the beginning of a great revival; it was, as has been justly said, a decisive moment in the history of religion in England.[3] Dunstan built a monastery, gathered disciples and gave them a rule of life based fully on the Rule of St Benedict.[4] The Rule itself, and perhaps some early Uses such as the *Ordo qualiter*, may well have been in the library at Glastonbury, and Dunstan had had opportunities of meeting those who had seen foreign houses, but every indication goes to show that in the early days at Glastonbury the particular shape taken by the life was due to its abbot, and we know that in exile his memory went fondly back to the fervour of those times.[5] National tradition, his own inclination and the absolute necessities of the time led him to give within the monastery the fullest and widest education possible, and he was fortunate in attracting a group of disciples of exceptional promise.

1 *Vita auctore B*, 14: "Tunc festinanter...ad se pontificem...vocavit...at ille visitando veniens consolatum et emendatum Deo monachum consecravit."
2 It is to this period that the construction of his "cell", if a genuine tradition, must be attributed.
3 Robinson, *Times of St Dunstan*, 85: "It was a turning point in the history of religion in England."
4 *Vita*, 25: "Saluberrimam sancti Benedicti sequens institutionem...primum scepta claustrorum monasticis ædificiis cæterisque inmunitionibus...munivit." For the condition of Glastonbury before 943 see Appendix II, *Glastonbury in 943*.
5 *Vita*, 35: "Constitutus in exsilio meminit quantam religionis celsitudinem in monasterio dereliquit."

Among these was Ethelwold, a man of about the same age, or perhaps somewhat younger, of distinguished birth and a native of Winchester. Like Dunstan, he had been first at Athelstan's court and then a disciple of Aelfheah, who ordained the two friends on the same day; afterwards, he followed Dunstan to Glastonbury, where he learned from him letters and divinity and became a monk.[1] There is more than one indication that Ethelwold was throughout life of a more austere and intransigent temper than Dunstan;[2] either for this or for some other reason which we cannot ascertain he became dissatisfied with Glastonbury and proposed to go overseas, presumably to Fleury. The queen-mother, Edith, however, prevailed with King Edred not to let such a brilliant subject leave the realm, and something of a compromise was effected, by which Ethelwold was given the derelict monastery of Abingdon to restore, taking with him, among others, three clerks from Glastonbury. This took place perhaps in 954.

We have no information as to how this move was regarded by Dunstan. He had been a chosen counsellor of King Edred, and a considerable portion of the royal treasures and archives was lodged at Glastonbury, but when, on Edred's death, Edwig succeeded, intrigues were set on foot which led to Dunstan's banishment, and in all probability Abingdon was deprived of most, if not all, of its lands. Dunstan found refuge first with Arnulf, count of Flanders, and then at the recently reformed monastery of Blandinium at Ghent. Here, for the first time, he was able to breathe the atmosphere of the vigorous continental monasticism, with its traditions of Charlemagne and Benedict of Aniane, its many relationships and its recent saints; although it seemed to him at times that all his work had been undone, his deeper conviction of final success never failed, and the foreign experience was to bear fruit in the years to come.

Recalled in 957 by Edgar, Edwig's brother, who had been set up as king of Mercia, Dunstan was consecrated bishop and given the administration of Worcester and later also of London; in 959 Edgar became king of Wessex also, and Dunstan became archbishop of Canterbury, vacant since the death of Oda "the good" in 958, and the king's principal adviser. Abingdon flourished once more, and Ethelwold, soon to be given the see of Winchester, had sent his trusted disciple Osgar to Fleury[3]

---

1 *Vita S. Aethelwoldi auct. Aelfrico (Chron. Abingd.* II), 257: "Didicit inibi grammaticam artem et metricam, et libros divinos... tandem monastici ordinis habitum ab ipso suscepit."

2 E.g. *Vita S. Aethelwoldi, loc. cit.*: "Fratres [at Glaston] semper ad ardua exhortans" [with reference to bodily austerities]; *ibid.* 262: "stultos verberibus corrigendo: eratque terribilis ut leo inobedientibus"; also Aelfric in his letter to the monks of Eynsham, 175, says he dare not tell them all he learnt in the years he was Ethelwold's disciple: "ne forte fastidientes districtionem tantae observantiae nec saltem velitis auditum praebere". His reason for going abroad (*Vita*, 257) was "se imbuendi...monasticis disciplinis perfectius", and a tradition survived that as bishop he contemplated retirement to the quasi-hermitage of Thorney (Will. Malmesb., *GP*, 327). Cf. also the allusion to him as "magnus Atheluoldus...boanerges [= son of thunder]" in the *Benedictional of St Aethelwold*, 4 verso.

3 *Vita S. Aethelwoldi*, 259: "Misit Osgarum monachum trans mare ad monasterium Sancti Benedicti Floriacense, ut mores regulares illic disceret."

and summoned monks from Corbie to give authority and unanimity to the method and practice of the ceremonial and chant.[1]

Meanwhile a third leader had come to join the two friends. Oswald, born of Danish family, was closely related to two archbishops, the saintly Oda and Oskytel of York. Probably he was considerably younger than Dunstan, for although he too as a young priest was at Winchester as head of one of the houses of "noble clerks" in the city, there is no mention of Bishop Aelfheah or of early acquaintance with Dunstan and Ethelwold, and his experience in the city was wholly discouraging.[2] Anxious for a more perfect life, he was sent by his uncle, Oda, to Fleury perhaps about the year 950; there he remained till 958, when the archbishop recalled him though he did not live to greet his return. At Fleury he would have known Osgar of Abingdon, and other young Englishmen were there also, among them Germanus of Winchester, who had followed Oswald. On his return he went to Oskytel at York, but Dunstan came to know him and, in 961, persuaded Edgar to give him the see of Worcester.[3] At once Oswald sent for Germanus from Fleury and settled him, with some disciples from Worcester, in a small establishment at Westbury-on-Trym near Bristol.

With three monastic bishops of outstanding ability thus in power, a great forward movement was made possible, and the character of the young king, only sixteen years old in 959, made him an active agent in the work. Edgar, as all his contemporaries agree,[4] was a man of ability and energy and his reign marks an important epoch in English history. He was besides devoted to religion, and his inborn zeal of temperament was stimulated by Ethelwold, who had exercised great influence over him from his early years. Before his accession he had, it would seem, made some kind of promise to restore Abingdon,[5] and as king he co-operated in every way with the three bishops, giving land for the foundation of monasteries both upon ancient sites and elsewhere. In one respect, indeed, he seems to have taken the initiative or, at the least, to have sponsored with enthusiasm a design of Ethelwold. Hitherto the monastic foundations had been made without the disturbance of vested interests, but the bishop of

---

1 *Chron. Abingd.* I, 129.

2 *Vita auct. anon.* (*Hist. York*), I, 410–11: "Monasterium quod est in Wintonia positum acquisivit, donando digno pretio.... Fulgebat quotidie in sericis vestibus, et epulabatur per singulos soles splendide."

3 His biographer emphasizes Dunstan's initiative, *op. cit.* 420: "sicut Christus negantem discipulum benigno respectu intuitus est, sic supremus episcopus humilem Oswaldum".

4 Cf. the poems in the *Chronicle, s.a.* 973–5 [A], the enthusiastic words of Oswald's biographer, *op. cit.* 425, and above all the tribute of the Hyde annalist, *Liber Vitae,* 7: "Eadgarus vir strenuissimus nemini priorum in temporali gloria vel divinitatis amore secundus."

5 For this incident, *v.* Cockayne, *Leechdoms,* III, 433 *seq.,* where it is related in a "postscript" to an English translation of the Rule. Robinson discusses the passage at length in *Times of St Dunstan,* 159 *seqq.* Ethelwold's early influence over Edgar is referred to in the Proem of the *Concordia,* 77: "Abbate quodam assiduo monente, ac regiam Catholicae fidei viam demonstrante, coepit [rex] magnopere Deum timere, diligere ac venerari."

Winchester was unwilling to tolerate the presence of clerks of irregular life in the cathedral and in King Edward's New Minster at the principal city of the kingdom. At the king's command, and by the agency of one of his principal ministers, Wulfstan of Dalham, the clerks were expelled from the cathedral and replaced by monks from Abingdon. A vivid account of the incident is given us by the great Aelfric himself, in his biography of his master Ethelwold. It took place on the afternoon of Saturday, the first in Lent, 21 February 964. The monks, waiting outside the church for the Mass to end, heard the clerks within singing the words of the Communion: "Serve the Lord with fear, and rejoice unto Him with trembling: get you discipline, lest ye perish from the right way." They took the text as an omen, and entered; the clerks were given the alternative of becoming monks or departing; all left, but three afterwards returned to join the new society.[1] This action has brought upon the memory of Ethelwold the severe judgments of modern writers, and even the latest historian of the reign of Edgar has shown himself chary of reversing them, though he pointed out with justice that to contemporaries Edgar, not Ethelwold, appeared as primarily responsible for the step.[2] Probably most English historians of the past have been swayed, at least unconsciously, by memories of persecution in the sixteenth century and of the dignified and gracious aspect of the cathedral close at Winchester in more recent times, but indeed the measure, if its causes and consequences are studied in contemporary documents, needs no elaborate defence.[3] The expulsion of clerks from the New Minster was effected in the next year, and followed by similar action in other places throughout the country.

In the years that immediately followed the number of monastic foundations steadily grew. As the narrative will have shown, they sprang from three distinct centres, Glastonbury, Abingdon and Westbury, each the work of one of the three bishops, and each with traditions of its own.

1 *Vita S. Aethelwoldi*, 260–1.

2 Robinson, *Times of St Dunstan*, 114: "We cannot acquit Ethelwold of responsibility for what appears to us high-handed action." Elsewhere (*ibid.* 44) he writes, very justly: "We can hardly say it [the expulsion] was unjustified, if what we are told of the clergy whom he found there is not a gross exaggeration." The *Chronicle*, *s.a.* 964 [A], has simply "Her dræfde Eadgar cyng þa preostas....꜓ sette hy mid munecan", whereas the [E] text *s.a.* 963 has "[Athelwold] draf út þa clerca of þe biscoprice". The Hyde account, *Liber Vitae*, 7, has: "extirpatis uitiorum tribulis, inertem nobilium clericorum turbam penitus eliminauit [Eadgarus]"; and the Proem to the *Concordia*, 77: "eiectisque negligentium clericorum spurcitiis...monachos...constituit [rex]". The personal responsibility of Edgar is thus made abundantly clear, but Oswald's biographer is doubtless right in assigning the initiative to Ethelwold, *op. cit.* 427: "Iste [*sc.* Ethelwold]...regem ad hoc maxime provocavit, ut clericos a monasteriis expulit [*sic*]...Relinquam erga sua beata gesta suis, etc."

3 For the misdemeanours of the clerks, besides the passages quoted in the last note, see the explicit testimony of Aelfric, *Vita S. Aethelwoldi*, 260: "Erant...malemorigerati clerici, elatione et insolentia ac luxuria praeventi, adeo ut nonnulli eorum dedignarentur Missas suo ordine celebrare; repudiantes uxores (quas illicite duxerant) et alias accipientes, gulae et ebrietati jugiter dediti." Cf. also the interesting anecdote concerning Eadsig, one of the expelled, in Aelfric's life of St Swithun in *Aelfric's Lives of the Saints*, ed. Skeat (EETS, 1881), I, 443–5. But these sources are, of course, "hostile".

Dunstan's group, we may suppose, had the simplest, most fully English practice; Ethelwold's, perhaps more austere in discipline, had elements borrowed from Fleury and Corbie; Oswald's was a pure reproduction of Fleury. The leaders, no longer able to exercise continuous supervision, were alike concerned for the future of their own establishments and apprehensive of the possibility of rivalry or schism, and their anxiety was shared by the king. At length it was decided to establish in common a way of life that all should follow, and to put the whole body, as well of men as of women, under the direct patronage of the king and queen. The suggestion of such an action may well have come from Oswald;[1] the means by which it was accomplished and its scope bears every mark of Dunstan's statesmanship; the actual instrument of union was the work of Ethelwold.

The meeting at which unity was attained took place at Winchester. Besides the bishops and abbots, the abbesses were also present, and it is possible that the occasion was the great Easter gathering of all the notables of the kingdom described so fully by Oswald's biographer.[2] We are ignorant of the precise date, but it must have been in the neighbourhood of the year 970. The procedure, and the form taken by the provisions of the synod, were modelled closely upon those of the meeting at Aachen under Louis the Pious and Benedict of Aniane in 817; and here again the character and continental relationships of the archbishop point to him as the one who thus consciously reproduced the past. Besides the English ecclesiastics, monks from Fleury and Ghent, personifying the two great foreign schools of monasticism, were at Winchester to give their advice,[3] and the outcome was the code bearing the comprehensive title *Regularis Concordia Anglicae nationis monachorum sanctimonialiumque*, which all the heads of houses present undertook to observe.[4]

III

The *Regularis Concordia* consists of a moderately long preface, setting out the reasons for the meeting at Winchester, its method of working and some of its particular resolutions, together with some recommendations made by Dunstan and approved by the king; this is followed by a series of chapters of varying length, giving in detail the liturgical functions of the day and year and the duties of some (but not all) of the monastic officials. It ends with elaborate prescriptions for the ceremonies and

1 So, at least, seems clear to me from the narrative in the *Vita S. Oswaldi*, 425.

2 The Proem to the *Concordia* (p. 77) gives us the facts: "Rex...Synodale Concilium Wintoniae fieri decreuit"; and notes the presence of bishops, abbots and abbesses. Cf. *Vita S. Oswaldi*, 425 *seqq.*

3 *Concordia*, Proem, 78: "Accitis Florensis Beati Benedicti, nec non præcipui cœnobii, quod celebri Ghent nuncupatur vocabulo, monachis."

4 *Ibid.*: "Unanimes voverunt, pactoque spirituali confirmaverunt, se vita comite...has adnotatas morum consuetudines communi palam custodire conuersatione."

suffrages connected with the death of a monk, and with a short postscript (contained only in one of the two surviving manuscripts) freeing the monasteries from the *heriot* due to the king at the death of owners of extensive property. The bulk of the document is therefore based on existing customaries; such parts as are original are written in the stilted Latin of the epoch, with a sprinkling of Greek forms in Latin dress, and the whole, though at first glance logically planned, abounds in repetitions, dropped threads, and paragraphs which appear to have been inserted without reference to the sequence of ideas, and in consequence it only yields all its information after careful and repeated inspection.

The explicit statement of Aelfric assigns the compilation to Ethelwold,[1] and from the text itself we can gather what were some of its antecedents and sources. All those acquainted with early medieval writings of any kind are aware how seldom they are entirely original; even the parts that on a first view seem wholly personal or occasional are found to be based upon writings of an earlier date. This is particularly the case with regard to legislation of any kind, and we should be prepared to find that very few of the prescriptions of the *Concordia* are due to Ethelwold or his assistants. It is beyond our province to examine all the sources here; the task has been accomplished in part, but is made more difficult by the disappearance of the customaries of Fleury and Ghent which we should expect to have been the documents used most frequently. Besides this, the medieval practice of copying phrases and sentences right and left from existing writings makes it exceedingly difficult, in such an amalgam as the *Concordia*, to distinguish between direct citations and family relationships, for all the Uses of western Europe were fundamentally similar. Speaking generally, traces of direct influence from Cluniac and Lotharingian Uses are frequent, and of the two the latter predominate. Besides these more recent sources, the compilers had before them the old monastic Use, common to all the West from the beginning of the ninth century, known as the *Ordo qualiter*, together with the *Rule for Canons* and *capitula* of Aachen.[2] It is clear from the preface that the synod made use also of the letters of Gregory the Great to Augustine preserved by Bede and of the *Regula Monachorum* of Isidore of Seville.[3]

The basis therefore of the monastic life of the English revival was the

---

1 *Letter to monks of Eynsham*, ed. M. Bateson, 175: "lib[er] consuetudinum quem sanctus athelwoldus uuintoniensis episcopus cum coepiscopis et abbatibus...undique collegit ac monachis instituit obseruandum." The Proem to the *Concordia*, it may be noted, while referring to Dunstan by name as *egregius hujus patriae Archiepiscopus*, refers to Ethelwold obliquely as *Abbas quidam*. In spite of this, the code was later attributed to Dunstan, cf. Anselm's letter (1, 31) to Lanfranc asking for a copy.

2 *V.* article *The Regularis Concordia* by Dom Thomas Symons in *DR*, XL (Jan. 1922), 15 *seqq.* Mary Bateson, in an article *Rules for Monks*, etc., in *EHR*, IX (1894), 690–708, signalized the presence of at least three MSS of the *Ordo qualiter* and four of the *Epitome Ludovici* in England *c.* 970.

3 *Concordia*, Proem, 78: "Sanctique patroni nostri Gregorii documenta...recolentes... [and a little later] ut beatus Isidorus hortatur."

normal use of western Europe, inherited in part, perhaps, from the traditions of Glastonbury and other English churches but chiefly through information and training received from Fleury and Ghent. In other words, the life, now set fully on a level with contemporary monasticism abroad, was primarily liturgical and claustral, and contained the accretions of psalmody and vocal prayer, together with the elaborate execution of the chant, that had become normal in Europe. Neither Dunstan nor his colleagues had any intention either of innovation or of returning to the distant past. The chief office of the monks was to be the solemn liturgy of the Church and intercession; the time for work that remained was in practice given to teaching, writing, illuminating and craftwork, though these are not mentioned explicitly in the *Concordia*. Nothing in the code suggests that any attempt was made to reproduce the simpler outline of the Rule or the missionary activities of the Celtic monasteries of the north. Any such ideas, indeed, would have been alien to the age. The monastic life to the English reformers as to their foreign contemporaries was not primarily a state in which the individual with a "special vocation" might devote himself wholly to God and receive guidance from a master of the spiritual life. It was rather a perfection of the clerical life and a discipline for the many, by which individuals might find salvation and the Church as a whole receive strength, dignity and order.

But though the *Concordia* differs little from other European customaries of the epoch there are a few provisions in which allusion is made to English practice. Thus a fire is allowed in a special room in winter, and the monks may work in shelter instead of in the cloister when the weather is cold;[1] the pealing of bells is to be prolonged in the national fashion on Christmas and certain other feasts;[2] processions are assumed as taking place not in the monastic buildings only, as came to be the custom abroad, but in the streets that lay between the monastic church and one of the town churches,[3] and (a practice still more peculiar to England) it is assumed that the people will assist at the chief Mass on Sundays and feasts.[4] Equally peculiar to the *Concordia* is the exhortation to daily Communion; it is difficult to say whether this was inspired by English custom or was directly due to the initiative of Dunstan and Ethelwold, perhaps recollecting the celebrated letter of Bede the Venerable.[5]

---

1 Cap. 2, p. 84.
2 Cap. 3, p. 85: "Ad nocturnam et ad vesperam, uti ad missam, sicut in usum huius patriae indigenæ tenent, omnia signa pulsentur, nam honestos huius patriæ mores ad Dominum pertinentes, quos veterum usu didicimus, nullo modo abjicere sed undique uti diximus corroborare decrevimus."
3 *Ibid.* with reference to Candlemas procession, with the "weather permitting" clause (*si aeris permiserit temperies*). There is a description of the Rogation procession at Ramsey in *Vita S. Oswaldi*, 447.
4 Cap. 1, p. 82: "Tertia peracta, mox signorum motu fidelem advocantes plebem."
5 *Ibid.*: "Fratres quotidie...regulari studio prorsus intenti, eucharistiam accipere non renuant."

Above and beyond these lesser regulations the English monasticism was given by its founders a bent quite peculiar to itself by the intimate connection established with the national life. The recognition of king and queen as *ex officio* patrons and guardians of the whole monastic institute,[1] though in a sense it only applies to English conditions the imperial theory of the relations of Church and State, has no exact parallel in medieval monastic history, and the special prayers for Edgar and his consort said after every portion of the Office save Prime, together with the offering of the Matin Mass for the same intention, are quite peculiar to England and must have given to the intercessory prayers of all the monks and nuns a strongly national sentiment. More remarkable still is the regulation in the preface which, after laying down the canonical procedure for a free abbatial election, subject to the royal prerogative, adds that where the monastic community serves a cathedral church it shall elect (if possible from its own body) the bishop, who shall conform his life in all respects to the monastic rule.[2] The inclusion of such a decree, affecting in an essential way the English episcopate, in a purely monastic code shows what great influence the primate and his two colleagues commanded, and also the favour shown to their programme by Edgar, who was certainly a party to the measure. Its significance has not been fully recognized by historians of the Church in England; though without any parallel in the Western Church of the time it was not wholly an innovation, but was based upon a reading of the constitution set up by Gregory in his letter to Augustine, familiar to all lettered Englishmen from the frequent allusions in Bede. There is, however, a subtle difference between the new formula and the old, introduced probably not of set purpose but simply with a view to existing circumstances. The original constitution was that the bishop (*ex hypothesi* a monk) should live in common with his clerks, and that these should conform in broad outline to the regular life; the question of election did not enter in. In the *Concordia* it is assumed that the place of the clerks has been taken by a fully organized monastic community; they will therefore enjoy the monastic privilege of electing their superior, and he, when elected, must still live as a monk. Intended as a practical measure to guarantee permanence to the cathedral communities, this regulation was destined to affect in an important way the future history of the English Church. It is remarkable evidence of Dunstan's independence

---

1 Proem, 77: "Regali itaque functus officio veluti pastorum pastor solicitus...oves, quas Domini largiente gratia studiosus collegerat, muniendo [a lupis] eripuit, conjugique suae Alphridae sanctimonialium mandras, ut impavidi more custodis defenderet cautissime præcepit; ut videlicet mas maribus, femina feminis sine ullo suspicionis scrupulo subveniret."

2 Proem, 78: "Episcoporum quoque electio, uti Abbatum, ubicumque in sede Episcopali Monachi regulares conversantur...eodem modo agatur...concordi Regis et fratrum, quibus dedicari debet, consilio eligatur. Qui ordinatus videlicet Episcopus in omnibus eundem morem regularem cum Monachis suis, quem Abbas tenet regularis, diligenti cura...custodiat."

of judgment as a statesman, for Abbo of Fleury, the friend of Dunstan and Oswald, and the spokesman and leader of the monastic party in the controversies of the time abroad, while equally persuaded that salvation could only come to the Church through the victory of the monastic ideal, aimed at securing this end by complete emancipation from the diocesan organization and control.[1]

In the event, the monasticism governed by the *Concordia* came to be very different in character from the foreign model. In the past of England the monastic body had had a share in the national life without parallel elsewhere, and the characteristics of the past revived in the century before the Conquest during which Church and State in England intermingled their functions in a manner wholly unique.[2] During that century, the majority of the bishops were monks, and their presence, and that of the abbots, in the Witan, which was the supreme consultative and legislative body in matters temporal and spiritual, made the monastic body predominant in the Church. The orientation towards external, public activity given by the example of Dunstan, Ethelwold and Oswald, and continued by their successors, led to enterprises farther afield, and a stream, small perhaps in volume but none the less powerful, flowed from the monasteries of England to the Scandinavian countries, where English monks either as simple missionaries, or as bishops and royal protégés, helped to Christianize the north. On the other hand, the influence and manifold relationships of the monastic body in the country took from it much of its distinct character as an order; there was no monastic party in the country at odds with the bishops or the king, and this close connection with public, national life was doubtless one of the reasons for the relaxation of discipline which we shall note as occurring before the Norman Conquest.

Within the walls of the monasteries, also, there was a difference between England and the Continent. The close relations in the early years with Fleury, which shortly before the time of Abbo and under his influence had a tradition for learning unique among the monasteries deriving from Cluny, might have been expected to influence England, and indeed there is clear evidence, especially at Ramsey, where the exiled Abbo stayed and taught,[3] that this was the case, but the artistic work of the English monas-

---

1 For a fuller discussion of this point *v. infra*, ch. XXXVI. For Abbo, cf. the judgment of Sackur, *Die Cluniacenser*, I, 298: "Die Verteidigung des Mönchtums gegen den Episcopat war die Tendenz, die ihn beherrschte."

2 Cf. the judgment of Böhmer, *Kirche und Staat in England*, 56: "Die englische Kirche hat sich. . . viel eigentümlicher, viel nationaler, entwickelt, als die übrigen abendländischen Landeskirchen. Sie weist daher in ihrer territorialen Organization, ihrer Verfassung und in ihrem Verhältnisse zum Staate noch Zustände auf, wie sie auf dem Kontinente etwa in der Zeit den ersten Karolinger herrschten."

3 Abbo was at Ramsey from *c.* 986 to 988 when he became abbot of Fleury, but he had visited England previously, *c.* 970, and may indeed have been present at the synod of Winchester.

teries, and still more the literary work of Aelfric and others directed to those outside the walls of the monastery, has no exact parallel in the contemporary monasteries of France. The monasteries did not indeed originate the schools of illumination and decorative work which reached such a high level of creative skill in the tenth and early eleventh centuries; the skill was endemic in England, and manifested itself wherever it had favourable surroundings. The monasteries did, however, provide the soil and the fertilizing agency, and for some fifty years at least attracted to themselves and focused almost all the available talent. It is clear from a number of indications and from such surviving masterpieces as the Alfred jewel, the Durham stole and a number of illuminations that great artists were at work before the monastic revival had begun. But the foundation of the monasteries, by giving centres of peace, leisure to work, expert tuition and criticism, and a steady demand for objects of beauty and price, focused and developed the talent of the country in a way that no other institution in the society of those times could have done. In the art of illumination a number of the monasteries, and in particular the two Winchester houses, the two at Canterbury and St Albans, harboured schools of artists whose works take rank as masterpieces of creative genius, and the work in all kinds of precious materials, which became something of a national industry, would seem to have received its impetus in large part from the same sources.[1]

In the sphere of letters, the example of teaching given by Dunstan and Ethelwold made their foundations the home of all the learning possessed by England between the days of Athelstan and those of the Confessor. In the half century that elapsed after the synod at Winchester a blossoming took place at Winchester and Ramsey which must have exceeded the most sanguine expectations of the founders. At Winchester Ethelwold's pupil, Aelfric, and at Ramsey Byrhtferth, taught by the exiled Abbo, are eminent as the most learned men of their day after Abbo himself. Their achievement, and that of their lesser contemporaries, is mentioned here only in passing, to complete the outline of the picture; it will be discussed at greater length in a later chapter.

In assessing their achievement it is not easy to avoid the danger of unjust depreciation without seeming too enthusiastic in awarding praise. They were men of their period, and it was a period before the reawakening of constructive, independent thought and scientific reasoning. We look in vain to Aelfric, and more vainly still to Byrhtferth, for an original, genial idea or for any of that intellectual self-possession and clarity of criticism that comes in with Anselm and Abelard. Both Aelfric and Anselm draw deeply upon St Augustine, but while Anselm penetrates and transmutes the inmost thought of his model, Aelfric is content with translating

1 The literary and artistic work of this period will be described more fully in the second part of this work.

or paraphrasing. Yet in one respect Ethelwold's disciple, and his contemporaries who took up in the monasteries the national task of chronicling, have an absolute greatness. In the art of language, in sensitiveness to fine shades of feeling, in the matching of words to thoughts, in that style which is the echo of a noble soul Aelfric and his fellows surpass all the chroniclers and letter-writers of twelfth-century England, and anticipate by more than three centuries the achievements of the latest English prose writers of the Middle Ages.

Thus far we have considered only the external manifestations of the monastic life of the tenth century; the spiritual life that lay behind all but eludes scrutiny. Apart from the lives, all too brief, of the three great bishops, and the few anecdotes of daily life with which they provide us, we have no intimate revelation of the life of an individual or the interior of a monastery till we reach the times of Wulfstan of Worcester and Aethelwig of Evesham,[1] and no directly monastic spiritual writings at all. Here again Dunstan and his colleagues were men of their period, a period content to live on such fragments of the past as had survived, supplemented by the immediate practical teaching of a man of holy life when such could be had. Neither in legislation nor in doctrine did the framers of the *Concordia* take any step forward or add to the inheritance from the past. Their achievement was to give to Englishmen what they had almost wholly lacked for more than a century, an ordered scheme, based on the soundest traditions of the past, for a life devoted to the service of God. They gave this in an epoch which for the rest of Europe was very dark, and almost a century before the Gregorian reform and the intellectual renaissance began to transform the Western Church. The homilies of Aelfric and Wulfstan, the history of the times, and the careful researches of modern historians show us how few of the means of moral and spiritual perfection were available in England during that century; that there were any centres of light and life at all was in large part due to the work of Dunstan, Ethelwold and Oswald.

IV

The half century that followed Dunstan's recall from exile in 957 saw the growth of the monastic movement from two or three houses to what was to be all but its maximum before the Conquest. More than thirty monasteries of men and at least half a dozen important abbeys of women sprang into being, and a writer at Winchester at the end of the tenth century could speak of his country as a new Egypt.[2] Speaking very generally, all the

1 There are, however, a few intimate details in Aelfric's *Life of St Swithun*, ed. Skeat, 443–5, 451–7.
2 *Hyde Liber Vitae*, 7: "ut Anglicae nationis monachorum coetus intuenti diligentius alter uideretur Aegyptus." The phrase was a commonplace, and must not be taken too literally.

houses founded under this impulse can be divided into three groups, according as they descended directly or indirectly from the three original plantations of Glastonbury, Abingdon and Westbury and owed some kind of spiritual allegiance respectively to Dunstan, Ethelwold and Oswald, but there was no direct system of filiation as with the Norman, Cluniac and Cistercian foundations, and though the natural procedure was for a band of monks to go from an existing house to a new plantation, it was not uncommon for a group of clerks and other aspirants to be given two or three teachers, or even a single master, at a new centre.[1] The limits of a bishop's jurisdiction in England had always been somewhat in-definite, and were to become wholly so immediately before the Conquest; we need not therefore be surprised to find all three of the founders con-stantly visiting and administering their foundations even when lying far outside their own dioceses; but while Dunstan and Oswald appear to have confined themselves to a few monasteries in which they were especially interested, the activities of Ethelwold were more general, and some of his most intimate disciples are found ruling houses within what might be thought to be Glastonbury's "sphere of influence" in Wessex, or in the Avon valley in the diocese of Worcester where Oswald was paramount. As the establishments made in these years endured as the most celebrated monasteries of England for more than five centuries, it will be well to pass them briefly in review.

The beginnings of Glastonbury may be set, as we have seen, about the year 943. Ethelwold had unquestionably departed to Abingdon before Dunstan's exile, but no other foundation can with certainty be dated before his return in 957. Between the latter date and the synod of 970, Dunstan was instrumental in the revival of Malmesbury, Bath and Westminster,[2] and the plantations at Milton and Exeter, both of which received Glastonbury monks, probably occurred during this period.[3] There would seem to be no authentic account of the foundation of Muchelney, but it appears in existence in Edgar's reign; whether any kind of regular life had lingered on at Athelney cannot be ascertained, but as, together with Muchelney, it appears later in a position of quasi-dependence upon Glastonbury, these two *monasteriola* may both be reckoned as daughters of their powerful neighbour. Towards the end of Dunstan's life came the four western foundations of Cerne, Tavistock, Horton and

1 Thus Oswald set Germanus on his return from Fleury over a dozen English priests and clerics (*Vita*, 423–4), and Aelfric addresses his monks at Eynsham as "nuper...ad monachicum habitum ordinati" (ed. M. Bateson, 174).

2 For Malmesbury and Bath, *v. supra*, p. 34, notes 4 and 5. Dunstan is found as archbishop visiting Bath and Glastonbury in *Vita auctore B*, 46–7. As regards Westminster, there is no reason to doubt the statement of Will. Malmesb. (*Gest. Pont.* 178) that "Dunstanus cum esset Lundoniae episcopus [Wlfsinum] abbatem apud Westmonasterium fecerat, instructo ad xii monachos cenobiolo." It is borne out by a charter of c. 971 in Birch, *Cart. Sax.* 1048.

3 For Milton, *v. Chronicle*, *s.a.* 964 [A] and *Monasticon*, ii, 348–9; also J. A. Robinson, *The Saxon Bishops of Wells*, 47.

Cranborne. The first of these was given by its founder, Aethelmaer, to Dunstan and Aelfheah, Ethelwold's successor at Winchester, and received from the Old Minster Aelfric as its first abbot.[1] The other three presumably derived from one or other of the houses of the West, and to them may probably be added Buckfast. Finally, shortly after Dunstan's death his disciple, Wulfsige, probably a monk of Glastonbury and later abbot of Westminster, made the church of Sherborne into a monastery on becoming bishop in 993.[2]

Besides the abbeys in the West and the foundation near London which dated from his administration of that see, the circumstances of his life brought the archbishop into close relationship with the two Canterbury churches, but the history of both at this time is extremely obscure. St Augustine's may, as has been suggested, have preserved more of the monastic framework than any other house in England, but strangely enough it is mentioned in connection with Dunstan only rarely and incidentally, though his interest in it must have been great, and a disciple of his, Sigeric, is said to have been appointed by him as abbot.[3] As regards Christ Church a long controversy has kindled fires of which the embers are still smouldering. The story told by its monastic historians after the Conquest was that it had been originally a monastery, but had fallen into the hands of clerks in the ninth century; these were replaced by monks at the command of the pope by Archbishop Aelfric (995–1005). Historians of the last century adopted the position, not yet abandoned by all, that it was never monastic at all before the days of Lanfranc, but a more recent and careful treatment of the question has proved beyond reasonable doubt both that in its early days the community was at least quasi-monastic under a monk-archbishop and that monks were at Christ Church during the whole of the eleventh century. Somewhat strangely, Dunstan's name is not connected with the story of their introduction, which is attributed to Aelfric or Sigeric, but indications are not wanting that some monks, at least, were at Christ Church in his day, and it is possible, perhaps even probable, that he proceeded like Oswald at Worcester by a method of gradual introduction beginning with his personal and official assistants, and respecting vested interests, and that one of his first successors hastened the process by a formal change.[4]

The great impulse that came from Abingdon did not begin till Ethelwold was bishop of Winchester. The introduction of Abingdon monks into the Old and New Minsters in 964–5 was rapidly followed by foundations at Peterborough (966), Ely (970) and Thorney (972).[5] To these may perhaps

1 For Cerne cf. charter in *Monasticon*, II, 625–6, from *Cart. Ant. Wint.* 16.
2 So Will. Malmesb., *GP*, 178, and *Vita S. Dunstani*, in *Memorials*, 304.
3 *V.* Stubbs, *Mem. St Dunst.* 388. n. 3. Sigeric had, it is probable, been a monk at Glastonbury; *v.* the letter to him of Aelfward, abbot of that house, in *Mem. St Dunst.* 400–4.
4 See Appendix III, *Christ Church, Canterbury, before the Conquest.*
5 For these three *v.* Aelfric's *Vita S. Aethelwoldi*, 261–2. They had as their first abbots

be added Croyland (*c.* 966), St Neots (*c.* 974) and Chertsey (? 960), where Ordbricht, a monk of Glastonbury and Abingdon, is found as abbot,[1] though they are not explicitly mentioned by Ethelwold's biographer. The case of St Albans is still more obscure; its reform (? 969) is attributed to Oswald by his biographer, but the first abbot, Aelfric, was probably a monk of Abingdon.[2] Finally, Eynsham, founded by Aethelmaer twenty years after Ethelwold's death (1005), had as its first abbot his most celebrated pupil, Aelfric, who wrote for the guidance of his family of novices an abbreviation of the *Concordia*.

Oswald's monastic plantation began with the small community of a dozen at Westbury-on-Trym near Bristol (*c.* 962). The bishop was never satisfied with the position of the monks there, apparently because the property belonged to the church of Worcester and he was apprehensive as to the action of his successors.[3] He approached Edgar, who offered him three sites, of which Ely and St Albans were two; Oswald inspected them, but for some reason made no immediate decision. It was at this juncture that he received from Aethelwine, son of Athelstan the Half-King, whom he met at a funeral at Glastonbury, the offer of the fertile island of Ramsey. He gladly accepted, and when the monastery was founded there (*c.* 971) the majority of the Westbury community would seem to have been drafted thither, and the earlier plantation ceased to have any significance.[4] Ramsey became a flourishing and model house; from it sprang Winchcombe (? 972), which had as first abbot Germanus, Oswald's friend long before at Winchester and whilom prior of Westbury, Pershore (*c.* 972) and Worcester, where monks were gradually introduced *c.* 974–7 under Winsige, a priest of the city who had been sent for training to Ramsey.[5] Pershore, it may be noted, had as abbot Foldbricht, one of those who followed Ethelwold in his migration from Glastonbury, and

Aldulf, Brihtnoth and Godeman respectively, all sometime monks of Abingdon; the two last are among the earliest names in *Hyde Liber Vitae*, 24, and perhaps came from that house.

1 Chertsey is one of the foundations attributed especially to Edgar; cf. *Chronicle, s.a.* 964 [A], where Ordbricht's appointment is noted, and *Vita S. Aethelwoldi* of Aelfric, 258, for his provenance. For Croyland, *v.* Ordericus Vitalis, II, 281–2, where it is described as an independent venture of Turketil, a cleric of London.

2 So Eadmer, *Vita S. Oswaldi* (*Hist. York*, II, 22), but this may be mere confusion; though we know from the anonymous *Vita S. Oswaldi* (*Hist. York*, I, 427) that Edgar offered Oswald St Albans.

3 *Vita S. Oswaldi auct. anon.* 424–5: "Collegit eosdem in quadam parochia sui episco-patus quae Westbirig dicitur...tanta eis contulit...in potu, et cibo, necne vestimentis, ut absque murmuratione servire Deo perseveranter potuissent...dubitavit quid de illo vellet qui post eum culmen sublime scanderet agere."

4 *Vita S. Oswaldi auct. anon.* 425–31. The first abbot of Ramsey was Aethelnoth, a priest who had been the most notable member of the group at Westbury; Germanus was at first prior (*nostri monasterii decanus, ibid.* 435), and then sent to Winchcombe as abbot (*Hist. Rameseien.* 42; cf. 29).

5 *Vita S. Oswaldi auct. anon.* 425–35: "Illis qui sub eo erant in civitate [*sc.* Wigornensi] anteposuit Wynsinum...qui erat apud nostri coenobii gymnasium eruditus, cui annexuit quosdam fratres ex nostro choro." For the whole process *v.* Robinson, *St Oswald and the Church of Worcester*.

another of his companions, Frithegar, is found as abbot of Evesham *c.* 975, but this last house, too, may perhaps be counted as Oswald's work.[1] When archbishop of York, Oswald may have replanted Ripon (? 980)[2] and Deerhurst was almost certainly another of his foundations (*c.* 970), thus completing the tale of seven houses in Mercia assigned to him by his biographer.[3]

Thirty-four monasteries are accounted for in this summary. To these were added, before the Conquest, another half-dozen, but it is altogether impossible to arrive, even by 1005, at the total of forty said by Oswald's biographer to have been founded under the influence of Edgar. It is indeed possible that one or two may have languished leaving no trace, but the statement is a very definite one, and is probably intended to include abbeys of women, of which six or seven date from the tenth century.[4]

The last five years of Edgar's reign were a kind of apogee for the monastic movement. The three great leaders, together with abbots, abbesses, monks and nuns, were invited by king and queen to take part in the various important gatherings of those years which Dunstan would seem to have encouraged in order to cement the nation's unity. The author of Oswald's *Life* describes two such meetings, most characteristic of the England of that day, the one, which we have considered as the preliminary to the synod of Winchester, at which massed choirs of monks and nuns sang vespers in the king's presence in the cathedral, and the other, the king's coronation at Bath on Whit-Sunday, 973, at which again abbots and abbesses, monks and nuns, assisted and were together entertained to a banquet by the queen.[5]

Such a harmonious state of things could not endure for ever. The *Regularis Concordia* was the production of a single great occasion. It aimed at creating no machinery of government, and alike in the purely

1 For Foldbricht, *v. Vita S. Oswaldi auct. anon.* 439. He, we are told, *durus visus est hominibus qui nesciunt secreta intueri*—a trait which seems to recall the school of Ethelwold. It must be added that domestic tradition regarded Ethelwold as the refounder of Evesham; cf. *Chron. Evesh.* 78: "Atheluuoldus...ad istum locum venit et Osuuardum abbatem hic constituit."

2 *Vita S. Oswaldi auct. anon.* 462; this passage, however, is ambiguous; Ripon is not explicitly named, and Prof. A. H. Thompson (*Bede*, 98) may be correct in supposing the allusion to be to Worcester, not Ripon.

3 *Vita S. Oswaldi auct. anon.* 439: "Sunt denique in provincia Merciorum...septem monasteria constructa." These words do not necessarily imply Oswald's initiative.

4 *Vita S. Oswaldi auct. anon.* 426: "Plusquam quadraginta jussit [rex] monasteria constitui cum monachis." The reference of Orderic to the abbey of Peakirk (OV, II, 284), which was amalgamated with Croyland *c.* 1048, warns us that other such minor houses may have existed. Possibly Hereford was another, and Bedford also (*v. Chron. Ang. Petr., s.a.*).

5 *Vita S. Oswaldi auct. anon.* 426: "Cuncti abbates cum monachis suis, atque omnes abbatissae cum monialibus suis properabant pedetemptim et ordinate ad vespertinam horam, quam ante conspectum cælestis regis et terreni debebant modulanter concinere." *Ibid.* 438 (at Bath): "Regina cum abbatibus at abbatissis convivium habuit." The Proem to the *Concordia* (p. 78) expressly lays down that "Ad Regis obsequium et Reginae Patres Monasteriorum Matresque quotiens expedierit...humiliter accedant".

personal undertaking of the heads of houses present and in the personal bond between the monasteries and Edgar and the nunneries and Aelfthryth the concordat was in essence transitory. In the event, the *concordia ordinum* of monarch, nobles, bishops and religious was even more transitory than might reasonably have been hoped, with a king not yet thirty. Edgar died in 975, and the complete harmony of his reign was never restored. In Mercia, indeed, there was almost at once a violent, though temporary, anti-monastic reaction, and a number of the landowners, whose relations had doubtless been among the communities of noble clerks, and who had seen with displeasure considerable estates passing to the monks, expelled the latter from the monasteries in the Avon valley and reintroduced the clerks. Germanus of Winchcombe and his community were among those so treated, Pershore was for a time dispersed and Deerhurst ceased to be an abbey, but in the east Aethelwine remained a firm supporter, and in the south Dunstan's influence in public affairs continued at least till the accession of Ethelred "the Unready".[1]

As long, indeed, as the great triumvirate was intact, commanding the dioceses of Canterbury, York, Winchester and Worcester, and with a growing number of monk-bishops in other sees, the new order could not be seriously disturbed. Besides their activity in purely religious matters Ethelwold and Oswald were men of unusual foresight and ability in secular administration. At Worcester, Oswald, with patient care, built up and organized the estates of his church into the three irregular hundreds known as Oswaldslaw, which long preserved their economic and administrative peculiarities. Ethelwold, for his part, besides his activities at Winchester, took constant interest in Ely and Peterborough, and here, also, immunities were obtained which gave private jurisdiction to the monks over a considerable territory.[2]

Ethelwold was the first to die, in 984. His biographer, who knew him intimately, gives us a vivid picture of his energy in his last years in constructing and visiting the monasteries he had founded, most of which lay far from Winchester, in translating books into English—among them, the Rule of St Benedict for nuns—and in teaching his young disciples.[3] His physical sufferings were great, but he spared himself not at all, nor departed from the monastic Rule in regard to food. He left behind him

---

1 For the anti-monastic movement *v. Chronicle, s.a.* 975 [E] and *Vita S. Oswaldi auct. anon.* 443–9.

2 As Armitage Robinson, *The Times of St Dunstan,* 131, remarks: "The number of charters issued by Oswald has no parallel for any other Church." And of Ethelwold, *ibid.* 120: "To read the *Liber Eliensis* is to obtain an amazing picture of the activities of St Ethelwold." Cf. also the interesting pages devoted to the subject in *Camb. Med. Hist.* III, 375–9 by the late W. J. Corbett, where, however, too much is made of the disintegrating effects of Oswaldslaw, and Maitland, *Domesday Book and beyond,* esp. 267 *seqq.,* 303 *seqq.*

3 *Vita auct. Aelfrico,* 263: "Dulce namque erat ei adolescentes et juvenes semper docere, et libros Anglice eis solvere." For his translation of the Rule, made (probably for nuns) at the request of Queen Aelfthryth, *v.* A. Schröer, *Die angelsächsischen Prosabearbeitungen der Benedictinerregel* and J. A. Robinson, *Times of St Dunstan,* 121–2.

a reputation for austerity and severity, but also of fatherly care and sympathy for the unfortunate and the oppressed;[1] the records of his life show him a lover of the chant and a skilled craftsman, and the Benedictional which bears his name stands as a monument to his patronage of the art in which his countrymen excelled. In his last days he was visited and counselled by Dunstan, and a fortunate accident has left us with an eye-witness's account of the meeting, at which, in the presence of monks from both the Winchester houses, their founder and bishop ratified an agreement of union and concord between them.[2]

Dunstan died four years later, in 988. His last years had been given almost wholly to the pastoral care of his diocese and to the direct service of God. From the many living touches of his earliest biographer a very real portrait of this great and eminently holy man emerges, though the traits are so many and so minute that a reader can scarcely analyse the whole for himself, still less transmit the impression to others. The sympathetic, receptive nature which in his early manhood made him the friend and guide of so many varied characters, the unshakable strength of his later years which made him to the end the master even of Ethelwold,[3] the wisdom and statesmanship which enabled him to be the counsellor and friend of successive kings and one of the creators of a united England, the gift of artistic creation of the highest order which is perhaps the most remarkable of all his gifts, and, finally, the mature sanctity which in his later years transcended and superseded his other activities and characteristics—all these, revealed to us in this way or that, make of Dunstan a figure of singular attractiveness, whose final and lasting impression is one, not of brilliance and fire, but of a calm and mellow light. His final illness came upon him shortly after Mass, at which he had preached thrice, on the feast of the Ascension, a season already associated in the memories of Englishmen with the last moments of the Venerable Bede. He lingered till the Saturday morning of 19 May when, immediately after receiving Viaticum at a Mass celebrated in his presence, he passed away. His last words, according to a tradition which has every claim to belief, were

1 *Vita S. Aethelwoldi*, 263: "Mitibus et humilibus mitior columba...viduarum consolator et pauperum recreator."

2 Cf. the letter of Eadwine of the New Minster, written *c.* 1056, describing how "the lord St Ethelwold lay sick and the holy Dunstan of Canterbury came to sit with him" (*Hyde Liber Vitae*, 96 *seqq.*). Probably also the record of Ethelwold's last visit to Canterbury, first given by Osbern in his *Vita S. Dunstani* in *Memorials*, 115, rests upon a genuine tradition.

3 *Vita S. Aethelwoldi*, 263: Ethelwold eats meat *jussu Dunstani archiepiscopi*; 258, Dunstan is *quasi columna immobilis*. Aelfric in his *Life of St Swithun*, ed. Skeat, 470, characterizes Dunstan as "the resolute" [anraeda]; to Wulfstan of Winchester he appeared *canitie niveus et angelicus* (*PL*, cxxxvii, 109). Cf. also the very impressive references to Dunstan in *Vita S. Oswaldi auct. anon.* 420 *et al.* While feeling that some recent writers in their eulogy of Dunstan's ability in secular affairs have attributed to him political aims and genius which he neither possessed nor could in that age have possessed, I cannot agree with W. J. Corbett (*Camb. Med. Hist.* III, 379) that his retirement from public life was due to failing powers.

those of the Psalmist: "The merciful and gracious Lord hath made a remembrance of His marvellous works; He hath given food to them that fear Him."[1]

Oswald, the youngest, survived till 992. His memory has fared well in subsequent ages, partly because his supposedly greater gentleness and moderation have been contrasted with the more violent methods of his colleagues.[2] Actually we have few details out of which to form his portrait. A Dane by blood, physically robust and with a magnificent voice,[3] he does not seem to have shared the artistic gifts of Ethelwold and Dunstan, though his career at Fleury and his reception of Abbo at Ramsey are evidence that he shared their love of learning. Like Ethelwold, he was tireless in visiting his monasteries in Mercia and the fens, but it is as bishop and father of his people that he stands out in the pages of his biographer. Though archbishop of York for twenty years, Worcester was always the church of his predilection; it is with its land that his name is linked, and there he died, as he had wished.

In November 991 he paid a notable visit, which he knew would be his last, to Ramsey. It was an annual custom for Oswald and Aethelwine, the founder, to meet there as guests, and the writer of the archbishop's life, who was present, gives a vivid and interesting description of the scene in the abbey during Oswald's Mass on this occasion, and of the banquet, given by Aethelwine, that followed it. Two days later Oswald took leave of the monks, after asking their blessing and bestowing his own, with a prayer that they might all meet in heaven.[4] He spent the winter months at Worcester, in ordinary health; and entered upon the season of Lent and the beginning of spring, a time always precious to him, with all his ordinary practices. Among these it was his custom to wash the feet of twelve poor men daily. On the last morning of his life, which was also the last day of February, he accomplished his usual task, reciting as he did so the Gradual Psalms. When, at the end, all knelt before the crucifix for the doxology, the archbishop's spirit passed away.[5]

The memory of the three great bishops was cherished by their countrymen. The records of those who had known them, so often quoted in these pages, show that they received at once the veneration of all classes; a

---

1 This account appears first in Adelard's *Vita* (*Mem. St Dunst.* 65–6). Robinson in his account of Dunstan's death (*Times of St Dunstan*, 89–90), following Stubbs, strangely enough deprives this last utterance of all appositeness by making no mention of the occasion (his reception of the Eucharist) and by failing to translate from the Vulgate.

2 Oswald's character was clearly a most lovable one. Cf. *Vita S. Oswaldi*, 411: "(as a young man) erat...amabilis et affabilis omnibus amicis suis...affabilis sermone"; 416: "habebat pacem cum proximo"; 421: "(as bishop) omni populo amabilis...vulgus [eum] praeamavit...pauperes eum dilexerunt"; 470: "(when dying) ut erat jocundissimus conviva".

3 *Vita S. Oswaldi*, 416: "Erat robustus corpore...fortis viribus"; 417: "habebat... vocis pulchritudinem...suavitatem...et altitudinem".

4 *Vita S. Oswaldi*, 463–7.

5 *Ibid.* 470–2.

century later we can find Wulfstan of Worcester, at a crisis of his own career, seeking strength in the example given by his two saintly predecessors; fifty years later again William of Malmesbury, with that true sense of values that underlies his superficial lack of discrimination, devotes to them words of reverent admiration such as he reserves for the greatest alone. They and their work, however, have failed to receive due recognition in modern times, for while the generality of English historians of religion have allowed themselves to be wholly occupied with the Norman monasticism and the *éclat* of Lanfranc and Anselm, the romantic school of writers on monastic history has turned more readily to the previous centuries of Aidan, Wilfrid, Aldhelm, Bede and Boniface; moreover, the darkness of the ninth century has in the past been rendered still more treacherous by the pages of the pseudo-Asser and the pseudo-Ingulf, so that the absolute break between old and new has not been adequately realized. When the strong new life of monastic England in the reigns of Edgar and Ethelred is seen in a true light, the achievement of the three, and especially of Ethelwold and Dunstan, can be more justly assessed. As has been said, they left no new impress on the form of monastic life; they changed nothing, nor did they enrich the blood of the religious world by their writings or spiritual doctrine. But in another respect they did everything: they called the dead to life; they created a great and flourishing system upon vacant soil; and to Dunstan especially, as to Augustine of Canterbury before him, are due in a very real sense the titles of patron and father of the monks of medieval England.

CHAPTER IV

ENGLISH MONASTICISM BETWEEN DUNSTAN AND THE CONQUEST

I

The eighty years that passed between the death of Ethelwold and of Dunstan and the Norman Conquest were years of continuous stress and insecurity in England, broken only by the interval, less than twenty years long, of strong and peaceful government under Cnut. In the last decade of the tenth century began the series of Danish expeditions and invasions which disturbed and ravaged the country, culminating in the fierce warfare which gave control of England to Sweyn and obtained the crown for his son, Cnut. Then after an interval of peace came the disturbed reigns of Cnut's sons, Harold and Harthacnut, followed by the longer reign of Edward the Confessor during which so many conflicting forces were at work.

During all this period the organization of the Church in England, which for two centuries at least had been extremely loose, and which had attained under Dunstan a unity and cohesion which depended upon the personality of the archbishop rather than upon the strength of the system itself, tended steadily to become less and less defined. From the earliest times, but especially since the days of Alfred and Edgar, there had been a merging and intermingling of national and ecclesiastical government hardly paralleled abroad; the state of things which resulted was in many ways paradoxical, for while the bishops never acted as an independent body, held few synods whether national or diocesan, and came to have less and less directly spiritual authority within their large and often ill-defined dioceses, they, and the abbots with them, were among the most powerful men in the land, both as owners of property and as counsellors of the king. In consequence the interests of religion, or what were conceived to be such, were almost uniformly consulted, while the strictly ecclesiastical and hierarchical functions of the episcopate received less attention. The full history of this period has yet to be written. Those who have hitherto attempted to describe the Church in England immediately before the Conquest, have for the most part been moved by apologetic considerations of one kind or another, while the German school, and in particular Heinrich Böhmer to whom we owe so much, concentrated their attention so closely upon the racial and institutional features of religion as to lose sight of the deeper spiritual and doctrinal life behind.[1]

1 The best full account of the English Church immediately before the Conquest is still that of H. Böhmer, as given especially in the section on England before 1066 in *Kirche und*

From the point of view of the historian of monasticism these eighty years may be divided into three periods of almost equal length: from the death of Dunstan to the great Danish invasions *c*. 1015; the period of Danish domination; and the reign of Edward the Confessor. During the first of these the impetus of the monastic revival attained its maximum force and then gradually became stationary; the chief bishoprics and abbacies were occupied by the ablest disciples of the three leaders; within the monasteries the religious and intellectual life developed along the lines laid down by the founders, and both abbots and bishops received support from a number of the most powerful landowners. It was the generation of Aelfric and Byrhtferth, of Wulfstan of York and Aelfheah of Canterbury. During the second period, introduced by the long years of invasion, there was little change, no essential growth, and perhaps a slow decline in some quarters, but under Cnut the monastic bishops were still supreme in council, the material possessions of the monasteries grew, and there were important new foundations. During the third period, the reign of the Confessor, a number of influences and movements opposed one to another were at work. The majority of the new bishops were not monks, several of the smaller monasteries suffered from encroachments of one kind and another and some of the greater houses showed signs of relaxation. On the other hand, the reign saw the first infiltration of the Norman monasticism; the Confessor was a benefactor and friend of monks, both English and Norman; and an important and wholly spontaneous revival took place in Worcestershire.

II

The last twenty years of the tenth century witnessed the growth to full stature of the monasteries founded in the reign of Edgar. The generation taught by Dunstan, Ethelwold and Oswald was everywhere in authority. No trustworthy and connected history of any individual house has come down to us, and we have therefore to form our judgment from a variety of indications and sources, from isolated contemporary notices and from

Staat, 42–79; in the monograph *Das Eigenkirchentum in England* in the collection of *Texte und Forschungen* presented to Felix Liebermann on his seventieth birthday (Halle, 1921); and the relevant pages in his essay *Das Germanische Christentum* in *Theologische Studien und Kritiken* (Gotha, Jan. 1913), 165–280. Böhmer's mastery of the sources was unrivalled, save perhaps by Liebermann, whose interests were, however, somewhat different, and the majority of his judgments are reliable within their own sphere, but, as is suggested in the text, he was interested almost exclusively in the social, phenomenal, quasi-material aspects of religion; also, his work (like that of Ulrich Stütz) is tinged by his conception of the Nordic, Germanic, racial characteristics as the master-key to the problems of medieval history. I may perhaps be permitted to say that this chapter was written before the appearance of a most valuable article by Dr R. R. Darlington with the title *Ecclesiastical Reform in the Late Old English Period* (*EHR*, LI (July 1936), 385–428). The similarity, therefore, between many of Mr Darlington's conclusions and those expressed in the following pages may be taken as evidence of their truth.

the remains of the literature and art of the time, but the general impression given by all these is one and the same, that in many of the monasteries a many-sided life of great richness was being lived. Pre-eminent among the houses, it would seem, were Abingdon, the two Winchester minsters, Ramsey, Ely, and, a little later, Peterborough.

On the material side, these were years of constant acquisition and consolidation of property. By the Conquest the monasteries had come to possess a very large proportion of the landed wealth of England, and a still greater proportion of its treasure in works of art, and much of this was already theirs by the millenary year. In the case of a few houses such as Ely, Abingdon and Worcester it is possible to watch the process of growth, and both there and elsewhere its rapidity is truly amazing.[1] The invasions and repulses of the Danes in previous generations had no doubt decreased very considerably the number of those owning and exploiting the land and enriched in proportion the conquerors and survivors; kings therefore and magnates were able to part with large areas without undue sacrifice. In the days of Edgar especially we find the king able to dispose freely of estates situated in every part of the country, and the greater part of the monastic property in the epoch of expansion came directly from royal gifts and from a small number of great aldermen and thegns whose names recur in the narratives and charters. One such was the alderman Aethelmaer, the friend of Aelfric and the founder of Cerne and Eynsham, another Aethelwine, son of Athelstan the Half-King, friend of Oswald and founder of Ramsey; others were Aelfwold, brother of Aethelwine, Brihtnoth, patron of Ely, and Wulfric "Spot", founder of Burton-on-Trent.

Along with the growth of property went the construction and decoration of the minster. Artistic talent of every kind had for long been latent in the soil of England, but the unsettled state of the times and consequent lack of scope for the arts of construction had restricted work in the fine arts to jewellery and embroidery. With the foundation of so many monasteries and the occupation of cathedral and pilgrimage churches by the monks an impetus was given to construction and decoration of every kind. Ethelwold was a great builder wherever he went, and brief accounts remain of his buildings at Abingdon and of Oswald's considerable church at Ramsey;[2] there is a more elaborate notice of Aethelgar's tower and chapels at the New Minster.[3] All these edifices, indeed, however magnifi-

1 Cf. *Liber Eliensis, Chronicon Monasterii de Abingdon* and Hemming's *Chartulary* (ed. T. Hearne), *passim*.

2 *Vita S. Aethelwoldi, Chron. Abingd.* II, 259: "Erat Aethelwoldus magnus aedificator." For the church at Abingdon, *ibid.* 277–8; for Ramsey, *Vita S. Oswaldi (Hist. York)*, I, 434.

3 For New Minster, *v. Hyde Register*, 9–10: "Turris mirae altitudinis eximiaeque uenustatis. . .cui nec ipsis temporibus priscis aliqua extitit hujus patriae consimilis et multiplicium peruagatoribus regionum sanctorumque locorum apparet singularis." Commentaries on these and other architectural descriptions of Saxon buildings will be found in Mr A. W. Clapham's *English Romanesque Architecture before the Conquest* (1930).

cent they may have appeared to enthusiastic contemporaries, were small in scale compared with the vast Norman structures which replaced them, and the monastic buildings were probably still more modest in proportion, but even in the purely architectural field the most recent investigators have passed more favourable judgments on the Saxon work than were common a few decades since.[1] The English excelled, however, rather in decoration than in planning and construction; in painting, carving and every kind of work in gold and silver and gilded wood the greater Saxon churches were supreme in western Europe, and their treasuries were stocked with every kind of gold and silver vessel, richly embroidered vestments and hangings, and jewelled and illuminated service books. The work of the monks in some of these arts will be considered on a later page; here, in order to form some idea of the setting of the life in the greater monasteries, it is sufficient to recall the lists of treasures that have survived from Winchester, Abingdon, Peterborough, Glastonbury and Ely.[2]

From the first the leaders of the revival, in full agreement with the monastic tradition of recent centuries, had set the solemn performance of the liturgy in the forefront of their design. One of the chief motives for the expulsion of the secular clerks from the Old and New Minsters was that the offices might be more worthily accomplished. There is clear evidence that at the two great centres, Winchester and Ramsey, the elaborate rendering of ceremony and chant was a feature of the life at least during the generation of Aelfric and Byrhtferth.[3] From Winchester, besides the service books that have survived, we have the two "tropers" which show that in addition to the full body of plain chant the English monasteries made use not only of the elaborate additional modulations which interpolated and prolonged the important parts of the chant of the Mass and Office, but also of a system of *organa* or polyphony which indeed shows a greater development in England than anywhere abroad. In addition, the English monasteries, as is clear from several indications, made much of organ music[4] and of the treble voices of the children of the cloister, both in contrast to the voices of the monks and in polyphonic combination.[5] In all this, it must be remembered, there was nothing un-

1 So especially Clapham, *op. cit.*, followed by subsequent students.
2 For Abingdon, *v. Chron. Abingd.* II, 278 *et al.*; for Winchester (Old Minster), *Annales Wintonienses* (*Ann. Monast.* II), *s.a.* 1035, 1040, 1043, 1047 (New Minster), *Hyde Register*, 9–10; for Peterborough, Birch, *Cart. Sax.* 1128–31 and *Hugonis Candidi Coenobii Burgensis Historia*, ed. Sparke (1723), 42–5; for Glastonbury, Will. Malmesb., *de Ant. Glast.*, in Hearne, *Adam de Domerham*, I, 92 *seqq.*; for Ely, *Liber Eliensis*, 249–50, 282–3. Cf. the words of William of Poitiers (*Hist. Norm. Script. antiqui*, ed. Duchesne [Paris, 1619], 210): "Chari metalli abundantia multipliciter Gallias terra illa vincit."
3 Cf. especially *Vita S. Oswaldi* (*Hist. York*), I, 426, 463–5.
4 For the organist at Ramsey, *v. Vita S. Oswaldi*, 464: "Magister organorum...ascendit...in altis sedibus, quo tonitruali sonitu excitavit mentes fidelium laudare nomen Domini."
5 For a fuller discussion of the chant at Winchester and elsewhere, with references to the sources, *v. infra*, ch. XXXI.

couth or embryonic; the plain chant was a developed art-form of extreme flexibility, subtlety and beauty, and the music of Winchester in the days of Aelfric was in all essentials identical with that of the Vatican gradual and antiphoner of the present day. From the descriptions in which the Ramsey monk, the anonymous author of the life of Oswald, takes especial pleasure we can see that equal richness of liturgical life prevailed in the houses which derived from Fleury. English treble voices have ever been celebrated for their purity and sweetness of tone, and all who took part in the choral service had been trained from their earliest years in the Gregorian chant. The Mass and Office on high festivals must have provided a musical feast of great richness, and we can readily understand the admiration with which Cnut, in the well-known story, heard across the water the singing of the monks of Ely.[1]

During the half-century that followed the expulsion of the clerks from the Old and New Minsters the two houses of the royal city were in many ways the cultural centre of England,[2] and it was St Swithun's that gave his formation to the most considerable figure of the period following the death of Dunstan. The name of Aelfric, often styled, somewhat inaptly, "The Grammarian" to distinguish him from his many namesakes, has already been mentioned more than once, and his position in the history of English learning will be discussed on a later page; for the moment we are concerned only with his life and the character of his influence.[3] Born probably between 950 and 955, and first taught by a priest who was not a monk, he early became a monk and the pupil of Ethelwold at the Old Minster.[4] Nothing is known of the external circumstances of his life till, in 987, he was sent by Aelfheah, Ethelwold's successor at Winchester, to instruct the monks of the new foundation recently made by Aethelmaer at Cerne in Dorset.[5] From thence till his death Aelfric, besides his task as teacher and ruler, put out a continual stream of writings, the fruits of his

---

1 *Liber Eliensis*, 202–3. There is no reason to doubt the truth of this story. The occasion was shortly before the feast of the Purification. On that day (2 Feb.) began the annual period during which the abbot of Ely was "chaplain" to the king (*Lib. Elien.* 194–5).

2 Cf. the words of Edmund Bishop, *Liturgica Historica*, 241: "In the last years of the tenth century both the Winchester houses...were a busy hive...painting, architecture, goldsmiths' work, music, history and grammar, verse-making and homiletics, even science, the vulgar and the learned tongues were alike cultivated."

3 For the dating of Aelfric's works I have followed in general the very full account given by Skeat in his introduction to vol. II of Aelfric's *Lives of the Saints* (EETS, 1900), xxv–l. There is an excellent short account, also based largely on Skeat, by Westlake in *Cambridge History of English Literature*, I, ch. vii, and still more precision has been given by Mr K. Sisam in a series of articles *Aelfric's Catholic Homilies* in the *Review of English Studies*, VII (1931), 7–22; VIII (1932), 51–68; IX (1933), 1–12. The article by the Rev. W. Hunt in *DNB* needs some revision.

4 It is sometimes stated (e.g. in *DNB*) that Aelfric was a monk of Abingdon. He never tells us this himself, and the dates of his life make it unlikely.

5 In the English preface to his first homilies Aelfric says (the paraphrase is that of Thorpe, *Liber Sermonum Catholicorum* [Aelfric Society, 1844–6]): "I Aelfric, monk and mass-priest ...was sent, in bishop Aethelred's day from bishop Aelfheah, Ethelwold's successor, to a minster which is called Cernel at the prayer of Aethelmaer the thane."

study in the past, but almost without exception composed at the direct request of one of his friends. As it was his habit to introduce his books with a short preface giving the circumstances of their origin, they can in most cases be dated with fair accuracy.

His first publications from Cerne were two series of homilies covering the Sundays and feast days of the year, dedicated to Sigeric, Dunstan's pupil and successor at Canterbury; the first series is largely doctrinal, the second historical in character; both were written to be preached or read by priests to their people. These homilies were followed by a venture of another kind, perhaps composed after the writer had returned to Winchester; a Latin Grammar, based on Priscian, a Latin-English Vocabulary, and the celebrated Colloquy, intended to give in a small compass and in a form that could easily be committed to memory the common words of every-day life in Latin for the benefit of the boys of the cloister. These books, wherever written, were the fruit of Aelfric's experience at Winchester; they were followed, c. 997, by a third series of homilies, this time on the lives of those saints who received commemoration in the monastic offices rather than in the calendar of the English Church; among them is one on St Swithun, which contains some interesting details of the miracles claimed to have been worked in such profusion at Winchester during Aelfric's own monastic life there.[1] This series has as preface a dedication to Aethelweard, the "beloved", the father of Aethelmaer. It was at Aethelweard's request, also, that Aelfric, c. 998, undertook to translate, or rather to paraphrase, the Old Testament for the benefit of those who had to preach to the people. In this task he was assisted by others, and modern criticism has been able to separate with some degree of certainty the master's contribution from those of his collaborators; not all the Bible was trans-lated; besides the Pentateuch, extracts were given from Judges, Job, Esther and Judith. Contemporary with this work of translation is a long pastoral letter written in 998 at the request of Wulfsige, bishop of Sherborne and previously abbot of Westminster, a disciple of Dunstan. This letter, and that written later for Wulfstan of York, show Aelfric the theologian at his best, conscious of his grasp of the traditional teaching of the Church and of his duty to pass on full and unchanged what he had received.

In 1005 Aethelmaer called Aelfric to be the first abbot of his new founda-tion at Eynsham, near Oxford, where he himself retired to end his days as Athelstan the Half-King had retired to Glastonbury. A literary result of this new undertaking was the letter, already referred to more than once, in which he gave to Eynsham a shortened version of the *Concordia*, and at about the same time, or a little before, he composed, in the years 1005–6,

---

1 In the *Lives of the Saints*, ed. Skeat, vol. 1 (EETS, 1881), 451–7, he tells us that as many as two hundred were on one occasion healed within ten days, and that the monks, commanded by Ethelwold to sing a *Te Deum* for each cure, grew slack from fatigue, and were rebuked by the bishop.

his life of Ethelwold. A few years later came a treatise on the Old and New Testaments, based on St Augustine's *De Doctrina Christiana*, and a letter strongly urging the celibacy of the clergy, both addressed to Sigeferth, a thane living at Asthall in the neighbourhood of Eynsham. Another correspondent of Aelfric's at the time was another thane living at Ilmington, not far from Stratford-on-Avon. Finally, *c.* 1014–16 he wrote another long pastoral letter, which he also translated into English, for Wulfstan, bishop of Worcester and archbishop of York, and probably himself a monk of Winchester. Aelfric wrote no more; he himself tells us that many years before he had desired to leave the work of translation and composition for his own reading and spiritual exercises. He was now an old man and England was passing through a crisis of war and invasion in which Wulfstan of York saw the divine wrath working upon the negligent people of the land. We know nothing of his last years or of his death, which probably took place *c.* 1020.

This brief summary, in which only the more important writings have been mentioned, will have shown how wide was the range of Aelfric's learning and of the circle of his relationships. The history of his posthumous fame is a curious one. Held second only to Bede by his countrymen so long as a knowledge of literary Anglo-Saxon remained common in England, he passed during the later Middle Ages into almost complete oblivion, from which he was rescued first by controversialists of the Reformed Churches, who considered that they had found in his writings the expression of their own teaching on the Eucharist, and more recently by students of early English literature, who see in him a great master of language. Neither party has wholly succeeded in paying adequate tribute to Aelfric, nor in obtaining for him the recognition due to his eminence. Strange as it may seem, the very fact that his most characteristic writings are in his native tongue has probably had much to do with this neglect, as has the entire absence of any account of his life in contemporary documents. Aelfric's real significance and greatness is as a monastic theologian and teacher of his countrymen second only to Bede and in direct spiritual descent from him. He did not, like Bede, add to his works of learning anything of national history; had he done so, he would have been far more familiar to succeeding generations; nor had he the peculiar greatness of Bede's critical judgment and personal sanctity which secured remembrance of another kind. But in his diligent absorption of the inheritance of the past, in the sobriety and breadth of his teaching, in his responsiveness to all calls made upon him, in his strong national feeling and in the quiet life passed within the walls of a monastery, he inevitably recalls his great forerunner, and is, when all his gifts are taken into the reckoning, one of the most distinguished figures in the history of Western theological learning in the centuries immediately before the renaissance of the eleventh century. In the task of rebuilding the intellectual and spiritual life of England he was a true successor to Dunstan and his own master, Ethelwold, though with the important difference—in which again he resembles Bede—that in a time of national misfortune Aelfric, so far as we can ascertain, took no part in the public life either of the Church or of the nation, and regarded it as his task to teach within the walls of the monastery or to supply materials for those who were working outside. Probably he had not by nature the gifts of a great leader or administrator, nor had he the uplifting power of sanctity, and it cannot be wholly accidental that there is scarcely a single reference to him in contemporary writings, still less did any tradition survive at Winchester of his sanctity. No one, however, can read his works without receiving a most pleasing impression of the character of their author, and more than one critic has left on record his judgment of Aelfric's deep sincerity and moral worth.[1]

If Aelfric is thus inspired by the ideals of Ethelwold, to whom he refers so often, as embodied in the early traditions of the Old and New Minsters, Byrhtferth is the most eminent English representative of the traditions of Fleury and the school of Abbo. His works, for the most part scientific in content, whether mathematical or philological, and written with few exceptions in Latin, are in contrast to the more spiritual and directly practical writings of Aelfric, of which the most important are in the vernacular. Byrhtferth would appear to have lived and worked all his life at Ramsey, where he certainly came under the direct influence of the exiled Abbo, but did not, so far as appears, ever visit Fleury.[2] Aelfric and Byrhtferth, though the most notable, are not the only representatives of their generation. Wulfstan of Worcester and York, formerly perhaps a monk of Winchester, wrote a number of homilies *c.* 1005–15 in the most celebrated of which, the *Sermo Lupi ad Anglos*, the vices and misfortunes of his flock are severely handled in impassioned language. Like Aelfric, he is a master of words,[3] though he has not the other's wide learning. Another Aelfric, a monk of Bath, translated the gospels into English, and yet a third Aelfric, "the Bat", a disciple of his great namesake, republished the *Colloquy* with additions of his own; Wulfstan of Winchester wrote on music, and gave a description of his own home, and Lantfrith of Winchester related the miracles of St Swithun; Aelfward, abbot of

1 Thus, e.g. Skeat in *Lives of the Saints, ut sup.*, vol. II, introd. liii: "It is impossible not to see in Aelfric a man of humble, honest and upright heart." M. R. James, in *Cambridge Medieval History*, III, 537: "Skill in narrative, beauty of thought, goodness of soul, are there."

2 The assertion (cf. *DNB*) that he was a monk of Thorney rests only on a statement of Leland's informant, Talbot; that he visited France (as stated in *DNB*) is equally untrue (cf. Prof. G. F. Forsey, *Byrhtferth's Preface* in *Speculum*, III (Oct. 1928), 510).

3 Prof. R. W. Chambers, in his essay *The Continuity of English Prose* (Oxford, 1932), lxi, refers to "the cultured prose of Aelfric; the utterly different eloquence of Wulfstan, amazing in its vehemence, which reminds us of an Old Testament prophet". For his career *v. A Note on the Career of Wulfstan the Homilist*, by Miss Dorothy Whitelock in *EHR*, LII (July 1937), 460–5.

Glastonbury, addressed a lengthy letter of advice to Sigeric of Canterbury (990–4).[1] All these, whether written in English or Latin, are of the school of Ethelwold; the long and anonymous life of Oswald, written by a monk of Ramsey, probably Byrhtferth, is in tone and style wholly a product of the school of Fleury. To them must be added the anonymous but often extremely gifted contributors to the *Chronicle*, who were for the most part, if not entirely, monks, and who were especially active at Winchester, Abingdon and Worcester. They, when they reveal their personality, are entirely English, and remind us of Wulfstan rather than of Aelfric in their insistence on the sorrows of their land.

Besides liturgy and learning, Dunstan and Ethelwold had looked to their monasteries to provide leaders of the Church in England. The archbishop's earliest biographer, writing about the year 1000, noted that many of Dunstan's disciples at Glastonbury had become bishops and archbishops throughout England.[2] He did not exaggerate; by that time, only twelve years after the saint's death, two Glastonbury monks had succeeded him at Canterbury and at least seven others had been, or were still, in occupation of other English sees.[3] Indeed, from the middle of Edgar's reign onward it became normal to fill all vacant sees from the monasteries. At first this may have been due to the direct initiative of the archbishop and Ethelwold, but it soon became the inevitable course to take. From the days of Edgar till the last years of the Confessor no centres of learning existed apart from the monasteries, and no "higher" clergy existed among the priests of the country until Cnut first began to surround himself with a "chapel" of educated secular clerks, mostly of foreign origin; apart from the monks, the "mass-priest" in country or town was often merely the functionary of an *Eigenkirche* or chapel, and those who, in the country districts, approximated to the rank of a parish priest were often married and transmitted their office to their sons. In the monasteries alone, therefore, could be found men able to teach and counsel, and when once the body of bishops in the Witan became predominantly monastic, they would naturally advise the sovereign to choose from their own order, especially as the majority of recruits for the more

1 Lantfrith's work is still unpublished in Brit. Mus. MS. Reg. xv, c. 7. His letter of introduction and Aelfward's letter are in Stubbs, *Mem. St Dunst.* 369, 400.

2 *Vita auct. B, Mem. St Dunst.* 26: "Plurimi ecclesiarum pastores documentis illius et exemplis instructi, ad diversas jam civitates...petebantur, electi ut essent...abbates, episcopi, etiam archiepiscopi."

3 The careers of the seven are of interest as showing how widespread was Dunstan's influence. Aethelgar, m. of Glastonbury, Abingdon and New Minster, b. Selsey (980–8), archb. Canterbury (988–90); Cyneward, m. Glastonbury, abb. Milton, b. Wells (974–5); Aelfstan or Lyfing, m. Glastonbury, abb. Chertsey, b. Wells (999–1013), archb. Canterbury (1013–20); Aelfwold, m. Glastonbury, b. Crediton (988–1008); Ethelwold, m. Glastonbury, abb. Abingdon, b. Winchester (963–84); Sigegar, m. Winchester, abb. Glastonbury, b. Wells (975–97); Sigeric, m. Glastonbury, abb. St Augustine's, b. Ramsbury (989–90), archb. Canterbury (990–4); Wulfsige, m. Glastonbury, abb. Westminster, b. Sherborne (992–1001). To these William of Malmesbury would add Aelfheah of Canterbury, but it is not certain that he was ever at Glastonbury.

celebrated monasteries came from the landed and often from the most powerful families. Consequently, from *c.* 970 to the accession of the Confessor the majority, probably the overwhelming majority, of the bishops were monks. During that period, considerably more than half the occupants of the sees of England can be shown to have been monastic, and only two or three individuals in the whole period are known to have been secular priests; the provenance of the remainder is unknown, or at least unattainable without exhaustive research, but where no evidence exists, there is the strongest presumption of monastic origin.[1] The clerical members of the Witan, therefore, whether bishops or abbots, were for the most part monastic, and from the days of Dunstan to the arrival of Stigand at Canterbury in 1051 both archbishops were monks.

Between the death of Dunstan and the Danish dynasty the number of monasteries continued to grow, though the period of rapid expansion ceased before 1000. After that year, new plantations were rare. One such was Eynsham, as has already been mentioned, and from Eynsham probably *c.* 1005–16 a small community was settled at Stow, near Lincoln.[2] In Mercia, Burton-on-Trent was founded by Wulfric Spot, 1002–4, though details are wholly wanting, and in Wessex Buckfast may date from this time. We should in any case hesitate to suppose that the *Concordia* was in all cases taken to a new monastery as its code; that document was the fruit of a single great occasion, and it was not in the genius of tenth-century England to conceive of a number of separate bodies as governed by an abstract code. Actually, we have the precise statement of Aelfric himself that Eynsham, after some years of existence, knew nothing of the *Concordia*, and that he himself hesitated to apply all its provisions to the house of which he was abbot.[3] The normal course, no doubt, was for the outgoing body of colonists, or the chosen instructor of the young group, to carry to the new house the customs of a previously existing one, which would reproduce the main lines of the life as described in the *Concordia*.

That piece of legislation, as we have seen, was intended by Dunstan as a bond of unity among the monasteries, which were themselves to form an important binding force in Church and nation. We can see this conception retaining some of its power in the first generation of his disciples, and then gradually disappearing. In the *Liber Vitae* of the New Minster are inscribed the names of those who from its foundation joined themselves to the house in friendship and union of prayers. In the early years, besides

---

1 See Appendix IV, *Monastic Bishops, 960–1066*.

2 For Stow *v.* Dr H. E. Salter's article on Eynsham in *VCH, Oxfordshire*, II, 65, and his edition of the *Cartulary of Eynsham Abbey* (Oxf. Hist. Soc., vol. I, no. XLIX, 1907).

3 *Letter*, ed. M. Bateson, 174–5: "Ecce video vobiscum degens vos necesse habere... instrui ad mores monachiles dictis aut scriptis; ideoque haec pauca de libro consuetudinum... scriptitando demonstro, eo quod hactenus predictus libellus vestrae fraternitati incognitus habetur...sed nec audeo omnia vobis intimare, quae in schola ejus [*sc.* Aethelwoldi] degens multis annis, de moribus seu consuetudinibus didici."

kings and great men, almost all the bishops of England, numerous abbots, and the entire communities of Abingdon, Ely and Romsey are so recorded.[1] But by c. 1020 this ceases; bishops, abbots and monks of other houses disappear, and the list becomes one of those friends and benefactors who had private relationships of affection with the New Minster. Unions of prayers and privileges, many dating from the earliest times, continued, but here again mutual assistance between the communities as individuals replaces corporate solidarity as the end in view. Indeed, when the monastic body had attained a position of predominance, and members of the order held the bishoprics of the country, it began, inevitably and insensibly, to lose alike its sense of solidarity and its exclusively monastic stamp. The houses developed traditions and interests of their own, often differing from those of others, and there was a tendency visible in a few cases to lose some of the distinguishing marks of full monastic observance and approximate more nearly to the way of life of a community of clerks.

There remains one more field of external activity to be mentioned, into which a number of English monks, small perhaps but influential, passed. Dunstan and his colleagues cannot have been ignorant of the apostolic labours of Boniface and other Anglo-Saxon monks in the past, but no explicit statement of any biographer connects their names with the English mission to Scandinavia. This, indeed, has been strangely neglected by English historians, ancient and modern, and though it receives due notice in the pages of all Danish, Norwegian and Swedish histories, no exhaustive research, so it would appear, has hitherto been made that might establish with any certainty the careers of the missionaries and pronounce on the share taken in the work by the English monasteries.[2] The first expedition, at the time of the baptism of Olaf of Sweden, is said to have taken place c. 1000 under the leadership of bishop John or Sigurd or Sigfrid;[3] a little later another party under Gotbald were received by Sweyn in Norway, while others, including two, David, the apostle of Västmanland and traditionally first bishop of Västerås, and Eskil, who are

---

1 *Liber Vitae*, 12 *seqq.*

2 My attention was called to the subject by a passage (p. lxxv) in Prof. R. W. Chambers' essay *The Continuity of English Prose*. The only quasi-contemporary chronicler to mention these English missionaries is Adam of Bremen, *Gesta Hannaburgensis Ecclesiae Pontificum* in *MGH, SS*, 7; he wrote from c. 1068, and the only Scandinavian works I have been able to consult, viz. A. Taranger, *Den Angelsaksiske Kirkes Indflydelse paa den Norske* (Christiania, 1890), and Toni Schmid, *Sveriges Kristnande* (Stockholm, 1934), do little more than quote the familiar passages of Adam. Since this chapter was written C. J. A. Oppermann's *The English Missionaries in Sweden and Finland* has appeared. This gives a lengthy account of all that is known about the activities of the English in the missions, but should be used with caution. *V.* also M. Ashdown, *English and Norse Documents*, 289.

3 Adam of Bremen, II, 319, ch. 78: "Alii dicunt olim et tunc [*sc. c.* 980] ab Anglia quosdam episcopos vel presbyteros evangelizandi gratia egressos a domo...quorum praecipuus esset quidam Joannes episcopus." *Ibid.* IV, 383, ch. 242: "In Nortmanniam primus ab Anglia venit quidam Joannes episcopus." Taranger, *op. cit.* 167 note, identifies John with another bishop Sigward or Sigurd; he appears as Jón-Sigurd in Icelandic sources, and Oppermann, *The English Missionaries*, 61, note 231, identifies him with St Sigfrid.

said to have been monks, evangelized Sweden and met in many cases with a martyr's death.[1]

The earliest stream, therefore, was to Norway and Sweden. After Cnut's conquest of England, however, there was a steady flow to Denmark, though probably most of these missionaries were of Danish blood; Aethelnoth of Canterbury consecrated at least one bishop, and the introduction of various candidates from England into Danish sees aroused the opposition of the existing archbishop of Hamburg.[2] A little later Olaf of Norway (1015–30) introduced a number of missionaries to Norway, including one Grimkil, apparently a nephew of the older bishop John-Sigfrid; these passed through Sweden and carried the gospel to Gothland and the other islands.[3] Later still came an Englishman, Wulfred, who preached to the heathen in Sweden and was martyred.[4]

How many of these were monks it is quite impossible to say, but in view of the condition of the Church in England at the time all the probabilities are that apostles of distinction and enterprise would come from nowhere else but the monasteries. Sigfrid may be claimed with some confidence for Glastonbury on the strength of the tradition recorded by William of Malmesbury; David was certainly an English monk and, even if he did not actually found a monastery in Sweden, was probably accompanied by others.[5] Whatever may have been their provenance, it was to the English monasteries that several of the Scandinavian bishops retired; thus Ralph, mentioned as one of the companions of Sigfrid, found a home at Abingdon when deprived of his office in Norway, and an Osmund from Sweden settled at Ely about the same time (c. 1055).[6] The connection between the Church in England and the new plantations in Norway, Sweden and Denmark was thus in origin very close, and was reflected in the institutions of Scandinavia, which were modelled almost entirely upon those of England.[7] It was all but broken at the Norman Conquest,

1 Adam of Bremen, II, 320, ch. 82: "Tunc [c. 1000] etiam Gotebaldum quendam ab Anglia venientem episcopum in Sconia posuit [Suein]."

2 Adam of Bremen, II, 325, ch. 92: "Episcopos ab Anglia multos adduxit in Daniam." The names he gives, Bernard, Gerbrand and Reginbert, are not English.

3 Adam of Bremen, II, 326, ch. 94: "Habuit secum [Olaph] multos episcopos et presbyteros ab Anglia...quorum clari doctrina et virtutibus erant Sigafrid, Grimkil, Rudolf et Bernard." Sigafrid is presumably the Sigefridus Norwegensis episcopus, monachus Glastoniae whose obit is noted by William of Malmesbury, de Ant. Glast., ed. Hearne, ap. Adam of Domerham, I, 94; Grimkil was a nephew of bishop John (Taranger, op. cit. 167 note); Rudolf was no doubt the "Rodulfus quidam longaevus...qui episcopatum apud Norweiam gentem diu moderans", retired to Abingdon as abbot c. 1052 (Chron. Abingd. I, 463); Bernard was probably a German.

4 Adam of Bremen, II, 327, ch. 97. Cf. also IV, 383, ch. 242.

5 For Sigfrid and Glastonbury v. supra, note 3. David was said to have founded a monastery at Munktorp c. 1030 (Oppermann, 113, note 460, with references); the term Cluniacensis given to him and others by later writers does not, of course, indicate that he came from a Cluniac house; it is no more than the equivalent of "black monk".

6 For Ralph (Rodulf) v. supra, note 3. For Osmund v. Liber Eliensis, 220–1.

7 The Anglo-Saxon influence on the Norwegian ecclesiastical constitution and practice is set out very fully in Taranger, op. cit. chs. v–vi, pp. 203–412.

but even when England became politically one with northern France the abbey of Evesham, and later the Cistercian houses of Fountains and Kirkstall, made foundations in the northern lands, and both Canterbury and St Albans had relations with Denmark.[1] In the twelfth century many Swedish diocesan bishops were Englishmen; thus Stephen an English Cistercian of Alvastra was first archbishop of Uppsala in 1164, and another Englishman Henry, also archbishop of Uppsala, ranks as an apostle of Finland.[2]

This record of varied activities tells us little or nothing of the inner life of the monasteries and of the spiritual life of the monks who never passed into public positions, and in default of all intimate record it is useless to make any pronouncement. It would appear certain, however, that no one arose in the second generation to take the place of the three great leaders, nor were close relations maintained with Fleury or the Netherlands after *c.* 1000.[3] The monasteries of England were thus left in isolation; without any great figures of their own and without any kind of bond of government, they received no fresh stimulus either from within or from without, and we may suppose that the eager life at Ramsey, modelled so closely on that of Fleury, of which we are given so vivid a glimpse by Oswald's biographer, would rapidly lose something of its rhythm when the sources of its inspiration had ceased to flow. More than this, the sources of our knowledge do not permit us to say.

III

The Danish raids and invasions, though so widespread, had remarkably little permanent effect upon the material prosperity of the monasteries. In the early years, the houses in Devonshire suffered most; Tavistock was burnt as early as 997,[4] but soon recovered; Exeter, however, and Bedford silently disappear from existence between 1000 and the Conquest. In 1011 Aelfmaer, abbot of St Augustine's, was taken prisoner by the Danes along with Aelfheah the archbishop, Godwin, bishop of Rochester, and Leofryn, abbess of St Mildred's,[5] and in 1016 Wulsig, abbot of Ramsey, was among those who fell at the battle of Ashingdon in Essex.[6] There was,

1 The Danish connections of Evesham and St Albans will be mentioned later. From Canterbury went Aethelnoth, the biographer of St Olaf (*Acta SS*, July, III, 127–42).

2 *V.* Oppermann, *The English Missionaries*, 178, 200.

3 In the early years Womar, abbot of Ghent, had visited the Old Minster, and had commended himself also to the prayers of the New (*Liber Vitae*, 24). Ramsey perhaps maintained relations with Fleury somewhat longer. A Ramsey Benedictional (Paris, B.N. lat. 987) was presented to the French house *c.* 1010 or 1020. An earlier gift, also probably from Ramsey, was the "Sacramentary of Winchelcombe" (Orleans, MS 105).

4 *Chronicle*, 997 [E]; for Exeter, *v.* 1003 [C].   5 *Chronicle*, 1011 [E].

6 *Chronicle*, 1016 [E, D, F].

however, no kind of general harrying and ravaging of the monasteries. Cnut, once in power, showed himself not only a strong and able ruler, but a patron of the monastic order and the friend of Aethelnoth of Canterbury and other monk-bishops. His reign shows no change in the policy of appointing monks to vacant sees,[1] and Cnut and his chief magnates appear as benefactors to a number of important houses. In East Anglia, hitherto bare of monasteries, two great foundations owed their origin to the Danish king, St Benet's of Holme, near the coast not far from Norwich, and Bury St Edmunds. Both of these received colonists from Ely, a house for which Cnut always entertained a particular affection, and Bury in particular was from the beginning so richly endowed with land, churches and immunities both secular and ecclesiastical that it took rank at once among the greatest monasteries of the land—a position which it never lost. In the midlands, Abingdon and Evesham had peculiar connections with the Danish dynasty, and in the case of the latter the connection had important results in later years. Besides Bury and Holme, there was little new growth between 1020 and 1042. Wulfstan of York, towards the end of his long episcopate, established a small monastery at Gloucester,[2] but the house did not flourish, and soon ceased to exist. In the south, the small monastery of Abbotsbury probably dates from this period, and is in any case the work of one of Cnut's followers; among contemporary losses must probably be put Exeter, Bedford and perhaps one or two more insignificant houses.

As has been said, Cnut continued to appoint and to be advised by monastic bishops, and the episcopate so recruited, which was not affected by the Danish invasions, undoubtedly helped to preserve the monasteries and the Church at large from change during the political changes of the period. Few figures of any importance stand out among the bishops, and none among the abbots. The most distinguished is Aethelnoth of Canterbury, son of Aethelmaer and spiritual son of Dunstan, who had been dean of Christ Church and before that monk of Glastonbury. He was Cnut's chief adviser throughout his reign, and left a memory of benediction.[3] The fame of his most distinguished contemporary among the bishops, Lyfing, the eloquent pluralist who combined the sees of Crediton and Cornwall and also held Worcester for a number of years, is more equi-

1 J. A. Robinson, *The Saxon Bishops of Wells*, 52, writes: "The king's mass-priests became under Cnut and Edward the Confessor the usual source from which bishoprics were filled." True of Edward, this is scarcely true of Cnut; perhaps the only examples of such appointments in his reign are those of Dudoc of Wells (1033–60)—it was this which occasioned Dr Robinson's comment—and Eadsige of Canterbury (1038–50) who, however, was probably a monk at the time of his appointment.

2 *Hist. Gloc.* (RS), I, 8.

3 Aethelnoth, a son of Aethelmaer (Fl. Wig., *s.a.* 1020) had been baptized by Dunstan (Will. Malmesb., *de Ant. Glast.* 93), and became a monk of Glastonbury (*ibid.*). Later dean (i.e. prior) of Christ Church (*Chronicle*, 1020 [E]), he became known as archbishop as "se góda"; the *Chronicle* tells us (1038 [D]) that Aethelric of Selsey prayed that he might not live "aefter his leofan faeder".

vocal. Before his elevation he had been abbot of Tavistock, and as such had accompanied Cnut to Rome.[1]

IV

If under Cnut the Church in England, and with it the monastic order, showed few, if any, changes, the reign of Edward the Confessor brought into play a number of new forces, and saw also a rebirth of old life. Along with the first Norman monks, who came into England either as friends and counsellors of the king, or to take possession of properties which he had bestowed on them, and of whom Robert of Jumièges was the most eminent in the early part of the reign and Baldwin of St Denis in the later years, Edward also added to his predecessor's group of trained clerks who were not monks, the nucleus of the royal "chapel". These, in origin Lorrainers or Netherlanders, gradually took the place of monks as the king's nominees to vacant bishoprics, and thus transformed the whole character of the episcopate as a body.[2] At the same time there came from Italy and from the reformed papacy the first infiltrations of a new movement, the institute of regular clerks or canons, and perhaps also rumours of the monasticism of the school of Camaldoli and Peter Damian.

Yet Edward's employment of secular clerks and his fondness for Norman monks did not imply unfriendliness towards the English abbots and their houses. We hear of at least four abbots who were among his closest advisers or whom he employed on various missions of importance —Wulfric of St Augustine, who was one of the delegates of the king at the council of Reims in 1049, Aelfwine of Ramsey, who was Wulfric's companion at Reims and who was also sent on a diplomatic mission to Denmark, Leofric of Peterborough and Aethelwig of Evesham—and the

---

1 Lyfing "se wordsnotera" (Chronicle, 1047 [D]) held Worcester and the united sees of Devon and Cornwall. Another monastic bishop of doubtful fame was Spearhafoc, abbot of Abingdon and appointed (but never consecrated) to London; for him v. references in Chronicle and Chron. Abingd. 1, 462–3 et al.

2 The following are the Confessor's secular and monastic appointments:

1043	Stigand (Elmham)	
1044		[Robert of Jumièges (London)]
1045	Herman (Ramsbury)	
1046	Leofric (Crediton)	
1047	Heca (Selsey)	
	Stigand (Winchester)	
1050	Ulf (Dorchester)	
1051	William (London)	[Robert of Jumièges (Canterbury)]
		Kinsige (York)
1052	Stigand (Canterbury)	Leofwine (Lichfield)
1056	Leofgar (Hereford)	Aethelwine (Durham)
1058	Herman (Selsey)	Siward (Rochester)
		Aethelric (Selsey)
1061	Walter (Hereford)	Ealdred (York)
	Giso (Wells)	
1062		Wulfstan (Worcester)

The only bishop unaccounted for is Wulfwig of Dorchester (1053).

king and queen appear as visitors and benefactors to Abingdon. Nor was
his appointment of clerks to bishoprics part of a set policy, for monks
were appointed when they seemed the obvious choice.[1] Rather it would
seem that, as under Edward the episcopal office lost still more of its pastoral,
diocesan character, he naturally chose for the position those clerks who
had been useful to him in the past and would continue to be so. Nothing,
perhaps, in this enigmatic reign is more perplexing to the modern reader
than the arbitrary treatment of spiritual offices by a most devout king.
Edward, while naturally retaining the English conception of the king as
patron and protector of the sees and monasteries, would seem to have
blended with this as a result of his Norman upbringing the fully developed
feudal idea in which the ecclesiastical fief and its income had long been
regarded as something quite distinct from the spiritual charge of a diocese
or the religious headship of a monastery. Whatever the reason, the
accumulation of benefices of all kinds was more frequent in the Confessor's
reign than before. Among the bishops, Stigand, Ealdred and Herman
were the principal examples, and Stigand, besides holding the two cathedral
monasteries of Canterbury and Winchester, though himself not a monk,
also had the administration of Gloucester and, for a time at least, Ely and
perhaps other houses. Ealdred, for his part, besides York, held Worcester
until compelled to release it by papal legates, and administered for a time
Hereford and Ramsbury, and the abbey of Winchcombe.[2] Among the
abbots, Leofric of Peterborough, nephew and namesake of the great earl
of Mercia, obtained from the king the administration of no less than four
other houses, Burton-on-Trent, Coventry, and the two neighbouring
monasteries of Croyland and Thorney.[3] Edward's own foundation of
Westminster shows the same tendencies at work. Its history, as that of so
much in the Confessor's reign, is singularly fragmentary and uncertain,
but it is clear that he intended it to be a royal "private" abbey, on the
model of Caen and other Norman houses, and to be directly dependent
upon the king in a more explicit way than any previously existing house.
It was richly endowed, largely at the expense of Pershore in Worcestershire. The principal benefactions of the king, however, were to the
Norman abbeys, which began to acquire lands and churches throughout
southern England and the midlands.

With such a number of independent forces at work, developing, so
far as can be seen, without co-ordination or control, it is impossible to
say that monasticism in England as a whole either developed or declined

---

1 As the preceding note shows, the later years show an increase of monastic bishops.

2 For Winchcombe *v. Chronicle*, 1053 [D], and Fl. Wig., *s.a.* 1053, 1054. For a defence
of Ealdred *v.* R. R. Darlington's article, *Ecclesiastical Reform*, 399–400.

3 *Chronicle*, 1066 [E]. It is to be noted, however, that according to the Croyland tradition,
as received by Orderic (OV, II, 285), the abbey was ruled by Wulfketel: "Burgensis
ecclesiae monachus [qui] Crulandiae regimen a rege Eduardo, jubente Leofrico abbate suo,
suscepit."

during the reign, or to predict what would have happened had there followed no change of dynasty. On the whole, perhaps, the observance continued slowly to decline, especially in the cathedral monasteries of Canterbury and Winchester and a few other southern monasteries, but no account of the Confessor's reign would be complete without mention of two centres, one in the fenland, the other in Worcestershire, where, in different ways, a new era of prosperity was opened.

Leofric of Peterborough, who has already been mentioned, became abbot in 1052. Himself no doubt originally the inheritor of wealth and attracting benefactions by his high connections, he increased the already considerable property of his abbey and enriched it in every way with gold and silver ornaments and vestments, so that the place gained the name of the Golden Borough.[1] We can gain some indication of its wealth as well from the Domesday record, where it stands fifth (or, if Christ Church be excepted, fourth) among the monasteries of England, as from the list of Leofric's benefactions in the chronicle of the house and from the description of the precious things that fell into the hands of the Danes in 1070.[2] Among them were two gold and nine silver shrines, fifteen large crosses of gold and silver, the golden helmet and footrest from the great rood and countless other treasures in precious metals and vestments and books. As the greater part of our information about Peterborough under Leofric comes from local sources which did not take their final form till many years later and are consistently tendencious in tone,[3] it is not possible to ascertain the state of discipline and observance that prevailed, but it is evident that Leofric's rule was the culmination of an epoch of influence and prosperity, during which the house supplied a bishop to Durham and was the recipient of benefactions from two archbishops of York, Aelfric and Cynsige, who elected to be buried there.[4] Leofric would seem to have been an able and popular administrator in the course of his comparatively short period of office, and as Peterborough had a large territory of private jurisdiction he must also have been a person of importance in the public life of the country, but of this side of his activities no record has survived. His eminent position would have made him a figure of importance after the Conquest; fortunately, perhaps, for the Conqueror his policy and fortunes were very different from those of Aethelwig of Evesham. Leofric in 1066 came out strongly for Harold and was present in the army at Hastings. He fell sick there and returned to Peterborough, where he

1 *Chronicle*, 1052 [E]: "Man hit cleopede þa Gildene búrh."
2 *Hugonis Candidi Coenobii Burgensis Historia* (ed. Sparke, 1723), 41–3. *Chronicle*, 1070 [E].
3 The [E] (Peterborough) text of the *Chronicle*, which alone contains the long passages referring to this house, dates in its present form from 1121. The Latin Chronicle of Hugo Candidus was written about the middle of the twelfth century and based upon it or a common source.
4 *Hug. Cand.* 45. The main facts of this chronicler are probably correct, but his interpretation of them is anachronistic.

died on 1 November,[1] thus leaving his abbey and its dependencies in an unfavourable position with regard to the Conqueror—a position rendered still more unfavourable, as will be seen, by the conduct of his successor and the disturbances of the following years. Very different were the fortunes of Evesham and its abbot, and the history of this house and its near neighbour, the cathedral monastery of Worcester, in the crucial years before the Conquest is so interesting as to demand separate attention.

V

In these Worcestershire monasteries we find a vitality which in many ways had no parallel in the rest of England. No judgment on Saxon monasticism in the middle of the eleventh century would be complete which did not take notice of the state of things in the Severn and Avon valleys and which did not give some account of two men, contemporaries and near neighbours, who both rose to positions of importance some years before the Conquest. Had there been no Conquest, neither Wulfstan of Worcester nor Aethelwig of Evesham would have played his peculiar part in English history, but both were men of mature character and fully developed powers at the death of the Confessor, wholly the product of the English Church and its monasticism, and would in any circumstances have been centres of new life.

Wulfstan[2] and Aethelwig[3] were almost exact contemporaries,[4] each was for a considerable period head of a monastic establishment which increased in numbers and resources under his rule, and both men, though wholly English in mind and character, were faithful agents of the Con-

1 *Chronicle,* 1066 [E].

2 Our chief authority for the life of Wulfstan is the *Vita Wulfstani* of William of Malmesbury. This, though not composed in its present form till after 1124, is little more than a faithful translation of the English life by the monk Coleman, who was Wulfstan's chaplain for fifteen years and also his chancellor. Coleman's original is not known to exist, and as it is all but certain that it was sent to Rome early in the thirteenth century in connection with the process of canonization, it possibly never returned to England. Malmesbury's translation, however, has all the authority of Coleman's work, which was clearly a sober and solid piece of biography. It has recently been edited in full for the first time by R. R. Darlington for the Royal Historical Society (Camden Society, 3rd series, vol. XL, 1928); this edition, with its valuable introduction and notes, is a model of its kind, and I have consulted it frequently. The *Life* has been translated into English from Mr Darlington's text by J. H. F. Peile (Oxford, 1934). The only other contemporary account, a very brief one, is that given by the Worcester monk Hemming in his *Chartulary* drawn up under Wulfstan's direction (ed. Hearne, 1723, 403–8).

3 No formal biography of Aethelwig exists, but Mr Darlington, in two important articles (*Aethelwig, abbot of Evesham, EHR,* XLVIII (1933), 1–22, 177–98), has shown conclusively that the pages in the *Evesham Chronicle* (ed. Macray, Rolls Series) which cover the abbot's rule are by a contemporary, and perhaps originally formed an independent account of his life and work. Corroboratory references to Aethelwig occur in the *Anglo-Saxon Chronicle* and Hemming. For further remarks on the *Evesham Chronicle v.* Appendix VIII.

4 Wulfstan died in 1095, *anno aetatis circiter octogesimo septimo* (*Vita Wulfst.* 61); he was therefore born *c.* 1008. Aethelwig died in 1078, not, it would seem, in advanced years; he was probably born *c.* 1010–15.

queror and held under him positions of administrative importance such as were entrusted to no other native Englishmen. While both were alive, the great administrative abilities of Aethelwig somewhat overshadowed Wulfstan, but after the abbot's death the wisdom and sanctity of the bishop gave him a place apart in the kingdom, and he, too, showed himself a prudent administrator in the reorganization of Worcester estates and the rebuilding of his cathedral; Aethelwig, for his part, though not a saint, was a wise father of his monastic family and a man of great practical charity.

At the middle of the eleventh century the monasteries of Worcester and Evesham were both small in numbers.[1] Both had suffered considerably since the days of Oswald, for, apart from the troubles of the time and the inroads of lay landowners, the church of Worcester had suffered from the almost continuous union with that of York,[2] and from a great harrying under Harthacnut in 1041,[3] while Evesham had fallen more than once completely under lay control and only attained final liberty c. 1014 with the appointment of Aelfward, monk of Ramsey and afterwards bishop of London, as abbot.[4] Evesham, however, from Aelfward's day onwards had within it the seeds of a new and fervent life. The notices of this time preserved in the chronicle of the house are all too few, but they are authentic, and we obtain a glimpse of a prior Aefic, the friend and spiritual guide of Leofric and Godgifu, and the friend also of Cnut. He came, as did so many monks of the time, from the landed class, and his influence and holiness of life drew attention to Evesham; from his day and that of Ailward, a blood relation of Cnut, dated the close connection between Evesham and Denmark. Aefic was not alone in his reputation for holiness at Evesham; in his day the abbey produced three who lived as hermits in the neighbourhood—Wulfsig (Aefic's brother), Basing and Aelfwin.[5] Anchorites, common enough a century later, are rare in the England of the Confessor; almost the only others of which record exists are connected with Worcester, and it is natural to suppose that there was something peculiar to the houses of Worcestershire and north Gloucestershire which fostered this austere spirit, for we shall see others attracted to it and ultimately going forth from the midlands as founders to the north. Though no direct connection can be traced between Worcestershire and Italy, the life which began at Evesham and Malvern c. 1050 and spread to Durham and Yorkshire twenty years later is undoubtedly a manifestation—the first to appear in England—of that great movement towards simplicity

1 At Worcester there were only a dozen monks c. 1050 (cf. the Alveston charter in Hemming, 418 and *Monasticon*, I, 599), and at Evesham the same number in 1058 (*Chron. Evesh.* 96).

2 The sees were united 972–1023 and again for a year or so c. 1040 and from 1061 to 1062.

3 *Chronicle*, 1041 [C]; Fl. Wig., *s.a.* 1041, 1042.

4 *Chron. Evesh.* 81 *seqq.* He was *consanguineus* of Cnut (*ibid.* 83).

5 For Aefic *v. Chron. Evesh.* 83–5. For Wulfsig and his fellows *v. ibid.* 83, 322. To these should be added the sacrist of the time, Aelsig, *maximae strenuitatis vir* (*ibid.* 321).

and austerity of life in which St Peter Damian, St Romuald, William of Chaise Dieu and Herluin of Bec are outstanding figures, and from which, both now and a little later, sprang the new monastic and eremitical orders.

Evesham's vitality, which had its origin under Aefic, continued under Mannig, who was abbot 1044–66.[1] Mannig, like Dunstan, united in himself a number of diverse artistic gifts; he added to Evesham's material prosperity and decorated and consecrated the church, where the shrine of St Egwin had become one of the principal resorts of pilgrims in England. The community remained small, but it contained, besides the saintly sacrist Aelsig, at least one member of unusual gifts.

Aethelwig, a man of high birth, was early distinguished by his legal knowledge and practical ability.[2] He attracted the attention of Ealdred, bishop of Worcester, who, some years before 1059, had given him charge of the properties of his see, presumably during one of his many absences from England,[3] and during the abbacy of Mannig administered the estates of Evesham.[4] The abbot, stricken with paralysis, asked King Edward to appoint Aethelwig as abbot; this was done, and henceforward, besides attending to the interests of Evesham, he was a constant counsellor of the Confessor[5] and later of Harold. When Ealdred was commanded to provide a successor to himself at Worcester, he hesitated between Wulfstan and Aethelwig, and according to the Worcester tradition the latter did not scruple to canvass for himself.[6] His activities and responsibilities under the new *régime* will be mentioned in their place, as also the more intimate aspects of his life within the monastery; here it is enough to record that under his rule, and before the Conquest, Evesham flourished as a well-ordered and highly disciplined house.

During the same period of years a very similar growth was taking place in the neighbouring cathedral monastery of Worcester. Here, as at Evesham, we have few details which do not refer to the actions of the man who was chiefly responsible for the fame of the house, but the fact that

1 For Mannig *v. Chron. Evesh.* 86–8; he also left a reputation *mirae sanctitatis et probitatis* (*ibid.* 321).

2 *Chron. Evesh.* 87: "Tam generis nobilitate quam divina lege ac saeculari prudentia plurimum valentem." All the sources—friendly, hostile and neutral—agree as to Aethelwig's wisdom in the things of this world; e.g. Hemming, 271: "Ingenio et calliditate et scientia secularium legum, qua sola studebat, cunctos praecelleret." *Vita Wulfst.* 18: "Maxime quantum ad seculum prudentie." *Chronicle*, 1078 [D]: "Aegelwig se woruld snotra abb on Eofeshamme."

3 It is unthinkable that Aethelwig was in episcopal orders, and in the English Church immediately before the Conquest the bishops did little in the way of spiritual administration. Probably, therefore, Aethelwig's position as deputy of Ealdred was purely temporal. *Chron. Evesh.* 87: "Qui multo antea tempore episcopatum Wigornensis ecclesiae sub Aldredo archiepiscopo [this word is probably an anachronism] laudabiliter rexerat." No exact parallel can be quoted (for the case of Siward of Rochester is different), but the hierarchy was in a chaotic condition and Ealdred was absent in 1048 (Rome), 1049 (Flanders), 1058 (Hungary, Jerusalem) and 1061 (Rome).

4 *Chron. Evesh.* 87: "Jure praepositi totius abbatiae hujus curam agebat."

5 *Chron. Evesh.* 88: "Inter primos necessarios [Edwardi] consiliarius habebatur."

6 *Vita Wulfst.* 18.

Wulfstan, when already a priest of exemplary life, should have wished to join the community, and the account given us of the simple life he was able to live there, show that at Worcester also the monastic order was observed.[1]

Wulfstan had a direct family connection with St Oswald,[2] and was born when the great archbishop's memory was still green; the example of his two saintly predecessors was always before him as bishop, and we know that even in late life he read the lives of Oswald and Dunstan at a moment of crisis.[3] Born at one of the Itchingtons in the heart of Warwickshire, he received his earliest training at Evesham and his fuller education at Peterborough, already a prosperous house, where one of his masters, Erwin, later abbot, was an illuminator of note. As a young man he joined the household of Brihtheah, bishop of Worcester (1033–8) and sometime abbot of Pershore. The bishop ordained him priest, and for a time he held the church of Hawkesbury near Chipping Sodbury in Gloucestershire;[4] then, wishing for a monk's life, he entered the priory of Worcester, whither his father had preceded him, and became successively childmaster, precentor, sacristan and provost. His biographer, the monk Coleman, who lived for years in daily contact with him, gives a number of details of his life in these years, which are a valuable evidence of English monasticism at its purest. We read of the many psalms which he added in private to those of the office, of the frequent visits by day and night to the numerous altars and churches of the town, and of sleep on the floor of the church. All this finds a parallel in the lives of the monastic saints of other countries at this epoch; peculiarly English, however, is the part taken by Wulfstan as prior in baptizing, preaching, confessing and directing those who came to the church at Worcester, among whom, even thus early in Wulfstan's life, were such eminent men as the Earl Harold.[5] Like Aethelwig, Wulfstan left his mark upon the estates of Worcester; a lasting memorial is Hemming's chartulary, composed at his insistent request when bishop. During Ealdred's lifetime the scope of his achievement was limited, and Worcester tradition regarded Aethelwig as a powerful neighbour who had encroached, but in his last years Wulfstan was able to secure for his church the possession of almost all the lands which she claimed to have lost in the previous half century.

1 *Vita Wulfst.* 8. It is indeed stated (*ibid.* 11) that when prior he strengthened the discipline within and without the house, but a man of Wulfstan's energy and holiness of life would do this in any community.

2 R. R. Darlington (*Vita Wulfst.* xxii) inclines to the view that his father was the *vir fidelis* to whom the archbishop granted land at Itchington in 991.

3 E.g. during the dispute with Thomas of York in 1072. "Habebat tunc in manibus vitas beatorum pontificum Dunstani et Oswaldi, qui ambo quondam diversis temporibus Wigornie presederant; quorum ut imitabatur vitam, sic tuebatur sententiam" (*Vita Wulfst.* 25).

4 It was there that the familiar incident of the roast goose occurred (*Vita Wulfst.* 47).

5 *Vita Wulfst.* 13.

When Ealdred, promoted to York in 1061, applied at Rome for the pallium, it was refused him by Nicholas II till he should have pledged himself to surrender Worcester, and in 1062 two cardinal legates visited England charged, among other business, with supervising the election of a substitute. Ealdred, as has been said, had thoughts of Aethelwig, but the cardinals, impressed with the strict life and charity of the prior of Worcester, who was their host during the whole of Lent, and extended to them the bounteous hospitality of England while himself going far beyond the canonical measure of fasting,[1] urged the merits of Wulfstan, who had also the support by this time of Ealdred and Harold. His public life as bishop and his services to the Conqueror belong to the story of later years, but it is interesting to learn that before the Conquest he acted with success as Harold's emissary in keeping the north to its allegiance.[2]

At Worcester, as at Evesham, there were aspirants to the eremitical life. Whatever be the facts concerning Werstan, said to have gone from Deerhurst into the wild country near Malvern c. 1050, it is certain that shortly after the middle of the century Aldwin, an unlettered monk of Worcester, settled there with Wulfstan's approval and, after despairing of success, was encouraged to persevere by the bishop.[3] Here, as at Bec not many years previously and as in the north at almost the same moment, the band of anchorites ended by adopting the Rule of St Benedict and the customs traditional in the old houses.

VI

The foregoing pages may have conveyed some general impression of the state of the monasteries immediately before the Conquest. They will at least have shown that no broad judgment can be made covering all. While a few of the smaller ones were apparently dwindling to extinction, and two or three of the greatest houses—in particular the cathedral monasteries of Winchester and Canterbury—had become relaxed, the majority were, it would seem, living a life distinguished from all save the most observant Norman houses, not so much by degrees of departure from the monastic rule as by the national characteristics of a less enclosed life and wider external relationships, though there is evidence that regular silence and regular food had to some extent given way to relaxations. At a few, and especially at Evesham and Worcester, a standard of fervour was maintained upon which the Norman model could not improve.

Before passing to describe this new monasticism from overseas, a word

---

1 *Vita Wulfst.* 17: "Nihil pretermitte[bat] quo minus Anglorum...liberalem dapsilitatem experirentur. Ipse interea...tribus in ebdomada diebus omnis cibi abstemius, etc."
2 *Vita Wulfst.* 23.   3 *Vita Wulfst.* 26.

must be said of the judgments passed on what had gone before by the monastic writers of the new generation, which have too often been repeated without modification by historians whose interests have not taken them behind the Conquest. Three of the most celebrated of these chroniclers speak in terms of the most sweeping condemnation of the old life, and as their words appear to be corroborated by notices in more than one chronicle, it is natural for those who have paid attention only to post-Conquest literature to accept their judgments without question; they must therefore be examined a little more carefully.

The three chiefly concerned are Eadmer, precentor of Christ Church, Canterbury, the intimate and biographer of St Anselm; the great historian, William of Malmesbury; and the Anglo-Norman monk of St Évroul, Ordericus Vitalis. All three belong to the generation that had grown up after the Conquest; Eadmer, the oldest of the three (he was born c. 1064), who had most opportunity of hearing of the past, was wholly of the school of Lanfranc and Anselm. His testimony, however, may be accepted in broad outline; it refers to a single house, his own, Christ Church. He gives two accounts of the life there before the reforms of Lanfranc, one, the more detailed, written several years before the other. In the first he states that the monks of Christ Church had lost their discipline as a result of the Danish invasions which culminated in the martyrdom of Aelfheah in 1012, and that previous to the Conquest they were living expensively and luxuriously, indulging in music, riding and hawking.[1] The second account is much more summary.[2] We can well imagine that, whatever may have been the effect of the Danish invasions, the years between Stigand's appointment in 1052 and Lanfranc's arrival in 1070 were most demoralizing, for the income of Christ Church (if, indeed, Stigand did not appropriate it all) was very considerable. Besides Eadmer's account, we have some vignettes of life at Canterbury given us by Osbern, his predecessor in the precentor's office. These neither corroborate nor contradict the other; they suggest only the hard, harsh life of the children of the cloister,

---

1 Eadmer, *Vita S. Dunstani* (*Mem. St Dunst.*), 236: "Quos [*sc.* monachos eccl. Christi] a tempore Danorum qui beatum Aelfegum occiderunt, cessante disciplina, in saeculari videbat [Christus] conversatione ultra quam debebant jacere." He then describes a miracle worked by St Dunstan on a demoniac monk, and continues (237–8): "Sciunt quippe quia qui prius in omni gloria mundi, auro videlicet, argento, variis vestibus ac decoris cum pretiosis lectisterniis, ut diversa musici generis instrumenta, quibus saepe oblectabantur, et equos, canes et accipitres, cum quibus nonnunquam spatiatum ibant, taceam, more comitum potius quam monachorum vitam agebant." He adds: "Nos quidem, qui qualiter ea tempestate res agebantur novimus indubitanter, etc." Eadmer would have been perhaps ten at the time; the episode of the demoniac is dated *c.* 1072–3 by the reference to Lanfranc's building operations.

2 Eadmer, *Historia Novorum* (RS), 12. Referring to Lanfranc's buildings and reforms at Canterbury, he alludes to the monks as raised by him "a saeculari vita, in qua illos invenit plus aequo versari". The *Vita Lanfranci*, based here on Canterbury tradition, has "Coenobialis ordo, qui omnino ad laicalem prolapsus fuerat dissolutionem, ad probatissimorum reformabat [Lanfrancus] disciplinam monasteriorum [i.e. by his *Consuetudines*]" (*Lanfranci Opera*, ed. Giles, I, 296).

of whom the writer had been one, under the old *régime*.[1] In any case, the changes made by Lanfranc were certainly great. Malmesbury's judgment, which again refers directly to Canterbury and is clearly based on Eadmer, is extended by a quasi-parenthetical remark to all English monasteries.[2] A criticism of this kind, made more than sixty years after the period to which it applies, cannot by itself carry much weight. That of Orderic, which again resembles that of Eadmer so closely in tone as to suggest some kind of dependence,[3] occurs in a long sketch of English monastic history which contains a number of inaccuracies, and in which the salutary influence of Fleury in the tenth century and of Norman monasticism in more recent years is duly, if not excessively, stressed.

The evidence of these three, therefore, would seem of itself to do little more than prove the relaxed state of Christ Church, a house which on any showing had had a chequered existence and had never had the advantage of possessing a superior of its own with full powers. Of the chronicles, those which give details of important disciplinary changes under the Normans come from Winchester and St Albans. Both in their present form are the work of later chroniclers writing over earlier material, and that of St Albans yields very little precise information.[4] At Winchester more details are given, and we may perhaps suppose that here, too, the years from 1047 onwards during which Stigand held the bishopric were demoralizing to a rich house at the centre of the chief city of the country.

Besides historians and chronicles, two other sources give us some information as to the state of the monasteries at the Conquest. Very little, however, can be gathered from the decrees of the reforming synods over which Lanfranc presided in the early years of his rule. Besides general exhortations, the only abuse against which they proceed is the holding of

1 *V.* especially *Mem. St Dunst.* 140–2.
2 Will. Malmesb., *GR*, ii, 304–6. He says that the monks before the Conquest "subtilibus indumentis et indifferenti genere ciborum regulam ludificabant"; also that "religionis normam, usquequaque in Anglia emortuam, adventu suo [Normanni] suscitarunt". In *GP*, 70 he is more precise: "monachi Cantuarienses, sicut omnes tunc temporis in Anglia, secularibus haud absimiles erant, nisi quod pudicitiam non facile proderent. Canum cursibus avocari; avium predam raptu aliarum volucrum per inane sequi; spumantis equi tergum premere, tesseras quatere, potibus indulgere; delicatiori victu et accuratiori cultu; frugalitatem nescire, parsimoniam abnuere; et cetera id genus, ut magis illos consules quam monachos pro frequentia famulantium diceres." The first of these passages should be read in its context; it occurs in a long and rhetorical comparison of the two races, Norman and English, immediately after the battle of Hastings. The second is in part a highly embroidered paraphrase of Eadmer; whether the dice, etc., are derived from some other document, or oral tradition, or Malmesbury's own sense of the likelihood of things, cannot be said. That his general statements cannot be taken literally can be shown from his own works. [After writing the above paragraph and notes I was gratified to read an almost exactly similar judgment in Dr Darlington's article *Ecclesiastical Reform*, p. 403, note 2.]
3 Ordericus Vitalis, ii, 208: "Per longum itaque retro tempus Transmarinorum monachatus deciderat, et parum a saecularitate conversatio monachorum differebat."
4 *Gesta Abbatum S. Albani*, i, 52, 59; *Annales Wintonienses* (*Ann. Monast.* ii), s.a. 1082.

private property by monks.[1] This probably refers to the retention of personal effects within the monastery without the permission of the abbot, but the Domesday survey gives us a glimpse of another and more serious kind of private possession, that of land, which though the examples are rare deserves examination. The Abingdon chronicler, indeed, tells us that before the Conquest it was common for monks to inherit property of which they had the usufruct and testamentary disposition.[2] This is an exaggeration, if not a wholly inaccurate statement, for we are fortunately able to check from *Domesday* itself the very case which prompted the chronicler's comment, and find nothing necessarily irregular,[3] but it is certain that before the Conquest it was by no means uncommon for properties to be settled upon monks for their support, and for the administration to be entrusted to the beneficiary. Normally, the income and ownership would be considered as belonging to the abbot and monastery, and this is sometimes explicitly stated in the Domesday account, but a few cases exist where the individual monk appears as the holder.[4]

We may say, then, that the monasteries of England, on the day when King Edward "was alive and dead", were as a body living and powerful. There is no trace of serious moral decadence, nor of that lay encroachment which in previous centuries had had such disastrous consequences both in England and abroad. At the majority of the important houses the

1 Among the decrees of the synod of London, 1075, are the following (Wilkins, *Concilia*, I, 363): "Ut monachi ordinem debitum teneant; infantes praecipue et juvenes in omnibus locis deputatis sibi idoneis magistris custodiam habeant; nocte luminaria ferant generaliter omnes....Si quis vero aliquid proprii sine praefata licentia habere in morte fuerit deprehensus...nec signa pro eo pulsentur, nec salutaris pro ejus absolutione hostia immoletur, nec in coemeterio sepeliatur."

2 *Chron. Abingd.* I, 477: "Consuetudinis apud Anglos tunc erat ut monachi qui vellent pecuniarum patrimoniorumque forent susceptibiles, ipsisque fruentes quomodo placeret dispensarent [from the context the last word would seem to mean 'give, grant away']."

3 Dd. I, 59 b (Sparsholt): "Edricus qui eum tenebat deliberavit illud filio suo qui erat in Abendone monachus, ut ad firmam illud teneret et sibi donec viveret necessaria vitae inde donaret, post mortem vero ejus manerium haberet."

4 I have noted the following cases of irregular ownership: Dd. 90 a (Pilton, near Glastonbury): "de terra quae non geldat tenet Alnodus monachus 1 hid liberaliter de abbate concessu regis"; 174 b (Defford, near Pershore): "de ista terra T. R. E. tenuit Alcot monachus 1 hid et faciebat servitium quod ei praecipiebatur"; 196 a (Bottisham, near Cambridge): "Alricus monachus habuit 2 hid quas non potuit dare vel vendere absque licentia abbatis de Ramesy cujus homo erat [!]"; he also had a share in three and a half hides nearby; 202 b (Tadely, Cambs.): "Walterus monachus tenet"; 155 a (Eynsham, Shipford and Lesser Rollright): "Columbanus monachus tenet de Ep. Linc." Here presumably a single monk was holding what had been the abbey of Eynsham. The fully regular state of things is noted in the following cases: 173 a (Washbourne, near Worcester): "Elmer tenuit et postea monachus factus est; Ep. ut terram suam recepit"; 239 a (Newbold-on-Stour, Warwicks.): "Ulvinus monachus tenuit et ipse dedit ecclesiae quando factus est monachus"; 336 a: At Lincoln Peterborough has the church of All Saints and its land because Godricus became a monk. The burgesses say this is unjust and that it could not be given away *extra civitatem nisi concessu regis*; a relation of Godric claims it. To these may be added the case from the Canterbury *Domesday Monachorum* translated from Christ Church MS. E 28 by Prof. Nellie Neilson in *VCH, Kent*, III (1932), 255–69. On fol. 9 (p. 263) Abel the monk holds land by order of the archbishop (c. 1086) at East Farleigh, etc.—Abel the monk holds it, and pays farm to the monks.

liturgical and cultural life inaugurated a century before was still in being, if somewhat less intense. No great spiritual leader, however, whether bishop or abbot, existed, for the genius of both Wulfstan and Aethelwig was for direct, practical, local action, and there was little or nothing in England of the new intellectual life of France, while the English abbeys wholly lacked the great and regularly planned churches and conventual buildings that had sprung up all over Normandy within the last generation.

CHAPTER V

THE NORMAN MONASTICISM

I

In the foregoing chapters we have seen how the revival of English monasticism, wholly spontaneous in its origin under Dunstan at Glastonbury, drew its further inspiration from two centres of new life abroad. From Fleury came the impulse of Cluny, modified by its passage at second hand and by the peculiar characteristics of Abbo and others; from Ghent came the spirit of the Lotharingian reform. Together these two sources sent to England what may be called the first of that series of waves of foreign influence which succeeded each other in the course of three hundred years, culminating in the coming of the friars in the first half of the thirteenth century.

As has been seen, the overseas influence in the tenth century was temporary. English monastic life, having once received in 970 the impress of foreign traditional practice in the *Regularis Concordia*, continued thenceforward to develop its own traditions and characteristics without any further communication with monasteries abroad. Between the sojourn of Abbo of Fleury at Ramsey in 986–8 and the first Norman heralds of the coming invasion under Edward the Confessor there is no trace of continental influence in English monasticism.[1] The second wave, that of the Norman tradition, was to be far more pervading and permanent in its effects, and in order to appreciate the changes which it brought about, we must glance at the antecedents and history of the body of monasteries from which it drew its origin.[2]

In the lifetime of Dunstan, and fifty years after the foundation of Cluny,

---

1 Even in the reign of the Confessor foreign influence was restricted to Westminster and Bury, where Baldwin became abbot in 1065. We hear of the presence of a foreign monk at Worcester before the Conquest (*Vita Wulfstani*, 14), and Wulfric, abbot of St Augustine's, Canterbury, was influenced by foreign architecture, especially by that of St Bénigne at Dijon. But these instances do not amount to a movement, or even to a current of thought, in England.

2 On the development and spread of Cluny and its influence the monumental work of E. Sackur, *Die Cluniacenser* (Halle, 2 vols. 1892, 1894) has not been superseded, though unfortunately the story is not carried beyond the death of Odilo (1049). Sackur's book makes singularly dry reading, consisting as it does almost entirely of a mass of data, but it is accurate in the extreme and based on a thorough acquaintance with all the sources. Sackur is at his best when enumerating the men and monasteries influenced by Cluny; he is less successful in depicting the spirit and constitution of Cluny herself and her immediate dependencies. By far the best brief account of the Norman monasticism, 1000–66, is in Böhmer, *Kirche und Staat in England und in der Normandie*, pp. 5–13. Böhmer, like Sackur, is thoroughly reliable (with the reservations noted above, p. 58, note) and is more successful in analysing movements and tendencies. There is much useful information, and a copious bibliography of several Norman monasteries in *Les privilèges d'exemption...des abbayes normandes* by J. F. Lemarignier (Paris, 1937). Also *v. infra* ch. VIII.

the territory of the Duke of Normandy was still largely heathen, and organized ecclesiastical life, and above all monastic life, was scarcely existent. Indeed, *c.* 930 no monastery of any kind existed in the land of the Normans, and the first foundation, that of Jumièges on the Seine below Rouen, made *c.* 940 with monks from Aquitaine, remained isolated and without influence. A more fruitful attempt was made by Duke Richard I who, between 961 and 963, refounded the ancient house of St Wandrille near Caudebec, between Jumièges and the mouth of the Seine, and settled monks at Mont St Michel and St Ouen at Rouen. These three houses did not derive from the group of Cluny, but from the Lotharingian monasticism of Ghent, where, as we have seen, St Dunstan was almost at this very moment in exile; they remained alone for forty years, since the endeavours of Duke Richard to introduce Cluniac monks to Fécamp failed, and it would seem that they gradually declined in vitality.

The decisive moment in the history of Norman monasticism is therefore the year 1001, when Duke Richard II invited the celebrated William of Volpiano, known more generally as St William of Dijon, to supplant the college of clerks at Fécamp with a community of his own. William, at the time abbot of St Bénigne at Dijon, is a figure of considerable importance in the religious history of north-western Europe.[1] William of Dijon (961–1031) is a figure of considerable importance alike in the monastic life of the time and in the history of the intellectual revival of north-western Europe. By birth a Piedmontese of noble family, when already a monk in north Italy he made the acquaintance of Maieul of Cluny and sought admission to the great abbey, where he speedily became the trusted disciple of the abbot, who in 989 sent him with a small group to reform St Bénigne at Dijon. Under Maieul, as under Odo, Cluny exerted her widespread influence by radiation rather than by absorption, and although William took the Cluny customs with him to Dijon and handed them on to his other foundations, he became himself the leader and centre of a widespread monastic reform which was Cluniac only in a wide sense of the term, and had a number of characteristics which Cluny did not share. William of Dijon, besides his spiritual gifts and his great administrative and diplomatic ability, was a man of considerable and varied intellectual attainments. He was skilled in music and an expert physician and geometrician, with a keen interest in architecture and the arts.[2] Above all, he founded schools at a number of his monasteries in

---

1 For William *v.* Sackur, *op. cit.*, esp. II, 126–33, 207–13, and the *Vita* by his disciple Rodulphus Glaber, Mabillon, *Acta SS, OSB*, saec. vi, I, 286 (*PL*, CXLII, 697 *seqq.*); also the article *William of Dijon* by Mr Watkin Williams in *Downside Review*, October 1934, 520–45. Sackur, II, 211–13 has a good sketch of his character: "Wilhelm war vielleicht die markanteste Erscheinung unter den Führern des Mönchtums. Er hat etwas rauhes, stacheliges in seinem Auftreten.... Dabei lebte in ihm ein Schatz von Liebe und Milde, u.s.w."

2 For William's medical, musical and other attainments *v.* Rodulphus Glaber *ap.* Mabillon, 294, *Chronicon S. Benigni Divion.*, *PL*, CXLI, 864 and Sackur, *op. cit.* II, 351–8. The organ at Fécamp later gave rise to controversy; cf. Mabillon, *Ann. OSB* (1713), V, 505.

which the monks gave instruction and in which not only the children of the cloister but aspirants to the clerical life and, it would seem, all who might desire to come, even the poorest, received education.[1] In all this, William differed from the tradition of Cluny; it must be remembered that he was an Italian by birth, and that in the cities of northern Italy education was already beginning to revive and to be alike more general in its scope and more widely diffused than in northern France. Probably, also, it was in the monasteries of northern Italy and southern and central France that the schools chiefly flourished to which the biographer of William refers. But the wide interests of William of Dijon had a lasting effect upon the houses which derived from his tradition, especially in Normandy; from them came some of the most eminent physicians of the next generation, and a school of chroniclers, biographers and writers of all kinds appeared amongst them from the beginning.

Fécamp, as has been said, was entrusted to the abbot of Dijon in 1001, and he ruled the house for more than a quarter of a century, without however relinquishing the abbacy of Dijon and the general superintendence of the numerous other monasteries whose reform had been committed to him. From Fécamp his influence went out, directly or indirectly, to almost all the Norman monasteries. Although no new foundations were made till the very close of his life, the three existing houses—Jumièges, Mont St Michel and St Ouen—were refounded or reformed earlier by the abbot of Fécamp. Then, between 1025 and the Conquest (nor did the stream cease then), the chief barons of Normandy, inspired by the example of the Dukes, made foundations in numbers all over the land.

The first, Bernay in the diocese of Lisieux, whose church was destined to provide a type for Romanesque architecture in Normandy and England, was made by William of Dijon himself c. 1025–7; all the others, with the important exception of one great house and her daughters, sprang directly or indirectly from the five previously existing monasteries, Fécamp, Jumièges, St Wandrille, Mont St Michel, and St Ouen of Rouen, of which group the last-named proved the most fruitful, giving birth to no less than nine filiations, direct or indirect. The growth, once it began, was rapid. Six foundations were made in the decade 1030–40; three in the following ten years; eight between 1050 and 1060 and at least four more between 1060 and the autumn of 1066. Then, as was to be expected, the pace slackened, for many of the great benefactors were absent among the *conquistadores*, and the monasteries themselves were providing a transfusion of some of their best blood for England, but foundations continued sporadically till c. 1130. In all, therefore, between twenty-six and twenty-

---

1 Rod. Glab., *PL*, CXLII, 709: "Instituit scholas sacri ministerii...quibus instarent fratres....[ut] gratis largiretur cunctis doctrinae beneficium ad coenobia sibi commissa confluentibus, nullusque qui ad haec vellet accedere prohiberetur: quin potius tam servis quam liberis, divitibus cum egenis, uniforme charitatis impenderetur documentum."

eight abbeys were in existence in Duke William's dominions when he landed in England.[1] Of these at least twenty-one derived their tradition, spiritual and intellectual, from William of Dijon and his immediate disciples, though in one or two cases it was blended with the kindred spirit of Richard of Verdun and the school of Lorraine, or even (as at St Évroul) with a new and direct inspiration from Cluny. A small group of three houses—St Wandrille and her daughters—had imbibed Dijon and Lorraine traditions in more equal proportions, but these four monasteries had little influence on England. Three others, Bec and her two daughters Lessay and St Étienne of Caen, stood in origin and spirit wholly outside the family of Fécamp, though they may have borrowed many customary details from this or that house. As the influence which two of them—Bec and Caen—exercised upon England was so decisive, their history and spirit will be touched upon in greater detail on another page.

William remained in active charge of Fécamp till 1028, when he appointed as his deputy and successor a disciple only less celebrated than himself, who had an even more widespread and lasting influence within the monastic order in France. This was John of Fécamp, Joannelinus as he was called, like his master an Ultramontane (he came from Ravenna), who learnt from William to be an expert in medical science and who occupied a position as spiritual guide and writer unique among his contemporaries. His very fame has obscured his memory with posterity, for some of his compositions, at first attributed by copyists to St Ambrose or St Augustine and later consigned to anonymity, have only been restored to their author in our own day—in particular by the careful investigations of Dom Wilmart, whose keen criticism has been instrumental in establishing the authorship of the beautiful and solemn prayers in preparation for Mass, familiar throughout the Church for many centuries owing to their inclusion in the Roman Missal, where they pass under the name of St Ambrose. Dom Wilmart, indeed, does not hesitate to call John of Fécamp the greatest spiritual writer of the epoch before St Bernard, and those familiar with his prayers will scarcely question this judgment; their clarity of thought and strength of language mark them as one of the first undoubted productions of the European renaissance.[2]

Norman monasticism thus drew its origin from all that was most vital in the immediate past and in the present, from Cluny and from the new current of life that was flowing in northern Italy. The framework of its organization differed little from that of the great Cluniac houses of the epoch of Maieul, before Cluny had entered upon its final phase of constitutional and liturgical elaboration, but there was no one code for all the houses. Customs passed from mother-house to daughter, and individual

1 V. Appendix V, *The Norman Monasteries 940–1066, with dates of foundation.*
2 V. the two articles by Dom Wilmart, *L'Oratio sancti Ambrosii du Missel Romain,* and *La complainte de Jean de Fécamp sur les fins derniers,* in *Auteurs spirituels,* 101–25; 126–37.

abbots might draw inspiration from observant monasteries outside the
bounds of the duchy of Normandy. That this could be the case even after
the advent of William I is seen from what occurred at St Évroul, and it is
worth glancing for a moment at the origin of that house, both because its
history is well known to us from the accounts given by its celebrated son,
Ordericus Vitalis, and because it provided, as we shall see, a considerable
number of heads of houses for England after the Conquest.

The monastery of St Évroul at Ouche in the diocese of Lisieux was
founded from Lisieux in 1050. Abbot Thierry, who died c. 1059, had sat
at the feet of abbots William of Dijon (†1031), Richard of Verdun (†1046)
and Thierry of Jumièges (†1028), and had handed on their doctrine to
those who came to join him at the new foundation. These traditions, so
we are told, were still faithfully preserved when Ordericus wrote, more
than half a century later.[1] Thierry was succeeded in 1059 by Robert de
Grentmesnil. He, when young, had with Thierry's permission paid a
visit to Cluny, then ruled by the young St Hugh, and had brought back
with him a distinguished monk of Cluny to teach St Évroul the ways of
his mother house.[2] There is no reason to suppose that the history of
St Évroul was altogether exceptional, and we shall be justified in supposing
that many of the Norman houses thus made their own traditions, coming
from a wide variety of sources.

The Norman monasticism, then, was of the same mould as Cluny, and
ultimately derived the greater part of its customs and liturgical observance
from Cluniac circles, but from the beginning it had a character of its own,
which racial and political circumstances made more and more distinct.
In growing measure, and especially under the long rule of William I,
Normandy became a political and ecclesiastical unit, sharply divided from
neighbouring lands, and more highly organized than her neighbours by
a fully developed military feudalism, in which every member was bound
by the closest ties to the Duke. William, for his part, had taken in hand the
reform and strengthening of his *Landeskirche* before the advent of Leo IX
at Rome. In this reform the monasteries were for him a most powerful
instrument; he used them as such, and encouraged his barons to make and
endow numerous foundations. The monasteries of Normandy, therefore,
while they received the benefactions of the Duke and his vassals, were
from the beginning caught up into the social and feudal organization

---

1 Ordericus Vitalis, II, 68: "Religiosa quoque instituta, quae ipse [Teodericus] ex
doctrina venerabilium abbatum Ricardi Veredunensis et Willermi Divionensis atque
Teoderici Gemmeticensis didicerat, et novellae ecclesiae sibi commissae fideliter tradiderat,
diligenti studio usque hodie observant [monachi S. Ebrulfi] et novitiis ad religionis con-
versationem conversis solerter insinuant."

2 OV, II, 69: "Justas observationes, quas pius praedecessor ejus instituerat, non solum
non imminuit, sed etiam...auctoritate majorum, vel exemplo vicinorum percussus aug-
mentavit. Ipse quidem, dum adhuc neophytus erat, permissu venerabilis Teoderici Cluniacum
perrexerat...Unde...Bernefridum...secum adduxit; eumque ut mores Cluniacensium
Uticensibus intimaret...retinuit."

depending upon him as head. His permission was necessary for their establishment; he appointed the abbots and received custody of their possessions during an interregnum; and some years before the Conquest a number of the houses had come to hold of him by military service.[1]

Side by side with this political development went the intellectual and moral growth of the Norman character. Cluny, from the beginning of the eleventh century, continued to develop on her own lines, which ran in many ways counter to the European revival. For whatever reason, intellectual and literary pursuits had never found a congenial home there, and as the strict observance of a most exacting daily round of choral duties came to be regarded more and more as her *raison d'être*, there was no room for the new methods of learning. The Norman monasteries, on the other hand, had from the beginning received a different bent from William of Dijon, and many of them lay near that district of central France, south and west of Paris, which became the home of the northern intellectual revival.

The Norman monks, besides, had all those characteristics of energy, enterprise and domination which distinguished their race. If in purely intellectual qualities the Normans of the mid-eleventh century were inferior not only to the Italians, but also to the peoples of central and eastern France, and if in the more delicate arts they were far surpassed alike by the sculptors of southern France and by the artists and craftsmen of England, they excelled in their ability to conceive and to execute great buildings, and to organize and administer great estates. It was in the circle of the monasteries of Normandy before the Conquest that there was evolved the typical plan of a large monastery with its cloisters and offices, and above all with its vast church, planned on a scale far more magnificent than anything that had been seen in the West for centuries.[2] It was there also that all the machinery necessary for such constructions was organized and in a sense standardized, and that the first beginnings were made towards creating the staff of a wide monastic estate.

II

In this brief account of the rise of Norman monasticism no mention has been made of the abbey which, even in a company of celebrated names, stands out among the monastic houses of Normandy *quantum lenta solent inter viburna cupressus*. Of all the Norman monasteries one must take pride of place alike in the weight of its influence upon England and in its significance in the history of Western religion and thought. Bec in the

1 The feudal obligations of the Norman monasteries will be considered in a later chapter. For Normandy at this time *v.* especially C. H. Haskins, *Norman Institutions*. The relationships between the monasteries are set out in Appendix, Table II.

2 The first typical Norman Romanesque church would seem to have been that of Bernay (? 1017–45); cf. Clapham, *English Romanesque Architecture after the Conquest*, 5 *seqq.*

days of its greatness—and its greatness endured for at least a century—had that rare fortune which comes now and again to a city or a university of attracting to itself, refining and handing on to the world around it all that is best and most characteristic of an age. It was not only that Bec had at one time within its walls two of the most powerful intelligences, and more than two of the most saintly men, of a great formative epoch. It was rather that the house had in a high degree that power—which we call the *genius loci*—of inspiring and moulding and bestowing, and that it had this power at a moment when new and wide fields were being opened to the reception of its seed.

The circumstances of its origin sharply distinguish the early history of Bec from that of the other monasteries of Normandy. These were, as has been seen, largely the result of an earlier movement at Cluny which sprang into new life at centres such as Dijon and Fécamp, and considered as individuals they owed their existence to the initiative and fostering care of the Dukes of Normandy and their great vassals. Bec was a new and independent birth, almost a new order, and in its origin it is clearly seen to be one of that series of attempts to regain solitude and simplicity and austerity of life which are visible all over north-western Europe at the middle of the eleventh century, and which culminated at its close in the congregations of Tiron and Savigny and the order of Cîteaux. Had it not been for the arrival of the illustrious Lombard, it might well have remained an insignificant house, to disappear or to be merged in the life around it. Instead, after passing rapidly through phases of growth that normally fill many decades, it became the most typical black monk monastery of its day and exercised a widespread influence which has been felt, at least indirectly, throughout monastic history from that time to this.

Its founder, Herluin, whose name it bears, was not a child of the cloister.[1] Of noble birth, excelling in arms and all physical pursuits, he lived for some twenty years—till past his thirty-seventh birthday—the life of a soldier in the retinue of Gilbert, count of Brionne. At the age of thirty-seven, about the year 1032, apparently as a result of some dangerous military adventure, he resolved to turn from the world and give himself to God.[2] For some reason he did not immediately decide to become a

---

[1] For the early history of Bec there are the brief *Chronicon Beccense* (ed. Porée for Société de l'Histoire de la Normandie, 1883), frequent references in Ordericus (esp. II, 244 *seqq.*), and above all Gilbert Crispin's *Vita Herluini*, which is a first-hand witness of unimpeachable authority. A critical text is printed by J. Armitage Robinson at the end of his *Gilbert Crispin, Abbot of Westminster* (Cambridge, 1911), 87–110. An inferior text is given by Giles, *Lanfranci Opera* (1844), I, 260 *seqq.*, where are also lives of Lanfranc, Anselm, Boso, Theobald, etc. The many English accounts of Lanfranc and Anselm, such as those of Maitland, Church and Armitage Robinson, have made Bec's story familiar.

[2] The dates would seem to be as follows: 1034, Herluin becomes a monk (OV, II, 306); 1039, foundation at Bec (Porée, *Histoire de l'Abbaye du Bec*, I, 43); 1041–2, arrival of Lanfranc (Porée, *op. cit.* I, 47, *Chron. Becc.*), who, born certainly after 1000 (Macdonald, *Lanfranc*, 1), left Italy c. 1036 (*ibid.* 9); ? 1057, arrival of Anselm, who was born c. 1033 (cf. authorities in Macdonald, *op. cit.* 57, note); 1063, Anselm becomes prior (*ibid.*).

monk. Remaining nominally a member of the circle of knights about the court of his lord he took every occasion for withdrawal and prayer, spending many hours in churches and fasting rigidly. He sought direction in vain from the priests and prelates of Normandy, who were at this time for the most part ignorant or worldly; failing to find what he sought, he resolved to give himself to the direct guidance of the Holy Spirit, obtained his release from his lord, and retired to an estate of his own where he spent his days in building a chapel and much of his nights in learning to read the psalter. After some two years, that is *c.* 1034, he decided to visit a number of monasteries in order to learn a monk's mode of life. At the time, only half a dozen houses existed in Norman territory, and it is possible that Herluin turned south to the older monasteries; in any case, his standards were doubtless exacting and he would at this period of his life have had little sympathy for an elaborate or wealthy institution; his experiences were therefore unfortunate enough, and he encountered worldly behaviour and rough treatment. Such a deep impression, we are told, did the sight of these disedifying lives make upon him in one abbey that he was on the point of despair, when an incident occurred which his biographer and disciple notes as an example of faith greater than miracles. In the depth of his discouragement Herluin remained after the night office praying in the church, as he thought, alone. There he saw one of the monks, who, like himself, imagined that the church was empty, remain instant in prayer from the depth of the night till full daylight. The example did its work.[1] Leaving other houses unvisited, he returned to his own lands, was ordained priest, and with two others began his monastic life in complete poverty and seclusion. The little group worked all day clearing land, farming, gardening and building; as yet they had little in common with the tradition of Cluny or Dijon, and their beginning might well have been that of Tiron or Cîteaux, or of the early Carmelites in a later century. Recruits came, but the community remained simple, poor and laborious; the mother of the founder lived nearby and washed the garments of her son's followers. Herluin himself felt deeply his inability to guide the growing family. This is a significant trait, for it shows not so much that he was a man of humility as that he had no definite programme of the monastic life to oppose to that current in France at the time, and that the simplicity of the early life was in a sense accidental. What would have become of his venture had his prayer for help received a different answer cannot be said. As it was, the whole history of the community was changed by one who sought admission about the year 1042, and who made of Bec for a short while the intellectual centre of Europe north of the Alps.

1 *Vita Herluini*, 92. As Armitage Robinson well remarks (*Gilbert Crispin*, 3): "That monk's prayer may even be said to have changed the course of history." It was the hour of the night when, during these very years, Wulfstan of Worcester likewise remained alone in the church in prayer (*Vita Wulfst.* 54).

Lanfranc, like Herluin, came to the monastic life late, though with very different antecedents.[1] He was perhaps thirty-five years old when, after a successful career as teacher of law and letters in Lombardy, he crossed the Alps and, after a short period of teaching at Avranches, turned from the world to the solitude and, as he thought, to the obscurity of Bec.[2] For three years he remained obscure; then, to aid in supporting the rapidly growing community, he began to receive pupils. The step was a surprising one for Herluin to take, and is another clear indication that he had no conscious design of departing from contemporary monastic tradition in the direction of an eremitical life. Indeed, it seems clear that he was a man, despite his early habits, of great flexibility and adaptability of mind and with a genius for leadership. He had by now taught himself letters and grammar, and made himself deeply conversant with the Scriptures. The reverent devotion shown to him by Lanfranc, even when archbishop of Canterbury, might indeed be attributed to the humility of a disciple, but we have the repeated witness of his biographer not only to his eminent ability in government, but to his knowledge of secular law as well as the Scriptures,[3] and above all to his appreciation of Bec as it became in the days of its greatest celebrity, and to his ability to discover in the young a zeal and talent for learning.[4] It is no small evidence of the genius as well as of the holiness of one who had lived the unlettered life of a knight that he was able to remain the real and effective head of his house not only in its days of simplicity and toil, but later, when it became an intellectual centre of the first importance, and later still when as a rich, splendid and populous establishment it was sending out its sons to rule churches and abbeys on either side of the Channel.

With Lanfranc's opening school the poor and primitive monastery of Herluin's first years embarked definitively upon a wholly different career, and it needed only the arrival of Anselm, some fifteen years later, attracted by Lanfranc but surpassing his master alike in sanctity of life and in purely intellectual gifts, to set the seal upon the new order of things. Thus Bec, in a little over a quarter of a century, from being a wholly obscure venture

---

1 According to the list of professed monks of Bec, printed by Porée, *op. cit.* from MS. Vat. Reg. 499, as an appendix to his first volume, I, 629 *seq.*, Lanfranc was the thirty-fifth to make his profession at Bec. Anselm was the sixty-eighth, his name occurring between those of the two future bishops of Rochester, Gundulf and Ernulf.

2 *Vita Lanfranci* (by Milo Crispin), ed. Giles, *Lanfranci Opera*, 283: "Rogavit [viatores] ut vilius et pauperius coenobium quod in regione nossent sibi demonstrarent. Responderunt 'vilius et abjectius monasterium nullum scimus quam istud [*sc.* Bec]'." *Vita Herluini*, 97: "Vixit [Lanfrancus] solitarius, gaudens quod nesciebatur."

3 *Vita Herluini*, 96: "Abbas peritus erat in dirimendis causarum saecularium controversiis, prudens in eis quae ad exteriora pertinent....Legum patriae [no doubt *le droit coutumier*] scientissimus." The words might have been written of Aethelwig of Evesham.

4 *Vita Herluini*, 104: "Sedulus enim perquirebat quis omnium eorum qui erudiebantur acutioris ingenii esset, quis tenacioris memoriae existeret, quis vehementius instare cuivis studio valeret....Litteratus aliquis volens monachus fieri...qua exultatione suscipiebatur, quae suscepto benignitas et veneratio exhibebatur!"

which was in a sense a reaction from the monasticism around it, came to rival and to surpass its neighbours in their most typical activities and to be the model and mistress of Norman monasticism, and its prior, instead of a solitary, became the trusted counsellor of Duke William, abbot of the Duke's foundation at Caen and finally Primate of England, called to re-organize the Church and the monastic life of a whole nation. Retaining little of her beginnings save a spirit of fervour and purity which endured for more than half a century, Bec by the time of Anselm's period of office had adopted all the chief features of the liturgical practices and monastic uses of her neighbours, while as an intellectual power she rose far above them all. She did, indeed, set up what was almost a new type of black monachism, for the culture and spirituality of Bec, seen so clearly in the life and writings of the saint who was the first great teacher and spiritual director of the new age, has remained a powerful influence over the centuries, most of all in the country of its origin, where it was before the eyes of the early Maurists in the seventeenth century and served as a distant model for the revived Congregation of France a century ago. Thus Anselm, like Bernard in the next generation and like Teresa and John of the Cross in a later epoch, has a significance in the history of the Church quite apart from his actions and achievements in his own age; he remains in per-petuity a living doctor from whom the intelligence and spirit continue to draw light and warmth.

III

If we now consider the Norman and English monastic bodies side by side, as they existed c. 1060, we see indeed very great differences, and yet also very marked similarities, both in the life within the monasteries and in their relations to society around them. In both countries there were numerous and powerful abbeys, endowed by the royal and noble families and with manifold relationships to the landowning classes, independent of each other and uncontrolled by any effective ecclesiastical authority, and in all of these the normal method of recruitment was from the oblate children of the cloister, who had received all their education within the walls of the monastery; in both countries, though for different reasons and in different ways, they were an integral part of the life of both the national Church and the State, thus forming a strong contrast alike to the early monasticism of Egypt and Italy, which stood wholly apart from all secular and ecclesi-astical organization, and to the reforming orders of the eleventh century in Italy and of the twelfth century in northern Europe, which had no relations with the State but were closely linked to the central government of the Church. In both countries the sovereign occupied a position of great and immediate influence over the monasteries; in both countries the broad framework of the monastic life and the general conception of its ideals were the same. Had these great similarities not existed it would have been wholly impossible to superimpose the one upon the other without violent change, as was in fact done by the Conqueror and Lanfranc, and to effect a fusion of the two within a short lifetime.

But within the similar framework the differences were very great. In England the bond between the monasteries and their abbots and the king had in it much of personal loyalty and past memories; alike between monasteries and monarch, monasteries and great landowners, monasteries and bishops the sense of relationship and interdependence was mutual— all were parts of the life of the country,[1] and in all departments of that life the limits of temporal and spiritual functions and jurisdictions were vague in the extreme. The sharp oppositions which had existed intermittently for two centuries abroad between the ecclesiastical and the secular power, and which had inspired the compilers of the False Decretals in the ninth century, Abbo in the tenth, and Cardinal Humbert in the eleventh, were entirely absent from England. Of the two great evils with which the Italian and Lotharingian reformers had long been at grips, simony and "nicolaism" or incontinence on the part of the clergy, the former scarcely existed in this country, while the latter was not felt as a public evil owing to the monastic provenance of almost all the influential churchmen.

In Normandy, on the other hand, all was in strict subordination to the feudal suzerain. Not only were the abbots appointed by him, but they were his vassals, bound by their homage to fidelity and in many cases also to military service. Here, as in England, the Duke acted with supreme power and unrestricted freedom in the regulation of ecclesiastical affairs, but nothing in Normandy corresponded to the mutual relationships and co-operation in national affairs that in England bound together king, bishops, abbots and great landowners. The people of Normandy, so lately heathen, had been Christianized, but until half way through the eleventh century the lower clergy and the bishops were unlettered and for the most part unworthy; William I, still more than his predecessors, consciously took in hand the task of reforming the Church of his dominions and directed to this end all the moral and intellectual resources of the monasteries. By the example of their lives, by their learning and by their direct influence as bishops the monks were to raise the whole level of the Norman Church. Both the Norman and English Churches, therefore, during the decades when the Roman reform was beginning, were self-contained, self-ordering *Landeskirchen*, but whereas in the English Church the organization was loose, undefined and traditional, in Normandy all the threads were held firmly by a ruler who was resolved of set purpose to raise the whole level of ecclesiastical discipline in his dominions.

1 It is perhaps significant that before 1066 the monastic chroniclers of Normandy were chiefly concerned with the annals of their own houses while those in the English monasteries were almost exclusively interested in the history of the nation.

Within the monasteries, also, the differences were as striking as the similarities. English monastic life was on the whole slackening in fervour, and in some of the monasteries a spirit of latitude and ease prevailed; in all the Norman monasteries, though doubtless differing greatly among themselves in degrees of observance, there was a spirit of enthusiasm and expansion, and in a few cases the highest levels of zeal and holiness were found. Still more striking were the intellectual and material differences. In England there was quiescence or slow movement; in Normandy rapid and ambitious growth, showing itself particularly in vast churches and monastic buildings; in England the intellectual influence of the monasteries, great under Dunstan, Ethelwold and Aelfric, was practically non-existent in the reign of the Confessor. Above all, what life there was of mind and spirit in England drew its inspiration from the past and continued the laborious transmission of an attenuated legacy that had been exploited for five hundred years; in Normandy the intellectual life in the monasteries was the keen new life, combative, eager, progressive. Anselm of Bec and Wulfstan of Worcester began to occupy responsible offices in their monasteries within a few years of each other, and thirty years later, when both were bishops, their paths crossed; they wore the same habit, and shared the same Rule and spiritual ideals, but they represented two epochs, two cultures; Wulfstan differed in outlook little, if at all, from the Saxon bishops of three and four centuries before, from Chad or Wilfrid; Anselm's mind reaches back to communion with that of Augustine, and anticipates the clarity of Aquinas. Certainly, it must not be forgotten that the four greatest names of Norman monasticism, William of Dijon, John of Fécamp, Lanfranc and Anselm of Bec, are those of ultramontanes from Volpiano, from Ravenna, from Pavia and from Aosta, and that Anselm's mind soared to heights reached by no contemporary; it is not easy to find in Normandy of that or the next generation men of their stamp.[1] But in Brittany, in the valley of the Loire, to the east of Paris, and in the schools of Normandy itself were to be found, by the middle of the century, teachers and disciples of a calibre which France had not known since the fourth century, and this life was shared in large degree by the monasteries. Of this England knew nothing.

IV

Since, in addition to the new spiritual impulse and the gifts of government and organization which the invaders brought to England, the cultural influence of Norman monasticism was so great during the seventy years following the Conquest, it is necessary to analyse it in some detail. When doing so, however, it should be borne in mind that we have very little

1 Böhmer, *Kirche und Staat*, 27, justly remarks: "Allein diese Kultur hatte nichts spezifisch Normännisches. Ihre Träger waren die auswärtigen Mönche."

first-hand knowledge of the interior of a Norman monastery (with the exception of Bec) before 1066. The chief sources of our information are either the original literary productions of monks, Norman or English, almost all of which date from after 1070, or the accounts contained in the lives of the abbots of Bec and in the writings of Ordericus Vitalis, all of which belong to the end of the eleventh or to the early twelfth century. Yet this lack of contemporary sources is of less significance than might at first appear; partly because the recollections of the writers and their informants go back to the middle of the century, still more because new and direct impulses continued to arrive in England until the second and third decades of the twelfth century through the agency of the distinguished Norman monks who were appointed to office in this country. Nevertheless, caution is necessary in forming a judgment as to the level of culture reached within the Norman houses. In the past, pronouncements have often been made by those interested primarily in political history or monastic antiquities, who were comparatively unacquainted with the theological, philosophical and legal writings of the time. This has led at times to an exaggerated enthusiasm for the monastic historians, such as Ordericus and William of Malmesbury, and to an acceptance at face value of the estimates made by them of their predecessors and contemporaries. Great as are the merits of these two writers, they cannot bear comparison as critical and philosophic historians with the great authors of antiquity or of the modern world; nor is their judgment as to spiritual and intellectual values to be accepted without reserve. There were, however, men of that generation and of the previous one—Anselm, Abelard, Ivo of Chartres, Bernard, to name but a few—who were of a stature to challenge comparison with the most eminent thinkers and writers of any period. We must therefore preserve some distinction between what was absolutely and what was only relatively excellent in the Norman monastic culture of the period, and, speaking generally, a broad distinction may perhaps be made between Bec and all other monasteries. At Bec, from the arrival of Lanfranc c. 1041 till the departure of Anselm in 1093, there were present in succession two minds of the first rank, two men of supreme ability as teachers, who were both (though in different ways and degrees) leaders of the thought of their epoch. At the other houses the calibre and the scope of the teaching was in every way inferior.

The diffusion of Norman monasticism from 1030 onwards coincided almost exactly in time and partially in locality with the intellectual rebirth which had its chief seats in the cathedral schools of Lorraine, the valley of the Meuse, Champagne and north-western France between the Seine and the Loire. Both Lanfranc and Anselm left Italy, which was itself witnessing a renaissance, in order to seek in northern France the foremost teachers of the day. During those early days of the revival, when the monasteries were still the chief repositories of the material resources of learning, and when the school was created by, and followed, the teacher, it was still possible for a monastery to be a centre of culture. This Bec was *par excellence* under Lanfranc, who taught all comers and attracted many of the best intelligences of Europe, and continued to be to a lesser degree under Anselm, whose influence was somewhat more restricted, being exercised chiefly upon the monks of Bec (themselves numerous and undoubtedly something of an *élite*) and those whom he reached by means of his letters and treatises. During all this time Bec was, if we may use the phrase, abreast of the most progressive thought of the time,[1] and the training there given in letters, in dialectic, in scripture and probably also in canon law was equal to the best given in any contemporary school of northern France. It cannot be an accident that it is precisely at the English monasteries most influenced by Bec—at Christ Church, which knew Lanfranc and Anselm, at Westminster, where Gilbert Crispin was abbot for thirty years, at St Albans, where Paul, Lanfranc's nephew, was abbot—that we find alike in letters and in theology a higher level of attainment than at any other houses.

Historians throughout the ages have dwelt with satisfaction upon the heyday of Bec under Anselm, who added to the eminent sanctity of his life a genius both as thinker and spiritual guide which made him a figure apart from and superior to all of his age, the most luminous and penetrating intellect between Augustine and Aquinas.[2] Anselm, for all his connection with Canterbury, is outside the purview of these pages; in England only those few who, like Eadmer, lived in his intimacy could feel his magnetic power; he belongs rather to the wider history of the thought and spirituality of Europe. An account of the spirit of Norman monasticism would, however, be scarcely complete which did not contain the passage in which Herluin's biographer narrates the zeal for letters of the self-taught founder of Bec.

If [he writes] he came upon one of the brethren who was neglecting regular discipline and the study of letters...he would say: "Of what use is a man who is ignorant of letters, and of the commandments of God?"...Many were

---

1 Many passages in Anselm's writings make this clear. Cf. especially the prefaces of the *Cur Deus Homo* and *Monologion* (*PL*, CLVIII, coll. 361–2; 143), and his comments on his own methods in *De fide Trinitatis*, cc. 2–4 (*ibid.* 265, 271–2).

2 For St Anselm, and references to the voluminous literature he has inspired as saint, theologian and spiritual guide, see above all the articles in *DHG* (by P. Richard, 1924), *DTC* (by J. Bainvel, 1909) and *DS* (by Dom M. Mähler, 1934). Writers of the most diverse outlook and opinions have noted both the singular charm of Anselm and also the impression he gives of soaring in genius far above his age. His qualities of soul were shared by others; his mind "was like a Star, and dwelt apart". Cf. R. L. Poole, *Illustrations of the history of medieval thought* (London, 1st ed. 1884), 104–5: "A thinker of immensely larger capacity than Lanfranc, Anselm, like his predecessor in the see of Canterbury, belongs in spirit to the past.... Unlike Lanfranc, he belongs also to the far future....His serene vision overlooks the chasm of scholasticism; he is not engulphed in it. Some of the questions on which he meditated are so alien from the temper of his time that one cannot but ask whence he derived the impulse. To this question, however, no answer has yet been given"; and J. de Ghellinck, *Le Mouvement théologique du XIIe siècle* (Paris, 1914), 59: "Saint Anselme

incited to study rather by his encouragement than by a love for learning, for he inquired carefully who among the whole body of those being taught were possessed of keen minds and strong memories, who were making the most eager progress, and in what subjects of study....If a man of letters came to him with a desire to become a monk, how gladly did he receive him, with what loving care and reverence did he entertain him![1]

Anselm, as prior and abbot, surpassed his predecessor alike in intellectual power, in the gifts of discernment and sympathy, and in the capacity for inspiring in others a desire to follow him. Few in the whole history of education can have equalled him as a teacher whose influence covered every activity of mind and will, and for whom his pupils never failed to feel a love which was greater even than their admiration. Here, at least, we may acquit Ordericus of undue enthusiasm, when, in a long and cele-brated passage, he speaks of the school of Bec, which made of all its monks philosophers.[2]

No other monastery had a history or an influence comparable to that of Bec, but during the middle decades and even in the latter half of the eleventh century, what may be called the specialization of higher education had not been carried so far as it was a few years later by the great masters of Chartres, Orleans, and other centres, and a number of monasteries, which before the Conquest and for some years afterwards attracted to themselves many who had taught and learnt in the cathedral schools, were able to provide within their walls a training for the young monks equal to any save that given by the most eminent masters outside. St Évroul, the home of Orderic of which he has left us such a vivid and glowing picture, is an excellent example of this, and may well have been *primus inter pares* after Bec. Within its cloister, during the half century that fol-lowed its foundation in 1050, not only the skilled copying and illuminating of manuscripts, but a high level of achievement in Latin prose and verse writing, the composition of homilies and the lives of saints, the minor fine arts, music and medicine were taught and practised.[3] The historian tells us that Thierry, the first abbot, used often to tell his young monks of "a certain brother in a certain monastery" who, though remiss in monastic discipline, escaped final condemnation by the amount and quality of his output as scribe;[4] one of his successors, Osbern, who was

dépasse complètement son époque....Son œuvre s'offre aux regards comme un fier pro-montoire qui se détache tout à coup, isolé, de la ligne régulière des collines." De Ghellinck, *op. cit.* 58, is not the only one to call him "ce génie, qui n'a pas son égal en Occident entre l'époque de saint Augustin et celle de saint Thomas".

1 *Vita Herluini* in *Gilbert Crispin*, by J. Armitage Robinson, 104.

2 OV, II, 246: "Ingens in ecclesia Beccensi liberalium artium et sacrae lectionis sedimen per Lanfrancum coepit et per Anselmum magnifice crevit....Sic ex bono usu in tantum Beccenses coenobitae studiis litterarum sunt dediti...ut pene omnes videantur philosophi."

3 Of the many accounts of Orderic and his *milieu*, the best is still probably that of L. Delisle in his introduction (1855) to the fifth volume of Le Prévost's edition of the *Historiae Ecclesiasticae*. References are given so copiously there and in other standard works that they may be dispensed with here.   4 OV, II, 49–50.

abbot at the time of the Conquest, used himself to prepare writing materials and wax tablets for the children of the cloister, and insist on the performance of a daily task.[1] Yet the catalogues of the libraries of St Évroul and her sister abbeys, dating from the twelfth century, are modest indeed, and warn us of the need of due perspective in interpreting the enthusiastic language of Orderic and others.[2] On the other hand, we may add to the credit side of the account, both at Bec and elsewhere, a quality which, strangely enough, is rarely mentioned by contemporaries, namely, the appreciation of great architectural designs and, to some extent at least, the ability to conceive them.

It will have been noticed that neither dialectic nor canon law figure in the activities of St Évroul as they do in the life of Bec. By the second half of the eleventh century the one was becoming increasingly the province of the cathedral schools, and the other was finding a natural home in the entourage of the bishops, and with the gradual emergence of dialectic and law, canon and civil, as the higher education of Europe and the corresponding development of the career of the professional master, the gulf grew ever wider between the meditative, literary culture of the Norman monasteries and the speculative and practical learning of the schools, which were dependent in a peculiar degree upon the personality of the master and the free play of debate among the students.[3] Medicine continued to find a home in the monasteries of northern Europe for some fifty years after dialectic had passed to the schools; in most cases it was practised and taught, as at St Évroul in the early days and as later at Malmesbury and St Albans, by one who had himself learnt at Salerno. Gradually, with the rise of Montpellier[4] and other medical schools nearer home, this too became the pursuit of a professional class, and was ultimately forbidden to monks.[5]

Thus the Norman monasteries were in a position to give to England a literary culture and an enthusiasm for at least a modest amount of learning to which no parallel, even the remotest, could be found at home, and which alike in richness of content and depth was wholly different from

---

1 OV, II, 94–5. Osbern had been a canon of Lisieux and subsequently a monk of St Trinité, Rouen, and Cormeilles. His career, which is typical, shows the many formative influences at work in any one house.

2 *V.* the catalogues of St Évroul, Fécamp and Lire printed by L. Delisle, *op. cit.* vii *seqq.*

3 The subject of monastic schools will receive fuller treatment in a later chapter. On the gradual transference of education from the monastery to the cathedral school see Rashdall, *The Universities of Medieval Europe*, 2nd ed. by F. M. Powicke and A. B. Emden, I, c. 2, with literature cited; C. H. Haskins, *The Renaissance of the Twelfth Century*, and *La Renaissance du xiie siècle: Les écoles et l'enseignement*, by G. Paré, A. Prunet and P. Tremblay, 15–55. The two last books, excellent for the twelfth century, fail, it may be thought, to do full justice to the progress achieved in the eleventh.

4 The medical school of Montpellier was celebrated by *c.* 1135 and soon equalled that of Salerno (Rashdall, *op. cit.* III, 119–20).

5 The teaching of law and medicine by monks was forbidden by Alexander III at the Council of Tours in 1163 (G. Paré, etc. *op. cit.* 43, with reference).

that developed almost a century before by Aelfric and Byrhtferth. The progress and scope of the revival effected by them in England will be considered in due course in a later chapter.

The Norman monasticism occupied, then, on the broadest view, an intermediary position between the new and the old, and was for this, if for no other reason, an important phase in monastic history. By its acceptance of the traditional scheme of life, as handed down from Benedict of Aniane and beyond, and in the simplicity of its organization, by which the various houses were wholly autonomous and depended for their internal economy upon nothing more formal than a body of custom, it might seem to be but one more of the many new branches that during five centuries had come into leaf upon the great tree which drew its life from the Rule of St Benedict. Yet because it came into being at a moment and in a land that harboured some of the most powerful beginnings of the new intellectual life and which was the fatherland of a race born to conquer and to organize, the group of Norman houses developed in an atmosphere of mental activity to which the past could show no parallel. Even before the Conquest the Norman monasteries, though united by no constitutional bond, had a greater solidarity than those of any other country owing to their strict dependence upon the Duke; the Conquest added to this solidarity that other which is common to all conquering and colonizing bodies; they were thus able to exercise a very great formative or transformative influence in England, and circumstances combined to place in control of this influence the greatest teacher of his age and a number of his most gifted disciples.

CHAPTER VI

THE NORMAN PLANTATION

I

At the time of the Norman Conquest there were in existence in England some thirty-five autonomous monasteries of black monks.[1] There were no other monastic houses in the country, and none of the existing abbeys had any connection with a foreign mother-house; neither had they any dependencies under their control. Nor did any kind of federation or interdependence exist between the English houses; indeed, so far as the scanty evidence goes, even the bond of common origin or tradition which, less than a century before, had to a certain extent grouped together the filiations of Glastonbury, Abingdon and Ramsey had by 1066 ceased to have any kind of influence.

These monasteries were as a body very wealthy. It has been calculated that their aggregate income was £11,066, or almost a sixth of the total actual revenue in England in 1086,[2] though the potential wealth of the country, and even to some extent its actual wealth, was much greater than appears in *Domesday*, for the Great Survey takes no real account of the lands north of the Humber and Mersey, and in every English county there were very considerable tracts of land lying uncultivated, which were exploited in one way or another within the two following centuries. As it was, however, the monasteries possessed a very considerable portion of the land, and to their wealth in land must be added their wealth in treasure and ornaments of every description, which made of their churches

1 This is the number of the pre-Conquest foundations owning land in *Domesday*, and is made up as follows: Abbotsbury, Abingdon, St Albans, Athelney, Bath, Buckfast, Burton, Bury, Canterbury: St Augustine's and Christ Church, Cerne, Chertsey, Coventry, Cranborne, Croyland, Ely, Evesham, Glastonbury, Gloucester, St Benet's of Holme, Horton, Malmesbury, Milton, Muchelney, Pershore, Peterborough, Ramsey, Sherborne, Tavistock, Thorney, Westminster, Winchcombe, Winchester: Old and New Minsters, Worcester. There are also traces of a monastery at Swavesey (Cambs) and St Neots (Hunts). Thus it will be seen that of houses known or supposed to have existed since the revival the following had ceased to exist: Bedford, Deerhurst, Exeter, Eynsham, Hereford, Peakirk, [Ripon] and Westbury; of these Deerhurst had come into the possession of St Denis of Paris, Westbury was owned by the bishop of Worcester, Eynsham by the bishop of Lincoln.

2 The *Domesday* figures given here and elsewhere are based on my own calculations made a number of years ago. As all who have worked over *Domesday* know, the task of arriving at satisfactory results is not a simple one, as a number of decisions regarding methods of reckoning have to be made. Quite apart, therefore, from errors due to oversight or faulty arithmetic—by no means easy to avoid in such a complicated record—independent investigators may well arrive at different totals, and I give a few such in the course of the following notes. As, however, the only interest of these figures lies in the broad relations of one sum total to another, it is perhaps sufficient that a uniform method should have been used for all. W. J. Corbett, in the *Cambridge Medieval History*, vol. v, ch. xv, p. 509, gives the proportion quoted in the text; he gives the total for all England as £73,000. His sum total is for the monasteries slightly higher than mine, viz. £11,200.

a wonder alike to Danes and Normans. Several of them, indeed, were richer than important bishoprics, and four of them were situated in cathedral churches, including the two most important sees in the country, Winchester and Canterbury, the one the political, the other the ecclesiastical metropolis.

These thirty-five monasteries were distributed very unevenly over the face of the country. There was no monastic house in 1066 west of the Severn, nor north of a line drawn from Worcester to Burton-on-Trent and thence to the Wash; in the large Danish counties of Lincoln, Norfolk, Suffolk and Essex there were only Cnut's two recent foundations of Bury and Holme. In the rest of England, Sussex—on the whole a barren, wooded county—had none, nor had Oxfordshire and Buckinghamshire; in the extreme west Cornwall had no house. On the other hand Wessex— or rather the group of five counties Berkshire, Wiltshire, Hampshire, Somerset and Dorset—had a considerable number fairly evenly distributed, including a large group of nine in Dorset and south Somerset. Another group of five considerable houses lay in the basin of the Severn near its junction with the Avon. A third group, also of five houses, three of them very rich, lay in the fens between the Welland and the Ouse.

The monastic wealth was very unequally divided.[1] Glastonbury, the richest house, had an income of £828; Horton, the poorest, had £12.[2] Between these two extremes is found every degree of affluence and poverty; there is no kind of "average", though if the arbitrary figure of £100 annual income be taken, it will be found to divide the monasteries almost equally, seventeen having an income greater than that figure, eighteen having less. But the inequality between the extremes is greater than this division might imply; while seven houses have £600 or over, five have under £40. In view of subsequent history, it may be worth while to survey the list rapidly, and it may for this purpose be divided into four groups, three at least of which have a real geographical and a certain historical basis, viz. the Wessex, Mercian and East Anglian groups, to which must be added the houses at Canterbury and in or near London.

By far the largest was the Wessex group. It included some seventeen houses, or half the total number of the houses of men, and six out of the nine nunneries of England,[3] and stretched from Malmesbury in north Wiltshire and Abingdon in Berkshire to Winchester in the east, Glastonbury in the

---

1 We are fortunate in possessing, in the Domesday Survey, a fairly complete record of all monastic property, together with income from rents and dues as these stood in 1085–6; the *valuit* of 1066 for the same properties is also given. In what follows the figures quoted are those of 1085; in other words, they show how the monasteries stood after the shock of the Conquest; but, as is mentioned later, there was no great loss of land after 1066, and in many cases the value of estates had appreciated.

2 A complete list of the monasteries and their value will be found in Appendix VI.

3 The Wessex nunneries were: Amesbury, Romsey, Shaftesbury, Wherwell, Wilton and Winchester. Outside Wessex were: Barking (Essex), Chatteris (Cambs) and Leominster. There were a few other groups of nuns of a semi-private nature.

west and Abbotsbury in the south, with two outposts in Devon. Considered as financial units, these abbeys exhibit great contrasts of affluence and poverty. Among them is Glastonbury, the richest house in *Domesday*, and the three poorest, Buckfast, Athelney and Horton, and while the six richest houses, all with incomes over £150, make an aggregate of £2615, the nine poorest total only £484.

The Mercian group was smaller and exhibited less contrasts of wealth and poverty. Of its seven houses five lay within a circle of fifteen miles' radius with its centre at Tewkesbury (where as yet no abbey existed); the two excentric abbeys, Burton and Coventry, were later foundations, and at the time of the Conquest were in some sort appanages of Peterborough. The five original houses had moderate incomes, ranging only from the £129 of Evesham to the £72 of Winchcombe. Coventry, well endowed by Leofric, was richer (£157); Burton was poor (£38).

The East Anglian group, also of seven houses, was as a whole very wealthy. Ely, with an income of £768, was second only to Glastonbury, and Bury (£639) and Ramsey (£358) were amongst the dozen richest. There remain four important houses—or, if Chertsey be included, five—which belong to no group. They are St Albans, Westminster and the two Canterbury monasteries. All these four were very wealthy: Christ Church (£688), St Augustine's (£635) and Westminster (£584) were among the very richest, and St Albans had a comfortable income of £270.

If the incomes of the monasteries varied greatly, a striking dissimilarity is seen also in the distribution of their estates even thus early in their history—a factor that would tell in their exploitation, for a compact and handy estate would be easier to control and to enjoy than a number of scattered and distant ones. Here the extremes may be seen in St Augustine's, Canterbury (one of the wealthiest), which had no land at all outside Kent, and most of its estates between Canterbury and the coast of Thanet, and the artificially endowed Westminster, with no great demesne, and properties in no less than fifteen counties.[1] Speaking generally, the abbeys of large and moderate income usually had a large *bloc* of lands round or near the abbey, representing the nucleus of the original endowment, and a number of scattered estates at a distance, but for the most part even the scattered estates have some regional connection with the monastery; Westminster, the work of the Confessor, in this respect as in others stands by itself as an anticipation of the practice which became normal after the Conquest, by which estates great or small, lying in every corner of the country, were bestowed upon some distant monastery in which the benefactor was interested.

---

1 Viz. Beds, Berks, Bucks, Essex, Glos, Hants, Herts, Lincs, Middlesex, Northants, Staffs, Surrey, Sussex, Wilts, Worcs. Of all the counties, Kent and Wilts contained by far the greatest value in monastic land; Derby, Notts and Cornwall had the least (excluding the northern counties).

The monasteries therefore were a social and economic factor of the first importance in the Conqueror's reckoning, and a factor unique in character. While the lay proprietors could be dispossessed by right of conquest, and the bishoprics, even apart from deprivations, would fall naturally one by one into the king's hand, the monasteries housed large and wealthy bodies of Englishmen who for reasons of every kind could not be dispossessed or replaced *en bloc*.

II

When Duke William landed at Pevensey all the English monasteries, with the partial exception of Westminster, were wholly national in sympathies. The majority of the monks were, as has been noted, of the class of landowners, great and small; their connection with the national life and with the royal family, for whom they doubtless still offered daily prayers, was very intimate, and many of them were under the patronage, or ruled by members, of the leading families of the land. Thus Aelfwig, abbot of the New Minster, was a brother of Earl Godwin;[1] Fritheric, abbot of St Albans, was a relative of Cnut;[2] Leofric of Peterborough was a nephew of Earl Leofric of Coventry, as was also Leofwin, till recently abbot of Coventry and in 1066 bishop of Lichfield;[3] Brand, Leofric's successor, was uncle of Hereward the Wake;[4] Aelfwine, abbot of Ramsey, had been a trusted ambassador of the Confessor, and had been to Denmark on the king's business; Wulfric of Ely was a relative of the Confessor.[5] It is natural, therefore, that a number of houses should be found taking an active part in the national resistance to the Duke of Normandy. Especially was this the case, it would seem, at St Augustine's, Canterbury, at the New Minster in Winchester, and in the powerful group of fenland houses. Abbot Aethelsig of St Augustine's joined Stigand and the thanes of Kent in organizing Kentish resistance;[6] Aelfwig of the New Minster was in the field at Hastings and died there, though it is not certain that he was there as a combatant, and the story that he was accompanied by a dozen of his monks who fell with him has been shown to be a fabrication;[7] Leofric of

1 *Monasticon*, II, 428, but cf. 437.

2 *Gesta Abbatum S. Albani* (RS), I, 41: "Frethericus...ex veteribus Saxonibus...et Dacis, Cnutoni Regi fuit consanguineus, et linealiter descendendo propinquus."

3 For Leofric v. *Chronicle*, 1066 [E].

4 *Chron. Ang. Petrib.*, s.a. 1069: "Brand patruus dicti Herewardi le Wake." *V.* also *Hug. Cand.* 43–8.

5 *Domesday*, 208 a. Ramsey has land at Broctone "propter unum servitium quod abbas Alvinus fecit ei [*sc.* regi Edwardo] in saxonia". Other land was lost while the abbot was in Denmark. For Wulfric v. *Lib. Elien.* 215.

6 So *Chronicon Willelmi Thorne*, ed. Twysden, 1787, but this chronicle is often demonstrably incorrect, and there is much uncertainty about the later career of abbot Aethelsig.

7 For the story v. *Monasticon*, II, 437. The abbot's death (with no record of any companions) is given in *Hyde Liber Vitae*, 35, with the information, added in a later hand, that he died at Battle. The rest of the story was incisively criticized by Round in *VCH, Hants*, I, 417–19.

Peterborough also was out with Harold, and was stricken with his last illness while in his train;[1] Aelfwold of St Benet's of Holme was placed by Harold in some kind of authority on the east coast;[2] Fritheric of St Albans was in the counsels of the magnates and prelates who were opposed to the Conqueror;[3] Brand, Leofric's successor at Peterborough, fell foul of William by approaching Edgar the Atheling upon his election.[4] There may have been other cases of initial opposition to the Conqueror, and it may have been for some such reason that William took Aethelnoth of Glastonbury with him out of England within a year of his landing, along with Stigand, Edwin, Morkar, the Atheling and other notabilities.[5]

William's victory placed these whilom opponents in an awkward position. A few, it would seem, took to flight. Aethelsig of St Augustine's may have gone to Denmark, and Fritheric of St Albans betook himself, a few years later, to Ely.[6] Others were imprisoned by the Conqueror; this was the fate of Godric of Winchcombe, who was ultimately entrusted to Aethelwig of Evesham,[7] and of Aethelnoth of Glastonbury, who was lodged at Christ Church[8]

Besides initial opposition, the various risings that marked the first ten years of the Conqueror's reign naturally involved some individuals among the English abbots. It was probably after the revolt of the West in 1067–8 that Sihtric of Tavistock took to piracy, that is, perhaps, joined Gytha at Flat Holme or the sons of Harold in the Irish seas.[9] Ealdred of Abingdon, who had originally made his submission, but whose tenants had been embroiled with the Normans, was accused, justly or unjustly, of conspiring with the Danes, no doubt c. 1069, and was imprisoned, first at Wallingford castle and later with Walkelin at Winchester, where he died.[10] In the autumn of the same year a Danish fleet, under Jarl Osbiorn and the sons of Sweyn, having with them Christian, the bishop of Aarhus, arrived at Ely, where the abbot was Thurstan, a nominee of Harold,[11] and a long tradition of friendship with the Danish royal house

1 *Chronicle*, 1066 [E].
2 *Chronicle of John of Oxenede*, 293: "[Abbati] a rege Haraldo marina committebatur custodia, qua de causa a Willelmo conquaestore postea non parva sustinuit discrimina."
3 So *GASA*, I, 44, but the narrative there given is confused and contains many errors. For an attempt to discuss it *v.* L. F. Rushbrook Williams, *History of the Abbey of St Alban* (London, 1917), 33–6.
4 *Chronicle*, 1066 [E].   5 *Chronicle*, 1066 [D].
6 For Aethelsig *v. Thorne*, 1787, "in Daciam navigio affugit, nec usquam comparuit". But cf. *Hist. Rames.* 177. For Fritheric's flight *v. GASA*, I, 50, and *Lib. Elien.* 227, where he appears as Egfridus. For Aethelsig *v.* also art. by H. Thurston, S.J., in *The Month*, July 1904, 1–15.   7 *Chron. Evesh.* 90.
8 Eadmer, *Epistola ad Glastonienses* (ap. *Mem. St Dunst.* 420), says Aethelnoth was *in quadam captione positus* at Christ Church.
9 Will. Malmesb., *GP*, 204, says merely "sub rege Willelmo piraticam·aggressus religionem polluit", and gives no details of the exploits of this compatriot and predecessor of Drake. For Gytha, who had with her a priest-tenant of Abingdon, *v. Chronicle*, 1067 [D], and *Chron. Abingd.* I, 484.
10 *Chron. Abingd.* I, 485–6; II, 283. The first is the more trustworthy account.
11 So *Lib. Elien.* 221.

existed. At about the same time Brand of Peterborough died (27 November) and the Conqueror, realizing that strong government was necessary in the fenland, sent thither Turold of Fécamp, at the time abbot of Malmesbury, a man whose combative qualities had embroiled him with the monks and whom William translated to Peterborough with the remark that, since Turold behaved like a soldier rather than a monk, he would provide him with somebody to fight.[1] The news of his arrival at Stamford with a large body of Norman men-at-arms precipitated a crisis at Peterborough.[2] Hereward, apparently a tenant of the abbey, invited the Danes from Ely to take the treasures of Peterborough before the Normans did so. On arrival, they met with resistance from the monks, who had sent urgent messages to Turold, and therefore proceeded to break their way in by setting fire to the monastery buildings, which were almost wholly destroyed, and to sack the church, which was prodigiously rich in ornaments and treasures of every kind. In the subsequent carousal this also was set on fire. The Danes then departed, taking the spoil with them by ship to Ely, together with the relics of St Oswald and such of the monks as had not fled. When Turold arrived he found the buildings in ashes and only one sick monk in the place, but those who had fled returned, and when the Danes departed the captives from Ely made their way home, having stolen the body of St Oswald and lodged it at Ramsey. The Ramsey monks declared their intention of retaining it, but Turold, true to his character and showing a consideration, unusual in a Norman abbot, for a native saint, promised to burn up their abbey unless it were returned.[3]

Meanwhile Ely had become a centre of the rebellion which takes its name from Hereward. The outlaws, who were joined by Morkar, by Fritheric of St Albans and perhaps also by Stigand, lived in and about the abbey for a year. The local historian gives a vivid picture of their life, and tells us that they ate with the monks, their weapons standing against the wall.[4] When at last the Isle was taken a heavy penalty was exacted from the monastery, and the abbot only obtained pardon after a journey with a number of his monks to Warwick, and the payment of a thousand pounds.[5]

One more rising remained to come, that of the Earls in 1075. The chronicler states that a number of abbots were at the forbidden bride-ale where the conspiracy was formed.[6] Their names are not given, but one

1 Will. Malmesb., *GP*, 420: "'Per splendorem,' inquit, 'Dei, quia magis se agit militem quam abbatem, inveniam ei comparem, qui assultus ejus accipiat.'"

2 The Peterborough [E] text of the *Chronicle* gives a vivid contemporary description of the whole affair, *s.a.* 1070: "Hereward ⁊ his genge...herdon sæcgen þet se cyng heafde gifen ꝥ abbot rice an Frencisce abbot Turolde wæs gehaten. ⁊ ꝥ he wæs swiðe styrne man. ⁊ wæs cumen þa into Stanforde mid ealle hise Frencisce menn, etc."

3 *Chronicle*, *loc. cit.*; *Hug. Cand.* 51: "Turaldus abbas minatus est arsurum se esse monasterium, nisi reddidissent quod eis commendatum fuerat."

4 *Lib. Elien.* 224–41.

5 Cf. an unprinted Ely Chronicle, Brit. Mus. MSS. Cott., Domitian XV, n. 2, fol. 5 v.: "Thurstanus elyensis usque Warewick pedes egressus cum XIIII monachis...gratiam regis obtinuit datis M libris."

6 *Chronicle*, 1075 [E].

of them would certainly have been Wulfketel of Croyland, a friend of Waltheof who subsequently obtained possession of the earl's body and buried it in his abbey.[1] This would suffice to account for the suspicion under which he fell, though it was not till 1086 that he was deposed by Lanfranc and lodged in custody at Glastonbury.[2]

Besides these cases in which abbots were involved in resistance or rebellion to William, a few were deposed for causes unknown to us. William's policy with regard to native lay landowners was probably extended to them—at the first plausible occasion those against whom any suspicions were entertained were removed. Aethelnoth of Glastonbury fell thus in 1077–8, and Wulfric of the New Minster in 1072;[3] these, together with the abbots of Croyland and Winchcombe mentioned above, would seem to have made up the total of degradations.

III

Clearly the Conqueror, even had he had no directly ecclesiastical policy, would have been obliged to take measures to ensure the loyalty of the monasteries. They controlled a large part of the land and wealth of the country; moreover, in the system of tenure and service which he was about to organize so completely the greatest abbots would be among the most important tenants-in-chief. Added to this, the abbeys were still, and would become increasingly, centres of educated life and nurseries of ideas and sentiment, and the heads of such establishments could not be allowed to be neutral. But William, as a statesman to whom the religious life of his dominions was of paramount interest, intended to do far more than safeguard or control the monasteries as might a modern secular government. He intended to renovate them, and the Church in England through their agency, by pouring into them the new life which had sprung up so wonderfully in his native country.

The task was clearly not an easy one. In the case of the bishoprics, rebellion, canonical faults, pluralism and death allowed the Conqueror to replace the old English hierarchy gradually with Normans, and there was no conservative social organization on the spot to oppose the change; but the abbeys were very different. The communities were jealous of tradition

---

1 Ordericus Vitalis, ii, 285: "Ab aemulis accusatus est...et Glestoniae claustro deputatus est." Orderic derived this information from Croyland.

2 V. Latin *Acts* of Lanfranc printed as Appendix B to vol. 1 of the *Chronicle* (ed. Earle and Plummer), i, 290.

3 *Ibid.* 288. A number of chroniclers state that many—*plures*—were deposed, but I can only trace six English abbots, viz. Abingdon, *c.* 1069; Croyland, at council of Gloucester, 1075; Glastonbury, at council of London, 1078; Malmesbury, *c.* 1068–9; New Minster, at council of Winchester, 1072; Winchcombe, before 1075. Matthew Paris, *Hist. Angl.* (RS), *s.a.* 1070, asserts that William "multos viros ecclesiasticos huic constitutioni pessimae [*sc.* of military service] rebelles et contradicentes a regno fugavit", but it is not easy to find an abbot to whom these words apply.

and had long memories. The business was not finished with the death or removal of an abbot. The stranger who replaced him had to live among and govern an alien body of men, buried, it might be, in the depths of Devon or Norfolk. We shall see in due course some of the difficulties with which he might meet.

From the very beginning of his reign William began the task of re-organizing the whole Church in England on the model of Normandy. He appointed a number of Normans to vacant abbacies and remodelled the episcopate with the aid of papal legates. For a moment he had thoughts of giving Cluny a leading part in the new life, and applied to the abbot, St Hugh, for a dozen of his best men. Hugh declined to furnish them; it was not part of Cluny's policy.[1] Thrown back thus upon his own resources, the Conqueror summoned from Caen the man who had for some years been his trusted adviser and whom, in the very year of the Conquest, he had made abbot of his own foundation of St Stephen's. From Lanfranc's arrival in England in 1070 till his death in 1089 his was the paramount influence in the monastic world of England. It is therefore necessary to form some idea of his character and policy, the more so because this great man has suffered a certain neglect at the hands of historians, who have devoted their attention almost exclusively to the Conqueror or to Anselm, and in so far as they have treated of Lanfranc, it has been as statesman and ecclesiastic rather than as monk and spiritual leader.

Lanfranc,[2] like his abbot, came to the monastic life comparatively late, as has been noted on an earlier page, and with a character and a mind already formed and exercised. We should, therefore, be justified in supposing, even if we had not the whole tenor and flavour of his acts and utterances to guide us, that he remained to the end, both as monk and prelate, distinguishable from one who had spent all his years from child-hood or boyhood in the cloister. If the traditional date of his birth is correct, he was at least thirty-five when, after a successful career in law at Pavia, he left Italy and came to Normandy, where he taught at Avranches and attracted numerous pupils.[3] Dissatisfied with this life, he resolved to

---

1 *Vita S. Hugonis, PL*, CLIX, 923; also Hugh's letter to William, *ibid.* 927.

2 The principal authority for Lanfranc's early years is Gilbert Crispin's *Vita Herluini*, of which a critical text is printed by J. Armitage Robinson at the end of his *Gilbert Crispin, Abbot of Westminster* (Cambridge, 1911), 87–110. It has been cited already as an authority for the early history of Bec. An inferior and incomplete text is given by Giles, *Lanfranci Opera* (1844), I, 260 *seqq.*, and in the same volume there is a later (? *c.* 1130) *Vita Lanfranci* by Milo Crispin (*ob.* Bec, c. 1150). The title of this, *Vita Lanfranci secundi abbatis* [*sc.* of Bec], which Giles prints repeatedly without comment, is presumably the cause of a mistake, very common in textbooks and works of reference, which makes Lanfranc abbot of Bec. A critical edition of the letters and whole Lanfranc *corpus* is badly needed. Dr A. J. Mac-donald's *Lanfranc* is a careful collection of all the known facts.

3 Dr Macdonald, *op. cit.* I, appears to accept the traditional date *c.* 1000–5 for Lanfranc's birth. Even if born in 1005, he would have been eighty-four when he died; yet there is, I think, no reference to this extreme old age, and he remained exceedingly alert and active to the last. A date *c.* 1015 would be more acceptable.

turn to solitude and obscurity, and chose Bec, then in its infancy, as the monastery most likely to provide him with both. For three years he lived there unknown; then, for whatever reason, the life ceased to please him and he decided to leave Bec and become a hermit. Herluin discovered his intention, and persuaded him to abandon it; it is impossible to be certain what took place between them, but the moment was decisive alike for Bec and for Lanfranc. He gave up wholly his desire for a solitary life, became immediately prior of Bec and opened a school there in which he taught all comers, among them several of the most influential churchmen of the next generation, one of them being the future Alexander II.[1] The story of his growing fame, of his share in the condemnation of Berengarius, of his opposition to William's marriage in 1058 and of the subsequent reconciliation by which he became his intimate counsellor, is part of the history of Europe and need not concern us here. It is more important to seize some of the traits of Lanfranc's firm and energetic character.

Wisdom was the quality that seemed most to distinguish Lanfranc in the eyes of his contemporaries,[2] and by wisdom they perhaps understood that elevation of mind and calm foresight which enabled him to impose order upon men and institutions, for great as was his reputation as theologian[3] even his own age realized that his disciples, rather than his writings, were his best monument.[4] Yet we cannot read his letters, with their short, lucid, decisive sentences and their sane, masculine judgments, without submitting to his mental power. Out of the strong could come forth sweetness, as we can see if we care to read his letters to Anselm at Bec or to his monk nephews, but strength was dominant even in his love.[5] There is something Roman in his character and mind; a clarity, an order, a keenness, a granite strength. As a young man, his agility of thought and speech had won him many victories, and even in later life the brilliant ultramontane used his gifts at the expense of the duller Normans.[6] This

---

1 *Vita Herluini*, 95–9; *Vita Lanfranci*, passim.

2 *Vita Lanfranci*, 291: "Homo...sapientia omni aevo memorabilis." *Ibid.* 292: "Sapientes et religiosi pontifices metropolitani, nec non et abbates...tremuerunt sapientiam Lanfranci." Armitage Robinson, *Gilbert Crispin*, 26, quotes an anonymous monk's judgment: "Anselmum mitem, Herluinum devotum, Lanfrancum sapientem."

3 An interesting letter (*c.* 1088–9) of the antipope Clement III to Lanfranc was printed by F. Liebermann in an article, *Lanfranc and the Antipope*, in *EHR*, XVI (1901), 328–32. In it Clement speaks of the archbishop as "illuminator ad edocendas Latinorum mentes... magister atque doctor sollertissimus novi ac veteris Testamenti...stella splendidissima Europae, etc." The writer, however, had his reasons for such language.

4 Will. Malmesb., *GP*, 73: "Vir, cujus doctrinam in discipulis ejus stupebit Latinitas.... Nam ipse pauca ingenii monimenta reliquit."

5 Cf. his letter to his nephews (*ep.* 53, Giles, I, 70–1): "Quo impensius amicum diligo, eo amplius majorem contra eum iram pro parva etiam culpa concipio." That he could inspire deep love is clear from his relations with Herluin; cf. *Vita Herluini*, 105, 107: "Abbas Herluinus eum supra omnes mortales amans, et ab eo amatus."

6 For Lanfranc's contemptuous treatment of Arfast at Bec *v.* Will. Malmesb., *GP*, 150, with its reference to Lanfranc's *Italica facetia*. But the story may well be merely *ben trovato*.

characteristic, and the manner of his endeavour to quit Bec, show that the natural man remained long in Lanfranc; we may perhaps detect in more than one of his actions as archbishop a prudence of this world that contrasts with the direct candour and simplicity of Anselm. Yet his relations in late life with his aged abbot, his avoidance of all display when he revisited Bec, and the affection with which he was regarded by the children of the cloister, combine to show that by self-discipline he had made mellow what was harsh. Gilbert Crispin, who knew him intimately, speaks of his loving-kindness,[1] and we have the most weighty testimony to his benignity at Christ Church, Canterbury, and to the fatherly care with which he ruled his English monks. He noticed at once if one was sad, spoke to him immediately and elicited the reason. It was by love, not by force, that he accomplished the necessary reforms, for he was a most skilled ruler of the hearts of men.[2] Eadmer, who as a child and young monk had known him well, gives us details at first hand of Lanfranc's delicacy and generosity. He never suffered parents of his monks to want, and was accustomed to give them assistance by the hands of their children. There is a touching story of one such mother and her son—it may well have been Eadmer himself—and of the great archbishop sitting in the cloister and noting the monk's sorrow.[3] Such incidents speak for themselves; if we wish confirmation, we may find it in Malmesbury's eloquent praise of the community of Christ Church as a living memorial of Lanfranc's charity and devotion,[4] or in the words used by an anonymous English chronicler to note the final departure of the venerable father and protector of all monks.[5]

It has, indeed, been hinted by more than one recent historian that Lanfranc's monasticism was only a phase of his life, which passed from his mind when he became immersed in the high problems of a statesman;

1 *Vita Herluini*, 105: "Benignitatis exhibitione ad amorem Dei aetatem invitans, quae sermonis sui capere nequibat altitudinem." *Ibid.* 107, at his departure from Bec: "omnes eruperunt in lacrimas; parvuli non valebant consolari."

2 Will. Malmesb., *GP*, 70–1: "Sciebat enim artis artium, id est regiminis animarum, peritissimus,...manet nec in aevum abolebitur communis in omnes, singularis in unumquemque, illius caritas."

3 Eadmer, *Historia Novorum*, 12–13: "Erga fratres autem ipsius ecclesiae quam bonus, quam pius, quam beneficus extiterit!" The sincerity of Eadmer's eulogy is apparent in every line.

4 Will. Malmesb., *GP*, 71: "Plurimus inest eis adhuc Lanfrancus, multa viri memoria, ingens in Deum devotio, pulcra in advenientes familiaritas."

5 *Chronicle*, 1089 [E] (the entry was probably written at St Augustine's, Canterbury): "On þisum geare se arwurða muneca feder ꝺ frouer Landfranc arcꝱ ge wat of þissum life. ac we hopiað ꝥ he ferde to ꝥ heofanlice rice." Recent studies of Lanfranc, and in particular those of Dr Z. N. Brooke and Dr Macdonald, have shown a reaction against the unfavourable judgment pronounced by Böhmer and others. Admittedly, there is room for more than one reading of his character; on a later page (*infra* 142–3) certain reservations are made regarding his political action and the case of forgery connected with his name is still *sub judice*. The paragraph in the text above does no more than reproduce the impression given by his own writings and those of his intimates.

such a view is hard to reconcile with his actions or with what is told us by Eadmer, and we need not doubt the sincerity of the archbishop's own words, when, writing to Alexander II, he speaks of the life in the monastery as that which he holds dearest in the world.[1] Lanfranc and Anselm differ much in character and mind, the one energetic, realistic, mastering every new task that is put upon him, the other gentle, excelling in speculation, remaining his calm, consistent self amid the rough chaos of events, but it is clear from the letters which they exchanged that in their conception of the monastic life they were at one. As a young man, Lanfranc must have been familiar with the kind of life advocated by Romuald and Peter Damian, and the vision of a hermit's life remained with him during his first years at Bec. That was not his vocation, nor would he have been drawn to the life of Cluny as it was brought to fullest development. His ideal was the Bec he had helped to create: a regular, liturgical life, with scope for study, and with the duty of raising the standard of religious life both by teaching and, when need arose, by going out to govern. This policy he developed as archbishop; the monasteries were to be the great powers in reorganizing the spiritual life of England, and he drew unsparingly upon Bec and Caen when he needed men for bishoprics, abbacies and for the good of Christ Church. In his conception of the monastic life, Lanfranc thus held something of a *via media* between the reformers of Italy and the tendency in England before the Conquest. He wished for a strict, ordered, cloistered monasticism, but not for one wholly separated by physical barriers from the life of the rest of the Church. Nowhere, perhaps, is his mind more clearly seen than in his organization and extension of the cathedral monasteries.

This monastic policy suited exactly the needs and situation of the Norman and English Churches as they were under the Conqueror: national churches, controlled with a very real, though undefined, power by a monarch anxious for reform. It was the exact counterpart of Lanfranc's attitude as primate, in which again he held in practice to a *via media*. With the full Gregorian programme of centralized and direct government from Rome, which implied a reduction of the jurisdiction of metropolitans, the possibility of all cases going on appeal to the Pope, and the growing exemption of monasteries from episcopal control, he had little practical sympathy.[2] He had left Italy before the reformed papacy had begun to take the lead in the reform of the Church, and in Normandy, where the Emperor was unknown and where simony, at least under William I, was non-existent, the ideal condition of things appeared to be a strong hierarchy under a powerful primate and powerful king. In England, as

---

[1] *Ep.* 3 (Giles, I, 20): "Vitam coenobialem quam prae omnibus rebus diligo."
[2] Cf. the judgments on this point of A. Fliche, *La Réforme grégorienne* (Louvain, 1924–37), vol. II (index *s.v.* Lanfranc), and Z. N. Brooke, *The English Church and the Papacy* (Cambridge, 1931), esp. 127–31.

in Normandy, regeneration was to be effected by the example and influence of the monks.[1]

IV

In his work of securing the monasteries of England for the new *régime*, the Conqueror had a powerful instrument in the royal prerogative of appointment to a vacant abbacy, which had even from the time of Edgar been recognized by all in a modified form, and which the Confessor, with Norman feudal practice in his memory, had exercised as a matter of course. Once William was *de facto* king of England the traditional routine brought the gift of all the abbacies of the country under his control.

From the very first he exercised it by appointing monks from across the Channel, and in one case at least the procedure would seem to have been irregular,[2] but it was only with the coming of Lanfranc that the plantation became systematic. Even under the old *régime* the primate, as chief ecclesiastic in the Witan, must have had great influence in appointments; in the Conqueror's early years the influence of Lanfranc would seem to have been wholly paramount. Unfortunately, complete and trustworthy lists of the abbots of a house only exist in a few cases; for the others the *fasti* can only be established from scattered references, and the provenance of the new superior is frequently omitted. Any statistics, therefore, have only a relative accuracy, but a few figures will perhaps show more clearly than general statements how methodical the plantation was, and whence the new abbots were drawn.[3]

As has been seen, the number of English abbots who fled the country or were deposed did not greatly exceed half a dozen. Those who remained were left in peace; there was no clean sweep; in 1073 there were still a dozen English abbots ruling in the twenty odd houses of which we have complete records, and eight of these were still alive in 1083, but in the year of the Conqueror's death there were only three English abbots (outside the Wessex group referred to below) still ruling, and only one of these saw the next year out.[4]

1 Cf. the judgment of Böhmer, *Kirche und Staat*, 17: "So war Dank den direkten Eingriffen der Mönche in die kirchliche Verwaltung und dem unermesslichen moralischen Einflusse, den sie auf alle Schichten der Bevölkerung ausübten, in der Normandie...eine fast alle Organe umfassende Regeneration...eingetreten."

2 Viz. at Malmesbury *ante* 1070. Will. Malmesb., *GP*, 420: "Turoldum...qui eum magnis demeruerat obsequiis, viventi Brihtrico intrusit."

3 These figures and references, and those which follow, supplement and in some places correct those given by Böhmer, *Kirche und Staat*, 107 *seqq.*, and by the present writer in an article, *The Norman Plantation*, in the *Downside Review*, XLIX, 141 (October, 1931), pp. 441 *seqq.*

4 The three veterans were Elsig of Bath (*ob.* 1087), Aelfwold of Holme (*ob.* 1089) and Aethelsig of Ramsey (*ob.* 1087). Ingulf of Croyland (1086–1109) and Leofwin of Coventry, instanced by Böhmer, *Kirche und Staat*, 107, note 2, are not cases in point, for Ingulf, though English by race, was a monk from Normandy, and Leofwin, whatever the date of his death, had ceased to be abbot of Coventry before the Conquest, and was succeeded in his bishopric in 1072.

There were, as has been said, some thirty-five monasteries in being in 1066. Four of these—Canterbury, Winchester, Worcester and Sherborne —were cathedral monasteries and need not detain us. The two first were immediately Normanized under Lanfranc and Walkelin with priors from Bec and St Ouen; Worcester under Wulfstan was left to itself; Sherborne, a small house, remained in obscurity under Herman and Osmund, and ultimately became autonomous in the reign of Henry I. A fifth, Bury, already had a foreign abbot, the royal physician Baldwin, a monk of St Denis, Paris. Thirty remain. In the case of fourteen of these there exists, so far as I am aware, no precise information as to the succession of their abbots immediately after the Conquest. It is not without significance that nine of these are small houses in the heart of Wessex, poor also for the most part, and that we have little or no information as to their abbots before the early years of the next century.[1] Everything tends to show that they were left in peace by the Conqueror, and in consequence continued to stagnate. In the remaining sixteen houses the total number of appointments during the reign of William I was twenty-four, and it is from these that his policy can be ascertained. Of the twenty-four, two are recorded as Normans in the sources without further precision, and one came from Marmoutier. The remaining twenty-one were drawn from nine different Norman monasteries, of which Jumièges supplied no less than six and Fécamp, Mont St Michel and Caen three each. That Bec should supply only one implies no neglect of that house, for apart from the fact that the Caen monks were probably all among the original colonists from Bec, that house, besides Lanfranc, gave two bishops to Rochester during the Conqueror's reign, besides a prior (subsequently abbot of Battle) and a number of monks to Christ Church and a contingent for the foundation of Rochester. In after years, besides two more archbishops of Canterbury and a number of abbots, Bec founded the abbey of Chester and helped to reorganize that of Colchester; in all, during the reign of William I and his two sons, the Caen-Bec society provided some fifteen heads of houses for England, besides bishops, and if our information were complete, this figure could probably be increased considerably.

If for a moment we interrupt the order of the narrative to follow the process of Normanization after William's death, it can be seen continued spasmodically by Rufus and methodically again by Henry I, who showed especial preference for monks of Bec, Caen, St Évroul and Séez. In all, between 1066 and 1135 notices remain of over sixty overseas abbots appointed to some twenty English houses, and there is no reason to suppose that the monasteries for which we possess no information stood permanently on a different footing from the rest.[2]

---

1 The nine are Abbotsbury, Athelney, Buckfast, Cerne, Cranborne, Horton, Milton, Muchelney and Tavistock. William did not wholly neglect them, for some were assessed for small quotas of military service, and the abbots were tenants *in capite*.
2 *V*. Appendix VII for complete analysis of the provenance of Norman abbots.

Ordinarily, so far as we can tell, William was content to appoint a Norman abbot and let the situation adjust itself by degrees, but in a few cases he or Lanfranc reshuffled the community. Thus some of the monks of Ely, of Glastonbury and of St Augustine's were dispersed to other monasteries, at least for a time, in 1072, 1083 and 1086 respectively, and besides the draft from Bec which went to Christ Church, we hear of a group following Simeon to Ely from the Old Minster and of a plantation from Christ Church at St Augustine's.[1] But in all these cases there were exceptional circumstances, and we need not assume that there were any other such rearrangements; nor can it be shown that English monks were ever sent abroad to drink in Norman traditions at the fountain head, though a single ambiguous, but interesting, reference in Orderic might be taken to imply this.[2]

V

Taken as a group, the new rulers appointed during the Conqueror's reign were an unusually able and exemplary body of men. This is, indeed, what we should expect when such a man as Lanfranc had the duty of choosing, but when the many calls, at home and abroad, that were being made upon the young Norman monasteries is borne in mind, the number of men of outstanding ability available for England is truly remarkable. Five or six, either by merit or the accident of plentiful record, stand out from the rest—Paul of St Albans, nephew of Lanfranc and monk of Caen, who set his house, hitherto comparatively undistinguished, in the high intellectual and religious position which it was to retain for centuries;[3] Serlo of Gloucester, a monk of Mont St Michel, who rebuilt on a grand scale the abbey which he had found almost extinct, and was responsible for the spirit of sobriety and observance which characterized it in the following century;[4] Simeon of St Ouen, prior of Winchester and abbot of Ely, who guided both houses through a period of transition and won their love and veneration;[5] Scotland, another from Mont St Michel, whose treatment of a difficult situation at St Augustine's receives praise from both the historian of the house and Orderic;[6] Henry of Bec, the trusted prior of

1 For St Augustine's *v. Chronicle*, Appendix B, 1, 292; for Glastonbury, Will. Malmesb., *de Ant. Glast.* 332; for Ely, *Chron. Ang. Petrib.*, *s.a.* 1072 and *Lib. Elien.* 261.

2 OV, II, 208: "Aliquanti abbates a rege noviter ordinati sunt, et complures coenobitae in monasteriis Gallicis competenter edocti sunt."

3 *GASA*, I, 52: "Facta est ecclesia S. Albani quasi schola religionis et disciplinaris observantiae per totum regnum Angliae." An *ex parte* statement, no doubt, but still largely correct.

4 Will. Malmesb., *GP*, 293: "Nota est Gloecestrensis religionis discretio...hoc illis signifer intulit Serlo." It is interesting to find Lanfranc (*ep.* 62, Giles, 1, 78) already praising Gloucester as a *regularis locus*.

5 *Annales Wintonienses* in *Annales Monastici*, II, *s.a.* 1082: "Simeon vir virtutis amator." *V.* also *Lib. Elien.* 253, 261. He died a centenarian (*ibid.* 279).

6 W. Thorne, 1787, praises Scotland, as does OV, II; 209: "Famosus abbas scientia et bonitate pollens."

Lanfranc and Anselm and finally abbot of Battle;[1] Gilbert Crispin, also of Bec and beloved of Anselm, the able and learned abbot of Westminster[2] —these do not exhaust the list of eminent Norman monks who came to England in the early years and who had at their head, besides Lanfranc, the saintly Gundulf of Bec and Rochester, and Remigius of Fécamp and Lincoln.

Three only would seem to have betrayed the trust put in them. The first of these was Geoffrey of Jumièges and Westminster, of whom little is known save that his appointment was probably the Conqueror's act, and that, proving unworthy, he was censured by Lanfranc and finally dismissed.[3] The second, Turold of Fécamp, Malmesbury and Peterborough, was likewise not one of Lanfranc's choosing. It would seem that he had done some service to the Conqueror, who recompensed him with the abbacy of Malmesbury, from which Brihtric was ejected;[4] Turold fell foul of the monks (no details are forthcoming) and was translated to Peterborough, under the circumstances related above. There he ruled for twenty-eight years, but the chronicler has little good to say of him, and it would seem that he continued to conduct himself after the fashion of William's military followers, for he saddled Peterborough in perpetuity with a military service—almost without parallel among the religious houses—of sixty knights.[5] There are, however, no charges against either his private character or his treatment of his monks.[6]

For the third bad choice, Thurstan of Glastonbury, Lanfranc must bear a share of responsibility, the more so as he hailed from Caen. His name acquired notoriety owing to an act of violence, unique of its kind, which profoundly shocked contemporary opinion. The monks of Glastonbury, a stronghold of tradition, were probably not a body of men easy to handle, and Thurstan, like Turold, appears to have resembled a Norman baron rather than an abbot in temperament and methods. Even if the charge against his private character be dismissed as mere scandal,[7] his behaviour

---

1 *Vita Herluini*, 103: "Arbor alta atque fructuosa extitit Henricus Cantuariensis ecclesiae decanus...vir ecclesiasticis omnibus disciplinis optime instructus."

2 Armitage Robinson writes of him, *Gilbert Crispin*, preface, ix, as "one of the greatest of the line [of the abbots of Westminster], distinguished alike by his high character [and] the fame of his learning".

3 Flete, *History of Westminster*, ed. J. Armitage Robinson (Cambridge, 1909), 84.

4 *V.s.* pp. 105 and 111 note 2.

5 Hugo Candidus, *Coen. Burg. Hist.* 64, concludes a long account of his rule with the words "iste abbas per viginti et octo annos abbatiae magis obfuit quam profuit". But the facts that can be ascertained of Peterborough's material prosperity do nothing to substantiate this judgment.

6 A curious adventitious celebrity has come to Turold as a candidate for the authorship of the *Chanson de Roland*. The attribution is a mere hypothesis, without plausible reasons; cf. the article *Turold* in *DNB*.

7 It occurs only in William of Malmesbury's earlier accounts in *GR* and *GP* (*v. infra*). As his editors have shown, Malmesbury in his earlier writings lets fall a number of irresponsible charges, many of which were omitted in subsequent redactions. This one is not so omitted, but it does not appear in his account in *de Ant. Glast.*

at Glastonbury was unreasonable, if not brutal. An *impasse* was finally reached over a question of ceremonies and chant, the abbot insisting on the substitution of the methods of the Dijon school for the Gregorian tradition of which Glastonbury claimed to be inheritor. One day in chapter, after mutual recriminations, Thurstan, losing control of himself, called in his men-at-arms to overawe the monks. The latter fled into the church, which was still the small edifice of the Saxon minster, and barricaded themselves in the choir. The men-at-arms, whose racial antipathies were no doubt aroused, endeavoured to force their way in and were met by resistance from the monks, who armed themselves with benches and candlesticks; some of their number therefore climbed into the gallery, common at the west of the transept in Saxon churches, and shot down upon the monks who took refuge near and even beneath the altar. The rood was pierced with arrows, which narrowly missed the hanging pyx, and a number of the monks were gravely wounded. Meanwhile, others broke into the choir and attacked them with spears. In all, at least two were killed and a dozen wounded. The matter was taken to the king, and Thurstan was sent back in disgrace to Caen, while a number of the monks were distributed among other houses. The abbot, however, was not formally deposed, and under Rufus bought his return, though he did not venture to live at his abbey.[1] A letter written to him by Lanfranc, in answer to one soliciting counsel, has been taken to imply that the archbishop's sympathies were with Thurstan, but we do not know the date of the letter, or the accuracy of Lanfranc's information at the time; his words are studiously non-committal, and if their tone, and the formula of salutation used, are compared with those employed in other letters to abbots found in the correspondence, they will be seen to be positively cold.[2]

The only other case of serious disturbance at an English monastery may be mentioned here for the sake of completeness, though it occurred in the following reign. Here again, though the occasion was ostensibly a quarrel over ancient traditions and rights, racial feeling would seem to have been at the root of the matter. The scene of the trouble was the great and

---

1 This Glastonbury scandal, doubtless on account of its sensational details, is narrated in a number of sources, among them the *Chronicle*, 1083 [E], the *Annales Wintonienses* (*Ann. Monast.* II, 33), Florence of Worcester, II, 16, William of Malmesbury (thrice), *GR*, 329, *GP*, 197, *de Ant. Glast.* ed. Gale, 332, and Ordericus Vitalis, II, 226. The most reliable of these accounts would seem to be that of the *Chronicle*, which is probably almost contemporary, and Malmesbury's notice in the *de Ant. Glast.*, probably composed at Glastonbury itself; Florence, however, adds some original details. Orderic's account is very vague. Malmesbury twice gives the casualties as two killed and fourteen wounded; the *Chronicle* has three and eighteen; the Winchester annalist three and fifteen. As even the Conqueror recognized Thurstan's guilt, it would seem unnecessary to defend him with Böhmer, *Kirche und Staat*, 120: "aber selbst diese Roheiten entsprangen nur aus übergrossem Reformeifer: Thurstan von Glastonbury hatte an sich löbliche Bestreben, in seinem Kloster an Stelle des gregorianischen Kirchengesanges die neue bessere [!] Singweise...einzuführen."

2 *Ep.* 59 (Giles, I, 77). Böhmer, *op. cit.* 121, note 4.

ancient abbey of St Augustine's, Canterbury, the near neighbour of the archbishop and his recently Normanized community, and possessed of secular traditions of independence and patriotism. Several years before, the house had received as abbot the capable Scotland, and all had apparently gone well; but on his death, which occurred within a few days of that of the Conqueror, the aged archbishop apparently appointed a Norman monk of Christ Church, Wido by name, and endeavoured to introduce him upon a community which, with the fear of the Conqueror removed, sought to assert its right of free election. When Lanfranc, supported by Odo of Bayeux, appeared with his nominee, there was an exodus of almost all the monks, and the archbishop was left to perform the ceremony of installation in an empty church. Having sent an ultimatum to the dissidents he received to pardon those who returned, imprisoned the English prior, Aelfwin, and another, Ailred, together with a few ringleaders, and temporarily dispersed those who still protested. The following year trouble broke out again, and one of the monks, Columbanus by name, admitted his intention of murdering the abbot; he was publicly scourged and degraded at the archbishop's orders, and again peace reigned for a while. It was broken at Lanfranc's death in 1089, and this time the malcontents raised a riot of the citizens, who attacked Wido's lodging and forced him to flee to Christ Church. The matter was taken up by Walkelin of Winchester and Gundulf of Rochester; the monks were scourged and their lay accomplices blinded and the community dispersed, this time apparently in permanence, for twenty-three monks of Christ Church, under their subprior, were introduced in their stead.[1]

These are the only instances of serious trouble in the English houses. The very chroniclers of the next generation whose criticisms of the old English monasticism have already been scrutinized and found to be exaggerated are also responsible for general statements as to the number of English abbots unjustly degraded and supplanted by tyrannical Normans.[2] These assertions, like the others, when tested by contemporary evidence, are seen to be exaggerations. It was natural that a few cases of real injustice and a number of changes and losses incidental to the Conquest should go the rounds and lose nothing in repetition. The wonder is that

---

1 A full account of this episode is preserved in the short and well-informed Latin *Acts* of Lanfranc, which are found as a continuation of MS Ā of the *Chronicle* and are printed by Plummer, I, 287–92. The MS is of Augustinian origin (*ibid.* II, introd. xxvii) and the tone, which is favourable to Lanfranc, indicates that it was written by one of the Christ Church monks introduced by him. Wido's Christ Church provenance is noted (292, *ad matrem ecclesiam fugit*) and is corroborated by Gervase of Canterbury (*Opera*, RS, I, 71); these two sources, which thus give a comprehensible account of the trouble, must certainly be preferred to the story of the late and often untrustworthy Augustinian historians Thorne, 1792 *seqq.* and Elmham (RS), 345–6, where it is stated that Wido was elected by the monks, who claimed their rights in opposition to a candidate forced on them by Lanfranc. The real origin of the trouble was probably personal and racial; I cannot here agree with Plummer's criticism (*Chronicle*, II, 316) of the opinion of Freeman (*Norman Conquest*, IV, 413).

2 E.g. OV, II, 225–6; Flor. Wig. II, 5.

serious friction was so rare, for relations between a Norman abbot and his English monks must often have been most difficult to maintain upon a sympathetic basis. Incidental references show us Lanfranc himself recoiling from the prospect of dealing with an alien people in an unknown tongue,[1] and the wise and gentle Anselm condoling with the archbishop's nephew, Paul, on being sent to St Albans to live among uneducated natives.[2] There was, indeed, enough of coarseness and stupidity among the English, as there was of rapacity and brutality among the Normans, but the great gifts and enlightened culture of the best Norman abbots were speedily recognized by the receptive and intuitive English minds, and their power of requiring and inspiring obedience sufficed, in the majority of cases, to make the period of transition peaceful.

Tangible complaints against the new *régime* recorded in the monastic chronicles may be reduced to two or three headings. There is, first, the charge that William or the Norman abbots robbed the houses, or allowed them to be robbed, of land or treasure or precious objects. As regards the Conqueror's share, it is certain that in 1070, when revolts had not yet ceased and the country was unsettled, there was a fairly widespread harrying of the monasteries, during which a considerable quantity of treasure was removed.[3] During the years that followed the Conquest, those of any wealth among the English had deposited their money and treasures in the abbeys of English sympathies, and the requisition of 1070 was intended to deprive possible rebels of the sinews of war. Doubtless in more than one case besides Abingdon some of the monastery's own wealth and even precious objects from the sacristy went the way of the deposits of others. In a few cases, also, it is probable that Norman abbots presented the monasteries of their origin with treasures of English art.[4]

As regards large losses of land and depreciation of property, the *ex parte* statements of chronicles and cartularies are not always borne out by a careful examination of *Domesday* and similar records. Rich as the greater houses were before the Conquest, there was no wholesale deprivation to benefit the new holders of the great fiefs. Glastonbury, Ramsey, New Minster lost some lands in the re-allotment, but gained others, even

---

1 Cf. *ep.* 3 to Alexander II (Giles, I, 19): "excusatio incognitae linguae gentiumque barbararum."

2 *Ep.* I, 71, *PL*, CLVIII, coll. 1141–2: "Quamvis enim barbaris vestra praelata sit sanctitas, quos verbis docere propter linguarum diversitatem non potestis."

3 *Chron. Ang. Petr.*, s.a. 1072: "Multa monasteria, tam de propriis pecuniis quam de alienorum apud ipsos depositis, ad quadrantem ultimum spoliata." *Annales Bermundes.* (*Ann. Monast.* III), s.a. 1070: "ii non. Aprilis...W. rex monasteria totius Angliae perscrutari et [pecuniam] in aerarium suum jussit deferri." Cf. also Flor. Wig. II, 5, and above all *Chron. Abingd.* I, 486, where a more detailed account is given of the action of the sheriff of Berkshire.

4 I have noticed two cases only, viz. Abingdon, where *quidam sacrista*, a Norman, is charged with carrying off a number of treasures to Normandy (*Chron. Abingd.* II, 278), but this passage occurs in an untrustworthy context; and Peterborough, where two of Turold's sacristans *de ultra mare* are similarly accused (*Hug. Cand.* 63–4).

in the Conqueror's reign; Evesham was robbed by Odo of Bayeux, and Aethelwig of Evesham was accused of robbery by Hemming of Worcester. Only a careful analysis of *Domesday* could give precise figures of the balance of gain or loss over the whole country, but one or two important cases have been examined,[1] and the verdict of one who knew *Domesday* extremely well was that on the whole the monasteries gained as much as they lost between 1066 and 1085, and the steady flow of benefactions in the next half-century far outweighed any losses.[2] In this matter, the statements of domestic historians must be received with the utmost caution; they never reconciled themselves to a loss, however inevitable, or forgave an alienation, however justifiable, nor do they distinguish between the loss of a few movable treasures or sums of money, and that of land together with all the real and personal rights that went with an estate.

Besides a few cases of downright loss in the troubled years after the Conquest, the monasteries as a whole suffered from the necessity of having to provide lands from their estates to support the knights who performed military service for them. The assessment for this was made soon after 1070 and its incidence was most uneven. The causes of this will be discussed later; here it is sufficient to remark that the domestic historians are often most unjust in blaming an abbot for an arrangement which in many cases was none of his choice. Only rarely—Turold of Peterborough and Thurstan of Glastonbury are cases in point—is it likely that the magnitude of the assessment depended directly upon the abbot's personal behaviour. Along with the charge of giving abbey lands away to knights went in a few cases the added charge of nepotism.[3] This, too, was often unfair. Once granted that an abbot had to support a group of knights, it was natural that if he were of a family whose members belonged to the military class a number of his relatives would attach themselves to him and be among the recipients of land. Cases of undue favouritism and dilapidation may have occurred, but not so frequently as the records suggest.

A third grievance, quite as widespread, is more curious. The Norman abbots, it seems, frequently outraged the feelings of their monks by their disrespectful attitude towards the old English saints. Here Paul of St Albans was at fault. He slighted the tombs of his predecessors, and

---

1 E.g. Evesham by Dr R. R. Darlington in his article *Aethelwig of Evesham*; New Minster by Round in *VCH, Hants*, I, 417–19 who concludes: "The alleged confiscation of its manors, on a colossal scale, at his [the Conqueror's] hands, must now be relegated to the realms of fiction"; and St Albans by L. F. Rushbrook Williams, *History of the Abbey of St Alban*, 33–6, who remarks: "this tradition [*sc.* of St Albans losses] is hardly borne out by sober history." Elsewhere (*ibid.* 245) Mr Williams shows that the total value of St Albans rose from £278 to £284 between 1066 and 1086. The present writer, when examining *Domesday*, noted that at Peterborough, for all the chronicler's laments, the value of land had markedly appreciated. *V.*, however, F. M. Stenton on Holme in *EHR*, XXXVII (1922), 225–35.
2 So W. J. Corbett in *Cam. Med. Hist.* V, 509.
3 Cf. *Chron. Abingd.* II, 283–4; *Chron. Evesh.* 96–8; *Hug. Cand.* 52.

referred to them as uneducated simpletons.[1] Athelelm of Abingdon held similar language, refusing to allow any feast of St Ethelwold or St Edmund to be kept, on the grounds that the English were boors.[2] Even the great name of St Cuthbert was not proof against Norman scepticism.[3] At Malmesbury Abbot Warin was so surfeited with the relics of English saints that he turned a number out with a jest; he retained St Aldhelm, however, and treated him with reverence.[4] At Evesham after Aethelwig's death Abbot Walter, acting on the advice of Lanfranc, examined all the relics and put doubtful ones to a kind of ordeal by fire.[5] The reference to Lanfranc is interesting, for it agrees perfectly with an incident related by his biographer. When on one occasion, he tells us, Anselm visited Canterbury, the archbishop deplored the English cult of worthies of questionable sanctity, alleging St Aelfheah as a case in point. It is characteristic of Anselm that he should have shown his veneration for Aelfheah, as he had previously done for Dunstan, and he succeeded in converting Lanfranc.[6] The latter certainly came to appreciate some, at least, of his saintly predecessors, for the hagiographers Osbern and Eadmer worked at his bidding.

VI

In almost every case the first task to which the newly appointed Norman abbots addressed themselves was the gradual provision of spacious and carefully planned monastic buildings and offices together with a large church. Coming as they did from a land which had recently witnessed an extraordinary efflorescence of ecclesiastical architecture and from monasteries complete with all the buildings necessary for the common life of a large body of men, the small proportions and irregular arrangements of the monastic buildings in England must have seemed to them to foster a corresponding irregularity and mediocrity of life. As in almost every case the income at their disposal was more than sufficient for the maintenance of the establishment, and as (to judge by the *valets* and *valuits* of *Domesday*) no radical reforms were necessary in the exploitation of their estates, they were rarely under the necessity felt by almost all great abbots in later

1 *GASA*, I, 62: "Tumbas venerabilium antecessorum suorum abbatum nobilium—quos rudes et idiotas consuevit appellare—delevit."

2 *Chron. Abingd.* II, 284: "Dixit enim esse Anglicos rusticos." Again a suspicious passage.

3 Flor. Wig. II, 53. The body of the saint was exhumed: "ob quorundam abbatum incredulitatem."

4 Will. Malmesb., *GP*, 421: "Tipo quodam et nausia Sanctorum corporum ferebatur." In this he has Böhmer's sympathy (*Kirche und Staat*, 121): "Jene Abte wollten ihre neuen Münster nicht zu einem Kirchhofe unheiliger Gebeine machen."

5 *Chron. Evesh.* 323–4, 335–6. At Glastonbury also there was trouble.

6 *Vita Lanfranci* (ed. Giles), I, 310: "Intimavit abbati [*sc.* Anselmo] antistes Cantuariensis quasi conquerendo, quod homines illius patriae colerent quosdam sanctos, quos ille non affectaret, et maxime, ait, quemdam Elfegum." He was convinced by Anselm's answer.

centuries of devoting all their energies for a number of years to financial and economic reorganization; they were therefore free to take a leading part in the work of material construction which produced a revolution in the art of building in England to which no parallel can be found at any other period of history.

It would be wholly outside the scope of these pages to attempt a detailed account of monastic architecture and its chronology, and indeed few departments of the life of the time have received fuller or more competent treatment at the hands of expert archaeologists.[1] It is sufficient to note that in almost every case, whether in the cathedral monasteries or elsewhere, building on a grand scale began as soon as the first Norman abbot felt himself firmly in the saddle. Besides the impulse towards great building, which was part of the genius of the race, the intrinsic necessities of a rapidly growing community almost always forced on the issue; very frequently, also, a catastrophe of some kind, whether fire or the fall of a tower, hastened on the business. Thus Lanfranc, on his arrival at Canterbury, found his cathedral and monastery partly in ruins as a result of the fire of 1067, and began to build immediately. Besides a large church, he erected the main monastic buildings and surrounded the whole group with a wall, thus introducing into England the norm of the great monastic enceinte.[2] His example was followed all over the land. At St Albans his nephew Paul began almost immediately upon his arrival to construct a church upon a magnificent scale;[3] simultaneously work of a similar kind was going forward under Baldwin at Bury,[4] Gundulf at Rochester[5] and Scotland at St Augustine's,[6] while Serlo began at Gloucester as soon as he had formed a community and organized its administration.[7] Conversely, the Englishman, Aethelwig of Evesham, though he had money to spare, continued to use it in decorating his church in the English style, whereas his successor, the first Norman, Walter, immediately began to build in the new style,[8] and at Ely nothing was done till the arrival of the first

1 Reliable monographs on the architectural remains of almost all the great religious houses may be found in the Journals and Proceedings of national and regional archaeological and architectural societies such as *The Proceedings of the Society of Antiquaries of London, The Antiquaries Journal, The Archaeological Journal, Archaeologia, The Builder*, etc., and in the volumes issued by the Royal Commission on Historical Monuments. There is still room, however, for a careful synthesis of all the data by a historian who is also an authority on architecture. For the Romanesque period an excellent and scholarly conspectus is given by A. W. Clapham, *English Romanesque Architecture after the Conquest*.

2 Eadmer, *Historia Novorum*, 12: "Quorum aedificiorum [*sc.* the new monasteries] constructoribus ipse primus exemplum praebens ecclesiam Christi Cant. cum omnibus officinis quae infra murum ipsius curiae sunt cum ipso muro aedificavit."

3 *GASA*, I, 52–3.

4 *Memorials of St Edmund*, II, 289.

5 *Textus Roffensis* (ed. Hearne, Oxford, 1720), 143: "Ecclesiam S. Andreae...novam ex integro...aedificavit. Officinas quoque monachis necessarias...omnes construxit."

6 Gocelin, *Historia translat. S. Augustini*, II, c. 2 (*PL*, CLV, 15).

7 *Hist. Gloc.* (RS), I, 11.

8 *Chron. Evesh.* 97. Walter was *recenti opere* [i.e. style] *delectatus* (*ibid.* 55).

Norman abbot Simeon from Winchester.[1] Only rarely did the first impulse, as at Canterbury, embrace in its scope the whole group of buildings and achieve its end at once; where it did so, it was doomed in part to disappear when the expanding establishment outgrew what had seemed to be the magnificent proportions of the early design. As from the nature of the case the church, even when absorbed or supplanted by later work, has left more traces above and below ground than the other buildings, we are dependent for the chronology of early domestic construction almost entirely upon literary evidence; but it seems probable that in almost every case, above all in the cathedral monasteries, the church was the first care of the new builders, and in the church a beginning was naturally made with the eastern limb and the transept, which gave accommodation for the essential liturgical and choral functions. This was followed by the central tower and nave, while the completion on a corresponding scale of refectory, chapter-house and dormitory was often the work of the next generation at the beginning of the twelfth century. Only those who have lived in a great and growing establishment can fully realize the effect upon the mind of expansion into spacious buildings from small. The sight of such constructions going forward, and the prospect of entering gradually into the enjoyment of new advantages, and of a dignified and magnificent place of worship, must have helped above all other means to take the minds of the English monks from past regrets and to reconcile them to the disciplinary and liturgical innovations which the new buildings must have seemed to justify and even to demand.

For along with the material changes the Norman abbots brought a new discipline and a new, or at least a revitalized, observance. It is a commonplace among the annalists and chroniclers—and in particular of those who looked back from the next generation—to refer to the reforming activities of Norman abbots.[2] As has already been seen, the need for reform varied greatly in degree with different houses. Nowhere, perhaps, was it more needed than at the two chief cathedral monasteries, where also it naturally received the greatest publicity.[3] In general, it would seem to have taken the shape of a return to what had been the norm a century before in such matters as regular silence, regular food, and the strict observance of community of property; of the material wastefulness and moral laxity that were attacked by so many critics and reformers in later centuries there is no mention in the sources of the early Anglo-Norman period. Indeed, the number of precise indications of the nature of the Norman reforms is

1 *Lib. Elien.* 253.

2 A reader unfamiliar with monastic annals often attaches undue weight to such phrases as *ordinem sollicite reformavit* or *auxit*. It is a mere commonplace, said of every good abbot.

3 Details of these changes will be discussed later. The chief sources of information, besides those given for Canterbury on a previous page, are *GASA*, I, 52, 59–60; *Annales Winton.*, s.a. 1082; *Lib. Elien.* 261.

surprisingly small; the majority of chroniclers content themselves with general statements, which have been repeated by historians.

We are on surer ground, and on a subject of more significance for monastic history, when we pass from discipline to observance, and ask whether the Norman abbots imposed a new rule of life upon their subjects, and, if so, whether it was identical throughout England, or varied from house to house. What we have already seen of the character of Western monasticism and of the origins of that of Normandy in particular will have prepared an *a priori* answer which an examination of the records will in great part bear out. As no constitutional bond existed between the Norman monasteries or between the English monasteries or between the new abbots and any major superior, there could be no question of the application of a single clear-cut code, new or old. As, on the other hand, the Norman houses had a common family tradition which was itself related to that still surviving in England, the observance brought from abroad was, in all essentials, uniform and, also, capable of growing upon the existing tree. The situation was, however, slightly modified by the racial and psychological solidarity which held the group of new arrivals together, and by the accidental circumstance that an archbishop, himself a monk, exercised a power of supervision and direction far beyond that belonging to his office as such, and to which an earlier parallel can be found only in the case of Dunstan.

These various influences are reflected in the sources. The norm was that each abbot introduced, so far as possible, the customs and observances of the house from which he came. Thus we have precise information that Gunter of Marmoutier enforced at Thorney the observance of his mother-house;[1] a little later, Herbert Losinga gave the customs of Fécamp to his foundation at Norwich,[2] and it is clear that Thurstan of Glastonbury was endeavouring, however unskilfully, to give the use of Caen to his monks.[3]

Probably in these and similar cases there was every variety of procedure between the *ipse dixit* of an abbot and the handing over of a written body of customs, such as would have been necessary in a completely new foundation. In any case, all the codes that were thus drawn up have perished, with one important exception. At no house was the break with the past so complete as at Christ Church, and the organizing genius of Lanfranc, together with his desire that the metropolitan church should set a standard of life and liturgy, prompted him to draw up constitutions

1 OV, IV, 282: "Hic monachilem Torneiae conventum ordine Majoris Monasterii regulariter instituit."

2 *Epistolae Herberti de Losinga* (ed. Anstruther, Brussels, 1846), 69. According to Bale, *Index Britanniae Scriptorum* (ed. Poole, Oxford, 1902), 169, he gave a written code: "Herebertus Nordovicensis episcopus scripsit Constitutiones monachorum." But probably he merely gave the Fécamp customary.

3 Will. Malmesb., *GR*, II, 331: "Qui dum conventui multa de antiquis et approbatis consuetudinibus subtraheret, quaedam etiam pro more suae patriae transmutaret."

which were not merely those of Bec, but which embodied all that he considered desirable in the practice—and especially the liturgical practice—of the monasteries with which he was familiar.

The scope of Lanfranc's *Consuetudines*[1] has given rise to some discussion in recent years.[2] It has in the past been very commonly stated that they were intended to apply to all the monastic houses of England; such a view reflects a conception of monastic uniformity and legislation with which the age of Lanfranc was wholly unfamiliar, and the title to the *Consuetudines* in the earliest printed edition, which was urged in its support, has been shown to rest on no manuscript authority.[3] Nor does the language of the introductory letter to the monks of Christ Church, if carefully weighed, indicate that Lanfranc's original intention was to provide a code for universal application; indeed, he explicitly states that one monastery cannot in all respects resemble another. But once the *Consuetudines* were compiled, it was natural that they should be given by the archbishop to any superior whom he directly appointed or who approached him for help; natural, also, that Lanfranc's fame should give them a permanent authority. Consequently, their observance at other houses is noted by chroniclers and can be inferred from the existence of manuscripts. Paul of Caen, it is explicitly stated, introduced them at St Albans,[4] and they passed thence to Croyland in the following century.[5] It may be presumed that they went to Lanfranc's plantation at Rochester, and with the group of colonists to St Augustine's after the trouble; besides these houses, both Durham and Worcester are known to have possessed copies,[6] and their influence has been traced in some later customs of Westminster.[7]

1 Lanfranc's *Consuetudines* or *Statuta* were first printed by Dom Clement Reyner, *Apostolatus Benedictinorum in Anglia* (Douai, 1626), appendix, *pars tertia*, 211 seqq. Thence they passed to D'Achery, *Lanfranci Opera*, 1628, Giles, *Opera Lanfranci*, I, 85–191 and Migne, *PL*, CL.

2 *V.* J. Armitage Robinson, *Lanfranc's Monastic Constitutions* in *JTS*, x (1909), 375–88; Dr Rose Graham, *The Relation of Cluny to some other Movements of Monastic Reform*, *ibid.* xv (1914), 179, reprinted in *English Ecclesiastical Studies* (London, 1929), 1–29.

3 The title *Decreta D. Lanfranci pro ordine S. Benedicti* was given by Reyner; in it *ordo* = religious order, whereas in Lanfranc's introductory letter it = ordered way of life.

4 *GASA*, I, 52: "[Paulus] attulerat secum Consuetudines Lanfranci, et Statuta Monastica, a Domino Papa merito approbata, conscripta." 58: "Consuetudines approbatas et approbandas, auctoritate Lanfranci...in ecclesia S. Albani, eliminatis antiquis reprobandis, constituit observari." 61: "Hic quoque Consuetudines, quas transmisit scriptas Lanfrancus Abbati Paulo, approbavit et conservari persuasit." Matthew Paris, *Hist. Angl.*, *s.a.* 1077: "Consuetudines approbatas coenobiorum ultramarinorum in claustro S. Albani inviolabiliter observari constituit." *Ibid.*, *s.a.* 1089: "Usque nunc...tam Lanfranci quam Anselmi vigent indelebiliter statuta et consuetudines approbatae." It must be remembered that the *Gesta Abbatum* were touched up by Paris, and at an epoch when constitutional changes were a living issue. Some of the above phrases have a ring of anachronism, in particular the reference to papal approval.

5 *GASA*, I, 121: "Qui [*sc.* Godfridus] ordinem hujus domus, cum consuetudinibus, ibidem constituit observari."

6 *V.* articles of Armitage Robinson and Dr Rose Graham cited above, and for Worcester also C. H. Turner, *Early Worcester MSS* (Oxford, 1916).

7 Armitage Robinson, *Gilbert Crispin*, 28, writes: "We can hardly doubt that this code, which Gilbert must have seen in force at Canterbury [where he had lived *c.* 1079–85], was

Thus there is a reasonable certainty that they were applied in eight houses and probably a few more received them directly or indirectly, but there was no question of a general edict binding all.

The *Consuetudines* were not merely the customs of Bec. Lanfranc himself in his introductory letter tells us that he had done a work of selection, and it has been shown conclusively that references to them by later chroniclers as Bec customs are due to an interpolation without authority.[1] Their author describes them as customs "extracted from those monasteries which in our own time are of the greatest fame". "I have added (he continues) some few things and changed others", but he himself allows for changes in the future, "since no church can exactly imitate another".[2] Thus Matthew Paris is perfectly accurate in his description of them as "the approved customs of monasteries across the Channel".[3] Actually, an examination of the *Consuetudines* shows a close resemblance throughout, especially in the non-liturgical portions, to Cluniac customaries, and in particular to those compiled by Bernard. Only a few usages come direct from Bec.[4] But taken by and large, they differ very little from the observance of the *Regularis Concordia* and could easily have been substituted for the earlier code; they show a slight development of ceremonial, but do not approach the contemporary usage of Cluny in elaboration. While they are in some ways more explicit in details of monastic life, they lack the touches of spiritual feeling which are found in the *Concordia*, and, save in the short introduction, throw no fresh light on the mind of Lanfranc himself. In other words, they contain nothing that is new either in legislation or spiritual doctrine; their unique interest lies in the exact evidence they provide of the first Norman observance in England.

VII

Besides their architectural and disciplinary activities, the Norman abbots and the monks they brought with them introduced the overseas culture into the English monasteries. Those who crossed from Normandy in the reign of the Conqueror were almost all of the generation that had grown to maturity in what may be called the golden age of the Norman houses,

brought by him to Westminster...considerable portions are embodied word for word in the thirteenth-century customary of Abbot Ware."

1 Milo Crispin, *Vita Lanfranci* (Giles, 1, 308) has: "Ibi [i.e. at St Albans] ordinem, et ecclesiastici officii usum instituit [Paulus], sicut cernere est hodie." Robert of Torigni, *Chronicle* (RS), 49, has "Ibi ordinem Becci et." This interpolated sentence was copied, *hodie* and all, by Ralph of Diceto, *Abbreviationes Chronicorum* (RS), 1, 215.

2 Giles, 1, 85: "Consuetudines...quas excerpsimus ex consuetudinibus eorum coenobiorum, quae nostro tempore majoris auctoritatis sunt in ordine monachorum. Addidimus quoque perpauca, et mutavimus nonnulla...nulla fere ecclesia imitari aliam per omnia potest."

3 *V.s.* note 4, p. 123.

4 So Dr R. Graham, *art. cit., English Ecclesiastical Studies*, 8.

before the new learning had left the monasteries for the schools and when Bec, under Anselm and Lanfranc, was the intellectual mistress of northern Europe. Consequently, they brought to England an education in letters far deeper and wider than anything they found in possession; above all they brought a culture which gave to those who imbibed it the ability and the desire to express themselves with ease in fluent and idiomatic Latin, and thus, while silencing the vernacular literature, made of England a province of the commonwealth of Latin Europe, which for a century and a half was to form a cultural unit more potent to unite than were racial differences to dissolve. From the beginning the great abbots are noted as collectors of books, and the process of building up the English libraries on continental lines continued for fifty years.[1] The greater English monasteries were thus gradually given the means of acquiring a literary culture which, in the case of abler subjects, could in time base itself on a comparatively wide reading, and by the beginning of the twelfth century at least half the English houses must have come to resemble the Norman in this respect. St Albans under Paul, Evesham under Walter, the Old Minster under Prior Godfrey[2]—even such monasteries of the second rank as Bath,[3] Thorney and Croyland[4]—came one by one under the influence of abbots of distinction, and by the reign of Henry I only the smaller houses or those which had suffered in some peculiar way remained outside the new life, remarkable for their lack of letters.[5]

Some particular aspects of this culture will be discussed on a later page. Here it is sufficient to note that it was rarely more than a literary culture. The Norman monasteries, and still more the English, gradually fell out of the main current of intellectual life that was to issue into the fuller renaissance of the twelfth century and to develop so greatly the study of philosophy, canon law and theology. Nor could an abbot, with his administrative duties and frequent absences, be the master of a school. But here again we can see a difference in the English houses which fell directly under the influence of Bec. Lanfranc, as archbishop, could not set up a school, but he had his old pupils under him, and we can see in Eadmer and others how great a power he exercised. It was to Lanfranc that Wulfstan of Worcester sent his monk Nicholas to be trained, and from Nicholas the school of Worcester—Coleman, Florence and John—was derived.[6]

---

1 *GASA*, 1, 58. *Chron. Evesh.* 97: "Multos libros fecit." For a fuller treatment of this point, *v. infra*, pp. 523–4.
2 Will. Malmesb., *GP*, 172: "Religione et litteratura insignis fuit."
3 Will. Malmesb., *GR*, 195: "[Bathonienses] qui sunt scientia litterarum et sedulitate officiorum juxta praedicabiles."
4 Both Thorney and Croyland later received an abbot from St Évroul, and the latter monastery was visited by Ordericus. Thorney's first Norman abbot was Fulcard of Séez, of whom Orderic writes (IV, 281): "Hic...fuit...grammaticae artis et musicae peritissimus."
5 E.g. Coventry, Will. Malmesb., *GP*, 310.
6 Will. Malmesb., *Vita Wulfst.* 57.

Similarly, at Westminster Gilbert Crispin inspired a group, of which Osbert of Clare is the most distinguished member, which added to letters the interest in purely theological questions which was a characteristic of Bec. With Anselm's familiar disputations at Christ Church and Gilbert Crispin's more controversial activities in London a chapter of monastic history was closed.[1]

Letters, music and medicine came with individual abbots to England. Baldwin of Bury and Faricius of Abingdon were in successive generations the two most celebrated practitioners in the country, and there are references to experts in other monasteries.[2] Among musicians in the first generation after the Conquest Paul of St Albans and Fulcard of St Bertin, Séez, the first Norman abbot of Thorney, receive special mention,[3] but every large house came gradually, in one way or another, to share in the developments of the liturgy and chant that had taken place on the Continent during the past century.

VIII

The immediate result of the transfusion of new blood into the monasteries of England was a great and rapid growth in the number of aspirants to the life. General references to this abound, and the scale of the new buildings corroborates the general statements, but precise figures are to hand for more than one important house. We do not know how many Lanfranc found at Canterbury, but all references suggest a community of very moderate proportions; when William of Malmesbury wrote in 1125 it was the largest house in England, and the figures we possess for other monasteries and for Christ Church itself a little later prove that this implies a hundred monks or more. Evesham rose from twelve to thirty-five odd under Aethelwig; Worcester from twelve to fifty under Wulfstan; Rochester from twenty-two to over sixty under Gundulf[4] (1077–1108); Gloucester from ten to a hundred under Serlo (1072–1104)[5]; and Gilbert Crispin left provision for eighty at Westminster[6] (ob. 1117). When the large number of wholly new foundations is taken into consideration, these great increases become all the more striking.

The new recruits came in part from the invaders and their children; this was especially the case in houses near the centres of administration such as Christ Church, Westminster and the two at Winchester; in the

---

1 V. Gilbert's *Disputatio Judaei cum Christiano* and *Disputatio Christiani cum gentili*; also Armitage Robinson's remarks (*Gilbert Crispin*, 74) on the "philosophers' club" in London.
2 E.g. at Malmesbury, Will. Malmesb., *GP*, 438.
3 For Fulcard v. OV, IV, 281: cf. *Mem. St Edm.* I, 70, for other influences from abroad.
4 *Text. Roff.* 143. Actually Gundulf found only five canons; the monastic plantation was with twenty-two. For further figures v. Appendix XVII.
5 *Monasticon*, I, 543; *Hist. Gloc.* I, 13.
6 Flete's *History of Westminster*, 87; cf. Robinson, *Gilbert Crispin*, 30.

New Minster in the last-mentioned city we can trace the process by the gradual introduction of Norman names into the *Liber Vitae*; in remote monasteries the change was not so marked, but in the majority the Norman or at least the Anglo-Norman element came gradually to predominate, and the chronicler of St Albans notes the dying out of the English "party".[1] A few houses, however, remained long predominantly English. Worcester was naturally one; another was Peterborough, where a patriotic and strangely melancholy spirit pervades the entries in the last text of the old English chronicle.

1 *GASA*, 1, 66. There is a reference, *à propos* of the accession of Abbot Richard in 1097, to *Normanni* as *jam multiplicati* and to *Angli* as *jam senescentes et imminuti*.

CHAPTER VII

THE DEVELOPMENT OF THE RELIGIOUS LIFE BETWEEN 1066 AND 1100

I

THE NEW FOUNDATIONS

Hitherto mention has been made only of the methodical transformation of the existing English monasteries into something of the Norman model. This, however, was far from being the sole result of the Conquest, for besides reorganizing and developing the old, the Normans created new centres of monastic life of various kinds throughout England. These new foundations owed their origin to every variety of circumstance, and cannot be treated in detail here. One, however, the first in point of time as of importance, deserves individual mention. This was the Conqueror's own foundation of S. Martinus de Bello, or Battle abbey, made upon the very spot where the last English king had fallen, in consequence of a vow made by the victor.[1]

It is remarkable that for this, his own monastery, the Conqueror sought a community not from among the monasteries of Normandy, but from Marmoutier on the Loire. Lanfranc was not yet archbishop, and this step, together with the application to St Hugh of Cluny at almost the same time, would seem to show that William had not settled upon a fixed policy of plantation. Battle was in every sense a foreign foundation. The community came from beyond the seas; so did the stone for the buildings and the workmen for the stone. In addition, the house was from the first set in a class by itself. Richly endowed and surrounded by a compact estate, it was a royal *Eigenkloster* with wide if ill-defined civil and ecclesiastical immunities that were to be a source of much litigation in the sequel. Apart from this litigation, Battle was in every way one of the most fortunate abbeys of England for more than a century, and more than one able and spiritual abbot helped to keep its first purity untouched. Founded with a large community as a monument of Norman victory, and for long recruited, we may suppose, from Norman blood, it remained in a sense apart from the monastic life of England more than any other autonomous

---

1 Preparations for the foundation of Battle began in 1067. An account of its early years may be found in the *Chronicon Monasterii de Bello* (ed. [by J. S. Brewer] Anglia Christiana Society, 1846), 1–30. This chronicle, of which a more satisfactory edition is greatly to be desired, has been criticized by H. W. C. Davis, *The Chronicle of Battle Abbey*, in *EHR*, XXIX, 426 *seqq.* It was composed c. 1170, but the compiler had earlier records before him, and the narrative may be taken as reliable; not so the early charters, which will be discussed on a later page. For Battle *v.* also Dr Rose Graham, *The Monastery of Battle*, in *English Ecclesiastical Studies*, 188–208.

house, though it successfully resisted all attempts on the part of Mar-moutier to keep it in tutelage.

Besides Battle, the later decades of the century saw the establishment of five or six other important houses: Selby, Shrewsbury, Chester, Spalding and Colchester.[1] The story of Selby is in part legendary,[2] but not without interest; the foundation of Shrewsbury was in part due to Odeleric, father of the historian Orderic Vitalis, whose five-year-old brother Benedict was given to the monks as an oblate, while the father in old age took the habit as a monk;[3] Chester was a plantation from Bec under Anselm. Finally, at the end of the century, the first Norman abbot of the small abbey of Cranborne, Gerald by name, transferred the bulk of his community to a distant property at the confluence of the Avon and Severn in Gloucestershire and thus established what was to become the rich and celebrated abbey of Tewkesbury.[4]

II

THE CATHEDRAL MONASTERIES

Besides the autonomous monasteries under an abbot, Lanfranc as arch-bishop was called upon to decide what part the cathedral monasteries should have in the new *régime*. In Normandy, as we have seen, monastic influence upon the life of the Church, though very great, was exercised almost wholly from within the walls of the monasteries. A monk bishop was a rarity; the bishops were either members of great families or chosen from among the circle of the Duke's chaplains, and the reformers among them aimed at surrounding themselves by a *familia* of canons and officials from among the clerks of their entourage. In England, however, there was in existence the institution, peculiar to the country, of cathedral monasteries, due in its present form at least to Dunstan and his friends, and affecting in 1066 four cathedrals, Canterbury, Winchester, Worcester and Sherborne. At the outset, therefore, Lanfranc found himself as arch-bishop at the head of a monastic foundation which performed all the liturgical functions in his cathedral. There is no likelihood that he ever contemplated a change. His *esprit de corps* as a monk, the policy of using

---

1 For Colchester *v. Monasticon*, IV, 607–9. Cf. also *Cartularium Monasterii S. Johannis Baptiste de Colecestria*, ed. S. A. Moore for the Roxburghe Club, 1897. The narrative of the foundation and the early charters have been subjected to criticism by Round in *Geoffrey de Mandeville*, 423–7, and *The early Charters of St John's Abbey, Colchester* in *EHR*, XVI, 721–30; also by J. Armitage Robinson, *Gilbert Crispin*, Additional Note A, 158–66.

2 *Historia Selebeiensis Monasterii*, reprinted from Labbe, *Nov. Biblioth. MSS. Librorum* (1657), I, 594–626, by J. T. Fowler in *Selby Coucher Book* (Yorks Archæological Society: Record Series 10 [1891]).

3 Ordericus Vitalis, II, 415–22; III, 425; V, 134.

4 Cf. *Registrum Theokusburiae*, Brit. Mus. Addit. MS. 36,985, which supplements the narrative printed in *Monasticon*, II, 59 *seqq.*, followed by Dr Rose Graham in *VCH, Glouc.* II, 61.

monasticism as a principal instrument of reform, his natural disposition of mind, shown in so many actions, to preserve existing institutions in England, and especially those connected with the archbishopric—all these influences combined to make him accept what he found with readiness, and in fact all his energies seem from the first to have been directed towards making Christ Church a model monastery. At Worcester, with Wulfstan, there could be no question of change; Sherborne, with which Herman had previously been dissatisfied, was, when the see had been moved to Ramsbury and Sarum, a bishop's monastery rather than a cathedral monastery. Over Winchester, however, there was a contest.

The new bishop, appointed in 1070 by agreement between William and the papal legates, was Walkelin, a priest of great ability who had been recommended to the Conqueror by his former patron Maurilius of Fécamp, archbishop of Rouen.[1] Walkelin entered upon his duties before Lanfranc's arrival in England; he was not a monk, and he found his cathedral occupied by monks with strongly national opinions and a certain laxity of life; only a few yards distant from the cathedral was another large monastery, whose abbot had died on the field of Hastings. Walkelin, familiar with the normal diocesan organization of the party of reform on the Continent, proposed to introduce canons instead of the monks, and succeeded in obtaining the sanction of the Conqueror. There is no reason to see in this any direct hostility to the monastic order as such; Walkelin, the *protégé* of a monk-bishop, had himself a brother in the abbey of St Ouen; the statement of a later writer that all the secular bishops wished to expel monks from their cathedrals is probably an anachronism.[2] It would, however, seem probable that the Conqueror's first group of bishops—Walkelin, Arfast, Thomas of Bayeux—contemplated a regularizing of the English Church on the continental model, and regarded the monks of Winchester and Canterbury as intruders, for they must have learnt, if they did not previously know, the history of the times of Dunstan. But before Walkelin could achieve his end Lanfranc was primate, and opposed the change; meanwhile, also, representations had been made at Rome on behalf of Canterbury, and Alexander II, Lanfranc's old pupil and a strong supporter of the monastic order, had written commanding him to safeguard the monks. With that, Walkelin's opposition ended. His brother became prior of St Swithun's, and he himself lived with his monks in perfect goodwill, leaving behind him a memory of benediction.

---

1 Will. Malmesb., *GP*, 172.

2 For this controversy *v.* letter of Alexander II to Lanfranc (ed. Giles, 1, 27); Eadmer, *Historia Novorum*, 18–19; *Annales Wintonienses, s.a.* 1098; Will. Malmesb., *GP*, 71–2. If Alexander's letter is genuine, it would seem to be Eadmer's chief source, but the incident as related has several suspicious details, e.g. that Walkelin had forty canons ready dressed [!] to enter, and no date is given. From the text of the papal letter it would seem that others, not Lanfranc, carried the matter to Rome, and it is indeed not easy to suppose that an attempt would have been made against Christ Church with Lanfranc there.

In the years that followed circumstances brought about a considerable extension of monastic influence in the cathedrals of England. The small and ancient see of Rochester, the occupant of which depended in a peculiar way upon the metropolitan, and had often in the past been little more than a *chorepiscopus*, was filled in 1077 by Gundulf, a monk of Bec. He and Lanfranc soon decided to revive the long vanished monastery of Rochester, and accordingly a community was settled there and endowed, mainly from lands given by the archbishop.[1] In the north the first Norman bishop, Walcher, though himself a secular clerk, found traditions of the past, and perhaps also a number of monastic customs, in his *familia* at Durham. He contemplated introducing monks from among the new-comers from the south, but met with a violent death before he could achieve his end. His successor, however, who was a monk, William of St Carilef, formerly abbot of St Vincent, established in his cathedral a community drawn from the group of new arrivals who had refounded Jarrow and Wearmouth under circumstances to be described later. In this he was no doubt influenced by the ancient traditions of Lindisfarne, where Aidan and Cuthbert had ruled as bishops surrounded by their monks; but the new life was consciously based upon that of Lanfranc's Canterbury, for Durham received a copy of the *Consuetudines* from the hands of bishop William, probably upon the introduction of the monks.[2]

Canterbury, Worcester, Durham and Rochester were thus monastic houses under monk-bishops, and it is probable that Lanfranc conceived that things would always thus remain, and that bishop and monks would continue to influence the Church in England in the direction of reform. Another tendency, initiated by the Conqueror with Lanfranc's support, had as its indirect consequence a still further extension of the system of monastic cathedrals. This was the transference of sees from their old situation in small, decaying and unprotected places to new centres of population which were capable of military defence. In almost all these cases the bishops disposed of incomes considerably less than the greater monasteries within their jurisdiction, and in default of any other means of improving their position a number of them contemplated the possibility of transferring their see to a monastic church. Herman of Ramsbury-Sherborne had endeavoured to annex Malmesbury in this way before the Conquest;[3] the transference of the see to Old Sarum c. 1075, and its

---

1 For the foundation of Rochester *v.* MS. Bodl. Hatton 54, quoted by N. E. S. A. Hamilton in his introduction (p. xxiv) to the *Gesta Pontificum* of William of Malmesbury; cf. also the *Gesta*, 72. For a list of monastic bishops, 1066–1215, *v.* Appendix XII.

2 Symeon of Durham, *Historia Dunelmensis Ecclesiae in Opera* (RS), I, 122 *seqq.* For the Durham MS. *v.* article, *The Earliest List of Durham MSS.*, by C. H. Turner in *JTS*, XIX (1918), 121–32.

3 Will. Malmesb., *GP*, 182, 420. For Baldwin *v.* the document quoted by V. H. Galbraith in his article *The East Anglian See and the Abbey of Bury St Edmund's* in *EHR*, XL (April 1925), 222 *seqq.* "Rex ut episcopus fieret et in Beodriches villa episcopalem cathedram sibi reformaret instanter laboravit" (p. 227).

occupation by St Osmund, who gave his cathedral its celebrated constitution, had the double effect of saving Malmesbury for a season and of giving a greater independence to Sherborne. In the east, Arfast of Thetford, after a determined attempt to occupy Bury St Edmunds, settled at Thetford, though there is evidence that the Conqueror subsequently urged Abbot Baldwin to accept episcopal office and make his abbey church the cathedral. The struggle with Bury continued into the reign of Rufus, and ceased to be a living issue only when Herbert Losinga, a monk of Fécamp whose reputation had hitherto been none of the best, removed again to Norwich, where he established and endowed a community of monks c. 1100 on the lines of Canterbury and Durham.[1] In the west, at the death of Giso of Wells, who had instituted a flourishing *familia* of canons in that remote settlement, John of Tours removed to the more important town of Bath and succeeded, apparently with Lanfranc's warm support, in occupying the abbey there. John had been given the town of Bath in 1088; the place had recently been ravaged by Roger de Mowbray and the monastery, whose English abbot had died in 1087, had no doubt suffered. The change was at first detrimental to the monks, but in the event prosperity revived, though Bath, with its dual capitular organization, was long in establishing itself as a cathedral priory on a level with the earlier members of the class.[2] In the midlands, a similar result was reached by more irregular means. Peter, the first bishop of Lichfield after the Conquest, had moved thence to Chester c. 1075; the diocese, which had suffered from the Conqueror's harrying, was poor, but contained the wealthy abbey of Coventry, which had provided a bishop for Lichfield previous to 1066. Peter's successor, Robert of Limesey, invaded the place in Lanfranc's last years, and though the archbishop protested vigorously, succeeded, at least after his death, in holding it, though, like John of Tours, he did not transfer the see entirely from Lichfield and after more than a century of disputes a dual organization not unlike that of Bath and Wells was set up.[3]

Another and more important cathedral narrowly escaped a monastic constitution. Remigius, formerly a monk of Fécamp, the first Norman bishop of Lincoln, had refounded Stow in the neighbourhood of his cathedral city, no doubt with the intention of introducing the monks later into Lincoln itself. He died without making the change, and his successor, the secular Robert Bloett, removed them, as being a burden to him, to Eynsham, the old home of Aelfric, which lay within his diocese.[4]

---

1 *Monasticon*, IV, 15; Will. Malmesb., *GP*, 151–2.

2 Will. Malmesb., *GP*, 194–5. Cf. charter of confirmation, *Monasticon*, II, 266: "Lanfranco archipraesule machinante." There seems no reason to doubt the authenticity of this, for which cf. *Calendar of Wells Diocesan and Cathedral MSS.*, I, 13. Cf. also *Chron. Ang. Petrib.*, *s.a.* 1088.

3 Will. Malmesb., *GP*, 310; letter of Lanfranc to Robert (*c.* 1087–8), *ep.* 32 (Giles, I, 51–2).

4 Will. Malmesb., *GP*, 313. The passage is not in the text as printed by the editor, but is given in a footnote.

One more change, though not effected till the reign of Henry I, may be mentioned here for the sake of completeness. The wealthy abbey of Ely, in the decades after the Conquest, showed every sign of developing its privileged position into a complete independence similar to that of Bury. Instead, the very opposite happened. By an arrangement of which Anselm approved, a new diocese was carved out of the vast territory of Lincoln, and the first bishop was given a portion of the revenues of Ely, with what had been the abbey church for his cathedral.[1] *En revanche*, however, another bishop relinquished a monastery he already possessed. Roger of Salisbury, whose general practice it was to absorb abbeys, loosed his hold upon Sherborne for some reason, and the house became autonomous.[2]

Thus within fifty years of the Conquest the number of cathedral monasteries had risen from three (or four if Sherborne be included) to nine, among the seventeen existing English bishoprics, and in 1133 the establishment of an Augustinian bishop and community at Carlisle made a tenth. As has been seen, they were not in origin a homogeneous group; speaking very generally, in six the end desired had been the presence of monks at a cathedral, in three it had been the acquisition of a wealthy church by a bishop. Their peculiar organization will be described later; here it is only to be remembered that two tendencies, one intrinsic the other extrinsic, came more and more to lessen their significance and modify the distinctions between them. On the one hand, monasticism of the traditional black monk kind ceased soon after 1125 to be the only or even the chief spiritual influence in the English Church; on the other hand, the occupation of almost all the sees by secular bishops and the canonical organization of chapters tended to separate the bishop from the cathedral monastery, and to level the differences among the cathedral monasteries, while giving to the prior and community various rights and obligations which had no bearing upon the monastic life as such. Whereas in the early years the great monastic bishops had been the effective spiritual rulers of their houses, later all internal administration, both spiritual and temporal, tended to pass more and more to the prior. There is nothing to indicate what conception of the future lay behind Lanfranc's actions which perpetuated and extended a system peculiar to England; probably here as elsewhere he should be seen as a practical statesman working for the immediate interests of religion rather than as a far-sighted monastic legislator. In the event, though the peculiar situation of the cathedral monasteries had less essential influence either on monasticism or on the Church in England than might have been expected, it led to a series of embittered controversies which bulk large in the external history of the times and cannot but have affected for the worse the communities engaged in them

1 Will. Malmesb., *GP*, 325; Eadmer, *Hist. Nov.* 195.
2 Will. Malmesb., *GP*, 175: "Scireburnensis dudum episcopatus, nunc per Rogerum episcopum Saresberiensem consensu Henrici regis facta abbatia monachorum."

whether as agents or patients. But these could scarcely have been foreseen by Lanfranc and his contemporaries.

III

DEPENDENT PRIORIES AND CELLS

Besides the foundation of numerous great monasteries, the Normans were almost wholly responsible for the plantation in England of an exceedingly large number of small and inchoate houses.

The Rule of St Benedict presupposes throughout that the monastic community for which it is making provision is self-contained and autonomous; in other words, the monastic family of the Rule is a single group, residing within the walls of a single house, and under the immediate direction of the abbot. At the time of the Conquest, with scarcely an exception, the old English monasteries satisfied these conditions. But in the reign of the Confessor came the first seeds of a new growth which increased very speedily after the Conquest: a large class, that is, of satellites to the independent houses, varying widely in size and in degree of monastic development from the small establishments which formed the residence of one, two or three monks to a fully organized monastery in miniature, but all lacking the final perfection of autonomy. Before the end of the twelfth century there were some two hundred such scattered throughout the length and breadth of England and South Wales.

These small monastic houses did not all originate in the same manner, or follow one and the same process of development; they may be conveniently divided into three groups. In the first fall the houses, originally independent, which had decayed and been subsequently absorbed by others, or which had been abandoned by the majority of their former inhabitants. In such cases both tradition and the economic conditions of the time made it natural for a small body of monks to be left to carry on the liturgical services of the existing church and to live upon and exploit the lands with which it was endowed. With no adequate system of transport or marketing the only alternative to a direct exploitation of the demesne lands of a distant estate was the uneconomical and more troublesome method of letting it out to farm. Houses such as these, however, were comparatively few; an example may be seen at Cranborne whence, as has been noted above, the bulk of the community were removed to Tewkesbury, but which continued to support a small body of residents, and at Horton, which was absorbed by Sherborne; in the north, some of the ancient sites, such as Jarrow and Wearmouth, were reoccupied for a time before the monks were concentrated at Durham, Whitby and York, and remained possessions of the new foundations, which maintained small communities in them.

A second class, larger than the first, but still of no great size, was made up of houses professedly founded as monasteries in miniature, daughters of some large abbey. The majority of these came into existence shortly after the Conquest. A benefactor, anxious to establish a monastery as a kind of *Eigenkloster* on his new estates in England, but unable to give land sufficient for a large community, made an agreement with one of the large houses to establish a dependency of a fixed number of monks with certain rights *vis-à-vis* the mother-house. In the early years of the Norman reorganization, it was probably intended by the founding abbey that such communities should grow and become independent, but a whole group of causes—such as the interests of the mother-house and the diversion of benefactions to new orders—arrested this growth in almost every case, and the dependency remained undeveloped, like some biological species left behind in the gradual evolution. Dependent priories of this type were by no means general. Many of the old abbeys, including some of the greatest, such as St Augustine's, Canterbury, the two Winchester houses and Bury, had none at all; others had one or two; a few, such as St Albans and Durham, had a numerous family of more than half a dozen, some of them far distant from the mother-house.

The third class was by far the most numerous, and indeed contained more than five-sixths of the total number of minor establishments. The allotment of lands all over England to the Norman followers of the Conqueror took place at the moment when members of the Norman baronage were vying with one another in founding monasteries. Consequently it became the fashion to bestow lands in England upon abbeys in Normandy, and as the lands of the king, and fiefs of the great tenants *in capite*, were widely scattered, it was not uncommon for gifts of land to a single house to be scattered also. Every student of *Domesday* will have been struck by the number of these isolated possessions of English and Norman monasteries even as early as 1086. Thus Grestain had land in six English counties, and the two Caen foundations in four and three respectively. The realization of the revenues from these cross-Channel properties was always difficult, and necessitated the presence, at least from time to time, of a member of the religious community to which they belonged. Gradually the practice became common of establishing a small group of monks in England to live on the produce of the land and collect the rents; in many cases such residences developed into small priories where the liturgy was carried out and monastic observance kept; others remained little more than residences with a chapel. Very often, also, in the early decades after the Conquest, the new owners of *Eigenkirchen*, in obedience to the Gregorian decrees against lay proprietorship of churches, made over their property of this kind to a monastery.

All these dependencies came gradually to be known by the generic name of "cell"; those belonging to overseas houses were later called "alien priories". Except in the case of those belonging to an English abbey whose chronicle has survived (St Albans is a case in point) little is known of their early history save for isolated charters of gift and an occasional enquiry into troubles which had arisen. Gifts to foreign houses continued to be frequent at least until the middle of the reign of Henry II, but the majority of the English dependencies date from the end of the eleventh and beginning of the twelfth centuries. Natural as was the process by which these small houses came into being, their appearance must be pronounced one of the most unfortunate by-products of the Conquest in England; save for a few of the larger priories, they served no religious purpose whatever, and were a source of weakness to the house that owned them. In the course of time they became the most considerable of all the elements of spiritual decay in the monastic life of the country.

IV

THE NUNNERIES

In comparison with the monasteries, the nunneries of England had little importance in the religious life of the country at the epoch of the Conquest and during the period of reorganization. In the modern world, the number of religious women exceeds, in most countries, the combined numbers of the regular and the secular clergy; in the Middle Ages this was not the case, owing in great part to the absence of the great nursing, teaching and missionary organizations of modern times; but even in the Middle Ages, as in more recent times, a Hilda, an Etheldreda, a Gertrude, a Hildegarde or a Mechtilde and their followers—as more recently a Teresa, a Jane Frances or a Thérèse of Lisieux—could be among the greatest spiritual forces of their age. In England, after the Conquest, this was not so, and indeed the whole of the eleventh and twelfth centuries in this country passed without giving birth to a single woman religious who attained any wide celebrity.

There were in 1066 only nine fully organized monasteries of women in being, four of which were very wealthy;[1] six of the nine were old Wessex foundations. Besides these, there are traces in *Domesday* of a few other families of religious women, and, in particular, several of the monasteries had among the number of their dependents a small group of *moniales* who in some cases attended to the sick among the travellers, pilgrims and recipients of alms.[2] The Conquest, so far as can be seen, had little immediate influence upon the organization or increase of the nunneries, but the

1 For these, *v.* Appendix VI. Wilton and Shaftesbury had approximately the same income (in the neighbourhood of £250) as St Albans, and considerably more than Malmesbury, Coventry, Evesham and other abbeys.

2 Thus in the well-known list of the dependents of Bury in 1085 (Dd. II, 372; the passage is printed in full in *Mem. St Edm.* I, 339, and with facsimile in *Corolla sancti*

greater houses fell naturally into the net of the Conqueror's system of land tenure, and this must have implied a certain amount of surveillance. The abbesses of the nine houses held in chief of the king, and thus formed a majority in the small class of women landholders in *Domesday*. Two only, the wealthiest, Wilton and Shaftesbury, were called upon for knight-service, and there is no explicit mention of Norman abbesses being appointed to England, but it is significant that Norman names appear very soon upon the lists.[1]

The nunneries, even more than the monasteries of men, were at this period preserves of the upper class. Several of them had been founded or endowed by royal ladies, and during the second half of the tenth century there is more than one instance of a princess of the blood taking the veil. The tradition continued in the next century. It was to Wilton, the home of St Edith, daughter of King Edgar, that Queen Edith, daughter of Godwin and widow of the Confessor, who had rebuilt the church there, retired for a time after the Conquest, c. 1072, and she would seem later to have been the object of a kind of *cultus*.[2] Gunhild, daughter of Harold, was a nun of the same place, though she ultimately failed to persevere.[3] Wherwell, also in Wiltshire, was the scene of Queen Edith's temporary retirement in 1048.[4] At Romsey Christina, sister of the Atheling, took the veil in 1085, and to her care c. 1093 Queen Margaret of Scotland, her sister, entrusted her two young daughters, Edith (later Matilda, wife of Henry I) and Mary;[5] early in the twelfth century the abbess there was Avicia, daughter of Robert fitz Haymon, earl of Gloucester.[6] Shaftesbury had still more illustrious connections, for Cecily, another daughter of the earl of Gloucester, was succeeded as abbess later in the century by a half-sister of Henry II, the poetess Marie de France.[7]

After the victory of the Conqueror in 1066 a number of Englishwomen, no doubt the wives and daughters of the chief supporters of Harold, took

Eadmundi (ed. Lord Francis Hervey, London, 1907), 615–16) occur "xxviii inter nonnas et pauperes qui quotidie pro rege et omni populo christiano deprecantur". In the Evesham list of 1095/6 (*Monasticon*, II, 37) occur five *moniales* (cf. *Vita Wulfstani*, ed. Darlington, 28), and there was at least one supported by Worcester (*infra*, p. 160, note 2). A group of nuns is found also at St Albans in 1140 (*GASA*, I, 81).

1 E.g. Eulalia of Shaftesbury, c. 1074; Beatrix and Alice of Winchester, c. 1084 (*v. Annales Wintonienses, sub annis*).

2 *Vita Aeduuardi Regis* (in *Lives of Edward the Confessor*, ed. Luard (RS), 418–21). This *Life* has been subjected to searching criticism by M. Marc Bloch in *Analecta Bollandiana*, XLI (1923), 17–44, and his thesis, that it was composed after 1103, and probably at Wilton, in order to join Edith to her husband in general veneration, may be accepted as proved. Apart from the objective arguments, the whole style of the piece reflects a date later than 1070–4, the date previously accepted. Queen Edith had been educated at Wilton (*Vita Aeduuardi Regis*, 403).

3 Will. Malmesb., *Vita Wulfstani*, 34, and Anselm *epp*. III, 157 (*PL*, CLIX, 189–94); cf. Dom Wilmart in *RB*, XXXIX (1926), 331–4, and *infra*, p. 139, note 1.

4 So *Chronicle*, 1048 [E], which must be preferred to the *Vita Aeduuardi Regis*, loc. cit., which gives Wilton.

5 *Chronicle*, 1085 [E]; OV, III, 399.   6 *Registrum Theokusberiense*, 14 v.

7 *V*. Bibliography for notices of Marie by J. C. Fox.

refuge in the nunneries from fear of the Normans, and ten years later
Lanfranc was called upon to pronounce on the nature of the obligation
they had thus incurred.[1] This, added to the instances already given, must
have tended to perpetuate the English personnel and sentiment of the
nunneries; Wilton, above others, would seem to have remained attached
to past memories, for there, according to all probability, lived the aged
clerk of Queen Edith who composed the *Life* of the Conqueror.[2] Consequently, the nunneries were behind the monasteries in adopting the
new style in architecture, and the beautiful abbey church of Romsey was
not begun before *c.* 1120.[3]

The great nunneries were in the early Norman period seats of a very
considerable culture. It is probable that they served as places of education
for the daughters of noble families more than the monasteries, though they
were in no sense schools. It is in any case certain that some of the inmates
attained a considerable proficiency in letters. William of Malmesbury bears
explicit witness to this in the case of Romsey and Wilton,[4] and his words
receive confirmation from more than one source. Wilton was the home of
the poetess Muriel, Shaftesbury later had Marie de France,[5] and Amesbury,
Shaftesbury, Wilton and Winchester contributed copies of hexameter
verses to the "bede rolls" which were circulated at this time.[6] Wilton
was also the original home of Eve, who later went over the Channel to
become a recluse with Goscelin.[7]

The vocation of the dedicated virgin to be the Bride of Christ, with all
that such a life implied, had from the earliest ages proved more capable
of expression in spiritual literature than its monastic counterpart. Bishops
and abbots had always been found to be directors of nuns, but it is somewhat surprising to learn that Lanfranc was chosen as her spiritual father
by Margaret of Scotland, who, though no nun, was a saint, and he sent
two monks of Christ Church to her at her request;[8] later, as we shall see,
Turgot of Durham acted as her director. Anselm's receptive and intuitive mind gave him a peculiar advantage in guiding women; several of
his letters to English abbesses and nuns survive and are among the most
attractive pieces of his correspondence. Eulalia of Shaftesbury and Alice
of Wilton were among his spiritual daughters, and we find him called upon
to rebuke the nuns of Romsey for venerating as a saint one who was not—

1 Eadmer, *Hist. Nov.* 121–6 (*à propos* of the case of Matilda); *Lanfranci ep.* 35 (ed.
Giles, I, 53–4). The letter is addressed to Goisfrid, bishop of Chichester, 1077–8.
2 So M. Bloch, *art. cit.* Cf. R. R. Darlington, *Vita Wulfstani*, 34.
3 So Clapham, *English Romanesque Architecture after the Conquest*, 45.
4 Will. Malmesb., *GR*, 493. Matilda, he says, was educated at Wilton and Romsey,
where *litteris quoque foemineum pectus exercuit.*
5 For Muriel, *v.* J. S. P. Tatlock, *Muriel the earliest English poetess*, in *Publications of the
Modern Language Association of America*, XLVIII (1933), 317–21; for Marie *v.s.*, p. 137, note 7.
6 *Rouleaux des Morts*, ed. L. Delisle (*v.* index under names of these houses; there are
also interesting lists of nuns' names).
7 *V.* Dom André Wilmart, *Eve et Goscelin*, in *RB*, XLVI (1934), 414–38; L (1938), 42–83.
8 Lanfranc, *ep.* 41 (ed. Giles, I, 59–60).

a trait in convent life of which other centuries can show examples; most beautiful of all his letters, perhaps, is that in which he recalls a fallen nun to her better self.[1]

The reigns of the Conqueror and Rufus saw very few additions to the number of the nunneries. Elstow, in Bedfordshire, which may have existed before the Conquest, was certainly founded by 1075, and Hinchin-brook in Huntingdonshire c. 1080. Almost the only other foundation before 1100 was the more important one of Malling in Kent, founded by Gundulf of Rochester in 1090 and the object of the bishop's peculiar care.[2] The great increase in the number of nunneries throughout England did not come till the reigns of Stephen and Henry II, and the total absence of any houses north of the midlands helps to account for the mission of Gilbert of Sempringham and its success in the middle of the twelfth century.

V

THE REGULAR CANONS BEFORE 1100

The history of the various bodies of regular canons in England does not strictly fall within the scope of this volume, but the paths of monks and canons crossed so often during the twelfth century that a few paragraphs on the origin, diffusion and character of the institute will not perhaps be out of place. The way of life that ultimately developed into the various families of regular canons was at first and for many centuries a parallel movement to monasticism in the Church, and although monasticism is in its essence a regular life apart from the world, and does not of itself imply the clerical state, whereas the canonical life was intended for clerics and above all for those living at the great centres of population, the two institutes in the course of centuries underwent so many modifications, and influenced and replaced each other so frequently, that the history of the one necessarily impinges upon that of the other.[3]

In the West, even before the days of St Benedict, it was common for the clergy surrounding a bishop to depend upon a common purse and share a common life; to this was added in some cases, of which that of St Augustine of Hippo is a notable example, a code of disciplinary and

1 For letters to English nuns, v. Anselm, epp. iii, 51, 70, 125, 127, 157 (*PL*, CLIX), and Dom A. Wilmart, *Une lettre inédite de S. Anselme à une moniale inconstante* in *RB*, XLI (1928), 319–32.

2 *V. Vita Gundulfi* (*PL*, CLIX), *passim*, esp. c. 830.

3 No adequate history of the growth of the regular canons in the eleventh century exists, and all except the most recent foreign work by canons of to-day is vitiated by an *esprit de corps* which seeks to trace back the regular institute in an unbroken tradition to the early Middle Ages and beyond. For England the best accounts are those of W. H. Frere, *The Early History of Canons Regular*, in *Fasciculus J. W. Clark dicatus* (Cambridge, 1909), 186–216, and of Prof. A. Hamilton Thompson in *Bolton Priory* (Thoresby Soc., xxx, 1928), 3–49; there are valuable incidental references in the various works of Dr H. E. Salter, esp. *Chapters of the Augustinian Canons* (Cant. and York Soc., 1922), xliv–xlv, 268–79, and in other monographs of Prof. A. H. Thompson.

spiritual directions. In the sixth and seventh centuries, the old canonical discipline of the urban centres of the Roman West was on the whole waning, whereas the monastic rule, to which Gregory the Great had given such encouragement, was spreading everywhere, even among the churches and basilicas of cities. In the eighth century, however, during the period of reorganization in the Rhineland preceding the age of Charlemagne, one of the chief means for the reform of the clergy employed by St Boniface and Chrodegang, bishop of Metz (742–66), was the organization of bodies of priests living a common and regular life; for these Chrodegang compiled *c.* 755 a Rule, based largely upon the Rule of St Benedict. The movement spread to various countries and even reached England with the visit of papal legates in 786–7, though there is little trace that anything came of it, save possibly at Canterbury. Henceforth, in the northern countries of Europe, the conception of a regular, quasi-monastic life for the clergy always remained present in the background and was revived by a series of reforming bishops, especially in south Germany and Lorraine, of whom Burchard, bishop of Worms from 1000, is a conspicuous example; it was regarded as the chief weapon to be used against simony and "nicolaism" or clerical incontinence.[1] Thus during the centuries from the eighth to the eleventh there were three degrees of community life in existence—the fully monastic, the canonical and the merely collegiate, and it can easily be understood that bodies of men could pass, in times of stress and isolation, down the scale; we have seen that in England under Alfred and Athelstan the English monasteries had, almost without exception, become merely collegiate, and that in cases such as that of the foundation of the New Minster under Grimbald it is not easy to say whether the life was fully monastic or simply canonical.

The canonical institute inevitably received a great impetus from the reform movement that was ultimately to pass under the name of Gregorian. Peter Damian and others saw in it a chief resource for raising the level of clerical life and evading lay control of churches, and the fourth canon of the council of Rome of 1059 contained an exhortation to the clergy in general to adopt a common and regular life.[2] Henceforward the canonical institute developed and spread steadily. At first, and especially in Italy, it took shape owing to the spontaneous action of collegiate bodies, such as that of the Lateran basilica, in reforming themselves and adopting a code of discipline; later, and especially north of the Alps, it became common for bishops and lay proprietors of churches who were anxious to conform to the spirit of the Gregorian decrees against private ownership to hand over groups of churches to the care of a community of regular canons. The "rules" for these communities were in origin local and vague,

---

1 For Burchard and his views, *v.* esp. Fournier and Le Bras, *Collections canoniques en Occident*, I, 390–6.
2 *PL*, CXLIII, 1316. Cf. Mabillon, *Annales O.S.B.*, IV, 585.

though with a strong family resemblance, and were composed either by the bishop or the leading spirit of the venture. Gregory VII himself composed one of considerable strictness.[1] Towards the end of the century, however, it became more and more common for new foundations to adopt *en bloc* the customs of an already celebrated body, and for all to take as the spiritual charter of their life the so-called Rule of St Augustine. Thus by 1100 the regular canons of northern Europe were beginning to be a body in the Church alongside of the monastic order and in many ways similar to it, alike in their liturgy and discipline, and in the independence which each house enjoyed.

In England, though colleges of clerks had been common from very early times and still existed in some numbers at the time of the Conquest, there was, till shortly before 1066, no life that could be called strictly canonical. In the reign of the Confessor, however, and even perhaps earlier, a number of bishops had begun to enforce a common disciplined life upon the clergy of their cathedrals and a few other bodies of clerks serving important churches; these became the so-called "secular" canons, who in the cathedrals and at Beverley, Southwell and other places continued in being throughout the Middle Ages. Harold's foundation at Waltham, into which entered a strong Lotharingian element, was possibly canonical in origin, though it became "secular" in course of time and fully Augustinian only in 1177.[2]

The Conquest retarded rather than hastened the spread of regular canons in England. The chief centres of their diffusion *c.* 1050–80 were Rome on the one hand and south Germany and Lorraine on the other, and one effect of the Conquest was to include England within the ring-fence of the Norman *Landeskirche*, thereby preventing for a time the infiltration of other influences. William and Lanfranc relied on monasticism as the great regenerative force; the most enlightened secular bishops, such as Thomas of York and Osmund of Sarum, were familiar with a less communal *régime* of prebendal houses. Nevertheless, a few communities were founded before 1100: St Gregory's at Canterbury by Lanfranc himself to serve the hospital and teach,[3] and perhaps St Giles's at Cambridge (later Barnwell) to serve a group of neighbouring churches;[4] Huntingdon, where

---

1 Cf. text printed by Dom G. Morin in *RB*, XVIII (1901), 177–83.

2 Giso of Wells, Leofric of Exeter, Ealdred of York and perhaps others had organized a community life for their cathedrals before 1066, and the last-named had extended his activities to Southwell and Beverley. Cf. R. R. Darlington, *Ecclesiastical Reform*, in *EHR*, LI (July 1936), 404. For Waltham, *v. The Foundation of Waltham Abbey*, ed. W. Stubbs (Oxford, 1861).

3 For Canterbury, *v. Annales Anglo-Saxonici*, ed. F. Liebermann in *Ungedruckte Quellen*, 4; H. Böhmer, *Die Fälschungen Erzbischof Lanfrancs von Canterbury*, 173; Eadmer, *Hist. Nov.* 16; Will. Malmesb., *GP*, 72. The last two state that the canons lived *regulariter*, but this need not mean that they had a complete rule, still less that they were Augustinian.

4 Cf. Frere, *op. cit.* 192; J. Hodson, in *Archaeological Journal*, XLI, 374 seqq.; XLII, 96, 215, 331, 440, shows that only some 37 out of 254 Augustinian churches in England were parochial in the later medieval period.

a song school is known to have existed,[1] and perhaps also Colchester, probably the first house to have its observance based completely on a French model. But it is uncertain how far any of these were fully "regular" in origin, and the great diffusion of the institute in its fully regular and Augustinian character belongs to the reigns of Henry I and Stephen.

VI

THE DEATH OF LANFRANC

The great archbishop died on 24 May 1089, after a short illness and with his mind clear to the last, as he had always hoped. Despite his extreme old age, he had been active till the last, as is seen by the leading part he took in the proceedings against William of St Carilef in the spring of 1087.[2] More than fifty years had passed since the young, but already celebrated teacher had arrived in the valley of Bec, and during that half-century Lanfranc had shown his consummate ability in adapting himself to the most varied needs and circumstances, and in remaining always a dominant figure, whether as the foremost doctor of Europe against Berengar, or the representative of Norman monasticism, or the reorganizer of the English Church, or the principal upholder of the Conqueror's *régime* in England. Yet he remains in the end something of an enigmatic figure to us, not by reason of any complexity of character or change of policy, for throughout all his actions the strong, direct, realist mind is apparent, but because even with all the material at our disposal it is not easy to make a single, living whole or to reconcile the various estimates of his contemporaries with each other and with his character as revealed by his actions and his correspondence. The vicegerent of William at Norwich, the energetic opponent of St Carilef, the archbishop who deferred to the Conqueror's opinion on more than one occasion seems at times a different man from the devoted friend of Herluin and Anselm, and the kindly father of the childhood's memories of Eadmer. We cannot fail to miss in Lanfranc that simplicity of outlook, that single aim, that is reflected in every recorded action and word of Anselm, and it is hard in the last resort to avoid the conclusion that in the realm of the pure intellect Lanfranc had agility and versatility rather than depth and intuition; that in the art of government he was a supremely able administrator and organizer of the plans and needs of the moment rather than a creative genius who could keep his eyes fixed upon the lodestar of a single end; and that on the deepest plane of the spirit, for all the strength of his religious conviction and his real nobility of soul, he

1 *V*. note by Mary Bateson, *The Huntingdon Song School*, in *EHR*, XVIII (1903), 712–13.
2 Cf. the tract *De injusta vexatione Willelmi*, probably compiled by Symeon of Durham and printed among his *Opera*, vol. I. Almost the only reference to the archbishop's advanced age occurs there, where (p. 187) Robert Piperel alludes to him as *vetulus ligaminarius*.

remained an ecclesiastic dependent upon and moved by the changing, temporary circumstances of the time rather than a saint who, with whatever limitations of mental outlook, directs his every action to the forwarding of a kingdom not of this world. It is certainly noteworthy that although recognized as such a dominant personality in the Europe of his day, neither in the sphere of learning, nor in the monastic life, nor in high ecclesiastical policy did Lanfranc anticipate or direct the minds of men to the ideas that were to be the moulding forces of the near future.

But though Lanfranc was essentially a man of his age, whereas Anselm is for all time, there can be no doubt which of the two had the greater influence upon the framework of the Church in England. Though the two widest of Lanfranc's aims—the subjection of all sees in the British Isles to Canterbury,[1] and the direct and uncontrolled government of his province by the metropolitan primate—failed of realization, the one because of its inherent impracticability, the other by reason of the victory of Gregorian ideas, it may be doubted whether of all the eminent men who filled the see of Canterbury between Augustine and Cranmer any individual, save only Theodore of Tarsus, had a greater share than Lanfranc in organizing the Church in this country. And as the propagator of the monastic order in England and of its conversion to the Norman model he holds a place among the archbishops which only Dunstan can challenge. When he died, every important abbey in England was held by a Norman, the Norman architecture observance and economic system were everywhere taking root, the number of monastic houses had increased by a half, the number of monks in the country had probably more than doubled, and the monasteries as a whole had entered the feudal system. For all this Lanfranc, under William, was very largely responsible. He was, in a very real sense, the "father of monks".[2] His letters that survive can be but a fraction of his correspondence, but they show him with a solicitude for all the churches, defending the monasteries against unjust aggression, overseeing nunneries, counselling abbots, and watching over the interests of private individuals.[3] Here indeed he held a position without parallel among the archbishops throughout the centuries. No other, not even Dunstan, had such universal powers of surveillance and control; neither before nor after did any individual so regulate the affairs of houses and persons among the black monks until, in other circumstances and for other ends, powers still greater were entrusted to the King's Vicar-general, Thomas Cromwell.

The years between the death of Lanfranc and the accession of Henry I have little significance, as a period, for the history of the monasteries.

---

1 *Ep.* 26 (Giles, I, 47–8).
2 *Chronicle*, 1089 [E]: "[Lanfranc] se arwurtha [venerable] muneca fader ꝺ frouer [protector]." The writer, a monk of St Augustine's, was probably the author of the celebrated character sketch of the Conqueror.   3 *Epp.* 22, 32, 34, 62, 63.

Taken as a whole, the tendencies and forces already at work continued to act; William II had no direct interest in the monasteries or policy regarding them; his personal attentions were confined to Battle; for the rest, he exploited the royal and feudal rights by retaining many vacant abbeys in his own hands or those of Ranulf Flambard and by endeavouring to raise sums of money upon the appointment of superiors.[1] These actions, though they brought financial hardships and some disciplinary relaxation upon the houses concerned, had no more than temporary and superficial consequences. William's nominees, when ultimately he made appointments, were of the same provenance as hitherto and continued the work of organization, and during his reign foundations great and small, both Anglo-Norman and Cluniac, continued to be made. Thus Chester, Colchester, Norwich and Pontefract were either actually founded or at least planned in these years, and at Bermondsey, Durham and other monasteries the work of building and organization went steadily forward.

Similarly, though for different reasons, Anselm's tenure of the see of Canterbury has no such significance for monastic history as has Lanfranc's. The time of great changes within the English houses was past; the new stream from abroad had not yet begun to flow; and in any case the violent controversies in which Anselm became engaged and his long absences from England would have prevented the development of a continuous policy. For these pages, Anselm's only significance is the clear-cut, wholly visible embodiment that his life gave of all that was best in the wisdom and sanctity of contemporary monasticism, and in the glimpses which his letters give us of the spiritual needs of communities and individual souls in England.

1 For the significance of Rufus' action, *v. infra*, pp. 435, 612–13, and also the important essay by R. W. Southern, *Ranulf Flambard and Early Anglo-Norman Administration*, in *Transactions of the Royal Historical Society*, IV Ser., XVI (1933), 95–128.

CHAPTER VIII

THE CLUNIACS IN ENGLAND

I

The developments recorded in the preceding pages do not exhaust the list of new movements set on foot by the Normans, for no mention has as yet been made of the Cluniac foundations. The influence of the great monastic reform which took its rise and maintained its seat in the celebrated Burgundian abbey had already twice affected the course of English monastic history before Cluny herself had any dependencies in this country. The revival under Dunstan had received a deep impress from Fleury, which in its turn owed its renaissance wholly to Cluny; similarly, the Norman monasticism, with the partial exception of Bec and her daughters, could trace a large measure of its spirit and almost all its uses back through William of Dijon to Maieul and Odo of Cluny. But while it is true to say that almost all black monk houses south of Lorraine and the Rhine owed their new life, or a large part of it, to the stream that had its rise at Cluny—and recent scholarship has shown the Cluniac affinities of almost all French customals of the late tenth and early eleventh centuries[1]—yet it is equally true to say that what these various centres received was not any specific variety of black monk life, but simply the life and observance typical of the epoch in its most active form. In other words, before the beginning of the eleventh century Cluny did not stand out clearly as the head of a new constitutional organization or as the representative of tendencies peculiar to herself, but simply as a monastery concerned to impart to others the great essentials of the liturgical monastic life as they were conceived and expressed by her. Nor did she, before the end of the tenth century, bind to herself by any external constitutional framework the abbeys which she had reformed.[2]

Under Odilo, abbot from 994 to 1049, a change gradually came about. Partly because experience showed that monasteries at the death of a reforming abbot or of his immediate disciples fell back into disorganization or came under the control of secular rulers or proprietors, but more because the whole of society was becoming conscious of capabilities for closer organization, Cluny now began to bind to herself in varying degrees of dependence the monasteries over which her abbot had been

---

1 In particular Dom Bruno Albers, in his volumes of *Consuetudines Monasticae*, and Dr Rose Graham, in her most valuable article, *The Relation of Cluny to some other Movements of Monastic Reform*, reprinted in *English Ecclesiastical Studies*, 1–29.
2 Cf. the judgment of Sackur at the end of *Die Cluniacenser*, II, 439: "Die Reform hatte sich zuerst in voller Freiheit vollzogen; man war zufrieden, wenn man die Hauptübel beseitigt hatte...in nebensächlichen Dingen war man offenbar nachsichtig."

given reforming power or which desired to adopt Cluniac customs, and whereas in the tenth and early eleventh centuries the abbots of Cluny had been content to reform by imposing Cluniac uses and by temporary supervision, the tendency grew to deprive monasteries of their autonomy, and even to draw back into the system houses previously reformed, but left independent. What was first noticeable under Odilo developed under Hugh, often called the Great, and in his long reign (1049–1109), which may in many ways be taken to cover the apogee of Cluny's long course of splendour, and during which the chief English plantations were made, the constitution of the Cluniac system of government reached something of an equilibrium.[1]

That system has often been described, though too often an account has been given of the state of fullest development in the later twelfth century without any notice of the gradual stages by which it was evolved. In its fullest extension, indeed, it was not wholly of domestic inspiration, but had adopted several important features, such as a general chapter and visitations, from the reform movements of the twelfth century. To describe it therefore *sans phrase* as a fully developed religious order and as the first of its kind in the Middle Ages, with the abbot of Cluny as General,[2] is not strictly true of even the latest stage, and is historically misleading. In its eleventh-century form, when it was still a growth untouched from outside, it was in no sense an order, but rather a body of head and members loosely knit together by bonds resembling those of contemporary feudal institutions. Its constitution was not a scientific, logical, legal creation like that of the Cistercians and their imitators, but a hierarchy of relationships culminating in personal dependence upon the abbot of Cluny. There was no balance, no co-ordination in it, still less any anticipation of the elective and judicial elements of the later orders of friars. It is not even possible to say that it was a stage in the evolution of the "order", save that the existence of the vast Cluniac body showed at once the possibility and the dangers of the dependence of a large number of houses upon a single head.

In the second half of the eleventh century the widespread Cluniac organization was made up of four classes: Cluny herself, with her satellite

1 No adequate history of Cluny between 1050 and 1150 has yet appeared. Sackur's account, as has been said, closes with the death of Odilo and does not even give a thorough analysis of the tendencies then maturing; for these *v.* Dom Besse, *L'Ordre de Cluny et son gouvernement*, in *Revue Mabillon*, 1905–6. Pignot's *Histoire de l'Ordre de Cluny* is very disappointing, and the recent works of M. Guy de Valous cannot be regarded as definitive (*v.* Bibliography). The scope of Dr Joan Evans' *Monastic Life at Cluny, 910–1157*, is indicated by the title; so far as it goes, it is a useful book. Dr Rose Graham's article, *Life at Cluny in the Eleventh Century* (*English Ecclesiastical Studies*, 30–45), is excellent; her long-awaited monograph on the English Cluniacs is, it is understood, in an advanced stage of preparation. Aspects of Cluniac life are treated in the *Millénaire de Cluny*; especially useful is Dom Léon Guilloreau's contribution, *Les Prieurés anglais de l'ordre de Cluny* (1, 291–373). Printed sources for a full history abound, in particular the vast collection of Bernard and Bruel, *Recueil des Chartes de Cluny*, and, for England, Sir G. Duckett's *Charters and Records of Cluny*.
2 So Abbot Butler in his article *Cluny* in *Encyclopaedia Britannica*, ed. 11, 1911.

cells depending immediately upon her; a few monasteries belonging to the system and sharing Cluniac uses and privileges but retaining abbots of their own; priories, which in importance and numbers were the equals of large abbeys but which received their superior at the hands of the abbot of Cluny; and, finally, lesser priories and cells depending as a rule upon their founding house in the same way that the latter depended upon Cluny. The monks of all these houses ranked as monks of Cluny and when at Cluny were considered children of the house; there was, however, a distinction between those of the second and those of the third and fourth classes. Novices of one of the abbeys were clothed and professed by their own abbot; novices of a dependent priory were received to the habit there with the permission of the abbot of Cluny, but could be professed only by the abbot of Cluny himself. In theory, therefore, the vows were taken to the abbot of Cluny and pronounced there in his presence, and even as late as Ulrich's day, c. 1070, the custom continued of novices coming up to Cluny on the feast of SS. Peter and Paul to make profession,[1] though they were allowed three years' grace in which to do it.[2] Distance clearly made this impossible of observance in all cases, and alternatively the novices could be professed or at least receive the blessing of their habit at the hands of the abbot of Cluny when on his rounds of the dependencies.[3] But in such cases they still had to present themselves at Cluny to make or repeat their profession to the mother-house, thus vowing "stability" a second time—an anomaly which did not escape criticism at the hands of the early Cistercians.[4] The unwieldiness of this system caused frequent and wholesale transgressions, and Peter the Venerable, in the first half of the twelfth century, records both the widespread, unauthorized reception of novices and a delay of ten or even thirty years in proceeding to Cluny for blessing or profession.[5]

Over all houses the abbot of Cluny exercised in theory at least supreme, plenary and immediate power, and was therefore constantly occupied in journeys and visits, but the frequency and procedure of these visits were fixed by no kind of legislation, nor did any machinery exist by which the responsibility and labours of the abbot could be lessened by means of a

---

1 Cf. the *Epistola* preceding Ulrich's *Consuetudines*, *PL*, CXLIX, 638, where he describes a prior who "singulis annis ad memoriam sanctorum apostolorum pro benedictione quantos potuit [novitios] misisset".

2 *Petri Venerabilis Statuta*, *PL*, CLXXXIX, 1036, n. xxxviii: "Extra Cluniacum novitii recepti usque ad primum vel secundum aut plus tertium annum ad benedicendum Cluniacum adducantur."

3 Ulrich, *epist. cit.*: "Hoc anno venit [Hugo ad cellam] et uno die lv novitiis [the accumulation of four years] habitum nostrum vel benedictionem dedit."

4 Ulrich, *Consuetudines*, II, 1 (col. 700), gives the case when the novices "benedictionem jam a domino abbate acceperunt, professione interim dilata et ad nostrum locum usque reservata". Peter the Venerable, *Statuta* xxxviii, gives a case when they were sent "ad obedientiam rursum in Cluniaco coram fratribus [promittendam]". For the Cistercian criticisms, v. Petri Ven., ep. I, 28, *PL*, CLXXXIX, 135–6.

5 *Petri Ven. Stat.* xxxv, xxxviii, coll. 1035–6.

delegation or devolution of powers. In practice, therefore, a very great measure of independence was left to local superiors, especially those at a distance from Cluny, and in England, if nowhere else, founders often succeeded in inserting clauses ensuring a certain degree of freedom into the charter of gift. And, although vows were taken to the abbot of Cluny, the monks of dependent priories remained for all practical purposes under the jurisdiction of the local superior all their lives; there was no constant interchange of personnel as in the later centralized orders.[1] Finally, the custom grew up of exacting from the houses founded or adopted by Cluny a yearly tribute, varying in amount and in itself of no great significance, but which in the aggregate brought in a considerable sum. This was the equivalent of the *census* paid to the Holy See by the churches throughout Europe which were in a special way under its protection.

Such in brief outline was the organization of the Cluniac body during the later years of St Hugh—supreme and immediate (though often limited) control by the abbot of Cluny; appointment by him of the superiors of all houses immediately depending upon Cluny; profession of all to Cluny and (in theory at least) at Cluny; and the payment of a small annual tribute. The whole body was bound together by a common acceptance of the customs and uses of Cluny and by the decrees of successive abbots.

Alongside of this constitutional development there was evolving at the same time a very definite spirit or programme within the mother-house, which inevitably spread in greater or less degree to her dependencies. Considered from the point of view of observance, this took the form of an increase in the number of psalms and prayers recited daily, together with an ever-growing elaboration of ceremonial in the performance of the liturgy; considered from the point of view of discipline, it consisted in extreme attention to regularity and uniformity in the performance of all corporate duties. Together, the observance and discipline of Cluny eliminated all extra-liturgical activity for the monks following the life of the greater houses, and thus Cluny had little or no share in the educational and intellectual revivals of the period, and her monks produced little artistic work within the cloister. A climax was reached in the central period of the long reign of St Hugh; alike in splendour of ceremonial, tireless activity in performance, and regularity of large masses of monks, Cluny in the third quarter of the eleventh century presented a spectacle without parallel in Europe, and the larger dependencies and those influenced most directly by her shared these characteristics in their measure, and indeed continued to exhibit them when a decline had begun to set in at Cluny herself.

But at the time of the Conquest, despite the great size to which the body had already attained, the heart would seem still to have been possessed of remarkable soundness. In 1049 Cluny had received as abbot, in succession

1 Here again Abbot Butler's account in the *Encyclopaedia Britannica* is misleading.

to the long-lived St Odilo, the young priest Hugh, of the highest nobility in blood and, as it already seemed to all, of predestinate sanctity, who although only twenty-five at his election had already been for some years in supreme charge of the discipline of the house as grand prior. He was in the event to rule for sixty years, during which period both he and his abbey were invested with an aureole of veneration comparable to, though very different from, that surrounding Clairvaux and its abbot in the fifty years that followed Hugh's death. The impression of sanctity given by Hugh and his community, at least until *c.* 1080, is vouched for by such weighty testimony of contemporaries that it is unnecessary to take space to record it. The enthusiastic praises of Peter Damian, the veneration to which Gregory VII gave expression on more than one occasion in public and private, the reverence with which the Conqueror regarded Hugh, the impression produced by Cluny on William de Warenne and his wife—these are but a few typical instances out of the many that could be adduced. In assessing their force we must, however, remember that in the fifth decade of the century the current was only just beginning to set in the direction of reform at Rome, that the monasteries of Romuald and John Gualbert and Peter Damian made no display to the outer world, and that the new Norman religious life was as yet unknown to Europe at large. Everywhere, and especially in the most populous parts of Germany and north Italy, "nicolaism" and simony were rife, and the spectacle of Cluny, a little world in itself given wholly to the worship of God in a setting of incomparable splendour and untouched by secular intrigue, must have been dazzling enough to those who in Italy and elsewhere were striving in the dust and darkness for better things.

Moreover, the ideal for which Cluny stood, its message to the world, was one not hard to comprehend. It was the regular, tireless, all but ceaseless liturgical service carried out by the great numbers of a highly disciplined army, using every means of chant, of ceremony and of ornament available to render that service more solemn and more splendid. This tireless, disciplined service—the *districtio ordinis* of so many witnesses—was, and remained for a century, the distinguishing note of Cluniac monasticism. To this, we have explicit testimony over the whole period. When, about 1059, the young Anselm, full of the desire for learning, was debating whither to turn in the religious life, he rejected the possibility of Cluny on account of the *districtio ordinis* prevailing there—that is, not the physical austerity or spiritual fervour of the life (for both of these were to be found at Bec also) but the rigorous observance which kept the monks occupied in choir and therefore rendered study impossible.[1] Some four years later we have the witness of Peter Damian. Using the same phrase (*ordo districtus*) he observes that when he was at Cluny, at midsummer, 1063, the monastic duties, and particularly those of the

---

1 *Vita auct. Eadmero*, I, i in *PL*, CLVIII, 53.

choir, were so prolonged that even in the longest days of the year, when sleep according to the Rule would have been shortest, the monks could hardly find half an hour's free time in the day at their disposal. He praises such a system, remarking that with their time so occupied the monks could scarcely commit any sin save one of thought.[1] Ulrich's *Consuetudines*, committed to writing some fifteen or twenty years later, enable us to verify Peter Damian's statement with precision. Speaking of the same days of midsummer, he tells us of the continuous sequence of offices which reduced the time for sitting and speaking in the cloister to a vanishing point; the whole framework and clock-time of the day, indeed, was artificially dislocated in the interests of the liturgy: Ulrich tells us that the night office on the feast of SS. Peter and Paul (29 June) began by daylight on the evening previous and lasted till daybreak; in order to obtain the requisite hours of sleep everything on the previous day after the High Mass was telescoped, and compline on the vigil was sung at the hour of sun-time (c. 2.15 p.m.) at which on the following day the monks were singing none.[2] On days of any solemnity, indeed, there was little if any cessation of conventual duty (in the main choral) between mattins, which often began before midnight, and the end of High Mass the following day about noon.[3] With such a horarium in mind we shall not wonder at the anecdote told by the Cluny chronicler of Abbot Hugh and Peter Damian: that when the latter praised all at Cluny save the quantity and quality of the food and drink, which exceeded that allowed by the Rule, he received the reply that before making such a criticism he should himself spend a week in following exactly the daily order of life, and that he would then confess that it could not be executed on such sparing fare.[4]

This, then, was the life which, still lived with enthusiasm and still attracting those with the highest aspirations in central and southern France, passed under chosen leaders to Bermondsey and Lewes in England and which, when the twelfth century had passed its second decade, still evoked the admiration of William of Malmesbury and King Henry I.

---

1 *Petri Damiani ep.* VI, 5, *PL*, CXLV, 380: "Nam tanta erat in servandi ordinis continua jugitate prolixitas; tanta praesertim in ecclesiasticis officiis protelebatur instantia, ut in ipso cancri, sive leonis aestu, cum longiores sunt dies, vix per totum diem unius saltem vacaret horae dimidium, quo fratribus in claustro licuisset miscere colloquium." Cf. also *ep.* VI, 2–4.

2 Ulrich, *Consuetudines*, I, 18, 41 (*PL*, CXLIX, 668, 688).

3 Cf. Ulrich, *passim*, and the heartfelt admissions of the later (c. 1125) Cluniac in *Une riposte de l'ancien monachisme* (ed. Dom A. Wilmart) in *Revue Bénédictine*, XLVI, 296–344, especially lines 532–641: "cum noctem fere in explendis matutinis protraxerunt...cum in voce psalmi...in protensa lectionum serie, in missis...usque ad nonam sequentis diei, etc."

4 *Vita Hugonis auct. anon.*, *PL*, CLIX, 925–6. The Cluniac quoted in the previous note (*loc. cit.*) says the same; the daily *hemina vini* of the Rule would be wholly insufficient to quench the drought caused by much singing.

II

As we have seen, William I, soon after the Conquest, had applied to St Hugh for twelve eminent monks, whom he engaged to promote to bishoprics and abbacies. Nothing came of this proposal; it had ceased to be Cluny's policy to despatch individuals in this manner, and Hugh might well fear both that distance across the seas might strain the bonds of union and that the Conqueror's desire to have supreme control in his own hands would render the mission useless. Indeed, even the first and most celebrated Cluniac foundation in England only came into being after much hesitation on the part of the abbot of Cluny. William de Warenne, one of the Conqueror's most trusted supporters, had, in consultation with Lanfranc, decided to found a monastery upon his land in Sussex. Before anything could come of his intentions, it happened that he and his wife Gundreda, while travelling on pilgrimage to Rome, were hindered from reaching their destination and were entertained at Cluny. Greatly impressed with both the fervour of the life and the hospitality of the monks, they resolved to take thence brethren for their foundation.[1] Hugh was absent and when, some time later, the request reached him he demurred. Only after receiving the fullest assurance as to material resources and royal and episcopal support did he grant the favour. Even then he assented with hesitation. Only three monks were sent at first; their leader Lanzo, indeed, was a distinguished man, but after a short time he was recalled to Cluny and kept there for a year. Disheartened, the founder had thoughts of sending his companions back and of applying for a colony to Marmoutier, a house which was energetically organizing the neighbouring foundation of Battle. Finally, however, after an interview with St Hugh, all was arranged, and a promise was even extracted that Cluny would always appoint as prior of St Pancras the holiest and wisest monk available, excepting the grand prior of Cluny and the prior of La Charité-sur-Loire, and at the same time a considerable degree of independence was guaranteed.[2]

The subsequent career of more than one prior of Lewes during the twelfth century would seem to show that this promise was honoured;[3] certainly, the abbot of Cluny can have had at his disposal few, if any, to surpass in virtue Lanzo, the first prior, who ruled the house for more than thirty years. Fifty years after its foundation, the reputation of Lewes still stood very high, and William of Malmesbury instances Lanzo, together with Serlo of Gloucester and Godfrey of Winchester, as the equal in sanctity of Robert of Arbrissel and Bernard of Tiron.[4] The account of his

---

1 Cf. charter of foundation of Lewes in *Monasticon*, v, i, 12.　　　　2 *Ibid.*
3 Thus Hugh, Ansgar and another Hugh left Lewes to become abbots of Reading in 1123, 1130 and 1186 respectively; the first later became archbishop of Rouen, and the third was elected abbot of Cluny.
4 Will. Malmesb., *GP*, 207: "Lanzo quidam [? quidem] Cluniacensis monachus in supremo religionis cacumine locavit. Efficatiam viri sullimitas praetendit loci, adeo ut

last hours, which Malmesbury transcribed from a document before him doubtless composed at Lewes as a "death-bill" to be circulated with a request for prayers, survives in the pages of the *Gesta Regum*. A few sentences deserve quotation, as both highly characteristic of the period and indicative of the manner of life of their subject. Lanzo was taken ill on a Thursday. In the early hours of Saturday he appeared to be dying and was anointed, after which, though instantly expecting death, he insisted on standing to receive the last embrace of all his monks. At dawn he was carried to the chapter-house and there absolved and blessed all his sons, receiving their blessing in return. Sunday was spent more peacefully, but on Monday morning he was clearly dying:

And having his hands washed and his hair combed, he entered the church to hear Mass; and receiving the Body and Blood of the Lord, retired to his bed.... Being entreated by the brethren to be mindful of them with the Lord, to whom he was going, he affectionately assented, bowing his head.... He beckoned for the crucifix to be presented to him which, adoring... and clasping with his hands, he kissed, as was apparent, with joy and fond affection.

When the moment of death was near

being caught up in the arms of those about him, he was carried, yet alive, into the presbytery of the church, before the altar of St Pancras [i.e. the high altar].... Here he departed to Christ pure and freed eternally from every evil.[1]

Of the other Cluniac foundations in England, only Bermondsey attained to something of the stature and celebrity of Lewes. This house was an offshoot of La Charité-sur-Loire, and was founded by an Englishman of London, Alwin Child, between 1082 and 1089, when the first monks, four in number, arrived.[2] Although in time it passed out of the Cluniac family and became an autonomous abbey, it was a member of the system throughout the period covered by these chapters, and had a number of distinguished priors, several of whom became abbots of important black monk houses at home and abroad.[3] William Rufus gave the monks land at Bermondsey and this, together with its situation in view of the city, attracted many rich benefactors. Although its annals for this period are a bare record of outstanding events, it is clear that it flourished greatly both materially and spiritually; from it, in 1148, were drawn the community and first abbot of Stephen's foundation of Faversham in Kent.

veraciter asseratur nullum omnino monasterium posse illud vincere religione ad monachos, etc." *GR*, 513: "Qui [*sc.* Lanzo] ea aetate nullo inferius sanctitate floruit."

1 Will. Malmesb., *GR*, 514. Cf. the traditional account of the death of St Benedict: "deferri voluit in ecclesiam: ubi, sumpta Eucharistia... inter manus discipulorum efflavit animam" (*Brev. Monast.* 21 March).

2 *Annales Bermunds.* (*Ann. Monast.* vol. III) and *Lewes.* (MS. Cott. Tib. A x fo. 163), *sub annis.*

3 E.g. Clarembald, abbot of Faversham, 1148; Roger, abbot of St Ouen, 1157; Adam, abbot of Evesham, 1161; Roger, abbot of Abingdon, 1175; Werric, abbot of Faversham, 1178; Henry, abbot of Glastonbury, 1189.

There is no need to rehearse the list of Cluniac foundations, great and small, which, beginning with Lewes in 1072–7, continued to grow until the middle of the following century.[1] Besides Cluny and La Charité, St Martin-des-Champs and Ste Foy-de-Longueville made plantations, and Lewes and her daughters formed a numerous family. Chief among them, after Lewes and Bermondsey, were Thetford (1104), Castle Acre (1089), Wenlock (c. 1080–1) and Pontefract (c. 1090). The growth was quite haphazard, depending entirely on the accident of gifts of land, and it was the Cluniac practice to occupy an estate with half a dozen monks or less, who had no stable existence or the power of receiving recruits. Some of these—Castle Acre is an example—might very soon develop into fair-sized religious houses; others dragged on a more irregular existence throughout a century without the full organization ever being completed. Consequently, even from the first, the Cluniac family consisted of houses in every stage of growth from such splendid institutions as Lewes, which rivalled a great abbey in size, to isolated cells inhabited by six or three or even a single monk. In all, there were some thirty-six members of the family, great and small, in existence by 1160, after which the growth practically ceased; of these only a dozen or so were fully organized monasteries. The small priory or cell was not indeed, as we have seen, exclusively or even predominantly a Cluniac growth, and the overseas Norman monasteries must bear an even greater share of responsibility for it, but Cluny added very considerably to the numbers of the class.

The sporadic and gradual evolution of the group in England, its isolation from public, national life, and the insignificance of the majority of its houses prevented it from exerting any noticeable influence, as a group, upon English monastic history. Lewes and Bermondsey were for long important as centres of religious influence, whence superiors could be drawn, but the Cluny of St Hugh gave nothing permanent to England, and the chief direct influence of the Cluniac spirit was in the twelfth century through individuals who came to occupy positions of eminence. Against the example of regularity, observance and hospitality given by Lewes, Thetford and a few other monasteries must be set the loosely knit aggregation of mediocre and half-alien houses, with many of the disadvantages of dependence and few of the advantages of centralization, a source of weakness rather than of strength to the monastic body, as future centuries were to show.

[1] A scheme of the houses, with dates of foundation and filiations, will be found in Table III, after the Appendices.

III

CLUNIAC ORGANIZATION IN ENGLAND

During the period between the Conquest and the death of Henry I, the Cluniac system in England was thus something of a half-way house between the entire absence of constitutional bonds among the English black monk houses and the fully developed union of the Cistercians, and if compared with the black monks it appears to be an "order", when compared with the white monks under the *Carta Caritatis* it is seen to be only a loose federation, depending in every case upon a series of individual acts and capitulations. Indeed, a close study of the relations of the English houses to each other and to Cluny leads to a very considerable modification of the general statements still frequently made or repeated as to the supreme and plenary jurisdiction exercised over all dependencies by the abbot of Cluny.

The normal procedure in almost all English Cluniac foundations was as follows. The would-be founder, having approached the abbot of Cluny or the prior of one of her important dependencies in France or England, received at first a small company of monks, who took possession of the estates and built (or occupied if built) a small church and offices. The numbers of the group, if all went well, were increased by new drafts till enough were gathered together to carry out the full regular and liturgical life; finally, when the community had taken shape, it could begin to receive its own novices, with due permission from the founding house. Thus the Cluniac procedure was more haphazard than the normal practice of the Anglo-Norman monasteries, where, as a rule, a fair-sized group of a dozen or more was sent all together from the mother-house, in order that a regular, self-contained life might at once begin,[1] and it differed, of course, still more from the Cistercian rule (framed precisely to avoid Cluniac failures) of sending out a complete new community of twelve under an abbot only after the necessary conventual buildings had been erected. In many of the English Cluniac foundations we can trace the whole procedure. Thus in the case of Lewes itself, where we should have expected every precaution to have been taken to ensure success, only three monks were sent with Lanzo, though William de Warenne was willing to support twelve. The project thus all but miscarried.[2] That this was not due solely to St Hugh's dislike of transmarine ventures is clear, for similar small beginnings are seen elsewhere. At Castle Acre in Norfolk William de Warenne had a few monks in his castle hoping for some years

---

1 E.g. Battle, Chester, Norwich, Rochester: contrast, however, the mission to the north. As we have seen, the black monks of England after the Conquest also had priories and cells; but after *c.* 1100 small and distant gifts were as a rule accepted simply as "cells" with no idea of development, whereas almost all Cluniac plantations began on a small scale.

2 Cf. charter of foundation in *Monasticon*, v, i, 12–13.

to make a foundation;[1] at Daventry (c. 1107) four monks replaced an equal number of canons, two of whom subsequently took the monastic habit;[2] at Mendham (c. 1140), a dependency of Lewes, the foundation charter stipulates that a few monks are to be sent at first, then gradually more, until full regular observance can be set up.[3] Perhaps the only exception that has left any trace is Thetford, whither Lanzo of Lewes, at the request of St Hugh, sent twelve monks and a prior to inaugurate the new foundation.[4]

Each new Cluniac house had certain relations of dependence upon its founding monastery. This scale of relationships is asserted with particular care in the charter of foundation of Mendham, a Suffolk dependency of Castle Acre. Mendham, it is laid down, is to be to Acre as Acre is to Lewes and as Lewes is to Cluny.[5] This subordination was of different degrees, according to the degree of organization of the new house; until it was large enough to be a unit by itself it depended, at least in theory, entirely upon the mother; afterwards it had power to carry on its own life subject only to certain permissions and supervisions. However, compositions of all kinds between the founder or his descendants and the founding house were common at every stage of its growth; these were directed towards limiting the absolute powers of the mother priory. Thus at Mendham an arrangement was made c. 1190 between Roger de Huntingfield and Prior Hugh of Acre; according to this eight monks at least were to be maintained there, and in the case of a death Acre must supply the deficiency. A monk in an official position (in obedientia) was not to be recalled to Acre without a clear need or cause; Mendham could of its own authority clothe a dying man with the habit (i.e. ad succurrendum), but novices in health must receive the approval of Acre and be trained there until Mendham was of full stature.[6] In the case of Prittlewell, an Essex dependency of Lewes, where the church given to Lewes was held by three priests who retained their rights for life, the charter of foundation asserts that the prior of Lewes is to have in perpetuum powers of correction and government there as if the monks were his own.[7] Similarly, at Farley the prior of Lewes has powers of correction, but he can only remove the

---

1 *Monasticon*, v, i, 12.
2 Register of Daventry in *Monasticon*, v, i, 178.
3 *Monasticon*, v, i, 58.
4 Cf. the fragment of a History of Thetford in *Monasticon*, v, i, 152.
5 *Monasticon*, v, i, 58.
6 Cf. extracts from the Register of Castleacre in *Monasticon*, v, i, 59.
7 *Monasticon*, v, i, 22–3: "Prior de Lewes de monachis suis ordinabit ibi libere et sine alicujus contradictione priorem et conventum monachorum...habebit autem prior de s. Pancratio imperpetuum emendationem et ordinationem et subjectionem de priore et monachis de Pritelwell tanquam de suis propriis secundum regulam s. Benedicti et ordinem de Cluniaco." So far as the words of this charter go, it would seem that Prittlewell was from the start intended to remain always undeveloped. Perhaps by the date of its foundation (c. 1130) it was realized that there was little hope of developing any more large Cluniac houses.

local prior for a just (i.e. provable as such) cause.[1] Over Thetford, Lanzo of Lewes had absolute powers, but they were personal, and expired with his death.[2] As for Lewes itself, William de Warenne, no doubt with the support of the Conqueror and Lanfranc, endeavoured to obtain for it the maximum amount of freedom, and the great foundation charter stipulates that the abbot of Cluny shall only interfere in disciplinary matters when the prior is unable to deal with the situation, and that the dependencies of Lewes shall be under her own control.[3]

Above all, in the matter of the election of a prior founders endeavoured to limit the absolute powers enjoyed by Cluny abroad, though often more from a desire to retain for themselves the rights of an *Eigenkirche* than from a preoccupation to safeguard the principles of the Rule. William de Warenne, as has already been noted, obtained from Hugh of Cluny an undertaking that Cluny would always appoint as prior of Lewes the wisest and holiest monk available after the great prior of Cluny and the prior of La Charité-sur-Loire; the prior so appointed was irremovable unless demanded for some exceptional position in the Church.[4] At Methwold, a cell of Acre, the founder claimed the appointment for himself. In the case of Monk Bretton, a daughter of Pontefract (*c.* 1153-4), the prior of La Charité in accepting the foundation gave the election of a superior to the community; the foundation charter gave the right of appointment to Pontefract; another charter of the founder allows for a domestic election in which Pontefract could interfere, and in the event a composition was reached allowing for a joint election between Pontefract and her daughter.[5]

The agreement just mentioned is perhaps an early example of what appears to have been almost a general movement among the founders and priors of Cluniac houses to limit the rights of the founding house—a movement due, no doubt, to a number of causes, such as the decline of Cluny's prestige, the growth of legal capitulations of every kind, and the strong contemporary tendency to assert the *jus patronatus*. Thus at Mendham *c.* 1190 it was agreed that the deposition and election of a prior should be effected by the priors of Acre acting with the *advocati* (including, it would seem, the founder's kin) of Mendham;[6] at Farleigh, a Wiltshire house of Lewes, a dispute between the mother-house and Henry de Bohun, earl of Hereford, the lineal descendant of the founder, was accommodated in 1208 by an agreement that on a vacancy the earl or his agents

1 *Monasticon*, v, i, 27.
2 *Ibid.* 152.
3 *Ibid.* 13: "Abbas [*sc.* de Cluniaco] de nulla ordinatione domus se intromittat super priorem nisi de observantia vel emendatione ordinis ubi prior non potuerit per se." Throughout the Cluniac charters (as here) a great vagueness of phraseology in constitutional matters is apparent; this must have tended to confusion when disputes arose.
4 *Ibid.* 13.
5 *Ibid.* 122-3 (Pontefract); 136-9 (Monk Bretton).
6 *Ibid.* 59.

with two monks of Farleigh should go to Lewes, where the prior would nominate two candidates, taken from any Cluniac house; of these the representatives of Farleigh would select one as superior.[1] This controversy is an interesting reflection of what had lately happened in the case of Lewes. There a long quarrel between the earl of Warenne and the abbot of Cluny had at last, in 1201, come before papal judges delegate, Hubert Walter of Canterbury and the bishops of Ely and Chichester. The decision was that on a vacancy the earl's agents and some Lewes monks should go to Cluny, where the abbot would put before them the two best men he had available, saving the grand prior and the prior of La Charité; of these, they must choose one, who, once appointed, was to have full powers of administration and to be irremovable save for a demonstrable reason.[2]

Every Cluniac foundation from Lewes downward paid a yearly tax to its founding house. This is specifically mentioned in William de Warenne's charter, where it is fixed as fifty English *solidi*;[3] in the controversy of 1201 it is given as double that amount.[4] The increase may have been made at the time of Cluny's distress under Peter the Venerable when, as we shall see, the financial system was overhauled by Henry of Winchester. Lenton and Thetford paid a silver mark each year to Cluny.[5] In the second generation the same procedure is seen: thus Farleigh paid a silver mark to Lewes; Monk Bretton a mark to Pontefract; and Horkesley half a mark to Thetford;[6] and just as Cluny was to be visited each year on the feast of the Apostles, so Lewes was to be approached on the patronal festival of St Pancras, when payment was made.

Of immediate control from Cluny there is very little trace during the period and there are only rare notices of a visitation from the abbot of Cluny or of a summons to Cluny. Peter the Venerable toured England in 1130,[7] thus arousing the apprehensions of patriots at Peterborough. It is not stated what his business was, but it is natural to suppose that it was some kind of survey preparatory to his summons to Cluny of all the priors of the order in 1132. There is no direct evidence that representatives went from the English houses, but no doubt they were present; the familiarity of Thurstan of York in the summer of that year with what had happened at Cluny was probably the result of information from the prior of Ponte-

1 *Monasticon*, v, i, 27.

2 There is a full account of this incident in *Rad. de Diceto*, II, 173. The normal procedure of appointment is seen in Gilbert Foliot's letters: *ep.* 254 (La Charité and Bermondsey); *ep.* 257 (Cluny and Lenton in 1161).

3 *Monasticon*, v, i, 13: "Constitutum est inter nos et abbatem, quod Cluniacum habeat omni anno l. solidos."

4 *Rad. de Diceto*, II, 173: "Nec poterit abbas Cluniacensis exigere nisi antiquam pensionem c. solidorum."

5 *Monasticon*, v, i, 113, 152. At a later period Lenton paid fifty *solidi* and Thetford two marks. *V. Millénaire de Cluny*, I, 341, where Dom Guilloreau quotes MS. lat. 17. 717, fol. 11 *recto* in Bibliothèque Nationale.

6 *Monasticon*, v, i, 27 (Farleigh); 122–3, 136–7 (Bretton); 157 (Horkesley).

7 *Chronicle*, s.a. 1130 [E text].

fract.[1] Seventy years later, we again hear of an abbot of Cluny on tour, and again his visit caused patriotic reactions at an old English house.[2]

Apart from praises of Lewes, Thetford, Reading and a few other important houses, there are very few references to Cluniac observance in this country in the English sources. It was doubtless modelled on that of Cluny, but a small community could not go far towards reproducing the ceremonial and choral splendours described by Ulrich; we hear at Horton, a cell of Lewes with some dozen inmates, that three Masses must be celebrated daily, with a deacon at the principal one, and that there must be reading in the refectory at dinner.[3]

Thus an examination of the Cluniacs in England confirms all that has previously been said of the "order". It was constructed on feudal, personal ties of dependence, not on legal relationships, and the strong centrifugal tendency, visible from the early days of the plantation in England, developed steadily during the twelfth century.[4]

1 *Memorials of Fountains* (ed. Walbran), I, 22.
2 *Jocelini Cronica* in *Memorials of the Abbey of St Edmund*, I, 322.
3 *Monasticon*, V, i, 35.
4 Besides the works already cited, reference may be made to Dom Besse, *L'ordre de Cluny et son gouvernement*, in *Revue Mabillon*, 1905, pp. 5 *seqq.*, 97 *seqq.*, 177 *seqq.*; 1906, pp. 1 *seqq.* A detailed account of the English Cluniacs by Dr Rose Graham is, I understand, shortly to appear.

CHAPTER IX

WORCESTER, EVESHAM AND THE NORTHERN REVIVAL

I

In the general eclipse which overtook almost all the ecclesiastical notabilities of English blood in the years that immediately followed the Conquest, two monastic superiors, near neighbours and friends of each other, had no permanent part. Aethelwig of Evesham is found almost at once occupying a position of responsibility and influence such as was held by no other Englishman, and Wulfstan of Worcester, after a short interval of trial, appears as a trusted agent of the Conqueror and as ultimately acquiring a prestige, due to his personal sanctity of life, such as was enjoyed by none of his contemporaries. In consequence, the two houses governed by them, together with a few neighbours and dependencies, stood for a long time outside the stream of Norman monastic influence, and developed their life along the lines which, as we have seen, were being already followed under the Confessor. This fact, besides its domestic significance for the two monasteries concerned, was destined to have a further and greater importance, for it enabled Evesham to take part in two enterprises of colonization which are wholly without parallel in the history of the period.

The Conquest found Wulfstan still in somewhat of an equivocal position at Worcester, overshadowed by the reputation and varied activities of Atchbishop Ealdred, and although, like his metropolitan, he supported the Conqueror after Harold's defeat, it was not till the claims of Thomas of York had been set aside in 1070 that he attained complete freedom of action. In any case he would seem to have avoided of set purpose all purely secular business.[1] His true vocation was found as a diocesan bishop, and the picture of his life as such, with its manifold duties, its wide beneficence and its private devotion, was drawn in all simplicity and fidelity by his chaplain Coleman, and has been preserved for us by William of Malmesbury.

As bishop, he retained so far as possible the monastic rule of life. Much of his time was occupied in visiting his diocese and in travelling to or from court, and other periods were spent at one or another of his manors, but when at Worcester he followed in large part the monastic horarium, singing the conventual Mass each day to make up for his many absences,

---

1 Hemming, *Cartularium* (ed. Hearne), 271: "Nec ullo modo, cum plurimum posset, secularibus negotiis implicare se vellet."

and in the evening attending the collation and compline.[1] As was to be expected, the community grew in numbers under his rule; according to his own statement in a charter at the end of his life he had found about twelve monks at Worcester; these had now grown to fifty, and it is probable that this figure does not include the smaller priory of Westbury.[2] He had himself been master of the children, and Coleman's *Life* and other writings,[3] together with the work of Hemming, a text of the *Chronicle*,[4] and a number of Old English manuscripts of Worcester provenance,[5] are evidence that the priory under his rule was a home of culture, and that the traditional culture of the England of the past. He also had the greatness of mind to appreciate the Norman learning; he sent the young Englishman Nicholas, one of his most intimate disciples, to learn from Lanfranc at Canterbury.[6] It is possible that Nicholas rose to be subprior and precentor at Christ Church;[7] in any case, he returned at length and was the centre of a flourishing group of pupils, among whom we may doubtless count Florence and John of Worcester.

Worcester under Wulfstan grew in numbers sufficiently to be able to refound Westbury, the ancient cradle of Oswald's disciples,[8] and the bishop gave his support to his monk Aldwin in his endeavours to found a congregation of hermits at Malvern;[9] probably, also, the first foundation

---

1 *Vita Wulfstani* (ed. Darlington), 54: "Quando erat Wigornie missam majorem cotidie fere dicebat...fertur enim solitum dicere...monachum se loci esse; septimanam ut ceteros ecclesie debere; ideoque quod suo explere nequiret ordine suppleret pro adventus tempore."

2 Cf. Alveston charter (Hemming, 418; *Monasticon*, I, 599) of 1089. There is an interesting corroboration in *Domesday*, where it is noted that a hide of land at Grimanleh "est de dominico victu monachorum sed praestita fuit cuidam Edgidae moniali, ut haberet et deserviret quamdiu fratres voluissent et carere potuissent. Crescente vero congregatione T. R. W. reddidit" (Dd. 173 b; cf. *VCH, Worcs*. I, 295).

3 In *Vita Wulfstani*, 11, William of Malmesbury refers to a *Life* of St Gregory: "quod a Colemanno in patriam linguam ut pleraque alia versum", etc.

4 It is usually assumed that the [D] text of the *Chronicle* had its origin at Evesham, Pershore or Worcester (*v.* Plummer's introduction and the edition of the [D] text by E. Classen and F. E. Harner). The depreciatory reference to Aethelwig, *s.a.* 1078, would seem to exclude Evesham, and there is no evidence of any literary activity at Pershore at this time.

5 Cf. W. Keller, *Die Litterarischen Bestrebungen von Worcester in Angelsächsischen Zeit* in *Quellen und Forschungen* (1900), 64, and *Zur Litteratur...von Worcester* (1897), 20. I owe these references to Prof. R. W. Chambers.

6 *Vita Wulfstani*, 57: "Mox ut plena informationis perfectio in eum conflueret, Cantiam misit; sub disciplina Lanfranci aliquamdiu militaturum."

7 There is a somewhat obscure reference in Eadmer, *Vita S. Dunstani* (*Mem. St Dunst.* 163–4) to an Aegelredus, subprior and cantor at Christ Church, who subsequently "Wigornensi ecclesiae...prelatus erat". There appears to be no vacancy among the priors of Worcester; either, therefore, *prelatus erat* = only "held official position", or Aethelred was another name of Nicholas, or was written in error. Dr Darlington, *Vita Wulfstani*, xxxviii, note, inclines to the identification, but it is not easy to suppose that Nicholas, a young man, would have quickly come to occupy such important posts at Christ Church, or would have had earlier connections with Aethelric of Selsey (*Mem. St Dunst.* 164), while his speedy return to Worcester seems to be indicated by the number of incidents in Wulfstan's life which he witnessed. However, there is a Nicholas, but no Aegelred, among the Worcester monks in the Durham *Liber Vitae* (facsimile ed., Surtees Soc., 1923, 22).

8 Westbury would seem to have been refounded shortly before 8 Sept. 1093, the date of the charter giving it to the monks of Worcester (Hemming, 421–4). Coleman, the first prior, was still chancellor of Wulfstan in 1089 (*ibid.* 420).

9 *Vita Wulfstani*, 26; Will. Malmesb., *GP*, 285–6.

of Gloucester in 1058 had come from Worcester.[1] References to Wulfstan's friendly relations with the other houses of his diocese—Evesham, Pershore, Winchcombe—are scattered through the pages of his *Life*; Serlo of Gloucester was his friend, and he seems to have attached particular importance to unions of confraternity in the old English style, for two such organized by him have survived, the one embracing all the houses of his diocese, together with Chertsey and Bath,[2] the other joining Worcester to its mother-house Ramsey.

But although Wulfstan continued as bishop to follow what part he could of the monastic order of life, and gave his support in every way to the spread of monasticism, he belongs rather to the class of great bishops than to that of the purely monastic saints. The distinction may seem subtle or useless, for Wulfstan's frugality of life and love of solitude and prayer were no doubt greater than those commonly to be found in monasteries; but the reader of his life feels instinctively that his significance in the history of religion is not that of Anselm, of Bernard or of Ailred. His concern was to give the law of Christ to all classes of men in matters of direct government and counsel; he was not concerned primarily to be an apostle or a reformer of the monastic life, nor to direct others by his writings or guidance to the highest degrees of union with God. In this he has a strong family resemblance to Dunstan and his two associates, and if his significance in history is less than theirs (for he originated and changed little in the external framework of the Church in England), he is their equal in sanctity and, thanks in large measure to Coleman, his portrait stands out more clearly before our eyes. He is, indeed, a most attractive figure, too little known to his countrymen, as we watch him at his life's work in the quiet villages beneath Bredon and the Cotswolds; the last, and certainly one of the greatest, of the bishops of pure English blood and culture.

Although there is no record of concerted action between Wulfstan and Aethelwig at the time of the invasion of 1066, it is not easy to suppose that they came independently to the important decision of supporting William with all their power, for the abbot was the bishop's penitent, while Wulfstan in the years after the Conquest often made use of Aethelwig's help.[3] The abbot of Evesham, in the years of life that remained to him, held a unique place among the abbots of England, with wide authority

---

1 The first superior was Wilstanus, ex-provost of Worcester.

2 It is noteworthy that the heads of all these houses were English, save only Serlo of Gloucester.

3 *Chron. Evesh.* 89: "Saepissime ad se convocans [Wulfstanus Athel.] et ipse ad illum veniens ejus consilio atque auxilio utebatur." *Ibid.* 90: "Et quoniam episcopus erat...pater suarum confessionum, etc." This last statement makes it clear that nothing in the nature of enmity existed between them. Besides the Evesham *Chronicle*, a few notices of Aethelwig occur in the *Vita Wulfstani* and Hemming's *Cartulary*, esp. 270–3. The latter is bitter in tone towards Aethelwig and does him less than justice, whereas the Evesham *Chronicle* has nothing but good to say of Wulfstan.

within Gloucestershire, Worcestershire, Shropshire, Staffordshire, Warwickshire and Oxfordshire—the counties of Mercian law [1]—and was able
to make many within and without his sphere of power beholden to him.
He thus overshadowed Wulfstan in the public life of the country, and all
records agree that he acquired influence and property on a large scale; we
need not disbelieve the Evesham writer's statement that in the case
against York and in other pleas he was of the greatest service to the
bishop of Worcester, and that he lent and gave him money. This sense of
obligation may well explain the confusion of rights and properties between
the two neighbouring churches, deeply resented by the monks of Worcester
and only settled by formal judgment after Aethelwig's death. Hemming's
insinuation, however, that a long quarrel had been smouldering between
the two is not corroborated by the language of Aethelwig's biographer
nor by other information that we possess. [2]

Besides the precious, if brief, indications of his abbot's part in public
life the Evesham chronicler describes also a side of his character of which
the other sources give but a glimpse. [3] Aethelwig's care for the aged
Abbot Mannig, his bounty to the sick and poor, and above all, his personal
attention to their wants, in which, like Wulfstan, he washed and kissed
the feet of the outcast and the leprous, are clearly described by one who
had been an eyewitness and show that Aethelwig, however fully occupied
with secular business, was in no sense a merely secular ecclesiastic. Above
all, his generous reception of the refugees from the areas of the north and
west harried by the Conqueror shows that his support of the new *régime*
was not the policy of a time-server, and that he was ready to use his great
influence to protect and assist his countrymen in distress. The town of
Evesham, indeed (and doubtless also Worcester), became a kind of relief
camp for these homeless unfortunates, who added their numbers to the
swarms of pilgrims from England, Ireland and France who came to visit
the shrine of St Egwin, and over whom Aethelwig set his young prior
Aelfric as almoner. [4] He himself supported thirteen pensioners and fifty

---

1 *Chron. Evesh.* 89: "Commisit ei [rex Willelmus] curam istarum partium terrae, videlicet, etc." Cf. Hemming, *Cartulary*, 270–1, 279. R. R. Darlington, *Aethelwig of Evesham*, 14,
remarks: "the abbot appears to have been in fact if not in name the king's justiciar within
the Mercian law", and adds (p. 22): "few men can have taken so important a part in the
settlement of the difficult problems to which the Norman Conquest gave rise".

2 Hemming, *Cartulary*, 272: "Cum autem in longum de his terris inter ipsos altercatio
protraheretur abbas ipse...defungitur, suo pontifici nec pacatus nec absolutus ab ipso."
Taken literally this is hard to reconcile both with the honourable references to Wulfstan in
the Evesham *Chronicle* and with the bond of confraternity into which the bishop entered
with Aethelwig in the last years of the abbot's life. Possibly the fact behind Hemming's
statement is simply that on the question of these lands Wulfstan had decided to waive his
claim during Aethelwig's lifetime. Hemming is often demonstrably loose and unfair in
his statements.

3 Coleman's *quantum ad religionem non minime* [*prudentie*] is a valuable corroboration
(*Vita Wulfstani*, 18).

4 *Chron. Evesh.* 91: "Jacebant miseri homines per totam villam tam in domibus quam
deforis, nec non et in coemeterio isto languidi....Hunc [Alfricum] abbas constituit, ut

poor day by day, and was constant in all his religious duties. Besides Evesham, he had for a number of years the administration of Winchcombe committed to him, and, although his biographer does not record the fact, to Aethelwig must almost certainly be given the credit of encouraging in its beginnings the enterprise of the prior of that house and his two companions, monks of Evesham, who set out to restore the shrines of the north. Under Aethelwig, Evesham prospered in every way; when he became abbot there were only twelve monks, when he died in 1077 there were over thirty, and the numbers continued to grow;[1] during his lifetime, he acquired property, both personal and for his house; and though after his death some of this was taken away from the abbey, it continued to be a house of wealth and importance.[2]

With Wulfstan and Aethelwig the old English monasticism had a worthy phase of splendour in the vale of the Severn, while elsewhere it was being gradually transformed. Though the position of each was exceptional, due both to circumstances without precedent and unique personal qualities, yet both were prepared by their early life and the examples of their predecessors to enter the public life of the country and to employ their communities upon works of charity. They were the last representatives of the old monastic life, peculiarly national in outlook, which naturally and without reflection took its place as part of the Church in England, expecting to give its leaders to the country's councils and to the rule of bishops' sees. Its spirit was in this different from that of the Norman monasticism, which stood rather as an exemplar to transform the ideals of other orders of the church, and still more different from that of southern France and Italy, where the *sacerdotium* was sharply divided against the *imperium*, and the monastic life against the world.

II

Evesham, as has been said, took part, while still an English house, in two ventures of distant colonization. The second of these in point of time may be first recounted, since so little is known of the manner in which it came about. Ailward, originally a monk of Ramsey and later abbot of Evesham and bishop of London, was, as has been previously noted, a blood relation of Cnut, and the Danish royal house had been among the benefactors of the abbey. Friendly relations were thus perhaps maintained with Denmark

omnes supervenientes peregrinos et pauperes devote susciperet, atque necessaria vitae sollicite administraret eis.... Solebant illis temporibus multi peregrini de Aquitannia, de Hibernia, ac de aliis terris plurimis huc venire, quos omnes iste suscipiens necessaria praebebat."

1 *Chron. Evesh.* 96 (but cf. Thorpe, *Diplomatarium*, 615-17, where in the letter of confraternity 32 monks appear, not 36 as in the Evesham *Chronicle*); for 56 c. 1090 (which included 12 at Odensee) v. Dugdale, *Monasticon*, II, 37.

2 Cf. the remarks of R. R. Darlington, *Aethelwig of Evesham*, 22.

even after the Conquest, though there is no record of them. In any case, when King Eric of Denmark, at the instance of Hubald, bishop of Odensee, proposed to found a monastery in that town and colonize it with monks from England, it was to Evesham, then under the rule of Robert, formerly a monk of Jumièges, that he applied. The request was met favourably, and a community of twelve went to Denmark, apparently with the approval of Rufus.[1] It is natural to suppose that this move may have been welcomed as a way of removing from Evesham some of those still attached to the old English traditions, but there is no positive evidence to countenance such a suggestion. Odensee, after a period of success, ceased to flourish, and application was again made to England for help in the second half of the twelfth century. Evesham long retained its connection and rights; as late as 1174 a prior of Odensee was elected at the mother-house, and a union of confraternity and privileges continued to endure not only between Evesham and the house in Denmark, but also between Odensee and St Mary's, York.[2] With the exception of the foundations made by Fountains and Kirkstead at Lysekloster and Hovedö in Norway fifty years later, Evesham's overseas priory was the last considerable event in the long history of the Christianizing of the northern nations from England.

The first group that went forth from Evesham, twenty years before the foundation in Denmark, though still smaller in number and more indefinite in its aim, was destined to influence profoundly the whole course of religious history in northern England, and to sow the seeds of a life that endured for almost five centuries. The names of the three monks who set out from the Vale of Evesham for an uncertain bourne deserve an immortality of memory which they have hitherto failed to inherit. Few indeed of those who stand in the choir of Durham cathedral, or who muse

---

1 Our scanty knowledge of the actual foundation comes from three Danish charters, two of Waldemar, king of Denmark (1157–82), and one of the bishop of Odensee contemporary with him. They are preserved in a manuscript at the British Museum (Cott. Vesp. B. xxiv, foll. 19–20 v.) and have been printed by W. Holtzmann in *Schriften des Vereins für Schleswig-Holsteinische Kirchengeschichte*, IX, 610–14. As I could not obtain access to this publication, I quote from the MS. Waldemar states (19): "cum avus meus pie memorie Ericus [1095–1103] apud Othensei monachos habitare disponeret, suggerente et constituente Hubaldo tunc ibidem episcopo, edificatores primos de ecclesia Eveshamiensi et monastice religionis institutores accepit." An Evesham MS. printed in *Monasticon*, II, 37 professes to give a list of monks *temp. Roberti abbatis* [ob. 9 Sept. 1096, according to a Register of Christ Church, Brit. Mus. Arundel 68] which includes twelve sent by William II to Denmark. Thus the foundation can be fixed (if these documents are trustworthy) within the limits 1095–6. The town of Odensee was reputed to have had an earlier connection with St Albans, *v. Gesta Abbatum S. Albani*, I, 13–19, and L. F. R. Williams, *History of the Abbey of St Alban*, 23–4.

2 The second charter of Waldemar referred to in the last note is an appeal to all religious in England for help for Odensee. It is natural to connect this with the election of William as prior of Odensee at Evesham in 1174 (*Monasticon*, II, 25). Other documents connected with Odensee will be found in the *Monasticon*, Evesham docs. xxix, xxx, xxxi. Cf. also *Chron. Evesh.* 325 and introd. xliii *seqq.* For another Englishman in Denmark, Aethelnoth of Canterbury, *c.* 1085–1110, *v.* his life of St Olaf in *Acta SS*, 10 July, III, 127–42. He may have been a monk or prior of Odensee.

upon the past in the ruins of Whitby or St Mary's, York, or who contemplate the beauties of arch and woodland at Fountains, are aware that the first impulse that set in being the monastic body in the north came from the vanished monastery of Winchcombe, on the slopes of the Cotswolds, and from the aspirations of a single monk, Aldwin the prior.[1]

Northumbria, at one time the home of English monasticism in its golden age, the land of Aidan, of Cuthbert, of Hilda, of Benet Biscop and of Bede, had seen its monasteries submerged, towards the end of the ninth century, under the flood of Scandinavian invasion, and though since the age of Edgar monks from the south had often filled the sees of York and Durham, no attempt had been made, with the doubtful and in any case short-lived exception of Oswald's foundation at Ripon, to revive the monastic life north of the Trent and Humber. At Durham itself, whither the body of St Cuthbert had been conveyed, after much wandering, at the end of the tenth century (the traditional date is 995), a college of clerks guarded the saint and fulfilled the liturgical offices, retaining, so we are told, many of the monastic uses which had been handed down the generations from Lindisfarne, but not constituting a monastic body in the full sense of the term.[2] For all the disappearance of former glory, however, two very powerful influences kept the north and its past alive in the memories of English monks of the south; the one was the *Historia Ecclesiastica* of Bede, read wherever books were treasured, and the other, due partly to Bede's writings, was a strong devotion to St Cuthbert and his shrine. More than one incident shows that this devotion was at its height in the years immediately preceding the Conquest at one of the chief centres of religious life in southern England. About the year 1056 Eadwine, monk and childmaster of the New Minster, having failed to obtain his abbot's permission to make a pilgrimage to Durham, whither he conceived himself to have been called by St Cuthbert in a vision, set out nevertheless for the north and visited the shrine, where he is said to

---

1 A wholly trustworthy account of this episode is given by Symeon of Durham (*Opera*, ed. T. Arnold, Rolls Series). Symeon, whose name appears thirty-eighth in order in the list of Durham professions (*Symeon*, I, 5), was born c. 1060 and was probably a monk of Jarrow before the transference to Durham. He was familiar with the choral customs of Durham previous to the change (I, 58), and was present at the examination of the body of St Cuthbert in 1104 (cf. *Capitula de Miraculis et Translationibus S. Cuthberti*, I, 247 *seqq.*, and Reginald of Coldingham, *Libellus* [Surtees Soc. 1835], 84); he is given the title of precentor of Durham in one MS. He died probably c. 1128. He was thus an exact contemporary of the first half-century of monastic life in the north, and his narrative is, so far as can be ascertained, accurate. Besides older editions and the volumes of the Rolls Series, his works have been edited for the Surtees Soc. LI [1868], by H. Hinde. Further details of the early history of the northern houses are to be found in the *Memorial of the Foundation of Whitby* (ed. J. C. Atkinson, *Cartularium Abbathiae de Whiteby*, Surtees Soc., LXIX [1879], 1–7), and in two narratives of the early history of St Mary's, York, printed in *Monasticon*, III, 544–7, and reprinted by Atkinson, *op. cit.*, introd. xxxiv–xxxix. There is no mention of the expedition of Aldwin in the Evesham *Chronicle*.

2 *Symeon*, I, 9, 57–8: "Unde tota nepotum suorum successio magis secundum instituta monachorum quam clericorum consuetudinem canendi horas, usque ad tempus Walcheri episcopi, paterna traditione observavit, sicut eos canentes saepe audivimus." Cf. *ibid.* 106.

have opened the tomb of the saint.[1] At almost the same time Aelfwold, bishop of Sherborne and sometime monk of Winchester, made a similar pilgrimage, and he, also, opened the tomb in which St Cuthbert's body was said to lie incorrupt.[2]

When Walcher, the first Norman bishop of Durham, took possession of his see in 1071, he found the clerks of the cathedral living a life which was certainly not fully monastic, but following many of the old monastic rites; these he changed into those common to bodies of secular canons.[3] He too, however, had read, if we may trust the chronicler, of the past history of his see in Bede, and prayed that the ancient monastic regularity of life might be restored there. The answer to his prayers came from an unexpected quarter.

A certain Reinfrid, a knight in the service of the Conqueror and apparently of a distinguished land-holding family, one of whose members, Reinfrid's son Fulco, held the important office of *dapifer* in the household of Alan de Percy,[4] visited the site of St Hilda's monastery at Whitby, probably during the northern expedition of 1069–70, and was greatly affected by the desolation which reigned there.[5] He determined to become a monk, and sought admission at Evesham, then under the rule of Aethelwig. We are given no hint why Evesham was chosen; there were, of course, no northern houses, and the fenlands were in a state of unrest; the connection between the sees of York and Worcester would naturally turn Reinfrid's attention to the Mercian monasteries, and he may have heard of the high reputation of Evesham under Aethelwig, and of the solitaries who had been members of its family. Whether Reinfrid had from the beginning an intention of returning to the north is not clear; he was not a man of clerical education, and so would belong to the class of monks called among the Normans *conversi*, who did not proceed to orders. Symeon of Durham gives us rather to understand that the mover of the scheme for a return to the north was the prior, Aldwin, of the neighbouring monastery of Winchcombe, which during these years was administered for a time by Aethelwig, who had Godric, the last English abbot, under his surveillance at Evesham.

Aldwin, who, like Reinfrid, would appear to have been a man of substance before becoming a monk, had read Bede's *Historia* and conceived a desire to visit the northern shrines and lead there a life of solitary poverty. He proceeded to Evesham and was there joined by Reinfrid and by Aelfwig, a monk and deacon of the house. The three obtained leave from

1 *Hyde Liber Vitae* (ed. Birch), 96–8.
2 Will. Malmesb., *GP*, 180.   3 *Symeon*, I, 106.
4 *Memor. Whitb.* 1: "Reinfridus, cum esset miles strenuissimus in obsequio domini sui Willielmi." Atkinson, introd. liii–v, and references there given, shows his connection with the family of de Arches. Freeman's unfortunate description of him as "seemingly a lay brother" (*Norman Conquest*, IV, 665) has led several subsequent writers into error.
5 *Memor. Whitb.* 1.

Aethelwig to set out for the north, Aldwin being appointed superior, and they left Worcestershire on foot, taking with them only an ass to carry the vestments and liturgical books. Their intention seems to have been to live in poverty and solitude, not primarily to reproduce the monastic life of the south;[1] they are therefore an English example of that widespread movement towards a simpler, more solitary form of religious life which had found expression in the previous half-century at Camaldoli and Vallombrosa, and was at the very moment about to develop at Tiron, Savigny, Cîteaux and the Grande Chartreuse.

The three companions left Evesham, it would seem, in 1073-4. Reaching York, they applied to the sheriff, Hugh FitzBaldric, for a guide to Monk-chester (the later Newcastle). Finding no trace there of the ancient monastic establishment, they passed to Jarrow, where ruins remained, and there they decided to settle, having received the approval of Bishop Walcher, who gave them the ruined walls of Benet Biscop's foundation. They found the church roofless and no domestic buildings standing, and themselves put a roof of unhewn timbers over the church and built a hut in which to sleep and take food, content, says one who shared their life, to live in poverty and discomfort though they came from rich abbeys of the south.[2] The district had lost all its memories of the art and learning of the past; such churches as existed were of wattle and thatch and the monk's dress appeared as a novelty. Gradually, however, the inhabitants came to the aid of the newcomers; Waldef, the earl of Northumberland, gave land for a monastery at Tynemouth,[3] and recruits joined them, though the majority of these were men from the south who, hearing in some way of the northern venture and perhaps regarding it as more national in prospect than the monasticism of the rest of England, chose, says Symeon of Durham, like Abraham, to leave their land and kindred and the house of their fathers. To these Aldwin was instructor, and Symeon, who must have known him well, gives high praise to his virtue and discretion. He was, he writes, "patient in adversity, modest in prosperity, acute and provident, weighty in word and deed, always yearning towards heavenly things, and taking thither such as would follow him".[4] The bishop seconded their efforts by gifts of land and constant support.

Among the recruits of these early years was one whom past adventures and future distinction mark out among his companions.[5] This was a cleric named Turgot, of one of the leading English families of Lincoln-shire, who, soon after the Conquest, had been imprisoned along with

1 *Symeon*, I, 108: "Aldwinus...qui paupertatem...cunctis seculi honoribus ac divitiis praetulerat. Didicerat ex historia Anglorum...desideravit...ad imitationem illorum pauperem vitam ducere."

2 *Symeon*, I, 109. 3 *Symeon*, II, 209. 4 *Symeon*, I, 110.

5 Turgot's story, which is not given in the *Historia Dunelmensis Ecclesiae*, written while he was still prior (i.e. *ante* 1109; *v.* I, 111, note), appears in the *Historia Regum*, written *c.* 1120 after his death (II, 202–3).

other hostages in Lincoln castle. Escaping by bribery, he made his way to Grimsby, where he found a merchant ship loading cargo for Norway. The Scandinavians stowed him away in the hold, but his escape was all but frustrated by the chance that emissaries from the Conqueror to Norway took passage in the same ship. His rescuers, however, refused to yield him up, and arriving in Norway he soon attracted the attention of the devout King Olaf, who took him as master in learning psalmody[1] and gave him a considerable sum of money. He had many thoughts of leaving the world, but gradually fell away from his desires; they were, however, to be fulfilled, almost in spite of himself, for, returning after a time to England, he was shipwrecked with the loss of all he had. Making his way to Durham, he told his story to Walcher, who immediately sent him to Aldwin at Jarrow, where he remained as a cleric under probation.

Shortly after this Aldwin, either from a desire of greater solitude, or, as Symeon says, from a desire to spread the monastic life elsewhere, left Jarrow under the rule of Aelfwig and, taking Turgot with him, proceeded north to Melrose, another long-abandoned shrine, and settled there.[2] Difficulties, however, arose with King Malcolm, while Walcher was instant in his requests and commands that they should return, and after a short stay they retraced their steps and took possession of the bishop's gift of Wearmouth, where Turgot received the habit and whence Aldwin frequently journeyed to visit Walcher, who began to conceive a desire to restore monks to his cathedral. As at Jarrow, so at Wearmouth there was a steady flow of recruits, for the most part men of the south.

The settlement at Wearmouth may have been c. 1076–8.[3] At about the same time the third member of the original trio, Reinfrid, left Jarrow on a new quest. He had approached William de Percy, in the service of whose family his son Fulco was, and had been given land at Whitby, the scene of his first conversion; there, also, recruits came in plenty.[4] The early history of Whitby is not altogether clear of confusion.[5] We hear of Danish incursions, and after a short time Reinfrid was accidentally killed by falling timbers. He was succeeded as prior by Serlo, a member of the Percy family, who in his turn was succeeded by his nephew William de Percy, the first to appear at Whitby with the abbatial title.

1 *Symeon*, II, 202–3. The reference to the superior English culture is noteworthy: "audito itaque quod clericus de Anglia venisset, quod magnum tunc temporis videbatur, etc."
2 *Symeon*, I, 111–12.   3 *Symeon*, I, 124; II, 260–1.
4 So *Memor. Whitb.* 2; *Symeon*, I, 111.
5 So far as I am aware, the first attempt to disentangle the matter was that of the Rev. J. C. Atkinson, in his introduction to the Whitby cartulary. Though his pages lack lucidity, his general conclusions would seem to be correct, viz. that the *Memorial* is a fairly reliable document, whereas the account (printed also in *Monasticon*) purporting to be written by Stephen, first abbot of York, is quite untrustworthy. This indeed has the appearance of being a composition of a much later date. Difficulties, however, still remain, and it would appear that there were troubles and family rivalries at Whitby which we cannot hope to understand with the scanty evidence we possess. It should, moreover, be added that W. Farrer (*Early Yorks. Charters*, II, 198–200) inclines to prefer the account of Stephen to that of the *Memorial*.

Meanwhile, in 1080, Walcher of Durham had met with a violent death before he had been able to carry out his project of reintroducing monks into his cathedral. His successor, appointed after a short interval at the end of the year, was one of the most distinguished of all the Conqueror's nominees. William, monk of St Carilef and afterwards abbot of St Vincent, was an excellent representative of the observant and lettered foreign monasticism; he was also a man of outstanding ability. Symeon remarks upon his clear intelligence and his wonderfully retentive memory; his mental and moral powers were indeed displayed to all in his controversy with the king and Lanfranc, and a letter of his to the monks of Durham shows him as a monastic superior of the type of Gundulf and Losinga.[1] Within a little over a year of his arrival at Durham he began negotiations for restoring monastic life in his cathedral. Having obtained all possible information as to local tradition and the history of St Cuthbert and Lindisfarne, he approached Lanfranc and the Conqueror, and ultimately proceeded to Italy to consult Gregory VII. The pope, as was to be expected, willingly consented, and wrote in that sense to the king and the archbishop.[2] The matter was ratified in England, and at the end of May 1083 St Carilef brought twenty-three monks from Wearmouth and Jarrow to Durham, and on Whit Sunday (28 May) received a renewal of their profession and vow of stability at the shrine of St Cuthbert. Three days later he appointed the officials of the house, setting Aldwin as prior, and assigned lands for the support of the monks.[3] Thus began the life of the great cathedral priory of Durham, destined to remain till the Dissolution one of the most celebrated and observant houses in the land; and with this settlement the enterprise of Aldwin of Winchcombe, which had broken away from the settled course of black monk life, re-entered the main stream of contemporary tradition.

The development of Durham may be told in a few words. Relations between the young community and St Carilef continued to be most

---

1 The most interesting tract, *De injusta vexatione Willelmi episcopi primi*, is printed by Arnold in *Symeon*, I, 170 *seqq*. If, as would seem to be the case, it is entirely genuine it must have been based on copious notes taken during the actual proceedings. Dr A. J. Macdonald, *Lanfranc*, 235–43, 267, ranks the bishop of Durham very high—perhaps too high: "It would be too much to claim that the Conqueror could not have found another man to do the work that Lanfranc did, and to do it well.... William of St Carilef, although coming late in the period of the Conquest, showed that Lanfranc was not *sui generis*." For a far less favourable estimate, *v.* the article (by Mandell Creighton) in *DNB*, which is based on Freeman, and is biased.

2 Jaffé-L. 5255–6; cf. Z. N. Brooke in *EHR*, xxvi (April 1911), 225–38. Gregory's letter has not survived. What purports to be it, together with a number of other letters and confirmations of the authorities concerned, is printed by J. Raine in *Dunelm. Scriptores Tres*, Surtees Soc., vol. 9 (1839), Appendix nos. i–xiv. Their authenticity was attacked in detail by W. Greenwell in his introduction to *Feodarium Prioratus Dunelmensis*, Surtees Soc., vol. 58 (1872), and his general conclusions seem certain, viz. that a body of meagre documents was wholly rewritten in the interest of the monks during their controversy with the bishops in the early twelfth century. For a further note *v. infra*, p. 629, n. 4.

3 *Symeon*, I, 123.

cordial. Prior Aldwin survived his promotion by less than four years; on his death he was succeeded by his disciple, Turgot. The latter, on St Carilef's return from the journey he had undertaken as a result of his breach with the king, joined with the bishop in 1093 in laying the first stones of the noble fabric which still remains, and must have taken many decisions affecting its rapid construction. He had not yet, however, done with change. If, as seems most probable, he was the author of the simple but exquisite life of St Margaret of Scotland,[1] he must, during his early years of office, if not previously at Melrose, have made the acquaintance and been admitted to the intimate confidence of that *âme d'élite*. This near and trusted friendship with the royal house of Scotland would serve to explain why, in 1107, Alexander chose Turgot as bishop of St Andrews. Unfortunately for his peace, a series of controversies followed his insistence upon recognizing the metropolitan supremacy of York, in which Anselm, Ranulf Flambard and King Alexander were involved; he was not consecrated till 1109 and was ultimately forced to proceed to Rome. His health broke down under his calamities, and obtaining leave to retire to Durham, he first celebrated a last Mass at Wearmouth where, some forty years previously, he had been clothed with the monastic habit, and then, yielding to his illness, he died, as he had prayed that he might, in the house of St Cuthbert, with the words of the psalm on his lips: "His dwelling is in peace and his habitation in Sion."[2]

Durham, where the new architecture of the Normans received such remarkable development, and where the library and the works of Symeon, Turgot and the later subprior Maurice showed the influence of Norman learning, long retained a strain of other aspirations. Besides Godric of Finchale and the ex-prior Bartholomew of Farne, others of its number passed to hermitages[3] and the first Cistercian houses, thus repeating in their own lives the history of their founders, and the place had, at least until the thirteenth century, a spirit of simplicity and earnestness that set it apart from the other great houses of the black monks.

To complete the story of the northern revival it is necessary to return to Whitby. Here, after the early troubles, the house prospered. It would seem, however, to have been discord, not prosperity, that led to a group leaving Reinfrid's foundation for York *c.* 1078. There they founded the abbey of St Mary, within a short distance of the minster. Such a move, even more than the settlement at Durham, was contrary to the ideal of seclusion and poverty which the three pilgrims from the south had set

---

1 The *Vita S. Margaretae*, originally printed in *Acta SS* from a continental MS. which has disappeared, was reprinted by H. Hinde in his edition of Symeon, I, 234 *seqq.* Turgot's authorship would seem all but certain.

2 *Symeon*, II, 205.

3 Besides Bartholomew, who went to Farne, and Maurice the subprior, who joined Rievaulx, Thomas, prior of Durham, joined Bartholomew on Farne *c.* 1163 (*Symeon*, I, 307).

before themselves, and it is noteworthy that it was here, less than half a century later, that the reaction took place which led to the foundation of Fountains. Whatever the circumstances of the move to York, St Mary's and Whitby remained closely united, and both long retained a connection of friendship and federation with Evesham.[1]

The expedition of the three from Worcestershire c. 1074 had thus, in a little over a decade, borne abundant fruit. Three large monastic families, together with a number of dependent houses, had taken root in the north, and, by their acceptance of the customs and observance current throughout England, seemed to be indistinguishable from the rest of the monastic body. The north was, however, profoundly different in spiritual outlook from the south, and it remained so. The traditions of the past, the early years of Aldwin and Reinfrid at Jarrow, Wearmouth and Whitby, the lives of the many northern hermits, whether at Finchale, at Farne, or at Knaresborough, the characters of the archbishops Thurstan and Henry Murdac, have all something more austere in them than their counterparts in southern England. The Anglo-Norman monasticism, though satisfying to the full the love of learning and the memories of Bede which had survived all the harrying of the land, did not fully meet the spiritual needs of this race. It is not surprising that the Cistercian movement found such a fertile soil there, nor that it drew away from Whitby, Durham and York a number of the most able and most fervent of their inmates.

1 Thomas of Marleberge wrote (c. 1220) in the Evesham *Chronicle*, 256: "Quod monasterium [sc. York] a fundatione sua ita confoederatum est monasterio Eveshamensi ut quasi unum corpus et una ecclesia reputentur." Evesham owned the church of Huntington near York, and two abbots of Whitby, John I (c. 1214) and William VI (c. 1501) bore the surname de Evesham (Atkinson, *Cart. Whitb.* introd. lxxxvii).

CHAPTER X

THE ENGLISH MONASTERIES UNDER HENRY I

I

The long reign of Henry I was for the Anglo-Norman monasticism of England a period of external and internal well-being. The reign of the Conqueror had been a time of conflict, of readjustment, of new beginnings; that of Rufus, especially in its later years, had brought material and moral disturbances which, had they continued, would have seriously affected the future; in that of Stephen, new political and religious developments were to change in almost every department of their life the condition of the black monk houses. But under the comparatively peaceful reign of Henry I, when the period of plantation was over,[1] the seeds sown by the first generation of Norman abbots could bear flower and fruit. During these thirty-five years the prestige of the monasteries, regarded as a body, was great and unchallenged. The old English stock, with its customs and memories of strife, had passed away; the monks attaining maturity in 1100 had received the full benefit of the new discipline and teaching, both moral and intellectual; there was still a real solidarity among the houses, not yet seriously undermined by the *esprit de corps* of individual monasteries, by rivalry with the new orders, or by the great jurisdictional controversies which were to occupy so many minds and dissipate so much energy in the course of the century. In a word, the Anglo-Norman monasteries were still the main spiritual and intellectual reservoirs of the country.

It was, like the period that had gone before, a time of great buildings. The few Saxon churches which remained (Peterborough is an example) were replaced by vast structures in the new style; Norman work still incomplete, as at Durham and at Ely, received additions, and in a few cases, such as Canterbury, was remoulded on a larger scale; a glance at any chronicle or a plan of one of the greater abbeys shows that the domestic buildings and offices were steadily completed or increased. It was, to a still more striking degree, a time in which the movable possessions and treasures of the monasteries were accumulated. Vestments, church plate, service books were acquired, libraries were extended, and all the furniture of the church and conventual buildings gradually set in place. It was above all the period of flowering of the Norman culture on English soil. Between 1100 and 1140 appeared almost all the works of Eadmer, of William of

---

1 No black monk houses of any importance were founded under Henry I save the semi-Cluniac Reading (1121) and two or three Cluniac priories such as Thetford (1104), Lenton (c. 1106) and Bromholm (1113).

Malmesbury, of Florence and John of Worcester, of Symeon and Turgot of Durham, of Osbert of Clare, of the anonymous first historians of Evesham, Battle and St Albans, and, we may add, of the English-born Orderic Vitalis. The period was brief, for during these same years the attraction of the new learning of the schools, which could no longer be found in monasteries whether English or foreign, was beginning to draw away the most enterprising part of the youth of England to the schools of France, whence they returned (if they returned at all) to masterships or bishoprics or the royal and episcopal households; but while it lasted it was brilliant. To a dozen monastic historians we owe a tradition of past records and a knowledge of domestic and foreign events for the period 1070–1140 such as are available in no other country of Europe, and their labours were imitated and used as a basis by the multitude of chroniclers, monastic or secular, who flourished in the following centuries.

Yet to the monastic body of the time the reign of Henry I did not appear a time of complete rest and peace. The early years, during which the Church in England suffered the consequences of the prolonged struggle over investiture, were for a number of monasteries a time of disturbance owing to the questionable status of their abbots who had either given money to Rufus or accepted investiture from Henry upon entering office, and in the event no less than nine were deprived of their rank for one reason or another at the council of London at Michaelmas, 1102.[1] Moreover, throughout the reign there were several occasions when Henry I held important abbeys vacant in his hand for a long period, and a number of bishops, either acting without scruple, as Roger of Salisbury, or through a growing consciousness of their diocesan rights, encroached upon monastic freedom of action and set in motion controversies which were to endure for many decades.

Nor was the reign a time in which institutions, within or without the monasteries, remained fixed. On the contrary, during the first half of the twelfth century the black monk abbeys entered definitively upon the path they were to pursue to the end. It was during the reign of Henry I that a number of abbots, clear-sighted in temporal matters, took steps to discount the evil consequences of prolonged vacancies *in manu regis* by drawing a sharp line between the revenues of abbot and monks, so that the latter might enjoy the administration of their full income even if the king held the feudal barony for a prolonged period. This was undoubtedly the most important stage in a contemporary movement of financial decentralization which developed between 1090 and 1150 and led in time to the complete separation of the households and revenues of abbot and monks and to a departmentalizing of all the revenues and expenditures of the houses,

---

1 Viz. the abbots of Bury, *Cerne*, Ely, *Milton*, Muchelney, *Pershore*, Peterborough, *Ramsey* and *Tavistock*. Only those in italics were accused of simony; several succeeded in regaining their position. *V.* Eadmer, *Hist. Nov.* 142.

which were split up and entrusted to a growing number of "obedientiaries".

Concurrently with this went the gradual crystallization of "customs" at the individual abbeys. During the first decades after the Conquest the Norman abbots, under the surveillance of Lanfranc and the Conqueror, had been chiefly concerned with imposing the norm of observance and discipline with which they were familiar, and in abolishing, so far as was practicable, domestic or national peculiarities and relaxations. In the years following the death of Lanfranc, when the individual abbots were left wholly without check or supervision, and when the movement of reform had slackened, there grew up at each house an unwritten body of customs governing the liturgical celebration of various feasts, which carried with them relaxations on points of diet and discipline; these were now committed to writing and successive abbots added their gifts and days to the list, which came gradually to be regarded as a charter of rights.

Thus in a number of ways the houses, from being members of a body united in sentiment and ideals by common interest, tradition and surveillance, and by the interchange of superiors, began slowly to develop into corporations independent of each other and of all supervision; there was an almost imperceptible hardening of outlook which made their inmates less susceptible of new spiritual influences from without, and at the same time social and economic conditions were causing them to sink, as it were, deeper into the soil of the country. But of this little was apparent at the time.

While the Anglo-Norman monasticism had thus attained its fullest expansion and was settling into middle life, a number of external developments were taking place. One of these was the arrival of a second wave of the Cluniac influence, due largely to the personal friendship existing between Henry I and Cluny, and the king's family connection with Cluniac monks in eminent positions. This second wave took a different direction from the first. Plantations were no longer made directly in the family of Cluny or one of her daughters. Houses such as Reading (and later Faversham) were founded by a body of Cluniacs and with Cluniac uses, but existed from the first as autonomous abbeys; or alternatively, leading Cluniacs were set over English houses without the latter losing their independence. It is a noteworthy fact that whatever may have been the feeling in circles affected by St Bernard's polemics, in England the reputation of the Cluniac monasticism had never stood higher than in the last decade of the reign of Henry I.

But this phase of foreign influence was only transient; within a few years Cluniac and Anglo-Norman monasticism were to merge, for all practical purposes, into a single way of life. Far more important was the gradual infiltration of the stream of reformed monastic and canonical life which, though it did not become a torrent till the reign of Stephen, began to attract attention before 1135. The first indication of the coming flood was a rapid growth in the number of regular canonical establishments. Previous to 1100 these had been few in number and small in size, with vague rules and founded to meet some direct practical and local need—the service of a hospital or a large church or group of churches. Now they became more numerous, with larger communities and a stricter rule of life, based in general either directly or indirectly upon some celebrated model at home or abroad, with the "Rule" of St Augustine as their spiritual code, and offering to aspirants a quasi-monastic life which often equalled that of the strictly monastic houses in liturgical elaboration and seclusion. These houses of regular canons were of all types. Some were founded and remained mere groups of priests serving a church; others, such as Dunstable, Merton and St Osyth's,[1] became centres of letters and education; others again, like Llanthony in the Black Mountains[2] and Kirkham and others in the north, were places of strict monastic solitude. Among the multitude of these foundations dating from the reign of Henry I were several which soon rose to eminence in the religious life of the country, such as Cirencester (1131), Dunstable (c. 1132), Llanthony (– 1108), Merton (1117), St Osyth's (– 1118), Oxford, St Frideswide's (1122), the London houses of St Bartholomew's (1123) and St Mary Overy, Southwark (? 1106), and the important northern group, including Hexham (1113), Bridlington (c. 1113), Guisborough (1129), Kirkham (1121) and Carlisle (c. 1133). The new significance of the canons is strikingly shown by the appointment of one, William of Corbeuil, prior of St Osyth's, to the primatial see in 1123, and that of another, Aldulf, prior of Nostell, the king's confessor, to that of Carlisle in 1133.

Finally, it was Henry I who, in his last years, was responsible for the introduction of the Cistercians alike into the south at Waverley (1128–9) and the north at Rievaulx (1131–2). They had been preceded by the monks of Savigny at Tulket in 1123.

For all this, the reign of Henry I remains a period when the traditional Anglo-Norman monasticism still dominated the religious life of England. The abbots of the greater houses were as a rule men of proved capability coming from celebrated Norman monasteries or from the two or three chief nurseries of Norman observance in England, and their principal aim was to lift their community to an equality with the best they had known in earlier life and to model it, spiritually and intellectually, upon the Bec of Anselm, or the Canterbury of Lanfranc or the St Évroul with which Orderic has made his readers so familiar. No clearer or more significant

---

1 For St Osyth's *v.* esp. Will. Malmesb., *GP*, 146: "Erant ibi et sunt clerici litteratura insignes, eorumque exemplo talis habitus hominum laeta, ut ita dicam, totam patriam vestivit seges."

2 For Llanthony, *v.* its *Historia* in *Monasticon*, VI, 128 *seqq.*, and the praises of Gerald of Wales, esp. in the *Itinerarium Kambriae* (RS), 37–41.

witness of this could be desired than the greatest of the English monastic historians, William of Malmesbury. Throughout his pages there runs a double thread of confidence, alike in the spiritual and intellectual training he had himself received, and in those who followed this way of life in the monasteries up and down the land. Still more noteworthy, perhaps, is the praise, without a tinge of jealousy, which he gives to others, whether Cluniacs, canons or Cistercians.[1] Malmesbury's spiritual judgments, it is true, often lack discernment, and are due to good nature rather than to deep insight, but he wrote as a black monk and for his order, and it is not conceivable that his attitude of confidence and sympathy could have been maintained at a time of bitter rivalry or when the traditional monasticism was on its defence. We can do no better, if we wish to see the abbeys of England in their prime, than accompany Malmesbury in the brief survey, based often upon first-hand knowledge, which he gives of the country in the *Gesta Pontificum*, written c. 1120.

II

We may begin, as does the chronicler, with the cathedral monastery of Christ Church, Canterbury. Throughout the period with which we are concerned this house had an altogether unique position among its fellows. The largest of all in numbers,[2] its situation at the metropolitan church, with the primate always nominally and in origin effectually its religious superior, involved it constantly in the public life of the Church in England, and therefore also in the frequent and intensely heated controversies of the century. Not only was the community of Christ Church warmly partisan on behalf of Anselm in his struggles with Rufus and Henry I: it also took a leading part in assisting successive primates in their endeavours to obtain professions of obedience from the archbishops of York and the abbots of the neighbouring monastery of St Augustine. Besides this, the monastery served as a guest house to all the most distinguished travellers of the epoch on their way to or from the Continent, and when, later, the archbishop came to be surrounded by a group of distinguished canonists and men of letters, Christ Church felt this influence also. Placed thus at the centre of things, it naturally became a nursery whence, often at the suggestion of the primate, superiors were drawn for other houses, and even occasionally bishops for sees over which Canterbury desired to

---

1 For Malmesbury's praise of Cluniacs, *v.* esp. *GP*, 193 (Reading) and 207 (Lewes); for canons, *v.s.* p. 175, note 1; for the Cistercian order, "quae nunc optima via summi in caelum processus et creditur et dicitur", *v.* esp. *GR*, 380 *seqq.*

2 So Malmesbury, *GP*, 71. Gervase of Canterbury, *Actus Pontificum* (*Opera*, II, 368), tells us that Lanfranc "processu temporis centum monachos apposuit: sic prudenter instituens ut in ecclesia Christi monachi essent septies xx vel centum et L". Presumably the number was maintained, if not increased, during Malmesbury's lifetime.

secure influence.[1] It is not surprising, therefore, that the priors of Christ Church rarely held office for long. During the opening years of the century, the community still had the advantage of being ruled by Anselm, and his impress, confirming the still weightier mark of Lanfranc, remained till Malmesbury's day; the observance, so the historian tells us, equalled that of the Cluniacs.[2] Of the religious spirit and level of learning of his home Eadmer may well stand as both pattern and witness.

Within a short distance of the cathedral monastery was the abbey of St Augustine, also wealthy and populous. As has already been seen, its history after the Conquest had been troubled, and throughout the twelfth century its peace was continually disturbed by the struggle for exemption against the archbishop. It would seem to have lacked the distinction of its neighbour, though the evidence of manuscripts shows that it was a home of letters, and besides the domestic records and muniments which formed the basis for later historians, it probably housed, till early in the twelfth century, one of the chief versions of the Old English *Chronicle*, and perhaps also the writer of the celebrated character study of the Conqueror.[3]

Of Rochester we know little, save the details of its economy preserved in the *Textus Roffensis*. It had attained a fair size under the saintly Gundulf,[4] and his successors, Ralph (1108–14), sometime abbot of Séez and later primate, and Ernulf (1115–24), a monk of Beauvais, were both intimate disciples of Anselm, and Ralph the prior, a monk of Bec and Caen, who became abbot of Battle in 1107, was a man of eminent ability and piety. Presumably, therefore, Rochester reflected the life of the most fervent Norman houses.

But the English abbey that most resembled its sisters overseas at this time was probably the Conqueror's foundation of Battle. Richly endowed, and under the especial protection of the king, the house prospered even under Rufus. In 1107, as has been said, it received as abbot Ralph, prior of Rochester, and the words of the chronicler that under his rule the abbey "was judged second to none in England for observance, goodness, gentleness, charity and charitable deeds" are probably true, even if written by one who was not a contemporary.[5] Nor did the quarrel with the bishop of Chichester over exemption cause as yet much disturbance.

---

1 I have noted at least twelve monks of Christ Church who became abbots of other houses in the course of a century; eight of them were priors. They are (a) *Priors*: Henry (Battle), 1096; Ernulf (Peterborough), 1107; Conrad (St Benet's, Holme), 1126; Geoffrey (Dunfermline), 1128; Odo (Battle), 1175; Benedict (Peterborough), 1177; Alan (Tewkesbury), 1186/7; Roger Norreys (Evesham), 1190. (b) *Monks*: Warner (Battle), 1125; William (Evesham), 1149; Ralph (Shrewsbury), 1175; Roger (St Augustine's), 1175/6. To these may be added the bishops, viz. Donat O'Haingly (Dublin), 1086 [*Chronicle*, vol. 1, Appendix, 290]; Ernulf (Rochester), 1115; Eadmer (St Andrews), 1121; Richard (Canterbury), 1174; Herluin (Leighlin), 1204 [Liebermann, *Ungedruckte Quellen*, 167].
2 Will. Malmesb., *GP*, 71: "Religione Cluniacensibus non impares."
3 *V*. Plummer's introduction to the *Chronicle* and notes *ad locc.*
4 The *Textus Roffensis* (ed. Hearne), 143, states that there were more than sixty monks at Rochester in 1108.   5 *Chron. Bell.* 52.

Abbot Ralph, who died in 1124 at the advanced age of eighty-four, had known Bec in the days of Herluin and Anselm, and himself embodied its finest spirit:

> Vigilant in his care for all that was without, let it not be thought burdensome if we relate how zealously he forwarded the salvation of souls....Ever did he adapt himself to the characters of those under him, never did he give orders as a master. He bore with the infirmities of others and led them on to great things. He himself practised what he preached; he lived what he taught. Saying that one should hasten to the divine service, he was there before younger men even though himself aged and leaning on a staff. First in choir, he was the last to depart....A Daniel in his sparing diet, a Job in his sufferings, a Bartholomew in his prayers, he ever bent his knees in prayer though he could scarce bend them when he walked. He recited the whole psalter every day, and abandoned this and his practice of kneeling at prayer scarce three days before his death. Neither a racking cough, nor haemorrhage, nor old age, nor a body shrunk to a skeleton could break him or bend him from his way of life.[1]

Despite some conventional phrases this account, which concludes with a detailed description of his last moments, is clearly the work of one who had known Abbot Ralph, though it is embodied in a later writing. It is fully corroborated by the notice of Orderic, written while the abbot was still living.[2]

Winchester, the old political capital of Wessex, which during the first decades after the Conquest was the scene of frequent Courts and till 1090 the seat of the royal treasury,[3] had, like Canterbury, two great religious houses, the cathedral priory of St Swithun and the New Minster which in 1100 was still adjacent. Both were wealthy and large communities, but, as at Canterbury, the cathedral monastery naturally had an advantage over the other and there was jealousy between them. St Swithun's was second only to Christ Church as a nursery whence abbots were drawn for monasteries all over England.[4] We have seen in a previous chapter that it was reorganized on Norman lines by Prior Simeon, brother of Walkelin; he was succeeded by a monk Godfrey of Norman birth who combined great literary gifts with holiness of life, and is ranked by Malmesbury with Lanzo of Lewes.[5] Godfrey died after a long and painful illness; he was

---

1 *Chron. Bell.* 59.

2 Ordericus Vitalis, II, 164: "Rodulfus...studio sanctitatis et salutaris doctrinae sibi multisque coessentibus prodesse sategit, et bona in senectute spiritualibus studiis adhuc insistit." A notice of his death follows; possibly the reading should be *institit*.

3 *Annales Wintonienses, s.a.*

4 I have noted the following, ten in all: (*a*) *Priors*: Simeon (Ely), 1082; Geoffrey (Burton), 1114; Ingulf (Abingdon), 1131; Robert (Glastonbury), 1173; Walter (Westminster), 1175/6. (*b*) *Monks*: Geoffrey (Burton), 1085; Hugh (New Minster), 1100; Ernulf (Malmesbury), 1106; Hugh (Chertsey), 1107; Robert (Malmesbury), 1187. Also the following bishop: Malchus (Waterford) [Eadmer, *Hist. Nov.* 76].

5 Will. Malmesb., *GP*, 172–3: "Religione et litteratura insignis fuit....Quid omne divinum officium, quod vetustate quadam obsoletum, nativa exculta vetustate [*leg.* venustate] fecit splendescere. Religionis et hospitalitatis normam pulchre inchoatam delineavit in monachos, qui hodie in utrisque....Godefridi formam sectantur." Cf. also *GR*, 516.

venerated as a saint at Winchester and miracles were reported at his tomb.[1] In the year of his death William Giffard became bishop. He was a man of determined character and in his first years by no means favourable to the monks; the chronicler describes the feud which came to a head in 1122–4. The later years were more peaceful, and Giffard was in the habit of dining and taking his siesta with the monks; at the end he received the habit and died in the monks' infirmary. He was succeeded by Henry of Blois.

The neighbouring New Minster had less distinguished and less prosperous times. It had suffered both from the intrusion of Robert Losinga, father of the simoniacal and afterwards repentant Herbert, and from the depredations of Ranulf Flambard.[2] In 1100 a monk of St Swithun's became abbot, and when the close proximity of the two houses continued to cause friction, the New Minster was in 1111 moved out to Hide. But even there its career was not wholly happy.

The history of the monasteries of Dorset and Somerset is all but a blank for this period. The Dorset trio of Abbotsbury, Cerne and Milton were poor and uninfluential; Milton, at least, to judge by the names of abbots that have survived retained an English character into the twelfth century.[3] Two of the Somerset houses, Athelney and Muchelney, were satellites of Glastonbury, little more than *monasteriola*. Malmesbury gives short descriptions of both, based probably on his own observation. Athelney, he tells us, though not an island in the sea, was so surrounded by lake and marsh that it could only be reached by boat. A thicket of alders gave a home to deer and other animals; the solid earth was only some two acres in area, and on it was a minute church and cloister; the church itself rested on wooden piles. The monks were few and poor, but content with their poverty and solitude. Of Muchelney he merely remarks that, like Athelney, it was extremely difficult of approach, and in winter was accessible only by water.[4] Of Tavistock in Devon he can only tell us that many fish are caught there, and that the river flows under the monastic buildings and carries off the refuse.[5]

Glastonbury, at the time of *Domesday*, had been the wealthiest abbey in England. It was not an island, but its remote situation among the

---

1 Rudbourne, *Hist. Wint.* (*ap.* Wharton, *Anglia Sacra*, I, 285): "dilectus Deo Godfridus, qui miraculis coruscat...qui humatus est in domo capitulari...miraculis coruscans." Such attributions are far rarer than is often supposed by those who have only a superficial acquaintance with monastic literature of the time.

2 For Robert *v.* Flor. Wig. II, 41 and Will. Malmesb., *GP*, 151: "Patre suo Rotberto... in abbatiam Wintoniae intruso." For Flambard *v. Ann. Wint.*, *s.a.* 1088.

3 An Aethelwine was abbot in 1075; he was succeeded by a Modred (*Chron. Abingd.* II, 286) and an Aethelric (Will. Malmesb., *GP*, 119).

4 Will. Malmesb., *GP*, 199–200. For a plan of the church at Athelney, *v.* Clapham, *English Romanesque Architecture before the Conquest*, 147–8; Hodgkin, *History of the Anglo-Saxons*, II, 613.

5 Will. Malmesb., *GP*, 202. A river was similarly utilized at Fountains and elsewhere.

marshes made it unattractive to Malmesbury,[1] who made a prolonged stay there, and though so celebrated and possessing still so many relics of past glory and a splendid library, its history since the Conquest had been little but a record of misfortune.[2] The dilapidations of the last Saxon abbot Aethelnoth, who was deposed by Lanfranc, were followed by some losses of land to enfeoff a large number of knights.[3] Then there were the troubles with Thurstan, the dispersal of part of the community, and the existence of the remainder without an abbot or with Thurstan returned and living in the neighbourhood. The abbots who followed him did not apparently succeed in putting all to rights, and it was not till Glastonbury was held for forty years by Henry of Blois that its finances were satisfactorily settled, and Henry, excellent administrator and generous benefactor though he was, cannot have fully exercised, either himself or through others, the duties of abbot in the midst of his many occupations and adventures.

Very little is known of Bath at this time.[4] Of the neighbouring ancient house of Malmesbury we know more, though not so much as we might expect, from the pages of its distinguished son. In William's youth Godfrey, a monk of Jumièges, was abbot (1081–1105) and founded the library of which the historian was later in charge. Besides William, Malmesbury had given a home for some years to Faricius, the celebrated abbot of Abingdon, and from references in the *Gesta Pontificum* and *Gesta Regum* we learn of other lettered monks of the house. The church contained the shrine of St Aldhelm, a place of pilgrimage and miracles.[5] In 1117, however, the abbey fell into the clutches of Roger of Salisbury, and its development was for a time paralysed.

More is told us of the history of Abingdon. At the accession of Henry it was suffering, along with others, from the exactions of Rufus and the dilapidations of the monk Modbert who was acting as royal steward.[6] Henry appointed almost at once as abbot Faricius, an Umbrian by birth and at the time cellarer of Malmesbury. Faricius was undoubtedly one of the greatest abbots of his age, and possessed almost all the qualities necessary for good government. To his contemporaries he was known pre-eminently as the most skilful physician of his time in the king's dominions; the king himself, Queen Maud and many of the most distinguished in the realm were his patients. Himself a man of wide culture,

---

1 Will. Malmesb., *GP*, 196: "Glastonia...nec situ nec amenitate delectabilis." He would not have subscribed to a description of it as "Deep-meadow'd, happy, fair with orchard-lawns And bowery hollows". The vine, however, flourished there in his day.

2 Will. Malmesb., *GP*, 196: "Ceterum, nescio quo infortunio, semper post adventum Normannorum pessimis infracta rectoribus, nec in novis edifitiis nec inhabitatorum compendiis profecit."

3 Will. Malmesb., *de Ant. Glast.* (*ap.* Gale), 330: "Willelmus...quamplures ex suis commilitonibus ex Glastoniae feudavit possessionibus." For Aethelnoth *v. Chronicle*, II, 316 and *Acta Lanfranci, ibid.* I, 289 and for the process of enfeoffment *v. infra* ch. xxxv.

4 Will. Malmesb., *GP*, 195; *GR*, 387.

5 Will. Malmesb., *GP*, 433–43.

6 *Chron. Abingd.* II, 42–3, 284–5.

he was tireless in providing Abingdon with books of every kind, hiring scribes in addition to the monks; he settled the liturgical observance of the place and adorned the church. In addition, he was prudent and energetic in administration;[1] he received not a few gifts from grateful patients, and organized, supervised and increased the revenues of the house. This enabled him to receive more monks, and indeed during the sixteen years of his rule the population of the abbey was tripled.[2] With all this, he was a man of patience and gentleness, indulgent to others though himself sparing in diet and insensible to extremes of temperature;[3] when he came to die he had upon his lips the words of the psalmist: "Lord, I have loved the beauty of thy house."[4] It is not surprising that on the death of Anselm Henry, who admired Faricius greatly, should have wished to make him archbishop. The design failed, partly because the majority of the bishops wished for one who was not a monk or at least not one of Faricius' determined character, partly, it may be, from dislike of his great influence, and a compromise was effected by the choice of the more amenable Ralph of Rochester. Faricius was succeeded at Abingdon by Vincent of Jumièges and Ernulf of the Old Minster, both men of character and learning.

In the valleys of the lower Severn and Avon there were in Malmesbury's lifetime seven monastic houses, the abbeys of Gloucester, Tewkesbury, Pershore, Evesham and Winchcombe, the cathedral priory of Worcester, and the priory of Malvern. Then, as now, the wide, level expanse of country bounded by the range of the Malvern Hills, the isolated Bredon Hill and the northern escarpment of the Cotswolds displayed a landscape of rich fertility and beauty, and Malmesbury had doubtless often paused to contemplate its peaceful expanse from the ridge of the hills above Birdlip on his way to Gloucester or Worcester.

From that city the whole district is called the vale of Gloucester. Everywhere the land is rich in crops and prolific in fruit; in some places the nature of the soil alone, in others careful cultivation achieves this, so that the idlest are incited to work upon land where the reward is a hundredfold. The high roads are lined with fruit trees, planted by nature, not by man; the earth of its own accord breaks into fruit—and that the best in the land for appearance and flavour.... The vines there are more numerous, more fruitful and sweeter than anywhere else in England, and the wines they produce are little inferior to those of France. It is a land of populous towns, thickset villages and great abbeys.[5]

1 Will. Malmesb., *GP*, 126: "Vir ingentis acrimoniae et insignis industriae ad ea quae cepisset explenda."

2 For Faricius *v. Chron. Abingd.* II, 44 *seqq.*, 285 *seqq.*, and many references in other sources. In 1100 there were twenty-six (or twenty-eight) monks; Faricius made the number up to seventy-eight (or eighty). *Chron. Abingd.* II, 49, 148, 289.

3 Cf. the story (true or not) of the monk and slices of pork (*Chron. Abingd.* II, 287) and the chronicler's judgment (*ibid.* 146): "vir per omnia mansuetissimus...vultu ut semper erat jucundo."   4 *Chron. Abingd.* II, 290.

5 Will. Malmesb., *GP*, 291–2; there is an interesting description of the Severn "bore" in this passage. From the *Vita Wulfstani*, 169, we learn that the roads in this fertile district ran between hedges.

At Gloucester itself, at the beginning of the reign of Henry, the long and beneficent rule of Serlo was drawing to a close. He, along with Godfrey of Winchester and Lanzo of Lewes, is singled out for praise above all other English superiors by Malmesbury. He had found only two monks and eight children in 1072, and left behind him a family of a hundred.[1] Gloucester, which became the monastic home of a number of cadets of great families, had for long a steady record of prosperity.

Within a few months of the death of Serlo the abbey of Tewkesbury came into being under circumstances already detailed. Abbot Gerald, the prime mover, after a rule of some years in which he laid foundations for the future and saw his community increase rapidly,[2] was accused, falsely as it would seem, on grave charges by one of his monks who had the ear of the king. Rather than undertake the labours and expenses of a formal defence he retired to end his days in seclusion at Winchester, his old home.[3] Orderic's account leaves no doubt that Gerald was among the ablest and most devoted superiors of his day, and Tewkesbury, like Gloucester, continued to flourish.

In contrast with their history in the previous period, little is known of Worcester and Evesham at this time, though it was during the early years of Henry that the accounts of the past at both places were brought to completion. At Worcester the tomb of Wulfstan was a centre of inspiration and devotion, and the house, besides being the home of the historians Florence and John, enjoyed the friendship of Malmesbury and Osbert of Clare. Farther north, the once fortunate abbey of Coventry continued to suffer from controversies with the diocesan.

In the east, the five fenland abbeys, Ely, Peterborough, Thorney, Ramsey and Croyland, had recovered from the disturbances of the early resistance to the Conqueror. The island of Ely, at that time the largest mass of dry land in the Fens, was surrounded by meres abounding in fish and waterfowl. The rich abbey was ruled by Norman abbots, who began to construct the vast fabric of the church, parts of which still remain as the most magnificent of all the buildings of the time, but the troubles would seem to have left a mark on the place, and the numbers did not grow. Instead of following the normal course of development it became, in 1109, the seat of a bishopric, and for many years its importance as a monastic house was small.

Of the history of Peterborough we have fuller record, due in the main to two chroniclers, the one being the vivid writer of the continuation of the old Saxon *Chronicle* from 1122 to 1154, who has left us the celebrated

---

1 Cf. Chronicle in *Monasticon*, I, 543; *Hist. Gloc.* 13.

2 *Registrum Theokusburiae*, foll. 1v.–3v.; 11v. In *Monasticon*, II, 81 (no. 87) the total is given as fifty-seven in 1105. This would seem very large for such a young community.

3 So OV, III, 13–16. *Ann. Wint.*, s.a. 1109, say: "regis animum nolens nec valens saturare muneribus."

description of the anarchy of Stephen's reign, the other his younger contemporary, the monk Hugh the White.[1] Both, alike in personal outlook and in their descriptions of events, have an individualism which has no parallel elsewhere. Intensely national in sympathies, they combine a love of the marvellous and the weird with a singular power of conveying emotion and portraying character. Peterborough, in the early part of the reign of Henry, was fortunate enough to have as abbot Ernulf, who had been a pupil of Lanfranc at Bec and subsequently a monk of Beauvais, which he left in order to become a disciple of Anselm, who appointed him prior of Christ Church.[2] He was taken from Peterborough to be bishop of Rochester, and the monks, so the annalist tells us, were deeply grieved, for he was good and gentle, and did good within and without the house.[3] In the *Chronicle* of Hugo Candidus, there is a digression after an account of Ernulf's buildings by one who wrote after Hugh's death, describing the chronicler and his early life. There were, he tells us, in the time of Abbot Ernulf (1107–1114), and for thirty years in all, two sacristans at Peterborough, Wictric and Reinald the Sprite. Reinald, the younger, owed his surname to his diminutive figure and his angelic character; he had, so we are told, the spirit of prophecy.[4] This Reinald attracted to the monastery his younger brother, Hugh, surnamed the White by reason of his pale and handsome face. As a boy he suffered from haemorrhages which brought him to the point of death; he was preserved, his biographer believed by miracle, and lived to extreme old age, beloved not only by his abbots and his brethren, but throughout the neighbouring houses.[5] He rose to the office of subprior and wrote his history, drawing largely upon the *Chronicle*.

Towards the end of the reign of Henry I, Peterborough suffered from the strange episode of the intrusion of Henry of St Jean d'Angely (1127–32). Henry was a Cluniac, and his appointment would appear to have been due to the king's favour for Cluny, shown in so many ways about this time. His arrival aroused the susceptible minds of the English at Peterborough, and their apprehensions, it would appear, were justified by the hard and selfish behaviour of the new abbot. The incident was recorded within a year or so of its occurrence by entries in the *Chronicle* which deserve quotation by reason of the vivid and even macabre power of language which they display:

This same year he [the king] gave the abbacy of Peterborough to an abbot called Henry of Poitou, who kept in his hands the abbey of St Jean d'Angely; and all the archbishops and bishops said that it was against right, and that he might not have two abbeys in his hands...he besought the king, and said to

---

1 For the Peterborough annalist *v.* Plummer, *Chronicle*, 1, 250–69 and notes.
2 Will. Malmesb., *GP*, 137–8.   3 *Chronicle*, 1114 [E].
4 Hugo Candidus, 67: "Wictricus senior erat et socium diligebat...Reinaldus vero Spiritus ita vocabatur quia parvus erat et spiritualis."
5 *Ibid.* 70.

him that he was an old man and a broken, and that he could not endure the great injustice and hostility there was in his own land...and the king obtained it [the abbacy of Peterborough] for him because he was his relative....Thus miserably was the abbacy given him in London between Christmas and Candlemas, and he came to Peterborough, and there he dwelt just as a drone does in a hive. All that the bees take in the drones devour and carry out. So he, all that he might get within and without, from learned and unlearned, he sent overseas; and he did no good there and left no good there.

Let no man think the truth we tell is strangely told, for it was very well known over all the land that as soon as ever he came there...then soon thereafter many men saw and heard a many hunters hunting. The hunters were black and huge and hideous, and they rode on black horses and black goats. This was seen in the very home park in the town of Peterborough, and in all the woods between that town and Stamford, and the monks heard the horn blown that they blew in the night. Trustworthy men who watched them in the nights said that, as it seemed to them, there might well be twenty or thirty horn-blowers. This was seen and heard from the time that he [the abbot] came thither through all that Lenten tide till Easter.[1]

The monks did not get rid of this incubus till 1132, though during one of his absences in 1131 they had elected an abbot of their own. Henry was finally persuaded to depart by the bishops of Salisbury and Lincoln, the two powerful brothers, and even so the abbey nearly went to Henry of Winchester, another Cluniac who already held Glastonbury. Ultimately Martin, a monk of Bec, at the time prior of St Neots, was appointed; he was an excellent abbot, as was shown in the days of Stephen.[2]

The neighbouring monastery of Croyland was at that time on an island, accessible only by water, though it lay upon a trade route and had many visitors.[3] It possessed, in the body of Waltheof, a relic reputed to work miracles, which remained an object of bitter controversy between Normans and native English even till Malmesbury's day. In 1109 the place received as abbot Godfrey of Orleans, then prior of St Évroul, who had been through the schools and had considerable literary talent. At Croyland he encouraged learning and began the new church. During his abbacy his old *confrère*, Orderic Vitalis, spent at his invitation five weeks at Croyland, and while there composed a short life of St Guthlac at the request of the monks,[4] to which he added a brief history of the place. Godfrey was succeeded by an abbot of very different origin, Waldef, brother of Cospatric, earl of Dunbar; he was a monk of the house, to which doubtless he had been attracted by family ties.

---

1 *Chronicle*, 1127 [E]. The version is mainly that of Stevenson, *Church Historians of England*, II, i, 160–1. The passage, as the annal for 1128 shows, is absolutely contemporary with the events; the same story is given by Hugo Candidus, 74, and is as insipid in Latin as it is effective in English—a point always to be borne in mind when reading Latin chroniclers of the time.

2 OV, v, 16.   3 Will. Malmesb., *GP*, 321.

4 OV, II, 268: "Fratrum benigno rogatu, cum quibus quinque septimanis Crulandiae commoratus sum, venerabilis Goisfredi abbatis caritativo jussu."

Near Peterborough also lay Thorney. To judge by the words of admiration which he lavishes upon it, Malmesbury had visited the place and found it more to his taste than the marshes of Glastonbury.[1] Like its neighbours, Thorney was an island, and its privacy was jealously guarded. Both Malmesbury and Orderic state that no woman was allowed to visit it save to pray at its shrines; even the servants left the island on feast days. Malmesbury describes its natural beauty as resembling a paradise on earth. Lofty trees, stretches of green turf, fruit trees and vines occupied every foot of the land. Thorney had been exceptionally fortunate in its Norman superiors. To Fulcard, a man of letters and a musician, had succeeded in 1083 Gunter, a monk of Battle.[2] Gunter, who was thirty years at Thorney, formed his community upon the observance of Marmoutier; he built the church, and entered the presbytery in 1098; by 1108 the whole building was complete.[3] He was succeeded by Robert, a monk of St Évroul and friend of Orderic, who states that he surpassed Gunter in learning, being famed throughout England for his eloquence.[4] Nothing, perhaps, in all the records brings before us more vividly the force of the new life that came to England from the Norman monasteries than the pages which the historian devotes to the eminent men who endeavoured to impart, in the solitude of the fens, what they had learnt in the schools and great abbeys beyond the Channel.

Ramsey, between Peterborough and Ely, rivalled the fertility of Thorney. The richness of the soil is, indeed, still shown by the acres of fruit plantations that lie between Earith and Cambridge, but familiarity with an England that has everywhere been disciplined for centuries, and a desire for hills and undulating woods and swift rivers cause us to read the glowing descriptions of the Ramsey chronicler with surprise, for the country round Ramsey, on the edge of the fens, is now comparatively bare of trees, and the horizon is unrelieved by hill or wood. It is strange to contrast these pages with the almost contemporary Cistercian accounts of the *loci horroris et vastae solitudinis* where we now admire the exquisite beauty of the valleys wherein lie the ruins of Fountains and Rievaulx. Ramsey, however, for all its natural advantages, had been less happy than its neighbours in its superiors, and was destined to remain an unfortunate house till towards the end of the twelfth century.

East of the fenland lay the great abbey of St Edmundsbury, where was the shrine of the martyred king who, at least before the death of St Thomas,

---

1 Will. Malmesb., *GP*, 326: "Paradisi simulacrum, quod amenitate jam coelos ipsos imaginetur." OV, IV, 281, remarks on the variety of the trees.

2 *Chron. Bell.* 31–2.

3 *Annales Mon. de Thorney*, Brit. Mus. Cott. MS. Nero, c. 7, *sub annis*.

4 OV, IV, 282–3: "Rodbertus autem . . . eruditione sublimior exstitit et ingenti constantia necne [= necnon] facundia inter praecipuos totius Angliae praelatos emicuit. . . . [He adds] His itaque dictis de amicis et notis sodalibus, etc."

was the national saint of England.[1] Richly endowed in land, with estates and churches up and down the eastern counties, it was surpassed by none in buildings and rich ornaments.[2] But although there are fair records of Bury during the struggle for exemption before 1100, and from Jocelin's time ample material for a view of the house, little is known of its life and fortunes during the reign of Henry, though the protection of the distinguished nephew and namesake of St Anselm for twenty years as abbot (1121–48) must have guaranteed steady growth.

Norwich had been founded at the very end of the century by the reformed Herbert Losinga, and carefully ruled by him. A doubtful authority speaks of more than sixty monks there in his day;[3] we have Malmesbury's word for it that they were numerous twenty years later, and he speaks in warm terms of their observance and hospitality.[4]

On the edge of the land, among what we now know as the Broads, lay the abbey of St Benet's of Holme. It received, in 1127, another of the *confrères* of Orderic as abbot, William Basset of St Évroul, but it was never a place of much importance. Farther south, the young abbey of Colchester was under the long rule of Gilbert, a monk of Bec (1117–40).

Two houses of the first rank remain to be mentioned, Westminster and St Albans. We are strangely ignorant of the history of Westminster until the end of the twelfth century, and even the dates of the abbots are uncertain. Gilbert Crispin's long term of office lasted till 1117; he represented the purest traditions of Bec, and the English-born Osbert of Clare is in the next generation a proof that letters and theology were still honoured in the house. Westminster was not yet the centre of royal and national activity that it became later, but its proximity to London and its privileged position brought it early into conflict with the diocesan.

St Albans, which claimed and vindicated for itself the premier place among all the black monk houses of England, may be regarded with some justice as the house which showed the fullest combination of all the characteristics of its order. In its liturgical observance, in the splendour of its architecture and decoration, in its encouragement of learning and the arts within and without its own body it holds a place above all others in the twelfth century, and during at least the first half of that period it was a centre of fervent spiritual life. In other respects, also, it has a place apart. We know more about its dependent priories and cells, more about the school it maintained, than we know of those elsewhere, and the rich-

1 Cf. Will. Malmesb., *GP*, 152–3: "Sanctus Edmundus...qui quasi rex et princeps patriae compatriotarum sanctorum primus palmam laudis vendicaret."
2 *Ibid.* 156: "Edifitiorum decus, oblationum pondus, quale et quantum in Anglia nusquam." Bury's material prosperity was largely the work of Baldwin.
3 Cf. Norwich MS in *Monasticon*, IV, 15: "lx et eo amplius."
4 Will. Malmesb., *GP*, 151: "Monachorum congregationem numero et religionem percelebrem instituit [Losinga]." 152: "Tam nobile monasterium...in quo nichil frustra desideres vel in edifitiorum spetie sublimium vel in ornamentorum pulchritudine, tum in monachorum religione et sedula ad omnes karitate."

ness of material accumulated by its historiographers, and especially by
Matthew Paris, allows us to trace the character and methods of government of its abbots, and their relations with the community. Many of these
points will be glanced at in later chapters; here it is only possible to sketch
the outline of the whole.

Neither the pre-Conquest history of St Albans nor its financial position
in *Domesday* explain the pre-eminence to which it attained.[1] Its success
was rather due to a succession of great abbots, all of whom except Paul,
the first, were monks of the abbey, to a steady influx of distinguished
recruits, to one or two strokes of fortune such as the elevation to the
papacy of Nicholas Brakespeare, and to a number of imponderable causes
which created a *genius loci*. The birth of the twelfth century found Abbot
Richard at the beginning of his rule. His accession had marked the victory
of the numerous Norman party in the house over the diminishing native
English.[2] Richard himself was a Norman of noble birth, the relative of
Robert Bloet of Lincoln and the friend of St Anselm. Under his rule the
possessions and the influence of St Albans grew steadily; other monasteries
received superiors from it and copied its institutions.[3] The abbot enriched
it with a mass of precious objects, hangings and books; he dedicated the
new church built by his predecessor in the presence of the king and queen
and numbers of bishops and barons in 1115. He was succeeded by Geoffrey,
also a Norman of distinguished family, kinsman of Robert de Lucy, whom
he introduced to the royal circle;[4] his early history is not without interest.
Summoned from Maine by Abbot Richard to take charge of the school in
the town he delayed, and the post was given to another. He therefore set
up a school at Dunstable till the place should fall vacant again; while there
he chanced to organize a miracle play in honour of St Katharine, and as
part of the properties borrowed a number of copes from the sacrist of
St Albans. His house was burnt down, and with it the copes, and Geoffrey,
at a loss how to make reparation, "offered himself as a holocaust to God"
in the monastery. For that reason, notes the chronicler, he was most
diligent when abbot in making copes, and it is interesting to note that he
established St Katharine's day (on which he was blessed as abbot) in the
calendar of St Albans.[5] Abbot Geoffrey made a whole series of liturgical
and dietary regulations; he also founded a hospital for lepers on the

1 Eleven houses were richer than St Albans; its income of £269 was exceeded three times
over by the richest, Glastonbury.
2 *GASA*, I, 66: "Determinata lite quae in conventu exorta fuerat inter Normannos, qui
jam multiplicati invaluerunt, et Anglos qui, jam senescentes et imminuti, occubuerant."
3 *Ibid.* 69: "Et floruit ordo monasticus, emanans a claustro S. Albani, ita ut aliae, quasi
candela a candela, illuminatae informarentur." I have noted seven abbots chosen from St
Albans during the century—a number surpassed only, I fancy, by the cathedral priories
of Canterbury and Winchester, viz. Bernard (Ramsey), 1102; Walter (Eynsham), 1129;
Godfrid (Croyland), 1138; Laurence (Westminster) and Germanus (Selby), c. 1150;
Nicholas (Malmesbury), 1183; Acarius (Peterborough), 1200. To these may be added
Samuel O'Haingly, bishop of Dublin, 1096 [Eadmer, *Hist. Nov.* 73].
4 *Chron. Bell.* 65.   5 *GASA*, 73, 75.

London road, and built a large guest hall, with a special chamber, called the Queen's Room, for the queen, who was the only woman permitted to lodge there. He also built a convent for some enclosed nuns at Sopwell, supervised the greater part of the construction of the magnificent shrine of St Alban, made by Anketil, a monk goldsmith, and caused the body of the saint to be solemnly translated on 2 August 1129. The chronicler of the house, in two long passages, gives a list of the ornaments and vestments of stuff and jewels, the metal work and precious illuminations which were the gift of Abbot Geoffrey; they give even to the printed page something of the opulence of a blaze of colour.

During his long rule (1119–46) three persons, reputed to be of unusual sanctity, affected the life of St Albans. These were Roger the hermit, originally a monk of the house, Christina, a recluse at Markyate, and Sigar, a hermit at Northaw. Unfortunately, the notices of their lives have not come down to us in their contemporary form; that of Christina, however, was clearly based on a document written shortly after her death.[1] Roger, like others of the period, especially in the north, taking literally the words of the Rule,[2] had left the monastery for a hermitage on the Dunstable road, where he was joined by at least five others. After some years Christina, a girl of wealth and position at Huntingdon, left her parents to become an ancress and put herself under his guidance; she was enclosed in a cell alongside of Roger's.[3] For more than four years she lived thus, and it is interesting to learn that the great Thurstan of York, who entered the lives of so many of the holiest of that age, was the friend of Roger, who consulted him concerning Christina's way of life and who introduced her to the archbishop.[4] After Roger's death Christina inherited his hermitage and was joined by some companions; Abbot Geoffrey knew her well, and though at first sceptical,[5] was in time so deeply impressed by her sanctity that he asked her advice on all matters of spiritual and practical importance.[6] In time, he founded the nunnery of Markyate

1 *GASA*, I, 97–106. As the editor remarks (p. 97, note 1) these pages do not occur in Paris' version, but are an addition made by one of the continuators. The facts, however, are clearly not the invention of a later hagiographer, and a *Life* of St Christina is referred to, *ibid*. 105. Roscarrock's *Life of St Christina*, printed by C. Horstman in *Nova Legenda Anglie*, II, 532–7, adds little of interest; it contains, however, the probably authentic statement that it was Thurstan who annulled the marriage into which she had been forced.

2 *Reg. S. Benedicti*, i, 5–13.

3 The following detail is clearly authentic. After a vision which seemed to imply that the conclusion of her suffering was near: "'Laetare mecum', ait [Rogerus] sermone vulgari, 'myn gode Sonendayes doghter'—id est, mea bona Dominicae diei filia—quia vestra tribulatio est in proximo terminanda."

4 *GASA*, I, 100: "Eo tempore venit ad partes Thurstanus, archiepiscopus Eboracensis, amator et fautor castorum studiorum, et Rogero, propter sanctitatem suam, fidus et devotus amicus."

5 *Ibid*. 102: "Abbas Normannorum more mox ad hoc intumuit, et ancillae Christi ne somniis crederet remandavit."

6 *Ibid*. 102–3: "Christina, igitur, tanto studio Abbatis invigilabat saluti ut...si facto vel verbo Deum offendisset, illa per spiritum in momento cognosceret." The writer refers to Christina as the "dilectrix" of the abbot, and the latter is quoted as referring to her as

for herself and her companions; she seems to have outlived her protector, for we are told that when Abbot Robert, soon after the accession of Adrian IV in 1155, repaired to Rome, he took with him many precious gifts and "three mitres and some sandals of exquisite workmanship, which had been most carefully prepared by" Christina. The Pope refused the other gifts, but accepted these, because the workmanship was so marvellous.[1] Of Sigar the hermit we only know that he came nightly from his hermitage to St Albans for the night office and that he and Roger were buried in the abbey near the monks' choir, where their tombs were venerated by pilgrims, gentle and simple. Whatever may be thought of the miraculous element in the lives of Christina and her associates, none familiar with the religious life of the age will overlook the real historical importance of such documents. The existence of such types of sanctity in the vicinity, and the encouragement of them by St Albans and its great abbot, are a sure proof that the things of the spirit had a real value within its walls.

III

The foregoing survey of some of the principal abbeys of England will enable the reader to make a number of general observations. It will have been seen that the period was on the whole one of expansion and development within a framework already existing, and that at the same time this development was in almost every case of importance due to men who came from abroad and aimed at realizing in their new homes and imposing on their family the spiritual and intellectual formation they had received in flourishing monasteries abroad; there was thus a continuous influx of new and higher life, which prevented stagnation and the isolation of the individual monastic families. Other tendencies there were, as we have already seen, making for a more static and self-centred life, and these were in time to prevail. For the present, however, the latter were less powerful than those making for growth and for the sharing of a common ideal. The great abbots were still primarily the teachers and leaders of the minds and spirits of their monks, concerned to give the twofold formation of spiritual doctrine and letters. Later, they were to become rather the representatives of their communities in external relations, and trustees of the manifold interests concerned, but so long as they were primarily teachers, the monastic order still remained for the majority of the inmates of the monasteries a way of life and a formation of spirit and mind directed primarily towards the perfecting of the individual, within which he could live and grow continually. This was to change later, when the

---

dilecta domina mea; the sanctity of both was well known. We think of Francis and Clare of Assisi, and of another Francis and Mme de Chantal.

1 GASA, 127: "Quia admirabilis operis."

monasteries lost their position as unique centres of culture and when their inmates became more and more occupied with the administration and exploitation of their varied possessions and obligations. Indeed, the cultural work of the great Anglo-Norman abbots of the early twelfth century was doomed for a twofold reason to have only a transient influence: the culture they gave, the literary, meditative culture of the "monastic centuries", had ceased to be the chief intellectual power of Europe, and, even had the future been with it, no intense culture could survive in so many scattered and remote centres. A teacher from St Évroul, ruling a Thorney or a Croyland, might create a circle of light among the young monks, and give to a few of the more gifted some of his own zeal and accomplishments, but no long succession of teachers could be hoped for which might preserve the tradition at its height; that could be expected only at a very few of the greatest houses. And while the lead in culture was passing from the black monks—and indeed the English flowering under Henry I was in a sense a "lag" from the past—they were ceasing also, for other reasons, to be the spiritual leaders of north-western Europe. Despite all the new life which the Norman revival had created in France and England, the Anglo-Norman monasticism was no more than a lineal descendant of the life which had been traditional since the age of Charlemagne. It was a life primarily liturgical, in which neither manual work nor solitary prayer had any large part; it was also a life in which contact of all kinds, administrative, social and intellectual, with the world at large was frequent. In England more than in any other country at the beginning of the twelfth century this life was still animated by real spiritual fervour and satisfied the highest needs, but abroad this was not so, and the English monasteries were soon to witness the invasion of a new form of the monastic life which was destined directly and indirectly to affect every department of their life and history.[1]

[1] For a table showing the increase in the number of religious houses between 1100 and 1175 v. Appendix XIII.

CHAPTER XI

THE NEW ORDERS

I

Between the age of Alfred and the opening of the twelfth century the history of monasticism in England is the record of a series of impacts from neighbouring countries across the Channel which brought different interpretations of a single way of life which had its roots deep in the medieval past. The impulses from Fleury and Ghent under Dunstan, from Normandy at the Conquest and from Cluny shortly afterwards were each a wave of a single tide. With the end of the century this tide reached its high-water mark; within a few years a confused mass of waters was seen to be approaching from a new sea, the flood tide of the European renaissance of the twelfth century.

Hitherto, since the decline of the ancient civilization, the spiritual and intellectual revivals in the West had been regional in origin and scope; even that under Charlemagne is scarcely an exception to the rule. In England, the ages of Alfred and of Edgar are examples of such a rebirth, but the most striking of all is also the last in point of time, the intense development within the ring-fence of the Norman territories. This, indeed, which has too often been studied in isolation, could only have reached such a perfection because the minds of the men who moulded it belonged to a new age, and the very decades which witnessed the evolution of this last great self-sufficient, self-contained *Landeskirche* saw also the growth of a new culture which transcended the bounds of kingdoms and duchies, and of minds capable of grasping and applying principles of wide and unified government. In monastic history, as in the history of learning and of the papacy, this new life showed itself first in numberless isolated strivings towards an ideal imperfectly grasped, and next in a series of attempts, growing more and more successful, to embody this ideal in an institution whose influence should reach beyond the nation to all Christendom. Alike in its spiritual, intellectual and political manifestations, this renaissance is clearly distinguishable from the smaller movements that had gone before by two characteristics—an increased intensity and clarity of vision, and a new appreciation of the legacy of the distant past. Just as in dialectic and theology minds such as those of Anselm and Abelard were of a calibre and temper that had not been seen for centuries, and just as the civilians, canonists and philosophers went back to Justinian, Gelasius, Plato and Aristotle for foundations on which to build, so in the circles of monastic reform a Peter Damian, a Romuald and a Stephen Harding had a clarity of vision and a resolution of aim wholly different

from those of Odilo, Dunstan or William of Dijon, and consciously
turned back to the past, as seen either in the bare text of the Rule of St
Benedict, or in the earlier doctrine of the deserts of Egypt and Syria.

Seen in a bird's-eye view the new monastic movement falls quite clearly
into two great tides, each having its rise in Italy and flowing north,
separated by an interval such that when the first is reaching northern
France the second is in flood south of the Alps. In the first individuals or
small groups leave the world, or long-established monasteries, to live
under conditions of extreme simplicity either as hermits or in groups
under no supreme authority; in the second, a series of attempts is made
to organize a new form of life, more solitary and more austere than contemporary monasticism, at first informally, under the authority of a
single leader, later more definitively under a written rule and within a
framework sanctioned by Rome. Logically regarded, the first tide should
have merged into the second, and this did indeed often come to pass, but
very often the individual ventures died away without fruit, and not infrequently, as it were in the gap between the tides, even the most earnest
of the community ventures reverted to type after a period of life in isolation, and became new centres of normal black monk life. Such was the
case at Cava in Italy; such, as we have seen, was the course taken by Bec
in Normandy, and Jarrow, Whitby, Selby and Malvern in England.

The new monastic movement, considered as a historical phenomenon,
had its origin in Italy a little before the year 1000. Italy, always a land of
many cities and of wild but habitable mountainous districts, had in the
fifth and sixth centuries been a land of hermits. Existing before St Benedict
and surviving the cenobite call of the Rule, the race had perhaps never
wholly died out, even in the north and centre of the peninsula, and in the
south, which still formed part of the Byzantine Empire, anchorites and
Basilian monks continued to live in considerable numbers. At the end of
the tenth century, a time of decadence in the social life of the cities of
Lombardy and among the clergy high and low, preachers of penance
and the eremitical life began to appear afresh. The revival which they
heralded had a twofold current; there was the call to a solitary, penitential
life, and the conscious recall to the spiritual legacy of the East.

One of the first who revived the memory of the past in central Italy
was St Nilus (c. 910–1005).[1] A Calabrian by birth, familiar with the
Greek Fathers and monastic saints, and himself of austere life, he visited
Cassino and Rome and ultimately founded the Basilian monastery of
Grottaferrata, which still exists on the slopes of the Alban Hills within
sight of the papal city. He was only one of many disseminators of Greek

---

1 For Nilus v. *Acta SS*, September, VII, 262 *seqq*. He knew the works of St Gregory
Nazianzen, Theodoret and the Fathers (*ibid*. 272); cf. *Life*, § 2: Ἠγάπα γὰρ ἀεὶ τῶν ἁγίων
πατέρων τοὺς βίους ἐκ νεότητος αὐτοῦ, Ἀντωνίου φημὶ δή, Σάββα τε καὶ Ἱλαρίωνος, and
§§ 15, 47. For his visit to Cassino and Rome v. pp. 303, 313, 317.

traditions at the time, for the Turkish invasion of Asia Minor sent large numbers of refugee bishops and monks to Europe, who settled in north Italy and southern France, especially near Dijon and Lyons, and even penetrated to England.[1]

The other, more eremitical, movement may count as its first important figure St Romuald of Ravenna (*c.* 950–1027). Although we have the advantage of possessing a life of Romuald written within a few years of his death by his great disciple, Peter Damian, the chronology of his career is highly uncertain.[2] He belongs to that large group of reformers, almost peculiar to the eleventh century, who after beginning the religious life in some old-established monastery, left the old ways in search of greater solitude and severity and passed many years of wandering in which they influenced several groups of disciples, dying at last without leaving any fixed or permanent institute of their creation to survive them. Such, in outline, was Romuald's story; and if the sequence of events is obscure, his main purpose is clear. Becoming after his conversion a monk of the Cluniac house of San Miniato at Ravenna, he steeped himself in the literature of the desert fathers, and wished to restore to the monastic life its earliest traditions of solitude and asceticism;[3] at the same time, by what seems to us something of a paradox, he desired to preach the monastic vocation to all as the one haven of salvation.[4] He left behind him, in embryo and far from the retreat in which he died, the institutes of Fonte Avellana, a congregation of hermits in the Apennines, and of Camaldoli, a community of monks near Arezzo living as hermits within a single group of buildings, but coming together for the liturgical prayer and on certain days for meals in a common refectory. In both communities silence was all but perpetual, and the fasts were of great severity. Fonte Avellana soon came under the influence of Peter Damian, but it was not for more than half a century after Romuald's death that the practices of Camaldoli were stabilized as a Rule, and that the order was made a double one by the addition of houses of cenobites following St Benedict's Rule interpreted literally and strictly.

1 Cf. the bishop *natione Graecus* who endeavoured to buy Ely in 970 (*Liber Eliensis*, 106), and the Greek monk Constantine at Malmesbury *c.* 1030 (Will. Malmesb., *GP*, 415–16); also Sackur, *Die Cluniacenser*, I, 324, 348, for the Armenian hermit Simeon and others.

2 *PL*, CXLIV, col. 953 *seqq.* It was written (col. 953) *tria fere lustra* after Romuald's death, i.e. *c.* 1042.

3 Cf. a very illuminating passage in the *Vita*, col. 962: "Contigit autem ut aliquando [*sc.* Romualdus in initio suae conversationis] librum de vita Patrum legens, in illum locum incideret ubi continetur quod quidam fratres, per continuam hebdomadam singulariter jejunantes [the reference is probably to Palladius, ch. 24 and ch. 106], Sabbatorum die pariter convenirent, etc. Quem vivendi ordinem statim Romualdus arripuit, et in eo quindecim fere annis...continua austeritate permansit." Cf. also col. 1002 for a clear imitation of Nitria.

4 So Damian tells us, doubtless somewhat rhetorically (*Vita*, col. 988): "totum mundum in eremum convertere, et monachico ordini omnem populi multitudinem sociare." For another side of Romuald's piety, *v.* his prayer (col. 983): "chare Jesu, chare, mel meum dulce, desiderium ineffabile, dulcedo sanctorum, suavitas angelorum."

A younger contemporary of Romuald, and one influenced by him, was St John Gualbert of Florence (*c.* 990–1073). After the striking and familiar episode which led to his becoming a monk at San Miniato, he left that monastery, desiring greater perfection, and stayed for a time at Camaldoli. Ultimately, however, he left the eremitical life and went to live at Vallombrosa near Florence, where he founded a cenobite monastery following the Rule of St Benedict but defining its scope very strictly and giving it precision and limits in favour of a purely contemplative life. Thus silence was perpetual, enclosure absolute and manual work forbidden. In order to secure quiet for the monks by taking business administration out of their hands he added to them a body of non-clerical *conversi*, and thus may probably be taken as the first to give formal sanction to a system which in one form or another was to influence so profoundly the future history of monasticism and of the religious life in general.

Neither Romuald nor John Gualbert wrote a Rule, still less did either found an order. Indeed, to attribute to any leader before the end of the eleventh century the conception of an order—that is, an articulated religious institute with a peculiar form of government and supra-regional extension—would be anachronistic, for such a body demands as a *sine qua non* a Church in which are functioning centralized powers of government and control, and such a state of things did not exist till the epoch of Gregory VII. But both Romuald and John Gualbert established bodies which later became orders, and though these both remained small and for all practical purposes cisalpine, the reputation and ideals of both travelled far and wide. At Camaldoli we can see present almost all the elements that reappear less than a century later north of the Alps at the Grande Chartreuse and later still at Grandmont; Vallombrosa, besides giving to almost all subsequent religious bodies the system of lay brethren, served also as an inspiration for those who wished a life of greater seclusion within the four corners of the Rule.

The greatest single influence, however, in what may be called the campaign of propaganda for a severely ascetical, quasi-eremitical monastic life was that of Peter Damian, who alike in writings, words and actions stands in something of the same prophetical relation to his age as does St Bernard to the age that followed a century later. Damian, at least until recent years, has probably been the object of less study and more misunderstanding than any other medieval figure of equal magnitude and significance.[1] His fame has suffered both from the scantiness of records

---

[1] Although Damian touched contemporary history at a number of decisive points, no adequate contemporary *Vita* or modern life exists, and the various biographical articles and other accounts, such as those in the *Dictionnaire de Théologie catholique* and the *Cambridge Medieval History*, are little more than a string of facts or a synopsis of his theological treatises. There is an excellent account of his activities as one of the pre-Gregorian reformers in A. Fliche, *La Réforme grégorienne*, vol. 1; in English, by far the most illuminating account is

of the time, and from the reputation he acquired of an intransigence amounting to ferocity. When his activities and writings are regarded more closely, however, his mental and spiritual powers appear at better advantage; not only is his title of Doctor of the Church seen to be merited by his sane and central position in the controversy concerning simoniacal ordination, but his spiritual outlook while opening, so to say, in one direction upon the desert, can be recognized as including in its scope much of the devotional sentiment of the new age of which Anselm and Bernard were to be the masters.

Peter Damian, like Romuald and Gualbert, came from a city family of Ravenna. Unlike them, he had as a youth entered fully into the new intellectual life of the schools of Lombardy before his conversion and entry into the Romualdine hermitage of Fonte Avellana, and this circumstance probably explains, as in similar cases throughout the ages, his frequent harshness of tone and exaggeration when criticizing the career he had abandoned. He early became a vehement advocate of a monasticism at once more austere and more eremitical than that of St Benedict and, trained as he had been in the schools that were so soon to develop into the universities of law, did not hesitate to defend his position with every kind of argument. More than once he met the critics who referred him to the words of the Rule which praise the common life by asserting roundly that the cenobitical life was a *pis aller* and had been recognized as such by the great legislator himself.[1]

Damian, like the Jerome to whom he bears some resemblance, wrote and acted with the fire of the moment rather than with the cold elaboration of logic, and in spite of his outspoken rejection of the traditional monastic life and his numerous controversies with abbots and monks, he retained a deep friendship and admiration for individuals and communities of the old model. One such was Monte Cassino itself, where in Damian's later life Desiderius, his colleague in the cardinalate, was abbot; another was Cluny, which he visited as papal legate in 1063, and to whose abbot and monks he wrote several letters of the warmest affection and praise.

---

that by Prof. J. P. Whitney in an article in the *Cambridge Historical Journal*, 1, 3 (1925). Damian's letters and spiritual treatises are, in the words of Dom Berlière, *L'Ascèse Bénédictine*, 78, "une mine trop peu exploitée pour la spiritualité [monastique]".

1 For Damian's method and programme *v.* especially his *ep.* xii to an abbot who had accused him of receiving the monks of another contrary to the Rule. He replies by quoting the first and last chapters of the Rule, and adds (*PL*, CXLIV, 393): "ad perfectionis igitur summam tendenti monasterium [as opposed to a hermitage] dicitur [*sc.* by St Benedict] esse non mansio, non habitatio, sed hospitium; non finis intentionis, sed quaedam quies itineris." 394: "Velut in convalle primae conversationis incipiat, deinde...tanquam a lacte ad solidum cibum transiens, verticem perfectionis ascendat." 395: "Dispensative constituit [Benedictus] prius monasterialis vitae planitiem, ut...jam facilius eremi conscendamus ad arcem.... fratres itaque in monasterio immobiliter permanentes, tolerandi sunt; ad eremum vero... transmigrantes plausibus ac praeconiis efferendi." It need scarcely be remarked that although the words of the Rule are not free from ambiguity, Damian's interpretation wholly falsifies the thought of St Benedict.

Besides these letters we have, in an account of the journey composed by his travelling companion, a still more detailed record of his appreciation of Cluny and its abbot, Hugh "the Great", but Damian was only at Cluny for a few days, and it was his nature to respond impetuously to a new impression; for all his generous appreciation, Cluny's way was not his, and there is evidence that even in his short visit he criticized some aspects of the life;[1] certainly years had not brought a change of outlook, for in a letter to his nephew, written later than his visit to Cluny, we find all the old fiery exhortation to penance, and depreciation of the easy life of a community as compared with the strictness of a hermitage.[2]

Damian, indeed, was not one of those spiritual teachers who build up a scheme for the soul's patient growth in perfection. His genius was to exhort and impel to the heroic, to praise striking achievements and to record edifying examples.[3] Yet in him, as in Romuald, along with much that recalls past ages and other climates, the reader meets with many traces of the new intuitions and an intimacy of devotion to the mysteries of Christ's life on earth and of his Mother's.[4] There are many sides to Peter Damian, as his hymns show—in particular the magnificent *Anglorum jam apostolus* to St Gregory the Great—and an extraordinary moral force burns in all that he wrote.

In monastic history Peter Damian's life and writings are of twofold significance. They show, first, a clear decision to return to the desert and its ways, not shrinking, if needs be, from the admission that the Rule of St Benedict is a mere propaedeutic or an easier way. Secondly, the hermit's life is held up to all souls of good will as the most perfect way of following Christ; no distinction is made or implied between different vocations, or between that to the active and that to the contemplative life. Few were found, in the age that followed, to hold these drastic opinions so fully and so explicitly. However individuals might act, the great monastic reformers north of the Alps were content to restore the cenobitical life to a supposed original purity, and the founders of the eremitical

1 Cf. *epp.* VIII, ii–v, and above all the tract *De Gallica profectione Domni Petri Damiani, PL,* CXLV, 865–79. These have already been quoted *supra,* p. 150. It is significant that even here the standard of comparison is the desert; e.g. col. 873: "veraciter ibi [at Cluny] multos reperi Paulos [i.e. eremitas], plurimos vidi Antonios, qui etsi solitudinis habitationem non incolunt, anachoritanum praemium imitatione operum non amittunt."

2 *Ep.* xxii to Damian (*PL,* CXLV, col. 405): "ad eremum ergo, charissime fili, sub omni celeritate revertere, ne dum monasterialis adolescentiam tuam latitudo delectat, eremi districtio...in odium veniat."

3 The personal reminiscence of an individual—"I knew a monk who..."—is characteristic of Damian; cf. *opusc.* xiii, *de perfectione monachi* (col. 325), for a monk who recited the whole psalter four times a day, and on four days a week neither ate nor drank; and *opusc.* li, *de vita eremitica* (col. 754): "porro autem duo in ejus cellula serpentes jam per plures annos, ut fertur, familiariter [!] spatiantur." The life of St Dominic Loricatus, Damian's companion, may also be consulted for similar curiosities of asceticism.

4 He was one of the most energetic advocates of the "Little" office of the Blessed Virgin. Cf. *epp.* VIII, xxix, xxxii, where he records the objection of a tepid monk: "satis superque sufficere quod sanctus praecepit Benedictus."

orders came to regard their institutes as meeting the needs of a peculiar and uncommon vocation.

Damian's direct influence north of the Alps was small. There is no evidence that his writings spread rapidly to a distance, and it is not to be supposed that he inspired all, or even any, of the numerous hermit bands of France, England and the Rhineland. These were commonly less logically consistent in their aims than the recluses of Camaldoli and Fonte Avellana. As in Italy itself, where the hermitage of Alferius at Cava near Sorrento became an abbey of the traditional type, so in France the hermit group under Robert of Chaise-Dieu (*ob.* 1067), and even the Vallombrosan foundation of Chézal-Benoît near Bourges became in time normal black monk houses. In all these cases, and in many others, we see the fervent individual, dissatisfied with contemporary monasticism, beginning anew in simplicity and attracting others of a like mind; then follows the rapid growth of the house, until its founder, who had not desired the eremitical life as such, and who certainly had no theoretical quarrel with the Rule, adopts almost *en bloc* the customs of an existing monastery, Cluny or another, having given to the monastic life an infusion of new vigour but no change of direction. It is the story of Benedict of Aniane repeated a hundred times, but the hour was now at hand for a new chapter to be written.

II

Under Gregory VII the various movements of reform, which in all countries save the Norman dominions were also movements towards independence of secular control, had found an abiding centre and leadership in the papacy, and in the same decades the desire for a simpler form of the monastic life than was presented by the wealthy houses of southern and central France was becoming more articulate, together with the sense that some sort of organization was needed that should perpetuate the benefits of a new start. The time had in fact come when the Western mind, here as in all other spheres of mental activity, was able and anxious to replace custom and tradition by law, and to rise from a system of personal dependencies to one of articulated government.

The transition was effected chiefly in two centres of independent origin which in time interacted upon each other in ways which can occasionally be traced and more often suspected, and the men who brought it about were of a different mental calibre and of a more elaborate training than their predecessors. The vague and often unintelligent and contradictory accounts of their lives must not cause the reader to forget that Bruno, Robert of Arbrissel, Vitalis of Mortain and Stephen Harding were the contemporaries, the equals and in some cases the friends of Anselm, Abelard, Ivo of Chartres, William of Champeaux and the other great masters of the intellectual revival, and were themselves men capable of making a wide search and a careful synthesis, no longer content to take without question the best available from the recent past. The two centres in which their action developed were in northern Burgundy, between Langres and Dijon, and on the confines of Maine and Brittany to the west.

The Burgundian focus, which had ultimately the preponderant influence, was also slightly the earlier in point of time to develop. The original nucleus, the grain of mustard seed which was to grow into such a vast tree, appears to have been a group of hermits, one of many such, living in the woodland of Colan, not far from Langres. These, hearing of the fervour of one Robert, a black monk who after early promotion and efforts at reform had become abbot of St Michel de Tonnerre, at first invited him to become their leader and subsequently obtained letters from Alexander II appointing him abbot. He removed his new community to Molesme, and there, c. 1075, they began life once again in huts made of boughs. The career and character of Robert are enigmatic; his many changes of habitation and returns to places he had left earned him a reputation for fickleness with some of his contemporaries and baffle the modern enquirer who has only inadequate sources of information;[1] the history of Molesme and of the early days at Cîteaux would seem to show at least that his clarity of vision and talent for organization were not above those of previous reformers and that, if he had not attracted disciples of another temper, not only Molesme, but Cîteaux itself, would have gone the way of similar ventures in the past. Molesme, indeed, so far as its history can be traced, seen perhaps through eyes somewhat dazzled by the later splendours of its offspring, appears to have rapidly degenerated when recruits and wealth arrived, and to have adopted the uses of monasteries around it.[2] In its early days, however, it was something of a cynosure, and lying as it did not far from the great roads connecting Paris and Lorraine with Lyons and Italy, attracted numerous visitors. Two of these were men destined to have permanent influence upon monastic life in the West. The one, Bruno, a well-known master in the schools and chancellor of Rheims, who had taken a vow to leave the world, stayed in the neighbourhood for some time c. 1080–2 in doubt whether to join the new foundation. In the event he passed on, to settle near Grenoble and lay the seeds of the order which others were to define and organize, but two of his companions, Peter and Lambert, remained, and we may perhaps

---

1 Thus Hugh, the celebrated archbishop of Lyons, writing to Robert, bishop of Langres, says what is to be done: "si deinceps eandem ecclesiam solita levitate deseruerit" (*Hugonis Lugdunensis archiepiscopi Epistolae et Privilegia* in *PL*, CLVII, 524). For an account of Robert somewhat differing from that above, *v.* W. Williams, *St Robert of Molesme*, in *JTS*, XXXVII, 148 (Oct. 1936), 404–12.

2 *Exordium parvum* (ed. Guignard), 68: "Depositis quorundam monasteriorum consuetudinibus."

recognize the former as one of the seven who urged for the move to Cîteaux.[1]

The other, to whose clear grasp of principle and tenacious will was due almost all that followed, arrived, we may suppose, somewhat later than Bruno. He was an Englishman, Stephen Harding, sprung from Sherborne in Dorset, who had left his native country in search of learning and of the perfect life. He had made a pilgrimage to Rome, and it was on his return that he joined Robert.

The community at Molesme soon found itself in the difficulty that awaited all such ventures. It had property and numbers; the simple day-to-day life under the direct command of the abbot was no longer possible; current uses were adopted and a number wished to interpret them as in other contemporary houses. Thus the original aim of simplicity and perfection was endangered; there was opposition to Robert and he retired for a time to a hermitage. In this crisis the decisive move came from Stephen Harding, the subprior, and Alberic, one of the original hermits of Colan, the prior.[2] A new move was proposed, in order to found a house in strict poverty and seclusion, with a literal observance of the Rule. Along with five companions, they put the matter before Robert, who apparently showed himself once more as willing to co-operate but unprepared to lay down a programme. After a final attempt to carry the whole house there was a secession in 1098, twenty following Robert into the forest of Cîteaux. The negotiations that followed are a well-known story and need not be recounted here. In the end, Robert returned to Molesme, and Alberic became abbot of Cîteaux with Stephen Harding as prior. This period lasted for ten years (1099–1109). The original purity of aim and internal observance was maintained, a new habit of grey-white was adopted, the accretions to the liturgy were dropped, manual work became normal, and papal approval was secured, but the simplicity and seclusion of Cîteaux like those of Molesme were threatened by the acquisition of property and treasures and by the presence of powerful benefactors. How far the peculiar and original features of the white monk economy—lay *conversi* and the "grange-system"—developed under Alberic cannot be decided with absolute certainty. When in 1109 Alberic died and Stephen was elected abbot, the new institute had at last at its head a man capable of conceiving, formulating and adhering to a coherent and complete programme of legislation which was calculated to make a break with past history and to provide a framework of great elasticity for developments which could not possibly have been foreseen.

1 *Exordium parvum*, 62: "Roberto...Alberico, Odoni, Joanni, Stephano, Letaldo et Petro." Alberic was one of the hermits of Colan.

2 The primary source for the story of the secession is the *Exordium Cisterciensis coenobii* (known later as the *Exordium parvum*) composed by Stephen Harding (ed. Guignard, *Monuments primitifs de la Règle cistercienne*, Dijon, 1878).

For the moment, however, it was not breadth and clarity of vision that appeared in the new abbot, but a more negative and less genial severity of view. Stephen refused to allow any of the powerful benefactors to stay at or near Cîteaux, and he decreed that in every department of the life the utmost simplicity should obtain. This simplicity, like the observance of the Rule *ad literam*, became a dynamic idea among the white monks; each was an easily comprehensible war-cry and in the hands of Bernard "the thing became a trumpet", but each was also easily misconceived: "literal observance" could easily become Pharisaism, and material simplicity Puritanism. Neither was peculiar to Cîteaux, or the greatest part of its true achievement.

For thirteen years Stephen held to his course in extreme poverty and hardship and with dwindling numbers. The collapse of Cîteaux seemed inevitable and imminent. The sudden change of fortune that came in 1112 when the young Bernard brought to the gate of the abbey, along with thirty companions, that portent of light and fire that was himself, is one of the most familiar incidents of medieval history. From that moment the future of Cîteaux was assured and the grain of mustard seed shot forth its luxuriant growth; indeed, it may be thought that the genius of Bernard effected not only an expansion, but a subtle and profound modification of the new order. But for the moment the assurance of growth impelled the less portentous, but scarcely less pregnant genius of Stephen Harding to legislate for the future. The issue of his thought took shape in the *Carta Caritatis* of 1119 and in the original *Uses*. Something will be said of these epoch-making documents in the following chapter; having seen Cîteaux become firmly established we must now consider the second great centre of revival.

III

There, in the woods and heaths of the marches of Maine and Brittany, a large congregation of solitaries had been formed. They were not, like the hermits of Colan, a single small band, but a heterogeneous assembly following various inspirations and leaders. A contemporary could compare them to the solitaries of the Thebaid in number; like those, also, they had a loose system of federation, meetings and conferences, and a routine by which recruits were assigned to a definite master; they had among their leaders a number of the most remarkable figures of their time—Bernard, later the founder of Tiron, Vitalis, the founder of Savigny, Ralph de la Futaye, founder of St Sulpice at Rennes, and Robert of Arbrissel, celebrated as an itinerant preacher and afterwards as the founder of Fontevrault.[1]

1 For these *v. Vita beati Bernardi Tironensis*, by Gaufridus Grossus, one of his monks, in *PL*, CLXXII, 1367–1446 (from *Acta SS*, April, II, 220 *seqq.*); *Vita b. Vitalis Saviniacensis*, by Stephanus de Fulgeriis, a chaplain of Henry II, later bishop of Rennes (*ob.* 1178), ed.

These men and their followers had been brought together by a common dissatisfaction with existing conditions among clergy or monks and a common desire for a way of perfection, but they were too diverse in character and aim to form for long a single family or to join in a single order.

Bernard (c. 1060–1117), originally a monk of St Cyprian at Poitiers, had a troubled and varied career not unlike that of Robert of Molesme, of which his biographer gives us glimpses without supplying the links of causality that might join the disconnected episodes. He appears now with the solitaries of Brittany, now alone at Chaussey on the coast opposite the Channel Islands, now as abbot of St Cyprian, now with Robert of Arbrissel and Vitalis on their journeys of preaching up and down the country. The final crisis of his life came when, as abbot of St Cyprian, he put up a determined resistance to the abbot of Cluny (the aged Hugh), who claimed jurisdiction over the place.[1] He retired for a second time to Chaussey, but soon gathered disciples and emerged from his solitude to found Tiron in 1109, meeting with warm encouragement from the great Ivo of Chartres. By this date Cîteaux had been in existence for more than ten years, and it is impossible that Bernard should have been ignorant of the aims and troubles of its first fathers. His own ideals were very similar. Besides the fervour and love of simplicity common to all the reformers, Bernard, like the Cistercians, wished to restore manual work to its (supposedly) original place in the monastic life, and was prepared to make room for it by abandoning all accretions of psalmody.[2] From another source it may be gathered that he differed slightly from the white monks in the scope he assigned to this work; instead of concentrating on field-labour, his monks (as, indeed, the monks of St Benedict's Monte Cassino) practised all the arts and crafts, and lay brothers were not an original part of the economy.[3] Tiron prospered, and rapidly became the mother of a considerable family which even for a time (so it would appear) included

E. P. Sauvage, in *Analecta Bollandiana*, I (1882), 355–90; *Vita b. Gaufridi* (the successor of Vitalis) probably composed some years later, ed. Sauvage, *op. cit.* 390–410; *Vita b. Roberti* [de Arbrissel], written soon after Robert's death for Petronilla, abbess of Fontevrault, by Baldricus, bishop of Dol, in *Acta SS*, February, III, 603–8; also the *Extrema Conversatio b. Roberti* (*ibid.* 608 *seqq.*), written by Andrew, a monk of Fontevrault, Robert's disciple and confessor. Details of the life in the forest of Craon *c.* 1096 are given in *Vita Roberti*, 1380–1; cf. *Vita Vitalis*, 381. A charter of Henry I, dated March 7, 1113, confirming the gift of the forest of Savigny to "Vitalis the hermit", will be found in *Calendar of documents preserved in France* (ed. J. H. Round), I, 287–8.

1 The outspoken criticism of the Cluniac system of government, alleged to have been pronounced by Bernard in the presence of Paschal II, *c.* 1105, is, even if not wholly authentic, a valuable indication of the feeling against Cluny, and that during the reign of Hugh (*Vita Bernardi*, 1401–2).

2 *Vita Bernardi*, 1404. It is significant that this act of retrenchment is attributed to a divine revelation. Nothing less could bring Bernard to take such a revolutionary step.

3 Robert of Torigni, *Tractatus de Immutatione Ordinis Monachorum* (written *c.* 1154), *PL*, CCII, 1312: "Hic [*sc.* Bernard at Tiron] omnes ad se venientes suscipiebat et artes quas noverant legitimas infra monasterium exercere praecipiebat." Needless to say, the reference is to common craft-work, not to artistic production.

Savigny and her daughters.[1] Owing to its situation in the north-west it attracted attention in Normandy and England sooner than Cîteaux and, as we shall see, sent a colony across the Channel as early as *c.* 1113. How far in these early years Tiron had a system of visitation and chapters approaching in perfection that of the white monks does not appear,[2] but in the event it resisted the attraction of Cîteaux and remained a congregation apart.

The foundation of Vitalis had a success still greater. Born near Bayeux, he became a clerk in the retinue of Robert, son of the Conqueror, and was afterwards a hermit, though he appeared not infrequently as a preacher, visiting London at the time of the council of 1102. After several years in the wild country near Craon he passed *c.* 1105, in search of greater solitude, to the forest of Savigny. Here he was joined, as Bernard at Chaussey, by disciples to whom he gave a rule of life; the establishment of Savigny as an abbey is probably to be dated 1112, the very year of the other Bernard's arrival at Cîteaux. Vitalis had not been a monk in the past; it is therefore all the more probable that he modelled his foundation consciously upon Cîteaux, which Savigny undoubtedly resembled much more closely than Tiron, as an almost contemporary observer noted.[3] Agricultural work, lay brothers and a system of visitation and general chapters appear very early. Vitalis, who died in 1122, was succeeded by his compatriot Geoffrey, who had been a monk of Cérisy; we are told that the observance was made more strict,[4] and to him was due the institution of an annual general chapter on the feast of the Trinity.[5] Savigny had a great vogue in the north of France and in England, where indeed its houses were from the first almost indistinguishable from those of the white monks, and among its sons were a number of saintly abbots. It lacked, however, leaders of the calibre of Stephen Harding and Bernard, and documents of the logical clarity of the *Carta Caritatis*, in which wheels engaged upon wheels with such precision. The machinery of Savigny worked less smoothly, and within less than fifty years of its inception the centrifugal tendencies were only arrested by a fusion (in 1147) of the whole body with Cîteaux.

1 *Vita Bernardi*, 1416, 1427. The (late) account of the foundation of Furness (*Furness Coucher Book*, ed. J. C. Atkinson, Chetham Society IX, (1886), 8; cf. *ibid.* 11) speaks of the house as belonging to the *Ordo Savigniacensis, i.e.* [? vel] *Tironensis*.

2 There was a triennial chapter at Tiron before 1120; it took place at Whitsuntide. Cf. charter of which a translation is given in *Calendar of Documents preserved in France*, I, 353–4.

3 Robert of Torigni, *Tractatus de Immutatione*, 1312: "Vitalis eremita optimus semini-verbius [preacher]…monasterium aedificans, modernas [i.e. of the new model] institutiones in aliquibus Cisterciensibus similes, monachis suis imposuit."

4 *Ibid.*: "[Gaufridus] multa monasteria aedificavit, et consuetudines prioribus arctiores Saviniensibus imposuit."

5 *Vita Gaufridi*, 405.

IV

Cîteaux, Tiron and Savigny, though a new model, were clearly branches of the tree of Western monasticism, and still held to the Rule as a basic code. More than one new order sprang from the centres of reform to break altogether new ground in this way or that, though remaining strongly tinctured with the tradition of the Rule. It has been noted that Bruno passed through the hermitage of Colan before settling at Grenoble and later in Calabria. The Chartreuse, which did not become an organized body for several decades, was long in arriving in England; it will form the subject of a later chapter.[1] The Vallombrosan plantation at Chézal-Benoît (1093), though its regional success was at first considerable, never colonized across the Channel. An eremitical order, however, which, whatever its precise derivation, had much in common with the Camaldolese and Carthusians, made later in its history a few settlements in England. This was the order of Grandmont, founded by Stephen of Muret *c.* 1100 near Limoges.

The chronology of Stephen's life and the influences that moulded him are alike uncertain, and it is no part of these pages to investigate them.[2] His order, which was strictly contemplative in character, though it remained fully cenobitical, had two peculiar features, one affecting its spirit, the other its organization. The one was a note of extreme, we may almost think ruthless, severity and poverty, joined to a silence and abstraction as absolute as that of the Carthusians. In a series of prohibitions Grandmont renounced not only churches, tithes and treasures, but lands, animals and fixed revenues; nor were the monks ever allowed to leave the enclosure. Cîteaux had secured simplicity of life, but had not abandoned the basic elements of a sparing livelihood; Grandmont carried the process *à l'outrance*, and in the event these severe regulations, after securing to the order a period of great celebrity, were the cause of bitter controversies. The second characteristic was the position given to the lay brethren. Already at Vallombrosa, the Chartreuse and Cîteaux the *conversi* had been used to do work and external business in order that the choir monks might be more free to devote themselves to spiritual duties, but hitherto the supreme administration had always been in the hands of monastic officials. Grandmont, here as elsewhere, carried an idea to its extreme logical limit, and gave to the lay brethren all the business administration of the house, and all but complete responsibility. Such an arrangement could not survive, and before the century was out a series of unfortunate

---

1 *Infra*, ch. XXII.
2 The *Vita S. Stephani* (*PL*, CCIV, 1065–72), composed by the seventh prior of Grandmont, is neither contemporary nor reliable; the so-called *Regula S. Stephani* (*ibid.* 1135–62) is not the work of the saint. There are two excellent critical articles on him and his order by Dom Raymund Webster in the *Catholic Encyclopedia* (1st ed.).

experiences caused its gradual supersession, but in early days the experiment was imitated elsewhere, and in particular, as will be seen, by Gilbert of Sempringham in England.

One more quasi-monastic institute must be mentioned, that of Fontevrault. This was the creation of Robert of Arbrissel, one of the leaders in the wilderness of Craon. Robert himself, who was not a monk in origin but a leading cleric of Rennes, was a preacher and spiritual guide of extraordinary energy and originality who directed his attacks against the current evils of the Church. After some time spent as a hermit, he founded a congregation of canons, but dissolved it to return to preaching; finally he became the head of a multitude of disciples of both sexes, and founded Fontevrault as a community of priests, lay workers and women on the model of the apostolic church.[1] The difficulties of the situation in which he was placed set, from time to time, somewhat of a cloud on Robert's reputation, and he met with severe criticism; Fontevrault nevertheless had a phenomenal success and gradually became a fully organized order with three members—the contemplative nuns, who were its centre, the lay sisters, and Robert and his priests, who served as chaplains and directors. The house became the most celebrated nunnery in northwestern France, and sent a colony to Amesbury in England, but its chief significance for this country is the inspiration it gave to Sempringham. The abbess of Fontevrault had jurisdiction over both nuns and monks; the latter dedicated themselves solemnly to the service of the former, and received from them their livelihood.[2] The superficial resemblance between this system and the double monasteries of the same neighbourhood four centuries earlier is very striking, but the differences between Whitby under Hilda and Fontevrault are very great, and the peculiar constitution of Robert's foundation was probably due to the situation and character of the founder, who had under his direction a number of able and high-born women, for whom he could only provide priests of humble rank and moderate attainments. In the sequel, Fontevrault, which was from the first organized on Cluniac rather than Cistercian lines, had a career of great prosperity for a century; it was founded c. 1100, and already at the death of Robert the community with its dependencies is said to have contained several thousand souls.[3] It early became, and long remained, a house in which daughters of the royal family and high nobility took the veil, and in this it was resembled by its English colony of Amesbury.

All the orders hitherto mentioned were at least in part monastic. On a

---

1 *Vita Roberti*, 605.

2 *Extrema Conversatio b. Roberti*, 609: "Quicquid in mundo aedificavi, ad opus sanctimonialium nostrarum fieri, eisque potestatem omnem facultatum mearum praebui: et, quod his majus est, et me et meos discipulos, pro animarum nostrarum salute, earum servitio submisi."

3 So *Vita Roberti*, 607: "Servos et ancillas Dei plusquam ad duo, vel circiter ad tria millia congregavit."

previous page something has been said of the Augustinian or "black" canons, whose life, though in broad outline monastic, was not directly based upon the Rule, and whose employment was often in teaching and the service of a public church. Midway between the Augustinian canons and the strictly monastic orders was the institute of "white" Norbertine or Premonstratensian canons. They owed their origin to Norbert (c. 1080–1134), a native of the Rhineland and a friend of St Bernard. Of high birth and great mental powers, a cleric converted to a fervent life, Norbert's own vocation was primarily missionary; he founded his order at the desire of Calixtus II near Laon in 1120 to provide for his numerous disciples. In its genesis the constitution of the white canons was eclectic, reflecting alike Norbert's own bent, his admiration for Clairvaux, and the contemporary spirit of simplicity and poverty. To preaching and spiritual ministration were joined a certain amount of manual work and a more severe observance than was customary in the general run of Augustinian houses; the order was strictly organized from the start on Cistercian lines, with Prémontré as the mother house. It had an immediate and great vogue in France and the Rhineland, attracting brilliant recruits and supplying the sees of the Continent with many bishops. In England, its arrival was tardy, and as late as 1170 only half a dozen houses were in existence. In the last decades of the century, however, it enjoyed a second spring of exceptional purity which lasted fully fifty years; in this the active, apostolic element was overshadowed by the monastic, and a number of abbeys were founded, frequently in desolate or remote situations, several of which long retained their reputation for fervour.

Finally, a word must be said of a purely English institute which arose out of the practical needs of the country, but which nevertheless borrowed almost all its constitutional framework from abroad.[1] Gilbert of Sempringham, when a parish priest in Lincolnshire, found himself in the position of director to a number of dedicated women; at the suggestion of William, first abbot of Rievaulx, who happened to stay with him while upon a journey, he added to his nuns a second branch of the order, that of the lay sisters.[2] Next, it was found that as the houses grew in possessions regular labour was needed to safeguard the cultivation of the land and the collection of the revenues. Here again Cistercian influence was at work,

---

1 The *Vita, Institutiones, Canonizatio, Miracula* and *Epistolae* of Gilbert are preserved in three MSS., viz. Brit. Mus. Cott. Cleop. B, I; Brit. Mus. Harl. MS. 468 and Bodl. MS. Digby 36. A considerable part of the *Vita* and *Canonizatio*, together with the *Institutiones*, is printed in the *Monasticon* (ed. Caley, etc., 1830), VI, ii, as an intercalation (pp. v–xcvii) between pp. 946 and 947, but many passages are omitted without any indication. The *Epistolae* have been printed as an accompaniment to an article by the present writer, *The Revolt of the Lay Brothers of Sempringham*, in *EHR*, L, 199 (July 1935), 465–87. Dr Rose Graham's valuable *St Gilbert of Sempringham and the Gilbertines* contains an excellent account of the saint and his institute.

2 *Gilberti Institutiones*, p. xxix: "Consilio abbatis primi Rievallis per me transeuntis et propositum meum laudantis."

for Gilbert was solicited by those who had seen or heard of the white lay brothers at work and wished to imitate their example. He therefore attached *conversi* to his nunneries.[1]

The order grew with unexpected rapidity. For a time Gilbert was alone in his responsibility for the spiritual and temporal administration, helped only by his lay brothers. Feeling himself unable to control the growing body and greatly admiring the white monks, he crossed to France in 1147 and proposed to the general chapter at Cîteaux that they should make themselves responsible for his order. It was, however, no ordinary year at Cîteaux; Eugenius III was present in chapter, and the Savigniac family was being received under its jurisdiction.[2] It is not surprising that the fathers were averse to further commitments, especially where women and lay brothers alone were concerned.[3] Gilbert was therefore confirmed in his administration by the pope himself, and decided to add a fourth member to his order by grouping together a number of chosen priests as canons who should be chaplains to his nuns. Finally, at a still later date, he consented to assume the office and title of Master.

For the rules governing the inner life of his communities he was content to take over what was already in existence; the nuns received the Rule of St Benedict, the canons that of St Augustine, and the lay brothers a very slightly modified version of the Use of the *conversi* of Cîteaux.[4] The written contribution of the Master consisted in little more than the careful and ingenious description of a double monastery which should give no occasion for scandal, and the elaboration of a scheme of government by Master and general chapter which gave the nuns a real voice in the settlement of their own affairs. Here, as in his liturgical dispositions[5] and elsewhere, Gilbert drew from many sources, and while the Cistercian constitutional documents are expressly cited as exemplars,[6] he had clearly studied besides the practices of Grandmont and Fontevrault.

His order continued to increase throughout his long life and beyond; at the time of his death in 1189, besides numerous hospitals for lepers and orphanages, he had founded more than a dozen monasteries of which

1 *Instit.* xxx: "Assumpsi mihi mercenarios, dans eis habitum religionis qualem habent fratres Cistercienses." Cf. *ibid.* lix and *Vita*, xi.
2 *Vita*, xi: "Ubi [*sc.* in capitulo] forte tunc aderat bonae memoriae Papa Eugenius." This gives us the date.
3 *Vita*, xi: "Dominus autem Papa et abbates Cisterciae dixerunt sui ordinis monachis aliorum religioni et praesertim monialium non licere praeesse."
4 *Vita*, xii: "Monialibus regulam beati Benedicti, clericis vero regulam Sancti Augustini tenendam proponens." Cf. *ibid.* xiii and *Instit.* xxx. Also *Instit.* lix: "Fratres nostri laici in modo victus et vestitus sequantur formam fratrum ordinis Cistercii qui morantur in grangiis"; and the charter of Alexander of Lincoln in *Monasticon*, VI, ii, 948.
5 *The Gilbertine Rite* has been edited for the Henry Bradshaw Society (2 vols. 1921–2) by Canon R. M. Woolley. The editor remarks (pref. xxv) that the "Use is generally speaking Cistercian. The body of the Missal is evidently copied directly from the Cistercian Rite... but on the other hand a considerable amount of variation [shows] great eclecticism as to the sources from which the various forms were derived."
6 *Instit.* xcvi: "Volumus Cisterciensis capituli vestigia sequi."

some ten were "double" houses of nuns and canons.[1] All the nunneries had a considerable staff of lay brothers and large communities of sisters. The cardinal legate Hugh, writing to Alexander III in 1175, reckoned the total of the nuns as high as fifteen hundred,[2] and the author of Gilbert's *Life* put the aggregate of the order at two thousand two hundred.[3] This was perhaps an exaggeration, but at some early period in its history it was found desirable to put a limit to the numbers of nuns and lay brothers by assigning quotas to the fourteen existing houses; the total allowed was 496 lay brothers and 960 nuns;[4] to these must be added the comparatively small groups of canons. All contemporary witnesses unite in praising Gilbert's nuns,[5] and there can be no doubt that from *c.* 1140 to the end of the century their houses enjoyed pride of place for fervour and observance among the monasteries of women in England.

The foregoing brief catalogue, though it may seem to have little to do with English monasticism, was necessary in order to give some idea of the ferment of new life in Italy and France which was soon to have influence upon this country. For the first time in the history of the western Church religious leaders and monastic reformers, instead of being content to adopt the Rule and traditional usages, were consciously breaking with the past and constructing new systems, and thus between *c.* 1100 and 1130 a striking change came rapidly over the various movements of new life; they took legal, formal shape; the framing of constitutions became widespread, and the decades which saw the civil law restored to honour under the influence of a newly revealed legacy from Rome, and the canon law receive a precision ever greater, saw also an activity in framing new systems of religious life to which a distant parallel may be found in the sudden impetus given to the framing of civil constitutions by the outbreak of the American and French Revolutions at the close of the eighteenth century.

1 Will. Newburgh, *Historia*, I, 55.
2 The letter is in *EHR*, L, 199, p. 483.
3 *Vita*, xiv.
4 *Instit.* xcvii.
5 E.g. Ailred, *Sermo II de Oneribus* (*PL*, cxcv, 370); cf. also *ibid.* 789 in the treatise on the nun of Watton, and the letter of the legate referred to above, note 2.

CHAPTER XII

THE NEW MODEL OF CÎTEAUX

I

THE CONSTITUTIONAL FRAMEWORK

Of the many ventures in reform and renovation of which mention has been made in the preceding chapter, one, that of Cîteaux, stands in a place apart. The extraordinary rapidity and extent of its growth and diffusion, and the influence which it exerted during the greater part of the twelfth century on the life of the Church, public and private—an influence which was largely the work of a single man, Bernard of Clairvaux—these would alone suffice to give the Cistercians a significance possessed by no other contemporary body. They have, however, a still further importance for the history of the religious life, for their success and influence rested upon a written code and constitution of great originality, which inspired numerous imitations from the first and which has helped to mould, to a greater or less degree, the organization of all subsequent monastic or quasi-monastic bodies. It may be added, also, that while none of the other new orders affected in any marked degree the religious history of England, the Cistercians, from the first years of their arrival until the Dissolution, exerted a great and powerful influence over the religious and social life of the country. It is therefore necessary, before examining the history of the first foundations, to consider in what way the institute of the white monks differed from that of the black.

Bernard entered Cîteaux in 1112; Clairvaux was founded in 1115, as one of the four "first" foundations; the *Carta Caritatis* was completed in 1119; within a few years the white monks were everywhere. The expansion and cohesion of the body would alike have been impossible had it not been already in possession of documents which served both to enunciate its ideals and to safeguard by legislation the principles of internal and external economy.[1] These documents are three in number,

---

1 The essential documents for the early history of Cîteaux have often been printed; the best text is that of Ph. Guignard, *Monuments primitifs de la Règle cistercienne* (Dijon, 1878). Besides the Cistercian text of the *Rule*, a *Kalendarium* and appendices, Guignard prints: (i) *Exordium Cisterciensis cenobii* (later called *Exordium parvum*); (ii) *Carta Caritatis*; (iii) *Consuetudines*, embracing (a) *ecclesiastica officia*, (b) *instituta generalis Capituli*, and (c) *Usus conversorum*. The only important piece not printed by him is the *Exordium magnum*, written c. 1180 and containing the early history of Clairvaux and other houses (*PL*, CLXXXV, 995 *seqq.*). Of the numberless short accounts perhaps the best is Dom U. Berlière's chapter in *L'Ordre Monastique*; for a more detailed appreciation *v.* the same writer's article *Les Origines de Cîteaux* in the *Revue d'histoire ecclésiastique*, I (1900), 448–71, II (1901), 253–90. For a still more detailed analysis, *v.* the articles by P. Gregor Müller in *Cistercienser Cronik: Die Entstehung der Charta Charitatis* and *Das Exordium parvum* (1897); *Gründung der Abtei Cîteaux* (1898); *Cîteaux unter dem Abte Alberich* (1909); *Cîteaux in dem*

and to them may conveniently be added a fourth, which took final shape a little later. The first is the *Exordium Cisterciensis Cenobii*, a documented account of the secession from Molesme and the early years at Cîteaux up to *c.* 1115. Though anonymous in form, it may be accepted with confidence as the work of Stephen Harding, the last paragraph being a later addition.[1] The second is the list of *Consuetudines* for monks and lay brothers. These would seem to have been chiefly the work, or at least to date from the rule, of Alberic, second abbot of Cîteaux (July 1099–26 January 1109). The third is the *Carta Caritatis*, a short but exceedingly important constitutional document which, composed before the order had spread widely, legislated for all inter-relations and inter-dependencies of the various houses, and for the election of all the officials. This also was the work of Stephen Harding.[2] To these may be added the *Instituta* or definitions of the annual general chapters, first codified in 1134 and reaffirmed with a few additions in 1152.[3] The earlier prescriptions do little more than put existing practice into formal language. Of these four documents, the first three mark with sufficient clearness three stages in the development of the Cistercian idea.

The exodus from Molesme was made with no thought of founding an order; the one aim of the group was to lead a life of evangelical perfection in congenial surroundings. Their motives are made quite clear by the narrative of the *Exordium*. They felt a deep conscientious conviction that life under conditions governed by the customs traditional in monasteries of their province was a constant transgression of the monastic profession as defined by the Rule of St Benedict; they therefore desired a life at once more severe and more retired. To secure this, they sought to place themselves first under the protection of the Ordinary of the diocese, and later under that of the papal legate, Hugh, archbishop of Lyons.[4]

Jahren 1109–1119 (1916). Dom J. M. Canivez, in *Statuta Capitulorum Generalium Ordinis Cisterciensis*, vol. I (1933), prints the *Carta Caritatis* (pp. xxvi–xxxi) and the early statutes (pp. 12–33); his text is the same in essentials as that of Guignard.

1 The self-effacing reference to Stephen as *quidam frater stephanus nomine anglicus natione* (*Exordium*, ed. Guignard, 73) has usually been taken as proof confirming the tradition that Stephen was its author. The extremely simple, abrupt, yet powerful style in which the narrative is cast bears this out. The *Exordium* was probably written before 1119, but the reference to twelve foundations in the penultimate paragraph fixes the final redaction between 22 March and 18 October 1120, the dates of the twelfth and thirteenth foundations (Guignard, préf. xxxiv). The last paragraph, describing the visit of (the late) Eugenius III in 1148, is an addition, *ad perpetuam rei memoriam*, which has no connection with the rest.

2 The *Carta Caritatis*, solemnly approved by Calixtus II on 23 December 1119, was probably composed before October 1118, the date of the first foundation by one of the "elder daughters".

3 So Guignard, préf. xv. St Raynard is usually credited with the collection.

4 Cf. the letter of the legate Hugh, archbishop of Lyons, to Pope Paschal II, in *Exordium* (ed. Guignard), 68: "Exeuntes propter artiorem et secretiorem vitam secundum regulam beati benedicti." Hugh, it may be remembered, was an intransigent, ultra-Gregorian reformer. "C'est un réformateur convaincu….Une prodigieuse activité, qui s'allie à une extraordinaire rigorisme, tel est le trait dominant de son caractère" (A. Fliche, *La Réforme grégorienne*, III, 205).

When once the external severance was complete, it was necessary to decide two questions of the utmost importance. First, what form was their rejection of the customs which had grown up against or beside the Rule to take? Secondly, what changes were to be made in the economic organization of the house in order to secure the degree of austerity and retirement for which they longed, and to prevent the recurrence of the abuses which they deplored? The answers given to these questions mark the difference between Cîteaux and all similar ventures in the past, and made of the place a new model. They can perhaps best be analysed in tabular form.[1]

I. They rejected radically all sources of luxury and wealth, as well domestic and artistic as economic and ecclesiastical.

(a) All articles of clothing and common use; and all foodstuffs not specified in the Rule, were abandoned. These rejections included cloaks, shirts, warm hoods, drawers, bedspreads and combs, as well as all food not specified in the Rule and the manifold extra dishes, flesh-meat and lard that had been introduced in many monasteries.

(b) Every kind of ornament or superfluity in the liturgical life was rejected. Crucifixes were to be of painted wood, not gold or silver; candelabra were to be of iron, thuribles of copper, chasubles neither of fustian nor of linen, nor with precious decorations; albs were to be of linen, not silk; chalices of silver, not gold; copes, dalmatics and tunicles were abolished. This particular legislation, we are given to understand, was largely due to Stephen Harding,[2] and was clearly directed against contemporary exuberance; it is familiar to all from the early diatribes of St Bernard.[3]

Although so often stressed by historians, this part of the negative legislation of Cîteaux has no peculiar significance, save in its thoroughness; it was part of the programme of every contemporary monastic reform.

(c) They renounced all possession and exploitation of feudal sources of wealth, such as manorial bakeries, mills, fairs, courts and serfs.

(d) Still more vehemently they renounced all income from the possessions of the Church, such as private churches, advowsons, rights to customary offerings, altar and burial dues, and all tithes.

---

1 The whole of what follows will be found set out with admirable terseness and completeness in *Exordium*, 71–4. The *Consuetudines* and decrees of chapter do little more than gloss the text. It is, however, noteworthy that while the changes affecting personal life and economic arrangements occur under, and are attributed to, abbots (Robert and) Alberic, those referring to art and decoration are explicitly attributed to Stephen Harding (73–4).

2 *Exordium*, 73: "Hujus [*sc.* Stephani] temporibus interdixerunt fratres una cum eodem abbate, etc."

3 E.g. *Bernardi Apologia ad Guillelmum* (*Bernardi Opera*, ed. Mabillon, Paris, ed. 1836, II, 1221–46); *Ailredi Speculum Charitatis*, II, 23–4 (*PL*, CXCV, 571–2).

II. They resolved to choose and receive for their foundations only land far from habitation, to be tilled and exploited solely for the uses of the community, and principally by its own labour. It was here that their practice and legislation, for all its simplicity, was an original creation, whatever its models in the past; it had also dynamic force. Faced with the need of securing labour, and of escaping from the evils of the normal system of rents, revenues and serfs, with all the complicated machinery of organization and administration, they made two great innovations. As even in the more spacious horarium of Cîteaux it was clearly impossible for the choir monks, while accomplishing all their spiritual duties, to devote the number of hours necessary each day to performing the field and farm work of a large estate, they introduced lay brothers to do the bulk of the work.[1] And, in order to cope with the stocking, storage and exploitation of extensive properties without resorting to the farm-rent, they established an altogether new system of isolated centres of exploitation (*curtes*, later *grangiae*) on the lands at a distance from the abbey, to be staffed by lay brothers.

III. Along with the destruction of obstacles and the constructive reorganization of the material and economic life of a monastery, went an even more important readjustment of its internal life. The primary aim of the fathers of Cîteaux was a spiritual one, to secure for the individual the means of sanctification; and although the legislative documents do not explicitly criticize the normal black monk horarium, the time table that was evolved shows clearly that they were convinced that it left far too little time for serious work and private prayer.[2] The tripartite division of St Benedict had, as we have seen, long given place to a life of two parts, prayer and study, or even (in the case of Cluny) to one of a single employment, liturgical service. In this matter the work of Cîteaux was drastic. All the accretions of centuries to the *Opus Dei* were thrown aside, save for the conventual Mass and the relatively short office of the dead, which was recited on certain days only. The office of all saints, Litanies, processions, visits to altars, Gradual and "prostrate" psalms, even the early or "chapter" Mass (save on certain days), all went, and with them all the elaborations of chant and ceremonial. To pass from Ulrich's long description of the day at Cluny *c.* 1090 to the Cistercian *Consuetudines* gives the reader something of the sensation of passing from a stale and heavy atmosphere into the fresh air. Once more there is space to move about in.

To take the place of the abandoned vocal prayer and ceremonial, both work of the hands and reading—the *lectio divina* of the Rule, not study or

---

1 From the very beginning hired (not serf) labour was also permitted when needful.
2 In the letter of Archbishop Thurstan to William of Canterbury, written in 1132, Prior Richard of York is quoted as saying: "certa quidem tempora ordinavit [beatus Benedictus] lectionis et orationis instantiae, certa quoque tempora laboris industriae" (in *Memorials of Fountains*, ed. Walbran, Surtees Society, XLII, 14).

artistic work—became once more a reality, and the *Consuetudines* expressly state that private prayer is allowed in the church at will during the periods allotted to reading.[1] On Sundays and some fifty other days during the year no manual work was done by the choir monks; reading and prayer took its place, and on these days there were two community Masses. In addition to these changes, a number of very important innovations affecting the whole life were made from the first in practice, and later embodied in legislation. One of these, that all recruits should make a regular noviciate of a year, was not strictly an innovation, but a return to the Rule, but in Cluniac and some other quarters the contrary custom was so normal that the Cistercian prescription had all the appearance of originality. More truly original was the decision that there should be no school of oblate children in a monastery, and that no one should enter the noviciate under sixteen. This ran counter to the Rule and to the practice of centuries; but it was a salutary change, and besides making the monastic life a real choice and vocation it was in harmony with the sentiment of the new age. The Cistercian monastery thus had no semblance of a school, and the pursuit of literary or scholastic fame was attacked in another regulation which forbade the writing of books without the consent of general chapter—a prohibition of which the effect was largely nullified in a short time by the activities of Bernard, Ailred and other distinguished authors among the white monks.

By this thorough, scientific reorganization of the internal and external life of the monastery the Cistercians solved with conspicuous success the problems that had beset all who had previously wished to break with the past and present. Within, they had achieved a way of life which disciplined and nourished all the physical and spiritual powers; without, they had created a self-sufficient economic unit which had the further advantage of enlisting and spiritualizing the labour of a great class of men hitherto excluded from the monastic life. There remained the old danger that all would vanish with expansion, and that either the centrifugal forces would rend the unity of the body or lack of control would lead speedily to decadence. It was for Stephen Harding and his counsellors to show that here, too, in the constitutional order, they were capable of evolving a masterpiece.

IV. For a masterpiece the *Carta Caritatis* assuredly is. With a rigid economy of words, and the utmost clarity of thought, it created in a few pregnant pages[2] all the machinery of a great order and defined the spirit that should inform its action, and while its prescriptions had all the simplicity that makes a new revelation seem but the enunciation of a

---

1 *Consuetudines* (ed. Guignard), 172: "Ad orationem vero ire possunt in ecclesiam non solum tunc [*sc.* after chapter] sed et omni tempore lectionis, et ad omnia intervalla."

2 The *Carta Caritatis* contains some 1680 words, and occupies but six pages in Guignard.

familiar truth, they were so comprehensive and so peremptory that no essential additions were ever needed in the sequel. It is one of the small group of documents that have influenced, in the course of the Church's history, the constitutional history of all religious bodies subsequent to their composition.

Hitherto, outside the family of Cluny, the only bond of discipline between monasteries had been the temporary and personal authority of a reformer. Cluny, in the later phase of her development, had made the personal authority of the arch-abbot permanent; but she had evolved no legal or administrative machinery to implement his rule, and experience had shown that while the efficient exercise of such wide powers was beyond the capacity of a single man, the mere existence of such a central authority paralysed the healthy and necessary action of those dependent upon it. Cîteaux therefore had a twofold end to secure—efficiency in central government combined with an autonomy of the members without which their spiritual and social welfare would be endangered.

The primary desire of the framers of the *Carta Caritatis* was to secure the permanence of the achievement of Cîteaux in all her offspring, or, in other words, to guarantee a uniformity by which, as the *Carta* itself says, "the abbeys in different parts of the world might be indissolubly united in soul, even though parted in body".[1] In so doing, the autonomous life of each house was safeguarded, and no monarchic position was given to the mother; at the same time Cîteaux retained her place as the fountain-head and was distinguished as the only place of assembly for all.

Uniformity was guaranteed by the imposition, not only of a single body of *Consuetudines* (i.e. a complete disciplinary and liturgical directory), but also of identical service-books for all community exercises. This, though a novel institution, was in itself only a negative safeguard. The two supreme contributions of the *Carta Caritatis* were the provisions for a yearly visitation of each abbey by the abbot of the founding house,[2] and for a yearly assembly of all heads of houses for general chapter at Cîteaux.[3] The maintenance of a uniform discipline was thus secured, as fully as

1 *Carta Caritatis* (ed. Guignard), 79: "Elucidaverunt et statuerunt suisque posteris reliquerunt quo pacto quove modo immo qua caritate monachi eorum, per abbacias in diversis mundi partibus, corporibus divisi animis indissolubiliter conglutinarentur."

2 *Ibid.* 81: "Semel per annum visitet abbas majoris ecclesiae per se vel per aliquem de coabbatibus suis [i.e. the abbots of the four first foundations] omnia cenobia quae ipse fundaverit." The system of regular visitation was not of course novel. It had been instituted for the cenobites of Egypt by Pachomius (292–346), *v. Historia Lausiaca* of Palladius (ed. Butler), I, 234 *et al.*, and from early times (e.g. the First Council of Orange) the yearly canonical visitation of his diocese by a bishop had been taken to include monasteries, though the custom had fallen into desuetude. Reforming bishops had always claimed the right, e.g. Burchard of Worms (*Decreta*, VIII, 67). The novelty was that monastic superiors should visit and should have a minute code on which to base their examination.

3 *Ibid.* 81: "Omnes abbates de ordine nostro singulis annis ad generale capitulum cisterciense omni postposita occasione convenient." This, also, had been a practice in the Pachomian monasteries, and the Fathers of Cîteaux may well have derived the idea thence. In more recent times it had been unknown.

human wisdom could provide, by means of a single code enforced by visitation, examination and additional legislation, and if in isolated cases disciplinary measures failed, it might reasonably have been hoped that the constant interchange of meetings and contact with the living spirit of the order as seen in the body of reigning abbots would supply the necessary moral force. Besides these two great creative prescriptions, the *Carta Caritatis* contained exact instructions concerning abbatial elections and resignations, together with various questions of misbehaviour and precedence, and arrangements for the visitation of Cîteaux herself by her four elder daughters.[1] Finally, just as the general chapter of abbots was given full power to enforce discipline and compel the resignation of unworthy abbots, so the four abbots of the elder daughters were given similar authority over the abbot of Cîteaux. This was undoubtedly a precaution taken not only to avoid a *débâcle* such as that of Pons at Cluny, but also to prevent the abbot of Cîteaux aspiring to any kind of monarchy.

The early definitions of general chapters did little but interpret aboriginal tendencies and define existing tradition. Thus the very first statute decrees that Cistercian foundations are not to be made in cities, fortified places or villages; another, ordering that monks shall live by their own work, legislates for granges, stating that they must not lie more than a day's journey from the mother-house and that choir monks shall not be in charge of them or reside in them;[2] yet another lays down that the abbot of each daughter-house should pay a "return" visit to report on his charge to the founding abbey;[3] and a number apply the principles of uniformity and simplicity to particular points.

The monastic life that flourished under this body of legislation was very different from that of the traditional, long-established black monk abbey. As regards the choir monks, the particulars already given will have indicated much of its character. It was a life of greater seclusion, simplicity and uniformity; it was also a life in which the day was divided between vocal and liturgical service in church, spiritual reading together with silent prayer, and hard manual labour out of doors. It was thus a life ordered solely for the spiritual good of the individual monk, and the pioneer character of the first half-century of plantation, especially when inspired by the clarion call of Bernard, made of this life a wholly new vocation of which something will be said later.

Alongside of the choir monks were the *conversi*, often the more numerous body; and as the Cistercians were the first to legislate in detail for lay brothers, it may be well to glance at their special *Uses* which, like the rest of the early documents, bear all the marks of clarity, sanity and

1 The four "elder daughters" were La Ferté (17 May 1113), Pontigny (31 May 1114), Clairvaux and Morimond (25 June 1115).

2 *Instituta capituli generalis*, c. lxviii (Guignard, 269).

3 *Ibid.*, c. xxxiiii (Guignard, 260): "Semel in anno saltem matrem ecclesiam per abbatem suum si sanus fuerit visitet filia."

wisdom. It is presupposed that the *conversi* are wholly illiterate,[1] and it is expressly forbidden that they should possess books or learn anything save the *Pater, Credo, Miserere* and a few other simple formularies that made up their daily vocal prayer, and even these they were to learn by heart, not in writing. Their sleep was somewhat longer than that of the choir monks; their food of the same quality but slightly larger quantity within the monastery and considerably more plentiful in the granges. They visited the church for a short period before beginning the day's work, and again before retiring; they had short and simple prayers, consisting of the *Pater* and *Gloria*, for each canonical hour; on some thirty or forty days in the year besides Sunday they·attended one Mass, and on some of these days two, but they only received Holy Communion seven times a year; they worked in silence save for strictly necessary conversation about the work in hand. It was thus a hard life of extreme simplicity, and presupposed the existence of a large class of men wholly illiterate. In England at the present day it is hard to reconstruct even in the imagination the social conditions of the twelfth century, but in the rural districts of south Germany and elsewhere in Europe lay brothers in great numbers may still be found living the same life of absolute simplicity. In the early twelfth century the appeal made by this vocation to the illiterate, who had for many centuries been neglected by monasticism, was immediate and widespread.

The seclusion and uniformity of the life of the choir monks, the absence of all servants, and the presence of lay brothers, made of the white monk abbey as an architectural, social and economic unit something quite different from one of the greater black monk houses. Whereas the latter was normally at or near a centre of population or pilgrimage, and indeed often created such a centre where it did not already exist, the Cistercians invariably settled in a remote or at least an unencumbered site, and never (while faithful to the original ideal) allowed it to become a secular resort. And whereas in a black monk abbey the monastic cloister and offices were surrounded by an outer ring of courts and buildings for the reception of guests, pilgrims, poor and stores of all kinds, the whole enclosed within a ring-wall outside which lay the houses, streets and fields, a white monk abbey consisted of the necessary monastic buildings, with simpler, if extensive, ranges of offices within a precinct-wall, the whole lying among·the meadows and arable owned and worked by the monks.

Considered as an economic unit, a black monk house was for all practical purposes exactly on a par with the barony of any other lay or ecclesiastical lord. That is to say, its lands consisted mainly of manors, each with its demesne-land worked by the service due from the various classes of the rural population, and a residue held by tenants. The actual

---

1 *Prologus in capitula usuum conversorum* (Guignard, 278): "Qui simpliciores et sine litteris esse noscuntur." This prologue is written in the first person: "Miror", etc.

labourers were in every case men of all grades from serfs to those completely free.

In contrast to this, the ideal aimed at by a white monk community (that is, one faithful to the original ideal) was to settle on undeveloped land, and, instead of owning a number of scattered manors and smaller holdings, each of which was a centre of independent life, to be possessed of a single great *bloc* of land, in which the only centre of economic life was the abbey, the granges being little more than depôts. With all necessary reserves, a comparison may be taken in the modern world from the property of a great corporation such as Trinity College, Cambridge, which comprises farms, fields, cottage holdings, city houses, glebe, advowsons, and funds of all kinds, as contrasted with the vast single area of a cattle or sheep ranch in the Argentine, with its one ranch house and its scattered and isolated huts, stores and byres. In a white monk estate, all the exploitation was effected, not by the casual population, but by the choir monks, by the lay brethren, and by a certain number of hired labourers when necessary.[1]

Finally, the Cistercian grange was a very different thing from the black monk "cell". The latter was a small settlement of choir monks (from a single individual to half a dozen or more) on land at a great distance from the mother-house; often, indeed, the Channel lay between. Its purpose was simply to supervise distant estates or secure the possession or service of an important church, and theoretically it was a monastery *in parvo*. The grange, in contrast, was merely a collection of farm buildings with a small oratory and common dining and sleeping accommodation, which served as a subcentre and depôt for the exploitation by lay brothers of land in the neighbourhood of the abbey, but too distant for it to be practicable for the labourers to walk each day to the scene of their work. The lay brothers there in residence, besides being changed from time to time, returned to the mother-house for great festivals and at other fixed seasons.

Such, in brief, were the aims and institutions of the new order that was to sweep like a tide over Europe, and in particular over England and Wales, in the course of the twelfth century. If the Cistercian movement is to be understood, the vital principles must be grasped, together with a realization of the novel element they contained, before any attention is given to the personalities and controversies that were so soon to emerge. Before the influence of Bernard made itself felt, Cîteaux had, in addition to its vast reserve of spiritual force, a clear-cut programme and a constitutional framework eminently adaptable to the needs of a growing order.

---

[1] Students of medieval institutions may perhaps feel that the above paragraphs simplify unduly a complex fabric in order to emphasize a contrast. No doubt most Cistercian abbeys, especially in agricultural regions, had from the first scattered lands and quasi-feudal commitments. It remains true, however, that the first fathers made a resolute attempt to escape from "feudal" economics.

II

THE INFLUENCE OF BERNARD

As has been said, Bernard had no share in the original spiritual impulse and the body of legislation of the Cistercians, and although his arrival at Cîteaux marks the moment when the miraculous expansion began, it is conceivable that another occasion might have supplied a more normal impetus to a religious body which possessed all the essentials for fruitful increase. Tremendous as is the figure of Bernard, it must not be allowed to occupy the whole canvas in a picture of the early twelfth century. The epoch was one of the most varied growth: schools, tribunals, commerce, town life were all in a ferment of new movement, and the renaissance of letters, of law, of philosophy and of science, was proceeding apace, accompanied by a rapid development in the arts of architecture and sculpture. To think of the age as in any sense dominated by the monastic ideal would be wholly misleading.[1] Even within the sphere of ecclesiastical history ample room must be left for other men and other forces. Besides the other new orders, several of which had a success that would have been phenomenal fifty years previously, there were in the high politics of the Church several groups that remained both powerful and antipathetic to, or at least quite distinct from, the spirit of Clairvaux. In particular, there was the group of bishops and cardinals, some of whom were constantly employed on important legations, belonging to the family of Cluny—Henry of Winchester, Gilbert Foliot, Matthew of Albano, Imar of Tusculum and many others. And it was an age of eminent and learned bishops, from Ivo of Chartres and William of Champeaux and Orleans to the Lombard of Paris and John of Salisbury and Chartres.

But when all reserves have been made, the impact of Bernard's dynamic personality on his age still appears tremendous.[2] Indeed, it is difficult to name any other saint in the history of the Church whose influence, both on the public life of an epoch and on the consciences of a multitude of individuals, was during his lifetime so profound and so pervasive. This influence, if coldly analysed, is seen to have lain primarily in direct contact by means of the spoken and written word with Bernard's galvanizing energy. Great as has been the power of his thought on all succeeding

1 Some idea of the luxuriant life of the century may be gained from such books as *The Renaissance of the Twelfth Century*, by C. H. Haskins (Cambridge, Mass., 1927), *La Renaissance du xiie siècle: Les écoles et l'enseignement* (G. Paré, etc., Paris and Ottawa, 1933) and the works of Pirenne and Halphen.

2 For Bernard E. Vacandard's *Vie de S. Bernard* (2 vols. 1895–7 and subsequent editions) is still essential. It may be supplemented by the same writer's article on Bernard in *Dictionnaire de Théologie catholique* and by the more recent one by Dom Anselme Le Bail in *Dictionnaire de Spiritualité*. In English, the fullest account is that by Watkin Williams, *St Bernard of Clairvaux* (Manchester, 1935); on Bernard's spiritual doctrine *v.* relevant sections in Butler, *Western Mysticism*. There are many vivid and penetrating appreciations in Dr G. G. Coulton's *Five Centuries of Religion*, vol. I.

ages of the Church, especially in the sphere of the devotional and spiritual life, Bernard is not among the greatest of philosophers or theologians, nor among the great monastic legislators. The unique quality of his genius was to excite spiritual energy and set it in motion, and it is for this reason, perhaps, that the movements of which he was the centre lost almost all their momentum with his death. But within his own monastic body his personality, active for almost forty years, altered the whole scope and focus of the institute, and when it disappeared circumstances had so changed that it is idle to speculate what would have been the subsequent history of the white monks had Bernard never been, and had they numbered fifty houses instead of three hundred in 1153.

Briefly, Bernard may be said to have affected the Cistercian order in three ways. In the first place, it was Clairvaux, not Cîteaux, that was primarily responsible for transforming a small, fervent centre of reform into a way of salvation for the nations, attracting to itself numberless *âmes d'élite* from among the higher clergy and other religious bodies as well as hosts of the less spiritually gifted, whose vocation to that particular form of life was far from imperative. Cîteaux thus lost, once and for all, the possibility of remaining, like the Chartreuse, a way of life for individuals with a very peculiar and strong call, and it became instead an ark containing every kind of living thing, a net holding every manner of fish. The strain that this expansion imposed on every joint of the constitutional fabric of the order was terrific; it survived, but without any reserve of elasticity and resistance.

Secondly, Bernard was largely responsible for the missionary and controversial activities in which the white monks so speedily became involved. Here again, something of the kind was perhaps inevitable, but Bernard's natural genius, like that of Napoleon, shone brightest in a combat, and he had a gift of inspired leadership and of triumphant propaganda which gave to his words, as to those of a Demosthenes or a Tertullian, an intoxicating efficacy.

Finally, his growing prestige, together with the spread of the white monks, made it possible and perhaps inevitable that he should become a great and growing force in the public life of the Church, and that he should use his order and its leaders as his marshals and storm-troops. During the last twenty years of his life, and above all during the last ten, when his old disciple Eugenius III was pope, his life and that of the Cistercian body was closely interwoven with that of the papacy and of ecclesiastical reform, as understood at Clairvaux, in all the lands north of Rome. In this campaign he was undoubtedly greatly aided by the Cistercian fabric of government, for which he was in no way responsible. The system which bound the daughter so closely to the mother made of the prolific Clairvaux a centre of greater power than Cîteaux, while the annual general chapter provided a platform whence attacks of all kinds might be launched.

It would be outside the scope of these pages to essay any kind of estimate of the profit and loss that accrued to the reputation of the white monks throughout Europe as a result of Bernard's life-work. The above brief analysis of the character of his influence was necessary, if only because it will be seen at work in the same directions in England.

III

THE CISTERCIAN VOCATION

When we consider the wide extent and the phenomenal rapidity of the development of the Cistercian order, and the vast number of individual lives involved, it is natural to enquire what was the nature of the appeal that exercised such power, and to seek for an answer in the documents of the time. Setting Clairvaux aside and considering only the outstanding personalities in England—Henry Murdac, master and teacher at York; Richard, prior of the great abbey of St Mary in the same city; Ailred, friend and favourite of King David of Scotland; Waldef, the nobly born prior of the canons of Kirkham; Maurice, scholar and subprior of the cathedral monastery of Durham—what, we ask, led these men, and a great company of others less celebrated and less gifted, to leave all and enter the Cistercian noviciate?

Throughout the history of the Church, the great monastic corporations and the religious orders have professed, at root, but one thing, the perfect following of the precepts and counsels of Christ in the gospel. They invite men, that is to say, to aim at, to tend towards, not the natural perfection of a life in a human society, but the supernatural perfection of a life of abnegation of self and imitation of Christ; without exception they presuppose at least the external, material observance of the three great abnegations to which Christ called—that of property, that of marriage and that of the individual's liberty of external action. Yet since every man can fail, to a greater or less degree, to follow what he knows to be righteousness and justice, and since not only individuals, but corporations, classes and even nations and civilizations can and do (within certain limits) wax and wane in moral and spiritual force, the great religious bodies, in general and in particular, pass through accesses and declines of fervour. What may be called the normal state is one neither of marked fervour nor of scandalous decadence. The life as lived accords with the profession of Christianity; duties, spiritual and temporal, are on the whole efficiently and reverently discharged, and though there may be a number of individual lapses and apostasies, there are also a number who rise above the average to the level of conspicuous virtue. This normal state admits of infinite degrees between hot and cold, but it is, to a general observer of history, a real and recognizable thing.

At each extreme of normality there is another very recognizable state. There is complete decadence, when a religious body, great or small, no longer stands before the world as in any sense realizing its high ideals, and at the other end of the scale there is the state of fervour, when not only isolated individuals, but whole institutions, realize in themselves something very near to the ideal at which they aim. Such a condition often obtains at the origin of a religious order, or at a time of healthy rejuvenescence. Generally it is of no long continuance; but where and while a centre of sanctity exists it is the most powerful of all magnets. Such a magnet was Cîteaux, such Clairvaux in the first years; such were Rievaulx and Fountains and (in their degree) many other Cistercian houses in England thirty years later. For a brief space they gave, as fully and as unhesitatingly as can be given here below, an answer to the question: "Good Master, what shall I do that I may possess eternal life?" Bernard of Clairvaux, William of Rievaulx needed to answer no more than: "Enter here: live as we do: this do, and thou shalt live."

That this, for a brief space of years—some twenty or thirty—was the peculiar and irresistible attraction of the best and purest Cistercian houses is amply shown by the documents of the time. It was the case with Bernard himself: we can see it in those who left all so suddenly in England. The spectacle of Rievaulx was the spark that set the tinder ablaze at York in 1132; a year or so later we hear the same of Ailred: when he heard from his friend at York[1]—Waldef, it may have been—of the recent arrival of the white monks and of their way of life:

"Ah," said he, "what way leads to those men?...greatly do I desire, ardently do I thirst to look upon them and to see the fortunate spot of which you speak."....He hastened to the archbishop [Thurstan], longing for what was to come, and having received his leave and blessing returned in speed to his lodging, took horse without delaying to enter the house, and, scarcely saluting his hosts, pressed on his beast to go he knew not whither.[2]

Nor did his great hopes fail. Ten years later Ailred could put into the mouth of one of his novices words which, though enthusiastic, were a sincere and truthful statement of what his soul had found:

Our food is scanty, our garments rough; our drink is from the stream and our sleep often upon our book. Under our tired limbs there is but a hard mat; when sleep is sweetest we must rise at a bell's bidding....Self-will has no scope; there is no moment for idleness or dissipation....Everywhere peace,

1 Cf. the words of Prior Richard of York (*Memorials of Fountains*, I, 20): "Intueamur saltem...monachos Clarevallis, qui nuper venerunt ad nos; quam clare revixit evangelium in illis; ut, si dici fas est, utilius sit eos imitari, quam evangelium recitare."

2 *Vita Ailredi*, in *Ailred of Rievaulx and his biographer, Walter Daniel*, by F. M. Powicke, p. 86. This singularly important and attractive study, for which I may be permitted once and for all to express my warmest admiration, first appeared in the *Bulletin of the John Rylands Library*, VI, nos. 3 and 4, July 1921–January 1922. It was reprinted at Manchester in 1922; the reference *Vita Ailredi* denotes the article, *Ailred of Rievaulx* the reprint.

everywhere serenity, and a marvellous freedom from the tumult of the world. Such unity and concord is there among the brethren, that each thing seems to belong to all, and all to each.... To put all in brief, no perfection expressed in the words of the gospel or of the apostles, or in the writings of the Fathers, or in the sayings of the monks of old, is wanting to our order and our way of life.[1]

Seldom, if ever, has the exultant call of one who has found what his soul desired been uttered so clearly as in Bernard's summons to the two Englishmen of Yorkshire—Thomas of Beverley, who closed his ears to the enchanting voice and died within a short space, and Henry Murdac, who followed the call and died archbishop of York.[2] Weighed merely by vocabulary and concordance, there is little difference between the language and scriptural allusions of Bernard and those of many a contemporary monk or bishop, but the reader must be deaf indeed to the accent of sincerity who cannot distinguish between the easy platitudes of others and the burning conviction of the abbot of Clairvaux:[3]

He who has ears to hear, let him hear Him calling aloud in the temple: "He that thirsteth, let him come to me and drink: Come to me all ye who labour and are heavy laden, and I will refresh you." Dost thou fear to faint by the way, when Truth promises that He Himself will refresh thee? Truly, if the dark water from the clouds of the sky so delights thee,[4] how much more wilt thou delight to drink of the untroubled waters of the Saviour?

Oh! if thou mightest but once taste a little of that richness of the corn, with which Jerusalem is filled to plenty!...How gladly would I give thee of that warm bread which, still smoking and drawn straight from the oven, Christ of His heavenly bounty so often breaks for His poor ones! Would that God might in His goodness let fall upon his poor servant a drop of that rain of his free choice which He keeps for His own inheritance, that I might pour it over thee and hear from thee in return how its touch had moved thee! Believe one who has experienced it. Thou wilt find among the woods something that thou didst never find in books. Stones and trees will teach thee a lesson thou didst never hear from masters in the school.[5] Thinkest thou that honey cannot be drawn from the rock, and oil from the hardest stone? Do not the mountains drop sweetness and the hills flow with milk and honey, and the valleys abound with corn?[6]

1 Ailred, *Speculum Caritatis*, I, 17 (*PL*, CXCV, 562–3). Such language is quite consistent with the admission that faulty individuals, such as the *Vita* shows us, existed at Rievaulx.

2 Cf. *ep.* 106 to Murdac; *epp.* 107, 411 to Thomas of Beverley, whose death is announced in *ep.* 108.

3 Bernard's earnest sincerity is beyond question; but it is permissible to note that he ever remained a consummate artist in words. In the early writings his art verges on rhetoric; this is not so in his later years, but even his later style is very different from the direct simplicity of the gospel.

4 The *tenebrosa aqua in nubibus aeris* (Ps. xvii, 12, Vulgate) is Murdac's book-learning, contrasted with supernatural enlightenment.

5 "Experto crede: aliquid amplius invenies in silvis, quam in libris. Ligna et lapides docebunt te quod a magistris audire non possis." A celebrated passage, often misinterpreted. Bernard, it should not need saying, was not a "nature mystic", nor does he refer to "sermons in stones"—the simpler, truer thoughts to which natural beauty gives rise—but to the Spirit of God Who will instruct the soul in solitude and desert places.

6 *Ep.* 106.

To those who answered such a call with all the strength of their soul the entry into Clairvaux or Fountains would indeed be a homecoming. Perhaps in no letter even of Bernard's is there more eloquence than in the one where, in phrases taken almost without exception from the Scriptures, he tells the worldly prelate, Alexander "the Magnificent" of Lincoln, that he will never see one of his prebendaries again. He had left England on pilgrimage to Jerusalem; he had found a city not made with hands. Bernard opens with an address that is itself a challenge, and begins his letter without a word of introduction:

Your Philip, eager to set forth for Jerusalem, has found a shorter way and swiftly reached his goal. Speedily has he crossed this great and wide sea, and with a prosperous voyage has now reached the shore he desired, and put in to the harbour of salvation. Now, yes, now his feet stand in the courts of Jerusalem; and that which he had heard of in Ephrata, he has found in the fields of the wood, and he adores with joy in the place where his feet have stayed. He has entered the holy city and has found his inheritance with those of whom it is rightly said: Ye are no more foreigners and strangers; ye are fellow citizens with the saints and the domestics of God. Coming in and going out with them, as one of the saints, he glories with them, saying: Our conversation is in heaven. He is, then, no mere curious beholder of Jerusalem, but a devout dweller and a citizen enrolled there, not indeed of this earthly Jerusalem, to which Sina a mountain of Arabia hath affinity, which is in bondage with her children, but of the free Jerusalem which is above, which is our mother.

Yes; if you would know, it is Clairvaux. She is Jerusalem, joined to that which is in heaven with all the power of her mind; she imitates the life above, she shares it by spiritual kinship. This is his rest, as the Lord promises, for ever and ever; he has chosen it for himself as his dwelling; for there he finds, if not the vision, yet at least the expectation of true peace, even that peace of which it is written: the peace of God, which passeth all understanding.[1]

In addition to the simple and potent appeal of evangelical perfection, the early Cistercian house held much to attract a hesitating aspirant. There was the life of patient and useful labour, which showed its gradual but enduring result as the original "waste howling wilderness" by the banks of Rye or Aire, or in the marshes of Howden or Lindsey, began to bud and blossom as a Carmel. All early observers speak of this. Orderic singles it out for mention; the Meaux chronicler tells of its influence upon the country people.[2] Then there was the absolute identity of treatment and occupation,[3] which contrasted strongly with the hierarchy of officials and

---

1 *Ep.* 64; written *c.* 1129.

2 OV, III, 445; *Chronicon de Melsa*, 83: "Stolidus enim populus gentem admirabatur cucullatam quibusdam temporibus divinis obsequiis insistentem et aliis temporibus operibus rusticanis occupatam." The quotation *locus horroris*, &c. (Deuteronomy, xxxii, 10) is a commonplace.

3 *Vita Ailredi*, 85 (the words are attributed to Ailred's friend): "Personalitas idemptitatem parit singulis unam ipsamque omnibus similem, nec est erga quemlibet excepcionis indicium preponderans equitati." Ailred, *Speculum Caritatis*, II, 17 (*PL*, CXCV, 563): "Et quod me [a novice is speaking] miro modo delectat, nulla est personarum acceptio: nulla natalium consideratio."

obedientiaries among the black monks, separated as the communities were, a little later, into the officials on the one hand and the "monks of the cloister" on the other. Also, there was the peace of these lonely yet populous houses, which could not but stand in contrast to the disorders of Stephen's reign, and to the eager controversies over rights and privileges that were beginning to occupy the minds of so many in the old abbeys.

There was, moreover, another appeal that must have been very strong in individual cases, an appeal that came from Clairvaux rather than from Cîteaux. This was the invitation to the mystical life which Bernard never ceased to make in his later years; the call to all who would hear among his sons to seek that union with God which is the theme of his sermons on the Canticle. It has not, perhaps, been sufficiently noted what a new thing such an appeal was in contemporary monastic life. Individuals, indeed, in every age had taken this path, but neither Cluny nor the monastic reforms of the eleventh century had preached it, nor was it an essential part of the Cistercian vocation, which was the more general one to the monastic, not to the purely contemplative, life. In certain cases, even, one who followed such a way might doubt whether Cîteaux were for him; William of St Thierry, whose call was even clearer than that of Bernard, died a white monk, but he had more than once lifted up his eyes to the hills where dwelt the solitaries. But the vocation could be satisfied under a Bernard, and in England we shall find more than one who followed it at Fountains.

When to these many appeals were added the incalculable advantages of a clear, uniform and comprehensive rule of life, of a system of government of unrivalled excellence, and of the presence in their midst of the man who was the greatest spiritual force of his century, and when all these advantages existed in a virile and unfolding society that, from Rome to Edinburgh, Hungary to the Pyrenees, was becoming more and more homogeneous in culture and institutions, the *succès fou* of Cîteaux was all but inevitable. As in all such movements, there was a time-lag of some twenty years between the moment when the thing was at its best and the moment when this was recognized by the world, and the best had been in the silence and obscurity of Cîteaux before Bernard; but when the world discovered the Cistercians men flocked to them as, in the middle of last century, a smaller host flocked across ocean and prairie to the goldfields. Three times within eight years did Fountains send forth more than fifty sons to new foundations.[1] Rievaulx under Ailred housed six hundred souls.[2] Clairvaux under

1 The foundations were: Louth Park and Kirkstead in 1139; Woburn and Lyse in 1145; Vaudey and Kirkstall in 1147. The regulation number for a foundation was twenty-five, and we may reasonably suppose that if fifty were sent out, more than that number remained; indeed, an early statute required that no house should found unless it contained sixty monks (*Statuta*, ed. Canivez, I, 22, footnote to statutes of 1134).

2 *Vita Ailredi*, 97.

St Bernard, despite its never-ceasing fecundity, rose to seven hundred. It could be said that the world threatened to become one vast Cîteaux.[1]

In the history of almost every religious order the original period of intense fervour is relatively brief. Such a vast affluence of the multitudes ensured that Cîteaux should be no exception to the rule. As early as *c.* 1135 Orderic, in a familiar passage, spoke of the tares among the wheat, and of those who wore the habit and affected the manners of a profession which they did not honour.[2] We do not need his word to tell us that many out of such a great number would fail to reach the high spiritual level of the early days under Stephen Harding. In a later chapter something will be said of the beginnings of the falling-off in England. From the moment that Cîteaux ceased to be a retreat from the world and became in a sense a world-movement, its peculiar purity was doomed, even if the personal influence of a number of men of eminent sanctity maintained its reputation for a lifetime, and the introduction of its spirit to distant lands prolonged the revival for a century. The few religious institutes which have endured through centuries with their purity all but unimpaired—the Carthusians and the nuns of the Teresian reform are examples—have done so, humanly speaking, because to a rigid observance and an unchanging Rule they have added a most rigid and exclusive selection and probation. They have therefore remained always relatively few in number, a *corps d'élite*. This, we may surely suppose, was the thought of the first fathers of Cîteaux; but the circumstances of the time and the genius of Bernard overbore all designs, and the white monks, like the friars a century later, became for a time one of the decisive factors in European society.

V

Clairvaux had been founded in 1115; in the autumn of 1119 the new order numbered already fourteen houses, and in the decades that followed it continued to increase by a kind of geometrical progression, as each generation in turn gave birth to children and spread its influence in circles ever wider and wider. Meanwhile a new significance had been given to the appearance of the white monks by the polemics in which Bernard had become engaged. The story and exact chronology of these need not be pursued here in any detail;[3] it is enough to note that the first passage of

1 *Omnia Cistercium erat.* A familiar phrase, the source of which I have not traced.

2 OV, III, 435: "Voluntaria paupertas...ut opinor, in plerisque fervet ac vera religio, sed plures eis hypocritae seductoriique simulatores permiscentur, ut lolium tritico." *Ibid.* 446: "Mixti bonis hypocritae procedunt, candidis seu variis [*sc.* the brown monks of Tiron] indumentis amicti, homines illudunt....Veris Dei cultoribus schemate, non virtute, assimilari plerique gestiunt, suique multitudine intuentibus fastidium ingerunt." The writer's bias appears in his words, and it will be noted that he comprehends all the new orders in his criticism.

3 The fullest of the many accounts of this episode is in Vacandard's *Vie de S. Bernard*, vol. I; the latest is that of Dom A. Wilmart in his article *Une riposte de l'ancien monachisme*

arms between the abbot of Clairvaux and a representative of Cluny occurred as early as *c.* 1116–19,[1] whereas the first exchange of letters between him and Peter the Venerable, and the celebrated *Apologia ad Guillelmum*, did not take place before *c.* 1125–7.[2] The last-named piece, which was certainly intended when published to reach beyond the friend to whom it was addressed, had something of the effect of ranging the white and black monks (and especially those closely bound to Cluny) into opposing camps, and the literary controversy continued in one form or another for half a century. It also occasioned a searching of heart in many monasteries of the *ancien régime*, and this, too, had a practical issue in more than one centre. Thus the black monk abbots of the province of Rheims held an informal general chapter in 1131 and passed a series of reforming regulations, forbidding the eating of flesh-meat and doing away with recreative conversation. This embroiled them in turn with the staunch and conservative Cluniac, the cardinal legate Matthew of Albano, and the friction which ensued must have served still further to advertise the uneasiness in French monastic circles.[3] At the same moment Peter the Venerable, without doubt as a result of his collision with Bernard, was embarking upon the first of his attempts to restrain abuses and reform lax customs throughout the great family of which he was head. He spent several months in England in 1130, and it is natural to regard this as part of his preliminary investigation. In 1131 he decided upon drastic and novel action, and summoned all the heads of Cluniac houses, more than two hundred in number, together with a miscellaneous company of others interested to the number of a thousand, to assemble at Cluny *ad audiendum verbum* in March 1132.[4] The statutes there promulgated were, like those of the abbots at Soissons, directed chiefly towards securing the fasts and silence of the Rule; some of them were modified under pressure, although Peter continued his legislative activity until his death. Thus while the expansion of the Cistercian order ensured that it would arrive in England before many years had passed, other events had made of its programme something of a challenge.

We are fortunate enough to possess a long notice of the white monks from the pen of the most representative black monk historian of the time

in *RB*, XLVI (July, 1934), 296–344. Dom Wilmart gives ample references to all the literature on the subject. There is still room for a critical study of Bernard's *Apologia* (*Opusculum*, v, in *Opera*, II, 1221 seqq.) and its satellite letters; the *Apology*, as all careful readers must note, is a composite document, and the date and precise aim and occasion of its publication are alike uncertain.

1 This was the familiar *ep.* 1: "Ad Robertum nepotem suum, qui de ordine Cisterciensi transiebat ad Cluniacensem."

2 Vacandard, *Vie de S. Bernard*, I, 115 (note), dates the *Apology* 1123–5. In his article "Bernard" in *DTC* (1910) he dates it 1127.

3 For this incident *v.* Bernard, *ep.* 91; also Dom U. Berlière, *Documents inédits pour servir à l'histoire ecclésiastique de la Belgique* (Maredsous, 1894), I, 92–102, and the same author's *Mélanges d'histoire bénédictine*, 4 série (1902), 52–171.

4 For this meeting *v.* OV, v, 29 seqq. Orderic himself was there.

in England.[1] William of Malmesbury wrote *c.* 1125–6, before the arrival of the Cistercians in England and the *émeute* at York had introduced an element of partisan feeling. Always a generous, if sometimes undiscerning, admirer of the merits of others, and proud of the English origin of Stephen Harding, he begins with a sincere tribute to the loftiness of the new ideal,[2] and, after an elaborate and accurate account of the observance of Cîteaux and of its literal dependence on the Rule,[3] ends with a warm word of praise.[4] If Malmesbury may be taken as speaking for others, the reputation of Cîteaux stood very high in England when he wrote, and no bitterness of feeling existed. It is noteworthy that his judgment is clearly based on the life of Cîteaux; Bernard and controversy had not yet entered the English field of vision; Malmesbury is therefore able to regard the white monks dispassionately as a separate order offering a different way of life to aspirants. But even when the Cistercians were settling all over England, there was an all but total absence south of the Trent alike of the friction and of the passage of black monks and canons to their ranks that so distinguished the movement in Burgundy. Only at York and in its neighbourhood did the history of Cîteaux and Clairvaux repeat itself in a series of arresting incidents.

1 Will. Malmesb., *GR*, 380–5.
2 *Ibid.* 380: "Ingenua mens est si bonum in alio probes quod in te non esse suspires."
3 *Ibid.* 383: "Ita regulae incubantes, ut nec iota unum nec apicem praetereundum putent."
4 *Ibid.* 385: "Sunt hodie monachi Cistellenses omnium monachorum exercitium, studiosorum speculum, desidiosorum œstrum."

CHAPTER XIII

THE CISTERCIANS IN ENGLAND: I

THE FIRST FOUNDATIONS

RIEVAULX AND FOUNTAINS

I

Although Cîteaux was in existence before either Tiron or Savigny, the latter were the first to increase. Both were situated on territory subject to Henry I, and Vitalis, the founder of Savigny, and Geoffrey, his immediate successor, both Normans by birth, were known to the king.[1] It is not surprising, therefore, that the brown monks and the grey should have been the first harbingers of the great invasion. The first to come were the monks of Tiron. Robert fitz Martin, c. 1113–15, approached Bernard of Tiron and received from him a group of twelve under an abbot, Fulchard; these he settled in west Wales on the banks of the Teifi near Cardigan, and constructed for them the abbey that became known as St Dogmael's.[2] This, together with its two cells of Caldey and Pill, founded later, was the sole offspring of Tiron in England and Wales, and its remote situation effectually prevented it from attracting attention or securing influence. Fifty years later, St Dogmael's had a close bond with the Cistercians of the neighbourhood, and thus entered into the life, and incurred the hostility, of Gerald of Wales.

Almost equally remote was the first plantation from Savigny. This was at Tulket, near Preston in Lancashire, on the land of Stephen of Blois, count of Boulogne and later king of England. Negotiations had apparently been begun with Vitalis, but the settlement was made under his successor, Geoffrey, in July 1124. Three years later the monks were given a more extensive and promising holding in Stephen's forest of Furness, and here they settled in the July of 1127.[3] The first abbot, Ewan or Yvon "of Avranches", was possibly an Englishman by birth, and he was subsequently

1 Vitalis preached in England (*Vita*, ed. Sauvage, 374–5); Geoffrey: "gratiam... maxime apud Henricum regem Angliae seniorem inven(er)it" (*Vita*, ed. Sauvage, 402).
2 *Vita b. Bernardi Tironensis*, 1426 (the date is there given as c. 1115); Symeon of Durham, *Hist. Reg.* (II, 247) gives 1113. For further information regarding Tiron and St Dogmael's, v. *The History of St Dogmael's Abbey*, by E. M. Pritchard, and an article by H. M. Vaughan, *The Benedictine Abbey of St Mary at St Dogmael's*, in *Y Cymmrodor*, XXVII (1917), 1–25. The erection of the priory into an abbey took place in 1120; v. *Calendar of Documents preserved in France*, I, 353–4. Kelso in Scotland, near the Border, was an early plantation from Tiron.
3 Symeon of Durham, II, 267.

for a time third abbot of Savigny itself.[1] Furness was to enter in more than one way into the religious history of the north, and to be mother of a numerous family, but for the moment the situation of the place, with the high moors between it and Yorkshire and the midlands, caused it to remain unnoticed. In the next twenty years a number of other Savigniac colonies came to England and south Wales. Several of these houses became later well known when they had joined the white monks, but their scattered forces, arriving at the same time as the more numerous Cistercians, produced no independent impression at the time.[2]

Contemporaneously with the first arrivals, a movement in the inverse direction was beginning to take place. From the outset Englishmen had been found among the groups of reformers abroad, and the fame of Stephen Harding must have served as an attraction to his countrymen. We do not know when the first Englishman entered Clairvaux, but William, the future first abbot of Rievaulx, must have been there in very early years, for he was Bernard's amanuensis for the celebrated letter to his nephew, Robert of Châtillon, c. 1116–19.[3] It is possible that he is to be identified with the William, a whilom pupil of Henry Murdac at York, who joined with Ivo, a fellow-pupil and later a fellow-monk at Clairvaux, in saluting their old master, to whom Bernard addressed the eloquent invitation quoted in the preceding chapter.[4] Murdac, as is well known, responded and became one of the most distinguished Cistercians of the age. If the suggested identification be not correct, there were two Englishmen named William at Clairvaux, and the second may also have returned later to his native country.[5] Ivo, for his part, persuaded Bernard to write to another friend, Thomas, the young provost of Beverley, inviting him to leave all and become a monk. Thomas promised, but in spite of a second long and warm letter failed to keep his word.[6] Yet another northerner of distinction to find a home at Clairvaux was Richard, a native of York, who after following Henry Murdac as third abbot of Vauclair, succeeded him again as sixth abbot of Fountains;[7] and mention has already been

1 Evanus de Abrincis appears first in the list of abbots in the Register printed in *Monasticon*, v, 246; cf. *Furness Coucher Book*, I, 8–10. The observations of the late compiler of this list (p. 10) are based on some misconception. Robert of Torigni, *de Immutatione Ordinis Monachorum* (*PL*, CCII, 1312 *seqq*.), speaks of "Evanus Anglicus, qui parvo tempore eidem monasterio [*sc*. Savigny, *c*. 1139] praefuit". The *Chron. Manniae, s.a.* 1134, gives his name as Yvo, and it is possible that Torigni's adjective refers merely to his sojourn in England.

2 The following were the Savigniac houses: Furness (1124), Neath (1130), Basingwerk (1131), Quarr (1132), Combermere (1133), Buildwas, Calder, Rushen [Isle of Man], Stratford Langthorn, Swineshead (1135), Buckfast (1136), Byland (1138) and Coggeshall (1140).

3 *Bernardi Vita Prima*, I, xi (*PL*, CLXXXV, 255).

4 *Ep.* 106. The date is perhaps *c*. 1125.

5 In *ep*. 320 [ed. Mabillon] a *frater Willelmus, qui est filius noster dilectissimus*, is sent to Fountains in 1138–9. The Trinity College Gale MS., however, followed by Walbran, and the Brit. Mus. MS. Arundel 51 read *Gualterum* (*Memorials of Fountains*, 82).

6 *Ep.* 411, addressed *Bonae spei juveni Thomae*, and *ep*. 107. The date cannot be fixed.

7 *Mem. Fount.* 108. He was Precentor of Clairvaux, according to this account.

made of Philip, the prebendary of Lincoln.[1] Circumstances had thus brought it about that among Bernard's most trusted disciples was a small group from York and its neighbourhood, and this goes far to explain why the distant north was chosen for the first transmarine foundation of Clairvaux.

From more than one point of view the north of England was a field ready for sowing. Despite the spread of monasticism after the Conquest, it was still largely virgin soil. If in 1130 a line had been drawn across England from the mouth of the Welland to the estuary of the Mersey, the district north of it would have been found to contain only five abbeys, the cathedral priory of Durham, and two or three smaller houses. And if much of the land was moor and crag, the wide dales and wooded valleys offered many sites peculiarly suited to the pioneer cultivation of the Cistercians. In the north, too, the spiritual atmosphere was congenial. In the early decades of the twelfth century a renaissance, intellectual and religious, was taking place at York itself and other centres, which were at last recovering from the Scandinavian invasions and the more recent harrying of the Conqueror, and the earnest, somewhat stern northern piety, which until the Reformation and afterwards was to remain a different thing from the religious sentiment of the south, was beginning to find an outlet, first in the revived monasticism and its hermitages, and then in the foundation of a number of strict houses of regular canons.

The first of these was perhaps Hexham, where the priest Eilaf, son of the treasurer of Durham who had had to yield place to the monks in 1083 and father of Ailred of Rievaulx, was in possession. The change was due to archbishop Thomas II in 1113; it was gradual, and the archbishop died early in the following year; the real transformation came when Anketil, a canon of Huntingdon, became prior.[2] Thurstan, the new archbishop-elect, after short visits to his diocese, was for several years occupied in his resistance to Canterbury and remained abroad; when he finally returned in 1120 he was active in his encouragement of regular canons. Thus Nostell, c. 1114, where the king's confessor, Aldulf, was prior, Bridlington, c. 1113–14,[3] Kirkham, founded from Nostell[4] by Walter Espec c. 1130, and Guisborough came into existence. Thurstan's character was one of unusual energy and determination. The same dominant traits appear in the three important episodes that distinguished his rule—his resistance to the primate and (later) Henry I on the question of profession (1115–20), his encouragement of the reformers at York and Fountains (1132–3), and his conduct in the campaign against the Scots (1138). Though he was a

1 *Ep.* 64.
2 For the refounding of Hexham, *v.* Richard of Hexham's *History*, and Ailred *On the Saints of Hexham*, in *The Priory of Hexham*, ed. J. Raine (Surtees Soc. XLIV (1865), 173–203; *v.* also I, 54 *seqq.*, 190–4). Also Symeon of Durham, II, 247.
3 Both Bridlington and Bredon (a foundation from Nostell) were in existence by 1122 (*v.* L. Delisle, *Rouleaux des Morts*, 330, 314).   4 *Monasticon*, v, 280; cf. *VCH, Yorks*, III, 219.

native of Bayeux, there is a striking similarity between his enthusiastic and ascetic temper and that of typical northerners such as Richard, first abbot of Fountains, and Henry Murdac. Himself a man of austere life, he had in early years vowed to devote himself as a monk at Cluny; in his old age his thoughts turned again to this and he consulted Bernard, who deprecated a change of life but hinted not obscurely that if change there were, it should be to Clairvaux.[1] In the event, Thurstan remained at his post, but when death drew near he proceeded to Pontefract where he died in the habit of Cluny, having previously taken part in a Dirge which he caused to be recited round his bed. He was thus one who might be expected to welcome the new monasticism, and to give his somewhat impulsive enthusiasm free rein in patronizing its expansion.[2]

Actually, however, the distinction of first introducing the white monks to England belongs, not to Thurstan and Clairvaux, but to L'Aumône and William Giffard of Winchester. The site chosen was Waverley, near Farnham in Surrey, in what was then a somewhat remote locality away from the main lines of travel. The abbot and community from L'Aumône were presumably foreigners, and settled down unostentatiously to their regular life at the end of 1128.[3] Waverley, though it grew steadily and made a number of foundations, attracted no recruits of renown, and Ailred, perhaps with a tinge of patriotic bias, could speak of it as hidden away in a corner.[4] The foundation that truly marked the beginning of the invasion was that of Rievaulx, near Helmsley, some thirty miles north of York. The founder was Walter Espec, acting in close concert with Thurstan; nothing is known of the previous negotiations, but it is natural to suppose that the group of Yorkshiremen round Bernard had had their share in forwarding the project. In any case, Bernard took all possible care to ensure success. The way was prepared by a characteristic letter to Henry I,[5] and at the head of the band of colonists was the Englishman, William. The gift of land was apparently made in 1131; the foundation dated from 5 March 1132.[6] Less than three weeks later the great assembly of black monks met at Cluny to hear the reforming regulations of Peter the

1 *Ep.* 319.
2 All the northern chroniclers devote space to describing Thurstan's character, and there are many other incidental references to his piety. The fullest and most eloquent account of his character is that given by Prior Richard of Hexham in his *History of the Church of Hexham* (ed. Raine), 57: "Hic inter innumeras et gravissimas adversitates, quibus diu et creberrime pulsatus est, animum invictissimum et constantissimum gerebat. His igitur tandem superatis et optato fine consummatis, celebrem cognitionis famam et magnae venerationis laudem apud plurimas gentes merito probitatis suae adeptus est. Erat quippe vir magnae castitatis et prudentiae, honestatis et justitiae, et multarum virtutum fulgore perspicuus."
3 *Annales Waverl.*, s.a. 1128.
4 Ailred, *de Bello Standardii* (PL, CXCV, 704; also in *Chronicles of the reign of Stephen*, III, 184): "Waverlenses...quasi in angulo latuerant." 5 *Ep.* 92.
6 This, the correct date, is given by *Chronica de Mailros* (Bannatyne Club, 1835), 69. The charter rehearsing the foundation, printed by J. C. Atkinson in *Chartularium Rievallense* (Surtees Soc. LXXXIII (1887), no. XLII, 16–21), states that the founder acted *consilio et consensu Turstini*. For Bernard's relations with England *v.* Appendix IX.

Venerable, and before the monks of Rievaulx had passed many weeks in their lonely valley, their presence had precipitated a crisis, fraught with important consequences for the religious history of the north, in the abbey of St Mary at York.

II

St Mary's, as has been related, was founded, under circumstances imperfectly described in the records, as a kind of schism from the community of Whitby, in 1078. Unfortunately, less is known of the place in the forty years that followed than of any other abbey of equal importance in England. The account of its first years, purporting to be written by Stephen, the first abbot, and the *Chronicle* giving a list of the early abbots with their dates, are alike wholly untrustworthy. Indeed, there may be said to be absolutely no reliable information about the house in the twelfth century before the crisis of 1132. The events that then took place show that by that time the spirit of simplicity which animated the Northern revival had given place to latitude. The abbey, which lay under the walls of the city and near to the busy river and the bridge-head, had become wealthy in land, churches and tithes; it had adopted the traditional modifications of the Rule. In this it did not stand apart from the other black monk houses, but it seems certain that the discipline of St Mary's had become relaxed, and that a majority of the monks had come to be satisfied with such a state of things, which was largely due to the aged and ineffective Abbot Geoffrey.[1] Whether anything gravely scandalous existed cannot be said with certainty; some remarks of Prior Richard, reported by Thurstan, leave the question open.[2] At the same time, there were in the house a group of men who had preserved the fervour of early years and were besides, as the event showed, exceptionally gifted in many ways. This group included several of the chief officials of the abbey: prior, subprior, sacrist and almoner. The abbey was in close touch on the one hand with Thurstan and the circle of able ecclesiastics by whom he was surrounded, and on the other with the monks of the neighbouring priory of the Holy Trinity and of the Cluniac house of Pontefract; it is therefore

---

1 There is considerable uncertainty as to the dates of Geoffrey's term of office. According to the MS. printed in *Monasticon*, III, 569 (cf. *Chronicle of St Mary's, York*, ed. Craster, Surtees Soc. CV, 1933, p. 1), he was elected in 1131 and died on 17 July 1132. Neither of these dates can be accepted. He appears as abbot in 1123 (Hugo Cantor, *Hist. York*, II, 199; *Historia Selebeiensis* [24]) and 1128 (*Hist. York*, III, 52), and was certainly alive in October 1132. According to the reliable John of Worcester (ed. J. R. H. Weaver), 48, the abbacy was "bestowed" in 1138; the vacancy may well have been caused by Geoffrey's death. The monk Serlo alludes to him as "vir grandaevus et etate confectus" (*Mem. Fount.* 7); Thurstan (*ibid.* 13) describes him more fully as "vir utique pro sensu et ingenio suo honestus et bonus, nimium tamen simplex et illiteratus".

2 *Mem. Fount.* 17: "Inter haec [*sc.* relaxationes] periculose, ni fallor, servatur pudicitia. Hinc quippe peccatis nostris exigentibus vix sufficiunt laternae [*sc.* circatorum] vel custodiae, cum personas honestiores excedant plerumque numero suspectiores. Si vero privata omnia interim bene procedant Deus novit, et nos experimento didicimus."

natural to suppose that the more alert among the brethren were well acquainted with the Cistercian movement, with Bernard's controversy with the black monks, and with the reaction of reform in Cluniac circles. Thurstan, at any rate, showed himself well informed on all this in the autumn of 1132.[1] The actual division of opinion at St Mary's, however, would seem to have been the direct result of the arrival of the white monks in Yorkshire, when they would no doubt have passed through the city and visited the archbishop.[2]

Our knowledge of the episode which followed is derived in the main from two chief sources, each of which has a high degree of reliability.[3] One is a long and strictly contemporary letter of Thurstan to William of Corbeuil, archbishop of Canterbury. The other, though composed rather more than seventy years after the event, is of a peculiar interest and value. A certain Serlo was at York in 1132; a native of the district, he had been educated at the abbey,[4] and was related to more than one of the group which seceded. He was an eyewitness of the events that accompanied their exodus; possibly he was a clerk of the archbishop, or one of the functionaries in the *curia* of the abbot. He was at the time some twenty-five years of age. Five years later he himself became a monk at Fountains, and although he was comparatively late in taking the habit, he was destined to survive all his contemporaries and to live far beyond the common span.[5] He was sent to Kirkstall, a daughter of Fountains, and

1 Thurstan in his letter (*Mem. Fount.* 22) refers to the recent reforms of Peter the Venerable: "Ipsa Cluniacus nova mutatione probavit quod multa sint inter suas consuetudines quae merito deberent emendari." He quotes the parallel of Molesme (*ibid.* 29) and is familiar with Cassian (*ibid.* 28). Prior Richard's manifesto has in it much of the spirit of the new dialectic.

2 Thurstan, writing *c.* 8 September, says (*Mem. Fount.* 11): "Ante dimidium ferme annum...ceperunt...agitari." That would have been precisely when the white monks arrived. Serlo (*ibid.* 5) says: "Cepit eos subito taedere, etc.", and the fact that the first movers and Prior Richard were mutually ignorant of each other's sentiments and that Richard *expavit de novitate rei* (*ibid.* 13) shows that dissatisfaction came to a head suddenly.

3 The *Narratio Fundationis: de fundatione Fontanis monasterii*, incorporating Thurstan's letter, was printed in the *Monasticon*, v, 294–6, from Dodsworth's transcript (MS. Bodl. Dodsworth 26) of an original which has not been identified; this gives a somewhat abridged version of both narrative and letter. Both were printed in full for the first time by J. S. Walbran in the volume of the Surtees Society, so often quoted (*Memorials of Fountains*, I, 1–128); the *Narratio* from Gale MS. O. 1. 79 in the library of Trinity College, Cambridge, of the early fifteenth century, the letter from a MS. in the library of Corpus Christi College, Oxford. The latter MS., of the twelfth century, had once belonged to Fountains. "The ingenious Mr Walbran", as a fellow-antiquary calls him, collated other MSS. and editions, and added very valuable notes, but he had had no training in the methods of exact scholarship, and his text contains a number of obvious inaccuracies. Thurstan's letter was reprinted by Mabillon from the *Monasticon* as an addition (*ep.* 477) to Bernard's letters.

4 Serlo says of himself (*Mem. Fount.* 2–3) that he was "apud eos [the monks of York] etiam nutritus".

5 *Mem. Fount.* 2–3: "Tum ille [*sc.* Serlo] sicut est in dicendo serius: 'sexagesimus', inquit, 'et nonus annus hic est a diebus conversionis meae, et eram tunc, ut memini, incipiens quasi annorum triginta, cum me primo Fontes contuli, sacro illi conventui sociandus'." Serlo took the habit at Fountains *c.* 1137–8 (*ibid.* 57); he therefore dictated his reminiscences *c.* 1206 at the age of ninety-eight. He was one of the group that founded Kirkstall in 1147 (*ibid.* 93). His narrative ends with the death of Abbot William in 1190.

there, when almost a hundred years old, he narrated the story of the origins and subsequent history of his first monastic home to a monk who had been charged by the then abbot of Fountains to compose a permanent record. He asserted, and with justice, that his memory retained unfaded the impressions it had received of the momentous events of his youth.[1] His account was dictated to Hugh, a monk of Kirkstall, who had before him, and embodied in his narrative, a copy of Thurstan's letter and of several from Bernard.

The arrival of the Cistercians from Clairvaux, we are told, brought forcibly to the minds of many at St Mary's that they were not following the Rule of their profession, and the teaching of the gospel on which it was based, in anything resembling entirety. After much discussion among themselves they at last approached the prior, Richard— clearly a man at once more capable and more spiritual than the abbot— whom they had at first avoided for fear lest he might quash their attempts. They discovered that he shared their convictions and he at once threw in his lot with them and took the position of leader to which his rank and ability entitled him; he was, besides being a man of deep spirituality, a prudent administrator; he had also influential friends, among whom was Archbishop Thurstan.[2] The matter was by now public property in the house, and the group were accused of levity and disobedience. At length, on 28 June, Richard the prior and Gervase the subprior laid the whole question before the abbot. His first reaction took the shape of grief that such a subversion of peace and order should have taken place in his days, when he was stricken in years. He warned them to desist from their enterprise, recollecting that as professed monks they had no longer any right to dispose of themselves or of their future.

To this Richard replied at length. He and his companions, he said, were making no innovation. They wished solely to observe the Rule, or to speak more accurately, the gospel which lay behind all rules.[3] The Rule had been written to guarantee the gospel to all, not to provide an ideal for individuals. As St Gregory had said, it was remarkable for its discretion; it appointed times for prayer, for reading and for work; moreover, it appointed a regular fare. But at St Mary's little of this was observed. Daily conversations had taken the place of the silence of the Rule; the food and drink were varied and excessive; and many were sent out of the

---

1 *Mem. Fount.* 3. Serlo's narrative is, however, occasionally confused, and in one or two places inaccurate.

2 Prior Richard is described by Serlo (*Mem. Fount.* 6) as "homo religiosus et timens Deum, et prudens in exterioribus, amicus potentium, fuit enim pro se [*sic*] reverentia religionis omnibus amori et honori, familiaris et notus Pontifici [*sc.* Thurstano]". The archbishop says (*ibid.* 13) that on him "tota pene monasterii cura pendebat".

3 *Mem. Fount.* 13: "Nil rude, O pater, novumve inducere contendimus, verum antiquam regulam beati patris nostri Benedicti, immo potius antiquissimum Evangelium Christi, quod omnes regulas antecedit...observare debemus."

monastery to live upon the estates of the house.[1] They were, nevertheless, pledged to evangelical perfection, and if the words of the gospel, heard so often, seemed utopian, they had the example of the Cistercians before them, in whose life the gospel was a living reality. If the proximity of the city made some features of the Cistercian life impossible of realization, they might at least perform the part that lay within their power.

Prior Richard spoke with the fire of new conviction, and used strong language; it is not surprising that Abbot Geoffrey heard him without enthusiasm.[2] Instead, however, of taking a clear decision, he asked the prior to furnish him with a written scheme of the reforms he suggested. Richard complied with alacrity, and produced a programme which reorganized the whole establishment in things temporal and spiritual. The Rule was to be kept strictly as regards silence and food; churches and tithes were to be handed over to the archbishop, and the monks were to live on the produce of their lands.

Meanwhile, news of what was afoot had spread through the community and caused a fresh outbreak of indignation. The prior, it was said, was attacking, not only his own house, but Cluny, Marmoutier, Canterbury, Winchester and St Albans. Richard, for his part, countered by again approaching the abbot with a request that he should either reform St Mary's or give to those who desired it opportunity to follow their profession. The abbot promised to give a full answer on the feast of the Nativity of Our Lady (8 September), after he had taken advice. But meanwhile feeling was running very high in the abbey; it was agreed that anyone who discussed the obligations of his profession should be excommunicated, and several of Richard's associates now left him, moved by fear or favour, to be received by their opponents only after a confession that they had erred. Richard therefore took the decisive step of appealing for assistance to the archbishop.

Thurstan's first step was to summon abbot, prior and subprior to a conference in the presence of witnesses. Richard once more made his petition: to follow Christ in voluntary poverty and bear His cross; to be allowed to observe fully the gospel and the Rule.[3] He begged the abbot to help him. The abbot replied that the loss of so many of his leading assistants would be a very serious one to him; that he and the rest of the community wished simply to live by the customs that were traditional to them; that in any case he could not promise help without the consent of his chapter. A day was therefore fixed on which the archbishop should visit the abbey and hear the matter discussed.

In the interval the abbot, who was clearly not a man of strong character,

---

1 *Mem. Fount.* 17: "Velint nolint omnes plerumque fit custos villarum."
2 *Mem. Fount.* 21: "Quae verba domnus abbas non satis jocunde [!] suscepit."
3 *Mem. Fount.* 23: "Quatinus pauperem Christum in voluntaria paupertate sequerentur, et Christi crucem in corpore suo portare, itemque Evangelicam pacem regulamque plene beati patris Benedicti observare non impedirentur."

called to his support monks from the priories of Holy Trinity and Ponte-fract. The archbishop, for his part, arrived on the appointed day surrounded by a group of notable ecclesiastics, among whom may be recognized several whose names afterwards became celebrated in the religious and literary history of the times. Hugh the dean was there, soon to be the first distinguished recruit and benefactor of Fountains; William Fitzherbert the treasurer, destined, as Thurstan's successor, to meet Richard the sacristan as his accuser before the pope, and to receive, after a troubled life, the honours of a saint; Hugh the archdeacon, better known as Hugo de Sottovagina or Hugh the Chanter; William of St Barbara, the future bishop of Durham on whose word were to depend the fortunes of Fitzherbert; Serlo (not the narrator), a canon, who like his namesake was to find his way to Fountains; and others. At the door of the chapter-house the abbot came to meet the archbishop, denying him entrance unless he dismissed some of his clerics. When Thurstan expostulated, a clamour was raised by the monks, some of whom showed signs of using violence. The archbishop, obtaining a hearing, proceeded to lay an interdict upon the abbey, whereupon a monk named Simeon exclaimed that a century of interdict was better than episcopal interference, and the cry was raised that Richard and his companions should be seized and imprisoned. They in turn crowded round Thurstan, who withdrew with them into the church, which was blockaded by the abbey's servants, the archbishop on his side barring the door which led into the cloister. Finally, Thurstan was able to return to his house, carrying with him the thirteen appellants. It was 17 October 1133.[1]

Abbot Geoffrey, though apparently at first condoning the exodus,[2] did not remain idle. Having written to the king and other notabilities, he took to the road in order to enlist allies to his cause.[3] It was to counteract his propaganda that Thurstan wrote to William of Corbeuil, then papal legate, the long letter which has formed the source for much of the preceding story.[4]

The group of monks enjoying the protection of the archbishop, originally thirteen in number, contained no less than seven future Cistercian abbots,[5] but before its departure from York it underwent a slight change.

1 So *Narratio* (*Mem. Fount.*), 10.

2 Bernard, *ep.* 313: "Sunt...sicut ipse testaris, te absolvente quandoque dimissi."

3 *Narratio* (*Mem. Fount.*), 10: "Abbas...nuncios ad regem dirigit...scribit etiam... episcopis, abbatibus, etc." Thurstan writes (*ibid.* 26): "Abbas vero nescio quid acturus iter arripuit."

4 William had been the determined opponent of Thurstan's claims, but there was no private enmity between them. Thurstan, indeed, had given evidence on behalf of William prior to his election in 1123 (Hugo Cantor, *Hist. York*, II, 199).

5 All agree that thirteen followed Thurstan (*Narratio*, 9; Thurstan's letter, 26: "presbi-teros duodecim et subdiaconum unum"; *Chronica de Melsa*, I, 74), but the names do not tally. From a comparison of the various lists it would seem that Robert of Whitby, though given as one of the thirteen by Serlo, joined later, as did also Adam of Whitby. The seven abbots were: Richard the prior (Fountains); Richard the sacrist (Fountains); Robert

Abbot Geoffrey did not cease to command and to implore his whilom subjects to return to their allegiance, and two of them, Gervase and Ralph, deterred by the prospect of material and spiritual hardship, returned to St Mary's. Their return gave the occasion for the entrance upon the scene of the abbot of Clairvaux. Strangely enough, the appeal to Bernard did not emanate from the group in Thurstan's house, but from the abbot of St Mary's, apparently at the suggestion of the uneasy consciences of the two defaulters, who were anxious for a decision from a master of the spiritual life. Bernard wrote twice to Geoffrey, and both letters belong to the weeks immediately following the exodus.[1] Their tenor was what might have been expected. Bernard brushed aside the complaints of the abbot and the pleas of the two waverers, recognized the work of God in the movement, warned Gervase and Ralph that having chosen the best, the second best was no longer lawful for them, and laid upon the abbot the responsibility of assisting by all the means in his power those of his sons who were aiming at perfection. A third letter, written about the same time, warmly thanked Thurstan.[2] In the event, Gervase rejoined his friends at the archbishop's house, while Ralph remained at St Mary's, but his place was taken about this time by a worthy substitute, a monk of Whitby who may have been residing at York, Robert, who was to become celebrated as St Robert of Newminster, and before they left York yet another Whitby monk joined them, Adam, the future first abbot of Meaux.[3]

Richard and his companions remained with the archbishop for almost three months. Then, at Christmas, Thurstan took them with him to Ripon, where he had extensive estates, and bestowed on them land in Skeldale; he presided at the election of an abbot, and blessed Richard the ex-prior, who was elected. He was, as the chronicler remarks, an abbot of monks without a monastery. The land by the Skell was totally uncultivated, and for the first winter the community was dependent on what the archbishop continued to supply. There was a large and spreading elm between the river and the steep side of the valley, which here was very narrow; under it they constructed huts; round it they began to cultivate a garden. Such was the origin of the abbey of St Mary of Fountains, as it was named from the pure springs abundant on the slopes of Skeldale.

The little group soon felt that their position was anomalous. The only motive for the departure from York had been dissatisfaction with black monk observance, and they feared lest, by remaining wholly independent, they might fail to escape the perils of private judgment and error. They

(Kirkstead); Gervase the subprior (Louth Park); Walter the almoner (Kirkstead); Ranulf (Lyse); Alexander (Kirkstall). To them were added Robert (Newminster) and Adam (Meaux) from Whitby.　　1 *Epp.* 94, 313.　　2 *Ep.* 95.

3 Adam is not mentioned in the account of the exodus; his Whitby provenance is given in the *Chronica de Melsa*, I, 74. Probably Whitby and York had a union of confraternity (*v. infra*, p. 475). For St Robert, *v.* his *Vita* in *Analecta Bollandiana*, LVI (1938), 343–60.

therefore decided to apply to the abbot of Clairvaux for permission to join the Cistercian order. A letter was drafted, detailing the history of the past year; it was accompanied by a warm recommendation from the archbishop and carried to Clairvaux by two of the band. Bernard replied with a letter of congratulation, and sent as bearer of his letter one Geoffrey, a monk now in his old age, whom he had often employed as a director of communities who had transferred themselves en bloc to Clairvaux.[1] By him the monks of Fountains were taught the Cistercian manner of life, and already they were beginning to receive recruits in considerable numbers.[2] Nevertheless, their material prospects showed no signs of improvement—it must be remembered that they were without lay brothers at the start—and after two years the situation was so desperate that Abbot Richard proceeded to the abbot of Clairvaux to beg him to assign them a home in France. Bernard acceded, and gave them Longué, a grange of Clairvaux, which subsequently became an abbey. But while Richard was on his mission, the tide had turned at home. Hugh, dean of York, and a man of property and culture, decided to offer himself as a novice at Fountains, and besides his money and lands, carried thither the nucleus of a library.[3] Shortly after, he was joined by two rich canons of York, Serlo and Tosti, and the long list of benefactions to Fountains had worthily opened. It was at this time, about five years after the exodus from York, that the other Serlo, at whose dictation many of the above facts were recorded, entered Fountains, and he comments with deep feeling on the fervent life he found there—a fervour which was still in existence when he spoke.[4]

Though the beginnings of Fountains, born into the Cistercian family as it were out of due time, had been so laborious, its story, and the character of its first abbot, soon attracted attention, and it rapidly became the mother of children. Something will be said of these later; for the moment it will be best to carry its domestic history forward. As early as 1138 Abbot Richard was sufficiently well known in high places to be chosen by Alberic, cardinal bishop of Ostia and legate in England, to accompany him on his tour of visitation.[5] When Alberic returned to

1 Bernard, *ep.* 96; cf. Walbran's notes, *Mem. Fount.* 46.
2 *Mem. Fount.* 48: "Adjunxerunt se eis clerici septem et laici decem recepti in novitios."
3 *Mem. Fount.* 53: "Erat autem homo dives...in libris scripturarum sanctarum quos... multis sibi sumptibus et studio comparaverat. Et hic primus qui armariolum de Fontibus felici auspicio suscitavit." It must have been about this time that Bernard addressed a letter to King David of Scotland soliciting his assistance for Fountains. The letter, an unfamiliar one, is to be found only in *Der heilige Bernard von Clairvaux*, by G. Hüffer (Münster, 1886), 233, no. x.
4 *Mem. Fount.* 57–8: "Deus bone, quanta tunc apud Fontes vitae perfectio!...Patres nostri...studuerunt...posteris suis...formam relinquere quae, favente Deo, usque hodie illaesa perdurat."
5 *Mem. Fount.* 71. This account is borne out by John of Hexham in his continuation of Symeon of Durham's *Historia Regum* (ed. Raine), 121, and by Richard of Hexham, *de Gestis Stephani* (ed. Raine), 98.

Rome, Richard accompanied him to act as representative of Thurstan at the Lateran Council of Lent, 1139, and to negotiate for the archbishop's retirement in favour of his brother Audoen.[1] It is possible that the legate intended to recommend him to the pope for preferment in the Curia but, to use Serlo's phrase, the Lord made better provision for him, and the first abbot of Fountains died in Rome on the last day of April 1139.

The orphan community addressed themselves to Bernard, and, on his advice, elected as abbot the other Richard, once sacrist of St Mary's, who had been the spiritual leader of the exodus which had been directed by the more active genius of his namesake.[2] The two Richards might, indeed, be taken as embodying the two vocations, of Martha and Mary, which existed alongside of one another in the early Cistercian houses, and which Bernard in a measure possessed in combination. The second abbot of Fountains was a contemplative, with unusual insight and prudence in the care of souls. The aged Serlo, who had passed the years of his spiritual formation under his care, speaks with deep feeling of his wisdom, and of his power to read the secrets of the heart. The external cares of office had little attraction for him, and his post was indeed no sinecure, for in addition to the three English foundations made at this time, Richard could not escape becoming involved in the controversy over the York election of 1141, and had ultimately to make the journey to Rome. Thrice in his brief term of office he begged Bernard, whom he would have met at the season of the annual general chapter, to relieve him of his burden and allow him to retire to Clairvaux. Thrice the saint refused; on the fourth occasion, when Richard called at Clairvaux on his return from Rome in 1143, Bernard wrote to the monks of Fountains that if they did not refuse, he would permit their abbot to resign his office. Richard returned joyfully home, and produced the letter, but the community, who found an eloquent spokesman in one Hugh of Matham, refused to allow him to depart. The abbot sadly accepted the verdict, but told his sons that they would not long enjoy their triumph. In the event, he died before a year was out at Clairvaux, whither he had been taken by his journey to chapter.[3] Thus within a little more than ten years of the departure from York the two leaders of the appellants had passed away.

As Abbot Richard had died at Clairvaux, it was natural that Bernard

---

1 Serlo (*Mem. Fount.* 71–2) says: "Peracta legatione renitentem trahit ad curiam volens hominem in majoris administrationis gradum promoveri." Richard of Hexham, however (ed. Raine, 104), says that he was sent out by Thurstan: "et propter Concilium et propter quaedam alia privata negotia quae per illum facere disponebat". He goes on to give these private reasons. His account is borne out by John of Hexham (ed. Raine, 124).

2 Serlo's long memoir of Richard, whom he knew well, is an eloquent and moving tribute (*Mem. Fount.* 73 seqq.). The statement that this Richard was the prime mover at York is his (*ibid.* 73).

3 *Mem. Fount.* 75–8. As abbot of a daughter-house of Clairvaux, Richard would have the duty of visiting Bernard every year; the natural time would be on his way to or from chapter.

should take steps to allot a successor. His choice fell upon a remarkable man. Henry Murdac was a native of the north of England and had held preferment under Thurstan;[1] from his position as a teacher of repute he had followed the call to Clairvaux, where he was the companion and friend of the future Eugenius III, and whence he passed to be abbot of Vauclair. Knowing, as Bernard did, that the infant community had lost the two outstanding men who had led it into the wilderness, and that it had become entangled in the fierce controversy over the York election, he may well have felt it to be imperative that a man of energy and experience should be sent north. In any case, Murdac arrived with a letter of warm recommendation,[2] nominally to join with the abbot of Rievaulx in holding the election, actually, to be elected himself.[3] He doubtless found a number of old friends at Fountains, and was duly chosen as abbot.

With Murdac's election in 1143–4 the first chapter of the history of Fountains, and the one peculiar to that house among all the Cistercian foundations in England, came to an end. The new abbot was by temperament a consuming fire, and temperament and circumstances alike were to stimulate his combative spirit in Yorkshire. Clairvaux with all its uses in their purity was his *mot d'ordre*; he made an end once and for all of any lingering customs from the past that had survived among the ex-black monks; he also entered with energy into the contest against the archbishop elect. Before giving any account of this it will be well to consider the growth of the other great Cistercian abbey of the north.

III

The land given to Abbot William and his companions in the valley of the Rye, not far from Walter Espec's castle at Helmsley, fully satisfied the Cistercian requirement of solitude and was, when the monks arrived, wholly uncultivated. The first years must have been full of the hard work of breaking up the land and constructing conventual buildings. Yet from the first the monks of Rievaulx appear to have attracted far more notice than their cousins at Waverley. Had they done no more than give the impetus to the group at York their coming would have been memorable, but within a few years they attracted to themselves numerous recruits, among them men of the highest distinction, such as Maurice, subprior of the cathedral monastery of Durham, known to his contemporaries as a

---

1 John of Hexham (ed. Raine), 150: "Excellentia quidem generis sed potius praecellentem frugalitate conversationis, ante monachatum sub venerabili archiepiscopo Turstino tam in Eboracensi ecclesia quam in circumjacenti provincia ex dono parentum honoribus et divitiis locupletatum, etc."

2 Bernard, *ep.* 320, to the prior, Alexander, and the monks of Fountains: "sic audite eum [Murdac] in omnibus tanquam me ipsum. Imo et tanto amplius quanto ille et prudentia et meritis antecessit."

3 *Ep.* 320. In *ep.* 321 he exhorts Murdac to accept the verdict if elected.

second Bede in his learning and sanctity,[1] and Waldef, stepson of King David of Scotland and prior of the Augustinian canons of Kirkham, destined to become first abbot of Melrose and a saint.[2] Another new-comer, who arrived within two or three years of the foundation, was destined to fill a still more important position in the history of the English Cistercians.

Ailred of Rievaulx, the "Bernard of the north", is a singularly attractive figure whom, thanks to the records left by a disciple and still more to his own writings, we can see as a living man in some completeness.[3] No other English monk of the twelfth century so lingers in the memory; like Anselm of Bec, he escapes from his age, though most typical of it, and speaks directly to us, as, in fuller measure, Augustine and Teresa speak, of his restless search for One to whom he might give the full strength of his love. As we read, a corner of the veil that hides the past from us seems to lift, and we catch a momentary glimpse of Rievaulx in its first eagerness— a glimpse that reveals something unexpected, at once most real and yet most alien to our habits of thought.

A true Cistercian in his simplicity and austerity, Ailred is also a true disciple of Bernard in the warmth of sentiment which makes more than one of his pages a counterpart of the Sermons on the Canticle. He re-sembles Bernard, also, in his ability to administer and organize, and in the attractive power of his mind, which made of him the counsellor and confidant of many in high places far from Rievaulx. Like Bernard, too,

---

1 For Maurice, v. John of Hexham (ed. Raine), 55, 150, and Walter Daniel, *Vita Ailredi* (ed. Powicke), 93–4: "Mauricius magne sanctitatis vir et preclare prudencie utpote qui potaverat a puero vinum leticie spiritale in claustro Dunolmensi, et ex pane Cuthberti viri Dei refectus creverat in sublime ita ut a sociis secundus Beda cognominaretur; cui revera erat in tempore suo tam vite quam sciencie prerogativa secundus." Prof. Powicke has collected all that can be known of Maurice in his article *Maurice of Rievaulx* in *EHR*, xxxvi (January 1921), 17–25. He notes there that a subprior, Maurice, of Durham, witnessed a charter in 1138, and very reasonably concludes this to be the future abbot of Rievaulx. To me it seems all but certain that it was to this Maurice, not to his namesake the prior of Kirkham, that Walter Daniel wrote the letter prefixed to the *Vita Ailredi*.

2 For Waldef, v. *Vita S. Waldeni*, by Jocelin of Furness, in *Acta SS*, August, I, 248 *seqq.* Jocelin wrote c. 1210, but had reliable sources before him. Cf. also Prof. Powicke's *Ailred of Rievaulx, passim.*

3 Ailred's works are printed in *PL*, cxcv, 209–796, with the exception of the Sermon *On the Saints of Hexham*, printed by Raine (v.s. p. 229, note 2), the *Regula Inclusarum*, printed by the Maurists as an appendix to Augustine and reprinted *PL*, xxxii, 1451 *seqq.*, the tractate *De Jesu Puero Duodenni*, printed by the Maurists in Bernard's works and reprinted *PL*, clxxxiv, 849, and some shorter meditations attributed to Anselm (nos. 15–17), for which see Dom André Wilmart's article, *Les Homélies attribuées à S. Anselme*, in *Archives d'Histoire doctr. et litt. du Moyen-Age*, II (1927), 5–29. A chronology of his life and works is given by Prof. Powicke, *op. cit.*, Appendix A, 477–80 (67–70 of the reprint), which needs a few slight corrections in view of more recent work. His unfinished treatise *De Anima*, hitherto un-printed, exists in more than one English MS., the best being perhaps that in the Durham chapter library, MS. B IV 25. Besides Walter Daniel's *Vita* and Ailred's autobiographical passages, and scattered references in chroniclers, there is a valuable appreciation of his mind and character by his friend Gilbert, abbot of Swineshead, written on hearing of his death. *V. Gilberti Hoilandensis Serm. 41 in Canticum*, printed in Bernard's works by Mabillon, v, 287. *V.* also the sketch by Jocelin of Furness in *Vita S. Waldeni, ut sup.*, 257.

he had a wide correspondence, and preached and wrote in the meditative, discursive manner that was so soon to give way to the new discipline of the schools. But Ailred cannot be wholly described in terms of Bernard. He lacks altogether the triumphant and compelling force, as also the consuming zeal, of the abbot of Clairvaux; he has, on the other hand, something altogether his own, a delicacy, an intuition which, from being a gift of mind alone, gradually came to be a reflection of the whole spirit, and which makes of his later years of rule at Rievaulx an episode altogether *sui generis* in English monastic life. It is not easy to think of another in that age—unless it be Abelard—who so arouses and baffles all our endeavours to comprehend what comes so near to us and yet remains so far away.

Ailred was by birth completely English, with an ancestry that gave him connections with the Church stretching far back into the Northumbrian past (for his father was "hereditary" priest of Hexham), and with the landed families between Hexham and Durham.[1] Though he was not trained in the schools as were his contemporaries who crossed to France, he had clearly been well taught, probably at Hexham,[2] by one who was familiar with the new humanism, and when still in the impressionable years of late boyhood he became one of the court circle of the Scotch king and ultimately held the post of steward or seneschal.[3] At that period, the rivalry between the Scotch and English had little of the racial significance it afterwards came to acquire. The kings of Scotland were of the blood royal of pre-Conquest England, and were in a sense the legitimate sovereigns of Englishmen; David had an earldom in the south, and was often at the court of Henry I; the district between the Humber and the Cheviot was still debatable ground. If the Scotch king claimed sovereignty over counties soon to be wholly English, the archbishop of York, on his side, claimed metropolitan rights far north of the Tweed, and more than one Englishman had tried his fortune in a Scottish see. Ailred had been brought up with David's son, Henry, and there was, therefore, nothing unusual in his presence at the Scotch court, as there was nothing strange in the Scotch king's English stepson, Waldef, entering a religious house in Yorkshire. The author of Ailred's *Life*, and Jocelin of Furness who composed the *Life* of Waldef, dwell naturally upon the temptations of

---

1 Ailred's family connections are described very fully by Prof. Powicke, 30–3, with ample references, especially to Richard of Hexham (ed. Raine), 55–6, and Ailred's own sermon *On the Saints of Hexham* (ed. Raine).

2 He was educated with Prince Henry, son of King David. Cf. *Genealogia Regum Anglorum*, PL, cxcv, 736–7: "Cum quo [Henrico] ab ipsis cunabulis vixi et puer cum puero crevi, cujus etiam adolescentiam adolescens agnovi, etc." Prof. Powicke does not mention this passage. The prior of Hexham, it should be remembered, was Anketil of Huntingdon, where a school of repute existed.

3 *Vita Ailredi*, 83: "Erat...echonomus domus regalis...mense regalis dapifer summus." Cf. Bernard's letter, PL, cxcv, 501–2: "Cui...in regia domo carnalium ciborum fuit credita dispensatio." V. also Prof. Powicke in *Scottish Historical Review*, XXIII (1925), 34–41.

court life. These were doubtless considerable, but the Scottish court had during the past fifty years been something of a nursery of saints. The exquisite St Margaret, King David's mother, herself a grand-niece of the Confessor, had in her husband, Malcolm, and still more in her son, David, and daughter, Matilda of England, a family not unworthy of her. In the next generation David's second wife, besides bringing him a stepson later to be venerated as St Waldef, brought also traditions of the boy's grandfather, the Earl Waltheof whom nationalist sentiment had invested with the halo of martyrdom. In addition to its tradition of sanctity, the Scottish royal house was distinguished by personal courage and administrative ability of a high order, so that the atmosphere, even if there was little culture in it, must have been morally bracing to a degree for a generous and receptive nature. Certainly Ailred, impressionable from a child, became deeply attached to David,[1] and his biographer tells us that the king intended him for the highest ecclesiastical preferment in his dominions.[2] This, however, was not to be. Already, as a young man of about twenty, he must have been stirred by the action of his friend Waldef, the king's stepson and brother of Simon, earl of Northumberland, who about 1130 became an Augustinian canon at Nostell, then under the rule of Aldulf. Within a few years the distinguished young canon became prior of Kirkham, a house founded by Walter Espec only a few miles from the still desert valley of the Rye, and there Ailred was soon to find his friend again, and his own heart's home.

Gentleness, radiance of affection and wide sympathy are not the qualities which most would associate with the early Cistercians, but they are assuredly the outstanding natural characteristics of Ailred. As a child and boy, his whole life had been given to his friends:

When I was still a boy at school, the friendship of those around me was my greatest joy, and in all the occupations and dangers of those years I gave myself wholly up to my affection for my friends, so that to love and to be loved seemed the most delightful thing in the world, and nothing else seemed of any profit at all.[3]

Cicero's *De Amicitia* was put into his hands as a text-book. He read it eagerly, and felt regret that his own friendships seemed to fall so far short of the grave and measured standards required by the philosopher.[4] As a

1 Ailred had a faithful memory, and twenty years after he had left Scotland and with the war of 1138 between he wrote shortly after hearing of David's death (1153) the eloquent lament for his *dulcissimus dominus et amicus* at the head of his work *Genealogia Regum Anglorum* (*PL*, cxcv, 713–16). At the end of the same treatise he speaks of David as one "quem prae cunctis mortalibus dilexi" (*ibid.* 737).

2 If this is exact, Ailred must have decided upon a clerical life while still at court, before his mission to York.

3 *De Spirituali Amicitia*, Prologus (*PL*, cxcv, 659–60). Ailred's *amari et amare* is of course an echo of Augustine's description of his early life in *Confessions*, ii, 2: "Et quid erat, quod me delectabat, nisi amare et amari?"

4 Laurence, Ailred's friend, gave a copy of the book to Durham (Powicke, *art. cit.*, 36) and Ailred takes it for granted that Ivo also had read it as a boy (*De Spirituali Amicitia*, 661–2).

boy and young man at David's court his heart still gave itself readily, perhaps all the more readily because his friends had the glamour of a higher birth than his own. His years in Scotland were sour-sweet days. They gave him a loving admiration for his patron David which never faded from his mind, and a deep friendship for David's son, Henry[1]—a friendship which had, indeed, roots still deeper in the past—and his stepson, Waldef, but they were years of a long struggle which he records in the cadences, and almost in the phrases, of the most familiar pages of Augustine. Here, again, besides an anguish the nature of which we can but surmise,[2] it was his heart that kept him from his heart's true rest:

The ties of that life among friends held me, and above all the knot of one friendship, dear to me above all the delights of the life that then was mine.... Those about me, seeing what I possessed, but ignorant what was passing within me, said: How well it is with him! They little knew how ill it was with me within, where alone true joy can be.[3]

The contest was so bitter that for a time death seemed to him the only solution that might rid him of his burden.[4] Whether the break with the past in his soul was accomplished before his arrival at Rievaulx, he does not tell us, but the manner of that homecoming is related by his biographer. Ailred was sent south, about 1134, on a mission from King David to Archbishop Thurstan. He heard from a friend, probably Waldef, of the white monks who had arrived two years before at Rievaulx, though it can scarcely have been the first time he had heard of those whom King David had helped.[5] Anxious to visit them, he was taken by his friend to Helmsley, where they stayed the night with Walter Espec and passed the next day at the new monastery. After another night with Espec, Ailred was setting out for Scotland when, riding along the ridge of the hill above Rievaulx, he could no longer resist the Spirit. Again he presented himself at the door, and this time he had come to remain.[6]

In his early days at Rievaulx he was still most sensitive to the affectionate influence of those about him. Among them was the monk Simon, younger than himself, who died still young shortly before Ailred wrote the *Speculum*

1 *V. Genealogia Regum Anglorum*, 736–7: " Quem [Henricum] juventutis flores pulsantem sicut patrem suum quem prae cunctis mortalibus dilexi...corpore quidem, sed nunquam mente vel affectu reliqui."

2 Cf. the autobiographical passages in the *Speculum Charitatis*, I, 28 (531–2) and *De Institutis Inclusarum*, c. xxvii (*S. Augustini Opera*, ed. Benedict. (Paris, 1836), I, i, 1392–3); also the *Vita*, 78.

3 *Speculum Charitatis*, I, 28 (*op. cit.* 531–2). Was this friend the prince Henry? The whole passage contains verbal and rhythmical reminiscences of Augustine, *Confessions*, VIII, II *et al.*

4 *Speculum Charitatis, loc. cit.*: "Nisi cito admovisses manum [he is addressing God]... forte pessimum desperationis remedium adhibuissem."

5 King David had assisted Rievaulx at the beginning. Cf. letter of Bernard referred to above, p. 237, n. 3. Writing *c.* 1134 he says: "Fratres nostri qui sunt Rievallibus senserant primi viscera tue pietatis" (Hüffer, *op. cit.* 233).

6 *Vita Ailredi*, 84–7.

Charitatis eight years later, and whom he laments in pages which, though they owe something to Bernard's lament on his brother composed some three years previously, and still more to those in which Augustine mourned Nebridius and Monica, are no less a revelation of his own deep emotion:

> I remember (he writes) how often, when my eyes were straying hither and thither, the mere sight of him so filled me with shame that, returning suddenly to myself, I sternly repressed my lightness of mind, and recollecting myself, began to think of something of more profit. The rule of our life forbade us to talk together, but his countenance, his gait, his very silence spoke to me.[1]

Almost twenty years later, the memory of Simon was still fresh; for Ailred was faithful in his love:

> I recall two friends (he says) who although they may have passed from this life yet live to me and always will live. The first I took as my friend when still young at the beginning of my religious life; our tastes, our characters were something similar.... He was snatched from me at the very beginning of our friendship, when he had been chosen, but not fully proved....[2]

Ailred's years in the court circle of King David had doubtless given a distinction to his bearing, and we know him to have been, as a young man, unusually handsome.[3] Abbot William soon singled out the young monk whose past history and qualities of mind, added to his growing holiness, must have distinguished him to any discerning observer, and in 1142 we find him sent as the abbot's representative to Rome in the matter of the York election.[4] It can scarcely be doubted that he met Bernard as he passed through France, and that it was at this meeting that the abbot of Clairvaux first made the request that Ailred should write on Charity— a request which he repeated shortly with such compelling force.[5] His letter found Ailred novice master at Rievaulx, and it was answered by the *Speculum Charitatis* written, as his biographer tells us, in the *probatorium*. A year later he was appointed abbot of the new foundation of Revesby in Lincolnshire.

1 *Speculum Charitatis*, I, 34 (539–46). The whole passage is perhaps the most eloquent in Ailred's works, and a most vivid glimpse of the Rievaulx noviciate. It was written 1142–3; St Bernard's lament on his brother Gerard (*Serm. in Cant.* xxvi, ed. Mabillon, III, 2816–27) was delivered in 1138. For Ailred's fidelity, cf. *De Spirituali Amicitia*, III (681): "Semel a me receptus in amicitiam, a me nunquam poterit non amari."

2 *De Spirituali Amicitia*, III (698–702).

3 His biographer (*Vita Ailredi*, 88) thus describes him on the day of his profession, *aet.* 24–5: "Quoniam aliquantulum rufus erat ut David, pulcher et decorus aspectu plurimum delectationis intuencium oculis ingerebat." A sentence of which St Stephen Harding would scarcely have approved.

4 *Vita Ailredi*, 89. This, as is learnt from the history of the York dispute, was in 1142.

5 This letter, which appears as an introduction to the *Speculum Charitatis* (*PL*, cxcv, 501–4), bears the title *Epistola Gervasii Parchorensis* [i.e. Louth Park] *Abbatis*. Dom André Wilmart, in his article *L'Instigateur du Speculum Charitatis d'Aelred abbé de Rievaulx*, in the *Revue d'Ascétique et de Mystique*, xiv (October 1933), 369–94, has shown conclusively from MSS. evidence that the writer is Bernard—and indeed the style *clamat dominum*.

Even so early the growth of Rievaulx had been phenomenal. When Ailred was master of novices Abbot William had already no less than three hundred souls under his rule.[1] Maurice, the "second Bede" of Durham, was there, and shortly after Ailred had left for Revesby the prior of Kirkham, Waldef, who also had been involved in the disputes of York, decided at last that his vocation was to the severer life of the white monks. For a time it seemed that many of his sons would follow their prior, and a draft agreement was actually framed by which the monastery of Kirkham was transferred to the monks of Rievaulx, who undertook to build a new home for the remaining canons at Linton, but the arrangement was never executed, and Waldef went out alone or nearly so.[2] He began his new life at Wardon, a foundation of Rievaulx in the south, but soon returned to the mother-house, where he remained till he returned to Scotland as abbot of Melrose.

William, first abbot of Rievaulx, had thus fully justified the confidence which Bernard reposed in him. Within a dozen years his sons had increased from twenty-five to more than three hundred, Rievaulx had become the mother of daughters and the abbot, besides taking part in public affairs of Church and state, had had a large part in moulding the vocations of Ailred and Waldef. When he died, in 1145, William was buried under the floor of the chapter-house, and venerated among the white monks as a saint.[3] Fragments of his tomb still remain, and we know that Waldef, on his customary visits to Rievaulx as abbot of Melrose, used to pray there.[4] His death, like that of the second Richard at Fountains two years later, ends the first period in the history of his house.

---

1 *Speculum Charitatis*, I, 17 (563): "Trecentis, ut reor, hominibus unius hominis voluntas est lex." Even if (as does not seem likely) some *mercennarii* are included in the number, the growth in a decade is stupendous.

2 *V*. no. cxlix of the *Rievaulx Cartulary* (ed. Atkinson), 108–9. Prof. Powicke, *Vita Ailredi*, 54–5, and *VCH, Yorks.* III, 219–20, give the correct explanation of this curious document. Cf. also *Vita Waldeni*, 257.

3 *V*. the description of the remains of William's tomb by Sir Charles Peers in *Archaeological Journal*, LXXXVI (1929), 20 *seqq.* For William's character *v. Vita Ailredi*, 93; John of Hexham (ed. Raine), 109: "vir consummatae virtutis et excellentis memoriae apud omnes posteros", and *ibid.* 149; and Bernard's letters to him.

4 *Vita Waldeni*, 264, 265.

CHAPTER XIV

THE CISTERCIANS IN ENGLAND: II

THE PERIOD OF EXPANSION

I. THE YEARS OF GROWTH

1135–1153

Nothing in the history of the Cistercian order, whether in the land of its origin or in the British Isles, is more striking than the rapidity with which it increased and multiplied both in the number of its subjects and in its new foundations.[1] This widespread increase, which was not confined to any one district of England, has often caused astonishment to modern readers. It is indeed truly remarkable that in a country already containing so many great estates in the hands of monks, where other religious foundations, such as those of canons and nuns, were also multiplying at the same time—and that too in decades marked by bitter civil strife—so many benefactors should have been found to establish the white monks on their lands. Further reflection, however, may help in some measure to modify our astonishment. To found a Cistercian house, it must be remembered, was a far less onerous undertaking than to found a black monk abbey. The latter, if it were to be set in running order, needed, besides a large group of buildings furnished with some elaboration, an extensive group of manors already fully exploited and sufficient to bring in produce and revenues for the support of monks, servants and dependents and for the upkeep of church, buildings, library and the rest. Such a gift, with its alienation of income and rights, meant a serious sacrifice to a benefactor. In the case of a Cistercian house the business was very much more simple. All the white monks needed was a sufficient area of waste land, capable of being cultivated for the needs of a group of men which did not in the beginning exceed thirty. Buildings were of course necessary —indeed, the Cistercian constitutions were explicit on the point—but it

---

1 For the dates and family relationships of Cistercian foundations the work of Dom L. Janauschek, *Origines Cistercienses* (Vienna, 1877), is still indispensable. It is an admirable piece of laborious scholarship, and needs correction only in isolated details. As regards the English houses, a valuable paper by Alice M. Cooke, *The Settlement of the Cistercians in England*, appeared in *EHR*, VIII (1893), 625–76. Unfortunately this took the story only down to 1154. Precision has been added in various volumes of the *Victoria County Histories* and in cartularies, etc., which have been printed in recent years; owing to the breadth of the field covered in this chapter it is impossible to be certain that all the relevant literature has been consulted. For a list of all Cistercian houses in England and Wales, with dates and derivations, *v.* Appendix XI and Table IV *infra*.

was enough that these should in origin be of wood or wattle work. Thus the sacrifice and outlay on a Cistercian foundation might well be almost negligible.

All depended, in fact, on the existence of great spaces of unexploited land of the type desired, and of these there was no lack in England in the first half of the twelfth century. Indeed, all over western Europe there was a movement towards bringing under cultivation great stretches of waste and forest land; of this movement the Cistercians formed part, and in the first fifty years of the order's existence the plantation of an abbey in the midst of a forest, or by moors and marshes, might well prove an asset of great value to the lands that lay round it. Save in rare cases, of which Byland and Kirkstall may perhaps be examples, there was in these early years none of that suppression of existing farms and villages, and substitution of pasture for arable, which later became a grievance against the white monks.[1]

The Cistercians, more than any other order before or since, regarded the growth of their body as that of a family tree, in which relationships by foundation were all-important. Consequently, though tables of dates and maps are not without interest, the only true analysis of a number of Cistercian foundations is that which separates them into families of common origin. The importance of such a division is, as it happens, very clearly seen in England, for, if we except the group of Savigniac houses, most of which were planted directly from Savigny, all the English abbeys up to 1153, some thirty-six in number, were, with only four exceptions,[2] descended from the three original houses of Waverley, Rievaulx, and Fountains.

Regular life had begun at Rievaulx in the early days of March 1132. In a little over three years the abbey was prepared to make its first foundation far south on land given by Walter Espec at Wardon in Bedfordshire.[3] The origin of this house shows clearly, what we can suspect in many cases where no precise information exists, that the site of a new foundation and the provenance of the first colonists were matters depending solely on the choice of the founder and his previous knowledge of a particular community. A few months later a second group of monks was sent out as far to the north to Melrose, a house destined to be among the most famous, and to be familiar to many in after centuries from the beauty of its architecture and of its surroundings of hill and wood, as also from the

---

1 These early cases, together with others, will be discussed later; v. infra, 350–1.
2 The four were Boxley (Kent) from Clairvaux, Dore (Hereford) from Morimond. Tintern (Monmouth) and her daughter Kingswood (Glos) from L'Aumône. In Wales, before 1153, Clairvaux had founded Whitland, as will be noted.
3 The date of Wardon's foundation is not certain. The original donation seems to have been in 1135 (*Monasticon*, v, 372), but probably regular life did not begin till 1136. Simon who, as Walter Daniel tells us (*Vita Ailredi*, 87), was Ailred's novice master, was almost certainly the first abbot; v. Powicke, *Vita Ailredi*, 43, n. 1, for references.

associations which its name gathered in history and in romance. The family of Rievaulx continued to grow, and the mother saw her children's children; before twenty years had passed she had become the source of eleven flourishing houses, of which the southernmost was Sibton in Suffolk, and the northernmost Kinloss, not far from Inverness on the Moray Firth.

But noble as was the progeny of Rievaulx, she was outdone in fecundity by the abbey which herself was without a Cistercian mother. Despite the hardships which she had endured, the controversies into which she had been drawn, and the frequent change of abbots, Fountains continued to send out colonies until in 1150, only eighteen years after her origin, she had a family of twelve, including the celebrated names of Newminster, Kirkstall and Woburn, and more than half of those who had left St Mary's, York, had been entrusted with abbatial rule. Among these foundations was a somewhat unusual venture. As has been seen in the history of Evesham and of the first northern revival, there was still occasional connection between England and the Scandinavian countries. In 1146 Sigward, bishop of Bergen, was in Yorkshire. He visited Fountains, and after his first acquaintance with Cistercian life, asked Murdac for a foundation in Norway. The request was granted, and Ranulf, one of the group from York, was sent out to the Lysekloster, on the fjord near Bergen.[1] The abbey prospered and gave bishops to the Norwegian church; the year after its foundation Kirkstead, a daughter of Fountains, sent a group to Norway, where they settled at Hovedö, an island site in the fjord of Oslo.[2]

It would be tedious, and serve no good purpose, to follow in detail the derivations of all the Cistercian abbeys of England. A word may, however, be said of the third important group. In spite of the opinion of Ailred that Waverley only became active when glory was reflected upon her from the north, it is a fact that several colonies had gone out in the south before the two northern abbeys had sent forth swarms in any number. Yet it remains true that the Waverley generation, unlike the others, *crevit occulto velut arbor aevo.* Save only for Ford in Devon, which acquired and retained a certain fame as the home of Baldwin of Canterbury, this numerous family never achieved more than local celebrity. Waverley herself gave birth to five daughters;[3] her eldest born sent forth two, of which the elder again was fruitful.[4] In a little over twenty years, therefore, she saw her children's

1 *Memorials of Fountains,* I, 89–90. The name of the Norwegian bishop is thus given in a note quoted by Leland, *Collectanea,* IV, 105; cf. Walbran, *Mem. Fount.* pref. xiv. Janauschek, *Origines,* 88, has Sigurdus or Sivard.

2 For subsequent friction between Fountains and the Lysekloster, *v.* the Cistercian *Statuta* (ed. Canivez), I, 406 (1213), no. 11; 422 (1214), no. 24, and *infra,* ch. XXXVIII, p. 658.

3 Garendon (1133), Ford (1136), Thame (1137), Bruerne (1147) and Combe (1150).

4 Garendon's daughters were: Bordesley (1138) and Bittlesden (1147); Bordesley founded Stoneleigh (1141), Merevale (1148) and Flaxley (1151).

children to the fourth generation, a sight which it was given to no other English house to see. With the single exception of Ford, all these were in the midland counties of Gloucester, Worcester, Warwick, Leicester and Oxford.

A few more plantations, independent of these three great fountain-heads, were made from time to time from overseas. First among them in date was a sister of Waverley, a second English daughter of L'Aumône, the Monmouthshire house of Tintern (1131), an abbey whose ruins, by reason of their architectural perfection and exquisite natural surroundings, and from their association with one of the greatest poems in the language, have won a celebrity little inferior to that of Fountains or Rievaulx. The history of Tintern, however, has in it little that is noteworthy, nor was she the mother of a numerous family.

Not content with supervising the careers of the two great houses of the north, Bernard sent from Clairvaux more than one other colony across the Channel. The earliest of these was Whitland or Alba Landa in Carmarthenshire (1140), a house that has left the scantiest traces for the antiquary, but which was destined to be the mother of most of the abbeys founded in the second half of the century in central and north Wales. In 1146 Clairvaux again sent a colony to England, this time to Boxley in Kent, and in the following year a group went to Margam in Glamorganshire. In the latter year, also, Morimond, one of the four elder daughters of Cîteaux, sent her single colony to Dore in Herefordshire, later, as will be seen, to incur along with her Welsh neighbours the strictures of Gerald of Wales.

Only one of the Savigniac abbeys had enjoyed a reputation at all comparable to that of the three great Cistercian mothers of families. Furness, the origins of which have already been described, remained for many years the only religious house north of the Mersey and west of the Pennine chain; it attracted many subjects, made a number of foundations, and came to the notice of the king of Man, who gave to its abbot the right of choosing the bishop of the Isles.[1] Furness was also the mother, even if the unnatural mother, of an abbey which became third in the illustrious trio which the historian, William of Newburgh, links together and entitles the three luminaries of the north. His words had already been written when Philip, third abbot of Byland, himself a stranger from beyond the seas, set down in 1197 what he could gather of the story of the first years of his house from those who had often listened to the recollections of its first fathers.[2]

1 V. the article by F. M. Powicke in *VCH, Lancs.* II, 116–17, and authorities there noted. The whole article is extremely valuable.
2 For Byland and Jervaulx, v. the narratives in *Monasticon*, V, 349–54, 568–74. There is no reason to doubt the substantial accuracy of the account there given, though certain dates and details are suspicious. A critical edition, long-needed, of these chronicles and of the Byland cartulary is being prepared by Miss Phyllis Auty for the Yorks. Arch. Society.

In 1134–5 Furness, at that time still a Savigniac abbey, made a foundation at Calder in Cumberland, under Abbot Gerold, who took with him twelve monks. They remained at Calder till 1137, when an incursion of King David and his Picts of Galloway so ravaged their land that they were forced to return to seek shelter at Furness.[1] This was refused, either (as one story, probably the true one, went) because Furness was herself in fear of being reduced to want by the presence of extra numbers or (as others, doubtless at Furness, related) because Abbot Gerold was unwilling to lay down his office and merge his community once more with the mother-house. Whatever the cause, the monks of Calder were forced to depart, carrying with them nothing but their clothes and a few liturgical books in a wagon drawn by eight oxen. They decided to cross the moors to York and ask help of Thurstan who, as they were aware, only six years previously had befriended another band of exiles from home. On their way to York the monks fell in, near Thirsk, with the steward of Gundreda, widow of Nigel of Albini and mother of Roger de Mowbray, at that time still a ward of King Stephen.[2] The steward invited them to his mistress's castle, and as they approached on foot with their wagon the lady, looking out from an upper window, pitied their condition and promised them help. For the time being, the best she could do was to send them to a relative of hers, Robert de Alneto, a Norman by birth and a monk of Whitby, who was living as a hermit at Hood, near Thirsk. He welcomed them with reverence and soon asked for the Cistercian habit.

The numbers at Hood increased rapidly and it soon appeared that their holding of land was too small for the buildings and fields of a great abbey. They therefore approached Roger de Mowbray, and he came to the rescue by giving them (Old) Byland in September 1143. Here, in the valley of the Rye, near and almost in sight of the abbey of Rievaulx, they erected small buildings, but the inconvenience of the situation was so great that it is hard to account for such a gift having been proffered or accepted. The new site, in itself none too satisfactory, was so near Rievaulx that each community could hear the other's bells, and casual encounters of all kinds must constantly have occurred. Although Rievaulx had as yet no means of enforcing on the Savigniac house the Cistercian regulation as to the distance between abbeys, common sense and neighbourly feeling, perhaps also rumours of the coming subjection of Savigny to Cîteaux, suggested another move to Stocking, near Coxwold.

The year 1147, in which the transference took place, was one of great moment in the history of Savigny. The machinery of the order was not

---

1 *Monasticon*, v, 349.
2 Roger de Mowbray, according to the narrative, *Monasticon*, v, 349: "de novo susceperat cingulum militare." This receives interesting confirmation from Ailred, *Relatio de Standardo* (*Chronicles of Stephen*, III, 182–3), where it is stated that Roger, *adhuc puerulus*, was brought into the army in 1138 and bore himself well.

working smoothly, and the English houses in particular, numbering some fourteen in all and forming a good half of the whole congregation, were discontented, some of them wishing to return to France, and the majority evading the duty of visiting Savigny for general chapter. Serlo, the abbot of Savigny, had his heart with the Cistercians, and especially with Bernard at Clairvaux, whither in the event he retired to end his days. Details of the previous negotiations are wanting in the sources;[1] in the event, the order of Savigny submitted itself to Cîteaux at the Cistercian general chapter of September 1147, at which Eugenius III was present in person. The step would seem to have been largely the personal action of Serlo, no doubt supported by the daughter-houses in France; it was from the first resisted or disregarded by the majority of the English houses, and no changes were made even at Byland for more than a year. For this reason, doubtless, the union was solemnly promulgated at the Council of Rheims in March 1148, and a strongly worded bull was issued by Eugenius III a few days later, in which the English houses were enumerated as depending upon Savigny.[2] In spite of this, Furness stood out, and the abbot, Peter, a native of York, travelled out in person to Eugenius III, to whom he had appealed. A commission was appointed to try the case; Peter was commanded to make submission and did so, having relinquished his office.[3]

Thus ended the English schism in the family of Savigny, and the abbot of the mother-house circularized all his subjects in England, ordering that they should change the grey habit for the white and accept the Cistercian constitutions. It was shortly after this that Byland sent a colony across the vale of Yorkshire to Fors in Wensleydale, in the romantic circumstances of which an account survives, and from Fors after a few years they moved to Jervaulx.[4] The mother-house, which had already thrice changed its home, made a fourth and final move in 1177 from Stocking to a site a few miles farther up the valley, and there, after long labour in clearing and draining the land, a great church and monastic buildings were at last erected where the fragments of their ruins still stand.

1 Surprisingly little information exists concerning the move towards union. The Byland narrative mentions the restlessness of the English houses owing to poverty, and their remissness in attending chapter, which is also recorded in the chronicle of Peregrinus Fontanensis abbas in D'Achéry's *Spicilegium*, II, 575. But nostalgia for Clairvaux certainly played a part.

2 This is the bull of 10 April 1148 (JL, 9235), printed in *Acta SS*, Oct., VIII, 1018.

3 For this episode cf. the *Historia Fundationis* of Furness in *Monasticon*, V, 246 and *Furness Coucher Book* (Chetham Soc. IX (1886), I, 1 *seqq.*). This account is a late compilation, and untrustworthy, as was indicated by Prof. F. M. Powicke in his article on Furness in *VCH, Lancs.* II, written many years ago. The three letters of the judges delegate, Hugh, the Cluniac archbishop of Rouen, and the celebrated Arnulf of Lisieux, are in the Savigny cartulary. They were printed in Latin, with an introduction by Léopold Delisle, in the *Journal of the Archaeological Association*, VI (1851), 419–24, under the title *Documents relative to the abbey of Furness, extracted from the archives of Savigny*. An English abstract is given by Round, *Documents preserved in France*, vol. I, nos. 813–15. Unfortunately, the letters are not dated.

4 *Monasticon*, V, 571–4.

The year 1147, in which the affiliation of Savigny to Cîteaux was effected, witnessed a greater number of Cistercian foundations in England —seven in all—than any year before or after. It was besides the year in which Henry Murdac became archbishop of York and Ailred abbot of Rievaulx. It marked, indeed, in many ways the apogee of the new order considered as a force working upon the Church and society.

The summer solstice of Cistercian growth was not of long continuance. It came to an abrupt end some six years later, when the prohibition by general chapter of promiscuous foundations in the future[1] was followed within a year by the deaths of the Cistercian pope and of the abbot of Clairvaux. As regards England the year 1152 marks, for all practical purposes, the end of the era of propagation; Wales, however, still largely virgin soil, received its quota of white monk foundations in the fifty years which followed.

II. THE CISTERCIANS IN PUBLIC LIFE

1138–1153

One of the primary aims of the original band of monks who seceded from Molesme had been to escape from that contact with the life of the world around them which had become inevitable for the officials of a great black monk house, and was shared in a lesser but real degree by all who lived in monasteries which were being constantly swept into the life and controversies of the day. This aim of solitude was prosecuted with success by Cîteaux and her first foundations, and, as has been seen, was a potent motive with many of those who in other regions were among the originators of the monastic reform. The desires of the group who left St Mary's, York, were identical with those of the first fathers of Cîteaux; they desired only to live "the world forgetting, by the world forgot".

This ideal of complete freedom from contact with contemporary life, which the Carthusians have always so jealously maintained, soon ceased to be an integral part of the Cistercian tradition. Here, as elsewhere, if we would assign the reason for the change, it is to the abbot of Clairvaux that we must turn. The extraordinary personal ascendancy and activity of Bernard, which gathered force year by year in the second and third decades of the century, not only set a precedent for lesser men but attracted to Clairvaux and its daughters many of unusual administrative and mental

---

1 The decree, which in its original form appears to have been absolute (*Statuta*, ed. Canivez, 1, 45; but cf. Guignard, *Monuments primitifs*, *Instituta*, lxxxvi, p. 273), was soon regarded as merely throwing the decision upon the chapter. It had a clear effect, however, in England; if we except Tiltey (1153), which doubtless fell under the year's grace specifically allowed for abbeys under construction, the years 1152–1216 saw the foundation of only seven houses in England, whereas the mean rate of the years 1128–52 was between two and three *per annum*. For a list and tables of Cistercian abbeys *v.* Appendix XI and Table IV.

abilities, and thus made of the Cistercian order at once a nursery from which rulers of churches might be taken and a centralized organization standing for purity of administration and ready to serve any reforming prelate or pope who might wish to use it. Thus for a brief space in the twelfth century the Cistercian order (or, to speak more exactly, the family of Clairvaux) filled the rôle which the Society of Jesus vindicated for itself in the Counter-reformation of serving and, if need be, of initiating the most varied movements of renewal and reform. In this phase of Cistercian activity the personal influence of Bernard was paramount; it was not his genius to follow, but to lead; the policy of reform, therefore, as understood at Clairvaux, was not necessarily the same as that of the Curia or the high Cluniac ecclesiastics; with the latter legal and political considerations might have weight, with Bernard the only consideration was the absolute purity, as he saw it, of the Bride of Christ. In consequence, when his personal eagerness to inspire and support was overcome by death, there ceased, almost at once, to be a Cistercian party and policy of reform. But it so happened that circumstances in the north of England were peculiarly favourable for the intervention of such a party during the twenty years that passed between the foundation of Rievaulx and Fountains and the death of Bernard.

Henry I of England, as is well known, succeeded in maintaining the Church within his dominions almost wholly as the *Landeskirche* of his father. The reforming and canonical activities of the papacy were on the whole successfully excluded. With his death, followed a year later by that of William of Corbeuil, the situation changed entirely. Stephen, not by nature a strong character and beholden to the pope for recognition as king, promised in return what was in effect a transference of practical surveillance from king to pope.[1] In 1138, for the first time for almost seventy years, a papal legate entered England with unrestricted powers. The legate was Alberic, one of the group of strongly Gregorian Cluniacs who are found in the papal service at this period; he had as his companion the abbot of Molesme.[2] His business was to visit the chief religious and episcopal centres of England and Scotland, to hold a council in which the recent reforming decrees might be applied to England, and to supervise the election of an archbishop of Canterbury. Arriving in England, he proceeded to select two assessors to help and advise him—one, as it would appear, from each province. In the south he chose the strict Augustinian Robert of Hereford, who often appears as a judge delegate trusted by the papacy in the various trials and controversies of the period. In the north he would certainly have consulted Thurstan, known to be a reformer;

1 For the relations of king and pope with the Church in England during this period *v.* the relevant chapters in Böhmer, *Kirche und Staat*; Tillmann, *Päpstlichen Legaten in England*; Z. N. Brooke, *The English Church and the Papacy*; and L. Voss, *Heinrich von Blois.*

2 References to Alberic have been given above, p. 237, n. 5. John and Richard of Hexham give the fullest account of his mission.

Thurstan was old and infirm, and hoping shortly to retire; the bishop of Durham was undistinguished; it was therefore natural that the archbishop should indicate his friend, the able and energetic Richard, abbot of Fountains. Richard was consequently taken by Alberic as his assistant, and accompanied him on his prolonged tour in the north of England and Scotland; he was with him on his return to Rome, as has been mentioned, as envoy from Thurstan on the subject of his meditated resignation of the see of York. Thus after only six years of Cistercian life, the abbot of Fountains had been drawn into the full current of the ecclesiastical life of England, and had he not died in Rome would undoubtedly have continued to occupy a leading place.

The next intervention of the white monks in public affairs was due to initiative from Rievaulx, and was more deliberate and voluntary. William of Rievaulx, an intimate disciple of Bernard, resembled his master in energy and zeal; indeed, in the exercise of the latter virtue even Bernard considered him to need on occasion a restraining hand.[1] Within a few years of his arrival at Rievaulx he had been used as agent by Walter Espec and had become known to David of Scotland in the quality of negotiator.[2] He was in close touch with Bernard, had watched his conduct of the episcopal election at Langres, and knew of his approval of the decree of the Lateran Council of 1139 that *viri religiosi* of the neighbourhood should assist the diocesan chapter at episcopal elections. Consequently, when the see of York fell vacant early in 1140, he was prepared to take a share in the proceedings, the more so because it was essential to the white monks that their infant communities should have a bishop favourable to the reform, while at the same time the ecclesiastical situation in the kingdom made it likely that political and partisan considerations would influence the electors. Richard, second abbot of Fountains, was by temperament far less inclined to take an active part in public life, but his associations in the past had made the personnel of the York chapter well known to him, and events took a turn which made of that knowledge an important factor in deciding his conduct.

It is unnecessary to relate in detail the complicated story of the York election and the subsequent controversies.[3] Waldef of Kirkham was among the candidates, and he no doubt had the warm support of the Cistercians; he was vetoed on political grounds by Stephen, and after prolonged negotiations William Fitzherbert, treasurer of York, was

---

1 *Ep.* 353 (autumn, 1143): "Propterea sciens zelum vestrum, ne forte plus justo ferveat, temperamentum scientiae non admittens, etc."

2 On 11 November 1138, Abbot William was at Wark-on-Tweed, arranging for the surrender of Espec's castle to David. Richard of Hexham, 100; John of Hexham (ed. Raine), 118.

3 I may be permitted to refer to an article, *The Case of Saint William of York*, in the *Cambridge Historical Journal*, v, 2 (October 1936), 162–77, 212–14, where a detailed narrative is given, with full references to the sources and previous literature on the subject.

elected under circumstances which gave serious grounds for charges of intrusion and simony. The elect had, besides, a reputation for unchaste living which Richard of Fountains, who had known him well in the years at York, considered to be wholly merited. Consequently, the two abbots gave full support to the party which appealed to Rome against the election, and William of Rievaulx sent out as his procurator with the deputation to Rome in 1142 no other than Ailred, whose conduct of the affair won him great credit and attracted the notice of Innocent II. The case was postponed for a year, and when in Lent, 1143, the parties again met in Rome, the two abbots William and Richard were among the York appellants;[1] during all this time Bernard, by letters to Rome and England, was taking the foremost part in an affair which he had made wholly his own.

In the autumn of the same year, 1143, Richard of Fountains died at Clairvaux on his way from general chapter, and a few months later Bernard sent to Yorkshire his trusted disciple Henry Murdac, himself a man of York, to be elected abbot of Fountains; the prime motive of this choice was certainly a desire to strengthen the hands of the Cistercians, who had recently seen William Fitzherbert put in possession of his see by the papal legate, Henry of Winchester. Murdac, a man of strongly ascetic life, was by temperament inclined to drastic and imperious action; he was a reformer *in manu forti*, a consuming fire. His arrival at Fountains was signalized by a number of disciplinary measures described by Serlo in a series of scriptural phrases: he cut down the groves, destroyed the high places, searched Jerusalem with lamps, swept out the house and scoured off the rust that still clung to the sides of the vessel.[2] In other words, he enforced the full observance of every Clairvaux use and tradition *au pied de la lettre*. This was in 1144. In 1145–6, owing largely to the unremitting attacks of Bernard, William Fitzherbert was first suspended and later deposed by the Cistercian pope, Eugenius III (1145–53), who had been the friend and fellow religious of Murdac at Clairvaux; whereupon the friends and relatives of William in the north, regarding his misfortunes as being due largely to the hostile action of the abbot of Fountains, raided the abbey and inflicted a considerable amount of damage, though they failed to meet with the abbot, whose death, according to Serlo, was the object of the attack.[3] When early in 1147 final sentence of deposition had been pronounced on the archbishop of York, another election was held at Richmond on 24 July, at which Murdac received the votes of a

1 Bernard refers twice (*epp.* 235, 236) to the *miseri, pauperes abbates* who have been compelled to come to Rome from the ends of the earth.

2 *Mem. Fount.* 85.

3 *Mem. Fount.* 101: "Abbatem de Fontibus Henricum...strictis gladiis perimere moliti sunt." The attack on the abbey is described in detail. John of Hexham, 152, speaks of the attack as on a grange of Fountains, but Serlo, a monk at the time, can scarcely be in error on this point, and he is supported by the *Chronica de Melsa*, I, 115.

weighty group, though some pronounced for Hilary, later bishop of Chichester. The matter was referred back to Eugenius, who confirmed the election of Murdac, whom he consecrated himself on 7 December of the same year.

With such antecedents, it was not to be expected that he would have a quiet reign. The whole country was disturbed; the deposed archbishop was still living, though he remained in retirement at Winchester with his uncle, Henry of Blois, and the majority of the York clergy, supported by the king, refused to receive his successor. He therefore spent much time, perhaps for the greater part of three years, on the archiepiscopal manor of Ripon.[1] Here he was within a few miles of Fountains; he would naturally not have resigned his abbey until his consecration, and it seems that owing to the peculiar peril under which Fountains lay he was advised by Bernard to retain some control over its government. Serlo states that he proceeded thither on his return to England and appointed a monk of Rievaulx, Maurice, probably to be identified with Ailred's predecessor at Rievaulx, as abbot.[2] Maurice resigned after a few weeks, and Murdac once more took a monk of Rievaulx, Thorald by name, who, like Maurice, was distinguished for his learning. He remained two years at Fountains, and acted with independence—in fact, with an independence too great to satisfy Murdac, who removed him from office with some violence to Cistercian custom. Both parties appealed to Bernard who, though without enthusiasm and refusing to take any responsibility for the change, decided that the archbishop must have his way.[3]

In the short space of less than three years, which was all that remained between the full recognition of Murdac in his diocese and by King Stephen in January 1151 and his death in October 1153, the archbishop's stern and resolute character showed itself in a number of reforming activities. He enjoined strict observance upon the canons of Carlisle and Hexham, introduced Augustinians from Lanthony into the church of St Oswald at Gloucester, which was the property of the see of York, and was only prevented by death from making a similar change at Beverley.[4] Nor did he hesitate to use all his powers over the black monks of his

---

1 *Mem. Fount.* 103.

2 *Mem. Fount.* 104. The identification is accepted as all but certain by Prof. Powicke (*EHR*, XXXVI, 17–25 and *Ailred of Rievaulx*, 26), and has certainly much to commend it, though there might well have been another monk of that name among the hundred at Rievaulx. If at first sight it seems unlikely that one who had resigned the charge of his own house only a few months previously would so soon undertake that of another, the rapid resignation at Fountains is certainly characteristic of Maurice of Rievaulx.

3 *Ep.* 306, to the Cardinal of Ostia: "Et quidem qui promovit, ipse et amovit; non negaverim: qua ratione hoc fecerit, viderit ipse. Nam multis displicuisse factum cognoscitur, nempe nec rationem, nec ordinem, nec consuetudinem in ejus amotione cernentibus. Tantum archiepiscopus sic voluit; et ne contristaremus eum [*sc.* Murdac] nostro hortatu iste [Turoldus] in pace cessit, et dedit locum irae." This letter, written when Bernard was ill and nearing his end, has a tone of restraint and diffidence that contrasts strongly with the buoyant confidence of earlier utterances.   4 John of Hexham (ed. Raine), 166.

diocese, as his conduct at Whitby and Selby showed; at both these houses abbots were elected in accordance with his wishes.[1] He also took a share in the affairs of the kingdom, for Stephen, making use of his connections with Eugenius III, sent him to Rome in 1151 as envoy to arrange for the recognition of Eustace as heir to the English throne. The last six months of his life were consumed in resisting the election of Hugh Puiset, a king's man and his old opponent, to the see of Durham. He died on 14 October 1153, a few weeks after Bernard and Eugenius, and with his death the identification of the northern Cistercians with the reforming programme of Clairvaux ceased.

Dissimilar in character as he was to Ailred, the latter revered Murdac profoundly. In his last years a crucifix which had belonged to the archbishop was among the handful of cherished objects preserved in the oratory of the abbot of Rievaulx,[2] and Ailred's narrative of the case of the nun of Watton, whatever may be thought of that strange document, is another witness to his opinion of Murdac's sanctity.[3] With the limited information at our disposal, it is not easy to judge whether his influence upon the white monks of the north was wholly beneficent; he certainly affected their history, brief as was his life among them, and he, even more than Thurstan and William of Rievaulx, must be held responsible for setting them in the full light of public controversy. Serlo, who was at Fountains when he was elected and knew him as abbot, characterized him as a man of high spirit, invincible in a just cause, ready to suffer for justice's sake rather than that justice should suffer,[4] but it is perhaps not an accident that almost all references to him are concerned with controversies in which he was engaged. Nor is it surprising that the experiment of seeking an archbishop of York from among the Cistercians was not repeated.

III. AILRED OF RIEVAULX: 1147–67

I

After Henry Murdac's death another Cistercian, with a character and mind of very different mould, filled for a number of years an important position in the ecclesiastical life of the north, and extended his influence far beyond the boundaries of the province by his presence and his writings. Ailred

---

1 *Whitby Cartulary* (ed. Atkinson), 8–9; *Historia Selebeiensis Monasterii*, [44].

2 *Vita Ailredi*, 107: "Paruulam crucem quae fuerat bone memorie archiepiscopi Henrici Eboracensis."

3 Ailred, *de Sanctimoniali de Wattun* (*PL*, cxcv, 791): "Pontificante...sanctae ac piae recordationis Henrico." The *dénouement* of the situation there described is occasioned by an apparition of Henry Murdac. The tract is appended by John of Hexham to his chronicle (*v.* ed. Raine, 172) but not printed by the editors of the Surtees Society and Rolls Series volumes.

4 *Mem. Fount.* 85: "Homo magnanimus, et in causa justitiae omnino invincibilis, eligens magis pro justitia periclitari quam justitia, eo praesidente, periclitetur."

became abbot of Rievaulx in 1147, when he was some thirty-seven years of age, and held the office till he died, a man whom long illness had made prematurely old in body, in the first days of 1167. The period of his rule, a little more than nineteen years long, was one of very great prosperity for the house in things material and spiritual, and one in which Ailred's great and in many ways unique gifts of mind and soul came to full maturity.

The material growth of Rievaulx can be traced in the record of benefactions provided by its cartulary[1] and the reconstructions that have been made of the plan of its early buildings, but the personal direction of Ailred effected its most striking work in the building up of the family of the house. He was, his biographer tells us, "of extreme delicacy of feeling, condescending to the weakness of all, nor did he think that any who besought him for charity's sake should be saddened". Hence:

In receiving those who desired to come to religion he made as though he would have gone further,[2] that the prayers of the brethren might press him, as one unwilling, to consent; hence it came about that many were received of whom he had no real knowledge, for he often left it to the judgment of the community to receive whom they would.[3]

A result of this condescension was an enormous increase of the numbers at Rievaulx. If we may receive as definite Ailred's own figures and those of Walter Daniel, the community which in 1132 may have numbered only twenty-five had risen to three hundred by 1142 and to six hundred and fifty by 1165.[4]

Ailred's biographer, in a vivid phrase, describes the crowded church on feast days, when the majority of the *conversi* would be back from the granges, as packed with monks as closely as a hive with bees; so close that they cannot stir, and resembling crowded choirs of angels as pictured by devout fancy.[5] The coming of such large numbers to Rievaulx was not merely the response of the north to the call of Cîteaux, still less was it due to a good-natured *laissez-faire* on the part of the abbot; it was Ailred's explicit desire and invitation. He never tired of repeating that the supreme and singular glory of Rievaulx was that it had learnt, beyond all other houses, to bear with the weak and to have compassion on those in need:

All (he said), strong and weak alike, should find in Rievaulx a haven of peace, a spacious and calm home...of it should be said: Thither the tribes go up, the

---

1 Cf. also the remarks of the editor, introd. lxxiv–v.

2 The reference is to Luke xxiv, 28–9: "He made as though he would have gone further. But they constrained him, saying: Abide with us, etc."

3 *Vita Ailredi*, 97. But it must be remembered that the biographer of a saint often fails to grasp his inmost thought.

4 For the figure of 1142–3 v. *Speculum Charitatis*, I, 17 (*PL*, cxcv, 563): "Trecentis, ut reor, hominibus." Walter Daniel (*Vita*, 97) says that Ailred at his death "reliquit monachos bis sepcies decem et decies quinquaginta [so the original reading] laicos fratres". Elsewhere he refers to him (*Vita*, 80) as "certe centum monachorum patrem fratrumque laicorum quingentorum".

5 *Vita Ailredi*, 97: "Tanquam in alueolo apes...constringi et conglomerari."

tribes of the Lord, unto the testimony of Israel, to give thanks unto the name of the Lord. Yea, tribes of the strong and of the weak. For that cannot be called a house of religion which spurns the weak, since: Thine eyes have seen mine imperfection and in thy book are all written.[1]

And so there flocked to Ailred men of every type from near and far:

> Was there ever (asks Walter Daniel) anyone weak in body or character expelled from that house unless his evil ways gave offence to the whole community or ruined his own hope of salvation? Hence there came to Rievaulx from foreign nations and distant lands a stream of monks who needed brotherly mercy and true compassion, and there they found the peace and sanctity without which no man can see God. Yea, those who were restless in the world and to whom no religious house gave entry, coming to Rievaulx the mother of mercy and finding the gates wide open, freely entered therein.[2]

Clearly for Ailred the Cistercian way of life was no garden enclosed, in which only rare and pure souls would find green pasture, but rather something in its way as catholic as the Church, a home for souls of every kind who should find each the help most suited to him. And it must not be forgotten that three out of every four who came were simple, unlettered, stolid labourers, come to swell the ranks of an army of *conversi*. The dangers accompanying such a policy as Ailred's are obvious, and must have been so to his own clear mind. But the influence of such a man as he was can scarcely be over-estimated, and all the evidence that exists points to the maintenance at Rievaulx of a sustained fervour for many decades after his death.[3] Ailred's condescension was not weakness or compromise; the strict rule of Cîteaux was honoured, and the latter years of the abbot's life, when his physical suffering was all but unceasing, must have made it abundantly clear that the way of mercy was not the way of delicate living.

More than two-thirds of the family of Rievaulx were made up of the *conversi*, and it is certain that of the choir monks many, no doubt the majority, were men of no refinement or intellectual gifts. Yet all the sources reveal the existence, alike at Rievaulx and the other houses of Ailred's family, of a numerous class of monks who had passed through the new humanist discipline of the schools and retained, even within the framework of the Cistercian life of labour, silence and simplicity, a warm eagerness of mind and heart which few who visit the ruins of Rievaulx would associate with its walls. It was with these that Ailred's relations were at once most characteristic and most individual. Hard though it be to fill in the details of the picture, the main outlines are given us, clear beyond the possibility of misconception, by Gilbert of Holland, Walter

---

1 *Vita Ailredi*, 96–7.   2 *Ibidem*.
3 E.g. William of Newburgh, writing *c.* 1193 (1, 52), speaks of the fame of Rievaulx for regular discipline.

Daniel and Ailred himself.[1] We see him, the Cistercian abbot, the centre of a group of listeners and interlocutors, engaged in one of those discussions, half Platonic, half scholastic in character, which in one form or another absorbed for more than two centuries the interests and energies of so many in Western Europe. With Ailred, especially in his later years, the aim was primarily spiritual, not intellectual, but the young monks who surrounded him had, like himself, steeped themselves in Cicero and followed the young Augustine; they had even given themselves to a newer spirit, that of the Arthurian romance;[2] they had much to learn and to leave before they could follow Ailred with the fourth gospel to the Cross. We can watch him treating with one such, the young monk Gratian, to whom two of the three dialogues *De Spirituali Amicitia* are principally addressed, and who is introduced to us in words put by Ailred in the mouth of no other than Walter Daniel as:

One whom I might fitly call friendship's child; for his whole occupation is to love and to be loved.[3]

Ailred had learnt much since the days at David's court. He now defines friendship with his eyes upon the later chapters of St John's gospel: All things which I have heard of my Father, I make known unto you; and: You are my friends if you do what I command you.

"By these words (he continues), as St Ambrose says,[4] he gave us a way of friendship to follow, that we should do the will of our friend, that we should lay bare the secrets of our heart to our friend, and know his in return.... A friend hides nothing. If he be a true friend, he pours out his soul, as the Lord Jesus poured forth the mysteries of the Father." Thus Ambrose. But how many do we not love, to whom it is unwise to open our soul and pour forth all that is within! Either their age or their understanding is unable to bear it.[5]

1 The novice, Ailred's interlocutor, in the *Speculum Charitatis*, II, 17 (562), says: "Tribus solum hominibus, et hoc rarissime, et vix de necessariis loquimur." This was the rule, the three being abbot, prior and master of novices. Yet we have several pictures of Ailred as the centre of an animated group, e.g. *De Spirituali Amicitia*, I (661): "In turba fratrum me residente, cum omnes undique circumstreperent, et alius quaereret, alius disputaret; et iste de Scripturis, ille de moribus, alter de vitiis, de virtutibus alter quaestiones ingererent, tu solus tacebas." *Vita Ailredi*, 98: "Venientes ad illud [Ailred's cell] et in eo sedentes uiginti simul vel triginta singulis diebus conferrent ad inuicem...super grabatum illius ambulantes et decumbentes loquebantur cum eo ut paruulus confabulatur cum matre sua." Gilbert of Holland had often witnessed similar scenes (*In Cant. Serm.* 41, in *Bernardi Opera*, ed. Mabillon, v, 287): "Memini me frequenter illum, cum coeptum de assidentibus aliquis interrupisset sermonem importune, etc." It is unnecessary to dwell upon the combination of qualities, natural and spiritual, essential to the successful conduct of such reunions.
2 *Speculum Charitatis*, II, 17 (565): "In fabulis, quae vulgo de nescio quo Arcturo finguntur." Cf. Prof. Powicke's interesting notes, *Ailred of Rievaulx*, 66.
3 *De Spirituali Amicitia*, II (672): "Quem ipsius amicitiae alumnum jure dixerim: cujus totum studium est amari et amare." The scene of Book I is laid at (?) Wardon; in Book II (675) there is a reference to the schism of Octavian, which began 7 September 1159. Ostensibly, and perhaps actually, many years had elapsed (670, *plures praeterierunt anni*) since the first Book was written, and Ivo, the original interlocutor, had died. The dialogue of the third Book took place the day after that of the second (692, *hesterna die*).
4 Ambrose, *De Officiis*, III, 21.   5 *De Spirituali Amicitia*, III (691).

To this Walter Daniel replies:

This friendship is so sublime and perfect that I dare not aspire to it. Gratian here and I are content with that described by your favourite Augustine[1]—to talk together, to laugh together, to do each other services, to read together, to study together, to share things trifling and serious; sometimes to disagree, but without passion, as a man may do with himself, and by such disagreement to season the numberless judgments which we share together; to teach and learn the one from the other, to feel the want of our friends when absent, and welcome their coming with joy. Such signs of heart-felt affection as these, translating themselves upon the countenance, or in the speech and eyes of those who love each other, and in a thousand affectionate gestures, are like tinder to set hearts on fire, and to make of many one mind and heart. This it is that we think to be lovable in our friends, so that our conscience seems guilty, if we do not return another's love, whether he or we first gave it.

To which Ailred:

This is the friendship of the flesh and above all of the young, as were once the writer of these words and the friend of whom he spoke. Yet, saving trifles and deceits, if nothing evil enters in, it may be tolerated in hopes of more abundant grace to come, and as the foundation of a more holy friendship. As one grows in the religious life, and in spiritual discipline, together with the gravity of maturer years and the enlightenment of spiritual understanding, such friendships pass easily into higher regions, as the affections become purified. For we said yesterday that it was easy to pass from man's friendship to God's, by reason of the resemblance between them.

This passage has been quoted at length, as showing Ailred at his most characteristic. In its outspoken humanism and serene optimism it recalls the atmosphere of the Academy or of Tusculum, and indeed the two chief treatises of Ailred are documents not yet perhaps sufficiently familiar to historians of the culture and religious sentiment of the times. The later dialogue, from which the quotations have been taken, ends with a long account of two of Ailred's own friendships.

I recall two friends (he says) who, although they have passed from this life yet live to me and always will live. The first I took as my friend when still young. [This, as we have seen, was the monk Simon.] The other[2] was chosen by me when he was still a boy; I tested him in many, many ways, and when I was now growing old I took him into my most intimate friendship. The first I chose as friend and companion in the joys of the cloister and the delights of the spirit which I was then tasting for the first time; I had no burden of the care of souls upon me yet, and no anxiety over temporal things. I asked nothing, I bestowed nothing, but affection, and the loving judgment which affection gave. The other I took, when he was still young, to a share in my solicitudes, and had him as my helper in this work of mine. So far as my memory serves to judge these two friendships, I would say that the former rested more on

---

1 *Tuus Augustinus*. The reference is to *Confessions*, IV, 8.
2 The second friend, who came from abroad and was ultimately subprior (699), cannot be identified.

affection, the latter on reason, though in the latter there was affection too, and the former was not without reason. But while the one friend, who was taken from me in the very beginnings of our friendship, could be chosen, as I have said, but not tested, the other was spared to me from boyhood to middle age and loved by me, and passed with me through all the stages of friendship.

And Ailred, after describing their life together, ends:

And thus, beseeching Christ on behalf of one's friend, and for the friend's sake desiring to be heard by Christ, the attention and affection are all directed to the friend; but suddenly and unawares love changes its object, and being so near touches the sweetness of Christ and begins to taste and feel how sweet he is. Thus rising from that holy love which reaches the friend to that which reaches Christ, he will joyfully pluck the rich spiritual fruit of friendship...and this friendship, to which few are admitted, will be poured out upon all and returned by all to God, when God shall be all in all.[1]

II

The writer of these lines was not a philosopher, writing at ease on his terrace, untroubled by the hard realities of life, nor even an Augustine among his pupils in peaceful, sunny Cassiciacum, but an infirm, tireless abbot, the ruler of a vast household, the counsellor of bishops and kings, who snatched time, between his solitary prayer and the visits of those who needed his help, to add a few sentences to the roll in his bare and comfortless cell. Besides the responsibility for all things material and spiritual at Rievaulx, Ailred had no rest from the obligation of long and regularly recurring journeys. The framers of the *Carta Caritatis*, writing for a small group of houses situated in a single region of one country, little realized when they wrote what a ceaseless labour of journeying to and fro was to be the lot of the abbots of mother-houses in the near future. By their regulations, increased by later statute, every Cistercian abbot had to visit every year both Cîteaux, for the general chapter in September, and the abbey of which his own was a filiation.[2] He had also to perform the regular yearly visitation of all the daughter-houses of his own home. Thus Ailred, in the course of each year, had the obligation of visiting Cîteaux, Clairvaux, Woburn, Revesby, Rufford, Melrose and Dundrennan, and though no doubt dispensations or sheer impossibility relieved him from time to time of some of these visits, there is evidence from a number of sources that none of his charges were neglected, and that he was continually on the road. Clairvaux was doubtless taken on the way to or from Cîteaux, and the three English houses could be visited on the same

---

1 *De Spirituali Amicitia* (698–702).
2 Bernard, it would seem, never in person visited Rievaulx or any of the Clairvaux foundations in the British Isles, nor have I met with any reference to substitutes sent by him to Rievaulx.

journey with little waste of time, but it was a long circuit to Melrose and Galloway (there is evidence that Ailred made this journey in the early spring), and the two absences must have accounted for some three or four months of a year.

These regular appearances of such a distinguished man as Ailred, the intimate friend of the king of Scotland, at the centres of life along the great roads, must have served as an incitement to many to make use of his counsel or his eloquence, and he became more and more a public figure, one of the most considerable in the north of England. David of Scotland was his friend, and in England, among others, Robert, earl of Leicester, the justiciar, and Gilbert Foliot, the active bishop of Hereford and London. He had addressed a work to Henry II before 1154[1] and the acquaintance ripened in after years; we are told that his advice had the greatest influence over the king in determining him to support Alexander III against the antipope Octavian in 1159.[2] His presence as arbitrator or adviser was desired by religious superiors and communities of every order, and he came to be sought after as a preacher for great occasions. As early as 1147 he arbitrated on a question of the prior of Durham's precedence;[3] in 1151 he gave judgment in the dispute between Savigny and Furness for jurisdiction over Byland; in 1155 he preached at Hexham on the occasion of a solemn translation of relics; in 1163 he was present at the council at Westminster that decided the question of exemption between St Albans and the bishop of Lincoln,[4] and in the same year he preached at the translation of the relics of Edward the Confessor, recently canonized;[5] in 1164 he attested an important agreement between the orders of Cîteaux and Sempringham.

No doubt his good offices were often solicited also by individuals. A casual reference shows him visiting, in company with a young monk from the neighbouring monastery of Durham, the celebrated Godric of Finchale,[6] and he himself tells us how he was called in by Gilbert of Sempringham to advise in the case of the strange happenings at Watton.[7]

Along with these external activities went a steady output of writing. If in 1142 it had required the direct and reiterated command of Bernard to make him break silence, in later life he gave himself more readily to

1 Cf. introductory letter to *Genealogia Regum Anglorum* (711–13).

2 *Chronicon Angliae Petriburgense*, 98: "Inductus ad ejus obedientiam...maxime viva voce s. Alredi abbatis Rievallensis." It is probable that the compiler of this late work had before him some Cistercian source, perhaps a chronicle of Wardon.

3 For references to all these events, *v.* Powicke, *Ailred of Rievaulx*, Appendix A, 67–70.

4 *Registrum Antiquissimum of Lincoln* (ed. C. W. Foster, Lincs. Record Society, 1931), vol. 1, no. 104, pp. 64–6.

5 The *Chron. Ang. Petrib.*, *s.a.* 1163, states: "S. Alredus abbas huic translationi interfuit, offerens vitam regis et homeliam." The abbot of Westminster was a relative of Ailred and the date (13 Oct.) would have fitted well with the return journey from chapter at Cîteaux.

6 Reginald of Durham, *De Vita et Miraculis S. Godrici* (Surtees Soc. xx (1845), 176–7).

7 *PL*, cxcv, 796.

composition of all kinds, and even became something of a historian laureate.[1] His first venture in this field would seem to have been his account of the Battle of the Standard; it was followed by his *Genealogy of the Kings of England*, written in 1152–3, which was addressed to the future Henry II when Duke of Normandy and celebrated the union of the Norman and old English royal lines; by a patriotic account of the saints of Hexham a year or two later; and by a life, destined to become standard,[2] of Edward the Confessor composed *c.* 1163. In another category are the monastic conferences and the sermons on Isaiah, which belong to the same years, together with the more characteristic and elaborate dialogues on Spiritual Friendship and the Soul, the latter of which was unfinished at his death;[3] nor did he refuse a request such as that of his sister, from her anchor-hold, for a rule of life. Literary activities of a theological or devotional nature, though a departure from the original scheme of Cîteaux, could find ample precedent in the life of Bernard, but the historical treatises of Ailred came *de son cru*, as the work of a northerner whose earliest memories were of traditions of Bede. They show, as do Ailred's discussions with a circle of his monks, that the *Carta Caritatis* and the Cistercian statutes, though in appearance so devoid of elasticity, were in practice capable of receiving new wine without being broken.

Besides these formal compositions Ailred began, at about the time of his first literary venture in 1143, to open a correspondence[4] which in time came to count among its recipients the pope, the kings of France, England and Scotland, almost all the bishops, and magnates such as the earl of Leicester.[5] Walter Daniel assures us, and we may believe him, that in these letters Ailred's spirit left its most living memorial; most unfortunately they have all disappeared, save for one or two epistles prefatory to his works.

Ailred was not a deep speculative or mystical theologian; he was not conversant with the dialectic that had developed so speedily in Europe during his lifetime, and he lacked Bernard's gift of grasping and expounding in magisterial manner a question of moral or spiritual importance. He had, indeed, an extremely sympathetic and alert mind, and the most superficial examination of his writings finds in them reflections of the

---

1 For Ailred's writings and their chronology, *v. Vita Ailredi*, 90, 99–100 and Powicke, *Ailred of Rievaulx*, 67–70.

2 Cf. the judgment of M. Bloch in *Analecta Bollandiana*, XLI (1923), 17–44.

3 So *Vita Ailredi*, 99, and the Durham MS. B IV 25 (f. 128 v.) confirms the statement. This dialogue, of which an edition would be welcome, contains an interesting allusion to the panorama of London, including Westminster Abbey, St Paul's and the Tower, with the Thames flowing beneath (f. 98 v.). I owe this reference to the kindness of Mr Richard Hunt, of Liverpool University.

4 *Vita Ailredi*, 90: "Per idem tempus [*sc.* when novice master] cepit scribere ad diuersas personas epistolas sensu serenissimas." *Ibid.* 100: "Epistolas...in quibus uiuentem sibi reliquit imaginem."

5 So *Vita Ailredi*, 100. To the sermons on Isaiah is prefixed a letter to Foliot which recalls the bishop's kindness to Ailred in London (*PL*, CXCV, 361–2).

thought of the time—in the earlier treatises of the Cistercian controversies[1] and Bernard's writings, in the later of the topics discussed by Hugh and Richard of St Victor[2]—but they are reflections and no more; Ailred was not of the schools and did not probe deeply into the mysteries of the faith. His unique position as a writer—wholly unique in England, and without exact parallel abroad—is due in part to the limpid sincerity with which he laid bare, in his wish to help others, the growth and progress of his own mind and heart from the human to the divine, and in part to the candid humanism of his most characteristic pages.

III

The demands which his various duties and employments made upon the mental and physical energies of the abbot of Rievaulx would have taxed to the uttermost the strength of one in perfect health. Ailred, during the last ten years of his life, was, like his master at Clairvaux, constantly ill and subject to recurring visitations of pain which left him prostrate and unable to stir. To a chronic disease which resembled gout or rheumatic fever in that it rendered him incapable of motion and acutely sensitive to the slightest touch, were added attacks of the stone in which he could do nothing but lie on a piece of matting by the fire in the infirmary, frail and twisted as a crumpled sheet of parchment.[3] During all these ten years he made use of a dispensation obtained from general chapter which permitted him to live in the infirmary and yet at the same time, whenever possible, travel about his lands and granges and take full part in all community duties. Walter Daniel gives a vivid description of the shed[4] which he caused to be constructed for himself alongside of the common infirmary, with two divisions. In one of these was his pallet, in the other his oratory; in the former he received his sons, who came to him in their numbers, sitting or standing about the room or on his very bed "as little children might on that of their mother"; in the other he wrote his letters and treatises, and spent many of the night hours in prayer. During the last four years of his life his austerities and prayers increased with his infirmities, and he ceased to care for the advice of physicians; he often returned from Mass so exhausted that he lay as one dead for an hour, yet he never failed to carry out effectively the administration of his house.

1 In *Speculum Charitatis*, III, 35 (608 *seq.*), he refers to a letter, resembling the first letter of Peter the Venerable to Bernard, on the questions at issue between the white and black monks. I have not been able to identify the writer.

2 E.g. *Sermo III in Isaiam* (367 *seqq.*) is clearly based on the doctrine of the Victorines.

3 The vivid simile is Walter Daniel's (*Vita Ailredi*, 80): "Quasi membrane folium juxta ignem appositum totum corpus in tantum contorsit ut inter genua caput prorsus habere videretur." It was when Ailred was in this condition that *quidam epicurus monachus* threw him into the fire.

4 He calls it a *mausoleum*, a *tugurium* (*Vita*, 98); it contained a *fovea in solo* in which Ailred used to sit (*ibid.* 104).

The last phase of his illness came upon him on Christmas Eve, 1166. A few days later he took a formal farewell of the community round his bed, and gave to them the small objects that had been so long and constantly used in his hours of vigil—a glossed psalter, Augustine's *Confessions*, a text of St John and Henry Murdac's crucifix.[1] His biographer more than once remarks on the charm which never left him, and on the love of his sons which brought them in crowds[2]—even to the number of a hundred—to his bedside. He adds, in a paragraph of singular beauty:

For myself, I must confess that while I felt a great awe as I stood by his bed during those days, yet I felt also a joy greater than the awe. For we heard him saying continually: "Hasten, hasten", and he often urged his request with the name of Christ, which he spoke in English, because Christ's name in that tongue is of only one syllable, and is easier to pronounce and more pleasant to hear. He kept saying, then, to give his very words: "Hasten, for Crist luve." And when I said to him: "What is it, father?" he lifted his hands towards heaven and his eyes, shining like fire, to the crucifix over against him, and said: "Suffer me to depart as soon as may be to Him, the king of glory, whom I see before me. Why do you delay? What are you about? What do you wait for? Hasten, for Christ's love, hasten." I say to all who shall read this page that never in all my life have I been so moved as when hearing those words so often repeated, uttered in a way that struck such awe, by such a man at such a moment, by a man of such holiness at the hour of his death. And these words were ever upon his lips for the space of three days.[3]

On the day before his death, 11 January 1167, Richard, abbot of Fountains, Roger, abbot of Byland, and almost all his choir monks, together with some *conversi*, were about him. He could not speak, but followed with his heart the Passion as it was read to him. Walter Daniel, who was holding the dying abbot's head in his hands, whispered to him, so low that no one could hear: "Father, look upon the crucifix; let your eyes be where your heart is." Ailred, who had not spoken for two days, at once opened his eyes, and gazing at the figure on the cross said: "Thou art my Lord and my God, thou art my refuge and my salvation, thou art my glory and my hope for ever. Into thy hands I commit my spirit." He did not speak again.[4]

---

1 *Vita Ailredi*, 107; cf. 104: "Et maxime confessiones Augustini in manibus portabat assidue, eo quod illos libros quasi quasdam introductiones habebat cum a seculo conuerteretur."
2 *Vita Ailredi*, 105: "Dulciter me intuens, ut erat dulcissimus." 108: "Sic vehementer amatus est a nobis amator ille omnium nostrum."
3 *Vita Ailredi*, 108.
4 *Vita Ailredi*, 109.

CHAPTER XV

THE BLACK MONKS BETWEEN 1135 AND 1175

I

The death of Henry I was taken in a previous chapter as a convenient date for ending a period in the history of the black monks of England. Under the Conqueror and his sons they had enjoyed and profited by a protection, a sheltering, which had no parallel in the rest of Europe. The isolation in which the Norman kings had maintained their dominions, together with the encouragement given to what was best and purest in the religious life, had made of England a garden enclosed; the vigorous young Norman monasticism, grafted upon the old English stock or planted to grow alone, had been sheltered from attack and protected from the danger of being choked or strangled by other growths. With the death of Henry I all this was changed. The cessation of his firm rule left the garden exposed to the inroads of all kinds of enemies, the lowering of the barriers that separated England from Europe allowed the entrance of new seeds, and, to carry the simile to the end, the original plantation, left to itself, began to grow irregularly and in some cases to revert to the wild. Such metaphors, and the ideas that lie behind them, must not be pressed too rigidly. The year 1135 is a convenient date, no more; the processes of change had begun before, and did not fully develop till years after, nor were the black monks, as a body, bound by a single law or measure. Unlike a "province" or "congregation" of the modern religious world, unlike even the contemporary Cistercian family, the individual houses, like the trees of a forest, could exhibit as individuals every kind of healthy growth or stunted development. Nevertheless, certain general tendencies can be observed, and it is with them alone that these pages are concerned. In the paragraphs that follow we shall review the effect upon the black monks of the competition from the new orders, the material damages suffered during the disorders of the reign of Stephen, the various circumstances that involved so many of the old monasteries in protracted and vexatious litigation with the bishops, and, finally, the tendency of the houses to lose the bond of a common aim and drift towards isolation, each one becoming, alike in its external and internal policy, something of a law unto itself.

II

The direct influence of the new orders, that is, primarily, of the white monks, was in every way less in England than abroad. Although the Cistercians by degrees penetrated everywhere they caused, south of the

Humber at least, none of the controversies, the searchings of heart, the striking conversions in high places, the transferences of allegiance and the reactions of reform that were so common in central and north-eastern France.[1] This was owing, as has already been said, in part to the flourishing state of Anglo-Norman monasticism, in part to the complete absence of any figure of distinction among the white monks of southern England. Until the appearance of Baldwin of Ford in another generation, no white monk of the families of Waverley or Tintern is so much as known by name, save as one on the roll of the abbots of his house, and it is hard to quote the case of a single black monk, or even of a highly placed secular clerk—south, that is, of the Humber—who became a white monk or white canon before c. 1175. Nor is there any case, save for a single Cluniac pamphlet of uncertain but probably English provenance,[2] of the English monks taking any part or interest in the fierce controversies aroused in France by Bernard's *Apologia*. The monks of England would seem to have watched the quiet and gradual Cistercian plantation without any feelings of rivalry or hostility; the newcomers could exist alongside of the old without disturbance; there was room for this spirit and for that.

Nevertheless, the white monks, and to a lesser degree the canons white and black, could not but affect the others indirectly if not directly. Even if the majority of their recruits were local, there must have been a certain number, and those among the most fervent, who deliberately chose the new instead of the old, and thereby deprived the old of valuable accessions. And the Cistercians, however peaceful their arrival, claimed to stand for a stricter, purer monastic life; the black monks could no longer regard their way as the one royal road of salvation, and the knowledge that others were taking the kingdom of heaven by violence may have tended to modify aspirations and diminish enthusiasm among those who followed a more beaten path. And this competition in the purely spiritual sphere came at the very moment when the monasteries, for altogether different reasons, were losing the intellectual leadership of the Church in England, and when many of the most gifted of the younger generation, who twenty years before would have gone to Winchester or Canterbury, were now going overseas in search of the new learning of the schools, and returning to be bishops or bishops' officials.

III

The sufferings of the population of the countryside during the anarchy under Stephen, and the outrages inflicted on all who had property that

---

1 For a list of monks and canons who became Cistercians, *v.* Appendix X.
2 Published by Dom André Wilmart in *RB*, xlvi (July 1934), 296–344. Dom Wilmart tentatively suggests that the author was Hugh, prior of Lewes, abbot of Reading (1123–9) and archbishop of Rouen.

could be turned into ransom-money, are vividly described by more than one monastic chronicler. In particular, a celebrated page of the Peterborough continuator of the Old English *Chronicle* has long been a *locus classicus* which all historians have quoted or paraphrased.[1] Towards the end of the last century, indeed, there was a tendency to question the extent of the anarchy and the consequent suffering, and to confine it to the fen country[2] and the surrounding districts, but a careful review of all the evidence did much to confirm the traditional account.[3] Certainly, so far as monastic records go, the spoliation and terrorism would seem to have been widespread and thorough, and few monasteries escaped without suffering material damage of one kind or another; their situation at the centre of important towns, such as Gloucester and Winchester, or at points of strategic importance, such as Evesham and Abingdon, made them peculiarly liable to attack, and their wealth and rich lands made them a desirable prey.

Three groups of monasteries suffered most severely, those in the west midlands, those in central Wessex, and those in or near the Fens. In the midlands the damage caused was as a rule a consequence of the situation of the abbey in a town or at a bridge-head. Both Worcester and Winchcombe were attacked and sacked by Miles of Gloucester on behalf of the Empress in 1139, and Tewkesbury was attacked by Stephen in the same year;[4] the abbeys must have incurred damage, at least to their properties. Three years later, in 1142, Coventry, always an unfortunate house, was seized and turned into a fortress by Robert Marmion.[5] Evesham, for its part, suffered from the ravages of William Beauchamp, who broke down the wall of the abbey graveyard, plundered its goods, and established a castle at the bridge-head of Bengeworth.[6] Farther south, Robert Fitzhubert, one of the most unscrupulous and lawless of the freebooters of the time, took possession, on the death of Roger of Salisbury at the end of 1139, of the castle which the bishop had erected at Malmesbury, entered the chapter of the monastery in arms, and threatened every kind of violence.[7] In the west, the town of Bath was held in a state of siege for

---

1 *Chronicle, s.a.* 1137. This long entry was not written till after the death of Stephen. Very similar language is used by William of Malmesbury, *GR*, 561 *seq.*, and by the author of the *Gesta Stephani* (*Chronicles of Stephen*, III, 50 *seqq.*).

2 So, in particular, H. Round in his *Geoffrey de Mandeville*.

3 Cf. the article by H. W. C. Davis, *The Anarchy of Stephen's Reign*, in *EHR*, XVIII, 72 (October 1903), 630–41.

4 *Chronicle of John of Worcester*, ed. J. R. H. Weaver (*Anecdota Oxoniensia*), [56–7], [60–1].

5 *Chronicle of John Oxenede, sub anno.*

6 *Chron. Evesh.* 100: "Willelmum de Bello Campo et complices suos qui muros coemeterii destruxerant et bona ecclesiae tempore werrae rapiebant...excommunicavit [abbas]...etiam castellum quod erat Bengewrthe ad caput pontis...funditus destruxit." William Beauchamp figures also as a plunderer of Gloucester abbey. Cf. G. Foliot, *ep.* 66 (ed. Giles).

7 Will. Malmesb., *GR*, 561–3.

the king, and the district round plundered by the soldiers of fortune who had occupied Bristol. There is also mention of the siege of a castle at Cerne.[1]

In central Wessex, the district round Winchester was a theatre of operations from 1140 to 1143. Wilton Abbey was one of the many places ravaged by Robert Fitzwalter in 1140;[2] that year was one of widespread misery for Wessex, of which the climax was the seven weeks' fighting in Winchester during August and September 1141, in which Henry of Winchester held the east, and the Empress the west, of the city. It was during this time that fire-bearing arrows, employed by the bishop, set fire to Hyde abbey and the nunnery of Winchester.[3] Hyde was reduced to ashes, and the monks were thus confirmed in their opposition to the bishop, which his various schemes to turn their house into an episcopal monastery had aroused.[4] Meanwhile, the nunnery of Wherwell had been burnt by William of Ypres, on the grounds that it had given shelter to supporters of the Empress.[5] Two years later Wilton was turned into a fortress by Stephen.[6]

Abingdon, whose abbot, in common with others of the west, had supported the Empress in 1141-2,[7] was subsequently plundered by Stephen, through the agency of William of Ypres, and its treasury was robbed both of money collected for the shrine of St Vincent and of that deposited for safe custody by neighbours;[8] there is record also of the wasting by William Beauchamp and others of the abbey's lands and of the erecting of castles.[9]

Worst of all was the fortune of the fenland houses that were at the centre of the operations of Geoffrey de Mandeville in 1143-4. The earl, soon after his revolt, seized the island of Ramsey, ejected the monks and used the abbey buildings and church as a barracks, from whence he harassed the surrounding district, giving the manors of the abbey to his followers.[10] Geoffrey's achievement was simplified by the state of chaos existing at Ramsey, where the abbot, Walter, had recently abdicated in favour of an unworthy monk, Daniel, who had previously been his right-hand man.

1 *Gesta Stephani* (*Chronicles of Stephen*, III), 58, 60 (Cerne); 109, 113, 114 (Malmesbury).
2 Will. Malmesb., *GR*, 563.
3 *Annal. Winton. s.a.* 1138-43; Will. Malmesb., *GR*, 581. For an account of this phase of the struggle, *v.* L. Voss, *Heinrich von Blois*, 28-9.
4 *Ann. Winton. s.a.* 1149.
5 Will. Malmesb., *GR*, 581.
6 Gervase of Canterbury, I, 125.
7 Will. Malmesb., *GR*, 573, records that the abbots of Abingdon, Reading, Malmesbury, Gloucester and Tewkesbury were among those who received the Empress at Winchester in March and April 1141.
8 *Chron. Abingd.* II, 210, where Stephen takes "quicquid in ecclesia custodiendi causa depositum fuerat". Cf. *ibid.* 292.
9 *Chron. Abingd.* II, 200, 231.
10 Cf. the account given by H. Round, *Geoffrey de Mandeville*, 209-23, based on *Monasticon*, IV, 142 and *Chron. Rames.* 325-36. Cf. also Henry of Huntingdon, 277: "Monachis expulsis, raptores immisit, et ecclesiam Dei speluncam fecit latronum."

It was no doubt during these months, until the earl's death in the following August, that the monk of Peterborough was enabled to observe at close quarters the horrors of which he has left such a graphic description. Ely, Ramsey's near neighbour, suffered scarcely less severely. Nigel, the bishop, had fallen foul of Henry of Winchester and Stephen, had negotiated with the Empress, and had betaken himself to Rome. His men at Ely were attacked by forces sent against them by Stephen and appealed for help to Geoffrey de Mandeville, who took possession of the Isle, which was then blockaded by the royal troops. The monks therefore had to watch their property on the Isle being wasted by Geoffrey, while that outside the Isle was ravaged by his opponents; much of their treasure had been taken by Nigel to help his cause at Rome; much of the rest was now sold for food.[1] St Ives, a dependent of Ramsey, suffered with the mother-house, and Thorney and Croyland cannot have escaped all damage. Farther south, St Albans, the scene of the arrest of Geoffrey de Mandeville in 1143, had been defended against the king by the knights of the abbey, but the abbot had been forced to convert many precious objects into money in order to buy off the king's agents, among whom William of Ypres is found once more, who threatened to burn the town.[2] To the east, Bury St Edmunds had its property wasted by Stephen's son Eustace.[3]

These scattered records of violence do not exhaust the list of misfortunes. Far up in the north, Durham was occupied by the intruded bishop, William Cumin, and Whitby was ravaged by Scandinavians,[4] and it is probable that an exhaustive search would reveal many other similar incidents. Throughout England famine followed war. We read of it in Wessex, in the Fens, and in Kent. As before in the time of the Conqueror, the inhabitants of the surrounding districts flocked to the abbeys. Ingulf of Abingdon gave treasures and revenues,[5] as did Walter of Ramsey, back in office,[6] and the monks of Canterbury;[7] at Evesham and Ely similar sacrifices were made, but apparently in order to feed the inhabitants of the abbey.[8]

Peterborough, situated so near to the scene of the most cruel sufferings, seems itself to have escaped the worst. After its misfortunes under the

1 *Historia Eliensis, ap.* Wharton, *Anglia Sacra,* I, 623.
2 Matthew Paris, *Historia Anglorum,* I, 271: "Milites...beati Albani, qui tunc, ad ecclesiae ejus custodiam et villae fossatis circumdatae, ipsum vicum qui juxta coenobium est, inhabitabant." *GASA,* I, 93–4: "Tabulam...ex auro et argento et gemmis...con-structam...abbas in igne conflavit et in massam confregit. Quam dedit Comiti de Warenna [and others] villam sancti Albani volentibus concremare."
3 *Chronicle* of Robert of Torigni, 176.
4 So Hugo Candidus, 86, *à propos* of the election of Prior Richard of Peterborough (a northerner) as abbot of Whitby in 1148.
5 *Chron. Abingd.* II, 214: "Ad hanc abbatiam pauperum multitudo istius provinciae confluebat infinita."   6 *Chron. Rames.* 335.
7 Gervase of Canterbury, I, 143. Gervase records this under date 1150.
8 *Chron. Evesh.* 99: "Crucem...pretiosiorem et culmen feretri...instante werra et urgente fame...monachi...auro et argento et lapidibus spoliaverunt."

intruder Henry of Poitou, it had in Martin, a monk of Bec, an excellent abbot who for more than twenty years, through all the stress of Stephen's reign, held a firm and wise rule. The monk of Peterborough, who composed his familiar description of these years after the king and abbot had both died, subjoins with unconscious art to his vivid picture of the horrors of torture and famine a paragraph in praise of the abbot:[1]

In all this evil time (he writes) held Martin his abbacy for twenty winters, half a year and eight days [actually, it would seem, from 29 June 1133 till 2 January 1155] with much toil, and found all that behoved for the monks and guests, and kept great cheer in the house, and withal did work on the church and assigned to it lands and rents, and endowed it well and caused it to be roofed...he made many monks and planted a vineyard and did many works, and altered the town and made it better than before, and was a good monk and a good man, and therefore he was loved by God and good men.[2]

This extract will have shown that even during the reign of Stephen a careful abbot could continue to build and decorate his house, and even at Ramsey, where after the death of Geoffrey de Mandeville Abbot Walter found no more than a single plough team on the demesne and a monastery burdened with debts, prosperity returned sufficiently before the end of Stephen's reign for him to build the great tower, and in the early years of Henry II to add to the monastic buildings.[3] The return to normality all over England was indeed, as has been shown,[4] speedy, but it is possible that some of the undertakings in these years, and the additional expense of upkeep which they entailed, were the cause of the gradual drift towards insolvency and indebtedness to the Jews that was such a feature of monastic domestic economy in the second half of Henry's reign.

IV

More lasting, and no doubt more damaging and demoralizing than the passing troubles of Stephen's reign, were the quarrels and lawsuits in which so many of the greater monasteries became involved during the first half of the century, and in which they continued to be engaged until its close and even beyond. These quarrels, almost all of which turned upon

---

1 A somewhat fuller account of the abbot's activities is given by Hugo Candidus, 76–89, who remarks that as *multi multa scripserunt* about the evils of the time he will be brief on the subject.

2 *Chronicle, s.a.* 1137. The last words, "and was god munec and god man, and forþi him luueden God and gode men", resemble in their rhythm and simplicity another celebrated passage of English prose, equally *simplex munditiis*, the last paragraph of *The Woodlanders*.

3 *Chron. Rames.* 333–4: "In omnibus terris dominicis totius abbatiae unam tantum carucam reperit et dimidium; reperit victualium nihil; debitum urgebat; terrae jacebant incultae, etc." Nevertheless (*ibid.* 336–7): "Circa finem...regni Regis Stephani magnam turrim ecclesiae...multis sumptibus fecit elevari."

4 By H. W. C. Davis, in the article referred to above.

the issue of jurisdiction and subordination, were by no means confined to England or to the monastic order. They were, we may say, endemic in Europe between the revival of the papacy in 1049 and the Lateran Council of 1216, and were fought out on every level—between emperor or king and pope, between pope and metropolitan, metropolitan and suffragan, king and bishop, bishop and monastery, bishop or monastery and beneficed cleric or private owner of churches. In the last century, when the original documents of these cases were being published independently by scholars and antiquarians all over Europe, it was common to treat each struggle in isolation, and to concentrate attention on the sequence of events and the personal characteristics of the disputants, and as the quarrel rarely had the attraction and nobility of a clear issue between liberty and tyranny, humanity and inhumanity, truth and error, the general impression gained ground that the ecclesiastics, and in particular the monastic communities of England, were peculiarly self-seeking, obstinate and acrimonious.

Motives of self-aggrandizement, together with folly and passions of every kind, did indeed have their part in many of these quarrels, and in some more than in others, but the true cause of the prevalence of these protracted disputes lay deeper, and is to be sought in the great movement of ideas that was changing European society. The reformers of the previous century, and especially the group of eminent ecclesiastics who surrounded or were inspired by Gregory VII, had found in the ancient canon law of the Church an instrument, as it were ready made and lying to hand, with which to accomplish all the regeneration they desired. This great *corpus juris* contained, as does the modern *corpus juris canonici* deriving from it, the most disparate elements; many of its enactments merely reiterated or applied essential principles and precepts of Christian teaching, while others laid down regulations valid and necessary for the functioning of discipline in any century, but there were a number which were the work of the fully organized Roman church of the Gelasian period and which reflected the life of a society very different from that of the feudal states of the eleventh century, and others still which, added subsequently by popes and councils, contradicted, at least in practice, some of the earlier decrees. All this mass of legislation, of which only a bare outline had been preserved in actual working, and which was in no sense the outcome of existing conditions, was now applied *ab extra* to an unsusceptible and in many cases recalcitrant society. Nor was this all. At first, the principal agent in the application of the canon law was the reforming papacy, and so long as this was so, under Gregory VII and those of his immediate successors who followed his policy, one and the same authority was concerned in promulgating, interpreting and enforcing the law. Gradually, however, this changed; the study, elaboration and diffusion of the canon law passed out of the immediate control of the papacy to various episcopal schools and households, and to the growing universities, and thus its interpretation became more formal, academic and doctrinaire, and certain schools pressed its interpretation from purely theoretical considerations, unhampered by any responsibility for its execution.[1] As a result, the papacy, which had always to deal with the Church in action, and which was often under the direction of men less determined and less clear-sighted than Gregory VII, tended to compromise between the existing state of things and the letter of the law, and to find a half-way house between the opposing claims of powerful disputants. Thus the supreme authority could not always be identified with the strictest interpretation and execution of the canons.

Over against the canon law there was the mass of feudal custom and national law, as well as every kind of aberration and abuse, and precisely because the papacy and the hierarchy had shared in the decline of previous centuries, some of these customs and laws were the outcome of efforts towards reform and strong control on the part of the secular authority, while others had resulted from the Church taking to herself what was advantageous to her cause in the society about her. To this mass of custom and national law (and we are here concerned primarily with England) the king stood in somewhat of the same position as the pope to canon law—that is, nominally and generally he stood by it and for it, but on occasion he was ready to compromise or even to act directly against it for reasons of personal or national policy. Thus there were, in almost all the quarrels of the twelfth century, two laws and two authorities concerned, and often the authorities and their courts departed altogether from the law or custom with which they were normally identified. When to this source of uncertainty was added the fact that things secular and spiritual were inextricably bound together in the life of the time, and that neither pope nor monarch was permanently strong enough to maintain supreme authority—and that the papal court was not yet one of first instance but of universal appeal, yet was always able to escape the odium of a decision by referring a case back to judges delegate at home—it will be seen that the material for protracted and futile judicial processes was superabundant.

The majority of the controversies in which the monastic bodies became engaged can be reduced to four classes: the invasion of the rights and property of a monastery by a bishop, with or without royal or papal permission; the attempt on the part of a monastery to secure or maintain complete independence of the Ordinary, in opposition to the jurisdiction normally given by canon law; the attempt to secure this independence for parishes and churches owned by the monastery; and, finally, controversies between the communities of cathedral monasteries and the bishop who took the place of abbot. Each of these classes will be discussed more fully in its proper place, but a brief enumeration of some of the more

1 For the history of this movement, *v.* Fournier et Le Bras, *Les Collections Canoniques en Occident*, t. II, *passim*.

important instances of each will show how general were these sources of disturbance to the monasteries.

The chief occupations of monasteries by bishops had already begun under Henry I. Roger of Salisbury had taken possession of Malmesbury *c.* 1125,[1] and held it till his death in December 1139; for part of the time he held also Horton and Abbotsbury. His neighbour, Henry of Blois, was from 1126 till his death in 1171 abbot of Glastonbury, and from 1129 onwards he was also bishop of Winchester. However beneficent his control may have been in many respects, it was weakening in others, and though it occasioned no litigation at the time, it set a precedent that was to cause Glastonbury much trouble in the future. Henry of Winchester also kept Hyde abbey without a superior for some seven years (1136–43), hoping to use it as a bishop's monastery in his schemes for reorganizing the sees of England in his own interest. Later (*c.* 1165–75) Geoffrey of St Asaph's held Abingdon.

Of the seven abbeys engaged first and last in suits for exemption, all save Bury were in the royal, episcopal or papal courts (and several in all three) between 1135 and 1175, and those of the six that held exempt churches were at issue likewise concerning these. Thus St Albans was occupied continuously in England and Rome, 1155–63; St Augustine's, Canterbury, from 1139 intermittently during the whole period (with inevitable repercussions at Christ Church, which always espoused the archbishop's cause); Battle between 1153 and 1157; Evesham *c.* 1139 and perhaps later; Westminster intermittently during the period; Malmesbury *c.* 1174. During the same years, many of the cathedral monasteries were at issue with the Ordinary, though here the great suits belong to the last quarter of the century. Nevertheless, at almost all the nine houses concerned, save Winchester and Norwich, some kind of controversy arose or was revived in the first half of the reign of Henry II.

To these large and quasi-public quarrels were added a number of smaller ones concerning the right to property, both civil and ecclesiastical. When once the way to the Curia on appeal had been thrown open under Stephen, and the papal practice of appointing judges delegate had become common, it was customary for the most insignificant cases to be referred to Rome and to travel from one tribunal to another. Examples of these private suits, many of which must have entailed litigation and other expenses out of all proportion to their intrinsic importance, abound in the cartularies and chronicles of the period; it was at this time that Samson of Bury, probably not yet a monk, made the journey to Rome in the matter of the church of Woolpit that nearly cost him his life.[2] The case of Woolpit

---

1 He is confirmed in his possession of Malmesbury, Horton and Abbotsbury by Honorius II in a charter of 1 January 1126 (Holtzmann, *Papsturkunden in England*, 2 Bde, ii, no. 7).
2 *Jocelini Cronica* in *Memorials of St Edmund's*, I, 252–4. For the volume of litigation cf. also list of judges delegate in *Cartulary of Oseney*, ed. H. E. Salter (Oxf. Hist. Soc., 1936), VI, 338–44.

was a simple one, but often the litigation was complicated and protracted; typical examples may be found in the cases of the churches of Mildenhall and Thurlow, and of the manor of Wye, that occupy so much space in the chronicle of Battle.[1]

V

Alongside of these external stresses must be set the developments of the internal economy of the monasteries. It was a period of devolution and separation in every department of administration within the house. From being a unit, financial and administrative, under the direct control of a single ruler, the abbot, the revenues, expenditures and executive powers were gradually separated into departments without any connection with each other, and most important of all, the abbot himself was separated from the convent and came to have lodging, household, officials, revenues and estates directly under his control, as distinct from those belonging to the community and administered by the officials of the house. The organization of this system will be discussed later; here it will suffice to note that whatever may have been its advantages (of which the chief was that of relieving the community of the feudal burdens and exactions that fell upon the estates of the abbot, especially during a vacancy) it had many disadvantages, even upon the purely material level, causing, as it did, a multiplication of servants and functionaries, increasing the chances of inefficiency, and giving rise to waste in departments where the income was abundant while in the same house other and less fortunate officials were resorting to burdensome expedients of borrowing money at exorbitant interest.

This reorganization of the offices and finances could not be secured without elaborate regulations, and in the middle of the twelfth century the large monasteries gradually came to be ordered by long and minute customs which settled not only the incomes and duties of the officials, but regulated the degrees of liturgical observance of feasts and appointed numerous additions to the regular fare in the refectory. Unlike the Cistercian Use, which was drawn up on logical principles to secure a uniform and precise observance in all houses, enforceable by the abbot and examined at times of visitation, the black monk customaries, though having a strong family resemblance among themselves, were enactments proceeding from the resolution, the devotion, or the indulgence of individual abbots, and in time they came to be so numerous and venerable as to shackle all attempts at change and to deprive the whole body of that flexibility, and the abbot of that initiative, that they had possessed in the early days of the Anglo-Norman plantation, and which the Cistercians preserved so long as they remained faithful to the spirit of their rule.

1 *Chron. Bell.* 113 *seqq.*, 170 *seqq.*

This enumeration of the misfortunes suffered by the black monks, and of the influences that tended to deprive them of the resources of spiritual initiative and receptivity, must not be taken to imply general disaster and decadence. On the contrary, the monasteries, regarded at least on the material level as great corporations, owning property and disposing of rights and occupying an important position in the life of the country, continued throughout the twelfth century to prosper and develop. Buildings, on an ever larger scale, continued to rise; libraries and sacristies became richer; estates were extended; and the whole institute, by reason of its very independence of all other authority and its multiple relations with the life around it, became more and more securely part of the national and local life. And although the monastic life had lost some of the regular simplicity of the first Norman monasteries, and was less strict and less sheltered than that of the early Cistercians, there was still full opportunity, as the chronicles and lives of abbots show, for many to live in a manner little differing from that of Anselm and Gundulf.

The last years of this period were rendered abnormal by the controversy between Henry II and Becket. This struggle had little direct influence upon the life of the black monks, save at Christ Church, Canterbury, where the community in the end supported the archbishop and suffered in consequence. The indirect results, however, were considerable, for the quarrel, followed by the death of Becket, threw all ecclesiastical machinery out of gear, and in particular affected abbatial elections. Between 1163 and 1175 very few appointments were made, and in the latter year at least twelve important abbeys were without superiors, and some had been vacant for a number of years.[1] At Abingdon and St Augustine's, in particular, where Geoffrey, bishop of St Asaph's, and Clarembald, a worthless monk from overseas, had respectively been in possession for many years, the long delay caused much damage. The great council at Woodstock in July 1175, attended by almost all the abbots of England, at which these vacancies were filled, may with reason be taken as opening a new period in the history of the black monk abbeys of England.

VI

The decades at the middle of the twelfth century were not so fruitful as those that had gone before in examples of great monastic superiors. There was, however, one such man, perhaps the greatest and most typical black monk abbot of his day, Walter de Lucy, abbot of Battle from 1139 till 1171. The son of a Norman baronial house, he was brother to Richard de

1 The following abbeys were certainly vacant in 1175, and probably others also: Abbotsbury, Abingdon (1164), Battle (1171), St Benet's of Holme (1168), St Augustine's (1161), Croyland, Hyde, Muchelney, Pershore (1174), Thorney (1169), and Westminster. The date is that of the demise of the last regular abbot, when this is known.

Lucy, the celebrated justiciar of Henry II, and the relationship stood him in good stead in more than one lawsuit. Originally a monk of Lonlé, prudent, eloquent and learned in secular and sacred letters, he had for some time been living with abbot Geoffrey of St Albans, a relative, and through him and through his brother, Richard, had become *persona grata* with the king and the court circle.[1] When his predecessor Warner, a monk of Christ Church, who had become involved in controversy with Stephen, resigned at the advice of the legate Alberic at the end of 1138, Walter was appointed to Battle, the legate's advice and the queen's interest having had influence with the king.[2]

In his account of Walter's rule the Battle chronicler is chiefly concerned with the series of important lawsuits in which the abbot vindicated the rights of his house. Chief among these was the long dispute over exemption with Hilary of Chichester, of which we are given a detailed and most interesting account, which will be discussed more fully in a later chapter. But there were other disputes of as great or greater financial importance to Battle, and we can watch the abbot, firm and prudent, pleading his case and demanding what seemed to him justice at Clarendon before the king, or before papal judges delegate at Staines.[3]

Walter de Lucy thus appears in the chronicle of his house chiefly as its representative in courts of law and as a prudent administrator, tireless in visiting his manors and the halls of great patrons. He is of the period of transition between the early Norman abbots, whose chief care was to construct the edifice entrusted to them, material, intellectual and spiritual, and the abbots of the type of Samson of Bury, great prelates whose business was with affairs of this world at home or in the kingdom. But Abbot Walter, though so occupied in external concerns, did not forget his new home:

Taking his pleasure (writes the chronicler) in the beauty of the house of God, he adorned his monastery with vestments, chasubles, copes, albs, dalmatics, tunics, hangings, bells and manifold ornaments the like of which, in number and beauty, had never been known in the times of his predecessors. He entirely pulled down the cloister, which had been built roughly in the first days of the house, and made another of marble walling and columns, shaped and polished.

1 *Chron. Bell.* 65: "Cum abbate s. Albani cognato suo Gausfrido nomine aliquandiu in Anglia manserat, fratrisque sui industria regiam cognitionem et procerum favorem obtinuerat."

2 *Chron. Bell.* 65: "Reginae suae...usus consilio." Walter would seem to have been equally in favour with the queen of Henry II in 1155; cf. *ibid.* 76: "Consilio reginae Angliae et Ricardi de Lucy fratris sui, etc."

3 The Battle chronicle introduces us to a variety of courts: in the exemption case we can watch chancellor Thomas, Hilary of Chichester, Richard de Lucy, Henry of Essex and the king arguing and interrupting; in the case of the manor of Bernhorne the king and Richard de Lucy give judgment (*Chron. Bell.* 105–10); the case of the church of Middehale introduces Richard of London and Jocelin of Salisbury as judges delegate (*ibid.* 113–15); that of the church of Trilawe comes before the episcopal court of London and the royal court (*ibid.* 115–19).

Having finished this, he engaged workmen to make a washing-place of the same material and design; death overtook him before the work was completed, but he earmarked a sum of money that it might be achieved.[1]

Nor was he forgetful of things more precious than rich cloisters:

His manner of rule was to be stern and severe with the disobedient and undisciplined, but forgiving and kindly towards the good and obedient.[2] He had an extreme pity for the poor; he fed them and clothed them. Above all he had compassion for outcast lepers and sufferers from elephantiasis; far from shunning them, he often served them himself, washing and wiping their hands and feet, and kissing them most gently and lovingly.[3]

For many years before his death he was partially paralysed, yet his last illness overtook him on a routine journey of business. Having received the last sacraments, he sent to Battle for the prior and some others to come to him. The chronicler who tells the story may well have been this prior:

When the prior and those with him had come at his bidding, he talked with him also of his soul [he had previously confessed to Abbot Clarembald of Faversham] and asked pardon of him and those with him for everything wherein he had caused them pain, with reason or no, and gave his own pardon to them. The prior and his fellows, in the name of the whole community, pardoned him all, and gave him the blessing of all; and he with fatherly love gave to all his blessing in return.[4]

Meanwhile his brother Richard de Lucy had arrived, and arranged that he should be carried to Battle. There he lay for two days when, bearing the signs of imminent death, he was carried into the chapter-house and laid on ashes and haircloth:

Suddenly he began to stir, though hitherto lying, as it seemed, still in death, and his lips moved. All the brethren were called, and those near him bent down to listen, but as they could catch only a whisper without words, nothing of what he wished to say could be understood. The night passed thus, and at dawn he gave up his soul into the hands and will of his Creator.[5]

1 *Chron. Bell.* 136.
2 A quotation from the Rule of St Benedict, ch. 11.
3 *Chron. Bell.* 135.
4 *Chron. Bell.* 137.   5 *Chron. Bell.* 138.

CHAPTER XVI

CLUNIAC INFLUENCE: HENRY OF BLOIS
AND GILBERT FOLIOT

I

In a previous chapter we have seen something of the history of the first Cluniac foundations in England.[1] They were comparatively few in number —less than a dozen in all, if only those houses are reckoned which attained the full stature of a regular monastery—and owed their origin to various private benefactors and admirers of Cluny or of one of the great Cluniac priories in France. Their plantation was not the result of policy on the part of the Conqueror, for though he may originally have looked towards Cluny as to a possible source for prelates to reform and govern the English Church, in the event his choice of Lanfranc and the coolness between himself and Gregory VII caused him to look exclusively to Normandy for monks to place over the English monasteries and to isolate the Church in England from all influences outside his dominions.[2] Consequently, the early Cluniac foundations were in the nature of private ventures and save for Lewes, whose first prior, the saintly Lanzo, gave his house an honourable reputation, and Bermondsey, they made little mark. Planted for the most part away from important towns and owing at least some sort of obedience to a religious superior outside the territory of the king of England, they could not expect to make the same mark in English life as the old and celebrated abbeys whose heads were regularly summoned to the royal courts and councils, and ranked among the important tenants-in-chief. They were founded almost without exception in the last quarter of the eleventh century, and though they continued after that date to send out groups to lesser priories their period of expansion, like that of the other black monks, had ended, for all practical purposes of reckoning, before the accession of Henry I. To regard the monasticism of England before the arrival of the Cistercians as influenced to any marked degree by contemporary Cluniac ideals or practice would therefore be wholly incorrect.

By contrast, the direct influence of Cluny in England between 1125 and 1175 was considerable, if sporadic. It came not so much from the existing Cluniac houses as from the personal predilection of Henry I and Stephen

---

1 *V.s.* ch. VIII.
2 To the best of my knowledge, no Cluniac was appointed to an English abbey under the Conqueror or Rufus. Serlo, the great abbot of Gloucester, whom the late *Chronicon Angliae Petriburgense, s.a.* 1113, calls *Cluniacensis*, actually came from Mont S. Michel (*Hist. Gloc.* 10).

for Cluny and radiated mainly from two royal foundations—Reading and Faversham—and from two eminent, influential and long-lived ecclesiastics, Henry of Blois, bishop of Winchester from 1129 to 1171 and Gilbert Foliot, bishop successively of Hereford (1148–63) and London (1163–87).

Since the days of Gregory VII the external prestige of Cluny, great as it was already, had steadily continued to grow. To modern students of the period, whose attention is caught by the polemics of St Bernard, and who find it hard to keep their eyes upon the background of the life of the times, the decay and inevitable decline of Cluny seem so strikingly clear that there is a tendency to regard its influence as insignificant after the death of St Hugh. Decline indeed there was, and most of all in the inner, spiritual life of Cluny, but, as so often happens in the life of great institutions, the fame of the house continued to grow for some decades after the summit of excellence had been passed, and the decline, which posterity can study in isolation in a few documents, was hidden from the eyes of contemporaries by the material splendour of the place and by the leading positions occupied throughout the Church by its distinguished sons. Cluny, in consequence, even after the rise of Cîteaux and Clairvaux, continued to bulk very large in the eyes of the great world.

II

The first event of importance in this second phase of Cluniac influence in England was the foundation of Reading by Henry I in 1121. The situation of the town on the navigable Thames, and at the division of the great western road along which flowed all the traffic from London and the Continent to Worcester, Oxford, Gloucester, Hereford, Bath and Bristol was bound to give the house importance;[1] in the history of English monasticism Reading's significance is twofold: it was the first black monk foundation of any importance for more than twenty years, and it was Cluniac. But though Cluniac, Reading was not a member of the Cluniac system. Cluny's policy was no longer that of Odilo and Hugh. The foundation took place under the rule (actually, during the absence from Cluny) of the unworthy Pons; unlike the dependencies of Cluny, such as Lewes, it had almost from the first an autonomous abbot as its head, and

1 William of Malmesbury, *GP*, 193, notes the importance of its situation: "loco ubi ad populosiores urbes Angliae omnium pene itinerantium posset esse diversorium". To-day Reading is too near London for its position to have the same significance; the river has ceased to bear trade, and cars on the road and expresses on the rail pass it by without halting, but it is still a junction of road and rail, and the volume of traffic that pours through its main streets and the Great Western Railway station by day and night is immense. Reading's foundation charter (*Monasticon*, IV, 40) takes a very unusual form, and doubts have been expressed as to its authenticity. Prof. F. M. Stenton, who was at one time inclined to think certain of its anomalies explicable (cf. *DR*, L (1932), 431), now informs me that he cannot regard the existing text as a genuine document of the reign of Henry I.

stood entirely outside the jurisdiction of the mother-house. Its community was composed of monks drawn partly from Cluny itself and partly from Lewes; the first superior was Peter, from Cluny, but after two years Hugh, prior of Lewes, was appointed abbot and Peter returned home.[1] Reading, therefore, although standing outside the Cluniac system, had the complete Cluniac observance and continued for many decades to draw its abbots from Lewes and relinquish them to fill positions in the Cluniac system abroad or in the hierarchy of France.[2] It was only in the thirteenth century that the abbey became more and more assimilated to her English sisters.

Whether the new abbot of Reading influenced the king, or whether the causes which had prompted the foundation of Reading were still at work, is not clear; in any case, five years later, in 1126, Henry took the important step, hitherto without parallel in England, of giving to a young monk of Cluny, his nephew, Henry of Blois, the great and potentially wealthy abbey of Glastonbury, recently left vacant by the elevation of Seffrid to the bishopric of Chichester. Contemporary authorities appear to leave little room for doubting that Henry was regularly consecrated as abbot, and not merely given charge of the house; if this is so, it is not clear how he justified his canonical position before the Curia when, three years later, he was appointed to the see of Winchester,[3] but Cluniacs, even the strictest, were strangely insensitive on the point of plurality of offices, and the papacy was more complaisant at the moment than later when Bernard stood behind it. However matters may have been accommodated, Henry of Blois was bishop of Winchester till his death in 1171, forty-two years later, during which time he was never even nominally resident in his abbey. Nevertheless, he took throughout his life a keen interest in Glastonbury. Besides his great work of material restoration there, he also took measures affecting the monastic discipline, and undoubtedly this was done along Cluniac lines both by himself and by Robert a monk of Lewes, whom he despatched to Glastonbury as his representative some time before 1136,

1 *Annales Radingenses*, ed. F. Liebermann (*Ungedruckte anglo-normannische Geschichts-quellen*), *s.a.* 1121: "Petrus Prior et vii cum eo fratres rogatu regis Henrici a Pontio abbate Cluniacensi missi in Angliam associatis sibi nonnullis fratribus de monasterio S. Pancratii Cluniacensis ordinis observantiam in monasterio Radingensi noviter tunc a rege fundato inchoaverunt xiv kal. Julii." *Ibid. s.a.* 1123: "Petrus prior Cluniacum redit."

2 Ansger (1130) and Hugh (1186), abbots of Reading, were previously priors of Lewes (Flor. Wig. II, 92; *Ann. Rading.* and *Ann. Waverl. s.a.* 1186). Hugh I became archbishop of Rouen in 1129 (OV, IV, 500); for his career, *v.* P. Hébert, *Revue des questions historiques*, LXIV (1898), 325–71; for his writings, *Dialogorum seu quaestionum theologicarum libri vii*, *v. PL*, CXCII, 1141 *seqq.* William became archbishop of Bordeaux in 1173 (Matthew Paris, *Hist. Angl. s.a.*); Hugh II, abbot of Cluny in 1199 (*Ann. Wint.* and *Ann. Waverl. s.a.*).

3 Adam of Domerham, II, 316, says that the matter was arranged *summi pontificis assensu*. Most sources refer to Henry as "abbas" *sans phrase*, but the usually well-informed Symeon of Durham, *Historia Regum*, II, 283, says that the king gave him the bishopric: "Adjuncta ei in augmentum honoris abbatia Glastoniae, quam prius ad procurationem sui a rege acceperat." In a passage *ex libro abbatis de Feveresham*, printed in the Red Book of the Exchequer, II, 752, it is stated that Henry was prior of Montacute (Somerset) previous to his appointment to Glastonbury. There is (so far as I am aware) no confirmation of this in other sources; it escaped the notice of Dr Voss.

in which year he obtained for him the bishopric of Bath.[1] Significantly, a later chronicle notes the presence at Glastonbury of a Cluniac consuetudinary,[2] but even if, as is likely enough, the abbey adopted certain Cluniac uses, it never ceased to be fully English in tradition.

Shortly after the appointment of Henry to Glastonbury, the king was persuaded to make provision at Peterborough for another connection of his, who had assisted him in the nullification of the marriage between William the Clito and Sibylla of Anjou. This was the ecclesiastical adventurer and erstwhile prior of Cluny Henry, abbot of St Jean d'Angély, whose presence at Peterborough, as we have seen, provided a theme for some of the most picturesque pages of the Old English chronicler.[3] In 1130, during his rule, Peter the Venerable visited England with the king's permission and was received everywhere with honour at the royal command.[4] He went to Peterborough, where the abbot assured him (so we are told) that he would succeed in placing the house under subjection to Cluny, even to the extent of reducing it to the rank of a priory. This, if actually said, may well have been merely an attempt on the part of the abbot to ingratiate himself with Peter; in any case, national sentiment and love of independence would have proved an insurmountable obstacle; as the chronicler remarked: "hedge abides that land divides".[5] The business dragged on for two years, for the king dallied with the proposal, under the impression either that the monks were willing or that they needed correction. In the event, Peterborough was rescued through the good offices of Roger of Salisbury and Alexander of Lincoln. On the evidence of the Old English *Chronicle*, the part played in the affair by Peter the Venerable reflects no credit upon him, but all our knowledge of the matter rests on local sources, the earliest of which is strongly national and querulous in tone.[6]

Stephen, as might be expected from his antecedents and from the in-

1 *Historia...episcopatus Somerset* (Camden Series, 1840), 23: "Robertus monachus coenobii de Lewes, quem bonae memoriae Henricus, episcopus Wyntoniensis, quomodo illinc acceperat et Glaston' miserat, uti rebus abbatiae disponeret, claris parentibus exstitit oriundus, vir religiosus et omnibus omnia factus."

2 *Johannis Glastoniensis Chronica sive historia de rebus Glastoniensibus* (ed. T. Hearne), Oxford, 1726, 435. I owe this reference to L. Voss, *Heinrich von Blois*, 77, note 36. At St Swithun's, Winchester, also, Henry drew up constitutions (*v. Winchester Cathedral Chartulary*, ed. A. W. Goodman, 1928, no. 176) and arranged a *mutua confederatio* with Cluny (*Registrum Johannis de Pontissara*, ed. C. Deedes, Canterbury and York Society, 1913-14, 622).

3 *V.s.* p. 184 for the state of Peterborough under his rule.

4 Hugo Candidus, 74: "Susceptus est per preceptum regis cum honore."

5 *Chronicle* [E], s.a. 1130: "To Burch he [Peter] com ꝺ þær be het se abbot Heanri him þ he scolde beieton him þone mynstre of Burch þ hit scolde beon underöed into Clunni. oc man seið to biworde, hæge sitteð þa aceres daeleth."

6 It would not, however, be entirely correct to say that only one authority lies behind the narrative. At least two hands seem to have been at work on the *Chronicle* in the years concerned, and Hugo Candidus, a younger contemporary of the events, has left a narrative which, though probably based on the *Chronicle*, adds several details. We have, therefore, the official Peterborough version of the affair.

fluence of his brother, the bishop of Winchester, was even more favourable to Cluny than Henry I had been, and a number of English houses received Cluniac abbots. In almost every case we can trace the agency behind the choice. In 1138 Robert, a monk of Cluny, was appointed to Winchcombe. John of Worcester states that he was said to be related to the king (and therefore to Henry of Winchester) and this was no doubt the case.[1] In 1139 a more fateful appointment was made, that of Gilbert Foliot to Gloucester. Here we can assemble details from more than one source. Foliot, though still a young man (he did not die till 1187), had already been prior of Cluny and of Abbeville, and his ability was unquestioned,[2] but the cause of his appointment was the advocacy of his near relative, the royal constable, Milo, earl of Hereford, who had already seen another of his nephews, Gilbert's brother Reginald, a monk of Gloucester, become abbot of Evesham.[3] In the following year Henry of Winchester as legate, having quashed the monks' election at Malmesbury, put there as abbot a *protégé* of his own who had for a time been prior of La-Charité-sur-Loire.[4] In 1148 Stephen, following the example of the Conqueror and Henry I, founded a royal abbey at Faversham in Kent. This, though not destined to become as important as Reading, followed in all respects the pattern of Henry's foundation; the community was drawn from the Cluniac house of Bermondsey and the prior of that house, Clarembald, became its first abbot.[5] Like Reading, it was a Cluniac abbey outside the Cluniac system, and, like Reading, it was the only black monk foundation of a reign that abounded in religious foundations of other orders.

Thus by 1148 at least six important English monasteries had a Cluniac as abbot. No additions were made to the number for more than a decade, but in 1160–1 Foliot, then bishop of Hereford, and apparently administering the vacant diocese of Worcester, was largely responsible for the choice of Adam, a Cluniac of La Charité and at the time prior of Bermondsey, as abbot of Evesham.[6] In the same year William, prior of St Martin-des-Champs, was appointed to Ramsey. The suggestion here appears to have come from an unexpected source, Thomas Becket, then still chancellor.[7]

1 Flor. Wig. II, 105: "Cluniacensi monacho, ut ferunt, regi propinquo."
2 Gilb. Foliot, *ep.* 269.
3 Flor. Wig. II, 91. "Reginaldus Foliot, nepos comitis Milonis Herefordiae", became abbot of Evesham in 1129. Like his brother, he was an able man and in 1139 was one of the English delegates at the Second Lateran Council (Flor. Wig. II, 114). Of Gilbert's election the same writer (114) says: "Rex Stephanus...petente constabulario suo Milone...concesserat praelationem Glaornensis ecclesiae."
4 The monks had elected one of their own number, John, but the king had been bribed to permit the free election (Will. Malmesb., *Hist. Nov.* ap. *GR*, II, 560) and Henry improved the occasion. John of Worcester (Flor. Wig. II, 129) gives some details of the second elect.
5 *Ann. Berm. s.a.* 1148: "Recessit prior Clarembaldus cum xii monachis."
6 Gilb. Foliot, *ep.* 254, to prior and community of La Charité, begging them to release Adam. The see of Worcester was vacant from 31 July 1160 till 23 August 1164 (Stubbs, *Registrum Sacrum Ang.*), and Adam became abbot on 15 April 1161 (cf. *Chron. Evesh.* 100). Foliot speaks as if he had authority—"quod nos probamus, etc."
7 William fitz Stephen in *Mat. Becket*, III, 24: "Cancellario Thoma suggerente."

William was a distinguished man, and left Ramsey to become abbot of Cluny;[1] he is of interest as being one of the last, if not actually the last, to be summoned directly from a monastery across the Channel to rule an autonomous English abbey.

But although the list of Cluniac superiors and connections is considerable, Cluniac influence, in the spiritual and even in the constitutional sphere, would seem to have been transient and superficial, save at Reading and Faversham, and even at those houses there was a steady drift towards the English norm. Cluny, indeed, at the time of the death of Peter the Venerable, had no spiritual doctrine to give that was in any way distinct from that of the other black monks of Europe. The advent of the Cistercians, coinciding as it did so nearly with the death of St Hugh, had marked the end of an epoch at Cluny. Peter the Venerable, admirable as he was and sympathetic to the deepest spiritual influences, not only had to spend his term of office fighting against financial distress and disciplinary relaxation, but was compelled again and again to abandon the purely spiritual sphere for that of high ecclesiastical politics. Cluny had still a constitutional discipline to give, as the various reforms she undertook especially in monasteries north of Paris show, and her distinguished sons had still an *esprit de corps*, but the rôle of mistress and missionary in the religious life of Europe had passed from her to others, never to return.

III

From 1070 to a little after 1120 English church history had been profoundly influenced by a group of bishops of the school of Bec. There was an interval of a few years during which no English see was held by a monk,[2] and for a moment it seemed that the turn had come of the regular canons. Then, between 1129 and 1187, the outstanding figures among the hierarchy were those of three monks, one of Bec, Theobald of Canterbury (1139–61), and two of Cluny, Henry of Winchester (1129–71) and Gilbert of Hereford (1148–63) and London (1163–87). Theobald, though his influence upon England was in some respects great and lasting, particularly in the encouragement he gave to the study and practice of canon and civil law, and in his patronage of able men of letters, found himself throughout his tenure of office forced constantly to be on the defensive against attacks upon his jurisdiction from various quarters, and rarely had the chance of taking the initiative of government; in his character and views he was an excellent example of the sober tradition of the mature Bec, but his actions in the monastic life of England were almost exclusively

1 Flor. Wig. II, 154; Robert of Torigni, 210, 287; Rad. Diceto, I, 424.
2 Strictly speaking, only from the death of Ernulf of Rochester (15 March 1124) to the consecration of Seffrid Pelochin of Chichester (April 1125). But the latter was a man of no mark. For monastic bishops, *v.* Appendix XII.

concerned with domestic controversies with Christ Church and St Augustine's. The two Cluniacs deserve fuller notice. Both were members of a class which has perhaps not received sufficient attention. From early times Cluny had been governed on monarchical rather than constitutional lines, and it had been the custom for abbots to choose their successors and important lieutenants young, and promote them from office to office. As the whole of Cluny, head and members, grew more and more unwieldy under St Hugh, any process of election or the gradual emergence of merit became more and more impracticable; the business of government consequently came to be entrusted more and more to a kind of *corps d'élite*, marked out for the purpose from their first entry into religion, young men of noble family and promise, *nobili ecclesiastici* destined for a career.

This career was at first confined to the Cluniac body, and it is possible to trace its stages, from subordinate office at Cluny or a lesser dependency to the headship of one of the great priories or abbeys of the Cluniac system, ending in a few cases in the twelfth century upon the abbatial throne of the mother-house. Towards the end of the eleventh century, however, a wider horizon opened for Cluniac activity. For fifty consecutive years, save for a brief interval, the papal throne had been occupied by monks (1073–87; 1088–1119), of whom Urban II had been prior of Cluny, and an increasing number of Cluniacs had been drafted into important posts as cardinals, legates and bishops. In the first half of the twelfth century the practice became still more common. Such names as those of Matthew of Albano,[1] Alberic of Ostia, Imar of Tusculum, Hugh of Reading and Rouen are only a few of those that could be enumerated; to their company belong Henry of Winchester and Gilbert Foliot.

Every student of Stephen's reign and of the Becket controversy necessarily makes the acquaintance of Henry of Winchester, but until recently no adequate presentation had been made of his various and widely separated phases and spheres of activity. The task has of late years been ably accomplished by a German scholar, and those interested have now before them all the materials necessary to form a judgment on Henry.[2] Like so many celebrated Cluniacs, he left the ranks of his brethren and entered public life at a very early age. He can scarcely have been more

1 For Matthew *v*. Dom U. Berlière, *Le Cardinal Mathieu d'Albano*, in *RB*, XVIII (1901), 113–40, 280–303; reprinted in *Mélanges d'histoire bénédictine*, IV (1902), 1–51.

2 *Heinrich von Blois*, by Dr Lena Voss (Berlin, 1932). This is a most satisfying and able monograph, in which relevant facts and references are given in full without tendencious interpretation. If the reader feels on occasion, and especially in the character sketch which forms the last chapter, that Dr Voss is carried away by enthusiasm for her subject, he may recollect that she has also provided on earlier pages the materials with which he may criticize her. My debt to Dr Voss in this chapter is very great, even if at times a different judgment is passed on the same evidence. May I add that one who uses the book frequently cannot but regret the absence of an index, and that a similar remark applies to the works of H. Böhmer and H. Tillmann? In this respect English publications, and especially those printed at the University Presses, have an honourable pre-eminence.

than thirty when he came to England to assume control of Glastonbury. Extremely active and extroverted by nature, he can have had little of a conventual vocation, and his early immersion in great affairs drove from his mind any desire he may once have had for the hidden life of a monk. Upright of life he always remained, and even when occupied with military or political schemes he was, with a few lapses, pre-eminently an ecclesiastical statesman, and in this he differed from such contemporaries as Roger of Salisbury and Alexander of Lincoln, but very few public actions recorded of him can be said to be typical of a monk, if by a monk we understand one who has at least in spirit and desire withdrawn himself wholly from the things of this world in order to follow the counsels of the gospel.[1]

The long public career of Henry of Blois falls naturally into two great divisions, separated by an interval of several years of transition. The first covers the period from his arrival in England in 1126 until the lapse of his legateship at the end of 1143. It is a period of great and ever-growing administrative and political activity. The three years before his episcopate began were spent in rescuing Glastonbury from its financial distress, in winning back lost estates and reorganizing the whole economic system of the great abbey. For assessing this work we have the advantage of possessing an account written by himself, in which he describes the abject condition in which he found the house, and some of the measures he took to re-establish its prosperity.[2] Appointed bishop of Winchester in 1129, and retaining his hold on Glastonbury, he gave constant proof of his clearsightedness and practical statesmanship, and acquired an influence in high politics. He was aided by the princely income which he drew from his two charges. At the time of *Domesday*, Glastonbury was by a considerable margin the wealthiest abbey in the land.[3] In 1166 it was still the richest.[4] Similarly in 1166 Winchester was, after Canterbury, the richest bishopric, and in *Domesday* St Swithun's stood seventh in the scale of wealth among the religious houses. The combined revenues put Henry in possession of enormous resources; he was an administrative genius of the first order and throughout his life, with all its reverses of fortune, he succeeded in remaining prodigiously wealthy.

1 Voss writes (p. 137): "Ist doch nie zu vergessen, dass er in erster Linie Geistlicher, ja, Mönch war." It is true that Henry was always an ecclesiastical statesman, and in later years an excellent bishop, but there is little trace of the specifically monastic. His gifts, etc., to his monks might well have been made by a Walkelin or a Giffard.

2 Henry's account is used by Adam of Domerham (II, 305) as part of his history of Glastonbury. His description of the abbey as he found it is: "Cum...regimen Glastoniensis ecclesiae suscepissem, inveni locum olim celeberimum priorum facta subsannantem, in tugurriis suis propinquam ruinam minantem, et...monachos necessariis indigentes." The truth of these words can be checked by William of Malmesbury's statements in his *de Gestis Pontificum* and *de Antiquitate ecclesiae Glastoniensis*, and also from the evidence of charters and papal grants.

3 In *Domesday* the income of Glastonbury was £827. 18s. 8d. Ely came next with £768. 17s. 3d., but had subsequently lost part of its revenue to the bishop.

4 *V.* assessment for *dona* in *Liber Niger Scaccarii* and J. H. Round, *Feudal England*, 236.

At the death of Henry I in 1135 he began his eventful career in national politics. Hitherto he had acted in secular affairs in an advisory capacity only; he now appeared in the double rôle of his brother's chief agent and of an ecclesiastical statesman with a supra-national policy. This policy was the Hildebrandine idea applied to a single kingdom and tinged with opportunism; the Church was to be in all essentials completely independent of the king, and reserved to itself the right of withdrawing its fidelity and support from a monarch who should be false to his promises.[1] For a short time Henry and Archbishop William worked together in Church affairs; William's death in 1136 left Henry as a paramount influence. There can be no doubt whatever that he both expected and desired the primatial office, to which indeed he was elected,[2] and which he administered for two years, but upon which he could not enter without papal permission to transfer from Winchester. His hopes were bitterly disappointed, but three months after Theobald, the candidate of Stephen and the papacy, had been appointed to Canterbury he was named legate by Innocent II, and thus for four years, besides suffering from the anarchy of the times, the Church in England was in the extraordinary situation of being under two masters—a situation to which a parallel can be found (though under very different circumstances) only during the years of Wolsey's greatest power.[3] Henry as legate presided over synods at which his metropolitan was present and promulgated canons and regulated church affairs over his head. From 1139 to c. 1141 he administered the vacant diocese of Salisbury, and from 1138 to 1141 that of London; the bishops of Bath and Exeter were his creatures, and several relatives, as has been seen, were imposed upon abbeys. He even conceived the extraordinary design of erecting Winchester into a metropolitan see with six suffragans covering Wessex and the west, and Bernard could allude to him as a rival pope.[4] During the greater part of these years he was in the midst of political intrigues and not infrequently engaged upon military operations. These, so far as he was personally concerned, may be said to have culminated in the summer of 1141, when he and the Empress entrenched themselves in opposite quarters of Winchester. This phase of his public life ended in part when his legateship expired at the death of Innocent II in 1143, but he continued in the forefront of affairs until the death of his brother in 1154.

---

1 Richard of Hexham (RS), 148 *seqq.* Böhmer, *Kirche und Staat*, remarks that by his charter at accession Stephen "erkennt die Kirche als eine halbsouveräne Körperschaft, als einen Staat im Staate, an". Cf. Voss, 14: "Die Kirche, ganz im Sinne gregorianisch-hochkirchlicher Ideen von jeder Einmischung weltlicher Gewalten befreit, stellte fortan einen Staat im Staate dar."

2 OV, v, 79: "Henricus frater Stephani regis ad regendam metropolim electus est."

3 For the date, *v.* Will. Malmesb., *Hist. Nov.* 550 and Tillmann, *Die päpstlichen Legaten*, 41, note 157.

4 *Ep.* to Lucius II, printed by G. Hüffer, *Bernard von Clairvaux*, i, 234–6, where he alludes to "vitis illa Wincestrie, immo ut vulgo canitur, vitis secunde Rome".

When Henry II came to the throne the bishop of Winchester left the country, not to return till 1158. During the thirteen years of life that still remained to him he appeared in a very different character. Age had moderated ambition and brought calm; under the new king there was no room or need for a military bishop; the aims and outlook of the papacy had changed and the generation of Cluniac ecclesiastics had almost all passed away. Henry could now fill the rôle of an elder statesman, the father of the hierarchy. He supported Becket quietly, but staunchly, as twenty years before he had supported his nephew, William of York, in his day of distress, and he, who twenty years before had been the opponent of the Cistercians of the north, and the object of Bernard's most violent invective, was now the advocate of the friend of the Cistercians, Gilbert of Sempringham. He was, indeed, universally respected, even revered, and the praise of Gerald of Wales, who knew him only in these mellow years of generous patronage, has secured his reputation with posterity.[1]

We are at one respect at a disadvantage in judging him. While his figure meets us at every turn for half a century, and while evidences and monuments of his activity are numberless, no collection of his letters has been preserved. Letters—a numerous and varied collection of letters—are the best of all mirrors of a man's character and mind and motives, whether he be a Cicero or a Bernard. We have only to recollect how much precious light is thrown upon Henry's contemporaries—Bernard himself, Peter of Cluny, Gilbert Foliot—by their correspondence to realize what such a collection would tell us of the bishop of Winchester. Failing this, we can but judge him by his actions, such as we know of them, and through his contemporaries.

Henry of Blois, though not precisely a complex character—for throughout all his activities there is the same stamp of energy and directness of purpose—was certainly a man of many-sided qualities. The commander who erected half a dozen fortresses in his diocese and burnt out his episcopal city, together with a great monastery and nunnery, was also the man who rebuilt Glastonbury on a grand scale, who re-established Cluny, who founded the hospital of St Cross, and who decorated his cathedral with the most precious and varied works of art, from the fonts which still remain to illuminations and enamels and masterpieces of the goldsmith's art which have almost entirely disappeared.[2] The patron of William of Malmesbury in the reign of Henry I and of Gerald of Wales in that of Henry II was also the friend of St William of York, of St Gilbert of Sempringham, of St Thomas of Canterbury, and—though not without

---

1 Giraldus Cambrensis, VII, 45.
2 For the gifts of treasures, relics and books to Glastonbury, v. Ad. Dom. II, 316–17. For those to Winchester, v. article by Edmund Bishop, *Gifts of Bishop Henry of Blois, Abbot of Glastonbury, to Winchester Cathedral,* in *DR,* III (1884), 41 *seqq.,* reprinted in *Liturgica Historica,* 392–401. For those to Cluny, v. Voss, 118, and references. Dr Voss remarks, very justly (p. 106): "seine Stärke war, in grossen Stil zu organisieren."

periods of coolness—of Peter the Venerable; while to St Bernard and Eugenius III he was the old enemy, the whore of Winchester.[1]

He was undoubtedly a man of extraordinary capacity for administration and organization. Not once only, but in at least four different theatres—at Glastonbury, at Winchester, both in the affairs of St Swithun's and in the administration of the diocese,[2] and at Cluny in 1156–7—did he rescue and restore to order the affairs of great corporations. At Cluny, moreover, when an exile and sixty years of age, he not only took the complex machinery of the whole economic administration into his hands, and produced a new scheme of "rationalization", but supported the entire community for a year out of his private resources.[3] In all these undertakings we see the same thorough methods, the same grasp of detail and of the whole behind the parts, and it is natural to see a kinship of mind between Henry of Winchester and those leaders of great industrial concerns who in our own day have been called at a moment of crisis from one department of industry or finance to another, and from private to national spheres of activity. Perhaps the greatest testimony to his supreme ability is the regard which the monks of Glastonbury always cherished for him. Great indeed must have been the practical benefits of his government which could outweigh the numberless disadvantages of having as abbot for forty years a foreigner and an absentee. Yet later generations at Glastonbury agree with William of Malmesbury in looking upon Henry's abbacy as a time of peace and prosperity. To the monks of St Swithun's and of Cluny, likewise, he appeared and remained a mercy and a benediction.[4]

As an ecclesiastical statesman, he left his mark on England chiefly by throwing the door wide open to intercourse and appeals from this country to the Curia, but in the evolution of ideas he is perhaps still more significant as being a Cluniac who held the full Gregorian conception of church government, but treated it as a political programme rather than as a moral ideal, and was therefore ready to concede and barter, just as he was ready to employ material arms in its execution or use it for personal aggrandizement. In all this, he stood at the opposite extreme, among the statesmen of the Church, to the school of reform that drew inspiration from Clairvaux. As to his wealth and magnificence, all witnesses at all periods of his public life are agreed.[5] To his princely buildings at Glastonbury,[6] at

---

1 Cf. Bernard's letter to Lucius II: "seductor ille vetus Wintoniensis, etc."

2 For Glastonbury, v. Henry's own account in Adam Domerham, II, 305 seqq.; for Winchester, v. above all Henry's "will" in *Registrum Johann. de Pont.* and Voss, 70–100, 108–19. The superb "Masters plaque" is probably a relic of his treasury; v. infra, p. 538.

3 Voss, 115 seq. The number of monks at Cluny was probably c. 400; Henry's expenses in a single year exceeded 7000 silver marks.

4 Voss, 70–90, and references.

5 William of Newburgh, I, 41: "Pecuniosus supra modum." *Gesta Stephani*, 73: "Omnibus Angliae magnatibus...divitiis...potentior." *Mat. Becket*, IV, 156: "Iste, cum omnimodis et infinitis supra omnes episcopos Angliae abundaret divitiis."

6 Ad. Dom. II, 304, 316.

Winchester and at Cluny, and his truly regal gifts to his English churches, must be added his own magnificent establishments, with their statues, their jewels, their gardens and their menageries.[1] He was the first amateur of art of his age, and his taste extended even to the remains of classical antiquity. Eloquent, persuasive, sagacious, and for all his drastic energy not without diplomatic tact and finesse,[2] he was above all a man of the firmest purpose where his interests were engaged.[3] Yet for all his strength, in which he far surpassed his brother,[4] he had at all times, but especially in his later years, a full measure of that amiability which all remarked in Stephen; it is noteworthy, and to the credit of all the three men concerned, that he never allowed his public quarrel with Theobald to embitter their personal relations, and that the cloud that passed over his friendship with Peter of Cluny was but temporary.

Such were some of Henry's admirable qualities; he had others which suited less with his office and his profession. Without question he was personally ambitious; he desired power and independence not principally for some higher end, but for themselves. From the moment that he eagerly entered the arena of secular politics till the death of Stephen he was in a false position from which no amount of sagacity or moderation could extricate him. The familiar and bitter phrase of Henry of Huntingdon was at bottom true, and nothing could redeem the combination of elements essentially hostile one to another.[5] Henry's acts of ruthlessness and tergiversation, so unlike his later and truer self, were indeed due to his position, but they were also due to his own choice. Even less susceptible of justification were his high-handed and selfish actions in the purely religious sphere. Strangely enough, no contemporary was found to blame explicitly his retention of Glastonbury during his forty years of episcopal life, but whatever excuses he may have found for himself from reasons of expediency such a practice was uncanonical, contrary to all monastic principle, and a precedent for the worst abuses.[6] Similarly, his persistent

1 Giraldus Cambrensis, VII, 45: "Opera mira, palatia sumptuosissima, stagna grandia, ductus aquarum difficiles."

2 The author of the *Gesta Stephani* uses *versute* (75) and *versutia* (79) of him.

3 He says of himself (Ad. Dom. II, 313): "nec prece nec pretio vinci nec flecti volui"; William of Malmesbury, *Hist. Nov.* 583, says of him "Legatus, immodici animi pontifex qui quod semel proposuisset non ineffectum relinquere vellet." A striking example of this was seen when his request for the erection of Winchester into a separate ecclesiastical province was refused by the pope. Henry proceeded to ask for exemption for his diocese from Theobald's jurisdiction, and when this was refused he asked for a personal exemption (cf. Voss, 66).

4 Voss, 138, rightly draws attention to "seine Sittenstrenge, seine männliche Selbst-beherrschung und sein edles Masshalten".

5 Henry of Huntingdon, 315: "Novum quoddam monstrum ex integro et corrupto compositum, scilicet monachus et miles."

6 The lack of adverse comment (cf. also Voss, 6, note 15) at Glastonbury is doubtless due to the abbey's earlier history. For decades its possessions had been raided or dilapidated, and Henry's reconstitution of its estates and his protection were felt as inestimable blessings. Also, bishops' monasteries were no novelty in England, though there is no other example (save while the vagrant Geoffrey of St Asaph held Abingdon) of the bishop being

and often successful efforts to obtain bishoprics and abbacies for his
relatives and supporters,[1] and his little less than outrageous schemes,
based purely on personal motives, for changing the whole framework of
the English hierarchy, betray an outlook very different from that of one
who considers only the spiritual end of a spiritual office. It was this subordination of the spiritual to a policy of alliance and personal influence
that drew upon Henry the vehement disapproval of Bernard, the Cistercians
of the north and Eugenius III who, it must be remembered, knew him
only in his years of ambition.[2] We do not, indeed, know the cause of the
coolness which existed between him and even Peter the Venerable during
some years of this period, but it is not unnatural to suppose that the abbot
of Cluny, though more tolerant by nature than the abbot of Clairvaux,
was out of sympathy with much in Henry's way of acting.[3] This estrange-
ment passed wholly, the great Cistercians died long before the bishop of
Winchester, and he himself mingled in the events of the next generation
with a character deepened and softened by age. His biographer distinguishes him more than once as the link between Anselm and Becket;[4]
Edmund Bishop, who never disguised his affection for Henry, signalized
him as the greatest English bishop between the two saints.[5] Yet though
the part he played was of great and often of decisive importance, Henry of
Winchester, we feel, fell short of absolute greatness, both as an ecclesiastical statesman and as a diocesan bishop. He was neither a Lanfranc nor
a Grosseteste. And the reason behind such a judgment would seem to be
that he lacked, during the years of his greatest power, both the intellectual

other than the diocesan. As for Henry, he could no doubt say during his early years that
Glastonbury was safer in his hands than another's, and during the last eight years of his life
when, to judge from his other actions, he might have been expected to feel more scrupulous,
to resign Glastonbury would have been to expose it to the fate of so many at the time, viz.
prolonged vacancy or occupation by a creature of the king's. But his action without question
paved the way for Savary later.

1 Böhmer, followed by Voss, 42–4 and notes, points out that at episcopal elections at
Bath (1136), Exeter (1138), Salisbury (1140, 1142), York (1141), Lincoln (1148) and
Durham (1153), and at abbatial elections at Winchcombe (1138), Malmesbury (1140) and
Cluny (1157), Henry did his best to put in relatives or *protégés*. Often he was successful;
if not, at least his native persistence made itself felt: thus at the Lincoln election of 1148
the claims of three relatives were pressed in succession, one of whom, Henry de Sully, had
previously been put forward at Salisbury and York.

2 Significantly enough, there is only a single letter from Bernard to Henry (*ep.* 93), and
that a short and non-committal note, written, it would seem, on his appointment to Winchester.
Later references during the York dispute are consistently hostile, e.g. *ep.* to Lucius II
(quoted above, p. 290, note 1,) and *ep.* 238 to Eugenius III:" Quid dicam de domino Wintoni-
ensi? Opera, quae ipse facit, testimonium perhibent de eo." Eugenius is related by Gerald
of Wales (VII, 46) to have said of Henry: "Potuit lingua sua duo regna corrumpere."

3 That such a coolness existed c. 1130–40 is clearly shown by Voss, 110–13.

4 Voss, xi: "Er steht gewissermassen als ein Mittelglied zwischen Anselm...und Becket."

5 *Liturgica Historica*, 394: "Henry...stands out, after St Anselm and St Thomas, as
the greatest English prelate of his century." If we take Henry as *homo inter homines*, in all
his activities, this judgment might stand, but considered *quâ* bishop, he was surely surpassed
by Theobald, Gilbert Foliot, Thurstan and perhaps others. Bishop elsewhere, in a letter
to Dean Armitage Robinson (*DR*, LII, 1934, 70), refers to "that princely person (a great
'admiration' of mine) Henry of Blois".

greatness needed for conceiving a policy and its means of execution, and the moral greatness essential in one who is to concentrate on a single aim devoid of personal interest. When, in his last years, he gave himself more fully to his spiritual duties and to the things of God, it was not by exercising his unusual gifts of administration or by satisfying his exquisite artistic taste, but rather by his withdrawal from external activities, that he regained something of his first vocation and found his true peace.

These pages on Henry of Blois may seem to have been of disproportionate length. It might be urged that it is not easy to give in brief an adequate outline of such a many-sided, long-lived man, but a truer reason for the space devoted to Henry is that he was for almost half a century a weighty influence in the religious and monastic life of the country, and, still more, that in his qualities and in his defects he was, to a quite remarkable degree, an embodiment and a reflection of the qualities and defects of the great abbey of which he had been a member, as it was in the days of its greatest outward magnificence, when its spiritual declension had already begun.

IV

Of a very different type of character and ability was that other Cluniac, Henry's younger contemporary, who like him held office for almost half a century first as religious superior and then as diocesan bishop, who shared, though with a difference, his conception of the relations of Church and state, and who for a quarter of a century was the only prelate who could compare with him in mental ability and permanent influence. Gilbert Foliot who, though he lived till 1187, must have been born at the latest before 1110,[1] came of a distinguished Anglo-Norman family which gave other sons to high ecclesiastical office.[2] Originally a monk at Cluny, he was, when still a very young man, appointed prior, and subsequently prior of Abbeville.[3] In 1139 at the motion of his relative Milo, earl of Hereford, and no doubt with the approval of Henry of Blois, he was made abbot of Gloucester, a flourishing house whence his brother had recently been taken to become abbot of Evesham. From this date till his death almost fifty years later we can follow his external activities in his voluminous correspondence.[4]

1 He had filled two important offices before 1139.
2 Reginald Foliot, abbot of Evesham, 1122–49: Robert Foliot, bishop of Hereford, 1174–86.
3 So Gilbert himself tells us in a letter written to Henry II c. 1173–4, in which he defends himself against a charge of ambition (*ep.* 269): "In promotione mea prima Cluniaci prior quidem sum constitutus in ordine, dehinc prior Abbatis Villae." There were several priors at Cluny; it is unlikely that Gilbert was first or "grand" prior.
4 Ed. J. A. Giles (2 vols. Oxford, 1845). Giles' text is reprinted in *PL*, cxc, 745 *seqq.*; it is very faulty, and the letters, which are not dated, are printed without any attempt at assigning a chronological order (*v.* Giles, introd. 1, xii).

As abbot of Gloucester his abilities speedily drew the attention of his contemporaries; we can watch him in his letters taking an increasing share in political and ecclesiastical affairs. While maintaining Gloucester at the high level of observance inherited from Serlo he took an interest in other houses, especially Cerne in Dorset, where he consistently both in public and private supported the party of reform under Bernard, a monk of his own abbey. In 1148 he was appointed bishop of Hereford directly by the pope, Eugenius III, to whom he was known as a supporter of the Empress, a strongly Gregorian ecclesiastic, and an upright man.[1] It is noteworthy that he endeavoured, but without success, to retain the abbey of Gloucester when bishop.[2] During his years at Hereford his influence continued to grow steadily; at the death of Theobald he was without question the most outstanding member of the hierarchy now that Henry of Winchester was settling to his quiet old age; he was the new king's spiritual adviser,[3] and it was freely said that he hoped for the primatial see.[4] If this were so, as it may well have been, he must have received some satisfaction when he was translated, at Becket's recommendation, to the important see of London. Friendly relations, however, between the two prelates, whatever their original sincerity, did not long endure. As is well known, Foliot was the leader of the party among the bishops which was opposed to the primate's sudden reversal of policy and subsequent refusal to compromise; in a moment of passion he told Becket that a fool he was and a fool he always had been, and in a long letter to the exiled archbishop in which the measured sentences, like points of steel, are driven home by the intense feeling of the writer, he travelled over the whole dispute.[5] We are not here concerned *tantas componere lites*, in which a strife of cold policies and warring personalities was inextricably interwoven. In the sequel, Foliot did not escape blame for Becket's murder, nor did he, two years later, fail to be an object of attack to those who saw in him once more an aspirant to the primatial see.[6]

Those who wish to estimate the character and influence of Gilbert Foliot will do so best by studying the whole range of his correspondence. They will find throughout a singular consistency of thought and action.

1 Joh. Sarisb. *Hist. Pont.* (ed. Poole), 48.

2 *Ibid.* "Disponebat auctoritate archiepiscopi retinere abbatiam suam cum episcopatu; sed monachi...Hamelimum...sibi...fecerunt in abbatem festinantius benedici."

3 Becket, *ep.* 129 in 1163 (*PL*, cxc, 602): "Cum dominus papa tibi specialiter curam animae domini nostri regis commiserit."

4 Becket, *ep.* 130 (*PL*, cxc, 606): "Potuit autem fieri aliquas ecclesiasticas personas ad eamdem promotionem ut solet aspirantes suspirasse, cum se sentirent ab ea quam conceperant spe decidere." Foliot's explanation (*ep.* 194) of his sighs was that he had been enabled by divine assistance to foresee the evils to come under the new primate: "Non nostram in vestra promotione repulsam planximus...sed...altis utique in Domino suspiriis ingemuimus et dolorum...praesagia certa quadam divini spiritus insinuatione... praesensimus." 5 *Ep.* 194.

6 *Ep.* 269 to Henry II (*PL*, cxc, 948–9): "Aiunt enim me ad archiepiscopatum Cantuariensem ambire."

Foliot was not many-sided, as was Henry of Winchester; he does not figure as patron and connoisseur, or as a great builder. His first appearance in England shows him as a zealous, even rigid, churchman, with a high ideal of religious discipline and a clearcut conception of the relations of Church and state, and of the sphere covered by the authority of the papacy and canon law.[1] We recognize in him one of the school of Alberic of Ostia and Matthew of Albano. In English history he is of significance as the greatest of that group of able bishops, which included Robert of Hereford, Hilary of Chichester and Bartholomew of Exeter, who were used by the Roman Curia to apply to England the system of papal courts delegate, which the legateship of Henry of Winchester and the teaching of Theobald of Canterbury had introduced into the country. We can trace him throughout the years as abbot, as diocesan, as judge delegate acting with strength, perseverance and principle in private cases, in monastic questions, in disputes between Cistercians and black monks, in matters of diocesan organization. His letters, without possessing the naked realism and power of Lanfranc's, are objective, lucid and unhesitating, and if they lack the deep spiritual ardour of Anselm and Bernard, they are equally distant from the rhetoric and verbiage of Osbert of Clare and Peter of Blois. Foliot was the friend of all religious who came to him for aid, the just arbitrator in innumerable disputes, and the long affair of Cerne shows with what loyalty and persistence he could support a cause which he had made his own. Nor should it be forgotten that though he was a Cluniac of the school of Matthew of Albano, he was yet the friend of Cistercians, and a kindly host to Ailred of Rievaulx, who dedicated to him his sermons on Isaiah in an introductory letter in which he addresses the bishop of London with exactly that measure of respect and restraint which might have been anticipated.[2] Gilbert himself, in old age, composed a commentary on the Canticle which he dedicated to his kinsman at Hereford;[3] it is a cold and correct exercise, lacking entirely the mystical insight and the doctrinal value of Bernard's Sermons.

In his personal life Foliot had been from his youth upright and ascetic;[4] in this, as in more than one trait of his character, we are reminded of another great High Churchman, once archdeacon of Chichester, and later cardinal; he was essentially measured, correct, and well-bred; we can therefore well appreciate the distaste with which he must have regarded alike the sudden rise and the seemingly violent impulses and swerves of Becket. But in almost every letter and recorded action there is an element of rigidity and a spirit which, while never superficial or secular, is yet

1 He states his position with admirable lucidity in *ep.* 194 (*PL*, CXC, 899–900).
2 *PL*, CXCV, 361.
3 *Ep.* 212.
4 The Gloucester chronicle tells us (*Hist. Gloc.* 18) that Stephen in 1139 appointed him "audita fama probitatis ejus eximiae". Walter Map has praise of Gilbert in *De Nugis Curialium*, 19.

formal, dry and external, not a little resembling that of the great Scots
judges of the golden age of Edinburgh, and which never touches the
deeply human and deeply spiritual depths of Bernard and Ailred. It is,
indeed, not hard to understand how he, the righteous man of so many
years experience of government, with a fixed and reasoned conception of
high policy, could fail at a moment of unexpected and intense crisis, and
amid the play of violent passions, to see that a vital spiritual issue had
suddenly emerged and was at stake.

V

The careers of Henry of Winchester and Gilbert Foliot have carried the
narrative somewhat beyond the limits which were on a previous page
assigned to the flood tide of the new orders; it will be well, therefore, to
return within those limits and review briefly the increase in the number
of religious houses in England and Wales during the years between the
death of Henry I on 1 December 1135 and the return to normality in
England after the disturbances of the Becket controversy c. 1175.

In fewest words, it may be said that during those forty years the
number of religious houses in England, already large, was almost doubled.
Moreover, all modern historians have noted—what did not, indeed,
escape remark from contemporaries—that by far the greatest part of this
increase, perhaps as high a proportion as four-fifths, took place during
the troubled reign of Stephen, during years which for the student of the
political, social and economic history of the country are full of waste and
anarchy. As will be seen, this period of violence and disorder, of which the
traditional account, even if painted in colours a shade too lurid, must
probably be accepted as substantially correct, did not pass without leaving
the marks of serious injury on English monastic life, but the brunt of the
attack fell almost wholly upon the wealthy and long-established houses
of the black monks; the new foundations, whether, as the Cistercians and
Premonstratensians, their houses were for the most part in remote situations and on virgin soil, or whether, as the Austin canons and the new
nunneries, they were situated in small villages, had in their first beginnings
slender means and few contacts with the great world; they were thus able
to grow to maturity in comparative peace. And, it may be, the very
spectacle of the harassed country sent many in refuge or reaction to these
new centres of order and calm.

The main cause of the increase, however, lay outside and above the
accidents of English political history and is to be found in the great
renaissance of the spiritual life and ecclesiastical discipline in north-
western Europe. England had begun to feel the wash of this tide before
1135, but the reign of Stephen, outwardly so unpromising to things of

the spirit, had, if carefully examined, more than one characteristic that aided the influx of new ways. During the greater part of the reign the door was open to papal and other foreign ecclesiastical influence, and the practical control of the Church in England vested in the hands of ecclesiastics, in a way that had not been known since the Conquest. Moreover, the outstanding bishops of the time—Theobald, Thurstan, Henry Murdac, Robert Bethune, Gilbert Foliot and (at least in his later years) Henry of Winchester—were all, even if in different ways, men of "European" outlook, with generous sympathies and a desire for spiritual reform, and in the north David of Scotland, whose reign covered all but a year of Stephen's, made it his care to multiply foundations of the new orders, some of which fell into districts under his rule which later formed part of England.

A glance at the statistics given on another page[1] will show how truly remarkable in English religious history were Stephen's twenty troubled years. William of Newburgh, writing at the end of the century, stated that more monasteries and nunneries were founded between 1135 and 1155 than in the hundred years before the earlier date—the century which had seen the Norman and Cluniac plantations—and if monasteries and nunneries are reckoned, to the exclusion of houses of canons, his statement is strictly accurate. In 1100 there were in existence in England some seventy monasteries of black monks (including Cluniacs) and about a dozen fully established nunneries; in addition, there were a few—perhaps eight or ten—houses of canons. The reign of Henry I saw little change among the black monks; the nunneries, however, increased slowly, and by the end of the reign numbered a little more than twenty. The most striking feature of the period was the spread of the Augustinian rule; between 1100 and 1135 some fifty houses of canons, some small, some important, came into being. Finally, in the last decade of the reign the invasion of the white monks began, and at Henry's death their foundations numbered seventeen.

Under Stephen, additions to the number of black monk houses were negligible, and could be counted on the fingers of one hand. Nunneries, on the other hand, multiplied. Even if the Gilbertines, no small family, are excluded from the reckoning, these twenty years saw more than thirty foundations, or considerably more than the number already existing in 1135. But more spectacular by far was the increase among the new orders. Between 1135 and 1155 the Cistercian family grew by thirty-six houses from seventeen, reaching a total of fifty-three; ten Gilbertine priories were added to the single existing house of Sempringham; six considerable establishments of Premonstratensians were made, and the already large number of Augustinian houses was increased by at least thirty new foundations. In all some 120 religious houses, at the very least,

1 *V.* Appendix XIII.

came into being under Stephen, almost all following rules of life that had
been sanctioned since the Gregorian reform.

Under Henry II the graph of increase rose less steeply. In the case of
the white monks, the legislation of 1152 and the death of St Bernard, both
of which events coincided so nearly with the death of Stephen, combined
to put a firm and immediate check; between 1153 and 1175 only five new
plantations were made, of which two were in remote Wales. The white
canons increased by only three or four houses; the Augustinians by more—
perhaps by twenty—and the nuns by a dozen or so, though only one or
two Gilbertine plantations date from this period. In all, the total number
of houses known for certain to have been founded between 1155 and 1175
was between thirty and forty, or about a quarter of the total of Stephen's
reign. No doubt what may be called "saturation point" was being reached,
at least in many districts. Yet the numbers continued to grow slowly for
another fifty years.

A few words may be said as to the geographical distribution of the new
foundations. This, absolutely speaking, was surprisingly even. If we
except the large tracts of country unsusceptible of cultivation, or closed
to it, such as the moors and mountains of northern England, central Wales
and Devon and Cornwall, the New and other forests, and the heaths,
downs and Wealds of Surrey, Sussex and Kent, almost all the counties of
England received a fair quota. The only localized order was that of
Sempringham which, especially in its full, "double" form, remained predominantly a growth of Lincolnshire and the contiguous districts. If,
however, the relative or proportional increase be considered, then it is
seen at once that the part of England north of Watling Street and the
fenlands was affected very differently from East Anglia, the midlands and
the south. The latter areas had their fair share of monastic and religious
life in 1100, if not in 1066; in the former, no monastic life was in being
in 1066, and even in 1100 the religious houses in all the vast area north of
the Welland and of Watling Street numbered but half a dozen. The fifty
years that followed the arrival of Thurstan at York in 1119 did much to
redress the balance. During that period some twenty Cistercian abbeys,
some forty houses of canons, the whole Gilbertine family, and a proportional number of other nunneries were established in the northern,
north-eastern and north midland counties. And, as will have been seen,
the new life in the north was inspired and directed by a sanctity and fervour
to which the contemporary south could show no parallel; indeed, the
religious houses of the north, and especially those of Yorkshire and
Lancashire, retained until the Reformation a character of their own,
which was to distinguish also the manner of their final dissolution.

CHAPTER XVII

THE BLACK MONKS FROM 1175 TO 1216

I

In an earlier chapter the forty years that elapsed between the death of Henry I and the return to something approaching to normality after the Becket controversy were characterized as a period of transition for the black monks, during which the most individual features of the Anglo-Norman monasticism grew less distinct, and the type of great religious corporation came into being that was to continue the same in its main lines throughout the remainder of the Middle Ages. In 1130 the black monk houses were still the only form available of the monastic life in England, and contained almost all that there was of fervour in the land; by 1175 they had become what they were to remain until the Dissolution, only one form among many, and that neither the most remote from the world nor the most austere. During the half-century that followed the Conquest a process of building and formation had gone forward on all sides; the monastic life of the country was remodelled and directed by a numerous group of able and spiritual abbots; it was a period of constant benefactions and not infrequent foundations. Such a state of change and development was, in the nature of things, only a phase; an equilibrium was gradually reached and a slow process of formalization began; the transition was rendered more speedy by the arrival of the new orders, and by the middle of the reign of Henry II the typical black monk house began to stand out primarily as a great corporation, an economic organization of great extent and complexity, a carefully graded society ruled by complicated custom in which everything tended, in the long run, to strike an average.

When the endeavour is made to go somewhat below the surface and to estimate the general condition of monastic life in the last quarter of the twelfth century, reliance must of necessity be placed on a comparatively few documents. A general impression, to be a true one, can only be gained by absorbing and tacitly criticizing a mass of detailed and intimate information, and this in the case of the majority of the monasteries is entirely lacking. In the case of five or six houses, however, we are fortunate enough to possess a fairly full record, and it is from these half-dozen, with a few additions from elsewhere, that the picture must be derived. As it happens, they are all houses of importance: St Albans, Battle, Bury St Edmunds, Christ Church, Canterbury, Evesham and Peterborough; and though their records are of very varying quality, there is a strong family likeness between them which encourages the belief that what is true of this group would be equally true of all other black monk monasteries.

Perhaps the first general impression that emerges from all these sources is that by 1200 the monasteries had become far more isolated from each other and uninfluenced by new life than a century earlier. Although no constitutional bond had ever existed among them, in the early days, when the Norman monasticism was a force, almost an instrument, for the Conqueror and Lanfranc to use, a strong feeling of solidarity existed and was intensified by the frequent interchange of superiors, by the diffusion of Lanfranc's *Statuta* and by the influence of a particular house, such as Evesham, or of a monastic bishop, such as Wulfstan of Worcester, upon a whole circle of neighbours. All this ceased as each house grew in numbers and wealth and developed its individual set of customs, and still more when the whole life of the country, religious, intellectual and social, became more highly complex and articulated. Towards the end of the twelfth century the history and outlook of the great monasteries of which we have the fullest record—a St Albans, a Bury, a Christ Church—has become wholly individual, even though the details and regulations of daily life are similar at each. We are reminded of the great public schools of England, bound by no union yet all organized in a uniform way; an unmistakable family and yet wholly distinct in individuality; producing a "type" of character and yet each with its own peculiar traditions and with an ebb and flow of prosperity quite distinct from any neighbour.

II

The gradual changes of life and organization that took place between the middle of the twelfth century and its end will be discussed in some detail later. In particular, the virtual separation, at most houses, of the finances and household establishment of the abbot from those of the monastery, and the devolution of expenditure and administration from one authority to many can only be grasped when studied at close quarters, though the effects upon the life of the body are clear to all readers of monastic history. Similarly, the growth and crystallization of "customs" which in many cases mitigated earlier rigour and hampered elasticity of movement can only be seen by a somewhat detailed process of comparisons. But, leaving these and other points for a further examination, one or two phenomena, common to all the monasteries at the opening of the thirteenth century, may be set out here.

One such is the new position which the abbot had come to occupy *vis-à-vis* his community. By 1200 this was something very different from that which had obtained in the Bec of Herluin and Anselm, or in the early Cistercian monasteries; the abbot was no longer the paterfamilias of the Rule, but is rather the prelate, almost the bishop of his monks, and the representative of his abbey to the outside world. In the Rule of St Benedict the immediate and ever-present paternal government of the abbot is presupposed on every page; the spiritual teaching of the whole document is built upon the direct and absolute responsibility of the abbot for each soul under his rule and presupposes the constant daily intercourse and ministration of father and sons, shepherd and sheep. At Bec and the Anglo-Norman monasteries of the eleventh century a daily intercourse and supervision was still practicable, under an able and spiritual abbot, but in the next century the growth of the communities and their offices, the responsibility for widely scattered properties, the many calls made upon the abbot by the public life of the country and by the duties of hospitality—all these, added to the separation of establishments due largely to feudal claims, tended to withdraw the father of the family from the life of the house, and to deprive him of any adequate knowledge of the characters and spiritual needs of his sons. Even the possibility of easy access to him tended to disappear, or was limited by the jealousy of his confidential officials; Samson of Bury found it necessary to assert in chapter that all were free to come to him, and the chronicler tells us that a spirit of constraint had arisen, owing to the behaviour of a clique who surrounded his predecessor.[1] Yet even under a Samson such a freedom was often limited by the existence of controversies between the abbot and convent, and its physical feasibility was further conditioned by the frequent absences from home of the abbot who, whether from genuine necessity or to avoid discordant and unpleasant incidents, might remain for a great part of the year upon one or other of his manors.[2]

Controversies such as have been alluded to were necessarily more frequent in the black monk houses than in the simpler Cistercian life; in a corporation owning large properties and controlling a mass of rights and dependencies there were continually coming up for decision questions, financial and other, in which the community had a voice. The wisest abbot might make mistakes, and a weak abbot could often dilapidate, through fear or favour, the inheritance entrusted to him. More than one chronicle, in summing up an abbot's career, sets against his good deeds his remissness in asserting rights or his thriftlessness in disposing of the property of the convent.

Such divisions of opinion and opposition of interest seriously affected the spiritual relationship of father and sons; a still more serious solvent was the power possessed by those abbots who controlled dependent

---

1 *Jocelini Cronica* (*Memorials of St Edmund's*, vol. 1), 242: "Illud autem dixit quia magnates nostri, tempore Hugonis abbatis, volentes nichil agi in monasterio nisi per eos, decreverunt nullum monachum claustralem debere loqui cum abbate, nisi prius ostenderet capellano abbatis quid et de qua re vellet loqui."

2 At Evesham, Roger Norreys spent more than a quarter of the year on his manors (*Chron. Evesh.* 105), and Jocelin alludes more than once to Samson's diplomatic absences from home.

houses to exile their subjects far from the mother-house. The power of physical punishment was the abbot's by the Rule, and was doubtless needed on occasion even in the twelfth century; the power of imprisonment was a development of this and employed not infrequently;[1] but banishment to cells or outlying properties, though in cases where a character or mind had become wholly warped it was perhaps the only ready solution of difficulties, might easily become an abuse. Samson and others had suffered from it at Bury under Abbot Hugh, who had been accustomed thus to rid himself of those who spoke freely to him,[2] but it is noteworthy that Jocelin never records such action of Samson himself. In the chronicle of St Albans the charge against abbots of having recourse to this expedient is recurrent, and was doubtless often well founded.[3] More than one of those so banished appealed, not without some reason, to the monastic vow of stability which he had taken.[4]

As a result of these and similar tendencies the monastic family in the greater abbeys came to lose something of its original unity and uniformity. The convent had interests and grievances as against the abbot and the officials directly responsible to him, and within the ranks of the community there was a sharp division between the obedientiaries and their assistants, whose life was one of variety, activity and responsibility, and who were exempted to a greater or less degree, either permanently or at recurring intervals, from community duties, and the monks of the cloister, who lived the common round of regular life and enclosure. It was the task of the ablest abbots, from the end of the twelfth century onwards, to re-establish the lost unity and guard against the abuses which had begun to be common as a result both of the claims of the community to a share in the government, and of the obedientiary system.

III

The internal harmony of the monasteries, threatened by these divisions of feeling, was often further jeopardized by material anxiety. In spite of their vast possessions, many of the great houses were seriously in debt in the last decades of the twelfth century. In the reign of Stephen the distress in which so many found themselves was due immediately to the warfare and brigandage of the times; later pecuniary difficulties were in

---

1 Samson, possibly when not yet a monk, had been in chains under his predecessor (*Jocelini Cronica*, 248), and himself had an opponent bound, though only for a day (*ibid.* 316).

2 *Jocelini Cronica*, 212: "Hugo prior noviter depositus est...et in exilium missus; Dionysius et H. et P. de Hingham de exilio nuper domum redierunt. Ego similiter [the speaker is Samson] incarceratus fui, et postea apud Acram missus, quia locuti sumus pro communi bono ecclesiae nostrae contra voluntatem abbatis."

3 *Gesta Abbatum*, I, 216, 223, 248, 251, 255, 258, 266.

4 *Ibid.* I, 248.

most cases due to less inevitable causes. Among the chief of these must undoubtedly be set the lengthy legal processes in which so many of the houses were involved. The chronicle of Battle abbey is peculiarly instructive on this point. Quite apart from the great exemption suit, we read of an almost unbroken chain of claims and suits regarding manors and churches, many of which came ultimately to the cognizance of king or pope. In almost every case, so far as can be judged, the pecuniary gain accruing from victory would be wholly absorbed in defraying the costs of travelling and litigation; yet it would not be true to suppose that abbots embarked on these suits through mere wantonness. It was an epoch of swift legal development in which law and life had not reached an equilibrium, and in which a violent or unscrupulous party acted as he pleased, leaving it to his adversaries to discover where the law lay and secure its application if they could. At such a time to abandon one claim as not worth the cost of a struggle would have invited other rivals to seize what they willed, and an able abbot such as Walter de Lucy of Battle doubtless hoped that a successful lawsuit would deter others from prosecuting their claims.

But private suits, costly as they may have been, were as nothing to the vast expenses of the *causes célèbres* in which so many of the monasteries were engaged. The amount of English wealth that must have poured into Rome during this period is quite incalculable. The chronicler of St Albans notes that in 1166 Abbot Robert at his death left a debt of six hundred marks, due in the main to litigation over exemption and the suits against Peter de Valoines and the earl of Arundel.[1] Fifty years later the Roman moneylenders at the end of the Evesham case claimed eleven hundred marks, although the abbot had already paid two hundred. In the event a composition was agreed upon for five hundred marks and some smaller debts, but this can have been but a fraction of the total cost incurred by the abbey, and Marleberge who, as early as 1202, had contemplated raising a thousand marks on mortgage or usury, is not likely to have over-estimated the probable expenses.[2] And the cost of the Evesham case must have been far surpassed by those of Glastonbury and Christ Church, Canterbury, during the struggles with Baldwin, Hubert Walter and Savary. All this expense was sheer loss without any material return whatsoever.

Another great source of expenditure was building. Constructions were as a rule embarked upon either by the abbot, who saved the sum needed out of his income,[3] or by the sacrist acting for the community, who often by a self-denying ordinance docked themselves of pittances to give an income to the building fund. Thus the tower at Evesham was built *c.* 1200 partly on the money that one of the monks acquired by practising in medicine, partly by what the community could save by renunciations of

---

1 The chronicler remarks (*Gesta Abbatum*, I, 183): "Excusabilis fuit [abbas] per omnia, propter tot arduorum causas negotiorum."
2 *Chron. Evesh.* 113, 230–1, 257.   3 *Gesta Abbatum*, I, 215.

various kinds,[1] and at Bury in 1198 Abbot Samson gave his whole store of sixty marks towards reconstructing the shrine of St Edmund and suggested that the monks should go without their pittances.[2] But for building, also, there was the temptation to raise money on loan, as had been done at Bury itself shortly before by William the sacrist under Abbot Hugh.[3]

Besides these extraordinary sources of expense, there was the ever-present possibility of maladministration, extravagance and waste. On paper, indeed, in 1175, the vast majority of the black monk houses would have appeared to be amply, and in some cases superfluously, endowed with wealth, and events showed that the time was not past when energetic administration could usually succeed in restoring order out of chaos and in setting an establishment again on its feet. But the current financial and administrative organization was, even when capably managed, very uneconomical. The scattered possessions, the absence of efficient transport, the methods by which rents and payments in kind were realized all tended to increase expense and wastage, and to widen the gulf between estimated income and actual returns. To these disabilities were added those of a divided financial control. Even the fundamental separation between abbot and convent, useful though it was in certain respects, created an unnecessary multiplication of machinery; far worse was the network of obediences which, by giving a large number of individuals charge not only of spending, but of realizing, revenues, made any kind of unity of control and method impossible and multiplied the chances that an office-holder would prove incompetent. When, under a weak or absentee abbot, the officials had *carte blanche* not only to spend, but to mortgage the resources and treasures of the house, a state of chaos was swiftly reached such as prevailed at Bury immediately before the election of Abbot Samson—and Bury, be it remarked, was possessed of potential resources amply sufficient for its needs and was far from being decadent in spirit.

As a result of the working of one or more of these causes a number of the greater houses are found in debt c. 1175, as were doubtless many others for which no record exists. Abbot Robert of St Albans, as has been said, left a debt of six hundred marks in 1166; this had increased to eight hundred by the death of his successor in 1183.[4] At Bury in 1180, as a result of sheer mismanagement without the excuse of any great lawsuits, the total debt had reached some £3000, to say nothing of the interest

---

1 *Chron. Evesh.* 108: "Convertentes redditus pitanciariae quandocumque eos habuimus et omnia alia quaecumque nobis subtrahere potuimus in opus illud."
2 *Jocelini Cronica*, 308. The sum is "totum thesaurum suum".
3 *Ibid.* 210.
4 *Gesta Abbatum*, I, 193: "Moriens, abbathiam suam aere alieno obligatam plusquam secentis marcis...sine aliis debitis, quae ad ducentarum marcarum et amplius summam excreverunt, dereliquit."

payable.[1] The greater part of the money in these and similar cases had been raised from the Jews, who consequently figure in a number of the chronicles. At Bury in 1180 we hear, among other creditors, of Isaac fitz Raby Joyce, of Benedict the Jew of Norwich, and of Jurnetus, and matters had reached such a pitch that the tribe had quartered themselves on the abbey, using its strong-room as a bank, lodging their women and children in the offices and wandering about the minster while Mass was being sung.[2] At St Albans in 1166 most of the debts were to Jews, and in 1183 Aaron the chief creditor made himself at home in the abbey, boasting that he had built the shrine of the patron saint.[3] Only a few years before, the abbot of Peterborough had endeavoured by force to extract the arm of St Oswald from its reliquary in order to pawn it for cash to the Jews;[4] thirty years later it was to the Jews that the monks of Evesham looked to raise the money necessary for their litigation; Canterbury had become engaged to them during the troubles;[5] and, as will be seen, even the Cistercians were in their clutches.

IV

The records of the most celebrated controversies of the period show several of the important monasteries in something approaching to a state of warfare. The picture may be supplemented by a glance at the more peaceful way of life of two of the most eminent English black monk abbots in the last quarter of the twelfth century, Odo of Battle (abbot 1175–1200) and Samson of Bury (abbot 1182–1211).

The figure of Odo of Battle is one of the most attractive of all those that appear in the literature of the time; he stands almost alone among his contemporaries as an inheritor of the spirit of Lanfranc and Anselm, and may be taken as the last abbot of whom any adequate account exists who belongs to the tradition of Bec and Normandy rather than to that of Samson and the great English administrative abbots of the late twelfth and early thirteenth centuries. It is thus all the more remarkable that he should have been a monk, and filled the office of prior, at Christ Church, a house above all others exposed to contact with the world and strife of all kinds. For when all allowance is made for *esprit de famille* on the part

1 Jocelin (*Cronica*, 210) gives a sample of the usury of the time. A debt of forty marks (£60) grew to £100; another of £100 was added to it and after some time this was recognized as a debt of £400. Four years later this had become by usury one of £880 (= 30 per cent. simple interest). These figures should be multiplied by twelve or fifteen to obtain the modern equivalent.

2 *Jocelini Cronica*, 210, 213, 218.

3 *Gesta Abbatum*, I, 183: "Multa enim Christianis, sed plura debebat Judaeis." *Ibid*. 193: "Aaron Judaeus...ad domum S. Albani in superbia magna et jactantia cum minis veniens, jactitabat se feretrum Beato Albano nostro fecisse."

4 Benedict of Peterborough, I, 106 (1175).

5 *Chron. Evesh.* 113; *Epp. Cant.* cccclxxxvii.

of the Battle chronicler, the impression given is still of one who both in his private life and in his acts of government set spiritual things before temporal and suited his actions to his profession. The chronicler records that at Battle he lived among his monks as one of them, present in the church at the Offices, eating in the common refectory and reading in the cloister with the rest during the day; he would even have slept in the common dormitory but for a physical disability. He was a man of unusual eloquence, deeply read in spiritual literature, and he willingly spoke to his monks and the people, to the former in Latin or French, to the latter in English. He was also a man of great charm of character, joined to administrative ability of a high order, and it was perhaps a real misfortune for the Church in England that the bishops succeeded in quashing the attempt made by the monks of Canterbury to elevate him to the primacy in 1184. Battle, during the twelfth century, was indeed fortunate in its abbots; had others cultivated the simplicity and sobriety of Odo the subsequent history of the monastic order in England would have been happier and more peaceful. It is to be regretted that the chronicle of Battle ends early in Odo's reign; from another source we know that he left behind him a reputation of sanctity and was in some quarters counted as a saint.[1]

The name of Odo is familiar only to a few students, that of Samson of Bury to all lovers of English literature. Probably, indeed, Samson is the single English abbot of the later Middle Ages of whom there is widespread knowledge among his countrymen, and in consequence he is still generally regarded as the type of a whole age of religion, and as the finest example of a class. Such an impression is due, apart from the accident of Carlyle's genius, to the rediscovery of his history at a moment when English sentiment, after several centuries of mistaken antipathy, and a shorter period of romantic admiration, was prepared to be more tolerant and more sane in its attitude towards the monastic life, and was delighted to find in Samson one whose worth and capability were unmistakable and shown in ways and with regard to matters with which men of every century and shade of belief are conversant; who made no demands, as does a saint and above all a saint of the monastic life, upon the reader's own powers of spiritual insight. In more recent years here, as in all other departments of medieval history, a more sophisticated and critical, if perhaps less warm-hearted, attitude has been adopted, and it has been recognized that Samson, though truly great as a man of many activities and as a ruler, was not a monk of the purest type—was not, in fact, a great spiritual power, still less a saint. He is, indeed, not at all typical of the monastic centuries that preceded his epoch, still less their brightest exemplar; he is, at least as known to us from the pages of Jocelin, no more than an able administrator,

1 Odo is the subject of a fairly full article in *DNB* by C. L. Kingsford; *v.* for his character *Chron. Bell.* 163.

a firm and just governor, and an upright, God-fearing man, and such have not been wanting to any profession or in any age. He is, however, an excellent representative of his own class in his own age, and since the process of crystallization which had developed so rapidly in the English monasteries was almost complete by 1200, he is also a true elder brother of the best and ablest abbots of the succeeding centuries. There were many Samsons between the reign of John and the Dissolution; it is not easy to find an Ailred or an Anselm.

Jocelin's *Chronicle* has achieved a world-wide celebrity in the pages of Carlyle; it is a celebrity not without its drawbacks, for what is in truth no more than a sketch of the superficies of a single type of monastic life at a single house during a particular epoch has been taken by the general reader to represent the whole of medieval monasticism. Despite this, one familiar with all the chronicles of the eleventh and twelfth centuries will probably allow Jocelin's fame to be deserved, for though the Battle chronicler has a loftier sense of his vocation, and Marleberge of Evesham a more connected and unusual story to tell, while the school of St Albans paints a richer and more varied canvas, yet Jocelin's keen personal observation and the moral worth of his hero give a unity to his diffuse records, and his work remains the only one which gives a clear picture of everyday life in a black monk monastery, as seen from the standpoint of the average monk. Even if the comparison sometimes drawn between Samson and Johnson be considered fantastic, Carlyle was right in thinking Jocelin and Boswell to belong to the same family; both have, together with keen sight and retentive memory, at once a just estimate of true worth and a *naïveté* when relating the words and actions of themselves and others which is the best guarantee of fidelity. Further than this, the comparison must not be pressed. Save for a few judgments of Samson, the sayings preserved by Jocelin have none of the moral and intellectual force that distinguishes the utterances of Johnson, and though Jocelin may well have been a better man than Johnson's biographer, Boswell was possessed of great mental sympathy and receptivity, wholly lacking in Jocelin, which go far to disguise in his pages the moral weakness of his character as we know it to have been. None of the conversation preserved by Jocelin deserves to live in virtue of any intrinsic excellence; it is merely the ephemeral stuff that passes in any group of men; its only value is that it shows us in photographic detail what otherwise could be reconstructed but vaguely in the imagination, and presents us with a glimpse of the daily life that is elsewhere concealed behind the conventional language of the typical letter-writers and chroniclers.

The Bury of Samson, as shown to us by Jocelin, is a corporate body which has taken firm and deep roots in the material and social world around it, and has adopted in much of its life the standards and aspirations of its environment. It is not rising, or being drawn, to some higher, spiritual goal, as were Bec, Clairvaux, Rievaulx and Witham. The circumstances which differentiate its religious sentiment from that of the common experience of the modern world—the prophetic dreams of the monks, the reputed miracles of St Edmund—are, whatever we may think of their objective truth, in the order of the marvellous, not in that of the spiritual. Whenever we see Jocelin and his contemporaries acting, speaking or reflecting, it is in a wholly human manner—part admirable, part petty, all comprehensible. It may indeed well be that in Jocelin's pages the picture takes a more ludicrous and infantile appearance than the existing reality would have shown; there must have been at Bury more than one of greater intellectual power and of deeper spiritual vision than the chronicler himself; there was undoubtedly in the community a strong core of honesty and good purpose, for they chose as abbot a strong and good man who had never striven to ingratiate himself with others, and in such cases the electors must be allowed to deserve the ruler whom they receive. To characterize Bury as an abode of mediocrity would therefore be unjust, if by mediocrity is understood all lack of enthusiasm or endeavour. Yet it would be true to say that, so far as can be seen, the purely spiritual ideal of the monastic life had been lost to view, and *esprit de corps* had come to occupy for many the position of a leading interest in life and guide of action. From this respectability the figure of Samson emerges, not in virtue of a more intense or spiritual ideal, but by reason of the native force and goodness of the man; the careful reader of Jocelin will observe that though he sometimes displays love of domination and arrives at his end by aid of finesse or cajolery, Samson's years of office are (so far as we see them) conspicuously free from acts of mere selfishness or high-handedness such as could seriously affect the welfare of individuals among his subjects, and such as occur in the records of the lives of several of the ablest of his contemporaries and successors. His government, though on occasion stern and even arbitrary, was always directed to the well-being of the governed, considered not only in the mass, but as individuals, and though Jocelin's *Chronicle*, which ceases some years before the abbot's death, gives the impression that his conduct became more arbitrary as the years advanced, another source testifies that he retained the love and even the veneration of his sons unimpaired at the moment of his death.[1] Familiar as may be the picture drawn of Samson by his chaplain, no account of English monastic life would be complete without it:

Abbot Samson was of medium height; his head was almost entirely bald; his countenance was neither round nor oval. He had a prominent nose, thick

1 *Annales S. Edmundi (Ungedruckte anglo-normannische Geschichtsquellen*, ed. F. Liebermann, 150), *s.a.* 1212: "Samson venerabilis abbas...ultimo filiis vale praesentato, a quibus benedictus in secula meruit benedici, astantibus omnibus non miserabilem sed mirabilem ejus transitum admirantibus...quievit in pace."

lips, eyes of glass-grey with a penetrating regard, ears wonderfully sharp, and shaggy eyebrows which he shaved frequently. A little cold made him speedily hoarse. At the time of his election he was forty-seven years of age, and had been a monk for seventeen; he then had a red beard with few white hairs in it, and fewer among the black hairs of his head, but before fourteen years were out he became white as snow in beard and hair.... He was extremely temperate and active and strong, and loved to go on horseback or on foot until age got the better of him; when he heard say that the Cross had been taken and Jerusalem lost he began to wear drawers of haircloth and a shirt of the same and to abstain from flesh-meat; he desired however that meat should be put before him at table, to increase the quantity of his alms. He preferred sweet milk and honey and such like things to any other food. Liars, drunkards and great talkers he hated, and he judged severely those who murmured at their meat and drink, especially if they were monks.... He was eloquent in French and Latin, attending rather to the order and matter than to fine words. He could read the Scriptures in English most attractively, and was wont to preach in English to the people in the dialect of Norfolk, where he was born and bred.... When abbot he gave the impression of preferring the active life to the contemplative, for he praised good obedientiaries rather than good cloistered monks, and he rarely expressed approval of anyone for his knowledge of letters only, unless he had a knowledge of affairs of the world; when he happened to hear of a superior who had resigned his charge and become an anchorite he had no praise for him.... He acted also as I have never seen another act, that is, he had a great affection for many without ever or at least without frequently showing it in his countenance.[1]

In the foregoing paragraphs no attempt has been made to reproduce or to outline the picture of life at St Edmund's under the great abbot. The majority of those who read these pages will no doubt be familiar with Jocelin. In any case, his vivid, racy memorial defies and eludes any process of analysis or synthesis; it will be used frequently elsewhere as a source of information on a number of detailed points of organization, but it must ultimately be left by the historian as one of the very few original sources of the period that every reader who is at all interested in medieval monastic life must read, and read more than once, for himself and in its entirety.

V

Of a character very different is the record of the acts of the abbots of St Albans. Taken, indeed, in their full sweep over the twelfth and thirteenth centuries they far surpass any other monastic chronicle in the wealth of information they give and in the data they supply for comparing epoch with epoch; in the case of no other house do we possess the materials for a *coup d'œil* in such abundance and variety, and it is most fortunate that the abbey concerned was the home of more varied interests and activities than any other. The value of the *Gesta Abbatum* is, however, greatly lessened by the lack of unity in composition. In its present form the work represents a

1 *Jocelini Cronica*, 243–7.

mass of earlier material worked over by Matthew Paris, but the celebrated historiographer made no attempt to reduce the whole to a straightforward narrative, and there are many displacements and "doublets" and contradictions of detail, while on the other hand the events of the past are sometimes stressed or criticized in the light of later controversy. The *Gesta Abbatum* therefore lack at once the spontaneity and the directness of sight of Jocelin; they have, however, in common with him the advantage of giving us, not a discreet, official narrative, but the unhampered personal view of a member of the community writing for his peers.

Life at St Albans at the end of the twelfth century was more vivid and varied than at St Edmundsbury. The three abbots whose reigns covered the space between the exile of Becket and the death of John were all men of considerable intellectual distinction and literary and artistic tastes. Simon, the first (1167–83), was a student; he had been a gifted scribe and continued as abbot to add books to a special collection made by himself in a cupboard in the church, and he maintained constantly two or three professional writers in his apartments. It will be seen elsewhere that he was in direct touch with the intellectual and theological movements of the Continent. He added much to the decoration of the church, but was no great administrator.[1] During the later years of his rule he had as prior Warin, who succeeded him. Like his predecessor Warin (1183–95) was a student, though of a different branch of learning; he was the leader of the group from Salerno who found a home at St Albans. John (1195–1214), who succeeded Warin, was a graduate of Paris who combined the intellectual interests of Simon and Warin, being skilled in both letters and medicine. More than either of his predecessors, however, he was a student before all else, and would seem to have lived in a retirement unusual for an abbot, giving over the charge of discipline and administration to his prior and cellarer. How far this retirement was the issue of a natural bent of character and how far due to motives of a spiritual order cannot easily be ascertained from the ambiguous language of the chronicle.[2] Clearly, however, Abbot John was of a very different type of character to Samson. Nevertheless, he was a greater builder than either of his predecessors, and it was under his rule that the artistic life of St Albans entered upon its golden age with the arrival of the Colchesters.[3]

As might be expected in a community where three such men had risen to posts of responsibility from which two, at least, had been chosen by the house as abbot,[4] there is full evidence that a rich intellectual, literary

---

1 *GASA*, I, 184–94.
2 *GASA*, I, 217–18: "Hic, more scholarium, rei familiaris ignarus, studium, contemplationem et orationum continuationem amplectens."
3 For the artistic work of St Albans, *v. infra*, ch. xxx.
4 Simon and Warin had been prior; John was prior of Wallingford when elected. Simon was one of three presented by the convent to the king; Warin was elected by all; of John's election nothing is known (*GASA*, I, 183, 195, 217).

and artistic life existed at St Albans. In this respect, indeed, as has often been remarked, the house surpassed all the other monasteries of England. Just as at Bury the best talent went to administration and the surveillance of estates, so at St Albans it went to letters and art. St Albans, for all its wide possessions, had not struck its roots as deep into the soil of Hertfordshire as had Bury into the countryside of Suffolk; the Athenian vivacity of the one is a contrast to the Bœotian atmosphere of the other. It was precisely this mental agility that caused disputes to arise over a series of issues between abbot and monks of St Albans, especially under the rule of Warin and John. When we come to analyse the monastic uses of the period we shall remark everywhere what a historian of St Albans has called a "constitutional movement" developing throughout the body of the black monks. Nowhere was this more notable than at St Albans, and during the whole period from 1183 to 1214 there was intermittent friction which broke out on occasion into flame. In such matters it is very difficult to separate fact from gossip, and we have no means of reading the story from the abbot's side, but neither Warin nor John was a born leader or ruler of men; both would seem to have relied on a group of officials and acted at times autocratically and even ruthlessly,[1] banishing to distant cells not only *mauvais sujets* but those also whom their gifts had rendered too eminent. Alongside of this exercise of absolute power there was a tendency to purchase contentment by means of relaxations of various kinds in the daily rule of the house. Here again the reader has to be on his guard against taking as an established fact the statement of the chronicler that all the changes were made solely for the sake of peace, for Paris was writing at a moment when the abbots of St Albans were leading the party of strictness in the thirteenth-century revival. The very pages that tell us of these controversies and relaxations tell us also of the deeply religious character of Abbot John,[2] and of the severe and observant life of his successor William of Trumpington. Yet even here there is hesitation; for the spirituality of the abbots of St Albans has not the luminous clarity and genial warmth that we recognize at Rievaulx or Sempringham; there is something in it of the equivocal, of the *manqué*, as in not a little of the spirituality of France in the seventeenth century; though here again the record supplies us only with contradictory indications, and with no means of resolving the apparent discord between them.

If these observations upon the life at St Albans seem themselves disjointed and inconclusive, they do but reproduce the impression created by

---

1 *GASA*, I, 196–7: "Multiplicati sunt igitur adulatores dicentes eum [*sc.* Warinum] beatum: quorum sermones, melliti super favum et molliti super oleum, ipsum deceperunt." Cf. *ibid*. 215: "Ipse igitur inexorabilis cum fratre suo, Domino Matthaeo, Priore, suspiciosissimo." Also Abbot John, *ibid*. 247–51.

2 *GASA*, I, 217: "Vir eximiae pietatis, amator ordinis et vigoris disciplinae claustralis." *Ibid*. 234: "Utpote praelatorum piissimus." 218: "Sic magis contemplativus, ut decuit, quam activus, etc."

the *Gesta Abbatum*, and in truth it is from a mass of such impressions, derived from fifty different sources, that a picture of the monastic life must be formed. The simplicity and regularity of Battle; the busy life and talk of Bury, absorbed in its own life and that of the countryside and town, under the strong government of Samson; the richer and less material interests of St Albans; the strivings and controversies of Christ Church and Evesham—all these must find a place and form a part of the synthesis. And if the *Chronicle* of Jocelin is the best of all correctives to a romanticizing imagination, it must not be thought to contain all that Bury knew of religion. When graver matters are in question Jocelin's language can become grave, and even below the froth of gossip, which amuses the reader and remains in his memory, we can see the daily round of observance and discipline going forward. And at St Albans Abbot John, if not a perfect ruler, left behind him a reputation which allowed the miraculous element to be associated with his name,[1] and the same witness who records his failings, or what were regarded as such by the convent, tells also of his regularity at the divine service and of his long hours of private prayer.[2]

1 *GASA*, I, 230–2. Abbot John is credited with a feat of memory which might have caused even Macaulay to blench—that of repeating the whole psalter verse by verse backwards by way of a *tour de force* ("quasi ad experimentum et exercitium"). The chronicler, who asserts his own incapacity to treat even the familiar *Miserere* in this way, does his best to substantiate the story ("fecisse ipsum meminimus...quod etsi verum, sit tamen incredibile") and indeed his previous narrative gives casually a good example of the ordinary memories of that epoch, for he tells us that the abbot's assistants were in the habit of reciting the twelve lessons and responsories of the Office of the Blessed Virgin in the dark.

2 *GASA*, I, 230: "In mansuetudine Deo in diebus et in noctibus singulis sine intermissione pensum reddendo cotidianum jugiter ministrabat."

CHAPTER XVIII

THE HOSTILITY OF THE BISHOPS TOWARDS THE BLACK MONKS

I

The last quarter of the twelfth century and the first decade of the thirteenth, or, to speak more accurately, the period between the death of Alexander III in 1181 and the Fourth Lateran Council of 1215, was a time of considerable disorder in the life of the Church in western Europe. Under a succession of short-lived and undistinguished popes the apostolic see lost the power of initiative and direction at the very moment when the great spiritual revival of the first half of the century was exhausted, while the intellectual renaissance, theological, legal and secular, was finding *foci* of growing importance at a number of widely separated points which were to become the medieval universities; at the same time the movement towards corporate, autonomous life, in the centres both of learning and of commerce, was developing very rapidly, and affecting the outlook of all groups and associations. There were, in fact, within the framework of the Church and nation, strong centrifugal forces drawing away from the central government towards lesser and more communal forms of control and association.

In England, this disorganization in the ecclesiastical sphere was increased by the trend taken by national events. The autocratic, strongly national government of Henry II had to a large extent withdrawn England in practice, though not in theory, from the control of the Curia and canon law; the group of curial, canonist bishops of the middle of the century had been succeeded by one composed of men less distinguished in themselves, with little experience of affairs outside the country, and appointed for the most part from the clergy surrounding the court; the absentee Richard I was succeeded by John, under whom all rational direction of affairs ceased and a complete and lasting rupture with the papacy ensued. Here we are not concerned at all with the social and constitutional results for England; as regards the life of the Church, order and fruitful growth returned in a large measure owing to the peaceful government of Henry III, to the legislation of the Lateran Council and the emergence of a number of eminent administrators among the diocesan bishops, to the arrival of the new orders of friars at the centres of population and intellectual life, and to the direction of the episcopate and the universities by the papacy which had been given a new life under the strong control of Innocent III. All this, however, took place outside the limits assigned to these pages;

here, we have only to consider the decades during which the centrifugal, disorderly forces were on the whole preponderant.

In the life of the monastic communities, and especially that of the black monks, the period was one of stress without and within. The growth of a powerful party among the bishops and their household clerks, opposed to the monastic body as such, and anxious to curtail its power, had its counterpart in the growth of a spirit—it might almost be called a school— of hostility and criticism among some of the ablest writers of the time. Besides these attacks from without, a number of the great monasteries found themselves engaged in long and most distressing domestic controversies, often issuing in violence, of which the most celebrated were the troubles of Christ Church with Archbishops Baldwin and Hubert, followed shortly by the strife subsequent to the Langton election, and the struggles of Evesham to obtain exemption and rid itself of its unworthy abbot. Quite apart from such *causes célèbres*, all the monasteries of the country suffered heavily from the anarchy and exactions of John's reign, while many were during the whole period seriously encumbered by debt. Finally, the absence of any strong control, either from Rome, or from the king, or from any religious superior outside the walls of the house, was beginning to lead in many cases to a decay of organization, of discipline and of spiritual life. Each of these various developments will be considered at some length in the following pages.

II

The last two decades of the twelfth century, as has been said, witnessed the growth of a sentiment hostile to the monastic order to which the previous age in this country can provide no parallel. Hitherto such hostility as had been incurred by individual houses, or by the monastic body as such, had been almost entirely due to personal ill-will or private quarrels. Monasteries had suffered, and suffered greatly, from hard treatment received from kings and bishops, and still more from the attacks of private individuals and from the lawlessness of the times. But in all these cases, the quarrel was not a calculated affair, and went no deeper than the particular issue; before 1150 no body of educated opinion in England was hostile to the monastic order.[1]

The absence of such educated criticism or hostility admits of a very simple explanation. On the one hand, the state of the monastic body in England between 1070–1150, taken in its bulk, did not justify serious or

---

1 The opposition of a number of bishops, first *c.* 1070 and later at the Canterbury election of 1123, does not really invalidate the above statement. Walkelin's opposition in 1070, as his subsequent extreme friendliness showed, was not based on any deep principle or prejudice, and on the second occasion the chief actors were a group of powerful and worldly bishops.

wholesale criticism; on the other, there was not in existence in this country before 1150 any body or class of men of learning or culture outside the walls of a monastery.[1] But by 1170–80 much of this had changed. The monks, and especially the black monks, quite apart from any deterioration of their own standard of life, had suffered a permanent loss of prestige from the competition of the Cistercians, and as the century wore on, monks both black and white had been to some extent outbidden by the strictly contemplative orders, such as the Carthusians and the second generation of Premonstratensians. Criticism could thus enfilade the black monks on either flank, by attacking them for their own shortcomings, and comparing their whole way of life unfavourably with that of others. Nothing, perhaps, has won more credence for the hostile judgments of Gerald of Wales than his reiterated praise of the regular canons and Carthusians.

Exposed as it thus was to attack, the monastic body found itself the object of the assaults of a new and large class of men, almost all clerks, who had enjoyed the advantages of an excellent literary and legal education in the schools abroad, who had then returned to England to enter the service of the king or one of the bishops, and whose interests and sympathies lay with the secular clergy and with the world of administration, of law and of letters as it existed at every great centre from Rome to York. Among this class there made itself felt, towards the end of the reign of Henry II, a spirit of polished satire and fluent criticism wholly without parallel in previous decades, but destined to find many adepts between the age of Walter Map and Gerald of Wales and that of Valla and Erasmus. This spirit was not confined to secular clerks; it had its adepts in the cloister also;[2] but from the nature of things it found greater scope in the eager, irresponsible circles of a royal or episcopal household.

Thus feeling against the monks came gradually to manifest itself in two movements only remotely connected in origin and aim, but which gave impulse one to the other and derived support from the same class of men. The one took the form of a concerted attack on the part of a number of bishops upon various monastic claims and rights; the other showed itself in the violent criticism of a group of literary men. The attack of the bishops was upon the black monks only and received considerable support

1 This statement is probably true, and for the whole kingdom, until c. 1120. After that date there was a gradual infiltration of clerks who had received a training in the foreign schools, and after another decade the number of native Englishmen who had gone abroad for their education begins to be considerable. But it was not till the middle of the century that these began to form anything like a class of mature minds, and the growth of such a class was hindered by the absence of any celebrated English centre of higher education. Probably before the days of Theobald the episcopal *curia* and schools of York and some other northern towns had a higher level of culture than anything south of the Humber, but although there was anti-Cluniac feeling at York, as evidenced by the writings of Hugo de Sottovagina (v. *Hist. York*, II, xiii), the flourishing state of the early Cistercians and canons kept the balance of opinion in favour of the monks.

2 The writings of the Winchester monk, Richard of Devizes, are a case in point.

from the Cistercians; the attack of the clerks was against the whole monastic order, black and white.

The patriarch of the anti-monastic party in the hierarchy of Henry II would seem to have been Roger of Bishop's Bridge, archbishop of York (1154–81). According to William of Newburgh, he was in the habit of asserting that the establishment of Fountains was the greatest stain on Thurstan's episcopate, and during his last illness his hatred of regulars of every kind appears to have amounted to a monomania.[1] It must be said, however, that the charters and other records of Roger's tenure of office do not give support to Newburgh's sweeping judgments.[2] The real attack came during the years in which Baldwin was archbishop of Canterbury.

Archbishop Baldwin has on the whole received kind, and perhaps even indulgent, treatment from historians.[3] His varied and eventful life received much incidental notice from chroniclers, but it is not easy to reconcile the various characteristics[4] and actions which they record, nor to ascertain what qualities in him led those who knew the man to assist so often in his promotion to high office, and what precisely were the defects that so repeatedly neutralized the unusual abilities that he must have possessed. Of those who speak at all intimately of him, the majority belong to the party of his adversaries in the Canterbury dispute, while Gerald of Wales who, as his familiar companion on a celebrated journey had every opportunity of studying him, creates more problems than he

1 William of Newburgh, I, 226: "Viros religiosos in tantum exhorruit ut dixisse feratur felicis memoriae Turstinum...nunquam gravius deliquisse, quam aedificando...monasterium de Fontibus."

2 He gave considerable countenance in his early years to the Cistercians, and later warmly supported Gilbert of Sempringham. On the other hand, he is almost certainly to be identified with one of the prelates who criticized the title of Ailred to sanctity (cf. Walter Daniel, *Vita Ailredi*, 71).

3 Stubbs set the tone: "Archbishop Baldwin...was a man of singular sanctity, courage and honesty....He was, in fact, a Cistercian of the best sort, a man who lived but little for the world, and that to make it better" (*Epistolae Cantuarienses*, introd. xxxiii–xxxiv). Higher praise could scarcely be given to an Ailred or a Hugh of Lincoln, and is scarcely consistent with the recognition by the same writer of "errors of temper, harshness, arbitrary severity, and want of tact, of which he cannot be acquitted" (*ibid*. xxxv), and with the "crooked ways" of his policy "in which a man cannot walk at once honestly and successfully". Stubbs, in fact, did not make a synthesis of the various judgments of contemporaries on Baldwin; he also mistakenly regarded the Cistercian type as a fixed one, and Baldwin as a palmary example. The writer (Rev. W. Hunt) of the article on Baldwin in the *DNB*, though less peremptory than Stubbs, leaves the reader equally unsatisfied. These two accounts have influenced almost all others, including those (likewise too indulgent) in the *DTC* and *DHG*.

4 Gerald of Wales, *more suo*, supplies us with contradictory data, e.g. in the *Iter Kambriae*, 149, he gives the well-known *mot* concerning Baldwin: "melior monachus simplex quam abbas, melior abbas quam episcopus, melior episcopus quam archiepiscopus", and in the *Speculum Ecclesiae*, IV, 76, he speaks of him as "morum lenitate nimia animique simplicitate praeditus immoderata...ob innatum omnino teporem nimium ac torporem...unde et eidem Urbanus papa quandoque scripsisse recolitur in hunc modum: 'Urbanus episcopus, servus servorum Dei, monacho ferventissimo, abbati calido, episcopo tepido, archiepiscopo remisso, salutem.'" In the same work (*ibid*. 106) Baldwin is described as "vir columbinae simplicitatis et innocuae...benignitatis".

solves by his judgments, even if we are willing to assume the substantial accuracy of what he says.[1]

Baldwin, a native of Exeter, came of humble stock, but obtained an excellent education, became himself a teacher of note,[2] and entered the service of the Church. Bartholomew, bishop of Exeter (1162–84), was led by his high reputation to make him his archdeacon,[3] in which capacity he would have acquired much knowledge and experience of a legal and personal kind, for the bishop was an energetic administrator and a celebrated canonist, whom Alexander III frequently employed as judge delegate. But the office of archdeacon was notoriously dangerous to the spiritual life of its holders, and Baldwin left the prospects of a career to become a Cistercian in the neighbouring abbey of Ford, on the borders of Devon and Dorset. There, after a very short time, the distinguished recruit was elected abbot.[4] In any estimate of his character, his late entry into religion and his speedy election to office must be borne in mind, for though he may well have appreciated intellectually and emotionally the Cistercian ideals, he can scarcely have been formed by them or have himself become a living exemplar of the hidden simplicity of the monastic life. As abbot, however, his reputation continued to grow; it was then, in all probability, that he composed the majority of his sermons and treatises;[5] he was also interested in the life of the saintly anchorite, Wulfric of Hazelbury.[6] In 1180 he became bishop of Worcester. The decade 1180–90 saw an unusual number of changes in the hierarchy;[7] the last of the great curial and canonist bishops disappeared, and the members of the episcopate in the later 'eighties could not at all compare in distinction with the bishops of the Becket controversy, a number of whom had occupied their sees for a long span of years. With the single, if brilliant, exception of Hugh of Lincoln (1186–1200) there was not one among those appointed after 1180 who could compare in ability with Henry of Winchester (1129–71), Gilbert Foliot of Hereford and London (1148–87),

1 Stubbs, *Epp. Cant.* introd. xxxiv, remarks with justice: "it is not easy to say how far he [Giraldus] speaks the truth."

2 Giraldus, *Speculum Ecclesiae*, IV, 81: "Diutius in scholis degens...scholarumque magister egregius." In 1150 Eugenius III appointed him tutor to Gratian, nephew of Innocent II (Jo. Saresb. *ep.* 292; cf. R. L. Poole, *Robert Pullen and Nicholas Breakspear*, in *Essays...presented to T. F. Tout* (1925), 61–70.

3 Gervase, II, 400.

4 Gervase, II, 400, says "after a few years". Gerald (*Iter Kambriae*, 148) says "within a year". Both had ample opportunity of knowing the facts, but Gervase is the more trustworthy, and his statement is intrinsically the more probable. Dom A. Morey, *Bartholomew of Exeter*, 121, shows that Baldwin probably resigned his post of archdeacon in 1169/70. He was abbot of Ford by 1175.

5 Printed in *PL*, CCIV. They show that Baldwin's theological learning was thoroughly abreast of the times, but have little originality or spiritual value. The art. *Baudouin de Ford* by Dom J. M. Canivez in the *DS* gives a useful list of MSS. of his works.

6 Cf. the *Life of St Wulfric* by John a monk of Ford, edited by Dom Maurice Bell for the Somerset Record Society, XLVII (1933).

7 In addition to thirteen deaths during the decade of bishops appointed before 1180, three appointed after that date died within a brief space and three more were translated.

Bartholomew of Exeter (1162–84), or even with Roger of York (1154–81), Hugh of Durham (1153–95), Hilary of Chichester (1147–69) and William of Norwich (1146–74). This absence of talent, together with the radical sympathy which Baldwin had with the secular clerks' outlook in Church politics, probably furthered his prospects as much as did his own recognized superiority, and goes far to account for the somewhat strange choice by the bishops of a Cistercian as their candidate in the customary dispute with the monks of Canterbury in the election of 1184.[1] The monks, for their part, put forward three of their own habit, Odo, prior of Christ Church and abbot of Battle, an excellent choice, Peter de Leia, a Cluniac of Wenlock, then bishop of St David's, and Theobald, abbot of Cluny.

Although Baldwin expressed his intention of ruling only if elected by the monks[2] and, when a satisfactory compromise had been effected, began his reign with a paternal exhortation to the brethren,[3] there was probably little sympathy from the beginning between one who combined the outlook of a clerk and a Cistercian and the jealous community of Christ Church, strong in their possession of the body and traditions of St Thomas and more concerned with the affairs of their own corporation than with the welfare of the Church in England or with the abstract principles of monastic life.

To Baldwin himself, and to his numerous recently appointed colleagues of the court party, the position of the monks at Canterbury and other cathedral monasteries must have seemed anomalous and their privileges undesirable. The history of the past was easily forgotten; Baldwin and his contemporaries had been brought up in the traditions of canon law, in which monastic cathedral chapters did not figure; the monks of Canterbury, in particular, claimed the right of being the sole electors to the primatial see, which the bishops had always wished to control; at every vacancy there was a bitter dispute, and the monks naturally put forward one of their own number. Although a bishop with a cathedral monastery had the advantage of possessing a body of ardent supporters if the rights of his see were impugned, he lacked the freedom of action in his cathedral and household that others possessed, he usually found himself sooner or later at odds with his monks, and he had less patronage at his disposal for the clerks and prebendaries of his entourage. This last consideration weighed heavily with the individuals concerned and made of them the strongest advocates of a change to the normal practice of a secular chapter.

The precise occasion of the open hostility which soon developed between Baldwin and his monks is not easy to ascertain. Peter of Blois who, as the archbishop's agent, must have known the inner history of the

---

1 Of the twelve English sees of the province of Canterbury (excluding Worcester), no less than six were vacant in December 1184, and Gilbert Foliot of London was too old a man to be a possible choice.

2 Gervase, I, 324.   3 Gervase, II, 401.

business as well as any man, sets out in a most tantalizing letter to tell the whole story in justification of his master, but fails wholly to achieve his purpose.[1] Moreover, as with Gerald of Wales, so with Peter of Blois, the reader is always chary of accepting any statement for which he is the only guarantor, and in this case, as in others in his correspondence, we are provided with a pendant to this letter in another written subsequently to the monks of Canterbury, in which he expresses his deep sorrow for the action he took against them, to which indeed he ascribes, as a scourge of the Lord, an illness from which he suffered.[2] He does however assert, what we know only from this source, that the real friction originated when Baldwin deprived the convent of their control of some property owing to the moral delinquencies of a few of the monks in charge.[3] This may have been so; but so far as can be ascertained from Gervase and other sources,[4] the first move in the struggle was when the archbishop deprived the convent of the Christmas offerings from their manors and from three churches which had been appropriated to the almonry. For this he had obtained, by subreption as the monks held, letters from Lucius III and Urban III authorizing him to act.[5] Appeals were duly threatened by the monks, but the matter was compromised, and the archbishop succeeded in ridding himself of the extremely able prior, Alan, by making him abbot of Tewkesbury.[6] This, however, was only the beginning of sorrows. Baldwin soon (autumn 1186) put forward a scheme which was destined to distract the reigns of himself and his successor, to provoke the unappeasable hostility of the monks, and to become a *cause célèbre* familiar to the whole of Christian Europe. This was a proposal to found a collegiate church at Hackington, a suburb of Canterbury, in honour of St Thomas and St Stephen. The project, it was alleged, was an act of piety in every sense, since a similar proposal had been dear to Becket himself, and it was

---

1 *Petri Blesensis Opera*, ed. Giles, *ep.* 216; *PL*, CCVII, *ep.* 211, coll. 492–5; *Epp. Cant.* Appendix, no. dlxxi, pp. 555–7. The difficulty of interpreting this letter is increased by the corrupt state of the text. Stubbs has improved greatly upon the version of Giles and Migne, but some words are still clearly faulty as printed.

2 *PL*, CCVII, *ep.* 233, coll. 534–5.

3 *Petri Blesensis Opera*, ed. Giles, *ep.* 216; *Epp. Cant.* p. 555: "Suos itaque filios cohibebat a firmis ruralibus quarum occasione quidam, pauci tamen, cum corporibus suis turpe foedus inierant."

4 Gervase, I, 332 (under date 16 December 1185); also the anonymous author of the contemporary introduction to the collection of *Epp. Cant.* (p. 2): "hujus autem tribulationis prima causa fuit, etc.", giving the same reason as Gervase.

5 To judge by this and a number of similar cases it was often possible for an energetic, astute or unscrupulous agent to persuade, stampede, delude or bribe officials of the papal chancery into issuing letters giving certain injunctions or powers, but containing no judgment on the facts or law of the case. These were used by the party concerned as useful weapons, but were recognized by all as in no way prejudicing future decisions. An example of two methods of obtaining such letters can be taken from the Evesham case. Marleberge, immediately upon arrival in Rome, obtained the pope's verbal engagement to issue important letters (*Chron. Evesh.* 142–3); the pope, however, was Innocent III and on second thoughts refused. Roger Norreys, on the other hand, was successful in obtaining by underhand means letters authorizing the expulsion of Marleberge himself (*ibid.* 145).

6 Gervase, I, 335: "Quasi in poenam suae constantiae." (This was summer, 1186.)

only fitting that an important church should be dedicated to him at Canterbury. But under this innocent exterior more grandiose aims were clearly envisaged. The king and all the bishops were to have prebendal stalls; they were to endow vicars, and funds were also to be raised from the churches of the city and by public subscription; the actual occupants of the foundation were to be clerks of learning. At the very least such an establishment, if it attracted and supported a college of eminent clerks at the gates of Canterbury and under the protection of St Thomas, would have been a permanent menace to the prestige of Christ Church, and such its promoters (if not Baldwin himself) doubtless intended it to be, but the monks saw in it also the thin end of a wedge by which a powerful body would be brought into being which would gradually supplant the chapter of Christ Church as the electors of the primate and as the clergy of his cathedral.[1] This indeed was probably the intention of the bishops who supported Baldwin, for not only does Gervase assert it,[2] but the contemporary northerner, William of Newburgh, gives it as the common opinion of his time ten years later,[3] and Gervase adds that all the bishops with monastic chapters bound themselves by oath to secure the introduction of secular canons in the room of the monks.[4]

How Baldwin was led into this scheme we do not know. Peter of Blois, in the palinode already mentioned, says that it was forced on him by the king,[5] and Gervase, in a long anecdote which seems to contain personal recollections,[6] gives striking corroboration to Peter, and throws all the blame on Henry who, it is suggested, hoped that such foundations would distract Baldwin and the bishops from any concerted action to secure their own liberty against the Crown. It is likely, also, that the archbishop was influenced by the scholars and clerks of his entourage, and by some of his colleagues who had private animosity to satisfy, for there is more than one reference to the influence exercised upon the archbishop by the scholars and clerks of his circle[7] and the subsequent conduct of several of the bishops is a sufficient proof of their feelings, but as both

1 So Gervase, I, 338.   2 Gervase, II, 402.

3 William of Newburgh, II, 392: "Idem [sc. Baldwin]...proprium eligendi pontificem jus et praerogativam transferre ab eis voluit." A little later he expresses his surprise that a man of such character (mirandum est tantum virum, etc.), himself a Cistercian, should prefer secular canons to monks. The passage would seem to have been written before Hubert Walter revived the scheme in 1196.

4 Gervase, II, 402. In his Chronica, I, 540–1, Gervase brings Henry II forward as advocating the introduction of secular canons alongside of monks in all cathedral monasteries.

5 PL, CCVII, ep. 233, col. 534: "Rex, qui semper voluit...archiepiscopum graves... discordias...habere...ut sic semper eum haberet...obnoxium sibi."

6 Gervase, I, 538–42.

7 E.g. Gervase, I, 332: "Subverterant enim quidam clerici seculares ipsius simplicitatem." Also Epp. Cant. no. clxx (letter of the community of St Denis to Clement III, 1188): "quorundam scholarium argutius archiepiscopi simplicitate abutentium." Simplicitas, it will be remembered, was the word used of Baldwin by Gerald of Wales. For a notice of the circle of clerks at Canterbury and elsewhere at this time, v. Stubbs, Learning and Literature at the court of Henry II in Lectures on Medieval and Modern History (1886), esp. 142–51.

Gervase[1] and William of Newburgh[2] state that the project had Henry's support from the start (he was, as has been said, to have a stall in the church) we may take it as certain that the king was favourable, doubtless largely with a view to future primatial elections.

Before the issue was irrevocably joined Baldwin spoke of the matter to Hugh of Lincoln, whom he admired. Hugh begged him to abandon the scheme. It would, he said, cause the primate infinite distress; Rome would not favour it, and it would bring about a fatal relaxation of monastic discipline at Canterbury.[3] His biographer, however, does not record any opinion of the saint on the intrinsic merits of the proposal. Despite this wise advice, Baldwin, who in more than one crisis appears as acting with great obstinacy after initial hesitation, proceeded on his way, and the battle was joined both in England and at Rome.

There is no need to recapitulate all the changes of fortune in the long struggle, of which a great historian has given a minute account.[4] The contest lacks both the unity and the legal and personal interest of a still longer controversy, the "Evesham case". As Bishop Stubbs remarked, the affair never came to actual trial either in England or Rome, partly because of the division of authority in the matter between king and pope, partly because the papal office passed rapidly through the hands of a succession of mediocre pontiffs,[5] most of all because both parties (and the Roman Curia also) found it simpler to rely on a succession of mandates which had little relation to each other. Save for a few whom the monks regarded with justice as interested traitors (the chief among them was Roger Norreys) the large convent presented an unbroken front to the enemy throughout the struggle, and whatever may be thought of Baldwin's scheme in itself, there can be little defence for the violence of method he used. For a year and a half (13 January 1188–12 August 1189) the community was imprisoned within the *enceinte* of the monastic buildings,[6] and for a great part of this time all liturgical service was suspended in the cathedral. A dozen or more of the monks were employed on missions

1 Gervase, II, 402.
2 William of Newburgh, II, 392: "Et archiepiscopus quidem favore regio fortior."
3 *Magna Vita Hugonis Lincoln.* 133–6.
4 Besides his long introduction to the *Epistolae Cantuarienses*, Stubbs prefixed to the letters a minute calendar (cxxi–clxvii). The whole volume, a monument of patient scholarship, is a good example of the solid and exact learning that lay behind all Stubbs' work, and which critics of his theories sometimes fail to appreciate. In this introduction he does indeed tend to note traces of national feeling and English law and custom where neither really existed, but his account of the events and his fairness of judgment on the characters engaged are excellent. The letters themselves and the long account in the *Chronica* of Gervase (I, 332–488) and other references permit a most exact reconstruction of the story. Gervase took a considerable part in the business, and was sacrist *c.* 1193–8.
5 Urban III (Nov. 1185–Oct. 1187); Gregory VIII (Oct.–Dec. 1187); Clement III (Dec. 1187–March 1191).
6 According to Gervase, I, 405, the convent was victualled during the whole of this blockade by the folk of the city, including even Jews. It was at this time that Roger Norreys made his escape to Baldwin *per cloacas*.

at Rome and elsewhere, and some six, including the prior Honorius, died of the plague in Italy. As the struggle wore on, the convent was at logger-heads not only with the archbishop and officials appointed by him, but with the king also, and perhaps the most remarkable feature of the whole episode is the freedom with which the monks opposed Henry's demands or suggestions of compromise, even in his presence. The spirit of Becket, like that of Caesar, lived on in power. All the influential ecclesiastics and monastic houses of Europe took one side or another, and a climax was reached when Baldwin, in October, 1189, by a kind of *coup d'état*, appointed the worthless Roger Norreys prior—a move which it is impossible to justify, and hard even to understand. The monks were reduced to despera-tion, but the death of Henry II had removed one great obstacle to peace, and in November 1189 the convent threw themselves on the mercy of the new king, who arranged a compromise in their favour by which Baldwin abandoned the project of a college at Hackington and dismissed Roger Norreys.[1] Within a few days Richard left England for the crusade and Baldwin, after acquiring land at Lambeth, announced his intention of transferring thither his foundation; in the meantime, he erected there the tents he intended to use in the Holy Land.[2] Early in the following March he, too, left the country, never to return. He died before Acre that same November, and the circumstances of his end probably account for much of the tenderness with which his memory was treated by contemporaries.

III

Meanwhile, several of Baldwin's colleagues had given evidence of the hostile attitude with which Gervase credited them. Of all the primate's associates and contemporaries the most bitter in his animosity towards the monks was Hugh of Nonant, who was consecrated to the see of Lichfield and Coventry in January 1188. Hugh was a nephew of Arnulf of Lisieux, and his contemporaries are agreed as to his astuteness, his gift of per-suasive speech, and his violence of method.[3]

According to Gervase of Canterbury who, however, only records hearsay, Hugh bought the monastery of Coventry off the new king and, after various moves against the monks, worked upon divisions in the community and finally broke into the place with an armed force, drove away the prior, wounded and imprisoned some of the brethren and

1 Gervase, I, 474–81, gives a vivid account of the final scenes at Canterbury. Cf. also Benedict of Peterborough, II, 97.
2 Gervase, I, 483–4.
3 Gervase sketches Hugh's character in his *Chronica*, I, 349. Gerald of Wales in his *Speculum Ecclesiae*, IV, 64–5, says: "erat vir singularis eloquentiae et admirandae facundiae... lingua facundissima." Cf. William of Newburgh, II, 394 and Ben. Pet. II, 215. There is a good article on Hugh by C. L. Kingsford in *DNB*.

exiled others.[1] Reliable details of the affair are irrecoverable, but some kind of fracas clearly took place in which it would seem that the bishop himself received some injuries which he did not fail to exploit, alleging that he had been attacked and wounded before the altar.[2] Shortly after, at the crisis of the Canterbury struggle, he asserted in the king's presence that in two months there would be no monks in any cathedral of the land, and added an imprecation to his words.[3] Having ejected at least a part of the community, whom he repeatedly abused in public, he destroyed the conventual buildings and prepared to establish secular canons; he followed his action up by a formal complaint lodged with the bishops assembled for a consecration at Westminster in October 1189.[4] He reminded his colleagues that in England alone did monastic chapters exist, owing to the partiality of St Augustine in the days of the first conversion, and he suggested that all bishops with monks in their cathedrals should subscribe to a fund for prosecuting his case at Rome. All, we are told, were willing, save Baldwin who hesitated; Hugh therefore abandoned the idea of joint action, but procured letters from all supporting his line of conduct at Coventry. He did not, as it would seem, go to Rome himself, but sent agents, who made his proposal more acceptable by announcing that prebends would be attached to certain cardinalitial churches. Clement III waited for six months for someone to come out to present the case of the monks, but they lacked the necessary funds, and could send no one; the pope therefore issued a mandate in the sense desired by the bishop. This was promulgated by William Longchamp, bishop of Ely and papal legate, at a council at Westminster on 16 October 1190, and the final clearance took place at Christmastide, the monks being dispersed.[5] The prior, Moses by name, was at last able to proceed to Rome, but his efforts were for the time unavailing, and secular canons were duly instituted. Gerald of Wales, who visited Coventry under the new *régime*, states that he found the change very much for the better;[6] William of Newburgh, who wrote before the monks had been restored, held a different opinion.[7]

The movement against the monks now became more general. In addition to the affair of Glastonbury, to be noticed later, we learn from

---

1 William of Newburgh, II, 394: "Denique inter priorem et monachos discordias serens vel nutriens...occasione captata, manu armata expulit universos."

2 Gervase gives the date as 9 October 1189. This is presumably the occasion to which Richard of Devizes, 387, alludes: "Hugo...querelam deposuit super monachis suis de Covintre, quod manus in eum violentas injecerant, et sanguinem suum fuderant coram altari. Maximam etiam partem congregationis ante querelam expulerat de ecclesia, etc."

3 Gervase, I, 470; *Epp. Cant.* cccxxix: "'Domine rex, si vultis mihi credere, infra duos menses in nulla sede episcopali in regno vestro erit aliquis monachus, quia justum non est,' et adjecit, 'monachi ad diabolos.'"

4 Richard of Devizes, 387. He is quite precise as to the date, *xi kal. Nov.*, i.e. 22 October.

5 Richard of Devizes, 392; Giraldus, *Speculum Ecclesiae*, IV, 64–8; Gervase, I, 489: "Monachos omnes et ordinem monasticum...ejecit...clericos instituens seculares... [monachi] per diversa vagantes dispersi sunt."

6 *Speculum Ecclesiae*, IV, 64–8.   7 William of Newburgh, II, 393 *seqq.*

a passage in the *Chronicle* of Jocelin that in the council held at Westminster in 1190 Longchamp proceeded to make a series of decrees affecting the black monks, directed especially against their going on pilgrimage and the lavish equipages of certain abbots; to this Samson of Bury replied that he would allow no one to interfere with his right to dispose of his monks as he wished, and that he needed all the horses he had for the king's business.[1] The moment, indeed, seemed so favourable for any action against the monastic body that Hubert Walter, lately appointed to the see of Salisbury, thought fit to bring up the old claims of the bishopric to the abbey of Malmesbury, and obtained letters from the king to the chancellor authorizing him to compel the abbot to answer in court to the bishop's demands. Abbot Robert, however, formerly a monk of St Swithun's, was not to be caught so easily and, fortifying himself with a contradictory letter from Richard, obtained a stay of proceedings till the king's return.[2] In the meanwhile, he revived the claim of Malmesbury to complete exemption, and secured a bull from Celestine III which confirmed this and gave a clear decision against the bishop's claims.[3]

As for Coventry, the secular chapter of Hugh of Nonant had no long life. The case had not yet been tried at Rome, and the monks were at length able to secure a mandate contrary to that previously issued. In 1197 Hubert Walter, Hugh of Lincoln and Samson of Bury were charged with the task of restoring the priory without any powers of reconsidering the merits of the case.[4] The king endeavoured to postpone their action, but Samson, at least, would have no delay, and on 14 January 1198 Hubert Walter and he formally reintroduced the exiles to Coventry.[5] Hugh of Nonant was at the time in France, stricken with the illness that was to carry him off; he died, we are told, repentant of his violence, and clothed with the monastic habit by the monks of Bec.[6]

1 *Jocelini Cronica*, in *Mem. S. Edm.* I, 259: "Cum cancellarius...quaedam decreta proposuisset contra nigros monachos, etc."   2 Richard of Devizes, 392.

3 JL, 16748 (30 August 1191); *Registrum Malmesburiense*, I, 359.

4 *Jocelini Cronica*, 295.

5 *Jocelini Cronica*, 296; Gervase, I, 550. Both give the date: "instante festo sancti Hilarii" (Jocelin); "iii id. Jan. [11 January]" (Gervase). Thus the restoration was made by authority of Celestine III, though in fact he had just died (8 January). The lively anecdote given by Roger of Wendover, I, 274, cannot be wholly authentic. According to this, there was at the time a monk of Coventry, Thomas, in Rome, who, approaching the newly elected pope boldly in consistory, presented once more his petition for redress. On Innocent's objecting that it had been rejected by his predecessors, Thomas replied: "Pater sancte, petitio mea justa est et omnino honesta, et ideo inaniter non exspecto. Exspecto enim mortem vestram sicut feci mortem antecessorum vestrorum." Innocent, turning in astonishment to the cardinals, exclaimed: "Nonne audistis quid diabolus iste dixit? Exspecto, inquit, mortem vestram...." Then, turning to Thomas: "Frater, per sanctum Petrum, mortem meam non hic exspectabis, exaudita est enim petitio tua." And he wrote immediately to Hubert Walter, who restored the monks *v kal. Feb.* The basis of fact behind this story is perhaps found in a short note of the Tewkesbury annalist *s.a.* 1191: "sed postea redierunt monachi, nolentibus adversariis, per monachum Romae degentem per septennium et semis nomine Thomam." Alan, abbot of Tewkesbury, was one of the commissioners appointed by Innocent in 1198, and would therefore know the facts.

6 Roger of Wendover, I, 274; Gervase, I, 552; Giraldus, IV, 70–1.

IV

Between the ejection of the monks of Coventry and their return the great Canterbury struggle, which might have seemed to be settled for good and all by the compromise of 1189 and to have been buried in the grave with Baldwin, broke out again in all its old force in 1196. The late archbishop's buildings at Hackington had been demolished soon after his death by papal mandate;[1] those at Lambeth had continued to rise slowly until the monks obtained injunctions against these too,[2] but in 1196, urged once more by the clerks of his household, Hubert Walter began to consider reviving the scheme.[3] In 1197, his offer of transferring the proposed college to Maidstone having been refused by the convent, he obtained all the necessary papal and royal permissions and opened negotiations with the monks, promising to make it a condition of the foundation that no canon should have a voice in the election of an archbishop or assent to any proposal for a translation of the body of St Thomas.[4] The monks, however, suspicious of all such schemes and reassured by their previous victory, refused, and both parties agreed to appeal to Rome. In the negotiations which ensued the archbishop would appear to have acted with more honesty than the monks, and the first mandate that was received, ordering the destruction of the church at Lambeth, was obtained by dubious means. Hubert Walter refused to act; the king entered in warmly on the side of the archbishop and the monks were once again deprived of the control of their property, which was seized by the royal agents; finally, to add to their bitterness, the Cistercian abbots and even some of the black monks wrote to Rome in opposition to their case.[5]

But the parties now had to deal with a pope capable of making a clear decision and of abiding by it,[6] and the monks had the advantage of the advocacy of Cardinal Ugolino, the future Gregory IX and friend of St Francis, who was to prove himself the friend, also, of Thomas Marleberge of Evesham.[7] Innocent III heard both sides and decided wholly in favour of the monks, ordering Hubert Walter to destroy his church and annul the

---

1 *Epp. Cant.* ccclvi–ccclviii.
2 *Epp. Cant.* cccxcvii (May 1192); Gervase, I, 534.
3 Gervase, II, 408.
4 Gervase, I, 545.
5 Gervase, I, 569; II, 408: "Scripserunt...nequius ceteris, abbates ordinis Cisterciensis, et abbates alii non tacuerunt." In the last words there is probably an allusion to the abbots of Chertsey and Waltham (*Epp. Cant.* ccccl). For the Cistercian letters, *v. Epp. Cant.* cccc|xii.
6 We need not attribute wholly to Innocent's previous or present favour the note of sincere admiration in the letter written home by Prior Geoffrey in December 1198 (*Epp. Cant.* dxi): "Revirescit enim in ecclesia Romana virga correctionis, jubar videlicet universalis ecclesiae, Innocentius, quem nec inclinat avaritia ad cujusquam injuriam, nec impedit segnities a correctione, quem virtutis amor in tantum possèdit, ut nihil quod bonum deceat pastorem praetermittat." Cf. Gervase, I, 550: "Consecratus [Innocentius] statim a curia omnes cupiditatis et avaritiae sordes exstrusit."
7 *Epp. Cant.* div, dix.

foundation.[1] On the first point the archbishop obeyed at once; as regards the second, he begged the pope's permission for a foundation at Lambeth on a new site. This was referred back to a commission in England and ultimately, on 6 November 1200, the judges delegate, transformed by consent of the parties into arbitrators of a compromise, decided that the archbishop might found a college, but it must be of Premonstratensian canons, and every guarantee must be given to the monks.[2] This was, in effect, to alter the whole scheme from the public establishment of a college of prebendaries, depending upon the archbishop and in direct opposition to the monks, to the private foundation of a quasi-contemplative religious house, and the permission thus granted was never acted upon.

We are not here concerned with the legal aspect of this long controversy, nor directly with the apportionment of responsibility or blame. It is not easy to excuse Baldwin's conduct, even if we suppose that in their different ways Henry II and Hugh of Nunant were the real instigators of the scheme; the archbishop's behaviour at the climax, and above all his support and installation of Roger Norreys, seem contrary to the dictates alike of prudence and the moral law, and on other occasions he would seem to have passed the bounds, or permitted others to pass them, where justice ceases and force or fraud begins. Hubert Walter, on the other hand, seems from first to last to have acted with honesty and considerable moderation, while the monks permitted themselves some very questionable actions; it is difficult, nevertheless, to comprehend why a man of such great practical wisdom should have so deliberately revived a proposal which had already caused such bitter and unprofitable strife.

On a larger view the harm that these struggles, and other lesser ones, did in overthrowing the discipline of regular life, in embittering the relations of subjects and superiors, and in sowing scandal far and wide, can scarcely be exaggerated and fully justified the warnings of Hugh of Lincoln. Only those who have perused with care the great *corpus* of *Epistolae Cantuarienses*, together with the polemics of Gervase of Canterbury and others, can form a just conception of the passions that were roused and of the mental and physical energy that was expended by the members of a religious family upon a matter which had nothing to do with the monastic life as such and which at best inspired a devotion that was private and partisan. Indeed, the marvel is that any real religious life survived at Canterbury, Coventry and the other houses that were the theatres of strife. Yet to regard these and similar controversies merely from their personal and moral aspects would, as has been suggested, be to see only a part of the whole. Both parties were in a sense the victims of circumstance, for the struggles could only have arisen, and endured so

1 Innocent's strong and clear letter is in *Epp. Cant.* ccccxcviii; Gervase, I, 576–84. *V.* also *Epp. Cant.* cccclix–cccclxx.
2 *Epp. Cant.* dxlvii–dxlviii.

long, at a period when rival jurisdictions clashed, and when judicial decisions and executive actions proceeded from no fixed principles and received no support from each other. It was indeed a time of crisis for the fabric of the Church's administration, and the parties to these suits, and above all the monks, suffered under a state of things which they could not directly control.

V

In the interval between the death of Baldwin and the revival of his designs by Hubert Walter, and while Coventry was still occupied by secular canons, yet another great monastery was caught in the toils of a struggle with its bishop. The wealthy abbey of Glastonbury, after fifty years of misfortune, had enjoyed nearly fifty years (1126–71) of peace and material prosperity under the protection of Henry of Blois, and at his death had received a regular and excellent abbot in the person of Robert, prior of the cathedral monastery of St Swithun's, Winchester.[1] Abbot Robert, however, died within nine years, and once more a series of misfortunes overtook the house. The precedent set by Henry of Winchester was an evil one; Henry II followed it by allowing no abbatial election and by "committing" the abbey to the charge of Peter de Marcy, a monk of Cluny who had influential connections in the Curia and was at the time the king's agent in Rome. Before he had been long in the west, there occurred a calamity of another kind. On 25 May 1184 the whole of the monastic buildings, including the church, were, with a few unimportant exceptions, consumed by fire, and along with them disappeared a large number of the precious objects amassed by Henry of Blois. Shortly after, Peter de Marcy died. He was succeeded in his charge by one of the king's household, Ralph fitz Stephen, and Henry, possibly feeling some responsibility for the community in its distress, treated the monks generously and allowed them the full use of their revenues for rebuilding; it is to the years 1185–6 that may be attributed the exquisite western Lady chapel that survives. Ralph fitz Stephen died at about the same time as his master; the new king appointed as abbot Henry de Sully, the Cluniac prior of Bermondsey, himself a relation of Richard and more interested in furthering his own career than in benefiting his abbey.

It was at this moment that an attack came from a new angle. Glastonbury, though not an exempt house, stood to the bishop of Bath in something of an exempt position, for it had inherited from the Saxon past a number of ecclesiastical immunities, including archidiaconal rights over

1 The chief authority for the narrative which follows is Adam of Domerham, *De rebus gestis Glastoniensibus* (ed. T. Hearne, II, 331–474). The story is told there fully and consecutively, so that detailed references are not necessary. Adam wrote at the end of the thirteenth century, but he embodies the original documents in his narrative, and may be taken as trustworthy.

a *bloc* of private churches situated in or near the Isle;[1] the house also exercised control over the two small monasteries of Athelney and Muchelney, and disposed of more property than the bishop. The latter, on his side, already held the monastery of Bath, but after Thurstan had vindicated his rights in the presence of Lanfranc at the council of the Parret there is no evidence that collisions between Glastonbury and the Ordinary had been at all frequent or violent. Among the entourage of Richard at the beginning of his reign was a certain highly connected ecclesiastic, restless and ambitious throughout his life, Savary de Bohun, a cousin of Jocelin of Salisbury, of Reginald fitz Jocelin of Bath, and of the Emperor Henry VI.[2] He had taken the Cross and accompanied Richard I on his journey towards the East; while in Sicily he obtained the promise of a bishopric. His design was that his cousin Reginald should be translated to Canterbury, still vacant after the death of Baldwin, and that he himself should have the succession of Bath; he secured his end—though Reginald died soon after his election as primate—and was himself elected and consecrated to Bath in 1192. Savary, who was familiar with the ecclesiastical situation in England and had considerable influence in the Curia, was aware that Richard had no rigid principles or policy in church government, and that Rome might grant a *transeat* to any change of organization that had influential support. He therefore took advantage of Richard's captivity, which gave him, as cousin of the Emperor, the rôle of negotiator, to extract from the king an arrangement by which Glastonbury should become a bishop's monastery, while Richard received in exchange the city of Bath. Henry de Sully complaisantly allowed himself to be appointed to the see of Worcester, and Savary secured testimonials from Hubert Walter and others, informing the pope that only by such means could the old feuds between the churches of Bath and Glastonbury be ended.

The details of the struggle that followed belong to local rather than to general history, and as such have been related more than once.[3] The majority of the monks resisted the change and appealed to Rome, and the customary series of delays and contradictory mandates ensued; the king, restored to liberty, declared that the arrangement had been extorted from him, though he refused to take immediate steps to revoke it. Savary, for his part, was indefatigable in Rome, and in the winter of 1196–7 obtained possession of Glastonbury. Nevertheless, a few months later (29 August 1197) Richard announced that he would take the abbey back into his own control, and allowed the election of an abbot, William Pica (25 November

---

1 For a fuller description of these, *v. infra*, p. 604.

2 There is a good article on Savary by the Rev. W. Hunt in *DNB*.

3 In particular by Dr J. Armitage Robinson, then Dean of Wells, in his papers on *The first Deans of Wells* and *Bishop Jocelin and the Interdict*, in *Somerset Historical Essays*, 68–70, 145–6. There is also an account by Chancellor Scott Holmes in his contributions to vol. II of the *Victoria County History of Somerset*.

1198). For this Savary excommunicated the elect and his supporters and laid an interdict on the house.

When Richard was succeeded by John and Celestine by Innocent the struggle continued. At first the new king supported the bishop, who entered into possession once more and ejected and maltreated his chief opponents among the monks; the new pope, on the other hand, took the side of the monks and revoked Savary's excommunications. Later, however, yielding to the representations of the bishop and apparently convinced that serious trouble had long existed between monks and diocesan, and that the monastery itself needed reforms, Innocent declared his intention of giving Glastonbury to the bishopric and entrusted to judges delegate in England the task of arranging the details along the lines of the existing cathedral monasteries. Meanwhile William Pica and some companions were carried off in Rome by an illness which their friends attributed to poison administered on behalf of Savary.

The commissioners, Eustace, bishop of Ely, Samson, abbot of Bury, and Geoffrey, prior of Christ Church, ultimately produced a schedule of arrangements by which the bishop was to have a quarter of the revenues and a proportionate share of other rights and patronage;[1] in the meantime Savary had embarked on another scheme, resembling that of Hackington and Lambeth, by which the collegiate chapter of Wells was to be used as a means of controlling other monastic bodies of the diocese, prebends being assigned to the bishop as abbot of Glastonbury, to the abbots of Athelney and Muchelney, and to the abbot of Bec as substitute for the newly arrived Cistercian abbot of Cleeve.[2] The restless bishop died, however, in 1205,[3] and the monks immediately appealed to John, who wrote to Innocent demanding a restitution of the *status quo* at Glastonbury, no doubt largely influenced by considerations of private interest. The king's letter was accompanied by numerous others from bishops, religious houses and magnates, and even from the chapters of Bath and Wells, begging for a restitution to the abbey of its old rights,[4] and it does not seem that the new bishop Jocelin ever made Savary's design wholly his own.

Innocent III, while allowing the monks complete freedom to reopen

1 Some points of interest in this arrangement will be discussed later, pp. 435, 627.
2 Cf. charter giving details of this arrangement from Bec in *Calendar of documents preserved in France* (ed. J. H. Round), vol. 1, no. 389.
3 Savary died in Rome. His epitaph records the impression made on his contemporaries:
    "Notus eras mundo per mundum semper eundo,
        Et necis ista dies est tibi prima quies."
4 The monks of Bath and chapter of Wells no doubt felt that a monastic cathedral chapter at Glastonbury would prove a serious rival. The reasons given for a return to the old state of things, including the *maxima pauperum et peregrinorum desolacio et detrimentum* (Adam of Domerham, II, 430) which several allege, may, however, be accepted as true. The letter from the monks of Worcester is of peculiar interest (*ibid.* 432–3), both because a cathedral monastery might have been expected to show less sympathy, and because it calls upon Innocent, who has saved the monks of Canterbury and Coventry, to do the same by Glastonbury.

their case, refused to pronounce before the see of Bath had an occupant, and any immediate progress in the suit was prevented by the troubles in England which culminated in the Interdict. Ultimately, in the winter of 1218–19, at a meeting between the parties held at Shaftesbury in the presence of arbitrators acting under mandate of Honorius III, a composition was effected by which Glastonbury regained its liberty, though it resigned to the bishop certain properties and patronage, including that of the abbey itself, which fell in consequence for a time into the same relations with the diocesan as obtained between Eynsham and the see of Lincoln and Selby and the archbishop of York. Thus here, as at Canterbury and Coventry, the bishop, after a long and weary struggle, failed to achieve his end. Whatever may be thought of the radical desirability of the immunities possessed by Glastonbury, the attack of Savary must be pronounced to have been interested and unprovoked; it was, in short, unjust, and there is no reason to suppose that its success would have been of any advantage to the cause of religion in the diocese. The evidence of the letters written by neighbours in support of the abbey, though they may not be wholly free themselves from motives of self-interest, shows clearly that there had been no unusual aggression on the part of the abbey in the past, and that the diversion of revenues to the bishop had deprived Glastonbury of the means of practising charity and hospitality.[1] The reversion to the original state of things was therefore regretted by none.

1 The letter of the *comites et barones Angliae* to the pope is peremptory on this point (Domerham, II, 428): "Quantum enim scandalum, propter status ejusdem ecclesiae permutacionem, in Anglicana ecclesia fuerit exortum; quam gravis discordia et dissensio inter ecclesias Bathoniensem et Wellensem et ipsam ob eamdem causam certissime videatur generari, quae semper ante tempora hujus mutacionis mutua pace gaudebant; quantum eciam pauperes et peregrini...sustineant dispendium, vobis ad plenam significare non sufficimus."

CHAPTER XIX

THE CASE OF EVESHAM

In the foregoing chapter an outline has been given of a number of controversies affecting monasteries and giving rise to litigation both in England and at Rome. All these quarrels had their origin in claims of one kind or another put forward by the bishop against monks within his diocese. During the same period yet another *cause célèbre* of a different kind was before the Curia from England, and its story has come down to us narrated in such detail and throwing such a vivid light on the life of the times that an account of it cannot be omitted from these pages, even though the story has been recently told elsewhere in considerable detail.[1]

The ancient abbey of Evesham, situated on falling ground at the foot of the main street of the town in a bend of the river Avon,[2] was in normal times a house of medium size with a competent, though not unusually large, income.[3] It had on the whole enjoyed good fortune, both temporal and spiritual, since the Conquest. Among its abbots since the days of eminence under Aethelwig had been Reginald Foliot, brother of the distinguished bishop, and William of Andeville, a notable member of the *familia* of Christ Church, Canterbury. For some thirty years (1161–89) it had been ruled by the Cluniac Adam, originally a monk of La Charité and subsequently (1157–61) prior of Bermondsey, and had prospered under him in every way.[4] He died at the end of 1189; within a few days of his death Archbishop Baldwin came to an agreement, in the presence of the new king, which brought to an end, as all thought, his great struggle with Christ Church, and as a part of the composition his creature and agent, Roger Norreys, was deposed from the priorship at Canterbury to

1 In particular, by Dr G. G. Coulton in his *Five Centuries of Religion*, II, 347–78. For many of the events in the narrative which follows the only authority is Thomas de Marleberge; where he can be checked, he will be found trustworthy, and his pages give an impression of honesty and precise statement, but it must constantly be borne in mind that his record is both highly personal and *ex parte*.

2 Of the monastic buildings nothing has remained above ground save the graceful detached bell-tower erected shortly before the Dissolution.

3 There were thirty-six monks in 1077 (*Chron. Evesh.* 96) and *c.* 67 in *c.* 1090 when twelve were sent to Denmark (MS. quoted in *Monasticon*, II, 37). In 1206 there were some forty (*Chron. Evesh.* 203; but cf. *ibid.* 136), and it is reasonable to suppose that the supply of recruits had dwindled during the troubles. In *Domesday* the income was £129, which set Evesham comparatively low in the scale of wealth.

4 *Chron. Evesh.* 100–2. Adam was a friend of Peter of Blois (*ep.* 97, *PL*, CCVII, 304–6). The editor (W. D. Macray) of the *Evesham Chronicle* gives the date of his death as 12 November 1191, quoting three MSS. The year must, however, be 1189. Roger Norreys was appointed by Baldwin (*Chron. Evesh.* 103), who left England for the Crusade on 6 March 1190; Gervase of Canterbury, I, 481, tells us that Roger was deposed from the office of prior at Christ Church on 30 November 1189, and blessed soon after 13 January 1190 (I, 484). *V.* also *infra*, p. 386, n. 1.

which he had been appointed a month previously.[1] No doubt the arch-bishop wished to lessen the appearance of a repulse and protect his instrument by finding office for him elsewhere,[2] and the vacancy at Evesham, a house which Baldwin would have known well when bishop of Worcester, seemed opportune. Speed was imperative, as both king and archbishop were shortly to leave the country, and within a fortnight of the Canterbury composition Richard had sanctioned Roger's appointment to Evesham without any form of canonical election, and before Baldwin departed in March the elect had been blessed and inducted.[3]

His appointment must always remain a dark stain on the archbishop's reputation. Roger was not only unfitted for this position in particular, but utterly unworthy to hold spiritual office of any kind. A man of great natural ability and ingenuity, he had become treasurer of Christ Church in 1187.[4] At about the same time he became Baldwin's agent and in consequence was appointed cellarer by him,[5] though the community refused to recognize the appointment and, treating him as a traitor for revealing to the enemies of the convent what had been said in chapter, put him in confinement, apparently in the infirmary building,[6] in September of the same year. From this durance he escaped, with more dexterity than dignity, at some time before March 1188,[7] and became the bitter enemy of his former brethren. Throughout his career he displayed a remarkable talent for ingratiating himself with those in power, and within a month or two of his escape he was in the royal favour[8] and it was soon rumoured that Baldwin intended to make him prior,[9] though there is no doubt that even at this period of his career his moral reputation was evil.[10] More than

1 Gervase, i, 481.

2 That this was the case is stated by Alan of Tewkesbury, sometime prior of Canterbury, in a fragment preserved by Marleberge in *Chron. Evesh.* 103: "Ob reverentiam archiepiscopi ne videretur et ipse in hac parte succubuisse, etc."

3 The king left England on 14 December, and all authorities agree that Roger was approved by him. Thus Alan of Tewkesbury (*ut supra*): "ipso rege id procurante"; and Marleberge records that Roger always maintained (*saepe dicere consueverat*) that the king had given him the post in return for services rendered: "quod dominus rex pro servitio suo dedit ei hanc abbatiam" (*Chron. Evesh.* 104).

4 *Epp. Cant.* xcvi, cxxi, 81, 94.

5 *Epp. Cant.* cxii, 89.

6 *Epp. Cant.* cxxi, 95: "Rogerum...ab officio suo depositum custodiae deputavimus arctiori, claustrali tamen." Cf. *Chron. Evesh.* 102–3 and *Epp. Cant.* cxxiii, 98, where, writing to their emissaries at court the monks say (September–October 1187) that if any questions are asked: "si verbum audieritis super Rogerum Noreis; quod vidistis, hoc testamini; videlicet vos ipsum in domo infirmorum, ut infirmum, reliquisse: quid postea acciderit ignorare."

7 *Epp. Cant.* ccviii, 193: "Rogerus Nories, qui quoniam nobis non erat necessarius per necessaria exivit immundus." *Chron. Evesh.* 103: "Egressus nescio per quae loca nudus." *Ibid.* 241: "Per cloacas." Gervase, i, 404: "Per cloacam." The episode was too piquant to be allowed to fade from memory, and Roger acquired the nickname *cloacarius*—"of the jakes", as Dr Coulton aptly translates it.

8 *Epp. Cant.* ccxl, 221.   9 *Epp. Cant.* cclxx, 252.

10 *Epp. Cant.* cclxxi, 253: "De cujus vita et moribus ad praesens melius est tacere quam loqui." Gervase, i, 382: "Erat enim ab adolescentia monachatus sui superbus, elatus, pomposus in verbis, dolosus in factis, cupidus praelationis, aspernator religionis, ad superiores

a year later the community of Christ Church were still living in fear of his appointment,[1] which in the event took place on 9 October 1189, the whole convent protesting by their absence;[2] he immediately came into residence with his friends on the monastery's manors.[3] Probably, as has been suggested on a previous page, the appointment was made to drive the monks to despair; if so, it was successful in achieving its end, and the unscrupulous action of the archbishop makes the subsequent transference to Evesham more comprehensible, though not more pardonable.

For some few years his behaviour in his new dignity in the midlands was not intolerable, at least so far as public appearances went,[4] but after a time he threw all restraints of religion and decency to the winds. The pages of Thomas de Marleberge, to whom we owe all our detailed knowledge, are the pages of a severe critic, but they are entirely without rhetoric and vague denunciation, and are in the main substantiated alike by the testimony of Gervase of Canterbury and Gerald of Wales,[5] and by the judicial issue of a legatine examination. From them we can form something of a living picture of this extraordinary man. Although wholly ignorant of the technicalities of the law,[6] he must clearly have been a man of great practical ability, and of still greater dexterity in seizing upon the weaknesses of those whom he wished to deceive or to placate; it was this latter talent, no doubt, that stood him in good stead with the credulous and lethargic Baldwin. Marleberge himself bears witness to his qualities as a lavish host and entertaining companion,[7] and to the energy with which he could throw himself into a course of action;[8] his appearance in Rome gave proof of a spirit as well as of an effrontery of no common order, and in the fluctuations of the long struggle it is more than once hard to resist feeling in his regard something akin to admiration. Morally, however, he must have been one of the worst men in the country. Openly and cynically impure of life, hesitating not at all in the face of adultery or sacrilege,[9] gluttonous besides and a drunkard,[10] he disregarded, even when within the monastery, every rule and custom of dress, food and decorum.

adulator, ad inferiores contemptor, gloriosus in veste, negligens in ordinis observatione, amicus foeminarum, amator equorum, iracundus ad correptiones, paratus ad detractiones, in omnibus etiam incorrigibilis." This was written probably *c.* 1199, when Roger was abbot and before the great storm had broken. I have quoted at length because Stubbs (*Epp. Cant.* introd. lxxv, note 2) suggests that Roger's evil qualities had not become manifest before he left Canterbury.

1 *Epp. Cant.* cccxxiv, 309.   2 *Epp. Cant.* cccxxvi, 311.

3 *Epp. Cant.* cccxxvii, 313: "R. Norreis per maneria nostra...et dona accipit et epulatur quotidie splendide." This is corroborated by *Chron. Evesh.* 103.

4 *Chron. Evesh.* 104: "Post paucos annos...quibus satis modeste erga conventum se habebat."   5 Giraldus, *Speculum Ecclesiae*, IV, 91.

6 *Chron. Evesh.* 109: "Juris civilis quam canonici ignarus." (The words are those of the expert Marleberge.)

7 *Chron. Evesh.* 109: "Ut erat dapsilis."

8 *Chron. Evesh.* 122: "Quasi tyro ut erat magnanimus viriliter praeparavit se."

9 Of sin, that is, with one under a vow of chastity.

10 *Chron. Evesh.* 119; cf. note 3 *supra*.

Surrounding himself with a few favourites, he abused and at times starved his monks, misappropriated the convent's property, and practised the most oppressive tyranny on his subjects. Under such a *régime* it was inevitable that regular life should collapse. The monks, not infrequently lacking food and its preservatives as well as fuel in sufficient quantity, accepted the hospitality of the townsfolk or wandered begging in the neighbouring villages, and at times even found themselves without the regular clothing necessary if they were to appear in choir or at the altar. The fabric of the monastery was neglected, and as a result only those portions of the church were weatherproof which had stone vaulting; hospitality and the relief of the poor were out of the question.[1] Doubtless all these misfortunes were not simultaneously and continuously acute, for Evesham, even during the misrule, could attract a recruit of distinction such as Marleberge, and he himself tells us that the tower of the church was built at this time largely out of money saved by the convent out of their income,[2] but the witness on oath before the legate in 1213 and the subsequent judgment must be held to substantiate all the charges brought by Marleberge against his abbot.

Matters may be supposed to have become serious *c.* 1195. Under normal circumstances the first person to have taken cognizance of the matter would have been the king, but Richard spent only a few months of his reign in England, and Roger Norreys had made friends among the great, including Geoffrey fitz Peter the justiciar.[3] Failing royal interference there was the Ordinary, but here two circumstances modified the course of events. First, the see of Worcester, after changing hands three times between 1190 and 1196, remained vacant from 1198 till 1200; secondly, Evesham had always had pretensions to exemption, and this would make a bishop chary of burning his fingers, while it also deprived the monks of their natural court of appeal, for claiming exemption they could recognize no authority short of a legate. To Hubert Walter, therefore, as such, they appealed in 1195, and the abbot was forced to make certain concessions; but the archbishop was a politician, not a spiritual man, and in any case his legateship ceased in July of that year, and things returned to their old state.[4] At some time during his short reign John of Coutances, bishop of Worcester (1196–8), succeeded in visiting the abbey, but according to Marleberge the abbot, by means of presents and renouncing his use of the *pontificalia*, was able to escape punitive measures.[5] Complaints were again made to Hubert Walter *c.* 1200, but he had on his hands the Lambeth quarrel, in addition to the care of the realm, and again the abbot, by timely concessions, warded off the evil day.

1 *Chron. Evesh.* 236–48.
2 *Chron. Evesh.* 108. The monks also renounced food, etc. to defray the expenses in Rome, and the "customs" which the abbot ultimately accepted have no trace of parsimony in them.
3 *Chron. Evesh.* 106.   4 *Chron. Evesh.* 106.   5 *Chron. Evesh.* 115–16.

At last, in 1202, matters came to a head. The church of Worcester had received as bishop Mauger, a learned and zealous prelate, well known in the Curia and a personal friend of Innocent III.[1] Learning of the plight of Evesham, he moved cautiously, and having equipped himself with a document from Rome authorizing him to visit the monasteries of his diocese, sent word to Evesham of his intention to come thither on 15 August. At this crisis it is questionable whether the abbey was fortunate in having in its midst a man with the intellectual antecedents, clarity of vision and tenacity of purpose possessed by Thomas of Marlborough. Had he not been there the bishop might well have succeeded in removing Roger Norreys, and Evesham, leaving to a future occasion its claim to the doubtful advantages of exemption, would have been spared ten years of trial and expense, and far greater losses in the things of the spirit. The abbot, indeed, if we may believe the chronicler, mistaking the purport of Mauger's letter, was for offering him ready hospitality, and it was only through Marleberge that the true issue was exposed.

Thomas of Marlborough had in 1202 been for less than three years a professed monk;[2] he had previously studied civil and canon law at Paris, where he had been a pupil of Langton and made the friendship of Richard Poore,[3] afterwards himself lecturing at Oxford.[4] If we assume him to have been near seventy at his death in 1236, he would have entered Evesham in the early thirties.[5] Outstanding alike in legal knowledge and vigour, he immediately took the lead among his brethren in the assertion of their claims. Many of the community, together with the abbot and his friends, fearing the difficulties and uncertainties of a struggle, or wishing for a quiet life, were for admitting the bishop. Marleberge and others were resolute in their opposition. They pointed out that Evesham had a strong case for exemption, that if it came to a test of financial resources a community, which was deathless, could raise more funds than a bishop, and that the favour which Mauger enjoyed at Rome would be offset by

1 Mauger, the physician of Richard I, had been elected bishop in accordance with the king's wishes (Roger Hov. IV, 78) though of illegitimate birth. Hubert Walter had scruples about consecrating him (*Ann. Wig.*, s.a. 1199) so the elect proceeded to Rome, where Innocent confirmed the choice and consecrated him (*Prima Collectio Decret. Innoc. III*, *PL*, CCXVI, 1193, 1195, 1196). Marleberge is candid in his praise of the bishop's integrity: "vir justus et timens Dominum...zelo bono ductus" (*Chron. Evesh.* 109). On p. 110 of the *Chronicle* the editor, in the account of the bishop's qualifications, reads and punctuates as follows: "valde favorabilis erat, utpote vir sanctus et in scientiis profundi pectoris, ecclesiae Romanae cardinalis, et a domino papa...dilectus, etc." He confesses (introd. xxiii, note 1) that he is troubled by this allusion to Mauger's cardinalate, as to which all other sources are silent. Marleberge, no doubt, wrote: "favorabilis erat....e. R. cardinalibus." The passive sense of *favorabilis* is not uncommon; indeed, an instance occurs a few lines below, p. 111.

2 So the continuator of the *Chronicle*, p. 264: "Anno tertio monachatus istius Thomae."

3 *Chron. Evesh.* 252.

4 *Chron. Evesh.* 267: "Rexit scholas...apud Oxoniam et Exoniam." There is possibly some corruption of the text here; cf. Rashdall's *Medieval Universities* (ed. Powicke and Emden, III, 18, note 1; 32, note 3).

5 In *Chron. Evesh.* 111 Marleberge is among those addressed as *vos juvenes*.

the unwillingness of the Curia to repulse an abbey which claimed the special protection of the pope. These arguments had weight, and the bishop was warned not to approach; when he nevertheless signified his intention of coming the abbot, after endeavouring to make terms apart from the community, retired to one of his manors, leaving the convent to face the storm.[1] Mauger duly arrived and was shut out by the monks, whom he suspended and excommunicated, despite their appeal to the legate. Marleberge, with whom the abbot refused to treat, sought Hubert Walter, whose interests were now at stake.

The case of the appeal was heard at Worcester (3 September), and again at Lincoln, and a third time at London (19 October), where the bishops of Ely and Hereford supported Mauger.[2] Meanwhile Marleberge and his friends had effected a *rapprochement* with the abbot, on the understanding that if he would take the lead in the suit for exemption they would under no circumstances make any accusations against him to the bishop; they then obtained from Rome the appointment of judges delegate —the abbots of Malmesbury, Abingdon and Eynsham—to decide the issue of the bishop's right to visit Evesham. Hubert Walter, relieved by this from the necessity of pronouncing a decision on the appeal to himself, allowed the papal delegates to act, but proceedings were stayed by Mauger's taking exception to the court as partial, being composed wholly of black monks. He straightway proceeded to Rome to press his appeal (winter, 1202), followed by two proctors on behalf of Evesham. Roger Norreys, thus freed from any immediate apprehensions, resumed his dilapidations and overbearing conduct, and Marleberge in desperation once more appealed to Hubert Walter, who eventually came to Evesham to make a settlement. Fearing, however, that by acting energetically he would provoke another appeal to Rome, he invited the abbot and community to choose arbitrators by whose decisions they would be ready to abide without appeal.[3] They agreed, the abbot selecting the abbot of Chertsey and the monks the bishop of Ely, but before the arbitrators met events had taken a fresh turn.

In the spring of 1203 (23 May) Mauger returned from Rome with letters establishing a second papal commission, composed of Geoffrey Muschamp, bishop of Ely, Jorbert, prior of Coventry, and the archdeacon of Northampton. The terms of reference were that they should hear the evidence on the question of exemption both for Evesham and its churches, decide on the present facts (*de judicio possessorio*) and report to Rome on the question of right and law (*de judicio petitorio*). The commissioners duly met and, as was usual, worked to a compromise by judging the bishop to have proved his actual jurisdiction over the abbey, and the abbey to have proved its actual jurisdiction over the exempt churches of

1 *Chron. Evesh.* 116.   2 *Chron. Evesh.* 123.
3 *Chron. Evesh.* 129.

the Vale.[1] But the bishop's lawyers had committed an error of judgment in their conduct of the case. Instead of delaying matters to the utmost by obtaining first a decision on the facts and then entering into possession, thus throwing on Evesham the onus of proving canonical exemption, they were swept into allowing all the evidence pro and con on the legal issue to be given at once. This allowed the commission to finish its work at once with a decision on the facts which left the parties at odds and resolute in going forward, and also to fix a day for the legal issue to be decided at Rome.

Mauger, indeed, having received jurisdiction over Evesham *pendente lite*, settled its affairs as best he could,[2] showed himself a just and kindly ruler, and endeavoured to persuade the monks to relinquish their suit, but when the turn events were taking in the court of the judges delegate became clear, and before their sentence had been promulgated, Roger Norreys and Marleberge had departed for Rome. The abbot was resolved to be well out of the way of Hubert Walter's arbitrators, should their commission be revived, and the convent could not trust him in Rome without an agent of their own to watch the proceedings in their interest. Marleberge in consequence left Evesham on 29 September 1204, amid the gloomiest prognostications from his brethren and with a resolve that, if he failed to win the suit, he would end his days in a monastery at Rome. Forty days later he arrived in the City and had his first encounter with Innocent III. Roger Norreys, for his part, had adventures on the road and only arrived at the beginning of the following Lent.

At first it appeared as if a complete breakdown of the case was inevitable; the abbot, apprehensive as to what might happen to him at the seat of supreme authority, refused to speak to Marleberge, endeavoured to obtain a papal brief enabling him to deprive him of the monastic habit, and even, so we are asked to believe, entertained designs against his life. The two were at length reconciled, and obtaining a loan of four hundred marks, spent some of it upon judicious presents in the Curia.[3] As the report of the English commission had not yet reached Rome, the winter and early spring of 1204–5 passed in complete inaction, save that a brief was obtained authorizing Evesham to use all its old privileges; in the late spring Marleberge, acting on the advice of Innocent and of

1 As Marleberge remarked (*Chron. Evesh.* 140) it is hard to see how, on legal principles, a non-exempt church could have any rights founded on exemption; but the commissioners were clearly anxious to avoid touching upon the canonical issue, realizing that wheels within wheels were at work. Moreover, the complex of ancient immunities out of which Evesham's claim grew had nothing to do with canon law. In fact, the decision favoured the abbey, for it retained jurisdiction over its churches (the recovery of which once lost would have been well nigh impossible) and every incentive was given to prosecute the claim for Evesham itself, by which its right over the churches ultimately stood or fell.

2 He could not, of course, take disciplinary action against the abbot, for the latter was appellant in the case about to be heard at Rome.

3 *Chron. Evesh.* 146.

Cardinal Ugolino, whom he had retained as patron of his cause, proceeded to Bologna, where for six months he studied canon law with great profit. Meanwhile the abbot returned to England and refused once more to admit the bishop into his abbey, relying on the brief recently obtained in Rome.

In October 1205 Marleberge returned to Rome, whither the report of the commission had at last arrived, citing the parties to appear before the Curia during the octave of St Martin. Once more Evesham was materially assisted by the straightforward but injudicious conduct of its opponents. Instead of acting upon the maxim (*beati possidentes*) that proceedings should never be started by those who are *de facto* in possession, they took the first step to bring on the hearing of the case; Marleberge, on the other hand, by a judicious *suppressio veri*, induced the pope to hear and decide the case of exemption before approaching that of the churches of the Vale; fortune, indeed, favoured him still further, for owing to a technicality his opponent was put in the disadvantageous position of plaintiff in the suit. The bishop's advocate, besides, committed a series of errors of method and was tactless enough to deliver elaborate speeches wholly distasteful to Innocent; Marleberge, on the other hand, himself cool and insinuating, was assisted by four of the most brilliant canonists in the Italian peninsula.[1] We need not here consider the nature and worth of his arguments. The case was developed in three sessions before the pope and his circle of cardinals, and Marleberge in a number of deft touches shows us the keen, realist mind of Innocent at work. When the pope declared that he would reserve judgment Marleberge betook himself to prayer, visiting the holy places, distributing largesse to beggars whether they solicited alms or no, and abstaining entirely from food for two days. On Christmas Eve, 1205, the day appointed for sentence, he embraced the feet of the cardinals as they went to consistory, and his obvious distress affected all the onlookers. When sentence was given, allowing Evesham full exemption, the relief from the strain, added to his physical weakness due to fasting, overcame him, and he fell fainting at Innocent's feet.

The principal legal question was thus settled for ever, but the process over the churches of the Vale remained to be heard. Marleberge was in high favour with the pope, who twice within the octave of Christmas sent him a present of venison,[2] but in other respects he was in difficulties. He had exhausted an additional sum of fifty marks which he had borrowed,

---

1 They were (*Chron. Evesh.* 153) Master Merandus of Spain, a pundit of Bologna, who had been the advocate of the bishops in the recent dispute over the Canterbury election; Bertrandus of Pavia, another Bolognese doctor, who had been the monks' advocate in the same case; Peter of Benevento, later cardinal; and Master William of the Chancery: the last two were experts in Curial procedure. He paid them at the rate, respectively, of fifty, forty, forty and twenty shillings of Provence *per diem*. When his adversary complained that Marleberge had exhausted the supply of counsel, Innocent remarked drily that no one in Rome need lack for that commodity.

2 *Chron. Evesh.* 184.

and as the merchants who had lent Roger Norreys over four hundred marks had failed to obtain repayment he could raise no more money and was even in danger of imprisonment—a fate which actually befell one of his colleagues, Ermesfrid by name, who died in custody.[1] He could therefore retain no advocate and was thrown upon his own resources; his documentary case was not strong and Innocent, in accordance with Curial practice, was clearly anxious to give the bishop what satisfaction he could to offset the recent adverse decision. When, however, it came to evidence from prescription Evesham was in a strong position, and Marleberge's opponent, Mauger's proctor, was driven to assert that he had learnt in the schools that no prescription against episcopal rights was valid. To this Innocent replied that Robert and his masters could have propounded and accepted such a doctrine only when under the influence of the national drink.[2] This sally was apparently appreciated, for the pope repeated it, but he was clearly unwilling to give a second judgment against the bishop, and as the Evesham evidence had serious gaps the whole matter was in February 1206 referred back to judges in England. Marleberge and his two companions, however, being insolvent debtors, were forbidden to leave Rome with their muniments, though they were sick and exhausted. In spite of the prohibition one of them returned with a document of the papal decision; news of this reached the creditors of the abbey and all the privileges of Evesham in Marleberge's possession were taken into pawn. He succeeded, however, in frustrating an attempt on the part of the bishop to obtain the deposition of Roger Norreys at Innocent's hands.[3] All other parties to the suit had now departed, but permission was still refused to Marleberge, according to his own account because he had failed to give to the cardinals the presents customarily expected from a victorious litigant. As he had no money his hopes of departing in the regular way were slight, and he failed to obtain a papal order for costs against the bishop; he therefore took French leave, obtained the blessing of Innocent in the midst of a crowd, and returned to Evesham in the late spring of 1206.

There he found that Roger Norreys, with his customary resilience, and considering himself now safe from all danger, had returned to his old ways of extravagance and oppression.[4] The agreement between convent and abbot having lapsed with the Roman decision, the monks delated their

1 *Chron. Evesh.* 184.

2 *Chron. Evesh.* 189: "Certe et tu et magistri tui multum bibistis de cerevisia Anglicana quando haec didicistis." Innocent had visited Canterbury (*v.* Powicke, *Stephen Langton*, 18), and doubtless had made personal acquaintance with the celebrated Kentish ale, for which cf. Giraldus, *De rebus a se gestis*, 1, 51.

3 *Chron. Evesh.* 199. Mauger had obtained complete evidence of Roger's misconduct and forwarded it to his procurator in Rome. Marleberge, knowing that his adversary had documents of importance, but ignorant of their contents, persuaded him, by a daring piece of bluff, to throw in his hand; he thus obtained his documents and destroyed them. This is surely the least creditable of all his actions, for he frankly states: "si vidisset [papa] inquisitionem in qua multa enormia continebantur, sine dubio eum deposuisset."

4 *Chron. Evesh.* 202–5.

superior to the cardinal legate John of Sancta Maria in Via Lata, who visited England in 1206 and came to Evesham. The legate appointed delegates, the Augustinian abbots of Lillishall and Haughmond, to settle the financial points at issue, reserving the spiritual question to himself, but while he delayed to act Roger Norreys succeeded in ingratiating himself with him, and bestowed an income on his nephew; the legate therefore departed leaving matters as they were.[1] The abbot now took steps to consolidate his position and expelled Marleberge and his ally, Thomas de Northwich, from the house. At this crisis Marleberge was loyally supported by his brethren and thirty of the community took to the road with him. They were pursued by the abbot and an armed party, and after a parley at Wickhamford a scuffle took place from which the monks, armed with staves, emerged victorious. They thereupon resumed their journey, and when they had passed out of the jurisdiction of the abbot near Child's Wickham another parley took place across the high road in which Roger capitulated on all the financial demands and undertook to attempt no reprisals against Marleberge and his associates. An allocation of the various revenues, which the legate had approved, was then sealed by the abbot and remained in force for the future, receiving confirmation from Innocent III during the Lateran Council.

When the legate was out of the country Mauger of Worcester cited the monks to appear before the papal judges delegate on the issue of the exempt churches of the Vale, and the case was heard at St Albans.[2] The monks (*beati possidentes*) used every means to stay and delay proceedings, and let it be known that they intended to apply at Rome for an order of costs against Mauger for the previous litigation, fixing the sum at two thousand marks. Roger Norreys, indeed, was willing to compromise by renouncing the claim for costs and by abandoning the churches situated on Evesham manors but beyond the limits of the Vale, but the monks would have none of this, and shortly after Mauger went into exile on account of the Interdict and died abroad before normal times returned. Thus the suit was suspended and only revived many years after the death of the bishop, when in 1248 a decision was given on the lines of the compromise proposed in 1207.

In other ways, also, the Interdict was fortunate for Evesham, for John in his displeasure arrested all Roman subjects in England and exiled them after confiscating their goods. Among those so treated were the Roman creditors of Evesham; the papal bulls which had been impawned were lodged in Corfe castle, and the abbey was relieved of any immediate necessity of finding the cash.[3] In the most important matter, however, Evesham suffered by the rupture with Rome, for there was now no possible method of getting rid of Roger Norreys. He had thus a respite

---

1 For John's legation *v.* Tillmann, *Päpstliche Legaten in England*, 92.
2 *Chron. Evesh.* 222.   3 *Chron. Evesh.* 225.

of more than seven years, for the Interdict was not lifted till the summer of 1213. Its suspension brought the Roman moneylenders back into the country, and Marleberge spent some months in bargaining with them at York, Northampton, London and Wallingford before he ultimately arranged a compromise very advantageous to the abbey.[1] Roger Norreys, however, refused to pay a penny[2] and this was the immediate cause of his final undoing, for Marleberge, who had been commissioned to carry his decision to the legate in London, took advantage of his journey to call upon his old friend Richard Poore, dean (later bishop) of Salisbury, and together they discussed the whole question of Evesham with their old master, Stephen Langton. But even Langton, whom Marleberge besought to visit the house and depose the abbot, was unwilling to engage upon a course of action in which the legal issue was far from clear.[3] Fortunately the papal legate *a latere* in England, Nicholas of Tusculum, was a man of energy and determined to make an end of the business. Dissembling his intentions, he appeared unexpectedly at Evesham within a few hours of the letter giving notice of his advent, and the moment of crisis had arrived. Marleberge, in a vivid page, describes the state of apprehension that reigned among all parties, the counselling and caballing that took place, and his own fears for the outcome. The monks had become inured to the scandalous life and oppressive conduct of their abbot, and their moral sense had doubtless long ago been blunted by their alliance with him in litigation; they had seen him emerge time and again victorious from situations which seemed desperate; they knew that he was now fighting for existence and would stick at nothing, and that unless utterly vanquished he would avenge himself on those who had attacked him by driving them out of the monastic order. When the legate summoned them to speak all, including Marleberge, remained silent, though the eyes of all his fellows were upon the old protagonist. But the cardinal of Tusculum was in earnest, and called upon Marleberge by name to rise and speak. The moment had come which he had long foreseen.[4] After a few words which showed clearly enough that he was not insensible to the dangers of his position, he broke into a long and reasoned accusation, giving on all points dates and the names of reliable witnesses. With admirable judgment he began by describing the decay of religious discipline at Evesham and the collapse of its finances; he then told of the antecedents of the abbot, of his intrusion upon the community and of his dilapidations; finally, when it was clear that he had the sympathy of the legate and his assistants, he denounced

---

1 *Chron. Evesh.* 230–1. The creditors claimed 1100 marks—400 for debts, 700 for forfeits and expenses; they were to receive 500.

2 *Chron. Evesh.* 231: "Jurans per reginam angelorum [a favourite oath: cf. 146] quod nunquam redderet inde unum denarium."

3 *Chron. Evesh.* 232–3. There was a doubt as to the validity of Langton's power to depose; it was argued that the pope alone had this right in the case of Evesham.

4 *Chron. Evesh.* 236: "Saepius enim super his mecum deliberaveram."

clearly and without rhetoric the manifold immoralities of which Roger
Norreys had been guilty. He ended by detailing the previous and unsuccessful attempts to carry investigations to an issue and declared that
if the endeavour failed this time also, the majority of the community
would in desperation abandon regular life.

When he had finished speaking the legate asked the monks one by one
if what he had said were true; all, save three, gave their assent. On the
following day Nicholas of Tusculum, assisted by the abbots of York,
Selby, Winchcombe and Gloucester, together with an Italian Cistercian,
called upon the abbot to make his defence. When nothing of any substance
was forthcoming the legate straightway deposed him and in his room
secured the election of the prior of Worcester, a native of Evesham. Roger
Norreys was exiled to take charge of the small and distant priory of
Penwortham in Lancashire, but in a few months was deposed from the
position by the legate. After five years of wretched existence as a wanderer
he was once more given Penwortham by Pandulf in 1218, and there he
died five years later, refusing to the end an oft-proffered reconciliation
with the monks of Evesham.[1]

As for Marleberge, the share he had taken in events had given ample
proof that he was a man of exceptional courage and resource; in the years
that followed he showed himself an excellent administrator and a beneficent
ruler. He was already dean of the Vale; in 1215 he accompanied the new
abbot to the Lateran Council, where he renewed old acquaintanceships
and succeeded in obtaining from Innocent certain confirmations and
privileges.[2] In c. 1217 he became sacrist and a year later prior.[3] Finally,
in 1229, he was elected abbot.[4] In all these offices he proved himself,
perhaps more than we should have expected from the tone of his narrative,
an administrator of wide and even magnificent aims. He developed the
estates of the abbey, built and decorated on a grand scale, enriched the
church with objects of beauty and the library with many volumes of law,
physic and liturgy. In the realm of things visible, indeed, he had deserved
well of his brethren, and there is evidence, besides his election as abbot,
that they were grateful. True to the end to his endeavours in the past, he
designed for himself a tomb of marble, with an effigy clad in the pontifical
vestments;[5] it is interesting to learn that he erected a memorial of equal
magnificence over the remains of a monk, John Denis by name, who for
thirty years and more—throughout all the trials and disturbances of the
reign of Roger Norreys—had lived a life of prayer and penance, giving
all that he could secure to the poor.[6] There is indeed clear evidence that

1 *Chron. Evesh.* 252–3.   2 *Chron. Evesh.* 266, 153, 205, 223.
3 *Chron. Evesh.* 266–7.   4 *Chron. Evesh.* 272–4.
5 *Chron. Evesh.* 275.
6 *Chron. Evesh.* 271: "De quo idem prior Thomas [*sc.* Marleberge] dicere consuevit
quod nunquam vidit hominem tam perfecte omne genus poenitentiae peragere sicut idem
Johannes peregit triginta annos et amplius, in jejuniis et orationibus, in lachrymarum effusione

long before the death of Marleberge Evesham had recovered the normal tenour of life which had been so rudely broken by the advent of Roger Norreys.

Such, in brief, is the narrative of the Evesham case. It has been retailed here in some completeness because it is only by watching how the original simple issue became cloaked and concealed with a luxuriant growth of litigation that we can form a true judgment on the conditions of black monk life in England at the time, and on the motives that swayed the principal actors in this singular drama. It may be well, by way of conclusion, to give in summary a few of the reflections to which the chronicle of Marleberge gives rise.

The principal and most painful impression that the casual reader of the Evesham chronicle receives is doubtless that given by the spectacle of an abbot of notoriously evil life, who not only remained in office for close on a quarter of a century, despite numerous attempts to dislodge him, but actually appeared in public at the centre of Christendom and retired untouched. No further reflection, indeed, can ever wholly efface this painful impression, nor that given by the compact between abbot and monks during the trial and by more than one action of Marleberge himself. Whatever palliating circumstances may be alleged in defence of the monks of Evesham, the reader is justified in feeling that, had the majority of them resolved firmly from the start to put spiritual things before material and temporal considerations, a more speedy relief could have been found without any undue sacrifice of their truest interests. Marleberge in particular, though a man of piety and good intentions, shows himself as one of no spiritual depth, to whom the temporal prosperity of his home, the *esprit de corps* of a great foundation and the combat of wits in the court of law, meant more than the peril to souls and the perfect following of the Rule and of the gospel.

But his narrative shows us very much more than this, and makes it clear that it was not solely moral weakness on the part of the subjects of Roger Norreys that caused the long scandal at Evesham. At least three accidental circumstances, quite independent of each other, were responsible besides. In the first place, Roger Norreys had been intruded into the abbey by the high-handed action of Baldwin, the superior ultimately responsible for Evesham, and a new and irresponsible monarch, both of whom immediately disappeared from the scene of action, Baldwin never to return and Richard never to see at close quarters the consequences of his appointment. Next, Norreys would in all human probability have been deposed by the energetic and zealous Mauger in 1202 had not the question of exemption, under the able lead of Marleberge, cut across the existing controversy and

et vigiliis, in corporalibus cruciatibus et frigoribus, in vestimentorum vilitate et asperitate, et ultra modum aliorum fratrum corporalium sustentationum subtractione, cunctis sibi subtractis bonis usibus et pauperum sustentationibus profuturis."

introduced a wholly new issue. Thirdly, he would probably have fallen in 1207–8 but for the application of the Interdict. Marleberge says so little of the affairs of the Church at large that it is possible for a reader, even though familiar from childhood with the story of John's misgovernment and its consequences, to forget that the later years of misrule at Evesham were years also of utter chaos in the political and ecclesiastical life of the country. Nevertheless, these accidental hindrances, real as they were, did not prevent a number of attempts being made on the part of various authorities to investigate and settle the troubles at Evesham; these attempts all came to nothing, and the reader of Marleberge's chronicle is justified in asking why, in the last resort, this was so.

As the ultimate event showed, it was not because the monastic institute, or contemporary society, was so decadent as to frustrate all individual attempts at reform. England in 1200 was far from being in the condition that part of Germany reached in 1500. The paralysis which overtook all authority as soon as it entered the electric zone of Evesham was due primarily to the excessive degree of independence enjoyed by the black monk houses and to the maladjustment of the legal and executive system of the Church at large, and the light which Marleberge's narrative throws on these points is perhaps its most valuable legacy to students of history. Gradually in the course of ages, and in England especially during the previous fifty years, the three authorities—bishop, monarch and neighbouring abbots—who in past ages of monastic history had been the normal guarantors of discipline, had ceased to have at their disposal, either by law, custom or public opinion, the powers essential to make their interference prompt and effective.[1] In particular, if the king lacked the ability or the desire to act, and the monastery laid claim to any sort of privileged position, the possibility of speedy settlement was wholly out of the question, for a series of appeals and references from England to Rome and from Rome back to England would be straightway set up. Had the law been something fixed and easily ascertainable, and the supreme authority prepared to apply it at once, exemption as such would not have affected discipline for the worse any more in 1200 than in modern times; but the process of adapting canon law to a society built on other lines was as yet far from complete, and although the papacy under a strong pontiff claimed the widest authority and was on occasion capable of making good its claims, there were many questions both of fact and of law, in the government of the Church, in which the Curia was as yet uncertain where the law, and the interests of the papacy, lay; it therefore preferred to evade a pronouncement as long as possible by reference to judges delegate, and by allowing a case to go through the longest form of trial.

The Evesham cases show clearly to the reader of to-day the need alike

---

[1] Before the Conquest the king and Witan acted; under the early Norman kings the king, archbishop and council; under Stephen legates.

of some more immediate control or union among the houses of the black monks and of an adjustment between the judicial and executive powers in the Church as a whole. Both needs were in part met within a short space of years: by the legislation of the Lateran Council, by the action of Gregory IX and others in their promulgation of Decretals, by the union for purposes of discipline among the English monks, and by the energy of a group of eminent pastoral and diocesan bishops. And though there is no record of the fact, it may well be that Innocent III, in applying to the black monks the system of general chapter and visitation, was made more firm in his resolve by memories of the long-drawn litigation and misrule at Evesham.

CHAPTER XX

THE CISTERCIANS FROM 1153 TO 1216

I

The legislation of the Cistercian general chapter of 1152, forbidding further foundations, followed as it was in less than a year by the deaths of Bernard and Eugenius III, marked the end in England of the epoch of rapid expansion for the white monks, and the end also of their influence as a body upon the ecclesiastical life of the nation. From that date till the end of the century very few houses were founded in this country—only some half-dozen in all[1]—and no Cistercian, save Baldwin, made any figure in public life. Later, at the beginning of the next century, King John's foundation of Beaulieu in Hampshire (1204), colonized directly from Cîteaux, was to bring a new and vigorous current of monastic life into England, and to become the mother of a small family which counted among its members the royal foundations of Hayles and St Mary Graces, London. But the history of these falls within another period.

There remained, however, in 1150, a large area of the island still almost entirely virgin soil to monasticism; in north and central Wales there were no houses of any kind of the black or white monks. Whereas in the south Brecon, Monmouth, Glamorgan, Carmarthen and Pembroke had in different degrees been brought under Norman rule and had received at first small colonies of black monks, and later some of the earliest plantations of the grey and white, and whereas in the Marches a few foundations had been made from Savigny, central and northern Wales, still wholly Celtic, contained no monastic foundations whatsoever[2] save the lonely outpost of Cwm Hir (1143), a daughter of Whitland, in Radnorshire, and a few families of Celtic culdees who still survived on Bardsey, on Priestholm off Anglesea, and at Beddgelert under the shelter of Snowdon.[3]

Among the early Cistercian abbeys of south Wales that of Whitland or Alba Landa near Carmarthen, a direct filiation of Clairvaux, at once

1 Pulton (Staffs.), ? 1153; Bindon (Dorset) and Stanlaw (Cheshire), 1172; Croxden (Staffs.) and Robertsbridge (Sussex), 1176; Cleeve (Somerset), 1198.

2 Basingwerk (Flint) is no exception. Its foundation as a Savigniac house *c.* 1131–3 (1132, *Louth Park Chronicle*, p. 30) was due to Ranulph, earl of Chester; it was only later patriotism that attributed it to Owen Gwynedd, who was probably a notable benefactor (*Brut y Tywysogion*, RS, *s.a.* 1164).

3 For Bardsey *v.* Giraldus, *Iter Kambriae*, 124: "Insula modica, quam monachi inhabitant religiosissimi, quos coelibes vel colideos vocant." For Priestholm (the modern Puffin Island), *v. ibid.* 131: "Insula modica...quam solum eremitae labore manuum viventes et Deo servientes inhabitant." For Beddgelert *v. Speculum Ecclesiae*, IV, 167: "Erat in Venedotia...domus clericorum religiosa sub pede montis Ereri [i.e. Snowdon]....Deo devote servientes sanctoque coetu in commune viventes...nulli quidem ordini monastico vel canonico specialiter addicti, sed tanquam coelibes sive colidei...dicti." For culdees in general *v.* A. Hamilton Thompson in *Bede: his Life, Times and Writings*, 87 seqq.

took pride of place. Well endowed from its origin, it was from the first a house of the native Welsh in which members of the chief families took the habit and became abbots;[1] from it, in the second half of the century, sprang a little family of foundations in central and northern Wales. It was a period of comparative prosperity and peace in the country, during which Rhys ap Griffith (*ob.* 1196) in south Wales and Owen of Gwynedd (*ob.* 1169) and Llewelyn ap Iorwerth, called "the Great" (*ob.* 1240), in the north, ruled with some firmness and beneficence, and during which, also, there was a brilliant rebirth of Welsh poetry. To Rhys was due the consolidation of Strata Florida, a daughter of Whitland originally founded in 1164, situated in an open valley of wide pastures between Aberystwyth and Lampeter,[2] while Llewelyn was the founder of Aberconway (1186) in the far north, a daughter of Strata Florida, and of Cymmer near Dolgelley at the head of the estuary of the Mawddach, a daughter of Cwm Hir. Two other abbeys, Strata Marcella near Welshpool, founded from Whitland in 1170 by Owen Kyveiliog, a prince of Powys and a poet of note, and Valle Crucis near Llangollen, a daughter of Strata Marcella, complete the tale of the plantations in northern Wales,[3] though Whitland subsequently sent two colonies to Ireland, and the total number of her daughters and grandchildren rose to eight.

These Welsh abbeys lay for the most part in situations very similar to those of their sisters in Yorkshire, on the strath or lower slopes of a river valley near the high hills or moors, where a narrow stretch of land in the neighbourhood of the monastery could be cultivated while the sheep were pastured on the sweet short grass of the moor or mountain. The visitor of to-day can scarcely fail to remark upon the great natural beauty and calm of the surroundings of Abbey Cwmhir, Valle Crucis and Cymmer; equally remarkable, from another point of view, is the evidence which their ruins provide of the strength of the tradition of uniformity in architecture among the white monks. Speaking generally, neither the Romanesque nor the early Gothic styles spread at all in the purely Celtic districts of Wales; the parish churches remained small, plain structures and only a very few of the larger churches, such as Bangor, ever attained to the stature of a complete Gothic edifice. But the Cistercian abbeys, alike in ground plan, design and detail of ornament, are indistinguishable from their contemporaries in England; Strata Florida and Valle Crucis, of which considerable remains exist, are particularly noteworthy in this respect.

1 An abbot Morvan died in 1146; Cynan in 1176; Rhydderch in 1184 (*Brut*, 175, 227, 233). For these Welsh abbeys *v.* also *Cartae...de Glamorgancia*, ed. G. T. Clark.
2 *Brut*, 203; Gerald of Wales, *Speculum Ecclesiae*, IV, 152 *seq.*: "Domus...opima...a nobili viro Roberto Stephani filio in pascuis pinguibus et amplis primum fundata... postmodum a dicto principe [*sc.* Rhys] terris fertilibus et grangiis plurimis abunde ditata, adeo quidem ut...cunctis domibus ordinis ejusdem Walliae totius, armentis et equitiis, pecoribus ac pecudibus, et opulentiis ex his provenientibus, longe copiosius esset locupletata."
3 For these *v. Brut*, 233, 251, 253, 257.

Of the early history of these houses little is known, save for a few notices in Welsh annals and numerous passing references in the works of Gerald of Wales and in the Cistercian Statutes. In the earlier part of his career Gerald was on friendly terms with Whitland and Strata Florida, but later, when he encountered opposition to his pretensions to the see of St David's, and when, if he may be believed, the abbot of Strata Florida had betrayed his trust, he became a bitter critic, and, as will be seen elsewhere, he draws a number of his examples of Cistercian misdemeanours and sharp practice from this group of Welsh abbeys. The evidence of the Cistercian Statutes, it must be said, goes far to corroborate the impression given by Gerald that the Welsh character found a difficulty in adapting itself to the discipline of the white monks; this, too, will be considered on a later page.

II

During the first fifty years of Cistercian life in England the economic and social significance of the monasteries underwent a very considerable development. In the sphere of material things, the great innovation of the white monks had been the introduction of agricultural work as an essential of the monastic life. In origin the move was largely due to a desire to escape from the possession of the complex sources of income of the black monks and to return to a simple life in which the community should live by the labour of its own hands. This, however, was soon recognized as being impossible once a family had passed the pioneer stage, for the hours of heavy labour needed for farm, field and forest work, especially if at any distance from the monastery, would have left insufficient time for the prayer and reading of the Rule. To escape from this difficulty the early fathers of Cîteaux had recourse to the employment, truly epoch-making in its consequences, of lay brothers. When the order was still in its cradle no eye could have foreseen what important economic consequences were to result from this system, and how these were to react in time upon the order itself. A small religious house, buried in the forest or in an upland valley, of which some members, not in orders, devoted the greater part of their time to rearing beasts and cultivating the scanty fields of the monastery, had as innocent an appearance as the first crude pieces of steam-driven machinery in the mills of the north six hundred years later. But when the houses of the order were multiplied a hundredfold, and when the monks and *conversi* in many of the larger ones could themselves be counted by the hundred, and when these powerful forces of labour could cease from reducing a wilderness to order and devote themselves to exploiting to the extreme limit all the resources of a territory already under cultivation, and when this territory, originally perhaps a waste, but now fertile and increased by gift after gift, was treated as a single economic unit and became something very considerable upon the map of the district, the full implications of the system were, if not fully realized, at least experienced far and wide. The wheel had come full circle, and the expedient originally devised to isolate the monastery from the life of the world was now something which affected at least indirectly the lives of all around. From being a small Christian household, exhibiting the dignity of toil and of direct production in the midst of a feudal society, the great Cistercian abbeys had become ranches, *latifundia*, the enemies of their small neighbours. In the districts of intense cultivation of vine and olive in the south of Europe, and even in the purely agricultural lands, harmful consequences were long in making themselves felt, but in north England and (though less notably) in Wales, circumstances combined to make of the white monks mass-producers of the raw material which formed the basis of much of the country's industry, trade and credit during the later centuries of the Middle Ages. All this came about in large part before the order had been established for a hundred years in England; later, the process was to go a stage farther when the class of *conversi* who had been its mainspring disappeared, leaving the Cistercian monks as capitalists in the full sense of the word. This rapid economic development is of such importance that its beginnings deserve to be traced in the scanty records of contemporary documents.

The *Exordium Parvum*, reaffirmed by the decrees of general chapter, laid down that the monks of Cîteaux might own land, together with all its natural freight of vegetable and animal life, with the exception of certain "luxury" animals. They were to live upon the fruits of their labour and the increase of their stock; the choir monks were to be assisted by *conversi*, and even, if necessary, by hired labour; they were not to possess any ecclesiastical revenues, or income of rent or toll from land, mills or any form of imposition, nor were they to receive any rents or services from dwellers upon the land.[1]

In the early beginnings of the order both the will and the possibility existed of observing all these decrees. The Cistercian foundations in England and Wales were, almost without exception, made in wild or waste districts, nominally the property of an overlord but economically undeveloped. The monks were therefore inserted, as it were, into the countryside without dislocation or disturbance of any kind; they proceeded to reduce the wilderness to cultivation and to live upon their labour. When they had developed the land within the immediate neighbourhood of the monastery, granges were constructed or adapted on more distant parts of the property, and the abbey became the centre of a wider economic unit, such as we can see by glimpses in working order at Rievaulx under Ailred. These granges multiplied rapidly. Meaux, founded only in 1151, had seven granges already by *c.* 1170, and Wardon twelve

1 *Exordium* (ed. Guignard), 71–2; *Consuetudines*, v, viii (ed. Guignard), 250–2.

by 1190,[1] and neither of these was an abnormally large house; Furness came gradually to be the nerve-centre of a far-flung system of exploitation.[2]

As the abbeys grew in population and reputation a twofold danger threatened their primitive simplicity. The growth in numbers, and especially the growth in the numbers of lay brothers, demanded more free land to occupy, and though the problem of finding it was in a sense lessened by the system of granges, which allowed bodies of *conversi* to live in buildings which formed the depots of estates at a distance up to twenty miles or more from the abbey, this very system aggravated the consequences of the growth for the surrounding population. At the same time their high reputation led to the diversion to the white monks of the gifts of developed land and all kinds of property that had hitherto gone to the older religious bodies, and among these gifts were inevitably such forbidden sources of income as vills, churches and tithes.

Even had all Cistercians possessed the strength and singleness of purpose to refuse all dubious gifts and hold unswervingly to the path of justice in all their transactions, it would have been well-nigh impossible for such a vast organization to avoid difficulties; as it was, the difficulties began to multiply almost at once, and although an examination of the early chronicles and cartularies shows that at first the gifts were mainly of land only, and that buildings were only accepted when they could be used for monastic purposes, it soon became more common for villages and groups of houses to be presented to the white monks.

Failing a resolute determination to accept none of these gifts and to limit the size of their communities and estates, there were, speaking broadly, two alternative courses of action possible, one which kept the letter of the statutes, the other wholly irregular. By the first, the gifts of developed and populated land were accepted, and the statutory conditions of personal labour and remoteness from the world were then satisfied by ejecting the inhabitants, allowing the houses to fall into ruin and thus converting or, as the technical phrase went, "reducing" the village to the status of a grange. This process, which perhaps aroused more protests from contemporaries than did the more irregular procedure, and which Gerald of Wales inveighed against so frequently, can be seen in action in many of the Cistercian records.[3] In isolated cases it was even applied to churches. Old Byland is a case in point; and another which has attracted more attention and received more obloquy than it deserves concerns the first foundation of what was later to be the house of Kirkstall at Barnoldswick. Here the parish church of the ejected tenants happened to be in the near neighbourhood of the monastery and within the "ring-fence" of

---

1 *Chron. Mels.* I, 178; *Monasticon*, V, 372.
2 *V.* art. by F. M. Powicke in *VCH, Lancs* II, 114 *seqq.*
3 Giraldus, IV, 206 (of Dore). Cf. the gift to Fountains *c.* 1200 of a vill: "quae amotis postmodum accolis redacta est in grangiam uberem frugibus" (*Monasticon*, V, 305; *Mem. Fount.* I, 124); cf. also *Chron. Mels.* I, 76, where a grange absorbed a common pasture.

the property; the abbot therefore destroyed it as disturbing the solitude of the monks, and was duly cited before the archbishop of York, who happened to be the Cistercian Henry Murdac; when Murdac upheld the action of the abbot both parties appealed to Rome, and the Cistercian Eugenius III decided that the greater good was more important than the lesser, and that an abbey, as a mother-church, might absorb the parish. The spectacle of a close circle of Cistercian judges, added to modern parish sentiment, has led antiquaries to animadvert severely on the case,[1] but there is no evidence that it served as precedent for a widespread suppression of parish churches, though such suppression appears among the general charges brought by Gerald of Wales half a century later against the Welsh abbeys.[2] Far more common was the destruction of villages, and the sight of hamlets disappearing within the ring-fences of the white monks, especially when the latter were becoming wealthy, and the arable was converted into pasture for sheep, caused widespread and adverse comment. How far this comment was justified and how far due to mere sentiment or to jealousy of the superior agricultural methods of the monks cannot be decided, at least so far as the twelfth century is concerned, owing to the absence of all statistics as to the frequency of such occupations and the hardships (if any) incurred by the former inhabitants.

In general, however, towards the end of the century, the Cistercians took the easier alternative of accepting gifts as they came, and by 1200 many abbeys were in possession of sources of income forbidden by the original statutes. Evidence of this, as regards revenues and services from land, is widespread and may be found in the cartulary of almost any English Cistercian house;[3] at some time between 1166 and 1179 Alexander III wrote a strong letter of remonstrance to Swineshead and Furness, who were said to own villages and serfs and courts,[4] and before the end of the century Gerald could point to a case where an abbey owned courts and used the income accruing therefrom exactly like the black monks.[5] Such extreme cases were perhaps isolated, and even as late as the accession of Henry III the irregular possessions of land in the hands of the white

1 For the Barnoldswick case v. Monasticon, v, 530, and Fundacio Abbathie de Kyrkestall (Thoresby Society, IV, 169 seq.). The text from Dugdale was reprinted with strictures by J. Walbran in Memorials of Fountains, I, and the author of the article on Kirkstall in VCH, Yorks III likewise passes judgment.

2 For Giraldus, v. Speculum Ecclesiae, IV, 177. An analogy in more modern times to the Cistercian practice may be found in the enclosures of the eighteenth century and the shifting of whole villages, such as Wimpole in Cambridgeshire and Milton Abbas in Dorset, away from the landowner's mansion. The tenacity of local sentiment in such matters may also be seen in the reactions to the practice and legislation concerning copyhold in the last century.

3 E.g. for the period 1180–1200 v. Chron. Melsa, I, 220 seqq.

4 Cf. the letter in Holtzmann, Papsturkunden in England, II, ii, n. 174: "Audivimus quod villas et rusticos habeatis et eos in causam ducentes notis pecuniariis condempnatis, et more saecularium dominorum jus patronatus in dandis ecclesiis vendicatis."

5 Giraldus, IV, 207. The abbey was Dore.

monks probably bore no large proportion to their total property; certainly no Cistercian abbey had as yet anything comparable to the complex of jurisdictions, tolls and revenues of which so many black monk houses were the proprietors. A breach, however, had been made in the primitive regularity, and the consequences were permanent and most unfortunate.

Apart altogether from any question connected with their constitutions or privileges, the Cistercians came, towards the end of the century, to have a reputation, in certain circles at least, for avarice and sharp practice in extending or improving their property at the expense of others. In part, no doubt, the charge was justified, and the chapter of Cîteaux implicitly acknowledged its justice by taking steps to escape the odium;[1] the Cistercian chronicles show clearly enough that the tenacious *esprit de corps* which made its appearance among the black monks at least as early as Hemming of Worcester had begun in time to take possession of the white. But in part also it was the reaction of rivalry to the successful and superior agricultural methods of the Cistercians, whose domestic organization gave to their enterprises many of the advantages possessed in the modern world by the multiple-branch concern or vertically controlled group-industry over the small manufacturer and trader. In particular, towards the end of the twelfth century, the white monks came forward as the leading producers of wool.

This branch of farming, which was to become such a source of wealth to the order, became their speciality largely by accident. Among the village communities of England previous to the thirteenth century there was little facility or incentive for sheep farming on any scale. In the great plain counties and the inhabited valleys of the west and south-west good enclosed pasture was reserved for horses and cattle, and waste land was either forest or heath; in the wolds and moorlands of the north the population was too scanty and conditions too unsettled for any exploitation of the grassland. But it was precisely in these desolate open spaces that the white monks first settled; wool was necessary for their habits and cowls, and it so happened that their sheep were set to graze upon the rolling pastures of Lincolnshire and Yorkshire, which ever since that time have proved among the best in the world for the rearing of noble sheep and the production of the finest fleeces. Sheep farming on a large scale, which had been utterly outside the purview of the small village cultivator, fettered as he was by divided strips, fold-service and labour-dues, was eminently practicable under the grange system of the Cistercian abbeys in the valleys of Lincolnshire, Yorkshire and, later, north Wales, and before the reign of John the annual yield of wool of their fleeces had become one of the assets of the country. In the thirteenth century it developed into a great export trade to Italy and the Netherlands, and for a time the white monks were the most considerable body of producers of wool in England, till

1 *V. infra*, ch. XXXIX.

gradually the graziers and merchants of Gloucestershire, Somerset, Sussex and East Anglia became supreme. But with these later developments we are not concerned.[1]

An early index of the growth of sheep farming is provided in 1193. In that year a collection was made throughout the country to ransom King Richard. In the case of prelates and churches and the old religious orders this took the form of a requisition of precious metals and jewelry; of this the Cistercians, so far true to their statutes, had little or none, so they were forced to give a year's yield of wool.[2] So keenly was the value of this contribution appreciated that Richard on his way home raised money on the security of the following year's crop (1194), and demanded the wool from the white monks. This would have spelt ruin, and they succeeded in commuting the demand into a sum of money.[3]

If this recognition of the importance of their wool-crop shows that the Cistercians were fast becoming a factor in the economic life of the country, other evidence points to financial transactions in a more unexpected quarter. The indebtedness of many of the greatest black monk houses to the Jews at this time has been already noticed; it is more surprising that the white monks should have been equally in the toils. At the death of that great financier, Aaron of Lincoln, in 1186, no less than nine Cistercian abbeys, and among them Rievaulx itself, were in debt to him for the gross sum of more than 6400 marks.[4] Aaron's assets reverted to the Exchequer, where they occupied the attention of what may almost be called a special department, and the Cistercians compounded for a thousand marks, Roche alone receiving remittance of 1300 marks from the king, doubtless the increment of years of usury.[5] From another source we learn that Meaux was in debt to Aaron in 1176;[6] the chronicle notes that this debt was at least in part due to the monks having received from benefactors land mortgaged to Aaron, together with the obligation to clear the mortgage and find the interest.[7] Such a transaction, apart altogether from

1 For a notice of the wool trade c. 1300 and a map showing the principal centres of production, monastic and other, v. H. C. Darby, *Historical Geography of England* (1936). It is noted there (p. 242) that c. 1300 the Cistercians produced only a sixth of the national wool-crop, but in 1200 their proportional share was certainly greater.

2 *Ann. Waverl.*, s.a. 1193: "Cum autem apud monachos ordinis Cisterciensis...non sunt inventae auri argentive possessiones, totam unius anni lanam dare compulsi sunt." *Chron. Melsa*, I, 233, 273: "Monachi Cistercienses et canonici Praemonstratenses omnes lanas suas unius anni...concesserunt." William of Newburgh, writing only a year or two later, is still more explicit (I, 399): "Quippe quod illis [sc. Cisterciensibus] in substantia praecipuum esse noscitur, et quod fere pro omni redditu ad usus sumptusque necessarios habere videntur, lanam scilicet pecudum suarum, exacti coactique resignarunt."

3 William of Newburgh, II, 416; Roger Hoved. III, 242: "Quia hoc facere erat eis grave et importabile."

4 *Memorials of Fountains*, II, 18. The nine were: Rievaulx, Newminster, Kirkstead, Louth Park, Revesby, Rufford, Kirkstall, Roche and Bittlesden.

5 *Monasticon*, V, 505: "[*temp.* abbot Hugh, 1179–84] Domus obligata [est] in magnis debitis in Judaismo. [King Richard] remisit...1300 marcas de Judaismo."

6 Pipe Roll, 9 Ric. I, 62. For Aaron v. J. Jacobs, *The Jews of Angevin England*, and *The Jewish Encyclopedia*, s.v.

7 *Chron. Melsa*, I, 173–4. Meaux was still in debt in 1197 (*ibid.* 306, 315).

its contravention of the Cistercian statutes, might seem of doubtful value as a business proposition, but at this period it was never part of the policy of a Jew to foreclose on a mortgage, and the abbey could hope that, being in a sense immortal, it might hold the land free or with a debt diminished by composition after the death of the creditor. Aaron, for his part, appears to have regarded the Cistercians as good debtors, for on one occasion he relaxed more than 500 marks of a debt in order to induce them to take it over.

Apart from such mortgages, the original loans were no doubt undertaken to raise funds for the buildings which all the houses were putting up at this time, and are therefore in a sense a witness to Cistercian poverty, for the white monks were as yet without the money revenues and gifts which the black monks could devote to the purpose. But in their deeper significance the records of such transactions make sad reading for those who have before their eyes the *Exordium* and first statutes of Cîteaux. And indeed, by the end of the century the wealth of some at least of these abbeys must have been very large, for besides debts paid off to the Exchequer and the loss of two years' wool-crop in 1193–4, they were mulcted by John during the Interdict of no less than 24,027 marks, the figure being given, not by a vague chronicler, but by the acknowledgment of the Exchequer.[1] Meaux alone, where the abbot was the object of the king's special animosity, was saddled with the immense fine of 1000 marks, which the house succeeded in this way and that in paying within a year.[2] Yet even so the white monks must not be reckoned as being by 1200 as wealthy as the black. Many of the houses had no sources of fixed income apart from the yield of their land and their savings, and when these were taken, or when harvests failed over a number of years, they were utterly ruined. Thus Meaux in the north and the celebrated Waverley in the south were twice forced to disband and seek asylum as individuals in other monasteries or where best they could until prosperity returned after a good harvest.[3]

Revenues from ecclesiastical sources such as churches, altars and tithes had been the object of explicit renunciation on the part of the first fathers.[4] Here again difficulties were not long in making themselves felt, for churches, advowsons and tithes were among the most common gifts to religious houses, especially on the part of the most scrupulous of the lay proprietors.

1 *Red Book of the Exchequer*, II, 772–3: "Recepta a Rege Johanne...tempore interdicti...de albis monachis 24,027½ marcae."
2 *Chron. Melsa*, I, 328–9: "De quibus [*sc*. mille marcis] cum maximo dispendio et inexplicabili detrimento domus nostrae, infra octavas S. Hillarii proxime sequentis satisfactum est regi."
3 Meaux had to disperse *c.* 1155 (*Chron.* 107) and again as a result of John's extortions (*ibid.* 353–4). On the latter occasion no Cistercian house was prosperous enough to receive them. Waverley were out in 1203 owing to bad harvests (*Ann. Waverl. s.a.:* "Pro nimia frugum penuria") and again in 1210 as a result of John's exactions.
4 *Exordium*, 72; *Consuetudines*, viiii (Guignard, 252).

In the early days in England, such gifts were occasionally refused. Thus *c.* 1143 Roger de Mowbray wished to give the Savigniac house of Byland the advowsons of Thirsk, Kirby Moorside and a third church, with the intention that they should ultimately put in vicars and draw the revenues. Abbot Roger, true to principle, refused, and the churches went to the canons of Newburgh.[1] Such careful self-denial, which was in fact the truest wisdom, was not general. Only after a careful analysis of many cartularies could any pronouncement be made as to the date when the possession of churches became common practice, but as early as *c.* 1170 Alexander III addressed a circular letter to the Cistercians in England ordering them to observe their constitutions, which he has heard that they have transgressed on this point,[2] and about the same time a council at Westminster passed a similar decree.[3] According to Gerald of Wales, the practice was becoming common on the border and in Wales at the end of the century,[4] and the chronicle of Meaux records a particularly clear case before 1200;[5] no doubt there were many earlier, and it seems probable that the English abbeys were in this matter the worst offenders in the whole order.

As regards tithes, the white monks were in a particularly delicate position. While their constitutions forbade them to accept as income those tithes which were treated as private property, they had received from Innocent II the privilege of exemption from payment of tithe on lands cultivated by themselves—a privilege deeply resented by bishops and clergy and attacked on theoretical grounds by not a few theologians, who contended that tithes had been instituted *jure divino*. The English Cistercians often found in practice that peace could only be bought by some form of composition in which a payment in money or kind of part of the value was accepted as a discharge of the whole;[6] on occasion, however, they did their best to exploit every legal resource by asserting their rights to a church and to income from tithe, while at the same time putting forward their privilege as a reason for not paying tithes to others.[7] In the sequel, the privilege was revoked by the Lateran Council of 1215 with regard to

1 Cf. *Historia fundationis* in *Monasticon*, v, 351. The abbot is described by his successor as "homo scrupulosae conscientiae pro cura animarum".

2 *PL*, cc (*ep.* 1152), col. 1004 [? 1162–75]. The pope has heard "quod vos jus repraesentandi clericos ad ecclesias, contra antiquam consuetudinem et institutionem ordinis vestri, emptionis titulo et modis aliis satagitis adipisci, ut sub tali praetextu vobis liceat habere ecclesias, et per vos et per alios detinere". This must stop. Cf. also the letter to Swineshead, *supra*, p. 351, n. 4.

3 Wilkins, *Concilia*, I, 474: "monachi albi...non praesument habere ecclesias contra statuta ordinis sui."

4 Giraldus, IV, 204, 207.

5 *Chron. Melsa*, I, 218. The abbey, which owned the advowson of Waghen, attempted to appropriate the church; the incident fell in the abbacy of Thomas (1182–97). Cf. a case at Sawley in *Monasticon*, v, nos. v and vi, p. 513.

6 *Chron. Melsa*, I, 218, 311–12; but cf. *ibid.* 380.

7 *Chron. Melsa*, I, 298, 320, 323.

all lands acquired in the future, but it stood for all received before that date, and an endeavour to interpret the earlier privilege as applying only to lands which the monks had been the first to bring under cultivation (*novalia*) was quashed, while on the other hand the monks were successful in bringing under this privilege all land so reclaimed after 1215.[1]

III

Thus by the end of the twelfth century an atmosphere of commerce and litigation was beginning to surround the white monks in England. As will be seen elsewhere, there is some reason to think that in this respect the Cistercians of this country were among the first to lose the original purity of their order. How far discipline and observance were affected for the worse is not so clear; this point, also, will receive further treatment on another page; here it may be sufficient to remark that the summary judgments that have sometimes been made do not sufficiently distinguish between century and century, house and house, and that in general the life of the order would seem to have been still vigorous at the death of John.[2]

The Yorkshire families, in particular, with all their ramifications, were still a powerful spiritual force in 1200. Rievaulx, Fountains and Byland were the luminaries of the north; Byland had only recently lost her founding abbot, Roger, and Rievaulx, which had called a succession of superiors from her daughter-houses to rule as abbots, was flourishing and observant. As for Fountains, the centenarian Serlo who could remember the first beginnings was able to assert *c.* 1206 that the spirit of the original fathers of the house still lived on there. This abbey, indeed, deserves more than a passing reference, for the origin of Fountains gives to it such a unique position among the Cistercian houses of England that it is of interest to follow its history to the end of the period with which we are concerned, so far as the scanty records permit.

Richard, the sometime precentor of Clairvaux whose arrival in the north followed the removal of Thorald by Murdac, ruled over the abbey till 1170. The schism which had marked the earlier years of his period of office became a thing of the past, and his latter years were peaceful; he died at Fountains, the first abbot to find burial there. He was followed by Robert (1170–80), previously abbot of Pipewell, and William (1180–90), who had been abbot of Newminster. The latter had been an Augustinian canon of Guisborough before he took the Cistercian habit under St Robert.

1 Cf. *Chron. Melsa*, I, 380–4.
2 Thus the judgment of K. Norgate, *Angevin Kings* (1887), II, 435, that by the end of the twelfth century "as an element in the nation's spiritual life the order of Cîteaux, once its very soul, now counted for worse than nothing", is far too severe; indeed it is wholly untrue.

Serlo, who during their terms of office was himself at Kirkstall, uses of them vague phrases of conventional praise which tell us little or nothing.

Of Ralph Haget, however, who came next, we have more information, due not to Serlo, but to the redactor of his narrative, Hugh of Kirkstall, who had received the religious habit at the hands of this abbot and to whom Serlo appealed at this point.[1] Ralph was the son of a well-known landed family in Yorkshire, and followed the ordinary career of a knight till his thirtieth year. Then, dissatisfied with the life he was living, he had recourse repeatedly for guidance to a lay brother of Fountains named Sunnulph, a man of unusual holiness of life. Sunnulph promised his prayers: "Do you pray also," he said, "and let not your deeds hinder our common prayers." Like Ailred before him, Ralph found it hard to break with the past. At last, rising one morning early in the dawn, with the spiritual crisis of his life upon him, he entered a neighbouring chapel and standing before the crucifix besought God to direct his path into the way of eternal life. He heard a voice from the figure on the Cross: "And why comest thou not? Wherefore delayest thou so long?" Falling to the ground he replied with all his heart: "Behold, Lord, behold, I come!" When day broke he made his way to Sunnulph, told him what had occurred, and promised to follow his advice. The old man was silent for a few moments, then replied: "At Fountains shalt thou take the religious habit, and there, when thy race is run, shalt thou die."[2]

Ralph followed the call, and took the habit in the first years of Abbot Robert. Even as a novice he received clear indications of a special calling. Two of the incidents in his life, related by him to Hugh of Kirkstall, are worthy of a place in the record of English spirituality. The first is told by Hugh as follows:

On one occasion the man of God was standing in prayer and lo! during his prayer his soul was filled with light. Wonderful to relate, he saw the fear of God, and himself feared not! "Nothing", he said, "could be thought of or told more terrible, more fearful, than this fear. Yet I saw this fear without fearing myself, and I warded off the weight of fear—that weight which hangs over those who are lost."[3]

The second of his experiences finds many parallels in the lives and writings of the saints:

I am about to tell (says Hugh) of what I have often heard him relate; I tell it not without hesitation, but I think it should not be concealed. One Sunday, when the community were at Lauds, the psalm *Confitemini Domino* [Ps. 117, Vulgate] was being sung. When the man of God was carefully attending to the meaning of that psalm, the hand of the Lord was upon him and he saw a great

1 *Memorials of Fountains*, I, 116–17: "Et me intuens [Serlo], 'Tu,' inquit, 'frater, quae de sancto abbate Radulfo dicenda sunt, diligenter resolve. Nosti hominem; quanta virtutum eminencia in divinis et humanis rebus enituit.'...Tum ego:...'Totum me illi debeo, semperque debebo.'" Ralph was abbot 1190–1203.   2 *Mem. Fount.* 120.
3 *Mem. Fount.* 120. Cf. St John of the Cross, *Living Flame* (trans. Peers), III, 60–3.

and glorious sight, the Trinity itself in three persons. I asked him under what form or appearance that revelation was made. He answered: "Nothing was there of form or figure, and yet I saw in a blissful vision three Persons in Unity. I saw and knew the unbegotten Father, the only-begotten Son and the Holy Spirit proceeding from both. The vision lasted while two whole verses of the psalm were being completed.[1] From that moment no misfortune, no sadness has ever come to me which could not be mitigated by the remembrance of that vision.... And such a confidence and hope was poured into my soul by this showing, that I could never after doubt of my salvation."[2]

Though a contemplative, Ralph was also a ruler, and c. 1183 was chosen abbot of Kirkstall. Here he had to meet with misfortune, criticism and some material failure, though Hugh, who was his subject, bears witness to his skill as master of souls. At one moment, owing to inroads upon the property of the house, the monastic family was dispersed among other abbeys.[3] The merits of Ralph, however, were recognized, for c. 1190–1 he was elected abbot of Fountains. There he was a zealous superior, though he met with criticism from the general chapter, and Hugh records the charity with which he and his monks employed all their resources to help the victims of famine and plague in 1194.[4] He was also the friend and correspondent of Peter of Blois.[5] Once it happened that he fell seriously ill at Clairvaux at the time of annual chapter. His companion despaired of his life, but the abbot consoled him. Sunnulph, he said, had told him that he would die at Fountains. And so it came to pass.[6]

Ralph Haget was succeeded by John, a native of York and abbot of Louth Park before his return to Fountains. He was a man of generous and lovable character, and an able administrator; under his rule the numbers rose and it was necessary to make provision for the Masses of the numerous priests of the house by beginning the construction of the eastern transept of nine altars. But with him there is, we feel, something of a change from the more intense life of the young Fountains. His rule was marked by King John's attack upon the possessions of the Cistercians; a large sum of money was extracted which left Fountains so impoverished that the community was for a time dispersed. The basic resources of the abbey were, however, so great that it could weather the storm with little permanent trace of loss, and within a few years Abbot John was able to begin the new buildings of the church. With his death in 1211 the detailed

---

1 The Cistercian recitation of psalmody was very slow, and a pause, sometimes sufficient for a *Pater Noster* to be said, occurred at the division of each verse.

2 *Mem. Fount.* 121–2. We may compare St Teresa, *Interior Castle* (ed. Zimmermann, London, 1912), VII Mansion, i, § 9: "By some mysterious manifestation of the truth, the Three Persons of the Most Blessed Trinity reveal themselves, preceded by an illumination which shines on the spirit like a most dazzling cloud of light." *Ibid.* § 12: "...whenever she reflects on it she feels the companionship of the Blessed Trinity." Also *ibid.* ii, § 13.

3 *Fundacio Abbathie de Kyrkestall* [Thoresby Soc. IV], 182–3.

4 *Mem. Fount.* 123.

5 *Petri Blesensis Epistolae*, ed. Giles, *ep.* xxxi; cf. *ep.* cv.

6 *Mem. Fount.* 123–5.

history of Fountains, which we owe to the memory of Serlo and the diligence of Hugh of Kirkstall, comes to an end.[1]

IV

During the last quarter of the twelfth century, when the monastic orders in England had all but ceased to increase the number of their foundations, there continued to be a steady growth among the regular canons. Of the Gilbertines something has already been said. The Augustinians, or black canons, continued during the reign of Henry II to maintain the reputation of earlier years; the worth of certain houses in particular, such as St Osyth, Osney, Cirencester, Llanthony and Holy Trinity, London, was recognized on all hands,[2] and it is noteworthy that the family for the royal foundation of Waltham was drawn in almost equal proportions from the first three of these.[3] In the court circle, in particular, the canons were in favour. Besides Waltham, converted from a secular into a regular establishment and re-endowed by Henry in 1177 as part of his satisfaction for the murder of Becket, Lesnes in Kent was founded in 1178 by his justiciar Richard de Lucy,[4] brother of Walter of Battle, and the founder was himself clothed with the canon's habit before he died; a still greater legal luminary, Ralph Glanvill, had a few years previously (1171) founded Butley in Suffolk.[5] The Austin canons, at once the oldest and the least united of all the canonical institutes, did not as a rule send out colonies spontaneously; new houses were more generally either formed from a group of clerics who adopted the uses of some celebrated house or assembled from one or more existing establishments by a bishop or lay founder. Thus in one of these two ways there was often a real dependence of origin among the canons, but it counted for far less than among the monks and the

1 *Mem. Fount.* 125–8. The tradition at Fountains as to the date of death of Abbot John of York was uncertain, both 1209 and 1211 being given (*Mem. Fount.* 133); that the later date is correct is shown by the *Chronica de Mailros*, which *sub anno* 1211 records the blessing of an abbot of Fountains.

2 For St Osyth, to which William of Malmesbury gave such high praise (*v.s.* p. 175, n. 1), *v.* John of Salisbury, writing as secretary of Theobald *c.* 1160 (*PL*, CXCIX, *ep.* 39): "ecclesia illa...totam insulam nostram irradiat, etc."; for Cirencester, *v.* Gilbert Foliot, writing as bishop of London after 1163 (*PL*, CXC, *ep.* 256): "vestrae conversationis opinio ipsa meriti sanctitate ad omnes longe lateque diffusa est." Cf. *ep.* 255, where he alludes to the *difficultas ordinis vestri* and *arcta observantia*. For Holy Trinity, London, *v. ibid. ep.* 299: "ecclesia quae...late claruit, et odoris boni suavitatem emittendo ex se caeteris sui ordinis ecclesiis velut speculum quoddam et defaecatae religionis exemplar emicuit."

3 Six came from Cirencester, six from Osney, four from St Osyth (Benedict of Peterborough, I, 174); the first prior was a canon of Cirencester (Rad. Diceto, I, 420), the first abbot, blessed in 1184, was a canon of Osney (*Ann. Osen. s.a.*). For Waltham in general, *v.* W. Stubbs, *The Foundation of Waltham Abbey.*

4 Rad. Diceto, I, 425; Gervase, I, 277.

5 *Annal. Colecestrenses* (ed. Liebermann, *Ungedruckte Quellen*), *s.a.* 1171, 1188. Giraldus (IV, 244) tells us, *more suo*, that Glanvill passed over the claims of the black monks as gluttonous, and of the white as too avaricious.

Premonstratensians, and carried with it no rights of supervision or visitation.

Yet though the black canons continued steadily to increase, the most remarkable feature of the regular life in England between 1170 and 1216 was the multiplication of the abbeys of the white canons of Prémontré. These, as has been said above, were at their origin modelled very closely upon the Cistercians, save that they added missionary and parochial work to manual labour and liturgical prayer; their polity also resembled that of the white monks, and had a similar system of general chapter and visitation, but they were more strongly centralized upon general chapter and the abbot of Prémontré. Their rule of life was stricter than that of the normal black monk house. They had been introduced early into Scotland by King David at Dryburgh and elsewhere, and had entered England *c.* 1143–6 at Newhouse in Lincolnshire.[1] From Newhouse a small family of half a dozen sprang almost immediately, all in the north-eastern and north midland counties, but between 1155 and 1175 only two or three isolated foundations were made. Between the latter date and 1200, however, there was a fruitful second spring in which at least fifteen abbeys had their origin, and the movement continued during the reign of John and after. This new plantation was not confined to a single district; the houses were far apart, from Shap in Westmorland to Torre in Devon, and from Tallach in Carmarthen[2] to Dereham in Norfolk, but it is perhaps significant that out of the comparatively small total such districts as Derbyshire, Suffolk and Sussex, where there were few existing monasteries, should have more than their quota. The white canons, like the black, were in favour at court; Ralph Glanvill founded Leiston in Suffolk in 1182 as a pendant to his foundation of Butley eleven years before;[3] Hubert Walter, a clerk in the royal service not yet a bishop, founded West Dereham in 1188 on family property in Norfolk,[4] and it will be remembered that Innocent III made the proposal that the Lambeth college should be abandoned in favour of a house of white canons. The Premonstratensians, unlike the Augustinians, were a fully organized religious order with family relationships. Almost all the English houses derived from Newhouse, either directly or through Welbeck, which became the mother of a large family; Newhouse itself derived from Lisques in the Pas de Calais. Alone of the English abbeys Bradsole in

---

1 Cf. *Chronicon Angliae Petriburgense, s.a.* 1143.

2 There has been considerable confusion over Tallach, which has often been reckoned as a black monk house; the statements of Gerald of Wales are, however, precise, e.g. III, 361: "pauperis coenobii cujusdam in Menevensi diocesi de ordine canonico et Pratomonstrato"; cf. also *ibid.* IV, 143–5, 150. The abbot Iorwerth or Gervase was elected bishop of St David's in 1215.

3 *Annal. Colecestrenses, s.a.* 1183.

4 Ralph of Coggeshall, 160; mention is there made of Hubert Walter's proposal to found a Cistercian house, which also formed a topic of deliberation in chapter at Cîteaux; cf. *Statuta,* ed. Canivez, I, 285 (1203), n. 5; 303 (1204), n. 36.

Kent and Bayham in Sussex would appear to have sprung directly from Prémontré.[1]

Unfortunately, there is a complete dearth of intimate documents from which to draw a picture of the life of the English white canons of this epoch.[2] Isolated references suggest that the English houses, at least, had withdrawn in large measure from the missionary work that had formed part of the programme of St Norbert, and closely resembled the white monks, even in their successful sheep farming. In the last decades of the century, when so many of the bishops were at odds with the black monks, and when the clerks of the royal and other great households, such as Walter Map and Gerald of Wales, were bitter in their attacks upon the Cistercians, it was a commonplace to contrast the sobriety and regularity of the canons with the avarice and laxity of the monks.[3] The justice of the charges against the monks need not be discussed here, but it may be remarked that both black monks and Cistercians, who were always regarded *en bloc*, offered a very large target to their critics, whereas in the case of the canons, and especially of the black canons, it was possible to concentrate attention upon a few well-known and flourishing houses. Moreover, the canonical establishments were all comparatively young, and followed a detailed body of uses which, while often strict, were not physically exacting and did not put before the inmates a Rule in which custom or necessity was continually making breaches. They were also for the most part establishments moderate in size,[4] without wide and scattered estates and a complex of rights and immunities, and therefore had less incentive to adopt an exclusive and litigious attitude towards all outside their body; they had also less administrative contact with the world around them. Finally, their connection, at home and abroad, with the new education, at least in its more elementary forms, and with the new theology and spirituality, together with the direct contact which many of them made with the religious life of the people, gave them for a short while something of the prestige which the monasteries had enjoyed a century earlier, as it also made them more amenable to the requirements of founders and benefactors. As the event showed, they, and especially the white canons, were to be the conduit through which a part of the monastic ideal passed

1 Abbot Gasquet, in his introduction to vol. I of *Collectanea Anglo-Premonstratensia*, which he edited for the Royal Historical Society (Camden Soc. Third Series, vol. VI, 1904), gave a brief sketch of the spread of the order, together with a table of derivations (p. ix), taken from the notes of the eighteenth-century antiquary, Francis Peck, but several of Peck's dates are erroneous, and this, together with our ignorance as to his sources, deprives his table and Gasquet's account of some of their value.

2 The veil is, however, partially lifted during the early decades of the thirteenth century by the Chronicle of Dale Abbey in Derbyshire.

3 Gerald's criticisms and comparisons are considered below, ch. XXXIX.

4 Glanvill's arrangements for thirty-six canons at Butley and twenty-six at Leiston are perhaps typical of the normal practice (Giraldus, IV, 244–5); Henry's desire for eighty or a hundred at Waltham (Benedict of Peterborough, I, 174) would, if ever realized, have been most exceptional.

on its way of evolution into the partly monastic, partly apostolic and partly intellectual life of the Friars Preachers.[1]

Along with the canons, the nuns continued to multiply, and here again the increase was chiefly among those who followed the rule of one of the new orders. Of the thirty odd Cistercian nunneries which were in course of time established in England almost one-half date from the period 1175–1215, and practically all the less numerous houses of Austin and Premonstratensian canonesses are of the same age.[2] Finally, it was in 1177 that the old-established community of Amesbury, one of the nunneries of the Edgarine revival, was partially disbanded in consequence of a serious scandal, and its place taken by an abbess and nuns from Fontevrault,[3] who made of the place a home for vocations from among the great families, resembling in this respect the mother-house in France.

1 Cf. the excellent article *Preachers, Order of*, by Père Mandonnet in the *Catholic Encyclopedia*, and more fully in the same author's *S. Dominique* (2nd ed. by H. M. Vicaire).

2 These rough calculations are based on the lists and dates given by Dr Eileen Power, *Medieval English Nunneries*, Appendix IV, pp. 685–92.

3 Benedict of Peterborough, I, 135, 165. Twenty-four nuns came from Fontevrault in 1177.

CHAPTER XXI

THE REIGN OF JOHN AND THE FOURTH LATERAN COUNCIL
1199–1216

I

The disastrous reign of John, so full of controversy and frustration, was to end an epoch in English monastic history, but the first years of the new king brought little change, so far as the black monks were concerned, from the conditions that had prevailed under Richard. Though the controversies in which Coventry and Christ Church were engaged had ended, or were on the point of ending, in 1199, Evesham was in trouble and about to embark upon its great struggle against bishop and abbot, St Augustine's, Canterbury, was still actively carrying on its secular warfare for exemption, and one or two more houses were occupied with suits of one kind or another. All, likewise, had to bear their share in the exactions made necessary by the foreign relations and wars of the king. But on the whole the life of the Church in England was more peaceful under the control of the Justiciar Geoffrey FitzPeter and the Chancellor Hubert Walter than it had been in the days of Richard.[1]

Christ Church, Canterbury, in particular, after almost fifteen years of wearing controversy, enjoyed a brief space of rest in which relations with the archbishop were not only tranquil but cordial.[2] The period of calm, however, was not to last, and the origin of the great storm was to be found again at Canterbury, and was to bring an even more severe visitation upon the house.

Hubert Walter, who had long been ailing, died after an affectionate parting with his monks on 13 July 1205.[3] John was in Buckinghamshire, but hastened with the utmost speed to Canterbury, and immediately visited the cathedral monastery to discuss the election. The long illness of the late archbishop had given all the interested parties time to decide upon their attitude, and the old claims and counter-claims of monks and bishops were at once put forward, the monks claiming to be the sole electors with the right of choosing one of their own body, while the

---

1 Gervase of Canterbury, *Gesta Regum*, II, 95: "Anglia...agente...Huberto et Gaufrido filio Petri tranquilla pace gaudebat."

2 Gervase of Canterbury, *Actus Pontificum*, II, 412: "Post tantam dissensionem...tanta dilectio inter eos data est ut per Dei gratiam essent quasi cor unum et anima una."

3 For the authorities of the narrative in the following paragraphs, which differs in several respects from that given by Stubbs in his preface to vol. II of the *Historical Collections of Walter of Coventry*, xlix–lv, and followed by other historians, I may be permitted to refer to my article, *The Canterbury Election of 1205–6*, in *EHR*, LIII (1938), 211–20.

bishops claimed a share in the election and desired an archbishop who was not a monk. John, doubtless, had already decided to do all he could to secure the office for John de Gray, bishop of Norwich, upon whose complaisant obedience he could rely. For the moment, he gave fair words to the monks, and arranged with both them and the bishops that the election should be postponed till the beginning of December; shortly after, both monks and bishops appealed to Innocent III on the question of the rights of election. Meanwhile, as would seem all but certain, John decided to make use of the interval by approaching the pope with diplomacy and bribery in order to procure an order to the monks to elect John de Gray; in this he probably acted in collusion with the bishops. When the monks got wind of this move they also departed from the course of straightforward dealing, and decided to hold a secret and conditional election, so that, if Innocent showed signs of yielding to John, they might present him with a *fait accompli*. Accordingly, they went through the procedure of nomination and election in their chapter, and the subprior, Reginald, appeared as the choice of the majority, though subsequent events showed that the community was by no means unanimous. Nevertheless, they held to their intention, and Reginald was given official documents of election, but at the same time was put under oath not to produce them unless it seemed likely that the pope was about to grant the king's request; he was then despatched to Rome with companions, ostensibly to forward the appeal against the bishops. On arriving at Rome, he immediately announced himself as the archbishop-elect and begged confirmation from Innocent, either because he and those with him sincerely felt that the interests of Canterbury demanded such a step or because, as seems more likely, he was personally ambitious for the archbishopric. His demand was met by the proctor of the suffragan bishops, who asserted that the election had been made after appeal and without the necessary co-operation of the hierarchy. Innocent therefore stayed proceedings and summoned evidence from England on the points in dispute.

While these things were happening in Rome, developments were also taking place in England. The king, having received information from his agents abroad of Reginald's action, demanded an account of the matter from the monks of Canterbury and used threatening language. They denied having made an election, and in order to substantiate their assertion and escape the consequences of John's displeasure, agreed to elect his candidate John de Gray. This second election took place on 11 December 1205, and a deputation left England forthwith to ask for confirmation from the pope. Arrived in Rome, they were confronted by Reginald, on whose behalf it was alleged that the second election had been made while the first was still *sub judice* and, moreover, that it had been transacted under the influence of fear. Innocent therefore quashed the election of de Gray, whereupon his supporters from Canterbury turned against Reginald and bore witness that his election had been conditional, and that the condition had not been verified. Baffled once more in his attempt to reach a conclusion, Innocent now summoned out to Rome a third deputation from Canterbury, who were to receive full powers from the convent to elect again should the subprior's election be declared void. In their presence, in December 1206, he first decided that the monks had the sole right of election; he then quashed the election of Reginald as made during an appeal and with conditions that had not been verified; finally, he called upon the delegates to elect once more. After considerable debate, their choice ultimately fell upon the English cardinal, Stephen Langton, whom Innocent, after a delay of six months in which he used every endeavour to recommend Langton to the king, consecrated himself and invested with the pallium.

The further history of the struggle, so far as it concerns John and Langton, belongs to English national history, but its consequences for the monks must be briefly told. Whatever their previous divisions, they held firmly by the action of their representatives in Rome; John therefore sent his agents to seize their properties and occupy their buildings, measures which either directly or indirectly drove all the able-bodied monks into exile, only a few aged and invalids remaining.[1] The body of the community crossed the channel and found refuge at St Bertin, a few remained in England, though not at Canterbury, and were regarded with suspicion by the rest;[2] all the possessions of the house were seized and wasted by the king. The ultimate outcome of his action was the Interdict of 23 March 1208. Thus Christendom was presented with the spectacle of the cathedral, so recently made a cynosure by the death and miracles of Becket, left desolate, for John's attempt to fill the choir with monks drawn from the neighbouring houses of St Augustine's, Rochester and Faversham,[3] even if at all successful, could have been no compensation for the wholesale removal of the lawful inhabitants. How long the exile lasted is not clear since, no doubt owing to the dispersal, the various memorials of the history of the house, hitherto so abundant, cease with the election of Langton and are resumed only in the reign of Henry III. But as the prior, Geoffrey, died in Rome in 1213, it may be presumed that full restoration was not made till the Interdict was lifted in that year, and this, indeed, is

1 Gervase, *Gesta Regum*, II, 100: "Expulsi sunt itaque omnes monachi...idus Julii et mari transito a conventu sancti Bertini honorifice suscepti sunt." Cf. also *Chronicle of Barnwell* (ap. Walter of Coventry, II, 199) and the anonymous *Canterbury Chronicle* (ap. Gervase, II, lxiii).

2 The *Ann. Winton.*, *s.a.* 1207, alone gives any figures; sixty-four monks are said to have been expelled. This number, even if correct, presumably does not include the invalids or those still at Rome.

3 This attempt is mentioned only by the Bury annals printed (no. xi) by Liebermann, *Ungedruckte Quellen*, *sub anno* 1207. According to these, monks from St Augustine's, Faversham and Rochester were drafted into Canterbury.

stated in general terms by some of the best informed of the chroniclers of the time.[1]

II

Meanwhile, the reign was proving a time of peculiar misfortune for the white monks. Indeed, to find any kind of parallel to the state of insecurity in which they found themselves, it is necessary to go back to the anarchy of Stephen's reign. If there was less actual armed violence under John, the moral and material losses were probably heavier and more general among the religious orders, and none suffered more severely than the Cistercians, who had hitherto succeeded in maintaining a privileged position of immunity save in the exceptional circumstances of Richard's imprisonment.

Their troubles began early in the reign. John, returning from Normandy in 1200, demanded an aid from the whole realm in order to pay a large sum to Philip of France for peace; it was levied at the rate of three shillings a carucate.[2] Being himself in the north, the king endeavoured to extract a contribution from a number of Cistercian abbots; they demurred, pleading constant precedent, and appealed to Hubert Walter, then chancellor and justiciar, who endeavoured with some success to placate the king; in June 1200, shortly before John left England, a lump sum of a thousand marks was offered on behalf of the order, but was indignantly refused by the king as insufficient. Shortly after, the general chapter at Cîteaux decided to address a request to Hubert Walter, begging him to assist by every means in his power in the preservation of Cistercian immunity. On John's return from Normandy at the beginning of October he proceeded to harass the white monks in every possible way, and gave directions that after a fortnight all beasts of theirs found pasturing within the royal forests should be confiscated. At this crisis Hubert Walter proved himself a steadfast friend to the Cistercians.[3] John was to be at Lincoln for the feast of St Edmund (19 November) in order to receive homage of the king of Scotland; the archbishop therefore summoned the abbots to meet him there, that he might lay their case before the king. When they met, their counsels were divided. Some wished to placate the king by the offer of money; others were unwilling to make any concession that might serve as a precedent. When they were hesitating, a leader came

1 [Gervase], *Gesta Regum continuata*, II, 108: "Monachi Cantuarienses a transmarinis redeunt, maneriis suis...plene restitutis." Cf. [Walter of Coventry], II, 213.

2 Radulphus de Coggeshall, *Chronicon Anglicanum*, 101. The author, whose autograph is preserved, was Ralph, abbot of Coggeshall from 1207 (cf. *Chron. Coggeshall*. 162–3); his narrative, which is full, is therefore entirely contemporary with the facts it records.

3 Whatever judgment may be passed on Hubert Walter's character and spiritual outlook, all the evidence goes to show that he stood by his word when once it was given. Cf. also Matthew Paris, *Chron. Maj.*, s.a. 1199: "Erat...archiepiscopus vir profundi pectoris, et in regno singularis columna stabilitatis et sapientiae incomparabilis"; *Statuta Cist.* (ed. Canivez), I, 259 (1200), n. 55: "tantum virum et Ordini nostro gratum et acceptum."

forward in the person of the abbot of Meaux, Alexander of Ford, the rival of Gerald of Wales and protégé and sometime secretary of Hubert Walter, who had long enjoyed the archbishop's patronage.[1] Producing a copy of the strongly worded letter of appeal from the general chapter, and no doubt assuring them that Hubert Walter intended to fight the case out, he persuaded them to be resolute in refusing to make any contribution.[2]

The meeting with John was postponed owing to political negotiations, and did not take place till 26 November. On that day, after prolonged discussions of which the chronicler gives a vivid picture, the king decided to waive all his demands, to beg pardon of the abbots for the damage he had caused, and, beyond this, to found an abbey where his body should ultimately find a resting-place. This unexpected issue to the negotiations, due in part to the advocacy of Hubert Walter, was attributed by contemporaries to another agency. Only a few days before the meeting between John and the abbots at Lincoln, Hugh of Avalon had died after a long illness at his London house (16 or 17 November) and his body was brought to his episcopal city and buried in the presence of the magnates already assembled there. Hugh's biographer, and doubtless others besides, saw in the unexpected clemency of the king an instance of the power of the saintly bishop, who had always been a peacemaker.[3]

The Cistercians had thus weathered the first storm, and John's promise was duly honoured by the foundation of Beaulieu in Hampshire, whither a community of thirty came from the fountain-head of Cîteaux at Whitsuntide, 1204.[4] For some years the white monks continued to enjoy good fortune, and were alone in escaping taxation as late as 1207.[5] When the Interdict was pronounced in 1208 they acted on the presumption of privilege and continued the liturgy as usual *januis clausis*, but after a year they were enjoined by Innocent to observe it in full, and the injunction was chronicled with some satisfaction by less privileged bodies, who go on to relate that when the ban was slightly relaxed in 1209, with leave for a

1 Rad. Coggeshall. 105: "Abbas de Mealse, quondam domni archiepiscopi notarius, et idcirco ei semper valde familiaris." Cf. also *infra*, p. 667.

2 Although the Coggeshall chronicler refers to the letter of general chapter as if it were a piece of news to the abbots, they can scarcely have been ignorant that a letter had been despatched, and indeed its receipt by Hubert Walter may be presumed to have supplied him with a motive for summoning the meeting. But until the abbot of Meaux, his confidant, took the lead they may well have been unaware of the archbishop's real intentions.

3 The author of the *Magna Vita Hugonis* implies (378) that explicit appeal was made to Hugh's memory in the negotiations: "Abbatibus Cisterciensis ordinis...exactionem pecuniariam...funditus ad honorem sancti...[rex] remisit." All agree that the issue was unexpected, e.g. *Ann. Margan*, *s.a.* 1200: "Non sine grandi admiratione omnium gratiam regis invenerunt."

4 Their arrival is recorded by various Cistercian chroniclers, e.g. *Chron. Stanlei.* (*ap.* William of Newburgh, II, 507): "Hoc anno [1204] circa Pentecosten venit conventus novus cum proprio abbate de Cisterciis in Angliam ad locum qui vocatur Belli-locus." Rad. Coggeshall. 147: "Conventum xxx monachorum fecit adduci de domo Cisterciensi." Cf. also *Ann. Waverl.*; *Ann. Margan*; *Chron. Jo. Oxenede*; *Chron. Ang. Petrib.*; Matthew Paris, *Chron. Maj.*, *s.a.* 1204. The thirty presumably included *conversi*.

5 *Chron. Stanlei.* (Will. Newb. II, 509).

weekly conventual Mass, the Cistercians were excepted by way of punishment for their previous contumacy.[1] Worse than this, however, was to follow. In 1210 John, now desperately in need of funds and unwilling to strain the laity any further, demanded an aid of the clergy secular and regular. The demand was put before the Cistercians at York, apparently before the Irish expedition of the summer of 1210, and was refused by the abbots as contrary to their liberties and to precedent,[2] whereupon John forbade them to go overseas to attend general chapter, where they might be likely to stir up disaffection.[3] On his return in the autumn he proceeded to drastic measures. Besides imposing a heavy fine or ransom on their estates, he ordered his justiciars and foresters to give no protection or rights to the Cistercians.[4] The gross amount extracted by way of ransom is given in widely differing sums by the various chronicles, and though we possess an official record of receipt, it by no means follows that this represents all that was forthcoming;[5] all agree that the burden was crushing, and in the few instances where the sums levied from individual abbeys are recorded, they are astonishingly large, even when considerably discounted. Only two houses escaped: Beaulieu, which John respected as his own foundation, and Margam, where he had twice that very year enjoyed Cistercian hospitality on his way to and from Ireland.[6] Rich as many of the abbeys were, it is not surprising that the exaction of these large sums brought them to the verge of ruin. One annalist, indeed, and that not a white monk, writes that John destroyed all the Cistercian houses and that

1 E.g. Jo. Oxenede, *s.a.* 1208: "Albi monachi celebrare praesumpserunt, unde excommunicati fuerunt." 1209: "Albi monachi hac privabantur indulgentia [*sc.* of the weekly Mass] quia in principio interdicti papa inconsulto celebrare praesumpserunt." *V.* also the relevant letters of Innocent appended to the Canterbury chronicle in Gervase, II, xcvi *seqq.* But cf. *Annals of Bury*, ap. Liebermann, *Ungedruckte Quellen*, *s.a.* 1209.

2 *Chron. Stanlei.* (Will. Newb. II, 510) records the meeting and demand at York and states that all royal charters were seized from the monks. The *Ann. Waverl.* and *Ann. Margan*, *s.a.* 1210, say "convenerat [rex] enim eos priusquam transfretaret de auxilio praestando", whereas his stern measures against them were only taken after his return. The Margam annals are particularly reliable for this year, as John was the guest of the abbey.

3 So Matthew Paris, *Chron. Maj.*, *s.a.* 1210. Only the abbot of Margam was allowed to go, as John Oxenede tells us, *s.a.* 1211: "Solus...abire...ad capitulum Cisterciense generale permittitur." This is an interesting confirmation of the Margam chronicle, *v. infra*, note 6. Gervase (II, 105) notes that even the abbot of Beaulieu was kept at home.

4 For the order to the justiciars *v. Chron. Stanlei.* (Will. Newb. II, 511).

5 E.g. *Eulog. Hist.*, *s.a.* 1210, 9,300 marks; *Ann. Margan*, *s.a.* 1210, 27,000; *Chron. Stanlei.* (Will. Newb. II, 512) and *Chron. Melsa*, 345–6, 30,000; *Ann. Waverl.*, *s.a.* 1210, 33,300 and over; *Ann. Bermund.*, *s.a.* 1210, 33,333 [!]; Jo. Oxenede, *s.a.* 1210, 40,000; Roger of Wendover, II, 57, "xl millia libras argenti". For the official receipt, *v. Red Book of the Exchequer*, II, 772–3: "Recepta a Rege Joanne...tempore interdicti...de albis monachis 24,027½ marcae." As for individual houses, Meaux is said to have paid 1000 marks (*Chron.* I, 328); Louth Park 1680 (*Chron., s.a.* 1210), which represented "summa dampnorum...in donis, depredationibus et jacturis"; Fountains 1200 (*Monasticon*, V, 305 n. L). It may be recalled that 1000 marks for the whole body was the original offer to the king in 1200.

6 *Chron. Margan*, *s.a.* 1210: "Duae tamen domus...ab hac exactione tunc immunes fuere, de Margan scilicet...eo quod hospitatus ibi fuisset rex cum exercitu...et de Bello Loco."

all the monks were dispersed.[1] This is the language of exaggeration; but it is certain that a number of the English houses, and those not the least important in the order, were unable to maintain themselves and had to disband for the time.[2] Among such extreme cases were the Yorkshire Meaux and the Surrey Waverley, the latter the first of all the Cistercian settlements in England and the mother of a numerous family. The exiles found homes where best they might with monks, canons, nuns and lay-folk; in the case of Meaux, where alone details are available, we are told that some went to St Mary's, York, which thus could heap coals of fire upon the grandchildren of its revolutionaries, others to the canons at Bridlington, others to Cistercian houses in Scotland, others finally to towns and castles up and down the country—for no other Cistercian abbey in England had substance enough to share with them.[3] As another class of the population, the Jews, had fared equally ill at John's hands, the unusual spectacle was provided of white monks and Hebrews begging alms simultaneously from all and sundry—a spectacle that would presumably have been viewed with some satisfaction by Walter Map.[4] This extreme indigence did not last long; in some cases the crops of the following year may have set the communities on their feet again;[5] but they had not yet done with troubles. In 1212 they were accused of hostility to the count of Toulouse, and besides a heavy fine they were forced to provide chariots and horses for the king.[6] Thus for the Cistercians the reign of John was one of almost continuous material misfortunes, though these were partly redeemed in the long run by the concession to them in fact of what they already had by right of privilege, the enjoyment of the tithes of all their lands.

The black monks did not, as did the Cistercians, incur any special displeasure as a body. They had, however, to make heavy contributions to the king, above all in 1209–10, and all suffered from the Interdict.[7] A

---

1 *Ann. Bermund.*, s.a. 1210: "[Rex] destruxit omnes domos alborum monachorum per totam Angliam...ita quod predicti monachi per diversas domos dispersi sunt."
2 *Chron. Stanlei.* (Will. Newb. II, 512): "Plurimae abbatiae destructae sunt." Jo. Oxenede, s.a. 1210: "A quibusdam eorum domibus quicquid haberent tulit."
3 *Chron. Melsa*, I, 353; cf. *Chron. Stanlei. loc. cit.*
4 Jo. Oxenede, s.a. 1210: "Hoc anno res inaudita contigit, scilicet monachi Cistercienses et Judaei...hostiatim sibi mendicabant victualia." For Map's oath to do justice to all save Jews and Cistercians, *v.* Giraldus, IV, 219, cited *infra*, p. 675.
5 Meaux was functioning again by 1 November 1211 (*Chron. Melsa*, I, 354).
6 Rad. Coggeshall. 164; *Ann. Waverl.*, s.a. 1212 (p. 268); *Chron. Stanlei.*, s.a. 1212 (Will. Newb. II, 513). Their serfs were taken away and each abbey had to supply one or more *carecta longa cum quinque equis optimis* (cf. *Ann. Dunstab.*, s.a. 1210; *Ann. Waverl.*, s.a. 1212). Individual houses suffered more severely still, e.g. Tiltey and Coggeshall (continuation of Ralph of Coggeshall, 177).
7 Reliable chroniclers assert that in 1209 John seized into his hands the property of all the black monks. E.g. *Chron. Barnwell* (*ap.* Walter of Coventry, II, 200): "omnium nigrorum monachorum possessiones a regiis ballivis quasi fisco describerentur." Cf. *Ann. Waverl.*, s.a. 1209, for details. According to Roger of Wendover (II, 57), who wrote *c.* 1235: "summa...excrevisse fertur ad c. millia libras sterlingas." Gloucester alone is said (*Hist. Glocestr.* 24) to have contributed: "DM et C [? marcas] caretas viii equorum", and to have sold some chalices. Cf. *Chron. Barnwell* (*ap.* Walter of Coventry, II, 200–1).

few houses suffered even more directly; thus John took St Albans "into his hand" as if vacant *c.* 1209 although an abbot was reigning,[1] and gave Thorney to the bishop of Ely, while Croyland had to stand an attack in the troubles of 1215–16.

III

During the fifteen years which elapsed between his election as pope and the issue of the bull *Vineam Domini Sabaoth* in 1213 convoking the Fourth Lateran Council Innocent III had had ample opportunity of observing the crisis in the life of the black monk houses in England and of studying its causes. As cardinal he had doubtless followed from his retirement at Anagni the long struggles of the monks of Canterbury, Coventry and Glastonbury against their bishops; as pope he had had to take repeated cognizance of the cases of Glastonbury and Evesham, as well as of less celebrated disputes, such as that between the monks of Durham and their bishop,[2] while the Canterbury election of 1205 had brought him once more into touch with the monks of Christ Church. Between 1190 and 1207, indeed, there can have been few months, save in the summer heats, when parties of monks from one of these or other houses were not in Rome. In all these cases very much must have been said behind the scenes and in the intervals of the courts, and Innocent's alert and retentive mind would have come by degrees to form something of a complete picture of the conditions in England. Thus in the Evesham case alone, though he allowed the legal issues to be slowly debated and made no disciplinary move, he must have known well all that Mauger could tell or gossip report of the character of Roger Norreys and of the futility of the various attempts made by the monks to bring him to book or to extract from him a capitulation. Nor can Gerald of Wales have been the only well-informed and hostile critic of the monks who rehearsed for the pope's benefit a catalogue of monastic misdemeanours and put forward some of the remedies which seemed to him desirable.[3] In the latter half of his pontificate English affairs bulked even larger at Rome, and though they were now ecclesiastical and political rather than monastic in character, they must have given many occasions for the discussion of the needs of the monasteries. In fact, during the whole pontificate of Innocent III it is not merely national vanity in historians that has led them to think that England, as at more than one other moment of our rough island-story, occupied a

1 *GASA*, I, 236.
2 Cf. *Innoc. Regist.* VII, 118 (*PL*, CCXV, 405).
3 Gerald was thrice in Rome between 1198 and 1203 when engaged in his assertion of metropolitan rights for Menevia, to which see he claimed to have been elected. He had several intimate conversations with Innocent in the gardens of the Lateran, and presented the pope with his *Gemma Ecclesiastica*, from the perusal of which, if the author may be believed, Innocent derived great satisfaction. Cf. Giraldus, *de Rebus a se Gestis* (*Opera*, I, 119) and *de Invectionibus* (*Opera*, III, 252, 266, 289).

place in the thoughts of a pope not in strict proportion to the size of the nation in the commonwealth of Roman Christendom.

The black monk houses, perhaps more than any other members of the religious commonwealth, were a prey to the centrifugal forces at work in all the degrees of English ecclesiastical life at the time.[1] Some were freeing themselves, or had already freed themselves, from the control of the diocesan; others had made some constitutional arrangement with their bishop (if they were at a cathedral) or with their abbot; all were wholly independent of each other and of any higher authority within the monastic body. Each, in all matters of discipline, observance and ritual, was a law unto itself, for no organ of legislation existed such as the white monks possessed in the general chapter at Cîteaux and the more recent orders of canons in a major abbot or Master and chapter, nor had there been in England any of those voluntary associations in imitation of the Cistercians such as had been seen among some of the monasteries of north-eastern France and Germany, and especially in the neighbourhood of Rheims and Sens, where a federation of houses had held general chapters with some regularity ever since their first meeting in 1131 which had so provoked the Cluniac cardinal Matthew of Albano.[2]

Yet already for several decades critics of the black monks had been calling out for the introduction among them of a system of visitation and legislation. Innocent himself had from the early years of his pontificate worked towards this end. Already in 1203 he had caused the abbots directly under his jurisdiction in Tuscany, the march of Ancona and the duchy of Spoleto to meet in chapter and appoint visitors, and in the same year he had approved of similar action on the part of the archbishop of Lund in Denmark. In 1210 he implemented a federation of the canons regular of the archdiocese of York.[3] Above all, he consistently strengthened

---

1 This disorder has received too little attention from English historians, who have been preoccupied by their interest in Richard's crusade and the political events of his reign and that of John. But the words of a German scholar, Dr Else Gütschow (*Innocenz III und England*, 17), are only slightly over-emphatic: "Die Kirche des Landes ist durch eine Reihe erbitterter Konflikte gespalten. . . . Jedermanns Hand hat sich gegen jedermann erhoben. Die Erzdiözesen. . . . sind durch eine mehr als hundertjährige Eifersucht getrennt. . . St David Ansprüche macht, zu einem dritten Erzbistum erhoben zu werden. . . . Die Suffragane sind nicht gewillt, sich den Metropoliten zu fügen. . . . Die Archidiakone wieder klagen bei König und Papst gegen die Übergriffe der Bischöfe. Am schlimmsten aber steht es um das Verhältnis der Klöster zu ihren Bischöfen. Jede Disziplin ist in den einzelnen Diözesen verschwunden."

2 For these and all early reunions *v*. Dom Ursmer Berlière, *Les chapitres généraux de l'ordre de S. Benoît* in *RB*, XVIII (1901), 364–98; XIX (1902), 38–75, 268–78, 374–411. These articles were reprinted in *Mélanges d'histoire bénédictine*, 4 série, Maredsous, 1902, 52–171. Outside the Rheims-Sens area the meetings before the pontificate of Innocent III are negligible. A shorter sketch of the movement is given by W. A. Pantin, *The General and Provincial Chapters of the English Black Monks*, in *Transactions of the Royal Historical Society*, 4th Series, X (1927), especially pp. 203–5.

3 For all these *v*. the most valuable articles of Dom U. Berlière, *Innocent III et la ré-organisation des monastères bénédictins* in *RB*, XXXII (1920), 22–42, 145–59; in particular the second article, pp. 157–8.

the hands of bishops throughout Europe whom he saw to be willing and able to exercise their primitive right and duty of visitation and correction;[1] thus Mauger of Worcester had received full powers in 1202, and Peter of Winchester, whom the pope himself consecrated at Rome in 1205, received a similar commission;[2] indeed, it was Innocent's policy to issue these and similar enabling powers to all bishops of whose zeal he had personal knowledge. But without the sanction of a Council he was in no position to impose or enforce new constitutional machinery on the monks in general.

When in 1213 he was able at last to issue the first bull of convocation to a general council, it was with a deep sense of the perils and needs, external and internal, of the Church, that he published the *Vineam Domini Sabaoth*. To most contemporary witnesses the external and political disturbances, both in Europe and in the East, may have obscured the inner crisis, but Innocent, though he had not the direct vision of a saint, had deepened in spiritual earnestness during his pontificate and seems to have realized, at least in large part, at once the danger that threatened the loosely knit body of Christendom of losing the order and uniformity that the rediscovered law had begun to give, and also the insufficiency of the methods of government by legates, appeals to the Curia and judges delegate which had been the chief instruments of the Gregorian party of reform a century before. In any case, in the Fourth Lateran Council he promulgated a whole series of canons containing no startling disciplinary or doctrinal developments, but making into law for all time what had hitherto been preached without sanctions as the normal Christian practice, and giving formally to bishops and other superiors the powers which had always been theirs by the Roman canons but which had so often lapsed through disuse or opposition.

When the Council met in November 1215, two years after the bull of convocation, it was attended by more than four hundred bishops and almost double that number of ruling abbots and priors. Innocent, who, though only fifty-five years of age, seems to have felt that his life was nearing its close, struck a peculiarly solemn note in the allocution which took for its text the words with which Christ prefaced His last charge to His apostles: "With desire have I desired to eat this Pasch with you before I die", and the pope opened his discourse with the phrases of the Apostle: "For me to live is Christ and to die is gain." The business had been most carefully prepared, and the fathers ratified in a surprisingly short time a multitude of propositions and canons covering a wide field of doctrine, morals and discipline. No record, unfortunately, exists of

---

1 The sentence in the text was written before reading the words of Dom Berlière, *art. cit.* 147: "C'est surtout par l'épiscopat qu'Innocent III veut mener à bonne fin le relèvement des monastères."

2 *Chron. Evesh.* 109; *Innoc. Regist.* VIII, 142 (*PL*, CCXV, 722).

the manner in which the schemata were produced or of those who took the lead in their formation. As regards the canon affecting the black monks, the alacrity with which it was received and applied in England, perhaps alone of all European countries, and the precise manner in which it met needs which had been long recognized, create a strong presumption that English minds had a share in its elaboration. Langton may well have taken a part in its remote preparation, as may one or two of the exiled bishops such as Mauger of Worcester; subsequent events show the abbots of St Albans, Bury, St Augustine's, Evesham and Tewkesbury (the last two monks of Worcester) as the leaders in its execution.[1] Several of these, and other English abbots, are known to have been in Rome for the Council or before and may have been consulted by the pope.[2]

The relevant canon, the twelfth in order, set up for both the black monks and the black canons a legislative and visitatorial organization, and made of the houses of each ecclesiastical province a single body.[3] A triennial general chapter was instituted, to be attended by all abbots and ruling priors. The first of the series, being a novel venture, was to have as presidents four abbots, two Cistercian invited by the black monks and two others co-opted by the two first, who were to order the business and see to the promulgation of the decrees. Besides issuing disciplinary measures the chapter was to appoint delegates to visit all houses of the province, whether of men or of women, following their common rule, and these delegates were to have full powers of correction; their authority extended as well over exempt as over non-exempt monasteries, but with regard to the latter the canon of the council presupposed a similar visitation from the diocesan. This legislation was confessedly based on Cistercian practice; in one important respect, however, the powers of chapter and visitors were to be less than among the white monks. Should the visitors consider the deposition of an abbot advisable, they had no authority to proceed with the case themselves; they were to advise the bishop; should he fail to act, they were to carry the matter to the Holy See.

By this legislation, which was duly put into execution within three years, the black monks of England became for the first time in their

1 For this and the early working of the new machinery v. *Chapters of the English Black Monks*, vol. I, ed. by W. A. Pantin for the Royal Historical Society (Camden Society, 3rd series, vol. XLV, 1931).

2 Cf. *GASA*, I, 261; *Chron. Will. Thorne*, 1866; *Chron. Evesh.* 205; *Ann. Wigorn.*, s.a. 1215, 1216.

3 Mansi, *Sacrorum Conciliorum Collectio*, XXII, 999–1002: "In singulis regnis sive provinciis fiat de triennio in triennium...commune capitulum abbatum atque priorum abbates proprios non habentium...ad quod universi conveniant...apud unum de monasteriis ad hoc aptum...capitulum aliquot certis diebus continue juxta morem Cisterciensis ordinis celebretur, in quo diligens habeatur tractatus de reformatione ordinis et observatione regulari.... Ordinentur etiam in eodem capitulo religiosae et circumspectae personae, quae singulas abbatias...vice nostra studeant visitare, corrigentes, etc....Porro diocesani episcopi monasteria sibi subjecta ita studeant reformari, ut cum ad ea praedicti visitatores accesserint, plus in eis invenerint quod commendatione quam quod correctione sit dignum."

history a canonically organized body, and the absolute independence and autonomy of the houses ceased, never to be resumed. Although the immediate results were not such as to arouse general attention, and though even the permanent effects, so far at least as the Middle Ages were concerned, were not considerable enough to counterbalance the general trend of social and religious life in England, the year 1215 must nevertheless be considered a most important landmark in monastic history; it was the moment when the *ordo monasticus* of the black monks, from being canonically no more than a way of life within the framework of the Church of the country, became in part, at least, an "order", a corporate group, however loose the bond and however great the freedom left to the constituent parts.

The circumstances of the decades that followed the death of John were to widen the gulf that separated the thirteenth from the twelfth century in England. The loss of Normandy, the long and peaceful reign of Henry III, the emergence of a new type of great diocesan bishops, the growing importance of the theological schools, the rise of the university of Oxford, the coming of the friars—all these were to have a great if indirect influence upon the monks. But the greatest single influence upon their domestic life was that of the twelfth canon of the Lateran Council.

CHAPTER XXII

THE CHARTERHOUSE OF WITHAM
AND HUGH OF AVALON

I

The tenth century, which saw the widest diffusion and the most elaborate development of black monachism, witnessed also a series of endeavours on the part of men who, in Italy and France, desired to find complete solitude and extreme austerity of life. These endeavours, as has been recounted, resulted at the very end of the century in the establishment at several centres (of which Molesme-Cîteaux was the most celebrated) of new monastic or canonical institutes alongside of the old which spread widely but which, while remaining at least for some generations stricter and more observant than the old monachism, nevertheless abandoned by degrees much of their primitive intransigence and exclusiveness, and modified their original aims. A few, however, of the earliest families belonging to the movement of return to the desert succeeded in establishing organizations which, though never attaining great numerical strength, changed little if at all from their original scheme of life. Such were the hermits of Camaldoli and the monks of Vallombrosa in Italy, who sent no colonies as far north as England; such, in southern France, were the poor brothers of God of the Chartreuse who, alone of the quasi-eremitical companies of the eleventh century north of the Alps, developed into a widespread order which, though never numerous, has never seriously threatened to decline from its first fervour, still less to become extinct.[1] These came late to England, and during the period covered by these pages were settled only at a single spot, and that a remote one far from the centres of national life. An account of their coming must nevertheless find a place here, for apart from the considerable significance which Witham came to have in the religious world of the day, it gave a great bishop and saint to the Church in England, and was the seed whence

---

1 The best English account of early Carthusian history is that given by Miss M. Thompson, *The Carthusian Order in England*; this is throughout a careful and reliable work. The indispensable sources for a study of Carthusian origins are *PL*, CLII, CLIII (Life of St Bruno and works of Guigo I, with Dom Le Masson's notes); the very rare *Storia critica-cronologica...del ordine Cartusiano* of Tromby (10 vols. Naples, 1773–9; this work is not in the library of the British Museum and was not used by Miss Thompson); *Annales Ordinis Carthusiensis* of Dom le Couteulx (8 vols. Montreuil, 1887–1901). Much has recently been done by Dom A. Wilmart to clarify the complicated history of early Carthusian documents, especially in the articles *La Chronique des Premiers Chartreux*, in *Revue Mabillon*, 2e série, no. 22 (1926), and *Les Écrits spirituels des deux Guiges*, in *Revue d'Ascétique et de Mystique*, t. 5 (reprinted in *Auteurs spirituels et Textes dévots*, 217–60). There is an unusually excellent article on the Carthusians, well-documented and critical, by Dom Raymund Webster in the *Catholic Encyclopedia*.

sprang a small but remarkable family destined to pass from the English scene with a singularly noble end.

The founder of the congregation of the poor brothers of God belongs to that numerous body of men who, between 1050 and 1100, left positions of security and dignity in great monasteries or churches to establish themselves in poverty and simplicity in the forest or waste. A canon and celebrated teacher at Rheims, Bruno left his career *c.* 1080 and joined for a short time the hermits of the forest of Colan, who had taken Robert of Molesme for their leader. Departing in 1084 with two others, he was established by Hugh, bishop of Grenoble, on the site which was to become renowned as the Grande Chartreuse. From there he was summoned to Rome, and after some years of service to the Apostolic See retired to Calabria, where he established other colonies of hermits and died in 1101, never having revisited his foundation in France. Bruno therefore, though he originated the community of the Chartreuse, was not the legislator of the Carthusians. At the time of his death his hermits differed little, if at all, from the many similar groups up and down France and Italy, most of which were destined to die away or to be absorbed by larger existing institutions; they had no code of rules and a certain latitude was left to individual choice. They were saved to the Church as a religious order by the fifth prior, Guigo I, who held office from 1110 till 1136. Guigo, the friend and correspondent of Bernard and Peter the Venerable, had a great capacity for attracting and training recruits; he founded six Charterhouses in France; above all, he committed to writing in full detail the Customs of the Grande Chartreuse, and these, modified but little by subsequent practice and the statutes of general chapter, have ever since been the basis of the Carthusian life.[1]

As is well known, the Carthusian order throughout the centuries up to the present time has retained, alike in form and in spirit, its original way of life more fully than any other medieval religious institute; it alone has never needed or suffered reform: *nunquam reformata quia nunquam deformata*. This long stability has been secured by a jealous and exact adherence to a code which from the beginning was in the main a written account of actual practice, not the enunciation of an ideal. Never since its early origins has the Charterhouse made any attempt to temper the wind of its discipline to the shorn lamb, or to adapt itself to the spirit of the age; the claim which was made as early as Ailred's day in the strict Cistercian monastery of Rievaulx, that an abbey should be a world in miniature, a haven of charity for every type of character, has never found an echo in a Charterhouse; throughout the history of the order failure to

---

[1] Guigo's *Consuetudines* are in *PL*, CLIII, coll. 635 *seqq.* Miss Thompson, *The Carthusian Order*, 20 *seqq.*, gives an adequate summary. The earlier and briefer customs of St Bruno's foundation at Squillace are in *PL*, CLIII, coll. 1149 *seqq.* The *Statuta Antiqua*, the early decrees of chapter, are *ibid.* 1125 *seqq.*; they also are analysed by Miss Thompson.

satisfy upon any point of the rule, even one least bound up with moral or spiritual principles, has always been fatal to the hopes of an aspirant. As a result, though the Charterhouse may have lost not a few recruits of seeming promise, it has ensured to itself a steady succession of subjects possessing all the bodily and spiritual qualities necessary in those who are to conform to a most exacting and unworldly discipline.

The student of religious history, seeking for the reason of the great and permanent, if necessarily limited, appeal of the Carthusian institute, will probably find it in the wise combination of cenobitic and eremitic elements in the life, and in the receptivity with which the nascent order absorbed at a fortunate moment the strong and clear-cut lines of organization that others had devised. While the black monks upheld their right to suit the Rule of St Benedict to the changing conditions of life, and the white monks aimed at a return to its literal observance, the early Charterhouse, together with the Vallombrosians and Camaldolese, consciously turned for inspiration to the earlier monachism of Syria, Palestine and Egypt. But while professedly striving after severe asceticism and a rigid solitude, the Carthusians avoided alike the extreme austerity and unbroken prayer and individualism of the desert, and their customs were a compound in which some elements were taken from the fathers of the desert, others from St Jerome, and others again from St Benedict.[1] The Charterhouse thus combined the eremitic and the cenobitic life, and, while shifting the emphasis, did not wholly destroy the tripartite division of a monk's life into prayer, reading and work which was of the essence of the Rule of St Benedict. It stands therefore, if the metaphor may be used, at one limit of the colours of the spectrum into which the passage of the centuries had split up the followers of the Rule, just as the earlier canonical houses stood at the other.

II

The Carthusian way of life has often been described,[2] but a short account must be given here, in order that its relation to other forms of monasticism

---

1 The letters of St Jerome and the Rule of St Benedict are explicitly referred to by Guigo as sources of Carthusian practice (*Consuetudines, prologus, PL*, CLIII); cf. the *Epistola ad fratres de Monte-Dei* of William of St Thierry (ed. Mabillon, *Opera S. Bernardi*, v, 419): "Fratribus de Monte-Dei, orientale lumen, et antiquum illum in religione Aegyptium fervorem tenebris occiduis et Gallicanis frigoribus inferentibus, vitae scilicet solitariae exemplar, etc." A number of close parallels may be noted between the language of the *Consuetudines* and that of the Rule, and much of the monastic ceremonial was borrowed. Miss Thompson, *The Carthusian Order*, 23, takes exception to Abbot Butler's judgment (art. *Carthusians* in *Encyclopedia Britannica*, ed. 11) that "the whole Carthusian conception, idea and spirit [is] quite different from the Benedictine", but it is certainly true if the comparison is between Carthusians and black monks throughout the centuries. It is true also in great part if taken as referring to the letter of the Rule, for certain essentials of St Benedict's scheme, e.g. the conception of the monastery as a microcosm, a family of many needs, and of the abbot as a *pius pater* who *multorum servit moribus*, finds no place in the Carthusian life.

2 *V.* in particular the article of Dom Webster, mentioned above, p. 375, note 1.

in England may be readily grasped. Briefly, then, it retained the three elements of liturgical prayer, *lectio divina* and manual work, but all three were given an eremitical colouring. Thus the monks came together in the church for only a portion of the daily Office—Mattins, Lauds and Vespers—the rest, together with additional psalmody and prayers, being recited in private in the cell. Moreover, there was, during the first age of the institute, no daily Mass, either conventual or private. Reading and work, likewise, took place (save in rare cases) in the cell or (at a slightly later period) in the monk's private garden; there was no question therefore of the claustral occupation of the black monks or of the agriculture of the white. An austere diet and personal mortifications such as the hairshirt were an integral part of the life, and the silence and solitude demanded were profound, but there was no question of a perpetual and speechless silence such as was inculcated at de Rancé's La Trappe, nor did study of a traditional theological cast receive any positive discouragement. The life, owing mainly to its marked element of solitude, was more "contemplative" than was that of the early Cistercians, but each house remained a true family, meeting together on certain days for meals and even for conversation.

In two important respects, however, the Carthusians, while remaining within the traditional monastic framework, modified existing institutions. From the first, the private cell, which in time came to be a miniature house, took the place of the common cloister, refectory and dormitory. The modern world has grown so used to the private cell, even among the strictest orders of religious (the reformed Cistercians are perhaps the only exception among orders of clerics in the Church of to-day), that the Carthusian cell is sometimes regarded as a development from the common life just as the modern house has grown out of the medieval family "hall". Actually, it was an alien, eremitical element, and must have differentiated the Carthusian life of the twelfth century very sharply from that passed in the large public offices of a monastery or canonical house. The Charterhouse was equally original in its treatment of the *conversi*. These, as has been seen, were unknown to the early black monks, and were introduced by the quasi-eremitical orders precisely in order to safeguard their solitude; the tendency, which in the event proved unwise, was to allow them an ever larger share in the administration and control of the temporal affairs of the community. The Cistercians, on the other hand, among whom they first became numerous, originally received them simply to do the heavy agricultural work for which the choir monks could not find time, but when Cîteaux became a world-movement the vocation of the lay brother was treated as an end in itself, and as a kind of apostolate to the unlettered.

The Charterhouse had from early days a clear conception of the functions of its lay brethren which combined the ideas of Vallombrosa and Cîteaux. The *conversi* existed to cultivate the land and to perform all the heavy manual tasks in order to safeguard the seclusion of the monks; they were never permitted to grow beyond a fixed number or to occupy responsible administrative positions; at the same time their life was fully recognized as a vocation, and was carefully regulated on lines similar to those of the monks, but with a more cenobitic complexion. In the early days of the order they had cells, offices and oratory wholly separate from those of the monks, and closely connected with the quarters of the guests, and the first Charterhouses, among which must be reckoned Witham, consisted of an "upper" and a "lower" house, the terms being adopted from the mother-house of the Chartreuse.

The Carthusians began to increase at a genial moment for the swift growth of an order's polity, and it is probable that elements of organization were adopted from Cluny as well as from Cîteaux. Strictly speaking, they were in no sense an order till 1142, when Anthelme, prior of the Grande Chartreuse, yielding to the requests of four other priors, instituted a system of general chapters; in this, from the beginning, the prior of the Grande Chartreuse was given a position akin to that of the General in later institutes. Subsequently, the Carthusians developed into an order more rigidly centralized than that of Cîteaux, for in the latter the individual communities remained in all essentials autonomous, there was no division into "provinces" for government or visitation, and save when general chapter was in session, authority proceeded from Cîteaux vertically by a process of devolution from mother to daughter, not horizontally over the whole order. The Carthusian polity, on the other hand, came in time to be much more akin to that of the later friars; in it all supreme power resided in general chapter and in the prior of the Grande Chartreuse, and there were provinces for visitatorial purposes, but the strictly enclosed and minutely regulated life made of this central control a very different thing from that of Cluny or of the later centralized orders. In the Cluniac system it tended to shackle the spontaneous development, material and spiritual, which is a part of the genius of black monk institutions; in the later orders it existed primarily in order that the forces of the whole body might, like those of an army, be used in the most effective and economical way. In the Charterhouse there was no place for spontaneous and individual development, nor were the forces of the order ever used for any purpose save to protect Mary from the advances and demands of her sister.

Thus the Charterhouse came very early to occupy the position which it still holds in the Church of a *ne plus ultra* in the enclosed monastic life for men; very early, too, it attracted to itself *âmes d'élite* from the laity, secular clergy and other religious orders and proved, also, a potent attraction to many who failed to satisfy the peculiar physical and psychological tests demanded by its rule. Few would have been clairvoyant enough to forecast such a future in the early days of the poor brethren of

God, when the little family seemed but one out of many such—Tiron, Cîteaux, Savigny, Grandmont and the rest. Had Cîteaux remained the Cîteaux of Stephen Harding it might well have been something of a competitor for pride of place with the Chartreuse, but when Clairvaux made of the Cistercian order a world-movement, a net holding all manner of fish, the tenacious exclusiveness of the Charterhouse prevailed, and it gradually came to be almost the sole representative north of the Alps of a peculiar ideal. To this fact, and to the clarity and wisdom of its constitutions, its long and glorious history may humanly speaking be ascribed.

One more characteristic, and that a spiritual one, remains to be mentioned. The Charterhouse began, as did so many other families of hermits, with no aim more specific than that of providing a life of abstraction and simplicity. The similar ventures south of the Alps drew their inspiration almost entirely from the earlier monachism of the desert and long retained many of its characteristics. The Charterhouse was from the beginning more fully in the stream of Western theological and spiritual tradition, and its situation and early superiors and associations all combined to make it an expression of the genius of France, and to give its spirit an affinity to that of the twelfth-century Augustinians and Victorines rather than to that of the solitaries of Cassian or to that of the later Carmel. And such, owing largely to the accidents of political divisions and historical revolutions, it has ever since tended to remain, possessed of the logical formality and uncompromising strength that are a part of the genius of the country of its birth.

III

The Carthusians spread but slowly, as was to be expected. At no time could such a way of life become common in northern Europe, and in the first half of the twelfth century the Charterhouse was but one of many similar ventures. Without some special invitation it was hardly to be anticipated that a semi-eremitical order, whose native seat was in southern France, would found a house in England. This special invitation, it would seem, came at the end of the Becket controversy. John of Salisbury, a firm if discreet supporter of the archbishop, spent a part of his time abroad during the trouble at the Charterhouse of Mont-Dieu, to which a few decades before William of St Thierry had addressed his "golden" letter, and he is known to have written to another Charterhouse explaining his position and defending Becket's action.[1] This letter, or others, may have reached the Grande Chartreuse; in any case, the Carthusians of the motherhouse took it upon themselves to write a letter of rebuke to Henry II.[2] A year or two later, in 1168, the prior of the Grande Chartreuse and

1 John of Salisbury, *PL*, CXCIX, 326–7 (*ep.* 286).
2 *Materials for the History of Becket*, VI, 165.

Anthelme, bishop of Bellay and ex-prior, were the bearers of a papal letter to Henry; he was therefore familiar with the order before Becket's murder.[1] A condition of his absolution was that he should make the pilgrimage to Palestine. Circumstances led him to abandon this design and his vow was commuted to the foundation of religious houses. It is the constant tradition of the order that two of these were Charterhouses, of which one was Witham.[2]

No special reason can be given for the choice of this remote spot in Selwood forest, near Frome, on the borders of Somerset and Wiltshire. Subsequent events would seem to show that the king took no great pains in the matter and assigned to the monks, who desired seclusion, a distant vill which could be lost without great sacrifice. The foundation was made c. 1178–9 and its beginnings were unfortunate.[3] The natives were suspicious, the prior of the newcomers, Narbert, was a man without practical ability, and the monks were distrustful of English food and manners. A second prior, sent to replace the first, died almost immediately. Both Henry and the brethren at Witham began to despair of the venture. It was at this juncture that the king, while abroad, heard from a nobleman of Maurienne to whom he had mentioned his perplexity of the merits of Hugh of Avalon, at that time procurator of the Grande Chartreuse.[4] He decided to invite him to England and, probably in 1180, Hugh came. In him, for the last time, the continent of Europe gave a saint to the English Church.

Hugh, the son of a house of eminent nobility, was born at Avalon in

---

1 *Materials for the History of Becket*, VI, 394–5 et al.

2 Le Couteulx, *Annales Carthusienses*, II, 449–52.

3 For the foundation of Witham v. *Magna Vita S. Hugonis*, ed. Dimock (RS), 52–3, and *The Foundation Charter of Witham Charterhouse* by J. Armitage Robinson in *Proceedings of the Somerset Archaeological and Natural History Society*, LXIV (1918), 5. Miss Thompson, *The Carthusian Order*, 53, points out that the earliest reference to the Carthusians in the Pipe Rolls is in that of 26 Henry II, p. 106 (Michaelmas 1178–Michaelmas 1179) and Le Couteulx gives the date as 1180–1. Dimock, *Magna Vita S. Hugonis*, 52, note 3 and 64, note 2, argues for 1175–6, but the reasons given by Miss Thompson are more convincing. She and Eyton (*Itinerary of Henry II*, 271) place the "foundation charter" in September 1186, as against J. A. Robinson's 1182—rightly, as it would seem. For the early history of Witham there is, besides the account in the *Magna Vita*, a fragment of a Witham chronicle, now in the possession of the Master of the (modern) London Charterhouse, first utilized by Miss Thompson and printed by her in *Bulletin of the John Rylands Library*, XVI (1932), 482–506.

4 The chief authority for the life of St Hugh is the *Magna Vita*. This was written c. 1212 (cf. pp. 221, 274) in response to requests from Witham (*ibid.* 1–4), especially on the part of Robert and Ralph, once monks of Winchester (*ibid.* 96). The author, Adam (*ibid.* 1), a monk of Eynsham (*ibid.* 315: "suus [sc. Hugonis] monachus"), was an inseparable companion of the bishop for more than three years (*ibid.* 47) and had doubtless known him earlier. His information as to events other than those that fell under his own observation was mainly derived from Hugh himself (*ibid.* 47); the *Vita*, in fact, whether it is judged on its external or on its internal credentials, is most reliable, and it is probable that not much of value has been lost with the disappearance of the earlier accounts which it supplanted. The author is probably to be identified with the Adam, abbot of Eynsham (1213–28), who was deposed from office (*Ann. Dunstapl., Ann. Monast.* III, s.a. 1228). The account given by Gerald of Wales, *Opera*, VII, 83–147 (ed. Dimock), is very meagre and disappointing. For Hugh's early life, the *Magna Vita* is less satisfactory, and is sometimes in error as to date.

Burgundy *c.* 1135. When still young, he became an Augustinian canon and as a deacon gave evidence of the apostolic zeal that was to distinguish his last years. Throughout his life his actions and words bore the stamp of an unusual delicacy of feeling, sweetness of temper and clarity of thought, and it is natural to trace the origin of these qualities in part to the blood that was in his veins and to the air which he first breathed. Eager for a stricter life, he passed to the Chartreuse and there in time became procurator, a post which he held for some ten or fifteen years until, against his inclination, he was sent as prior to Witham. On his arrival, he found no true beginning had as yet been made. The brethren were living in wooden huts, and no division had been effected between monks and *conversi*; moreover, the original inhabitants still occupied the fields. Hugh soon had the construction of a monastery in train and removed the peasants with compensation; as he was obliged more than once to visit the king, the two men came to know one another well, and the king in whom as a prince thirty years before Ailred had reposed such high hopes, and who was still the friend of Gilbert of Sempringham, came to love and admire the Carthusian with such warmth that during Henry's life and after his death it was freely said that Hugh was his natural son, a belief which received confirmation from some resemblance of feature. Witham, or a part of it, was soon built, and we learn from an incident of Hugh's later life that while the upper house was of stone and built round a cloister, the quarters of the lay brothers and guests were a circular group of wooden buildings.[1] The solitary Charterhouse soon became well known in English religious circles.[2] Partly, no doubt, this was due to the personality of Hugh and to his friendship with the king, partly to the lack of rivals. By this time the Cistercians, at least in the south, had ceased to be a cynosure, and the great black monk houses held no attractions for those whose vocation was to solitude. For a few decades Witham might have been to southern England something of what Rievaulx and Fountains had been to the north fifty years before, but Hugh was faithful to the spirit of his order, and resolutely preserved the strictness of the silent and enclosed life.[3] In this, as he found it, the newcomer must find peace, or go elsewhere; there could be no accommodation, none of that warmth of friendship and sympathy by which an Ailred might guide from the human to the divine, but which could find no place in a hermitage. And so Witham remained small, if numbers only are reckoned, but true to its primitive ideal.

1 *A fragment of a Witham Charterhouse Chronicle*, ed. Thompson, 499–500.
2 *Magna Vita*, 85: "Hinc subito, per omnes Britanniae fines. . .viri literatissimi, variisque redditibus ditati. . .sanctae et sincerae illius conversationis humilitatem. . .expeterent."
3 *Magna Vita*, 86: "Nec cito nec facile aperiebat pulsantibus." 91: "Zelabat per omnia suorum quietem, tanquam suam ipsius salutem."

IV

Hugh was not the only distinguished religious sent to England from the Grande Chartreuse. Bovo, who succeeded him at Witham, was influential enough in 1180 for his opinion as to Hugh's eminent qualities to carry weight.[1] Two also of the early *conversi* were men of unusual gifts. One, Aimard, whose past history had been full of incident, had been sent to assist new foundations in various parts of Europe, and was a centenarian, or nearly so, during Hugh's life at Witham. He became a celebrated character whose fame spread far beyond the walls of his monastery;[2] on one occasion, when Hugh, as bishop, was at Witham, he threatened to return to the Chartreuse and was only dissuaded when his old prior followed after him and declared that he would himself accompany Aimard home and relinquish his bishopric.[3] Another, Gerard, who seems to have been of gentle birth and of caustic speech,[4] did not hesitate to take Hugh his prior to task for what he considered to be remissness in applying to the king, and when on a later occasion both he and Hugh were in Henry's presence he addressed the opponent of Becket in words of objurgation so fierce that even Hugh, who was not wont to fear the person of man, related many years afterwards that he could never recall the episode without feelings of the most acute discomfort.[5] Nor are these the only ones mentioned in the early records as coming from abroad to a Witham which, with its surroundings of oakwood, bracken and heath, and its drenching gales, must have seemed indeed a place of horror and a vast wilderness to those born under the skies of Burgundy or of Provence.

We are fortunate in having information from more than one source of some of the aspirants who applied for admission to Witham either during Hugh's short tenure of office as prior, or during the years when as bishop he still kept up the closest connection with his old home. Among them was Robert fitz Henry, for some years prior of the cathedral monastery of St Swithun at Winchester, who resigned his office at an advanced age, but lived for some fifteen years in the Charterhouse, where Adam, Hugh's biographer, knew him well and remarked upon his calm and dignity.[6]

1 *Magna Vita*, 60. Miss Thompson, *The Carthusian Order*, 70, notes that in 1185 his signature to a charter occurs next after the prior of the Grande Chartreuse.

2 *Magna Vita*, 217: "De cujus hodie perenni memoria dignis et gestis et factis tanta per totam fere Angliam vulgata sunt [*sic*] celebri sermone, etc."

3 *Magna Vita*, 210–12. Hugh of course took this way of bringing home to Aimard, as words would not have done, that a lay brother, no less than a bishop, had a task committed to him, and a post which he must not abandon. Other actions recorded of Aimard show him to have been somewhat *entêté*.

4 *Magna Vita*, 74: "sanguinis generosi"; 71: "austeri ingenii".

5 *Magna Vita*, 74: "Referebat saepius jam episcopus talia eum et tanta prosecutum ut horum post tantum temporis ipse reminiscens totus inhorresceret." *V.* also the description of Gerard given by Peter of Blois, *infra*, p. 385, n. 5.

6 For Robert *v. Witham Chronicle* (ed. Thompson), 503, 506, and *Magna Vita*, 95–6: "Erat vultu placidus, corde serenissimus, canitie niveus, ore facundus, spiritu mitis, affectu suavis." Cf. also Richard of Devizes, *infra*, p. 387, n. 1.

With him, apparently, went Ralph, sacrist of St Swithun's.[1] But of all those who found a home at Witham, by far the most remarkable, after Hugh himself, was another Adam, formerly abbot of the Scottish Premonstratensian house of Dryburgh, and well known throughout his own order for his learning, ability and sanctity.[2] Having become acquainted with Hugh as bishop of Lincoln, and with the Carthusians of Val St Pierre during a journey abroad, he approached Hugh, obtained letters of recommendation from him, and joined the community of Witham, where he remained in spite of the efforts made by his friends and the abbot of Prémontré to procure his return to their order. He lived at Witham for some twenty-five years, and became the close confidant of Hugh during the bishop's many visits; Hubert Walter, also, who visited Witham on his way from Glastonbury, made the acquaintance of Adam, for whom he conceived a great admiration, and who wrote for him a meditation on the Lord's prayer. Adam also composed, as would now seem certain, a more celebrated treatise which had a considerable vogue in medieval Charterhouses at home and abroad. This was *The Quadripartite Exercise of the Cell*, a piece which, beginning with an apologia for the Carthusian way of life and with a statement of its *raison d'être*, passes on to describe in some detail the degrees of prayer.[3]

Besides those who found there a lasting abode, Witham also housed for a time more than one aspirant of distinction who failed to persevere. Among these was Walter, sometime subprior of the New Minster at Winchester, from which post he was called to be prior of the cathedral monastery of Bath. Though successful as superior, he left Bath *c.* 1190 for Witham, possibly stirred by the example of Robert of St Swithun's. He was not suffered to remain in peace; pressure was brought upon him to return and it may be he was all but forced to yield, for the bishop of Bath was Ordinary of the diocese in which Witham lay.[4] One Andrew, sacrist of the neighbouring abbey of Muchelney, had previously tried his vocation under Hugh; in his case the personal failure was clear, and he was bitter against the prior who had dismissed him.[5] Still more bitter was

1 *Magna Vita*, 96: "Radulfi quondam sacristae illius [*sc.* apparently, St Swithun's] ecclesiae."

2 For Adam, *v. Magna Vita*, 201–3, and *Witham Chronicle* (ed. Thompson), 496 *seqq.*; also Dom Wilmart: *Maître Adam* in *Analecta Praemonstratensia*, IX (1933), 207–32.

3 *The Quadripartite Exercise of the Cell* is printed in *PL*, CLIII, 799–884. The question of authorship was discussed by Dom André Wilmart in *Les écrits spirituels des deux Guiges* (*v. supra*, p. 375, n. 1) and more recently in a contribution, *Magister Adam Carthusiensis*, to *Mélanges Mandonnet*, II (1930), 145–61. Miss Thompson gives a good analysis of the work in *The Carthusian Order*, 354–67. The conclusions of Dom Wilmart and Miss Thompson as to Adam's authorship of the treatise, which was formerly attributed to Guiges II, are based upon a passage in the Witham chronicle, and may be taken as certain.

4 For Walter *v. Witham Chronicle* (ed. Thompson), 506; Richard of Devizes, 403, and *Ann. Winton.* (*Ann. Monast.* II), *s.a.* 1198. This annal was almost certainly composed by Richard of Devizes.

5 For Andrew *v. Magna Vita*, 87–8, 91: "Andreas utcumque modestius furebat" [*sc.* compared with Alexander].

Alexander of Lewes, a learned secular canon who poured forth his resentment in a comprehensive attack on the Carthusian institute.[1] His case is the more interesting by reason of an old friendship which existed between him and Peter of Blois, from whose letters we can supplement the notice given by Hugh's biographer.[2]

Alexander remained at Witham long enough to make his vows as a Carthusian,[3] then, beginning to tire of the solitude, he complained of certain regulations of the Charterhouse, in particular the absence of the daily Mass, and contemplated passing to the Cluniacs of Reading.[4] Some of his friends sympathized with him, and he wrote to enlist the support of Peter of Blois. But the archdeacon of Bath who, if we may trust the impression given by his works and letters, failed to realize his own highest aspirations, whether temporal or spiritual,[5] was yet able to pass a correct judgment on another, and replied to Alexander in no measured terms, condemning his levity and lack of courage. Passing on to consider his proposed migration to the Cluniacs, Peter gives an interesting criticism of the formalism of their liturgical life, which he contrasts not only with the Carthusians' gathering of the hidden desert manna, but with the austere and busy family life of the Cistercians. The letter bears every mark of having been written directly for its ostensible purpose of advising an individual and may therefore be taken as representing the writer's genuine views; moreover, as the event proved, his judgment on Alexander and his motives was correct. Its contents, however, became public, apparently through Peter's own lack of discretion, and not unnaturally gave offence in Cluniac circles. Among those who expressed disapproval was Adam, sometime monk of La Charité and prior of Bermondsey, and now abbot

---

1 For Alexander v. *Magna Vita*, 87–90. Adam calls him (*ibid.* 87): "secularis ut vulgus loquitur...canonicus, cognomen habens de Lewes, praenominatus magister". Cf. Petri Blesensis *ep.* 86 in *PL*, CCVII, 262 *seqq.*

2 *PL*, CCVII, 271: "Foedus amicitiae contraximus ab antiquo."

3 *PL*, CCVII, 269: "Nunc voti vinculo necessitati astrictus es."

4 *PL*, CCVII, 264: "Hoc in ordine Carthusiensi causaris et arguis, quod singulis diebus missas non faciunt." Originally the Carthusians, imitating what they supposed to have been the practice of the monks of the Thebaid, celebrated Mass only on vigils and feasts; cf. Guigo's *Consuetudines*, c. xiv in *PL*, CLIII, and Peter the Venerable, *de Miraculis*, lib. II, c. xxviii in *PL*, CLXXXIX: "festivis tantum diebus antiquorum eremitarum aemulatione... salutare sacrificium offerunt." Later, even when private daily Masses became the practice in the order, there was only one (the conventual) Mass on feast days, at which all communicated. That the rarity of celebration was difficult to maintain in the face of current practice outside is seen from the fact that Alexander himself obtained special permission (Petri Blesensis *ep. cit.* col. 267: "tibi fraterna charitas singulis diebus offerre hostiam... indulsit") and that Hugh, when bishop, celebrated daily at Witham (*Magna Vita*, 199: "missam devotissime...quotidie celebrabat"), though previously he had offered Mass only when allowed by the rule (*ibid.* 329: "monachus quoties de permissu ordinis licuit... episcopus, quoties possibilitati ratio concurrit, missas celebrare nullo tempore praetermisit").

5 Cf. the judgment of J. A. Robinson, *Peter of Blois* (*Somerset Hist. Essays*, 100). It is clear from another reference that Peter knew Witham at first hand. In his *Compendium in Job*, *PL*, CCVII, 815, he says: "nudius tertius vidi quemdam discipulum hujus sectae", and gives a long description of the Witham *conversus* Gerard (v. supra, p. 383).

of Evesham, and Peter felt called upon to sing a palinode.[1] By praising
Cistercians and Carthusians, he explained, he did not intend to disparage
the black monks. The beauty of the Church arises from the very variety
of the clothing of her children; in Jacob's sheepfold were lambs black and
white, and white and black grapes were in the vineyard of Sorec. Length
of psalmody, he willingly grants, may be most advantageous to the soul's
health, nor did he intend to suggest that manual labour was good for all.
As the prophet wrote: "strangers shall stand and feed their flocks; but
ye shall be called the holy of the Lord, ministers of God."[2]

For all his second thoughts, Peter's original remonstrance was wise; it
agrees perfectly with the judgment passed on Alexander by Hugh's
biographer, Adam of Eynsham, and was justified by the truant's subsequent career. Alexander had his way and passed to Reading, where
Abbot Hugh made much of him on account of his reputation for learning;
when the abbot was chosen to rule Cluny in 1199 the ex-Carthusian,
deprived of this consolation, tired of the community life of a large abbey
as he had tired of the solitude of Witham, and begged Hugh of Lincoln
to allow him to re-enter the Charterhouse. But this time Hugh, who had,
as he well knew, used every resource of his patience with Alexander in
the years past, was unyielding in his refusal.[3]

Alexander's complaint had been that the Carthusians spent the whole
day in dull and melancholy idleness, with nothing to look upon save the
walls of their own cells, yet maintaining that theirs was the only way to
heaven.[4] As the black monk, Adam, rightly remarked, such an opinion
was that of one who, having himself desired to attain to the land of vision,
had failed in the strength necessary for a soul that was to pass into the
darkness where God is to be found.[5] But the learned canon and the sacrist
of Muchelney were not the only critics of Witham. The attraction which
it exercised over many minds in black monk circles inevitably produced a
repercussion of hostility. A vivid reflection of this is seen in the writings
of a monk of St Swithun's, Richard of Devizes, whose prior, as has been

1 Petri Blesensis *ep.* 97, *PL*, CCVII, 304–6. No name is given in the letter to the abbot of
Evesham, but he was certainly the Cluniac Adam (abbot 1160 or 1161–89: for the latter
date, as against that of 1191 given by the editor of the *Evesham Chronicle*, 102, note 4, *v.*
Gervase of Canterbury, I, 484 and W. Holtzmann, *Papsturkunden in England*, I, ii, no. 269).
Alexander's departure from Witham must therefore have been before 1189, and his attempt
to re-enter during the last year of Hugh's life, 1199–1200.

2 This letter is a good example of the manner in which Peter and others could quote
Scripture quite as readily and as *mal à propos* as a Roundhead or Covenanter; it is interesting
to compare his method with the equally ready, but as a rule deeply significant, selection of
Bernard of Clairvaux. For another palinode of Peter, *v. supra*, p. 319.

3 *Magna Vita*, 89–90.

4 *Magna Vita*, 88–9: "Ecce soli sine solatio, prae accidia languidi et torpentes, neminem
totis diebus videmus quem imitemur, parietes solos quibus includimur intuemur." From
Adam's usual method of careful citation, one would suppose this to be an actual extract
from Alexander's letter.

5 *Magna Vita*, 86–7: "Declinabant vero cum Loth montem contemplationis arduae...
non valentes cum Moyse ad caliginem accedere in qua erat Deus."

seen, had passed to the Charterhouse, and whose monastery seems to have been peculiarly well informed as to all that passed at Witham.[1] Richard makes no attempt to conceal his rancour, and three times[2] his mordant wit plays upon the Carthusian way of life, which he affects to regard as the offspring of delusion and misanthropy. He records the sarcastic words of a monk of Hyde when on a visit to his quondam subprior, Walter of Bath, and he himself went to Witham to see his own ex-prior. Indeed he dedicates to him his history (which he professes to have been commanded to write by Robert himself) in a preface of studied irony which, if it was (as it purports to have been) sent to Witham, can only have been sent in a spirit of cold and bitter hostility.[3] And in distant East Anglia Samson of Bury, perhaps with Robert of Winchester in mind, delivered himself of an expression of disapproval towards those who left an abbey for a life of solitude.[4]

V

Hugh of Avalon was prior of Witham for some six years only. In the early summer of 1186, at the instance of the king, he was elected to rule the vast diocese of Lincoln which, even when shorn of Cambridge and Ely, stretched from Grimsby to Eton and from Oxford to Huntingdon, and which had been vacant, save for twelve months, for almost twenty years. But even when bishop, Hugh counted for much to Witham. To the end of his life he returned annually thither for a month or more, choosing for his visits the late summer, when he could dismiss his household to their own homes to help in gathering the harvest. At his old Charterhouse he lived in a cell like the rest and, as Wulfstan had done at Worcester a century before, took his turn as priest of the week, and used all the Carthusian vestments. Besides these long annual visits, and the celebrity which his prestige and reputation gave to his old home, Hugh seems to have retained to the end some kind of authority over Witham, for there

1 Richard of Devizes and companions visited Witham (Richard of Devizes, 381) as did a monk of Hyde (*Ann. Winton., s.a.* 1198), and the *Magna Vita* records the visit of another monk (93–4); there was also the affair of the Winchester Bible (*ibid.* 92–3).

2 Richard of Devizes, 381, 403; *Ann. Winton., s.a.* 1198.

3 Such, at least, is my opinion, and the editor (R. Howlett) of Richard in the Rolls Series characterizes some of his remarks as bordering on blasphemy. On the other hand, a translator of Richard's work, Rev. J. Stevenson (*Church Historians of England*, v, p. xi, 1858), sees no irony in what is said, and Miss Thompson, *The Carthusian Order*, 77, refers to his introductory letter as "sarcastic, but not wholly unsympathetic". The various references, however, to the Carthusian vocation as *fervor vel furor, dolor an devotio* (Richard of Devizes, Prologue and 403) and his use of the phrase applied in the gospel to the Prodigal Son—*ille ad se reversus*—(*Ann. Winton., s.a.* 1198) would surely have severely taxed the sense of humour of even the most genial Carthusian, to say nothing of the deeper aspects of the matter.

4 *Jocelini Cronica*, 245: "Cum audiret forte aliquem praelatum cedere oneri pastorali et fieri anachoritam, in hoc eum non laudavit."

is record of his deposing a prior, of his refusing to allow admissions and of his having a lay brother as his attendant at Lincoln.[1]

The career of Hugh as bishop scarcely falls within the scope of these pages, save in so far as he appears as the last example in English medieval history of a saintly monk-bishop. The first Carthusian, and the last, to occupy an English see, he retained as much of his old habit of life as was compatible with his new duties, and devoted all his energy to the spiritual functions of his office, refusing steadfastly to enter with his colleagues into the political life of the country. In consequence, his tenure of office left no mark on the external framework of Church history; his moral influence upon his wide and neglected diocese eludes assessment for other reasons. He did not, however, stand wholly outside the currents of life of the time. His relations with Henry II, for the short space that remained of his reign, were intimate, and he had almost equally close contact with Richard, when the king was in England or Normandy. He sought and obtained many of the best and most learned of the clergy of the new model for posts of teaching and administration at Lincoln and up and down the diocese. It also fell to him to take the decision of rebuilding his cathedral on a grand scale and in the new style, and his edifice at Lincoln, of which the transepts still remain, was the earliest work of such magnitude to be built in pure Gothic. His judgment and integrity soon singled him out as an ideal papal delegate, and between 1190 and 1200 he was constantly employed on judicial commissions, sitting at least once on the same board as Samson of Bury.[2] In his first years at Lincoln he must have often met the aged Gilbert of Sempringham, but no record of their intercourse survives save Hugh's sanction of a modification of the lay brothers' constitutions. Chance also threw across his path at Lincoln the two writers of the age who are at once the most representative of a new school and the most familiar to the modern reader, Walter Map, archdeacon of Oxford, and Gerald de Barri, the latter of whom wrote a life of the bishop soon after his death.[3]

Hugh was more fortunate in another biographer, Adam, a monk of Eynsham who had been his constant companion for years and who had absorbed, with his intellect at least, much of his master's spirit and doctrine; his *Life* gives a clear and living picture of the great bishop. Different as he was alike from Wulfstan, from Ailred and from Gilbert, with an order and

[1] For the powers given to Hugh in this respect by general chapter, and his deposition of Albert, *v. Witham Chronicle* (ed. Thompson), 505–6; for his refusal of Alexander when bishop, *Magna Vita*, 89; for "frater Petrus, conversus noster", *ibid.* 339.

[2] *Magna Vita*, 299: "Omnium sane difficiliores ac magis arduas negotiorum decisiones... episcopo delegabant Lincolniensi quotquot suis temporibus ecclesiae praesederunt Romanae pontifices summi" (cf. also *ibid.* 342). The records bear out this statement, which is made to explain why the pope thrice refused to allow Hugh to resign. Samson sat with Hugh in the business of the monks of Coventry in 1197; *v.s.* p. 324.

[3] Hugh's biographer quotes Gerald on the subject of the swan (*Magna Vita*, 115–17) and refers to Walter Map (*ibid.* 281).

lucidity of mind that are often reckoned characteristics of the French race, and with a quality of soul which his contemporaries loved to describe by the word "milk-white", Hugh was a saint indeed, as every page of his life testifies—that is, he was one who appeared to those who knew him best as a pure reflection of Christ, and as such able in a strength not his own to transcend the limits of human virtue and endurance. Though a devoted and typical Carthusian, he was in a sense a Carthusian of the second generation. A lover of absolute solitude and silence, he is yet in no way a reincarnation of the spirit of Egypt or Syria; there is not even in his character a resemblance to the saints of the forest of the previous century. He was by nature and vocation a man of action and an ascetic rather than a pure contemplative, and his singularly clear conception of Christian holiness found ready expression in his teaching as bishop. He had, says his biographer, absorbed most perfectly the sanity and humility inculcated by the founders of the Charterhouse, and attached little importance to prodigies and miracles. He related such as occurred in the lives of the saints and reverenced them, recounting them to others where they might help those who admired such things; for himself, the essential holiness of the saints alone served for miracle and example. In place of wonders, he had the constant and intimate sense of his Maker's presence, and of the marvellous and unsearchable variety of His mighty works.[1]

Though a Carthusian, Hugh could admire and respect the traditions of other and less austere orders; he had no illusions as to the essence of the teaching of the gospel. Layfolk, wondering at his sanctity, not infrequently complained to him of the hindrances they found to the service of God in the world. His reply was always the same:

Others (he said) besides monks and hermits will possess the kingdom of God. When God judges you He will not chide you for not being an anchorite or a monk, the charge against those who are found wanting will rather be that they have not been true Christians. Three things are demanded of a Christian; if one of these is lacking to a man when he is judged, the name of Christian will have no power to protect him; indeed, the name without the practice will rather prejudice than protect, for falsehood is the more atrocious in one who makes profession of the truth. Love in the heart, truth on the lips and chastity in the body: these a man must have to be in truth and in act a Christian.[2]

And he would go on to say that the married, without changing their vocation, might share in the glory of chastity and receive a crown of reward along with virgins and those wholly continent. He himself, as bishop, had no scruple in following common usage and admitting married women and widows to sit at his table; his biographer tells how he would

---

1 *Magna Vita*, 97: "Nam et in hoc etiam traditam a sancti ordinis Cartusiensis auctoribus gravitatem pariter et humilitatem altius...imbibebat, ut nihil minus quam miraculorum prodigia mirari aut aemulari videretur."
2 *Magna Vita*, 195–6.

sign their foreheads with the cross as they knelt before him, and gently press their heads between his two palms. "God", he would say, "well deserves to be loved by women, for He did not shun to be born of a woman. Marvellous and precious was the privilege He thus gave to all women; it was not granted to a man to be or to be called father of God, but it was given to a woman to bear God."[1]

The detailed account of Hugh's last visit to his own people in Grenoble, and to his early homes, both earthly and monastic, is full of interest; still more intimate is the account of his last days and death in London. There he lay ill for long before the end, and two months before he died received Viaticum and the last anointing. When the Host was brought into the room where he was lying:

He rose from his bed, clothed in his hair shirt, habit and cowl, with bare feet, and kneeling, prayed and adored for long.

After he had received the two sacraments he said to those about him:

Now my doctors and my diseases may fight it out as they will, I shall have little care for either. I have given myself to God; I have received Him, I will hold Him and rest fast in Him; it is good to abide fast in Him, it is a blessed thing to hold Him; he who receives Him and gives himself to Him is safe and sound.[2]

Among those who visited him during those weeks were King John and Hubert Walter; to neither did Hugh give any cause for self-congratulation. The king, who sat long by his bedside, was full of kind words, but Hugh knew that little trust could be put in him and wasted none on him in return. Hubert Walter, after offering to do anything in his power for his sick colleague, felt called upon to suggest that Hugh might wish to beg pardon for any hard or provocative words or actions of which he might have been guilty, and specifically with regard to his primate. Hugh replied that he remembered well enough the occasions the archbishop had in mind, and his only regret was that the words had not been stronger. He added that he had often been weak and complaisant through human respect; should he be restored to health he would endeavour to remedy the failing.[3] Among his last visitors was Geoffrey de Noiers, the architect in charge of the works at Lincoln. Hugh urged him to complete the altar of St John the Baptist, that it might be ready for a large gathering shortly to take place at Lincoln, and to have it consecrated at once. He had hoped to do this himself; that was not to be, but he would be among those present at the gathering he had spoken of.[4] The gathering was for his funeral, and his body was laid by the altar of St John, where it remained till his presbytery was taken down to make room for the Angel choir and for the feretory in which his relics reposed until the Reformation.

1 *Magna Vita*, 197.   2 *Magna Vita*, 333–4.
3 *Magna Vita*, 335–6.   4 *Magna Vita*, 336–7.

Hugh died in 1200, but there is every indication that Witham remained as he had formed it for some decades after his death, and that it passed beyond the limits of our period as a house which not only observed in their fullness the statutes of the Charterhouse, but which was a spiritual magnet attracting to itself a strong, if small, body of ardent life. It was, to recur to a metaphor used on an earlier page, the last, and in some ways the purest, of those successive waves of fresh monastic life which had drawn from France and broken upon the English shore. If this account of Witham and St Hugh has seemed disproportionately long, it may at least have served as an attempt to atone for the neglect that has overtaken the place with the passage of the centuries, and to call attention to a spot which was for a period one of the centres of the spiritual life of England. The numerous visitors to Rievaulx, to Fountains and to Tintern, to St Albans and St Edmundsbury, see at least some material traces of the habitations of the monks, and give at least a passing thought to their life, but only a mound—if even so much—marks the site of the cloister built by Hugh of Avalon, the scene of so many meetings between the great bishop of Lincoln and Adam of Dryburgh, and few of the many who pass by the place in the great expresses to or from the west realize, as their glance falls upon the unpretentious roof and small turret of Witham church, that they are looking upon all that remains of the first Charterhouse of England, and the home of the last of a long line of sainted monk-bishops.[1]

1 The name, Witham Friary, which the place bears, is not a modern misnomer, but a survival of the primitive style of the lay brothers' chapel. Perhaps it may be well to add that Hugh, though avoiding secular business, was firm in the assertion of his legal rights against the king in 1198; cf. *Magna Vita*, 78, 191, 248 (the last is reprinted by Stubbs, *Select Charters*, 255–6).

Part Two. Institutional

CHAPTER XXIII

THE OFFICE OF ABBOT

I

THE ELECTION OR APPOINTMENT OF THE ABBOT

Throughout the period with which we are concerned the right of electing or appointing the abbots of the English black monk houses was claimed, with varying degrees of insistency and success, both by the monks themselves and by the king. In this respect, indeed, abbatial and episcopal elections were equated in almost every way, and followed the same rhythm of freedom and control, save that two or three important circumstances made of abbatial elections an issue constantly living.

The Rule of St Benedict, itself based on older tradition, laid down that the abbot should be chosen by his monks from among their own number,[1] and this legislation passed into the canon law,[2] which never knew of any other practice. Gradually, however, as the monasteries, in common with all other ecclesiastical foundations, came under private ownership or patronage, the right of appointing the abbot was asserted by the founder and his descendants, or by the patron, or by the bishop, or by the king, and throughout the dark ages reformers were constantly struggling to recapture or maintain the freedom of the Rule. Thus in Northumbria Benet Biscop secured for his monasteries of Jarrow and Wearmouth a papal privilege which included a clause securing free election, and his last address to his monks contained a solemn exhortation to maintain their rights;[3] indeed almost every papal privilege to a monastery during these centuries repeated the words of the canons and the Rule,[4] and this freedom was one of the chief motives for commendation to the Apostolic See, both in earlier cases and above all in that of Cluny and her family.

1 *S. Benedicti Regula*, lxiv, 1–5: "In abbatis ordinatione illa semper consideretur ratio, ut hic constituatur quem sive omnis concors congregatio secundum timorem Dei, sive etiam pars quamvis parva congregationis saniore consilio elegerit." For further reservations, *v.* the rest of the chapter.

2 E.g. *Gratiani Decreti* Pars 2, C. xviii, qu. 2, c. 2 (ed. Friedberg, vol. 1, 830): "Abbas in monasterio non per episcopum aut per aliquem extraneorum ordinetur." *Ibid.* c. 3: "Abbatem cuilibet monasterio non alium sed quem...communi consensu congregatio poposcerit, etc."

3 Bede, *Historia Abbatum* (Plummer, *Baedae Opera*, 1, 375): "Juxta quod regula... Benedicti, juxta quod privilegii nostra continent decreta, in conventu vestrae congregationis communi consilio [abbatem] perquiratis."

4 E.g. the privilege (seemingly genuine) of Pope Agatho to Erconwald, bishop of London, on behalf of Chertsey (*c.* 678–81): "Eligendi abbatis licentiam soli congregacioni ejusdem venerabilis monasterii concedimus, etc." This privilege is preserved in Brit. Mus. MS. Cott. Vitell. A. xiii, 24.

In the early days of the revival under Dunstan, it was natural that the three great founders should appoint the superiors of the new houses, and so long as they lived each exercised this power to some extent over the group of monasteries for which he was responsible. In the *Regularis Concordia*, however, which here as elsewhere shows the practical and national outlook of its framers, a procedure was laid down which was destined to remain normal until the Conquest and beyond. Abbatial elections were to be made by the monks in accordance with the Rule, but at the advice and with the consent of the king; no other patron was to exercise any influence.[1] This, in practice, came to mean that abbots, like bishops, were appointed by the king, who might or might not have ascertained the wishes of the community, and the appointments usually took place at a meeting of the Witan, and with the advice of the monk-bishops and abbots who were members of that body. Detailed information as to elections is almost wholly wanting before the reign of the Confessor; possibly in many cases some form of election in the monastery marked out the candidate, and occasionally an infirm or aged abbot presented one of his monks to the king with the request that he might act as his assistant and successor. Under the Confessor the evidence becomes more explicit; in this, as in other respects, Edward moved a step nearer to the feudal practice of the Continent and "bestowed" abbacies. This was not, however, his invariable practice, and at least three different methods can be seen at work in his reign: the direct appointment of an outsider as a reward for services, as in the case of the ex-bishop Ralph from Scandinavia at Abingdon;[2] the presentation of the person of his choice to a group of monks summoned to court to "elect" him, as with Baldwin at Bury in 1065;[3] and the designation by an abbot of his successor, as with Mannig and Aethelwig at Evesham in 1059.[4] In the short reign of Harold there is an example of appointment at Ely, and immediately after the Norman invasion the monks of Peterborough held a free election and sent their choice to Edgar the Atheling for confirmation, supposing that he would succeed to the kingdom.[5]

Under the Conqueror there was no question of free elections. Accustomed as he was to a fully organized feudal state in which the abbeys held

1 *Regularis Concordia*, Proem (ed. Reyner, 78): "Abbatum...electio cum Regis consensu et consilio, sanctae regulae ageretur documento."

2 *Chron. Abingd.* 1, 463.

3 *Heremanni Miracula S. Edmundi* (ed. Liebermann, *Ungedruckte Quellen*, 245). On the death of abbot Fretheric: "cogitat...rex...quem ejus in locum subroget." He decides on Baldwin, his physician; the prior and *fratres personati* are summoned to Windsor; Baldwin is presented to them and *communi favore fit abbas electus*.

4 *Chron. Evesh.* 87–8: "Qua de re prudenti usus consilio quendam de suis monachis elegit [Mannius] ad id officium. Misit...eum...ad regem Aeduuardum. Rex...fecit... eum...ab Aldredo archiepiscopo...consecrari."

5 *Liber Eliensis*, 1, 221: "Mox accepto regno [Haraldus] Turstanum...constituit abbatem." *Chronicle* [E], *s.a.* 1066: "Ða cusen þa munecas to abbot Brand provost...] senden him þa to Aedgar aeðeling."

of the Duke and several of them by military service,[1] he was also concerned to secure his hold over the English monasteries, which in many cases were centres of national sentiment; over and above this, he shared with Lanfranc the view that the English monasteries needed refashioning on the Norman model. Consequently he appointed without a semblance of election, and his nominees were almost invariably foreigners. Occasionally, and above all at the beginning of his reign, the appointments were wholly his own, and were sometimes the reward of personal services, but soon Lanfranc made his influence felt, and many of the abbots were his personal choice, as Paul, his nephew, whom he brought from Caen to St Albans, and Gilbert Crispin, who passed from Bec to Westminster. From the case of Gerald of Cranborne and Tewkesbury it can be seen that appointments were often discussed and effected by the bishops during a meeting of the king's Council.[2] Yet though his practice was to appoint directly, even the authoritarian Lanfranc, when legislating for his monks, made no attempt to suppress the traditional formula which guaranteed a free election.[3]

Under Rufus the direct action of the king was still less subject to control in the years after Lanfranc's death. He sent his nominees over to England from Normandy and declared more than once that abbeys were his property as much as his private estates and that he would dispose of them as he chose.[4] Besides keeping many vacant for a long period he gave others to Ranulf Flambard to hold and enjoy. Peterborough, however, by means of bribery secured a free election and so probably did the other houses whose heads were subsequently deprived of office by Anselm on a charge of "simony".[5]

Henry I began his reign by appointing at least two foreigners to vacant abbeys on the day of his coronation. Both of these were subsequently removed by Anselm on the grounds of uncanonical election.[6] For the rest of his reign, even after the settlement over investitures, Henry's constant practice was to appoint, usually during a Council and with its

1 For the Norman practice c. 1066, v. Böhmer, *Kirche und Staat*, 31–2; Sackur, *Die Cluniacenser*, ii, 46; Ordericus Vitalis, ii, 39, 81–5; and Haskins, *Norman Institutions*, 8–14. Fuller details and references for English elections 1066–1216 will be found in an article by the present writer, *Abbatial Elections*, in *DR*, xlix (May 1931), 252–78.

2 *Registrum Theokusburiae*, fol. 2 recto: "Convocatis igitur apud Gloucestriam... magnatibus...Lanfranco...praesidente Rex Willelmus electos canonice personas [this is the late writer's account] nonnullis praefecit ecclesiis."

3 *Lanfranci Statuta*, ii, 232: "Abbas cum elegitur, omnes fratres, vel major et melior pars, in ejus electionem consentire debent."

4 *Chron. Will. Thorne* (ed. Twysden), coll. 1794–5: "Se velle omnes baculos pastorales per totam Angliam manu sua tenere, et de eis pro libito suae voluntatis disponere"; William of Malmesbury, *GP*, 85: "Abbatias suas esse, de his se facturum quod liberet, perinde ut ipse faceret de villis suis quod sibi in mentem veniret." The passage is printed as a footnote by the editor.

5 Cf. Hugo Candidus, 64, and *Chron. Angliae Petriburg.* 68; Eadmer, *Hist. Nov.* 142.

6 The two were Richard of Ely, *Liber Eliensis*, i, 284 and Robert of Bury, *Ann. S. Edmundi* (ed. Liebermann, *Ungedruckte Quellen*), 131. Cf. *Anselmi epist.* iv, 21.

advice, without the semblance of a free election. On occasion a deputation from the monastery was summoned to the royal presence, presumably to give some kind of assent to the choice; very rarely a chronicler claims a free election or notes the designation of his successor by an abbot.[1]

Stephen, in spite of his oath of 1136 giving freedom to the Church, continued during the earlier and more normal part of his reign to follow Henry's practice of appointment after consultation with his advisers. He often went to considerable pains to ensure merit in his nominees, and several of them were excellent abbots; as his political difficulties increased, however, he and his brother Henry of Winchester tended to put relatives and *protégés* into abbacies as well as into bishoprics.[2]

When control of the government passed from Stephen's hands in 1139, and Henry of Winchester as legate threw the English Church open to the influence of Gregorian practice and law, the question of elections, both episcopal and abbatial, immediately came to the fore. For a number of reasons the monasteries were more fortunately situated than the cathedral chapters: the electing body had a permanent existence and was accustomed to meet, deliberate and decide other business; it was vitally concerned in the issue of an election and could foresee and prepare for it; finally, the office of abbot was not, like that of bishop, the object of promiscuous ambition and had little political importance. Beyond this, the monks were familiar with the legislation of the Rule, and as unrestricted intercourse with Rome became for the first time a reality, they saw this repeated in the papal privileges which poured into the country in such numbers, especially during the pontificate of Eugenius III (1145–53);[3] no doubt, also, the influence of the white monks, who always enjoyed complete freedom, made itself felt. In any case, there is record of a number of free elections between 1140 and 1154. When the house concerned lay outside the sphere of Stephen's control, the election was wholly free, save when the legate interfered; when the king had power, freedom was often bought at a price.[4]

1 Eadmer, *Vita Anselmi*, 414–15, says that in 1107 the king "personas quae in regimen assumebantur per se [non] elegit", but there are many examples of the more normal method, e.g. *Chron. Bell.* 51 (1107): "Quendam suorum consilio asciscens Cadomensem monachum... praefecit." *Ibid.* 60 (1125), where deputies from vacant abbeys are ordered to France *ad suscipiendos praelatos*. The prior and three monks go from Battle: "rex consilio usus archiepiscopi Cantuariensis et episcopi Cicestrensis monachum Cantuariensem...delegavit."

2 For examples and references, *v.* Voss, *Heinrich von Blois*, 42–5.

3 Cf. the common papal form in a privilege of Eugenius III to St Albans in 1146. This appears in all bulls confirming property. "Obeunte te...nullus ibidem qualibet surreptionis astutia vel violentia praeponatur, nisi quem fratres communi consensu, vel fratrum pars consilii sanioris, secundum Dei timorem et Beati Benedicti regulam, canonice providerint eligendum."

4 Examples of free elections are Cerne (*c.* 1145), Foliot, *ep.* 13; Gloucester (1148), *Hist. Glocestr.* 19, and John of Salisbury, *Historia Pontificalis*, 48; St Albans (1146), *GASA*, I, 106. Money was given at Malmesbury in 1140, Will. Malmesb., *Hist. Nov.* ap. *GR*, II, 560; and at St Augustine's, Canterbury in 1151, *Hist. Pont.* 89. John of Salisbury, *Hist. Pont.* 91, remarks that "ea tempestate sub optentu libertatis redimendae symoniacam plurimi pravitatem palliabant".

The early years of Henry II saw a gradual reversion to earlier practice, in conformity with the king's policy in every department of Church government. Occasionally permission was specifically asked and granted for a free election under the presidency of a bishop, and so long as Theobald lived this was perhaps a usual course for events to take,[1] though even in his lifetime there are cases of abbeys being "bestowed" by Henry at the request of Queen Eleanor or Becket when Chancellor.[2] Gradually, however, the king asserted more and more consistently the powers exercised by his grandfather, and these were duly embodied in the Constitutions of Clarendon: the "election" was to take place in the king's chapel with the royal permission and upon the advice of the Council.[3] Such a procedure gave the electors just as much freedom in their choice as the king might wish, and in any case it removed all possibility of the whole body of the community being present and showing its wishes during the election. This remained the usual practice till the end of the reign; even when reconciled with Rome after the murder of Becket Henry paid no more deference to the canons than was shown by allowing the delegates to go through the form of an election. The monasteries on their side endeavoured to secure the candidate of their choice by holding a previous election of their own and pledging the delegates to propose and abide by the person so chosen. Sometimes, especially in the case of great abbeys such as Bury and St Albans, the move was successful; it was thus that Samson, who was personally unknown to the king, became abbot:[4] on other occasions the firmness of the monks resulted in some kind of compromise by which they secured an abbot of whom they approved; but more often the language of the chronicler or the provenance of the elect shows the election to have been in fact a royal nomination.

Richard I while in England or Normandy held to the same methods as Henry II, though showing himself more irresponsible; during his absence William Longchamp as Chancellor was still less scrupulous, and more than one abbot was forced in upon his community, though in other cases at least a show was made of observing the canonical procedure.[5]

There is little record of elections under John before the years of conflict

1 Cf. the Evesham election of *c.* 1161 where John of Salisbury writes for Theobald (*ep.* 37): "a domino nostro rege obtinuimus ut secundum institutionem sacrorum canonum pastorem idoneum vobis praeficere valeamus" (*PL*, CXCIX, 24). There is more about this election in Gilb. Foliot, *ep.* 254.

2 *Chron. Abingd.* II, 292: "Dedit rex abbatiam...interventu reginae Alienorae." *Materials...Becket*, III, 189.

3 Stubbs, *Select Charters* (1874), p. 140: "Et cum ventum fuerit ad consulendum ecclesiae, debet dominus rex mandare potiores personas ecclesiae, et in capella ipsius regis debet fieri electio, assensu ipsius regis et consilio personarum regni, etc."

4 *Jocelini Cronica* in *Mem. S. Edmund's*, I, 227 *seqq.*

5 Cf. the cases of Muchelney, Westminster and Chertsey in Richard of Devizes, 410, 411, 420 and *Ann. Winton.* ap. *Ann. Monast.* II, 65. For a more regular proceeding *v.* that of York in 1197 as given by Ralph of Diceto, II, 151: "Robertus...xiiii monachis cum capituli sui literis...directus...coram regni justiciario sollempniter electus est."

with Rome, and it so happened that several of the greater houses had
abbots whose reign extended over the greater part of the king's. Scattered
references indicate that the custom of election by delegates in the king's
presence continued the norm, but that a monastery often secured the head
it desired. From 1208 to 1213 the Interdict held up all elections in the
autonomous black monk houses, and as during the struggle one of the
chief points at issue between John and the papal party was the control of
episcopal elections, abbatial elections naturally followed the others in the
controversy. At the time of John's absolution in June 1213, at least nine
abbeys, besides several bishoprics, were vacant; the king claimed his old
rights, while the bishops of the papal party stood out for full canonical
freedom.[1] It so happens that the fullest of all the narratives of abbatial
elections of the period deals with the vicissitudes of these months of
struggle; it is that of the Bury election consequent upon the death of
Samson at Christmas, 1212.[2] In the following August John, recently
absolved, summoned deputies to come and elect in the royal presence,
according to the custom of the realm. Instead, the monks elected one of
their number, Hugh, and sent him off to the king for confirmation.
Rebuffed by John on the grounds that no alternative candidates had been
proposed, he proceeded to Stephen Langton, by whom he was warmly
received, and subsequently travelled about for two years, now abroad,
now at court, now with a papal commission which delayed of set purpose
to pronounce a judgment; finally his fortunes took him to Runnymede,
and there the final reconciliation with John took place. It is interesting
to note that the community of St Edmund's, at the height of the controversy, were divided almost exactly in half by the opposing claims of
allegiance to king and pope.

Before John had given any final undertaking on the election question
the legate Nicholas of Tusculum received instructions from Innocent III
in 1214 that he was to make appointments in concert with the king, and
this was accordingly done at a number of abbeys.[3] Finally, John made a
complete surrender, so far at least as written agreement went, and
guaranteed full canonical freedom, reserving to himself only the rights of
granting *congé d'élire* and of approving the elect, neither of which permissions was in practice to be refused.[4] The history of the subsequent
working of this system falls outside our period.

Thus over the whole epoch between Dunstan and John six main

---

1 So the *Barnwell Chronicle* ap. Walter of Coventry, II, 213.
2 *Cronicon de electione Hugonis abbatis* in *Mem. S. Edmund's*, II, 31 *seqq.*
3 *Barnwell Chronicle*, as above, II, 216.
4 Stubbs, *Select Charters*, 289: "De caetero in...monasteriis...liberae sint in perpetuum electiones...[He promises not to impede the elections] petita tamen prius a nobis
et haeredibus nostris licentia eligendi, quam non denegabimus nec differemus [if delay does
occur, the house can proceed to an election]...similiter post celebratam electionem, noster
requiratur assensus [which will not be refused]."

THE OFFICE OF ABBOT

divisions may be made: from Edgar to the Conquest the ultimate choice lay with the king, who usually acted upon the advice of the Witan given at a formal meeting, though the elect was often submitted by the monks: under the Conqueror and Rufus and in the first years of Henry I the appointments were almost invariably made directly by authority, with no formalities of election: from 1106 to *c.* 1139 the normal procedure was for a small number of delegates to "elect" in the king's presence a candidate proposed by him, usually at the advice of his Council: from *c.* 1140 to *c.* 1161 every type of election and appointment is found, but the full canonical election in the monastery itself predominates: from *c.* 1162 to 1208 the methods of Henry I are restored, though in practice many monasteries succeeded in securing their own choice, partly because the king no longer desired to appoint monks from overseas: from 1208 to 1215 controversy prevailed, issuing ultimately in the recognition of the principle of free canonical election by the monks.

On the whole, it cannot be said that the royal control of elections was a source of injury to the monasteries. It is true that almost every king was responsible for a few wholly bad appointments, either of relatives or of individual monks whose only qualification was some private service rendered to the Crown, but the great majority of the nominees were either members of the house whom the community had selected or monks of other monasteries at home and abroad whose abilities had made of them figures in the life of the Church. An important consequence of the system, and one which may be pronounced beneficial, was the constant introduction of new life into the monasteries. Under normal circumstances the monks in a free election would, like their descendants at the present day or the members of any fellowship such as a college at Oxford or Cambridge, almost invariably choose one of their own body; thus at St Albans and Bury, the two great abbeys which were most successful in securing domestic elections, a succession of abbots were sons of the house. The king and his advisers, on the other hand, would in most cases put forward one upon whom they had had their eyes for a considerable time, and had intended to promote to the first vacant post. In the days of the Norman plantation, and indeed until the end of the reign of Henry I, the great majority of such nominees were monks from Normandy, and without the royal initiative the monasticism of England would never have received so prolonged a spiritual and cultural impetus from abroad; after the death of Theobald the appointments were almost as invariably of Englishmen, but the inter-change between house and house, especially in abbeys of the second and third rank, did much to counteract the tendency towards isolation and stagnation which inevitably made its appearance at this time in the scattered and independent monasteries of England.

II

ABNORMAL CASES: THE MACHINERY OF ELECTIONS

Hitherto only autonomous houses of the normal type have been considered. These were by far the majority, and the largest extraordinary class, that of the cathedral monasteries, will receive particular notice later. Two abbeys, apart from these, stood in a class by themselves; these were the two bishops' monasteries of Eynsham and Selby, which were *Eigenklöster*, the former belonging to the bishop of Lincoln, the latter to the archbishop of York. In their case the bishop claimed and usually exercised the rights enjoyed elsewhere by the king of holding the election and bestowing the temporalities;[1] a bishop, however, would naturally allow more freedom to the electors, both from considerations of principle and because he had no power to summon a stranger to his monastery.

More irregular and less permanent was the curious case of Alcester. Founded in 1140 at the desire of a bishop of Worcester, with a Worcester monk for its first abbot, it had in its foundation charter a proviso for a joint election at Worcester by the two communities, confirmation and the pastoral staff being given by the bishop. This did not remain long unchallenged, and *c.* 1163, when a vacancy occurred, the monks of Alcester proceeded to an election at home. When the bishop of Worcester intervened they appealed to the archbishop, Becket, who upheld their action, declaring that the clause in the charter was uncanonical and contrary to the Rule of St Benedict, though it had been duly confirmed by Alexander III.[2]

Finally, in a very few cases during the reign of Stephen, the diocesan took the initiative in organizing and controlling the election. This was, in fact, a return to primitive practice, and it is natural to find that the only prelate who systematically and successfully acted in this manner was Henry Murdac of York, whose Cistercian theories, reforming zeal and independent situation moved and enabled him to exercise full authority in his diocese, as in the case of the Whitby election of 1148.[3]

For information as to the procedure followed by the monks when they made an election within the monastery we are dependent upon half a dozen narratives supplied by the chroniclers of four houses: St Albans,

---

1 For elections at Selby under Thurstan and Henry Murdac *v. Historia Selebeiensis Monasterii*, [31], [44]; for Eynsham cf. the *Confirmatio Fundationis* in *Monasticon*, III, 15: "A quo [*sc.* episcopo Lincolniensi] etiam honoris donationem... secundum canonum censuram adepturus est [abbas]"; and *ibid.* 16, where it is stated that the bishop has power "constituendi abbatem". Cf. also the *Magna Vita* of St Hugh of Lincoln, 189–92. For John and Eynsham *v. Barnwell Chronicle* ap. Walter of Coventry, II, 213.

2 *V. Carta Fundationis* in *Monasticon*, IV, 175: "Eligetur abbas in capitulo Wig. communi convenientia utriusque conventus...episcopo...curam animarum cum pastorali baculo tradente." The papal privilege of confirmation is in Holtzmann, *Papsturkunden in England*, II, 2, no. 109; Becket's judgment is in *Monasticon*, IV, 176.

3 *Whitby Cartulary* (Surtees Society), ed. J. C. Atkinson, 8–9.

Battle, Bury and Peterborough—but the strong family likeness shows that all followed a common traditional usage. The election seems invariably to have been effected *per compromissum*: that is, the actual choice was not made by a direct majority vote of the whole body, but by the decision of electors, seven, twelve or fourteen in number, chosen, directly or indirectly, by the chapter; these electors usually sounded the individuals of the community *in camera* as to their wishes.[1] This system was no doubt devised to satisfy the consecrated but ambiguous formula of the Rule and canons that the election was to be the work of the *major et sanior pars* of the electing body; the choice of electors and the expression of opinion to them safeguarded the interests of the majority, and the final election by a select few might be supposed to guarantee its "sanity". When the election in the monastery was not the definitive one, but was held only to instruct the delegates who were to go to court, the procedure was of necessity somewhat different. In such cases the whole body, or chosen electors usually other than the delegates, selected two or three candidates whose names were given to the deputation, sometimes under seal, and an oath was administered that one of these names, and no other, should be chosen in the king's presence.[2]

III

THE DEPOSITION OF AN ABBOT

The Rule and the canons assumed that an abbot, like a bishop, held office for life, and such was the invariable practice throughout the centuries with which we are concerned. From early times it had been the rule for the abbot-elect to be confirmed in his office and blessed by a bishop, normally the diocesan, and gradually the ceremony of this function came to resemble more and more in external appearance that of the consecration of a bishop.[3] In consequence, the abbatial office came to be regarded as possessed of much of the sacrosanctity of the episcopal, while, for wholly different reasons, the abbots became more and more intangible by the bishops, owing to the royal practice of appointment and the position which most of them had of tenants *in capite*. Thus the right claimed and exercised in early times by the bishops of deposing unworthy abbots was rarely asserted in practice in the eleventh and twelfth centuries in England; and as there was no monastic machinery available for the purpose among the black monks themselves, depositions were extremely rare during these centuries, in contrast with what happened among the white monks, where

1 For Bury, *v. Mem. S. Edmund's*, I, 227 *seqq.*, II, 31 *seqq.* For St Albans, *GASA*, I, 250-1. For Battle, *Chron. Bell.* 145-57, 193. For Peterborough, Hugo Candidus, 89-91.
2 This was done at Bury in the election of 1182 and at Battle in 1175.
3 The rite of benediction had, however, probably not attained full development by 1100; cf. art. *Bénédiction d'un Abbé* by Dom J. Baudot in *DAC*.

a visitor could advise and enforce a resignation. Since voluntary resignations were almost unknown, save when an abbot passed to another monastery or to a bishopric, almost all abbots, once elected and blessed, remained
in office till death. The rare depositions were the work either of the
primate at a synod (in the days of Lanfranc and Anselm) or of a papal
legate acting either alone or as president of a council, but the interlocking
of temporal and spiritual powers and allegiances was so complete that a
deposition was avoided whenever possible, as is seen in the palmary
instance of Roger Norreys of Evesham. The consequent disciplinary
dangers were serious, and it was to remedy them that Innocent III asserted
once more the powers of the diocesan in this matter, though the additional
mention of recourse to the Holy See shows that it was considered likely
that bishops would be unwilling to move.[1]

IV

THE SEPARATION OF ABBOT AND COMMUNITY

St Benedict in his Rule assumes that the abbot will live the common life
of the monastery, sharing in the work and prayer of the daily round, and
such, as shown in the *Dialogues* of St Gregory the Great, was the practice
of the legislator himself. The single exception allowed by the Rule, that
the abbot should dine apart from the common table with the guests, was
intended as a safeguard for monastic silence and abstraction of life, and
even this, owing to the abuses which so easily resulted, was repeatedly
disallowed by reformers. At the same time it was impossible for the
simple family life to persist once a monastery became a large organism.
The abbot was forced of necessity to be sometimes absent from home on
business connected with his family, even before abbots were caught up
into public life, and when at home the numerous interviews with visitors
and functionaries made it necessary for him to pass some hours, at least,
in a place where the coming and going of these strangers would not
interfere with the regular life of the house. The simplicity of the Rule,
however, was always looked upon as the ideal to be aimed at by all who
had the spiritual interests of the monastery most at heart, and every new
monastic movement tended to reproduce, so far as possible, its primitive
conditions. Thus Dunstan, in the early days at Glastonbury and again
with his friends when compiling the *Regularis Concordia*, clearly desired
that the abbot should live among his monks as their ever-present spiritual
father, and the same desire can be seen in the arrangements made by
Herluin in the first stages of the growth of Bec.

Between the days of Dunstan and the Conquest, although the English
abbots were frequently drawn into public life, there was no separation

1 For a list of abbatial depositions, 1070–1215, *v.* Appendix XXI.

between them and their monks when they were at home. They dined and presumably slept with the community, and attended the offices in church along with them. This was the practice also of Norman monasticism in the eleventh century; at Bec, fifty years after its foundation, when it was great and wealthy, the abbot still lived among his monks, and it can be seen from the descriptions of scenes at Canterbury that Lanfranc even as archbishop conformed his life so far as possible to that of the convent and even sat with them in the cloister. Indeed, until the end of the eleventh century it is clear that no essential separation of abbot from community had taken place. The vital change was made in the reign of Henry I.

The primary cause was the feudalization of the abbot's position, and above all the claim of the king, asserted brutally and unjustly by Rufus, to hold and enjoy the revenues of a vacant abbey. To avoid this, the abbey lands and income were divided between abbot and community, the abbot having complete responsibility and control of his share; this in turn brought into being a private household of servants and officials and, ultimately, separate quarters in which they and the abbot lived, and the new establishment was rendered still larger and more distinct from the convent by the many duties laid upon the abbot by the fully developed feudal system. The abbot's separate apartments, which at first had probably been little more than a room, gradually became a complete establishment with hall and chapel and court.

These new arrangements gradually took the abbot away, even when at home, from cloister, refectory, dormitory and choir. As early as *c.* 1110 Faricius of Abingdon dined apart from the community, for the chronicler attributes to him the introduction of the custom of inviting some of the monks to eat with him.[1] By the middle of the century the separation was universal, though on all the greater feasts the abbot dined in the refectory.[2] The custom of monks dining with the abbot did not obtain everywhere; Samson of Bury seems usually to have taken meals with his immediate attendants, entertaining guests on occasion.[3] Thus there were regularly three separate tables to cater for: those of the convent, the abbot's household, and the guests.

Presumably the abbot left the dormitory when he left the refectory. Lanfranc assumes that he will sleep with his monks,[4] and there are few, if

---

1 *Chron. Abingd.* II, 287: "Ab illo quoque die quotidie vocavit ad mensam suam x monachos vel xii." The passage is, however, somewhat suspect; *v. infra*, Appendix XIX.

2 It is to this that Marleberge refers in *Chron. Evesh.* 104: "per multos enim annos...in refectorio non comedit [Roger Norreys]."

3 There is no trace in Jocelin of monks from the convent dining with the abbot; on the other hand the twenty-four riotous young knights (*Jocelini Cronica*, 260) *manducaverunt omnes cum abbate.* An easy-going abbot was liable to have all kinds of dependents of great men settled upon him ("vel nuncios vel citharoedos", *Jocelini Cronica*, 246); Samson *a talibus superfluis se prudenter exoneravit* by going upon a journey.

4 *Lanfranci Statuta*, ii, 233: "de abbate. Quamdiu dormierit in lecto suo mane nullus sonitum audeat facere, etc."

any, explicit references to the change of custom, but by the end of the
twelfth century the abbot is found sleeping in his lodging.[1] Finally, the
custom grew up of his reciting the office there with his chaplains and of
celebrating Mass in his private chapel.[2]

This separation of the abbot from the community profoundly modified
black monk life and gave it a new character which it retained in part till
the Dissolution. Unlike similar developments in earlier centuries, this
had come to stay; the whole social economy of which it was a consequence
crystallized and became set; it expressed itself in terms of revenue and
money, and in bricks and mortar, and it affected the whole structural
design of the monastery; nothing, in fact, short of a cataclysm could have
swept it away.

A few houses clung for long to the old ways. As the change was largely
due to the exigencies of feudalism, it is natural to find that the monasteries
which fell least under that system were the slowest to change. At Battle,
for example, where there was no reason for dividing the revenues between
abbot and monks, the abbots continued to live and eat with the community until the end of the twelfth century and beyond.[3] Similarly the
Cluniac houses, which had no abbot and never held by knight-service,
kept for long the single establishment and abbeys such as Reading,
Cluniac in arrangement, followed the same practice,[4] as did also, at least
for the most part, the cathedral monasteries, where the priors long remained in something of their original subordination, and only emerged as
virtually independent superiors after the Fourth Lateran Council and the
consequent reorganization of episcopal methods in the thirteenth century.
Ultimately, all these monasteries adopted the separate establishment in
its main lines, but this final development falls outside the period with
which these pages are concerned.

V

ABBOTS IN PUBLIC LIFE

Concurrently with this separation of life and occupations within the walls
of the monastic buildings went a further separation of interests which
steadily drew the abbot away from the house altogether for shorter or
longer periods of constant recurrence. Besides the immediate and inevitable business of his abbey which took him away, and the financial
and economic motives which led him, when once his revenues were

1 *GASA*, I, 231.
2 *Ibid.* A later abbot of St Albans, however, is noted as having been regular in his
attendance in choir (*ibid.* I, 300–3).
3 Cf. the behaviour of abbot Odo, *Chron. Bell.* 162–3.
4 Cf. the foundation charter in *Monasticon*, IV, 41: "Quia abbas Radingiae non habet
proprios redditus sed communes cum fratribus, etc."

separate from those of the convent, to live for a considerable period of the year in and upon his manors at a distance from the abbey, his office and the very qualities which had led to his selection as abbot often made him a man of mark either in administration, or in things intellectual or spiritual. In the simple society of England before the Conquest he was among the few available counsellors of kings and magnates; in the more complicated feudal state he was among the chief vassals of the Crown and contributors to the revenue; in both he was the spokesman of his order, and his presence was expected at great ecclesiastical meetings and ceremonies. Such duties and interests were routine for all abbots; a commanding personality, a man of genius or sanctity—an Anselm, a Bernard, a Peter, a Suger—exercised a still deeper and wider influence over all those with whom he was thrown into contact.

The *Regularis Concordia* took care to insist that the superior of a monastery, even if he were a bishop, should follow in all things the monastic Rule and way of life,[1] but the very fact that from the first a number of heads of houses were bishops must have made the activities of public life familiar to monastic circles. The three great reformers, and especially Dunstan, were constantly travelling and engaged in diocesan and political affairs, and it must be confessed that their conception of the solidarity of Church and state and of the monks as an integral part of the nation's life made it natural for abbots as well as bishops to pass easily into public life. Very soon some, at least, became members of the Witan. However irregular the meetings of this body may have been, their connection with it gave to the heads of religious houses a permanent interest in the affairs of the kingdom, and the frequency of abbatial attestations to the important charters of the old English period shows that they were often in the company of the king, his bishops and his great men. To official relations personal qualities could add the bonds of intimate counsel and friendship: Wulfric of St Augustine's and Aelfwine of Ramsey represented the king of England at the Council of Rheims;[2] Leofstan, abbot of St Albans on the eve of the Conquest, is said to have been the friend and confessor of Edward and his queen and to have assisted the king on his deathbed;[3] his contemporary, the great Aethelwig of Evesham, was likewise a trusted counsellor of the Confessor, as well as acting as administrator for Ealdred of York in the diocese of Worcester.[4] Thus the tradition of public service of every description was very strong in the English monasteries during the first half of the eleventh century—stronger, indeed, than in any other country of Europe.

1 *Regularis Concordia*, Proem. 78: "Episcopus in omnibus eundem morem regularem cum monachis suis quem Abbas tenet regularis...jugiter sine intermissione teneat."
2 *Chronicle* [E], 1046.
3 *GASA*, I, 38: "Regis Eduuardi...familiaris, confessor et consiliarius, atque Reginae Edithae extiterat."
4 *Chron. Evesh.* 87–8.

Such a tradition was foreign to the Norman monasticism. In Normandy the duke ruled as head of a body of military vassals and there was no tradition of monastic bishops. An individual here and there—Lanfranc is the most eminent example—might have great personal influence outside his monastery, but the monasteries as a whole stood apart from political activity, though when their possessions increased, and especially when, after the Conquest, they became responsible for daughter-houses and cells in England, it was necessary for abbots to be frequently away from home for considerable periods, and Anselm's letters show him as often absent from Bec; but they show also that he was very little engaged in public life.

In England after the Conquest, however, the tradition of severance from external activity was not maintained. In the council of the king which took the place of the Witan all the abbots, so it would seem, or at least all who held of the king *in capite*, had a place; they, like the bishops, were affected by the Conqueror's ruling that all prelates and magnates should be present thrice a year at his crown-wearing at Winchester at Easter, at Westminster at Whitsun and at Gloucester at Christmas.[1] Besides these meetings of the royal Council there were, in the early years of Lanfranc's episcopate, a series of church councils in which the abbots had a place, and they were also present at the great pleas of which there is record. The courts and councils, which were so regular a feature of the Conqueror's reign, became less regular under Rufus and under Henry I; the abbots were apparently only present when some question of national importance had to be decided. Their presence, however, was expected at all great celebrations, such as the dedication of new abbatial or cathedral churches, and the continued frequency of their attestation of charters of all kinds is a proof of their constant visits to court.

Besides these public appearances which affected all as feudal tenants or ecclesiastical dignitaries, individual abbots were from the first employed by the king on special missions. At the very outset of the Conqueror's reign there is the striking case of Aethelwig of Evesham, unique of its kind, which has already been referred to more than once. Athelelm of Abingdon was sent by William I on an embassy to Malcolm of Scotland,[2] and Baldwin of Bury, besides constant attendance on the king and others as court-physician, was employed on a number of political missions.[3] In the following reign Rainald of Abingdon was in favour with Rufus and given the task of distributing the treasure of the Conqueror to churches and the poor in accordance with his will.[4]

1 *Chronicle* [E], 1086: "þænne wæron mid him ealle þa rice men ofer eall Englaland. arce biscopas. ꝼ leodɓs. abbodas ꝼ earlas, etc."
2 *Chron. Abingd.* II, 9.
3 *Hermannus de Miraculis S. Edmundi* (*Mem. S. Edmund's*, I, 72): "Baldwinus curis creberrime regalibus intentus, tam pro medecina regi regisque primoribus impensa, quam etiam circum circa terrarum legationis regiae fungens officia."
4 *Chron. Abingd.* II, 41.

In the next century abbots are continually found on public or diplomatic service of one kind or another. In 1114-15 John of Peterborough was one of the party sent to Rome for the Canterbury pallium, and in 1123 Anselm of Bury and Seffrid of Glastonbury were on the same errand;[1] Hugh of Chertsey had been sent to the pope with others in 1116, presumably to discuss the question of the admission of a legate into England,[2] and Symeon of Durham records that in 1123 the two abbots already mentioned, both near relatives of former archbishops, were commissioned to put the case of Canterbury in the dispute with York;[3] Stephen, abbot of St Mary's, York, acted in the same matter as representative of Thurstan.[4] When the case was further debated in 1125 the abbots of Sherborne and St Albans were with the archbishops.[5] Geoffrey of St Albans, indeed, seems to have been particularly in favour for such missions in this and the following reign, and was sent to Rome by Stephen to announce his accession and again a few years later,[6] while in 1138 Reginald of Evesham, brother of Gilbert Foliot, was one of the English delegates at the Lateran Council.[7] The troubled intrigues of Stephen's reign drew or forced a number of abbots into politics, and more than one source gives information of a number of heads of houses who supported the Empress and were with her when she was received at Winchester.[8]

From Stephen's reign onwards a new source of employment for distinguished abbots was found in the ever-growing number of commissions issued by the Curia to judges delegate in England. At first only bishops were employed, together with a rare Cluniac abbot, known to have been trained in canon law and Gregorian ideas, such as Gilbert Foliot of Gloucester,[9] but gradually it became the practice to employ well-known abbots with considerable regularity, and Jocelin records that Samson, though wholly unknown to the Curia before his election, received his first commission after only seven months of office.[10] Henceforward his name recurs as a judge delegate in a number of the *causes célèbres* of the time.

It would be tedious and unnecessary to give in any detail examples of the many occasions which brought a capable abbot into public life under Richard and John. Instances of all kinds abound in the chronicles of

---

1 *Chronicle* [E], 1114. 2 *Ann. Winton.*, s.a.
3 Symeon of Durham, II, 269.
4 *Historians of York*, II, 121.
5 *Historians of York*, II, 210.
6 *GASA*, I, 104. The chronicler tells us that Geoffrey was chosen four times to go to Rome, but was twice saved by the prayers of the ancress Christina. For another much travelled abbot, Robert of St Albans (1151–66), cf. *GASA*, I, 110–82. Böhmer, *Kirche und Staat*, 403 *seqq.*, gives a list of thirteen abbots who made the journey to Rome between 1136 and 1153.
7 Flor. Wig. II, 114.
8 Will. Malmesb., *GR*, 573; Flor. Wig. II, 130. Malmesbury was himself present.
9 Cf. Gilb. Foliot, *ep.* 23, for the case of Reading *versus* St Denis.
10 *Jocelini Cronica*, 238.

Gervase of Canterbury, Benedict of Peterborough and Ralph of Diceto,[1] and to these we must add the numerous lawsuits which took abbots to the court (often in France) or to the Curia, as also the private relations they might have with the king and his chief officers. An example of the latter at the end of the century may be found in Benedict of Peterborough, whom Richard called his father, and who during the absence of the king in the East was a close ally and counsellor of the Chancellor, William Long-champ.[2] Fragmentary as are the records of any one abbot's activities—for even of Samson we know relatively little[3]—the impression is nevertheless given that abbots of the greater houses were almost continually on the move, either round the circle of their manors or in distant journeys, and almost as continually occupied with external business, either connected with their feudal and economic position, or with the life of the Church and the nation. Few, under such conditions, can have remained true spiritual fathers of their monks.

1 Gervase, I, 358, 469, 545, 556; Benedict of Peterborough, I, 93, 112, 145, 221; Ralph of Diceto, I, 306–10.

2 *Hugonis Candidi continuat. Robert. Swapham*, 102: "Erat enim dicto regi valde specialis amicus et familiaris: in tantum ut ipsum dictus rex patrem suum vocare solebat...fuit idem abbas Willielmi...cancellarii...coadjutor et consiliarius."

3 Among Samson's more abnormal exploits were his assistance at the siege of Windsor at the head of his knights in 1193, and his journey out to Germany to visit the imprisoned Richard (*Jocelini Cronica*, 259).

CHAPTER XXIV

THE INTERNAL GOVERNMENT AND PERSONNEL OF THE MONASTERY

I

THE DEVELOPMENT OF THE CHAPTER

St Benedict, when setting up a system of monastic government, adapted to the needs of a religious family the broad and spacious constitution of the city churches of the ancient world under their patriarchal bishop, which found its typical and crowning achievement in the Church of Rome. Here, as always, the enactments of the legislator have that quality of eminent simplicity which, precisely because it is a simplicity superior to detail, is at once luminous in its wisdom and clarity and extremely difficult to translate faithfully into practice. The abbot is supreme in the monastery much as the bishop is supreme in his diocese and the pope in the universal Church: that is, there is no formal limit set to his competence save that he must himself follow and administer the Rule, which in its turn presupposes the immutable commands of God and the spiritual principles of evangelical perfection. He is, however, in no sense irresponsible, for besides his accountability as an individual soul to his God and his Judge, the Rule tacitly assumes throughout its pages that the abbot (as indeed any ruler under God), precisely because he is the head of a body, exists and acts for the good of that body, and has no power to act apart from it or to alter its character or to exploit it for his private ends. Besides these general principles, St Benedict also lays down certain broad instructions for the abbot. He is supreme; he alone decides and administers all things; but he will only decide wisely if he takes counsel, and therefore all the brethren are to be summoned to give their advice on matters of great moment, and in questions of less importance the seniors alone. All are to say freely what they think; the abbot is to weigh all that has been said and then to decide.[1] Simple as these directions are, they presuppose a single-minded humility and strength in both ruler and ruled that can rarely have been attained in practice. In so far as that humility and strength are failing in either party difficulties at once arise, and the freedom and simplicity become constraint. The abbot, instead of seeking guidance, seeks to dominate or to cajole, or else burkes the issue; the monks on their side fall into the position of a parliament that dictates, bargains and obstructs. Consequently, it became first the custom and later the canon law that on certain great issues affecting the life and fortunes of the house the abbot should

---

[1] *Regula S. Benedicti*, c. iii: "De adhibendis ad consilium fratribus."

not act without the formal consent of his community. In this matter, the final transition from custom to law was not fully made by 1216, but it is possible to watch the gradual evolution, during the twelfth century, of the conception of the community as a corporate body with certain fixed rights *vis-à-vis* the abbot.

Behind the formally expressed wishes of the monks lay two strong but imponderable forces which limited the freedom of the abbot's action in practice no less effectively. These were first, what we now call the public opinion of a community, and next, the elaborate body of customs governing the liturgical and economic life of the house which appeared in St Benedict's Rule in germ as the "practice of the elders" but which soon became codified, at least in liturgical and disciplinary matters. In matters financial and in all those concerned with the jurisdiction of the abbot over the life and fortunes of his monks, the codification only attained full development during the legal renaissance of the twelfth century.

In England before the Conquest there is little or no record of concerted or corporate action on the part of a community, save in its occasional choice or acceptance of an abbot. Long before the revival under Dunstan the daily chapter had become a traditional feature of the monastic horarium on the Continent. The monks left the church at the end of Prime and proceeded to a room near by; a portion of the Rule was read; the superior commented upon it, and breaches of regular discipline were confessed or alleged, and corrected; it was the natural occasion for announcements to be made affecting the life of all before a blessing was pronounced upon the day's work; from its most familiar element this meeting came to be known as the Chapter of Faults. Doubtless in the century before the Conquest English abbots consulted their monks "in chapter", and in some matters at least, such as the admission and profession of novices, some kind of formal consent was probably required, but the *Regularis Concordia* gives no instructions on the point, and the absence in the old English legal system of the conception of a corporate or collegiate body prevented the development of the chapter as a legal agent or witness. Lanfranc's *Statutes*, which devote a section to the daily chapter, are chiefly concerned with the meeting as a part of regular discipline. They state, however, that the consent of the body is necessary for the profession of a novice,[1] and when a monk of another house, or a lay person, or even a woman, is admitted to confraternity, the ceremony takes place in the chapter.[2]

During the first decades after the Conquest, when reorganization under Norman abbots directed by William and Lanfranc was general, the newcomers no doubt disposed of all things within and without their houses

---

1 *Lanfranci Statuta*, c. xviii, 244 (of the profession): "Interroget Abbas considentes fratres, quid inde sentiant? et utrum precibus ejus [*sc.* novicii] annuendum esse concedant? quibus respondentibus se libenter concedere, etc."

2 *Lanfranci Statuta*, c. xxi, 247, enacts that the kiss of peace is to be omitted in the case of women. The presence of women as donors in chapter is frequently noted during this period.

with very little reference to the wishes of their subjects, but gradually, as an equilibrium was reached, the multiplication of gifts and charters of all kinds, the organization of the feudal system, the development of national and the infiltration of canon law, the separation of establishments between abbot and monks, the emergence throughout Europe of corporate bodies, and of a spirit of controversial assertion of rights and liberties—all these various influences tended to transform the community "in chapter" into a deliberative body with certain customs and rights.

Among the primeval "rights" of the chapter was its voice in the profession of new subjects. This, which had its counterpart in the primeval consultation of the people as to the fitness of candidates for the priesthood and episcopate, was presumably always honoured, at least in theory. As regards the reception of a postulant to the habit, tradition and equity were less clear. The common practice was for the brethren to be asked their opinion, and for the abbot then to decide,[1] but while on the one hand the postulant might well be wholly unknown to all save the guest-master and abbot, the convent felt that his reception was as the thin end of the wedge opening the door to profession, especially in an age when the novitiate of a year's duration was not universally observed. There is consequently evidence that throughout the twelfth century communities were endeavouring to secure a right of decision on this point, but the matter remained undetermined.[2]

In the matter of the acquisition of property and its alienation, transactions often accompanied by a whole congeries of rights and restrictions for the parties, it was to the interest of all concerned to secure the assent and testimony of the whole community with a view to avoiding future controversies. It therefore became the custom for all charters, where possible, to be recited, signed and sealed in the chapter; instances abound in all the chronicles and the fact is often rehearsed in the charter itself; not infrequently the ceremony was followed by a symbolical livery of seisin before the high altar of the church.[3] Gradually, also, as the practice of sealing all engagements with the common seal in chapter grew up, this became a condition *sine qua non* in all important financial engagements, as on the one hand the creditors and lessees would accept no smaller security, and on the other the community could not allow their seal to be used save in their presence. It was long, however, before this rule was established, chiefly as a result of painful experience, and it was often broken. The

---

1 Cf. *Lanfranci Statuta*, c. xviii, 243: "Ostendatur res fratribus in capitulo, quorum audito consilio, si suscipiendum eum esse Abbas decreverit, etc." This, the procedure of the Rule in all matters, came later to be formalized into a consultative, as opposed to a decisive, vote.

2 E.g. one of the clauses of the capitulation suggested by Samson before the Bury election of 1182 was that everyone should swear, if elected: "ne aliquem monacaret sine voluntate conventus" (*Jocelini Cronica*, 225).

3 For a quit-claim at St Albans, *v. GASA*, I, 78–9: "Post capitulum, coram monachis ante maius altare stantibus, super altare, per unum cultellum, etc." For similar incidents *v. ibid.* 77, 224; *Chron. Abingd.* II, 124; *Chron. Bell.* 123, 127.

approval of the chapter was also asked for appointments to churches and for any kind of domestic regulation, such as the establishment of an anniversary, or the introduction of a new liturgical rite.[1] In all these matters, there was as yet nothing corresponding to the modern canonical and constitutional sanctions invalidating certain acts if performed without due permission, and complaints of monastic chroniclers that abbots failed to obtain the consent of the monks before alienating property are common; often, no doubt, the acts to which exception was taken were real abuses of power on behalf of relatives, friends and potentates, but very often abbots, upon whom fell the direct responsibility of all things and who had to meet demands on the part of the king which were often far from equitable, realized that their only hope lay in swift administrative action. On the other hand, abbots on occasion upheld the rights of chapter in order to secure support for measures of retrenchment or reform; thus Samson, when entering upon his task of establishing sound economy at Bury, proposed that no mortgages should be entered upon by officials, and no charters signed, without the consent of the chapter, and a little later he fixed the maximum of debt that could be incurred without this consent as low as £1.[2]

Among questions that afforded matter for controversy was the appointment of the major officials. Originally and radically, the appointment lay with the abbot alone, and long-lived abbots and vested interests made for long tenures of office, especially under a weak superior; but when the community became something of a corporate body divided against the abbot (and it must not be forgotten that the majority of the abbots were strangers to the house appointed by the king), a feeling rose that the convent should have some say in a matter affecting so intimately the daily life and finances of the monastery. This was one of the clauses of the capitulation proposed by Samson the subsacrist for acceptance by potential candidates in the election of 1182;[3] when he himself became abbot he had less democratic views, but in the account of the lengthy negotiations preceding his appointment of Prior Herbert it can be seen that, although Samson had his way, it was only after all the forms of a free election had been honoured.[4] Marleberge's constitutions for Evesham which, drawn up as they were by a civilian and a canonist who had been engaged in a long struggle with his abbot, must be regarded as reflecting extremely democratic views, though they were duly confirmed by a legate in 1206 and Innocent

---

1 *GASA*, I, 207 (an anniversary); 285 (daily sung Mass of Our Lady).

2 *Jocelini Cronica*, 235: "Prima die qua tenuit capitulum...proposuit edictum ut nullus de caetero ornamenta ecclesiae invadiaret sine assensu conventus, sicut solebat fieri, nec aliqua carta sigillaretur sigillo conventus nisi in capitulo coram conventu." *Ibid.* 243: "Prohibens ne aliquis officialis appruntaret aliquod debitum ultra xx solidos sine assensu prioris et conventus." At York in 1206 a hundred shillings was fixed by a similar regulation (*EHR*, XLVI, July 1931, 451).

3 *Jocelini Cronica*, 225: "Nec capitales obedientiales mutaret sine assensu conventus."

4 *Jocelini Cronica*, 322–7.

III in 1216, provide that fifteen or more officials should be appointed with the advice and consent of the chapter.[1] Other occasions on which the chapter's right of election was claimed were the appointments of priors of dependent houses and of coadjutor-abbots,[2] and the granting of rights of heredity and other privileges to servants.

Less controversial were a number of great questions where abbot and community made common cause in a matter deeply affecting the honour or well-being of the monastery. Thus in the Battle exemption claim we are told that the abbot made a point of obtaining the advice and support of his chapter,[3] and the whole community of St Albans gave their assent to the translation of the body of their titular saint;[4] it was in chapter, also, that Abbot Geoffrey of York met and resisted Archbishop Thurstan, who had announced his intention of investigating the causes of the disturbances in the abbey.[5] And when, at Bury shortly before the death of Abbot Hugh, the king's almoner appeared to enquire into the truth of the reports as to the abbey's insolvency, he was conducted into the chapter where the prior, in the name of all, assured him that nothing was amiss.[6] Finally, in an interregnum the chapter, under the presidency of the prior, acted as a kind of council of regency, and on several occasions of which record has survived showed considerable ability in conducting the preliminaries of an election.[7]

The gradual emergence of the community in chapter as a body with a certain competence of its own, whether in conjunction with or as opposed to the abbot, though it was in a sense only the translation into a legal formula of St Benedict's directions, had as its result a narrowing of the legislator's ideal, not only by putting certain limits, however vague, to the abbot's freedom of action, but by giving him a correlative sense of complete independence in all matters where no claim or obligation to consult the chapter existed. It was, perhaps, an inevitable result of the separation, under feudal conditions, of abbot from community, and of the development of black monk abbeys into vast and wealthy establishments whose resources could be employed, exploited and wasted in numberless ways by those entrusted with their administration; it was also in part a consequence of the great legal movement of the twelfth century. It is natural that the clearest traces of what may be called the juridical notion of the chapter should be found in abbeys such as St Albans, where intellectual interests and the study of canon law were common, or in individuals such as Marleberge of Evesham, whose private studies and personal history had inclined them to limit the powers of authority. As was to happen two

1 *Chron. Evesh.* 206: "De consilio et consensu conventus vel majoris et sanioris partis in capitulo." 2 Matthew Paris, *Historia Anglorum, s.a.* 1090, 1150.
3 *Chron. Bell.* 62, 82. 4 *GASA*, 1, 85.
5 *V. supra*, p. 235. 6 *Jocelini Cronica*, 211.
7 Cf. *Jocelini Cronica*, 223–5; *Chron. Bell.* 146 seqq.; 32, 58, 120, 123, 127; *GASA*, 1, 72, 77, 95, 96, 109, 119, 156, 206.

centuries later in the college of cardinals, those who as private individuals had been anxious to capitulate upon a ruler's rights often became strenuous defenders of absolutism when they were themselves in office, and doubtless other abbots besides John of St Albans, after promising to yield to the wishes of the community, turned their faces to the wall and died without signing the charter that guaranteed freedom.[1] In general, also, democratic movements within a monastery were apt to break ultimately upon the patriarchal authority of the abbot so clearly asserted in the Rule, and there is an air of futility about much of the agitation at St Albans and Bury. But it would be unhistorical to condemn all efforts of the monks to limit the independence of the abbot as so many attempts to escape regular obedience. The majority of black monk abbots, on their side, had already departed from the conception of their office outlined by St Benedict; by withdrawing from the common life and from the immediate daily responsibility for the spiritual well-being of their subjects they had impaired the equitable relationship between ruler and ruled which alone justified the claim to universal control. Innocent III realized this clearly enough, and in his efforts to reinvigorate the monastic order throughout Europe did not hesitate to sanction and impose upon various monasteries constitutions giving considerable power to the chapter in order to check the abuse of freedom on the part of abbots.[2] It was in pursuance of this policy that his legate, John of Ferentino, approved of the Evesham constitutions, and imposed others, still more drastic, upon the abbey of St Mary's, York.[3] In these two documents there is mention, perhaps for the first time in England, of the Council of Seniors as a body with specific functions, and of a regular inspection of accounts on the part of both abbot and chapter. Here, as in many other respects, the pontificate of Innocent opened a new constitutional era, and many of the measures then outlined passed into the canon law of the Church. But this development belongs rightly to the century after the Lateran Council.

Although the competence of the chapter was undefined on many important issues, it had one great advantage that was lacking to the various national parliaments in later centuries, for the constituent body met together every day independently of any initiative on the part of the abbot, and had constantly to be used in witnessing and agreeing to quasi-routine actions and transactions; it was therefore a simple matter to start a discussion.[4] A strong abbot like Samson might absent himself for a time from

---

1 *GASA*, I, 248. The date was 1214; the point at issue the exile of monks to distant cells.

2 For a full treatment, with references, *v.* Dom U. Berlière, *Innocent III et la réorganisation des monastères bénédictins*, in *RB*, XXXII, 22–42, 145–59.

3 *Chron. Evesh.* 202: for York, *v.* C. R. Cheney, *The Papal Legate and English Monasteries in 1206*, in *EHR*, XLVI (July 1931), 449–52.

4 There is no trace in the twelfth century of any special days being assigned or barred to general business in chapter. In modern black monk practice formal meetings of the chapter as a voting body are infrequent, and constitutions often enact that considerable previous notice must be given of any important business.

motives of policy, to allow passions to cool,[1] but only an utterly worthless abbot would wholly discontinue his attendance,[2] and his daily presence, with the possibility of considerable freedom of speech being used by the monks, was no doubt a salutary check upon irresponsible action.[3] The chronicles have preserved for us accounts of a number of scenes in which a wide liberty of criticism was allowed and used.[4] Normally, however, the checks of conscience and family respect, together with a love of peace, prevented serious friction.

The business of the chapter took place after the customary prayers which now form a regular part of the office of Prime. The presiding superior said: *Loquamur de ordine nostro*: after which he himself could address the brethren, or call upon offenders to confess their faults. After this, or in substitution for it, official business was introduced, and from Jocelin it can be gathered that voting by show of hands was not uncommon.[5] The meeting ended with a procession out of the chapter-room, accompanied by the chanting of a psalm, *Verba mea*, for the dead, and the intoning of this psalm by the presiding superior was on occasion a sign for the formal closure of a heated debate, comparable to the rising of the Speaker in the House of Commons.[6]

II

RECRUITMENT—*OBLATI* AND *CONVERSI*

St Benedict in his Rule allowed for two methods of recruitment to his monastery and, as a corollary, for two ways of instruction in the monastic life. The one applied to all who sought for admission when already past the age of boyhood. These were put through a year's training and supervision in special quarters set apart for the novices and then, if all was satisfactory, made their monastic profession.[7] The second covered the case

1 *Jocelini Cronica*, 316: "His dictis, statim recessit abbas de villa, et absentavit se octo diebus." But cf. also the sequel to this action.

2 *Chron. Evesh.* 104: "Per multos enim annos ante depositionem suam, septem vel amplius, capitulum non tenuit [Roger Norreys]."

3 When Samson, at the height of his power, swamped the lands of the cellarer to improve his fishpond, we are told that the injured official "convenit eum quandoque in pleno capitulo super damno tanto" (*Jocelini Cronica*, 328), and though he got little satisfaction in this particular case, such remonstrances doubtless often took effect.

4 In *GASA*, I, 255 and *Jocelini Cronica*, 316 we can see something of a storm in chapter.

5 *Jocelini Cronica*, 225: "Et hoc ipsum concessimus, omnes dextras erigentes in signum concessionis."

6 *Jocelini Cronica*, 316: "Cumque prior incepisset cantare *Verba mea* pro defunctis, sicut consuetudo est, restiterunt novitii, etc."

7 *Regula S. Benedicti*, c. lviii. Although St Benedict devotes a special chapter (lx) to the case of priests and clerics who may wish to join the monastery, it is not clear whether he intended them to go through a regular year's novitiate. Probably he did not: they took,

of children who were offered to the monastic life by their parents. This custom of child oblation, already in existence in both East and West before St Benedict's day,[1] was taken by him into the Rule as a normal procedure, and the account of his life by Gregory the Great gives more than one incident from the years at Subiaco illustrating his relations to such children. In their case, the solemn offering at the altar was accompanied by the formal promises made by the parent on behalf of the child and was held to dedicate the boy's life irrevocably; the subject passed through no definite period of subsequent probation, but was trained gradually under special regulations of discipline until he arrived at maturity. A close parallel to these two kinds of monastic profession, the personal and the vicarious, can be found in the two rites of baptism, for adults and for infants, with their promises; like the similar engagements of infant marriage and vicariously dedicated virginity such a disposal of a child's future was in perfect accord with the outlook of the time, and, indeed, with the manners and circumstances of European society throughout the first half of the Middle Ages.

These two methods of admission remained in vogue throughout the centuries between Benedict and Dunstan. Indeed, here as elsewhere, it is the twelfth century that witnesses the break with ways of thought that had been unchanged for six hundred years. The *Regularis Concordia* contains no detailed legislation for the novitiate and profession, and records of the kind before the Conquest are meagre in the extreme; the presence of a number of children and boys is, however, assumed throughout the document and throughout all the writings of Aelfric and his school, and such other references as exist go to show that after the early years of the revival the greater number, if not nearly all, of the monks had been children of the cloister. At the very beginning of the movement Dunstan is seen in charge of a group of boys at Glastonbury, and the reminiscences of Osbern and Eadmer at Canterbury c. 1060–80 give a similar picture; Thurstan, who became abbot of Ely in 1066 and had been in the monastery from his infancy, may be taken as typical of his age.[2] Exceptions, if indeed they were rare enough to be called such, there must always have been; in the early days there were many recruits of mature life and more than one great benefactor took the habit at a house he had endowed, while at the end of the Saxon period the case of Wulfstan of Worcester, who was a priest before becoming a monk, cannot have been wholly exceptional, but the norm was undoubtedly for future monks to enter the monastery as children or boys.

---

however, the vows of obedience to the Rule and stability ("promittunt de observatione Regulae vel [= et] propriam stabilitatem"). The latter promise was likewise made ("stabilitatem firmare") by stranger monks who might wish to join.

1 It is found on all sides in contemporary and earlier monasticism; cf. the *Rule of St Basil*, c. 7, quoted by Butler in note to *Regula*, c. lix, 22.

2 *Liber Eliensis*, 231: "In monasterio monachus factus laudabili conversatione vitam ab infantia huc usque servavit."

The Statutes of Lanfranc, which reflect contemporary Norman practice, give fuller information; they contain a few elements which would seem never to have become fully naturalized in England. The two classes, of children and late arrivals, are still assumed, but for each the legislation of the Rule is somewhat modified. Thus in the case of those who came into the cloister "from the world" a full year's probation was no longer demanded.[1] All depended, it would seem, upon the abbot and his advisers. This abandonment, common throughout Europe and above all at Cluny, of the year-long novitiate was due partly to the exceptional nature of such conversions, as opposed to the normal education in the cloister. Such an utter change of life, comparable to a change of religion by an Anglican clergyman at the present day, needed, as it seemed, no long period of trial to demonstrate its sincerity, since the position in the world had been abandoned once and for all. Partly, also, it was due to an almost entire absence of recruits of the age of adolescence. The system had its dangers, however, and formed one of the principal charges brought against the traditional monasticism by the Cistercians.

Conversely, in the case of children offered in infancy, this oblation was considered as the equivalent of clothing with the habit, not, as in the Rule, of final profession. Under Lanfranc's scheme, which merely repeated current practice, the boy brought up in the cloister made his final monastic promises only when he had attained adolescence.[2] There were, therefore, two groups in the monastery, the *monachi nutriti* and the *conversi*. But although Lanfranc, in the chapter already referred to, applies the term *conversus* to all latecomers, lay and clerical, his regulations make it clear that in Norman monasticism there was a cross division in the community separating those in orders from laymen, and as the majority of late vocations would be incapable of undergoing the training necessary for those proceeding to ordination, the term *conversus* came to be used, and is often used by Lanfranc himself, as a synonym of *monachus laicus*. At first sight, indeed, the reader familiar with the "lay brothers" of modern black monachism might easily suppose Lanfranc's *conversi* to be their equivalent, for they wear beards, sit apart from the clerics in choir, walk in a different rank in processions, and perform a number of minor duties as altar servers and candle bearers, which often fall to lay brothers at the present day.[3] Such an equation would, however, be incorrect, for these *conversi* were fully professed choir monks with all chapter rights and forming part of a single monastic family, though there would seem to have been

---

1 Lanfranc (*Statuta*, c. xviii, 244) says merely: "transactis plerisque diebus."

2 *Lanfranci Statuta*, c. xviii, 245: "Cum vero adulta aetate facturus professionem fuerit, etc."

3 Cf. the order of the procession on Palm Sunday (*Lanfranci Statuta*, c. i, § 4, 217): first servants (*famuli*) with banners; then a *conversus* with holy water and others with candles, etc.; then *laici monachi, infantes, ceteri monachi, Abbas. Ibid.* c. xviii, 244: "In choro si clericus est [novitius] ultimus sit in ordine clericorum; si laicus, laicorum."

a certain division of sentiment between the two groups.[1] In the event, the sharp distinction, which was foreign alike to the intention of St Benedict and the practice in English monasteries, seems never to have become normal in this country. It is hard to discover a single reference to these *conversi* or to any distinction between them and the *monachi nutriti* and *clerici* in the whole mass of indigenous monastic literature; we may therefore suppose that Lanfranc's Statutes did not succeed in perpetuating the Norman tradition in this respect.[2]

During the fifty years immediately following the Conquest the twofold method of recruitment continued in vogue and examples of both kinds are to be met with on every hand. One such, which may almost be called classic, is provided by the historian Orderic Vitalis who, born near Shrewsbury shortly after the Conquest, was at the age of ten given by his father to the monk Rainald to carry beyond the seas to a monastery, with the promise that eternal life should be his. At the age of eleven he was clothed and tonsured at St Évroul, and ordained in due course subdeacon at sixteen, deacon at eighteen and priest at thirty-three. As for his father, he took the other entry and lived the last years of his life at Shrewsbury, the house of his own founding, as a *conversus*.[3] Besides Orderic, most of the great names of Anglo-Norman monasticism are those of whilom children of the cloister; William of Malmesbury was one, it would seem; William Godemon, abbot of Gloucester (1113–30), had been offered to God and to St Peter at the age of seven,[4] and the Abingdon chronicle and cartulary contain a number of records of knights and townspeople who had given their children to the monastery, together with a gift of property that preserved the memory of their action.[5]

On the other hand there are numerous records of late vocations, either of simple changes of life on the part of a knight or priest, or of knights and merchants who became monks as a result of some signal warning or favour received at the hands of a popular saint.[6] Of the former class, a notable early case is that of Hugh de Fleury, a relative and follower of William I, who became a monk at St Augustine's, Canterbury, c. 1090 and was almost immediately appointed abbot by Rufus, though protesting

---

1 Cf. the illustration drawn by Anselm (Eadmer, *De s. Anselmi Similitudinibus*, c. 78, in *PL*, CLIX) from the distinction between *monachi nutriti* and *conversi*.

2 The only two exceptions to the statement in the text (to my knowledge) are the reference of Anselm (v. preceding note) and another in a Reading document (*Monasticon*, IV, 43). But Anselm, a monk of Bec, was speaking to those for whom Lanfranc had written his statutes, and Reading was modelled upon Cluny. Cf., however, Appendix XXIII.

3 Ordericus, II, 301; V, 133. Cf. *Chron. Bell.* 25: "[After the foundation] nonnullis illuc religionis desiderio confluentibus, quamplurimis etiam liberos suos in Dei instruendos servitio offerentibus, etc."

4 *Hist. Glocestr.* 15.

5 *Chron. Abingd.* II, 145, 169, 170, 207.

6 For cases of a *miles* becoming a monk v. *Chron. Bell.* 36; *Chron. Will. Thorne*, 1794. For the second class of vocation v. *Mem. S. Edmund's*, I, 77 (a knight of the Conqueror's); *ibid.* 185 (a rich merchant); Will. Malmesb., *GP*, 287 (a merchant *jam senectute fractus*).

his "illiteracy";[1] of a somewhat different type were the two goldsmiths, Godric and Anketil, who in middle or late life joined the communities of Evesham and St Albans respectively.[2]

Towards the middle of the century, however, a great change came about by slow and almost imperceptible degrees; the offering of children ceased altogether; the custom of all, or nearly all, proceeding to the priesthood became universal, and the majority of recruits were either boys sent by their parents without any formal oblation to be educated in the cloister or youths and young men who had received an education at one of the numerous non-monastic schools and (a little later) often also a university training abroad. Various causes contributed to this change. At the root of all was the development of a new social and intellectual order, of greater complexity than the old, which gradually replaced the more simple social fabric of the last five centuries. When the monks had ceased to be the only teachers and educated class it was inevitable both that monasteries should pay less attention to their children and that boys educated outside the cloister should wish to become monks. But there was also a more immediate reason. The early Cistercians, by allowing no one to join their order under the age of seventeen, and by their direct attack on the Cluniac novitiate, set up a standard which could not but influence, directly or indirectly, other monastic bodies, and within a very few decades the sentiment arose, to receive the sanction of an ecclesiastical decree after 1215, that infant oblation, regarded as imposing a life-long obligation on the subject, was undesirable and indeed unlawful.[3] This sentiment was no doubt encouraged in its growth alike by the increasing number of those who became novices when mature in years and mental training, and by the allurements offered by the other administrative and intellectual careers that now began to lie open to the educated. It is even possible to fix within ten or twenty years the change of feeling. The last, or one of the last, recorded cases of oblation at Abingdon is *c.* 1150.[4] Twenty years later, in 1168, the community of St Augustine's, Canterbury, is found protesting that infants recently at nurse have been clothed with the habit by their intruded superior, Clarembald, and procuring a papal injunction that none are to be received below the age of fifteen.[5] Within fifty years of this the Lateran Council abrogated the institution of oblation altogether, and the system which had been an inseparable part of black monk life since the age before the Rule was declared to be henceforth unlawful.

This decree, as a legal enactment, touched only the practice of oblation in the form of the solemn dedication of a child to the monastic life with

---

1 *Chron. Will. Thorne,* 1794.
2 *Chron. Evesh.* 86–7; *GASA,* I, 83–4.
3 *Corp. Jur. Can.,* Decret. lib. III, tit. xxxi, c. 8 (ed. Friedberg, II, 571).
4 *Chron. Abingd.* II, 207. The preceding page contains a record of a priest and his son becoming monks.
5 *Chron. Will. Thorne,* 1815: "Pueri vix ablactanei."

the intention of removing for ever his freedom of personal choice. It was still open to monasteries to receive boys or even small children for education with the moral certainty that they would in time take the habit. But the institution of oblation had gone, and it would appear that before 1200 the group of children (*infantes*) of the cloister had dwindled in some houses and disappeared altogether in others. The office of childmaster, so commonly mentioned in documents preceding and immediately following the Conquest, is seldom if ever alluded to after 1150, and there is in Jocelin's *Chronicle* no mention of *pueri*. Such a silence, even if it does not prove that there were no young boys at Bury, is at least very significant, and if such scattered evidence as exists for the period *c.* 1200 is marshalled, a general if vague impression results that the bulk of a black monk community at that time were natives of the district who had taken their vows after a number of years spent either in the intern school of the monastery or in the public school of some neighbouring town, but that in every house there was a group, greater or smaller, of those who had entered between the ages of twenty-five and thirty-five, men who had been at a university, or who were already priests, or who had begun to practise a trade, craft or profession.[1]

III

NOVICES

A reader at all conversant with modern religious life cannot fail to remark that the master of novices figures extremely seldom in the sources of the period. Partly, no doubt, this is because no revenues, which might necessitate documentary record, were attached to the office; partly, and especially before 1150, because the novice master would be of less significance than the master of the children; perhaps, indeed, the functions often coalesced. But even at the end of the century the office was regarded as of minor importance,[2] and some evidence goes to show that the black monk master, at least in England, did little more than teach the customs of the house and watch the external deportment of his charges.[3] Among the white monks, on the other hand, the master of novices was expected to give a spiritual formation which should influence a whole life.

While the children do not figure in Jocelin's pages the novices, who

1 Very few lists of communities before 1215 are in existence, and these few rarely give more than the name in religion and (occasionally) the office of the individual. In the "division lists" of the Bury election of 1214–15 (*Mem. S. Edmund's*, II, 75–6) five out of sixty-two names bear the title *magister*, one *sacerdos de hospitali*, and twenty-eight have a distinguishing local surname—almost all from East Anglia.

2 Thus we learn from an *obiter dictum* of Jocelin (*Cronica*, 212) that Samson had been his novice master, but the office is not mentioned among those held by Samson (*ibid.* 214); either it was held concurrently with another or not considered worthy of note.

3 Cf. *Jocelini Cronica*, 212: "[Magister meus] qui me docebat ordinem et cujus custodie deputatus sum." Too much weight, however, should not be attached to such isolated allusions.

rarely appear as a class in the earlier sources, are frequently in evidence, and the term would seem to have been used to cover a fairly long stage in a young monk's life, in something of the same way that the term "junior" or "cleric" is used at the present day, and to have been employed in reckoning seniority.[1]

IV

SOCIAL STATUS OF THE RECRUITS

Since until the multiplication of the houses of canons (c. 1100) and of Cistercians (c. 1135) the monasteries of the black monks offered the only available form of religious life, and since at the same time the classes of those free to devote themselves or their children to the cloister were limited in number, it would be natural to suppose a priori that the population of the monasteries between 960 and 1130 would be drawn exclusively from the various sections of the class of wholly free land-holders in town and country; closer examination, indeed, shows this to have been the case.

The three leaders of the first revival were men of distinguished family and high connections in Church and state, and their first disciples were probably of the same rank. When, between 960 and 1000, monasticism spread rapidly, it is likely that children from all the free classes of society entered the cloister, but so far as the scanty information extends it is clear that until the Conquest there was always a strong aristocratic element in the monasteries, especially, perhaps, in East Anglia, where so many houses received support from Cnut and his nobles. Thus Abbot Leofric of St Albans (c. 1000–1040) is said to have been a son of the earl of Kent, and Fritheric, abbot at the Conquest, was a near relative of Cnut;[2] Leofric of Peterborough (ob. 1066) was a nephew of the earl Leofric, the founder of Coventry;[3] Wulfric of Ely (c. 1045) was a kinsman of the Confessor, and Thurstan, abbot in 1066, was a noble;[4] Aelfwig, the abbot of the New Minster who fell at Hastings, was an uncle of Harold[5]; Prior Aefic (c. 1040) and Abbot Aethelwig of Evesham were both men of considerable property by inheritance.[6] There are even indications that in the East-Anglian houses some kind of birth or property qualification was demanded of

1 The presence of the *novitii* as a group in chapter (*Jocelini Cronica*, 316) is a proof of this, for a novice before profession was not admitted to discussions in chapter. Cf. also the criticisms of the *novitii* before the election of 1182 (*ibid.* 221) and the choice of *magister Hermerus tunc temporis novicius* as one of the electors (*ibid.* 223); also Gervase, I, 293, where Prior Alan, ex-canon of Benevento, is described as *quinquennis fere novitius*, and *GASA*, I, 215, where the phrase *novitii quinquennes* occurs. Cf. also *Mem. St Edmund's*, II, 86.

2 *GASA*, I, 28, 41: "Frethericus ex veteribus Saxonibus claram ducens originem et Dacis, Cnutoni Regi fuit consanguineus." Even if incorrect, these statements are significant.

3 *Chronicle* [E], 1066: "Se eorl Leofric þe waes his eam."

4 *Liber Eliensis*, 215, 231.

5 *Monasticon*, II, 437.

6 *Chron. Evesh.* 83 (Aefic), 95 (Aethelwig); *ibid.* 83, 325–6, where Aelfward, c. 1030, is called a *consanguineus* of Cnut.

aspirants, as in a number of south German and Italian abbeys at the end of the Middle Ages.[1] This influence of the old English aristocracy tended to cease after the Conquest, though one or two abbeys, and notably Croyland which honoured the tomb of Waltheof, kept up their connections with the great families of the past.[2] In Normandy the monasteries had been founded almost without exception by the great landowners, and many sons of these houses became monks and passed as abbots to England. It was not, however, to be expected that the old-established English abbeys would receive many recruits from among the first tenants-in-chief of the Conqueror and their sons, and when the new Anglo-Norman landowning class began to found religious houses in large numbers in the twelfth century the prestige of the black monks was somewhat on the wane. A number of men of the highest Norman families are indeed found as English abbots, but in the majority of cases they came direct from overseas.[3] Nevertheless, their presence is significant, and it is probable that during the first fifty years after the Conquest a large proportion of the inmates of the monasteries situated in the provinces (as opposed to the Canterbury and Winchester houses) were from the larger and smaller Anglo-Norman landowning and military families. After that, as English society gradually became more complex, the sons of all classes of free men were among the recruits, and no house remained in any sense a preserve of the aristocracy. Two groups, however, retained longer than others a community of predominantly Anglo-Saxon blood: the fenland circle of Ely, Peterborough, Thorney, Ramsey and Croyland, and the remoter Wessex houses such as Cerne, Milton, Athelney, Muchelney and Abbotsbury. Towards the end of the century the element drawn from the class of great territorial families tended to decrease; the great waves of conversion to the cloister had passed with the earlier fervours and enthusiasms; there were, besides, far more varieties of religious life now soliciting the choice of aspirants. Every indication goes to show that in the reigns of Richard and John the monasteries were recruited almost entirely from what may be called, at the risk of anachronism, the middle class: from families, that is, of small owners of land and traders in the town or district near the abbey, with a fair leaven of priests and university-trained clerks or masters

---

1 *GASA*, I, 31: "Nullum nisi genere clarum vel saltem legitimum in monachatum admisit [Leofric]." *Liber Eliensis*, 200: "[Leofsig, *c.* 1029] studuit... ut neminem in congregatione monachorum susciperent nisi electos in scientia et praeclaros genere."

2 A Waldef, brother of Cospatric, earl of Dunbar, and monk of the house, was abbot of Croyland, *c.* 1124–38.

3 The following may be given as examples of overseas abbots of high family: Hugh de Fleury (St Augustine's), *c.* 1091–1124; Richard de Essay (St Albans), 1097–1119; Hugh de Blois (St Benet's, Holme), *c.* 1138; Walter de Lucy (Battle), 1139–71; Robert, son of Hugh earl of Chester (Bury), 1100–2; Richard, grandson of Gilbert du Pin (Ely), 1100–7; Henry of Blois (Glastonbury), 1126–71; Gilbert Foliot (Gloucester), 1139–48; Gilbert Crispin (Westminster), *c.* 1090–1117; Gervase de Blois (Westminster), *c.* 1138–60; Serlo de Percy (Whitby), *c.* 1085. Reginald Foliot (Evesham), 1129–49, and Walter de Lacy (Gloucester), 1130–9, may possibly have been natives of England.

of the same social grade, who entered the monastery at the age of thirty or above. It is a community of this kind that the contemporary chronicles of such different types of house as St Albans, Bury and Evesham reveal by glimpses at the end of the twelfth century.

V

MONASTIC NUMBERS

It goes without saying that adequate statistics of the numbers are wholly wanting in the case of the majority of the monasteries, and that it is rarely, if ever, possible to trace the fluctuations in the strength of a community over the whole period. Sufficient indications, however, remain to permit of a few general judgments.

The houses of the old English revival would seem to have been, even in the epoch of their greatest prosperity, relatively small. If the lists of monks at the Old and New Minsters given in the register of the latter house are complete, some hundred and ninety and hundred and fifty respectively would appear to have entered between 965 and 1066, including in this figure the original colony of perhaps twenty.[1] This would give an average of about fifty and forty as the strength of the two monasteries, which unquestionably ranked among the most important houses of the land. By the time of the Confessor almost all the monasteries would seem to have been smaller than this; according to one source, there were twenty-six monks at St Benet's of Holme in 1020,[2] and Evesham and Worcester, though spiritually flourishing, were reduced to a dozen monks immediately before the Conquest.

All the sources agree that a great and wholesale increase in the numbers followed the Norman plantation, and the figures, which now become fairly plentiful, amply bear this out.[3] Almost all the more important monasteries appear to have risen in numbers to a figure between sixty and a hundred. The peak was attained during the reign of Henry I; within its limits Ely had fifty, Norwich, Peterborough and Rochester sixty, Evesham about seventy, Abingdon eighty, Gloucester a hundred and Christ Church, Canterbury perhaps a hundred and fifty monks. The last-named house, as unexceptionable testimony informs us, was the most populous in England;

1 *Hyde Liber Vitae* (ed. Birch), 22–9, 31–6.
2 Chronicle printed in extracts in *Mem. S. Edmund's*, I, 359.
3 As the matter is of some interest in enabling us to form an impression of the life of the monks, I have set out in Appendix XVII all the figures that I have met with during the period 960–1216. For purposes of comparison it may be mentioned that Downside and Ampleforth to-day have resident communities of about fifty and seventy (without any lay brothers); Solesmes (France) has some seventy choir monks in residence together with twenty-five lay brothers engaged on house and garden work; Beuron (Germany) has some ninety choir monks and over a hundred lay brothers, the latter being chiefly engaged, like medieval Cistercian *conversi*, on land work, though all are housed in the abbey.

there was thus nothing in this country among the black monks corresponding to the vast communities of Cluny and Cîteaux, or even to those of the northern Cistercians in the first decades, and it would probably be near the truth to allow for fifty to sixty as the average complement of two-thirds of the monasteries at the middle of the century.

The last decades saw a decline from this, due partly to the competition set up by the new orders and partly to the private troubles which came to almost every house at some time or another during the period 1150–1216. By *c.* 1200 there was probably no community larger than a hundred, and almost all had decreased from their maximum by about a third. Never again, it may be added, did they attain the size reached at the beginning of the twelfth century.

CHAPTER XXV

THE ADMINISTRATION OF THE MONASTERY

I

THE OFFICIALS

The power of an abbot was, within the limits of the Rule, absolute, and he was the only source of authority; no part of the administration was outside his ultimate control, and he could, and often did, take upon himself direct responsibility for this or that sphere of administration, in somewhat the same manner as a modern premier takes into his hands the portfolio of one or more ministries. But, even in the smallest monastery, some delegation of power was necessary, and gradually an elaborate hierarchy of officials was evolved.

The Rule of St Benedict legislates for but two lieutenants of the abbot. One of these is the second in command, the provost or prior, whom the legislator admitted with a certain reluctance, clearly preferring a scheme of government by deans over ten monks;[1] the other is the cellarer, who has complete control of all the material resources of the community.[2] Besides these there is passing mention of a master of the novices.[3] As a monastery grew in numbers and wealth, and doubtless in Monte Cassino itself during St Benedict's lifetime, a number of other offices would find place and gradually become traditional. In new beginnings, however, there was often a reversion to the simplicity of the Rule and in England, at least, it was not till the twelfth century that the highly complicated system of departmental administration became stereotyped throughout the black monk houses. Very early, however, two offices, which well reflected the development of the monastic order, came into being and rose to importance—that of the sacrist, and that of the precentor or cantor. Yet another official must always have existed, even if unnamed, the master in charge of the children of the cloister, and an interesting reference to the life at Fleury c. 960 mentions six major officials apart from the abbot, viz. dean, provost, librarian, cellarer, cantor and master of the school.[4]

1 *Regula S. Benedicti*, c. xxi: "de decanis monasterii." c. lxv: "de praeposito monasterii." In the latter chapter he observes (27–9): "si potest fieri per decanos ordinetur, ut antea disposuimus, omnis utilitas monasterii." Both systems had been in vogue in the East. The late Abbot Butler was in the habit of remarking that the prejudice of St Benedict against a prior was the solitary error in practical judgment of the Rule.

2 *Regula*, c. xxxi: de cellarario, 5–7: "Omni congregationi sit sicut pater. Curam gerat de omnibus."

3 *Regula*, c. lviii, 11–12: "Et senior eis [*sc.* noviciis] deputetur."

4 *Vita S. Oswaldi, auct. anon.* (*Hist. York*, 1, 423): "Pater monasterii [abbot]...decanus [? prior]...praepositus [? extern procurator]...armarius [librarian]...cellerarius...cantor ...magister scolae."

In pre-Conquest England, where the houses remained for the most part fairly small, the names of only five officials appear in the sources—provost, cellarer, sacrist, precentor and master of the children—and if the *cursus honorum* of Wulfstan of Worcester may be taken as normal, the sacrist's office was regarded as more important than the precentor's, which in its turn was superior to that of master of the children.[1] After the Conquest, the number of officials increased rapidly. The chief cause of this was no doubt the steady growth in numbers and wealth of all the greater houses in the first thirty years of Norman rule; this growth was accompanied by the erection of spacious conventual buildings, with offices and stores for the various needs, and the great establishment which came into being attracted more and more dependents, guests and poor and, in many cases, pilgrims. One by one a whole series of administrative departments sprang into being, each with its chief and assistants.

On the purely religious and disciplinary side were, after the abbot, a second in command, known usually as the *prior*, a third, the *subprior*, and, in the largest houses, a fourth, known as the *third prior*. Besides these, there were the *master of the novices*, the *master of the children* and an indefinite number of seniors charged with supervision in the cloister and dormitory, known as *circatores* or *custodes ordinis*.

In a position by himself stood the *cantor* or *precentor*. His office, though it came to have an administrative side, was chiefly concerned with liturgical and literary matters, and at the end of the eleventh century in England the literary side of the precentor's duties would seem to have gained ground at the expense of the musical; the post became the perquisite of the most gifted man of letters in the community, and was held by such eminent writers as Eadmer, William of Malmesbury, Maurice of Durham and Osbern of Canterbury, though the case of Uhtred of Worcester, Wulfstan's precentor, who was taken with his last illness when intoning an offertory in 1132, shows that at that date it was still normal for him to direct the choir, and Uhtred was succeeded by the chronicler, John, who was singing beside him as he fell.[2] The cantor had charge of all the writing and illuminating in the cloister, and of all the choral service of the church, as opposed to the service of the altar, which was the sacrist's department. Where the abbot and prior were not qualified or not interested, the precentor was the intellectual leader of the house who chose the books to be copied and directed the work and studies of the younger monks; in the early years of reorganization he sometimes had charge of the growing library, as had William of Malmesbury. As the office was concerned with the internal life of the monastery it could be, and not infrequently was, held by the

---

1 *Vita Wulfstani* (ed. Darlington), 9: "Fratres illius ecclesie...[eum] puerorum faciunt custodem, mox cantorem, postremo secretarium." The usual pre-Conquest terms in England were *magister* for *custos* and *aedituus* for *secretarius*; *precentor* gradually superseded *cantor*.
2 For Uhtred *v. Chronicle of John of Worcester* (ed. Weaver), 36.

prior or subprior, but this was not the normal practice. The precentor, like all the major officials, could have one or more *succentors* as assistants or deputies;[1] in course of time a *master of the book press* took from him a part of his responsibility.[2]

The chief need for subdivision of powers, however, was felt in the directly administrative offices, the receiving and spending departments. To the original *cellarer* had early been added a *sacrist*; gradually two other major offices grew up, those of the *chamberlain* and *almoner*. These four maintained their position as the four great departmental chiefs all through the twelfth century and beyond,[3] and all could have deputies; the *sub-sacrist* in particular, especially in the great pilgrim churches, was an official of considerable importance, and the post, as will be remembered, was held by Samson at Bury at the time of his election as abbot;[4] the *subchamberlain* also is thought worthy of mention on occasion. But it was out of the cellarer's sphere of activity that most of the new offices took their rise. Thus there were *intern* and *extern cellarers*, a *kitchener*, a *refectorer* and his *subrefectorer*, a *pittancer*, a *gardener*, a *hosteler* or *guest-master*, and a *wood-ward* in charge of the fuel. Besides these, there was always an *infirmarian*, and in the larger houses the infirmary had its own kitchener, chamberlain and pittancer. In the great age of building there was often, in addition to the sacristan, a *master of the works*, who controlled all additions or important renovations to the fabric of the church or monastery, and in those churches which housed a celebrated shrine there was a *warden of the shrine* and his deputy. Where the monastery, as at Evesham and St Albans, exercised spiritual jurisdiction over its own churches there was a *dean* or *archdeacon*. Finally, in all houses the abbot or prior had two or more *chaplains* or *secretaries*, and in many, as will be seen, a number of the monks were *wardens of manors*.

Thus in addition to the abbot some twenty-five monks in a large abbey would be holding an office of administration and responsibility, and these had in addition an indefinite number of assistants; in all, about half of the total community, including novices and the aged.[5] The duties of most are made clear by their titles. The *sacrist* had complete charge of the

1 *Chron. Evesh.* 206: "Nulli duo officia assignentur, sed cuilibet adjungatur socius, si opus fuerit." This document, however, dates from *c.* 1206. The *succentor* is mentioned in *Memorials of S. Edmund's*, II, 75.

2 *Jocelini Cronica*, 241: "Magister almarii et custos librorum."

3 Cf. the interesting letter of instruction of Innocent III to the commissioners in the Glastonbury controversy in 1202, where the sacrist, cellarer, chamberlain and almoner are specifically mentioned as the spending officials (Adam of Domerham, II, 417–18).

4 Samson had previously held the offices of novice-master, guest-master, pittancer and third prior (*Jocelini Cronica*, 212, 214).

5 The two most complete lists of officials in our period are those of Abingdon, *c.* 1185 (*Chron. Abingd.* II, 297–334) and Evesham, 1206–15 (*Chron. Evesh.* 205–21). To these may be added the references to the Glastonbury officials under Henry de Sully in 1189 (*Liber Henrici de Soliaco*, 1 *seqq.*) and the many references to those at Bury in Jocelin's *Chronicle*, 1180–1200, and in the narrative of the election of abbot Hugh, 1212–15 (*Mem. S. Edmund's*, vols. I and II). For a composite list of all these *v.* Appendix XVI.

service of the altar, of the vestments, and of all the internal decoration and repair of the church. Presumably he was, at least in our period, the directing master of ceremonies, though strangely enough the references to such an office are almost wholly wanting, and in some ceremonies, at least, the precentor had directive functions. Originally, the sacrist had complete charge of the church and its fabric, and in many cases he maintained this control, but when great building operations were in progress—and in many churches, such as Canterbury and Bury, building and rebuilding was all but ceaseless—the direction of them might be undertaken by the abbot or prior, or be delegated to a special official, the master of the works, but not uncommonly the sacrist or his deputy held this office also either in fact or name.[1]

The *cellarer* was the universal provider of all foodstuffs for monks, guests, poor and servants, save in so far as special contributions of food and drink came in directly to departmental officials from certain manors or tenants. It was his business to maintain the stocks of the great staples, such as flour, fish, beans and beer, from which the other departments drew; he had complete responsibility for housing all the servants and in general had charge of all that was not definitely allocated to others. But save in regard to the servants, and in some houses also the guests, his was, so to say, a wholesale not a retail function. The actual distribution and preparation of the food and drink was the task of others.

The *kitchener* was the immediate caterer for the monks. He received directly a number of perishable foodstuffs, such as honey, eggs and milk, from the farms;[2] the rest, such as flour and dry vegetables, he drew from the cellarer. He was in charge of the food from the time it entered the kitchen till it passed into the refectory; the actual cooking was of course done by servants.[3]

In distinction to the kitchener, the *refectorer* had charge of all within the refectory itself: of the table linen, furnishings, rushes, lamps and oil. The *pittancer* had charge of the provision of all materials for the pittances, or individual "extra" dishes, which, varying in number with the grade of the feast day, supplemented the "general" dishes of the Rule. As regards drink, beer, the staple, was controlled by the cellarer. The provision of wine and mead on certain days, which was known as a *caritas*, and grew in frequency to something approaching an average of two *caritates* a week, was laid as a charge on fixed days upon all the administrative officials.

The primary duty of the *chamberlain* was the clothing of the brethren and the provision of all necessary personal and domestic effects. Thus

1 Thus during the somewhat anarchic last years of Abbot Hugh of Bury, and during the interregnum of 1180–2, Samson as subsacrist, apparently holding also the post of *magister operis* ("S. subsacrista, magister super operarios", *Jocelini Cronica*, 217), collected money and undertook the building of the great tower.

2 *Chron. Abingd.* II, 306–9: "Vaccarius [dairyman] sub dominio est coquinarii de vaccaria sua."   3 *Chron. Evesh.* 207.

besides clothes, he had charge of the boots and shoes, of the fur capes, of the bedding and of the baths.[1] The *almoner* dispensed the charity of the house to regular and casual applicants for help; this might take the form of food, clothing or lodging. It was also his duty to visit deserving cases in the town or city and distribute alms. The *infirmarian* had complete charge of what gradually became a separate establishment, complete with its own kitchen, chapel, refectory and garden, and besides the material service of the sick he was responsible for providing them with Mass and the sacraments. As he had on his hands not only the diseased, but the aged and those in need of temporary relaxation, together with the groups of monks who were bled in rotation several times a year, the office was a taxing one; doubtless it was for this reason that at some houses (Abingdon is an example) special assistants were deputed to be his kitchener, chamberlain and pittancer. The *guest-master*, besides the social side of his activities, had to furnish the guest-rooms, and he was also responsible for shoeing and obtaining veterinary treatment for the horses of monks and pilgrims.

II

THE CONTROL OF REVENUES: THE "OBEDIENTIARY SYSTEM"

Though it may perhaps be thought that a number of the offices mentioned above were the result of unnecessary subdivision—in particular, those concerned with the provision of food—some such multiplication was inevitable in a great establishment whose members were occupied for many hours each day in religious duties, and of itself would not inevitably have modified the character of the monastic life. At the present day an almost equally elaborate hierarchy exists in many large monasteries and nunneries. What profoundly modified the life was the manner in which the revenues of the house were allotted to departmental officials and administered by them, and which resulted in a vast scheme of devolution that may conveniently be called the "obedientiary system".

The growth of this system in the English monasteries is not easy to trace in detail, though the main stages are clear. The Rule of St Benedict, as has been seen, committed all administration to the cellarer, under the abbot. At the revival under Dunstan at Glastonbury this was the arrangement followed, and there would seem to have been an attempt to avoid all extra-mural activity for the monks; Dunstan put his brother in charge of the estates of the monastery for this reason,[2] and the *Regularis Concordia*

---

1 *Chron. Abingd.* II, 299–301.
2 *Memorials of St Dunstan, Vita Dunstani auct. "B"*, 28, where the reason for this is given: "ne vel ipse vel quispiam ex monastica professione foris vagaretur."

contains explicit warning against monks travelling about on business.[1] At the other houses the simple arrangement of a single cellarer was doubtless the normal one, and such a condition of things lasted till the Conquest.[2] Meanwhile, however, a much more complicated practice had become common abroad, and in order to understand the nature of the changes effected by the Normans, it is necessary to glance briefly at the process of evolution at Cluny and in the Norman monasteries.

This process, here as in all departments of early medieval administration, was from the simple to the complex, from central control to devolution. Originally, the lands and goods of the normal monastery, usually forming a single *bloc*, had been administered by a single monastic official; as the original estates were plundered from 850 onwards, and new benefactions were later made parcel by parcel, the properties came to be situated at a considerable distance from the monastery and from each other, and it became the norm to set over each a steward (*villicus*) who represented the monks and collected the produce and rents. This office of steward, held originally by one of the serfs of the *villa*, came to be one of some consequence, carrying with it land and often becoming hereditary.[3] At the same time the difficulty of controlling distant stewards who were, in the ultimate resort, more concerned with their personal interests than with those of the monastery, led to the practice, common in the great French monasteries of the Cluniac movement, of administering properties through the agency of monks known as *decani*. This system was sometimes combined with that of stewards, sometimes wholly substituted for it. At Cluny an elaborate development of these "obediences", as they were called, existed by which the monk-stewards lived on a part of the proceeds of the scattered lands and sent only a percentage back to Cluny.[4] Other houses made use of stewards for some estates and monks for others, especially for those which had churches upon them.[5] A further step, taken very

1 *Regularis Concordia*, Proem. 79: "Villarum circuitus, nisi necessitatis causa magna compulerit...vagando nequaquam frequentent."

2 For Ely *c.* 980 *v. Liber Eliensis*, 167: "Brithnodus abbas...virum honestum ex eis [*sc.* monachis]...posuit...cui rei familiaris commisit praeposituram." For Ramsey, *c.* 980, *v. Hist. Rames.* 29, 40. For Evesham, *c.* 1050, *v. Chron. Evesh.* 87: "Et nunc sub eo [*sc.* abbate Mannio] jure praepositi totius abbatiae hujus curam agebat [Aegeluuius]." For Worcester, *c.* 1060, *v.* Hemming, *Cartulary*, I, 279: "Pius pater Wilstanus, tunc temporis prior hujus monasterii, et Wilstanus prepositus, qui postea fuit abbas Gloeceastre, cum venissent ad Alritune expetentes terras monasterii, etc." The matter is complicated by the use of the term *praepositus* (preost, provost) for any kind of official, but in the second and third of the above passages it seems clear that Aethelwig and Wilstan doubled the posts of second-in-command and cellarer.

3 For a description of the *villicus* and his duties, especially in houses of the Cluny tradition *c.* 1000, *v.* Sackur, *Die Cluniacenser*, II, 418 *seqq.*

4 Ulrich, *Constit. Cluniac.* III, 5. Cf. Sackur, II, 422 (notes) for examples from charters of Cluny and other houses, and de Valous, *Le Temporel...de Cluny*, 128 *seqq.*

5 Cf. a very clear statement (quoted by Sackur) in *Rodulfi miracula sanctorum in Fuldenses ecclesias translatorum*, in *MGH, SS*, XV, 330: "Quorum [praediorum] alia quidem per villicos ordinavit, alia vero et maxime illa, in quibus ecclesiae fuerant, presbyteris procuranda atque disponenda commisit." But were these *presbyteri* monks? The practice of sending

early by Cluny and other monasteries, was to send to these latter properties a small group of monks to perform the liturgical offices in the church and live on a part of the income; it was from this that the majority of "cells" abroad took their origin.[1] Even from an economic point of view this system, though it guaranteed the supervision of outlying estates and avoided the difficulties connected with the transport of large quantities of perishable stuffs, had grave drawbacks. It was impossible that all the scattered monks should be men of administrative capability and practical energy, and just as the religious life of the cells tended to tepidity, so likewise did the material administration become slack, and in any case a wholesale devolution of authority tended to weakness. At Cluny the whole economic system broke down completely early in the twelfth century.

Side by side with this method of exploitation by scattered groups or individuals was another often combined with it in various proportions. This was the "obedientiary system" which afterwards became the norm in England. As estates multiplied in the hands of the monastery and were devoted to some specialized product—vine, olive, fruit, corn, vegetable— it was natural to ear-mark the product or the revenues for specific purposes. Throughout Europe in the tenth and eleventh centuries it had become the custom to assign certain episcopal lands to the bishop's personal keep and expenses and others to the chapter, and among the monasteries some lands were generally assigned to the abbot, others to the feeding or clothing of the brethren.[2] Gradually, either for convenience or as the result of testators' wishes, more and more of the properties came to be assigned to specified purposes; these were sometimes pre-arranged with minute precision to provide, for example, an annual distribution of food, or wheat and wine for the service of the altar, or a lamp or tapers before a shrine.[3] When the destination of a large proportion of the revenues was thus pre-arranged, they could travel direct to the official concerned with their administration without passing through a central clearing-house; it was only a small step further to allot all properties to fixed purposes and give the various officials complete control of them from start to finish. Such a system was in action in many Continental monasteries as early as the beginning of the eleventh century; it was opposed on religious grounds by reformers, as encouraging a spirit of private ownership; it was also found to have its practical disadvantages both because it excluded the

monks to distant churches owned by the monastery was not, however, uncommon abroad, especially in the Rhineland in the ninth and tenth centuries. Cf. Imbart de la Tour, *Les paroisses rurales*, 246, and charters there quoted.

[1] These cells were not uncommon among the monasteries founded by William of Dijon. Cf. Sackur, II, 424, and charters quoted.

[2] Much information concerning episcopal finances and the bishop s *mensa* is to be found in Lesne, *Histoire de la propriété ecclésiastique en France*.

[3] Examples may be collected from any cartulary; cf. Sackur, II, 425.

possibility of strong central control and because the varying fortunes of different properties in unsettled times constantly upset the equitable distribution of revenues. In consequence, many abbots with a talent for administration endeavoured to centralize the incomes once more.[1] At Cluny a complicated method was evolved by which the produce and revenues of the various properties, administered for the most part by monks, were despatched to Cluny to the two major officials, the Prior (who received all imports in kind) and the Chamberlain (who received all moneys); these distributed the receipts to the various heads of departments within the house. In the Norman abbeys in general a modified form of the obedientiary system seems to have been common by the middle of the eleventh century, but as these monasteries were of recent origin and (at least before 1066) possessed fairly compact estates, the administration was a comparatively simple matter. Bec in particular and its daughters, being more recent and more simply organized than the group of houses deriving from William of Dijon, would seem originally to have had a very simple form of the obedientiary system which left the greater part of the control of the property in the cellarer's hands.

How far the subdivision of the revenues had gone in the English houses before the Conquest is not wholly clear. In *Domesday* a number of revenues (chiefly, but not solely, belonging to cathedral monasteries) are attributed to the upkeep of the monks (*de victu monachorum*), and in the case of Canterbury and the Old Minster at Winchester alone some lands are assigned specifically to provide clothing (*de vestitu monachorum*). A broad division was probably general by which some lands, above all the demesne and neighbouring farms, provided food, and the others money for clothing and necessaries, but the disposition of all was probably in the hands of the cellarer.[2] Aethelwig's arrangements at Evesham during the relief work of *c.* 1070 appear to presuppose the general control of the cellarer and the absence of any special revenues attached to the almonry and indeed of the very office of almoner.[3] Nor does the contemporary cartulary compiled by Hemming at Worcester, where wholly English institutions prevailed, show any clear indications of specific allotments,[4] and it does not appear that at Worcester the officials had as yet any great share in the exploitation and realization of the properties of the house;

1 Cf. the action of the abbots of Gembloux given by Sackur, II, 426.
2 Since lands in the Worcester entry are assigned *de victu monachorum* we cannot suppose that the division was first made by Normans such as Lanfranc and Walkelin. Cf. also Hemming, I, 286: "Precepit [Wulstanus] adhuc omnia privilegia et cirographa terrarum que proprie ad victum monachorum pertinent separatim ex his [of church of Worcester] congregari." For an arrangement of yearly "farms" cf. *ibid.* I, 98–100; for a similar method at Ely, *v. Liber Eliensis*, 201. Note also the gift of land by Queen Edith to Abingdon for the specific purpose of supplying the children of the cloister with morning milk (*Chron. Abingd.* I, 461).
3 *Chron. Evesh.* 91.
4 Cf. esp. Hemming, I, 289–91, where instead of any specific allotment the phrase recurs: "reddit...monachis v denarios, etc." Cf. also *Liber Eliensis*, 201.

this was in the hands, as it would seem, of lay reeves (*praepositi*), though the fragmentary nature of the records and the use of the term *praepositus* for a number of different officials make it difficult to reach complete certainty on the point.[1] The same uncertainty prevails with regard to the sacrist, for there is no record that offerings made by pilgrims or guests to the church at this period went directly into his funds.

In the years after the Conquest a great change came about, partly due to the introduction of Continental methods, partly to the initiative of abbots who found themselves faced with changing economic and feudal conditions. The change was only gradual; Lanfranc's *Statuta* of *c.* 1075, either because the author of set purpose adapted his regulations to English conditions or, as is far more probable, because he was following very closely the simple economy of Bec and Caen, assume that the cellarer will control the income of the house and that the other officials will be concerned only with domestic administration.[2] But as the properties of the monasteries grew through a multitude of small and scattered gifts of land, tithes, jurisdictionary rights, "half-churches", tolls and the rest it became increasingly difficult, in the elementary economic system of the age, for a single official to maintain a clearing-house through which all receipts might pass before distribution, especially as a number of the revenues were ear-marked by the donors for specific purposes. Still, it would have been possible, and the system of a single control was perhaps actually preserved at a few houses.[3] At the majority devolution set in, hastened by the feudal burden, new to England, by which the estates of a vacant abbey, like those of any vacant fief, passed into the king's hands during an interregnum—a custom which under William Rufus was greatly abused.

Owing to this last reason, devolution on a grand scale began with a division of all lands and revenues between abbot and convent, the abbot becoming wholly and solely responsible for his share, which was ad-

---

1 Cf. *Chron. Evesh.* 91 (*c.* 1070): "Praecepit etiam [Ageluuius] celerario et omnibus praepositis [*i.e.* reeves] abbatiae hujus ut ei [*sc.* priori] in omnibus obedirent et...omnem decimationem suam...abundanter ei redderent." Cf. also the well-known account of the town of Bury in *Domesday*, ii, 372, reprinted *Mem. S. Edmund's*, I, Appendix A, 339: "Praeter quos [servientes] sunt xiii super terram praepositi, qui habent domos suas in eadem villa." It is not easy to determine how many of the *praepositi* in Hemming (e.g. I, 254), the *Liber Eliensis* and the Abingdon *Chronicle* (e.g. II, 306) are officials directly controlled by the monasteries.

2 *Lanfranci Statuta*, c. ix, 237: "Pater totius Congregationis debet esse [cellerarius]."

3 As late as 1202 Innocent III states that the commissioners appointed in the Glastonbury case to investigate the financial system of the cathedral monasteries found: "in quibusdam illarum...unicum...et commune marsupium constitutum...ex quo ad·omnes usus monasterii, hospitum et pauperum...ministratur. In aliis vero separatas porciones habent et marsupia sacrista, celerarius, camerarius et elemosinarius" (Adam of Domerham, II, 417–18). This statement seems peremptory, but the investigation was confined to the cathedral monasteries, where the complete and early separation of the bishop's lands and the lack of a fully independent monastic superior would hinder devolution. There is no indication in the report as to which houses followed the one or the other practice.

ministered by his officers, who were not monks, under his supervision.[1] From the income accruing he supported himself, his officials, knights and servants, and usually a fixed proportion of guests.[2] These properties, and these alone, fell under the control of the royal officials during a vacancy. Next, the properties assigned to the convent were allocated to the various heads of departments, who varied somewhat in number according to the size and customs of different houses. The cellarer would seem always to have retained something of the privileged position accorded him by the Rule, for besides being responsible for a greater share than the others it fell to him to administer all that was not specifically assigned elsewhere, and he was in a peculiar way the universal provider—the father—of the monastery.[3] But in the manner of his administration there was no distinction between him and the other officials. All had certain sources of income—lands, churches, tithes, rents, dues—allotted to them and put completely under their control. Thus they not only disposed freely of the revenues, but also had full responsibility and initiative with regard to the exploitation of the property, which they could administer directly, or farm out as they pleased, and which they could exchange and even (though this was regarded as an abuse) mortgage; as regards the income, they were equally free to dispose of it in any way that enterprise might suggest within the sphere of their office.[4] The date at which this devolution took place varied somewhat from house to house; the process was often gradual. There are few traces of it before c. 1100, but from thence onwards the evidence becomes plentiful: thus the Abingdon chronicle explicitly attributes it to the great abbot Faricius (1100–1117)[5] and many allusions show the system

1 The ratio of the division is not easily ascertainable; perhaps the abbot normally had about a fourth part.

2 For different arrangements cf. *Jocelini Cronica*, 243: "Quando abbas est domi, ipse recipiet omnes hospites...praeter viros religiosos et praeter presbyteros...et eorum homines...si vero abbas non fuerit domi omnes hospites...recipientur a celerario usque ad tredecim equos. Si vero laicus vel clericus venerit cum pluribus equis quam tredecim, recipientur a servientibus abbatis...ad expensas abbatis." *Chron. Evesh.* 207: "Hospitibus... providebit celerarius; viris tamen religiosis coquinarius...exceptis abbatibus et capellanis eorum" [for whom the abbot presumably catered].

3 *Chron. Evesh.* 207: "Celerarius siquidem exterior...exceptis redditibus monachorum officiis assignatis, ad praeceptum abbatis totius abbatiae curam gerens, etc." In the constitutions of some modern monastic bodies it is enacted in a similar spirit that even if the disposal of moneys is permitted to other officials, there shall be but one banking account, under the control of the cellarer.

4 *Chron. Evesh.* 207: "Liceat praeterea monachis possessiones et redditus officiis suis assignatos veluti novalia faciendo et redditus augmentando et novos acquirendo ampliare, seu quibuscumque aliis justis modis meliorare, et alios pro aliis tantumdem valentibus...vel ad tempus vel in perpetuum commutare." The extent to which this freedom went under a weak abbot may be seen in Jocelin's *Chronicle*, e.g. 210: "Unde contigit quod quilibet obedientiarius haberet sigillum proprium, et debito se obligaret tam Judeis quam Christianis pro voluntate sua." Samson found no less than thirty-three monks in possession of seals, i.e. in the habit of making financial agreements on their own responsibility (*ibid.* 243).

5 *Chron. Abingd.* II, 289: "Providit et sacristae, cellarario, lignario, et caeteris obedientiariis omnia necessaria." Details of his allotment are on pp. 152–4.

functioning under his successor Vincent (1121–*c.* 1130);[1] the chronicler
of St Augustine's, Canterbury, attributes it there to Abbot Hugh (*c.*
1125),[2] and at Tewkesbury it was introduced by Abbot Gerold at the
advice of Robert fitz Haymon *c.* 1105.[3] By the second half of the century
it was firmly and completely established in all the great houses.

As the bulk of monastic property was in land, the officials were directly
concerned with all the duties of a landlord or land-agent; they had besides
to supervise the exaction and delivery of a large number of detailed dues
and services to which the modern system of tenancy affords no parallels;
finally, they had complete jurisdiction over "their men": that is, they, and
not the abbot, heard the pleas and exacted the fines pertaining to the feudal
overlord's court.[4] Under their control were the various degrees of villein
on the land, and besides workmen, bond or free, the major officials had
one or more personal servants with their horses. They, and not the cellarer
alone, travelled about the country to fairs to effect purchases.[5]

In addition to the regular offices of the convent, the practice grew up,
at least in a number of houses, of giving to individual monks, not necessarily officials, the task of administering manors. At the time of the
Conquest, as has been said, the normal practice was to lease these to lay
reeves or farmers (*praepositi*), who were responsible for a fixed return of
money or goods, thus absolving the monastery from further trouble.[6]
Later, keen administrators found that a higher income could be secured
by personal supervision; this, it will be remembered, was a chief means
adopted by Samson in restoring order to the Bury finances.[7] Yet another
expedient was to entrust manors, or groups of manors, to individual
monks.[8] How far this was carried in the twelfth century is not easy
to ascertain; it is probable that house differed greatly from house in
the matter, and that Bury, concerning which we have comparatively full

1 E.g. *Chron. Abingd.* ii, 290: "Dedit [Vincentius] et totam lanam suam unius anni pro
magno dorsario de x Virginibus. Omnes vero obedientiarii fecerunt dorsarium de Apo-
calypsi." Cf. also *Chronicle* (E) *s.a.* 1137 for Peterborough.

2 *Chron. Will. Thorne*, c. 1799.

3 *Monasticon*, ii, 81.

4 *Chron. Abingd.* ii, 299: "Ad camerarium enim pertinet omnes causas et negotia hominum
suorum audire et terminare, et delinquentes pro qualitate delicti poena pecuniaria con-
demnare; quam poenam non poterit abbas a camerario, vel sine camerario a condemnatis,
exigere....Si tamen camerarius excesserit...debet eum abbas...corripere et...cohibere.
De jure vero suo non debet ei aliquid detrahere." Cf. *Jocelini Cronica*, 302: "Sollemniter
curiam suam solebat tenere [celerarius] de latronibus et omnibus placitis et querelis...et
inde lucrum capere sicut praefectus capiebat ad portmane-mot." The whole passage,
302–4, should be noted, and *v. infra*, 616–18.

5 *Chron. Abingd.* ii, 300: "Item, si camerarius vadit ad nundinas de Winchelcumba...";
ibid. 327: "Si vadit ad feriam de Wintonia."

6 Cf. Hemming, i, 98–100, 254 *seqq.* and *infra*, pp. 442–3.

7 Cf. *Jocelini Cronica*, 238, where Samson makes £20–£25 out of a manor previously
farmed for £4; also *ibid.*: "Unum solum manerium...carta sua confirmavit cuidam Anglico
natione."

8 *Jocelini Cronica*, 320: "Galfridus Ruffus monachus noster, licet nimis seculariter se
gereret, utilis fuit nobis in custodia iiii maneriorum...ubi prius defectus saepe solebat esse
de firmis." When Geoffrey was deposed the manors were entrusted to two others.

information, was peculiarly immersed in the land. But the practice was widespread throughout the century,[1] and despite the prohibitions of reforming synods, which saw in it not only a kind of private ownership contrary to the monastic profession, but also an influence which took monks to live alone outside their monastery, it was too convenient and profitable to be wholly abandoned.[2] It is easy to realize how profoundly the obedientiary system, with the additional wardenship of manors, modified the whole monastic life, when and where it was developed at all fully. In time, more than half the total number of the community came to be engaged, either as chiefs or as subordinates, in the administration of estates, in the managing of money and in the application of revenues either to the day-to-day business of provisioning the house or to the completion of schemes of building or decoration. In addition, many of those not so engaged would be young monks, expecting to take their part in years to come. Save in monasteries, such as Winchester, Canterbury and St Albans, where strong intellectual or artistic interests existed, business of this kind was the career which absorbed all the talent of the house. When once the system had developed the obedientiaries, great and small, became a definite class, exempted by their duties from the normal life of silence, reading and writing in the cloister, and often excused from attendance at the liturgical offices in the church and absent for a number of days on a journey. Numerous references in the only familiar chronicle of the period, that of Jocelin, show us this sharp division in the community.[3] Regulations regarding the obedientiaries began to be introduced very early,[4] and were multiplied in the thirteenth century, but the system was part of the life and no regulations could essentially modify it. Some of its moral and spiritual consequences, as well as its effect upon the position of the abbot, will be mentioned in a later chapter.

The chief officials, as has been seen, had complete control of their departments, and a custom grew up and became established that, under normal circumstances, even the abbot should refrain from altering their sources of revenue or diminishing the dues and services they received. They were, however, like the abbot himself, amenable to protest and criticism in chapter; they were also liable to summary deposition at the abbot's hands. Moreover, the abbot could in extreme cases of mismanage-

---

1 As early as 1132 it had been one of the plaints of the reformers at St Mary's, York, that a majority of the monks were engaged in overseeing vills (*Mem. Fount.* I, 17).

2 What the councils directly attacked was the leasing of land to monks, who paid an agreed sum to the monastery and disposed of the profits like any other "farmer". Cf. *infra*, p. 442.

3 *Jocelini Cronica*, 245: "Videbatur quoque abbas activam vitam magis diligere quam contemplativam, qui bonos obedientiales magis commendavit quam bonos claustrales." Cf. also the reference (*ibid.* 267) to the days *quando pauper claustralis fuit Samson. Ibid.* 320, Geoffrey after his deposition from the wardenship of the manors is placed *in claustrum*.

4 E.g. *Chron. Evesh.* 206 (1206–15): "Isti officiales quotiens domi fuerint in congregatione jugiter permaneant, et conventum...sequantur."

ment suspend one or more officials and take the administration into his own hands; that is, he could collect and spend the revenues by the agency of monks, not officials, acting under him without power of initiative, or of members of his personal staff of servants and clerks. This was the course taken by Samson for a short time at Bury in 1197,[1] and a similar action, though from different motives, was one of the principal charges against Roger Norreys at Evesham.[2] But such a step, under whatever circumstances, was regarded as a disgrace, and could be no more than temporary, somewhat in the same way as the supersession of a defaulting municipal body by officials of the Home Office at the present day.

At the beginning of the thirteenth century we meet, in Marleberge's constitutions for Evesham, an attempt, perhaps the first of its kind in England, to establish a regular system of days of reckoning. It is provided that all obedientiaries shall present quarterly accounts to a board consisting of abbot, prior, and nine monks, six appointed by the abbot and three elected by the community. The kitchener is to present accounts weekly and the cellarer as often as the abbot wishes.[3] In the contemporary York statutes there is a similar quarterly audit.[4] Marleberge also enacted that the abbot and chapter should have power to transfer surplus funds from one department to another temporarily or in permanence; the York statutes, on the other hand, prohibit all such pooling or transference of a surplus.

III

SERVANTS

No account of the life of a black monk house would be complete which did not contain some notice of the servants and functionaries employed about the premises. They were very numerous. Lay brothers were unknown to the black monks in the Middle Ages; in the beginnings of the revival under Dunstan it seems clear that much of the domestic work was done by monks,[5] and in the Norman monasteries, whose tradition was for a time imposed in England by Lanfranc's Statutes, the *conversi* (that is, those who took the habit in maturity and consequently did not pass through the normal course of study and took no orders) performed some of the work of supervision usually given to servants; but the system of lay servants was firmly established before the Conquest. Already the

---

1 *Jocelini Cronica*, 289–93: "'Accipio', inquit, 'in manu mea celerariam vestram et expensam hospitum, et procurationem interius et exterius.'"

2 *Chron. Evesh.* 105: "Cameram et sacristariam et alias obedientias in manu sua quantum ei placuit tenuit."

3 *Chron. Evesh.* 206–7.

4 C. R. Cheney, *The Papal Legate and English Monasteries*, EHR, XLVI (July 1931), 450.

5 *V. Vita S. Aethelwoldi* (ap. *Chron. Abingd.* vol. II, appendix i) for monks building (p. 264) and cooking (p. 259). *V.* also Appendix XXIII.

staff of the greater abbeys had swollen enormously; the system of services accompanying tenure of land and the absence of fixed wages and vocational training doubtless prevented "rationalization" of labour, and when a host of customary corrodies, gifts and liveries sprang up, corresponding to the services due, the number of dependents, regular and casual, grew ever larger. Although only a few definite figures are available, those that exist allow us with practical certainty to draw the somewhat surprising conclusion that the number of servants and dependents who lived about the abbey and were either wholly or in great part supported by it always equalled and often exceeded the total number of monks. Thus at Bury at the time of the Domesday inquest there were seventy-five servants and workpeople of various grades;[1] this must have considerably exceeded the number of the monks, who at the death of Samson a century and a half later totalled some seventy odd. At Evesham *c.* 1090–5 there were fifty-five resident monks and sixty-five servants.[2] At Ely, twenty years later, the due complement of the house is put at seventy-two monks and an equal number of servants,[3] and at Peterborough, *c.* 1125, the number of servants stood at seventy-one. One of the fullest lists is that of Abingdon, where *c.* 1185, on the death of Abbot Roger, the royal proctor called upon all who received any kind of allowance from the abbey to make a statement of their claims. On such an occasion we may well suppose that absentees were few, but the enquiry was careful, and in most cases the office as well as the name of the beneficiary is recorded, and it appears that there were some seventy-seven regular servants and workpeople, together with a few casual dependents.[4] There is no record of the number of monks at the time; sixty years previously, in an epoch of prosperity, it had reached eighty or thereabouts.[5] Another, almost exactly contemporary with that of Abingdon and perhaps even richer in information, comes from Glastonbury; it is the document recording the customary services, payments, liveries and corrodies drawn up when Abbot Henry de Sully entered upon his office in 1189.[6] It ends abruptly, and from the absence of more than one important official, both lay and monastic, would seem to be incomplete, but the bulk of the servants are there, and the total is curiously near that of

---

1 *Domesday*, ii, 372 (reprinted, *Mem. S. Edmund's*, 1, 339): "Ubi sunt...lxxx minus v inter pistores cervisiarios sartores lavatores sutores parmentarios kokos portitores dispensatores; et hi omnes quotidie ministrant Sancto et abbati et fratribus." There were sixty-seven monks on the division-lists in the election of 1213 (*Mem. S. Edmund's*, 11, 75); to these must be added a few novices.   2 *Monasticon*, 11, 37.

3 *Liber Eliensis* (continuation ed. Wharton), 11, 617: "Numerus loci debitus scilicet lxxii monachorum ac servorum totidem." For the Peterborough servants *v. Monasticon*, 1, 351.

4 For the list *v. Chron. Abingd.* 11, 237–43.

5 *Chron. Abingd.* 11, 49, 148, 287.

6 *Liber Henrici de Soliaco*, ed. for Roxburghe Club by J. E. Jackson (1882). The format of this book has made it something of a rarity and consequently unfamiliar. One of the most interesting notices is that of Godfrey: "persona de Deverel [qui] tenuit quoddam misterium [*i.e.* ministerium] ad quod pertinet emendare ornamentum ecclesiae Glaston. et facere aurifragium" (p. 13). His son held it after him.

Abingdon. There are, roughly speaking, eighty minor officers and servants, and three major officials of the abbot's household; with regard to the last-named, it is natural to suppose that the long tenure of the abbacy by Henry of Winchester had delayed the full development of the abbot's establishment. As for the monks, they numbered seventy-two in 1162 and some sixty in 1200.[1]

Many of the details given in the Glastonbury document are extremely interesting and have not received the attention they deserve. It is, for example, remarkable how many of the minor officers and head servants enjoy hereditary tenure by charter; there are eight or more such, including the porter, the chief baker, two cooks, the butler (represented by an heiress), the gatekeeper, the scullion and the swineherd. In considering the number of servants, it must be remembered that besides monks, there were at all the large abbeys numerous guests and at some (such as Evesham and Bury) a continual stream of pilgrims, but when all allowance has been made for the amount of regular and casual work to be done, it is hard to resist the conclusion that there was a superfluity of hands to be filled and mouths to be fed. We know that at some large monasteries abroad, and in particular at Cluny, the presence of large numbers of half-idle and ill-organized servants seriously disturbed the silence and order of the monastic buildings and led to much waste; they hung about the offices, gossiping and shouting, and pilfered the provisions for the benefit of their relatives in the town.[2] Something of the sort may have taken place on a smaller scale at Glastonbury or Abingdon; in any case, the presence of so many individuals, bound by no religious discipline, must have tended to disturb the quiet of the courts and offices.

IV

ECONOMIC ORGANIZATION

Although the economy of the monastic estates was not in origin different from that of lands owned by lay proprietors, and belongs rather to the economic than to the religious history of the country, there is some evidence that the monasteries were among the first to introduce new methods into the exploitation of their property, and as these changes affected the domestic life of the houses concerned, a brief notice may be given of the systems in vogue during the early Anglo-Norman period.[3]

---

1 Adam of Domerham, I, 417–18.
2 Cf. *Petri Venerabilis Statuta Congregationis Cluniacensis*, nos. xxiii, xxiv (*PL*, CLXXXIX, 1032–3).
3 For the agricultural economy of the eleventh and twelfth centuries the main authorities are still F. W. Maitland, *Domesday Book and beyond*, and P. Vinogradoff, *English Society in the Eleventh Century*; intensive study in the last thirty years has been directed rather to the later centuries of the medieval period, when the records become more abundant. Of recent

In the century between Dunstan and the Conqueror the owner of a large estate had in general four potential sources of income from those living upon his land, viz. rent from the holding, right to a certain amount of service from the lower orders, various customary payments in money or kind, and the profits arising from rights of jurisdiction. The last, which were intimately linked with the holding of courts and hearing of pleas, were almost invariably received directly by the land- or office-holder concerned; the other three were assets which could either be exploited directly or leased out to a middleman. Before the Conquest, it may be said that in general all rents for land and most customary payments were made in kind: the owner of the property exacted in the course of the year a fixed quantity of beasts, fish, fowl, eggs, grain, honey, etc., which in the case of a monastery went directly to the support of the inmates of the house. Tenants of house-property in a town, on the other hand, usually paid a small annual money-rent, as did the priest of a church to its owner. Thus at Worcester, where the economic organization of the estates of the monastery can be seen with some clearness from Hemming's cartulary, these two divisions of revenue—that of food-rents from the country estates and that of money-rents from the town of Worcester—are the basis of the whole economic fabric, and the records of Abingdon, St Albans and Bury show an almost exactly similar state of things. Since, however, the monastery needed more money than was provided by house-rents, while on the other hand the gross income of perishable stuffs was hard to realize and exceeded the day-to-day needs of the monks; since, also, the direct exploitation of large and scattered estates was impracticable, there was a universal practice of leasing out individual properties to other landowners or to professional stewards or bailiffs, who paid either in kind or in money, usually the latter, an agreed annual rent considerably less than the potential value of the estate.[1] This was the farm-system which was ubiquitous throughout the eleventh and twelfth centuries; as will be seen, the "farmer" differed considerably from his namesake in modern England; while the latter cultivates the land himself for a fixed rent, the former was often rather in the position of a bailiff or agent who directed the cultivation and exploitation of a number of agricultural units without having a permanent interest in the land, though no doubt the bailiff often himself lived upon the demesne land of the property for which he paid rent. Moreover, the farm did not, as in the modern world, consist of open land alone, with a

studies on the economy of the early twelfth century, by far the most important are those of Prof. D. C. Douglas: *Social Structure of Medieval East Anglia; Fragments of an Anglo-Saxon Survey from Bury St Edmunds*, in *EHR*, XLIII (1928), 376 *seqq.*; and the introduction, pp. cxx–cxxxiii, to *Feudal Documents...of Bury St Edmunds*. Cf. also p. 618, note 1, *infra*.

1 Cf. Vinogradoff, *English Society*, 374: "The usual way of drawing income from estates, rights and privileges was to give them in farm to a bailiff or steward." Also J. H. Round, *The Burton Abbey Surveys*, in *EHR*, XX (1905), 275–89: "The abbey's most usual method of dealing with its manors was to grant them out at farm for two lives." I have observed this as the universal practice in all cartularies.

single farmhouse at its centre, but of the whole complex of one or more village communities or manors. These "farms" were leased to the *prae-positus* for a year, or for a period of years, or for a life, or for two lives; naturally, there was a tendency for son to succeed father, but the monastery usually took care, especially when demesne lands were concerned, to keep the lease short or even terminable at will.[1] When, after the Conquest, posts of every kind came to be held by charter and in heredity, the farmers endeavoured to secure this privileged position for themselves—an endeavour which energetic abbots did their best to thwart. The farm-system, though unavoidable, meant loss of potential profit to the landowner; hence the tendency, repeatedly attacked by reformers within and without the monastery, and as consistently reappearing on all sides, to grant the exploitation of estates to monks of the house, who might be supposed to be more zealous in extracting the utmost from the land and who in any case would not absorb the profits of a middleman.[2]

Within the bounds of the village, the agricultural system in England before the Conquest was, as has been repeatedly shown, extremely complicated. The numerous grades of the population, the rights and dues of labour-service, the intermingling of holdings and their small size, the elementary methods of cultivation and rotation of crops, all combined to prevent intensive and "rationalized" exploitation, and the farm-system, added to all other limitations, hindered the employment of capital on the land. Indeed, the monasteries were almost alone as agricultural capitalists, and there is some evidence that they were among the first owners of property in England after the Conquest to use their resources for the improvement of their demesne lands, and to organize the labour-service into something approaching a scientific system.[3]

The chief innovations brought about by the reorganization immediately after the Conquest were the gradual substitution of money payments for rents in kind and customary dues of foodstuffs, together with the exaction of more labour from the lower ranks of the population. The latter change was not peculiar to monastic estates; it was part of the movement by which the inferior classes of society fell in status under organized feudalism, and

1 Vinogradoff, *English Society*, 378, quotes from Dd i 377b, as typical of the treatment of demesne farms, the land of Croyland at Repinghale, leased by Abbot Wulfketel [? 1052– ? 1085]: "ad firmam Hereuuardo sicut inter eos conveniret unoquoque anno." Cf. also the land of Worcester at Grimanleh noted in *Domesday*, 173b as given to a nun for her use: "quamdiu fratres voluissent et carere potuissent." Later, manors were often granted out at farm for two lives (*v*. previous note: in the passage referred to Round also notes cases where the "men" of a manor farmed it themselves).

2 *V. supra*, p. 438. At Burton *c*. 1133 Edric the monk farmed two manors. For repeated prohibitions *v*. Council of London (1102), can. xxi: "ne monachi teneant villas ad firmam"; Westminster (1173), can. xxi: "monachi firmas non teneant"; Westminster (1195), can. xiii: "ne reditus, quos obedientias vocant, ad firmam teneant."

3 Cf. Vinogradoff, *English Society*, 356: "The great pioneers in this direction were the ecclesiastical institutions. We find on their estates the largest concentrations of capital and the most systematic combinations of peasant labour to support them."

has been described by all historians of feudalism and villeinage. The former was, however, largely the work of the monks, or at least appears most clearly on monastic estates; it is most remarkable upon the extensive properties of Bury, where its introduction can be precisely assigned to the twenty-five years immediately after the Conquest, and appears to have been largely the work of the great abbot Baldwin.[1] The superior convenience of money-rents, at least from the point of view of the proprietor, was obvious, and the monastic corporations throughout England did their best to introduce them wherever possible; to a certain extent, indeed, this movement checked the contemporary increase of labour-service on the lands concerned, and it became more and more the custom that all occasional, small services on the part of individuals otherwise free should be commuted for a regular payment in money. Finally, towards the end of the twelfth century there took place in East Anglia in general, and consequently on the estates of Bury and other houses, what has been called a contractual movement by which the peasants obtained tenements of land for a rent settled, not on the basis of customary valuation, but by individual bargains and separate contracts. Outside the lands of St Edmund this movement was widespread; within the eight and a half hundreds of the Saint it was kept in restraint so far as was possible.[2]

V

THE MONASTIC BOROUGH

The black monks in England, from the days of Dunstan onwards, made in general no attempt to put their foundations at a distance from centres of population. Indeed, the majority of the houses founded before the Conquest lay in the centre of such small towns as then existed, and since the remainder, with few exceptions, made no attempt to be economically self-contained or self-supporting, they soon attracted to their neighbourhood a settlement of artisans and small traders, in addition to the group of dependents who gave labour-services and rent to the monks. Thus even when, as was rarely the case, the monastery was founded in the open countryside, it soon became the nucleus of a small town, in something of the same way as have railway works or permanent military camps in modern England. A particularly clear instance of this can be seen at the post-Conquest foundation of Battle; there the monastery, erected on the

1 Cf. Douglas, *Fragments of an Anglo-Saxon Survey*, 377–8: "On the extensive lands of St Edmund's abbey... during the latter half of the eleventh century a wholesale transference seems to have taken place from an economy based upon the payment of food-rents to one dependent partly upon labour-service but also very extensively upon money-rents." Cf. also *Feudal Documents*, introd. cxxxiii: "The Norman Conquest and the reorganization of Abbot Baldwin were fatal to the great majority of food-rents.... By the middle of the twelfth century the Bury economy, except for a few sporadic survivals, depended upon cash payments."

2 D. C. Douglas, *Social Structure of Medieval East Anglia*, 60 seqq.; *Feudal Documents*, introd. cliii–iv.

open land which had been the site of the Conqueror's triumph, rapidly attracted and even invited a settlement of workmen and artificers, who were housed in what soon became a small town at the gates of the abbey.[1] Only a very few of the old monasteries, situated on islands in the fens or among the marshes of Somerset, remained isolated until, in later centuries, works of drainage made their environs habitable.

In cases where the town existed before the monastery came into being, as at Canterbury, Winchester, Worcester and elsewhere, municipal history had no essential connection with that of the monastery, which had no important proprietary or seignorial rights over the burgesses, but where the whole superficies of land on which the town lay formed part of the endowment of the monastery, or where the growth of the town was due to the presence of the abbey, the position of the monks *vis-à-vis* the population was similar to that of the Crown with regard to royal boroughs, and that of lay lords or bishops with regard to boroughs which they controlled, and the monastic borough, with close and peculiar relations to the convent, came into existence.[2] No full account will be expected here of such monastic boroughs; their history forms part of the history of the boroughs of England and has nothing of itself to do with monastic or ecclesiastical history. Moreover, even if the heterogeneous group of boroughs controlled by monasteries is treated separately, adequate materials only become available from the reign of Henry III onward. All that will be attempted here is to indicate some of the ways in which the rights and duties of proprietors of towns, like the feudal rights and obligations, affected the life and activities of the monks. For this, in the twelfth century, almost all the information available refers to Bury St Edmunds, and comes from the invaluable chronicle of Jocelin of Brakelond.

As ultimately more than twenty boroughs were owned by black monk houses,[3] and the majority of these were the towns immediately adjacent to, or surrounding, the monastic buildings, they are an element to be reckoned with in estimating the normal engagements of an abbey. Some of these

---

1 *Chron. Bell.* 11–21, especially p. 12: "Accitis hominibus quampluribus ex comprovincialibus quidem multis, ex transmarinis etiam partibus nonnullis, coeperunt fratres qui fabricae [ecclesiae] operam dabant circa ambitum ejusdem loci...mansiones singulis distribuere...cum consuetudinali censu vel servitio." A list of 115 houses follows, which may be taken to represent a population of 500 or more. The normal payment was 7*d.* per house per annum, and the service a day's harvesting, together with mill-repairing and malt-making. On p. 17 we are told that "homines villae...Burgenses vocantur", and that on the accession of an abbot they gave a relief of a hundred shillings *pro libertatibus suis.*

2 For these *v.* J. Tait, *The Medieval English Borough* (Manchester, 1936); N. M. Trenholme, *The English Monastic Boroughs* and M. D. Lobel, *The Borough of Bury St Edmunds.*

3 Trenholme, *op. cit.* Appendix I, p. 95, gives a list of twenty boroughs belonging to the black monks and five to houses of Austin canons. The monastic boroughs are: Abingdon, St Albans, Baschurch (Shrewsbury), Burton, Bury, Coventry, Elvet (Durham), Evesham, Faversham, Fordwick (St Augustine's, Canterbury), Glastonbury, Leominster (Reading), Malmesbury, Peterborough, Reading, Sandwich (Christ Church, Canterbury), Tavistock, Weymouth (St Swithun's, Winchester), Whitby, Winchcombe. To these should be added: Battle, Cerne, Milton, Pershore, Selby and probably others.

boroughs were among the first in the country to grow in prosperity after the Conquest, and until the reign of Henry II derived more profit from the protection and initiative of their proprietors than did other towns from their first steps towards freedom and self-government. From the reign of Henry II onwards, however, friction between the burgesses and the monks was frequent, not so much on account of any oppression or injustice, as by reason of the unwillingness of the monastery to make any change in the amount and character of the customary payments and services.

The borough, in the century after the Conquest, was regarded primarily by the monastery as a financial asset on a par with other sources of revenue. So far was it originally from being considered as of administrative import-ance that at the division of property and income between abbot and convent at Bury c. 1105 the borough was not reckoned as part of the abbot's barony but fell to the share of the convent. All the important obedienti-aries received rents of some kind from it, but the income and rights accruing from the inhabitants and their lands considered as a group went to the cellarer and the sacrist, the former becoming lord of the manor of Bury, and the latter the lord of the borough itself. Thus the cellarer, besides a number of rights over pasture and mill, and receipts in commuta-tion of labour, and various privileges of pre-emption and monopoly, had the judicial rights of the manorial court of the town. The sacrist, besides rents in the modern sense of the word, received several payments by way of tenement-tax, reliefs, tolls, market and fair dues, etc., and himself, with the permission of the convent, could levy taxes; he also had the rights and profits of controlling the court of portman moot and the leet court. Above all, he appointed the reeve or reeves of the borough (later known as bailiffs), to whom he farmed the town as such, and thus had the govern-ment of the place in his power; he was also archdeacon of the exempt *banleuca*, with vicarial jurisdiction in the abbot's ecclesiastical court, and the profits arising therefrom.[1]

Thus in the borough of Bury the abbot of St Edmund's had very little direct power in the twelfth century. He had, of course, indirect powers of importance. The free tenants of the borough pleaded at his court, the *curia S. Edmundi*, the court of honour, and in the last resort the sacrist and cellarer, being his nominees and holding office at his pleasure, were merely his vice-gerents; but unless a strong abbot wished to guide matters, or quarrels between the burgesses and the convent came before him as arbitrator, the routine administration went on without his direct action. At Bury, from 1182 onwards, disturbed conditions obtained, and con-sequently Samson took a leading part in the settlement of the difficulties which arose. The history of these, being part of the domestic story of a single house, cannot be recounted here, but the pages of Jocelin's chronicle show how large the affairs of the town bulked not only in the life of the chief

1 For details and references *v.* Lobel, *op. cit.* 17–59.

officials of the monastery, but in the minds of all the monks, whose routine might easily be disturbed by them and who had repeatedly to take cognizance of them in chapter.[1]

It is probably not wholly accidental that Bury is the only monastic borough of whose development much is known during the twelfth century. At most of the others either their smaller size, or the more uniform control of the abbey, or their situation at a distance from the monastery, made their development, with the friction consequent upon it, more gradual. But in all the cases where a borough lay at the gates of a monastery and was controlled by the monks, it formed one more element, and that an important one, among the many interests and responsibilities, wholly unconnected with religion, that absorbed the minds, and employed the various talents, of the members of the community.[2]

1 *V*. Lobel, *op. cit.* 118 *seqq.*, with references to Jocelin.
2 Several municipal questions were normally decided in the monastic chapter, e.g. the sacrist nominated the bailiffs there, to be approved by the brethren (*v.* Lobel, *op. cit.* 33).

CHAPTER XXVI

THE DAILY LIFE OF THE MONASTERY

I

THE HORARIUM

Every student of monastic history must on occasion feel something of a desire to see again the daily round of life in a monastery of the past and recapture the atmosphere that surrounded the events and personalities of the time. Many sketches have indeed been made of life in a medieval cloister, but the majority of them are as it were composite photographs, combining details drawn from different centuries and therefore lacking precision, and, since material for such reconstruction is provided more abundantly by the age immediately preceding the Dissolution, the picture is as a rule that of a house in the fifteenth century. Here we are concerned to know the outline of the daily life as it developed between the times of Dunstan and those of Stephen Langton.

At the basis of any description must lie a clear conception of the normal horarium in a black monk house, and here at the outset considerable difficulties present themselves. Although there is ample information as to the round of conventual duties each day, there is an almost complete absence of indication in terms of clock time as to the hour at which they began and the length of time occupied by each. Moreover, the main sources of our knowledge are official regulations such as the *Concordia* and Lanfranc's *Consuetudines* or *Statuta*, which present the day in the abstract, not as lived by the individual. There does not even exist, for the England of this period, a customary such as that of Ulrich of Cluny containing the reflections and criticisms of the author. Consequently, for all beyond a bare list of liturgical functions it is necessary to rely upon the occasional observations of monastic writers and chroniclers. Even official documents such as the *Concordia* and *Statuta*, which profess to give instructions for all occasions, are unexpectedly disappointing, for without exception they cease to give detailed information after the chief meal of the day has been reached, and are also, as has been said, without any adequate indications of time.

In approaching the matter of time-tables, it is necessary for a reader unfamiliar with medieval monasticism to bear in mind a few general principles governing every horarium, but seldom explicitly formulated. The most important of these is the variation of the time of meals and Office as between the seasons of winter and summer, and, in both winter and summer, between fasting days and others. If, on a broad view, we exclude such casual fast days as occurred during the summer and autumn, we may say that the framework of the day changed three times during the year: there was the winter horarium, the Lenten and the summer. The winter arrangement began on the thirteenth of September[1] and ran until Ash Wednesday;[2] its characteristics were an early retirement (with a long night's rest as a consequence) and a single full meal at about two in the afternoon. The Lent horarium was similar in general outline, save that the meal was taken later, after Vespers, at half-past five or six. The summer time-table differed considerably from both of these. Retirement was later, the night office somewhat earlier and shorter; consequently there was a longer space of time between the night office (Matins and Lauds) and the first of the day hours, Prime. It became customary to allow a second period of sleep here. A still greater distinction was made by the allowance of two meals, one at midday, the other at about six o'clock in the evening; and after the midday meal a siesta of some length was taken.

The whole scheme of these arrangements is so foreign to anything in modern life, even among religious orders,[3] and especially to anything in English life, that it is difficult, when reconstructing it in the imagination, to appreciate where its physical hardships lay, and where use had become second nature. Speaking in the most general way, we may say that the monastic day of the early Middle Ages ran in winter from 2 a.m. to 6.30 p.m., whereas in most modern religious houses it begins and ends some three hours later, and in the ordinary life of the country some five hours later. Even more foreign to modern experience is the assignment of the first meal to a time never less than ten, and throughout the winter about twelve, hours after rising. This arrangement, as a necessary corollary, threw almost all the duties of the day, and in particular all the liturgical duties, into the "morning"; consequently the tripartite division of the day, standard among all northern European and American peoples, into three roughly equal periods of morning, afternoon and evening, did not exist in a monastery. This medieval monastic horarium, which was uniform all over Europe and unmodified by any differences of climate or latitude, derived from the countries of the Mediterranean and, ultimately, from the

---

1 The date of the autumn change is very old, and no doubt goes back beyond St Benedict. In the Rule (c. xli) it is given as *ab Idibus Septembris* (i.e. 13 September) and this still holds in the Statutes of Lanfranc. Later, the feast of the Exaltation of the Cross, which fell on the fourteenth of the month, was taken as the marking date.

2 This general statement needs qualification in detail: thus (a) the liturgical change was not made on 13 September, but on 1 October (hymns) and 1 November (lessons); (b) from 13 September till 1 November sleep was still taken, as in summer, between Lauds and Prime (so Lanfranc, but not, apparently, the *Concordia*) and again in the siesta; (c) the abstinence of Lent began partially at Septuagesima and wholly at Quinquagesima.

3 Only the eremitical orders of medieval origin and (though in part only) the reformed Cistercians have preserved their original horarium unchanged, and their manner of life is so different from that of the black monks that a visit to Parkminster or Camaldoli gives little idea of conditions at St Albans in the twelfth century. All other orders, not excepting almost all the strictly enclosed and penitential orders of women, have greatly modified the medieval scheme by retiring later, rising later, advancing the meal, even on fast days, to midday, and by setting earlier the hour of the conventual Mass.

East. In particular, the summer change of time-table was conditioned by the hot summers of the south, where the siesta is all but a physical necessity and where the early autumn finds health and energies impaired, as does February with us.[1] The arrangement did not suit the British Isles, but the force of tradition was too strong to break by a direct and wholesale change; instead, breaches of one kind or another were made in it by custom and indirectly.

As a basis for a review of detailed points in the life, a short outline of the winter arrangement set out by the *Regularis Concordia* may be given.[2] The monks and children of the cloister slept in a common dormitory, wearing by night the habit, without the scapular. Rising a little after two, the monks proceeded to choir in their night shoes, recited certain prayers, and then waited while the children entered and repeated the same prayers. The fifteen gradual psalms were then recited, followed by Nocturns (or, as they are now called, Matins) and prayers for the royal house. Then, after a short interval, Matins (the modern Lauds) were begun, perhaps about five o'clock, and were followed by various prayers, and by Lauds of All Saints and of the dead. Prime followed immediately if the day had already dawned, otherwise there was a wait till the light came. This, a reasonable procedure in southern France and Italy, where the rising of the sun varies less, must have led to inconvenient periods of waiting in England. After Prime came three psalms, followed by the seven penitential psalms, litanies and prayers. If Prime began at six, the whole cannot have ended before a quarter to seven at the earliest. From thenceforward till eight o'clock was a time for reading in the cloister, and perhaps for the private Masses of such as were priests; at eight the monks returned to the dormitory, washed, and put on their day shoes; they then returned to choir for Terce and the morrow Mass. This would have ended a little before nine; it was followed immediately by the chapter, at which a spiritual conference was often given, and faults confessed and punished; it closed with five psalms for the dead. The end of chapter would have come between half-past nine and ten; next came a long stretch of work, manual, intellectual or artistic, lasting till about half-past twelve, when Sext was recited, with other prayers, followed by the sung High Mass. Then, while the community remained in choir, the servers and readers of the refectory broke their fast with a small quantity of bread and beer; when they returned to the church, None was recited, and then all went to dinner, at

1 Abbot Butler, in his sources for c. xli of the Rule, adduces St Jerome's preface to the Rule of Pachomius, where one of the reasons given for the summer arrangement is the *aestus gravissimi.*

2 For the monastic time-table in general *v.* Butler, *Benedictine Monachism*, ch. xvii, and Dom U. Berlière, *L'Ascèse Bénédictine* (1927), 51–4. For the horarium of the *Concordia*, cf. the article by Dom T. Symons, *The Monastic Observance of the Regularis Concordia*, *DR*, XLIV (July 1926), 157–71, and for a number of monastic and canonical time-tables set out in parallel columns *v. The Monastic Horarium*, by the present writer, in *DR*, LI (October 1933), 706–25. The horarium of the *Concordia* is set out *infra*, Appendix XVIII.

about two o'clock or a little later. Dinner was followed by the second long period of reading, from a little before three till about five. Then came Vespers, and Vespers and Matins of the dead, after which the monks put on their night shoes and performed the Maundy. Next, after a drink in the refectory, there was a short public reading in choir, followed by Compline, and at a little before seven they retired to the dormitory.

It will be seen at once that there was very little time during the day which was not occupied by liturgical or community duties of one kind or another. The only times for private reading or work were an hour in the early morning, some three hours between chapter and Sext, and something over two hours in the afternoon. Even this average of five hours, which on some ferial days may have been increased, must often in practice have been greatly curtailed, both by the elaborations of chant and ceremonial on feast days and by the numberless pieces of necessary personal business to be done by each individual, to say nothing of conversations. It is, indeed, quite impossible to calculate the time which was occupied by the ceremonies and chant, sung lessons and responds, "farced" Common and Proper of the Mass, and the rest. At Cluny and the greater Cluniac houses we know from first-hand evidence that on all feasts (and feasts were of extremely frequent occurrence) practically the whole day was filled up, and the manuscripts of chant which remain, even those which date from before the Conquest, and the elaborate regulations of Lanfranc's *Statuta*, show that the greater houses, at least, practised an extremely rich liturgical life.

Yet a few considerations may be brought forward to show that at some monasteries, if not at all, the day was not in practice so crowded as a glance at the official horarium would suggest. It is in the first place reasonable to suppose that the chant was often sung with the promptness of attack and ease and smoothness of rhythm (and consequent economy of time) which obtain to-day in the centres of execution best qualified to set the norm;[1] and as regards the psalmody, such few references as exist from the beginning of our period to the end suggest that precipitation was a more general fault than drawling.[2] Moreover (to speak only of the period before the Conquest), although such houses as the Old and New Minsters at Winchester had fairly large numbers and an elaborate life, when numbers fell, as they did at Evesham and Worcester and doubtless elsewhere, to ten or a dozen, elaborate chant and ceremonial were clearly out of the

1 Thus visitors to Solesmes and other houses of the Congregation of France frequently remark on the comparatively short time occupied in singing even the most elaborate Tracts and Graduals, though there is no impression whatever of haste. It is the "slickness" which characterizes all expert musical and theatrical production.

2 The *Concordia* in its proem warns monks that they provoke God to anger rather than to mercy *nimia velocitate psallendo*. A century and a half later, excessive speed was one of the abuses envisaged by the Cistercian reform, and *c.* 1185 Abbot Warin of St Albans abandoned some of the extra psalmody, which was recited *confuse, quandoque diffuse* (*GASA*, I, 212).

question. And in every house, and at all periods, there must have been a fair proportion of monks excused from some, at least, of the choir duties. Lanfranc's *Statuta* have more than one clear indication of this; they presuppose that, setting apart those on a journey, some will be absent from High Mass and that others, who have been engaged in business, will be taking a meal while the community are at Compline.[1] Later, in the middle of the twelfth century, the multiplication of officials and the extension of their activities virtually divided the community into two groups, those in obediences who attended the liturgical services partially and occasionally, and the "monks of the cloister" who "followed the convent".

Thus in a number of ways, which varied at different periods, the weight of the full horarium was modified in its incidence upon communities and individuals. As with all elaborate schemes of life for large bodies of men, it rarely affected all in its completeness. Yet when all allowances have been made, it is clear beyond all doubt that in the eyes alike of the reformers under Edgar and of Lanfranc and his contemporaries the monastic life was primarily a liturgical one: a life of the service of God by vocal prayer, chant and ceremony; and such a judgment holds true even if it is also freely acknowledged that the Anglo-Saxon and Anglo-Norman way was not, as was the way of Cluny, solely and exclusively liturgical. It was certainly more liturgical than any Benedictine life at the present day,[2] and it can be called a contemplative life only by a very wide extension of the meaning of that phrase.[3]

So far as official regulations went, the framework of the life of the monks changed very little between 970 and 1200. The legislation of Lanfranc, in all its main lines, follows very nearly the scheme of the *Concordia*, though slightly increasing the additional psalmody and the ceremonial complexity, and in the following century the only alterations took the form of additions made by this house or that to the number of feasts or the ceremonial with which they were celebrated.[4] The Cistercian movement produced no repercussions in English black monk circles comparable to the innovations

1 *Statuta*, I, § 1, p. 212: "Si vero alii sint qui pro utilitate ecclesiae majori Missae non possint interesse, etc."; XVI, pp. 241–2: "Completorium vero dum canitur, licet Priori, et eis qui per licentiam de completorio remanent, etc....loqui...tunc enim licet iis qui aliqua utilitate impediti [fuerint]...comedere."

2 The congregation with the fullest liturgical life to-day, that of France, has, as a general practice, no psalmody or vocal prayer beyond the Office and Mass; all "troping" is of course absent from the chant, and the Chapter Mass has fallen out as a conventual exercise. Though its place is more than taken by the private Mass and "meditation" of each priest, these latter are essentially individual exercises.

3 It is not possible to accept without reservation (at least for England) the judgment of Dom Berlière, *L'Ascèse Bénédictine*, 54: "La vie [monastique en IX–XII siècles] devient plus exclusivement contemplative." The life at Winchester *c.* 1000 or at St Albans *c.* 1100 was only contemplative in a very negative sense—that is, the house was not, as a body, engaged in external work. Its daily life had little of that simplicity, solitude and devotion to private prayer that characterized so many of the new movements of the eleventh and twelfth centuries.

4 Lanfranc's *Statuta* give an elaborate list of the various grades of feasts, *v. infra*, p. 541.

in central and eastern France which moved the Cluniac cardinal of Albano to such indignation; there is no trace of any attempt in this country to shorten vocal prayer and ceremonial, to increase silence and to give time for manual work. Later, indeed, c. 1190, a whole series of small curtailments are found at St Albans, but they were the work of Abbot Warin, a university-trained physician and scholar of the new type. Later still, c. 1220, at the same house, further alterations were made by Abbot William. These latter do not strictly fall within our period; they would seem clearly to have been part of the general movement towards reorganization and "rationalization" which was one of the *sequelae* of the great Lateran Council. The earlier changes were not inspired by any desire to follow the white monks, but were part of a personal programme elaborated by a man who belonged to the new school of learning and who in his years of training had seen a number of systems at work.[1]

II

SILENCE

Capital as is the point of silence in any monastic horarium, it is nevertheless curiously difficult to glean precise information as to its observance during this period, or indeed throughout the whole of monastic history previous to the detailed constitutions of the thirteenth century. In the Rule of St Benedict (which itself is not wholly free from ambiguity) it would seem that while no fixed time was allowed for any kind of social or recreative conversation, necessary speaking, concerning material or spiritual business, was permitted at any time during the day when the community was not engaged in a common exercise. Long before the age of the *Regularis Concordia* it had become the general practice to specify a certain fixed period or periods when talking was allowed in the cloister, and to set apart a room where necessary business might be discussed outside those times. So much is clear, but it is all but impossible to ascertain the exact length of the periods, and how far the conversation was intended or permitted to be merely recreative.

Normally, in customaries of the tenth and eleventh centuries, talking upon all matters of business and utility was allowed in the cloister, which was the common place of work and reading, once a day in winter, between the Chapter and the office of Sext which preceded the High Mass, and twice a day in summer, immediately after Chapter and after None, which came at the end of the siesta; in other words, talking was permitted only during times of "work". The reason for the double period in summer was the curtailment of the morning stretch of work by the midday meal. The

1 For Warin's changes *v. GASA*, I, 212–13; for the later changes, *ibid.* 292–5.

Concordia in several passages assumes this arrangement, as do the regulations for feast days, when no work was done, by expressly excluding talking.[1] Contrariwise, the time allotted to reading in the cloister (that is, in theory, all the time not spent by the monks in common prayer or common work) was a time of silence.[2] That this silence was only a "lesser" silence, and not inviolable, is shown by the provision that from the beginning of Vespers (perhaps about 5 or 5.30 p.m.) until the end of Chapter of the following day (9.30 a.m.) the silence shall be absolute, and any necessary conversation is to be conducted outside the cloister in a special place, the *auditorium*, and even there only in a low tone of voice.[3] Thus it would seem that there were three degrees of observance; first, the period or periods of work omitted on feast days, when general talking was allowed; next, the periods of reading when silence was in general to be observed, but when it could be broken for a reasonable cause, though not perhaps in the cloister; thirdly, the evening and early morning when it could be broken only rarely and in the parlour. It must, however, always be borne in mind that outside the *monasterium*, i.e. church, cloister, refectory and dormitory, the officials and those allotted to some special work would talk freely.

Lanfranc's *Statuta* altered very little. They specifically permit talking in the cloister after Chapter till Sext and again in winter in the interval after Sext.[4] In the summer, there is only one period in the morning, but no doubt the second after None remained.[5] As in the *Concordia*, no talking is allowed on feasts of twelve lessons; the reason for this was no doubt that on those days no manual or craft work was done which would call for discussion.[6] There is no mention of an *auditorium*, just as there is none of a "greater" silence beginning at Vespers; perhaps this implies that it was the practice at Bec to keep the shorter but wholly inviolable silence of the Rule from the end of Compline.[7] Gradually, however, two *locutoria* or parlours came to be part of all monastic buildings; one, near the chapter-house, was used by officials and private monks; the other, near the abbot's

---

1 E.g. *Concordia*, vi, 90: "Quicquid necesse fuerit etiam tunc [*sc.* after None in the summer] operentur, ceteris enim horis...silentium diligenti cura in claustro custodiant"; *ibid.* i, 82: "In diebus autem Festis, ob taciturnitatis studiique observantiam, etc."; *ibid.* "Tota autem die [*sc.* festiva] solemne silentium teneatur in claustro."

2 *Concordia*, vi, 90: "Tempus etiam lectionis tempus est taciturnitatis."

3 *Concordia*, vi, 90.

4 *Lanfranci Statuta*, I, § 1, p. 212: "Peracto Capitulo...loquantur in claustro....Post sextam nullus in claustro loquatur donec...minimus [infantum] alta voce *Benedicite* dicat."

5 *Lanfranci Statuta*, I, § 6, p. 227: "Una tantum vice loquantur in claustro [*sc.* in the morning]...id est, post Capitulum usque ad tertiam." The double period of talking in the morning in winter was no addition to the earlier scheme, since Lanfranc put the office of Sext in the middle of the spell of work after Chapter (*c.* 11 a.m.), whereas in the *Concordia* it came at the end, immediately preceding Mass.

6 *Lanfranci Statuta*, I, § 11, p. 231: "In omnibus festivitatibus duodecim lectionum, quaecumque sunt, et in omnibus diebus qui infra Octavas sunt in quibus in claustro non loquuntur monachi."

7 Cf. the incident related in *Liber Eliensis*, 262.

quarters, by the guests and the poor. At Abingdon both were constructed soon after 1100.[1]

It is quite impossible to trace the working of this formal legislation in everyday life. The two most illuminating documents of the twelfth century, the *Vita Ailredi* and Jocelin's chronicle, make it clear enough that even in the strictest Cistercian monastery, and under a saint's rule, there was abundant scope for the easy intercourse of master and disciple, and that in a black monk house there were numberless occasions for discussing all that was going forward. In the matter of silence, as in all else, the separation of abbot from monks and the multiplication of officials engaged in multifarious activities emancipated a large proportion of the community from the full observance of the regular life. For the others, the "cloistered monks", quite apart from lax discipline, a number of customs developed which amounted to periodical times of recreation. First in importance of these was the oft-recurring blood-letting or *minutio*.

The gradual regularization of this in England would seem to have been the work of the Normans. There is, as it would appear, no explicit mention of it in the *Concordia*; the practice, no doubt, existed, but took place only when supposedly necessary and was treated as any other small indisposition. In Lanfranc's *Statuta* it is still something personal and irregular; the individual, who may be alone, asks permission for the operation, which is to take place at a specified time, varying with the seasons; after it he stays away from choir until chapter on the following day and for two days takes the anticipated light meal or *mixtum*; there is no mention of any recreative talking. A century later, however, other customs had gradually developed. The *minutio* is no longer an individual "cure", but a regular event treated in effect as a kind of vacation. The earliest detailed enactments that have been preserved are those of Abbot Warin of St Albans (1183–95), who was himself a master of the medical university of Salerno. He extends absence from the night office to two days, allows earlier meals and expressly permits two periods of talking in the guests' parlour, the first after dinner and the other in the evening while the community are at Compline.[2] From being a purely medical measure the *minutio* is now clearly also a vacation, for Abbot Warin enacts that if the second day's relaxation is interrupted by the occurrence of a great

1 *Chron. Abingd.* II, 286: "Aedificavit [Faricius, abbot from 1100]...duo locutoria, unum ad orientem juxta capitulum, aliud ad occidentem sub capella abbatis." Similarly at Evesham a *privatum locutorium* was constructed by Abbot Maurice [1096–], and a *regula e locutorium cum capella* by Abbot Reginald (? 1122–49), *v. Chron. Evesh.* 98–9.

2 *GASA*, I, 207: "In locutorio hospitum divertant...licentiamque habeant loquendi, cum omni tamen gravitate"; *ibid.* I, 208: "Ipso die, ad completorium in supradicto loco conveniant, ibique loquantur, quamdiu Hospitali visum fuerit, aut hora permiserit." For a collection of references to the *minutio*, which would appear to have become regular under Salernitan influence in the twelfth century, *v.* Dom L. Gougaud, *Anciennes Coutumes claustrales*, ch. vi, "La phlébotomie monastique".

feast, it shall be made up on the day following.[1] As a living commentary from a neighbouring abbey upon these regulations we have the passing remark of Jocelin, who retails the election gossip of the monks when they met together at the time of blood-letting, "when monks of the cloister are wont to reveal each to the other the secrets of the heart".[2] A number of scattered notices and all later customals[3] allow the inference that a similar development of the *minutio* had taken place in black monk houses in general. The final step was to make blood-letting at fixed times a matter depending not upon personal initiative or the abbot's judgment, but on a process of routine, by which the whole community went in batches of ten or a dozen four or five times a year. This practice came in at Peterborough at the very end of our period; it may possibly have been introduced somewhat earlier elsewhere.[4]

III

THE NUMBER AND QUALITY OF THE MEALS

The arrangement of meals in medieval monasticism differed very considerably from the practice of the modern world. The times at which they were taken and the variations in their hour and number according to the seasons of the year are alike alien to the experience of the present day or of recent centuries. The monastic system was derived directly from the legislation of the Rule, which in its turn represented the practice of classical antiquity as modified by ecclesiastical and monastic tradition. Roman society of the Empire, besides an occasional light breakfast at about nine o'clock, took two meals, the luncheon (*prandium*) at midday and the dinner (*cena*) or principal meal about four o'clock. Ecclesiastical discipline had superimposed on this arrangement various periods and days of fasting, when no meal was taken till the late afternoon or evening. In the Rule, the year is divided into four unequal parts: in the winter *régime*, from 13 September to the beginning of Lent, a single meal was taken at 2.30 or 3.0; in Lent this was set later, at 4.30 or 5.0; from Easter to Whitsuntide two meals were taken, the first and chief (*prandium*) at midday, the second at 5.0 or 5.30; from Whitsuntide till 13 September the *régime* was as in Paschal time save for Wednesdays and Fridays, when a single meal was taken at 2.30, as in winter.[5] St Benedict does not specifically mention ecclesiastical fast days outside Lent, such as Ember Days and occasional

---

1 *GASA*, I, 208: "In nocte altera recompensetur."

2 *Jocelini Cronica*, 221: "Tempore minutionis...quo tempore claustrales solent alternatim secreta cordis revelare."

3 E.g. *Chron. Evesh.* 213, notes 6 and 11; *Chron. Abingd.* II, de Obedientiariis Abbendoniae, *passim*.

4 Rob. Swapham, *Historia Coenobii Burgensis* (ed. Sparke), 110. The regulation appears to have been one of the first acts of Abbot Robert in 1214.

5 *Regula S. Benedicti*, c. xli: "Quibus horis oportet reficere"; cf. c. xlii, 11; liii, 23, 24.

vigils, but presumably the Lent *régime* obtained on them when they occurred. The servers and the cooks received an additional portion of bread and wine an hour before the meal, as did the reader immediately before reading.[1] The children of the cloister and the aged had special indulgences and anticipated the hour of the first meal.[2]

These arrangements persevered in the main unchanged throughout the Dark Ages, and are assumed so clearly all through the *Concordia* and Lanfranc's *Statuta* that no particular references need be given. Two modifications, however, had been introduced, the one slight, the other more important, at least in its developments. The first of these, a drink in the evening in winter and at mid-afternoon in the summer, may have been the unrecorded practice even in St Benedict's day: the original measure of water became a draught of the standard beverage of the country, wine or beer, and by the time of Dunstan it had become customary on certain days to supply a finer wine or mead with an accompaniment of light bread or cakes. The second was the introduction of a second meal in winter on certain days, varying in number in different houses according to different uses, but including all Sundays and feasts of twelve lessons and octaves.

Traces of these two practices can be seen in the *Concordia*. The regular evening drink in the winter, no doubt of beer, is assumed as taking place in the refectory immediately after the change into night shoes before the short period of reading (*collatio*) which preceded Compline.[3] On certain days this drink was replaced by another, the *caritas*, probably accompanied by cakes, which was taken during the *collatio*, and formed a kind of mean between the simple drink and the second meal which, as is to be gathered from a passing reference, was allowed in winter on certain feasts.[4] There is no detailed instruction concerning the children; other uses permit them to breakfast during the monks' chapter, and there is a charming story told in the Abingdon chronicle of Queen Edith who, entering the refectory while the boys were eating and remarking that they had nothing but bread, gave some property to supply an income for better food.[5] A similar tradition at St Albans assigned a gift of land in Ethelred's day to the provision of cheese and milk for the children.[6]

Lanfranc's *Statuta* make no alterations in the scheme. They presuppose that two meals will be taken on certain days during the winter,[7] and they legislate for a mid-morning breakfast for the children and those monks

---

1 *Regula*, c. xxxv, 20; c. xxxviii, 22. 2 *Regula*, c. xxxvii, 7.

3 Cf. *Concordia*, i, 83, where it is described as *ad haurienda pocula*.

4 *Concordia*, i, 83: "Quotiescumque fratribus charitas interim dum collatio legitur praebetur"; *ibid.* viii, 91: "His tantum diebus festis, quibus coenaturi sunt fratres."

5 *Chron. Abingd.* I, 460–1: "Invenerunt in refectorio pueros monachos, ut moris est puerorum, propter aetatis infirmitatem ante refectionem fratrum cibum sumentes." The gift is elsewhere called a "breakfast", *matutinellum* (*ibid.* II, 283).

6 *GASA*, I, 54: "Ad alimenta monachorum juniorum lacticiniis alendorum."

7 *Lanfranci Statuta*, I, § 6, p. 227: "Ab idibus Septembris privatis diebus [i.e., not feasts] agantur continue jejunia quae regula praecipit." At Peterborough in the later twelfth century

who are unable to fast longer,[1] and so far as can be ascertained the arrangements for the common meals remained unchanged between 960 and 1216, modified only by the addition of more feast days in winter. How far the observance was relaxed in the decades before the Conquest and again in some quarters at the end of the twelfth century must remain, in default of full evidence, a matter of doubt.

Such being the number of meals, it is natural to proceed to a consideration of the quality and quantity of the food and drink, and, at the outset, to meet the capital question of abstinence from flesh-meat. On this point the Rule is peremptory, though by his use of the word quadruped St Benedict supplied matter for argument, and as a general rule the flesh of birds had come to be considered lawful fare.[2] The evidence as to English practice from the time of Dunstan onwards must be examined in some detail, owing to the views of certain scholars in recent times.[3]

The *Concordia* does not include a chapter devoted expressly to diet, but it is quite clear from the words of the proem, which announces that the Rule is to be followed absolutely, that its compilers, chief among whom was the austere Ethelwold, intended to adopt the traditional monastic programme,[4] and an incidental enactment, forbidding lard in Advent and between Septuagesima and Easter, shows that the current monastic discipline was fully kept.[5] Two casual references in contemporary sources show that abstinence from flesh-meat was assumed as normal. One occurs in Aelfric's *Colloquium*, written some twenty years after the *Concordia*. The pupil, a child of the cloister, when asked by his master to give an account of his diet, answers that he still eats meat, because he is still a boy in the school.[6]

two meals were allowed: (*a*) continuously until 1 October; (*b*) during the octave of St Martin; (*c*) from Christmas to the Epiphany; (*d*) on all feasts of twelve lessons, which included all Sundays.

1 *Lanfranci Statuta*, 1, § 1, p. 212: "Infantes Capitulum suum teneant et postea in refectorium pergant"; *ibid*. 1, § 5, p. 225: "(On Rogation days) post Tertiam sumant mixtum pueri et infirmi qui jejunare non possunt."

2 *Regula*, c. xxxix, 22–5: "Carnium vero quadrupedum omnimodo ab omnibus abstineatur comestio, praeter omnino debiles aegrotos." The tradition at Monte Cassino as early as 800 seems to have been in favour of eating the flesh of birds.

3 In particular O. Cockayne in *Saxon Leechdoms* (RS), III, 410, and Edmund Bishop in a paper printed after his death with the title *The Method and Degree of Fasting and Abstinence of the Black Monks in England before the Reformation*, in *DR*, XLIII (October 1925), 184–237. It is only right to recall that Bishop's paper, which is an example alike of his power of assembling the results of his wide learning in answer to a request for help and of his patriotic prejudices, was written *c*. 1883 and neither intended nor revised for publication. What follows in the text above corrects both his conclusions and those of a previous essay of the present writer, *The Diet of Black Monks*, *DR*, LII (April 1934), 275–90.

4 *Concordia*, Proem, 79: "Victum cum pondere, mensura et numero...jejunium, abstinentiam...quae Patroni nostri Benedicti traditione voluntarie suscepimus...totis viribus custodientes, etc." This decisive sentence escaped the notice of E. Bishop who remarks (*art. cit.* 188): "The *Concordia*...has practically nothing bearing on the subject."

5 *Concordia*, ii, 84: "In adventu Domini pinguedo interdicitur, scilicet lardi, nisi festivis diebus"; *ibid*. iii, 85: "In Septuagesima vero pinguedo intermittitur."

6 *Aelfrici Colloquium* (ed. B. Thorpe), in *Analecta Anglo-Saxonica* (2nd ed. 1868), 34: "M[agister]. Quid manducas in die? D[iscipulus]. Adhuc carnibus vescor, quia puer sum sub virga degens."

A second occurs in the same writer's life of Ethelwold, where the saint is stated never to have eaten flesh-meat, even when seriously ill, save twice at the command of Dunstan.[1] The rule and practice, therefore, of the first revival would seem beyond a doubt to have been the same as that of observant Continental monasticism.[2]

In the decline which affected certain abbeys before the Conquest, the eating of meat, together with other elaborations of diet, was introduced here and there, but it cannot be said with any certainty how widespread the practice became. It is asserted categorically of the Old Minster, ambiguously at Christ Church, and with still more ambiguity at St Albans; on the other hand, it is not easy to suppose that it existed at Worcester under Wulfstan or at Evesham under Mannig. For Christ Church, our informant is William of Malmesbury, none too reliable a witness, as has been seen, when he is making assertions about a state of things that existed half-a-century before he wrote.[3] At Winchester the first Norman prior, Simeon, found the brethren eating meat and weaned them from it by exquisitely prepared dishes of fish.[4] At St Albans Abbot Paul, Lanfranc's nephew, making use of similar methods, put a stop to the meat-eating of those who had been bled; a first reading of the chronicle, in the version that resulted from later editing, suggests that all, and not the invalids only, had been taking meat, but the words are not free from ambiguity.[5]

Lanfranc's *Statuta* naturally presuppose the observance of monastic tradition. Thus in the regulations for the sick it is laid down that when really ill they are to be allowed meat, but while on this *régime* they are to walk hooded and upon a staff, and when recovered are to ask pardon in Chapter for eating irregular food.[6] It is also assumed that the monks will abstain from lard from Septuagesima till Easter, and in Advent save on Sundays and feasts.[7] There can, indeed, be no doubt that complete ab-

1 *Vita S. Aethelwoldi, Chron. Abingd.* App. I, vol. II, 263: "Infirmabatur saepe... minime tamen esu carnium quadrupedum aut avium usus est, nisi semel, etc." The reference to birds, taken in conjunction with the practice of Wulfstan of Worcester, seems to indicate that the fathers of the *Concordia* reckoned their flesh along with meat.

2 For a discussion of the alleged Ethelwoldian dietary *v.* Appendix XIX.

3 Will. Malmesb., *GP*, 70–1: "Potibus indulgere, delicatiori victui, etc."

4 *Ann. Winton., s.a.* 1082: "Cum videret monachos in refectorio carnibus assidue vesci, fecit exquisita piscium parari cibaria et dari eis; illi autem delectati in his, rogabant hujusmodi eis donari cibaria et tunc velle abstinere a carnibus. Datae sunt autem eis pisces, et abstinuerunt a carnibus."

5 *GASA*, I, 59: "In conventu autem monachorum...esum carnium refrenavit, habitum commutavit; paulatim tamen ne repentinus impetus seditionem suscitaret....Minutis autem, qui de sua consuetudine pastillis carneis vescebantur, esus subtraxit inordinatos, et pro carne, de allece [herring] et liborum cedulis [*sic* the printed text] congestum quoddam ferculum (cujus solum remansit nomen) ipsis in communi cumulavit; quod more Normannorum karpie quasi kar en pie sophistice nominavit." There is considerable confusion and repetition in these pages, and it is possible that the first lines of the above extract refer to the same matter as the later ones.

6 *Lanfranci Statuta*, XXIII, p. 248: "De misericordia concessa debilibus."

7 *Lanfranci Statuta*, I, § 2, p. 213: "Dominicis et aliis festis quibus duodecim lectiones faciunt, adipem comedant."

stinence from flesh-meat, save in the case of definite illness, was the rule throughout the monasteries of England between 960 and 1216; there is not a single piece of trustworthy evidence to show that meat was ever allowed in the common refectory during that period.[1] But before the Lateran Council certain relaxations had begun to come in outside the refectory, and these must be considered in some detail.

First among them was the use of meat at the abbot's table. Both Ethelwold and Lanfranc suppose that the abbot will dine with his monks, but, as has been seen, the custom was introduced very generally at the beginning of the twelfth century of his dining with his household and selected guests, and at his table flesh-meat was served. Gradually another custom came in which had its sanction in the letter (though scarcely in the spirit) of the Rule. This was that the abbot should invite to his table certain of the brethren; they would then eat whatever was served there.[2] The Abingdon chronicler, in a passage of very doubtful authenticity, dates this development at his house from the rule of Abbot Faricius (1100–17); however uncertain the anecdote there related, the passage at least shows that the practice was regarded as an innovation.[3] Seventy years later, Jocelin presupposes as a matter of course both the separate table and the meat, but he does not mention any monks as invited to dine with Samson.[4] At the end of the century invitation to the abbot's table was sufficiently widespread to be subject of remark for St Hugh of Lincoln; according to his biographer the saint criticized those black monk abbots who did not afford their sons this relaxation.[5] A few years later the papal legate Nicholas is quoted by a Bury chronicler as recognizing the right of the prior, during an interregnum, to invite a small number of the brethren to

1 The word "meat" in the text is not intended to include the flesh of fowl. There is no peremptory evidence that this was allowed, but the very large number of birds that figure on all contemporary farm lists might seem to point in this direction, though the sick and guests must always be remembered. E.g. *GASA*, I, 75: "De Kayso, ad Natale...24 gallinae...de Rykemanwurthe...48 gallinae...Cudicote et Waldene...50 gallinae." Similar lists may be seen in Hemming's *Cartulary*, the *Abingdon Chronicle*, etc. A difficulty is also caused at first sight by the (relatively small) number of pigs and lambs that figure on these lists, but the flesh of these may well have been used for guests, servants and the sick, while the lard went to the monks. The St Albans list states explicitly that the items were to be shared by both cellarers (*inter duos cellararios*), i.e. intern and extern, and specific mention is made of guests and servants.

2 *Regula*, c. lvi: "De mensa abbatis." Cf. c. liii, 34. It is not to be thought that St Benedict intended his abbot and monks to eat meat.

3 It occurs in *Chron. Abingd.* II, 287. It is natural to suspect any incident at Abingdon concerning diet, but this one may rest on a basis of fact, all the more because it contradicts the apocryphal account of the dietary.

4 *Jocelini Cronica*, 244. Actually, Jocelin mentions flesh-meat only to say that Samson abstained from it after the fall of Jerusalem in 1187. "Coepit...abstinere...carnes tamen voluit sibi anteferre...ad augmentum...elemosinae."

5 *Magna Vita Hugonis* (ed. Dimock), 343–4. Hugh is reported to have said that black monks, who varied more than Carthusians in natural complexion, needed a greater variety of diet. That he spoke on the subject is doubtless true, but it must be remembered that his biographer, himself a black monk, wrote when the diet question was in full agitation.

eat meat in his private room.[1] As an alternative, apparently, to this, Abbot Acarius, a monk of St Albans and Samson's contemporary at Peterborough, adopted a system of sending each day special food from his table; to the monks he sent "regular" food, to the infirmary meat.[2] In the controversy of the thirteenth century both the existence and the legality of this widespread practice of eating meat with the abbot were admitted.

Meanwhile another custom had proceeded along parallel lines of development. The sick who were really in need of a fortifying diet had from the first received meat in the infirmary, though not before the infirmarian had taken upon himself the responsibility of asking permission.[3] Those who had been bled, on the other hand, though allowed to anticipate the hour of meals and to break certain fasts, ate regular food, and it does not appear that the eating of meat was ever allowed to them after the Conquest before 1216.[4] But by degrees a practice was introduced of allowing those who were ailing or weakly to eat meat in a room apart from the rest, thus keeping the letter of the Rule as regards the refectory itself. This practice, originally due to the action of an abbot in the case of individuals, naturally left little traces in the records until, as happened between 1225 and 1275, it was made a subject of disciplinary examination. In the case of St Albans alone can the date of its introduction be fixed; there it was due to the physician Abbot Warin (1183-95).[5] A quarter of a century later it was fairly general; thus at Peterborough the community, no doubt in batches, had three such periods of meat-eating during the year, besides any meals they might have with guests or with the abbot.[6] At Durham, according to an alleged "old custom" brought forward in 1235, ten yearly *recreationes* (subsequently trebled) were allowed,[7] and without a doubt the "eatings of flesh" customary at Bury in 1215 were similar in kind, unless indeed they were the indulgences permitted in some houses to obedientiaries.[8]

The discipline regarding flesh-meat may therefore be summed up as

1 *Electio Hugonis* in *Mem. S. Edmund's*, ii, 56. The legate [1216] is reported as saying: "et ego omnibus carnium commessationes prohibui...praeter quod prior, cum fuerit in camera, quos voluerit de fratribus ad se convocet per tres vel per quatuor."

2 Rob. Swapham, *Burg. Hist.* 107: "Qualibet die mitt[ebat] in conventum de dominico pane suo et de cibis regularibus ad consolationem fratrum...et...infirmis fratribus de cibis carnium." 3 This held good at St Albans as late as c. 1190 (*GASA*, i, 211).

4 Cf. *GASA*, i, 207-9; Rob. Swapham, *Burg. Hist.* 110 [c. 1220]: "Minuti reficiebantur in refectorio regularibus cibis."

5 *GASA*, i, 211: "Hic quoque primo permisit aliquibus fratribus...ut seorsum, scilicet in oriolo, carnem comederent: et hoc fiebat, Abbate compellente, et in virtute obedientiae praecipiente." These words have a tendencious sound, as if written during the food controversy.

6 Rob. Swapham, *Burg. Hist.* 110: "Conventus habuit trinam misericordiam per annum in domo ad hoc proprie deputata, ubi comedebant carnes, secundum quod Deus dabat [!]: similiter et in domo hospitum et alibi ubicumque comedebant extra refectorium vescebantur carnibus."

7 *Hist. Dunelmensis Scriptores Tres* (ed. J. Raine), Appendix, xliv.

8 *V.s.* n. 1. That such relaxations for officials existed we can gather from the statutes of the first General Chapter of 1218-19; cf. *Chapters of the English Black Monks* (ed. W. A. Pantin), i, 11-12.

follows. Lanfranc's statutes, agreeing with Norman tradition and the still earlier discipline of the *Concordia*, prohibited the eating of meat save by the sick in the infirmary. This was enforced and held good in practice everywhere for half a century and in some houses for much longer, but in the course of the twelfth century meat was allowed first to those dining with the abbot in his private room, next, also in a separate room, to those who were in poor health and finally, but still apart from the refectory, to obedientiaries, to those dining with the guests and (the final stage) to all the monks during certain fixed periods of "recreation" in the course of the year. Some or all of these practices can be traced before 1216 at Abingdon, Bury, St Albans, Peterborough and Durham; the reforming statutes a few years later imply that they were almost universal, but differed greatly in detail in various houses.[1] A few monasteries, of which perhaps Battle was one, held for long to the original observance and may have preserved it unimpaired up to the end of our period.[2]

A return may now be made to earlier years to consider other developments in the monastic diet. St Benedict decreed that the chief meal (*prandium*) should consist of two cooked dishes, doubtless of flour, beans, eggs, cheese and the like, and a third of fresh vegetables and fruit, if such were available; he also allowed an ample quantity of bread, a pound in weight. He nowhere expressly legislates for the second meal, but it may be supposed that it was a lighter version of the other, for a third part of the daily ration of bread was to be kept back for it.[3] No precise and authentic data exist for reconstructing the daily monastic meals of the times of Dunstan and Lanfranc; the Norman practice clearly allowed for some kind of scale in the dishes corresponding to the rank of the feasts, for not only does Lanfranc direct that the refectory shall be provided on great days with finer cloths and napkins, but he expressly mentions a custom that on the day (presumably thrice in the year) when the chapter of the Rule concerning the cellarer was read in public, that official should provide the community with feastday fare.[4] Nor need it be supposed that the ordinary diet, even in observant houses, was poor in quality or meagre in quantity. The boy in Aelfric's dialogue to which reference has already been made ate, besides meat, green vegetables, eggs, fish, cheese, butter, beans—everything, in fact[5]—and there is every reason to think that, apart from flesh-meat, all these articles of food, together with dripping, lard,

1 Cf. *Chapters of the English Black Monks*, I, 17 (statutes of 1219–25): "Secundum diversorum monasteriorum regularem consuetudinem."

2 Such is the implication of the Chapter of 1218–19, *ut supra*, p. 10: "Salvis consuetudinibus quarundam ecclesiarum in quibus major abstinentia hactenus exstitit observata."

3 *Regula*, c. xxxix, 10–12.

4 *Lanfranci Statuta*, I, § 7, p. 227. If the napery was of a better order no doubt the food was also. *Ibid*. IX, p. 237: "Honestum et festivum servitium ipsa die [faciat cellararius] fratribus in refectorio."

5 *Aelfrici Colloquium* (ed. Thorpe), 34: "M[agister]. Quid plus manducas? D[iscipulus]. Olera et ova, pisces et caseum, butyrum et fabas et omnia."

milk and honey, figured at the monastic table. England as a whole had all over the Continent a reputation, which perhaps was lost only within living memory, for heavy feeding. The observations of the Norman knight entertained as a prisoner at Ely during the siege, even if in reality the comments of a Norman monk, are a fair indication of current opinion,[1] and the wholly genuine, but none the less Gargantuan, dietary of the canons of Waltham corroborates all the suggestions contained in other sources.[2]

When information becomes plentiful, it is clear that, erected upon the basis of an ordinary day's fare of bread, cheese, vegetables and two or three dishes of cereals, beans or eggs a considerable fabric of customary or occasional dishes had sprung up. The most general form taken by these additions was the pittance, a small dish, that is, usually of fish or eggs, served to each monk or pair of monks in addition to the common dishes. At Glastonbury already at the beginning of the twelfth century the monks had two pittances on Sunday, Tuesday, Thursday and Saturday, and one on the remaining days of the week,[3] and the Abingdon dietary allows for one a day on ordinary days, the number rising to three or four with the degree of the feast. Towards the end of the century we have the well-known description of a dinner at Christ Church, Canterbury, from the pen of Gerald of Wales. He was a guest at the high table on Trinity Sunday, one of the greatest Canterbury feasts, and counted sixteen courses, cooked in the most exquisite manner; delicacies were also sent down by the prior from the high table to individuals.[4] Elsewhere Gerald speaks of the ten or thirteen courses commonly enjoyed by the black monks.[5] In this he is probably generalizing from a particular case, *more suo*, and even the Canterbury episode may be over-coloured in his narrative, but the chroniclers furnish plenty of evidence of the most ingenuous kind that the meals on feast days were far from frugal.[6] In course of time, as has been seen,

1 *Liber Eliensis*, 232. He says that himself and Hereward's men "cotidie cum monachis in refectorio suo habunde satis, more Anglorum, vesceba[ntur]".

2 *The Foundation of Waltham Abbey* (ed. W. Stubbs), 16. The whole page is of great interest. Besides the daily allowance the canons had pittances, three, two or one in number, on various feasts. "Erant autem tales pitantiae unicuique canonico:...aut xii merulae aut ii agauseae aut ii perdices aut unus phasianus." It must of course be borne in mind that at least one destitute man was supported out of each canon's allowance.

3 The *Consuetudines* of Glastonbury in Will. Malmesb., *de Antiquitate Glast.* (*PL*, CLXXIX, 1732), which are said to have existed under Abbots Thurstan and Herluin (1082–1118), allow for two and three *generalia* on alternate days. The *Abingdon Chronicle*, I, 345–6; II, 279, gives two dishes of vegetables, one (or two) *pulmenta* and one *generale*. *Pulmentum* was usually a dish of cereals or beans, etc.; *generale* one of eggs or fish; both were served to the whole table, in distinction to the *pitantia*.

4 Giraldus Cambrensis, *de Rebus a se gestis*, I, 51.

5 Giraldus, *Iter Kambriae*, VI, 46: "Isti [monachi nigri] de decem ferculis vel tredecim, quae sibi de consuetudinibus solo jure deberi contendunt, etc." Cf. I, 52.

6 The ordinary meal among seculars of the period would seem to have consisted of four to five courses; cf. Giraldus, I, 52, and Jocelin's statement that Samson as abbot regularly took a dinner of three or four courses, with the addition of game if anything had been taken in the hunt (*Jocelini Cronica*, 246).

a special official, the pittancer, was appointed with revenues of his own, to provide these extra dishes according to the scale established by custom. That they were, and remained, quite literally "extras" may be gathered from the circumstance that it was not uncommon for a community to vote away the pittancer's revenues to achieve some necessary piece of building. Thus at Evesham *c.* 1200 the church tower was built by this means,[1] and a few years previously the monks of Bury, at Samson's suggestion, were about to surrender their pittances for a year in order to repair the shrine of St Edmund, when the sacrist pointed out that such an action would show a lack of faith in the power of the saint to help himself.[2] In addition to pittances, the ordinary bread was replaced on feast days by a finer kind, or by spiced cakes.[3] But it need not be assumed that all made use of all the liberty of choice that was provided, or that Wulfstan of Worcester was the only one to abstain altogether from certain common articles of diet.

Feasts were divided for sumptuary purposes into four classes. The first and lowest included all Sundays and feasts of twelve lessons; these implied two meals and the eating of lard in winter. Above these were feasts "in albs", feasts "in copes" and half a dozen of the greatest feasts of all. But beyond these there gradually grew up a number of obits. The anniversaries of all abbots were celebrated not only with a Mass and almsgiving, but with a feast in the refectory, and sometimes this honour was extended to the memory of an official, who, like Adam the cellarer of St Albans, had deserved well of the commonweal.[4] Thus, speaking generally, on all Sundays and on an average of one or two days a week some kind of festal addition was made to the regular diet.

After food, drink. The basic beverage of Anglo-Saxon monasticism was, it may be assumed, beer. It is the drink of Aelfric's boy-monk, when he can get it; otherwise he drinks water. Wine is dear and is not for such as he.[5] But no doubt wine was drunk at the *caritas* mentioned in the *Concordia*, and mead on feast days. After the Conquest wine became more common, owing to increased commerce with the wine-growing districts of France and to a more intensive cultivation of the vine in England, especially in the fens, the Severn valley and the fertile land about Glastonbury. *Caritates* of wine at dinner and supper and *misericordiae* at other

1 *Chron. Evesh.* 108: "Turrim ecclesiae ereximus, convertentes redditus pitanciariae... in opus illud."

2 *Jocelini Cronica*, 308.

3 Cf. *Chron. Bell.* 131, for wastel bread, spiced with pepper, and simnel cakes.

4 *GASA*, I, 206: "Ita omni anno omnibus festive agatur [*sc.* anniversarium Adae] sicut solet honestius et honorabilius in anniversariis Abbatum nostrorum fieri; videlicet, in Psalmis, in Missis, in pauperibus recreandis...cellerarius...providebit...sufficientem et splendidam conventui in refectorio exhibitionem." *Chron. Bell.* 130–1, Abbot Walter's anniversary foundation. *Chron. Abingd.* II, 315–16, where eight such annual *obits* are mentioned.

5 *Aelfrici Colloquium*, 35: "M. Et quid bibis? D. Cerevisiam si habeo, vel aquam, si non habeo cerevisiam. M. Nonne bibis vinum? D. Non sum tam dives ut possim emere mihi vinum; et vinum non est potus puerorum."

times make their appearance with the pittances, following the scale of the feast. Before the Conquest wine would seem to have been regarded as a more uncommon delicacy than mead, but in the twelfth century it appears as a simple alternative.[1] The days on which wine was provided increased greatly; as early as *c.* 1132 these customary rounds of wine were among the gravamina at St Mary's, York;[2] Gerald of Wales noted at Christ Church an abundance of wines, mulled and clear, together with unfermented wine, mulberry wine and mead, and from the lists of wine days preserved in the Abingdon documents it would seem that at least eighty-odd feasts in the year were thus celebrated.[3] The chronicler of St Albans notes that Abbot John (1195–1214) succeeded in cutting away some at least of these occasions at his abbey;[4] but heavy drinking, like heavy feeding, was a national characteristic of England in the eyes of the rest of Europe, and such indications as to quantity which exist do nothing to prove that the black monk houses observed to the letter the provision of the Rule.[5]

IV

INCIDENTS OF DAILY LIFE

A few scattered notices bearing on the domestic life may be added here. The monks slept in their habits, and did not make their toilet on rising for the night office, but when they had changed into their day shoes before Terce. They then went to the washing-room and first washed their faces and hands, then combed their hair and beards; this order was always observed save by the priest and ministers at the midnight Mass of Christmas Day, for whom a fire and warm water were provided, and who combed their hair first and washed afterwards.[6] It were noted as an act of charity in Abbot Vincent of Abingdon that he daily filled the washing-troughs with water for the monks.[7]

There is no mention of baths in the *Concordia*, though it legislates for the weekly washing of feet that preceded the Maundy of the poor.[8]

---

1 That is, if the Abingdon dietary is here recording an old tradition; it allots mead to feasts in albs and copes, and wine to the greatest feasts. The Waltham statutes give mead on the greatest feasts, not mentioning wine. At St Albans Abbot Geoffrey (1119–46) provided a *caritas vini vel medi* every Saturday, and mead and wine were in evidence at Christ Church when Gerald dined there.

2 Cf. the letter of Thurstan, *Mem. Fount.* I, 16: "Dulcis et solemnis vicissitudo potionum."

3 *Chron. Abingd.* II, 312, 314–17. Actually seventy-six days are enumerated, but no doubt there were other "occasional" ones every year.

4 *GASA*, I, 235: "Procuravit efficaciter ut detestabiles ingurgitationes misericordiarum, in quibus profecto non erat misericordia, prohiberentur." But, once more, the tendencious nature of this source must be remembered.

5 *Regula*, c. xl, 6–7: "Credimus heminam vini [half-a-pint] per singulos sufficere per diem." This would, of course, have been mixed with water. For medieval quantities *v.* Appendix XX.

6 *Concordia*, i, 81; *Lanfranci Statuta*, I, §§ 1, 2, pp. 212, 214.

7 *Chron. Abingd.* II, 290. 8 *Concordia*, ii, 83.

Lanfranc, however, gives elaborate directions for shaving and bathing, which took place on fixed days five times a year. The head was washed after shaving.[1] Even so the bath would seem to have made its way but slowly to England, since its introduction at Abingdon is attributed to Abbot Vincent (1120–31), who appears to have taken a particular interest in such matters.[2] Hot water was, of course, provided, and rushes for the feet in the bathroom; the occasion was taken for a change of clothing.[3]

The *Concordia* informs us that a fire was provided for the monks from 1 November onwards (a day which then fell some ten days earlier in the season) and a special workroom in winter, by reason of the cold and damp of the cloister.[4] There is no such provision in Lanfranc's Statutes, but a fire was certainly allowed in the room afterwards known as the calefactory. The cloister, especially without any (or at least without adequate) glazing, must have been a cold place in the winter, even when, as was customary, the monks worked in the north walk which opened to the south and backed onto the high nave of the church. When, as at Canterbury and Gloucester, the cloister-garth lay to the north of the cathedral, it must indeed have been cold in the winter and many in England, like Orderic in Normandy, must have had to abandon their writing or illumination for the whole season, with hands unable to hold the pen.

V

MANUAL WORK

Work, that is, some fixed employment other than reading, is one of the three chief ingredients of the monastic life of the Rule. The precise scope of the work of monks in St Benedict's day has been often debated, not without heat, and has recently once again been matter for controversy among scholars; when all has been said it seems clear that while a great part of it consisted of housework and the exercise of all those useful crafts which could make the community self-sufficing, a certain amount of common garden work and even of agricultural labour was normal, and we have the precious witness of St Gregory the Great that there were occasions when the whole monastic household laboured in the fields, led by the abbot.[5]

1 *Lanfranci Statuta*, I, § 2, pp. 213–14; XII, p. 239. However, the bath appears to have been optional, for Lanfranc, in the first passage, says: "balneentur qui volunt balneari."
2 *Chron. Abingd.* II, 290: "Balnea monachorum instituit."
3 *Chron. Abingd.* II, 300; *Lanfranci Statuta*, I, § 2, pp. 213–14.
4 *Concordia*, ii, 84.
5 The question of work in St Benedict's day is discussed fully by Abbot Butler, *Benedictine Monachism*, ch. xvii (2nd ed. pp. 285–6), Abbot Chapman, *St Benedict and the Sixth Century*, 169–72 and Abbot Butler again in his article reviewing Abbot Chapman's book and bearing the same title in *DR*, XLVIII (October 1930), 192–4. Abbot Chapman endeavoured to show, relying on parallels from the monasticism of Cassiodorus, that scholarship, calligraphy, and the artistic crafts formed part of the monks' employment, and that field labour

In the Northumbrian monasticism of the time of Bede, which was in so many ways a replica of life in St Benedict's monastery, a *régime* of a very similar kind is found, and there is no suggestion that the work in field or garden has become formalized or the occupation of a few individuals.[1] By the ninth century, however, monastic customaries make a clear distinction between individual employments, usually of a quasi-sedentary kind in and about the cloister, and work (*opus*) in the fields or garden, which was performed in common. When this latter was to be done, special notice was given and the monks proceeded to it reciting psalmody, which was continued during the work. The work, therefore, had been gradually ceremonialized, and this is in itself an indication that it had become exceptional; Ulrich of Cluny, indeed, in the late eleventh century, describes it almost as an antiquary might describe the fossilized relics of a medieval custom, and even in the eighth century it was prohibited on all feasts and certain greater fasting-days.

Such was the common state of things on the Continent in Dunstan's day, and it is accurately reflected in the *Concordia*. If on a given day there is work to be done, the monks proceed to it singing psalms.[2] How often this was the case in the revived monasticism we have no means of knowing. Save for a statement that St Ethelwold caused his monks to help in some building operations[3] the sources are wholly silent, but all indications, and the current estimate of field work, go to show that little, if any, agricultural or heavy garden work was done by the monks. In Lanfranc's Statutes even these faint traces of the old tradition are wanting, and the distinction is no longer made between days on which common work is, and is not, performed, but between those on which talking during employment is allowed in the cloister and those on which complete silence must be observed and all employments give place to reading. In the twelfth century, so far as can be seen, there is not a single reference to field or garden work performed as a common exercise by the English black monks, nor did the Cistercian programme arouse any attempts at emulation in this country.

---

was altogether exceptional; Abbot Butler, however, was successful in proving that St Benedict's *artes* are the useful, not the fine, crafts, and that field labour, though not the only or even the constant employment of the whole community, was yet a perfectly normal one. Though St Benedict assumes that the harvests will as a rule be gathered in by labour other than that of the monks (*Regula*, xlviii, 16), work in the field and garden is so often referred to in the Rule that it must have been the common practice (cf. *Regula*, c. vii, 190; c. xli, 4, 8; c. xlvi, 2; c. lxvi, 14). The incident of the common field work is in St Gregory's *Dialogues*, II, 32.

1 *V. supra*, pp. 22–3.

2 *Concordia*, i, 82: "Si vero opus habuerint...cum decantatione canonici cursus et psalterii operentur."

3 *Vita S. Aethelwoldi, auct. Aelfrico, Chron. Abingd.* II, 259, 264.

VI

THE SACRAMENTS

It need hardly be said that the Mass and the sacraments of Holy Eucharist and Penance figured largely in the monastic life. In the normal horarium there were two Masses each day attended by the whole community; the recited morrow- or chapter-Mass and the sung High Mass. It would seem, however, that no English statutes or customaries of the period give any directions as to the period to be devoted to private Masses. In the Cistercian use, they were permitted whenever the monks were reading in the cloister during the early morning; at Cluny, owing to the size of the community, they were allowed during the chapter-Mass itself.[1] From an anecdote in the life of St Wulfstan, it may be gathered that the interval between Nocturns and Matins in summer and autumn was no uncommon time;[2] probably not every priest celebrated every day, though on the other hand the custom of offering Mass twice or thrice on a single day had not yet been wholly abolished.[3]

In the tenth and early eleventh centuries it was not yet the normal practice for all monks to be ordained priest, and even when, in the twelfth century, the custom became established there was often a lapse of many years between the reception of the major orders. In England, however, where there was an ancient tradition of monastic priesthood, it would seem to have been usual in the time of St Dunstan for the majority of the community to proceed to orders; indeed, it is probable that the English monastic families c. 1000 were more homogeneous in this respect than were the Normans fifty years later, for there is no trace in them of the special class of late vocations (*conversi; monachi laici*). On the other hand, the language of the chroniclers leaves it uncertain whether even such a distinguished monk as Aethelwig of Evesham was a priest,[4] and it is certain that his contemporary Baldwin of Bury (who was, however, of French provenance) was only ordained several years after his assumption of office when on a visit to Rome.[5]

A very interesting passage in the *Concordia*, wholly peculiar to that document and unquestionably due directly to Dunstan or Ethelwold,

---

1 *Udalrici Consuetudines*, I, 18 (*PL*, CXLIX, 668).

2 *Vita Wulfstani* (ed. Darlington), 54.

3 *Vita Wulfstani*, 49, which has been quoted in this connection, is not an example; but v. *Vita Gundulfi* (*PL*, CLIX, 822), where Mass is said twice.

4 In the long account of his virtues there is mention of his hearing several Masses daily, but none of his own Mass (*Chron. Evesh.* 93); contrast the account of Wulfstan's own Mass and the two he heard (*Vita Wulfstani*, 49).

5 *Heremanni Miracula S. Edmundi* in *Mem. S. Edmund's*, I, 61: "Romam profectus, illic etiam promotus a papa Alexandro secundo ad ordinem presbyteratus." But Baldwin was a French monk and a physician, i.e. possibly a late vocation.

exhorts the brethren to a daily reception of the Holy Eucharist;[1] probably, therefore, in England as abroad at this time, it was not uncommon for a monk who was a priest to receive Communion at the solemn Mass as an alternative to celebrating himself; in any case, the direction is a precious indication of the place taken by the Holy Eucharist in the spiritual life of the monastery. The *Concordia* also enacts that the sick, after receiving Extreme Unction and Viaticum, are to have the Sacrament carried to them every day;[2] we can see this injunction being observed in the case of Wulfstan of Worcester.[3] Lanfranc's code does not contain this explicit direction, but instances show that the frequent reception of the Eucharist after Extreme Unction was common.[4] It may be added that Communion under both kinds was common in religious houses till the thirteenth century.

From an incident in Dunstan's early life it may be gathered that he was in the habit of receiving sacramental absolution every evening.[5] In the *Concordia* a weekly confession, on Sundays, is enjoined on all, including the children, and apparently the normal confessor of all was the superior of the house.[6] In the Norman monasteries confessions were commonly heard in the chapter-house, and at any time when the monks were reading in the cloister. Lanfranc supposes that the novices and children will have, besides abbot and prior, a certain number of confessors allotted to them, but abbot and prior appear, at least at first, to have been the normal confessors of the whole community.[7] William of St Carilef presumes this at Durham, and Anselm at Canterbury and Bury.[8] Later, certain special confessors were appointed by the abbot, but they seem to have been few in number; there were only, it appears, four at Bury in 1182, and the new abbot, Hugh, in 1215 appointed only two.[9]

1 The relevant passage is worth quoting in full from *Concordia*, i, 82: "Post pacem fratres quotidie (nisi qui crimine se aliquo vel carnis fragilitate reos cognoverunt) regulari studio prorsus intenti eucharistiam accipere non renuant, attendentes illud quod ait Beatus Augustinus in libro de verbis Domini: quod, videlicet, in oratione Dominica non annuum sed quotidianum deposcimus panem, etc."

2 *Concordia*, xii, 93.   3 *Vita Wulfstani*, 61.

4 E.g. *Chron. Bell.* 137.   5 *Mem. S. Dunst.* 15.

6 This would seem to be the interpretation of *Concordia*, i, 82: "Fratrum unusquisque... patri spirituali vel ejus, si absens fuerit, vicario [confiteatur]." If by *pater spiritualis* (a phrase used of the abbot in the Rule) no more were meant than "confessor", it is not easy to see why his frequent absence should be anticipated.

7 *Lanfranci Statuta*, XVIII, XXII, pp. 244, 248.

8 Cf. William's letter to the monks, Symeon of Durham, I, 126: "Confessiones vestras frequenter priori faciatis." Cf. also *Anselmi Epp.* III, 89: "Domno priori [*sc.* of Christ Church] committam totam curam animarum vestrarum, secrete et publice"; III, 118 (to prior Alferus and monks of Bury): "Peccata...puro et simplici corde domno priori, aut cui ipse concesserit [the abbacy was vacant at the time] confiteatur" (*PL*, CLIX, 155).

9 *Mem. S. Edmund's*, I, 224: "Nominati sunt quatuor confessores [i.e. *the* four confessors]"; *ibid.* II, 123: Richard and magister Alanus are given *curam super confessionibus privatis exercendam*.

VII

PRIVATE PRAYER

Throughout the legislative literature of the Middle Ages there is a marked absence of reference to any set periods of what is now called "meditation" or "mental" prayer; in this there is a strong contrast both with the documents of Egyptian and Syrian monachism and with those of European spirituality from the end of the Middle Ages to the present day. In part this was no doubt due to the provision made in the Rule and in all early customaries for the periods of *lectio divina*, the meditative reading of the Bible and works of theology and spirituality, which would often pass naturally into prayer or be exchanged for it;[1] in part, to the reticence and wide discretion which St Benedict himself had allowed in the matter.[2] The question, as always where deep spiritual issues are involved, demands very delicate handling and a very fine sense both of the things of the spirit and of historical perspective; it is possible for a student, by restricting his view to the spiritual masterpieces of an epoch and to the lives of its saints, to portray a state of things wholly divorced from reality; it is equally possible, by confining the attention to chronicles and official documents, to lose sight of the spiritual forces which form the basis of all religious life that is not wholly decadent. Here, however, we are not concerned to assess the spirituality of an epoch, but merely to record the place that private prayer held in the lives of the general run of English monks of the time. In this matter it may be said, with all due reserve, that the multiplication of vocal, liturgical prayers in monastic circles before 1100 had had a certain effect in exalting the estimate of such prayer at the expense of private, silent, unspoken prayer, though a type midway between the two, that of the *meditationes* of St Anselm, seems to have been in common use.

The widespread movement towards solitude and simplicity of life, which impelled so many to become hermits in the eleventh century and gave rise to the congregations of Vallombrosa and the Chartreuse and to the orders of Cîteaux and Prémontré, was in part due to a reaction from an exclusively liturgical conception of the monastic life, and the tendency is seen more clearly in the writings of what may be called the second generation of the newcomers, among whom William of St Thierry holds an eminent place, who turn for guidance to the contemplatives of the Eastern desert and to the works of the pseudo-Denis. And while, throughout the twelfth century, it is constantly recorded that the saints and others distinguished for holiness of life spent hours in private and silent prayer, it

---

1 The anonymous apophthegm (*Lib. de spiritu et anima*, c. 50 in *PL*, XL, 816), reduced to lapidary brevity by the Carthusian Guigo II: "quaerite legendo et invenietis meditando; pulsate orando et aperietur vobis contemplando" (*PL*, CLXXXIV, 476), was taken as axiomatic by all, though there was the widest divergence in interpreting the final word.

2 E.g. *Regula*, c. lii, 5–7: "Sed et si aliter vult sibi forte secretius orare, simpliciter intret [*sc.* in oratorium] et oret."

must be acknowledged also that there is little mention of such private prayer in the official legislation or in the accounts, such as they are, of daily life in the monasteries of the black monks.

Three moments of the day were, however, particularly allotted to private devotions: the spaces before Nocturns and Terce when the monks were already in choir while the children were rising or washing and dressing for the day's work, and the time after Compline in the evening. During the two times of waiting the *Concordia* lays it down that the monks are to pray in silence, but significantly presupposes that they will be engaged in the recitation of some such part of the psalter as the penitential psalms.[1] The time after Compline, as is learnt from more than one source, was often spent in visits to the numerous altars dedicated to various saints. Besides these times, both the *Concordia* and Lanfranc's *Statuta* mention a period of silent common prayer after None and before the midday meal. We are not told how long it lasted; it is possible that it may have been a survival of the time of prayer after the Office mentioned by St Gregory and practised in some form at least by St Benedict.[2]

It goes without saying that the lives of the monastic saints of the period abound in references to long periods of silent prayer; sanctity, indeed, has never existed without an almost unbroken communion with God. But though it would be uncritical to attach too great a weight to the accounts of those who are describing what they cannot fully understand, and although throughout the ages it is a characteristic of hagiography to interpret the most elusive manifestations of sanctity in terms of more current experience, it is perhaps noteworthy that the frequent repetition of psalms, rather than silent absorption, is mentioned as typical of the great monks of the period. Thus it is recorded of Ralph, abbot of Battle (1107–24), that he recited the whole psalter each day with frequent genuflexions, and only abandoned the practice three days before his death;[3] of John, the devout abbot of St Albans (1195–1214), that he knew the whole psalter by heart; and of Wulfstan of Worcester and Lanzo of Lewes that they were accustomed to recite numerous psalms and set vocal prayers apart from the regular office.[4]

1 *Concordia*, i, 80, 81, 83: "(before Nocturns) Effundat preces magis corde quam ore ita ut illius vox per magnam animi compunctionem...aures misericordis Domini efficaciter penetret...(before Terce) prout Deus unicuique in corda eorum divino immiserit instinctu silenter ac tota mentis intentione opus suum...celebrent, horas canonicas vel septem poenitentiae psalmos vel aliud quippiam spirituale...psallendo...(after Compline) si quis post haec devotionis suae forte fervore, his diutius incumbere voluerit, etc."
2 *Concordia*, i, 82: "Pulsetur primum signum Nonae et agatur oratio." This *oratio* is clearly distinguished in the words which follow both from the office of None and from private recited prayers. *Lanfranci Statuta*, I, p. 212: "Post Missam pulsato signo agatur oratio." Cf. *Regula*, c. xx, 10: "In conventu omnino brevietur oratio", and *S. Gregorii Libri Dialogorum*, II, 4: "Cum, constituta hora, expleta psalmodia, sese fratres in orationem dedissent, etc."
3 *Chron. Bell.* 59: "Diebus singulis psalterium ex ordine totum decantans."
4 *GASA*, I, 232; *Vita Wulfstani*, 49, 95, etc.; Will. Malmesb., *GR*, 514.

CHAPTER XXVII

UNIONS AND CONFRATERNITY: HOSPITALITY AND CHARITY

I

AGREEMENTS OF UNION

Throughout the centuries it has always been the norm for monasteries following the Rule of St Benedict to exist as independent self-governing units. Although St Benedict wrote his Rule for a number of houses, if not indeed for the monastic order in general, he nowhere hints at any bond between abbey and abbey save that created by Christian charity and their common profession. In the course of the centuries a number of federations were made for the sake of restoring or preserving discipline, the most remarkable of which was that under Benedict of Aniane, but with the single, though important, exception of Cluny, which was based on feudal rather than on canonical precedent, none of these were more than temporary in duration. Even after the legislation of the Fourth Lateran Council, establishing national or provincial congregations, the autonomy of each fully constituted house of the traditional black monachism was preserved, and is at the present day defined by the codified Canon Law of the Church.[1] During the period with which we are concerned this radical autonomy was never seriously questioned in England; indeed, towards the end of the twelfth century the centrifugal, if not antinomial, tendencies were so pronounced as to provoke a reaction culminating in what was almost a *coup d'état* on the part of Innocent III. Bearing in mind, therefore, that the radical autonomy of each abbey was taken for granted, a review may be made of the various steps taken by all or some of the houses to unite for purposes of spiritual or temporal utility.

The revival under Dunstan had a somewhat abnormal beginning. It was not a plantation from an existing body, bearing with it documentary and traditional guidance in the monastic life, nor was it in origin uniform. Glastonbury had to some extent been created by Dunstan, assisted by survivals of old English practice; Ethelwold, though Dunstan's pupil, seems clearly to have desired a way of life more resembling Continental examples; Oswald had received his monastic training in a flourishing house abroad. Consequently there was a real danger of three parallel but

---

1 E.g. *Codex Juris Canonici* (1917), canon 488, n. 8, equates an *abbas monasterii sui juris, licet ad monasticam Congregationem pertinentis*, with the heads of other religious Orders and Congregations as a Superior Major, and gives him the title of Ordinary with regard to his subjects (canon 198, § 1). For a sketch of black monk constitutional history, *v.* Butler, *Benedictine Monachism*, chs. xv, xvi: "The Benedictine Polity" and "The Order of St Benedict".

dissimilar and in a sense rival movements growing up in the closest neighbourhood to each other, a situation quite without parallel in the early feudal states and opposed alike to the peaceful growth of the monastic order and to its influence in strengthening the national revival of religion and culture so dear to the heart of Dunstan.[1] The aim therefore of the discussions at Winchester, out of which issued the *Regularis Concordia*, was to agree upon a common basis of discipline and observance for all the houses already in existence. Nothing more was aimed at or achieved. No constitutional machinery of any kind was set up to give the union an external or permanent framework. The abbots and abbesses, by accepting the *Concordia*, implicitly took upon themselves the obligation of observing it in the sense recorded in general terms in the document itself.[2] Thenceforward each house entered upon its own life of growth or decline; the sole link established by the *Concordia* was a mutual announcement of deaths, with its corollary of suffrages, and even this was restricted to monasteries in the near neighbourhood of each other.[3]

The scope of Lanfranc's Statutes has already been considered in some detail. Their general aim was identical with that of the *Concordia*, but their promulgation and acceptation were even less general; they rested on no mutual agreement, explicitly allowed for some variety of practice and often, even where introduced, failed to supplant wholly an earlier usage. From the date of their composition until the Fourth Council of the Lateran no further attempt was made either from within or from without to legislate for the black monks of England as a body, and the individual houses steadily elaborated each for itself a body of customs.

But although the individual houses went each its own way unfettered by any official code, a number of private agreements and unions were framed between particular abbeys. These fall roughly into two classes, those concerned simply with the mutual discharge of spiritual good offices, and those giving in addition some kind of temporal confraternity.

The first class of engagement, of a type common to religious bodies throughout the history of the Church, appears to have been peculiarly common in the years immediately following the Conquest. Wulfstan of Worcester attached particular importance to them, and the original charter still exists by which the group of monasteries in his diocese, together with two others outside, agreed to foster the religious spirit, to intercede for the king and queen, and to pray for each other's dead.[4] A similar engagement

1 Cf. the words of the Proem to the *Concordia*, 77: "ne impar ac varius unius regulae et unius patriae usus probrose vituperium sanctae conversationi irrogaret."

2 *Concordia*, Proem, 79: "[Quae] palam cum magna examinis discussione jugi custoditis usu...solicite uti polliciti sumus."

3 *Concordia*, xii, 93: "Mittatur etiam epistola ad vicina quaeque monasteria."

4 *Vita Wulfstani* (ed. Darlington), 191. The houses were: Worcester, Evesham, Gloucester, Pershore, Winchcombe, Bath and Chertsey, and the date 1077. For the similar union of the two Winchester monasteries *v. Hyde Liber Vitae*, 47.

was made between Worcester and its original mother-house, Ramsey,[1] and yet another was already in existence between the two Minsters at Winchester. In the same sense Rochester, during the early decades after its re-foundation, entered into agreements concerning suffrages for the dead with some twenty-eight houses in England and Normandy. These engagements fall into no less than nine classes, varying each from the other as to the number of prayers and Masses to be offered, and the sum total must have represented a considerable burden upon the house.[2] Instances of this kind could be multiplied; doubtless almost every abbey had some undertaking of a similar nature.

The second kind of union, of which there are traces even before the Conquest, became extremely popular in the second half of the twelfth century. In its fullest development it took the form of a sharing of all rights. Not only did the monks of one house pray for those of the other as brothers, but the individuals of each enjoyed at the other all the domestic privileges of a full membership of the community. An early example of this type is the agreement made between the two Minsters at Winchester in the lifetime of Dunstan and Ethelwold, in virtue of which the monk Eadwine, of the New Minster, who had gone without permission on a pilgrimage to the shrine of St Cuthbert, was received on his return at the Old Minster until his own superior re-admitted him.[3] One of the most explicit of such documents in later years is that drawn up between Evesham and Malmesbury c. 1200. Besides several articles concerned with suffrages, it gives full right of entry to choir, chapter and monastery, and enacts that a delinquent monk of one house may be sent to the other to live, not as a prisoner, but as a monk of the cloister, and that if a monk flees from one house to the other he is to be received there, and the abbot is to use his good offices to effect a reconciliation. A somewhat similar and exactly contemporary engagement between St Augustine's, Canterbury, and Bury gives in addition full rights to all of voting and receiving votes at an abbatial election in either house. How far such privileges were exercised cannot be said; probably not at all. In the two cases just recorded it is hard to resist a suspicion that the agreements were a kind of insurance on the part of the communities of Evesham and St Augustine's, both of which were passing through a time of trial, and the suspicion is intensified by the existence of a somewhat similar Augustinian agreement with the powerful cathedral priory of Winchester.[4] Seen from another angle, all such engage-

1 *Vita Wulfstani*, 191. Cf. also the Durham *Liber Vitae* (SS 1923), XVIII–XIX, 48.

2 *Textus Roffensis* (ed. Hearne), 231–4. The most privileged class is of three houses— Christ Church, Norwich and Malling nunnery. The place accorded to Norwich would suggest that part of the original colony of that house hailed from Rochester.

3 *Hyde Liber Vitae*, 96–8.

4 For the Evesham document *v. Monasticon*, II, 19. It was framed *temp*. Robert of Malmesbury and Roger (Norreys) of Evesham, i.e. between 1190 and 1208. For the Canterbury-Bury agreement *v.* Thorne, 1843; the date here is 1200. For the Winchester agreement *v.* Elmham, 447; here the date is *c.* 1180–5.

ments are symptomatic of what may be called the democratic movement among the black monks of the time, by which the chapters, isolated from the abbot, were claiming to act as a body with definite rights. A network of these articles of union existed between Evesham and its neighbours and whilom daughters: Evesham was joined to Whitby, York and Odensee, Pershore to Whitby, York to Odensee, Worcester to Evesham, Pershore and Alcester.[1] In the event, the legality of a black monk having a stall in two choirs and a seat in two chapters was challenged at the Fourth Lateran Council, and the practice declared to be inadmissible.[2]

As has been said, the ostensibly wide opportunities of interchange offered by these documents were no doubt limited in practice by personal, social and religious considerations, much in the same way as they are at the present day in the analogous unions between universities and colleges. Beyond this, stability has always been an element of the monastic profession. Transference, however, was not unknown; apart altogether from the wholesale or group removals effected by Lanfranc for disciplinary reasons, there are a number of individual cases of free exchange; several occur in the annals of the single house of St Albans. Abbot Ralph (1146–51), so we are told, persecuted his prior, Alcuin, who took refuge at Westminster, where he ultimately attained again his old rank; Ralph's successor, Robert, was a Norman monk who had been attracted by the spirit of St Albans when on a visit to England; and at the beginning of the thirteenth century there is mention of a prior of Whitby who migrated to St Albans and ultimately became prior of Wymondham.[3] Record of all these cases has been preserved by reason of the distinguished careers of the individuals concerned; no doubt there were others of less fame, but St Albans, with its high reputation and wide outlook, cannot be taken as an example of common practice.

II

PERSONAL CONFRATERNITY

Throughout the early Middle Ages the monks were regarded as intercessors *par excellence* for the rest of the world; it was natural, therefore, that many laypeople should wish to share as intimately as possible in the benefits of their prayers for the living and the dead. It had always been recognized

1 The following is a list of some of the unions other than those mentioned in the previous note: St Benet's of Holme and Bury (*Mem. S. Edmund's*, III, 2); Evesham and Odensee (*Monasticon*, II, 26), and Whitby (*ibid.* II, 19 *seqq.*), and York (*Chron. Evesh.* 256: "quod monasterium a fundatione sua ita confoederatum est monasterio Eveshamensi ut quasi unum corpus et una ecclesia reputentur"; cf. also 258); Pershore and Whitby (*Monasticon*, I, 421); Peterborough and Ramsey (*ibid.* I, 395); Worcester and Evesham (*Chron. Evesh.* 255), and Alcester (*cart. fundat.* in *Monasticon*, IV, 175).

2 Cf. the words of Marleberge writing at Evesham c. 1225 (*Chron. Evesh.* 255): "tunc temporis [*sc.* 1213] bene licuit quod monachus in pluribus monasteriis haberet locum in capitulo et stallum in choro". 3 *GASA*, I, 108, 109, 111, 260.

that founders and benefactors had a special claim and part, but the desire for some tangible bond led, as early as the ninth century, to the reception of *confratres* who shared in an especial way in all the prayers and Masses.[1] Their names, inscribed in a book, were (at least in early times) recited by the deacon during Mass, and the volume lay upon the altar during the Canon;[2] at their death they were prayed for as members of the community. All classes were represented in these lists: the blood royal, great land-owners and benefactors, bishops, religious of other houses, local worthies, parish priests and layfolk from the immediate neighbourhood of the monastery. In England the institution was common before the Conquest and there are in existence several such early Books of Life, as they were called.[3] Lanfranc in his Statutes gave particular instructions governing the ceremony of admission to confraternity, and though he had in mind primarily monks of other houses, provision is made for layfolk of high and low degree, and for women.[4] Monastic cartularies, as well as special lists, bear witness to the great number of these *confratres*. Not infrequently the whole family of a benefactor was enrolled, and there are many refer-ences to the ceremony in the chapter-house, to which even women were admitted.[5] Two of the most distinguished instances date from the second half of the twelfth century: in 1184 Henry II claimed his right as *confrater* of entering the chapter-house to visit his brethren of St Albans;[6] only a few years before, in 1179, King Louis of France, no doubt from devotion to St Thomas, became a *confrater* of Canterbury, settling upon the house in return an annual gift of wine.[7]

The institute of confraternity, beginning early, continued in England until the Dissolution of the monasteries and is still common at Benedictine

1 The St Gall confraternity book begins in 810, that of Reichenau in 826. Cf. *MGH, Libri Confraternitatum Sancti Galli, Augiensis, Fabariensis*, ed. Piper (Berlin, 1884), and for the whole subject two papers of Edmund Bishop: *Some Ancient Benedictine Confraternity Books* and *A Benedictine Confrater of the Ninth Century*, in *Liturgica Historica*, 349–69. A number of distinguished English names appear in these lists, e.g. King Athelstan at Reichenau, Bishop Kenwald of Worcester at St Gall, etc.

2 So the proem of the *Hyde Liber Vitae* (ed. Birch), 10–11.

3 Above all the *Liber Vitae* of Durham, in which the first entries date from *c.* 800–850, though many refer to the earlier monastery of Lindisfarne. The Durham volume was first edited for the Surtees Society (no. XIII) in 1841; and again in photographic facsimile (no. CXXXVI) in 1923. Second in interest only to the Durham book is that of the New Minster, *Liber Vitae: Register and Martyrology of New Minster and Hyde Abbey, Winchester*, edited for the Hants. Record Society by W. de Gray Birch in 1892. It begins *c.* 1020–30.

4 *Lanfranci Statuta*, c. xxi, 247: "Si secularis persona fuerit...sin honorabilis persona sit...ad osculandum fratres, si mulier non sit, in circuitu pergat."

5 An early post-Conquest example is that of Hugh, earl of Chester, at Abingdon on 14 March 1089. In his confirmatory letter the earl asks: "ut frater vester sim, et uxor mea, et pater meus et mater mea, in orationibus vestris, et ut simus scripti omnes in Libro Commemorationum et ut sit factum tale obsequium pro nobis quale debet fieri pro uno fratre de ecclesia ubicumque moriamur" (*Chron. Abingd.* II, 20). Cf. *Chron. Abingd.* II, 36, 161, 170 (Ralph Basset the justiciar); *Hist. Rames.* 237–8, 240, 272, 309 (a woman).

6 *GASA*, I, 197: "Postulavit igitur in crastino Rex, ut intrans Capitulum fratres suos visitaret; fatebatur enim se esse confratrem Conventus et monachum S. Albani."

7 Gervase, I, 293.

houses. Connected with it in our period was the custom, common enough at the time but ultimately to pass away, of taking the monastic habit, *ad succurrendum* as the phrase went, either within or without the monastery shortly before death. The incentive to this practice was the aura of reverence surrounding the monastic state in the minds of all during the early Middle Ages. When society was divided sharply between "the world" and "the cloister", when the monastic profession and even the ceremony of clothing with the habit were regarded as having the efficacy of a second baptism, with all the retrospective virtue of cleansing from past sins,[1] and when it was a commonplace to apply to the monastic life the promise of Christ to Peter regarding those who had abandoned all things, it was natural that many who felt the need of some great conversion in their last hours, or who had long felt an attraction towards the monastic life, should wish to die clothed in the habit. So deeply ingrained, indeed, was the persuasion of the security of the monastic state that not infrequently those, whether barons or bishops, who had been the bitterest opponents of the monks during their lives, asked for the habit on their deathbeds.

Naturally, *confratres* had a special motive for such a request; in some cases it was stated on their first admission that they might take the habit when they willed, and some kind of tacit agreement of the kind probably always existed.[2] But most commonly the habit was only taken in mortal sickness. The individual, when he felt his end approaching, asked for admission to the monastic infirmary, was clothed with the habit, and remained there till death. As in the fully developed monastery of the twelfth century facilities for care of the sick were probably greater than in any other place in the kingdom, and as on the other hand the dying man was usually a benefactor, no material obstacles of any kind existed; in most cases the retirement took place at the close of a long life or after the warning of a stroke of paralysis, but there are records of some who recovered and lived on as monks.[3]

In the course of the twelfth century a number of bishops both of good and ill repute ended their days in the habit, and as the new orders came to England these too absorbed their share of deathbed recruits. The early Cistercians, indeed, legislated against both *confratres* and receptions *ad succurrendum*, but they are nevertheless found admitting bishops and others towards the end of the century. Among the prelates who died thus were William Giffard of Winchester, Thurstan of York, Hugh of Nonant

1 This is a commonplace of ascetic writers of the eleventh and twelfth centuries, e.g. *Petri Damiani opusc.* xiii de perfectione monachorum, c. 6 (*PL*, CXLV, 300): "Religiosam professionem secundum esse baptismum." With St Thomas, *Summa Theologica*, II IIae, Q. clxxxix, art. 3, ad. 3, it passed into current teaching; cf. Dom U. Berlière, *L'Ascèse Bénédictine*, 118–20, and Dom Germain Morin, *L'Idéal Monastique*, ch. iv.

2 E.g. *Hist. Rames.* 272. A priest is given a church belonging to the abbey, together with confraternity and the right of becoming a monk when he wishes.

3 Cf. Eadmer, *Hist. Novorum*, 430, where a priest mortally ill takes the habit, and recovers through the intercession of Anselm.

of Coventry and Mauger of Worcester, and the habit chosen by these and others is no unfair index of the current reputation of the orders and houses concerned.[1] Of all these deathbed receptions the one which has left most copious record and which has most interested historians is that of Thurstan of York, who in so many ways impressed his fiery personality upon the annals of the northern province. In his youth, on a visit to Cluny, he had taken a vow to become a monk, and later contemplated resigning his see and becoming a Cistercian. For whatever reasons, he never carried out these intentions, but when he felt himself to be a dying man he retired to the Cluniac priory of Pontefract.[2] There, in the presence of his diocesan officials, so soon to be at odds with each other, he disposed of his affairs and the monastic habit was put upon him with the customary ceremonies and blessings. When, a few weeks later, the end was near, he caused himself to be laid out as if for burial, with tapers around him, and summoned the monks to perform in his presence the Dirge, in which he himself took part, reciting the last solemn responsory *Libera me Domine*.[3]

Less spectacular but more common were such incidents as the death of Ralph Basset. A *confrater* of Abingdon, where he had expressed a wish to be buried, he was taken suddenly ill at Northampton and demanded the monastic habit. Asked what monastery he wished to join, he replied naming Abingdon and, having left that house a considerable legacy, he died and was carried for burial to the abbey of his choice, being laid to rest under the floor of the chapter-house.[4] As the reception of a wealthy *confrater* to the habit and sepulture usually implied a legacy there was, it would seem, on occasion a certain amount of competition between rival

1 The following is a list of those English bishops I have noted, but it makes no pretence of being exhaustive:

   1129   William Giffard of Winchester (Winchester: black monk). Rudbourne, *Hist. Winton.* 279.

   1137   William Warelwast of Exeter (Plympton: black canon). *Ann. Plympt.* (ed. Liebermann, *Ungedruckte Quellen*), s.a.

   1140   Thurstan of York (Pontefract: Cluniac). Will. Malmesb., *GP*, 266 *et al.* Thurstan's brother, Audoen, bishop of Evreux, took the habit of the black canons at Merton at about the same time.

   1182   Richard Peche of Coventry (Stafford: black canon). *Ann. Waverl.,* s.a.

   1184   Jocelin of Salisbury (Ford: Cistercian). *Chron. Ang. Petr.,* s.a.

   1191   Reginald fitz Jocelin of Bath, elect of Canterbury (Christ Church: black monk). Gervase, I, 512; cf. *Epp. Cant.* ccclxxxvii–ix.

   1198   Hugh of Nonant of Coventry (Bec: black monk). Roger of Wendover, I, 274.

   1212   Mauger of Worcester (Pontigny: Cistercian). *Ann. Waverl.,* s.a.

2 Symeon of Durham (cont. John of Hexham), II, 304: "Memorque voti sui quod juvenis apud Cluniacum fecerat." The references to this vow have escaped the notice of some modern writers, who have expressed surprise that Thurstan, who had shown himself such a fierce critic of the black monks, should ask for their habit when dying.

3 Symeon of Durham, II, 304. The episode is highly characteristic both of the age and of the stern asceticism of Thurstan, but those who see in it no more than a singular exhibition of the macabre do less than justice to the great archbishop. The major part of the antiphons and responsories of the Office of the Dead consists of the appeals and prayers of a soul awaiting judgment, and is perfectly applicable to one in expectation of imminent death.

4 *Chron. Abingd.* II, 170–1.

houses and orders. Gerald of Wales, as might be expected, has more than one story on this topic.[1] Less open to criticism is a narrative in the Abingdon chronicle concerning a priest of Oxford who had obtained from the abbey half the benefice of St Aldate's with the proviso that if he took the religious habit it should be at Abingdon. He was taken ill, and asked for the habit, and while unconscious was clothed (so the Abingdon account had it) by the canons of St Frideswide's. Coming to himself, he expressed the most lively indignation and repudiated the act, but died immediately and was buried by the canons.[2] True or not in all its details, this incident shows clearly enough what abuses the early Cistercians were anxious to prevent when they put a prohibition upon deathbed clothings.

HOSPITALITY AND CHARITY

GUESTS—PILGRIMS—POOR—SICK

Hospitality and almsgiving, presupposed by St Benedict as duties to be performed as a matter of course by his monks,[3] filled a considerable place in the daily life and economy of all monastic houses throughout the Middle Ages, and perhaps never more than during the eleventh and twelfth centuries. Indeed, in more than one foundation charter of the period they are specifically mentioned as a principal *raison d'être* of the monastery.[4] Whatever may have been the abuses connected with the entertainment of wealthy guests and indiscriminate charity at the end of the Middle Ages, when society was more complex and in some ways better organized, there can be no doubt that in the eleventh and twelfth centuries monastic charity and hospitality were indispensable elements of the life of the times; as regards hospitality, even if in the case of wealthier travellers a demand for accommodation might have created a supply apart from religious houses, the poorer sort and pilgrims would have fared ill indeed without them; as regards the relief of the diseased and indigent, whether sufferers from some general calamity of war or famine or individuals who through misfortune or physical debility lacked a livelihood, nothing in the England of the twelfth century could have replaced the monasteries.

I

GUESTS

In St Benedict's Rule it is laid down that the guests, "who are never wanting in a monastery", shall have quarters separate from the monks,

1 E.g. Giraldus, IV, 200.   2 *Chron. Abingd.* II, 174–5.
3 *Regula S. Benedicti*, c. liii, 30–1: "Pauperum et peregrinorum maxime susceptioni cura sollicite exhibeatur." *Ibid.* 35–6: "...hospites, qui nunquam desunt monasterio."
4 E.g. at Battle and Reading.

with a special attendant, and shall have meals with the abbot apart from the brethren. The last enactment was commonly obeyed in the centuries immediately following the lifetime of St Benedict, as it was again in the later medieval monastery, where the abbot had a self-contained establishment apart from the convent. In the *Regularis Concordia*, however, it was explicitly decreed that in the interests of religious discipline abbots should never take their meals outside the refectory.[1] Possibly this had as a corollary the custom that guests also should dine in the refectory; this is explicitly stated to have been the case at Ely during Hereward's sojourn there,[2] and although the occasion was extraordinary and the source of information not wholly reliable, it is likely enough that the better sort of guests normally took meals with the monks. The practice of the Norman monasteries was not far different. Lanfranc's Statutes presuppose that the abbot dines in the refectory with the monks, though at a special table; guests, however, normally ate in their own quarters, though on occasion those in orders were permitted to dine with the monks.[3] The custom, which gradually became general in England, and which was already common in France south of Normandy, that the abbot should dine separately, either with distinguished guests, or with his household, or with chosen monks, was in this country a result of that gradual separation of revenues and administration which affected all relations between abbot and community.

Lanfranc laid down exact regulations separating the monks from the guests, and these probably remained in force, as much from motives of convenience as from strictly religious considerations; only guests who were monks had free access to cloister and church. Ordinarily, the great majority of guests would be travellers without any interest in the monastery as such, not, as nowadays, relatives or friends of the monks, or laymen anxious to obtain some acquaintance with the monastic life, and their number would have varied very greatly from house to house. Monasteries such as Christ Church, Canterbury, and Westminster, which lay at the centres of national life, and had often to entertain royalty, and those, such as Reading and St Albans, which lay upon the great thoroughfares, must have received an incessant stream of visitors; at others, which lay away from a city or great road, guests would have been comparatively few; in any case, there is no means of estimating their number. As for the relations

1 *Regularis Concordia*, x, 92: "Hoc solummodo, quod sancti patres ob animae salutem virtutumque potius custodiam quam ad regulae contemptum synodali statuerant concilio, magnopere custodito ut videlicet in monasterio degens extra refectorium nec ipse abbas nec fratrum quispiam...manducet vel bibat."

2 *Liber Eliensis*, 232: "Miles [i.e. the soldiery] semper cum monacho ad prandium et ad coenam refecit...ad superiorem vero tabulam...abbas cum tribus praelibatis comitibus [sc. Edwin, Morkar and Tostig] et illi duo praeclari viri Herewardus et Turchitellus."

3 *Lanfranci Statuta*, c. ii, 233: "[Abbati] intraturo in refectorium duo fratres serviant ei"; *ibid.* "ad mensam abbatis quotidie..."; c. ix: "Si extranei clerici se dixerunt in refectorio velle comedere, etc."

of the monks, there is an interesting passage in the Abingdon chronicle which records that all those connected with the brethren who came to the monastery on the vigil of the Nativity of Our Lady (8 September) were given hospitality.[1]

II

PILGRIMS

In addition to guests of passage, a number of monasteries, which possessed the body of a saint reputed to work miracles, had another class of visitor; their churches were the resort of numerous pilgrims, sick and sound, whose presence at all times of the night and day must have considerably affected the freedom and privacy of the monks, though tangible compensation was given by their offerings at the shrine, which were a notable source of income and helped to erect and adorn the church. Chief among such places of pilgrimage immediately before the Conquest were Bury (St Edmund), Evesham (St Egwin and others) and Malmesbury (St Aldhelm), but other abbeys, such as Ramsey, a "holy isle", were places of considerable resort. All the shrines just named were at the height of their celebrity for half a century after the Conquest; in the second half of the twelfth century their reputation for miraculous cures declined somewhat, though they remained centres of pilgrimage, and popular enthusiasm was transferred to the shrines of St Edward at Westminster, St Wulfstan at Worcester and, eclipsing all, St Thomas at Canterbury.

Those who, at the present day, have visited Lourdes or Lisieux, or the abbeys of Montserrat in Spain or Monte Vergine in Italy, will be able to form, with the aid of contemporary narratives, something of a picture of the scenes which took place daily. The conditions at Evesham, Bury and Malmesbury are described by the chroniclers of the houses.[2] Pilgrims and sick came from all parts of England, and even from Ireland and across the Channel, and it seems to have been a common custom for them to spend the night in the church before the shrine, sleeping or waking; their presence made it necessary for the monastic wardens of the shrine to sleep alongside of their charge.[3] The church at Evesham was rarely without such visitors.[4] Besides sick and pilgrims, the feast days drew crowds of hangers-on and buffoons; William of Malmesbury, who describes more than one miraculous cure of which he had been a witness,

1 *Chron. Abingd.* II, 313: "In Nativitate sanctae Mariae parentes monachorum supervenientes habebunt necessaria sibi et hominibus et equis de curia in vigilia et in die festivitatis."
2 For Bury, *v. Heremanni de Miraculis S. Edmundi* (ed. Liebermann, *Ungedruckte Quellen*, 239–81), and Samson in *Mem. S. Edmund's*, I, 107–208; for Evesham, *Chron. Evesh.* 50–1, 62–7, 91; for Malmesbury, Will. Malmesb., *GP*, 412–43.
3 *Mem. S. Edmund's*, I, 78, 128–9; Will. Malmesb., *GP*, 427. Until very recent years, the women pilgrims used to spend the night in the church at Monte Vergine.
4 *Chron. Evesh.* 50.

gives details also of the less edifying aspects of these gatherings, and the accounts of the conditions at Canterbury and Worcester at the end of the century are very similar.[1] Nowadays, as may be seen at such pilgrimage abbeys as Einsiedeln in Switzerland or Monte Vergine, the visitors to the shrine give occupation to a number of the monks who administer the sacraments, but if there was any parallel to this in the Norman period it has left little trace in the records.

III

THE POOR AND SICK

The *Regularis Concordia* laid down that accommodation and livelihood should be provided by each monastery for a certain number of the poor, and that every day the monks in turn and the abbot should wash the feet of three such pensioners. Besides these, provision was to be made for poor pilgrims, who were to receive a gift of food on departure.[2] The examples of Wulfstan and Aethelwig at Worcester and Evesham show that these enactments were no dead letter, at least where the religious life was at all flourishing. Wulfstan's custom,[3] if it stood alone, might be attributed to his sanctity, but the practice of Aethelwig shows that the observance of the *Regularis Concordia* was traditional in England. At Evesham, indeed, abundant care was given to the poor. The whole passage in the contemporary chronicle deserves quotation:

In those days many pilgrims resorted to Evesham from Aquitaine, from Ireland, and from many other countries; all these he received and supplied with what was needful. And since our father Benedict in his rule bids that "the table of the abbot should be with pilgrims and guests" this abbot always gave bountiful provision from his own table[4] to thirteen poor men daily. In addition, until the day of his death, whether at home or abroad, he maintained twelve poor men for the Maundy,[5] who had food and clothing in all respects the same as a monk's. He or his prior, who had special charge of this under him, loved with all humility daily to wash the hands and feet of these men with warm water; some of them were lepers, but Aethelwig washed and kissed their hands and feet exactly as he did those of the others. Likewise at Christmas, Easter, Whitsun and all the principal feasts he gave presents of money to these and other poor people....Every year four or five days before Christmas and between Palm Sunday and Easter Day a great army of poor and pilgrims used to come to Evesham; all these Aethelwig succoured both in person and by means of trust-

---

1 Cf. esp. the *Miracula S. Wulfstani* which follow the *Vita* (ed. Darlington).
2 *Regularis Concordia*, c. x, 92: "Qualiter mandatum quotidianis diebus a fratribus exhibeatur pauperibus, et quo ordine Abbas erga peregrinos agat."
3 *Vita Wulfstani*, 57.
4 *De mensa sua*. This I take to mean that food equal to that served at his table was given, not that the poor dined with him.
5 *Ad mandatum* (S. John, xiii, 34: "Mandatum novum do vobis"). Cf. p. 451.

worthy monks and laypeople, giving bountiful alms, accomplishing the Lord's Maundy by washing their feet, giving clothes to some, boots to more, and money to many others.[1]

Such personal, direct service on the part of the abbot tended to disappear in the course of the following century, but where traditions remained purest, as at Battle, a great feudal abbot such as Walter de Lucy is found engaged in similar ministrations.[2]

The Anglo-Saxon system appears to have entrusted the care of almsgiving directly to the abbot or his representative. Norman monasticism brought with it the almoner as a regular official of the monastery and, as has been seen, he soon came to have a fixed income. Originally, if we may judge from Lanfranc's Statutes, the Norman almoner did not receive poor within the monastery precinct, but distributed alms on his visits to the houses of the poor and sick of the neighbourhood.[3] The English custom prevailed, however, and the almonry came to be an integral part of the monastic building scheme; that at Abingdon was built *c.* 1125 and that at Evesham almost contemporaneously.[4] The income of the almoner was gradually built up throughout the twelfth century; thus Abbot Walter of Ramsey (1133–60) gave a manor and two churches to the almonry;[5] Abbot Geoffrey of St Albans (1119–46) made a number of similar assignments.[6] At Abingdon by 1185 the almoner had very considerable revenues, with ten servants under him, and at Evesham, besides rents and tithes, he had a tenth of all bread baked or bought by the abbey and charge of the monks' garden to provide vegetables for the poor;[7] such arrangements are no doubt typical of the general practice.[8]

At Evesham, as has been noted, besides casual relief, there were two groups of twelve and fifty pensioners. The smaller of the two, in return for their livelihood, were expected to be present in the church at certain times and to intercede for their benefactors. At Bury, according to the Domesday entry, there were forty-three such dependents, each with a *bordarius* to serve him, and twenty-eight religious women and poor, whose task it was to intercede for the king and all Christian men,[9] and a similar group is found at St Albans. It was generally composed, no doubt, of those who

1 *Chron. Evesh.* 91–3.
2 *Chron. Bell.* 135–8: "Leprosorum...manus pedesque abluendo fovebat, et...blanda oscula imprimebat." 3 *Lanfranci Statuta,* c. ix, 238.
4 *Chron. Abingd.* II, 171. Abbot Vincent (1121–*c.* 1131) built "aula hospitum cum camera, granario, bracino, pistrino, duplici stabulo, eleemosynaria...". Abbot Reginald of Evesham (1122–*c.*1142) built "aulam hospitum cum camera et magnam coquinam" (*Chron. Evesh.* 99).
5 *Chron. Rames.* 303, 304, 335. 6 *GASA,* I, 59.
7 *Chron. Abingd.* II, 327–34. The servants are noted on p. 331. *Chron. Evesh.* 216: "Curam horti monachorum, ut inde habeat pulmentum ad refectionem pauperum."
8 Cf. Gervase of Canterbury, II, 401, for churches assigned *pastui pauperum et orphanorum.*
9 *Mem. S. Edmund's,* I, 339: "xliii elemosin. quisque eorum habet i bord[arium]...ubi sunt...xxviii inter nonnas et pauperes, qui quotidie pro rege et omni populo Christiano deprecantur."

had attracted the notice of the monks by some physical deformity or disability, or by the performance of faithful service in the past, or by inheriting some title to gratitude; in the case of Glastonbury in 1189 we possess the list of such names and titles as they were taken down by the abbot's agents: "a widow", "the sister of Adam Berra", "a cripple woman", "Stephen's mother", "Christiana of the graveyard", and the rest.[1]

In addition to regular pensioners, numbers were fed and clothed on certain days or for certain periods. Thus at Glastonbury early in the twelfth century thirteen poor men were entertained on the obits of kings, abbots and other benefactors; a century later it was usual for a hundred poor to be fed on the funeral day of a monk and the custom was widespread of maintaining a poor man in food and clothing for a year after each death.[2] At St Augustine's, Canterbury, thirty of the poor were entertained on the commemoration day of benefactors and as many on the anniversaries of abbots; during each Lent as many poor were fed as there were monks in the house;[3] similar provision for the entertainment of a hundred poor guests can be seen at Ramsey and St Albans,[4] and instances could be multiplied indefinitely.

Before the Conquest, perhaps as a result of the relaxation of the original regularity, the custom had arisen of each of the monks giving alms from any income he might have. This no doubt explains the action of Aethelwig of Evesham, who apportioned refugees in 1070 to such monks as could support them.[5] This was, strictly speaking, an abuse, for monks were forbidden private property, and Lanfranc acted on the more regular system of giving definite sums to his monks with instructions that they were to pass them on to their indigent relations.[6] But the old custom died hard. Samson, in 1182, when enforcing the rule of personal poverty, allowed each monk to retain a sum of two shillings for presents, to be bestowed on poor relations or other deserving objects.[7] Marleberge, on the contrary, decreed in his statutes that all alms were to pass through the hands of the almoner.[8]

To the monasteries, as to the only stable places of refuge, flocked the refugees from any extraordinary shock of war or famine. The fullest

1 *Liber Henrici de Soliaco* (ed. Jackson), 8 *seq.*
2 Will. Malmesb., *De Ant. Glast.* 333–4; Adam of Domerham, II, 440.
3 *Chron. Will. Thorne*, 1798, 1814; the latter enactment was by Abbot Silvester (1151–61); it is known that in 1146 there were sixty-one monks (*ibid.* 1807).
4 *Chron. Rames.* 335; *GASA*, I, 206, 284.
5 *Chron. Evesh.* 91: "Quibusdam fratribus ad hoc posse habentibus unum puerulum dominus abbas ut alimento corporis sustentarentur commendabat."
6 Will. Malmesb., *GP*, 71: "Ultroneus juvenibus offerr[ebat] denarios quibus necessitudinum propriarum inopiae occurrerent." Malmesbury doubtless has in mind the touching incident related by Eadmer, *Hist. Novorum*, 14, perhaps concerning his own mother.
7 *Jocelini Cronica*, 243: "Ita tamen ut in pauperes parentes vel in pios usus expenderentur."
8 *Chron. Evesh.* 206: "Et ut eleemosyna eorum [*sc.* monachorum] per manus eleemosynarii erogetur."

description of relief work of this kind is that embodied in the account of
Abbot Aethelwig of Evesham, so often quoted in these pages. The chronicler
there tells that after the Conqueror had harried the North and West,

a vast multitude of men old and young, and of women with their little ones,
came to Evesham in their distress, fleeing from famine; all these Aethelwig
supported as best he could. Many, who had long been starving, died after
eating ravenously, and the wretches lay sick throughout the town, indoors and
out and even in our cemetery, starving, and dying when they ate. And thus
many died for many days, so that five or six daily, sometimes more, who thus
died miserably, were buried here by the prior.[1]

The abbot's works of mercy towards these refugees have already been
mentioned. Scenes of a similar kind took place in any time of public
calamity. During the anarchy of Stephen's reign a particularly severe
famine is noted. The poor besieged the gates of Abingdon, and Abbot
Ingulf, exhausting other resources, stripped the precious covering off the
shrine of St Vincent to buy food; it was about the same period of lean
years that the ornaments of Christ Church, Canterbury, were alienated
for the same purpose, that Abbot Walter of Ramsey gave a tenth of all
his moneys to the poor and that Abbot Geoffrey of St Albans stripped off
the silver plates, which he himself had just caused to be laid on the shrine
of his patron, and melted them down into coin.[2] By contrast, it is related
of Abbot Alfred of Abingdon (1186–9) that, although very wealthy, he
neglected to feed the poor in a time of great famine.[3] It may well have
been this that Gerald of Wales had in mind a few years later when he
contrasted the charity of the white monks with the neglect of the poor on
the part of the black.[4]

Besides regular and occasional relief of this kind, the monasteries were
responsible for founding and (though more rarely) for maintaining a
certain number of hospitals. It is very difficult to trace institutions of this
kind before the Conquest; after 1066, especially when the towns began to
grow, they multiplied, but they were usually in the charge either of hired
attendants or of canons or, later, of the members of one of the orders of
hospitallers which came into being in the twelfth century.[5] The accounts
of the activities of Wulfstan at Worcester and Aethelwig at Evesham give
the impression that there was no kind of provision for the sick. At
Canterbury, Lanfranc was responsible for the foundation and endowment
of the hospital of St Gregory, which had no connection with Christ Church,

---

1 *Chron. Evesh.* 90–1.
2 *Chron. Abingd.* II, 214; Gervase, I, 143; *Chron. Rames.* 335: "Tanta vero in eo fervebat
caritas, ut non solum panes ad furnum, sed etiam omnes denarios suos ad usus pauperum
faceret decimari"; *GASA*, I, 82.
3 *Chron. Abingd.* II, 293.   4 Giraldus, *Iter Kambriae*, 46.
5 It is quite beyond the scope of these pages to consider the history of hospitals in
England, but it may be remarked that some of the collections of miraculous cures (e.g. those
in the *Vita Wulfstani*) contain descriptions of hospital life which have not yet been fully
made use of.

but was under the spiritual charge of regular canons. At some houses the older English system, under which monasteries had received a certain number of the sick, may have still survived.[1] Certainly the presence of a community of religious women in the almonry at St Albans when Abbot Paul arrived in 1077 suggests that nursing work as well as mere relief was done there,[2] and it is precisely at St Albans that there are the clearest indications of later hospital foundations. There Abbot Geoffrey (1119–46) founded and endowed out of the income of the house the hospital of St Julian for lepers,[3] and half a century later the institution received its complement by the separate establishment of St Mary des Prés as a quasi-monastic community of leprous women.[4] Such foundations by monasteries were not common in the twelfth century, though a case may be found in the well-known gift of Samson of Bury to the hospital of Babwell; this, however, would seem to have been more of a hospice than a clinic.[5]

1 Cf. the deformed boy who *pascebatur a monachis* at Malmesbury (Will. Malmesb., *GP*, 427). The sick pilgrim monk of Bermondsey, who was received in the monks' infirmary at Bury, is perhaps an exceptional case (*Mem. S. Edmund's*, 1, 203).

2 *GASA*, 1, 59: "Coetum quoque sanctimonialium [no doubt those mentioned in *Domesday*] quibusdam regulis...coartavit in eleemosynaria...collocando; ut...cotidie Mandatum facerent."

3 *GASA*, 1, 77.   4 *GASA*, 1, 202.

5 *Jocelini Cronica*, 252: "Dono...novo hospitali de Babbewell, in sustentationem pauperum et usum hospitalitatis."

CHAPTER XXVIII

THE INTELLECTUAL ACTIVITIES OF THE BLACK MONKS: I
EDUCATIONAL AND LITERARY

THE MONASTIC SCHOOLS

I

When considering the educational influence of medieval monasticism it is of the first importance to distinguish between various epochs and localities, and above all between the age previous to the renaissance of the eleventh century and that which followed it. The four centuries between 600 and 1000 were, as is universally acknowledged, peculiarly the monastic centuries. From the disappearance of the Roman tradition of secular education beneath the advance of the new northern nations until the intellectual adolescence of those nations shortly after the millennium, the only permanent depositaries of the resources of culture were the monasteries, and the part which they played in educating Europe and in preserving something of the heritage of the past has been generously appreciated and assessed by modern scholarship.[1]

The monastic revival associated with Dunstan and his colleagues was part of a general renaissance throughout the Church and nation of England, and the monasteries were from the first intended to be centres of cultural life. Dunstan himself, who had learnt as a boy at Glastonbury from both English and Irish, had in turn taught boys, perhaps even before his establishment as abbot at Glastonbury,[2] and it seems probable that the house continued to give education to others besides monks.[3] Ethelwold likewise, even when abbot and bishop, continued to teach and to translate

1 Cf. Dom Ursmer Berlière, *Écoles claustrales au Moyen Âge (Bulletin de la Classe des Lettres de l'Académie royale de Belgique* (1921), 550–72), which contains an exhaustive bibliography.

2 In many pre-Conquest documents it is not easy to decide whether such words as *clericus* or *scholasticus* are used as synonyms of *monachus* and *puer*, or are intended to distinguish lay from monastic pupils. We have the witness of Aelfric's *Vita S. Aethelwoldi* that the latter studied at Glastonbury: "didicit namque inibi grammaticam artem et metricam, et libros divinos seu auctores" (*Chron. Abingd.* II, 257). If, as seems to have been the case, he was of the same age as Dunstan (so J. A. Robinson, *The Times of St Dunstan*, 108) he must have been a man of thirty at the time. Dunstan's earliest biographer twice records incidents in which Dunstan and *se sequentes scolastici* or a *parvus scolasticus* figure (*Mem. St Dunstan*, 18, 28). The second passage certainly dates from his abbacy at Glastonbury.

3 All turns on the meaning given to certain phrases, e.g. *Mem. St Dunstan*, 25–6; *Vita S. Aethelwoldi*, in *Chron. Abingd.* II, 258; *Vita S. Aethelwoldi* by Wulfstan in *PL*, CXXXVII, 91, 95. The last, however, must be received with caution, as it is possible that the Life took its final shape after the Conquest (J. A. Robinson, *The Times of St Dunstan*, 107–8, and Additional Note B, pp. 168–70).

books from Latin into English.[1] As for Oswald, if he is not himself spoken of as a teacher, he was responsible for inviting the celebrated Abbo to his foundation at Ramsey, and there again it would seem certain that many of those whom he taught became priests outside the monastery.[2] The monastic system of education thus established bore abundant fruit in the next generation, in which Byrhtferth and Aelfric were only the most eminent among the many *alumni* of Winchester, Ramsey and the other houses. Primarily, no doubt, the monastic education was directed towards the instruction of the boys and youths of the cloister, destined to become monks. It had been one of the decrees of Benedict of Aniane that only those who were to become monks should be taught in the monastery, and it was part of his policy to isolate the abbey from the world, but even on the Continent such provisions were rendered inoperative by the real needs and urgent demands of the times,[3] and there is no evidence that such a conception had ever been part of the programme of Dunstan and Ethelwold. Rather, everything we know of their lives and activities suggests that they desired to use the educational resources at their command so as to influence the greatest possible number, though indeed in the England of 970–1066 the number outside the monasteries who would desire to make use of those resources must always have been small.[4]

The positive evidence for the presence in the cloister schools before the Conquest of boys who did not subsequently become monks is necessarily scanty, but it exists. How far the general tone and subject-matter of Aelfric's Dialogue and that of his disciple Aelfric Bata imply that many of their pupils were destined for life in the world must remain a matter of opinion, but the way in which the boys are addressed, and the care with which the great Aelfric compiled his Latin Grammar and Glossary for the boys of his time in general, indicate at least a very much wider aim than that of the monastic generations after the Conquest.[5] A few decades later,

---

1 *Vita S. Aethelwoldi, Chron. Abingd.* II, 263: "Dulce namque erat ei adolescentes et juvenes semper docere, et libros Anglice eis solvere." One of the books so translated was the Rule of St Benedict (*v.* J. A. Robinson, *The Times of St Dunstan*, 121); it has been edited by Schröer, *Die angelsächsischen Prosabearbeitungen der Benedictinerregel* (1888).

2 *Hist. Rames.* 42.

3 Dom Berlière, *L'Ordre Monastique*, 116, remarks: "Au ixe siècle, on accepta franchement l'évolution, et les écoles s'ouvrirent partout."

4 On the whole question of monastic schools, *v.* G. G. Coulton, *Monastic Schools*, in *Contemporary Review*, June 1913, reprinted as no. 10 of *Medieval Studies*; A. F. Leach, *The Schools of Medieval England* (a work to be used with caution; for a careful criticism *v.* A. G. Little in *EHR*, xxx, 525–9); R. Graham, *The Intellectual Influence of English Monasticism*, in *English Ecclesiastical Studies*, 146–87 (a careful and learned study, but the author herself would probably put her conclusions in another form to-day), and above all the essay of Dom Berlière referred to above, p. 487, n. 1. G. Paré, etc. in *La Renaissance du xiie siècle*, 42, note St Vincent de Metz and St Trond as the two solitary examples of monastic "external" schools on the Continent in the twelfth century.

5 Cf. *Aelfrici Colloquium* (Brit. Mus. MS. Cott. Tib. A 3), printed by B. Thorpe in *Analecta Anglo-Saxonica*, 18–36 (ed. 1868). A better edition is that of W. H. Stevenson in *Early Scholastic Colloquies (Anecdota Oxoniensia*, Med. and Mod. Series, xv (1929), 75–101). Dr R. Graham, in the work referred to in the last note (p. 155), considers that the *personae*

in the reign of Cnut, we hear of the son of a foreign noble receiving his education at St Albans,[1] and at about the same time the young Wulfstan, who had at that time no intention of becoming a monk or even a priest, was receiving his education at Evesham and Peterborough.[2] It would certainly be wholly alien to all we know of pre-Conquest monasticism to suppose that two carefully distinct schools, an intern and an extern, were maintained in the monasteries, and on the other hand there is, so far as can be seen, no evidence at all of the existence of other schools until the houses of canons began to spring up from c. 1050 onwards. Outside the monasteries, the only teaching available was that of a rare lettered country priest. Immediately after the Conquest, we find the half-English son of one of the newcomers, Orderic, learning from a priest, to whom he acted as *clericellus*, serving at Mass and other ceremonies, and living in his house. This, from the earliest days of the Church until the present time, has always been a natural way of education, especially for boys destined for the altar, but the priest whom Orderic attended seems to have been a man of exceptional gifts and perhaps of some social position.[3] Most probably, the monastic schools, while chiefly consisting of children of the cloister, gave education to a small number of the sons of the more considerable men of the neighbourhood. As for the life lived by the boys, the dialogues of the two Aelfrics can be supplemented by the passing references of the monks Osbern and Eadmer of Canterbury, both of whom were at school shortly before the coming of Lanfranc. The picture of all is the same: a life of some freedom, coarse and harsh; not unlike that of a grammar school a century ago.[4]

of various professions in this dialogue are boys at school destined for these callings. I confess this does not appear to me possible; they are rather characters introduced to provide the widest vocabulary. The *pueri* addressed later (*Colloquium*, ed. Thorpe, 33, 35) *in propria persona* are clearly the children of the cloister school, among whom may have been some who did not intend to remain as monks. It is equally clear, as against the view of A. F. Leach (*The Schools of Medieval England*, 88–91), that the master is a monk.

1 *GASA*, I, 91: "At rex [Cnut] misit illum ad sanctum Albanum ut ibi in tutela Abbatis commorans respiraret. Quod Abbas acceptans, eum ad Regis petitionem et delicate educavit et instrui civiliter praecepit." Although the source of this incident is a post-Conquest work, there is no reason to doubt the accuracy of the statement.

2 *Vita Wulfstani* (ed. R. R. Darlington), 4–5.

3 OV, V, 134: "Cum quinque essem annorum, apud urbem Scrobesburiam scholae traditus sum, et prima tibi [*sc.* Deo] servitia clericatus obtuli in basilica sanctorum Petri et Pauli apostolorum. Illic Siguardus insignis presbyter per quinque annos [1080–5] carmentis Nicostratae litteras docuit me, ac psalmis et hymnis aliisque necessariis instructionibus mancipavit me." Cf. II, 301: "Siuuardo nobili presbytero litteris erudiendis... cujus magisterio prima percipiens rudimenta quinque annis subjugatus sum." The attempts which have been made to claim Orderic as one of the first old Salopians are not convincing, despite the phrase *scholae traditus*; he was probably Siward's only pupil.

4 *Mem. St Dunstan*, 137–8, 140–2, 229–30. Cf. also the Colloquies of Aelfric Bata, ed. W. H. Stevenson, *Early Scholastic Colloquies*, no. IV, 27–66, for games, excursions into the town, gathering fruit in the garden, etc.

II

The Norman monasteries derived their inspiration ultimately from William of Dijon. He himself at the beginning of the eleventh century had created at Fécamp a system whereby education, and even free lodging, were given to all who came, both those who intended to be clerics and others.[1] To what extent the school at Fécamp was "double", how far it survived its founder, or was reproduced elsewhere, or was modified in the interests of monastic life, are questions seemingly unanswerable. So far as can be seen, only the schools for the children of the cloister, the oblates, survived in the Norman monasteries at the time of the Conquest, save in the case of one house, but the brilliance of the single exception was so great that it has put all else in the shade. Bec had always stood apart from its fellows by reason of its origin, but its fame as a school was due in the first place entirely to Lanfranc. He himself had been formed and had taught in the law school of Pavia, which alike in organization and intellectual subtlety was far in advance of anything then existing north of the Alps. Lanfranc's genius throughout life showed itself in an ability to use his great mental gifts for the immediately practical purpose. He taught at Bec because he was bidden to do so in order to earn money, and since as a monk he had turned his attention to Scripture and theology he was able to give instruction in those subjects. At that time, and until the age of Abelard, a single master made a school, and there is no evidence that Lanfranc was assisted by any others of the monks in his achievement of making Bec for a short space the most celebrated school of northern Europe. Anselm, like Lanfranc a stranger from the south, had learnt from the master before becoming a monk; unlike Lanfranc, he turned naturally to dialectic and theology, and his teaching would seem from the first to have been less that of a master "holding a school" than that of a monk who gave what he had to the boys and young monks and visitors at Bec, and to all correspondents who sought his help. With the lapse of every year from 1050 onwards the new system of education was developing and crystallizing in the cathedral schools of France, and the specialized knowledge and absorption involved in the career of a master was every year making it less feasible for a monastery to be a school. The celebrity of Bec during more than a generation as the home of the two greatest minds of Europe was almost wholly accidental; it did not at all represent the culmination of the monastic educational system; had it done so Bec would not have stood, as it did, alone. Indeed, very soon after the death of William of Dijon the

---

1 Mabillon, *Acta SS, OSB*, vi i, *Vita Willelmi*, by Rodulphus Glaber, § 14: "[Ut] gratis largiretur cunctis doctrinae beneficium ad coenobia sibi confluentibus, nullusque qui ad haec vellet accedere prohiberetur: quin potius tam servis quam liberis, divitibus cum egenis, uniforme charitatis inpenderetur documentum." This corrects the impression given by another passage, which might seem to restrict the scope to clerics: "instituit scholas sacri ministerii...quibus...instarent fratres."

stream of culture in northern France began to flow into two gradually diverging channels. The purely literary and historical studies, which were peculiarly fitted to thrive among the monks, reached for a time their fullest development in the cloister, at Bec, at St Évroul, at Mont St Michel and elsewhere; the dialectical, theological and scientific culture, which needed for its progress brilliant masters and a host of eager and capable disciples, after finding a passing home at a whole series of schools finally, at the beginning of the twelfth century, gained a focus at Paris and passed into the university. The monastery of Bec endured for some decades as a centre of speculation, of scriptural and canonical learning, but it was living largely on the reputation of its two great sons, and giving too freely of its best to England to keep its fame.

So far as can be seen, Lanfranc made no attempt to reproduce the external school of Bec at Caen, still less at Canterbury. His Statutes show a school for the children of the cloister, living the full liturgical life and rigidly disciplined, and there is no provision for a second school. And in fact there is no trace of a systematized lay or clerical education in the Normanized monasteries of England; the learning of Canterbury was famous, but it attracted monks alone. There are, however, a few indications, especially in the abbeys that retained most of the old traditions, that boys were occasionally accepted for education and brought up within the monastery with no intention of remaining there as monks. It is possible that this was a kind of private tuition reserved for the sons of distinguished neighbours or benefactors. Such indications are rare, but they warrant us in thinking that many other cases have passed unnoticed: there is the monk at Binham, a cell of St Albans, who had a scholar who acted as his minister;[1] there is the case of a boy accepted at Ramsey to be educated for a period of seven years;[2] there is the boy that Queen Eleanor sent to Abingdon;[3] above all, there is the case of Robert, earl of Leicester and Justiciar, who had received his education at Abingdon at the end of the eleventh century;[4] and, fifty years later, Gerald of Wales received his first schooling in the abbey of Gloucester.[5]

These must, however, have been in the nature of special cases; the majority went to school with the parish priest, if at all, or in one of the

1 *Heremanni Mir. S. Edmundi* (ed. Liebermann, *Ungedruckte Quellen*, 267). This *scolaris ac clericellus* was almost blind.

2 *Hist. Rames.* 268.

3 *Materials for the History of Becket*, I, 213.

4 Robert as Justiciar helped to settle a lawsuit *c.* 1160 in favour of Abingdon by giving his recollections of the market he had seen there *cum adhuc puer esset, et apud Abbendonam nutriretur regis Willelmi tempore.* There can be no question here of an "extern" or town school (*Chron. Abingd.* II, 229).

5 Giraldus, *Speculum Ecclesiae*, Opera, IV, 107: "Puerilibus olim in annis viridisque juventae diebus cum apud Gloucestriam sub viro literatissimo magistro Haimone studerem, in abbatia S. Petri quam tunc abbas Amelinus [regebat]." Here, again, the possibility of a "town" school seems excluded, though not, perhaps, the possibility that Giraldus was a child of the cloister who did not persevere.

multitude of new schools springing up all over the country which naturally, in an age when none but ecclesiastics had letters, made their first appearance in close connection with a cathedral or house of canons, or in a town near a great monastery. The last class were often generously supported by the monks, but there is, so far as would appear, no evidence that the schools in monastic towns such as Bury or St Albans derived from an "extern" section of the abbey's school. The very fact that Lanfranc established the canons who opened school at St Gregory's, Canterbury,[1] is against such a hypothesis, and when the school at St Albans first appears in the records c. 1100 it is in full and flourishing independent existence.[2] Of this school more information has survived than of any other in a monastic town. All through the twelfth century it appears to have maintained its position as one of the leading schools of England, and this was largely due to the patronage of the abbey.[3] Besides Geoffrey, later monk and abbot, we are told of two other celebrated masters, Alexander Nequam and Warin, a nephew of the abbot of the same name and an able civilian and canonist, and at the end of the century, as at the beginning, a master was willing to leave Dunstable for St Albans.[4] Of the school at Bury little is known till the days of Samson, who himself had been master before becoming a monk. In the course of his abbacy he provided funds first for the erection of lodgings for poor clerics and later for the payment of a master, thereby rendering the instruction entirely free.[5] In these ways, rather than by themselves teaching, the monks of England of the later twelfth century helped in the education of the country; within the cloister, the number of those taught would seem to have diminished, and the scope of the teaching to have narrowed.

THE LITERARY AND LEARNED WORK
OF THE MONKS

I

The literary and cultural history of English monasticism between the reigns of Edgar and John falls naturally into three divisions: the period of Anglo-Saxon culture; the period, lasting from the Conquest till the death

1 H. Böhmer, *Die Fälschungen Erzbischof Lanfrancs* (Appendix), 174: "Scolas urbis et viculorum ejus tam grammatice quam musice regi debere statuentes, earum regimen prepositis sacerdotum ipsius ecclesie et eorum dispositioni commisimus."

2 *GASA*, I, 73: "Iste [Gaufridus] de Cenomannia, unde oriundus erat, venit, vocatus ab Abbate Ricardo [1097–1119] ut scholam apud sanctum Albanum regeret. Et cum venisset, concessa fuit schola alii magistro, quia non venit tempestive. Legit igitur apud Dunestapliam, expectans scholam sancti Albani." As Geoffrey became monk and prior of the abbey, and ultimately abbot in 1119, his arrival cannot well have been after c. 1100.

3 *GASA*, I, 196: "Qua tunc temporis [c. 1170–80] vix inveniretur in Anglia schola melior vel fructuosior, aut scholaribus utilior vel copiosior." Allowance must of course be made for the patriotism of the chronicler.

4 *GASA*, I, 196.   5 *Jocelini Cronica*, 249, 296.

of Stephen, in which the English monasteries absorbed and developed the Norman monastic learning; and the period from the accession of Henry II onwards in which, while continuing to practise their characteristic studies and interests, they gradually became, what they were to remain for at least a century, centres of literary and historical pursuits alone, leaving to the growing universities the direction of the studies of theology, philosophy and law. In the first two periods, which together formed the last phase of the "monastic centuries", the monasteries had to all intents and purposes a monopoly of learning in England; in the last, the initiative had passed from them to the schools and the universities, and the most gifted and typical black monks of the time had as a rule themselves passed through a scholastic training.

The great trio whose names have so often appeared in these pages, Dunstan, Ethelwold and Oswald, were organizers and administrators rather than writers or thinkers. The first generation of their disciples, however, proved singularly rich in men of learning who were also masters of language. Indeed, the fifty years between 970 and 1020 saw an output of native prose and verse which alike in quality and quantity was unsurpassed for more than three centuries, and during that time the English language attained a dignity and beauty which no other native European tongue could attempt to rival before the age of St Francis of Assisi. The scanty nature of our knowledge of the history of these times, as compared with the Norman epoch, the unfamiliar form of the language, and perhaps also the religious quality of most of the compositions, would seem to have deterred all but professed students from making any acquaintance with early English literature, and even among scholars, until very recent years, much of the most important work had been done by German and (to a lesser degree) American students. Recently, however, the work of Thorpe and Skeat has been again taken up in this country, and a number of generous appreciations have been made of Old English literature.[1]

The three greatest names of that literature, Aelfric, Wulfstan and Byrhtferth, are those of monks of the revival. Aelfric, the first and greatest, was a monk of the Old Minster and, as he himself tells us, the pupil of Ethelwold. Aelfric's writings have already been mentioned in some detail, and the list need not be again rehearsed.[2] As a theologian he has little constructive or speculative power; like Bede, he did little more than translate relevant passages from the Latin fathers and Church historians, and above all from SS. Augustine and Gregory. As a practical moralist he has more significance; his earnest and reiterated plea for clerical celibacy, free as it is from the note of controversy or rigorism, stands apart from

1 The best account in English of the literature of this period, easily accessible to all, is still the excellent ch. vii of vol. I of the *Cambridge History of English Literature*, by J. S. Westlake.

2 *V. supra*, ch. IV.

anything of its date that appeared abroad. But it is as an educator and a publicist, and above all as a master of his native tongue, that Aelfric is of the first significance. He has been called, and with some justice, "the greatest [English] prose writer...[and] the most distinguished English-writing theologian in his own time, and for five centuries afterwards".[1] He lacked the critical acumen of Bede, nor do his writings transmit the charm of Bede's spirit, but it is certain that had not the language in which he wrote hindered him from influencing the Norman school, as it renders him a closed book to the majority of his countrymen to-day who find no difficulties in Bede's Latin, he would occupy—as indeed he deserves to occupy—a far more prominent place than in fact he fills in the memories of Englishmen. The evidence of manuscripts shows that he continued to be a force up to and indeed after the Conquest, and more than one historian of that Conquest (and the majority of the readers of history) would have done well, in forming a picture of English Church life immediately before 1066, to remember the breadth and quality of the works of Aelfric.

His contemporary Wulfstan, probably a monk of Ely and afterwards bishop of Worcester and archbishop of York, is known only by his homilies and by one in particular which describes the condition of England under the Danish invasions.[2] The third great name is that of Byrhtferth, a monk of Ramsey, Oswald's foundation, and a pupil of the learned Abbo of Fleury. Byrhtferth, though primarily a mathematician, was also a homilist and a man of wide reading; in width of knowledge and scientific temper of mind he is probably the greatest of the English monastic scholars; it is interesting to note that despite his training under Abbo, he shows as great an indebtedness to Bede as do Alfred and Aelfric. Byrhtferth has been singularly neglected by his countrymen. The only substantive works of his hitherto published are the commentaries on four treatises of Bede included in the Cologne 1612 edition of Bede's works, and the life of his great master, Oswald, which criticism of to-day has endeavoured to vindicate for him by stripping it of its secular anonymity.[3]

1 Westlake, art. cit. 127. We may take exception to "five" centuries, for Rolle, Hilton, the author of The Cloud of Unknowing, and Margery Kempe achieved an equal mastery of English prose. Westlake himself wrote on another page (136): "four hundred years elapsed before the vernacular was again employed with the grace and fluency of Aelfric." H. Sweet (An Anglo-Saxon Reader, 9th ed., 61) refers to "that command of the tender and pathetic in which he [Aelfric] excels...[the specimens given] are perfect models of style", and W. P. Ker (English Literature: Medieval, 55) speaks of him as "the great master of prose in all its forms. [He] works on principles that would have been approved by Dryden".

2 The Sermo Lupi ad Anglos quando Dani maxime persecuti sunt eos (dated 1014 in one MS. and 1009 in another) has been printed by Napier in Sammlung englischer Denkmäler, Bd. 4, 1880, by D. Whitelock (1939), and elsewhere. H. Sweet (An Anglo-Saxon Reader, 88) speaks of his "fiery, impassioned, half poetical language, which forms a complete contrast to the calm elegance of Aelfric's classic prose".

3 Stubbs amassed all the then available information concerning Byrhtferth in his intro-duction to the Memorials of St Dunstan, in order to disprove the identification with B. presbyter, the author of the first life of Dunstan. His authorship of the Life of Oswald has been (to my mind) convincingly demonstrated by S. J. Crawford in Speculum Religionis:

Besides these three outstanding names there are others: Wulfstan, precentor of Winchester and disciple of Ethelwold, Aelfric Bata, pupil of his namesake, who continued his dialogue in a somewhat coarser strain,[1] and a succession of nameless and scattered writers who bear striking witness to the diffusion of education and national sentiment in the Old English monasteries and who at divers times and places composed the *Chronicle*, the last monument of the language to be submerged beneath the waters. Great and small, they all have in varying degree the three characteristics of the literary work of the revived monasticism: its beauty and flexibility of form, its poverty of original and ordered thought, and its inspiring aim of reaching beyond the cloister to educate or to stimulate all such Englishmen as had ears to hear.

II

The culture that came into this country with the Norman monasticism was in basic essentials similar to that which it supplanted; that is to say, it was a culture typical of the first half of the Middle Ages, though possessed of greater strength and purity than its predecessors. It was not a culture which made new discoveries either in thought, science or language; rather it was a culture almost entirely literary in content, which aimed at assimilating and handing down the traditional stock of ideas and facts and literary forms that had been current for five centuries. The most typical products of the age, an Eadmer, a Geoffrey of Winchester, an Orderic, were another species of the family that had included Bede, Alcuin and Aelfric. Indeed, in one sense it was a retrogression from the culture of Aelfric and Wulfstan of York, for neither in language nor in scope was it fully national. The Latin of Eadmer, William of Malmesbury and the rest, though fluent and tolerably pure, has none of the idiomatic power and emotional subtlety of Aelfric's prose; it contains no seeds of development and in some degree fetters those who use it. The aim, likewise, of the Anglo-Norman literature was not expansive. It was intended primarily, if not entirely, for circulation among the peers of its authors, that is, in the circle of the monastic houses; it had no missionary or educational direction to those outside. The Anglo-Norman monks consciously regarded themselves as a class apart from the rest of society in a way unknown to their Old English predecessors. The monastic state, in the eyes of Dunstan and his school, was the highest state in society, but it

Essays presented to C. G. Montefiore (Oxford, 1929), 99–111, though Dr Armitage Robinson showed some reserve in the matter (*Byrhtferth and the Life of St Oswald*, in *JTS*, XXXI (1929), 35–42). For Byrhtferth's Manual, composed to assist the secular clergy, *v.* EETS, vol. 177 (1929); for his preface to Bede's *De Temporibus*, *v.* the article by Prof. G. F. Forsey in *Speculum*, IV, October 1928, 505–22.

1 Edited by W. H. Stevenson, *v.s.* p. 488, n. 5.

was a part of society and had a duty to enlighten and purify.[1] Norman and Anglo-Norman monasticism regarded itself rather as a state apart from "the world", with a duty of praise and prayer on behalf of others, but with no direct task of passing on to others what it might itself learn or create.

But if within the limits that have been indicated Anglo-Norman monasticism was a less powerful social influence than its predecessor in the days of flowering had been, and though the culture that it introduced was not wholly new in kind, its intellectual influence was in many ways far more powerful and durable than anything that had gone before. The Norman character and mind, though falling short of the finest type of the Old English alike in the range of its sympathies and in the delicacy of its powers of perception and creation, had a greater constitutional strength and vigour, and it would seem also that a greater proportion of those of Norman blood were capable of benefiting by an educational formation. Consequently, the Norman monastic culture imposed itself with immediate and permanent success everywhere, and if in many places it ousted a spirit more sensitive and artistically creative, it undoubtedly acted as a bracing wind upon the minds of the English in general. Yet it remains a noteworthy fact that almost all the great names of Norman and Anglo-Norman monastic literature are those of men not of pure Norman blood. When we have taken Lanfranc, Anselm, Osbern, Eadmer, William of Malmesbury, Orderic,[2] Symeon of Durham and Ailred of Rievaulx from the account, the quantity of monastic literature of any importance dating from 1050 to 1150 and issuing from Normandy or England is very small.

The *floruit* of the Norman monastic culture may perhaps be said to begin *c.* 1040, when Lanfranc arrived at Bec, and to cease with the deaths of Orderic, Malmesbury, Theobald of Canterbury and their generation from 1145 onwards. Henceforward on the Continent the schools, universities and lay *ateliers* took and retained the lead in almost all literary, intellectual and artistic activities. In England, the period of brilliance began *c.* 1070 and had no limit that is easily recognizable. In a sense, it may be said to have ended with the death of Stephen. Till then, almost all literary and artistic work was in the hands of the black monks; after that, it was shared by religious of other orders, by secular clerks, and by laymen. But the new dialectical and legal learning was slow in making its way into the fabric of English life, and even after the reign of John, when the uni-

1 Cf. the attitude of Aelfric in his *Colloquium* (ed. Thorpe), 30–2: "MAG. Quid dicis tu, Sapiens? Quae ars tibi videtur inter istas artes prior esse? CONSILIARIUS. Dico tibi, mihi videtur Dei servitium inter istas artes primatum tenere...[sed] sive sis sacerdos, sive monachus, seu laicus, seu miles, exerce temet ipsum in hoc: esto quod es, quia magnum damnum et verecundia est homini nolle esse quod est, et quod esse debet." Compare with this the motives of Orderic's father, and his promise to the child (OV, v, 133).

2 William of Malmesbury may have been wholly English; Orderic's mother was English, and he was born and bred as a child in England.

versity of Oxford was firmly established, a few great monasteries such as St Albans retained a national reputation for certain branches of learning and art which cannot be exactly paralleled in France. Nevertheless, the reign of Stephen marks with fair precision the end of the period in which the solidarity of Norman and Anglo-Norman monastic culture was maintained, and was alone in the field.

That culture, which was in all essentials identical in all the monasteries under Norman influence, found its most enthusiastic panegyrists in William of Malmesbury and Ordericus Vitalis, whose statements are corroborated by numberless passages in the chronicles.[1] It was primarily and indeed almost exclusively literary, and its artistic activities were in origin directly connected with the transmission and ornamentation of books.[2] Of the seven traditional branches of the old curriculum, Dialectic, the third member of the *Trivium*, had little place in the monasteries compared with that which it was beginning to hold in the schools and nascent universities, and of the *Quadrivium* only Music was at all generally taught. Such an exclusive attention to literature was only to be expected. A monk led a very stationary life; he could gain little by contact with fresh minds with a different outlook, for in England at least the only men of learning were monks like himself. He could not, like a studious recluse of the modern world, choose his subject and enjoy the riches of some great public or private library; he was, for all practical purposes, limited to the books contained in his own cloister, and these, at least till the twelfth century was well advanced, were comparatively few in number, while the stock of one monastery was as like that of another as at the present day are the stocks of the multiple branches of popular booksellers or circulating libraries. Having learnt to read a few of these books at the feet of one of the elders of the house, his working life was spent in reading more and in handing on to others a similar discipline. An exceptional mind, an Eadmer or a Malmesbury, might learn from his reading of the past to appreciate the significance of the present and seek to record it, or, drawn into public life as an abbot or bishop, might be compelled to counsel or to persuade by letter, but the whole training and tenor of a monk's life in the first fifty years after the Conquest was alien to the atmosphere of change and disputation in which the new thought was being born in the cities of northern Italy and the schools of central France. Anselm had neither predecessor nor successor in the cloisters of Normandy and England.

One of the first houses, perhaps the very first, to show the influence of the new learning was Lanfranc's community of Christ Church. Here more than one of those who were inmates of the monastery before the

---

1 The *loci classici* in Orderic are his eulogy of Bec in II, 244 *seqq.*, and his descriptions of his own life at St Évroul; Malmesbury's are to be found scattered throughout the *Gesta Pontificum*.

2 *Studium litterarum, peritia litteralis, bene litteratus* are phrases constantly recurring in Orderic and Malmesbury.

Conquest showed himself a willing and capable pupil. The oldest was Osbern, who had been a child of the cloister under the old dispensation, had gladly taken part in the revival under Lanfranc, and became in time subprior and precentor.[1] He wrote, with Lanfranc's approval, at least three biographies, all of archbishops of Canterbury: Oda, Dunstan and Aelfheah;[2] though praised by Malmesbury for both his Latin style and his excellence in musical composition,[3] he was castigated as a historian as well by Eadmer his *confrère* as by William, both of whom rewrote the life of Dunstan.

Of greater significance is his younger contemporary Eadmer (*c.* 1055– *c.* 1124). Like Osbern, Eadmer was a boy at Canterbury immediately after, if not before, the Conquest.[4] He seems, also like Osbern, to have become precentor and in later life was celebrated as the close companion and confessor of Anselm, and as archbishop-elect of St Andrews. All that we know of his life, corroborated as it is by his writings, shows him to have been a man of ability, judgment and high character. Like Osbern, he wrote or rewrote a series of lives of English saints—Dunstan, Bregwin, Oswald and Wilfrid—but he had the good fortune to be himself the confidant of a saint no whit inferior to the others, and his life of Anselm is in every way a work of far greater significance, and must always remain the primary authority for the later life and personal character of its subject. The life is, indeed, in a sense a companion to Eadmer's account of his own epoch, the *Historia Novorum* from the Conquest to *c.* 1120; this, like the life of Anselm, is sober and well documented, and William of Malmesbury declared that he could not improve upon it.[5] Eadmer has also a place, if a small one, in the history of theology, as will be seen on a later page.

Besides Canterbury, Westminster and Winchester, one of the most active centres of intellectual life in the fifty years after the Conquest was the cathedral priory of Worcester. Here two streams of learning flowed alongside of each other under the rule of Wulfstan. While the copying of Anglo-Saxon books continued here longer, or at least in greater bulk, than elsewhere,[6] and while as late as 1100 the life of Wulfstan was written in English by his chancellor, Coleman, Wulfstan had nevertheless sent his favourite disciple, Nicholas, afterwards prior, to complete his studies

---

1 Cf. the allusions in his *Vita Dunstani*, *Mem. St Dunstan*, 137–8, 142 and elsewhere.
2 The *Vita Dunstani* is in *Mem. St Dunstan*, 69–161, *PL*, CXXXVII, 413–74 and elsewhere; the *Vita S. Alphegi* in *PL*, CXLIX, 375–94 and elsewhere; the *Vita Odonis* perished in the fire of the Cottonian library in 1731. Other lives of old English saints, composed at this time, are those of Etheldreda, Ivo and Augustine, by Goscelin; and of Adulf, Botulf and John of Beverley, by Fulcard of Thorney.   3 Will. Malmesb., *GR*, 166, 389.
4 Cf. the allusion in *Mem. S. Dunstan*, 229–30.
5 Will. Malmesb., *GP*, 74, 113. For all this a careful reader occasionally catches Malmesbury trying to improve upon Eadmer; accuracy suffers under the process.
6 Cf. W. Keller, *Die litterarischen Bestrebungen von Worcester in Angelsächsischer Zeit*, in *Quellen und Forschungen* (1900), 64.

under Lanfranc, and the first after the Conquest to attempt a history of
the past and continue it in the present were the monks Florence of
Worcester (*ob. c.* 1118) and his continuator, John, who, though themselves of no great originality, served as a basis for future writers as
widely separated as Symeon of Durham, William of Malmesbury and
Ordericus Vitalis.[1]

The first of these three, Symeon of Durham (*c.* 1060–1130), though his
life presents no features of great interest, is of significance as the first of
the reborn northern school. He had been one of the earliest recruits to
join the refounded Durham, and he rose ultimately to be precentor of the
house. Inspired by Bede, he wrote first a history of the church of Durham
and later a general history of England; he continued his chronicle till 1129;
on his death, the work was taken up by two priors of Hexham, Richard
and John, who preserved the sincerity and objective outlook of their predecessor. Why the chronicle passed from Durham cannot be said; certainly
there would seem to have been no lack of literary talent there. In Symeon's
day Turgot, the prior, later bishop of St Andrews, had written a life
of his penitent, the saintly Queen Margaret of Scotland, which must take
a high place among the biographies of the time. Twenty years later
Maurice, known to his contemporaries as a second Bede, was subprior.
Durham long continued to produce literature; Geoffrey of Coldingham
wrote its history at the end of the century; he also composed a life of
Bartholomew, the anchorite of Farne, as another Durham monk of an
earlier day had written an account of the more celebrated Godric of
Finchale,[2] and to the influence of the school of Durham must also be
ascribed not only the chronicles of Hexham, but the historical works of
Ailred and, later, the history of William of Newburgh.

The second of the trio of historians, William of Malmesbury, is unquestionably the greatest figure in the English circle of lettered monks of
the time; he may even claim with justice to be the greatest English medieval
monastic historian after Bede;[3] for though Matthew Paris, a century later,
has in some respects a greater brilliance, it may be questioned whether his
work is either as truly original or as truly critical as that of Malmesbury.
The reputation of the latter has always stood very high. He is the only
historical writer of his country and generation who can be read with
continuous pleasure and with unflagging interest, and this circumstance,
combined with the love of truth which he sincerely professes and displays,

1 For the events of Orderic's life, and the date of composition of the various books of
his history, the invaluable *Notice sur Ordéric Vital* by Léopold Delisle, added to vol. v
(book 13) of Le Prévost's edition, should be consulted, especially pp. xlviii–xlix.

2 The *Libellus de Vita et Miraculis S. Godrici* by Reginald of Durham was excellently
edited for the Surtees Society, vol. xx, in 1845 by J. Stevenson. The editor compiled a
full index, and the volume as a whole is one of the most interesting and valuable of the
hagiographical pieces of the age. *V.* also the good article in *DNB.*

3 He makes this claim for himself. *GR,* II, 518: "Ipse mihi sub ope Christi gratulor,
quod continuam Anglorum historiam ordinaverim post Bedam vel solus vel primus."

has put him in the forefront as an authority. Malmesbury's work is full of individuality. Critical and reserved in his judgments of the distant past, as recent investigation has shown,[1] he has a clear-cut opinion on all the important actors of his own generation and of that which immediately preceded it, and while he cannot bear comparison with Bede, and falls far short in intellectual stature of Anselm, his mind has certain qualities of greatness which distinguish his work from that of all his rivals. In particular, he had a sense of proportion and design rare in those who came after him; his careful division of his matter both topographically into dioceses and biographically into the reigns of kings and bishops was as original as it was successful.

The *Anglo-Saxon Chronicle* had been begun as a national, official compilation, not as the work of monks; it found a home in the monasteries only with the revival under Dunstan.[2] To the last it preserved its interest in national affairs, and the passage written by one (probably a monk of St Augustine's, Canterbury) who had known the Conqueror well, and the later pages from Peterborough describing the miseries of Stephen's reign, are familiar to all. Both these writers deserve a mention in any account of English monastic letters. Whatever be thought of their language in its technical aspect, there can be no two opinions as to their ability to hold the attention and capture the imagination of the reader.[3] Say what we will of the style or truth of these passages, they remain deeper in our memories than any words written by even the greatest of the literary historians. The Peterborough chronicler in particular, with his penchant for the weird and the macabre, and with his deep despondency at the evils of the times, is unique among the writers of his age, living in a kind of twilight between the world of reality and that of folk-lore.

The Latin annals of this period, though invaluable by reason of their notices of new foundations, dedications, constructions, elections and the like, are scarcely to be classed as literature. The gap separating them from the historians and great chroniclers is very wide, and they do little more than provide a record of the fortunes of the houses in which they were composed.

1 In particular J. A. Robinson in his discussion of the *De Antiquitate Ecclesiae Glastoniensis* in *Somerset Historical Essays*.

2 The questions of provenance and interdependence of the various versions are so complicated that any discussion soon assumes the appearance of an essay in higher mathematics. For the present purpose it is sufficient to note that after the Conquest the *Chronicle* was being continued at (Worcester)-Evesham (+ 1079), Christ Church (c. 1100), St Augustine's (till 1121), and Peterborough (intermittently till 1154).

3 The indiscriminate praise of the final pages of the *Chronicle*, culminating in Freeman's reference (*Norman Conquest*, v, 284) to "all the matchless strength of our ancient tongue", received a cold douche from the Oxford editors of the work, who considered that they reached "the lowest stage of decline at which written literature is possible" (*Chronicle*, ed. Earle and Plummer, II, 306–7). Professor Chambers (*The Continuity of English Prose*, lxxxv–vi) in his turn reacts against this: "With this [*sc.* the Peterborough annal] the noble record of historical writing in English prose ends, and ends nobly." Of the *Chronicle* as a whole H. Sweet (*An Anglo-Saxon Reader*, 98) wrote that it was "one of the noblest pieces of prose in any literature, clear, simple and manly in style, calm and dignified in tone".

It will have been seen that practically the whole of the output of monastic learning between the Conquest and the reign of Stephen was devoted to hagiography and history. In both these departments of literature work of high merit was produced, but it was almost wholly esoteric in aim. Nothing, so far as can be gathered, was written for the benefit of those outside the walls of the monasteries, and English monastic literature has no direct connection with the contemporary theological and controversial literature of the Continent. Save for a reply to the *Apologia* of Bernard, issuing, as seems all but certain, from a Cluniac house and probably the work of a French monk,[1] England took no share in the debates of which the abbot of Clairvaux was the centre, and the English monasteries, so far as is known, contributed no page to the voluminous pamphlet warfare between Empire and Papacy. The monastic culture was the culture of an order, shared by and directly benefiting that order alone.

Reserving the development of the liturgy and chant for special mention, reference may be made here to a literary accomplishment typical of the rebirth of letters in central France. That rebirth, especially in the schools of Orleans, Tours and Chartres, manifested itself in an acquaintance with the great literary masters of the past, and a skill in imitating their compositions, such as was not again attained before the Italian renaissance in the days of Petrarch. Among the accomplishments of these schools was the writing of Latin verse, after the classical models, and the fashion spread to the Norman monasteries and was carried into England. The most celebrated exponent in this country was Godfrey of Winchester, who imitated Martial, and whose verses are graceful and smooth, though without the wit of his original.[2] The writing of verse clearly formed a part of the ordinary curriculum in the monastic schools and was very general; interesting evidence of this is given by the copies of memorial verses attached to the "death-bills" of eminent persons which were circulated through the religious houses in order to obtain prayers, and which gradually became booklets of some size. Two of these, dating from 1113 and 1122, contain between them verses from no less than fifteen black monk houses; some bear the annotation that they were composed by a young monk or a boy; there are besides copies of Latin verses from three abbeys of nuns.[3] It may be doubted whether the monasteries of England, in all their subsequent history after 1150, ever attained to such a fluency in classical composition. Skill, however, in verse composition by no means implies a poetic gift, and none of the surviving English work reaches the level of merit of a Hildebert of Tours or a Sigebert of Gembloux; only if the so-

1 Cf. Dom André Wilmart, *Une riposte de l'ancien monachisme*, in *RB*, XLVI, July 1934.
2 Godfrey's poems have been printed by T. Wright, *Anglo-Latin Satirical Poets and Epigrammatists of the Twelfth Century* (RS, 59, 2 vols.).
3 L. Delisle, *Rouleaux des Morts*.

called Rosy Sequence, the *Dulcis Jesu memoria*, is ever identified with certainty as the work of an English monk will the presence of a true poet be granted.

III

Between 1150 and 1170 there is a remarkable absence of monastic literature of any importance. The years, besides being a time of stress, were also a time of change. The literary culture of the monasteries had waned, and the new learning of law, dialectic and theology was attracting all the most alert minds to the nascent universities of Italy and France. From 1150 onwards an ever-increasing number of monks, and those the intellectual *élite*, owed their training to the schools, not to the cloister; they could no longer feel, therefore, as Orderic and Malmesbury had felt, that when they had mastered the contents of a good monastic library they were possessed of all the learning they needed. Naturally, it is impossible to compile even the roughest statistics of the change in education, but it is significant that from *c.* 1180 onwards an abbot is often a master, and he rarely stood alone among his monks in this distinction.[1] Bury was not, like St Albans, Christ Church or Winchester, a house with a reputation for intellectual pursuits, but already in 1183 it counted at least five *magistri*, including two in medicine.[2] Thirty years later the number had not increased; it still stood at five;[3] but probably St Albans could have numbered more.

It is in these two abbeys, Bury and St Albans, that we can trace the infiltration of the new learning of the schools most clearly. The process at St Albans seems to have begun under Abbot Simon (1167–83), himself a child of the cloister, especially during his later years of office when Warin was prior. Warin, with his family group of graduates from Salerno, has already figured in an earlier chapter; besides references to him in the chronicle of the house, a group of letters exists which shows that a close connection was maintained at this time between St Albans and the schools of Paris. In one of these, Abbot Simon sends a messenger to the celebrated Richard of St Victor asking for permission to copy all the works of Hugh of St Victor not yet in the abbey library.[4] At about the same time Prior

1 Besides instances given in the text, the following occur: (1174) Richard, monk of Christ Church, prior of Dover and archbishop of Canterbury, "de Normannia natus, artium liberalium scholas egressus, etc." (Gervase, II, 397); (1183) magister Nicholas of Wallingford, monk of St Albans and abbot elect of Malmesbury (*Jocelini Cronica*, 228); (1198) magister Anselmus, monk of Reading and elect of Pershore (*Ann. Winton.*, *s.a.*); (1199) magister Willemus Pica elect of Glastonbury (*ibid. s.a.*), etc.

2 *Jocelini Cronica*, 223. There may well have been others, for these five occur among the twelve electors.

3 That is, only five appear with the title *magister* in the division lists of summer, 1214, given in *Mem. S. Edmund's, de Electione Hugonis abbatis*, II, 75.

4 *Opera Richardi S. Victoris, PL*, CXCVI, 1228 (*ep.* 8): "Opuscula magistri Hugonis, quae in partibus nostris undecunque quaesita reperire potuimus, summo studio et exactissima

Warin was in correspondence with Richard, first with a letter of recommendation to Paris on behalf of his brother Matthew, then in grateful recognition of the kindness Matthew is encountering, and finally begging Richard to extend to his nephew Warin the same indulgence that he had shown to his brother.[1] This was the same Warin who had studied canon law at St Albans, his uncle buying the books. When these letters were written the abbey of St Victor, the solitary example of a religious house in the full life of the schools, was nearing the end of its period of theological influence,[2] and there is, it would seem, no trace of any other English abbey sending its monks thither, still less of any direct connection with the schools of Paris, but within a year or two of the writing of these letters—perhaps at that very moment—John de Celle, the successor of Warin in the abbacy of St Albans (1195–1214), was studying with distinction at Paris, where he became a master,[3] and the monk Nicholas was in controversy with the eminent Pierre de Celle, archbishop-elect of Chartres, on the subject of the Immaculate Conception. John de Celle, we are told, retained as abbot the studious habits of his early life, and the influence of himself and Warin over a period of thirty years, besides setting St Albans in a place apart among the abbeys of England, doubtless did much to prepare for the historical and artistic achievement of St Albans in the days of Matthew Paris.

In interesting contrast is the record of Bury St Edmunds. In early years after the Conquest it had been ruled by a series of foreign abbots of distinction, but from 1138 onwards a more national and even provincial spirit seems to have prevailed.[4] The Bury of Jocelin, so far as we can see it, was almost wholly absorbed in its own affairs and in the practical administration of its vast properties. The new learning of the schools was bound to enter; there were, as has been remarked, at least five *magistri* in 1183; but it was not welcomed with enthusiasm by all, and the house was clearly divided in its appreciation. In the vivid fragments of conversation recorded by Jocelin in connection with the election of 1183, while some were insistent that the future abbot should be a man of learning, such as were present in sufficient numbers in the house, others made sarcastic references to philosophers and clerks, and begged to be delivered from

diligentia...collegimus, et ex eis plurima in volumina nonnulla redegimus, etc." All this group of letters must date from before March 1173, when Richard died. They escaped the notice of the historian of St Albans, L. F. Rushbrook Williams.

1 *PL*, CXCVI, 1230 (*ep.* 10; the letters are in no order); *ibid.* 1228 (*ep.* 7): "Quia fratris mei M[atthaei] qui in partibus vestris amore scientiae peregrinatur, tam singulari gratia... curastis, etc."; *ibid.* 1227 (*ep.* 6).
2 "The famous monastery of St Victor had lost its reputation as a centre of learning [*c.* 1180]" (F. M. Powicke, *Stephen Langton*, 27).
3 *GASA*, I, 217: "Hic in juventute scolarum Parisiensium frequentator assiduus ad electorum consortium magistrorum meruit attingere." This must have been *c.* 1170.
4 Cf. *Jocelini Cronica*, 218–19: "Dixit quidam:...'Abbas Ordingus [1138–56, typical of the "good old times"] homo illiteratus fuit.'"

such inflictions.[1] Jocelin himself, he tells us, being young and foolish, said that for his part he would brook no one as abbot who was not skilled in dialectic.[2] In the event, Samson, the elect, was something of a compromise, for while he had taken degrees at Paris and taught school at Bury, had written an account of the miracles of St Edmund and composed elegiacs for the paintings in the choir,[3] and could express (in a moment of depression) his predilection for the office of librarian, all his preferences were on the balance for a life of activity, and the world of men and things was more to him than the world of ideas. His entertainment of the masters of Oxford no doubt gave him more satisfaction than any study would have done.[4] When, c. 1200, there was a question of appointing a prior at Bury, a similar division of opinion manifested itself,[5] and the phrase "much learning maketh him mad" appears to have acquired a cant significance;[6] even at St Albans, the unpractical habits of the studious Abbot John did not escape criticism.[7]

Something will be said later of Christ Church in connection with its special study of canon law. At Evesham, soon after 1190, arrived Thomas de Marleberge with a large collection of books covering all departments of learning in addition to civil and canon law. Marleberge had been a pupil of Langton in Paris, with Poore as his comrade, and had afterwards himself taught at Oxford.[8] His companion in Rome, Adam de Sortes, was likewise a master and ex-teacher, though in the arts alone,[9] and Evesham housed besides a celebrated physician. These numerous, if scattered, allusions are, when taken in the aggregate, most significant. They show clearly that in the last quarter of the twelfth century many, if not almost all, of the greater black monk houses contained a number of men who had passed through a university course in arts and often also in law, medicine and theology, and who in some cases had themselves taught at a university or school. In the nature of things these men would be the leaders in the

1 *Jocelini Cronica*, 219: "Respondit alter: '...absit ut statua muta erigatur in ecclesia sancti Aedmundi, ubi multi literati viri et industrii esse dinoscuntur.'" *Ibid.* "Dixit quidam de quodam: '...licet non sit tam perfectus philosophus sicut quidam alii.'...Respondit alter: 'A bonis clericis libera nos Domine.'"

2 *Jocelini Cronica*, 221: "Et ego quidem, tunc temporis juvenis, sapiebam ut juvenis, loquebar ut juvenis, et dixi quod non consentirem alicui ut fieret abbas, nisi sciret aliquid de dialectica, etc."

3 *Jocelini Cronica*, 247–8: "Magister in artibus, scilicet dialecticae et medicinae." *Ibid.* 217: "Samsone...historias picturae ordinante, et versus elegiacos dictante." Cf. also 241.

4 *Jocelini Cronica*, 245: "Raro aliquem propter solam scientiam literarum approbavit, nisi haberet scientiam rerum saecularium"; cf. *ibid.* 295.

5 *Jocelini Cronica*, 322–4: "Dixit aliquis:...'valde timendum est ne clerici literati habitum religionis de cetero dedignentur suscipere penes nos.'"

6 *Jocelini Cronica*, 219, 326.

7 *GASA*, I, 217: "Hic, more scholarium, rei familiaris ignarus, etc."

8 *Chron. Evesh.* 267: "Rexit scholas ante monachatum apud Oxoniam et Exoniam." Cf. also *ibid.* 147, 232. Marleberge, whose library shows him to have been interested in Arts and Scripture, doubtless studied theology under Langton, who did not teach canon law. Possibly this last was a private study.

9 *Chron. Evesh.* 147: "Magister Adam in literatura apprime eruditus qui antequam esset monachus rexerat scholas artium liberalium per multos annos."

communities they had joined, and thus the intellectual tone would be set by those who had not been reared in the traditional education of the cloister.

This gradual disappearance of the purely monastic culture was hastened by the tendency, already noted as general among the black monk houses, to lose the sense of corporate solidarity as every monastery became immersed exclusively in its own problems and controversies. At the same time the whilom monopoly of education had been lost; the new orders, monastic and canonical, had been nourished on the same literature, while the diffusion of education made it possible for secular clerks and men of every kind to profit by and continue the work of a Malmesbury. It is therefore no surprise to find that the great national historians of the latter half of the century are for the most part seculars, and that the chief exception is not a black monk, but a black canon.

IV

But if the monks could no longer feel that they were the depositaries of learning who had a task of enlightening contemporaries and instructing posterity, the spread and sophistication of education caused the rise of a large number of chroniclers who recorded the fortunes of their houses in times of controversy, or simply wrote from intense personal interest in what they had seen. During the fifty years after 1170 almost all the monastic chronicles become more elaborate and comprehensive, and writers of talent appear even in small and obscure houses, though more especially among the white monks and canons. In consequence, it would seem that by c. 1200 almost every monastery of any size possessed a chronicle.

Some of these remained mere annals, to which the official annalist added from year to year whatever events appeared to him to be of interest, without regard to literary form. Of this class the annals of Burton, Tewkesbury, Worcester and Winchester are good examples. All are patchworks, not only of the additions of numerous hands, but of borrowings from other chroniclers and writers, and all become noticeably fuller during the reigns of Richard and John, when the numerous political and ecclesiastical controversies, culminating in the Interdict and Magna Carta, supplied topics of general interest. These annals are almost invariably objective records, intended for all to read, and therefore colourless in style. A notable exception, however, is provided by the Winchester annals, which from the Conquest onwards contain a number of entries in the distinctive style of Richard of Devizes, who may be assumed to have become the official chronicler of St Swithun's.[1]

A second group is of the chronicles proper, continuous narratives

---

1 The identification was tentatively made by the editor (Dr Luard) of the Winchester annals for the Rolls Series, and has been widely accepted. The style is, indeed, all but unmistakable.

detailing the history of the house with judgments on events and personalities; in other words, literary productions. Some of these were clearly
inspired by a desire to perpetuate the memory of a great struggle. An
excellent example of this is the principal Battle chronicle, the work of an
anonymous writer (perhaps the prior of the narrative) who recast existing
material and added a more elaborate narrative of his own times. He was
especially concerned to record the great exemption case of his abbey, and
gives a clear and exceedingly interesting *procès verbal* of the pleadings in
that and other suits, as well as long characterizations of the two great
abbots he had known well. The chronicle is dignified in tone, and is
clearly the measured work of a trained mind, intended to be read by all,
and for that very reason supplying few of those glimpses of daily life and
passing sentiment that are given, intentionally or otherwise, by more
irresponsible writers.[1] Very similar in scope, though very different in
tone, is the chronicle of Evesham, so often alluded to in these pages.
Thomas de Marleberge, like the Battle chronicler, is writing officially for
his house, and while his principal aim is to retail the controversies of the
early years of the thirteenth century, he narrates with great care the past
history of the abbey, quoting, as seems certain, from earlier documents of
some fullness.[2] But though writing officially, it is for domestic eyes alone
that Marleberge caters; clearly the story of Evesham's sorrows was not
meant for the great public; he wrote that future generations might know
from what they had been rescued, and that they might be warned by the
knowledge. Although for the general reader the appeal of the Evesham
chronicle is lessened by the technical details of many pages and the un-
savoury quality of others, it deserves to rank, alike in the vividness of its
narrative and for the light thrown in every direction on contemporary life
and on more than one eminent man, as second only, if indeed second, to
the chronicle of Jocelin. Yet a third chronicle of an official, semi-apologetic
type is that of Gervase of Canterbury. Gervase, indeed, is in many ways more
of a historian than a chronicler, but his Canterbury chronicle, though less
personal and more annalistic than those of Battle and Evesham, is throughout
controlled by the *arrière-pensée* of the rights of his church and reaches a
climax in a full history of the quarrel with Baldwin and Hubert Walter.
With his work may well be linked the *Epistolae Cantuarienses*, a great collection of more than five hundred letters carefully assembled and preserved
by his monastic family as a permanent memorial of the great controversy.

1 The Battle chronicle was (perhaps unfortunately) among the first of such documents
to be edited in the last century before the inception of the Rolls Series. The edition (by
J. S. Brewer for the short-lived *Anglia Christiana Society*, 1846) has numerous palpable
errors, and the rare notes are often inadequate and sometimes incorrect. A fully critical
edition is needed; cf. H. W. C. Davis in *EHR*, XXIX (1914), 426–34, *The Chronicle of
Battle Abbey*.

2 On the early portion of the Evesham Chronicle *v.* R. R. Darlington, *Aethelwig of
Evesham*, in *EHR*, XLVIII (1933), 1–22, 177–98. The writer, so it seems to me, was in all
probability the prior, Dominic; *v. infra*, Appendix VIII.

A third group of chronicles is made up of those written from a still more personal point of view, no longer mere annals, or the official or corporate account of controversies, but the story of the years of a monastery's life as seen through the eyes of a private individual, who is not an office-holder of any kind, who finds many occasions to criticize the administration and indeed writes as a kind of representative of the general public, the *pauperes claustrati*. The Abingdon chronicle shows this tendency, as does also the Peterborough chronicle of Hugo Candidus and his continuators; it is equally the prevailing tone of a series of St Albans writers previous to Matthew Paris; they close the account of each abbot's reign with a summary of his good deeds and misdeeds, and air a number of grievances. Such compositions can scarcely have been left lying in the cloister as a book of reference for all and sundry; the reader cannot help feeling that they must have been kept private within the circle of the writer and his friends. It is from such records as these that we gain the clearest picture of everyday life in the monasteries of the time, though perhaps many readers of to-day are apt to forget that the deepest life of the writer, and still more the deepest life of his more spiritual contemporaries, find little expression in these pages.

In a place by himself among these chroniclers of private life stands the familiar figure of Jocelin of Brakelond. Accidental as his celebrity may be, there can be no question that he is the most vivacious and spontaneous of all monastic writers of this, or indeed of any, period of the Middle Ages. No other possesses in the same degree a *naïveté* combined with such powers of observation and memory and such a singular talent for preserving, out of an ocean of froth, just those opinions and judgments which are common to the varying types of character throughout the ages,[1] and no other has presented to his readers a single character of outstanding importance with the clarity shown by Jocelin in portraying Samson.[2] Yet the chronicler's ability must not blind us to the limits of his range. Even if we suppose, perhaps with more indulgence than circumstances warrant, that the fatuous and malicious criticisms, or the futile attempts at self-assertion, are only recorded as part of the whole and that the strong and energetic figure of Samson is a silent but real counterpoise, in some such way as an Othello or an Imogen is silent evidence that Shakespeare valued generosity and purity above all else, yet Samson remains a man of

---

1 Jocelin has in this respect a certain kinship with the fifteenth idyll of Theocritus, with the conversations of Bottom and his friends, with the talk of the company in the parlour of the *Rainbow*, and with that of the worthies of Mellstock, save that in all these cases the writer is also a critic; it is not here, but in the strokes which reveal Samson, that Jocelin approaches to the skill of a Cavendish or a Boswell.

2 There is, however, some evidence to show that a number of contemporaries were extremely skilful in reconstructing conversations and isolating the most significant points. Passages in the *Battle Chronicle* (esp. pp. 89–103), in the *Evesham Chronicle* (pp. 145–68) and the anonymous *Electio Hugonis*, a Bury document, but certainly not written by Jocelin, are little if at all inferior.

very moderate stature, with not a trace of the spiritual greatness of an Anselm or an Ailred.[1] The real significance of Jocelin is rather that he is the first example, at least in this country, of a man of no great attainments, of a man in the street, who feels compelled to record all that he has seen, and is able to do so.

Two black monks of this period may claim to have been historians as well as chroniclers. Though differing in their gifts they are both typical of the lettered class of monks of their age. Of the two, Gervase of Canterbury is the more substantial. Besides his various chronicles of Canterbury he compiled a *Gesta Regum* which has considerable value for its account of contemporary events. Gervase, though a diligent compiler who had a mass of material in the archives at his disposal, rarely displays any sympathy wider than an *esprit de corps*; he often passes by without notice events of great importance, and his style is colourless. Very different is Richard of Devizes, the monk of Winchester who wrote a very full account of the earlier part of the reign of Richard I. His narrative flows easily and is continually enlivened by personal expressions of opinion; though extremely partisan, a comparison with other authorities shows him to be in the main reliable on points of fact. Richard's is not a prepossessing mind; his brilliance has a metallic hardness, and in his recklessness of judgment and lack of moral gravity he has considerable kinship with Gerald of Wales, but of his literary knowledge and mordant wit there can be no question. It is not to him and Gervase, however, that we look for the most mature account of the events of the reigns of Richard and John, but to the annals, now grown full, of Barnwell, Burton, Meaux and elsewhere, and to the histories, composed outside the cloister, of Ralph of Diceto and the so-called Benedict of Peterborough.[2]

---

[1] Historians have, *malgré eux*, been somewhat dazzled by Carlyle's *bravura*, and have generally regarded Samson as the greatest monk of his century. Such a view is wholly misleading, as has been noted on a previous page.

[2] Since the above chapter was written an important paper by R. W. Hunt, *English Learning in the Late Twelfth Century*, has appeared in the *Transactions of the Royal Historical Society*, 4th series, XIX (1936), 19–42. The conclusions of the author are in agreement with those expressed in the text, with some interesting amplifications and full documentation; in particular, he notes the work of Senatus, prior of Worcester 1189–96. *V.* also M. R. James, *Two ancient English Scholars, St Aldhelm and William of Malmesbury* (1931).

CHAPTER XXIX

THE INTELLECTUAL ACTIVITIES OF THE BLACK MONKS: II

THEOLOGY, CANON LAW, MEDICINE, MONASTIC LIBRARIES

I

THEOLOGY

The part played by Aelfric and others in doctrinal instruction has already been alluded to more than once. Meritorious as was this work, it was in character evangelical rather than theological; the more learned monks of the revival aimed at handing on in a simplified form to their countrymen as much as they were capable of receiving of the doctrinal legacy of the ancient civilization; they made no attempt to develop or to discuss dogmas, and no controversies forced them into being apologists. Although on two points, the nature of the Real Presence in the Eucharist and the celibacy of the clergy, Aelfric put forward views which are still of interest to historians of dogma and discipline, in neither case did he intend to modify or to add to the traditional teaching as he found it in the sources before him, which were, in fact, the same few treatises of Augustine, Gregory and others which had for four centuries formed the principal food of all minds in western Europe. And in the event, the coming of the Normans with their new culture put an end to the influence of Aelfric's writings once and for all.

In like manner, though for very different reasons, the theological works of Lanfranc and Anselm need find no mention in a history of English thought. Lanfranc's one serious excursion into the field of theology, his controversy with Berengar, was over long before he came to England, and although Anselm's latest and most characteristic works, the *Cur Deus Homo* and the *Proslogion*, were composed when he was archbishop of Canterbury and probably first read by monks of Christ Church either in his company or at home,[1] there is no evidence that his theological teaching had the slightest influence upon his contemporaries in England outside the narrow circle of his intimates at Canterbury, some of whom were doubtless Normans by birth and training. Nor did the monks of England take any part in the slow development by which theological writing, which had been for so many centuries in the West largely a formless rehearsing

---

1 Thus the *Cur Deus Homo* was begun in England "in answer to many requests" (*PL*, CLVIII, 361) and *Ep.* iv, 104 is a long letter on the Trinity to monks of St Albans.

of familiar passages of Scripture together with meditative comment, was gradually brought under the discipline of Abelard's *Sic et Non* and became a matter for set disputation and for ordered display in such works as those of Peter Lombard and the other early Masters of Paris.

But there was one important topic in which, as it were by accident, the monks of England found their interests and sympathies engaged. Beginning as a movement of liturgy and devotion, it came in the twelfth century to be matter for theological discussion and during the whole period remained an interest peculiarly English. This was the question of the orthodoxy of the doctrine of the Immaculate Conception of the Blessed Virgin, which it fell to the monks of England to defend as traditional and expose as consonant with the Catholic faith.

The early history of this dogma cannot be set out here.[1] Familiar at least implicitly and in principle to Greek theological thought for several centuries, it had before the tenth century become the object of liturgical veneration both in the East and in the Greek settlements of southern Italy, and above all in the monasteries, in the form of a feast of the Conception of Mary on 8 or 9 December. In the Western Church both the feast and the teaching behind it were unfamiliar; the minds of all, cut off from connection with Eastern theology past and present, had been familiar with the peculiar bent given to all speculation on Grace and Original Sin by the Pelagian heresy and by the strongly personal idiom in which Augustine had in reaction expressed the traditional teaching on these and all kindred doctrines. Nevertheless, the evidence of pre-Conquest liturgical texts shows that at several monasteries, mainly of southern England, and above all at the two Canterbury houses, the two Winchester Minsters and Worcester, the feast of the Conception was being celebrated from *c.* 1030 onwards.[2] When attention was first drawn to this fact some fifty years ago by Edmund Bishop, he himself inclined to the view that the institution of the feast must be referred to Ethelwold; subsequent writers, while supporting this hypothesis, endeavoured to trace its introduction into England to Irish agencies.[3] More recent study has shown that neither of these opinions can be maintained, and it is now certain, as

1 It may be studied in the very full and scholarly article by X. le Bachelet and M. Jugie, *Immaculée Conception*, in the *DTC*, VII, i, 845–1218.

2 Cf. calendars of the Old and New Minsters, Brit. Mus. Cott. MSS. Vitellius E xviii and Titus D xxvii; a pontifical of Christ Church, Harl. MS. 2892; a martyrology of St Augustine's, and a calendar of Worcester in Corpus Christi College, Cambridge, MS. 391; cf. arts. of E. Bishop and A. W. Burridge in following note. Probably other instances could and will be discovered; no doubt Abbot Aethelsig introduced it from Canterbury at Ramsey—hence the legend.

3 E. Bishop, *On the Origins of the Feast of the Conception of the Blessed Virgin Mary*, in *DR*, April 1886, reprinted, with important additions, in *Liturgica Historica*, 238–59. Between the first and final appearances of this article, much important work was done by Fr Herbert Thurston, S.J., and others; all this is summarized, with a full treatment of Eadmer and Osbert of Clare, in the excellent article *L'Immaculée Conception dans la théologie de l'Angleterre médiévale* by Fr A. W. Burridge in *Revue d'Histoire Ecclésiastique*, XXXII (July 1936), 570–97.

Bishop himself demonstrated in one of his last writings, that the liturgical celebration was introduced to England from the Greek monasteries of central Italy in the first decades of the eleventh century. As has been seen on a previous page, there was about the year 1000 a great northward surge of a revived monasticism drawing its inspiration from the East; the Basilian or semi-Basilian monasteries of Grotta Ferrata and of SS. Alexius and Sabas in Rome were founded, and numerous Greek monks and hermits found their way to the cities of the Rhône valley, where some of them became bishops, and even to England.[1] During the same period, there were a number of solemn pilgrimages to Rome on the part of English celebrities between 1020 and 1030, in particular that of Cnut in 1027. To one of these, perhaps resulting in the emigration to England of Greek monks, the origin of the feast in England would seem to have been due; so far as can be seen it was restricted to five or six churches, all monastic, which were thus the first in the purely Latin Church, so far as the records show, to observe the feast of the Conception.

So matters stood till after the Conquest. When Lanfranc in his Statutes reorganized the calendar for his monks, the feast of the Conception disappeared along with those of the Old English saints; unlike these last, it depended upon a doctrinal support and found no advocates capable of pleading, and neither Lanfranc nor Anselm had any familiarity either with the theology or the liturgical celebration of the feast. The memory of its celebration remained, however, and in such matters the memories of a religious family are extremely tenacious, as has been shown times beyond number throughout the ages; ritual observances return, though flung out with a pitchfork. In this case the impulse came apparently once more from abroad; all early references connect the reintroduction of the feast into England with the name of Anselm, nephew of the archbishop and abbot of Bury from 1121 onwards.[2] Anselm had previously been abbot of S. Sabas in Rome, and it is impossible not to see in this circumstance the origin of his zeal in the matter. Within a few years of his arrival in England the institution or revival of the feast of the Conception is signalized at a number of monasteries: thus at Bury itself by Anselm, at St Albans by Abbot Geoffrey (1119–46), at Gloucester by Abbot William (1113–31), at Winchcombe in 1126 and at Worcester c. 1125.[3] At two other abbeys

1 V.s. p. 193 and Sackur, Die Cluniacenser, 1, 332–50.

2 Cf. esp. ep. 7 in Letters of Osbert of Clare (ed. E. W. Williamson), where Osbert writes to Anselm: "diligentia sollicitudinis vestre per diversa mundi spacia multos ad amorem...Marie ferventer accendit...et in multis locis celebratur eius vestra sedulitate festa conceptio, quam antiquitus apud patres veteres celebrare non consuevit christiana religio." This edition has a valuable biographical sketch of Osbert by J. Armitage Robinson, reprinted from the Church Quarterly Review, LXVIII, 136 (July 1909), 336–56. Anselm's institution of the feast at Bury is noted in Brit. Mus. Harl. MS. 1005, quoted by Bishop in his article p. 247, note 1.

3 For Bury v. charter no. 112 in Feudal Documents...of Bury (ed. D. C. Douglas), p. 113, with the editor's comments, introd. cxxxv–cxxxvii; for St Albans v. GASA, 1, 93; for Gloucester, Hist. Gloc. 1, 15; for Winchcombe, annals in Cott. MS. Tiberius E iv (quoted by

its celebration has particular features of interest. At Westminster it was introduced by the English prior Osbert of Clare *c.* 1127–8 during an interregnum, and was forcibly resisted by Roger of Salisbury and Bernard of St David's, themselves acting presumably during the vacancy of the see of London.[1] Osbert wrote for support to Abbot Anselm, and adduced as other partisans of the devotion Gilbert "the Universal", recently consecrated to London after being a canon of Lyons, and Hugh, the Cluniac abbot of Reading, who had recently instituted the feast in that newly founded royal abbey, with the warm support of Henry I.[2] Osbert begged Anselm to confer with these on the subject.[3] No record of any discussion has survived, but it is significant that less than two years later, at a legatine council held at London under John of Crema in 1129, the celebration of the feast was solemnly confirmed.[4]

Meanwhile, the question had been lifted from the devotional to the theological plane by Eadmer of Canterbury, who in the last years of his life wrote a treatise maintaining the sinless conception of the Mother of God which passed for centuries as the work of Anselm of Canterbury.[5] Though no precise occasion or date can be assigned to the work, it is natural to connect this also with the advent of Anselm the younger, whom Eadmer knew well; he was also acquainted with Rome, central Italy and Lyons, which he had visited in company with the exiled archbishop. The treatise is a work of solid theology, and must have been based on Greek materials known to the author either in translation or by word of mouth; the principal argument is drawn from Mary's privileged position as living temple of the Word of God and sharer in the work of the Incarnation and Redemption; it is, in fact, the first, as it remained for two centuries the most valuable, Western exposition of the doctrine, and it received throughout the later Middle Ages full recognition as such in its quotation by theologians and its reception into liturgical Offices. Eadmer died, in all probability, soon after its composition; within a few years, *c.* 1128, Osbert of Clare himself wrote a *Sermo de Conceptione* based principally upon Eadmer's treatise, but far less solid, and written throughout with a reserve due to the opposition which he knew to be entertained in certain

Bishop, p. 247, note 4); for Worcester, *Chron. Jo. Wig.* (ed. Weaver), *s.a.* 1129 and *Annales Monastici*, IV, 377 (but neither of these is completely cogent; cf. rather Osbert, *ep.* 13).

1 Osbert, *ep.* 7.

2 Osbert, *ep.* 7 (ed. Williamson), p. 67: "Vir vitae venerabilis, domnus Hugo abbas Radingensis, qui hanc festivitatem prece etiam regis Henrici solemniter celebrat." Hugh himself, however, apparently did not teach the Immaculate Conception (*v. PL*, CXCII, 1152).

3 Osbert, *ep.* 7: "Hortor ut cum eis [*sc.* Gilbert of London and Hugh of Reading] de hac eadem re sermonem instituatis."

4 *Chron. Jo. Wig.* [MS. G from Gloucester], *s.a.* 1129: "Inde in concilio apud Lundoniam congregato in presentia eiusdem regis Henrici ex auctoritate apostolica confirmata est festivitas Conceptionis Sancte Dei genitricis Mariae."

5 *Tractatus de conceptione S. Mariae*, in *PL*, CLIX, 300 *seqq*. For a better edition *v. Eadmeri monachi Cantuariensis tractatus de conceptione sanctae Mariae*, ed. H. Thurston and Th. Slater (Freiburg-im-Breisgau, 1904).

quarters.[1] Thus the revival of the feast, as its first introduction, together with the first attempts at a theological justification of the belief on which it rested, were the work of English black monks. Authorized by the Council of London, the liturgical celebration spread slowly in the country, and from England was carried, perhaps by Hugh of Reading, soon (1129) archbishop of Rouen, to Normandy, where it became common, and at about the same time it began to attract notice at Lyons.

The attack of St Bernard in 1140 in his letter to the canons of Lyons opens the period in the history of the dogma during which its true theological origins were largely lost from sight, and the silence of Western tradition added to unsatisfactory explanations as to the nature and manner of transmission of original sin seemed to some of the greatest teachers of the schools to be fatal to its admission, if enunciated without reserves. Before the time of the great scholastics, however, there is yet one more incident which gives an interesting glimpse of theological activity in the monastery of St Albans and shows the fidelity of the English monks to their tradition. This is the correspondence between Nicholas, a monk of the house, and Peter de Celle, one of the best known black monk writers and spiritual guides of his day in France: The friend of Bernard and Thomas Becket, the friend also and patron of John of Salisbury, originally a monk of St Martin des Champs, later abbot of Moutier-la-Celle (1147–62) and of St Remi at Rheims (1162–81), and finally for a short while bishop of Chartres (1181–3), he was a man of the type of Peter the Venerable, welcoming monastic reform while remaining a friend of the old order.[2]

The first letter of the short series that has survived, written some time after the murder of Becket, refers to a previous exchange of views on the question of the Immaculate Conception of Mary. Peter, who had thought Nicholas to be dead, rejoices to hear that he is still alive, and wishes to know whether his supposed death has had the effect which actual death would have had in converting him from his errors. If Nicholas has written anything since their old controversy, let him send a copy to his friend.[3] The reply of Nicholas has not been preserved, but it is clear that it took the form of a reiteration of his previous defence of the doctrine. Peter, who elsewhere in the letters refers to the English characteristic of hard drinking, replied by attributing the vain imaginings of Nicholas to the mists and waters of his native isle. He himself, with French solidity of mind, prefers to follow St Bernard. The feast of the Conception is novel, and has not the sanction of Roman authority. He grants that the Blessed Virgin never felt the motions of concupiscence, but holds that before the Incarnation she felt, though she did not succumb to, human weakness and the difficulty of well-doing. If she had had no original sin there would

1 For Osbert's *Sermo de Conceptione v.* A. W. Burridge's article and references.
2 Peter's works are in *PL*, ccii.
3 Petri Cellensis *ep.* ii, 169 (*PL*, ccii, 611–13).

have been no credit or merit to her in vanquishing these.[1] Nicholas replied by asserting that Bernard, saint though he was, had erred on this point; it was the one stain on his white habit. As for himself, he cannot understand what Peter means by feeling sin while remaining sinless.[2] Peter's reply, written when he was already bishop-elect of Chartres in 1181, is chiefly a long exhortation to Nicholas to check his praise of the Virgin Mother on this side idolatry, and to remain in the beaten path of the saints and sound tradition. He quotes the familiar verse of Genesis (iii, 15) to prove his original point; had Mary not felt the power of sin she could have had no contest with the Evil One; she felt it, but did not succumb. He ends with a renewed appeal for sobriety and for a patient refusal to go in advance of the pronouncements of Rome; many of the phrases of this letter anticipate to an extraordinary degree the views and expressions of more recent "inopportunists".[3] As will have been seen, the correspondence does not reach a high level either in tone or thought; of the two, Nicholas shows the greater subtlety and depth, though neither touches at all deeply upon the true foundations of the dogma or upon the speculative problems connected with it that exercised Aquinas and Scotus; Nicholas is moved chiefly by loyalty to national tradition and Peter by respect for Bernard. Nevertheless, the letter of Nicholas is not a mere devotional outpouring, and the episode, especially when set alongside of the correspondence between Warin of St Albans and Richard of St Victor, shows that there was at least one English abbey in 1170–80 which kept abreast of foreign speculation and which could provide an apologist to engage on equal terms with one of the leaders of the opinion of his age.

England, as is well known, remained true to her tradition. It was at Oxford, at the end of our period, that Alexander Nequam endeavoured in vain to protest against the celebration of the feast of the Conception, and, a century later, it was at Oxford that the "rarest-veinèd unraveller" taught and wrote,

Who fired France for Mary without spot.

1 Petri Cellensis *ep.* II, 171 (*PL*, CCII, 614): "Certe expertus sum somniatores plus esse Anglicos quam Gallos...insula enim est circumfusa aqua...non sic aquatica Gallia"; *ibid.* 619: "Credo siquidem quod saeva libidinis incentiva...numquam senserit [B.V.M.], vel ad modicum: cetera vero impedimenta humanae fragilitatis...ante divinam conceptionem [i.e. at Annunciation] sentire potuit...tolle pugnam, tolles et victoriam."

2 [Petri Cellensis] *ep.* II, 172 (*PL*, CCII, 625): "Dicis, eam sine peccato sensisse peccatum. Fateor me nescire quid velis dicere." Peter presumably meant that the Blessed Virgin, though immune from concupiscence, could feel the difficulty of performing *bona ardua*, and that this resulted from original sin. Nicholas means, though he fails to put it clearly, that immunity from concupiscence would imply (the greater implying the less) immunity from all the *sequelae* of original sin.

3 Petri Cellensis *ep.* 173 (*PL*, CCII, 630): "Sensit peccatum sine peccato. Sensit equidem non ad laesionem sed ad probationem...sensit extrinsecus, non intrinsecus." It is not easy to see how, on Peter's showing, the temptation of the Blessed Virgin differed from that of Christ. *Ibid.* 632: "Versa et reversa in quolibet statu venerationis et glorificationis, tecum vado, tecum sentio. Si vero extra communis monetae formam vis fabricare aliam, quam non approbaverit sedes Petri...pedem sisto."

II

SCRIPTURE AND CANON LAW

Before the development of the method of disputation, both oral and written, in the first half of the twelfth century, the teaching of theology was indistinguishable from that of Scripture, or, rather, there was no theological teaching as such, but only the study and exegesis of the inspired books. Here, as elsewhere before the renaissance of the eleventh and twelfth centuries, the teaching was strictly traditional, and as there was as yet no one *textus receptus* of the Latin Vulgate, the various great cultural divisions of Europe were represented by various typical texts, such as the Irish, the Alcuinian and the Imperial, and the introduction of one of these into a country implied far more than a merely academic substitution of one Latin text for another closely related to it. The revival under Dunstan, which in so many ways brought England into touch with all that was best abroad, introduced into this country the Vulgate text of the Continental schools, as used at Fleury. Manuscripts of the gospels that survive include one taken by Oswald himself to York and another given by Ethelwold to Thorney and many others written in the southern monasteries and based upon a common ancestor at Winchester. The text of these provides a curiously close parallel to the history of the styles of illumination; it is chiefly Continental, but with readings from the archaic Irish and from the English school of Alcuin.[1]

Lanfranc, who had devoted himself seriously to the study of Scripture at Bec, undertook also, with characteristic practical thoroughness, the castigation of the text of the New Testament with a view of bringing the English text into line with that traditional abroad; he inspired a number of his disciples, including Gilbert Crispin, to undertake the same work,[2] and when he came to England took steps to ensure that all the principal monastic churches were supplied with Bibles, for liturgical and educational purposes, which might provide a text agreeing with that in current use in Normandy and France and Italy. In this field, as in so many others, he left an abiding mark. Recent investigation has shown that "the Lanfrankian text...remained for about a hundred years the standard text in the larger English monasteries", and by this means the readers in those houses became familiar with the version of the Vulgate which gave a basis to the traditional exegesis of the Church and to the new learning of the Glosses.[3]

---

1 This paragraph and that which follows make use of the hypotheses of H. H. Glunz, *History of the Vulgate in England.*

2 *Vita Lanfranci, auct. Milone Crispin, PL,* CL, 55: "Et etiam multa de his quibus utimur nocte et die in servitio Ecclesiae ad unguem emendavit, et hoc non tantum per se, sed etiam per discipulos suos fecit. Qua de causa...merito illum Latinitas· cum honore et amore veneratur magistrum."

3 Glunz, *History of the Vulgate in England,* 169, 195–6.

Great as was Lanfranc's influence in giving England the standard Western text of the Vulgate, it was still greater in introducing the canon law that was proving itself at once the firmest support and the most efficient instrument of the reformed papacy. Careful investigation in the recent past has shown that he brought into England, almost certainly from Bec, a collection of the Decretals and a copy of the Councils which he joined into one volume and caused to be copied and circulated to the cathedrals of England, several of which, and those the most important, were monastic.[1] The impetus thus first given by Lanfranc was greatly increased by the third monk of Bec to become archbishop of Canterbury, Theobald, who had devoted himself to the study of ecclesiastical law in Normandy. In England, he established what was almost a school of canon law among his clerks at Canterbury, and although the majority of these were not monks, some of the members of the *familia* of Christ Church were among the archbishop's officials, and the library of the cathedral monastery gradually became well stocked with legal texts which were to prove of use in the many controversies in which the monks became engaged. With Theobald the direct influence of the legal traditions of Bec came to an end; the study of law was by now a highly technical affair and had been brought to perfection in the Italian universities; but for various reasons and from different sources the monastic libraries continued to be enriched with the works of the great commentators until the end of the twelfth century and beyond, and the monks had in their midst some of the ablest canonists of the country.[2]

III

MEDICINE

During the early Middle Ages the monasteries were the only seats of what medical learning had survived in western Europe from the ancient world. In England, however, more than in southern France and Italy, almost all traces of the Greco-Roman medicine had disappeared, and its place was taken by a mixture of traditional practice, herbal knowledge and popular magic. Neither Cluny nor Fleury was interested in medical science, and there is no evidence that in this department the revival under Dunstan brought new life into this country. The Norman monasticism, however, had inherited the traditions of William of Dijon, who, himself an Italian, had established first at his monastery in Dijon and later in many of his other foundations something like a serious study of physic deriving from the south Italian tradition which had already begun to break into new life

---

1 For all this *v*. Z. N. Brooke, *England and the Papacy*, esp. ch. v, Lanfranc's Collection. Dr Brooke's conclusions are accepted by Fournier et Le Bras, *Histoire des Collections Canoniques en Occident*, II, 227–30.

2 *V*. infra, p. 524.

at Salerno.[1] Consequently, from the first arrival of Norman monks in England until the end of our period there is a succession of monk-physicians, at first trained within the cloister, but later themselves graduates of Salerno or other medical universities.

The first of these was Baldwin, originally a monk of St Denis at Paris, who came to the court of Edward the Confessor as the king's physician.[2] Rewarded with the abbacy of Bury he continued his good offices with the Conqueror and was recognized as the leading consultant of the realm.[3] He was Lanfranc's physician, and the archbishop sent him other patients;[4] among those who consulted him was Arfast, bishop of Thetford, who had been seriously injured in the eye by the branch of a tree.[5] Baldwin died in 1098; his place at the head of the faculty was almost immediately taken by another abbot, the great Faricius of Abingdon (1100–17). Faricius was an Italian from Arezzo, and it is quite possible that he had studied at Salerno; in any case his reputation was very great. He became the trusted physician of both Henry I and his queen Matilda, whom he assisted in her first confinement, and the numerous royal charters of gifts and confirmations in his favour, often attested by his colleague Grimbald, presumably a secular clerk or layman, are evidence of his assiduity in attendance upon the king and of the success of his ministrations.[6] In addition to his activities at court, Faricius also acted as consultant to a number of the great families of England, and the Abingdon cartulary contains a number of charters of gifts bestowed in recompense for professional services, in particular from the families of de Vere, fitz Haymon and Crispin; indeed, when there was talk of his succeeding to Canterbury, his practice of medicine was one of the disabilities alleged against him by those who opposed his candidature.[7]

Faricius was not the only well-known monastic physician of his time. Hugh, a monk of St Swithun's at Winchester and afterwards abbot of Chertsey (1107–28), was a distinguished practitioner, and William of Malmesbury tells of a monk of his abbey, named Gregory, possibly a

1 *V. supra*, p. 84 and Sackur, *Die Cluniacenser*, II, 351 *seqq.*

2 *Heremanni Miracula*, in *Mem. S. Edmund's*, I, 56: "Medecina peritus, ex hoc quoque a rege Anglorum cum multa diligentia habitus." For other references, *v.* Douglas, *Feudal Documents…Bury*, introd. lxi–lxiii.

3 *Heremanni Miracula*, 58: "Placens regi [Willelmo] officio consuetae medecinae."

4 *Lanfranci Epp.* (ed. Giles), nos, 20, 21.

5 *Heremanni Miracula*, 63–4.

6 *Chron. Abingd.* II, 44–5: "Probatissimus officio medicus, adeo ut ejus solius antidotum confectionibus rex ipse se crederet saepe medendum"; *ibid.* 50: "Regia eam [*sc.* Matildam] primo contigit prole gravari. Mandatur mox medicis ei curam impendere…quorum primus abbas Faritius, secundus Grimbaldus, uterque gentis et linguae unius." That Faricius so often worked with another Italian strengthens the probability that he had studied at Salerno.

7 *Chron. Abingd.* II, 55: "Godefridus de Ver…abbatem medendi se gratia ad Faritium contulit"; *ibid.* 96: "Roberto filio Haimonis multa medelae beneficia abbas Faritius frequenter impenderat"; *ibid.* 97: "Milo Crispin, pro servitio quod abbas Faritius ei in sua infirmitate impenderat, etc." For the hostility to him on the part of Roger of Salisbury and Robert of Lincoln, cf. *ibid.* 287.

pupil of Faricius, who had been cellarer there; he also was a noted consultant.[1] Later in the century occurs the family group of distinguished physicians at St Albans, all trained at Salerno, at whose head was Warin, sometime prior and later abbot (1183–95). Warin's successor, John, was likewise a skilled physician, and had among his monks at least one other trained in medicine, by name William, later prior of Worcester.[2] Indeed, it would seem probable that a number of the greater monasteries counted a physician among their members; then as now a celebrated consultant could command a great price, and we hear of at least two such at the end of the twelfth century who materially assisted their community. Walter, almoner of Bury c. 1190, constructed the almonry from fees received, and Thomas of Northwick, a monk of Evesham and a physician with a wide reputation, assisted in building the tower of the abbey church c. 1200.[3] The lucrative nature of the profession, and the contact with the world that its practice implied, caused it to be banned to monks by conciliar legislation, but the prohibition, at least as regards England, was inoperative; circumstances combined to make the great monasteries almost the only places in the kingdom where medical books, traditions of treatment, and constant need for a physician's skill were present in combination, and even if those with a reputation could have resisted the desire for fame or gain, it would have been difficult to resist the claims of those in real need of healing. But though the monasteries, and especially the black monk monasteries, housed the ablest physicians all through the century and no doubt established for themselves a fairly efficient tradition of clinical treatment, it cannot be claimed that they did anything to forward the study of medical science for Europe in general. In so far as this can be said to have been accomplished by any teaching body in the twelfth century, it was the work of such universities as Salerno and Montpellier.

IV

THE SCRIPTORIUM

Throughout the early Middle Ages, as is well known, the copying of manuscripts was the fundamental claustral employment of the black monks; that is to say, it was the one regular work which all were capable of per-

---

1 For Hugh v. *Hist. York*, II, 143–4: "Hugo Certesiensis abbas et medicus." For *Gregorius probatissimus medicus*, v. Will. Malmesb., *GP*, 438.

2 *GASA*, I, 194–6: "Hic [Garinus] cum fratre suo Magistro Matthaeo...in physica apud Salernum eleganter atque efficaciter erudito." Four Salernitans became monks of St Albans. Abbot John was a Parisian; *GASA*, I, 217: "In Physica censeri potuit Galenus"; *ibid.* 246: "Experientissimus in arte medecinae erat." For William, *magister* and *physicus*, v. *GASA*, I, 246.

3 For Walter v. *Jocelini Cronica*, 297: "Frater noster Walterus medicus...multum apposuit quod arte medicinali adquisivit." Samson, also, was a skilled physician (*ibid.* 248). For Thomas v. *Chron. Evesh.* 108: "Per...bonum monachum, magistrum videlicet Thomam de Northuuic, qui per sapientiam suam et maxime physicam qua pollebat gratiam totius patriae sibi comparaverat, turrim ecclesiae ereximus."

forming, and which all did in fact perform unless or until they were transferred to some other form of activity. The boys of the cloister, and at a later period the novices, were instructed in all the technical details of the preparation of ink and parchment, and trained to follow with exactitude the particular form of script common at the time, and in due course were given a fixed task of copying to carry through.

The proportion of those actually engaged on this work varied from period to period. In the first decades of the revival under Dunstan, and again during the first decades after the Norman plantation, when the monasteries were devoted to a very intense intellectual effort, and when this and the ever-growing number of monks created a lively demand for books of every kind, the writing of manuscripts must have occupied the time and energies of a very large fraction of the total monastic population. When, on the other hand, numbers dwindled, or when, as in the later twelfth century, administrative duties absorbed so much of the energies of the monks, the task of copying books no doubt fell solely upon the young monks and a few incapable or not desirous of other employment.

The straightforward hack-work of writing was, however, only one of the departments of the scriptorium. Above it was the more careful writing of Bibles and service-books and the picking out of initial and capital letters in gold or colours; above this again, and the province of those with gifts purely artistic, was the painting and illumination of designs and miniatures; a corresponding occupation of those with exceptional literary talent was the composition and transcription of original work, or the compilation of a chronicle. At the head of all was the precentor, for in origin the chief business of writing had been concerned with books for the choir and altar; it was his duty to assign the work to be done and to provide the necessaries with which to do it, though it is natural to suppose that the senior monks pursued lines of their own, and had under them small groups of the younger.

In epochs of expansion the need for the multiplication of books was very great, and especially of service-books for the Office, Chant and Mass, and of Bibles for use in the choir and refectory; however solidly bound, these would often need renewing if in constant use. There was, besides, a need for the commonest text-books of instruction for the children, and when, after the Conquest, all transactions were recorded by charter and almost all official letters were both carefully written and copied, the routine work of this kind, and the compilation of cartularies and registers, implied a steady output of manuscript volumes. All the evidence goes to show that the diffusion of certain types of book at different periods was very rapid and widespread; thus Bibles and Gospels containing the Continental text and based on a Winchester tradition, and all written within a few years of the entry of the monks into the Old and New Minsters, are known to have been soon in the possession of many of the newly founded monasteries.[1] Under Lanfranc, Bibles[2] and texts of canon law were broadcast, and a little later there was great activity in the writing of large and sumptuously illuminated Bibles; later still, shortly after the death of Becket, and due in part to his influence and that of his biographer, the monk of Christ Church, Herbert of Bosham, the scholastic text of the Scriptures, together with the Glosses of Peter the Lombard and of the school of Anselm of Laon, was diffused throughout the monastic body.[3] The researches of specialists have already shown how often the impulse to a particular method or pursuit came from a single centre, and how often books of the same family can be shown to derive from a common ancestor and from a single scriptorium or school of illumination, and without question further investigation will identify more and more of such centres of intellectual life.

Where the demand for books was great it was sometimes necessary to add the work of paid scribes to that of the monks. Paul of St Albans, faced with the necessity of building up a collection of books for a community of English monks unable to write, or at least unable to write script that would satisfy a Norman, employed paid labour;[4] thirty years later Faricius of Abingdon (1100–17), who was responsible for a great increase in the numbers of his abbey, imported scribes for the service-books, while apparently reserving for the monks the transcription of theological and medical works.[5] Later, perhaps owing to the numerous other occupations which drew the monks off from the work, almost every great abbey had one or more permanent writers with a fixed corrody;[6] it is possible that these executed much of the purely routine and secretarial writing of the house.

The training in writing demanded of the learner an exact conformity to the style of hand current at the time; all individuality was excluded, so much so, indeed, that at the period when the culture of western Europe was most homogeneous during the first half of the twelfth century, not only the personal, institutional and regional individuality of the scribe disappeared, but even traces of national influence distinguishing England and France are very rare, and the differences of hand between Cîteaux and Durham are often so small as to be hard to detect.

1 H. H. Glunz, *History of the Vulgate in England*, 140, notes the presence of gospels derived from a common Winchester ancestor at St Augustine's, Bury, and possibly Christ Church and Ely.

2 E.g. the "Gundulf Bible" at Rochester and the "Carilef Bible" (Durham MS. A ii 4) at Durham. *V.* Glunz, *History of the Vulgate in England*, 181–2, 191.

3 Glunz, *History of the Vulgate in England*, 218–22.   4 *GASA*, I, 57–8.

5 *Chron. Abingd.* II, 289: "Instituit scriptores praeter claustrales, qui missalia, etc.... scribebant." It is possible that they also wrote the books of which a list follows, but the passage is not clear.

6 E.g. at Glastonbury in 1189: "Precentor debet habere scriptorem unum", and £1 *per annum* (*Liber Henrici de Soliaco*, 8); at Evesham *c.* 1203 the precentor provided ink, pigments and binding materials for the monks who were writing or illuminating, whereas the prior gave parchment and money to the hired scribes (*Chron. Evesh.* 208–10).

At the revival under Dunstan the formal Carolingian minuscule came into the monasteries of England, and gradually displaced the pointed English hand. The latter was retained for the native language till the Conquest, though it became firmer and more square under the influence of the foreign script which was used for all liturgical and Latin writing. With the Conquest the entry of the Continental minuscule was complete; in the early days a special variety of this, radiating from Canterbury, was common in the monasteries. Perhaps Lombardic in origin and brought north by Lanfranc, it certainly came to England from Bec under the influence of the archbishop; it has been called the "prickly" style on account of the many sharp and elongated points on the letters, and is usually found together with a peculiar shade of colour in the decoration.[1] In time, however, all such peculiarities tended to disappear, and the typical style of the twelfth century was evolved in France and England. This, which was largely the product of the scriptoria of the black monks, is probably the most exact and beautiful form of writing that has ever existed as common property to be used for all purposes.[2] The scribes throughout north-western Europe produced work of almost incredible regularity and perfect legibility, in which contractions were few and clearly indicated and every letter was formed separately. The writing was never suffered to deteriorate, whatever the subject-matter, and charters and cartularies of the time are as beautifully and clearly written as service-books or Malmesbury's autograph of his own work, so much so that the reader takes the excellence of the calligraphy for granted much as he would the clearness of modern print, and is only reminded of the quality of the work when he turns to a page added to the same volume in a hand of the fourteenth or fifteenth century. In England especially this style attained a perfection unrivalled in other countries, and the work of the great monastic scriptoria supplies almost all the surviving examples. As the century wore on, the absolute uniformity tended to disappear; together with a general tendency to a smaller writing, and with the beginnings of a "Gothic" appearance, minute peculiarities of the individual schools appear, and in the thirteenth century it becomes possible to attribute a book to Canterbury or St Albans from considerations of calligraphy alone.

1 Cf. M. R. James, *The Ancient Libraries of Canterbury and Dover*, introd. xxx: "I am unable to doubt that this remarkable school of writing is directly due to the influence of Lanfranc...the Lanfrancian script...lasted through a large part of the twelfth century. The books in which it is employed would, if gathered together, form no bad library in themselves." A reproduction of this script is given by Sir J. E. Sandys, *History of Classical Scholarship*, I, 523.

2 Such was the considered opinion of Sir E. M. Thompson in *Encyclopaedia Britannica* (11 ed.), art. *Palaeography*: "This style...for absolute beauty of writing is unsurpassed", and in the *Companion to Latin Studies* (ed. 3, 1921), §§ 1163–4, he remarks: "Perfect symmetry of letters, marvellous uniformity in structure...unerring accuracy...are all present. In no country was a more graceful hand written in the twelfth century than in England." As regards accuracy and clarity there can be no two opinions; aesthetically, some may prefer the earlier Anglo-Celtic or contemporary Lombardic script.

The production of books included their binding. This at first was elaborate only in the case of the books for the church, the most precious of which were encased in ornamental bindings, enriched with metals and gems, which were the work of artist craftsmen. Later, binding in thick parchment or vellum, or in boards covered with leather, became general for all books.

The work of writing was normally done in the north walk of the cloister: the walk, that is, that lay nearest to the church. If it happened, as at Christ Church and elsewhere, that the church lay to the south of the cloister garth, the walk of the cloister against the building was still used as the workplace of the monks, though the north aspect must have made it both cold and dark. References to the cold, and to the impossibility of working in winter, are not wanting; in pre-Conquest days, as has been seen, work was done in the room where there was a fire, and it is difficult to suppose that this practice was abandoned so long as the cloisters had no glass. At St Albans there is mention of a special room built as a scriptorium, and such may have been the case elsewhere.[1] Later, when the windows were glazed and wooden carols were provided, a walk with a southern aspect, in the lee of a great church, would not often have been intolerably cold; the first mention of carols is in the thirteenth century,[2] but they may have existed towards the end of the twelfth.

V

THE MONASTIC LIBRARIES AND THEIR CONTENTS

The contents of the monastic libraries of England in the Middle Ages have formed the subject of so many monographs during the last half-century that the materials for a synthetic study are probably now in print in sufficient quantity. No such study has, however, as yet appeared, and the mass of literature is too great, and too full of problems demanding detailed antiquarian and literary knowledge, to permit of anything of the kind being undertaken here; the reader must have recourse to the work, laborious and meticulously accurate but never inhumane, of that lamented scholar and friend of scholars who has put all historians of the Middle Ages under such a heavy debt to himself and who has left in so many paths and byways of English letters the memory of his genial presence.[3]

1 *GASA*, i, 57–8.
2 Viz. at Westminster *c.* 1260–70; cf. J. W. Clark, *The Care of Books*, 98.
3 The indispensable guide to the multitudinous and scattered writings of Dr M. R. James is the bibliography: *Elenchus Scriptorum Montacutii Rhodes James*, compiled by A. F. Scholfield (Cambridge, privately printed, 1935; this has been reprinted as part of *A Memoir of Montague Rhodes James*, by S. G. Lubbock, 1939). Failing this, students must consult the catalogue of the British Museum, or of the London Library. A fairly complete list to date (1911) is given by E. A. Savage in Appendix D to his *Old English Libraries*, a book of which the permanent value is chiefly to be found in Appendices B (list of classical authors found in medieval catalogues) and C (list of medieval collections of books), both of which

Few of the most ancient monastic houses preserved their original deposit of books to hand on to the revived monasticism of Dunstan. During the first decades after the mission of Augustine, and again in the days of Theodore, Adrian and Benet Biscop, books of every kind, including even a certain number of Greek codices, had found their way to England, and a stream had also flowed from Scotland to Northumbria and from Ireland to Glastonbury and Malmesbury, while the native scribes, both in Kent and in Northumbria, had added many to the treasures of the monasteries. Of all this, much had been lost in the invasions, or by fire, or by neglect in deserted or secularized sites; only Glastonbury and the two monasteries of Canterbury succeeded in preserving a great part of their libraries for future ages.

In the early days of the revival of monastic life there was once more a steady influx from abroad, this time chiefly from the monasteries of central France, and again the English monks copied books in great numbers, both the new importations and the original compositions, both Latin and English, of Aelfric, Byrhtferth, the homilists and the chroniclers. Before the Conquest, however, no library was really large or comprehensive in its contents; western Europe had not yet become a single cultural province within which ideas and books could circulate freely. The real impetus to the formation of libraries came from the early Norman abbots, who, besides causing books to be copied, imported them in large quantities and often bequeathed considerable personal collections to their houses. At St Albans, to which Abbot Paul gave twenty-eight "fine volumes",[1] at Evesham and at Abingdon we can see the process at work;[2] at Malmesbury Abbot Godfrey laid the foundations of a notable collection, of which William of Malmesbury soon had charge;[3] Lanfranc brought many books to Canterbury, and William of St Carilef gave more than fifty to Durham, the titles of which have fortunately survived.[4] No doubt the collections were still small, but too much emphasis has sometimes been laid on the passage in Lanfranc's Statutes where he lays down that at the beginning of Lent, in accordance with the prescription of the Rule of St Benedict, the brethren shall be given each a book from the collection possessed by the house, which shall be laid out on a carpet in the chapter room. On such an

contain full and accurate references. The principal works of Dr James dealing directly and solely with monastic libraries are: *On the Abbey of St Edmund at Bury*. I. *The Library* (Cambridge Archaeological Society, XXVIII, 1895), *The Ancient Libraries of Canterbury and Dover* [i.e. Christ Church, St Augustine's, and Dover Priory], *Lists of MSS. formerly in Peterborough Abbey Library*, *The MSS. of Westminster Abbey*, and *The Library of the Cathedral Church of Norwich*. His little book, *The Wanderings and Homes of Manuscripts*, is a marvel of condensed and illuminating information. For dates, etc., of these books *v*. Bibliography.

1 *GASA*, I, 58.
2 *Chron. Evesh*. 97: "[Walterus] Libros multos fecit"; *Chron. Abingd*. II, 289.
3 Will. Malmesb., *GP*, 431–2. An interesting passage.
4 *Dunelmensis Ecclesiae Cathedralis Catalogi librorum* (Surtees Soc. VII (1838), 117–18). For a twelfth-century list of 366 volumes *v. ibid*. 1–10. An elaborate description of the Durham MSS. by R. A. B. Mynors, with exquisite reproductions, has recently (1939) appeared (*v*. Bibliography).

occasion it would normally be a question of religious books for private reading; the service-books and Bibles would be excluded, together with all works of classical literature, history and the sciences;[1] moreover, those distributed the previous year are expressly ruled out.

Throughout the century the growth of the libraries was steady, and save for the frequent fires which devastated the monastic buildings, especially before the massive Norman constructions were complete, and which in some cases, such as that of Christ Church in 1067, we know to have caused the destruction of books and muniments, the manuscripts already on the shelves had no enemies. During the early twelfth century the gifts recorded are mainly those of church books; later the donations reflect the tastes and pursuits of the donors. Glastonbury received more than fifty books from Henry of Winchester c. 1150;[2] St Albans had a succession of literary abbots who supplied books of theology, canon law and medicine; Benedict of Christ Church took with him to Peterborough in 1177 a valuable private collection including classics and theology, but particularly rich in canon law;[3] twenty years later Thomas de Marleberge, the protagonist of the exemption suit, took with him to Evesham a small library of books, chiefly of civil and canon law and medicine, but including also a number of other books of all kinds.[4]

Thus between 1150 and 1200 most of the more important black monk houses found themselves in possession of libraries of a considerable size, and patient research during the last fifty years has provided many of the documents necessary for reconstructing their catalogues in whole or in part.[5] It need scarcely be said that very few monastic collections of books have survived *in situ*; two have, fortunately, at least in part: those of the cathedral monasteries of Durham and Worcester, which at the Dissolution became part of the respective chapter libraries, contributing each several hundred manuscripts; and by a series of chances a large section of the library of the Austin canons of New Lanthony passed into the possession of the archbishops of Canterbury at Lambeth. A number of others are represented by large or small collections of manuscripts that have remained together and have been given or bequeathed to the British Museum or one of the University or College libraries of Oxford and Cambridge; among such survivals are books from St Albans, Norwich, Bury and the

---

1 *Lanfranci Statuta*, c. 1, § 3, p. 216: "Custos librorum debet habere congregatos libros in capitulo super tapetum extensum, etc." Prof. C. H. Haskins, in the excellent chapter on libraries in his *Renaissance of the Twelfth Century*, seems to stress the passage unnecessarily. I have written "normally" above; for exceptions *v.* Dom Wilmart in *Revue Mabillon*, XI (1921), 92.

2 Adam of Domerham, II, 317–18, gives the list.

3 Robert Swapham, 98–9; the list is given in full by M. R. James, *Lists of MSS. formerly in Peterborough Abbey Library*, no. ii.   4 *Chron. Evesh.* 267–9.

5 A complete list of medieval library catalogues in print is given by T. Gottlieb, *Über mittelalterliche Bibliotheken* (Leipzig, 1890). Those dating from 1050 to 1250 and published since the appearance of Gottlieb's work are listed as an appendix to an article *The Ancient Classics in the Medieval Libraries* in *Speculum*, V (1930), 3–20, by J. S. Beddie.

two Canterbury houses. Others still, though in great part lost or scattered, have contributed isolated volumes to this or that public or private collection, and the provenance of the books has been discovered by the late Provost of Eton or other antiquaries. A few important libraries, and among them those of Glastonbury and Malmesbury, have disappeared almost entirely.

Failing the survival of the books themselves, the contents of the libraries can be ascertained from catalogues, where these have been preserved. Among the best and fullest of these for the twelfth and early thirteenth centuries are those of Christ Church, Canterbury, Bury and Peterborough;[1] these and more besides have been published in full; in the case of other houses (e.g. Glastonbury and St Augustine's) the earlier books must be extracted from the later catalogues. Finally, the chronicles contain a number of lists of books added to the libraries by abbots or given by individuals, thus giving precious contemporary evidence not only of the presence of a book, but of the very moment when it first made its entry into the library of a monastery and began to exert an influence there.

One of the largest, if not the largest, of the libraries was that of Christ Church; it has been computed that as early as c. 1170 there were at least six hundred volumes in the house, including in the reckoning the several copies that existed of all the books in greatest demand. That this figure is a conservative rather than an exaggerated estimate may be gathered from the fact that Lanthony at the same period or a little later possessed the surprisingly large total of nearly five hundred volumes.[2] Durham in the same century had almost four hundred books; Rochester c. 1202 about three hundred; Reading two hundred and thirty. The eighty volumes known to have been at Peterborough c. 1177 and the seventy at Whitby c. 1180 cannot be taken as the total of the collections of those abbeys, for even such a small priory as Leominster had more than a hundred books at the beginning of the thirteenth century, and the undistinguished Cistercian house of Flaxley in Dean almost a hundred.

In all the larger catalogues of the twelfth century, besides the liturgical books and the recognized text-books of grammar, rhetoric, music, history, medicine and the rest, all the major Latin fathers figure, above all, Gregory, Augustine and Jerome, together with some of the Greeks translated into Latin; besides these, the chief classical poets and prose writers of Rome are present in surprisingly large numbers; only Lucretius, Catullus and Tacitus are absent from the list of authors of the first and second rank. Horace, Virgil and Ovid are universal, and usually in several copies; of

---

1 For these, v. the works of Dr M. R. James mentioned above, p. 523 (footnote).
2 There are 223 titles in the fragment of the Christ Church catalogue of c. 1170 printed by M. R. James, *The Ancient Libraries of Canterbury and Dover*, 7–12, but the editor remarks, introd. xxxv: "We cannot allow less than from 600 to 700 volumes as the total extent of the collection." References to the sources for the figures which follow in the text will be found collected by E. A. Savage, *Old English Libraries*, 264–6; many of them have already been quoted in these pages.

the rest, writers of the Silver Age are more common than those of the Augustan or Republican period; Lucan, Persius and Seneca are ubiquitous, and Martial and Statius far from rare. It was no doubt constant reading of the authors of the early Empire, almost always brilliant, hard and sententious, and often bitter and satirical, that gave something of a similar tone to so many of the monastic and other writers of the epoch of Henry II; the undertones and overtones of Virgil, and the exquisite felicity of the *Odes* of Horace may have been appreciated at Chartres half a century before, but in England in the twelfth century Lucan and Virgil are put on a level, and the *Epistles* and *Satires* of Horace are more familiar matter for quotation than the *Odes*.[1]

From the evidence of surviving books, from catalogues and from isolated references, it is often possible to trace the penetration of a new influence into the monastic life of the country. With Lanfranc, as has been seen, came the earliest collections of the canons, and the modern text of the Vulgate. Bernard and Anselm reached Glastonbury in their most characteristic works, *de amando Deo* and *Cur Deus Homo*, at least as early as *c.* 1130–50 among the gifts of Henry of Winchester, and the same two went, in other works, with Abbot Benedict from Christ Church to Peterborough in 1177;[2] Hugh of St Victor was introduced to Glastonbury by Bishop Henry, and on a previous page we have seen how carefully Abbot Warin of St Albans completed his works *c.* 1180. Peter the Lombard and Gratian both figure on Abbot Benedict's list, and the Glosses of the Lombard began to spread from Paris *c.* 1170; the commentaries of the great Italian canonists were at Canterbury before *c.* 1175 and at St Albans *c.* 1170–80; they reached Peterborough with Abbot Benedict and Evesham *c.* 1190 with Marleberge. These examples have been taken almost at random; they might be multiplied indefinitely, and indeed it is only by careful and detailed research of this character that the spread of spiritual, intellectual and scientific movements can be ascertained with any precision.

The white monks, in their origin and for the first generations, eschewed on principle the collecting and reading of books simply for the sake of knowledge. Their libraries consisted for long solely of books of a theological, scriptural or spiritual kind, and as late as 1187 the general chapter at Cîteaux decreed that texts of the canons or Gratian, if owned by the monastery, should be kept in a private place separate from the common collection of books.[3] Their exclusiveness gradually broke down here as in

1 Cf. C. H. Haskins, *The Renaissance of the Twelfth Century*; J. S. Beddie, *The Ancient Classics in the Medieval Libraries* (*supra*, p. 524, n. 5); E. K. Rand, *The Classics in the Thirteenth Century* in *Speculum*, IV (1929), 249–69; also Appendix D in *Old English Libraries*, by E. A. Savage (*v.s.* p. 522, n. 3). William of Malmesbury, I have noticed, is very familiar with Lucan.

2 For references, *v. supra*, p. 524, nn. 2–3. Abbot Benedict's library included the *Meditationes Anselmi* and the *Sermones, de Incarnatione Verbi* and *Epistola ad Eugenium* of Bernard; he also possessed a Terence, a complete Martial and the letters and other works of Seneca.

3 *Statuta Capitulorum Generalium* (ed. J. M. Canivez), I, 108 (1188), no. 7: "Corpus Canonum et Decreta Gratiani apud eos qui habuerint secretius custodiantur...in communi

other matters, and the influence of such men as Ailred on the one hand, and Baldwin and Alexander of Ford,[1] and Ralph of Coggeshall on the other, must have tended to increase the variety of their reading. In any case, by the beginning of the thirteenth century their libraries in England, though probably smaller, were of the same general character as those of the black monks.[2]

VI

The original resting-place of the books of an ecclesiastical establishment in the early Middle Ages was a cupboard in the church or sacristy, and probably the majority of the books of the English monasteries were thus kept before the Conquest, for the small and irregular monastic buildings would have given less security for the more precious service-books and muniments.[3] The cupboard in the church survived as the home for some at least of the more valuable manuscripts at St Albans until the end of the twelfth century,[4] though a scriptorium with aumbries for books had been built long before; it was this original connection with the church that gave to the precentor charge of the books of the monastery.

When, under the Norman influence, spacious and solid cloisters were constructed, and these became the normal working-place of readers and writers, the books in general use came to be stored in presses in the north walk of the cloister, standing against the south wall of the church. This remained for centuries, and in some houses until the Dissolution, the sole or chief place for the storage of books, and such special rooms as were built for their reception in individual monasteries date without exception from a later period than the reign of John.

The Cistercians, in contrast to the black monks, made architectural provision for their books from very early days. This may seem surprising in view of the little importance they attached to study, but it was in fact part of their desire for rigid uniformity of practice. The accommodation thus provided was at first extremely modest in size, being no more than a cupboard or recess in the wall between the chapter house and the door into the church. Later, a small book room was provided by cutting off a portion of the sacristy, which lay regularly between the south transept of the church and the chapter house. Later still, a special and larger book room was incorporated as part of the plan between the chapter house and the church.

armario non resideant, propter varios qui inde possunt provenire errores." The Cistercians from the earliest days had a special room for writing; cf. *Statuta* of 1134, n. lxxxv (Canivez, I, 32).

1 Alexander, a *protégé* of Hubert Walter, is noted in the chronicle of Meaux (of which house he became abbot) as *librorum maximus perquisitor* (*Chron. Melsa*, 326).

2 Cf. the list of Rievaulx books given by M. R. James in his *Descriptive Catalogue of the MSS. in the Library of Jesus College, Cambridge.*

3 For all that concerns the housing of books in the Middle Ages, *v. The Care of Books*, by J. W. Clark. Excellent plans of Cistercian and other libraries are given pp. 84 *seqq.*

4 *GASA*, I, 184.

THE ILLUMINATION OF MANUSCRIPTS AND MONASTIC CRAFT WORK

I

THE ILLUMINATION OF MANUSCRIPTS

In a study such as the present no account will be expected of monastic architecture. The subject is wide, and falls within the provinces of the architect and the antiquary rather than of the historian; it has indeed been very minutely and copiously illustrated in monographs and in the publications of learned societies, though there is still wanting a full review of monastic architecture, making use of all the data amassed during the past hundred years, and composed by one who combines the qualities of an architect and antiquary with those of a critical historian capable of tracing developments and indicating relationships. Moreover, the monks, as monks, were not architects or masons, and though, like the governing bodies of colleges and universities at the present day, they were necessarily patrons of great architectural undertakings and not uninfluenced by the beauty and majesty of the buildings under whose shadow they lived, it was only by accident that an individual had a share in designing them, or exceptional gifts as a connoisseur of the art.

The case of illumination is very different. Throughout the period covered by these chapters it was the monastic art *par excellence* in England and all its masterpieces before *c.* 1220 were products of the cloister. Moreover, surviving examples of the art and modern reproductions and studies are alike less accessible and less familiar than is the case with architecture, and though no detailed history of manuscript painting can be attempted here, to leave it without any mention would be to neglect one of the highest creative achievements of the epoch. A brief account must therefore be given of the phases of its development in the English black monk houses.

Of all the activities of the cloister in the early Middle Ages that which occupied the largest proportion of the working hours of the monks and which has received fullest attention from historians was the copying of books. Springing naturally from this employment, but rising far above it as affording opportunity and incitement for the exercise of creative talents of a high order, was the art of painting and decorating manuscripts or, as it is usually called, the art of illumination. Exquisite as are the masterpieces of this art in themselves, they have an importance in the history of culture still greater than that given by their intrinsic excellence, for illumination, besides being the only art practised wherever higher civilization existed in western Europe, was (largely owing to this circumstance) the medium in which the various styles and motifs of Eastern and Western painting, sculpture and iconography were transmitted from place to place, and developed and blended in the process. In ages and lands where sculpture, architecture and painting languished or were non-existent illumination was often flourishing, and in an epoch when artists travelled little and no reproductions existed the only portable works of art were the products of a school of manuscript painting that were bought or presented across frontiers and seas, and influenced distant artists in other lands. Illumination, therefore, has been called with justice "the basic art of the [early] Middle Ages".[1]

Before the age of Dunstan the Anglo-Saxon monks had been celebrated for their artistic skill in this respect. The earliest derived their inspiration from the Celtic schools and their masterpieces, such as the Lindisfarne Gospels (c. 700), equalled or surpassed anything produced in the monasteries of Ireland. The artist of the Lindisfarne Gospels was probably Eadfrith, bishop of Lindisfarne; it is typical both of the eighth and tenth centuries that the most talented artists and craftsmen should be men found at the head of the administration of a church or an abbey. Illumination flourished in the south of England when the north had been over-run by the Danes, and c. 800 reached a high degree of perfection at Canterbury.[2] Here the style was a blend of insular and continental elements, and the motifs common in the Empire from the time of Charlemagne were combined with many of the forms of Irish art. After this, so far as can be ascertained from the evidence of manuscripts that have survived, there was little or no illumination. The art disappeared, and here, as in so many other departments of cultural life, the rebirth came in the days of Dunstan.[3]

That eminent man, as has been seen, was a creative artist of genius;[4] but the chief impetus towards the painting of manuscripts came from

1 O. E. Saunders, *English Illumination* (Florence and London, 1928, 2 vols), I, 1. For a general view of the subject, together with excellent reproductions and careful criticism of the selected examples, the following, in addition to the work of Miss Saunders, may be consulted: E. G. Millar, *English Illuminated Manuscripts from the tenth to the thirteenth centuries* (Paris and Brussels, 1926); O. Homburger, *Die Anfänge der Malschule von Winchester im X Jahrhundert* (Leipzig, 1912). Dr Millar's work contains a useful handlist of the chief English illuminated MSS., together with their place of origin.

2 The three chief examples of this southern English work are a book of the Gospels (MS. Royal I E. vi) and a psalter (Cott. MS. Vesp. A. I) in the British Museum, and the *Codex Aureus* of the Gospels at Stockholm. *V.* also Kendrick, *Anglo-Saxon Art*, ch. IX.

3 In embroidery, however, such a masterpiece of beauty and technical skill as the Cuthbert stole and maniple was produced c. 909–16, probably at Winchester; v. A. G. I. Christie, *English medieval embroidery* (Oxford, 1938), 45, and Mrs Christie and G. Baldwin Brown in the *Burlington Magazine*, XXIII (April and May, 1913). And even as regards illumination Dr Millar is perhaps too positive in stating (*English Illuminated Manuscripts*, introd. x and p. 2) that "there is in fact a complete gulf between the earlier and the later styles", and that the later style "drew its inspiration in the first instance from abroad". Mr Francis Wormald has pointed out to me that, e.g., the initials in Bodl. MS Junius 99 and Cotton MS Galba A. XVIII are directly descended from the "Canterbury" initials of the 8th–9th century; similarly, the early post-Conquest work at Durham is wholly English.

4 *Vita auct. B*, in *Mem. S. Dunst.* 20–1: "Hic etiam...artem scribendi...pariterque pingendi peritiam diligenter excoluit."

Ethelwold and was felt in his two houses at Winchester. Ethelwold, like Dunstan, had artistic gifts; he had looked abroad for his observance and his Chant, and had no doubt imported from Fleury and Corbie many painted manuscripts. Perhaps, also, illuminations had come from Reims, for some of the earliest English work shows affinity to the well-known Rhemish style, and with the Continental art there came also the beautiful Carolingian minuscule script. Ethelwold must have had at his disposal artists with singular powers of receiving and creating, for the first known manuscript of the celebrated Winchester school is the charter of King Edgar to the New Minster, dating from 966, only a year or two after the expulsion of the clerks from the two churches of the city.[1] The New Minster, rather than St Swithun's, seems to have been the centre of the highest activity in the art, and as early as 980, when Aelfric at the Old Minster was about to begin the composition of his Homilies, produced its most exquisite surviving masterpiece, the sumptuous Benedictional of St Ethelwold, of which the artist was possibly the monk Godeman, subsequently abbot of Thorney.[2] "Winchester" work long continued to reach a high level of excellence, as is shown by a magnificent Psalter, attributed in the past to Ethelwold himself[3] but probably executed in East Anglia, and by other examples, justly celebrated, such as the Missal or Sacramentary of Robert of Jumièges, and the so-called Benedictional or Pontifical of Archbishop Robert, both of which are now at Rouen.[4] The former was presented by Robert to his old abbey when he was bishop of London (1046–50) and therefore shows that the English school long retained its pride of place, and that a foreigner could esteem its work so highly as to send an example as a gift to one of the most flourishing abbeys of Normandy.

Other houses produced work of a similar style and may have reached an equal height of achievement; in particular, perhaps, Christ Church, Canterbury, the home of the Bosworth Psalter,[5] Bury St Edmunds[6] and Ramsey; but indeed the art was common property to all the monasteries. The original "Winchester" style is so distinctive as to be easily recognizable; it consists of grand compositions or single figures enclosed by the so-called

1 Brit. Mus. Cott. MS. Vesp. A VIII; reproduction in *British Museum Reproductions*, Series I. The illumination is probably a little later than 966.

2 It is now in the collection of the Duke of Devonshire at Chatsworth. For reproductions, *v. The Benedictional of St Aethelwold*, ed. G. F. Warner and H. B. Wilson (Roxburghe Club, 1910), and O. E. Saunders, *English Illumination*, i, plates 18–21; the first of these contains a valuable introduction on the Winchester school. Dr E. G. Millar (*English Illuminated Manuscripts*, 7) considers on the evidence of style that the work was produced at the Old Minster; J. B. L. Tolhurst, in *Archaeologia* LXXXIII (1933), 27 *seqq.*, makes out a strong case for Ely; both houses derived from Ethelwold and Abingdon.

3 Brit. Mus. Harl. MS. 2904.

4 For these two, *v.* the editions of H. B. Wilson for the Henry Bradshaw Society in 1903 and 1896 respectively. The Missal may be Ely work, *v.* Tolhurst, *art. cit.*

5 Edited by Abbot Gasquet and E. Bishop (London, 1908).

6 An example is the Psalter at the Vatican Library, MS. Regin. 12, though it is possible that this was executed for Bury at Winchester or Ely.

"Winchester border" with its outbreaking acanthus foliage. The technique of the designs and of the drawing of the figures is Carolingian, following especially the schools of Reims and Lorraine, which in their turn owed much to the past. The large illustrations of such subjects as the Ascension or the Entry into Jerusalem are more elaborate and successful in their massing and composition than anything that followed them; the style continued to be developed at Winchester till the Conquest and its latest examples show it still full of life,[1] though it never again equalled the masterpieces of the first decades.

Besides this monumental and subtly coloured style there was another equally widespread. This consisted of outline drawings of figure subjects on plain vellum, apparently executed with great speed and ease and resembling fine pen-and-ink or brush drawings of the present day. The origin of this style has often been found in the "Utrecht" Psalter, the provenance of which has given rise to much discussion,[2] and which is known to have been copied at least once at St Augustine's in the early years of the eleventh century, but there was an old tradition of good outline drawing in England. The style spread all over southern and eastern England and was practised at Canterbury, Malmesbury, St Albans and Bury. Whatever its origin, it was singularly suited to the native genius, reflecting in draughtsmanship something of the sensitive and imaginative spirit of the Peterborough chroniclers; at its best it is full of life and makes an instant appeal, in less skilful hands it becomes mannered and harsh.[3] The best original work in this style that survives comes from the New Minster and dates from the reign of Cnut; it is to be found in the *Liber Vitae*.[4]

As has been noted, it was characteristic of the revival under Dunstan that the most distinguished monks should be also artists, and this continued the case until the Conquest. Godeman of Winchester, who was perhaps the Master of the Benedictional of St Ethelwold, became abbot of Thorney; fifty years later, the teacher of the young Wulfstan at Peterborough was Erwin, a distinguished artist whose Sacramentary and Psalter, once the delight of his pupil, were given to Cnut and Emma, who in their turn

---

1 E.g. the Psalter at the British Museum, Arundel MS. 60; reproduction in E. G. Millar, *English Illuminated Manuscripts*, 31.

2 There is a general consensus of recent expert opinion for northern France in the ninth century. It was in England all through the Middle Ages, and afterwards for a time in the Cottonian Library.

3 Perhaps to this style, even more than to that of the Winchester school, may be applied the words of Prof. Haseloff in A. Michel, *Histoire de l'Art*, I, part 2, ch. vii (1905): "Dans aucune école du moyen âge, on ne trouverait autant d'originalité, de force expressive, de fraîcheur d'observation, que dans l'école anglo-saxonne...on ne saurait assez admirer la fécondité d'invention toute pétillante de vie, dont fait preuve ici l'artiste." Many, looking at these drawings, will be reminded of the elves, fairies and countrymen that appear in the background of Mr Arthur Rackham's illustrations to the plays of Shakespeare.

4 Brit. Mus. Stowe MS. 944.

presented them to the emperor Henry at Cologne;[1] twenty years later still, the illumination of manuscripts is mentioned among the other accomplishments which gave Mannig of Evesham his celebrity.[2] That the two last-named artists, whose reputation was high over all England, should hail from abbeys from which no work of any importance has survived is an indication that almost all the monasteries of England were homes of the art, and that apart from Winchester, known to have been mistress of all, pride of place should not be given without reserve to the houses represented most richly in the collections of the modern world.

The upheaval and break in traditional life caused by the Conquest and the Norman reorganization of the monasteries seems to have brought about a diminution of production for many years. The Norman work was different from the Old English, and less cultivated by the ablest men in the monasteries; few therefore of the new abbots were themselves practitioners or disposed to be patrons of native art. When illumination again became universal in England, forty years later, the style was changing; the light, free originality of the Anglo-Saxon artists was often ousted by a manner in which heavily outlined, forbidding and even positively ugly figures and faces prevailed, and in which a greater simplicity and brilliance of tint, often bordering on the crude use of the primary colours, had replaced the subtle blending of shades. Instead of the delicate "Winchester border", the most striking characteristic of the new style is to be found in the elaborate initial letters, often displayed with architectonic effect across a whole page, or containing within themselves an intricate design. The earliest work, as has been said, is harsh and sometimes grotesque, but gradually, as a new generation grew up, the native freedom and taste for blended colour was combined with the peculiar brilliance and monumental decision of the imported style, and at about the middle of the century a series of masterpieces was again produced equal to, though wholly different from, both the Lindisfarne Gospels and the Benedictional of St Ethelwold.

One of the earliest and most magnificent of these, alike in colour and design, is the Bury Bible, the work of Hugh, sacristan of Bury under Abbot Anselm (1121–48);[3] it had been preceded at Bury itself by the Life of St Edmund now in the Pierpont Morgan Library in New York, and at St Albans by the celebrated Albani Psalter now at Hildesheim. Second only to the Bury Bible is the so-called Lambeth Bible,

1 *Vita Wulfstani* (ed. Darlington), 5: "Habebat tunc magistrum Eruenium nomine, in scribendo et quidlibet coloribus effingendo peritum. Is libros scriptos sacrame[n]tarium et psalterium, quorum principales literas auro effigiauerat, puero Wlstano delegandos curauit, etc." Cf. *ibid.* introd. xxiii.

2 *Chron. Evesh.* 86–7: "Scriptoris, pictoris. . .scientia pollens."

3 Corpus Christi College, Cambridge, MS. 2, identified with the Bible described in the *Gesta Sacristarum* of Bury (*Monasticon*, III, 163) by M. R. James, *On the Abbey of St Edmund at Bury*, 7, and in *Catalogue of MSS. of Corpus Christi College, Cambridge.*

probably illuminated at Canterbury.[1] New Minster, so far as extant evidence goes, would seem to have ceased in productiveness after the Conquest, but St Swithun's remained a seat of art, as also of literary culture. The peak of its attainment in this second period was reached under Henry of Winchester, himself a collector and connoisseur of excellent taste, and the masterpieces that remain are two Bibles, very different in style and technique from the Bury Bible, but as undoubtedly in the first order of artistic achievement. The one which is complete is clearly the work of a number of artists, all men of genius, a fact that reveals both the richness of talent and the level of tuition at Winchester. It has been conjectured with some probability that the "Winchester Bible" now in the cathedral library of that city was the volume "borrowed" by Henry II as a gift for Witham and subsequently returned by Hugh of Avalon.[2]

Besides the southern and eastern abbeys, the northern also adopted the new style. Durham had begun to produce illuminations of an English type under William of St Carilef; the house continued throughout the twelfth century to develop its art, of which specimens remain in a magnificent Bible and other books.[3] Indeed, by the middle of the century skill in illumination seems to have been widespread; it continued to the end and beyond, though the style gradually developed, first under Byzantine influence, seen in a noble Westminster Psalter,[4] and later under the transformation, shared by contemporary architecture and sculpture, into the new Gothic idiom.

Nor did the native style of free outline drawing wholly disappear. The Utrecht Psalter was copied yet again at Christ Church in the middle of the century, as may be seen in the Eadwine Psalter at Cambridge, though the original idiom is here blended with the new Continental style.[5] More than twenty years later a masterpiece of drawing was produced at Croyland, otherwise quite unknown as a centre of art, in the Guthlac roll, which has been described as unquestionably "the high-water mark of English outline drawing".[6] It is characteristic of this, the Anglo-Norman period of illumination, that the artists are for the most part unknown "monks of the cloister". They are no longer, as in Anglo-Saxon times, found among the principal ecclesiastics of the kingdom, nor, with one or two exceptions, are they men distinguished for their achievements in a number of artistic fields. Rather, they are the patient specialists.

---

1 Vol. I of this is MS. 3 of Lambeth Archiepiscopal Library; vol. II is in the Maidstone Museum.   2 *Hugonis Magna Vita*, 92–4.

3 Cf. the Bible in Durham Cathedral Library, MS. A II 1. A Life of St Cuthbert is in the British Museum, Addit. MS. 39,943. For plates, *v.* Mynors, *Durham Cathedral Manuscripts*.

4 Brit. Mus. Royal MS. 2 A XXII.

5 The Eadwine Psalter has recently been sumptuously reproduced, with valuable introductory matter, by the late Dr M. R. James; *v.* Bibliography, *The Canterbury Psalter*.

6 So E. G. Millar, *English Illuminated Manuscripts*, 37. The Guthlac Roll (Brit. Mus. Harl. Roll Y 6) has been edited for the Roxburghe Club by Sir G. Warner (1928).

The second great period of illumination touched its highest level of excellence between 1140 and 1180. Until the end of the twelfth century the English work was not only indisputably superior to that produced abroad but also unlike it; after 1200, England and northern France tended more and more to form one artistic province, though for another twenty years the superiority of the English painting was still unchallenged. The English monastic art was to reach a peak for the third time with the school of St Albans, from *c.* 1220–70, but this falls outside the limits of our period.[1]

Altogether, the three great periods of productivity covered the greater part of three centuries, and for all that time the masterpieces of England were never surpassed abroad. The casual reader of the monographs on the art may be tempted to think that the warmth of the praise bestowed is due to the natural partiality of a specialist, and if he has only seen photographic reproductions of the early illuminations, or is familiar only with original work of the later Middle Ages, of which so many examples, often of very mediocre quality, are to be seen in all the public and private collections of Europe, his hesitation is comprehensible. But no one who has once examined at leisure the masterpieces mentioned in the foregoing pages, many of which are among the permanent exhibits at the British Museum, will wish to question the opinion of those most competent to form a judgment of the kind, that these illuminations are worthy to take their place among the supreme artistic achievements of the West.

II

MONASTIC ARTS AND CRAFTS

The share taken by the monks of the medieval world in practising and perfecting the various manual arts and crafts has been the subject of considerable misapprehension in the past century. The enthusiastic and often indiscriminate praise accorded to the monastic order by the early historians of the Romantic revival, of whom the most influential was Montalembert, was echoed with far less discrimination by a number of publicists and apologists of the religious, social, and aesthetic ideals of the Middle Ages, many of whom made no clear distinction between epochs, and applied to the monks of the fourteenth century judgments expressed by historians concerning those of the eighth. In consequence, a large number of those without first-hand knowledge of the sources of history came to believe that artistic work of all kinds was common to all monks of every period. More recently, in reaction from this, there has been a tendency in some

---

1 E. G. Millar, *English Illuminated Manuscripts*, 24, speaks of the talent which raised "English art in the...two centuries [1070–1270] to a height unsurpassed and rarely equalled by the contemporary art of any other country", and notes that "at the beginning of the thirteenth century English manuscripts were still supreme and were even in demand abroad" (*ibid.* 44–5).

circles to ignore the existence at any period of a peculiarly monastic art. The truth lies between these extremes, and on no point of monastic activity is it more necessary to distinguish between the various branches of the monastic order, and between times and places, in order to arrive at a correct estimate as to when and where the exercise of artistic craft work was general, or occasional, or wholly non-existent among the members of a particular institute.[1]

The century between the first revival and the Norman Conquest in England was undoubtedly one in which manual artistic and craft work of every kind was executed very generally within the monasteries, and far less generally outside their walls. In all the small-scale fine arts England held a position from the death of Athelstan to that of the Confessor above every other nation in western Europe.[2] Evidence for this fact is afforded by the judgments and descriptions of chroniclers, native and foreign, by the inventories that have been preserved of the ornaments and treasures at Waltham, Ely, Abingdon, Evesham, Peterborough, Winchester and elsewhere, and by such few material objects as have survived.[3] Under Athelstan, Edgar and his immediate successors the great monastic churches alone could provide a haven where work in the precious metals might be undertaken and preserved, and we know that at a number of the monasteries there were artists of the highest attainments, several of whom became abbots of their own or another house; the impetus and example were given by two of the great leaders of the reform.

Dunstan, besides his skill as a musician, illuminator and designer, was a metal-worker to whom Abingdon attributed two of its bells.[4] Ethelwold, who had been Dunstan's disciple at Glastonbury, was like him a skilled craftsman and even (if the term may be used) a mechanic. Among the treasures at Abingdon were many attributed to his hand, ranging from an organ and church bells to an elaborate hanging golden coronal or wheel,

---

1 A criticism might be made of the interesting work of R. E. Swartwout, *The Monastic Craftsman*, in this respect. Very many references are gathered with the greatest diligence, but it is not made clear to the inexpert reader that the characteristics of the various epochs differed widely. Less than justice, it may be added, is done to Mannig and his contemporaries of the late Old English period.

2 Two foreign judgments on the paramount excellence of English craftsmanship may be noted: William of Poitiers, in *Historiae Normannorum Scriptores Antiqui*, ed. Duchesne (Paris, 1619), 210–11: "Chari metalli abundantia multipliciter Gallias terra illa vincit... aerarium Arabiae auri copia [dicenda videtur]...egregie viri in omni valent artificio." Cf. also *Chron. Mon. Cassinensis, auctore Leone*, in Pertz, *MGH, SS*, VII (1846), 649, for the incident of the English shrine: "argento et auro ac gemmis Anglico opere subtiliter ac pulcherrime decoratus", for a relic at Monte Cassino c. 1020. I owe these two references to Prof. R. W. Chambers.

3 Cf. *The Foundation of Waltham Abbey*, 17–18; *Liber Eliensis*, 249–50; *Chron. Abingd.* I, 344–5; *Chron. Evesh.* 84, 87.

4 *Vita auct. B*, in *Mem. S. Dunst.* 20–1. For the Abingdon bells cf. *Chron. Abingd.* I, 345: "Fecit etiam [S. Ethelwoldus] duas campanas...quas in hac domo posuit cum aliis duabus majoribus, quas etiam beatus Dunstanus propriis manibus fecisse perhibetur." The accuracy of the attribution is not essential; particular frescoes are attributed, correctly or not, to Fra Angelico, not to Savonarola.

supporting lamps and little bells, and a precious retable of gold and silver, and if the attribution of some of these and other similar works of art is questionable, the fact that so many were claimed for his hand, whereas none of those at Ramsey was attributed to Oswald, is sufficient evidence that his reputation as a metal-worker was a piece of genuine tradition.[1] During the fifty years after his death the chief monasteries amassed a store of precious objects of all kinds, most of which must have been the work of the monks, and there are a number of indications that the traditions of Dunstan and Ethelwold were honoured by the most able among their spiritual descendants. Among these were three monks of Ely: Brithnod, originally of the Old Minster, a carver and goldsmith; Leo, provost at a later date, a silversmith, and Aelfsig, abbot from 981 to c. 1019, a worker in precious metal,[2] and the *Liber Vitae* of the New Minster contains the names of more than one monk so distinguished for his craft as to be known by its title.[3] Half-way through the century a monk of Bury, Spearhavoc by name, a skilled goldsmith, became abbot of Abingdon. We are told that he was commissioned to make a crown for the emperor, no doubt Henry IV who was crowned in 1053, and that having received the jewels and precious metals he levanted; whatever the truth of the latter tradition, the fact of the commission may be accepted, and is significant of the position held by English work and by the monks among English workmen at the time.[4] A still more celebrated contemporary was Mannig, abbot of Evesham, who executed commissions for Canterbury and Coventry, and made the shrine of St Egwin at his own monastery.[5] To skill in metal-work was added that in carving of every kind. All wooden carving of the

1 *Chron. Abingd.* I, 344–5; II, 278. It is not easy to be certain how many of these objects were made by Ethelwold, though some certainly were. The accounts in their present form date from the twelfth and thirteenth centuries, and some of the context is suspicious; also, the alternatives *dedit* and *fecit* are not without ambiguity. The list is as follows:

(a) A great golden chalice—*dedit* (I, 344).

(b) Three crosses of silver and gold—*dedit* (I, 344); *fecit* (II, 278).

(c) A precious carved retable of gold and silver—*abbas A. fecit* (I, 344); *fecit et sanctus A.* (II, 278); it was known as the *tabula sancti A.* (II, 163).

(d) The rotating coronal or wheel of gold—*fecit vir venerabilis A.* (I, 345); *ipse fecit* (II, 278).

(e) Two church bells and other objects—*fecit propriis manibus, ut dicitur* (I, 345); *fecit propriis manibus* (II, 278).

(f) The organ—*propriis manibus ipse feci* (II, 278); *struxit* (Wulfstan in *PL*, cxxxvii, 109–11).

2 *Liber Eliensis*, 114: "Fecit [Brithnodus] namque beatarum virginum imagines easque auro et argento gemmisque pretiosis texuit"; *ibid.* 168: "Crucem vero [Leo] fecit argenteam, quae crux Leonis praepositi nominatur"; *ibid.* 247: the statue of the Blessed Virgin with her Child, "mirabiliter fabrefactam, quam Aelfsinus abbas fecerat de auro et argento."

3 *Hyde Liber Vitae* (ed. Birch). At the New Minster Aelfnoth, *pictor et sacerdos* (p. 31), at the Old, Wulfric, Brihtelm and Byrnelm *aurifices* (p. 25) occur; all are monks.

4 *Chron. Abingd.* I, 462: "Monachum . . . aurificis arte peritissimum, nomine Spearhauoc." For the story of the imperial crown, *v. ibid.* 463.

5 *Chron. Evesh.* 86–7: "Cantoris, scriptoris, pictoris, aurique fabrilis operis scientia pollens super omnes alios fere hujus patriae magister optimus habebatur. Apud Cantuariam vero atque ecclesiam Coventreiam sicuti in multis aliis locis plurima opera tunc temporis valde laudabilia operatus est."

period has perished, but the few objects of ivory that remain, including a superb crozier, show that technique and design were alike of the first order.[1]

If in the first decades of the revival the monks had a monopoly of precious metal-work and carving, there are indications that by the reign of the Confessor a class of lay craftsmen was springing up, both native and foreign. Thus Mannig was assisted by a layman, Godric, but it is noteworthy that Godric's son became a monk and later prior of Evesham, and that Godric himself some years after took the habit in the house.[2]

With the Conquest came a change. Among the new Norman abbots there was no tradition of skill in the manual arts and in not a few cases the existing treasures were lost, either to the Danish invaders, as at Peterborough and other fenland houses, or to Norman freebooters and officials who often rifled them for their market value as stones and precious metal, or to satisfy the demands of the Conqueror. In addition, the majority of the newcomers would have had little appreciation for the unfamiliar style of such English art as was not executed in jewels or gold.[3] When again, forty years later, carvers and metal-workers were in demand to decorate the vast and bare new churches, the monastic craftsman is something of an exception, though it was not uncommon for an artist who had been employed upon work to join the community, and in such a case he might well train assistants among the younger monks. After Godric of Evesham the most notable early example of this class is Anketil of St Albans. He was an Englishman who c. 1100–10 had gone to Denmark at the invitation of the king and had there become a celebrated goldsmith and supervisor of the royal mint. Returning to England on a visit, he became a monk at St Albans and constructed the shrine of the saint for the translation of the body which took place in August 1129.[4] His chief assistant was a young lay craftsman, Solomon of Ely. Other cases of monk craftsmen in this period are rare, but they exist. One such would seem to have been Hugh, sacrist of Bury c. 1130–40, who carved the screen and cast the bronze doors and bell of the church;[5] another perhaps was Robert, sacrist of Abingdon, c. 1120–40, who is recorded to have cast a church bell and embroidered a vestment.[6] Other monasteries, however, employed resident lay workers;

1 For these v. H. P. Mitchell, *Two English Ivory Carvings of the Twelfth Century*, in *Burlington Magazine*, XLI (October 1922), and *Flotsam of Later Anglo-Saxon Art*, I and IV, by the same author in the same magazine, XLII–III (February 1923 and September 1923). There is a good illustration of the crozier in *English Art in the Middle Ages*, by O. E. Saunders, facing p. 37.

2 For Godric, v. *Chron. Evesh.* 44, 86–7. William of Poitiers (*loc. cit. supra*, p. 535, n. 2) vouches for Germans at work in England c. 1066.

3 There were, however, a few early exceptions, such as Theodwin of Jumièges, abbot of Ely 1076–9 (*Liber Eliensis*, 249). In general, however, the judgment of Mr Clapham cannot be gainsaid: that in the minor arts of England, at least, "the Norman Conquest was little short of a catastrophe" (*English Romanesque Architecture*, I, 77).

4 For Anketil, v. *GASA*, I, 83–7.   5 *Monasticon*, III, 162–3.

6 *Chron. Abingd.* II, 171: "Dedit [sc. abbot Vincent c. 1121] casulam purpuream, quam Robertus sacrista...auro obtexuit obrizo"; *ibid*. 291: "Emit [sc. Abbot Ingulph, 1130–c. 1158] magnum tintinnabulum...et quidam sacrista, Robertus nomine, fecit parem suum."

thus at Glastonbury in 1189 there is mention of Andrew the goldsmith, who held the post at the monastery in succession to his brother Turstin, appointed by Henry of Winchester, and enjoyed the possession of some land and a corrody; at Glastonbury, likewise, Godfrey, parson of Deverel, held the office of repairer of vestments and maker of orphreys which he had transmitted to his son.[1] With such extern craftsmen in mind, we shall perhaps be hesitant in attributing the superb work of the Winchester school of metal-workers responsible for the Masters Plaque and other pieces commissioned by Henry of Winchester for his cathedral to inmates of the monastery of St Swithun's, though the clear influence of the Winchester illuminations on the design of the great plaque of the Doom points to a very close connection between the artist and the monastery.[2] Still more enigmatic is the provenance of the superb Gloucester candlestick, forty years earlier. While expert opinion tends to assign this to an English hand, there is at present wanting any record of a group of lay craftsmen of the date (known to have been 1104–13) of its creation. The attribution to Anketil of St Albans is a tempting one, but lacks all confirmatory evidence.

Thus in the century after the Conquest work in the precious metals, jewelry and carving of all sorts, from being a speciality of the monasteries, and of the most eminent monks, had gradually passed into the hands of lay and commercial workers, though individuals still practised their crafts in the cloister. At the end of the twelfth century St Albans alone, perhaps, of the English abbeys still housed such artists; there one Baldwin, most probably a monk, made a great chalice of gold and precious stones, a smaller one of gold and two of silver, together with a golden hanging pyx.[3] Twenty years later, at the extreme limit of our period, began the connection between St Albans and the group of artists, three brothers and their nephew, Walter, William, Simon and Richard, called of Colchester, who executed a series of works of art of every description. Two of them, Walter and Richard, became monks, and the former was appointed sacristan.[4] Their history, however, more properly belongs to the years which followed the Lateran Council and the accession of Henry III.

1 *Liber Henrici de Soliaco* (ed. J. E. Jackson), p. 13: "Andreas aurifaber tenet misterium aurifabrice…Godefridus persona de deverel tenuit quoddam misterium ad quod pertinet emendare ornamentum ecclesiae…et facere aurifrigium."

2 For these cf. the articles of H. P. Mitchell in the *Burlington Magazine, Some Enamels of the School of Godefroid de Claire*, XXXIV–V (1919) and *English Enamels of the XIIth century*, XLVII (October 1925), in which the Masters Plaque is claimed for Winchester c. 1165. The writer justly remarks of the plaque of Henry of Winchester that "when freshly executed on the gilded ground its richness must have been astonishing".

3 *GASA*, I, 190–1. It is not explicitly stated that Baldwin was a monk, but a sacrist of that name occurs on p. 205, a few years later, and the identification is very probable.

4 *GASA*, I, 232–3, 279, 283, 286. Cf. also W. Page, *The St Albans School of Painting*, in *Archaeologia*, vol. LVIII, part i.

CHAPTER XXXI

THE LITURGY AND THE CHANT

I

The liturgy of the monasteries of the medieval Church, being as it is a subject altogether remote from the interests and experience of the general reader and of the majority of historians in this country, is peculiarly the province of specialists, and it lies outside the scope of these chapters. A few pages must, however, be devoted to giving a brief sketch of the daily liturgical practice of the English monasteries; it was the principal employment of the monks and was the constant, unbroken centre of the life of the monastery, compared with which all alterations of work and external occupations were in a sense peripheral.

The normal liturgical service of a black monk monastery may be considered in four divisions: the Office of the Day, that is, the celebration of Nocturns, Matins, Prime, Terce, Sext, None, Vespers and Compline; the community Masses, from the beginning of our period two in number, the Morning or Chapter Mass, originally recited, later sung, and the Conventual Mass, celebrated each day with ministers and full chant; the various additional Offices and prayers which had been added to the Office of the day; and, finally, some extraordinary but not infrequent ceremonies, such as processions of all kinds.

The structure of the monastic office in England in the period from the revival onwards was in essentials what it is to-day; that is to say, there was the same broad division into days of three nocturns and twelve lessons, comprehending all Sundays and many feasts, and days of two nocturns and three lessons, including both non-festal days, on which passages of Scripture or homilies on the gospel were read, and minor feast days. Moreover, the actual text of the lessons, responsories, antiphons and the rest was in England very similar to that of the modern monastic breviary; there was nothing corresponding to the extremely long lessons of the Cluniac observance.[1] The number of feasts of saints celebrated was very large. Already considerable at the time of the composition of the Benedictional of St Ethelwold c. 970, the *Sanctorale* received additions constantly, and was rarely, save at the revision of the calendar by Lanfranc, shorn of what it already contained. In the Worcester calendar of c. 1230,

---

1 All minor changes have been ignored in the above paragraphs. The only complete English black monk breviary hitherto printed is that of Hyde abbey c. 1300, recently (1932) edited for the Henry Bradshaw Society by Mr J. B. L. Tolhurst: *The Monastic Breviary of Hyde Abbey, Winchester*. The earliest breviaries known to survive are those of Winchcombe (twelfth century) in the library of Valenciennes, and of St Albans in the British Museum, MS. Royal 2 A X; cf. *JTS*, xxxvii (January 1936), 93.

which in all essentials may be taken as the equivalent of a twelfth-century list,[1] there are over a hundred feasts of saints and their octave days of twelve lessons; if to these be added the Sundays and feasts such as the Epiphany and the Ascension, and allowance be made for the occasional coincidence of Sundays and saints' days, it will be seen that on more than a hundred and fifty days of the year, or an average of three days a week, the long office of twelve lessons was prescribed.

Of this office a certain proportion was chanted each day. Probably at the greater monasteries the portions thus sung on all solemnities and feasts included the responsories to the lessons at Nocturns, together with the Invitatory, Hymn, Te Deum and Gospel when these were prescribed; the whole of Matins (the modern Lauds); the Hymns, at least, of the day Hours and the whole of Vespers. On this substructure was erected an edifice of greater or less elaboration of additional chant and ceremonial for the more important feasts.

Of the Masses nothing for the moment need be said. The Morrow Mass, originally recited, came in time to be sung; it took place at the choir altar; the daily solemn Mass was celebrated at the High Altar, with musical and ceremonial elaboration corresponding to that of the Office.

Mention has already been made of the additional offices and prayers, and no detailed account will be expected of the exact seasons at which they were varied or omitted.[2] They consisted, roughly speaking, of the thirty last psalms of the psalter, the seven penitential psalms, five psalms for the dead after chapter, a small number of psalms for relations and benefactors, the litany of the saints, the Office of All Saints and the Office of the Dead. Some or all of these were omitted on feast days of twelve lessons, during certain octaves and throughout Paschal Time. The Office of Our Lady does not figure either in the *Concordia* or the *Statuta* of Lanfranc; it was introduced gradually and sporadically during the twelfth century, one of the first houses to adopt it being Bury when under the rule of Anselm, the nephew of the archbishop and a ritualistic innovator in more than one direction;[3] it became widespread and in large part superseded the Office of All Saints, which was reduced to Lauds and Vespers. Of all these offices certain antiphons and responds were sung, to judge from the specimens of chant given in such books as the Worcester *Antiphoner*.

Processions of one kind or another were extremely frequent. In the pre-Conquest monasticism, they would seem to have been confined to the Sunday *Asperges* and the quasi-public processions inherited from the

---

1 Printed on pp. 29–40 of the introduction to the Worcester *Antiphoner*, for which *v. infra*, p. 553.

2 *V. supra*, p. 450, and references throughout that chapter.

3 Brit. Mus. MS. Harl. 1005, 218 v, note (quoted by E. W. Williamson, *The Letters of Osbert of Clare*, 198): "Cotidie...post canonicas horas alias in honore ejus [*sc.* B.M.V.] celebrandas decrevit." This was probably *c.* 1120. The office figures in the Worcester *Antiphoner*, written *c.* 1230.

Roman rite, such as those on Candlemas, the ferial days of Lent, the Rogations, and those to the font during Easter Week. In the observance of the *Concordia*, the old custom was maintained of assembling at some church of the neighbourhood and returning in procession to the monastery. In the Anglo-Norman monastic observance, modelled on that of the Norman monasteries deriving from William of Dijon, the number of processions was greatly increased, but, with the exception of those on Palm Sunday and the Rogation days, which at first went outside the enclosure, they were confined to the precincts of the monastery, and especially to the cloister and the nave of the church; as has been said, the need, or at least the taste, for ample processional room was a principal reason for the great length to which the nave of the typical Norman monastic church was extended. In the twelfth century, besides the regular procession at the *Asperges* or blessing of holy water before the Mass each Sunday, there were processions after Vespers and Lauds on the feast of every saint to whom an altar was dedicated in the church, and a more solemn one on the dozen or so greatest feasts of the year. Besides these, there were the bi-weekly and quasi-penitential processions of Lent and a procession to the cross in the cloister on Saturdays.[1]

The *Concordia* gives no explicit grading of feasts, beyond the division into those of three lessons and those of twelve, the latter being days of silence in the cloister, two meals and no official work.[2] But already Cluny had evolved an elaborate and gorgeous ritualism, and part of this came into England with the Norman monasticism and Lanfranc's Statutes, and became the normal practice. The principal innovation was the celebration of the most important feasts "in copes" and "in albs". On the days in the first class all the altars of the church were decorated, stalls in choir and chapter and benches in the refectory were covered with hangings, special cloths were on the tables and rushes on the floor, and all the lamps of the church were lighted. At the various Hours of the Office the cantors and hebdomadaries wore albs and copes, and for the procession and the principal Mass all the monks were so robed. On the days of the second rank the decorations were omitted and albs only were worn without copes.[3] In Lanfranc's directory only five feasts in the year belonged to the first class, and a comparatively small number to the second. At Worcester, a century and a half later, more than forty days in the year were celebrated "in copes" and another eighteen "in albs", and two smaller classes had been created of feasts "in copes", consisting of the greatest days of the year, on which certain additional elaborations took

---

1 A list of those at Worcester, extracted from the *Antiphoner*, is given in the introduction, p. 94.

2 *Concordia*, vi, 90.

3 *Statuta*, c. 1, §§ 6–8, pp. 226–8. In the *Concordia* there is no mention of copes as worn by all the community, but albs were worn by all at Mass on great feasts cf. iii, 84–6, and E. Bishop, *The Origins of the Cope*, in *Liturgica Historica*, 260–75.

place. As always in such matters, the progress is steady from complexity
to greater complexity, and by *c.* 1230 the group of the "Seven Feasts" at
Worcester, originally consisting of that number of the most solemn days,
had come to be a mere class-name, including thirteen days.[1]

II

While all the monasteries had a common basis for the greater part of their
calendar, every house observed a number of feasts on its own account.
In this matter the abbot and community were free of all control, and
notices of such additions are frequent in the chronicles and can be checked
in the calendars that have survived. Chief among such peculiar festivals
were those of the patron saints of the abbey, or of any whose bodies or
other relics rested there, but besides these local feasts there occurred a
gradual infiltration of devotions from abroad, which reflected the tastes
of an influential abbot or the spread of a fashionable cult. Thus the commemoration of all the souls still in Purgatory, rendered fashionable by
the example of Cluny, made its appearance at some houses during the
twelfth century, and was followed by a further special commemoration
of deceased relatives and benefactors.[2] Similarly, the observance of a
special feast of all the saints whose relics were in the church was a natural
consequence of the influx of new relics under the first Norman abbots.[3]
The introduction of the feast of the Conception of the Blessed Virgin has
already been noticed; that of her mother, St Anne, was peculiar to
Worcester cathedral priory, where its introduction was perhaps due to
Theulf or Simon, bishops who both came from the neighbourhood of
Bayeux, and was probably derived from a Greek source in Italy or elsewhere. The devotion to St Joseph, which accompanied the cult of St
Anne at Worcester, may possibly have come from Ireland with the pilgrims
to Worcester or Evesham.[4]

Already in the *Concordia* it was decreed that the principal Mass on
Saturdays should be a Mass of Our Lady when no feast occurred. Later,
it became the custom for a daily Mass to be said or sung *De Beata*. At
first this was probably a private Mass, not attended by the community,

1 Cf. Worcester *Antiphoner*, introd. 48–52.

2 Cf. *Chron. Will. Thorne*, 1798, for this at St Augustine's *c.* 1120 on 3 July.

3 It was introduced at Abingdon *c.* 1160, on the Tuesday after the second Sunday after
Easter (*Chron. Abingd.* II, 207–8); for its observance at Leominster, *v. Monasticon*, IV, 56.
At Worcester it was kept on 15 October (*Antiphoner*, introd. 38).

4 For St Anne at Worcester, *v.* Osbert of Clare, *ep.* 12 (ed. Williamson, 77–9, with the
editor's notes; he remarks, p. 211, that "the feast is almost unknown in the West before the
thirteenth century"). It is noteworthy that Osbert's correspondent, Prior Warin, is one of
the signatories to the foundation charter of Alcester in 1140; the new house had the extraordinary dedication to the Blessed Virgin, St Anne, St Joseph, St John the Baptist and St
John the Evangelist (*Monasticon*, IV, 175–6). Cf. also Dom André Wilmart's article *Les compositions d'Osbert de Clare en l'honneur de sainte Anne* (*Auteurs spirituels et Textes dévots*,
261–87), and F. Wormald, *English Benedictine Kalendars after 1100* (HBS, LXXVII, 1939), 97.

but gradually the custom was introduced of adding a third Mass to the existing two, in honour of Our Lady and known as the *Missa Familiaris* or *De Domina*.[1] Gerald of Wales notes as the first black monk house to adopt the practice Rochester, as the result of a request of William of Ypres in the reign of Stephen. Here, as usual, his information is probably inaccurate, but the date given is that at which the devotion was becoming common.[2] Finally, two or three peculiarly national customs connected with the liturgy may be mentioned. One such concerns the method of reserving the consecrated Hosts in the church. It would seem to have been the universal English practice, at least in the monasteries, for the Eucharist to be kept in a vessel hanging from the roof or a beam above the High Altar. The actual pyx in which the Hosts were kept was often made of gold studded with precious stones, and sometimes encased in a vessel of the shape of a saucer to which the chains or cords were attached; sometimes this took the form of a dove.[3] Before it burned constantly a lamp or taper, and in the middle of the monks' choir usually hung another circular holder of precious metal, supporting candles or lamps which were lighted in greater or less quantity on the various feasts.[4]

The composers of the *Concordia* noted as peculiarly English the custom of frequent and joyful pealing of bells and expressed their wish to retain it in monastic practice.[5] In all the accounts of the great ecclesiastical re-unions of the reign of Edgar and his successors the ringing of bells is mentioned;[6] the bell-turret of the Old Minster at Winchester was one of

---

1 The private celebration of such a Mass, together with the private recitation of Our Lady's Office, is mentioned as a devotion of Abbot Benedict of Tewkesbury, *ob.* 1137 (*Chron. Jo. Wig.*, ed. Weaver, *s.a.*). Anselm of Bury, *c.* 1129: "instituit cotidie unam missam de ea" (*loc. cit. supra*, p. 540, n. 3).

2 Giraldus, *Speculum Ecclesiae* (IV, 202): "Haec autem prima missa fuit, ut fertur, in Anglia cotidie de Domina solemniter celebrata, sed postmodum ad loca plurima...est derivata."

3 E.g. at Canterbury, on the opening of the new choir, the archbishop "suscepit a monacho quodam pixidem cum Eucharistia, quae desuper altare majus pendere solebat" (Gervase, I, 23); at St Albans *c.* 1166–83 Baldwin the goldsmith made "unum vasculum... ex auro obryzo et fulvo, adaptatis et decenter collocatis in ipso gemmis impretiabilibus diversi generis...ad reponendam Eucharistiam, supra majus altare Martyris suspendendum." Henry II, hearing of this, "unam cuppam...in qua reponeretur et ipsa theca immediate continens Corpus Christi...transmisit" (*GASA*, I, 190); at Battle, at the same date, a vessel of silver gilt was made: "habens in medio columbam, corpus Dominicum continentem" (*Chron. Bell.* 138). There can be little doubt that the "halig dome" at Glastonbury, towards which the Norman archers of Thurstan shot (*Chronicle* [E], *s.a.* 1083), was the reserved Host and not (as suggested by Plummer in his glossary) the relics.

4 Cf. the *corona deaurata, viginti quatuor sustinens cereos* at Canterbury (Gervase, I, 13) and the *argentea dependens corona* at Battle (*Chron. Bell.* 138, 167). The fullest and most accurate reconstruction of the interior of a monastic church in the twelfth century is that of Bury in M. R. James, *The Abbey of St Edmund at Bury ... The Church* (Cambridge Archaeological Society, 1895).

5 *Concordia*, iii, 85.

6 E.g. *Vita S. Oswaldi auct. anon.* [Byrhtferth], 426 (a gathering at Winchester *c.* 980): "aedituus templi ipsius cloccam person[abat] Altissimo"; *ibid.* 464 (Ramsey, Nov. 991): "aedituus strenue coepit ecclesiastica tuba filios invitare suos ad se" (this would seem to refer to a bell, as the organ is mentioned later).

the features of Ethelwold's new building, and a sketch of it appears in one of the illuminations of his Benedictional. Both he and Dunstan, it will be remembered, were credited with themselves having cast bells for Abingdon. The monasteries, to judge from the customaries, were faithful to the recommendations of the *Concordia*, and the ringing of bells, singly or in combination, was a feature both of the daily horarium and of certain special occasions, such as processions.

Gifts of bells were not infrequent throughout the twelfth century; they often bore names, or an inscription giving that of the donor or craftsman who had cast them.[1] The music of church bells, which remains one of the most cherished and characteristic sounds of the English countryside, and fills the closes and gardens of the cathedral cities with its gracious harmony, is thus one more of the many traditional things of the oldest Christian England that Dunstan and his associates preserved for future generations; it is not, as a great artist in prose suggests, a legacy from Norman or Plantagenet days, but comes from the still earlier age that had in so many ways a love for all that was precious and mellow in sight and in sound.[2]

Two extraordinary quasi-liturgical rites, both connected with the ceremonies of Holy Week, were practised by the English monks at different periods, and though probably neither was English in origin, each of them was given a peculiarly ready reception in this country. The first in time was the dramatic representation of the visit of the holy women to the sepulchre on Easter morning, and the announcement made to them by the angel of the Resurrection. This was performed by monks, one robed in an alb and three wearing copes, after the third responsory of Nocturns on Easter Sunday, on which day, and during the whole octave of the feast, the monastic office gave place to that of the secular clergy in the scheme of the *Concordia*, out of deference to the arrangements of the Roman anti-phoner attributed to Gregory the Great. The action was accompanied by appropriate singing, both solo and choral, and the long description of the rite is the fullest early mention of something that was later to blossom into the mystery-play.[3] The manner in which it is introduced and described in detail in the *Concordia* seems to suggest that it was something unfamiliar to England; it probably came from Fleury and France. In the earlier of the two Winchester tropers it appears in the same place in the liturgy; in the later one it has been transferred to Holy Saturday before the blessing of the Paschal Candle.[4] In Lanfranc's arrangement it disappears altogether, which is an indication that it was not known in the monasteries of Nor-mandy, and, so far as I am aware, there is no subsequent mention of it as a part of the monastic Easter.

1 For the bells at Evesham, *v. Chron. Evesh.* 98–100; for St Albans, *GASA*, 1, 60–1.
2 J. A. Froude, *The History of England*, links the melody of church bells, "that peculiar creation of medieval age", with the sight of recumbent effigies of knights in armour.
3 *Concordia*, v, 89–90. Cf. K. Young, *The Drama of the Medieval Church*, 249–50.
4 *The Winchester Troper*, ed. W. H. Frere (Henry Bradshaw Society, 1894), p. 17.

CHAPTER XXXII

THE PLACE OF THE MONASTERY IN THE FABRIC OF THE CHURCH AND OF SOCIETY

I

In order to understand at all the manifold relationships that existed between the monasteries and the kings and bishops of England, and between the monasteries again and the churches which lay upon, or formed part of, their property, and in order to appreciate the causes and the nature of the controversies to which these relationships gave rise in the twelfth century, it is necessary to have some conception of the social and ecclesiastical framework of the early Middle Ages, and of the development of the law and discipline of the Church during the centuries that elapsed between the dissolution of the Roman Empire and the simultaneous emergence of the perfect feudal state and of the movement of legal and disciplinary reform associated with the name of Gregory VII. This is all the more necessary since English ecclesiastical historians have for the most part neglected to study early Roman and Carolingian practice, and have therefore tended to ignore the immense legacy from the past that gives a character to so many institutions in this country, and have looked only at the superficial, proximate causes of much that happened under the Norman and Angevin monarchs. Before, therefore, approaching the study of the movement among the black monks towards exemption from the jurisdiction of the diocesan bishop, and of the parochial organization dependent upon the monasteries, a sketch must be attempted of the changes in the ecclesiastical fabric between the days of St Benedict and those of St Bernard, and of the consequent change in the relationship of the monasteries to the other members of the Church.

The monastery of St Benedict on Monte Cassino, where the Rule was written, stood, so far as can be ascertained, in a practical independence of all external authority, both civil and ecclesiastical. Situated at a distance from any city or group of great estates, virtually outside the boundaries of parochial and diocesan organization, the only links that bound it to the external framework of the Church were the need for a bishop's hand to ordain ministers for the altar, and the right and duty of the bishop within whose sphere of influence the abbey lay to take measures, should need arise, to safeguard the discipline of the monastic life.[1] Nor was there any possibility of collision outside the monastery, for the great majority of the monks of Italy in the sixth century were laymen, and though they

---

1 The only references to the bishop in the Rule are those which concern these points: e.g. *Regula S. Benedicti* (ed. Butler), c. lxii, 19; c. lxiv, 12; c. lxv, 8.

might on occasion preach to a pagan or neglected population, they had no cure of souls, or charge of churches. Between the monks and the decaying civil government there was an equal lack of relationship; the monastery was, to all intents and purposes, an isolated cell of life.

Great indeed is the contrast between this condition of freedom and isolation and the manifold relations and dependences and responsibilities of the black monk houses in regard to the Church and society of the later Middle Ages. The majority of these relationships, at least until the end of our period, owed their existence to the great social and racial movements of previous centuries, and especially to the claims of individuals, whether private proprietors or those holding positions of public authority, to own and dispose of Church rights and property of every kind. A brief account, therefore, must be given of the origin, development and decline of the system of private ownership and control of churches in western Europe; only so will it be possible to grasp the problems connected with the parish organization of the monastic churches, with monastic exemption, and with the absorption of the monasteries into the feudal system.[1]

II

When, at the time of Constantine, the Church became a recognized part of society, its possessions and the jurisdiction over them were regulated by a legal system based upon Roman law. This law, which had already

---

1 The whole system of the private ownership of churches (the *ecclesiae propriae* of contemporary documents) which is comprehended under the convenient German term *Eigenkirchentum* (with its cognates *Eigenkirchenidee, Eigenkirchenrecht,* etc.) has been the object of much research during the past fifty years. This has been especially the case in Germany, where its study has formed the life-work of Ulrich Stutz, whose early publications, *Die Eigenkirche als Element des mittelalterlich-germanischen Kirchenrechts* and *Geschichte des kirchlichen Benefizialwesens von seinen Anfängen bis auf die Zeit Alexanders III* (both Berlin, 1895), marked an epoch. The latter book, in particular, though at first sight of forbidding density, is a masterpiece of ordered and documented presentation. Stutz became head of a *seminar* of pupils, and general editor of a long series of monographs on this and kindred subjects, of which one dealing with the twelfth century, *Kurie und Kloster,* by Georg Schreiber (Stuttgart, 2 vols. 1910), will be often used in a later chapter, and his work influenced many other historians, above all Heinrich Böhmer, who contributed in 1921 a monograph on *Eigenkirchentum in England* to the collection of studies presented to Felix Liebermann on his seventieth birthday. *V.* also note at the end of this chapter.

Simultaneously, the French scholar Imbart de la Tour had been following a parallel course of research concerning the origins of the parochial system of the Middle Ages, the results of which appeared in *Les paroisses rurales du ive au xie siècles* (Paris, 1900), and common ground was also covered by Paul Thomas in *Le droit de propriété des laïques sur les églises* (Paris, 1906) and Mgr. E. Lesne, *Histoire de la propriété ecclésiastique en France* (? Paris, vol. I, 1910 onwards). Subsequent monographs and articles by these and other scholars have added precision to details, but have done little to modify the general conclusions that can be drawn from Stutz's original work, and the documentation printed by him and Imbart de la Tour render any new sifting of the sources superfluous. Stutz himself contributed an excellent summary of the whole question, together with a bibliography to date, in his article *Eigenkirche, Eigenklöster* in the supplementary volume (23) of Hauck's *Realenzyklopädie für protestantische Theologie* (1913). The subject has received far too little attention from English historians.

developed with great precision the conception of a society, a community and a corporation possessed of rights and owning property, exactly suited its needs. The "church" of a city was at once recognized as a *collegium* or corporation; the control of its property was vested in the bishop, and within the diocese or area administered by the city-church the bishop remained for long the only acting proprietor of church land and goods. These powers he enjoyed not as an individual or as the head of a family, but as the representative of the individual "church". Roman law had always recognized the competence of *personae morales*, and the concept of a church or of any religious institute as a *persona moralis* was natural and simple. When, side by side with the growth of public church property, belonging to the city community and controlled by the bishop, there grew up also gradually in the country districts and on large and distant estates a multitude of sanctuaries, oratories and chapels, built by the proprietors for their private convenience or devotion, the question of their status was considered and made the subject of legislation at Rome. Gelasius I, whose pontificate (492–6) coincided with the youth of St Benedict, laid down that for all consecrations of new churches constructed by private individuals permission must be asked from Rome; the bishop of the diocese was then to examine the case and receive from the builder the church and its endowment; the founder was to disclaim all rights save the right of access held in common with all his fellow-Christians;[1] the church itself was regarded as henceforth a *persona* with inalienable properties and privileges. The founder, however, and his heirs, might present to the bishop for examination, ordination and installation a cleric of their choice to serve the church. This concession, which was to have such far-reaching consequences, was in origin no more than the legalization of a common and convenient practice; in later centuries the private owners claimed it as an indefeasible right, while canonists wished to regard it as a pure concession.

This traditional system, centralized upon the city-church, upon the bishop and upon Rome, for which a careful legislation was slowly maturing,[2] was in great part shattered by the cataclysm of the barbarian invasions and by the course taken by the conversion of the northern nations. In the new countries dioceses were territories rather than cities, and bishops of necessity looked for support to their immediate temporal ruler rather than to canon law, or to their metropolitan, or to the pope.

1 Stutz, *Geschichte*, 57–62, and the many examples there given, e.g. J-E, 630, 679, 704, etc., especially 680: "Nihil tamen fundator ex hac basilica sibi noverit vindicandum, nisi processionis aditum, qui Christianis omnibus in commune debetur."

2 Cf. Fournier et Le Bras, *Histoire des Collections canoniques en Occident*, I, 14 [the writer of the section is M. Le Bras]: "Une Église parfaitement hiérarchisée, pourvue de lois précises, abondantes; tel est le résultat de l'activité organisatrice qui s'est déployée dans toute la chrétienté au temps même où se préparait la désagrégation de l'Empire." Cf. also *ibid.* 7: "Ce temps de brillante activité qu'inaugure le pape Gélase et qui s'achève par le pontificat d'Hormisdas", and P. Thomas, *Le droit de propriété des laïques*, 14: "La législation du pape Gélase qui constitue un point culminant...le but que [l'église] se propose avec Gélase, est de combattre le laïcisme, d'empêcher toute ingérence des laïques."

36-2

For the groups of city-churches was substituted the territorial church (*Landeskirche*), and for the corporate ownership a system of private proprietorship of all church property (*Eigenkirchentum*).[1] New places of worship were no longer constructed by the old communities of towns living under the rule of a bishop, but by the new possessors of the number-less *villae* of Italy and Gaul, and by the missionary enterprise of monks in the north and of Celtic monastic immigrants into the west and south of France.

Over all such new foundations the claims of private ownership were victorious. For the principle of canon law that a church carried with it its dower of inalienable land and revenue was gradually substituted the principle of Germanic law that all upon the soil fell under the dominion of the soil's owner. Along with the fabric of the church went the revenues: the income from the church lands, the tax, the oblations of the faithful, the tithes. When once churches were regarded as private property they fell to the level of all other private property, and as such could be given away, sold, exchanged and bequeathed.[2] Inheritance, when there was more than one heir, produced a further complication, and churches, that is, the income derived from them and the rights enjoyed by the owner, were split into two, three, four, eight, or even twelve parts. Among these private owners the king was naturally pre-eminent, but the bishops of the ancient dioceses, while losing their rights as public proprietors or ad-ministrators over the old parish churches, gradually became themselves owners in a private capacity of churches which they had built, or which had been given or bequeathed to them.[3] Monasteries also became owners of churches. In some cases these had been constructed by the monks themselves for the surrounding population; more often they were gifts, either a part of the original endowment of land by the founder, or presented by individual benefactors, or, finally, acquired by every kind of legacy and exchange. Along with the development of private ownership the right of presentation, secured to the founder in early days by canon and civil law, became a right of appointment, and the bishop's power of examination,

1 The various theories as to the origin of *Eigenkirchentum* will be found in the works already referred to. The subject, though apparently so remote from modern life, proved capable of arousing the patriotic susceptibilities of the scholars concerned. Stutz, in his general conclusions, saw in the creation and diffusion of the *Eigenkirchenidee* an achievement of the German race; in his later work the *Eigenkirche* became a key capable of unlocking a whole host of medieval problems; this impelled French scholars first to vindicate the institution of *Ecclesiae propriae* for the Latin races and later to minimize, unduly it would seem, their importance in history. In consequence, the savants of the two nations have made little use of each other's magnificent work.

2 Stutz, *Geschichte*, 140–50, with the numerous charters cited; Imbart de la Tour, *Les paroisses rurales*, 198: "L'Église rurale devient une *res privata*...elle peut être donnée, vendue, léguée. Contrairement au principe du droit romain qui fait de toute *res sacra* une chose publique, elle entre dans la propriété individuelle; elle a un maître."

3 Stutz, *Geschichte*, 296 *seqq.*; Imbart de la Tour, *Les paroisses rurales*, 233: "Ainsi, le pouvoir épiscopal recule peu à peu devant le pouvoir seigneurial"; and *ibid.* 229: "On peut dire qu'au xie siècle l'unité religieuse du diocèse n'existe plus."

rejection and substitution was reduced to a mere formality or disappeared altogether, in some cases through explicit renunciation. Thus while the bond between priest and lord became ever stronger, that between bishop and priest tended to disappear altogether.[1]

These changes from the old canonical scheme of things were almost entirely the outcome of new social and economic conditions, and were often due to the action of irrational, material forces. The gradual emergence of "feudalism", first as a customary disposition of things, next as an all-embracing framework of authority and finally as a logical, quasi-scientific form of political theory, altered the whole aspect of the Church in north-western Europe and deeply affected the *Eigenkirchenidee*. Churches, and especially the nucleus of land and income enjoyed by the priest, came to be regarded as any other fief or *beneficium* in the disposal of a lord, and to be treated as such; that is, to be bestowed for services rendered or antici-pated. Thus from being merely a piece of property capable of being disposed of by an act of private generosity or goodwill, a church became part of a greater complex, the holding of a landowner. At the same time the universal need and practice of "commendation" of small men to great to secure protection developed, between priest and owner, into feudal homage and service and led to the recipient of a church falling into the class of his lord's "men" from whom an oath of fealty was demanded before the *beneficium* was bestowed.[2] Thence, by a natural process, the bestowal of private churches came to take the form common to all feudal gifts, that of investiture, with its accompanying oath and the tradition of some of the insignia of office. Ecclesiastical benefices of all kinds were thus split into innumerable groups of honors, owing submission some to the king, some to bishops, some to monasteries and some to lay lords, and subject like all other fiefs to rights of appointment, performance of duties and fixed payments at a change of occupant or during a vacancy.

The final stage was reached when in the eleventh century the countries north and west of the Alps became capable of devising and maintaining a logical and universal theory of authority in the state. Under this, what the ancient and modern worlds have recognized as the public rights and powers of the monarch assumed the private character of a real eminent dominion, a real ownership of all the land and property which was

---

1 Stutz, *Geschichte*, 137–8: "Es ist das Jahrhundert, in dem der Metropolitanverband zerfiel...die kirchliche Disziplin sich bedenklich lockerte...kurz, jener Zeitraum, in dem der Zerfall der fränkischen Landeskirche sich vollzog"; Imbart de la Tour, *Les paroisses rurales*, 105: "Alors...commencent le désordre, l'enchevêtrement des institutions religieuses ...une même force mystérieuse et immuable travaillait partout à résoudre l'État et l'Église en petites groupes"; Fournier et Le Bras, *Les Collections canoniques*, 1, 22: "Les agents d'unité suspendent ou ralentissent leur activité...le risque d'une dispersion complète s'aggrave."

2 Imbart de la Tour, *Les paroisses rurales*, 234: "Il n'y a pas de différence entre la pro-priété d'une église et la propriété d'une terre"; 299: "La paroisse est absorbée par la seig-neurie...il ne reste plus au prêtre qu'à devenir l'homme du seigneur."

possessed and enjoyed by his subjects as a gift and fief from himself.[1] The wheel had now come full circle in the system of private ownership, and to the chaos and decentralization of Merovingian times from which it had sprung had succeeded, in such lands as south Germany and Normandy in the eleventh century, the perfect, compact feudal state which, however loosely knit according to both ancient and modern theories of government, had its only bond in the supreme dominion of the monarch over every yard of land and stick of property, with the consequent duties of fidelity and service from all holders. Almost insensibly the process was completed by the emergence of a powerful ruling house in Normandy and England.

Under this dispensation the old canonical relations of ecclesiastical authority and private owner were almost exactly reversed. The Roman decrees of the age of Gelasius I gave complete and supreme ultimate dominion to the Church, that is, to the bishop and finally to the pope. Private founders had no more than a *nudum jus*, if even that, to a church. They could present a cleric, but the actual choice and ordination lay with the bishop, who had complete and sole authority over the priest ever after. Now, in practice and in what there was of theory also, private owners had a complete *jus proprietatis*, and above them, and over all property, whether of monks, bishops or metropolitans, the monarch had dominion. He, and lay proprietors in general, now commended and bestowed churches, abbacies and bishoprics, and invested the nominees with their spiritual *beneficia*. To the ecclesiastical authority, if indeed it had any articulate voice at all, was left only a final transeat and ratification.

It was this state of things that precipitated the great conflicts of the eleventh and twelfth centuries, for in reality it was one and the same social and intellectual renaissance that made possible at once the creation of the unified feudal state and the resurrection of the ancient Church law and polity. From about 1000 onwards a new school of churchmen began to make its appearance which attacked the whole system of private ownership on the grounds alike of high principle and old law. At first this party was concerned with the reform of the coarsest abuses, such as simony and "nicolaism", and of acts of private iniquity, rather than with the system of secular ownership as such; later, under the leadership of the canonists who preceded and accompanied Hildebrand, an attempt was made to invoke ancient law and conciliar decrees against lay proprietorship of churches great and small; finally, the battleground was transferred by Gregory VII from *Eigenkirchen* to the Empire and became the celebrated

1 Cf. U. Stutz, art. *Eigenkirche* in *Realenzyklopädie f. prot. Theologie*, and Imbart de la Tour, *Les paroisses rurales*, 340: "C'est un des traits essentiels de ce régime que la puissance publique ait un caractère privé et qu'elle se traduise par un domaine éminent, une 'haute' propriété sur les terres qui dépendent d'elle."

struggle over the Imperial prerogative and supremacy, and over imperial and royal investiture of high spiritual office.[1] The phases of this conflict do not fall at all within the scope of the present study. It is sufficient to note that in the course of a century the victory of the Church over the feudal and political development of *Eigenkirchentum* was decisive in the realm of theory and law, though far from complete in practice. The classical canonists of the age of Gratian and Alexander III succeeded in placing the spiritual authority, and above all the authority of the papacy, in a position of supremacy which could be assailed by no forces which paid any regard to the traditional legislation of Christendom.

But the system of private ownership and disposal of the individual churches and church revenues of western Europe could not be so easily uprooted, either in the realm of law or in that of practice. It was not, like high feudalism, a theoretical claim concerning rulers alone, but was a dense growth of venerable antiquity with roots deep in the social and economic life of the whole of western Christendom, and directly affected the interests of every man of property, not excluding abbots, bishops and the papacy itself. The councils and popes who had first condemned lay investiture had also condemned lay ownership of churches, and a whole family of movements of reform, including the Cistercians and numerous bodies of canons regular and secular, had arisen pledged to honour the spirit and letter of their decrees. Half a century later the great canonists laboured to separate those parts of a church's revenue which were wholly spiritual in origin and destination from those which might lawfully pass into lay hands, and to reduce the lay right of the bestowal of a benefice to the ancient privilege of gratuitous presentation to the bishop.[2] But the massive and tenacious forces of resistance were too strong to permit of a complete restitution of the *status quo* of A.D. 500, and indeed a wholesale transference of such vast and manifold sources of wealth and influence to the trusteeship of the spirituality of Europe was neither possible nor desirable. In the event there was a sharp division of tendencies. On the one hand the churches possessed by religious bodies of all kinds fell more and more into what was called incorporation or impropriation. This, the process by which the owning body took to itself all revenues and rights and appointed (or presented for appointment) a stipendiary to hold office *in spiritualibus*, became later what has been called the "vicarage system"; it was in reality the perpetuation of the essential features of *Eigenkirch-*

---

1 The clearest accounts of this movement are in Fournier et Le Bras, *Les Collections canoniques*, vol. 2, and A. Fliche, *La Réforme grégorienne*, vol. 1.

2 U. Stutz, *Gratian und die Eigenkirchen*, art. in *Zeitschrift für Rechtsgeschichte*, XLV (1911), Kanonistische Abteilung 1, 1 *seqq.* Stutz remarks *ibid.* 27, note 1: "Die eigentlich wissenschaftliche und systematische Bekämpfung des Eigenkirchenrechts beginnt...erst mit Gratian." But as early as 1059 the synod of Rome under Nicholas II had decreed (can. 6): "ut per laicos nullo modo quilibet clericus aut presbyter obtineat ecclesiam nec gratis nec pretio" (Labbe, *Concilia*, IX, 1010).

entum under another name.[1] On the other hand, the enjoyment by lay proprietors of the revenues of churches was, in part at least, curtailed, traffic in churches and the splitting of the sources of income into fractions was no longer countenanced, and the right of dominion and bestowal of benefices was reduced to the right of patronage. How these processes affected in their development the monasteries of England will be discussed on a later page.

III

Having thus passed briefly in review the evolution of law and practice regarding the holding of church property in Europe between 500 and 1100, it is now necessary to return to the early days of Western monachism in order to examine the gradual change in the relationship of the monastery to both bishops and lay owners and suzerains.

In the countries where settled monastic bodies were numerous, and especially in Egypt, Asia Minor and the Greek islands, conciliar decrees and civil enactments had taken cognizance of them from very early times, and in particular the council of Chalcedon in 451 established broad principles which served as a basis for all future legislation. The monks, like all other Christians, were to come under the bishop's jurisdiction; it was for him to ratify their choice of an abbot, to consecrate the church, to appoint or approve its clergy, and in general to watch over the discipline of the establishment.[2] At the same time it was recognized that the monastic way of life and the monastic code or Rule (where one existed) was beyond the bishop's control; his function was to guarantee its observance. A similar function was his with regard to monastic property, though here there was more room for controversy. It is indeed self-evident that no explicit system of "exemption" from episcopal control could find a place in the Church until an articulate central authority legislated for a unified body; all Christians fell perforce under the external jurisdiction of the successors of the apostles in one way or another, and until there was in action a power that could remove the monks from the control of the local bishop and take them under its own supreme surveillance they necessarily remained subject to the diocesan.

In the West, it was not till settled and flourishing monasteries multiplied, partly as a result of the Rule, and till the reign of the first great monk-

1 As Stutz puts it in the article cited in the preceding note, p. 12: "So entstand als zweite Tochter des Eigenkirchenrechtes und als jüngere Schwester des Patronates die Inkorporation."

2 F. Homes Dudden, *Gregory the Great* (1905), vol. 2, ch. ix, gives references to pre-Gregorian conciliar activity; cf. also pp. 79, 80 and esp. p. 84, note 3. Still more abundant references will be found in E. Lesne, *Histoire de la Propriété ecclésiastique en France*, .I, ch. xi: "Les monastères propriétaires", pp. 124 *seqq*. A useful outline may also be consulted in *Le très ancien Droit Monastique de l'Occident* of T. P. McLaughlin (1935), especially pp. 130 *seqq*.

pope, that canonical legislation began to develop. Gregory I was the first pope to make the monastic order his peculiar care and to take frequent and direct action against bishops and monks who failed to respect their mutual obligations, and by means of numerous "privileges" issued to monasteries he did much to codify these obligations and to provide a basis upon which succeeding generations could erect a more elaborate edifice. Moreover, in his energetic remonstrances to encroaching bishops he showed that the papacy could be a very active court of appeal for the monks, and in at least one case he hinted that he would be prepared, should need arise, to take measures amounting to real "exemption".[1]

It is not therefore surprising that the first case of canonical exemption should have occurred within a few years of the death of Gregory the Great. This was the privilege issued in 628 by Honorius I in favour of the Celtic monastery recently founded by Columbanus at Bobbio near Genoa. The surrounding territory having fallen under the control of Arian Lombards, the pope withdrew Bobbio from the jurisdiction of the local ordinary and set it directly under that of the Apostolic See. The Bobbio privilege became common form, and appears as such in the papal *Liber Diurnus*;[2] it was repeated in isolated cases in the eighth and subsequent centuries, though it must be remarked that many of these documents have been questioned as forgeries. Thus papal policy, before the great invasions had wholly dislocated the ancient framework of the Church, was beginning to protect and to legislate for monks as a class more nearly pertaining to its care than any other.

The great changes which took place in the seventh century throughout Gaul, Germany and Italy, by introducing a new society composed of new races, put a stop to this slow canonical development and set in its place a complicated body of customary relationships and *de facto* dependencies. Under the ancient Empire, the monasteries had been completely free from secular control. The newly founded monasteries of the Merovingian Empire were regarded as being owned, at least radically, by the founder, and even in the case of monasteries previously or independently founded, spoliations and the gradual devolution of all authority led to a general subordination of the unprotected to the strong by a relationship of *commendatio*.[3] Gradually, all fell under the dominion of either bishops, kings or lesser lords, and as the king alone could guarantee complete protection and give the fullest freedom, more and more houses were commended to him and thus became his property, royal *Eigenklöster*.

1 Cf. F. Homes Dudden, who in the chapter referred to above gives an excellent account of Gregory's activity. The nearest approach to full exemption is in *Epp.* VII, 40 (quoted by Dr Dudden, 188, note 4; and McLaughlin, 184, note 3).

2 JE, 2017; *Liber Diurnus* (ed. Sickel), 82. Cf. also art. by Dom H. Leclercq, *Exemption monastique*, in *DAC*, v, i, 952–62.

3 A good account of this development is given by Lesne, *Propriété ecclésiastique*, i, 79–143, esp. ch. xi: "Les monastères propriétaires" and ch. xii: "Les monastères possédés".

In the ninth century this *commendatio* to the king or emperor, with its correlative of *tuitio* or protection, by which monasteries passed under the *mundium palatii*, was extended to all houses. Hence there gradually arose the state of things, familiar in England in its fullest development only after the Conquest, by which the king exercised eminent dominion over all monasteries. As the king owned the monastery he could give it to whom he wished; the sum total of property, the *abbatia*, could then be treated as a *beneficium*, and in the latter half of the ninth century this became the general principle on the Continent. Abbeys became ecclesiastical honors, given, like other honors, to faithful servants or officials, though in the Carolingian Empire spiritual autonomy, together with a fair amount of administrative freedom, was usually secured by the monks. When, however, the royal power grew ever more feeble under the successors of Charlemagne, the royal *tuitio* became less and less of a safeguard, and the abbeys began to fall once more entirely into the hands of private individuals or local rulers. All the movements of reform in the late ninth and early tenth centuries aimed at escaping from this subjection, but in the majority of cases, apart from Cluny and her family, the monasteries fell back either into complete secular ownership or into the less objectionable relationship of feudal *commendatio*.

During these varied phases of secularization and feudalization the old canonical control of the bishops lapsed, and was replaced by two equally uncanonical movements. On the one hand, bishops were among the most prominent and often among the most unscrupulous invaders of monastic rights, and obtained total or partial possession of a large number of abbeys; on the other, many monasteries succeeded in obtaining, as a part of their grant of immunity from the sovereign, a total or partial suspension in their regard of all episcopal rights, and thus were set in a kind of vacuum of ecclesiastical authority,[1] for there was during these centuries no question of the papacy exercising direct and effective powers of supervision.

Indeed, the papacy itself, by an adaptation of ideas at once strange and natural, had become a part of the new order of things. When all churches and monasteries were falling into private ownership and under lay suzerainty the Apostolic See came to receive churches and above all abbeys "commended" to its protection, which thus became the property and domain of the Roman Church, the *Eigenklöster* of St Peter.[2] This sub-

---

1 Lesne, *Propriété ecclésiastique*, II, ii, 14–15: "Une église royale, en effet, est en même temps une église parfaitement autonome....Un monastère ne peut, au sentiment des hommes de ce temps, être en la possession de la communauté qui l'habite et de ses abbés réguliers que sous le couvert de la propriété royale....L'autonomie dont jouit un établissement monastique est rattachée, suspendue en quelque sorte, au *dominium* royal." Cf. also *ibid.* II, i, 22–3, and the same author's article *Évêché et abbaye* (*v.* Bibliography).

2 U. Stutz, *Geschichte*, 313, where the common formula of the *Liber Diurnus*, the outcome of decentralization, is discussed. The terms *jus*, *dominium* and *proprietas* are commonly used, in all privileges of protection, of the position of the church of St Peter *vis-à-vis* the monastery "commended" to it.

jection to Rome brought with it none of the inconveniences of royal protection and proprietorship; the papacy had neither the power nor the inclination to interfere in the material and spiritual administration, and beyond paying a small tax on feudal analogy as a sign of subjection, the house lost nothing whatever. It gained, on the other hand, a very great liberty, for often the charter by which a founder or reformer gave the monastery to St Peter stipulated that neither king nor other lord might bestow the abbey as a benefice or possess it as such; often, too, any kind of encroachment on the part of a bishop was expressly prohibited. Thus, though on the plane of ideas the difference between the ancient canonical dependence on Rome and the new quasi-feudal relationship was immense, it was in fact a very natural transition from soliciting a privilege of the Gregorian type from Rome in the seventh century to commending a house to St Peter in return for a charter of liberty in the eighth or ninth, and the latter formula often employed phrases of the former. In this way there grew up between 850 and 1050, amid the manifold feudal relationships and groups of western Europe, a large class of monasteries "commended" to the Apostolic See. This class, which was such by virtue of no common legal or disciplinary bond, but by reason of individual acts and charters following the same broad pattern, was made up of all kinds of elements. Besides new foundations hoping thus to secure independence, and a certain number of powerful old houses linked by ancient tradition with Rome, it comprehended a large number of central and north Italian and Alpine monasteries, founded for the most part by Lombard kings and favoured with grants of complete royal "immunity", which at some time of their existence exchanged the royal for the papal eminent dominion, while retaining under the latter all the practical liberty they had enjoyed under the former sovereignty. From the early tenth century onwards a prominent place in the group was occupied by Cluny and her growing swarm of dependencies.

In the eclipse of papal prestige in the tenth century the protection of St Peter counted for little; the abbey, for its part, might decay or be despoiled, or find in some royal or local lord a more powerful protector than Rome. But Rome was immortal, and in very many cases the written charter remained, throughout all vicissitudes, in the archives of the house. When, in the course of years, the papacy once more became a paramount power with which all rulers had to reckon, the old privileges were drawn forth, studied, and it may be interpolated or rewritten in a new idiom, and became once more instruments of power.

When, therefore, in the first half of the eleventh century, the reviving papacy found its strongest ally in the monastic order and especially in the new monastic reform, Rome at once became active in ensuring to these centres of religion complete liberty of action by binding them to herself. At first she proceeded in the fashion most familiar to the ideas of the time, by multiplying the number of monasteries quasi-feudally commended to her and thus forming part of the property of St Peter. Many of the new families, such as the Camaldolese and Vallombrosians, slipped in this way from episcopal control and a number of old houses, rendered independent by a grant of immunity from some royal house long vanished, and now as it were resting on air, transferred themselves, with all their claims, to Rome. Besides these, when the victory of the papacy became evident at the end of the eleventh century, a host of monasteries secured from the Curia a charter of protection and a number of liberties, which, though usually falling short of complete independence at home, had their effect in bringing to the cognizance of the papacy the affairs of almost all existing monastic bodies. Finally, when the study and application of canon law became common, popes began to embody in confirmations of old privileges words and phrases which bestowed upon certain monasteries full canonical exemption from the jurisdiction of the diocesan.

Consequently, it was one of the many tasks undertaken by the great canonists and legislating popes of the twelfth century to discover or create amid this confused mass of individual grants some fixed principles and formulae with which to produce order, to settle disputes and, finally, to bring into being the system of exemption which, in the end, encouraged by the rise of centralized monastic institutions and still more by the appearance of the fully-fledged international orders of friars, became an essential part of the law and discipline of the Church. Some of the stages of this progress, so far as they affected English monasteries, must be considered in a later chapter; they were accompanied by bitter controversies and a considerable element of chicanery, and the monasteries involved, at least within the limits of our period, continued to wear the appearance natural to a group of individuals of disparate origin combined almost by force under the bond of a common formula.

IV

This long process of evolution and revolution affected the monasteries of Europe in yet another way. Besides being themselves property capable of suffering appropriation and possession at the hands of others, and besides being themselves proprietors capable of owning property (e.g. churches and tithes) originally spiritual, they were themselves a part of the spiritual organization of the Church, and thus stood in peculiar relations both to the churches they owned and to ecclesiastical authority.

A monastery that was more than a group of hermits included necessarily within its walls an oratory or church. This originally, like all other churches, depended directly upon a bishop not only for its consecration, but for its minister, for neither the monks of the East nor those of the

West were at the first clerics. Inevitably, however, it came about that priests became monks or that a member of the monastery was proposed by the abbot for ordination, and in the sixth century, as seen in the Rule[1] and the letters of Gregory the Great, it had become recognized that an abbot stood in the position of the founder of a church, only with enhanced dignity: he had, that is, the right of proposing his subjects to the bishop for ordination as ministers of the monastic church. In almost every other way, as has been seen, the monastic community, so long as its activities remained circumscribed by the walls of the monastery, was almost wholly independent of the diocesan.[2] Gradually, however, a more complicated situation began to develop. Almost all monastic communities became nuclei round which clustered a large population of servants, functionaries, sick, poor, guests, pilgrims and tradespeople, all living upon the monastic estates; the vast majority of abbeys, also, soon became possessed of churches. As regards the immediate dependents of all kinds, it was the custom from the first, and remained so throughout the Middle Ages, to supply their spiritual needs in a church separate from that of the monastery and usually through the ministry of a priest not himself a monk. By rights, such a church and priest should have fallen under the direct control of the bishop, but special privileges and the influence of the *Eigenkirchenidee* often resulted in securing for them a position of complete or partial independence, and in later centuries, if the monastery were "commended" to the Apostolic See, the extern church and the district served by it, which was often one enjoying various kinds of immunity, was included in the "property" of St Peter.[3]

As regards the churches owned by the abbey but not used by its dependents, the greatest variety of practice prevailed, governed in each case by the past history and special privileges of the place. The simplest case was where chapels had been constructed upon monastic lands for the needs of the population. These, which often developed into parish churches, usually followed the normal course of other such chapels and churches, becoming *de facto* private property, but retaining dormant relationships to the bishop which woke again to life when the episcopate wished and was able to urge its claims. A more complicated situation arose when a group of parish churches formed from the first a *bloc* of territory sharing some kind of immunity with the abbey. In south Germany and the Alps this was often due to the missionary activity of the monks in the days of the conversion; they had built churches served by themselves which, even when monks ceased to minister, remained closely dependent upon the

---

1 Cf. *Regula S. Benedicti*, c. lxii, 1–3: "Si quis abbas sibi presbyterum vel diaconem ordinari petierit [*sc*. ab episcopo], de suis elegat qui dignus sit sacerdotio fungi."

2 Thus St Benedict, on arriving at Monte Cassino, found the scattered population largely pagan, and himself destroyed two pagan shrines, erecting in their stead oratories of St John the Baptist and St Martin.

3 *V*. Schreiber, *Kurie und Kloster im 12 Jahrhundert*, II, 202, note 5; 203, note 1.

abbey. In other countries such a *bloc* was formed when the founder, who was either the immediate or ultimate lord of the land, created round the monastery a free territory protected against both secular and ecclesiastical encroachment. Such a district, if it succeeded in passing across from royal to papal protection, often received in its papal privilege a confirmation of independence of the bishop for its parishes; this might be either total or partial, and admitted of numerous modifications. A number of abbeys in Lombardy and central Italy controlled such districts; there, the secular authority broke down earlier than in the north and, in addition, several monasteries were presented by popes with papal *Eigenkirchen* which even after the transfer retained their independence of any other bishop. These Italian, Lombardic and Alpine houses were the originals of what became in time a class of holders of a jurisdiction unique in the Church, and indeed anomalous: they became what were later called *prelaturae nullius* [*sc.* diocesis], districts, that is, in which the religious superior exercised over the parishes belonging to his house all the spiritual and administrative powers enjoyed by a bishop, save those for which the episcopal character was necessary.¹ In the lands between the Rhine and the Pyrenees the distance from Rome and the more regular development of feudal society rarely favoured the growth of this type of immunity. In England, on the other hand, the first stage of the process, a monastery, that is, surrounded by its own churches and forming a territory enjoying royal "immunity", was often in being, and, as will be noted on a later page, a number of these, and in particular those already connected with Rome by "commendation", seized an opportunity sooner or later to carry their churches over into the immediate jurisdiction of the Apostolic See. Their history will form the subject of a later chapter.

1 Some of these, such as La Cava, Monte Vergine, Subiaco, Monte Cassino and Farfa-St Paul's in Italy, and St Maurice in Switzerland, have preserved their peculiar status throughout the centuries, winning for themselves in course of time particular mention in the *corpus* of Canon Law, and have served in recent years as models for *abbatiae nullius* in Asia, America and Australia. An interesting account of the origins of exemption in Germany will be found in the article by H. Goetting, *Die klösterliche Exemtion in Nord- und Mitteldeutschland* (*v.* Bibliography). The author notes (p. 108) that Fulda's exemption in 751 was "das erste und auf Jahrhunderte hinaus einzige Exemtionsprivileg auf deutschen Boden."

The above pages were already in the press when the valuable collection of historical essays, translated from the German by G. Barraclough with the title *Medieval Germany, 911–1250*, appeared (1938). This contains U. Stutz's inaugural lecture of 1894, *The Proprietary Church as an Element of Medieval Germanic Ecclesiastical Law*, and Hans Hirsch's essay, *The Constitutional History of the Reformed Monasteries during the Investiture Contest* (1913). These and the articles of Goetting and Steinwerder (*v.* Bibliography), contain full references to the literature of the subject in German. A full bibliography of Stutz's writings to date will be found in *Zeitschrift für Rechtsgeschichte* (Kanonistische Abteilung), 71, xxvii (1938), 686–760.

CHAPTER XXXIII

THE ORIGINS AND DEVELOPMENT OF EXEMPTION IN ENGLAND

I

BEFORE THE TIMES OF DUNSTAN

In the foregoing chapter an outline has been given of the gradual changes in the relationship between monasteries and other members and authorities of the Church and secular society in Europe between the days of St Benedict and the epoch of Gregory VII. We have now to consider somewhat more closely the English situation during the same period, for the movement towards canonical exemption in the twelfth century had its roots deep in the past. Too many modern students of medieval English institutions have failed to appreciate this, and, relying on a few *ex parte* statements thrown out in the heat of controversy, have treated the whole question of exemption as if it were a sudden attempt to repel authority, whereas it was in fact the last and most articulate stage in that evolution of privileged rights and jurisdictions, civil and ecclesiastical, which had gone on for centuries in north-western Europe.

In England, although the same two main forces were at work as on the Continent, the tradition, that is, of the Roman Church and the very different outlook and practices of the Germanic and Scandinavian invaders of the Empire, the Church history of this country between 596 and 1066 has a peculiar character of its own more distinctly marked than that of any region covered by the empire of Charlemagne. The manner of the replantation of Christianity in England by the mission of Augustine direct from Rome, followed as it was by several lesser Roman missions such as those of Paulinus and of Theodore and Hadrian, established a close connection with the papacy as the seat of authority and the norm of practice which endured as a vital force until the end of the eighth century and lived on as a powerful sentiment until the Conquest. At the same time the insular situation of the English Church and the later Scandinavian invasions hindered that steady evolution from tribal law and national customs to organized and scientific feudalism that took place in the lands united for a short time under the rule of Charlemagne.

The ultimate origins of the later canonical exemption must be sought in England, as elsewhere, in the independent actions of two very distinct authorities, the papacy and the local ruler.[1] Southern England, with which

---

[1] No single work exists setting out fully the early evolution of what later became "exemption", and until the present century no adequate investigation had been made of the relations between Curia and monasteries. Still less is there in existence any study of the development of the institution in England. Failing, therefore, any one authority to which

alone we are concerned in this matter, received the faith in 596 from the
pope who had carried both the centralization of government and the papal
control of the monastic order further than any of his predecessors, and
for a century and a half after the mission of Augustine England was in
closer touch with Rome than was any other part of the Church north of
the Alps. It is therefore extremely probable that some of the monasteries
of Kent, and especially that of St Augustine's at Canterbury, were recipients of the typical monastic privilege of the time.[1] These, while in no
sense giving canonical exemption, were in the nature of a charter of rights,
giving freedom of abbatial election, empowering the abbot to present his
subjects for ordination, and putting under anathema all, whether seculars
or ecclesiastics, who should invade the properties of the monastery or
interfere with its regular life. Privileges of this type continued to be
issued by energetic popes until the middle of the eighth century; that
obtained by Benet Biscop[2] from Pope Agatho for Jarrow c. 679 was
doubtless couched in the same terms as the extant ones of Agatho to
Chertsey, of John VII to Farfa in 705, of Constantine to Bermondsey
and Woking c. 710,[3] and of the less authentic (at least in their present
dress) letters of Deusdedit II and Agatho to St Augustine's, of Constantine
to Evesham, and of Sergius I to Malmesbury.[4] Modern historians have
dismissed these papal documents far too lightly, owing to certain diplomatic
flaws in some, and a few phrases of clearly later date in others; it is highly
probable that one or two have come down in their original form without
any change, and that the others are in substance perfectly genuine, but have
been interpolated by interested copyists in later controversies.[5] None of

the reader might be referred throughout, I can only indicate, as an excellent technical study
which has not hitherto been superseded, the work of a follower of Ulrich Stutz, *Kurie und
Kloster im 12 Jahrhundert* (2 vols. 1910), by Georg Schreiber, which contains a full biblio-
graphy to date, but which does not profess to treat fully of the early pre-history of exemption.
For the main facts of the individual controversies I may be allowed to refer to two articles
of my own in the *DR*, L (May and October 1932), 201–31; 396–436, with the title *The
Growth of Exemption*. The articles *Abbaye Nullius* and *Censuum Liber* in *DDC* are useful.
Other studies of varying merit on "exemption" are: A. Blumenstok, *Der Päpstliche
Schutz im Mittelalter*; P. Fabre, *Étude sur le Liber Censuum*; F. K. Weiss, *Die kirchlichen
Exemtionen der Klöster*; C. Daux, *La Protection apostolique au moyen-âge*, in *Revue des
Questions historiques*, LXXII (1902), 2 *seq.*; A. Hüfner, *Das Rechtsinstitut der klösterlichen
Exemtion*; G. Letonnelier, *L'Abbaye de Cluny et...Exemption*, in *Millénaire de Cluny*,
the same writer's fuller *L'Abbaye exempte de Cluny et le Saint-Siège*, and, above all, J. F.
Lemarignier, *Les privilèges d'exemption...des abbayes normandes* (1937), which appeared
after this chapter had been written. *V.* also *supra*, p. 574, n. 1.
  1 St Augustine's claimed to possess a bull of Boniface IV (c. 610). Elmham, 129; *JE*,
1997.
  2 Bede, *Historia Abbatum* (ed. Plummer, I, 369): "Benedictus non vile munus adtulit,
epistolam privilegii a venerabili papa Agathone cum licentia, consensu, desiderio, et hortatu
Ecgfridi regis acceptam." Cf. *Historia Ecclesiastica*, IV, xvi (*ibid.* I, 241).
  3 The letter of Agatho to Chertsey is in Brit. Mus. Cott. MS. Vitell. A xiii 24; for that of
Constantine *v.* F. M. Stenton, *Medehamstede and its Colonies* in *Historical Essays in honour
of James Tait* (1933), 313–26, where reference is given to the Farfa bull.
  4 *JE*, 2104, 2105 a (St Augustine's); 2147, 2149 (Evesham); 2140 (Malmesbury).
  5 As long ago as 1892 Paul Fabre in his *Étude sur le Liber Censuum*, 202, remarked:
"Le nombre de ces bulles, fabriquées en des temps et en des lieux très divers [Italy, France,

these instruments give, or profess to give, exemption; they merely safeguard the regular life according to the canonical formulae which became common form under Gregory I and his immediate successors; but by establishing a close connection between the abbey concerned and the Apostolic See they paved the way for further communication and concessions in the future.

Meanwhile, the English monasteries, like those on the Continent, had sought protection and guarantees also from the secular power. The celebrated letter of Bede to Bishop Ecgbert, written c. 734 in what is often called the golden period of Northumbrian monasticism, shows clearly what dangers threatened the monasteries, and how easily they could be absorbed, not only by a king, but by lay proprietors of every rank and by bishops.[1] It was therefore natural for them to seek, by "recommending" themselves to the king or the local ruler, a solemn guarantee of liberty which might form a pendant to the papal privilege, and we know, from the unexceptionable testimony of Bede himself, that such an assurance was frequently granted.[2] The effect of these two guarantees, papal and royal, would be to confirm the monastery as an autonomous house at the centre of a kind of vacuum of external authority.

The next stage in the development of liberty came from the secular power. As on the continent, so in England, the royal founder of a monastery often endowed it with very extensive liberties and immunities, which comprehended not only freedom from external control and taxation of every kind, but the authority to exercise the rights and enjoy the fruits of judicial and other administration on certain lands and estates. Two of the earliest alleged grants of this kind, those to St Albans and Evesham, are both connected with the name of Offa, and here again, though the charters in the form in which they are extant contain flaws and interpolations, there is no reason to reject the tradition of a transaction of the kind just indicated. As with contemporary papal privileges, exemption from episcopal control was not directly envisaged by grantor or recipient; the immunity was of a feudal, not of an ecclesiastical kind; the original canonical position of the bishops in England was tending in the ninth century to dissolve, leaving them on a level with other owners of land, and these royal charters aimed at keeping the monasteries free from all material aggression, from whatever quarter it might come.

England], l'identité de leur objet, leur attribution à une même très courte période [c. 675–725], et le témoignage d'historiens presque contemporains qui placent vers le même temps des actes très semblables *quoad substantiam*, tout cela constitue un ensemble qui doit faire hésiter à rejeter en bloc toute cette masse de documents." As regards Evesham in particular, the criticisms of M. Spaethen in his article *Giraldus Cambrensis und Thomas von Evesham*, in *Neues Archiv*, XXXI (1906), 629–49, have been largely invalidated by Dr R. L. Poole, *The Papal Chancery*, 147, note, and Dr W. Holtzmann, *Papsturkunden in England*, I, i, 112.

1 *Opera Historica* (ed. Plummer), I, 413–18; especially 413, where a monastery is to be made a bishopric *pontificali et regali edicto.*

2 *Hist. Ecclesiastica*, IV, xvi (ed. Plummer, I, 241).

The grant of royal immunities did not cease with the collapse of monastic life in England. The establishment which later became the monastery of Bury St Edmunds, and the church of Ramsey, together with some northern churches, preserved the tradition that their extensive franchises were due to King Athelstan (924–39), and those of other places, such as Glastonbury, Ely, St Augustine's, Canterbury and Croyland, may well have been received or confirmed at his hand.[1] These franchises were not primarily concerned with episcopal authority and had indeed no direct connection with the monastic life, but when regular monasteries were re-established in the churches which enjoyed them, the monks entered immediately into the existing condition of immunity, which was often confirmed or extended by later kings, such as Edgar and Cnut.

Direct disciplinary action with regard to the monastic life, following the old canonical forms, had practically ceased at Rome by the end of the eighth century. Instead, as has been seen, the papacy had adopted from the society around it the custom of receiving into its protection, and some-times into its proprietorship, churches and monasteries who hoped thus to secure some kind of liberty for themselves and their possessions. So far as can be ascertained, no English monastery, with the exception of St Augustine's, Evesham and Malmesbury, had taken this step before the collapse of monasticism at the end of the ninth century.[2] In the revival under Edgar and his immediate successors the privileged position of the new monasteries, the extremely loose diocesan organization, and the fact that the majority of the bishops were themselves monks, made it un-necessary for the monks to seek new safeguards or privileges for themselves at Rome, especially as the papacy was for most of this period at the lowest ebb of its influence. It is probable, however, that a few houses, possessed of ancient papal documents, took the opportunity, when their abbots were on pilgrimage or mission to Rome, of joining the ranks of "commended" or "tributary" abbeys; among those which may have so acted and which are found later in this class are Chertsey and St Albans.

At the accession of Edward the Confessor, therefore, the position was as follows: a number of the monasteries were in possession of extensive liberties and immunities granted by sovereigns, which rendered them in effect wholly free from episcopal jurisdiction; some, moreover, were surrounded by the highly privileged ring of land, usually a mile in radius, known later as the *banleuca*, from which the episcopal as well as the royal

---

1 M. D. Lobel, in *The Ecclesiastical Banleuca in England*, in *Oxford Essays in Medieval History presented to H. E. Salter*, 122–40, notes (p. 129) that tradition ascribed to Athelstan the liberties of Ripon, Beverley, Hexham, Bury and Ramsey. For his connection with Glastonbury and St Augustine's *v*. the early chapters of J. A. Robinson's *The Times of St Dunstan*.

2 St Augustine's was almost alone in claiming to possess, in two bulls of John XII (956), privileges of the tenth century. *V. JL*, 3678–9.

jurisdiction was expressly excluded by royal grant;[1] a few had a traditional connection with Rome, which in some cases amounted to membership of the class of "tributary" monasteries, but in general neither the need nor the opportunity had arisen for this connection to be exploited.

II

FROM THE ACCESSION OF THE CONFESSOR TO *c.* 1100

The accession of Edward the Confessor here, as in all other matters of government, altered the complexion of affairs. Edward perhaps brought with him from Normandy the more explicit and defined conceptions of the rights of a feudal monarch, which included the power of disposing of an abbey as a benefice upon a bishop and the corresponding one of possessing, as patron, a royal *Eigenkloster*. This, together with the tendency to appoint bishops from the royal chapel rather than from heads of monasteries, made the episcopal control a living issue, for in some cases the monks, and in others the king himself, became concerned to maintain the complete spiritual liberty of their houses. Moreover, the accession of the Confessor coincided with the re-entry of the reforming papacy into European politics, together with the accompanying recognition of the need of strengthening all existing bonds between monasteries and Rome, and in particular the relations between the Apostolic See and abbeys which were its "property". Consequently, the reign saw several incidents prophetic of much that was to come after, such as the attempt of Herman of Ramsbury to obtain possession of Malmesbury abbey, the concession to Aethelsig of St Augustine's of the right of using mitre and sandals by Nicholas II in 1063,[2] and above all, the peculiar status acquired by West-minster on its refoundation by the Confessor at the beginning of his reign. Here, although the early history of the house has not yet been cleared from a mist of legend, and all the early charters and bulls are suspect, there can be no doubt as to the founder's design. In the eyes of the Confessor, the abbey was a royal *Eigenkloster*, as directly under his control as the clerks of the chapel royal, and therefore outside the jurisdiction of the bishop of London. At the same time he was anxious, as a devout client of the Apostolic See, that his abbey should have a privileged status at Rome, and in con-sequence the English monastery of St Peter was put under the special patronage and protection of the papacy, thus giving in practice an example of the easy combination of two apparently irreconcilable notions, that of a monarch's *Eigenkloster* and that of an abbey commended in a special

---

1 For this *v.* the essay of M. D. Lobel referred to on the preceding page. The writer enumerates five ecclesiastical *banleucae*: Ripon, Beverley, Bury, Ramsey and Battle, but notes that other churches such as Ely, Croyland and Glastonbury had similar privileged territories.

2 Elmham, 89; Thorne, 1789; *JL*, 4541.

manner to Rome, if not actually committed to the proprietorship of the Apostolic See.[1]

At the death of the Confessor, therefore, in 1065, the position of the privileged monasteries was somewhat as follows. By ancient royal grants the abbeys of St Albans, St Augustine's, Bury, Croyland, Ely, Evesham, Glastonbury and Ramsey had extensive civil and ecclesiastical franchises, which they used in varying degree; out of this group, Bury, Croyland, Ely, Ramsey and possibly Glastonbury had, beyond other immunities, the rights later associated with the *banleuca*, which, besides its other liberties, implied the suspension, within a restricted area, of the bishop's power of excommunicating and interdicting. This suspension, however obtained, came in time to be regarded by the Roman Curia as one of the surest criteria of exemption. Finally, Westminster, though not possessing an enfranchised district, great or small, was a royal *Eigenkloster* or "peculiar".

Partly coincident with this group was the smaller class of monastic houses which were in some living way united to the church of St Peter at Rome. Of these, a group of only five or six in all, Chertsey, Evesham and Malmesbury were in possession of ancient papal privileges, but it is not clear that between their rebirth in the tenth century and the Conquest they had made any active use of this connection, or had in any way developed it.[2] Westminster, on the other hand, had almost certainly been received under the special protection of the Apostolic See during the reign of the Confessor, and St Augustine's had been recognized at Rome as a house belonging to the church of St Peter.

The advent of the Normans brought little change at first. The organization of the recently born Norman territorial Church, centred as it was upon the Duke, who effectively controlled both bishops and monasteries, did not include ancient and extensive franchises such as those of the East-Anglian monasteries, and gave still less scope for the development of privileged connections with Rome, though Fécamp had been freed from diocesan authority in 1006 by Dukes Richard II and Robert the Pious, and St Stephen's, Caen, from the bishop (but not from the metropolitan) in 1068, and both abbeys had been taken under the protection of the Apostolic See.[3] In England, the Conqueror's policy was to respect the *status quo* of the Old English institutions and, in increasing degree, to settle all con-

1 For Westminster *v. The Growth of Exemption* (i), 415–20, and for a criticism of some of the early documents, J. A. Robinson, *Flete's History of Westminster*, introd. xii *seqq.*, and Dr Holtzmann's notes to the bulls he published in *Papsturkunden in England*, 1, ii. The story of the clash between Robert of London and Abbot Wulnoth *c.* 1045–9, though first occurring in a bull of Paschal II of doubtful authenticity (Holtzmann, *op. cit.* 1, ii, no. 9), may well be true.

2 Malmesbury and Chertsey occur in the official list of Cencius (1192) of tax-paying churches (ed. P. Fabre and L. Duchesne, 1889–1910), but it is not known when they first paid tax.

3 For Fécamp and Caen, *v.* J. F. Lemarignier, *Les privilèges d'exemption...des abbayes normandes*, 32–43, 141–6.

troversies at home and prevent the papal movement towards centralization of government from gaining ground. It so happened, however, that one important controversy between a bishop and a monastery broke out early in the reign, before William and Lanfranc had fully established their policy, and before Hildebrand had become pope.

The Norman Arfast, appointed to the East-Anglian see which had its cathedral in the small village of Elmham, found himself poor and un-influential in East Anglia, while the abbey of Bury, besides holding a vast number of *Eigenkirchen* up and down the diocese, had an extensive franchise of eight and a half hundreds, and the smaller *banleuca* containing the town and abbey of St Edmund.[1] A movement was on foot, directed by the king himself, to remove sees situated in open country villages to strong towns, and Arfast, who contemplated transferring himself to Bury, began by claiming it as part of his diocese.[2] Baldwin, the abbot, met his claim by producing the abbey's royal charters of liberty, given by Cnut and confirmed by the Confessor; the king, on the other hand, would seem at first to have countenanced Arfast's design. As all parties recognized the need of permission from Rome for the transference of a see, Baldwin resolved to be before the bishop in proceeding thither, and as his personal relations with the Conqueror, whose physician he was, were excellent, he obtained both permission to do so and letters of recommendation from the king. Alexander II received him with distinction and, having satisfied himself as to Bury's privileged position by royal grant, took the oppor-tunity of uniting the abbey to Rome by receiving it into the most privileged class of papal monasteries, using the most elaborate formula then current to assert its independence of all episcopal authority in England and its direct dependence upon the Holy See.[3] This was too much for Lanfranc, who conceived that the metropolitan should control monasteries freed from their diocesan; he confiscated the papal document and apparently relaxed for a time his efforts on Bury's behalf.[4] Meanwhile, Arfast con-tinued to press his claims, and as barriers had by now been set up between England and Rome the case for Bury's independence was treated as a purely national affair and heard first at a plea before Lanfranc and a jury

1 Heinrich Böhmer, *Das Eigenkirchentum in England*, 332, calculated from *Domesday* that while Bury owned 65 *Eigenkirchen* in Suffolk, the bishop of East Anglia had only two-and-a-half. For Bury's other privileges, *v.* M. D. Lobel, *The Borough of Bury St Edmunds*; H. W. C. Davis, *The Liberties of Bury St Edmund's*, in *EHR*, xxiv (July 1909), 417–31, and above all Prof. D. C. Douglas, *Feudal Documents from the Abbey of Bury St Edmunds*, esp. introd. cxxxiv–clxxi.

2 There is a contemporary account of the struggle by Herman, sometime friend and secre-tary of Arfast, and later in the service of Bury, who wrote *c.* 1096. His *Miracula S. Eadmundi* was excellently edited by F. Liebermann in *Ungedruckte anglo-normannische Geschichtsquellen.* Prof. V. H. Galbraith has printed in *EHR*, xl (April 1925), 222 *seqq.*, a contemporary state-ment of the bishop's case with the title *The East Anglian See and the Abbey of Bury St Edmund's.* This contains (p. 227) the statement that after Arfast's death the king repeatedly endeavoured to make Baldwin bishop and fix the see at Bury.

3 *JL*, 4692.
4 Eadmer, *Hist. Nov.* 133; Gregorii VII *Epp.* i, 31; *JL* ,4803.

from nine counties, and subsequently at a royal council at Winchester in 1081. It was held to be proved, and a royal charter was issued reasserting Bury's complete liberty.[1] Meanwhile Lanfranc, in the case of St Albans, had combined a maintenance of ancient privilege with his conception of his metropolitan rights. The abbey, which had liberties of a kind less definite and far less recently confirmed than Bury, lay within the vast and disorganized diocese of Lincoln, but its neighbourhood to London, and the appointment of Lanfranc's nephew, Paul, as abbot, brought it readily within the sphere of influence of the archbishop. Though there is no precise record of what happened, it would seem that Lanfranc recognized its independent position, under his supreme jurisdiction, and that no objection was made by Remigius of Lincoln.[2]

One important addition was made in the reign of William I to the number of privileged houses. The Conqueror's foundation of Battle was treated by him from the outset as a royal *Eigenkloster*. The early documents purporting to contain his definition of its rights are forged in part, if not wholly, and it is probable that William I gave little thought to the ecclesiastical implications of Battle's freedom and relied on his direct action to safeguard its various privileges, but in practice Battle was from its foundation in a more secure position than even Westminster, for it lay at the centre of a *banleuca*, and had extensive jurisdiction over its large and compact property in Sussex.[3]

Of the other privileged abbeys little is heard before 1100. The peculiar circumstances of some, such as Evesham, and the misfortunes of others, such as Croyland, together with the general disturbances of the change of *régime*, and the strong royal control over bishops and abbots alike, were not favourable to the development of freedom either at home or through papal action. Glastonbury, at the Council of the Parret, appears

1 The giving of the charter is in Herman (ed. Liebermann), 257. The charter itself, no. 137 in Davis, *Regesta Regum Anglo-Normannorum* (cf. cognate nos. 138, 139), is also in *Monasticon*, III, 141, *Memorials of St Edmund's*, I, 347 and Douglas, *Feudal Documents*, no. 7. Davis considered the charter spurious, but the fact and substance of the transaction are undoubted; Prof. Douglas, *op. cit.* introd. xxxii–iv, is inclined to accept the document as genuine.

2 Eadmer, *Hist. Nov.* 37, states: "non solum Lanfrancus, sed et antecessores ejus habuisse noscuntur" the abbey of St Albans, which was confirmed to Anselm by William II in 1093.

3 The early history of Battle has yet to be definitively written; cf. H. W. C. Davis, *The Chronicle of Battle Abbey*, in *EHR*, XXIX (1914), 426–34 and *Regesta Regum Anglo-Normannorum*; H. Round in *Complete Peerage* (1896), VII, 322; R. Graham, *The Monastery of Battle*, in *English Ecclesiastical Studies*, 188–208; Dom D. Knowles, *The Growth of Exemption* (i), 218–25, (ii), 431–6, embodying, pp. 431–2, some valuable observations communicated by Prof. F. M. Stenton.

Two of the Battle charters compare the abbey to the royal chapel and to Westminster: "sicut mea dominica capella, et signum Angliae coronae per quam ego regno" (*Monasticon*, III, 245; Davis, *Regesta*, no. 113); "sicut illa [ecclesia] quae mihi coronam tribuit" (Davis, *Regesta*, no. 262). Cf. the description of Westminster in a bull of Innocent II (1133) printed by Dr Holtzmann, *Papsturkunden in England*, I, ii, 241: "ecclesia que regni tui extat corona." These phrases, even if the charters are forged, show clearly enough the current conception of the two monasteries as royal *Eigenklöster*.

to have received a confirmation of its liberties, and at both Ely and St Augustine's there is record of abbots elect standing out for their alleged right of applying for consecration to a bishop other than the diocesan, together with its corollary of making no profession of obedience to the latter.[1] At Ely a compromise was agreed to before a decision had been reached on the legal issue; at Canterbury the issue was confused both by domestic troubles and by Lanfranc's unwillingness to admit a claim which would have left St Augustine's subject to no superior save the pope.

Thus in the reigns of William I and Rufus little or nothing, save in the case of Bury, was done to define or clarify the status of the privileged monasteries, least of all in their relations with Rome, and collisions between them and the bishops concerned were for the most part obviated either by the direct control of the king, or by absence of any desire on the part of the first Norman bishops to exercise all the various canonical rights and perform the various duties which had fallen into desuetude in the Anglo-Saxon Church, but were being energetically asserted and performed by the bishops throughout Europe wherever the spirit of the Gregorian reform found entry. With the beginning of the twelfth century a new ecclesiastical era began gradually to open in England also, and the question of exemption was brought to a head alike by the infiltration of canon law and canonical practices and by the direct action of the Roman Curia, which now became for the first time for centuries a power to reckon with in every section of the life of the Church. Before glancing at the development in the field of events it will be well to consider briefly the new canonical conception of privilege, which had reached a fair degree of definition.

III

During the century that passed between the election of Gregory VII in 1073 and the death of Alexander III in 1181 the Roman Curia and (during the twelfth century) the canonists of north Italy were engaged almost without respite in deciding cases of alleged monastic privilege and in bringing under formulae that could be recognized by canon law the multifarious grants and charters couched in semi-feudal language. Their task, considered in its legal, theoretical bearings, was twofold. First, the Curia had to decide which, out of the vast and ever-increasing number of monasteries commended to the protection of the Holy See, were to be considered as papal *Eigenklöster*, and as exempt from the jurisdiction of the diocesan; and secondly, what, out of the complex of privileges and liberties that were possessed in combination or isolation by innumerable monasteries, were to be considered criteria of such freedom. In the sphere

1 For Glastonbury v. Will. Malmesb., *de Ant. Glast.* 331; *Vita Wulfstani* (ed. Darlington), introd. xxix; 26, 79. For Ely v. *Liber Eliensis*, 1, 253–86 and Davis, *Regesta*, nos. 151–3. For St Augustine's, *The Growth of Exemption* (ii), 403–6.

of practical decision the task was likewise twofold, for the Curia had not only to decide upon its treatment of the various houses bound to it by privileges of different kinds, but it had to decide under what circumstances it was prepared to allow the *Eigenklöster* of kings and other potentates, freed by them from episcopal jurisdiction but not "commended" to Rome, to pass directly under the control of the Apostolic See.[1]

The first achievement of Rome was the gradual substitution of the canonical conception of reserved jurisdiction for the feudal one of papal *Eigenkirchen*. The monasteries under papal protection were gradually separated into the two groups of "commended" and merely "protected"; the former were almost all held to be freed from the bishop, the latter almost as invariably not. Similarly, the tax-paying houses were divided according as the tax was paid as a sign of liberty (*ad indicium libertatis*) or merely of protection (*ad indicium protectionis*). By slow degrees, certain words and formulae were settled upon as legally decisive; thus when a house was declared in a privilege to belong in an especial way to Rome (*ad jus et proprietatem beati Petri* specialiter *pertinere*), and when for the phrase *salva in omnibus diocesani episcopi reverentia* at the end of a bull was substituted the one *salva in omnibus Romanae ecclesiae proprietate* or the more canonical *salva sedis apostolicae auctoritate*, these were held to be criteria of freedom from episcopal jurisdiction. Finally, the great canonist Alexander III put an end to all ambiguities of form by the insertion of the two decisive words *nullo mediante* in the formula which declared the monastery to be in a special way under the jurisdiction of the Apostolic See.[2] In this way the process was gradually completed which transformed an undefined assertion of protection, proprietorship and privilege into the clear-cut canonical limitation of jurisdiction, but it was not till after our period that the term "exemption" with its cognates became the common, technical form.[3]

During the century which witnessed this canonical development the policy of the Roman Curia changed more than once with regard to the monastic order. In the first half of the eleventh century, when popes and reformers saw in the monasteries, and especially in Cluny and the north Italian reforms, the chief source of strength against the evils in the Church, they were lavish in their grants of privileges, and seized every opportunity of uniting the monasteries to Rome by bulls granting protection and liberty; this attitude continued to prevail until the beginning of the twelfth century. From thence onwards the policy of the papacy fluctuated. The

---

1 Schreiber, *Kurie und Kloster*, I, 40: "Die Scheidung der nicht kommendierten Klöster in exemte und nicht exemte vollzog sich vor und in unserer Periode [12th century] mühelos." For a list of Continental royal *Eigenklöster* which became exempt *v. ibid.* 41.

2 E.g. for Westminster, *JL*, 12,734: "...Qui nullo mediante ad jurisdictionem beati Petri et nostram specialiter pertinere noscuntur." *V.*, however, the article of H. Goetting.

3 Schreiber, *Kurie und Kloster*, I, 28, note 1, gives a list of the cases, only three or four all told, in which *eximere* is used in papal documents of monasteries before *c.* 1189.

rise of the new orders, and especially of the white monks, who professed to be fully incorporated in the diocese, but who soon came in practice to be wholly outside the control of the bishop, and who possessed a number of valuable privileges, chief among which were those absolving them from the payment of tithes and the observance of interdicts, caused the episcopate to tighten their hold, wherever possible, upon the black monks. Moreover, a new hierarchy sprang up throughout Europe inspired by many of the Gregorian ideas and conversant with canon law; they, and no longer the monks, were the power to which the papacy now looked for support and sound administration, and it became necessary to maintain for the bishops their ancient canonical rights of supervision and scrutinize closely any claims or petitions for privilege. Finally, the reduction into canonical form of the various degrees of liberty tended to transform what had previously been an unfettered exercise of papal prerogative into the hearing and decision of suits on strictly legal merits. It is possible to note an important moment in this evolution with the accession of Hadrian IV in 1154. Save in isolated cases, such as the personal one of St Albans, the English pope showed himself very chary of countenancing monasteries in their claims against a diocesan, and his policy was largely maintained during the long reign of his successor, Alexander III (1159–81).

IV

The complex of privileges ultimately comprehended by the concession of exemption was large and heterogeneous. Setting aside for the present all question of churches and franchises possessed by a monastery, a general summary of the purely canonical privileges may be given as follows:

(1) The abbot on election would normally be blessed by the diocesan in his cathedral and make profession to him of canonical obedience. Papal privileges freed him from this in varying degrees:

(a) In all cases he was exempt from the oath of obedience.

(b) He might be permitted to be blessed in the abbey church.

(c) He might be given free choice of the officiating prelate.

(d) He might be allowed to apply for consecration directly to the pope.

(2) The monastery became free from the bishop's excommunication and from general interdicts.

(3) The abbot might invite any bishop to perform ordinations and consecrations which required the episcopal character in the officiant.

(4) The bishop could not claim hospitality for himself and his retinue when on his official visitation of his diocese (*procuratio canonica*), nor the right of celebrating a solemn Mass and holding ordinations in the church.

The first of these episcopal rights implied also that of disciplinary visitation, though this practice had fallen into total desuetude in many countries.

(5) The abbot was freed from attendance at the diocesan synod, from observing its decrees, and from paying its tax.

(6) The abbot had the right of wearing some, or all, of the seven garments or articles comprehended under the term *insignia pontificalia*.

These privileges, and some other less important ones, had been granted to monasteries by Rome for three hundred years in various combinations and subdivisions, and many secular grants of immunity had equally implied the possession of some of the more important of them.[1] Before c. 1155 there was no clear conception, either at Rome or elsewhere, which of these rights implied complete withdrawal from the bishop's jurisdiction and which carried others along with themselves; it was the task of popes, curial officials and canonists gradually to define these and other questions; but it may be remarked provisionally that the basic rights were freedom from profession of obedience and from excommunication at the hands of the bishop. To the modern world, as to the ancient canon law, these rights appear exclusively spiritual and ecclesiastical, but it was precisely because, in the early Middle Ages, feudal conceptions and secular control had cut across them, that the most paradoxical situations arose in the controversies between monks and bishops, both elsewhere and especially in England.

It is quite beyond the scope of this chapter to give any narrative of the complicated suits and conflicting pronouncements that accompanied the struggle for freedom of the seven English abbeys that ultimately became exempt houses, and of the two or three others that failed to attain to that status, but some of the general characteristics of the succeeding periods may be briefly given.

V

1100–1154

The reign of Henry I saw a number of collisions between the monks of privileged houses and bishops. Some of these were caused by bishops using or abusing feudal conceptions to obtain possession of an abbey: thus Herbert Losinga of Norwich endeavoured in 1101 to make good the old claim of the East-Anglian bishops to Bury St Edmunds. He failed, and Bury never again suffered in this way. A little later the two brothers Roger of Salisbury and Alexander of Lincoln each attempted to gain an abbey. Roger was successful, and held Malmesbury from 1117 to 1139; Alexander's designs on St Albans failed, though the house had cut itself away from the jurisdiction of the archbishop of Canterbury, and had fallen to a certain degree under the control of the diocesan.[2] Meanwhile Ely, with the

---

1 They may all be studied in detail in Schreiber. Cf. also Appendix XIV.
2 *GASA*, I, 71–2.

approval of both Henry I and Anselm, had been made the seat of a new bishopric, and thus passed permanently from the ranks of aspirants to exemption. Chertsey also, an unimportant house with no royal immunities and no unequivocal papal privilege, after an unsuccessful attempt to assert independence, ceased to prosecute its claims.[1]

In the case of all the other abbeys with traditions of freedom, friction of one sort or another arose with the bishop. The most general occasion was a demand of profession of obedience as a condition of consecration from an abbot elect, for this was at once a crucial and inevitable test, though long tenures of office and long vacancies of sees might well postpone the conflict for half a century. Another source of friction was provided by the revival of diocesan synods, to which the abbot was summoned. It is rarely possible to ascertain exactly what happened in these early trials of strength, for neither party was fully aware of the implications of its actions and verbal compromises were often made of which each side gave tendencious accounts later. Concurrently, also, the monasteries concerned were acquiring a series of new and more extensive privileges from Rome, especially during the pontificates of Innocent II and Eugenius III, though these were as a rule couched in the old ambiguous phraseology of "commendation" and "protection". In this way the middle of the century was reached before any house save Bury had firmly established its freedom.

VI

THE REIGN OF HENRY II

In the early years of Henry II the crisis came for more than one abbey. The English episcopate now numbered among its members several energetic bishops familiar with canon law and curial practice, and thoroughly prepared to assert their rights; at the same time the new king was ready to take active cognizance of any important case, and decide it according to the precedent of his grandfather's reign. Thus for one reason or another four houses, St Albans, St Augustine's, Battle and Westminster, found their status challenged.

St Albans[2] had had in 1154 the good fortune to see a native of their soil elected pope as Hadrian IV, and in 1155–6 the abbot proceeded to Rome, where he secured, in the bull *Incomprehensibilis*, privileges equalling or surpassing those of any other English abbey; on a second visit he received the gift of the *pontificalia*. These grants were challenged by Robert of Lincoln, who made a formal appearance as Ordinary at St Albans, where he was refused admittance; he then approached both pope and king, obtaining from the former the appointment of judges delegate, and from the

---

1 For Chertsey's attempt *v. Chron. Abingd.* II, 291–2.
2 For the narrative and references *v. The Growth of Exemption* (i), 213–18.

latter the erection of an ecclesiastical commission to discover the status
of the abbey under Henry I. After various delays the case was heard by
the king himself, who was later a confrater of St Albans, at a Council at
Westminster in 1163, in the presence of Thomas of Canterbury and Roger
of York; the abbot of St Albans produced the alleged charter of Offa and
the more recent papal bulls, and as the bishop had no documentary evidence
the king advised a composition highly favourable to the abbey, and himself
issued to St Albans a notification that the house was free from the jurisdiction of the bishop and taken under the royal protection as if it were an
Eigenkloster.[1] Set thus in possession of their liberties by both papal bulls
and royal charters, the monks of St Albans had little difficulty in maintaining their position, and later obtained from Clement III a further bull which,
by the use of the technical phrase *nullo mediante*, finally established their
exemption.[2]

St Augustine's, Canterbury,[3] which ever since the time of Lanfranc
had been engaged in desultory warfare with successive archbishops over
the question of the profession and consecration of abbots as well as on
other matters, was in a position at once strong and vulnerable: strong by
reason of the undoubted and ancient bonds which united the abbey to
Rome as the "property" of the Holy See, weak owing to the immediate
neighbourhood of an Ordinary who was also metropolitan and often
papal legate, and was in any case the most powerful ecclesiastic in the
kingdom. During the first half of the twelfth century the abbots elect had
generally yielded in practice and made profession, with or without a
saving clause, while at the same time the abbey had secured bulls from each
successive pope confirming and adding to their existing privileges. Under
Theobald an attempt was made to reach a decision both at Rome and in
England; all the Roman documents were in favour of the liberty of the
abbey, while at a royal Council at Northampton in 1157 a pronouncement
was made in favour of Theobald, for St Augustine's had no royal charters
of immunity comparable to those of Bury and St Albans by which Henry II
might be moved. This, however, was far from ending the controversy; it
broke out again in 1176, when the two chief actors, Richard, archbishop
of Canterbury, and Roger, abbot elect of St Augustine's, were both in
origin monks of Christ Church. A temporary settlement was arranged at
Rome in 1179 and 1183; the abbey was recognized as depending directly
upon the pope, and Roger was blessed in Rome, but the house lost its
spiritual jurisdiction over Thanet.

In the same year that Theobald and the abbot of St Augustine's appeared
before the king, Henry II took cognizance of the interesting case of Battle.

---

1 Cf. the documents printed in the *Registrum Antiquissimum* of Lincoln, ed. Foster
(1931), nos. 104, 254, pp. 64–6, 202. In the first charter Henry II writes: "et abbatia sicut
mea dominica ecclesia in manu mea in perpetuum libera remanebit."
2 Cf. *JL*, 14,725, 16,174–5.
3 *The Growth of Exemption* (ii), 401–15.

This abbey, founded, as has been said, as a royal *Eigenkloster*, had had several brushes with previous bishops of Chichester, but the issue was only joined in earnest during the episcopate of Hilary (1147–69), an expert canonist who had held a position for some years in the Curia.[1] Battle had no papal privileges of any kind, and the bishop had no difficulty in obtaining from Eugenius III and Hadrian IV instructions to the abbot to submit himself to the diocesan. Walter de Lucy, however, relying on the support of his brother and the old traditions of his house embodied in a number of charters of very questionable authenticity, appealed to the king, and the case was finally heard at a Council at Colchester in May 1157, at which a leading part was taken by Becket as Chancellor. Hilary based his case on the axiom of canon law that only direct papal action could withdraw a monastery from the jurisdiction of the diocesan, whereas Battle had no papal documents at all. Unanswerable as this argument was from the point of view of a canonist, it had no weight with Henry II, who was further alienated by the ill-timed exposition of the relations between Church and State to which he was treated by the bishop. The king decided to maintain to the full Battle's immunities as a royal "peculiar", confirmed all the old charters and extracted from both Hilary and Theobald a submission to his will. Battle, therefore, emerged in the paradoxical position of an abbey declared exempt from the bishop's jurisdiction by the king, against both the common law of the Church and the explicit pronouncement of the pope.

The privileges of the royal *Eigenkloster* of Westminster[2] do not seem to have been the object of direct attack during the reign, though, as will be seen later, Gilbert Foliot of London asserted his claims over St Margaret's; it continued, however, to solicit and obtain bulls of increasing definition. Guaranteed as it was by both king and pope, Westminster by steady degrees acquired all the privileges ever granted to the most favoured monasteries by Rome. Besides these four houses, Malmesbury,[3] which since its restitution to independence in 1139 had also been exploiting at Rome its traditional position as a tributary to the Apostolic See and the "property" of St Peter, had amassed a collection of papal bulls which stood it in good stead when its position was challenged by the bishop of Salisbury *c.* 1174. Here again the occasion was the consecration of an abbot elect; the bishop asserted his right and demanded profession of obedience, while the abbot refused and obtained consecration from the bishop of Llandaff. Richard of Canterbury, who was himself at odds with St Augustine's, took up the case, but the abbot appealed to Rome; Alexander appointed judges delegate, who presumably decided in favour of the abbot. The case is of some historical importance, as it was in con-

---

1 Symeon of Durham, *Historia Regum*, cont. John of Hexham, II, 321.
2 *The Growth of Exemption* (ii), 415–20.
3 *The Growth of Exemption* (i), 225–31.

nection with it that Peter of Blois, acting as secretary to Richard of Canterbury, wrote to the pope a letter of some length in which he deplored the prevalence and evils of exemption from the diocesan.[1] This letter, and the statements it contains, have more than once been taken at their face value by historians unacquainted with the remote origins and legal development of monastic exemption; actually, it is the *ex parte* presentation of a case from the pen of one known from his other writings to have lacked both a sense of responsibility and a judicial temper of mind.

Had its domestic fortunes been different, Glastonbury might well, during the reign of Henry II, have shared something of the royal favour shown to Battle and St Albans. Like the latter house, it had considerable immunities deriving from royal grants, but, unlike St Albans, it had never stood in any special relations to Rome. Actually, the long tenure of the abbacy by Henry of Blois as bishop of Winchester (1129–71) prevented both diocesan interference and assertions of independence, and before the abbey had found its feet after its long tutelage it was swept into the long struggle for autonomy against Savary and Jocelin of Bath.

By the death of Henry II, therefore, all save one of the group of privileged abbeys had achieved something approaching to their final status of exemption, either by royal decision or papal privilege or a combination of both. The first half of the reign had been marked by the king's interference to grant freedom by his charters and pronouncements; after the Becket controversy such formal royal pronouncements ceased, and it was left in the last resort to the monasteries and bishops concerned to conduct the controversies along the lines laid down by canon law and curial practice.

VII

1189–1216

Between the death of Henry II and that of John the chief development was the application to the English "exempt" houses of the full Roman formula of liberty, perfected by Alexander III, together with the crowning privilege of exemption from visitation at the hands of any legate not sent *a latere*. This last had now become a very valuable liberty, owing to the activity of the archbishops of Canterbury since 1174 as legates in visiting monastic houses in general, and in particular those that were exempt from the diocesan. Bury obtained this favour temporarily *c.* 1176 and permanently under Samson *c.* 1198;[2] Westminster and Malmesbury equivalently in 1189 and 1191;[3] St Albans and Battle retained without serious opposition the freedom they had gained. Only one house was in the Roman courts

---

1 *Petri Blesensis Epp.* (ed. Giles), no. 68 (*PL*, CCVII, 1456–9).
2 *Jocelini Cronica*, 212, 260, 284.
3 Holtzmann, *Papsturkunden in England*, I, ii, 262; *JL*, 16,748.

on a plea for exemption during the pontificate of Innocent III; this was Evesham, the story of whose troubles has already been told in part and need not be repeated.[1] The history of Evesham's immunities in the past century had been very similar to that of St Albans, save that the former had neither enjoyed any peculiar papal or royal favour, nor come into serious collision with the diocesan. It is not easy to say what would have happened to its privileges had not the scandal of Roger Norreys attracted the disciplinary notice of Mauger of Worcester; as it is, Evesham stands alone as the solitary case of an English abbey fighting for exemption in order to escape from a bishop's visitation.

At the end of our period, therefore, seven abbeys appear as exempt: St Albans, St Augustine's, Canterbury, Battle, Bury St Edmunds, Evesham, Malmesbury and Westminster. Of these, three, viz. St Albans, Bury and Westminster, owed their freedom in almost equal measure to both king and pope; in each case the original immunity was a royal grant, and in each case the abbey had, so to say, taken out a counter-insurance by commending itself to Rome as the property of the church of St Peter. Three others, St Augustine's, Evesham and Malmesbury, owed their success all but entirely to their own efforts at Rome, based as they were upon an intimate ancient relationship with the Apostolic See. One, Battle, owed its exempt status entirely to the king, and did not pass across into the number of canonically exempt houses until several decades had passed.

Summary and yet complicated as the above account may perhaps seem, it will at least have served to show that to treat the growth of exemption as a phenomenon of the twelfth century, caused by a desire to escape disciplinary control, is to misunderstand the whole nature of the connections that existed between monasteries and Rome during the early Middle Ages, as well as to ignore the consequences of *Eigenkirchentum* in England and abroad. In every case, save that of Battle, the connection with Rome was either extremely ancient or directly encouraged in its origin by the king of England; in every case, save perhaps those of St Augustine's and Malmesbury, the original basic immunity came from a secular grant; and in every case the Curia, though not infrequently guilty of ambiguous and contradictory pronouncements, based its new grants carefully upon older documents. And whereas after *c.* 1175–1200 freedom from disciplinary visitation at the bishop's hands was perhaps the most important privilege conferred by exemption, before that date such freedom had little significance, since the episcopate had not as yet seriously begun to assume its ancient responsibility and reassert its canonical rights.

1 *V.s.* ch. XIX and *The Growth of Exemption* (ii), 396–401.

CHAPTER XXXIV

THE MONASTIC CHURCHES

I

EIGENKIRCHEN IN ENGLAND

In a previous chapter we have seen something of the process by which, throughout Europe, church property and spiritual rights of all kinds passed into the hands of private owners between the times of Gregory I and Charlemagne. In England this process developed late, and along somewhat different lines. The first early country churches after the coming of Augustine were in the nature of missionary posts controlled by the bishops, and it is usually supposed that these were gradually converted into parish churches and that some sort of parish organization was in existence over the greater part of England south of the Humber by the time of Theodore or at latest by that of the Council of Cloveshoe (747).[1] It must always be remembered, however, that very large areas of the country were desert or very sparsely populated, either as moors, downs, fens or forest, and that not only in Northumbria but in Mercia and parts of Wessex monasteries and *monasteriola* had supplied centres of religion to the countryside in a way different from that obtaining in the Frankish Empire. Moreover, even Northumbria of Bede's day, the home of such an advanced and apparently widespread literary and artistic culture, shows a contrast which we should hardly have expected between the intense and wholly traditional religious life of Jarrow, Wearmouth and elsewhere, and the inchoate, unorganized state of affairs revealed by Bede's letter to Egbert. It is in any case perfectly clear, both from that letter and from other passages in Bede's works, and later from the laws of Alfred,[2] that private ownership of churches and church lands was common in England before the end of the eighth century; as common, perhaps, as in any other country of Europe. Certainly, by the time of Alfred, after the Danish invasions had done their worst, it is probable that all ecclesiastical property in the parts of England still Christian was in the hands of private owners. The number of "abbots" whose names occur in the Saxon charters during the century before King Edgar as masters of sites not known otherwise to have been monastic, and which certainly had on them at the time nothing approaching to a regular monastic community, is a witness to this, as is also, from another angle, the record of the gift of estates, known to have

1 Cf. the conclusions of R. H. Hodgkin, *History of the Anglo-Saxons*, II, 425–7.
2 H. Böhmer, *Das Eigenkirchentum in England*, 336.

been once the property of monasteries, by lay magnates to the reformers under Athelstan, Edgar and their successors. Materially speaking, therefore, the churches of Saxon England, great and small, were as fully private property as on the Continent.[1] Formally regarded, however, they were not so fully laicized; for while abroad a real legal compromise had been struck by the decisions of powerful rulers, culminating in the capitularies of Charlemagne, between *Eigenkirchentum* and the ancient canon law, in England the old canonical discipline had been obliterated by the stress and strain of events, not by a body of legislation or recognized customs, and at every revival, such as that under Alfred or that under Edgar and Dunstan, the claims of the Church were reaffirmed in something like integrity. For the most part, however, these claims were restricted to the disciplinary control of the priests as spiritual functionaries and private individuals; no attempt was made to change the system by which the church itself, that is, the actual fabric of the individual church together with the land assigned to the support of the priest and the income accruing from tithes, dues and oblations, was in large part private property.

In this matter, recent careful study,[2] based chiefly on the record of *Domesday*, has shown that in the century that ended with the death of Edward the Confessor the churches and chapels of England had each an "owner", who might be either the king, or a great landowner, or a bishop, or a monastery, or a small proprietor, or (in a few cases) the priest of the church concerned. The rights of this owner varied from period to period, but throughout he had the radical possession of the church, which he could give, sell, bequeath or mortgage like any other property. He had also the right of appointing a priest to serve the church, of receiving the entrance fee on that occasion, and subsequently of commanding the priest's services. He enjoyed, finally, the receipt of a tax or due, apparently first imposed by Cnut and not very considerable in amount in England before the Conquest.[3]

The inevitable consequences of this system had resulted in England as abroad. When a church had been founded by more than one person, or had devolved upon more than one heir, each of these was considered to possess "half a church" or a third of a church. Examples occur in *Domesday* of fractions as small as a twelfth of a church or (when a second subdivision had occurred and the number of beneficiaries was uneven) of

1 Böhmer, *Das Eigenkirchentum in England*, 317: "Wie auf dem Kontinente, haben damals auch in England alle Kirchen einen 'Eigentümer'. Alle Kirchen sind *propriae ecclesiae*, Eigenkirchen." *V*. also W. Page in *Archaeologia*, LXVI (1914–15), 61–102.

2 Above all, that of Heinrich Böhmer, quoted in the previous note, a wonderfully thorough and convincing piece of work which must, however, be supplemented by studies which take account of other administrative and spiritual activities, such as those of J. Armitage Robinson, and above all, the article by R. R. Darlington, *Ecclesiastical Reform in the Late Old English Period*, in *EHR*, LI (July 1936), 385–428.

3 The tax, a penny or twopence per acre per annum, was probably imposed by Cnut (so Böhmer, *Das Eigenkirchentum*, 320).

as many as seven or eleven owners holding "half a church", and in later decades tithes and dues were similarly held in fractions.[1]

As for the priest, all the evidence goes to show that during the period ending with the Conquest he had gained or maintained a position of greater personal independence than his fellows abroad. As regards his relations to the proprietor, he had only to perform the recognized spiritual services (in practice, little more than Mass and infrequent sacraments and sacramentals, for there was little preaching) for the owner and his dependents, to pay a lump sum on obtaining his post and a small annual rent thereafter. All stole-fees, Mass offerings, Easter offerings and tithes were his, and he had the enjoyment of a house and a fair-sized piece of land. As regards the bishop, the priest would seem to have become all but wholly free in the decades before the Conquest. The holding of synods and the payment of contributions to the bishop or archdeacons had very generally lapsed, and in many cases the only regular connection between priest and Ordinary was the annual application for the holy oils. The priest of a larger church was usually married and in many cases the office was regarded as all but hereditary. The bishops, for their part, devoted more attention to the churches which they owned as proprietors, whether within or without the limits of their diocese, than to the diocesan churches as such.

This system (if system it can be called) led to a very great multiplication of churches and chapels, and to a neglect of parish organization. When a man of any property wished to secure for himself the rites of the Church, he constructed a small church or chapel of his own and established a priest.[2] Suffolk alone had some four hundred churches and chapels noted in *Domesday*; Norwich had twenty churches and forty-three chapels, and Winchester probably had still more. But, as has been said, a church, beyond its spiritual convenience, was of no great pecuniary value to the owner as an asset; it was the source of a small income and some influence, no more. In Normandy, on the other hand, the proprietor received from the incumbent at least a part of the tithes, offerings and burial dues; more than in England, therefore, churches formed a complex of pecuniary assets, and the new owners of the land after the Conquest proceeded to apply to their possessions the customary processes with which they were familiar abroad. The effects of this change, especially in the case of churches owned by monasteries, and the modifications introduced by the Gregorian movement of reform, will be considered below.

1 Böhmer, *Das Eigenkirchentum*, 317, cites as a palmary instance of transfer, from *Domesday*, I, 208a, the church of St Mary at Huntingdon, originally belonging to the abbot of Thorney, which was successively mortgaged to the townspeople, given away by the king to two priests, sold by them to Hugh the chamberlain, and sold again by him to the priests of Huntingdon. For "a twelfth" of a church *v. Domesday*, II, 211b, 410.

2 Cf. the case of Stori at Derby in *Domesday*, I, 280b (quoted by Böhmer, *Das Eigenkirchentum*, 322, note 3): "quod sine alicujus licentia potuit sibi facere ecclesiam in terra sua et suam decimam mittere quo vellet."

II

MONASTIC *EIGENKIRCHEN*

Whatever may have been the case in the early days of the conversion of England, and again during the Celtic monastic missions in Northumbria, it may be taken as a principle throughout the centuries covered by these chapters that the monks of England took no share whatever in the work of preaching or administering the sacraments to layfolk outside the walls of the monastery. Although the distinction between priests who were also monks and the secular clergy was less emphasized in pre-Conquest England than in later times, and although it is probable that isolated monks, and in particular the priors of cathedral or pilgrimage churches, took a share in administering the sacraments on occasion to visitors, especially before the Conquest,[1] the normal abbey church and cathedral monastery was intended primarily for the use of the monks, and was in no sense a parish church. Similarly, the cases in which monks can be shown to have acted as officiating clergy in any save conventual or quasi-conventual churches are so rare as to be negligible.[2] In the present chapter, therefore, we are concerned, not with the work of the monks as priests, but with their conduct as owners of churches in which the rites were performed by secular clergy.

The monasteries of England naturally figured among the owners of churches even before the Conquest, but it would appear certain that monastic ownership in Saxon England was far from attaining the scale it had reached on the Continent. The complete disappearance of the monasteries as active agents between 850 and 950 was no doubt a partial cause of this; in any case, a church, which had little value in this country as a pecuniary asset, was not often bestowed as an isolated gift. Most of the monasteries, however, had a certain number of churches that had followed gifts of land or had been bestowed in free alms.[3] Thus Bury had a great

---

1 Thus we read of Wulfstan of Worcester hearing confessions and baptizing when prior (*Vita Wulfstani*, ed. Darlington, 12–13). Elsewhere, however, the cathedral might not be a baptismal church; at Canterbury, e.g., the font was at St John's. Wulfstan's preaching was severely criticized by a foreign monk, Winrich, as *contra regulas* (*Vita Wulfstani*, 14).

2 I have noted only a few cases, dating as a rule from the early decades of the Norman plantation, e.g. at Colchester, Eudo's foundation charter (a very doubtful document as it stands), in *Monasticon*, IV, 609, records the following gift: "omnes proventus omnium capellarum in maneriis meis citra fluvium Tamesyae, maxime in praecipuis festis; ita tamen, si monachi aliquem de suis ibi transmittant, qui diebus festis ibi servitium Dei faciant." But no doubt at many of the lesser priories and "cells" the sacraments were administered to the few who worshipped in the churches; cf. the letter of Eugenius III to Hilary of Chichester in 1149, ordering him to expel the evil-living clerics from Arundel and replace them by monks chosen by the abbot of Séez, the owner of the church (Holtzmann, *Papsturkunden in England*, II, ii, no. 59). For cases of monks acting thus in Normandy *v.* Böhmer, *Kirche und Staat*, 10, note 4.

3 Some thirteen of the seventy Bury churches in Suffolk are thus designated in *Domesday* (Böhmer, *Das Eigenkirchentum*, 349). Later the monasteries succeeded in exploiting these also.

bloc of seventy in Suffolk, and Westminster had a number in Worcester-shire, while others, such as Glastonbury, Evesham, St Albans and St Augustine's, had a small group on their land belonging to them in an especial way, as will be mentioned later. But the overwhelming majority of the churches of England before the Conquest, and especially those in the eastern counties, were owned by small thegns and freemen; a careful analysis of the Domesday record has shown that in the comparatively rich and populous county of Suffolk some two-thirds of the total number of four hundred and twenty-two churches were owned by men of this type, a few by the king, queen and great men outside the county, twenty or more by the abbot of Ely, some seventy by the abbot of Bury, and only two by the bishop of the diocese.[1]

Churches, therefore, do not figure to any great extent in the administra-tive life of the old English monasteries. Doubtless, when an estate was given to an abbey the church often passed with it, but the monastery would get little from it save the small tax, and if it were given *in elemosina* would in theory and pre-Conquest practice get nothing at all. It was only in the days of the Confessor that a beginning was made of treating churches primarily as assets, and bestowing them freely on great ecclesiastics and religious houses.[2]

The process was completed after the partition of the spoils of the Conquest, and at the same time the Norman owners introduced all the practices of their native land, taking to themselves or bestowing on a monastery the greater part of the various ecclesiastical dues, in particular the regular oblations, burial fees and tithes. Henceforth charters of gift enumerate all the various sources of income familiar to the church-owners of the Continent, and the exploitation of privately-owned church property in the centralized manor and fief, and with the keener methods of the Normans, became very intense. Some of these methods will be considered in a moment, but first it will be well to consider another tendency that came in with the invaders, and proved equally profitable to the monasteries.

The reform movement with its centre at Rome had in the middle of the century attacked both the marriage or concubinage of the clergy and lay ownership of churches.[3] A number of the new Norman landowners endeavoured to satisfy its demands or ideals by making over their larger churches to monasteries on the understanding that a small group of monks should be sent to carry out the rites there. It was this motive that led to the foundation of a number of small dependencies by English and overseas

---

1 Böhmer, *Das Eigenkirchentum*, 332.

2 Thus the Confessor, besides many gifts to Stigand, endowed Westminster and several foreign monasteries with churches; Queen Edith and abbesses were also owners. Cf. *Domesday*, I, 337 d, 59 d and Böhmer, *Das Eigenkirchentum*, 315.

3 Cf. canon 6 of the Synod of Rome (1059): "Ut per laicos nullo modo quilibet clericus aut presbyter obtineat ecclesiam nec gratis nec pretio." For developments and modifications cf. Synods of Rome (1078), c. 2; (1080), c. 1; Council of Poitiers (1100), c. 3; Council of London (1125), c. 4, and P. Thomas, *Le droit de propriété des laïques*, 134–6.

abbeys during the first fifty years after the Conquest; such small priories or cells were already in existence in large numbers abroad, and probably many, if not the majority, of those established in England before *c*. 1110 were due to a desire on the part of the owner of the land to establish monks in his church in the room of an English priest, whom he might condemn as married and ignorant; at the same time he would rid himself of the responsibility of "owning" a church. The chronicle of Battle abbey, a wholly Norman foundation, notes three such gifts of important churches, the first near Exeter, the second at Brecon, the third at Carmarthen. In each case the same procedure was followed: first, one or more monks were sent to take charge of the churches; next, as affairs went well, other gifts came, more monks were sent, and Exeter, Brecon and Carmarthen became regular priories dependent upon Battle.[1] A similar method of acting may be seen at Abingdon and other houses.

Clearly, however, monks could not be sent to all churches bestowed on the monasteries by generous or scrupulous owners, especially as these gifts became still more frequent when the reform movement, abandoning the root and branch attack on private ownership, endeavoured, with slow but increasing pertinacity, to vindicate at least all revenues from oblations, stole-fees and tithes for religious purposes by condemning their possession by laymen. Monasteries, being spiritual foundations, did not fall under this ban, and although the spread of the reform was slow, especially in England, a knowledge of the prescriptions of Roman synods and canon law had a growing influence over the more religiously minded. Nor did the practice of bestowing churches on monasteries, so familiar to Norman sentiment, arouse any kind of opposition among the bishops, at least before 1100;[2] the more zealous, whether monks or secular, may well have considered that monastic owners were more likely than others to secure the appointment of devout and lettered clerics and above all to break the traditions of a married and hereditary rural clergy; in any case, the bishops, and even the secular bishops, were among the most noteworthy benefactors of the monasteries in this respect. Thus in one way or another, the monasteries and other religious houses of England and Normandy became possessed, by the end of the first century of Norman domination, of perhaps a quarter of the total number of churches in England.

While the monasteries thus profited, materially speaking, from the consequences of the Gregorian reform, they profited equally from the new methods of exploitation of church property introduced by the Normans into England. Briefly, these resulted in substituting for the Old English conception of a private church as no more than a tax-paying asset giving

---

1 *Chron. Bell.* 31–2 (Exeter); 34–5 (Brecon); 55, 61 (Carmarthen).

2 Anselm endeavoured to keep the movement within regular bounds; cf. Council of London (1102), c. 22: "ne monachi ecclesias nisi per episcopos accipiant neque sibi datas ita expolient suis redditibus ut presbyteri ibi servientes...penuriam patiantur."

through its priest all spiritual and some personal services, the Norman conception of a church as a nucleus of revenues enjoyable by the owner, to whom the priest stood in the relation of a dependent stipendiary. Here we are concerned only with the share taken by the monasteries in this process, and a few typical examples may do duty for all. The end aimed at, consciously or unconsciously, was always the same, viz. to substitute for the priest who enjoyed full rights for life in the church, less only a small tax, one who paid an annual pension, scaled according to the value of his income, and in any case considerably higher than the tax, and who had no radical ownership. As the monastery had complete freedom in appointing to vacancies it was able to drive a hard bargain, and the pensions were increased, sometimes as much as fourfold, by a keen man of business.

An example of the change of treatment occurs in the very well-informed chronicle of Abingdon.[1] The monastery had for some time before the Conquest enjoyed two-thirds of the tithe of the royal vill of Sutton and a hide of land which was held of the abbot by the priest. William II, for a consideration of £20, made over the church of Sutton to Abingdon with the proviso that the priest who held it was to continue in all his rights, but that after his death the monks were to be full owners. In the event, the monastery agreed to allow the priest's son to succeed him in full enjoyment, for which concession the priest made over the chapel-of-ease of Milton with all its revenues to the monks. Fifty years later, Abingdon was in full possession of Sutton.[2] Thus by stages, and with little disturbance of existing rights, churches passed from the Anglo-Saxon status to the Norman. The incumbent remained for his lifetime; the owner (in this case the king) received £20 for a benefaction which cost him nothing, and Abingdon, for the payment of this premium, entered ultimately into full radical possession of the revenues. At Battle, during the same years, the same agencies were at work. William II, who was present at the consecration of his *Eigenkloster* in 1095, gave a number of churches from his lands in East Anglia with the proviso that the existing incumbents were to remain in possession, paying ten shillings per annum to the monastery and giving two nights' hospitality to visiting abbots; at their demise, Battle was to possess the churches.[3] Some fifty years later, the great abbot Walter de Lucy was able to raise the pensions of the incumbents, in one case to a sum four times that of the original agreement.[4]

Pensions, however, especially when derived from distant, scattered, and

---

1 For this episode *v. Chron. Abingd.* II, 27–8. It was not uncommon for owners before the Conquest to give their tithes away from the parish church, especially to a monastery; this practice must be distinguished from that of the owner enjoying his own tithes as private revenue.

2 Cf. the charter of Stephen, *Chron. Abingd.* II, 179.

3 *Chron. Bell.* 41–2, 119–20, 128–30.

4 *Chron. Bell.* 128–9. The passage is of particular interest, because the chronicler, writing *c.* 1175, criticized the abbot's action in the light of more recent practice; nowadays, he says, appropriation would be regarded as a wiser procedure.

small churches, were difficult of collection, and as conflicting claims or refusal to pay often entailed litigation they might easily become assets of very doubtful value. Consequently, monasteries tended to realize their property in other ways. One such was suggested by a practice already current for other sources of revenue: the system of farm. This was, in its early form, merely an extension of the pensionary method. Instead of the incumbent paying a pension, a third party, usually one who had interests in the locality, paid to the monastery an annual sum by an agreement made for a fixed term of years. He then appointed to the church a priest without fixed tenure, paying to himself a yearly pension greater than the farm which went to the monastery. Alternatively, and with increasing frequency of application as the century advanced, the farmer, especially if he himself were a cleric, received all the revenues of the church and appointed a salaried *vicarius*, who thus did not directly touch any of the income. From this to appropriation was only a short step, and when farming, a peculiarly English practice,[1] fell under conciliar condemnation, appropriation, which was not unknown on the Continent, became more and more common.[2]

By this process the abbot and community took the whole benefice to themselves as their own property, becoming, either as a corporation or through one of their officials, the rector or *persona* of the church. They then put in a vicar receiving a salary fixed between the parties, and wherever possible with no right of permanent possession. So long as the conception of the *Eigenkirche* was still potent, and before the bishops had become familiar with canon law and the principles of diocesan reform, the change was accomplished as a simple administrative act on the part of the monastic owners, and they were able to exploit their property by appointing a vicar removable *ad nutum* and supported upon the smallest salary that competition for the post might make acceptable. The bishop lost nothing personally by the change, and no doubt the priests appointed by a capable and God-fearing abbot were superior in quality to the general run of the lower clergy. Thus the church of Warboys was given *c.* 1150 to the almonry of Ramsey; two priests had a life interest in it and were to pay a pension to the almoner; when they both died, he was to have the rectory and all the income. Robert of Lincoln (1148–60) confirmed the arrangement.[3] Towards the end of the twelfth century, however, when the control of the bishops grew firmer, signs began to appear of the struggle which

1 Schreiber, *Kurie und Kloster*, II, 12, refers to "die für das englische Recht charakteristische Form, die *datio ad firmam*", and remarks that it is seldom found abroad. He notes various conciliar condemnations.

2 Imbart de la Tour, *Les paroisses rurales*, 247–8, where an example of incorporation is given from Le Mans at the beginning of the eleventh century; he adds, however, "toutefois, cet usage est loin d'être général" [*sc.* at this date].

3 *Chron. Rames.* 301–3. The bishop's charter runs: "Volumus itaque ut eleemosinarius Rames., quisquis fuerit, ejusdem ecclesiae personatum obtineat et tanquam persona omnibus rebus illius ecclesiae pro voluntate sua disponat."

only became general under the great diocesan bishops of the thirteenth century: first, to assert the necessity of episcopal permission for appropriation; next, to uphold the right of the bishop to full jurisdiction *in spiritualibus*; and finally, to insist that the vicar should have tenure for life and an income fully adequate for his maintenance. Thus Samson of Bury would willingly have impropriated the church of Woolpit, but fearing a collision with the bishop, he appointed instead a pensionary vicar;[1] about the same time the monks of Battle, who had temporarily appropriated their parish church, appointed a rector for similar reasons.[2] In the same period Nicholas of Llandaff (1148–83) confirmed various churches to Tewkesbury on the understanding that when the rectors should die or depart, the abbey should institute vicars with a reasonable income,[3] and a little later Hubert Walter (1194–1207) confirmed a grant to the Cluniac Horkesley on condition that a decent allowance should be made for the vicar.[4] But the alternative pension system lasted long, and it is often possible to trace a series of stages in the transition from a rector with full rights to a pension-paying rector, and from him through a pension-paying vicar to a stipendiary vicar who receives little or nothing from his church, but an allowance from the appropriating monastery. In the sequel, the majority of churches belonging to religious orders were impropriated; it was, as keen administrators realized, the most lucrative course to take, and in many cases, at least in the twelfth century, the priest lost nothing, for the complex of tithes and offerings had been for many decades in lay or monastic hands. For the most part, therefore, bishops contented themselves with maintaining a hold on all church property nominally owned by lay proprietors, and reducing the owner's rights to the single right of patronage; they allowed the monasteries, as religious bodies, to remain in the enjoyment of all the fruits of their possessions.

III

MONASTIC PECULIARS[5]

Hitherto the monasteries have been considered simply as one among the several classes of owners of churches. It is now necessary, for the sake of

---

1 *Jocelini Cronica*, 254. Samson says to his monks: "Integram libentius vobis eam [ecclesiam] darem, si possem; sed scio, quod episcopus Norwicensis mihi contradiceret.... Faciamus ergo quod de jure possumus facere; ponamus clericum vicarium, qui episcopo respondeat de spiritualibus et vobis de decem marcis."

2 *Chron. Bell.* 166–70.

3 *Monasticon*, II, 67. Here we have the vicarage system coming in.

4 *Monasticon*, V, 157. The monograph of R. A. R. Hartridge, *A History of Vicarages in the Middle Ages*, may also be consulted, though it is almost wholly concerned with the period after 1216, and devotes little attention to the crucial decades of the late twelfth century. Prof. F. M. Stenton has some valuable observations in his article, *Acta Episcoporum*, in *Cambridge Historical Journal*, III (1929), 1–14.

5 I have used this term, though it was not, it would seem, introduced until after the Dissolution (so exx. in *New English Dictionary*, s.v.). It is unfortunate that it is restricted

completeness, to glance at those few cases where abbeys claimed not only financial and patronal rights, but partial or complete spiritual jurisdiction over some of their churches.[1]

In this country, as elsewhere during the epoch of secularization, kings had on occasion endowed monasteries with estates to which immunity from all interference, secular and ecclesiastical, was attached. This immunity was not originally considered as ecclesiastical, or as directly affecting the churches situated on these lands, but by preventing bishops from exacting dues of hospitality and from holding solemn meetings within the franchise it had the effect of keeping them at a distance; moreover, those offences against the laws of the Church which by law or custom rendered the offenders amenable to judicial decision and pecuniary punishment passed gradually, if not at once, under the jurisdiction of the spiritual holder of the immunity. The growth of these private ecclesiastical franchises, relatively few in number and almost always attached to some celebrated monastery or shrine, has an exact parallel in the corresponding franchisal jurisdictions in civil affairs, which formed such a feature of English legal history throughout the Middle Ages and beyond.[2] It was encouraged by the loose organization of the dioceses, especially in England north of the Thames; from the earliest times there had been continual trespassing on the part of neighbour bishops in the wide and townless eastern Midlands, as is shown by conciliar legislation;[3] when during the eighty years previous to the Conquest, the organization of the Church in England was even looser than before, it became the custom (if indeed it had not long been so already) for a bishop who owned churches in another diocese to perform for those churches all those acts (such as consecration) which required the episcopal character, and to give to his parishioners any canonical permissions and dispensations that might be required. This was the situation found by Lanfranc on taking charge at Canterbury; the archbishop of Canterbury owned a number of churches in the dioceses of London and Chichester, and Lanfranc, for all his reforming policy, decided not to change the existing state of things and energetically maintained his rights in the diocese of Chichester, claiming complete jurisdiction save in the matter of holy oils. A similar *bloc* belonging to the

in English ecclesiastical law to a single species, viz. the churches wholly outside the control of the Ordinary, of the genus *Eigenkirche*, as it would otherwise provide an exact equivalent for the German term and for the Latin *propria ecclesia*. This subject, like the kindred one of monastic exemption, has not yet been fully studied; for the present, reference can only be given to Schreiber, *Kurie und Kloster* and (for England) to my article, imperfect in many respects, [*Monastic*] *Parish Organization*, in *DR*, LI (July 1933), 501–22.

1 A full and valuable examination of similar private jurisdictions in Normandy will be found in J. F. Lemarignier, *Les privilèges...de juridiction ecclésiastique des abbayes normandes.*

2 For this, *v.* W. O. Ault, *Private Jurisdiction in England* (Yale Historical Publications, 1923), who does not, however, give all the cases, nor treat fully of the origins.

3 Cf. Council of Hertford (673) in Bede, *Historia Ecclesiastica*, IV, 5 (ed. Plummer, I, 216): "Ut nullus episcoporum parrochiam [= diocese] alterius invadat, sed contentus sit gubernatione creditae sibi plebis."

archbishop of York lay round Hexham in the diocese of Durham. The maintenance of these episcopal peculiars by Lanfranc and Anselm was not without its effect in securing the survival of monastic peculiars.[1]

Another kind of ecclesiastical immunity was introduced or standardized in England under the Confessor, if not before. This was the royal chapel, consisting of the group of clerks chosen for their literary or administrative ability, who formed a body of chaplains to perform the rites of religion for the king and assist him in various functions of government. They, and the church in which they officiated, were the royal *Eigenkirche par excellence*, and completely outside the jurisdiction of any bishop; they served as an exemplar of freedom for the royal *Eigenklöster* of Westminster and Battle.

Before, therefore, any kind of papal sanction had been obtained, there were in England a few monasteries owning churches over which they had all but complete jurisdiction *in spiritualibus*. Among them were Evesham, which had the churches of the Vale; St Albans, which had fifteen churches in the countryside of Hertfordshire; St Augustine's, which had the churches of the Isle of Thanet; Glastonbury, which had the churches on the adjacent islands; and two or three of the fenland sanctuaries. Bury St Edmunds was in a somewhat different position. Here, no spiritual immunities were claimed for the numerous churches up and down East Anglia possessed by the abbey, but the town of Bury, with any churches it contained, lay within the *banleuca* over which the bishop of Elmham had expressly renounced all rights.[2]

If we now turn from England to southern Europe and Rome, we shall see that similar franchises had arisen abroad and had obtained gradual recognition from the papacy in the case of those abbeys which were recognized as papal *Eigenklöster* and which formed the class around which the canonical conception of exemption crystallized. Once again, it must be remembered that in this matter the law was the clothing put upon an existing state of affairs, and that although popes and canonists endeavoured to establish principles and reduce a mass of individual immunities and privileges to order, every kind of anomaly continued to exist. Thus exemption of itself did not necessarily imply a status of freedom for any of the abbey's churches, still less for all,[3] while on the other hand, and with still greater anomaly, cases existed where the abbey never attained ex-

---

1 Eadmer, *Hist. Nov.* 21 and *Lanfranci Opera* (ed. Giles), I, 50 for his letter to Stigand of Chichester which served as starting-point for Böhmer's study of English *Eigenkirchen*. Lanfranc's conduct in this matter is an interesting pendant to his eclectic treatment of canon law. Even Anselm, after consulting Wulfstan of Worcester, upheld the traditional rights of the archbishopric.

2 *Mem. St Edmund's*, I, 359–60 (Appendix E). At Glastonbury it was the tradition that the immunity came from King Ine and had been confirmed to Dunstan by Brihthelm of Wells.

3 Schreiber, *Kurie und Kloster*, II, 191: "Irrig wäre die Annehme, dass mit der Exemtion des Klosters auch immer eine Befreiung der Eigenkirchen gegeben war."

emption, but succeeded in retaining the spiritual jurisdiction over its churches which it had acquired by an ancient royal franchise. But speaking generally, the Curia at the beginning of the twelfth century was familiar with four classes of monastic "peculiar", which may be compared to four concentric circles each with larger radius than the last. First, the (secular) priests ministering to the servants and other dependents of a monastery might be set outside the control of the bishop or (what was practically the equivalent of this) immunity might be secured for the public church erected within the abbey precinct. This degree of freedom existed in the case of almost all houses pertaining directly to the Apostolic See, and ultimately came to follow automatically upon the grant of "exemption". Next, the whole town or village round the monastery might be similarly exempt. This was very common wherever the abbey lay at the centre of its own lands and was the cause of the concentration of population. Thirdly, an abbey might have rights of various kinds, falling short of complete jurisdiction, over some of its churches and priests. Finally, it might have all ordinary jurisdiction over a solid territorial *bloc* of churches.[1]

England, in the course of the twelfth century, came to provide examples of all four of these classes. In the first were Malmesbury and Westminster. Neither of these owned churches endowed with an old royal franchise; consequently, they had only the rights common to all monasteries ultimately recognized as pertaining to the jurisdiction of the Apostolic See. In the case of Malmesbury it was laid down in the final settlement with the bishop of Salisbury that the bishop's jurisdiction extended everywhere outside the enclosure of the abbey.[2] In the case of Westminster, there was a controversy over St Margaret's. Though situated within the limits of the abbey cemetery, it had apparently in early days been treated as falling under the jurisdiction of the bishop of London; when canonical practice became standardized under Alexander III and his successors, the monks obtained a bull giving to the church that freedom accorded to all buildings in the precincts which followed automatically upon the recognition of exemption.[3]

The second class, familiar to the Curia from many Continental instances, was that of the exempt town or village round the monastery. Of this Bury provided an English example, for all within the four crosses of the *banleuca* was free of episcopal jurisdiction. As for Battle, it is not entirely

---

1 For examples, *v*. Schreiber, *Kurie und Kloster*, II, 185–207.
2 A clause in the definitory decree (1219) of the judges delegate in the case between Malmesbury and the bishop of Salisbury runs: "Salvae autem sint dicto episcopo et successoribus suis per Sarum diocesim in omnibus ad dictum monasterium pertinentibus, extra ambitum monasterii et cimiterii ejusdem, lex et jurisdictio diocesanae" (*Sarum Charters*, 90).
3 Gilbert Foliot, bishop of London 1161–76, endeavoured to secure control over St Margaret's (*ep*. 266, ed. Giles). The bull of Clement III, confirming its freedom, and dated 20 July 1189, is in Holtzmann, *Papsturkunden in England*, I, ii, no. 262.

clear whether it should be classed with Bury or with Westminster or with neither. The abbey, like Bury, lay at the centre of a *banleuca*, or, as it was there called, a *leuga*, but there was no town with its churches in existence before the foundation, and the inhabitants of the village that sprang up came at first to the abbey church for worship, and enjoyed the ministrations of a priest, kept by the abbot as his chaplain, who lived in the precincts at the expense of the monks. After a time, the presence of the people and their special services in the church proved irksome to the monks, and a chapel was built for them outside the abbey walls, to be served by a priest appointed by the abbot. For a time the bishop claimed jurisdiction over this chapel, but *c.* 1122 it was recognized as free of all customary dues and fines by bishop Ralph of Chichester.[1] The bishop, however, would appear to have retained radical jurisdiction over it, as subsequent incumbents received the benefice at the hands of his successors.[2]

Glastonbury, Ely and perhaps Ramsey had somewhat more extensive rights. These three houses enjoyed franchises covering originally the several islands upon which they lay, together with those adjacent in the case of Glastonbury. This carried with it to the abbey the right of receiving the fines and holding the ecclesiastical courts in lieu of the bishop's arch-deacon; as, however, for different reasons none of these three houses became exempt, their control over the privileged territory never became so complete as did that of Evesham, though it would seem that the archi-diaconal rights continued to be exercised by the monks at Ely even after the bishopric had been erected there, and at Glastonbury even though the abbey was not exempt.[3]

To this group should perhaps be added St Augustine's, Canterbury. Here the monks claimed similar rights over the isle of Thanet, which they held together with its churches. In the early decades after the Conquest, when there were troubles at St Augustine's and the house was largely re-colonized from Christ Church, and when the strong-willed Lanfranc, whatever views he might hold with regard to his own *Eigenkirchen*, was not predisposed to let a part of his diocese remain outside his control, the claims of the abbey were in part allowed to lie dormant, and during the twelfth century the question of the churches of Thanet was often lost to sight behind the much more important one of the radical exemption of the abbey itself. Later, the monks obtained papal privileges in their favour, but in the final composition with the archbishop, arranged in the presence of King Henry II, they agreed to abandon all their claims in Thanet, and the churches were reduced to the level of the general run of monastic

1 *Chron. Bell.* 27, 56–7; *Parish Organization*, 504–5.
2 *Chron. Bell.* 170: "A quo [*sc.* episcopo] personatum ecclesiae curamque animarum suscipiens, ad sacerdotii gradum est promotus."
3 At Ely the sacrist "archidiaconi vices in insulam gerit" (*Liber Eliensis*, 169) and at Glastonbury there is mention of the archdeaconry (Adam of Domerham, II, 345). For monastic archdeacons in cathedral monasteries, *v. infra*, 629–30.

Eigenkirchen.[1] All that was saved from the wreck was a limited immunity for five churches only.

There remain the two abbeys which successfully asserted their claim to a complete spiritual jurisdiction over a group of churches. These originally differed in no essential from the others just enumerated, but by a more pertinacious maintenance or assertion of rights the monks extracted either from bishop or Curia or both an express recognition which set their exempt territory on a level with those abroad which vindicated for themselves a place in canon law and became ultimately *abbatiae* or *prelaturae nullius diocesis.*

With St Albans it was a question of fifteen churches in the countryside near the abbey and in the town itself.[2] Owing no doubt to the distance from Lincoln and the protection of Lanfranc and Anselm, the monks were able to act with greater freedom here than elsewhere; they not only exercised archidiaconal rights, but the sworn testimony of witnesses in the final enquiry of 1163 established the fact that they had constantly in the past invited bishops other than the diocesan to perform episcopal consecrations at their churches. They had moreover obtained from Hadrian IV a bull commanding the clergy and laity of the Hertford district to make their annual Whitsun procession at St Albans, not at Lincoln, and confirming all the powers of the monastic archdeacon. When the final suit between bishop and monks took place before Henry II in 1163, and St Albans was successful in establishing its claim to freedom from the jurisdiction of the bishop, the fifteen churches were separated from all the others held by the abbey and declared to be equally free.[3] For all episcopal functions and consecrations the abbot might invite any bishop he chose, his priests and clerics attended a synod of his own summoning, and they and their parishioners were amenable, for all matters connected with the courts christian, to the abbot's archdeacon, a monk.

As for Evesham, when the abbey was in the Roman courts in the first years of the thirteenth century, Thomas de Marleberge attempted with success to demonstrate that the like rights had been claimed and exercised over the churches of the Vale.[4] In his chronicle, indeed, he traces the office of dean (here equivalent to archdeacon) of the Vale back to one Avicius in 1016; nor can this be dismissed as an impossible claim.[5] Certainly in the first half of the twelfth century the abbey was acting in a similar manner to St Albans, and, like that house, obtained bulls from Innocent II

---

1 *Parish Organization,* 515–17 and references.
2 *Parish Organization,* 517–19.
3 *Registrum Antiquissimum of Lincoln* (ed. Foster), no. 104, p. 65: "Volo quod de cetero liberum sit monasterio beati Albani et xv jamdictis ecclesiis crisma sibi et oleum…a quo voluerint episcopo accipere." This is the king's notification of the agreement of 1163. Cf. *GASA,* I, Appendix A.
4 *Parish Organization,* 519–22.
5 *Chron. Evesh.* 83, 195–6; cf. 264, together with the remarks of R. R. Darlington in *Vita Wulfstani,* introd. xxxv, note 2.

and Alexander III, the latter of whom in 1163 decreed that the abbot might invite any bishop to perform episcopal acts for his churches and clerics. It is, indeed, this introduction of the stranger bishop, the surest evidence of liberty, that distinguishes the cases of Evesham and St Albans from the others, Bury alone excepted, and whatever inconsistencies there may have been in practice, there can be little doubt that from 1163 to 1204 the abbey enjoyed practically complete jurisdiction *in spiritualibus* for the churches of the Vale, settling all ecclesiastical cases, and holding the solemn Whitsun procession for its people at Evesham.[1] Even the bishop's advocate at the Roman trial admitted that the abbey had proved prescription.[2] Innocent III, as has been related, was unwilling to decide this, the second great case, against the bishop, but Evesham remained in possession of its churches, and its rights were confirmed by the decision of papal judges delegate in 1249. Had there been in England, therefore, no great social or religious cataclysm sweeping away all boundaries, it is probable that at the present day Evesham and St Albans, like Monte Cassino, La Cava, and other ancient monastic foundations, would stand in the privileged position of *abbatiae nullius*; as it was, their peculiars survived as exempt from the diocesan control until the middle of the nineteenth century.[3]

The possession of all or some of the rights and perquisites of spiritual jurisdiction implied the holding of private courts christian; consequently, as has been mentioned in passing, one of the monks held the office, and usually the name, of archdeacon. Usually, it would seem, these functions were exercised by the sacrist; and it has been noted in the case of Bury, for which we possess the fullest information, that unlike the diocesan archdeacon, the monastic official never acquired ordinary powers, but remained the abbot's vicar.[4] In other respects, at least at the three abbeys of Bury, Evesham and St Albans, where the exemption was complete, he was the exact equivalent of the bishop's official, and took cognizance of all offences against the ecclesiastical law, giving judgment in all cases of which the courts christian took cognizance, and imposing fines, public penances and excommunications.[5] In all these matters his jurisdiction was rendered less extraordinary in appearance by the concurrent exercise, by himself and other officials, of plenary secular powers in the abbey franchise.

1 *Chron. Evesh.* 187.
2 *Chron. Evesh.* 189: "Et dominus papa, taedio affectus, conversus ad adversarium nostrum, dixit.... 'num praescripserunt?' Et dixit magister Robertus, 'Revera praescripserunt'."
3 *V.* Macray, *Chron. Evesh.* introd. xxviii, note.
4 For a full account of the archidiaconal functions of the sacrist at Bury, *v.* Lobel, *The Borough of Bury St Edmunds*, 41–7. He usually acted through an officer appointed by himself, the *decanus Christianitatis*.
5 At Evesham the *decanus Vallis* was a secular cleric from *c.* 1050 until Marleberge undertook the office (*Chron. Evesh. ut supra*, note 1). For Bury *v.* last note. At St Albans monks held the office of archdeacon, *GASA*, I, 149 (cf. the bull of Clement III, *ibid.* Appendix C, p. 500); Giraldus, *Speculum Ecclesiae* (*Opera*, IV, 95). Cf. also p. 604, n. 3. For foreign examples *v.* Dom U. Berlière, *Les Archidiaconés...de monastères*, in *RB*, XL (1928), 116–22.

CHAPTER XXXV

THE MONASTERIES AND THE FEUDAL SYSTEM

I

KNIGHT-SERVICE

The English monasteries before the Conquest and their heads, though occupying an important position in the social and national life of the times, had none of the duties and obligations associated with the feudal system, based on tenure by military service and on direct control by the king, which was introduced shortly after the Conquest. Speaking very generally, it may be said that before 1066 any part taken by an abbot in the administration or service or support of the nation was either due to his personal choice and influence, or was identical with that taken by all his countrymen of a similar social rank. It is to be presumed that abbots, at least on occasion, took part in the courts of shire and hundred; the career of Aethelwig of Evesham immediately after the Conquest, the assistance of abbots at a number of the great pleas in the Conqueror's reign at which two or three shires met to adjudicate on territorial or jurisdictional rights, and the presence in the monasteries of men distinguished by their knowledge of the laws and customs of the country[1] all suggest that this was so. And, of course, the abbots, as landowners, controlled extensive personal rights over those commended to them, and had the advantages and obligations that came from holding sake and soke. But the abbot, *quâ* abbot, had no civil jurisdiction and was trustee for no corporate burdens. It was even specified in the *Regularis Concordia* that religious houses were not bound to the heriot of a thegn,[2] though just before the Conquest they had had, in isolated cases, to support housecarles on their land.[3]

In Normandy, on the other hand, many, though not all, of the abbeys had been drawn fully into the system of tenure by military service perfected by Duke Robert "the Devil" and inherited by Duke William "the Bastard". Careful examination has shown that only some eight of the Norman abbeys of men owed this military service, and of these all except St Évroul were founded before 1050. The other monasteries in existence before that date were either dependent houses or not yet fully organized, and the later foundations had no obligations, save for St Étienne at Caen, which was not assessed as a barony, but on account of a fief which had

1 Especially Aethelwig of Evesham and two monks, brothers, of Abingdon, of whom it is stated (*Chron. Abingd.* II, 2) that "tanta secularium facundia et praeteritorum memoria eventorum inerat, ut caeteri circumquaque facile eorum sententiam ratam fuisse...approbarent. Sed et alii plures de Anglis causidici per id tempus in abbatia ista habebantur."

2 *Regularis Concordia*, Conclusion (p. 93): "Rex [Edgarus]...jussit ut nemo abbatum vel abbatissarum sibi locellum ad hoc thesaurizaret....ut solitus census, quem indigenae *Heriatua* [*sic.* Reyner] usualiter vocitant, [daretur]."

3 *Chron. Abingd.* II, 3.

come into its possession.[1] The conclusion has therefore been drawn that the imposition was made under Robert the Devil and not extended, at least to any notable degree, by Duke William.[2] The quotas were in all cases relatively small, and it will have been noticed that Bec and (for practical purposes) Caen did not fall under assessment, but the principle had been established, and was capable of application to England.

After the Conquest the greater number of the abbots of English monasteries were put on a level with other tenants *in capite* by being made responsible for providing knights to serve in the feudal host or to take turns in castle-guard. Some fifty years ago, when Round demonstrated that knight-service was first introduced very shortly after the Conquest and its incidence determined by the arbitrary decision of the Conqueror, it so happened that almost all the proofs he offered were drawn from monastic sources.[3] The lapse of time and subsequent research have but confirmed his conclusions, and his marshalling of evidence regarding the monasteries is so complete and masterly that there is no need to repeat it here.[4] It is accepted on all hands that round about 1070 the Conqueror made a series of agreements with his chief followers and tenants as to the numbers of knights due from each, that at first these knights (who formed the military escort and companionship of their lord) were stipendiaries in the household of the great man concerned, and that gradually a process of subinfeudation took place by which hereditary knights' fees were established. All the stages and developments of this organization have been noted in the case of the religious houses by Round and his successors, and need not be dwelt on.[5] Some particular points, however, concerning the monasteries have not been emphasized by historians of feudalism, and deserve some mention.

We possess, in the returns made to the Exchequer in 1166 by the tenants *in capite*, exact information as to the amount of knight-service due from each, and there is little doubt that the quotas assigned by the Conqueror

1 *V.* art. *Knight-Service in Normandy in the Eleventh Century*, by Prof. C. H. Haskins in *EHR*, xxii (October 1907), 636–49, the general conclusions of which are embodied in the same writer's *Norman Institutions*. Fécamp, Bernay, Jumièges, St Trinité, Rouen, Mont St Michel, St Évroul, St Wandrille, St Ouen (and Caen) were the houses giving knight-service (*art. cit.* 638).

2 Haskins, *art. cit.* 639–40.

3 *The Introduction of Knight-Service into England, EHR*, vi (1891), 417–43, 625–45; vii (1892), 11–24, reprinted in *Feudal England* (1895), 225–314; cf. also *The Knight-Service of Malmesbury Abbey*, in *EHR*, xxxii (1917), 249–52.

4 "This [i.e. recent] work has only confirmed Round's main position" (F. M. Stenton, *English Feudalism, 1066–1166*, 122). The chief texts used by Round were Matthew Paris, *Hist. Angl.* I, 13; *Chron. Abingd.* II, 2–3; *Liber Eliensis*, 274–6; *Chron. Evesh.* 91–6.

5 *V.* in particular Stenton, *op. cit.* ch. iv: Thegns and Knights, and ch. v: Knight's Fees and the Knight's Service, and H. M. Chew, *The English Ecclesiastical Tenants-in-chief and Knight-service* (1932), esp. chs i, iv and v. For the development and organization of scutage reliefs *v.* Miss Chew's article *Scutage* in *History*, xiv (Oct. 1929), 236.

had remained substantially unchanged.[1] Round printed in tabular form the services due from the religious houses, but he was not concerned to make more than the most general remarks upon the list.[2] There are, however, two peculiarities in it which impress the reader at the first glance: the absence of any assessment for certain houses, and the extreme inequalities in size between the various quotas. As regards the first of these two points, it is clear at once that no house founded after the Conquest appears on the list. Thus Bardney (1087), Battle (after 1067), Bermondsey (after 1082), Colchester (1095), Selby (1069), Shrewsbury (c. 1083), Tewkesbury (after 1086) and the northern group in general never held by military service. Battle and Selby, the two earliest, were peculiarly connected with the Conqueror. Battle was his own church and in Selby also he had a certain personal interest.[3] The others were all founded later than the date at which knight-service was introduced into England, and the fact that none of them was assessed is one more proof that the quotas were fixed once and for all. There are, however, a few of the older houses also which appear never to have held by military service; they are Athelney, Burton, Croyland, Gloucester, Horton and Thorney. In default of any positive evidence, it may be supposed that in each case some peculiar circumstance hindered or dissuaded the Conqueror from assessing them; what this was can be conjectured with some probability with regard to all. Athelney was an insignificant settlement among the marshes of Somerset; it was moreover closely bound to Glastonbury, where there were knights in plenty. Burton, Croyland and Thorney were held, at his death in 1066, by Abbot Leofric of Peterborough; Peterborough had (along with Glastonbury) the highest assessment on the list, and it may be supposed that the position of its sometime dependents had not been fully regularized by 1070; the two near neighbours, indeed, may have contributed to the upkeep of Abbot Turold's knights.[4] Gloucester, where Serlo became abbot in 1071 or 1072, had only a handful of monks, and William, who visited the town each year for one of his solemn gatherings of magnates, may well have been unwilling to burden the new abbot and his struggling family. Horton also was in a state of decay from which, unlike Gloucester, it never recovered. Thus in all these cases the fact of their omission from the number of abbeys maintaining knights, and their permanent exemption, are a strong corroboration of the view that knight-service was fixed arbitrarily by the Conqueror early in his reign.

The inequality of the quotas is no less remarkable than the omission of

---

1 The *cartae* of 1166 are printed in the *Red Book of the Exchequer* (RS), ed. H. Hall, I, 186–445.

2 Round, *Feudal England*, 251, 278. *V*. Appendix XV for the list of quotas, and *dona*.

3 It is reasonable to suppose (even setting aside the charters as in large part forged) that Battle was founded free from such burdens as knight-service. For Selby *v. Selby Coucher Book* (Yorks. Archaeological Society Record Series, 10), I [15–18] and II (charter I).

4 For Leofric's pluralism, *v. Chronicle* [E], 1066.

certain houses. Twenty-three abbeys of men (excluding the cathedral monasteries, then only four in number) gave knight-service; of these four supplied forty knights or more; six maintained numbers ranging from thirty to ten; and thirteen sent six or less. In other words, the sum of the quotas of the four first houses on the list considerably exceeded the aggregate of the remaining nineteen. Nor does the scale of service follow that of the extent or value of land possessed by the abbey. It is true that the four sending the largest quotas are among the richest in *Domesday*, and those sending only one or two knights are among the poorest, but a number of the wealthiest houses were assessed very lightly, and one of the poorest (Tavistock) received a heavy burden.[1] Two of the greatest and wealthiest in particular, Ramsey and St Albans, escaped very lightly indeed. Once again, the only explanation of these figures would seem to be that the assessment was made very early, before the Domesday inquest and before the plantation of Norman abbots was complete or the country fully at peace, and that it was based not so much on the potential capacity of the house as on the actual situation there, that is, on the actual number of *milites* retained at the moment (1070–5) by the abbot. It is significant that in the case of four out of the five abbeys providing the largest contingents there is explicit evidence that during the Conqueror's reign the abbots maintained for their own protection a large escort of Norman men-at-arms. At Peterborough the warlike Turold, sent there in 1070 to hold the place against Hereward and the Danes, entered the town with a hundred and sixty armed followers;[2] at Glastonbury Thurstan had an armed band of Normans whom he ultimately used against his monks;[3] at Abingdon the first Norman abbot, Athelelm, had a similar retinue.[4] As for Ely, that centre of disaffection, the chronicler records that the first Norman abbot, Simeon, was ordered by the Conqueror to board a number of knights, probably those already on garrison duty there,[5] and possibly Baldwin of Bury received similar instructions. And it is natural to account

---

1 This may be seen at a glance by comparing the list of quotas with that of the incomes n *Domesday* set out *infra*, Appendix VI. St Albans provided only six, Ramsey four and Malmesbury three knights. If what appear to be the original assessments are taken, Peterborough (60), Glastonbury (60), Ely (40) and Bury (40) = 200, very considerably exceed the total of all the remaining houses = 163 (including Bath). A difficulty in reckoning is caused by the three houses, Ely, Bath and Sherborne, of which two became and the third ceased to be bishoprics between the Conquest and the earliest lists. Presumably Ely, which only became a bishopric in 1108, retained its original assessment, but it is possible that all the Bath quota came from Wells, and part of the Salisbury quota from Sherborne.

2 *Chronicle* [E], 1070: "Đa com Turold abbot ꝺ aehte siþe twenti Francisce men mid him ꝺ ealle full wepnode."

3 *Chronicle* [E], 1083 alludes to Thurstan's *Frencisce men*; cf. Will. Malmesb., *de Ant. Glast.* 330: "Willelmus...quamplures ex suis commilitonibus ex Glastoniae feudavit possessionibus."

4 *Chron. Abingd.* II, 3: "In primordio autem sui adventus in abbatiam, non nisi armatorum septus manu militum alicubi procedebat."

5 *Liber Eliensis*, 275: "Habuit ex consuetudine, secundum jussum regis, praetaxatum militiae numerum infra aulam ecclesiae"

for the relatively large number debited to the mediocre house of Tavistock by supposing that the first Norman abbot needed some kind of military protection against the inroads of his predecessor, the English Sihtric who had joined the marauding exiles.[1] In default of all evidence, it is not easy to conjecture why St Albans and Ramsey escaped so lightly, but it is significant that both long held aloof from the new *régime* and received Norman abbots only in 1077 and 1087 respectively. Taking the abbeys as a group, therefore, it would appear that the Conqueror took large knight-service from those abbots who actually retained large escorts, and on the rest set a very moderate quota bearing some proportion to the capacity of their resources.

Round and more recent scholars have demonstrated, largely from the evidence of the bishoprics and abbeys, that the *milites* were in origin stipendiaries, boarded in the abbey, and that the expense and discomfort of this arrangement led to gradual subinfeudation.[2] This in its turn led often to feelings of grievance, and it is not uncommon to find abbots charged with exploiting their position in favour of Norman kinsmen.[3] The charge may on occasion have been well founded, and kinsmen would naturally be found among the knights of an abbot who sprang from some great family, but monastic chroniclers were extremely and often unreasonably jealous of any alienation or apparent diminution of property. Faced with the unpopular necessity of maintaining Norman knights an abbot would naturally adopt subinfeudation which, though as a "book-entry" it might appear a serious loss of property, was often less expensive than the board and lodging of a household, and far less disturbing. The process of this subinfeudation, common to all honors lay and ecclesiastical, was not wholly complete in 1166; several of the *cartae* of that date, especially among the small Wessex abbeys, still refer to knights supported on the demesne.[4]

Knight-service was thus a burden unequally distributed upon the monasteries. In the case of the half-dozen upon which it pressed most heavily it was a permanent source of very real hardship. Besides the loss of land to military tenants, the abbot was always liable to be in difficulties in extracting money or service from his knights, especially when the fees were scattered or fractional; Samson of Bury was forced to cross the

1 Will. Malmesb., *GP*, 204: "[Abbas] Sihtritius postea sub rege Willelmo piraticam aggressus."

2 Round, *Feudal England*, 300 *seqq.*; Stenton, *English Feudalism*, 135 *seqq.* The clearest passages in the sources are *Chron. Abingd.* II, 3; *Liber Eliensis*, 275; *Vita Wulfstani*, 55: "habebat ipse in curia sua milites multos"; Dd, II, 372 (Bury). For the enfeoffments at Bury, made soon after the Conquest, *v.* Douglas, *Feudal Documents*, lxxxii–cv.

3 *V.* Round, *Feudal England*, for the relevant passages, several of which have been quoted above, ch. VI, p. 118.

4 E.g. in *Red Book of Exchequer*, I, 210 (Milton): "ecclesiam nostram nullum militem feffatum habere...sed servitia...de dominio suo persolvit." Cf. also Abbotsbury and Cerne (*ibid.* 211–12).

Channel in 1198 and bargain with the king over a question of four knights, and was in danger of being disseized of his barony;[1] on another occasion he had a vexatious controversy with the whole body of his military tenants,[2] and it was as leader of his contingent that he took the field in person at Windsor during Richard's imprisonment, thereby incurring adverse criticism.[3] Still more damaging was the constant drain of expenses, either by way of service and scutage, or by way of grants of all kinds, which were exacted on the basis of knights' fees. For the regular scutage, indeed, an abbot could recoup himself in whole or part from his tenants, but at the beginning of the reign of Henry II a heavy *donum* was levied (1159) from ecclesiastical tenants-in-chief holding by military service.[4] A few houses without knights' fees were called upon for *dona*, for the most part small in amount, and the quotas in general show a departure for the first time from the basis of service, and appear to be an endeavour to frame an assessment based on capacity for payment.[5] The impost was not repeated immediately, but proved a useful precedent for exactions half a century later.

II

THE WARDSHIP OF VACANT ABBACIES

Along with knight-service, in the case of lay fees, went the feudal claims for reliefs, wardships and marriage as between king and tenant-in-chief, and similar claims on the two latter counts as between tenant-in-chief and under-tenant. At first church fees escaped these payments to the crown; then, under William II, Ranulf Flambard made a double claim: that of annexing the temporalities of a church fee during a vacancy and that of extracting from the under-tenants a relief corresponding to that paid by lay tenants on a change of overlord.[6] The latter exaction did not become a permanent institution, and attempts on the part of the king to obtain a *quid pro quo* on the appointment of an abbot or the grant of a free election were from the days of Anselm onward regarded officially by the Church as simony. The custom, however, of the temporalities reverting to the Crown during a vacancy persisted.

There does not seem to be any direct evidence to show what was the practice before the Conquest in this matter; presumably the revenues were

1 *Jocelini Cronica*, 288: "Timens ne amitteret saisinam baroniae suae pro defectu servitii regis."

2 *Jocelini Cronica*, 269–71.

3 *Jocelini Cronica*, 259.

4 For this *v.* Round, *Feudal England*, 276 *seqq.*

5 Thus St Albans (6 knights) and St Augustine's (15) gave 100 and 220 marks; Peterborough (60) and Bury (40) 100 and 200; Gloucester and Battle (no knights) 120 and 60 marks (*Red Book of Exchequer*, I, 16 *seqq.*).

6 Round, *Feudal England*, 308–13. For the relief extracted from the Worcester tenants in 1095 cf. Hemming, *Cartulary*, I, 79–80.

administered by the prior and his advisers. The statement of Orderic that the bishop of the diocese took charge may be true of isolated cases, but can scarcely represent a general practice.[1] The entire absence of complaints during the Conqueror's reign is of itself strong evidence that he did not annex the revenues during a vacancy, and the explicit statements of the reliable Abingdon chronicle and of William of Malmesbury, as also of Orderic, that the custom of applying to religious houses the procedure of lay fees was introduced by Rufus at the suggestion of Ranulf Flambard, may be accepted as giving the truth.[2] The move was dictated by motives of avarice, whatever feudal analogies might be urged; Rufus claimed to have the absolute disposal of the abbacies and made no attempt to fill most of the vacancies. The usual procedure was for Ranulf Flambard as justiciar to have the custody of the abbey; a monk, not necessarily of the house, was then appointed warden and all surplus revenues went to Flambard or William. At the death of Rufus at least eleven houses were thus held in farm by the king.[3]

Henry I at his coronation renounced his claim to such revenues,[4] but some years later it was his customary practice to annex them, and often to keep the abbacy vacant for a number of years. At the demise of an abbot, royal clerks were sent by the justiciar to take an inventory of treasures and income; a sum was assigned to be paid annually to the king, and a monk, either of the house or a stranger, was given charge of the temporal administration during the vacancy. Thus Abingdon was held vacant for four years after the death of Faricius in 1117, the king taking roughly two-thirds of the income;[5] Peterborough was similarly treated in 1125.[6] At Battle, which did not hold by military service, a still more comprehensive procedure was customary on the score that the abbey was a royal *Eigenkloster*. There, from 1102 onwards, the house was administered in things temporal and spiritual by Geoffrey, a monk of St Carilef, and

1 Ordericus Vitalis, III, 313: "Antequam Normanni Angliam obtinuissent, mos erat ut, dum rectores ecclesiarum obirent, episcopus coenobiorum, quae in sua diocesi erant, res sollicite describeret, et sub ditione sua, donec abbates legitime ordinarentur, custodiret."

2 *Chron. Abingd.* II, 42 [1097]: "Ea tempestate, infanda usurpata est in Anglia consuetudo, ut si qua praelatorum persona ecclesiarum vita decederet, mox honor ecclesiasticus fisco deputaretur regio." Cf. Will. Malmesb., *GR*, 369. Ordericus Vitalis, III, 313, supplies the Flambard's name. *V.*, however, the essay on him by R. W. Southern (*v.* Bibliography).

3 *Chron. Abingd.* II, 42: "Motbertus, ecclesiae hujus monachus, curam rerum infra extrave ministrabat, non ecclesiae provectibus, sed regii marsupii mercibus." Cf. *Ann. Winton.* 36–7 for the Flambard as *custos* of the New Minster, Canterbury and Chertsey; Eadmer, *Hist. Nov.* 26, describes the straits of the Canterbury monks. Henry of Huntingdon, 232, gives the number as eleven.

4 Stubbs, *Select Charters*, 100: "Nec mortuo...abbate aliquid accipiam de dominico ecclesiae vel de hominibus ejus donec successor in eam ingrediatur."

5 *Chron. Abingd.* II, 158–9 (1115–19): "Omnes res sive redditus hujus ecclesiae mox describuntur, trecentis libris fisco regali per singulos annos deputatis. Reliqua usibus ecclesiae conceduntur."

6 Hugo Candidus, 72 (1125): "Rex misit justiciarios suos Ricardum Basset et Walterum archidiaconum et...descripserunt omnes thesauros ecclesiae et omnem abbatiam, et quicquid erat intus et foris, et attulerunt ad regem, rex tenuit abbatiam in manu sua."

Gunter, abbot of Thorney, formerly a monk of the house, successively; in 1124 wardenship of the temporalities was given by Roger of Salisbury as justiciar to Aelward, a monk of Battle; in 1171 Richard de Lucy appointed two of his officials as procurators.[1] Although in some cases ample funds were left to the monks, the practice naturally tended to encourage long vacancies and was exploited by such men as Roger of Salisbury who, besides Malmesbury, held Milton for five years and Abbotsbury.[2] It also made possible the gift of wardenship to a prelate not a monk, as happened at Abingdon in 1164 when Henry II commended the abbacy to the bishop of St Asaph, thus providing an early English example of what later became a common practice abroad.[3]

Against long vacancies the monks could only appeal to the conscience of the king or, if circumstances were favourable, demand a canonical election. Against the misfortunes of administration by a royal proctor or favourite they devised the system by which abbatial revenues were completely separated from those allotted to the convent, and claimed that the former only should fall to the Exchequer during a vacancy. The precise moment at which this was done is not often specified, and probably varied from house to house; a division of this kind must usually have preceded the settlement of incomes upon the obedientiaries, which took place in the first quarter of the twelfth century, and at Bury the change is known to have taken place under Abbot Robert II (1103–7).[4] It was not till the reign of Henry II, however, that the claim based on this division became general and successful. It would seem to have been so at St Albans in 1166, and was certainly so at Bury in 1180.[5] At Abingdon, on the death of Abbot Roger in 1184–5, the royal proctor arrived, made an exhaustive enquiry into income and charges, and stated that he had been given charge of the whole abbey. The prior and others thereupon set out to visit Ralph

---

1 *Chron. Bell.* 47 (1102), 60 (1124), 139 (1171).

2 *Red Book of Exchequer,* I, 210–11.

3 *Chron. Abingd.* II, 234, with Henry's charter: "Godefrido...cui commendavi abbatiam de Abbendona tanquam abbati."

4 Cf. the charter printed by H. W. C. Davis in his article, *The Liberties of Bury St Edmund's,* in *EHR,* XXIV (July 1909), 417–31, no. vii: "Notum sit vobis quod volo et precipio ut particio facta a Roberto abbate sancti Edmundi de omnibus redditibus abbatie sit imperpetuum; ut abbas scilicet s. Edmundi libere habeat omnia maneria sua et redditus suos per se, et prior et conventus habeant liberam disposicionem omnium maneriorum et reddituum suorum. Et regales ministri tempore vacantis abbatie nullam sibi attrahant in maneriis predicti conventus." Cf. *Jocelini Cronica,* 283, 291, for references to this disposition of Abbot Robert. Davis (*art. cit.*) dates the charter 1100, taking the witness Th[oma] arch. Ebor. to be Thomas I, thus making the abbot Robert I. The date, however, of the anniversary of Robert II, alluded to by Jocelin, *Cronica,* 289–91 (cf. *Mem. St Edmund's,* I, 356), shows that he was the one responsible; the signature must therefore be that of Thomas II, and the date 1109–14. The charter has been printed again by Prof. D. C. Douglas, with date 1108–14, in *Feudal Documents from...Bury St Edmunds,* p. 69, n. 35.

5 *GASA,* I, 182: "Tota abbatia confiscata ex praecepto judicis regni [*sc.* Robert, earl of Leicester]; sed ejus cura omnis Priori...commissa est." *Jocelini Cronica,* 215–16: "Impetraverunt literas [monachi] ut res et redditus conventus, qui separati sunt a rebus et redditibus abbatis, essent integri in manu prioris et conventus."

Glanvill, whom they informed of the division of the accounts of the obedientiaries from those of the abbot, and stated that ancient usage, going
back to the days of the Confessor, gave the monks control of their share
during a vacancy. Their claim was allowed, largely owing to the advocacy
of the great justiciar, though it can scarcely have been historical in the
form in which it was urged.[1] The arrangement, in itself equitable, seems
to have met with no formal resistance on the part of the Crown, though it
may occasionally have been disregarded in practice; it became standard in
the last quarter of the century.[2]

III

THE ABBOT'S HOUSEHOLD

The various administrative and judicial duties of a great honor could be
discharged by the lord only with the aid of a number of officials. The
complexity of this organization was from the beginning considerable;[3]
indeed, it would appear that the machinery became simpler rather than
the reverse during the course of the twelfth century. How early the
black monk abbots began to surround themselves with the customary
officials retained by a great lord is not clear, but all indications go to show
that it was not primitive, but a part of the tendency towards a feudalization
of the abbatial dignity and office which set in during the reign of Henry I.
No attempt has yet been made, even in the case of lay barons, to reconstruct the normal lord's household at that time from the scattered references
in charters, and the task would be still harder where abbots were concerned,
for they doubtless made use of clerks, servants and even monks to a
greater or less degree where lay lords employed officials with a title. A
description of the household of the abbot of Westminster, dating from
1215, shows that he was normally accompanied on his visits to his manors
by seven principal officers, the seneschal, chamberlain, pantler, butler,
usher, cook and marshal.[4] In the list of monastic servants and functionaries at Glastonbury in 1189 it is possible to trace a seneschal, dispenser,
cook and porter.[5] Of these officers the seneschal or *dapifer* was the most
important, for besides other duties he acted as justice and legal representative of his lord, and the office was commonly hereditary towards the
end of the twelfth century. Thus Samson, on his election in 1182, was

1 *Chron. Abingd.* ii, 297: "Propositum est [by royal proctors]...ut tam obedientias
nostras, quam possessiones ad cameram abbatis pertinentes, in manu domini regis seisiret."
2 Interesting details may often be found in the entries of the Pipe Rolls, e.g., in Pipe
Roll 31 Henry II (vol. 34 of *Pipe Roll Soc.*), 29 (Abingdon), 77 (St Mary's, York etc.).
3 Stenton, *English Feudalism*, 65: "It is easy to underestimate the complexity of the
organization required for the administration of a great honour in the twelfth century."
4 Published by Stenton, *English Feudalism*, Appendix no. 17, pp. 267–8.
5 *Liber Henrici de Soliaco*, ed. J. E. Jackson (Roxburghe Club, 1887, 10): "Galterius
portarius...debet ire cum abbate. Gillelmus Pastorel magister cocus est...debet ire cum
abbate, etc."

presented with a young man not yet a knight who claimed the stewardship of St Edmund's by charter right, and though he was not accepted a *locum tenens* was taken for him. The incident shows that in the past the abbot of Bury had supported (also by charter) no less than ten attendants for the steward.[1] These, and the others required by the other functionaries, must be added to the list of monastic servants in order to arrive at the full complement of dependents upon an abbey.

IV

COURTS

What we call the feudal system introduced into England a practice and machinery of feudal law and jurisdiction which superimposed itself upon the original local system of justice. Consequently, side by side with the shire and hundred courts there were the manor courts or halimots and the *Curia domini*, the court *par excellence* of the honor. The monasteries as landholders, and their abbots or priors as their representatives, thus became charged with the responsibilities and possessed of the income accruing from the administration of justice and the settlement of innumerable disputes. The history of these courts, manorial and honorial alike, is at present very little known as regards the twelfth century, and no attempt can be made here to give details. No review, however, of the activities of a monastic house and its abbot would be complete without a brief reference to them.

These feudal courts, great and small, being an inseparable adjunct to every holding of land, existed on the estates of all religious houses which held *in capite* of the king, whether or no they held by knight-service. It so happens that one of the earliest accounts of a process before the honorial court of an abbey occurs in the Battle chronicle. Battle never held by military service, but however suspect may be the account of the gift of the court by the Conqueror,[2] and the charter from which that account derives, there can be no doubt that the abbot and monks of Battle exercised by 1100 over their *bloc* of manors the same rights as were enjoyed by the lords of other honors. The case referred to occurred in 1102. The abbacy, which was vacant, was being administered by a monk, Geoffrey of St Carilef, who charged the reeve (*praepositus*) of the important manor of Wye with maladministration. He cited him at the manorial court,[3] but the defaulter, Robert by name, had powerful friends and refused to give satisfaction; he was therefore summoned to attend the court of Battle.[4]

1 *Jocelini Cronica*, 232–3. For the abbot's 'council' a little later *v.* Levett, *Studies*, 31 *seqq.*, 153 *seqq.*

2 *Chron. Bell.* 23–4: "Huic ergo ecclesiae s. Martini de Bello hanc imprimis regali auctoritate dignitatem concessit et dedit, ut habeat curiam suam per omnia et regiam libertatem...et justitiam per se tenendam, etc."

3 *Chron. Bell.* 48: "Convictum in ejusdem manerii curiam compulit, etc."

4 *Chron. Bell.* 48: "Praecipiendo apud Bellum curiam adesse."

The case was discussed before Robert, his friends and other "barons", and the whole community, young and old.[1] Robert appealed to his shire court, but Geoffrey asserted that the court of Battle was the king's court, to which all were amenable, and had his way.

References to the monastic honorial courts are frequent in the latter part of the century. An interesting case of the conflict of jurisdictions occurred at St Augustine's, Canterbury, in 1176. The men of Thanet claimed that they were not bound to come to the honorial court of the abbey to plead or receive judgment, but could do all in their halimot in Thanet; the appeal went to the shire court of Kent, presided over by the sheriff's deputy, and the decision was given for the monks, though the men of Thanet gave more trouble later.[2] Besides the courts of manor and honor, the monasteries which controlled a borough had also the administration of the borough court or leet, and where they had the right of holding a fair they also had control of the court which came into existence to try the offences of strangers and settle trade disputes, and later became known as the court merchant.[3] An early example of this last jurisdiction in embryo is seen at Glastonbury in 1189, where Robert the reeve or steward (*praepositus*) appears as in control of the fair at Glastonbury and holding all the pleas.[4]

At Bury St Edmunds a peculiarly complicated network of jurisdictions existed, all enjoyed by the abbot: the *curia abbatis*, the honorial court for all the abbot's tenants; the *curia S. Aedmundi*, the central court of the franchise, with a general jurisdiction over eight and a half hundreds, and a more particular one over the *banleuca* of the town which included all pleas of the Crown; thus Samson vindicated his rights against the archbishop of Canterbury, who held a manor within his hundred, and also against the bishop of Ely, who claimed a criminal for the *curia S. Aetheldredae*, the court of Ely's five and a half hundreds. Besides these, there was the borough leet, and also a special court known as the portman moot.[5] At Bury, as at other abbeys, the abbot retained the revenue of fines from the manorial courts of his own manors, and allowed to the chief officials, such as sacrist and cellarer, the court rights on the manors allotted to them as representatives of the convent.[6]

At St Albans, with its large Liberty of St Edmund, there was a somewhat similar, though less complicated, organization: the free court

---

1 *Chron. Bell.* 48: "Non solum seniores fratrum sed et juniores interesse procura[vit]."
2 *Chron. Will. Thorne*, 1827, 1842, where there is reference to *capitalis Curia b. Augustini*. The *halimotum in Thaneto* was clearly something more than a manorial court.
3 *V.* N. M. Trenholme, *The English Monastic Boroughs*, 82–6; M. D. Lobel, *The Borough of Bury St Edmunds*, 95 *seqq.*
4 *Liber Henrici de Soliaco*, 13: "Robertus prepositus est prepositus fori Glaston.... omnia placita habet."
5 *Jocelini Cronica*, 255–6, 265–6, 331–3; Lobel, *The Borough of Bury St Edmunds*, 95 *seqq.*; Douglas, *Feudal Documents*, clv–clxx.
6 *Jocelini Cronica*, 301–5.

or *curia de abbathia*, of which the character is not wholly clear, and which does not appear to have been precisely a court of the honor; the halimots, which met on various manors or were summoned to St Albans to meet "at the ash tree"; and the courts leet. The president of the Abbey courts was, at least in the thirteenth century, the abbot's *dapifer* or seneschal, a lay official; the halimots were controlled in general by the external cellarer acting as representative of the abbot; in the manors belonging to the various obedientiaries the officials concerned held their courts.[1]

Within a few days of the abbot's blessing he received homage from all his tenants; this was an occasion which enabled him to confirm or revise the many customary engagements with which the whole fabric of his establishment was enmeshed, to settle any questions of knight-service and to receive an aid. Thus Samson acted at Bury, receiving his men on Easter Wednesday after his own reception by the monks on Palm Sunday, 1182; and thus Henry de Sully in 1189 at Glastonbury received homage within a week of his blessing.[2]

1 The above paragraph has been added in order to call attention to the important work of the late Prof. Elizabeth Levett, which did not appear till this chapter was in the press: *Studies in Manorial History* (Oxford, 1938). In particular, *v.* Essay II, Baronial Councils and their relation to Manorial Courts, pp. 21–40; III, The Financial Organization of the Manor, pp. 41–68; and IV, Studies in the Manorial Organization of St Albans Abbey, pp. 69–368. In the last, there are interesting statistics and a map of the liberty. Reference may also be made to an article by the same author, *The Courts and Court Rolls of St Albans Abbey*, in *Transactions of the Royal Hist. Soc.*, 4th Series, VII (1924).

2 *Jocelini Cronica*, 232–3; *Liber Henrici de Soliaco*, 1.

CHAPTER XXXVI

THE CATHEDRAL MONASTERIES AND THE BISHOPS' ABBEYS

I

The English black monk monasteries of which the inmates performed the offices in the cathedral church, having the bishop in place of an abbot, and enjoying from the middle of the twelfth century onwards all the rights of the capitular body, formed a group almost unique in the medieval Church.[1] It was at the time assumed by the monks of these foundations and by others,[2] and has repeatedly been asserted by historians, that the system was initiated by Augustine in the very first years of his mission to England. Historically speaking, this was not precisely the case; still less was it true that the metropolitan church had always housed a monastic community; but it is most probable that in the first decades of the seventh century there were monks at Christ Church, and it may well be argued that the later arrangement was originated by those who supposed Augustine to have been before them and who were influenced by what they conceived to be his example.

If the celebrated answers of Gregory the Great to Augustine may be taken as undoubtedly authentic,[3] the early history of the church of Canterbury can be reconstructed as follows.[4] Augustine arrived at the head of a small band of monks; for some time they were his only companions and clergy, but very soon he began to gather round him clerics who were not monks. It was respecting these that his first question to

1 Among the rare contemporary examples outside England are Monreale in Sicily, where the abbey was made the see of a bishop in 1176, perhaps with English precedent in mind, and Downpatrick in Ireland, where monks from Chester were imported to form a cathedral monastery on the English model c. 1185. It is noteworthy that in Sicily in 1176 the archbishops of Compsa, Syracuse and Palermo were all Englishmen (cf. Stubbs, *Lectures on Medieval and Modern History*, 134).

2 E.g. by the monks' enemy, Hugh of Nonant of Coventry; v.s. p. 323.

3 Bede, *Historia Ecclesiastica*, I, xxvii (ed. Plummer, I, 48–9). As is well known, both the matter of these answers and the manner of their tradition by Bede have given rise to doubts as to their authenticity; among recent scholars of the first rank, however, there is a consensus in their favour; thus F. H. Dudden, *Gregory the Great*, II, 130, note, writes: "The genuineness of this document is now generally admitted", and J. Armitage Robinson (v. next note) assumes this without discussion. More recently Dr W. Levison, in his chapter in *Bede* (ed. A. H. Thompson), 128, n. 2 and 139, n. 2, shows more reserve, relying on M. Müller, *Zur Frage nach der Echtheit und Abfassungszeit des "Responsum b. Gregorii ad Augustinum episcopum"*, in *Theologische Quartalschrift*, CXIII (1932), 94–118, but Müller's arguments, which are directed chiefly against Gregory's answers on points of marriage and morals, are not, to my mind, convincing as to the probability of the letter being a forgery of the eighth century, and it is in particular impossible to see what a forger could hope to attain by the first answer concerning the bishop's *familia* at Canterbury.

4 For this, v. J. Armitage Robinson, *The Early Community at Christ Church, Canterbury*, in *JTS*, XXVII (1926), 225–40.

Gregory was addressed, and the pope replied that Augustine, being a monk, must live the common life with his clergy. This answer, if its terms are carefully weighed, does not imply that the new clergy were to be monks; indeed, it assumes that they were not, and the result of Gregory's arrangement seems clearly to have been the establishment of a body of clergy, living a common life with Augustine, alongside of the existing family of monks. For the latter, the archbishop soon founded the monastery of SS. Peter and Paul (later St Augustine's) under an abbot who had been one of his original companions, while the clergy of the cathedral of St Saviour's (later Christ Church) continued to live a quasi-regular common life.

A few years later, however, a change took place. Augustine's successor was Laurence, himself undoubtedly a monk. In 610 Mellitus, bishop of London, also a monk, went to Rome on business connected with the English Church. While there, he obtained from Pope Boniface, who was at the moment engaged in regulating the monastic life in Italy, a letter[1] assenting to the request of King Ethelbert that such of the original companions of Augustine as remained at the cathedral church of Canterbury should have power to receive others as monks there. In this way, no doubt, the community became for a time wholly monastic, on the contemporary Roman model, though in the course of a century it probably fell back into something more nearly resembling a family of canons.

In the north, however, a totally different form of ecclesiastical government had been introduced with the mission of Aidan. Aidan and his companions, like the band with Augustine, were monks, but they were familiar with churches ruled from monasteries of which the abbot was the effective head, and the bishop a subordinate, and although it is probable that from the first Aidan and his successors were in control and even that they had around them a number of clergy who were not monks, the custom remained that the bishop of Lindisfarne should be a monk and live with his monks. Bede took this arrangement for granted as the natural one, and even suggested, in his well-known letter to Ecgbert, that new bishoprics should be erected in monasteries on the model of Lindisfarne.[2] This was not done, but Lindisfarne remained monastic, and even after the removal of the see, after many wanderings, to Durham in 995 the traditions of the past remained, however much the monastic regularity of the life may have tended to disappear.[3] Durham, however,

---

1 This, in the form handed down to us, is the first document in the celebrated Eadmer-Malmesbury "forgeries". It is printed in Eadmer, *Hist. Nov.* 261 *seq.*; Will. Malmesb., *GP*, 46–7; and H. Böhmer, *Die Fälschungen Erzbischof Lanfrancs*, 145–6. For a discussion, which aims at establishing its substantial authenticity, *v.* art. by the present writer in *Journal of Theological Studies*, XXXIX (1938), 126–31.

2 For this, *v.* Bede, *H.E.* IV, xxv (Plummer, I, 268–70); *Vita Cuthberti*, xvi (ed. Giles, IV, 257 *seqq.*); *Ep. ad Ecgbertum*, § 10 (Plummer, I, 413).

3 For this, and a valuable discussion of the Celtic episcopal system, *v.* Prof. A. Hamilton Thompson in *Bede*, 72–92.

distant and decayed as it was, cannot possibly have had any direct influence on the arrangements of Dunstan and his associates; on the other hand, the writings of Bede, which implied that the Northumbrian church had for long been familiar with monastic bishops living as monks in their monasteries, and that this system was similar to that initiated by Augustine at Canterbury and maintained there for an unspecified leng·h of time, undoubtedly had the greatest influence on future generations.

The first introduction of monks into a cathedral church in the south, and the seed from which sprang the whole family of cathedral priories, was due to the action of Ethelwold at Winchester in 964. Here the bishop's intention was simply to secure for his cathedral the full liturgical service carried out by men living the edifying monastic life, to whom he, who had previously been abbot at Abingdon, would continue to stand in the relation of spiritual father; holding, as he did, that the monastic life was the only way in which the Church in England could be regenerated, he intended this arrangement to abide; his successors were to be monks, and they were to be as abbots in the monastery attached to the cathedral; Ethelwold could not be expected to foresee that social and ecclesiastical developments would in the future complicate a system which appeared to him essentially simple. His example was followed almost immediately by Oswald at Worcester, and a little later at Sherborne and Canterbury. There the movement ceased, and nothing happened between 997 and 1066 either to alter the equilibrium or to suggest that the number of cathedral monasteries would either increase or decrease in the future.

The appointment of Lanfranc to Canterbury had the effect of giving the system a new lease of life. Like Ethelwold and Dunstan, Lanfranc was a monk who looked to the monastic order as the chief instrument of reform; although there were no cathedral monasteries in Italy or Normandy, he willingly accepted the English situation as he found it. Like Ethelwold, also, he acted in all respects as abbot, and unquestionably supposed that his successors would be monks and continue so to act. Once again, the concentration of the supreme government of both Church and State in the hands of the king, and the absence of any large body of diocesan officials, effectually prevented clashes of jurisdiction and concealed the potential difficulties of the arrangement.

When the organization of Canterbury as a monastic cathedral had thus been accepted and developed by Lanfranc, other Norman bishops who were monks took the further step of introducing such arrangements where they did not already exist. An account of this process has already been given, and need not be repeated. Within fifty years of the Conquest the number of cathedral monasteries rose from four to nine; in other words, nine out of the existing sixteen sees had monks in the bishop's church; and though the group was far from homogeneous in constitution, and each house was governed by its own arrangements with the diocesan, the monks in every case occupied the place of a chapter, or shared rights with another capitular body, and when under the restored canon law cathedral chapters became a power to reckon with, the monks were there to claim equal rights. No further additions or subtractions were made in the number of cathedral monasteries between the reign of Henry I and the Dissolution; the remote see of Carlisle, restored to English influence and given to Aldulf, a black canon, and an Augustinian chapter in 1133, had in some respects a parallel history, but had no importance during our period.

II

It had been the intention of the framers of the *Concordia* that the monk-bishop should live the regular life with his community and fill the place of an abbot.[1] Ethelwold himself, though often taken away by court business, and Oswald, though similarly distracted by his tenure of the archbishopric of York, did their best to rule their monks directly, and no doubt their early successors did the same. It was, however, inevitable that a bishop should be frequently absent, and gradually the second in command, the dean or provost, came to be the effective monastic superior.[2] At Worcester the almost continuous union of the see with that of York, and at Canterbury the pluralism of the secular Stigand immediately before the Conquest, must have completed the evolution of offices, and the account of Wulfstan's life, when prior of Worcester, shows him as the effective superior of the monks who determined the policy and prosperity of the community.

Lanfranc, both in his daily practice and in the decrees of his *Statuta*, clearly intended once more to set the diocesan in the place of abbot. He explicitly equated bishop and abbot,[3] and imposed this conception upon Christ Church and the houses, such as Rochester and Durham, that were modelled upon it. More than a century later Gervase could write, perhaps somewhat tendenciously, that it was the age-long custom at Canterbury that all things within and without the house should depend upon the nod

---

1 *Concordia*, Proem. 78. It is noteworthy that the *Responsum* of Gregory to Augustine is alluded to a few lines above this passage.

2 In pre-Conquest documents he appears often as dean or provost. For Canterbury, cf. *Chronicle* [E], *s.a.* 1020, where Aethelnoth is *munuc and decanus*; for Winchester, *Ann. Winton.* (*Ann. Monastici*, ed. Luard, II), *s.a.* 1082: "Simeon...ex praeposito Wintoniae, quem nos priorem vocamus, etc."; for Durham, Symeon of Durham, I, 129: "beatus Cuthbertus successit in praepositi, id est prioris, officium." For Worcester, *v.* the kalendar preceding the *Homilies of Wulfstan* in Brit. Mus. MS. Hatton 113, where the *obits* of four *decani* (= priors) occur.

3 Cf. Lanfranc's *Statuta*, Preface, 211: "Quorum [*sc.* monachorum] per abbates frequentius quam per antistites vita disponitur; quamvis et ipsi antistites, si paternam curam vice Christi subjectis suis impendant, non absurde abbates...appellari queant." For Lanfranc's practice cf. Eadmer, *Hist. Nov.* 14.

of the archbishop.[1] When Lanfranc was succeeded by Anselm, the arch-bishop's rule was even more immediate and paternal. Whatever judgment may be passed on Anselm as archbishop, all are agreed that he excelled as abbot of Bec; to his new family in England, many of whom were in origin Norman, he seems to have given himself fully as father and spiritual guide, and among his most exquisite letters of advice are those written to his prior and individual monks. He speaks throughout as abbot, confirming the reception of novices in his absence, reasoning with an apostate monk, gently reproving three of the brethren who wished to follow him, their guide, beyond the seas. When departing, he delegates all his care of souls *in foro interno et externo* to the prior, whom the monks are to obey as himself.[2] Eadmer, the precentor, was his confidant and confessor, and Anselm was never more at home in the last years of his life than when speaking familiarly to his sons in chapter.[3]

At Durham William of St Carilef acted no differently. The contemporary chronicler tells us that he ruled his monks as the most loving of fathers and was loved by them to the full in return. Although he gave a great measure of responsibility to his prior, Aldwin, he was nevertheless instant with his own words of counsel, and a letter of his exists, exhorting the monks to frequent the choir and the sacraments, which was to be read in chapter every week during his absence.[4] At Rochester, the few details given of Gundulf show that his rule was after the same pattern. He was, so his biographer tells us, the example, the correction and the support of his monks.[5] At Worcester, Wulfstan when at home acted as abbot. He attended the choir, noticed absences from the night office and regarded himself as responsible; he refounded Westbury-on-Trym and sent thither monks and a prior of his own choosing; when at Worcester he performed the duties of *hebdomadarius* or priest of the week and gave the blessing at Compline.[6]

Finally, at Norwich Herbert Losinga, who had been like Anselm an

1 Gervase, I, 30: "Haec est...Cantuariensis ecclesiae ab antiquis temporibus usque in praesens...consuetudo, scilicet ut omnia intus et extra...sui archiepiscopi, immo et abbatis, nutum attendant." This passage occurs in Gervase's *Imaginatio quasi contra monachos*—that is, a hypothetical presentation of Baldwin's case against the monks—and the writer would not necessarily have admitted all the claims put forward. But presumably the archbishops would have maintained them.

2 *PL*, CLIX, *Anselmi epp.* IV, 41, III, 144, 108, 89.

3 Cf. Anselm's words in chapter (Eadmer, *Vita Anselmi*, 364): "Sicut bubo dum in caverna cum pullis suis est laetatur et suo sibi modo bene est...ita et mihi."

4 Symeon of Durham, I, 125–6: "Nimium eos [*sc.* monachos] diligens, nimium ab eis diligebatur, etc." Symeon had been at Durham from 1083 onwards. In view of the ultimate hostility between Lanfranc and St Carilef, it is noteworthy that the *Statuta* of the arch-bishop were among the collection of books given to the church of Durham by the bishop himself, probably at the foundation of the monastery; cf. the catalogue in article by C. H. Turner in *JTS*, XIX (1917–18), 121–32.

5 *Vita Gundulfi, PL*, CLIX, 821: "His [*sc.* monachis] Gundulfus vivendi speculum, his totius religionis factus est documentum, etc."

6 *Vita Wulfstani*, 51, 54.

abbot, speaks throughout his letters as the father of his monks. He wishes their knowledge and love of him to be as intimate as possible; he is "anxious with a father's apprehensions and apprehensive with a father's anxiety"; he writes to individuals a word of praise or blame; he examines the children of the cloister on what they have learnt. When leaving Norwich he uses language which is the exact equivalent of Anselm's to his prior; he writes to Ingulph that he commends to him the church of Norwich and the work of the church and his, the bishop's, own work. It is no surprise to learn that he composed a set of monastic constitutions.[1]

Such relationships could only exist when the bishop was a monk who himself had had some experience of ruling souls in religion. At Winchester a different state of things existed from the Conquest onwards; both Walkelin and William Giffard quarrelled with their monks at the beginning of their episcopate, and although in both cases a total reconciliation took place and (if the monastic annalist may be believed) the former loved his monks as if they were angels, while the latter often took his siesta with them in the common dormitory and ate at the novices' table,[2] such manifestations of affection are a different thing from the constant rule of a monastic superior. In the event, the golden age of patriarchal rule in the cathedral monasteries was of short duration. At Canterbury the best was over with Anselm's death, though his successor, and perhaps Theobald a little later, were in the same tradition. At Rochester the rule of monastic bishops continued till 1124, but at Norwich the death of Herbert Losinga in 1119 and at Durham that of William of St Carilef in 1095 marked the end of the short epoch. For the future the Winchester of Walkelin, not the Canterbury of Lanfranc, was the type towards which all tended to conform. The prior became the effective religious superior and the bishop, from being abbot in all but name, came to hold nothing but a formal jurisdictional position of prelacy. Even in the few cases where monks were bishops, as William of Norwich (1146–74) and Henry of Winchester (1129–71), their position was one of patron rather than father, and the external occupations, the growth of the episcopal *familia* and the separation of revenues and interests all combined to make the bishop a stranger to his monks and often an opponent.

1 As it is not easy to obtain the Latin text of the letters (ed. Anstruther, Brussels, 1846) the references are to the translation given in the *Life, Letters and Sermons of Herbert de Losinga* (ed. Goulburn and Symonds), as follows: vol. 1, letter xv, p. 135; lvii, 204; xxiii, 192; xliii, 196; lvii, 206; xv, 135. Bale, *Index Britanniae Scriptorum* (ed. Poole), 169, is the authority for the constitutions: "Herbertus Nordovicensis episcopus scripsit Constitutiones monachorum." It is to them no doubt that the bishop refers in a letter to the abbot of Fécamp (ed. Anstruther, 69, quoted by Berlière, *L'Ascèse Bénédictine*, 31, n. 4): "usus et consuetudines...in quantum potuimus extrahere a Domno Balduino vel in quantum eas ego ipse possum recolligere, etc." They were presumably the Fécamp customs, pure and simple.

2 *Ann. Winton.* (*Ann. Monastici*, ed. Luard, II), *s.a.* 1098, 1128.

III

As the bishops after the Conquest all held by military service, and had a household and many official expenses to provide for, the separation of episcopal lands and revenues from those of the monks was accomplished earlier than the equivalent division in the autonomous abbeys. Already before the Conquest, as is made clear by *Domesday*, some division, or at least a permanent allocation, had been made, though the arrangements differed in different churches and probably followed the type common throughout western Europe by which certain lands were assigned to the *mensa* of the bishop and others to his clerks. In the case of Canterbury, though the record of all the lands begins with the words *ipse archiepiscopus tenet*, the properties appear under separate entries as *Terra archiepiscopi* and *Terra monachorum archiepiscopi*;[1] occasionally the land is further earmarked for a particular purpose, such as clothing (*de vestitu monachorum*).[2] At Winchester also there are separate entries, first *Terra Wintoniensis episcopi* and then the heading: *hae terrae infra scriptae sunt de victu monachorum Wint*.[3] At Sherborne, not yet autonomous, there is the same procedure; first the bishop of Salisbury's land and then that of the monks, consisting of nine manors followed by the rubric: *haec novem descripta maneria sunt de victu monachorum Scireburn*.[4] In the case of Worcester the hundred of Oswaldslaw is described as demesne land of the church of St Mary held by the bishop and there is no separate heading for the monks, though some of the manors of the hundred are noted as being *de dominico victu monachorum*. Hemming's cartulary gives a similar account, though in it properties outside as well as inside Oswaldslaw are assigned to the monks.[5]

In the three new monasteries careful provision was made from the start. At Rochester Lanfranc himself divided the property and endowed the monks with some of his own land, and there is record of his making a purchase of territory to give to them.[6] At Durham, according to Symeon, who usually shows himself trustworthy, William of St Carilef made exhaustive enquiries as to the ancient relations between bishop and monks before completing his own establishment. Under the Lindisfarne system the property would have been held conjointly by bishop and monks; Symeon states that before the Conquest a formal separation had been made between the properties, and though his assertion has been questioned, if not disproved, the proceeds of various estates must in practice have been

---

1 *Domesday*, 4b, 3a.
2 *Domesday*, 16b (Odintune and Petchinges).
3 *Domesday*, 41a.   4 *Domesday*, 77a.
5 *Domesday*, 172b; Hemming, I, 289, II, 493–4.
6 *Vita Gundulfi*, in *PL*, CLIX, 824: "Placuit episcopo, placuit et Lanfranco, ut episcopus res suas seorsim, monachi vero et ipsi possessiones suas haberent seorsim." Cf. Will. Malmesb., *GP*, 72, 137, for Lanfranc's gifts.

traditionally earmarked between bishop and clerks. In any case, St Carilef made a complete separation on the lines of that at Canterbury, though energetic attempts to reverse the arrangement were made by his immediate successors.[1] At Norwich Herbert de Losinga did the same; to the monks he gave lands from his private property, not from the scanty possessions of the bishopric, in order to avoid any claims on the part of his successor.[2]

Bath and Coventry were at first in a different position, for here the bishops obtained possession of the whole abbey by forcible means, and for a time at least gave the monks an insufficient dole with no fixed property. The community were therefore forced to struggle for a constitution, which they obtained with difficulty and by degrees. At Ely a clear division was made in 1109, but the monks alleged that the bishop had taken the lion's share, and quarrels over revenues occurred more than once in the sequel.[3]

IV

The appointment of the prior everywhere rested with the bishop, and, in the early days under monk-bishops, the appointment also of all the officials of the monastery. Attempts were made in some houses to make the post of prior wholly elective, but they were not successful, though the wishes of the monks were usually consulted;[4] as regards the other officials, the practice under later bishops varied in the different cathedrals. At Canterbury for long the archbishop appointed all, even the least important;[5] later, Theobald retained for himself the right of appointing prior, sub-prior and precentor while apparently giving to the prior and convent the disposal of the other offices, and this arrangement was confirmed by Alexander III;[6] later, however, Urban III confirmed a different one accord-

1 Symeon of Durham, I, 123–4: "Terrarum possessiones illorum...a suis segregavit." The editor (Canon Greenwell) of the *Feodarium Prioratus Dunelmensis* (Surtees Soc. LVIII, 1872) endeavours to prove (introd. xiv–xxiv) that the lands of the monks and clerks were not separate from the bishop's before the Conquest. The reputed charters of William of St Carilef printed by J. Raine in an appendix to *Historiae Dunelmensis Scriptores Tres* (Surtees Soc. IX, 1839) are conclusively shown by Greenwell (introd. xxxi–lviii) to be forgeries of the early twelfth century.

2 Will. Malmesb., *GP*, 152. Cf. also the charter of foundation in *Monasticon*, IV, 13–16.

3 For Bath, *v.* Will. Malmesb., *GP*, 195; for Coventry, *ibid.* 310; for Ely, *ibid.* 325.

4 For the customary procedure cf. Symeon of Durham, I, 127: "Turgotum communi fratrum consilio episcopus surrogavit"; *Ann. Winton.*, *s.a.* 1111: "Episcopus Gaufridum priorem deposuit, et assensu conventus substitutus est Gaufridus [alter]"; also the letter of Urban III to Christ Church, 8 April 1187 (in Holtzmann, *Papsturkunden in England*, II, ii, n. 251): "prior...communi consilio et assensu archiepiscopi vestri et vestro prefici debeat." Alexander III had previously guaranteed to Christ Church the free election of their prior *sede vacante* (letter of 30 March 1174, Holtzmann, *op. cit.* 131). Coventry had by false pretences obtained free election, which was revoked by Urban III (18 June 1186–7, Holtzmann, *op. cit.* 243).

5 Gervase, I, 30 (*Imaginatio contra monachos*): "Ad eum omnimodo pertinet...positio et depositio prioris, subprioris, caeterarumque personarum ecclesiae."

6 Letter of Alexander III of 28 May 1163 (Holtzmann, II, ii, n. 110); Urban III, 8 April 1187 (*ibid.* n. 251).

ing to which the prior, subprior, sacrist, cellarer and chamberer were appointed by the archbishop, with the advice and consent of the monks, who had the right of appointing to the other offices independently of the primate. At Winchester, soon after the Conquest, Walkelin is recorded to have appointed the cellarer, and William of St Carilef at Durham appointed a sacrist;[1] probably it was usual for the bishop to retain his rights over the two or three major offices, and in fact the commission set up by Innocent III to investigate the conditions at the cathedral monasteries, with a view to framing a constitution for Glastonbury, reported that the bishop universally had the right of appointing the prior, and in most cases also the sacrist, cellarer, chamberer and almoner, always supposing that the convent gave its assent.[2]

The cathedral priories, like other houses, could have dependent priories and cells, usually, but not always, situated within the diocese of their bishop. On all questions of business where the affairs of the monastery alone, and not the see, were concerned, the usual negotiator was the prior, not the bishop. Even in Anselm's time the prior of Canterbury is represented as taking the initiative in building, and this he and his fellows continued to do throughout the century.[3]

Ethelwold, when framing the *Concordia*, had laid it down that the monks of a cathedral monastery were to have the right of electing their superior, who was also bishop.[4] This enactment, unfamiliar to most historians of the twelfth century, must always be borne in mind when judgment is passed on the action of the monks in the various election controversies; it was but a logical application of the general principle that the bishop was to live with his monks and be in all things their abbot. Evidence is almost entirely lacking as to how far the provision was honoured in practice between the death of Ethelwold and Oswald and the Conquest; probably the king and Witan appointed with little reference to the monks. There is, however, record of the monks of Canterbury electing one Aelric in 1050, though the choice was set aside by the Confessor in favour of Robert Champart.[5] Lanfranc's *Statuta* are silent on the point of a cathedral election;[6] in theory and as a monk, he could not but have stood for the right of election, but on the other hand he knew that in practice the king would uphold his prerogative of appointment. Actually, in every Canter-

---

1 *Registrum Theokusburiae* (Brit. Mus. Addit. MS. 36,985), 2; Symeon of Durham, I, 123.
2 Adam of Domerham, II, 418.
3 Cf. *Chron. Bell.* 148, where prior Odo of Canterbury is at court on important Christ Church business; and Will. Malmesb., *GP*, 138: "Ernulfus prior Cantuariae...partem ecclesiae...splendide reerexit."
4 *Concordia*, Proem. 78: "Episcoporum quoque electio, uti Abbatum, ubicunque in sede Episcopali Monachi regulares conversantur...cum Regis consensu et consilio sanctae regulae ageretur documento."
5 *Vita Aeduuardi*, in *Lives of Edward the Confessor* (ed. H. R. Luard), 399–400.
6 He lays down the general principle (*Statuta*, c. 2, p. 232): "abbas cum eligitur, omnes fratres...in ejus electionem consentire debent."

bury election after Anselm's death, a deputation from the monastic chapter either freely elected or at least went through the form of choosing the archbishop. Anselm's immediate successor, Ralph of Rochester, was a compromise between Faricius of Abingdon, whom Henry and the monks desired, and a secular demanded by the bishops.[1] The next election, at midwinter 1138–9, was exceptional owing to the presence of the legate Alberic; a deputation of the monks elected, and although the candidate was proposed by the king, Theobald, abbot of Bec, was in every way acceptable to them.[2]

Very little information is obtainable as to the manner of election to the other monastic sees before the reign of Stephen, when the emancipation of the Church and the application of the canon law in full regarding episcopal elections brought the claims of the monks to a point. The canons and the recent Lateran Council of 1139 gave the right of episcopal election to the chapter assisted by the *viri religiosi* of the neighbourhood; as, where the chapter was secular, this was taken to give certain rights to outstanding abbots of the diocese, so in the case of monastic chapters the leading secular clergy were admitted. At Durham, in 1143 and 1153, the election appears to have been made by the archdeacons and some of the higher clergy under the presidency of the prior of Durham;[3] at Norwich, in 1146, the monks must have been chiefly responsible for the choice of Prior William de Turbe. Some years later, Hadrian IV issued a series of bulls, numerous enough to indicate a settled papal policy, to the cathedral monasteries giving or confirming their rights: thus at Norwich, in 1155, the election was given to the monks and clergy together, presided over by the prior as dean; at Durham, in 1157, the monks and archdeacons under the prior were denoted; at Canterbury, in 1158, the election was given to the monks alone.[4] The monks had, indeed, in the eyes of the Curia a double title to elect: they were the chapter of the cathedral, and the bishop stood to them *in loco abbatis*. An exception, however, was made of Rochester, where the bishopric was recognized as being in the free gift of the archbishop of Canterbury,[5] and at Bath and Coventry the monks shared the election with the other capitular bodies of Wells and Lichfield. Whatever the rights of Canterbury, they curtsied to great kings, and the monks did nothing but give a transeat to the appointment of Becket.[6]

1 Eadmer, *Hist. Nov.* 222. The writer was one of the deputation of electors.
2 For Theobald, cf. Gervase, I, 109; II, 384.
3 John of Hexham, *ap.* Symeon of Durham, II, 314, 320.
4 The letters are in Holtzmann, *Papsturkunden in England*, II, ii, nos. 85 (Norwich), 94 (Durham), 102 (Canterbury).
5 So Alexander III to Archbishop Richard in 1174 (Holtzmann, II, ii, 136): "ita quod decedente eiusdem loci episcopo in tua sit dispositione et successorum tuorum episcopum tanquam proprium capellanum ibidem instituere secundum antiquam ecclesiae tuae consuetudinem." On the other hand Gervase, who holds no brief for Rochester, describes the *antiqua consuetudo* differently; according to him (I, 132–3): "[debet] eligi in capitulo Cantuariensi ex dono archiepiscopi et electione conventus Roffensis ecclesiae", the abbot of St Augustine's also voting.   6 Gervase, I, 170.

Perhaps for this reason they were careful, when on the crest of the wave in the early years of his posthumous glory, to obtain bulls from Alexander III guaranteeing the election to them and recommending that the person chosen should be a monk of Christ Church whenever possible.[1] When these bulls were issued the monks had recently anticipated the provisions of both by electing Richard, monk of Christ Church and prior of Dover, but in spite of the papal documents the monks' rights were strenuously challenged, and the elections of Baldwin in 1185 and Stephen Langton in 1206 were the outcome of stormy scenes familiar to all readers of English history. Previous to Langton's election Innocent III, after exhaustive enquiry, had confirmed the monks as sole electors,[2] but in spite of the right enjoyed by the cathedral monasteries, it is noteworthy that between the death of Henry I and that of John only five black monks were elected to these sees, and of these only two or at most three were elected solely and directly by the monks.[3]

The prior of these houses, as has been mentioned, took the place of the dean of a secular chapter, presiding over elections and perhaps also over synods and courts christian in the bishop's absence. Besides this, at Durham and Worcester he or another monk exercised the functions of archdeacon. At Durham this was probably an inheritance from the clerks of St Cuthbert whom the monks had ousted; prior Turgot was given the office for the whole diocese by William of St Carilef, and it was confirmed to his successors.[4] As it happened, Turgot quarrelled with Ranulf Flambard in the exercise of his functions and was sent out of the way to become bishop of St Andrews, and almost immediately the secular clerks Rannulph and Robert are found as archdeacons.[5] Secular archdeacons

---

1 Letter of 20 December 1174 (Holtzmann, II, ii, 142).

2 Cf. the article by the present writer, *The Canterbury Election of 1205–6*, in the *English Historical Review*, LIII (1938), 211–20.

3 The five were: Robert of Bath (1136–66; a Cluniac, put on by Henry of Winchester), Theobald of Canterbury (1139–61; primarily a royal choice), William of Norwich (1146–74; probably elected freely), Walter of Coventry (1149–60; perhaps free), Richard of Canterbury (1174–84; free).

4 Symeon of Durham, I, 129: "Vices suos...[Turgoto episcopus] injunxit, ut scilicet per archidiaconatus officium, Christianitatis curam per totum ageret episcopatum, ita statuens, ut quicumque illi successores fuerint in prioratu, similiter succedant et in archidiaconatu." Cf. Will. Malmesb., *GP.* 273: "Quin et priorem loci hoc insigni extulerit, ut in toto episcopatu decanus et vicedominus esset." Apart from any diplomatic considerations, the authenticity of the bull of Gregory VII and of St Carilef's original charter as given in *Hist. Dun. Scriptores Tres*, Appendix, nos I and III, can be wholly disproved by external arguments, viz. (a) Both documents decree (sc. in 1083) the appointment of the prior as archdeacon. But this was only effected by St Carilef in 1093, when Symeon attributes it to his own initiative. Possibly until that date the previous dean, who alone of the clerks had become a monk in 1083 (Symeon, I, 122), had continued to exercise his functions. (b) The bull decrees free election of the prior. But St Carilef in 1083 not only appointed Aldwin as an act of plenary power (Symeon, I, 123) but also previously appointed a sacrist. (c) No trace of the prescriptions of the bull appears in Symeon. (d) At the arbitration of 1147 by Ailred no reference is made to any papal or episcopal document, but only to traditional practice as remembered, among others, by Ailred himself.

5 Will. Malmesb., *GP*, 273–4; Symeon, II, 312.

continued to be appointed, and at the time of the controversy as to the prior's right of precedence over his colleagues, decided in 1147 by a board of arbitrators under the presidency of Ailred of Rievaulx, there was no mention of his claim to the sole exercise of archidiaconal functions. At Worcester the prior had archdeacon's rights over all the churches of the city belonging to the monks.[1]

V

When once the age of monastic bishops had passed, the relations between the monks of the cathedrals and their bishops were frequently strained and even openly unfriendly. The various troubles of Canterbury have often been noted in previous chapters: Winchester, where the reigns of William Giffard and the still more beneficent Henry of Blois covered almost three-quarters of the century, was more fortunate, and there is little record of trouble at Norwich and Bath, both of which churches had an able monk-bishop for thirty years. At the other cathedrals, there was a succession of quarrels. Rochester was at odds with John of Séez, who had granted away some of its churches, and the litigation came to an end only in the court of the legate, Imar of Tusculum,[2] in 1145; the trouble broke out again under Gilbert de Glanville (1185–1214). At Durham, the convent suffered under Ranulf Flambard and later under the intruded William Cumin; later still there were controversies with Hugh de Puiset and his successor.[3] Worcester had trouble with Bishop Simon (1125–50) over rights to property, and was in distress at the end of the century.[4] As for Coventry, one misfortune succeeded another, culminating in the expulsion under Hugh of Nonant.

Indeed, troubles only ceased when, in the thirteenth century, an equilibrium was reached by which the provinces of bishop and monks were clearly defined; the monastery became almost entirely autonomous internally and entered with the abbeys into the chapter and visitation system, while it took a smaller share in the affairs and controversies of the diocese. In later centuries the cathedral monasteries were among those which best preserved their life, both spiritual and intellectual, and thus the institution

---

1 Wulfstan's charter, drawn up in 1092, "a document beyond suspicion" (Darlington, *Vita Wulfstani*, xxxv, n. 2), has the clause: "concessit [*sc.* St Oswald] etiam illi [the provost or prior] omnibusque suis successoribus prioribus hujus ecclesiae, decanos esse super omnes ecclesias suas [*sc.* the *Eigenkirchen* of the priory] et presbiteros ita videlicet quod nullus decanus nullus archidiaconus de monachorum ecclesiis seu clericis se intromittat nisi per priorem ecclesiae" (*Monasticon*, I, 610). The witnesses at the synod go on to say that this had been observed ever since St Oswald's day. Cf. *Chron. Evesh.* 227: "Ecclesia Wigornensis habet priorem qui fungitur vice decani."

2 The decision of Imar is given by Holtzmann, *Papsturkunden*, II, ii, n. 45.

3 Symeon of Durham, I, 148; *Hist. Dunelm. Scriptores Tres* (Surtees Soc. IX, 1839), 8, 21–3.

4 Gervase, I, 530.

of Ethelwold and Lanfranc, though it developed into something other than that foreseen by its founders, did not altogether fail in its functions. What failure there was had its origin principally in the radical fault of the system, which was not apparent at the beginning; the establishment, that is, of a monastery under a superior who did not live solely with and for his monks.

VI

For the sake of completeness, a few words must be said of the two episcopal *Eigenklöster*, Eynsham and Selby. Eynsham had been revived or refounded on a modest scale by Remigius, and thither, as has been noted above, his successor Robert Bloett removed the monks from Stow near Lincoln; it was from the first and remained the property of the bishops of Lincoln, who exercised the right of appointing the abbot and bestowing the temporalities.[1] Hugh of Lincoln, at the end of the twelfth century, successfully vindicated his claims as against Richard I, sending a clerk to exercise the wardenship on the death of Abbot Geoffrey in 1195–6, and subsequently holding the abbatial election;[2] later, the Barnwell chronicler noted as one of King John's enormities that he held the abbey of Eynsham in his own hand, just like the others, though it belonged to the bishop of Lincoln.[3]

Selby, which came to belong to the archbishops of York, had been founded on land belonging to the Conqueror, and was given by Rufus to Archbishop Thomas in 1094, along with the church of St Oswald at Gloucester, in compensation for the disallowment of his claim that Lincoln and Lindsey formed part of the province of York.[4] As may be seen from the annals of the house, the archbishops took an active part in elections and in maintaining discipline at Selby, as did Hugh of Lincoln at Eynsham, but at both monasteries the abbots, once appointed, had complete freedom in the administration of all things temporal and spiritual. In other words, the bishops concerned exercised little more than the right of patronage.

1 *Monasticon*, III, 15, 16.
2 *Hugonis Magna Vita*, 189–92. The writer, it will be remembered, was a monk of Eynsham and described himself as "Hugh's monk" (*suus monachus*).
3 *Barnwell Chronicle*, ap. William of Coventry, II, 213.
4 *Selby Coucher Book* (ed. J. T. Fowler), introd. ix, gives the charter of William II, who gives "archiepiscopo Thomae et successoribus ejus abbaciam Sancti Germani, sicut archiepiscopus Cantuariensis habet episcopatum Rofensem" (a curious comparison). Cf. also *Ann. Winton., s.a.* 1094, and the life of Archbishop Thomas by Hugh the Chanter in *Hist. York*, II, 105–6.

CHAPTER XXXVII

THE INSTITUTIONS OF THE WHITE MONKS

I

INTRODUCTORY

The reader who has had the patience to follow the account of the complex organization which surrounded the life of a black monk house will be in a position to appreciate the freedom enjoyed by the early Cistercians. Many historians, whose aim has been to give a brief survey of monastic history, have been at pains to emphasize the rapidity with which the white monks became assimilated to the older monastic bodies, and have perhaps for that reason failed to show clearly enough the very real contrasts that existed for many generations. It is indeed true that to one viewing together the five centuries following the Conquest, and especially to one viewing them from our own day as it were in perspective, the distinctions between the black monks and the white seem to fade rapidly into something like similarity: the white monks lose their austerity, their solitude and some of their most characteristic features, such as the lay brothers, while the black monks adopt some elements at least of the Cistercian organization. But during the period with which alone we are here concerned the distinction between the two bodies remained very great, and was not lessened by the progressive complexity of the black monk relationships and the centrifugal tendencies which continued to operate before the Fourth Lateran Council.

In the spheres of constitutional and economic life the essential difference between the original Cistercian monasteries and the typical abbeys of black monks is to be found in the detachment of the former from the social life of the country.[1] The Cistercian abbey was in theory, and remained for several generations in practice, an entirely self-contained unit, severed from all alien influence whether ecclesiastical, politico-feudal or social, whose members and officials existed solely for the common life of the family. In recent years, stress has often been laid upon the autonomy of the black monks as compared with the numerous disciplinary and constitutional links which bound the white monks into an "order"; considered merely from the viewpoint of monastic political theory, this distinction is a true one and has survived and become more marked with the lapse of centuries. But in the twelfth century, with which alone we are dealing, the lack of complete autonomy and the measures taken to secure unanimity of ob-

---

1 Certain aspects of Cistercian life and development have already been treated at some length, v. supra, chaps. XII–XIV.

servance were undoubtedly a liberating rather than a shackling force, and in practice fettered the religious life of the white monks far less than did the complex of domestic customs and external relationships in the case of the old abbeys. All the mass of administrative detail, all the multiple engagements, all the duties of surveillance and exaction which occupied the officials of the older bodies were virtually non-existent for the early Cistercians. With them the sole task was the organization of their own body for labour and the collection and distribution of the produce; there was thus no occasion for the financial and administrative devolution of the obedientiary system, which was indeed contrary to their principles, and they were able to concentrate all into the hands of a single cellarer. Instead of other officials equal in rank to himself, he had as subordinates of a lower grade the overseers among the lay brothers who had been appointed to the headship of the various granges, and instead of manorial complexes, tenant holdings and labour dues, he had to deal simply with land—forest, field and furrow—which could be exploited without any restriction in any way that might be feasible and economically most profitable. The Cistercian estate, therefore, granted that the territory was capable of agricultural or pastoral development, and that the initial hardships of *défrichement* had been overcome, was clear of all the encumbrances of situation, labour and distribution which made of the vill and the manor such intractable units, and as in early days the monks needed scarcely any commodities which were not found upon their lands, contact with external traders was altogether unnecessary.

Their civil, feudal independence was as complete as their material. As has been seen, the majority of black monk abbeys held by military service, several of those which did not so hold were tenants-in-chief of the Crown, and almost all had some sort of seignorial jurisdiction over their own tenants in manor or hundred, or in districts of sake and soke. Of all this the Cistercians were free. Holding invariably in frank almoin, they had no direct relations with the Crown, and (in early days at least) having no tenants, and no organized and populated territories under their control, they had no jurisdictional rights.

They were equally free as regards the ecclesiastical authority of the country. Their entry into a diocese did indeed depend upon the goodwill of the Ordinary, but this sanction, when given, was understood to imply an acceptance on the bishop's part of all the *corpus* of Cistercian legislation, and especially that section which governed the election of abbots and the visitation of monasteries. As the period of Cistercian expansion occurred before the bishops claimed any disciplinary control of religious houses this acceptance meant little or no renunciation of rights, while it effectually forestalled all subsequent claims; and as on the one hand the economic and financial unity of a white monk establishment offered no crevices or fissures upon which the fingers of avarice could lay hold, and on the other the communities of Cistercians were never the chapters of cathedrals, the occasions of friction in early days were very rare. The prohibition against possessing churches or tithes, though it rapidly became inoperative in England, was effective at first and thus left the white monks completely clear of the parochial system, and it goes without saying that no Cistercian abbey in early days owned a group of independent *Eigenkirchen*. Hence, by what appears at first sight a paradox, the white monks, who had first at Cîteaux and later, in the person of Bernard, at Clairvaux, protested so energetically their submission to the bishop and their detestation of exemption, found themselves in fact as independent of episcopal control as the most favoured black monk abbeys, without any of the toil and disturbance suffered by the latter in erecting, maintaining and defending against repeated attacks the bulwarks of their liberty. The Cistercians received their orders and their holy oils from the diocesan; apart from this they were to all intents and purposes exempt from his control.

II

RECRUITMENT AND THE NOVITIATE

The first fathers of Cîteaux abolished of set purpose both the oblation of infants and the education of boys within the monastery. In other words, entry into a Cistercian house was what entry into the religious life is to-day, the solemn and deliberate act of one fitted to make the choice between life "in the world" and a life dedicated to the service of God in the cloister. An early statute, giving precision to the *Consuetudines*, decreed that no novice was to be received under the age of fifteen, and no boy taught in the monastery, unless he were already at least a novice.[1] Another decree laid down that if the founder of a house, layman or clerk, desired to receive the habit, he must pass through the regular course of probation.[2] The division of the choir-monks into *nutriti* and *conversi* thus vanished; all Cistercians were in the old sense of the term *conversi*, but the name was transferred by them to the new class of labouring monks which they introduced into northern lands and came to bear the meaning which it has ever since retained. One consequence of this change was to give the novitiate an importance which it had ceased to have in many monasteries of black monks. It became once more a year's searching test for all recruits, and in the twelfth century at least the Cistercian discipline was such that it meant a total change of life. The austerity, the hard labour, the silence, the absolute uniformity which prevailed made of it a real year of trial, even

1 *Statuta*, c. lxxviii, in Guignard, *Monuments primitifs de la Règle cistercienne*, 272. The age was raised to eighteen in 1175 (Canivez, *Statuta*, I, 84, n. 26).
2 *Statuta*, c. xxiii (Guignard, 256).

for those who came young, still more for those who came in middle life, leaving a career in the world, or some ecclesiastical preferment, or the easier way of another religious institute. References to the exercises of the novitiate[1] in England are all too few, but the precious accounts of the experiences of Ailred and of his friend Waldef in the *probatorium* of Rievaulx, and the choice of Ailred himself for the post of novice-master when already clearly distinguished for his mental and spiritual gifts, form a marked contrast to the insignificance of the novitiate in contemporary black monachism, and the Cistercian novice-master, at least during the first decades of the plantation, had to deal with men of widely differing characters and antecedents.

The influx of *âmes d'élite*, however, save in the case of a few northern houses, was markedly less in England than in France, where the magnetic influence of Bernard attracted to the cloisters directly depending upon him no small proportion of what was best in contemporary society. So far as can be gathered, only a few English abbeys such as Rievaulx and Fountains in the north and Ford in the south-west had more than a local reputation, and the mass of the novices were drawn from the small land-holders and clerics, with a scattering of men of more distinguished family. But for all, during the twelfth century, to enter a white monk house was to embark upon a life of hard and frugal service with no prospect of such varied occupations as were offered in the various obediences of a black monk monastery; still less was there any such atmosphere of intellectual activity and keen controversy and contact with the great figures and currents of the country's life as surrounded the monks of a dozen of the greater abbeys and cathedral monasteries.

The reform of the novitiate and the abolition of the "monachization" of children were in themselves such wise measures and were so consonant with the new sentiment of Europe that they remained the norm; it was otherwise with the ban on the reception of outsiders to the habit *ad succurrendum* when aged or dying;[2] in this matter contemporary sentiment and personal, material interests combined to modify the original rigidity of practice. Gradually the custom reappeared, though for a while the letter of the law was kept by ostensibly admitting the invalid to the habit and the novitiate, when in fact he passed directly into the infirmary, and by avoiding any kind of death-bed profession ceremony.[3] But whatever

1 The clearest, indeed the only, picture of the *probatorium* in England is that of Walter Daniel in his life of Ailred. Those who wish for an English version of the relevant passages, set in juxtaposition with the contemporary methods of Bernard at Clairvaux and those of Caesarius of Heisterbach almost a century later, should consult Dr G. G. Coulton's *Five Centuries of Religion*, vol. I, ch. xviii: St Bernard; ch. xix: Clairvaux; ch. xxiv: A Novice's Soul; ch. xxv: The Novice and his Master.

2 *Statuta*, c. xxvii (Guignard, 257). This decrees that the dying may be received in the monastery, but not admitted to the order.

3 Cf. *Chron. Melsa*, I, 96 (*c.* 1155): "Amandus... qui obiit novicius apud nos... Robertus apud nos factus novicius, secundus fuit qui in monasterio nostro in noviciatu est defunctus."

technicalities might be observed, the process by which such bishops as Jocelin de Bohun of Salisbury and Mauger of Worcester,[1] to say nothing of Welsh princelets,[2] died in the Cistercian habit was indistinguishable from the age-old institution of *ad succurrendum*. Gerald, indeed, asserts that the white monks had begun to tonsure and clothe dying ladies,[3] and an entry in the Welsh chronicle for 1209 would seem to confirm his statement.[4]

III

INTERNAL POLITY: THE ABBOT AND HIS OFFICIALS

The early Cistercians were fortunate in all matters of domestic organization, for they possessed clear-cut legislation and enjoyed freedom from interference. This was especially the case with regard to abbatial elections. The first fathers had decreed that at the election of an abbot of any house save Cîteaux the abbot of the mother-house should preside, and if necessary advise or even decide upon the person to be chosen; in addition to the monks of the house, the abbots of all its daughters were to be present and to vote, and the new abbot was to be chosen either from the house itself or from its descendants.[5] The last recommendation was not always observed; departure from it was most frequent when the abbey had no daughters.

These precise constitutions left no room for the interference of a bishop who had accepted the *Carta Caritatis*, and the Cistercians of early days, having no part in secular life, provided no motive for royal action. Consequently, the elections were entirely free. Indeed, almost the only cases of direct interference which are recorded are those of the monopolizing ex-abbot of Fountains, Henry Murdac, who as archbishop of York made and unmade successive abbots of his old home, not without protest. But Murdac, the confidant and agent of Bernard, might claim that his position was exceptional. In later decades, the Cistercians fortified themselves with papal privileges which gave them a freedom with regard to abbatial blessings all but as extensive as that enjoyed by St Albans or Evesham, but this was rather to make assurance doubly sure in situations where (as at Meaux) the monks were wrangling with the Ordinary over some question of property or tithe, than to obtain an independence which they did not already possess.[6]

For later cases *v. ibid.* 303, 321, 365, and especially 233, where William Rule, the parson of Cotyngham, "qui in infirmitatem, unde et mortuus est, decidens, factus apud nos novicius, plusquam ducentas libras argenti secum afferebat."

1 *Ann. Waverl., s.a.* 1184; *v. supra*, 478, n. 1: "Dimisso episcopatu, factus est monachus ordinis Cisterciensis [Jocelinus]." 2 *Brut y Tywysogion*, 227, 251, 255–7.
3 Giraldus, IV, 200. Once more Dore is the offending house.
4 *Brut*, 266. Mahalt de Bruse receives the habit.
5 *Carta Caritatis* (Guignard, 82–3).
6 *Chron. Melsa*, I, 329–31, *tempore Innocentis III.*

Within the monastery the appointment of the officials and the assignment of their duties was the direct prerogative of the abbot, and as none save the cellarer had charge of moneys or contact with outsiders, the whole scheme was very simple. It is noteworthy that whereas the Customs of the black monks deal chiefly with the revenues and rights of the obedientiaries, the constitutions of the white lay down in broad outline the basic duties of each official, which are in all essentials the same as in Cistercian monasteries of to-day. It is significant also that the master of novices appears in a position of importance immediately after the subprior.

In the case of the black monks mention has been made of a tendency on the part of the monastic chapter to become something of a parliament in embryo, wherein acts of the administration were criticized and voting rights asserted. The Cistercian chapter, alike from religious considerations and from the greater simplicity of the life, was, at least in the first generations, primarily an assembly of the family for spiritual conference. It was laid down that the superior should each day comment upon the passage of the Rule that had been read,[1] and abbots often took this occasion for delivering those long discourses of which so many examples survive in the works of St Bernard, and in the Sermons of Ailred of Rievaulx and Gilbert of Holland; with Bernard, however, it is clear that many of his conferences were delivered in the evening. After the abbot's discourse came the commemoration of the dead and the declaration and punishment of faults, and only at the end was provision made for the discussion of business such as the reception or profession of novices. Towards the end of the century, however, there is evidence of the chapter organizing itself for votes, protests and appeals, and in a privilege of Innocent III it is laid down that certain actions can only be taken after the approval of a majority vote.[2]

IV

VISITATIONS AND GENERAL CHAPTER

Perhaps the most distinctive and valuable contribution of the *Carta Caritatis* to ecclesiastical discipline was its institution in clear and simple decrees of a system of regular visitation. The evidence of Cistercian sources, of casual references and of hostile criticism all combines to show that this system, during the first century of the plantation in England and Wales, worked regularly and efficiently, and continued to be an effective instrument for maintaining or restoring discipline. The white monks had indeed every advantage here over the black. They possessed a clear and

1 *Consuetudines*, c. lxx, Guignard, 169: "Et dicto Benedicite ab illo qui capitulum tenet, exponatur sententia [sanctae Regulae] etiam in parasceve" [i.e. not even on Good Friday is this to be omitted].
2 *Chron. Melsa*, I, 298 [c. 1200]: "Plurimis tamen...a capitulo se retrahentibus et reclamantibus, sed prius in capitulo appellantibus." Cf. *ibid.* 309. The privilege is that referred to on p. 636, n. 6, *supra*.

detailed code, uniform throughout the order, with which existing conditions could be compared and according to which extravagances of any kind could be repressed by the visiting abbot, without precipitating a collision with the hydra heads of immemorial and individual custom which so impeded changes in the old abbeys. Moreover, the white monks were bred up in this system and knew no other, and, perhaps most important of all, the legislation left no loophole for appeals, which in all other departments of the life of the Church proved such a hindrance to decisive action in the twelfth century. A glance through the lists of English Cistercian abbots provides plentiful evidence of visitatorial activity. It is easy to find a dozen deposed by visitors before 1215, and a still greater number, feeling themselves unequal to their task, freely resigned during a visitation. In this the reminiscences of Gerald of Wales corroborate the Cistercian sources, for he tells of a number of cases where offenders of one kind or another were brought to book. Of the numberless cases where a visitation did no more than remedy small defects and reinvigorate the life of the house there is naturally no record. Over and above the ordinary visitation from the founding abbot, there was always the possibility of the abbot of Cîteaux and the general chapter intervening on receipt of a sufficiently serious representation. Gerald of Wales lodged a successful complaint at Cîteaux against an abbot of Whitland, and there is record of the descent in 1188 of special visitors upon England, sent by general chapter; among other results, they effected three changes of abbots.[1] Indeed, during this first century of the order the system of visitation would seem to have achieved the end for which it was instituted, and to have kept the Cistercians, in broad lines at least, to the observance of their Rule. Visitation is too often regarded by historians as no more than a remedy for crying abuses; if it achieves this result alone it will not be a life-giving power, and it was because episcopal and other visitations in the later Middle Ages came to be something of a police enquiry that they failed to assist the spirit of true religion. The Cistercian visitation was originally conceived as something positive, as the periodical infusion of new life, and as such it endured and was successful for several generations.[2]

Something has already been said of the labour and time involved in the annual journeys of the abbots to general chapter; as originally conceived, it was a meeting of the monks of a province, not of a great continent, and Cistercian settlements in Ireland and Scandinavia created unforeseen difficulties. It was, however, a most necessary mainspring in the Cistercian machine, and it was essential that as many abbots as possible should be present. The annual journeys therefore continued throughout our period and beyond. References to them are frequent, and more than one abbot died either at Cîteaux or on the road.

1 *Ann. Waverl.*, s.a. 1188.
2 Cf. the wise directions for a visitation in *Statuta*, c. xxxiii (Guignard, 259).

As the order spread into distant lands, it became necessary often to grant temporary or permanent dispensations from attendance to individuals, and as early as 1157 the abbots of Scotland as a body, numbering some five houses, obtained leave to come only every fourth year.[1] A similar concession was secured by the Irish abbots, also few in number, in 1190,[2] but when the English abbots put in a petition to the same effect in 1201 it was peremptorily refused.[3] There were at the time some seventy English abbeys in existence, and to absolve such a large and influential fraction of the order would indeed have deprived the annual chapter of much of its authority. Henceforward, references to defaulting English abbots are frequent in the statutes; the offenders were reprimanded by chapter through the agency of colleagues who had made the journey to Cîteaux.

As the supreme executive and judicial power among the white monks resided in general chapter, not in the abbot of Cîteaux and his assistants, it soon became necessary to devise some means of instituting enquiries and securing the observance of decisions after the chapter had dissolved. The custom therefore grew up, no doubt modelled upon the Curial practice, of appointing in chapter two or three abbots delegate with powers of examining a case or executing a sentence. The Statutes contain numerous examples of English abbots so appointed, and the business and additional travel which these tasks implied must have added very considerably to the duties of an abbot whom the chapter had found reliable and therefore frequently commissioned. Some instances of the business thus delegated will be given on a later page.

V

THE HORARIUM

The horarium of the white monks is set out in their early legislation with a fullness and simplicity that leaves nothing, save the addition of clock hours, to be desired. It contains several important changes from the standard practice of the black monks. The introduction of manual and field labour as the norm for all split the day sharply into the original three divisions of St Benedict—those of liturgical prayer, private reading (for which private prayer could at all times be substituted) and regular labour. This last, again following the prescriptions of the Rule, varied between summer and winter as regards the length and position of the time allotted to it; in the winter it formed a single spell of some four hours between chapter (which followed Mass and Terce) and dinner, in the summer the single period was split into two, the earlier and longer taking place after

1 Canivez, *Statuta*, I, 67 (1157), n. 62.
2 Canivez, *Statuta*, I, 122 (1190), n. 17.
3 Canivez, *Statuta*, I, 272 (1201), n. 45: "Petitio...nullatenus admittitur."

chapter (which followed Prime) and lasting some two hours and a half until Terce and Mass, the second, an hour and a half in length, following the siesta and preceding None. Exceptional arrangements prevailed during the hay and grain harvests: Mass followed the chapter and the work continued till midday or beyond; it might also be begun before the chapter. To clear the day sufficiently for these long spells of work two drastic changes were made in the traditional usage: the majority of accretions to the canonical office were swept away, together with many elaborations of chant and ceremonial, and the second Mass was dropped, thus enabling the single conventual Mass to be thrown back into the early morning.[1] Such was the normal day's round, varied only as to the hours of meals by the ecclesiastical and monastic fast days.[2] It was, however, fairly frequently cross-cut in both summer and winter by another arrangement caused by the incidence of feast days. St Benedict in the Rule had legislated for these, though they were presumably rare in his age; he decreed that the Office should follow the arrangement of Sundays,[3] though he does not explicitly tell us whether Mass was celebrated and work suspended on all of them; doubtless the greater feasts were so observed.[4] Cîteaux, though sufficiently drastic in clearing the calendar, could not, of course, abolish all the landmarks of the liturgical year, and made a considerable concession to the liturgical tradition of the monastic centuries by retaining on festal days the two conventual Masses. Even here, however, an important division was made; only on the greater feasts, some forty-five in number, was there a cessation from work and a full celebration of the second Mass; on the remaining festal days work was done as usual and the second Mass, which took place almost immediately after the first, was treated as of secondary importance, and the priests of the house were allowed to say their private Masses concurrently. On feasts when no work was done the time left free was devoted to reading or prayer.

1 The one original survival was the office of the dead, which maintained its place on all non-festal days (with a few exceptions); cf. *Consuetudines*, c. 1 (Guignard, 137–9) and William of Malmesbury, *GR*, 383: "Nulla appenditia extrinsecus adjicientes, praeter vigiliam pro defunctis." This office, however, occupies very little time, scarcely half an hour, when recited without chant immediately after the canonical hours. A more considerable addition, made very early, was the Little Office of Our Lady (for arrangement of this *v*. Canivez, *Statuta*, 101–2 [1185], n. 28); but even this, when monotoned immediately after the canonical hours, does not make a serious inroad on the day, as those will recollect who have followed the routine of a modern Cistercian abbey.

2 In the black monk Uses these fast days caused a liturgical variation in the hour of Mass; apparently this was a constant with the Cistercians, as in the Church to-day.

3 *Regula*, c. xiv: "In nataliciis sanctorum qualiter agantur vigiliae."

4 On some at least Mass is presupposed; cf. *Regula*, c. xxxv, 24: "In diebus sollemnibus usque ad Missas sustineant [servitores]."

VI

FOOD AND DRINK

Since the white monks aimed at keeping the Rule *ad literam*, the main outlines of their dietary are simple, being those of the Rule both as to the quality and quantity of food. In winter there was a single meal, consisting of the pound of bread and two *pulmenta* or dishes of eggs, fish, cereals and vegetables, and in the evening the drink of water in common. In summer there were two meals, the *prandium* and the *cena*. As has been mentioned, St Benedict nowhere gives instructions as to the composition of the second meal, save in his enactment that a third of the bread is to be reserved for it. It has often been assumed that *pulmenta* were provided for it as at the *prandium*; this may have been the case, but the Cistercian statutes did not so interpret the text. They decreed that in summer this evening meal was to consist of the bread, together with fruit and uncooked vegetable (the "third dish" of the *prandium* in the Rule), and that those who needed it might have an extra quantity of coarser bread.[1] During hay-making and harvest time this arrangement was altered, and a single *pulmentum* provided at each meal.[2] The only regular addition to these meals was the *mixtum*, a breakfast of four ounces of bread and a little wine taken by the cook and the reader; it was also allowed to the young monks and to some of the lay brothers.[3]

Meat and lard were never eaten in a Cistercian house save by those seriously ill and by the hired workmen. The diet was therefore confined to bread, vegetables, and dishes made from fish, flour, eggs, milk and cheese, with honey as an exception. Throughout Lent and Advent, and on certain vigils, eggs and cheese were banned, as were all kinds of imported spices.[4] Three kinds of bread were distinguished: white, eaten only by the sick and those recently bled; the ordinary brown bread; and a still coarser kind given when an extra quantity was needed.

This diet may be considered sparing enough, especially as no addition or variation was made on feast days; it is, however, a little surprising to find allowance made even in the earliest legislation for pittances, which had proved so baneful an influence in black monk dietaries. The most explicit references to them occur in the directions for blood-letting, which took place four times a year and immediately before the *prandium*. At the

---

1 This seems clear if *Consuetudines*, c. lxxxiiii (Guignard, 190), is compared with the chapter which follows and with c. cxvii, 240: "Illis qui ad prandium usque ad terciam partem panis comedunt, ad cenam de grossiore pane ubi habetur superaddere [debet]."

2 *Consuetudines*, c. lxxxiiii (Guignard, 191). This arrangement, clearly intended as an extra concession during hard work, would seem to prove that the two *pulmenta* of the *prandium* were considered as alternatives, not as complementary. In other words, only in times of hard work did the monks partake of both; this would certainly seem to have been St Benedict's intention.

3 *Consuetudines*, c. lxxiii; *Usus Conversorum*, c. xv.

4 *Instituta Capituli Generalis*, xxiiii, xxv, lxiii, in Guignard.

meal which followed the patient received a pittance and an extra half-pound of white bread; on the two following days, if in winter, he had a pittance and a pound of white bread for a breakfast in addition to the usual *prandium*, if in summer, he had for three days an extra pound of bread and pittance at dinner, and a pittance at supper.[1] Pittances were also given to the sick at the abbot's discretion, and to visiting monks on the first day of their stay.[2] In all this there is no great relaxation, but it is perhaps strange that the white monks should have retained at least a vestige of black monk customary usage by allowing the prior to distribute on occasion special dishes, which the recipients could share with their next neighbours after rising and bowing to the superior.[3] We recognize here the practice which, carried to ridiculous excess, was to form the subject of one of the favourite and most vivid reminiscences of Gerald of Wales. These regulations on diet, which William of Malmesbury regarded with such admiration within a few years of their establishment, were maintained all but intact throughout the period with which we are concerned.[4]

VII

SILENCE, PRAYER, AND THE SACRAMENTS

The Cistercian statutes follow the Rule in making no provision for general or recreative conversation at a particular hour of the day; in this they differed from the customaries of the black monks. The text of the *Consuetudines*, however, and all that we know of life at such observant houses as Clairvaux and Rievaulx in their heyday, make it quite clear that there was no intention of securing a perpetual silence, as of the grave, such as was in part aimed at by de Rancé at La Trappe. Questions about the matter to be read or chanted and the mode of execution might be asked by those concerned as they sat at reading in the cloister; business matters might be discussed with the prior and another monk in the parlour during reading time; questions about the work were allowed at the scene of labour, as were quiet conversations with the infirmarian in the infirmary.[5] Monks might also speak with their confessor, and of course with the abbot, and novices with their master. The glimpses of the life of the golden age as seen in the biographies and writings of Bernard and Ailred show that opportunities for frank and full discussion of all individual needs and of speculative questions of spirituality were even more frequent than might be expected from the letter of the legislation.

1 *Consuetudines*, c. xc, "de minutione".
2 *Consuetudines*, cc. lxxvi, cxvii.   3 *Consuetudines*, c. lxxvi.
4 Will. Malmesb., *GR*, 380–5. The evidence of Gerald of Wales is contradictory; at the most it shows the occurrence of failures at individual houses. Contrast *Speculum Ecclesiae* (*Opera*, iv, 208–9, 215) with *Itin. Kambriae*, 46. For the abuse of beer-drinking, *v*. the following chapter, pp. 656–60.
5 *Consuetudines*, cc. lxxi, lxxv, xcii, Guignard, 173, 178, 202.

In reviewing black monk life some difficulty was experienced in ascertaining how frequently the sacraments were received. The *Consuetudines* leave us in no such doubt regarding the Cistercians. It is laid down explicitly in the first place that priests may say private Masses on any day of the year either during the time of reading or, if prevented then, after the offertory of the conventual Mass; if on a Sunday they elected not to celebrate they might, if they wished, communicate.[1] Those not priests were exhorted to receive the Holy Eucharist every Sunday; if a Sunday were missed, another day during the week might be chosen; this communion was under both kinds.[2] Lay brothers communicated more rarely, that is, only seven times a year except at the special bidding of the abbot.[3]

Confessions were normally heard in the chapter-house, either after chapter, or during any period of reading; the references presume frequency and a certain informality, and it is even laid down that absolution may be given during work in the fields at a distance from the house.[4]

Private prayer in the church was allowed, as has been mentioned, at any time when the community were engaged in reading.[5]

VIII

INTELLECTUAL ACTIVITY

Literary work in all its branches, the artistic copying as well as the composition of books, was alien to the austerity and simplicity of the primitive Cîteaux, and the writing of them was indeed forbidden by statute.[6] The aim of this was probably to prevent a monk from devoting himself to such a life of reading and digesting as is seen with William of Malmesbury and Orderic, rather than to prohibit writings called for by an immediate occasion. It was, however, clearly decreed that no member of the order should write a book without the permission of general chapter, but whatever may have been opinions on the point, the appearance in the bosom of the family of such a literary genius as Bernard must have gone far to discount any deterrent effect such a prohibition might have had, and we know that Bernard himself urged Ailred to write. The voluminous works

1 *Consuetudines*, c. lviiii, Guignard, 156–7; cf. c. xiiii, 105 and lxvi, 160–1. In all these passages considerable choice is left to the individual, e.g. c. lviiii, 156: "Potest cantare missam usque ad nonam, et in quadragesima usque ad vesperas qui voluerit et cui vacuum fuerit"; *ibid.* c. lxvi, 160–1: "In eorum sit potestate [die dominica] communicare vel non."
2 *Consuetudines*, cc. lxvi, lviii.
3 *Usus conversorum*, c. v, Guignard, 281.
4 *Consuetudines*, cc. lxx, lxxv, Guignard, 172, 178.
5 *Consuetudines*, c. lxxi, Guignard, 172: "Ad orationem vero ire possunt in ecclesiam non solum tunc [*sc.* after chapter] sed et omni tempore lectionis et ad omnia intervalla"; *ibid.* c. xv, 106: "Et ideo omni die [in Lent] unusquisque fratrum certa consuetudine orationem privatam tempore lectionis in ecclesia Deo offerat."
6 *Statuta*, c. lviii, Guignard, 266: "Nulli liceat abbati nec monacho nec novitio libros facere, nisi forte cuiquam in generali abbatum capitulo concessum fuerit."

of Bernard are, however, largely made up of sermons and letters; those treatises which can be described as "books" do not form a half of the whole *corpus* and were mostly composed for a special occasion at the demand of an individual. Nothing in them corresponds to the historical, scriptural and theological work of contemporary black monks and canons, still less to the works of Gratian and the Lombard.

A more real contravention of both letter and spirit of the statute is to be found in the writings, and especially in the historical works, of Ailred of Rievaulx. Like Bernard, Ailred was a prolific writer of letters and sermons, but his most original and characteristic work falls into two collections each without exact parallel in the writings of Bernard or any other contemporary white monk. The long spiritual treatises composed in the form of dialogues are not, like Bernard's spiritual works, the outcome of a compelling practical necessity, and their form owes far more to literary models, to the *de Amicitia* of Cicero and to the *Confessions* of Augustine. Despite the repeated and doubtless sincere assertions that he is writing with diffidence and under compulsion, Ailred has a genius and certainty of touch and an originality in self-expression beyond any English black monk of his day, and inferior only to Anselm, Bernard, William of St Thierry and a few others in the spiritual literature of his age. But besides his spiritual writings, which the early fathers of Cîteaux might have tolerated at a pinch, Ailred put out a number of works which nothing but the unique position and reputation of the author can have justified at general chapter. His accounts of the saints of Hexham, and his *Life of Edward the Confessor*, though both in a real sense hagiography, are also both pieces of national history based on a fairly wide reading and inspired by an interest in past and present politics, and have no connection with the religious life. Still less connection is visible in his account of the campaign of the Standard, which is frankly nothing but a piece of national history, and in all this Ailred belongs to the Northumbrian rather than to the Cistercian school. As has been remarked, Rievaulx, with Ailred, Maurice, Walter Daniel and (later) Nicholas, was *sui generis* as a home of letters, and there is some evidence that this was realized in the order, not with unmingled satisfaction. Thirty years after Ailred's death, William of Newburgh, in the letter to Abbot Ernald (1189–99) which stands before the preface to his history, records that the abbot has laid on him the charge of writing, though there is no lack of talent at Rievaulx, in order to safeguard his own monks from disturbance.[1]

The writing of the life of a saintly abbot by a disciple was never considered to come under this ban. Two such lives exist of the two saints connected with Rievaulx: Walter Daniel, an intimate disciple of Ailred,

[1] The attitude of chapter to the study of canon law in 1188 has already been noted (*v.s.* ch. XXIX, p. 526, n. 3). In 1198 it proceeded against a Spanish monk reported to have learnt Hebrew, and in 1199 against monks *qui rhythmos fecerint* (Canivez, *Statuta*, 227, n. 27; 232, n. 1).

wrote his master's life shortly after his death; Waldef, Ailred's comrade at the court of David, and later monk of Rievaulx and abbot of Melrose, remained for some forty years without an adequate biography, when at last the want was supplied by Jocelin of Furness. Of the two, Walter Daniel's, as might have been expected, is the more vivid. Though it contains a certain amount of sententious moralizing,[1] it contains also a number of passages which bring us very near to the living Ailred and the unique atmosphere which he created around himself, and it must on the whole be pronounced one of the best biographies of our period. Jocelin's is naturally far less intimate, and Waldef's was no doubt a less arresting personality, but the narrative is straightforward and reliable, and is valuable as supplementing in numerous ways our knowledge of the early days in Yorkshire. To these two lives may well be added the work of Hugh of Kirkstall, who persuaded the aged Serlo, once of Fountains, to dictate his reminiscences, and who supplemented them by his own account of the saintly abbot Ralph Haget.

Ailred had more than one successor as a homilist among the English white monks. Mention has already been made of the most celebrated, Gilbert of Holland, who had the temerity to continue the exposition of the Canticle at the point reached by Bernard when overtaken by death. Another Cistercian spiritual writer of some fame was Stephen of Sawley,[2] and a little later Baldwin of Ford had a wide reputation, though most of his theological writings were probably composed when he was still a secular clerk; later still Ralph of Coggeshall, the chronicler, was to all appearances the author of a kind of *Summa* of some importance.[3]

Towards the end of the twelfth century, indeed, there are signs that the studied illiteracy of the Cistercians was beginning to break down everywhere. Abbots are spoken of as collectors of books[4], and there is a widespread development of chronicle literature, in addition to a number of interesting accounts of the early days of famous houses, such as that of the wanderings of the community from Furness that settled finally at Byland, and the laborious beginnings of Kirkstall and Jervaulx. In the reigns of Richard and John the Cistercian chronicles, like those of the black monks and canons, became increasingly elaborate; the Coggeshall book, the work of the theologian Ralph, who became abbot in 1207, is a primary source for many of the events of John's reign, and there was abundant material at the disposal of the later Meaux chronicler, who worked over the history of his house from its origin.

1 Prof. F. M. Powicke, by his judicious cuts, has done Walter's reputation a considerable service.

2 For Stephen, *v.* the article of Dom Wilmart, *Les méditations d'Étienne de Salley*, in *Auteurs spirituels*, 317–60.

3 Cf. the article by Dom G. Morin in *RB*, XLVII (1935), 348–55, *Ralph de Coggeshall*, etc.

4 Cf. *Chron. Melsa*, I, 326: "Librorum fuerat maximus perquisitor" [Abbas Alexander, 1197–1210].

IX

ART AND ARCHITECTURE

The zeal of the fathers of Cîteaux, and later of Bernard, for an absolute material simplicity and their avoidance of all that was precious and splendid and ornamental is familiar to all. It is therefore useless to search among early Cistercian records for traces of any school of art or illumination. The statutes, indeed, besides prohibiting precious vestments and vessels, specifically decree that the books written by the monks shall be in ink of one colour and without bright or illuminated capital letters, and though there are indications that this had ceased to be binding even in observant Cistercian houses before the end of the twelfth century, it effectually prevented the emergence of a school of manuscript painting.[1] Yet in one department of art the white monks were *malgré eux* a potent influence and left to after generations monuments of a singular grace and purity. Neither the strictures of Stephen Harding nor the satire of Bernard could undo the past and prevent the natural evolution of an art-form. They succeeded, however, or, to speak more accurately, the spirit to which they gave expression succeeded, in originating a type of architecture of reaction, *simplex munditiis*, which ultimately, by a strange fortune, gave the go-by to ornate Romanesque and became one of the direct ancestors of the most beautiful Gothic.[2]

A whole series of considerations combined to make the original Cistercian churches extremely plain. It was indeed a matter of principle with them, both as a conscious reaction from vanity and as a consequence of the strict view which they took of monastic poverty. It was, besides, a matter of convenience, not to say necessity, for the circumstances of many foundations were at first very straitened and as a general rule the white monks, unlike the black, were independent of external labour in their building operations; the heavy mason's work was done by the *conversi*,[3] the overseer's and perhaps even the architect's task was undertaken by choir monks who had the talent.[4] In addition, many of the plantations were made with no more than the regulation thirteen choir

---

1 *Statuta*, lxxx (Guignard, 272): "Littere unius coloris fiant et non depicte." In the *Miracula* of Godric of Finchale (ed. Stevenson, Surtees Soc. xx, 466–8) the story is told of a young monk of Fountains abbey whose brightly coloured folios of Godric's life were scattered by the wind in the cloister, and reassembled by the saint.

2 The best account of Cistercian architecture is still Dr J. Bilson's *The Architecture of the Cistercians* in the *Archaeological Journal*, LXVI (1909), 185–280; this contains excellent illustrations and plans. Cf. also A. W. Clapham, *English Romanesque Architecture*, II, 74–83.

3 This would seem certain; it is the judgment of Dehio and von Bezold, *Die Kirchliche Baukunst des Abendlandes*, I, 521, quoted and endorsed by Dr Bilson, and suits all that is known of the early plantations.

4 One such was Adam, a monk of Whitby who joined the group of seceders from St Mary's, York, and himself became first abbot of Meaux. Before this foundation he had been engaged "in aedificiis construendis monasteriorum, videlicet [Kirkstead, Woburn] et praecipue de Valle Dei" (*Chron. Melsa*, I, 76).

monks and twelve lay brothers. Consequently, the first churches of the white monks were in many cases mere oratories or chapels of wood or rough stones,[1] but the practical requirements of regular life in a growing community, and the influence of the spirit of an age remarkable above all others for the revolutionary grandeur of its architectural conceptions, combined to produce large Cistercian churches with a style and plan of their own.

The principal notes of this architecture, in the heyday of its flower, were simplicity of plan, omission of ornament, abandonment of the triforium, and a universal use of the pointed arch.[2] As has been said, Cistercian planning and construction, like all else in their life, was at first uniform throughout the order, and the family resemblance between their churches in Burgundy, the Rhineland, Wales and Yorkshire cannot fail to impress even the most superficial observer.[3] Towards the end of the twelfth century this uniformity began to disappear,[4] and even earlier the northern English builders, by making frequent use of pointed barrel vaults in stone, greatly accelerated an evolution of the first significance in the history of English architecture. These developments, however, and the discussion of the technique of Cistercian construction, belong properly to the history of architecture, not of monasticism, and cannot be pursued further here. Of the surpassing beauty of the early Cistercian churches there can be no two opinions.[5]

X

THE CHANT

If in the realm of architecture the influence of the white monks was powerful, beneficent and widespread, in another branch of art the changes they introduced were baneful, though fortunately restricted to their own body. The zeal for simplicity in the liturgy and for a return to the norm of earlier centuries showed itself during the first years at Cîteaux in a

---

1 For the first churches at Tintern, etc. *v.* Clapham, *Romanesque Architecture*, II, figs. 25–6; there are some excellent illustrations of Fontenay, the exemplar of all later churches, in Dr Coulton's *Five Centuries of Religion*, vol. I.

2 Cf. Bilson, *The Architecture of the Cistercians*, 236: "The vaults [of the church at Kirkstall, *c.* 1130–40] are among the very earliest examples in England of the complete solution of the Gothic problem, so far as vaulting is concerned."

3 In Great Britain the churches of Newminster (Northumberland), Whitland (Carmarthen), Quarr (Isle of Wight) and those of Rievaulx (*c.* 1132), Kirkstall (*c.* 1152) and Valle Crucis (*c.* 1201) are similar in all essentials.

4 The large church built on a virgin site at Byland *c.* 1175 is representative of the later Cistercian plan (Clapham, *Romanesque Architecture*, II, fig. 27). H.M. Office of Works has in recent years obtained possession of a number of the most celebrated Cistercian sites, and by skilful and discreet repairs and the removal of all creepers and rank weeds has restored much of the original appearance of purity and order.

5 Dr Bilson, *The Architecture of the Cistercians*, 280, remarks with justice: "The eastern parts of Fountains [and] Rievaulx are distinguished by a purity of design which was rarely equalled and never surpassed in the thirteenth-century architecture of northern England."

movement to reduce the multiplicity of hymns and to return so far as possible to the simple cursus of the week's hymnody attributed to St Ambrose. Stephen Harding took the matter in hand with characteristic directness and inflexibility of purpose, allotting a single ferial hymn even to solemnities, thus giving occasion for some pointed criticism from Abelard.[1] Unfortunately, he adopted for his hymns the Ambrosian or Milanese form of chant, under the impression that it was orthodox and venerable, and this was, for a time at least, imposed upon the family of Cîteaux.[2] Stephen Harding himself recoiled before the heavier labour of purifying the Antiphoner and Gradual, but forty years later the general chapter entrusted the task to the intrepid abbot of Clairvaux, who had already made an excursion into the field of the chant with his *Regulae de arte musica*.[3] Bernard and his disciples accordingly attacked both liturgical books and corrected them by *a priori* methods, treating as corruptions all departures from the principles of music which they had laid down for themselves, and all elaborations of which they did not approve. Besides revising the musical text in the interests of simplicity they altered a number of melodies in the Gradual which went outside the octave of the mode concerned, and excised many of the *jubila* of the Alleluias; their reform was, however, less drastic and complete than they could have wished owing to protests raised by other abbots of the order against certain modifications of the familiar tonality.[4]

Doubtless the English white monk houses received and adopted the revised Antiphoner, together with Bernard's introductory letter. Here, as in other respects, Rievaulx and her family stood peculiarly near to the fountain-head, for William, the first abbot, was an expert musician who had often discussed problems of the chant with Bernard at Clairvaux; to him, indeed, was later addressed the theoretical treatise on music by Guy of Cherlieu, a leading member of the committee responsible for the Cistercian revision of the service-books.[5] In default of contemporary evidence, however, it is not possible to say with certainty how far the English houses attained unanimity in the matter; certainly they had no influence on the black monks, and there are indications that early in the thirteenth century Cistercian severity in the chant was yielding in places to the secular fashions of the day.[6]

1 Cf. his letter in *PL*, CLXXVIII, 339.
2 For Stephen Harding's action and his justificatory letter, *v*. the article by Dom P. Blanchard, *Un monument primitif de la Règle cistercienne*, in *RB*, XXXI (1914), 35–44.
3 For a summary account of this curious episode *v*. Vacandard, *Vie de S. Bernard*, II, 104–7, and the remarks of Wagner, *Einführung in die Gregorianischen Melodien*, II, 450 *seqq*.
4 For this, *v*. the *Tractatus de cantu*, a *pièce justificative* accompanying the Antiphoner and having as preface a letter of Bernard (*Opera*, II, 1529–42).
5 *V. Tonale S. Bernardi* in *PL*, CLXXXII, 1154.
6 Thus the chapter of 1217 noted that at Dore and Tintern: "triparti vel quadriparti voce, more saecularium, canitur, ut dicitur" (*Statuta Cap. Gen. Ord. Cist.*, ed. J. M. Canivez, I, 472, n. 31).

CHAPTER XXXVIII

THE MAINTENANCE OF DISCIPLINE

I

THE BLACK MONKS: EPISCOPAL SURVEILLANCE AND VISITATION

The Rule of St Benedict presupposes the existence of no external authority responsible for maintaining discipline in the monastery. St Benedict legislated for a household, a self-contained unit under its abbot; beyond this he did not go. The bishop, in his scheme and in his age, had no direct concern with the monastery, save in so far as some of its members were in holy orders.[1] The Rule does, however, envisage the case arising when a community has elected an unworthy abbot, whose actions have become a public scandal. Should such a state of things come about, the bishop, together with neighbouring abbots and layfolk, is to step in and appoint a fit superior.[2] In all this St Benedict, while reflecting the usage of his day, gives to the bishop a somewhat more vague position than the decrees of councils might warrant, for from very early times the right and duty of the bishop to visit a monastery for disciplinary purposes had been asserted.[3] In the event, however, the relations between an autonomous abbey and the diocesan remained very indeterminate throughout western Europe during the first half of the Middle Ages, for, speaking generally, the periods of monastic decadence coincided with periods when the hierarchy also and the priesthood were decadent, and the situation rarely arose in which the bishops of a land were in a position to demand or to secure a reform of the monasteries. Nevertheless, the old legislation stood, and was re-asserted with energy in the early eleventh century by reforming prelates such as Burchard of Wurms;[4] monastic bishops, on the other hand, preferred to act in virtue of their personal influence rather than to open the door to indiscriminate interference.

As detailed treatment has already been given to the cases where full immunity from control was claimed by a few houses, a brief outline may suffice of the gradual reintroduction of the ancient canonical practice of diocesan control. In the revival under Dunstan the new life in the Church came from bishops who were also monks, and until the Conquest the majority of the bishops sprang from the monasteries. Consequently,

---

1 *Regula S. Benedicti*, c. lxii, "de sacerdotibus monasterii".
2 *Regula*, c. lxiv.
3 Cf. canons of the First Council of Orange (441).
4 *Burchardi Decretum*, VIII, 67 [c. 1010]: "Non semel, sed saepius in anno episcopi visitent monasteria monachorum, et si quid corrigendum fuerit, corrigant."

the case never arose in England before 1066 of a secular bishop claiming a right to interfere in monastic matters in virtue of the canons. In the first years of the revival, as in previous situations of the same kind in Europe, the leaders held themselves responsible for the houses which had sprung from their own foundations, and exercised wide but wholly personal and informal powers of visitation and correction.[1] When they passed away no one took their place, and if, between 1000 and 1066, any individual considered himself responsible for maintaining monastic discipline, it was a conscientious and energetic king such as Cnut, acting in concert with his Witan of bishops and abbots. An abbot, when elected and blessed, presumably continued to take the canonical oath of obedience, but in the loose state of diocesan organization in the Saxon Church this had become a mere formality, much as have a number of professions and promises in the ecclesiastical life of England at the present day.

The advent of the Norman bishops under Lanfranc did little at first to alter the existing state of things. Lanfranc, as the powerful primate of the new *Landeskirche*, took upon himself very great but wholly undefined powers of surveillance; he and the Conqueror, not the diocesan bishop, were responsible for dealing with the various disciplinary problems that arose, such as the case of Glastonbury, but there is no sign that Lanfranc or any other bishop made any attempt to institute regular or systematic visits to the monasteries. Anselm, who was seldom at peace in England, exercised less powers of general supervision than his predecessor, and at his death the monasteries were once more for a space wholly abandoned to their own independence, under the supreme control of the king.

New forces were, however, by this time at work within the Church which were destined sooner or later to effect a change. The most important of these, though its influence in England was tardy, was the rise of a number of new orders, above all that of the white monks, in whose system great importance was attached to regular disciplinary visitation. From the beginning the salutary effects of this in practice offered a strong weapon to critics of the black monks in France and the Rhineland, and provoked some attempts at imitation, but in England the political situation and the flourishing state of the old houses allowed the existing order of things to remain wholly unchallenged. Next, there was the movement, rapidly attaining momentum in the post-Gregorian Church, to apply the centralizing, unifying principles of canon law to diocesan affairs. It was this that in several cases caused the question of immunity to become a living issue, and although before c. 1190 the efforts of the bishops were directed almost exclusively towards an assertion of their strictly diocesan

1 Thus we are told that Dunstan "loca sacrorum coenobiorum [sc. Bath and Glastonbury] ob animarum aedificationem circuibat sollicitus" (*Mem. S. Dunst., Vita auct. B.* 46–7). Ethelwold "circuit...singula monasteria, mores instituens, etc." (*Vita auct. Aelfric*, in *Chron. Abingd.* II, 262–3). Oswald "idem qui fuit in visitatione monasteriorum quae instituerat, semper extitit" (*Vita auct. anon.* in *Historians of York*, II, 496).

rights of control over parishes, rites and synods, it was inevitable that sooner or later the old equivocal status of the abbeys—neither freed from the bishop nor controlled by him—must give place to full exemption or complete subjection. Inevitable as it was, this process was very slow in England owing to the strength of tradition and the private and political activities of most of the bishops; the beginning made by the Cistercian Henry Murdac of York (1147–53) had little consequence for more than twenty years.[1] Thirdly, there were the sporadic appearances of papal legates in England, whose universal jurisdiction was admitted by all and who were from the first men familiar with the visitation system. It was at the hands of these that the English black monk houses first became aware of the realities of visitation.

The earliest of these legates to make a regular survey of the English monasteries would seem to have been John of Crema in 1125.[2] In 1138 a similar tour was made by Alberic of Ostia, a Cluniac, who took with him as assessor the Cistercian Richard, first abbot of Fountains.[3] A few years later Imar of Tusculum, another Cluniac, despatched a certain amount of monastic business during his visit in 1145.[4] Had such legatine visitations continued with the same frequency subsequent developments might have been very different; as it was, they were interrupted, partly by the political situation in England, but still more by the appointment of a resident legate in the person of Henry of Winchester, and later of successive arch-bishops of Canterbury. At first these resident legates did not exercise any supervisory jurisdiction over the monasteries, but under Richard of Canterbury (1171–84) a new phase began. More active in this than in some other directions, he visited Peterborough and deposed the abbot in the autumn of 1175[5] and between that year and 1180 threatened to visit Bury, an exempt house, in his legatine capacity.[6] In all this he may have been stimulated by the example of the cardinal legate Hugo Pierleoni, who made a visitatorial survey of the country in 1175–6.[7] Henceforward legatine visitations by the primate and others became common. William Longchamp of Ely was making them in 1191[8] and Hubert Walter, a few years later, was particularly active. In 1195, acting on instructions from

1 For Murdac's dealings with the black monks v. supra, ch. XIV, p. 257.
2 Chronicle [E], sub anno: "He ferde ofer eall Englalande to ealle þa biscop rices ⁊ abbot rices."
3 John of Hexham, 169. Alberic, inter alia, assisted in bringing about a change of abbots at Battle (Chron. Bell. 64–5), deposed Waldef of Croyland (Chron. Ang. Petr., s.a. 1139) and probably also the abbot of Shrewsbury (John of Worcester, 53). He also dealt with Coventry (Holtzmann, Papsturkunden in England, II, ii, no. 18).
4 Textus Roffensis, 204; Holtzmann, Papsturkunden in England, II, ii, no. 45.
5 Radulph. Diceto, I, 402; Benedict of Peterborough, I, 106. It is likely, however, that in this he was acting merely as the instrument of Henry II, whose motives were interested (Hugo Candidus, 93).
6 Jocelini Cronica, 212: "Auctoritate legatiae suae."
7 Benedict of Peterborough, I, 106: "[Hugo] iter...fecit...per abbatias Angliae ad visitandum eas tanquam legatus apostolicae sedis."
8 Benedict of Peterborough, II, 143.

Rome, he deposed Robert of Thorney,[1] and in the same year took drastic action at Worcester[2] and announced his intention of visiting St Augustine's.[3] He took cognizance of the troubles at Evesham, though his legateship expired before any serious action had been taken,[4] and made an attempt, thwarted by Samson, to visit Bury.[5] He would seem even to have visited houses in the province of York, where he deposed the abbot of St Mary's.[6]

Hitherto all episcopal visitations had been either legatine or made in obedience to royal commands, but at the very end of the century there are indications that diocesan bishops were beginning to assert the right of visiting non-exempt religious houses. The desirability of such visitations was becoming a commonplace among the contemporary critics of the monks, of whom Walter Map and his friend Gerald of Wales were the most vocal,[7] but it is noteworthy that neither of these strengthens his case by insisting on the canonical powers possessed by the Ordinary. The earliest notice of a purely diocesan visitation is apparently that concerning Hugh of Lincoln in 1191, but the words are vague and need not necessarily refer to monastic houses.[8] Marleberge tells us that John of Coutances, bishop of Worcester (1196–8), promulgated some decrees in the chapter-house at Evesham, but here again the words do not make it absolutely certain that these were monastic and not merely diocesan regulations.[9] The first undoubted case is that of Mauger of Worcester in 1202 when, in the course of a general visitation, he appeared before the gates of Evesham and precipitated a crisis. But even here Mauger had thought it advisable to fortify himself with a papal rescript authorizing him to visit houses subject to the diocesan.[10] Finally, England was twice visited in the reign of John by papal legates who made a tour of many of the monastic houses; John of Ferentino in 1206 drew up a series of articles for St

1 Gervase, I, 530; Radulph. Diceto, II, 151.
2 Gervase, I, 530: "Videns...quod...ordo monasticus in parte plurima deperisset... quosdam ex ipsis misit Cantuariam et alias per Angliam; duosque ex Cantuariensibus misit Wigorniam."
3 *Epp. Cant.* ccccxii.
4 *Chron. Evesh.* 106.
5 *Jocelini Cronica*, 283–7. Samson countered by procuring a privilege exempting Bury from visitation from anyone save a *legatus a latere*.
6 Radulph. Diceto, II, 147; Roger Hoveden, III, 294; cf. *Jocelini Cronica*, 285.
7 Cf. especially Giraldus, IV, 93; W. Map, *Poems*, 184.
8 Benedict of Peterborough, II, 231. It is described as "visitatio per domos virorum religiosorum diocesis suae", but the only example given of Hugh's action is the ejection of Rosamund's bones from Godstow nunnery, and he may have only visited his *Eigenkloster* of Eynsham and some houses of canons. Despite its vast extent, the diocese of Lincoln contained very few black monk houses.
9 *Chron. Evesh.* 115.
10 *Chron. Evesh.* 109: "Iste...indulgentiam a domino papa maxime propter correctionem status nostri...impetravit, videlicet ut liceret ecclesias diocesana lege sibi subjectas, appellatione remota, visitare." He had already been to Gloucester (*ibid.* 109–10). The words of the chronicler do not make it absolutely clear whether the point of the permission was to allow the visitation or merely to cut off the possibility of appeal.

Mary's, York, and endeavoured to settle affairs at Evesham, and Nicholas of Tusculum in 1213 dealt finally, among other cases, with those of Roger Norreys and the abbot of Bardney.[1]

Thus during the pontificate of Innocent III everything was tending towards a general application to all religious institutes of the now familiar system of visitation. Legatine action, common criticism and, perhaps, the simultaneous occurrence of two or three notable and abiding scandals, helped to bring about the legislation of the Fourth Lateran Council, which allowed, in the case of the black monks who were not exempt, for two visitations, the episcopal and the regular, but threw stress on the former by expressing a hope that the bishop would so order matters that the monastic visitors, when they came, would find that all was well.

In the absence of any system of visitation, together with its records, it is extremely difficult to give a detailed account of the maintenance of discipline in the black monk houses during the period 1135–1216. Before the earlier of these two dates the frequent appointment of eminent Norman or Anglo-Norman monks to all the English abbeys, the creative spirit which continued to overflow from Norman monasticism, and the solidarity which bound the various houses together under the supreme control of the king all combined to keep the body sound; after 1216 the visitation and chapter system, with the records it has left behind, allows us to draw, at least roughly, a graph of good discipline or evil. During the eighty years between 1135 and 1216 the monasteries, as has often been noted above, enjoyed a degree of immunity from all control such as had not been theirs before and was never to be theirs again. On the whole it appears that almost all, save under circumstances of unusual stress, maintained at least a respectable level of discipline. In the medieval as in the modern world, a large institution with many external contacts and with a personnel largely composed of educated men, has so many natural safeguards of publicity and incitements to efficiency that it is able, like a moderately healthy body, to expel without extraordinary difficulty the germs of disease. The fullest chronicles, those of St Albans and Bury, both indicate the presence of unworthy and even gravely immoral individuals from time to time in the community; they also show that public sentiment was shocked, and that in time the offenders were brought to book. The cases of a whole house standing in need of reform are very rare; perhaps there are less than half a dozen in all during the period under consideration. One such would seem to be the case of Cerne in Dorset c. 1147, which is a subject of frequent allusion in the correspondence of Gilbert Foliot when still abbot of Gloucester; but the sequence of events is not easily followed

1 For the legatine visitations at the end of John's reign cf. Flete, *History of Westminster* (ed. J. A. Robinson), 100; *GASA*, I, 252 (Gualo), 257 (Nicholas); *Chron. Evesh. ut supra*; *Mem. St Edmund's*, II, *Electio Hugonis, passim*; also C. R. Cheney, *The Papal Legate and English Monasteries in 1206*, in *EHR*, XLVI (July 1931), 443–52. For the later history of visitation in England *v.* C. R. Cheney, *Episcopal Visitation*.

from the fitful glimpses thus given, and of the origin of the trouble and its final resolution we are quite in the dark.[1]

Apart from the case of Cerne, and that of Worcester at the end of the century, where the archbishop of Canterbury, Hubert Walter, took action as legate, scattered some of the community to other houses, and set two monks of Christ Church in charge,[2] the distresses of the black monks were without exception caused or displayed by the excesses of unworthy abbots, many of whom were near relatives or favourites of the royal house. On another page[3] there will be found a list of all the cases where an abbey appears to have reached a serious state of distress not through any material or quasi-political misfortune, but through the misrule of an abbot. Such cases can only be recognized by notices of deposition, and the abbatial *fasti* are not complete, but the very frank references of contemporary chroniclers make it probable that record has survived of the majority of the public scandals that occurred.

II

THE WHITE MONKS: ACTIVITIES OF GENERAL CHAPTER

The white monks, on the point of maintenance of discipline, were in many respects at an advantage when compared with the black. They had a detailed code governing their whole life, and a system of visitations by which all deviations from this code could be checked and corrected; the visitors had full power to depose any unworthy officials, not excluding the abbot himself, and behind all lay the absolute control of general chapter.

At the same time the Cistercians were in other respects less fortunately placed than their older brethren. While many of the greater abbeys, such as Waverley, Rievaulx and Fountains, had the same advantages of a large community, counting among its members many of ability and mental distinction, and having therefore a public opinion which stood for respectability and sheltered higher aspirations, there were from early days

1 No edition of Gilbert Foliot's letters attempts any chronological arrangement. Böhmer (*Kirche und Staat in England*, 393, note 2) arranges the letters referring to Cerne in the following order, which appears to me to be correct: 13, 15, 20, 37, 30, 32, 67, 38, 39, 43, 44, 50, 92, 72, 52, 1. There are, however, a few indications of date regarding which Böhmer is not wholly accurate: e.g. *epp.* 20, 37 refer to the recent arrival of Imar in England, probably in January 1147; *ep.* 72 was written shortly before 1 June 1174; *epp.* 52 and 1 before March 1148.

2 Gervase, I, 530: "[Archiepiscopus] videns...quod...ordo monasticus in parte plurima deperisset, et inter monachos frequenter essent litigia, quosdam ex ipsis misit Cantuariam et alias per Angliam; duosque ex Cantuariensibus misit Wigorniam, qui ordinem et res dissipatas in bonum statum reformarent." This took place between the death of Henry de Sully of Worcester (autumn, 1195) and the appointment of John of Coutances in 1196. There is no mention of the incident either in the Worcester annals or in the Evesham chronicle, and Worcester appears as flourishing *c.* 1205.

3 *V.* Appendix XXI. The above paragraph does not, of course, apply to the smaller houses.

many smaller houses where very different conditions prevailed. In the upland abbeys of England, and still more in those of Wales or the Marches, all recruitment came from the locality, and few of the aspirants were men of any education. In the monastery itself they would receive no intellectual training and their mental outlook would remain confined. Moreover, the choir monks, who were at least literate, must often have been outnumbered by the lay brothers, who were wholly uneducated and uncultured. In consequence, once the fervour of the original plantation had cooled, it was possible for the whole house to take on the colour of the locality and become narrow in spirit and uncouth in manners; regular visitations and the arrivals of extern abbots no doubt helped to keep the current of life moving, especially when the mother-house was a great and flourishing abbey; but when the monastery concerned was of the second or third generation, and had for parent a small, provincial abbey, the stimulus provided by visitation must have been small and the safeguards given by external observation and internal enlightened public opinion of little strength. As will be seen there is evidence that certain houses in England and still more especially in Wales were almost from the first a source of anxiety to the order.

As the early Cistercians were divided into no national provinces or congregations, and as no visitatorial records exist, the only official source of information as to the state of discipline in the order is the series of statutes of general chapter. In the Cistercian constitution the annual general chapter was the supreme legislative and executive body; no smaller conciliar group existed, and there were no permanent administrative superiors comparable to the General and Provincials, Assistants, Consultors, Diffinitors and the rest, of later orders. Consequently, it fell to the annual general chapter to take cognizance, in the ultimate resort, of matters affecting the well-being or reputation of individual houses and of the whole body. From the beginning, or at least as early as c. 1140,[1] questions of all kinds were canvassed and debated with great freedom at Cîteaux, and the practice existed, as has already been noted, of deputing two or three abbots to execute the capitular decisions regarding individual houses, but the early statutes are few in number and consist almost entirely of important pronouncements or reaffirmations of earlier statutes. From c. 1180 onwards, however, the annual declarations become very much more numerous and are more frequently directed against current abuses; besides this, it became the custom to include in the statutes all the penalties decreed against defaulting abbots and to record the appointment of commissioners to investigate cases of misdemeanour or to execute capitular decisions. It is therefore possible from c. 1180 to obtain a very fair conception of the weaknesses and distresses of the order, and to see

---

1 Cf. the notices of the discussions relative to Byland c. 1142 in the *Registrum Bellal.* in *Monasticon*, v, 568 *seqq.*

in what houses or groups of houses decay of discipline most frequently caused anxiety.

This evidence, it may be said, goes far to substantiate the charge of avarice brought by Gerald of Wales and Walter Map against the white monks, as also the statement of the former that the English houses were on the whole less fervent than those of France.[1] The first acknowledgment that the charge of avarice is well founded occurs in a solemn pronouncement of the five major abbots and others in 1190. In order to restrain the desire for possessions, they say, and to repel the charge of constant acquisition of property under which the order labours, it is decreed that none save poor monasteries are to buy lands or immovables of any kind, and that no novices are to be received for a year in order to make new acquisitions of property unnecessary.[2] At the same chapter the grave debts of certain houses, which had been the subject of a decree in 1188, gave rise to an enactment that no loans were to be taken up on usury and that none of any kind were to be received from Jews.[3] Solemn as was the statute against buying it was, nevertheless, impracticable; it was repeated in identical words the next year.[4] It is difficult not to see an allusion, in the reference of the fathers to adverse criticism, to the group of officials and clerks at the court of Henry II, where the charge of avarice was a commonplace and was made even by a responsible officer such as the justiciar, Ralph Glanvill.[5] The statute, it appears, was not observed, for it was repeated in 1205 and in 1206, to be binding for one year only, and again in 1214 and 1215. In 1216 it was formally repealed.[6]

Another abuse, that of owning churches and advowsons, was peculiarly English. Alexander III, as early as c. 1170, had addressed a bull on the subject to the Cistercians of England, but the practice, as has been seen, continued to gain ground.[7] It appears first in the statutes of general chapter in 1214, and was repeated in the following year, but the question may well have been debated many years before.[8] Still more peculiarly national was the irregularity of beer-drinking, shared in full measure by the abbeys of Wales. The chapter of 1190 noted that beer had been drunk

---

1 *V. infra*, pp. 670, 676.

2 *Statuta Capitulorum Generalium Ordinis Cisterciensis* (ed. J. M. Canivez), vol. I (1116–1220), p. 117 (*s.a.* 1190), no. 1: "Ad temperandam cupiditatem et notam semper acquirendi qua impetimur repellendam proposuimus firmiter tenendum ab omnibus ut...ab omni emptione terrarum et quarumcumque possessionum immobilium abstineamus." Cf. also p. 118, no. 2.

3 *Statuta*, 120, n. 14.   4 *Statuta*, 142 (1191), n. 42.

5 So at least Gerald says, *Speculum Ecclesiae* (IV, 244): "Dicebat enim quia nullius ordinis viros totiens coram ipso in foro publico pro tribunali sedente, super cartis falsis et sigillis adulterinis, super terminis terrarum metisque finalibus dolose transpositis, multisque cupiditatibus aliis valde detestandis, convictos invenit." This is clearly the language of exaggeration, but the basis of fact is probably beneath it.

6 *Statuta*, 306–7 (1205), n. 5; 321 (1206), n. 9; 427–8 (1214), n. 54; 448 (1215), n. 65; 449 (1216), n. 2.

7 JL, 12, 412 (the date can only be given as 1162–75). *V. supra*, p. 355, n. 2.

8 *Statuta*, 428 (1214), n. 57; 448 (1215), n. 63.

in the granges of Margam;[1] two years later it is enacted that in English abbeys where the *conversi* are incorrigible offenders in this respect no more lay brethren are to be admitted;[2] in 1195 another statute decrees that no beer is to be drunk in the granges of the Welsh abbeys, and that no *conversus* is to be received until this regulation is observed.[3] The last enactment was reaffirmed in the following year, and in the same chapter order was given that the grange given to Garendon by the earl of Leicester for the purpose of providing beer for the *conversi* should be converted to other uses or returned to the donor.[4]

Of the English abbeys in whose regard general chapter took disciplinary action between 1180 and 1216 only four present cases of any interest or importance. Furness, the eldest-born of Savigny in England, was in trouble more than once. Already *c.* 1170 Alexander III had had occasion to reprimand the abbots of Swineshead and Furness for owning villages and serfs and churches;[5] in 1193 the abbot of the latter house is penanced for disobedience to the abbot of Savigny and in the following year one of his monks, who has illicitly procured consecration as bishop of Man, is excommunicated and expelled from the order.[6] Two years later the chapter was occupied with the affair of Garendon. This abbey, an early plantation from Waverley in Charnwood Forest, under the patronage of the earls of Leicester, had been for some years in an unsatisfactory condition. Gerald of Wales has a story, which may or may not be true, of a monk of the house becoming a Jew, and another of a murderous attack on a rich testator.[7] The decree of general chapter already mentioned shows that there had been irregularity among the *conversi* as regards beer-drinking, and it may have been this that brought about the resignation of Abbot William in 1195. He was succeeded by Reginald, previously abbot of Merevale in Warwickshire, and it may be supposed that measures of reform were applied, for in less than a year the *conversi* attacked and wounded the abbot in the dormitory.[8] It was this that brought Garendon to the notice of chapter and a resolution was passed that letters should be written to King Richard, Hubert Walter and the earl of Leicester, and that all the *conversi* should be expelled to remote houses of the order;[9] the occasion was taken, as has been noted, for animadverting upon the earl's gift of a grange for brewing beer. In spite of this decree, action was delayed, and

1 *Statuta*, 123 (1190), n. 21.   2 *Statuta*, 149 (1192), n. 16.
3 *Statuta*, 193 (1195), n. 76.
4 *Statuta*, 199 (1196), n. 9; 202, n. 25: "grangia quae data est a comite pro cervisia conversis facienda in eos usus de cetero non expendatur."
5 Holtzmann, *Papsturkunden in England*, II, 2, n. 174 (1166–79): "audivimus si quidem, quod villas et rusticos habeatis et eos in causam ducentes notis pecuniariis condempnatis et more secularium dominorum jus patronatus in dandis ecclesiis vendicatis."
6 *Statuta*, 169 (1193), n. 58; 179 (1194), n. 51.
7 Giraldus, *Speculum Ecclesiae* (IV, 139); *ibid.* (IV, 241). In the second case the name of the abbey can only be conjectured from the provenance of the alleged victim.
8 *Annales Waverl.*, *s.a.* 1195, 1196.
9 *Statuta*, 202 (1196), n. 24.

in the following year the abbots of L'Aumône and Boxley were commissioned to proceed to Garendon and execute the punitive measures; this time, it seems, the matter was carried through.[1]

Another English house to occupy the attention of the abbots in chapter at this time was Fountains. This, at first sight, is somewhat surprising, for the abbot of Fountains from 1191 to 1203 was the saintly Ralph Haget, but as the matter for which he received reprimand more than once was a controversy with the archbishop of York, Geoffrey Plantagenet, it may well be that the abbot was in the right and that the chapter acted in his absence on information received from the party of the archbishop.[2] This is the more likely in view of the second charge made against an abbot of Fountains, Ralph's successor, John I. He was accused in his absence at the chapter of 1210 of having failed to visit the Lysekloster in Norway in person, and of having sent monks who abused their powers; he was given a penance, as was also the abbot of Kirkstead, who had not visited his overseas daughter Hovedö.[3] In 1211 two Scandinavian abbots were commissioned to visit Lyse and report on the doings of the visitors from Fountains;[4] they presumably did so, for in 1212 the two English monks who were alleged to have misconducted themselves were expelled from their abbey, and John II of Fountains was directed to visit Lyse either in person or through another abbot.[5] Apparently he appealed against this decree, for in 1212 Lyse was taken from Fountains and given as daughter to Alvastra, on the ground that visitation from England was impossible.[6] If the story ended there it would be natural to suppose that Lyse was altogether the injured party, but in 1214 its abbot (though not present in person) was on the tapis at Cîteaux, accused of refusing to receive the abbot of Hovedö as visitor and of other unspecified misdemeanours, and the abbots of Fountains and Kirkstead were commissioned to investigate, Lyse being restored to the family of Clairvaux.[7] With this notice the record of the incident ends.

Finally, the abbot of King John's new foundation of Beaulieu earned an early notoriety. He was from the first used as an agent by the king, and this may have put him in the way of temptations, as it certainly won him enemies. Already in 1208 rumours were abroad concerning him, and the abbot of Cîteaux, the mother of Beaulieu, was ordered to investigate.[8]

1 *Statuta*, 216 (1197), n. 32. The entry in the Waverley annals (p. 657, n. 8) implies that the dispersal took place.

2 *Statuta*, 232 (1198), n. 48; 244 (1199), n. 57; 253 (1200), n. 24. The controversy lasted after Ralph's death; cf. *ibid*. 377 (1210), n. 42.

3 *Statuta*, 375–6 (1210), nn. 33, 35.

4 *Statuta*, 387 (1211), n. 41.

5 *Statuta*, 396 (1212), n. 32: "monachi de Fontanis...qui multa enormia occasione visitationis in domo de Lisa commiserunt, emittantur de domibus propriis, etc."

6 *Statuta*, 406 (1213), n. 11.

7 *Statuta*, 422 (1214), n. 24: "de abbate de Liza qui noluit recipere visitatorem abbatem... et...de quo multa alia sunt audita, etc."

8 *Statuta*, 354 (1208), n. 41: "de abbate Belli loci...de quo multa dicuntur, etc."

His report was presumably satisfactory, for in 1213 the alleged culprit was given a commission by chapter, though he failed to execute it and was duly penanced the following year, and was also accused of failing to observe the decisions of commissioners in a suit with Stanley.[1] In 1215, however, the charges once more came to a head; the abbot of Beaulieu was accused of drinking wassail with three earls and forty knights, of having his bed guarded by a watchdog on a silver chain, of eating off silver plate and of receiving the ministrations of obsequious secular attendants; he was ordered to present himself without fail to undergo examination at the next chapter, or, if he defaulted, to suffer deposition.[2] The picturesque details of these accusations give the impression that a certain proportion of legendary matter had added itself to the basis of fact, and the impression is borne out by a decree of the chapter of 1216, ordering the abbot of Cîteaux in general terms to deal with the case.[3] The issue of this investigation, if it ever took place, is not recorded, but we know from other sources that Abbot Hugh was in fact deposed before 1218, and that soon after his public services were rewarded with the bishopric of Carlisle, where he left behind him a somewhat equivocal reputation.[4]

With the exception of these cases, and of glimpses of controversies between the English houses and the wool merchants of the Low Countries,[5] there is little referring to England in the statutes, and the darkness which covers the life of the majority of the abbeys may be taken as an indication that their discipline was healthy. It is otherwise with the abbeys of Wales and the Marches; though a group relatively small in numbers, one or more of them came up for reprimand at Cîteaux almost every year, thus bearing out the indications received from other sources, that they were among the most unsatisfactory members of the order. Indeed, it could hardly be otherwise. The clear-cut, rigidly uniform character of the Cistercian institute, evolved in one of the most cultured and sophisticated provinces of Europe to meet the needs of those who wished for simplicity in the midst of a complicated feudal society, was not easily applicable to the restless, uncultured, half pagan inhabitants of the remote valleys of Wales. As might be expected, it was the *conversi* who gave most trouble. The first notice is of Margam in 1190–1. There the devout Abbot Cunan,

---

1 *Statuta*, 414 (1213), n. 51; 420 (1214), n. 10; 443 (1215), n. 41.

2 *Statuta*, 445 (1215), n. 48: "abbas Belli loci in Anglia qui coram tribus comitibus et quadraginta militibus inordinate se habuit in mensa, scilicet bibendo ad garsacil, et qui habet canem cum catena argentea ad custodiendum lectum suum, et qui adduxit secum servientes saeculares in equis qui ei, flexis genibus, ministrant, et qui in vasis argenteis de consuetudine facit sibi ministrari, et de quo multa alia dicuntur, etc."

3 *Statuta*, 460 (1216), n. 54.

4 *Ann. Waverl.*, s.a. 1218, 1223; *Chron. Lanercost* (Bannatyne Club, 1839), p. 30.

5 Cf. *Statuta*, 401 (1212), n. 55 where Dore, Kingswood, Mellifont, Fountains and Furness are at issue with Florence and John fitz Bartholomew, burgesses of St Omer, and *ibid.* 426 (1214), n. 45, where the English *conversi* are accused of buying wool to re-sell at a higher price.

praised by Gerald, had been succeeded by one of whom little good is heard.[1] Unspecified misdemeanours had occurred in the house, and the abbot was given forty days penance and ordered to send two of his *conversi* to Clairvaux to do regular satisfaction.[2] Four years later the abbot himself was summoned to Cîteaux to do penance, apparently for allowing beer to his *conversi*.[3] Eleven years later again another and more extensive *émeute* took place. The *conversi* arose in a body, threw the cellarer off his horse, attacked and pursued the abbot for a number of miles and barricaded themselves in their dormitory, refusing to provide the monks with the wherewithal to live. For this they were ordered to proceed to Clairvaux on foot previously to accepting dispersal at the direction of the abbot of Clairvaux.[4] It was a brave form of words; but no information exists as to the number of truculent Welshmen who submitted to the laborious pilgrimage in order to place themselves in the dock.

Meanwhile similar trouble had arisen elsewhere. In 1194–5 the *conversi* of the lonely abbey of Cwmhir had stolen their abbot's horses in revenge for his prohibition of beer; they were given a similar penance to that related of Margam.[5] It was in this very year that the abbot of the last-named house, together with the abbot of Strata Marcella, was summoned out to Cîteaux to do penance; in the following year the abbot of Whitland is ordered to investigate the excesses of the *conversi* at Strata Florida,[6] and the frequency with which internecine quarrels among the Welsh houses are recorded is evidence of the restlessness that prevailed. Among them all Aberconway would seem to have had an unenviable notoriety. Constantly engaged in litigation it produced more than one *mauvais sujet*, such as the monk Philip, who claimed to have been consecrated bishop without authorization, and the whilom subprior, Rotoland, who had apostatized from the order, and it is not altogether surprising to hear that the abbot, along with the abbots of Caerleon and Valle Crucis, was accused of rarely celebrating Mass or receiving the Holy Eucharist.[7]

Yet in all this it must be remembered that the statutes of general chapter give but one aspect of the situation of the order. They are concerned solely with disciplinary action; it was not the function of general chapter to single out the good for praise and the holy for admiration. Of

1 Giraldus, *Speculum Ecclesiae* (IV, 129 *seqq.*).
2 *Statuta*, 123 (1190), n. 21; 138 (1191), n. 23.
3 *Statuta*, 193 (1195), n. 77.
4 *Statuta*, 324 (1206), n. 23: "conversi de Margan qui, conspiratione facta, insurrexerunt in abbatem, et cellerarium de equo ejecerunt, et insequentes armata manu abbatem usque ad xv milliaria, qui etiam se incastellaverunt in dormitorio suo...ad portam Claraevallis pedites veniant, etc."
5 *Statuta*, 191 (1195), n. 66: "conversi Walliae qui abbati de Guthlimur [apparently Cwmhir] equos abstulerunt quia cerevisiam eis inhibuerat, etc."
6 *Statuta*, 193 (1195), n. 77; 199 (1196), n. 8.
7 *Statuta*, 262 (1200), n. 70 (Philip); 281 (1202), n. 34 (Rotolandus); 281 (1202), n. 35: "de quibus dicitur quod rarissime celebrant et abstinent ab altari."

the gradual work of civilization accomplished by the Welsh abbeys there is no mention, but there is something little short of magnificent in the spectacle of a body of men, far away in central France and bound together by no permanent tie of administrative routine, applying their strict law to remote Welsh abbeys and issuing commands to individual monks and lay brothers, and though some of their precise instructions may have been disregarded, there is plenty of evidence that the disciplinary system was still in its main lines efficient. The faults recorded of the Welsh monks are those of untutored lawlessness, not of effete decadence, and on the whole, in the twelfth century at least, the law and its sanctions were victorious among the white monks, even in Wales.

CHAPTER XXXIX

THE CRITICS OF THE MONKS:
GERALD OF WALES, WALTER MAP AND
THE SATIRISTS

I

In an earlier chapter some account was given of the active hostility shown towards the monastic body by a group of influential bishops in the last decades of the twelfth century. At the very moment when the opposition of the secular clergy in high places was thus making itself felt, another and hitherto unprecedented form of attack began which was to continue intermittently in one form or another until the Reformation. This was the criticism of the monastic life of the country by members of the new class of highly educated clerks who filled various administrative or magisterial posts in the royal and episcopal households or in the various schools, some of which were to develop into universities. The literary education of the day, based as it was on Latin models, and including among its most familiar text-books the satires of Horace, Persius and Juvenal, and the epigrams of Martial, gave to those with a talent for writing a bent towards the satirical and critical, and there was throughout the Middle Ages, especially in the universities of France and Italy, a floating population of men at once brilliant and irresponsible, occupied with matters of religion and yet without depth of feeling, to which earlier and later centuries afford no exact parallel. This type made its first considerable appearance in the literature of Europe in the works of two clerks who moved in the highest English ecclesiastical circles at the end of the reign of Henry II. That Gerald de Barri and Walter Map did not stand alone, but were the representatives of a whole movement of taste and sentiment, can be seen from many incidents and personalities of the time,[1] but they may not unfairly be taken as the most eminent members of their class. Both were severe and persistent critics of the monastic body, and as their writings, not without influence in their own day, continue to be sources from which modern students derive both facts and opinions, it is necessary to consider in some detail the nature and truth of the charges which they bring against the monks.

[1] Hugh of Nonant, bishop of Coventry, eloquent, witty and bitter, is clearly of the same family; so is Richard of Devizes, monk of Winchester. One can see the type evolving in such men as John of Salisbury, Peter of Blois and Gerard la Pucelle. There had, of course, been satirists of the monks in an earlier age, such as Adalberon of Laon, who attacked Cluny in the eleventh century in his *Carmen ad Rotbertum regem* (ed. G. A. Hückel, *Les poèmes satiriques d'Adalbéron*) and Hugo Sottovagina of York, who also wrote a poem against Cluniacs (*Hist. York*, II, xiii), but there had been as yet, in England, nothing like the concentrated attack of Gerald and Map.

II

Gerald of Wales is probably of all the writers of the twelfth century the one most familiar to English readers, and he has been consistently fortunate in the friends he has found among editors and biographers.[1] His excursion into the realm of Irish history and ethnology has ensured to him celebrity of one kind, and it so happens that of his other works, the book in which his amiable qualities appear to the best advantage and his failings are inconspicuous is one which by reason of its subject has appealed during the last century to innumerable lovers of the beauties of Wales. Gerald de Barri belongs to that small class of writers which counts in its ranks the illustrious name of Cicero and is made up of those to whom the world listens most readily when they speak about themselves. Vain and naïve to a degree, he provides us in his pages with a whole arsenal of weapons with which to attack him, yet he has always succeeded in exciting in his readers an interest which has in it more of affection than dislike. He is, indeed, a medieval member of the fraternity to which belong Cellini and Pepys and Creevey, and has the peculiar advantage of having written in an age of which the abundant literature is for the most part serious, formless and colourless; his extreme facility, his vivacity, and his love of anecdote have therefore all the charm of contrast. He has besides a number of characteristics which give him a kinship with the modern world: a love, or at least a sense, of natural beauty and wild landscape; a warm affection for his home and for his native land; a keen memory for friendships that had meant much to him in the past; a curiosity for the marvellous and the uncanny; a ready, if often ineffectual, aspiration towards the ideal; and a genuine admiration for nobility of character. It may be added that these qualities, as has already been suggested, are seen at their best in the two or three books which are most readily accessible in translation and which deal with subjects of general interest; in much of his later work the facility

---

[1] Gerald, if fortunate in his friends, has not been wholly fortunate in his copyists and editors. Some of his principal works exist only in a single manuscript: e.g. the *Speculum Ecclesiae* only in Brit. Mus. MS. Cott. Tib. B xiii, a manuscript from which several chapters were missing even before it suffered damage from the fire of 1731; the *De Invectionibus* only in MS. Vat. Regin. 470. The eight volumes of the Rolls Series containing his works are far from satisfactory, especially those edited by J. S. Brewer; the text is often untrustworthy, there are no historical or topographical notes of value, and the introductions leave much to be desired. An advance was made in one direction by the edition of the *De Invectionibus* by W. S. Davies in *Y Cymmrodor*, vol. XXX (1920), but even this text is not fully critical and the introduction somewhat tentative. Recently an excellent translation has appeared of the *De Rebus a se Gestis* (*The Autobiography of Gerald of Wales*, translated by H. E. Butler, with an introduction by C. H. Williamson, London, 1937). The article in the *DNB*, which relies too much on Brewer, gives little light. The best short account is that given by Prof. F. M. Powicke in a lecture, *Gerald of Wales* (*Bulletin of the John Rylands Library*, XII, 2, July 1928, 389–410, reprinted in *The Christian Life in the Middle Ages and other Essays*). There is room for a complete critical and annotated edition which should both settle the text, indicate (where possible) Gerald's inaccuracies, and draw attention by means of cross-references to his many repetitions. For his use of the term *Cluniacensis* v. Appendix XXII.

becomes mere fluidity and utter formlessness, and the love of anecdote sheer sculduddry.

Gerald's life was one of movement, disturbance and controversy, and it put him in a position to know well many of the most eminent figures of his day; he was, indeed, acquainted with almost all those whose names have recurred so often in these pages: the kings Henry II, Richard and John; the archbishops Hubert Walter, Baldwin and Stephen Langton; Hugh of Lincoln, Innocent III, Walter Map and many others. In the final event, his was a life of disappointment, frustration and waste, and this declension is unquestionably reflected in his works. The writings of his early days, before the death of Henry II, have in them freshness and generosity of appreciation; then came the years of adventure and strife, and the books that deal with them have a tinge of strain and bitterness, and all is regarded from the angle of a personal quarrel; the keen observer of earlier years is still there, but he is no longer tolerant and receptive. Finally, the last books, and in particular the *Speculum Ecclesiae*, fall in tone below the level demanded of any serious work of history or criticism; the chapters flow out like water from a spring, or like the words of a man talking to himself with little or no inflexion of the voice, and the matter is as fluid as the manner. Yet even here Gerald's gift of vivacity does not wholly desert him; the reader may at times feel indignation, or disgust, but his attention is held; Gerald never falls into mere dullness.

III

The *Itinerarium Kambriae*, describing his tour with Baldwin in 1188, is the earliest of his works in which Gerald discusses the monastic orders, and it is by far the most sober. He is led into the topic at the beginning of the book by the visit paid to Llanthony, a house of Augustinian canons situated almost at the head of a lonely valley in the Black Mountains.[1] It was a house dear to Gerald from early days, and he remarks on its solitude and simplicity of life. Its daughter, New Lanthony near Gloucester, had a different ideal, so he tells us, and its grasping spirit had caused losses to the mother-house. But in both the rule was well kept.[2] He goes on to contrast the canons with the monks, black and white, and the theme is introduced which, with certain variations, is developed and repeated in all that he wrote after. For the black monks he has little praise. They are

---

[1] The picturesque ruins of the church still exist; the site of some of the domestic buildings is occupied by an hotel, well known to anglers. The abbey is on the north (i.e. the sunny) side of the narrow valley, and Gerald bears witness to the healthiness of the place (*Itinerarium Kambriae* in Rolls Series, *Opera*, VI, 37 *seqq.*). In strong contrast is the site, still farther up the valley, chosen by Father Ignatius at the end of the last century; this is on the south side, dark and damp.

[2] *Itinerarium Kambriae*, 41: "Utrinque tamen, tam hic quam ibi, quae aliis hodie cunctis praeminet ordinibus, ab Augustino instituta canonica servatur disciplina."

rich, yet their riches serve no good purpose, for in part they are wasted in
luxurious living, and in part they slip between the fingers of the many who
have a share in their administration. The white monks, on the other hand,
are excellent men of business and all is centred in the hands of one procurator; they do not live on rents and charges, but on their own work;
they are most sparing in their diet and therefore able to practise the most
abundant works of charity to the poor and travellers.[1] Their fault is a
grasping anxiety to acquire more and more land. The methods of the two
bodies, Gerald continues, are utterly opposed one to the other. If you
were to make a present to a community of black monks of a fully equipped
abbey in the enjoyment of ample revenues, it would be dilapidated and
poverty-stricken in a very short time. Give the Cistercians a wilderness or
a forest, and in a few years you will find a dignified abbey in the midst of
smiling plenty.[2] Consequently, whereas the black monks will let a crowd
of paupers starve at their gates rather than give up one of their thirteen
courses, the white will abandon one of their two scanty dishes rather than
see a single poor man in want. Best of all, and combining the good
qualities of black and white monks, are the canons.[3]

Apart from this long passage, Gerald has little to say on the subject of
monasticism in the *Itinerarium*. He has, however, some warm words of
praise for the charity and hospitality shown by the abbot of Margam,[4]
and tells for the first time the story of the disgraced abbot of Strata
Marcella.[5] Before he had occasion to treat of the white monks again, the
circumstances of his own life had brought him into collision with several
members of the order. There was, first of all, William Wibert, cellarer and
later abbot of Bittlesden. Gerald met him first at the court of Queen
Eleanor in 1192.[6] He had then recently been deposed by visitors from the
post of cellarer and accused of peculation, mismanagement, and a number
of other misdemeanours.[7] He attached himself to Gerald, who was then

---

1 *Itinerarium*, 43: "Hospitalitatis namque gratia, quam hujus ordinis viri, quanquam in
se abstinentissimi, prae aliis cunctis, caritate largiflua in pauperes et peregrinos infatiganter
exercent."   2 *Itinerarium*, 45.

3 *Itinerarium*, 46. It must be remembered that the Cluniac, Peter de Leia, had already
crossed Gerald's path.

4 *Itinerarium*, 67: "Prae aliis cunctis ordinis illius per Kambriam locis...caritativa
largitione laudatissimum."

5 *Itinerarium*, 59. This story in its various editions affords another good illustration of
Gerald's methods. The abbot, whose name was Enoc, *Speculum Ecclesiae* (IV, 168), not
Enatus as printed in *Gemma Ecclesiastica* (II, 248), was abbot after Ithel (*ob.* 1186) and before
Gruffudd (*ob.* 1196); cf. *Brut*, 233, 245. He was guilty of misconduct with a nun and
abandoned the habit. In the *Gemma Ecclesiastica*, written before *c.* 1200, Gerald tells the
story a second time and says that the culprit after many years (*pluribus annis*) returned to
Whitland, the house of his profession, and did full penance. In the *Speculum Ecclesiae*,
written *c.* 1216, the story is told for the third time, somewhat more fully, with no mention
of the repentance.

6 He gives the date in *Ep.* xxviii (I, 295): "Anno quo dominus rex in Alemannia detentus
fuerat."

7 Gerald gives the fullest list in his letter to the abbot of Cîteaux, *Ep.* i (I, 207–9). He
asserts that he ascertained William's misdeeds on enquiry after he himself had become

frequently employed as English emissary in Wales, and who admits or
professes that he was completely deceived as to his real character; the
connection, in any case, would seem to reflect either upon Gerald's
honesty or upon his perspicacity. After several journeys together,
William represented to people of influence that Gerald was playing false
to the English, and that therefore his, William's, constant surveillance
was necessary; moreover, if Gerald is to be at all believed, he persuaded
Peter de Leia, bishop of St David's, that there were hopes of his translation
to Worcester, meaning thereby to secure the vacant see for himself.[1]
This, indeed, we are told, was the motive for all his activity against Gerald.
In any case the archdeacon resolved to have his revenge;[2] William had,
by favour of the queen-mother, obtained the abbey of Bittlesden; Gerald
accused him both to the abbot of Garendon, the mother of Bittlesden,
and to the abbot of Cîteaux; they moved, if slowly; a visitation by the
abbot of L'Aumône was followed by another of the four abbots of
Fountains, Rievaulx, Wardon and Waverley in 1198, in which William
was finally deposed.[3] We are not reassured as to the sincerity of Gerald's
attitude or the truth of his allegations by his own assertion that he himself
had previously been reconciled to William Wibert and had offered to
write a withdrawal of his accusations.[4]

Whatever may have been the sincerity of his attitude, the affair embroiled Gerald with Hubert Walter, whose *protégé* William had been,[5]
and the abbot of Bittlesden, as he himself tells us, caused him to feel
towards the white monks the hostility which had been previously aroused
in him towards the black by the conduct of Peter de Leia.[6] These incidents
occurred before the St David's election of 1198. In that unfortunate
business Cistercians thwarted Gerald at every turn. In the first place,
Hubert Walter, who was justiciar as well as archbishop, happened to be
on the Marches when Peter de Leia died, and refused utterly, remembering

suspicious. William was clearly a man of bad character, but it is hard to believe that if he had
been formally deposed for these offences Gerald would have heard nothing of his evil
reputation during the months spent in his company.

1 *Ep.* xxviii (I, 300).

2 *Speculum Ecclesiae* (IV, 160-1): "Vindicis animi vitio et naturae Britannicae, quae
vindictam appetit, incontinenti forte contagio."

3 The date is given by *Ann. Waverl.*, which records the deposition *s.a.* 1198. The
abbot of Garendon was Reginald (*ibid.*, *s.a.* 1195); of Waverley, John (*ibid.*, *s.a.* 1196); of
Rievaulx, the distinguished Ernald, sometime abbot of Melrose (*Chron. Mailr.*, *s.a.* 1189);
of Fountains, Ralph Haget.

4 *Ep.* xxviii (I, 294): "Consului [Willelmo] quatinus Lincolniam veniens, litteras a me
retractationis praemissarum et excusationis acciperet."

5 *Ep.* xxviii (I, 293-4) and *De Rebus a se Gestis* (I, 95-6).

6 *Ep.* (I, 213): "Ob has igitur monachi istius, nec monachi tamen sed verius demoniaci,
alteriusque cujusdam Cluniacensem cucullam praeferentis [no doubt Peter de Leia]...
nequitias, quotiens litanias repeto...etiam hanc...deprecationem ingemino, cunctisque
fidelibus et amicis praecipue ac familiaribus ingeminandam in fide consulo: 'A monachorum
malitia, libera nos, Domine.'" The passage pleased Gerald, and he repeated it four years
later in a letter to Hubert Walter (I, 298), where the editor renders the Latin untranslatable
by printing *abbas* for *ob has*, and *demonachi* for *demoniaci*.

the business of William Wibert, to allow Gerald to administer the diocese during the vacancy.[1] Then the chapter of St David's, after nominating Gerald as first choice, added three other names, those of Walter, abbot of St Dogmael's, a Tironian,[2] Peter, abbot of Whitland, and Reginald Foliot; in addition to these the abbot of Dore decided to play for his own hand in the matter,[3] while Hubert Walter, for his part, put up yet another Cistercian as candidate, Alexander of Ford, for whom he had recently secured the abbacy of Meaux, together with Geoffrey, prior of Llanthony. Thus Gerald had among his opponents four Cistercian abbots and one grey monk.[4] But the worst was yet to come. Forced for the third time to make the journey to Rome, a lack of ready money drove him to raise cash on his library. According to his own story, this had been housed since 1198 at Strata Florida; he now approached the abbot, who agreed to take the books into pawn. When all had been arranged one of the monks persuaded the abbot that such a course was contrary to the Cistercian statutes; they might buy books but not advance a loan upon them. Faced with this emergency at the very moment of departure, Gerald had no alternative but to sell the books.[5] How far in all this Gerald's account of facts and motives can be trusted must always remain a matter of opinion; the hostile feelings that ensued are, however, beyond a doubt, and Strata Florida was added as fifth to the four other monastic houses, Bittlesden, Whitland, Dore and St Dogmael's, against which this resentment burned. To these must be added the community of Christ Church, Canterbury, which had espoused the cause of the archbishop in the suit against Menevia. The observant reader of the books written at this time (1198–1203) will not fail to see that, with certain insignificant exceptions, these, his personal enemies and their communities, are the only monks against whom he levels his criticisms. The same cannot be said of his last work, the *Speculum Ecclesiae*, though here, too, his personal enemies occupy no inconsiderable place. This book, which its author had projected as early as 1190, was receiving additions at least as late as 1215–16.[6] So far as is known, it exists only in a single manuscript, which contains notes made by Gerald himself, and it was perhaps never published during his lifetime. It is by far the most painful of his books to read. Lacking the cohesion which the narrative form imposes on much of Gerald's earlier work, it consists

1 *De Rebus a se Gestis* (I, 95).

2 He was a relative of Gerald, who calls him *consobrinus* (*De Invectionibus* (III, 34); cf. cognatum vestrum, *De Rebus a se Gestis* (I, 179)). Gerald further asserts that Hubert Walter put him up to draw off the support of other relations.

3 *De Rebus a se Gestis* (I, 104).

4 For the Cistercian abbots and Walter of St Dogmael's, Gerald's works should be consulted, *passim*. For Alexander of Ford, *v.s.* p. 367.

5 *De Rebus a se Gestis* (I, 117); *Speculum Ecclesiae* (IV, 154–5).

6 *Itinerarium Kambriae*, VI, 47: "Sicut in libro quem de ecclesiasticis ordinibus, Deo annuente, scripturi sumus, plenius explicabitur." In the *Speculum Ecclesiae* (IV, 94) there is a reference to the Fourth Lateran Council.

for the most part of a catalogue of instances of monastic corruption and depravity. *Quidquid agunt monachi*. . . . Yet for all the length of the book, Gerald deals with surprisingly few concrete, individual cases, and several even of these are related without names or with only the vaguest of references. Some of them can indeed be identified from his other works, for Gerald was no foe to the maxim that what is best will bear repetition, while his unfortunate experiences in the abbeys of Wales, and in particular the incident of the library lost at Strata Florida,[1] are constantly reappearing when least expected, in some such manner as does the consulate of 63 B.C. in Cicero's later speeches, or the memory of King Charles's head in the conversation of Mr Dick.

IV

When the historian comes to assess the value of Gerald's arraignment of contemporary monasticism a kind of paralysis invades him; he has a sense that he is hunting in a nightmare or grappling with wraiths. For to suppose that Gerald had the intention, similar to that of a later reformer or modern critic, of arraigning the monks of his time before the bar of the world's or posterity's judgment, is to attribute to his mind a consistency and a purpose which it did not possess. He was but a keen, critical, perhaps we may even feel at times a morbid, spectator;[2] he had moved for the greater part of his manhood in the circles of courts and schools whither gravitated all that was least settled in the intellectual life of the times, and where numberless acute minds, perpetually witnessing the intrigues of ecclesiastics and serving as a clearing-house for all scandals, were unhindered in all that they said or wrote by any responsibility of office or by the standards of sobriety which common consent, sanctioned by law, has imposed upon all who publish books at the present day. His criticisms, therefore, like those which a wronged or wounded man utters in private conversation, are often thrown out with no ulterior purpose whatsoever.

Beyond this, it is almost always singularly difficult to grip one of Gerald's stories and (to use the phrase) nail it to the counter. When is he telling the exact truth concerning an incident of which he has himself been witness? When is he recording a mass of hearsay accretions which have crystallized round a core of fact? When is he merely retailing a legend so remote from the facts as to be little more than a *fabliau* or a *ben trovato*? On occasion the reader can be tolerably certain of the answer to such questions; more often he is forced to leave the anecdote in a kind of penumbra which conceals the boundaries of fact and fiction.

1 Cf. *Speculum Ecclesiae* (IV, 161), where he says: "quae [*sc.* loss of the books] vix quidem a scriptoris et operis hujus auctoris mente recedit."
2 It is impossible not to feel that the struggle for Menevia left Gerald's mind morbidly sore on some points. And there would appear to have been a real psychological weakness where sexual matters were in question.

With regard to the black monks, the first and on the whole the most severe charges are brought against the cells where only a few monks, or even only a single individual, were in residence. Here it is probable that facts went far to justify the indictment. These small country priories and cells, unorganized as monasteries and accomplishing no work for the Church, had no sufficient spiritual *raison d'être*; inevitably their personnel was inferior, and their observance incomplete; under such conditions worse would often follow.

After the cells, Gerald criticizes the rich diet of the black monks. Excess in matters of food and drink has always formed a wide and attractive target for satirists from Lucilius and Juvenal to Dryden and Swift. Eighty years before Gerald wrote, the topic of Cluniac meals had supplied material for some of Bernard's most brilliant pages; the monastic good cheer was to continue as a commonplace until the Reformation and beyond, and the evidence of the chronicles of the twelfth century shows that in many, perhaps in most, of the great black monk houses the food was varied and doubtless excellently cooked, and that a hierarchy of feasts had been established with extra pittances and rounds of wine. It does not, however, strengthen Gerald's case that in a book not completed in 1215 he should take as his three palmary examples an incident at Christ Church in 1180, another at Winchester of the same date, and a third, apparently at Hereford, which may indeed rest upon a substratum of truth, but which reads like an adaptation of the fourth satire of Juvenal.[1]

After gluttony, incontinence. In this matter Gerald presents his readers with a few highly coloured stories concerning individuals, almost always unnamed, and a number of general charges. Thus after describing the worldly and luxurious life of an unnamed abbot, in language which reads like a romance,[2] he goes on to insinuate unnatural vice,[3] and continues to give in great detail, but with no names, two cases of this. He then passes to a consideration of the misdeeds of the three abbots of Evesham, Bardney and Westminster,. who were deposed by the legate Nicholas of Tusculum; in the case of Evesham, which can be checked from Marleberge's narrative, he is substantially correct, though he gives no adequate account of the previous history of Roger Norreys or of the detestation with which he was regarded by the communities of Christ Church and Evesham; of the other two he tells us nothing definite.[4] It must indeed be confessed that Gerald's method of procedure is in effect more odious than he perhaps

---

1 *Speculum Ecclesiae* (IV, 57); cf. the story of the turbot in Juvenal, *Sat.* IV.

2 *Speculum Ecclesiae* (IV, 86). He was a monk of St Augustine's *his nostris diebus* (this in Gerald's idiom would cover any date between 1170 and 1215) who became abbot by simony of a *magnus et opimus* convent. I have not succeeded in tracing him.

3 *Speculum Ecclesiae* (IV, 87): "Absit autem ut Sodomae vitio...congregationem sacram...contaminari posse credere quis praesumat."

4 For the abbots of Bardney and Westminster Gerald is our only source of information; the former he accuses of worldliness and incontinence; of the latter he says merely that he was "non minus caeteris duobus, ut fama ferebat, flagitiosum", *Speculum Ecclesiae* (IV, 92–3).

intended, for he insinuates that depravity was widespread, whereas the chronicles and other literature of *c.* 1200 allow no such general judgment to be passed, and while during his lifetime his attacks were read by a few friends only, they are at the present day in the hands of all interested in medieval history. We have, therefore, no contemporary rejoinder to his strictures, and few are sufficiently familiar with all the sources to criticize them adequately for themselves.

He proposes as a remedy the institution of a system of chapters and visitation, preferably by the Ordinary, on the Cistercian model. The suggestion was not original; as has been seen, it was familiar in Curial circles and was the goal at which Innocent III consistently aimed, and no doubt was a commonplace in all gatherings of clerks. Gerald undoubtedly exaggerates the probable efficacy of the system, while he ignores the causes, legal and historical, lying behind the instances of exemption which he so deplores. Nor does he seem to have reflected that the principal cases of scandal to which he refers were the outcome of the general antinomian struggle for independence of which his own assertion of metropolitan rights at Menevia was such a striking instance. In the event, he lived to see and welcome the application of the visitation system to the black monks.

With regard to the white monks, Gerald's judgments are in some important respects different from those he pronounces on the black. In the first place, as he himself remarks, the Cistercians had no cells, which were always a special object of his attack; next, they were in possession of visitatorial and legislative machinery of whose efficacy he himself had made more than one reassuring test.[1] Consequently, though some of his bitterest abuse is directed to the address of individual Cistercians of whom he had at one time or another fallen foul, there can be no question but that on the whole the white monks fare better at his hands than the black. If we set on one side the many stories of the misdeeds of Welsh abbots and the tale of his own wrongs, of which the whole litany from William Wibert to the lost library is rehearsed anew more than once,[2] and do not take too seriously some anecdotes of Cistercian good cheer,[3] the head and front of their offending is avarice, which leads only too often to injustice. To own fair acres in the neighbourhood of an abbey of the white monks, so Gerald gives his reader to understand, was to invite a repetition of the history of Naboth's vineyard, and he quotes more than once the appropriate line of Virgil.[4] As Whitland did by Tallach, and Strata Florida by

1 *Speculum Ecclesiae* (IV, 102): "Circumspecte vero Cistercienses in his et similibus cavendis sibi providerunt, dum et cellis per totum ordinem carent, et cuncta supervacua et honestati ordini contraria per visitatores et capitula resecare curant." Cf. *ibid.* 114, 121–4.

2 E.g. *Speculum Ecclesiae* (IV, 146–9, 156 *seqq.*, 161 *seqq.*, 232).

3 *Speculum Ecclesiae* (IV, 208–18). These stories, even more than the generality of Gerald's anecdotes, have a ring about them which suggests that they were old favourites or *raconteurs* in the circle of Map, and that they reposed upon the most fragile basis of fact.

4 Virgil, *Ecl.* IX, 28: "Mantua, vae, miserae nimium vicina Cremonae."

a poor nunnery under Plynlimmon, so did Aberconway by the simple culdees of Beddgelert.[1] Sometimes even the brood preys on itself, and he tells us of the absorption of Trescoit by the rich Dore and of the persecution of Neath by Margam;[2] more often parish churches are left desolate by the white monks. How far the particular stories, and the interpretation put upon them, are merely the issue of scandal or jealousy, it is quite impossible to determine. The Cistercians were excellent farmers, as all contemporaries admit and as Gerald himself in more than one emphatic passage asserts, and, as modern commercial life has repeatedly shown, it is not always easy to distinguish between the jealous complaints of inefficient competitors and the charges of real injustice brought against an all-powerful syndicate or a multiple-branch store. Gerald, we may think, like the children in the market-place, is not easy to satisfy: the black monks are a scandal to him by reason of their inefficiency, the white by their sound business methods. To modern readers in particular, too long familiar with a countryside where agricultural prosperity is a thing of the past, the picture so often given in his pages of the smiling, rich and well-ordered fields and pastures, which gave to the environs of a Cistercian abbey the appearance of a rose of Sharon in the desert, outweighs the charge of adding field to field, and although to-day we may feel deeply the loss of the smallest fringe of woodland, it is difficult to accept as a crime the deforestation of three hundred acres of a remote Herefordshire valley in the twelfth century, even though its sylvan charms and sporting possibilities are set out in some of the most vivid pages that Gerald ever penned.[3]

Yet for all his accusations and abuse, some of which is indeed harsh enough, and although he asserts more than once that the white habit has become black as soot[4] with stains that resist all the fuller's art and the strength of the most mordant lye,[5] Gerald retains a very deep reverence for the white monks and an earnest hope that all may yet be well. Whether this is merely the outcome of a desire to witness to the truth, or whether he never wholly forgot the pleasant associations of the distant past, and old friendship and kindnesses at Margam[6] and Strata Florida, we cannot

1 *Speculum Ecclesiae* (IV, 143–5, 152–3, 167).
2 *Speculum Ecclesiae* (IV, 205–6, 129–39; *et alibi*).
3 *Speculum Ecclesiae, passim*, especially IV, 186–93. It is unfortunate that the manuscript is greatly damaged in these pages; some of the descriptions show a real sense of natural beauty, e.g. (IV, 190): "tam proceris arboribus ilicibusque rectis et altis per totum robur inferius levibus ac planis, et in ipsa solum summitate frondosis, et tanquam in vertice crispatis, naturali artificio quodam ad delicias intuentium ordinate dispositis, etc."
4 He quotes more than once Ovid, *Metamorph.* II, 541: "Qui color albus erat nunc est contrarius albo."
5 *Speculum Ecclesiae* (IV, 117): "Tam tenaciter et tanquam inseparabiliter ordini sacro dictae maculae naevus adhaesit, quod nullo nitro, nulla fullonis herba, hactenus ablui valuerit aut deleri."
6 Gerald, it would seem, had often before 1188 enjoyed the hospitality of the learned and discreet abbot Cunan at Margam, *caritativa largitione laudatissimus* (*Itinerarium Kambriae*, 67), and more than once he relates of him something approaching to a miracle.

tell. Whatever the motive, the fact remains, and one of the most eloquent and sincere passages in the *Speculum Ecclesiae* is a prayer that the alms and works of charity of the Cistercians may even now bring about an outpouring of grace that shall leave the order in the snow-white purity of its origins.[1] Indeed, the more carefully his pages are studied, the stronger is the impression received that essentially the white monks were still true to the spirit of prayer, work and charity, and that Gerald realized this and wished to record it, as he recorded many times the vigilance and success of their system of discipline.

Besides his charges against the monks, Gerald makes one or two general judgments of considerable interest. Thus he states (or perhaps introduces another as stating) that the black monks on the Continent are far more remiss than their English brethren, while on the other hand the French Cistercians are stricter than the English. He adds as an incontrovertible fact that the monks who come from France to cells belonging to their abbeys are far worse offenders against their Rule than English monks in cells.[2] Here, as always, it is not easy to say whether Gerald is giving his mature and settled opinion. Probably, in this case, he is; probably, also, his opinion is tolerably correct. The reader of these pages will have had ample opportunity of forming a judgment on the black monks; as regards the Cistercians, no student of English monastic history in the twelfth century can have failed to remark on a certain absence of distinction in the annals of the white monks, with the important exception of the houses north of the Humber and the Ribble, with which Gerald had no first-hand acquaintance.

Gerald never wavers in his admiration for the Carthusians,[3] and he has a predilection (shared by Henry II) for the order of Grandmont, though in his account of the origins and constitutions of these he shows the same lack of exact information as in his narrative of the origins of Cîteaux. He has besides some characteristic personal likings. He had lived at Lincoln when Hugh of Avalon was bishop, and although there is nothing

---

1 *Speculum Ecclesiae* (IV, 117): "Forsan autem eveniet, gratia desuper inspirante, quod per ordinis orationes ac merita totius per orbem universum tam longe lateque diffusum ac dilatatum, praecipueque propter eleemosynas tantas et caritatis opera, necnon et hospitalitatis officia praeclara, quibus infatigabiliter cunctis praeeminet et praecellit, totum evanescet in brevi quod dedecuit, niveumque de caetero corpus indecens omnis et inconveniens, per Dei gratiam, menda relinquat." It is an interesting example of Gerald's methods of thought and consistency of opinion that this passage is found to be little more than an amplification of one written some twenty years previously in *Itinerarium Kambriae*, 43. A good specimen of his inaccuracy may be seen in his account of Cistercian origins, *Speculum Ecclesiae* (IV, 111–14).

2 *Speculum Ecclesiae* (IV, 45).

3 *V.* esp. *Speculum Ecclesiae* (IV, 248 *seqq.*), but his incidental references are all consistent e.g. (IV, 194) referring to Adam II of Dore, who had been a clerk and a black monk previously: "utinam...qui saltum duplicem...de statu clericali scilicet ad ordinem Cluniacensem, a Cluniacensi quoque ad Cisterciensem...tertium subsequenter in ordinis Cartusiensis carcerem, omni tam edacitatis nimiae quam cupiditatis multae [MS. mude] notabili naevo carentem, etc."

to show that he had close or indeed any personal relations with the saint, he must have had numberless opportunities of speaking with his entourage. It is therefore somewhat surprising that his brief life of St Hugh, though unexceptionable in tone, should be a colourless piece of work which adds little to our knowledge either of the saint or of his biographer.[1] More personal is his persevering memory of Baldwin's early kindness, repeated during their Welsh tour and never forgotten, though from time to time Gerald lets fall derogatory expressions concerning the archbishop.[2] His constant admiration for Henry of Winchester is less comprehensible. It is possible, though there is no explicit evidence, that Gerald himself had received some kindness at the hands of the old bishop in the mellow days at the end of his life; certainly he lavishes on him praise such as he gives to no other,[3] though Henry's conduct in the past had offended against so many of the monastic proprieties.

Gerald of Wales, throughout his works and in all the changes of his life, remains something of an enigma, a strange compound of prejudice and perspicacity, of superficiality and insight, of vanity and zeal, of fervent aspirations and unworthy utterances. He learnt nothing and forgot nothing, and though he was seventy or more when he revised his latest writings they are as inconsistent and irresponsible as his earliest works. It is perhaps this very characteristic of irresponsibility, joined to the vivacity which never wholly forsook him, that has caused almost all who have studied his pages to extend to him an indulgence usually accorded only to the warm and hasty aberrations of youth, and to allude to his prejudices, his obscenities and his calumnies in a tone of banter. Yet Gerald must bear the responsibility of having aspersed the fair fame of a whole class of men, the majority of whom were sincerely striving to follow a high ideal, and of having done so in a way which gave those whom he attacked no means of replying, and which has poisoned the ears of countless readers in later centuries. Lightly as all profess to treat him, more than one weighty writer on monastic history has insensibly adopted Gerald's opinions and conclusions, and he has thus come to occupy among the sources of history a position of importance which is out of proportion to

1 *Opera*, VII, 83 *seqq.* The editor, E. A. Freeman, remarks in his preface, p. liv: "In the life of St Hugh we see Gerald at once at his best and his worst. He is at his worst because he is at his best . . . because he was simply setting down what he had heard and read." The epigram is scarcely justified. The composition is neither Gerald's worst nor his best: it is colourless.

2 Gerald often speaks of Baldwin. Besides *Itinerarium Kambriae*, 148, v. esp. *Speculum Ecclesiae* (IV, 76–80 and 104 *seqq.*). In the last passage—a quintessentially Geraldic episode—there is the most pleasing portrait. The incident related must have taken place at least later than summer, 1180, for Baldwin was already bishop. Gerald therefore must have been at least thirty-four, yet he refers to Abbot Serlo's admiration for his fleeting youthful beauty: "eram autem tunc adolescens . . . facie quoque fragili . . . formae nitore praeclarus." In later life his large and bushy eyebrows were a distinguishing feature (*De Jure et Statu Menevensis Ecclesiae*, III, 293). Serlo was an Englishman *a Wiltunia* (Map, *Nug. Cur.* 70); he died in 1181 (*Ann. Waverl., s.a.*).

3 Esp. in *Vita S. Remigii* (VII, 43 *seqq.*) and *Speculum Ecclesiae* (IV, 80–1).

KMO

43

his worth. When all is said, it is not easy to account for his extreme animus against the monastic body. Had he himself, in his youth, felt the call to a perfect following of Christ, and chosen instead the ambitious career of preferment and celebrity?[1]

V

In any discussion of the literature that proceeded from the court circle of clerks the name of Walter Map is necessarily associated with that of Gerald of Wales. The careers of the two men had many points of similarity and contact. Both were by blood and birth connected with Wales;[2] both had studied in Paris;[3] both were archdeacons; both spent much time at court; both were familiar with the Lincoln of St Hugh;[4] both strove unsuccessfully for the office of bishop,[5] and they shared many of the tastes and opinions that counted for much in their lives.

Map, it would seem, was the older of the two by a few years. If less complex and less sympathetic in character than Gerald, he was possessed of a keener wit and a more decisive temperament. Gerald's admiration for him was very great, and we owe to this almost all that is known of Map's pursuits and qualities save what can be deduced from his own pages; indeed, it is possible that the brilliant, hard, cynical mind of the arch-deacon of Oxford had a moulding influence on Gerald's more receptive spirit.[6] Certainly, with his great natural talents and his friendship with Henry II, Map must have been a force of considerable power in creating a "public opinion" in the administrative circles where the highest figures

---

1 Gerald once in early life asked of a Welsh hermit to pray for him that he might under-stand Scripture. The hermit, whose Latin was weak, replied: "Och, och, noli dicere scire sed custodire; vana, vana est scire nisi custodire" (*De Rebus a se Gestis*, I, 90). He had perhaps judged Gerald more truly than he knew.

2 Map = Ap = 'son of'. It would seem to have been a current sobriquet for a Welshman. Walter appears to have come from the Herefordshire marches; cf. excellent article in *DNB*. I quote *De Nugis Curialium* from the Camden Society's edition, as being more accessible than the far superior text of M. R. James in *Anecdota Oxoniensia*, Med. and Mod. Series, 14 (1914).

3 Map had attended the lectures of Gerard la Pucelle (*N.C.* 73): "vidi...in schola magistri Girardi Puellae." Cf. Giraldus, *ep.* xxiv (I, 271).

4 Map was precentor of Lincoln before St Hugh's arrival; the collocation of characters is a strange one, but of the relations of the two nothing is known, save that on one occasion Hugh refused to forward Map's candidature for the see of Hereford.

5 Map was in the running for Hereford in 1199, and Gerald recommended him (some-what half-heartedly) for St David's in 1203, *De Jure et Statu Menev. Ecclesiae* (III, 321). I have not noticed any explicit statement that either Map or Gerald were in priest's orders.

6 Gerald's references are always laudatory, e.g. *De Jure et Statu Menev. Ecclesiae* (III, 335): "Duo viri literati plurimum et in scripturis affatim eruditi...scilicet mag. Robertus de Bello-fago...et mag. Galterus Mapus"; *Speculum Ecclesiae* (IV, 140): "Vir ille celebri fama conspicuus et tam literarum copia quam curialium quoque verborum facetia praeditus"; *ibid.* 219. How far the curious letter to Map, *ep.* xxiv (I, 271 *seqq.*) was serious is questionable.

in lay and ecclesiastical life met and mixed. If Gerald is more critical of the black than of the white monks, Map's hostility, so far as it can be traced in his book *De Nugis Curialium* and the few genuine poems, is reserved almost exclusively for the Cistercians, against whom he proceeds in a chapter of great violence, consisting, like similar passages in the *Speculum Ecclesiae*, of bitter general accusations, mingled with a number of isolated examples and a fair proportion of ribaldry, a compound which Gerald thinks fit to characterize as urbane and witty criticism, seasoned with the salt of wisdom.[1] As with Gerald, so with Map, the primary cause of this hostility must probably be assigned to the recollection of a wrong, real or imaginary, suffered at the hands of the white monks, for there is no reason to disbelieve the account his friend gives of the loss incurred by Map in his revenues from the church of Westbury in Dean as a result of the alleged encroachments of the neighbouring Cistercians of Flaxley.[2] It was in consequence of this supposed act of injustice that Map added to his judge's oath, by which he swore to do justice to all, an excepting clause covering Jews and Cistercians.[3] Of the two bodies, in fact, Map professed to prefer the former; when Gerald related to him a sad story of two white monks becoming Jews Map remarked that it was strange that, having decided to change their lives for the better, they had not made the conversion complete by becoming Christians.[4] These, and other still more bitter, coarse and heartless gibes were not mere flashes of wit or outbursts of passion, but the manifestation of a deep and implacable hostility[5] on the part of one who was no private satirist, but a man in high public office, who had the ear of the king himself.

Map's principal charge is one of shameless and remorseless avarice.

1 *Speculum Ecclesiae* (IV, 219): "Ad sales saporifero sapientiae sale conditos urbanasque reprehensiones...W. Mapi...vertamus."

2 *Ibid.*: "In primis causam commotionis et exasperationis hujus in ordinem istum palam proponere dignum duximus. Monasterium igitur quoddam...partem ecclesiae de Westburi grandem...in detrimentum ejusdem ecclesiae non modicum occupaverunt; propter quod maxime in domum illam ordinemque totum exacerbatus plurimum fuit et conturbatus." Cf. Map's own words in *N.C.* 57: "Ego autem de his...quod scio...loquor nec inexpertus."

3 *Speculum Ecclesiae* (IV, 219): "Semper adjicere solebat se cunctis...praeterquam Judaeis et albis monachis fidelem pro posse futurum."

4 *Speculum Ecclesiae* (IV, 140). Here again Map's enmity, or as Gerald calls it his *urbana eloquentia*, is attributed to the Flaxley incident. How far the story of the visits of the abbot of Flaxley and Map to each other urging conversion, when each in turn was supposed to be dying, is simply a *ben trovato* cannot be decided with certainty.

5 Cf. *Speculum Ecclesiae* (IV, 221) for a heartless, indeed blasphemous, action of Map which Gerald introduces with the statement: "noverat [rex Henricus] enim animum ejus huic ordini per omnia contrarium, cunctisque negotiis et agendis ejus quantum poterat adversarium." Map, whether he wrote them or not, would certainly not have disowned the verses (*Latin Poems attributed to Walter Map*, 56) *de Grisiis Monachis*:

> "Duo sunt qui nesciunt satis detestari,
> quae exosa sentio coelo, terra, mari,
> quibus omnis regio solet devastari,
> quibus nullo studio potest obviari,
> Pestis animalium, quae shuta vocatur,
> et Cisterciensium quae sic dilatatur."

The Cistercians will do anything to extend the boundaries of their land;[1] their rule requires that they should dwell in a solitude; if, therefore, they cannot find one, they make it for themselves;[2] they destroy villages and churches and allow the outcast inhabitants to die of want or earn a little bread by crime or shame; they forge their charters and cozen the rightful owners of the land, and the fields of waving corn cover the site of a populous village.[3] Map does not share Gerald's admiration for Cistercian hospitality and charity; as to the former, it is only bestowed on the great and the gullible, not on the children of Egypt; as for the latter, they dispense in alms to Paul far less than they have robbed from Peter.[4] They vaunt their hard labour, rough clothes and coarse food,[5] but the upland Welsh have a far more rough and laborious life than the white monks.[6] And Map passes to a piece of ribaldry on the abandonment of breeches by the Cistercians.

It would be uncritical to treat as a serious pronouncement such an outpouring as this. We are indeed justified in adding Map as one more witness to the undoubted tendency among the white monks throughout England, and especially perhaps in Wales, to carry their spirit of thrift and keen husbandry to excess, and to throw the cloak of obedience to the letter of their rule over actions whose real motive was *esprit de corps* and aggrandizement. But Map, perhaps even more than Gerald, lacked both balance of mind and ethical sobriety; to the deeper aspects of the Christian life he was quite blind, and therefore failed to see any of its manifestations in those around him.[7]

From Map, as from Gerald, a number of details can be gleaned. He also, but more correctly than his friend, describes the origins of Cistercians, Carthusians and Grandimontines.[8] Indeed, points of contact between the two are all but innumerable. They shared an acquaintance with Abbot Hamelin of Gloucester and Abbot Serlo of L'Aumône, an Englishman by birth; they both admired Baldwin, whom they had known when bishop of Worcester; both took an interest in hermits.[9] One of the most pleasing

---

1 Map (*N.C.* 53–4) mentions the tale, given in greater detail by Gerald, *Speculum Ecclesiae* (IV, 225–7), of the thorn-tree, a conspicuous landmark, shifted and replanted by the monks of Byland.

2 *N.C.* 48: "Et ut soli sint, solitudinem faciunt." Had the *Agricola* of Tacitus been known at the time, Map would have had a still more telling epigram.

3 *N.C.* 48: "Ut...dicere possis: 'Nunc seges est, ubi Troia fuit'" (Ovid, *Ep.* i, 53). For us, a sentiment exactly the reverse of Map's is evoked by such names as Chalk Farm or Shepherd's Bush.

4 *N.C.* 51–2.

5 *N.C.* 51. An interesting admission (here agreeing with Gerald) of the Cistercian discipline and observance. 6 *N.C.* 52.

7 One who could not only utter, with all its circumstances, but commit to writing some years later such a piece of obscenity as that in *N.C.* 42, can clearly make no pretensions to judge of spiritual things.

8 The two latter orders were patronized by Henry II. This probably accounts for the special attention devoted to them by the two court clerics.

9 *N.C.* 69, 70. Had Map also been to school at Gloucester?

passages in the *De Nugis Curialium* is an appreciation of the work of Gilbert of Sempringham, who was alive when the words were written, but Gilbert had influence with Henry II, and adverse criticism would not have been welcomed.[1]

VI

Gerald of Wales and Walter Map were but two outstanding figures in a whole army of contemporary satirists. The *genre* was fashionable among those who had passed through the training of the schools, and the mood suited the forty years between the murder of Becket and the death of John, a period full of disillusion without the great figures and ideals that had given their stamp to the first half of the century. To such an extent was satire, and satire of the monastic orders, the vogue in all polite circles, that a black monk is found among the leading practitioners. Nigel Wireker was a monk of Christ Church, Canterbury, an exact contemporary of Gervase and, like him, an active participant in the struggle between the convent and the archbishop.[2] He was the author of several satirical works in prose and verse which had a considerable reputation throughout the remaining centuries of the Middle Ages; chief among them is the *Speculum Stultorum*, which relates the adventures of a dissatisfied monk and gives his judgment on the various orders together with the reasons which prevented him from joining each.[3] His criticisms, compared with those of Gerald and Map, are restrained, and the striking similarity between the three in the points selected for satire, and the facility with which a black monk is willing to satirize the Cluniacs, indicates that there was a floating body of commonplaces from which all drew.[4]

Wireker accuses the Cluniacs of eating meat even on Fridays,[5] and of wearing expensive garments; the system of cells is also criticized, though with some ambiguity. The hardships of their life are the midnight office

---

1 *N.C.* 59.

2 The earliest authority for his surname appears to be Bale, and for his having held the office of precentor, Leland. His share in the controversies at Canterbury is clear from *Epp. Cant.*, and from his works it may be gathered that he was a client, perhaps a relative, of William Longchamp the Chancellor.

3 Nigel has been edited by Wright in *Anglo-Latin Satirical Poets of the XII century*, vol. I. The *Speculum Stultorum* or, as it came to be called, *Dan Burnel the Ass*, is the subject of an allusion in Chaucer which proves it to have been familiar in his day, as indeed is shown by the number of MSS in existence. Cf. *Nonnes Preestes Tale*, line 492, where "daun Russell the Fox" is introduced as saying:
"I have wel rad in daun Burnel the Asse."

4 As the context shows, Nigel refers to Cluny itself. Not only does he give the name of the mother-abbey in his first line (p. 83) on the subject:
"esse Niger Monachus si forte velim Cluniaci,"
but he goes on to describe aspects of the constitutional system of Cluny.

5 Ed. Wright, 83:
"Multotiens carnes et pinguia saepe vorare
in feria sexta saepe licebit eis.
Pellicias portant, etc."

and the exhausting chant.[1] The white monks provide the aspirant with nothing but the two dishes of the Rule, with much hard work and little rest;[2] they eat no meat, but include birds in their scheme of diet. Their vice is avarice, which tolerates no neighbour and is never content with plenty;[3] less space is, however, devoted to this fault than to a consideration of the advantages and disadvantages arising from their lack of breeches, a subject which proved an inexhaustible source of material for coarse pleasantry; the frequency with which it is exploited is a sufficient indication of the moral earnestness of the writer concerned. Nigel then passes the other orders in review, dwelling on the severity of the Carthusians and the Grandimontines; the black canons are reasonable, the white, rigorous and simple; for the secular canons he has nothing but hard words. Finally, the Gilbertines, here as in Map, are spoken of with a respect bordering almost on affection.[4] Of all the orders he makes the complaint that they have forgotten poverty and amassed wealth, but his language here, as indeed throughout the bulk of his work, is very general, and it is clear that he is merely developing a literary topic.

1 *Ibid.*: "Surgere me facient media de nocte, etc." A reference to the elaborate liturgy of Cluny, which led to all kinds of variations and anticipations in the hour of the night office.

2 *Ibid.* 84:

> "Si fuero monachus albus generalia dura
> hi pulmenta duo, sed bene cocta, dabunt.
> .   .   .   .   .   .
> sabbata rara colunt, male respondente coquina;
> est ibi virga frequens atque diaeta gravis."

3 *Ibid.*:

> "Agrorum cupidi nunquam metas sibi poni
> vicinis vellent pestis iniqua suis. . . .
> paucis contenti, non cessant quaerere magna
> et cum possideant omnia, semper egent."

4 *Ibid.* 94:

> "Est et adhuc alius nuper novus ordo repertus.
> quem bene, nam bonus est, commemorare decet.
> Simplingham dictus de simplicitate vocatus, etc."

CHAPTER XL

REVIEW OF THE PERIOD 943–1216

I

At the end of these pages, looking back over three centuries from a date which, though marked by no great catastrophe, is yet in a real sense a moment of division, a watershed which separates the epoch of religious and intellectual awakening in Europe from that of the maturity of medieval culture, it is permissible to gather up the threads of the preceding chapters into a single pattern, and to look at the monastic life of England as it lies spread out before us, from the early manhood of Dunstan to the death of Innocent III.

Between those two dates the numerical increase and diffusion of the monastic body in England and Wales had been truly prodigious. In 943 there was in existence scarcely a single fully regular monastic community; in 1216 there were over a hundred large monasteries of black monks, some seventy abbeys of Cistercians, and a multitude of lesser communities and groups, to say nothing of the quasi-monastic families of the regular canons, themselves almost as numerous as the monks. In default of any reliable data it is impossible to hazard a precise estimate of the total population of these houses; it probably attained its maximum *c.* 1150 and had already sensibly declined by 1216; but in the latter half of the twelfth century the number of black monks in the country cannot have been less than some figure between four and five thousand, while that of the white monks, including lay brethren, may well have been almost as great.[1] We may indeed think that the point of saturation had been reached or passed, that a number of the foundations, especially of the Cistercians, had been made to satisfy the wishes of benefactors rather than the intrinsic requirements of the religious situation, and that it would have been well to call a halt before 1153 and to safeguard the spirit of early fervour and observance. Certainly in later centuries, when the orders of friars had arrived and the influx of recruits to the monastic orders had slackened, the great number of houses in existence was a source of weakness rather than of strength. In all such matters it is more easy to be wise after the event than to perceive the moment for caution when the tide of success is still at the flood, but the apprehensions of the chapter of Cîteaux in 1152 and of Sempringham thirty years later show that even at the time the dangers of overgrowth were realized.

---

1 If the total number of monks and canons be put at *c.* 15,000 and the population of the country at three million, it will appear that the religious amounted to between 1 and 2 per cent. of the adult males of England.

The possessions of the monasteries in land and in every kind of wealth and influence were even greater than their numbers might seem to warrant. Already at the Conquest, as has been seen, the black monks owned roughly one-sixth of the cultivated land and actual rents of England south of the Humber and Mersey. After the Conquest their possessions, to which were soon added those of the white monks, steadily increased, and although the total wealth of the country was also everywhere increased by the reduction of waste to cultivation, by the development of sheep farming and by the growth of trade, the share of the monks in the whole was without doubt greater in 1170 than in 1066, and perhaps amounted to a quarter or even to a third of the total wealth of the country in lands, rents and dues. Above all, they had grown in wealth and influence in ecclesiastical property, and were the owners or patrons of perhaps a quarter of the churches of England. To this must be added the ownership of so many great fabrics and groups of buildings stored, at least where the black monks were masters, with precious objects of all kinds and housing almost all the artistic treasures and books of the land.

But while the graph of material and financial increase had continued to rise all but continuously from the time of Dunstan to the accession of Henry II, and continued to rise still, though less steeply, after that date, the significance of the monastic order, and its position in the life of society and of the Church had altered profoundly between 970 and 1154. The former date lies well within the limits of the "monastic centuries"; by the latter year the monastic order had all but ceased to have any directive or formative influence over the spiritual and intellectual life of the Church and nation.

Under Edgar and Dunstan the revived monasticism had been the very heart and soul of the rebirth of the country; from the monasteries came the rulers of the Church for two generations, and the same men were the controlling influence in the social and political life of their times. In the monasteries, from 950 to 1050, was all that was purest in the spiritual, intellectual and artistic life of England. They were, indeed, especially between 950 and 1000, the very core and kernel of the nation, and by their achievement in the transmission of the heritage of the past and in the execution of works of literature and art they have placed all succeeding generations in their debt.

This phase of their life had passed before the Conquest, largely because its own inner force was spent. It never exactly repeated itself, for the nations of Europe had begun another chapter in their history. Yet the position of the new Anglo-Norman monasticism from 1070 to 1135 was to all appearances as influential as before. The monasteries were more wealthy and more numerous, the abbots and monk-bishops were the most eminent men of their day, and within the abbeys there was a virile and dynamic intellectual and spiritual life which, at least till 1100, was almost the only refining and enlightening power in the land. To the Anglo-Norman monks, as to their Saxon predecessors, the debt of Englishmen is very great. Nevertheless, there was a subtle, if at first almost imperceptible, difference from the Old English era. The monasteries were no longer exclusively the soul of the country, if by the soul be understood the vital, informing principle of life and unity. Alongside of the monasticism was the feudal, secular organization, equally virile and dynamic, and capable of independent action and growth. Moreover, even in the purely ecclesiastical and spiritual realms the paramount influence of monasticism was on the wane. First, the reformed and reforming papacy, next, the new and lettered hierarchy, informed with Hildebrandine principles, and finally, the reawakened mind of Europe, which found expression above all in law and theology, slowly regained the initiative of government and teaching which they had held in the last centuries of the ancient civilization, and which they were never again to lose to the monks.

This new era had opened in all essentials before 1050 in Italy, and by 1100 had extended its influence over all north-western Europe outside the bounds of the Anglo-Norman *Landeskirche*. North of the Alps, however, the retreat of the monastic influence was arrested and to all appearances changed into a wholly victorious advance by the emergence of the Cistercians and their employment as the storm-troops of Christendom by Bernard. Bernard's exploitation of the zeal and organization of the white monks may seem, indeed, in some sense a *coup d'état* of the monastic body, but though to contemporaries Clairvaux appeared to inherit the mantle of Cluny, of Gorse, of Bec and of the other early centres of new life, Bernard was in fact fighting with new weapons—a rational organization and a new education—which were not peculiar, or even proper, to the monastic life as such, and the combat was for dominion in the purely ecclesiastical sphere, not in the cultural. When, in 1153, he and Eugenius III passed away, all specifically monastic influence upon the policy of the Church at large ceased at once and for ever. And at almost the same moment the monastic culture of England, which seventy years before had received from Normandy all that was best in the Europe of that day, began to languish in isolation and then to disappear before the new education of the schools. Henceforward the monastic order, and above all, in our period, the order of the black monks, crystallized slowly into what it was to remain in England until the Reformation, an element of great importance in the religious, social and economic life of the nation, but no longer its principal, still less its sole spiritual or intellectual force.

Simultaneously with the passing of the monastic culture there passed also the literary humanism of the first European renaissance. If in philosophy, canon law and theology, if in architecture, sculpture and the kindred arts the development followed a steady and unbroken course from the days of Bernard to those of Aquinas, the sentiment of Europe and the faculty of expression tended, at least in the higher circles of the Church, to lose much of their earlier warmth and flexibility. The great bishops and theologians of the thirteenth century were, as lawyers and thinkers, immeasurably more precise and profound than the contemporaries of John of Salisbury, but the cultivated minds of the earlier age were no less superior in their width of sympathy and in their ability to give measured expression to their emotions and dignified shape to their thought. The most celebrated masters of the schools could write no letters like those of Anselm, of Bernard, or of John of Salisbury, and the works of Matthew Paris, though perhaps more gaily coloured, show far less of classical form and true critical power than do those of William of Malmesbury. Whether the decline of humanism and broad refinement of mind among the educated classes was in any sense a remote consequence of the transference of cultural leadership from the monasteries is a question that cannot be answered here; it is at least certain that the monastic culture had been classical and humane, within its narrow limits, and that this humanity is not found in the fully developed universities of northern Italy, France and England.

II

Although the monasticism of Dunstan and his colleagues had so soon become a part of the national life, it was in origin a purely spiritual birth. It was the work of saints and, so far as its originators were concerned, made no compromise with interests that were not spiritual. The early monasteries of the revival were not entangled in any secular organization, and their rule of life was the pure Rule of St Benedict, modified only by the liturgical developments of the centuries. But, as has been said on an earlier page, they gave nothing new to monasticism, either in the purely religious sphere or in that of constitutional development or external employment. The houses of the *Concordia* were thus simply a variety of the species common to Europe and centuries old; they were a new growth on the old trunk.

The Norman monasticism, on the other hand, and especially that of Bec, though wholly traditional in spirit, did in fact establish a new model. A fervent spirituality, which gave birth to sanctity both recognized and hidden, existed here in the midst of a new culture capable of real achievement in the realm of thought and literature, and it found in John of Fécamp, Anselm and others, and later in such men as Hervé of Déols and Rupert of Deutz, minds capable of formulating and transmitting theological and spiritual teaching both for their own generation and for all time. Hence it is that Bec and the group of houses most nearly akin to it stand as one of the most majestic peaks in the long range of monastic history, and as an example, to which later generations have looked for guidance and inspiration, of the monastic life as lived in a perfection and purity as nearly ideal as is possible in things human. The life of Bec under Anselm was not that of Monte Cassino under Benedict, or of Wearmouth under Benet Biscop, or of Cîteaux under Stephen Harding; it was in many ways more complex, more sophisticated. But it was exemplary, and inasmuch as it was the perfection of a highly organized family, committed to a life in which elaborate ritual and intellectual work had a considerable place, it has served as an inspiration to houses of a similar type and in a similar position ever since its day, just as Cîteaux has been an inspiration to so many movements in the direction of primitive simplicity. England in its measure and for a period shared the spirit of Bec, and though no single house and no single monk could challenge the position of the Norman abbey and its second abbot, many English monasteries and Anglo-Norman abbots were of the same family, and when all allowance has been made for shortcomings here and there, the fifty years that followed Lanfranc's arrival in this country may undoubtedly be looked upon as one of the periods, relatively rare in monastic history, when not only are the external records of the monasteries of a land happy and their work beneficent, but the spiritual forces of the body also are genial and capable of influencing for good all who do not actively elude or repel their attraction.

This fortunate state of things passed in less than a long lifetime. But in the very decades of transition another focus of life appeared in the Cistercian abbeys of northern England. They, too, are a summit. Though in a sense they derived their spirit entirely from abroad, from Cîteaux and Clairvaux, and though the example of Yorkshire is in some ways less luminous and less durable than that of Burgundy, yet Rievaulx and Fountains were, in their measure and for a period, centres and true sources of life and light. With them may worthily be ranked the hermits of Finchale, Farne and the dales; in their rugged solitude and in the direct simplicity of their aim these northerners stood apart from the men of the south and gave to English religious life something without which it would have been the poorer.

III

The monastic vocation, in its primitive form, had been the quest of God, through the pursuit of moral and spiritual perfection, by the individual soul in the desert, "the world forgetting, by the world forgot".[1] This

1 Cf. the words of Abbot Moses, in Cassian's first Conference: "Finis quidem nostrae professionis regnum Dei est, destinatio vero (i.e. the immediate aim) puritas cordis, sine qua ad finem illum impossibile est quempiam pervenire."

aim was in a sense modified by St Benedict; the primary, immediate aim of the Rule is to set the norm and discipline of a regular and virtuous common life for the many. Nevertheless, the personal, individual note remains; the monastery is a training-school of the service of God for each monk; the end is still the progress towards perfection of the soul of the individual.[1]

This purely personal and spiritual conception of the monk's life had, by the time of Dunstan, been largely overlaid by one more material, more social, and more static. This arose, no doubt, in part from the universal practice of child oblation, which included within each monastic family all types of mind and character, and in part from the monopoly of culture enjoyed by the monasteries. Monks were regarded as a class of society, and their life as an *ordo*—an organized, disciplined round of duties. Even for the monk himself the purely spiritual conception of the soul's growth in the love of God had passed into the more superficial, material idea of the *servitium Dei*, the due and regular performance of external obligations. Throughout the early Middle Ages the monks were regarded by their lay contemporaries as the intercessors for the rest of society, divided against those who gave it livelihood by toil and those who defended it by arms. The monasteries therefore were not endowed solely as shrines of adoration or homes of charity, but as houses of public prayer, and when, in the perfected, self-conscious feudal state labour-service and military service were imposed and assessed as necessary functions of different classes, the monks were regarded as executing an equally indispensable social service of intercession. Lands, consequently, given to them "in free alms" carried with them in "tenure by divine service" the obligation of a *quid pro quo* every whit as real as that which derived from the gift of an honor or the assignment of a knight's fee.

For the monk himself, the monastic profession was often now regarded as the holocaust of a human life, made once and for all, and carrying with it an earnest of salvation. Such an attitude finds expression in the common practice of self-oblation by vow at a moment of danger or crisis, and still more characteristically in the dedication of a child. It was typical of the Norman rather than the English character; a classic instance is that of the child Orderic of Shrewsbury, sent by his devout father a sad ten-year-old exile to St Évroul beyond the sea, with the solemn assurance that if he became a monk he would enjoy paradise in the company of the innocent.[2] In such an outlook the emphasis is on the single action in the past, not on the ever-growing knowledge of God in the soul.

More typical of English feeling, though perhaps still more alien to

---

1 Cf. *Regula*, Prol. 116: "Constituenda est ergo nobis dominici schola servitii." *Schola* here, it may be noted, is probably to be understood in its late, military sense. Cf. also the reference (*ibid*. lxxiii, 5) to those who *ad perfectionem conversationis festinant*.

2 OV, v, 134: "Ipse me spopondit ex parte sua, si monachus fierem, quod post mortem meam paradisum cum innocentibus possiderem."

modern habits of thought, was the conception of profession at the shrine of St Edmund or St Cuthbert as a kind of "commendation" to the saint analogous to the commendation of a free landowner to a great lord. Nothing, perhaps, in the religious sentiment of eleventh- and twelfth-century England is harder for us to recapture than the awe with which the material remains of an all but mythical saint were sometimes regarded, and the devotion of those who regarded him as, in a real as well as in a legal sense, the owner of the lands and the protector of the material interests of his servants. Even so late as the close of the twelfth century, and in a mind so virile and realistic as Samson's, this sentiment was of enormous power, joined as it often was to a vivid, if not morbid, conviction of the guilt of sin.[1]

In so far as such accidental modes of thought and sentiment prevailed, they were the outcome of the mental climate of the age. In every century fashions of one kind or another have coloured the external expressions and manifestations of religion in all save the deepest and purest minds. In a Wulfstan, in an Anselm, in an Ailred they give place to the truer, unchanging conception of the monastic profession as the dedication of a soul to the perfect love of God, and it is not the least of the claims of Bernard to our respect that he should have explicitly made of the monastic life what it had been in the early ages, the quest of God by the individual. To this root idea Bernard himself, William of St Thierry and others added a still deeper call, again echoing the purest traditions of the past, and proclaimed the possibility of a real, intimate and conscious union of the soul with its Creator on this side of the grave.

IV

No one who has followed the story of the monks of England during the twelfth century will have failed to note the elements of weakness and of danger in the complex fabric of their organization. Of these elements the most striking, perhaps, is their great wealth and, still more, the source from which this was chiefly drawn, property in land. Wealth, whatever shape or form it may take, has always been and will always remain a most formidable enemy of the religious spirit, for it directly contradicts the standard of values proclaimed by Christ and, if not only used but enjoyed by the possessor, effectually prevents the perfect observance of His commandments. Regarded, therefore, from the spiritual point of view, the form taken by the wealth of the monasteries in the centuries after the Conquest was peculiarly baneful. The monks, and especially the black monks, were great capitalists whose income was not the result of any work or employment of the religious life as such, although its sources could be exploited and increased by the personal efforts of individual

1 For remarks on this v. Böhmer, *Eigenkirchentum in England*, 341 seqq.

monks. Consequently, the whole active employment of great numbers of religious lay in the direct administration of property and in the purely material care of extracting from the land and those who dwelt on it the maximum yield of natural wealth or of money; they were overseers and bailiffs, not tillers of the soil. If the judgment, pronounced originally by Stubbs and often repeated, that a monastery of the thirteenth century was composed of a group of country gentlemen,[1] be held far too summary, and misleading in more than one respect, it nevertheless contains more than one element of truth with which all historians of English monasticism must reckon.

For the possession of extensive properties in land, with all the complex of dues and rights that a manor or liberty carried with it in the Middle Ages, was a direct cause of that corporate selfishness and avarice which is one of the least pleasant features in the monastic literature of the time. *Un père de famille est capable de tout*, and the compiler of more than one monastic cartulary showed himself ready to overstep the bounds of honesty in the interests of his house. This spirit was not imported from Normandy, though far from uncommon there at the end of the eleventh century; it may be seen informing the work of Hemming of Worcester, in the palmy days of Wulfstan; it is the source of that bitterness of tone and harshness of judgment shown by so many monastic chroniclers towards rival bodies or authorities who disputed the claim of the house to property or privilege of any kind, and under its influence were perpetrated the numerous falsifications of documents which have confused the records of so many of the controversies of the early twelfth century. Even if the term "forger", which has acquired peculiarly odious associations, be considered too severe to apply indiscriminately to those who in many cases did but embody real rights and evolutions of privilege in earlier and simpler formularies, or who reconstructed with some freedom damaged or vanished muniments, yet their conduct, which had often received at least the tacit consent of the community and its head, deviated to a greater or less degree from the path of perfect probity, and gave rise to much of the unfriendliness with which a number of the greater houses were regarded by their neighbours.

Of another source of weakness something has already been said. The possession of small and distant dependencies, in which the full monastic life could not be lived, and which were often used as places of exile for *mauvais sujets* or psychological invalids, might seem an advantage to the eyes of opportunism, but was in fact more often deplorable. Innocent as was the origin of many of these priories and cells, founded by those anxious to relieve themselves of the ownership of *Eigenkirchen*, they were

---

1 *Epp. Cant.* introd. cxix. "Their inhabitants [i.e. of the monasteries] were bachelor country gentlemen more polished and more charitable, but little more learned or more pure in life than their lay neighbours."

rarely, in later centuries, an asset, though it must be remembered that a majority of the mere cells were the property of overseas houses, that many of the greatest English monasteries were without a single dependency of the kind, and that others secured a good observance in their priories. Observance, however, is not all; such houses, however regular, lacked a fully responsible spiritual head, and so could never fully realize the life of the Rule.

A third disability, which did not make itself acutely felt till after the limits of our period, was the lack of suitable regular work for the rank and file of a large and varied community. Manual work was a thing of the legendary past, and the purely claustral occupations of study and writing and illumination, which in the simpler society of Europe before c. 1100 had been found adequate, proved less satisfactory when monasteries were no longer the sole or chief centres of culture, and when the writing of books and even their illumination had become a professional and a commercial occupation. The attempts, and the general failure, to supply a substitute belong to later centuries; here it is enough to indicate the problem as it had begun to declare itself in 1216.

Besides the difficulties and dangers resulting from their position in the social and economic life of the nation, the English monasteries which had been caught up into the web of the feudal state had others which were at first peculiar to those holding by military service. Hard as it would have been for members of the Norman *Landeskirche* of the Conqueror and Lanfranc to resist this entanglement—and even such as Wulfstan and Anselm were unable to escape it—it nevertheless carried with it a close connection with merely secular affairs, and its consequences were unfortunate in the extreme. The two principal and most permanent modifications of the monastic life which ensued, the separation of abbot from community and the wholesale devolution of financial and administrative responsibility, have so often been mentioned in these pages that they need not occupy us here. Both were to prove sources of weakness until the Dissolution. Abroad, the former developed rapidly into the system of commendatory abbacies which proved such an obstacle to all domestic attempts at reform in later centuries; in this country the worst abuses were avoided, but the true spiritual character of the office of abbot could rarely be grasped in its full purity when the holder lived apart from his monks, surrounded by his officials and servants, and occupied with a host of cares, personal and public, which had nothing to do with the religious life of those over whom he exercised supreme authority as representative of Christ. Similarly, the obedientiary system, especially when it existed in an establishment from which the religious superior was to some degree separated, could not but tend to weaken the sense of retreat from the world, and the regard for that simplicity of life and community of possession which are essential to the monastic state.

V

A religious or monastic institute will in the last resort prosper or decline in exact proportion to its fidelity to the spirit of its Rule, which interprets and makes concrete for it the comprehensive directions of the gospel. It is, indeed, the function of a Rule to provide for those who obey it a precise directory which, if followed perfectly according to the spirit, and according to the letter also so far as true discretion demands, will lead the individual from strength to strength until he reaches the highest moral and spiritual development of which he is capable.

The *Regularis Concordia* and Lanfranc's Statutes, and the monastic bodies to which they were applied, however they may have differed in circumstances and surroundings from the less complex society of Monte Cassino in 530, were nevertheless faithful to the spirit of St Benedict. Even if it be granted that the life for which they legislate is not one of extreme physical or psychological tension,[1] yet there is no formal decline from the highest ideal, and no weakening of the essential features of the Rule.

The same cannot be said of the bodies of "customs" which were codified and sanctioned at so many houses in the course of the twelfth century. In two or three not unimportant matters, such as the regulation of diet, the standardization of certain exemptions and relaxations, and the entanglement of individuals or the whole body with purely secular interests, these customs did in effect make a serious breach in the Rule, and gave to the communities concerned a kind of charter of rights which might be conceived as mitigating an original severity. Incorporated as they were in documents fixing the life of the house, they lowered the standard of fervour by recognizing a respectable regularity as the norm for all instead of throwing the road open to a higher achievement, and by giving an all but explicit and official recognition to a frame of mind which often found expression in everyday life, that the present generation could not hope to attain to the performance of the past. In the sequel, even under the Lateran system of chapter and visitation, repeated attempts to secure unity and a return to the prescriptions of the Rule were to break themselves in vain against the "old and reasonable" customs of the individual monasteries.

VI

During the seventy years between the foundation of Waverley and the death of Richard I the Cistercian order in England had passed rapidly

---

1 Cf. the judgment of A. Hamilton Thompson in the *Cambridge Medieval History*, vol. v, ch. xx, p. 666: "Lanfranc, in issuing his ordinances..., had in view a well-ordered community, pursuing the life of church and cloister with exemplary decorum and following the Rule without extravagant professions of asceticism. The land-owning monasteries of Domesday...were certainly not homes of an excessively severe discipline."

through several phases of its development. From origins in poverty and obscurity the most celebrated abbeys had grown, almost overnight into vast establishments whose fervour had made them a cynosure; the propagation of the institute and its diffusion into every corner of the land had been spectacular in its rapidity. While many of the first fathers were yet alive the face of England was already covered with the regular and austerely beautiful architecture of the white monks, and her fields and moors tilled by their *conversi* or grazed over by their flocks and herds, and before all the original novices had passed away this vast body was being freely accused in court and cloister of avarice and ambition, and of having fallen away from its first fervour.

Modern writers are, perhaps, too apt to emphasize the contrast between 1130 and 1200. When painting the picture of the first settlements, they often unawares describe Waverley or Rievaulx in terms of the Cîteaux of 1090, ignoring the developments of the first forty years. Similarly, when considering the white monks under Richard I or John, their attention is caught by the strictures of Gerald of Wales or Walter Map, and by a few notorious cases of irregularity, and they neglect not only the scattered indications that have survived to show that real fervour still existed, but also the more abundant, if less striking, evidence that in many quarters a life of quiet and dignified regularity continued to edify and attract those who came into contact with it.

Yet when all exaggeration has been avoided, it remains true that the history of the white monks (and especially, perhaps, in England) appears to show a very rapid decline from the magnificent splendours of its dawn into the toneless light of common day. The pages devoted in earlier chapters to the Cistercians will have suggested that this decline was in part due to the inexorable working out of certain psychological laws. The perfect suitability of the Cistercian way to the social and economic needs of the early twelfth century, and the resounding appeal made by Bernard to the whole of Christendom, changed the gradual and normal increase of a fervent and primitive monastic body into what was in effect a world-movement. Under such circumstances it was inevitable that the vast new body should have more kinship to the society around it than to the nucleus of fervour which had been its first inspiration. The wholesale acquisition of churches, tithes and secular rights; the quest of property for its own sake, and its exploitation for gain, above all where sheep-runs were concerned; the undertaking of ambitious schemes of construction for which money was raised on usury or mortgage; these were all serious departures from the letter and spirit of the early legislation. On the other hand, save in individual cases, the spirit of luxury and relaxation had not invaded the white monk cloisters by 1200, and it was thus possible for the members of a community to achieve a high level of observance and even holiness, although the family to which they belonged

KMO

44

owned buildings and lands which the first fathers would have wished
away.

The Cistercian order had begun its career with three most valuable
assets: the evangelical spirit of the founders of Cîteaux; the detailed and
wise rule of life, exquisitely adapted to the needs of the time; and the
constitutional machinery of the *Carta Caritatis*. The first, the new spirit
of fervour, was at once the most precious and the most volatile. The
saints of Cîteaux, unlike the fathers of the desert or the reformers of
Carmel, left no body of purely spiritual doctrine to enrich the blood of
the Church, and this absence of systematic teaching, at an epoch when
law and theology were in process of codification, told more, perhaps,
than has been generally recognized on the later history of the white
monks.

The second great asset remained, and in absolute obedience to their
Consuetudines the new order would have found salvation. The experience
of the ages has shown repeatedly that fidelity to the rule, even at the cost
of a certain formalism and dryness, safeguards a religious order against
decay and makes a spontaneous rebirth of true life possible. We have
seen in previous chapters how long, and how far, such a fidelity obtained
among the Cistercians of England.

Finally, the constitutional, legal machinery of the *Carta Caritatis* continued in action, but of itself it was as powerless to prevent a spiritual
decline as had been the strong and balanced canon law of Gelasius and
Gregory to prevent the secularization and decentralization of the seventh
century. An abstract legal creation, however perfect, can be no more than
an instrument and means of government; it fails when governors or
governed no longer wish, or are able, to apply it. As a code, however,
it remains, like all abstract creations of the human mind, as a legacy for
future generations, and the main provisions of the *Carta Caritatis* have
been woven into the fabric of the constitutions of almost every religious
institute that has arisen in the West since the death of Stephen Harding.

VII

The monastic order in England approached the new era that was to open
after the death of John no longer as the paramount influence in the cultural
and spiritual life of the nation, but more happily situated than had seemed
possible a few years before. The attacks from without and, with the black
monks, the drift towards isolation within, had been to a great extent
arrested by the renovation of discipline in the Church in England, by the
new constitutional union, and by the more immediate supervision of the
Holy See, all of which were due directly to Innocent III and the legislation
of the Lateran Council. In the achievements of the thirteenth century

the monks of England were to have a share, even if not a formative and preponderant part, and in many ways the era following the death of John was a more healthy time than the fifty years before had been.

The reader of these many pages may perhaps have felt that very little that is definite has been said of the spiritual life of the rank and file of the English monks. The modern world is familiar with schools of spirituality, with histories of religious sentiment, and with works outlining the spirit and doctrine of eminent saints. Is it not as possible, with the great store of material that has survived, to obtain an idea of the spiritual life and discipline of the English monks of the twelfth century as it is to recapture the spiritual atmosphere of a Jesuit or Carmelite house in Spain under Philip II? The present writer cannot but answer, somewhat regretfully, that in his judgment it is not: partly because the traditional monastic *ascèse* has never lent itself to analysis or reduction to method, but still more because no English black monk between 970 and 1216 has left behind him either autobiography or body of spiritual doctrine or even so much as a treatise or collection of conferences or letters on matters of spirituality. The letters of Anselm, the letters and sermons of Bernard, the treatises and works of William of St Thierry, Peter the Venerable and Rupert of Deutz, give at least a fair indication of the kind of spiritual teaching and aspirations that were common at Bec, Clairvaux and else-where, but in England, if we put aside the Cistercians Ailred of Rievaulx and Gilbert of Holland, there is a complete lack of such literature. As historical writers, the English black monks had no rivals in Europe; as masters of the interior life of the soul, they were wholly mute. We have therefore perforce to be content with what we can surmise from the lives of a few outstanding individuals, and from what we know of the employ-ments of the day and of the resources of the monastic libraries. Of anything specifically English there is no trace; in this respect the twelfth century provides a contrast both to the eighth and to the fourteenth; and the reader who wishes to supplement his own conclusions from the data provided in previous chapters must look to the analysis of monastic spirituality in the countries of the Continent presented by Berlière or Pourrat. One observation, however, may not be out of place. Too few, it may be, of those who endeavour to reconstruct the mentality of the monks of this period make adequate allowance for the influence of the monuments and treasures of spiritual doctrine which were present in the round of every day's life. Before and behind all other teaching and literature the monk had the Bible in the simple, masculine prose of Jerome's Vulgate, the Psalter with all the associations which its verses had gathered in Christian tradition, and the magnificent treasure of the Roman liturgy in the year's cycle of solemnities and feasts, with all its calm, dogmatic formulas of prayer and praise, and the inspired and allusive beauty of its quotation and adaptation of the text of Scripture. With such

44-2

a background, and with the daily sacramental life, the monk faithful to his calling did not need the help of a system. *Erant omnes docibiles Dei*.[1]

VIII

The student of monasticism in this country, when he comes to pass his subject in a final review, has to beware of an attitude of mind to which the course taken by English history renders him peculiarly prone. The monastic life disappeared entirely from the purview of the English nation at the dissolution of the religious houses under Henry VIII; it is therefore natural for an Englishman to regard it, in its religious as well as in its social aspect, as something purely medieval, outliving by a century or more its due time, and passing with the changing world for ever.

Such an attitude fails to separate the temporary, external, accidental shape taken by monasticism from the essential qualities which distinguish a life apart from the world based on the counsels of the gospel. As a great and formative influence on the civilization of the West the monasteries of Europe are perhaps the most important factor in the spiritual and cultural life of the Church and society from the days of Gregory the Great to those of Bernard; though they had fallen from their paramount position before 1216 they continued as an important element in the social and economic life of nations until the Reformation in northern lands and until the Revolution in the countries which had remained Catholic. In the modern world they have become once more what they were in the beginning, a factor in the spiritual life of the Church working upon individuals and not upon society. But underneath the changes of the outward garment the monastic life, its aim and its ideal, have continued without change:

The Form remains, the Function never dies.

That life is in its essence neither ancient, nor medieval, nor modern, but of every Christian age, and though the institutions in which it is embodied change and decay, one and the same spirit and power has manifested itself in an ever-recurring rhythm by which new life appears where decay seemed final, as inevitably, though not (to our sight) as regularly, as the new bud is on the tree when the leaf falls in November.

The historian must therefore be careful to keep separate in his mind the external, social work of the monks from the inward, spiritual, individual achievement of their lives, and to judge the former in relation to the needs and conditions of medieval Europe and the latter by the abiding standards of Christian perfection, which do not alter with the centuries. And he must above all, if he be an Englishman, resist with all his power the siren

1 St John vi, 45.

voice of romanticism. Few indeed who have written with sympathy of the monks of medieval England have wholly escaped the spells of that old enchantress, who has known so well how by her magic of word and brush to scatter the golden mist of the unreal over the generations of the past.

In the opening pages of this volume an attempt was made to give an outline of the form of life imposed by the Rule of St Benedict. By the prescriptions of that Rule, understood not indeed with antiquarian literalness, but in full spiritual strength, must the monasticism of every age be judged. Unless it give to those who enter it an invitation to the highest perfection, together with the doctrine and discipline without which, in the normal course, that invitation cannot be followed, a religious institute must be pronounced a failure, and unless a monk, in his years of maturity, live in spirit apart from the world, with all his powers dedicated to the love of God, he must be pronounced unfaithful, in greater or less degree, to his profession. The words of Christ, from which alone the monastic life takes its origin, are valid for every age: "if thou wilt be perfect go, sell all thou hast, and come, follow me...for whosoever he be of you that forsaketh not all that he hath, he cannot be my disciple."[1]

By this test, and by such a standard, and by these alone, must the monastic order in any age and in any country be judged. It is for the reader of these pages to decide at what periods and to what degree the different families of monks in England between the times of Dunstan and those of Stephen Langton satisfied the demands of their high calling. In making his judgment he will do well if, while abating not a whit of the ideal of Christ, he remember also the warning of the ancient liturgy, and be mindful of his own proper state and condition.

[1] St Matthew xix, 21; St Mark x, 21; St Luke xiv, 33.

APPENDICES

I. THE EVIDENCE FOR THE DISAPPEARANCE OF MONASTIC LIFE IN ENGLAND BEFORE 943

King Alfred [writing *c.* 895] on the state of learning in England in 871, in preface to his translation of the *Pastoral Care* of Gregory the Great. The passage is quoted by W. H. Stevenson in his edition of Asser, p. 225, n. 2.

Asser, *De Rebus Gestis Aelfredi*, §§ 92–8 [written *c.* 893, referring to 887]: "In quo monasterio [*sc.* Athelney] diversi generis monachos undique congregavit...quia nullum de sua propria gente...qui monasticam voluntarie vellet subire vitam, habebat; nimirum quia per multa retroacta annorum curricula monasticae vitae desiderium ab illa tota gente...funditus desierat, quamvis plurima adhuc monasteria in illa regione constructa permaneant, nullo tamen regulam illius vitae ordinabiliter tenente" (ed. Stevenson, 80–1).

Regularis Concordia, Proemium, 77 [970]: "Comperto etenim quod sacra coenobia diversis sui [*sc.* Edgari] regiminis locis diruta ac pene domini nostri Jesu Christi servitio destituta neglegenter tabescerent, etc."

Hyde Liber Vitae, ed. Birch (Hampshire Record Society, 1892), in the account of the origin of the New Minster [written *c.* 990], speaks (p. 7) of *monasticae religionis exoriens norma* under Edgar.

Vita S. Dunstani auctore B (*Memorials of St Dunstan*), p. 25 [*c.* 1005]: "Dunstanus...primus abbas Anglicae nationis enituit."

Vita S. Aethelwoldi [by Aelfric, *c.* 1005], in *Chronicon Mon. de Abingdon*, II, 261: "Nam hactenus [*sc.* 965] in gente Anglorum ea tempestate non habebantur monachi nisi in Glastonia et Abendonia."

Vita S. Oswaldi auctore anonymo (*Hist. York*, I, 411) [*c.* 1005]: "In diebus illis non monastici viri, nec ipsius sanctae institutionis regulae erant in regione Anglorum."

"Postscript" to Anglo-Saxon translation of the *Rule* [after 1000] in Cockayne, *Leechdoms*, III, 439: "Before that [*sc.* 954] there was but a scant number of monks in a few places in so great a kingdom living by right rule. That was not more than in one place, called Glastonbury."

II. THE STATUS OF GLASTONBURY PREVIOUS TO DUNSTAN'S APPOINTMENT AS ABBOT *c.* 943

Apart from general statements, already quoted in Appendix I, which cover all English monasteries, the chief source of our knowledge for Glastonbury is in the account of Dunstan's first biographer, the priest "B", who wrote *c.* 1000 and had known the saint well. He tells us that Dunstan's parents "dignam sibi clericatus inposuere tonsuram officii inque famoso Glestoniensis aecclesiae sociaverunt coenobio" (*Memorials of St Dunstan*, 10)—a step which, it may be remembered, did not imply the monastic obligations (*ibid.* 13). His *praelatus* there was "quidam Glestoniensis aecclesiae diacon" (*ibid.* 15), who appears as a *juvenis* in the Canterbury Lives and a *monachus* only in William of Malmesbury (*ibid.* 263); during his residence there after he had taken monastic vows to Aelfheah of Winchester the Lady Aethelfleda constructed "casulas sibi commanendi in affinitate sacri templi ad plagam occidentalem" (*ibid.* 17). When King Edmund and Dunstan went to Glastonbury (*ibid.* 25) the king "ducens [eum] ad sacerdotalem cathedram et imponens illum in eam, dixit, 'Esto sedis istius princeps potensque insessor, et praesentis aecclesiae fidelissimus abbas, etc.'", and the narrator continues: "Igitur...praedicto modo...primus abbas [i.e. of that epoch] Anglicae nationis enituit"; and tells us that his first care was to construct monastic buildings. All this gives us a consistent account, bearing all the marks of truth, of a small *familia* of clerks at Glastonbury.

Osbern of Canterbury, writing shortly after the Conquest, added that Dunstan, between his monastic profession and reception of the abbacy, lived at Glastonbury as a solitary. This was the tradition on the spot, for Osbern had seen his cell (*ibid.* 83), and may well embody a certain amount of truth. That the story, thus related by "B" and embroidered by Glastonbury tradition, was the accepted one is shown by the words of William of Malmesbury when he describes the abbey in his *Gesta Pontificum* (196). He says that monks were there till the Danish invasions of Alfred's time: "Tunc enim, ut cetera, desolatus, aliquantis annis notos desideravit incolas. Porro...reparavit egregie Dunstanus, qui prius eo loco vitam solitariam monachus [some MSS. omit or alter this word] actitarat."

Confusion, however, was introduced by those at Glastonbury and elsewhere who supposed the description of "B" (reproduced by Osbern) of Dunstan as "primus abbas Anglicae nationis" to imply that Glastonbury had never previously had an abbot, or an English one. The monks therefore asked Malmesbury, when their guest, to refute the assertion; this he had no difficulty in doing from the muniments of the house, and the critical acumen shown in his researches has recently been vindicated by the late Dean of Wells, Dr J. Armitage Robinson. Not content with this, however, Malmesbury went on to demonstrate uninterrupted continuity of monastic life, by a series of identifications and hypotheses which cannot be regarded as probable. As nothing in the charters can be shown to disprove the traditional account given above (*v.* Robinson, *The Saxon Bishops of Wells*, 43), we are justified in regarding it as substantially correct.

III. THE COMPOSITION OF THE COMMUNITY AT CHRIST CHURCH, CANTERBURY, BEFORE THE CONQUEST

As mentioned in the text, widely divergent views have been held on this subject. Till recently, the opinion that Christ Church had never been monastic, and that it did not become so in the monastic movement of the tenth century, was very widely held. It was maintained by Miss Margaret Deanesly in her paper in *Essays in Medieval History presented to T. F. Tout* (Manchester, 1925), and in the following year a writer in the *Victoria County History of Kent*, II, 113–14, stated that: "from the foundation to the Conquest the cathedral establishment... consisted of secular clerks and not of monks". In the same year (1926), however, appeared the careful study of Dr J. A. Robinson (*Journal of Theological Studies*, XXVII, 107 (April), 225 *seqq.*), in which he proved beyond reasonable doubt both the existence of a quasi-monastic community in primitive times and the introduction of monks *c.* 1000. His conclusions were supplemented by a note in the following (July) number of the same Journal (pp. 409–11) by Dom Thomas Symons, O.S.B., pointing to the existence of a formula for the notification of monastic *obits* adapted to the needs of Christ Church and written *c.* 1000. Both Robinson and Dom Symons were content to endorse the traditional account which attributed this introduction of monks to Archbishop Aelfric, *c.* 997. *A priori*, we should expect it to have been the work of Dunstan, and, indeed, there are not wanting indications that he at least began to work towards this end. In the earliest Life by "B" we are told that Dunstan, when archbishop, heard a new anthem in a dream, which he at once dictated *cuidam monacho*, and when day broke taught *universos sibi subjectos, tam monachos quam etiam clericos* to sing it (*Memorials*, 41–2). There is also the provision, referred to in the text, in the preface to the *Concordia*, covering those monastic communities which served cathedral churches. It is difficult to suppose that Dunstan could have watched the action of Ethelwold and Oswald with no intention of doing the same in the cathedral for which the instructions of Gregory had been given to Augustine.

My own opinion (it cannot be more) is, therefore, that Dunstan began gradually to introduce monks, and that the process was formally completed by one of his immediate successors. On the other hand, it is my impression, derived largely from incidental allusions in Osbern and Eadmer of Canterbury, that the community never became, or certainly did not long remain, fully and purely monastic in spirit, and that, more than any other house, it became secular in outlook under the Confessor.

IV. MONASTIC BISHOPS, 960–1066

The names are taken, with a few alterations, from Stubbs, *Registrum Sacrum*, 2 ed.; I have printed those of monastic bishops in italics. A.R., *Sax. Bish.* = Armitage Robinson, *The Saxon Bishops of Wells.* F.W. = Florence of Worcester. *L.V.* = *Hyde Liber Vitae.* W.M. = William of Malmesbury.

CANTERBURY

Dunstan	960–988	Glastonbury
Ethelgar	988–990	Glastonbury; Abingdon; abb. New Minster [W.M., *GP*, 32]
Sigeric	990–994	Glastonbury [Will. Malmesb., *de Ant. Gl.* I, 92–4]; abb. St Augustine's
Elfric	995–1005	Glastonbury [Flor. Wig. 995 A]; abb. Abingdon [F.W. 1006 B; W.M., *GP*, 32; *Ch. Ab.* I, 416]
Alfheah	1005–1012	Bath
Elfstan	1013–1020	Glastonbury [W.M., *de Ant. Gl.*]; abb. Chertsey [A.R., *Sax. Bish.* 50]
Ethelnoth	1020–1038	Glastonbury [W.M.]; pr. Christ Church, Canterbury [*Chron.* 1020 E]
Eadsig	1038–1050	A monk [Plummer, *Chronicle*, II, 217, ref. Kemble, *Codex Diplomaticus*, vi, 190]
Robert	1051–1052	Abb. Jumièges
Stigand	1052–1070	King's priest

YORK
Oswald	972–992	Fleury
Aldulf	992–1002	Abb. Peterborough [*Chron.* 992 E]
Wulfstan	1003–1023	Abb. [F.W. 1002]; ? Ely [art. in *DNB*; cf. *Lib. El.* 205–6]
Elfric	1023–1051	Prov. Winchester [F.W. 1023]; ? New Minster [*Liber Vitae*, 32]
Kinsige	1051–1060	Abb. Peterborough [*Chron. Ang. Petrib., s.a.* 1051].
Ealdred	1061–1069	Winchester; abb. Tavistock [F.W. 1046]. N.B. not in *L.V.*

CORNWALL
Wulfsige	967–980	
Ealdred	980–1002	
? Burwold		
Lyfing	*c.* 1040	Glastonbury [W.M., *de Ant. Gl.*]; abb. Tavistock [Plummer, *Chronicle*, II, 225]

CREDITON
Sideman	970–977	Old Minster [*L.V.* 23]
Elfric	977–985	Abb. Westminster [A.R., *Sax. Bish.* 67]
Elfwold	988–1008	Glastonbury [W.M., *de Ant. Gl.*]
Eadnoth	1008–1019	
Lyfing	1027–1046	Glastonbury [W.M., *de Ant. Gl.*]; abb. Tavistock [Plummer, *Chronicle*, II, 225]
Leofric	1046–1072	King's chancellor

DORCHESTER
Eadnoth	*c.* 964–*c.* 975	Old Minster [*L.V.* 23]; Ramsey [*Ch. Rames.* 29 seqq.]
Aescwig	979–1002	Old Minster [*L.V.* 23]
Aelfhelm	1002–1005	
Eadnoth	1006–1016	Worcester [*Hist. York*, i, 423, 430]; prov. Ramsey [F.W. 1016]
Ethelric	1016–1034	Ramsey [*Ch. Rames.* 148]
Eadnoth	1034–1049	Ramsey [*Ch. Rames.* 148]
Ulf	1050–1052	King's priest
Wulfwig	1053–1067	

DURHAM
Elfsige	963–990	
Aldhun	990–1018	
Edmund	1020–1040	
Eadred	1041	
Ethelric	1042–1056	Peterborough [F.W. 1048; *v.* Symeon of Durham, *Hist. D.* I, xliv]
Ethelwin	1056–1071	Peterborough [F.W. 1056; S.D., *Hist. D.* I, xliv]

ELMHAM
? Elfric		
? Theodred		
Elfstan	995–1001	Not a monk [cf. *Lib. El.* 184–5]
Alfgar	1001–1016	Priest of Canterbury [*Mem. St Dunst.* 64; *Lib. El.* 189–90]
Alwin	1016–1022	Ely [*Lib. El.* 191–2]
Elfric	1023–1038	
Stigand	1043–1070	King's priest
Ethelmar	1047–1055	Stigand's brother

HEREFORD
Athulf	973–1012	Old Minster [*L.V.* 23]
Ethelstan	1012–1056	
Leofgar	1056	Harold's priest [*Chron.* 1056 D]
Walter	1061–1079	King's priest

LICHFIELD
Winsige	964–973	
Elfheah	973–1002	Old Minster [*L.V.* 23]
Godwin	1002–1008	
Leofgar	1020–	
Brihtmaer	1026–1039	
Wulfsige	1039–1053	
Leofwin	1053–1067	Abb. Coventry [*Chron.* 1053 C]

LINDSEY
Sigeferth	995–1006	

LONDON
Dunstan	959–961	Glastonbury
Aelfstan	961–995	
Wulfstan	996–1003	
Aelfwine	1004–1012	
Elfwig	1014–1035	
Elfward	1035–1044	Ramsey; abb. Evesham [*Ch. Ev.* 83, 85]
Robert	1044–1051	Jumièges
William	1051–1075	King's priest

RAMSBURY
Elfstan	970–981	Abingdon [*Ch. Ab.* II, 259; W.M., *GP*, 181]; Old Minster [*L.V.* 23]
Wulfgar	981–984	Old Minster [*L.V.* 23]
Sigeric	985–990	Glastonbury; abb. St Augustine's [*v.s.* Canterbury]
Elfric	990–995	Glastonbury; Abingdon [*v.s.* Canterbury]
Brihtwold	1005–1045	Glastonbury [W.M., *GP*, 182]
Herman	1045–1078	King's priest

ROCHESTER
Elfstan	964–995	Old Minster [*L.V.* 23]
Godwin	995–1046	
Siward	1058–1075	Abb. Chertsey [*Chron.* 1058 E with Plummer's note]

SELSEY
Ealdhelm	967–979	
Ethelgar	980–988	Glastonbury; Abingdon; abb. New Minster [*v.s.* Canterbury]
Ordbriht	989–1008	Glastonbury; Abingdon [*Ch. Ab.* II, 258]; abb. Westminster [A.R., *Sax. Bish.* 67]
Aelfmaer	1009–1031	Glastonbury [W.M., *de Ant. Gl.*]
Ethelric	1032–1038	
Grimketel	1039–1047	
Heca	1047–1057	King's priest
Ethelric	1057–1070	Christ Church, Canterbury [*Chron.* 1058 E]

SHERBORNE

Aethelsige	978–991	Old Minster [*L.V.* 23]
Wulfsige	992–1001	Glastonbury [W.M., *de Ant. Gl.*]; abb. Westminster [A.R., *Sax. Bish.* 67]
Ethelric	1001–1009	? Glastonbury [W.M., *de Ant. Gl.*]
Ethelsige	1009–1014	
Aelfmaer	1017–1022	Old Minster [*L.V.*27]; abb. St Augustine's Thorne, 1909
Brihtwy	1023–1045	
Elfwold	1045–1050	Winchester [W.M., *GP*, 179]
Herman	1058–1078	St Bertin *c.* 1055 [*Anal. Bolland.* LVI (1938), 37]

WELLS

Cyneward	974–975	Glastonbury [W.M., *de Ant. Gl.*]; abb. Milton [F.W. 973]
Sigegar	975–997	Abb. Glastonbury; Old Minster [W.M., *de Ant. Gl.*; *L.V.* 23]
Elfwine	997–998	? Glastonbury; abb. Westminster [A.R., *Sax. Bish.* 51, 67]
Lyfing	999–1013	Glastonbury; abb. Chertsey [*v.s.* Canterbury (Elfstan)]
Ethelwin	1013–1023	Abb. Evesham [A.R., *Sax. Bish.* 50]
Brihtwig	1024–1033	Abb. Glastonbury [W.M., *de Ant. Gl.*]
Dudoc	1033–1060	King's priest
Giso	1061–1088	King's priest

WINCHESTER

Aethelwold	963–984	Glastonbury; abb. Abingdon
Aelfheah	984–1005	Bath
Kenulf	1005–1006	? Old Minster; abb. Peterborough [*Chron.* 963 E]
Ethelwold	1006–1012	
Aelfsige	1016–1032	
Aelfwin	1032–1047	
Stigand	1047–1070	King's priest

WORCESTER

Dunstan	957–961	Glastonbury
Oswald	961–992	Fleury
Aldulf	992–1002	Abb. Peterborough [*v.s.* York]
Leofsige	1016–1033	Abb. Thorney [F.W. 1016 A]
Brihteag	1033–1038	Abb. Pershore [F.W. 1033]. Sister's son of Wulfstan of York
Lyfing	1038–1046	Glastonbury; abb. Tavistock [*v.s.* Cornwall]
Ealdred	?1044–1062	Winchester; abb. Tavistock [*v.s.* York]
Wulfstan	1062–1095	Worcester

Suffragan of Canterbury: Siward, 1044–1048; abb. Abingdon [*Chron.* 1044 C].

It will be seen that of the 116 occupants of sees listed above 67 (i.e. considerably more than half the total) are known to have been monks, while only some 14 are known to have been secular clerks; almost all the latter date from the Confessor's reign. If translated bishops and pluralists are counted once only, the figures retain almost exactly the same proportion. Some 33, or considerably less tnan a third, remain unaccounted for, and a glance at the lists will show that it is extremely probable that almost all these, save for one or two early bishops, were monks. We have very little information of the East Anglian and Mercian sees, but probably they were often filled from the fenland houses, and it is highly probable that Winchester always had a monastic bishop;

on the other hand we have full information for the Confessor's reign, when the presumption would be for clerks. It is, therefore, probable that for the whole period three-quarters of the total number were monks, and for the period up to, but not including, the Confessor's reign the proportion would be more in the neighbourhood of nine-tenths.

If the provenance of the monastic bishops is analysed, it will be found that out of 54, no less than 18 came from Glastonbury, 9 from the Old Minster, 5 from Peterborough, 3 from "Winchester" (most likely the Old Minster), 3 from Ramsey, 2 from Worcester and one each from Abingdon, Bath, Canterbury (Christ Church), Chertsey, Coventry, Ely, Evesham, Fleury, Jumièges, Pershore, Thorney, and Westminster, leaving one or two whose provenance is uncertain. These figures, however, are deceptive, for the ultimate provenance is often unattainable in the case of those who passed from abbacies to bishoprics, while in the early years almost all the Old Minster and Peterborough communities were monks trained at Abingdon, and several more bishops should therefore be credited to that house. The above figures, however, at least show how great was the influence of the *bloc* of houses directly founded by Dunstan and Ethelwold.

V. THE NORMAN MONASTERIES, 940–1066, WITH DATES OF FOUNDATION

(The name of the diocese is given after that of each house)

*Jumièges (Rouen)	c. 940	restored c. 1005
*St Wandrille (Rouen)	961–3	restored c. 1005
*Mont St Michel (Avranches)	c. 966	
*St Ouen (Rouen)	c. 970	restored c. 1005
*Fécamp (Rouen)	1001	
*Bernay (Lisieux)	1025–7	
*Ste Trinité (Rouen)	1030	
*Cérisy (Bayeux)	c. 1030	
Burneville-Bec (Rouen)	1034	
St Taurin, Évreux (Évreux)	1035	
La Croix St Leufroy (Évreux)	+ 1035	
Conches (Évreux)	c. 1035	
Préaux (Lisieux)	c. 1040	
St Pierre-sur-Dive (Séez)	1046	
Lire (Évreux)	c. 1046	
St Évroul, Ouche (Lisieux)	1050	
Grestain (Lisieux)	+ 1050	
Fontenay (Bayeux)	− 1055	
St Victor-en-Caux (Rouen)	1055	
Troarn (Bayeux)	1050–9	
Le Tréport (Rouen)	1059	
Lessay (Coutances)	1056–64	
St Vigor, Bayeux (Bayeux)	?	+ 1049 − 1082
St Martin de Séez (Séez)	1060	
Cormeilles (Lisieux)	c. 1060	
Beaumont-en-Auge (Lisieux)	1060–6	
*St Étienne, Caen (Bayeux)	− 1066	
*Montébourg (Coutances)	?	− 1087

* Foundations of the ducal family, to which the Duke appointed abbot.

LATER FOUNDATIONS: St Sauveur le Vicomte (Coutances), 1066; St Martin de Pontoise (Rouen), 1069; Ivry (Évreux), 1071; St Séver (Coutances), 1085; Bonne-Nouvelle (Rouen), 1107; St Georges de Boscherville (Rouen), 1114; Eu (Rouen), 1119; St Martin d'Aumâle (Rouen), 1130; Beaumont (Rouen), 1130.

VI. THE VALUE OF THE HOLDINGS OF MONASTERIES AND NUNNERIES IN *DOMESDAY*

The figures in the first column are my own calculation; those in the second column (unless otherwise stated) those of W. J. Corbett in the *Cambridge Medieval History*, vol. v, ch. xv, p. 509. Those in the third column show the number of knights at which the house was assessed, as given by Round, *Feudal England*, 249, 251, from the *cartae* of 1166 as shown in the *Red Book of the Exchequer*, ed. H. Hall (Rolls Series), 1, 186–445. The quotas of the cathedral monasteries are omitted, as they were (in part, at least) the quota of the bishop; at Ely, however, the original assessment probably remained.

HOUSE	GROSS INCOME IN *DOMESDAY*				QUOTA OF KNIGHTS
	£	s.	d.	£	
Glastonbury	827	18	8	840	40 [earlier 60]
Ely	768	17	3	790	40
Christ Church, Cant.	687	16	4	635	—
Bury St Edmunds	639	18	4	655	40
St Augustine's, Cant.	635	0	0	635	15
Winchester, Old Minster	600	1	0	640	—
Westminster	583	11	2	600	15 ?
Abingdon	462	3	3	—	30
Winchester, New Minster	390	4	0	—	20
Ramsey	358	5	0	†	4
Peterborough	323	0	8	—	60
St Albans	269	12	0	‡278	6
*Wilton	246	15	0	—	5
*Shaftesbury	234	5	0	—	7 [earlier 10]
Chertsey	198	14	0	—	3
Malmesbury	178	10	0	—	3
*Barking	162	19	8	—	—
Cerne	160	5	0	—	2 [earlier 3]
Coventry	157	3	0	—	10
*Romsey	136	8	0	—	—
Evesham	129	2	3	—	5
Gloucester	99	0	0	—	—
St Benet's of Holme	96	5	4	—	3
Milton	91	13	4	—	2
Winchcombe	82	0	0	—	2
Pershore	81	15	0	—	2 [earlier 3]

* Nunneries.
† No figure given by Corbett.
‡ Amount given by L. F. R. Williams, *History of the Abbey of St Alban*, 245.

House	Gross Income in *Domesday*				Quota of Knights
	£	s.	d.	£	
Bath	81	13	6	—	20
Tavistock	78	10	0	—	15?
Worcester	72	5	0	—	—
Abbotsbury	69	5	6	—	1
*Leominster	66	5	0	—	—
*Winchester	65	0	0	—	—
Sherborne	61	10	0	—	2
Muchelney	54	16	0	—	1
*Amesbury	54	15	0	—	—
Thorney	53	15	0	—	—
*Wherwell	52	4	0	—	—
Croyland	52	6	0	—	—
[Eynsham	40	9	0]	—	—
Cranborne	38	0	0	—	—
Burton	37	8	6	—	—
*Chatteris	20	10	4	—	—
Athelney	20	7	6	—	—
Buckfast	17	8	4	—	—
Horton	12	5	5	—	—
Swavesey	2	0	0	—	—

HOUSES FOUNDED AFTER 1066

House	Gross Income in *Domesday*			House	Gross Income in *Domesday*		
	£	s.	d.		£	s.	d.
Battle	212	3	2	Tewkesbury	18	0	0
Shrewsbury	61	10	0	Selby	8	0	0
Wenlock	34	5	4	York	2	18	0
Lewes	23	0	0				

HOLDINGS OF FOREIGN HOUSES IN *DOMESDAY*

House	Gross Income in *Domesday*			House	Gross Income in *Domesday*		
	£	s.	d.		£	s.	d.
Fécamp	200	0	3	St Ouen, Rouen	22	0	0
*Ste Trinité, Caen	107	0	0	Lire	21	0	0
St Remi, Rheims	94	13	0	Jumièges	20	0	0
Grestain	73	18	4	Cluny	18	0	0
St Étienne, Caen	73	0	0	Lonlé	16	16	0
St Denis, Paris	45	4	6	Préaux	11	0	0
St Wandrille	42	13	0	Bernay } Marmoutier }	10	0	0
*Almenèches	40	0	0	Montébourg	9	0	0
St Évroul	35	5	0	Tréport	4	5	0
St Valéry	34	8	8	Cormeilles	5	5	0
St Pierre, Ghent	30	0	0	St Taurin, Évreux	5	0	0
Mont St Michel	26	15	0	St Nicholas, Angers	4	0	0
Séez	26	0	0	La Croix St Leufroy	3	0	0
Troarn	25	0	0	St Pierre-sur-Dive	2	2	1
Bec	23	0	0				

* Nunneries.

VII. THE PROVENANCE OF FOREIGN SUPERIORS APPOINTED TO ENGLISH MONASTERIES, 1066–1135

N.B. These figures can only have a relative accuracy, since we do not possess information of all appointments, and fresh evidence may appear from sources not yet printed, or which I have failed to note. In the rare cases where a foreign monk passed from one English house to another as superior I have reckoned him twice, since each period of rule implied a new foreign influence for the house concerned.

House of Origin	– 1066	1066–1087	1087–1100	1100–1135	Total
In Normandy					
Bec	—	1	—	5	6
Bernay	—	1	—	—	1
Caen	—	3	—	4	7
St Évroul	—	—	1	3	4
Fécamp	—	3	—	—	3
Jumièges	—	5	1	1	7
Lire	—	1	—	—	1
St Ouen	—	1	—	—	1
Mont St Michel	—	3	1	1	5
Séez	—	1	—	2	3
St Wandrille	—	1	—	—	1
Anonymous	—	2	1	1	4
Other French Houses					
Cluny	—	—	—	2	2
Beauvais	—	—	1	1	2
Marmoutier	—	2	—	—	2
St Denis, Paris	1	—	—	—	1
Norman monks from					
Christ Church, Canterbury	—	1	2	2	5
Winchester, Old Minster	—	1	4	3	8
St Sabas, Rome	—	—	—	1	1
	1	26	11	26	64

Add following bishops	1	6	1	3	11
	Jumièges	Bec (4)	Fécamp	Séez (2)	
		Fécamp (1)		Beauvais (1)	
		St Carilef (1)			

VIII. DATE AND AUTHORSHIP OF THE *EVESHAM CHRONICLE*

Dr R. R. Darlington, in the article so often cited, has established beyond reasonable doubt that we have in the so-called *Chronicon Abbatiae de Evesham* (ed. Macray), pp. 86–96, a contemporary account of Aethelwig's life. Macray (introd. xl) and Edmund Bishop (*Downside Review*, XLIII (Oct. 1925), 188 note) had already drawn attention to tenses and phrases which clearly could not be attributed to Thomas de Marleberge (*ob.* 1236), the redactor of the chronicle.

The whole document needs careful critical examination; Dr Darlington is of opinion that the account was written immediately after Aethelwig's death, but there are a number of indications which make this improbable. Cf. the passages (86–7) "Godricus postea, tempore Walteri abbatis monachus factus, *plurimis annis* vivens in bona conversatione quievit in pace"; (90) "*Usque in hodiernum diem* anniversarius depositionis ejus [*sc.* Aethelwig] ibi in ecclesia illa observatur"; (*ibid.*) "Abbatia etiam de Gloecestre in primis, *venerandae memoriae* Serlone abbate [*ob. c.* 1102–4] ibi veniente, etc."; (89) "Iisdem namque temporibus *erat* vir religiosus simplex et rectus Wigornensis ecclesiae antistes, Wlstanus nomine." Unless we suppose these phrases to have been interpolated later (which seems improbable for more than one reason), it would seem that the whole account was written *c.* 1110. It is possible that the author was the prior Dominic, still alive in 1125, who is known to have written the account of St Egwin which forms part of the chronicle as printed. The style of pp. 69–70 is very like that of pp. 1–2, which we know to have been written by him. If he was a man of sixty, he might well have known Aethelwig himself, and veterans such as the ex-goldsmith Godric (pp. 86–7) could have told him about Mannig.

IX. THE INTERVENTIONS OF ST BERNARD IN ENGLISH AFFAIRS

The following table will give some idea of the extent of St Bernard's interest in English affairs; it does not claim to give an exhaustive list of his relationships with England.

ante 1120	Receives William, an Englishman, afterwards first abbot of Rievaulx, at Clairvaux	Bern. *Vita Prima*, I, 2
?	William and Ivo, pupils of Murdac at York, become monks at Clairvaux	Bern. *ep.* 106
?	Richard, a native of York, later abbot of Vauclair and fourth abbot of Fountains, becomes monk at Clairvaux	*Mem. Fount.* 107–8
ante 1130	Urges Henry Murdac to come to Clairvaux	*ep.* 106
ante 1132	Twice urges Thomas, provost of Beverley, to come to Clairvaux	*epp.* 411, 107
c. 1129	Writes to Alexander of Lincoln on behalf of his prebendary, Philip, at Clairvaux	*ep.* 64
c. 1131	Announces to Henry I forthcoming foundation of Rievaulx	*ep.* 92
c. 1132	Tentative letter to Henry of Winchester	*ep.* 93
1132	(autumn) Letters to Abbot Geoffrey of York, Archbishop Thurstan and Prior Richard on behalf of York seceders	*epp.* 94–6, 313
1133	(spring) Writes to Richard of Fountains, sending his monk Geoffrey	*ep.* 96; *Mem. Fount.* 46–7
	Writes to David of Scotland on behalf of Fountains	*ap.* Bernard *v.* Clairvaux, G. Hüffer, p. 233, no. x
	Writes to Henry I on behalf of Innocent II	*ep.* 138

KMO

1134	Offers monks of Fountains a site in Burgundy at request of Richard, who visits him	*Mem. Fount.* 51
c. 1138	Writes to Thurstan advising him not to resign his see	*ep.* 319
	(summer) Writes to Fountains, advising monks to elect Richard II	*Mem. Fount.* 73
1139–43	Repeatedly advises Richard II not to resign	*Mem. Fount.* 75
1140	Founds Whitland (Carmarthen)	
1140–53	Takes constant and energetic share in the controversies rising out of the election at York in 1141	
1141	(spring) Receives Robert Biseth, late prior of Hexham, at Clairvaux	*John of Hexham* (RS), II, 311
1143	Writes to Fountains on behalf of Richard II (letter not extant), who later in year dies at Clairvaux	*Mem. Fount.* 81; *epp.* 320–1
	(autumn) Sends Murdac to Fountains to be elected abbot	*ep.* 321
1142–3	Writes to Ailred of Rievaulx, bidding him write the *Speculum Caritatis*	*PL*, CXCV, 501–4
1144	Introduces John of Salisbury to archbishop Theobald	*ep.* 361
? *c.* 1145	Supports Robert of Newminster	*Vita S. Roberti*, c. 6
1146	Founds Boxley (Kent)	
1147	Writes to Eugenius III on behalf of Fountains, which had been burnt	*ep.* 252
	(summer) Advises Murdac how to proceed after his contested election	*Mem. Fount.* 103
	Founds Margam (Glamorgan)	
1148	(autumn) Gives advice concerning his order to Gilbert of Sempringham	*Vita Gilberti*, ix, in *Monasticon*, VI, ii.
1149	(September) Interests himself on behalf of Byland and Jervaulx, especially in general chapter	*Historia Bellaland.*, *Monasticon*, V, 571
c. 1149	Advises abbot Thorald of Fountains to give way to Murdac, and receives him at Clairvaux; sends Richard, his precentor, to be abbot	*ep.* 306; *Mem. Fount.* 105, 108
ante 1150	Obtains dispensation for William le Groos, on condition that he founds Meaux	*Chron. Melsa*, I, 76

X. A LIST OF BLACK MONKS AND REGULAR CANONS WHO BECAME CISTERCIANS BETWEEN 1132 AND 1200

I give all the names I have noted from 1132 to 1200. No doubt there were others, but it is significant that all are from the north of England; there was not in this country the widespread emigration that took place in central France and Burgundy.

I. Black Monks

Richard (prior)	1132	St Mary's, York	Fountains
Gervase (subprior)	,,	,, ,,	,,
Richard (sacrist)	,,	,, ,,	,,
Walter (almoner)	,,	,, ,,	,,
Robert	,,	,, ,,	,,
Ranulph	,,	,, ,,	,,
Alexander	,,	,, ,,	,,
Geoffrey	,,	,, ,,	,,
Gregory	,,	,, ,,	,,
Thomas	,,	,, ,,	,,
Hamo	,,	,, ,,	,,
Gamellus	,,	,, ,,	,,
Robert	,,	Whitby	,,
Adam	,,	,,	,,
Maurice (subprior)	c. 1139	Durham	Rievaulx
Robert de Alneto	c. 1143	Whitby	Byland

II. Augustinian Canons

Robert Biseth (prior)	1141	Hexham	Clairvaux
Waldef (prior)	c. 1143	Kirkham	Rievaulx
Everard	,,	,,	,,
William	c. 1165	Gisburn	Newminster
Nicholas	c. 1190	Warter	Meaux

Gerald of Wales asserts that Adam, abbot of Dore (c. 1200), was a Cluniac; v. supra, p. 672, n. 3.

XI. A LIST OF THE CISTERCIAN AND SAVIGNIAC FOUNDATIONS IN ENGLAND AND WALES, 1124–1437

For the authorities for the dates of the English houses, which in many cases differ from those given in the *Monasticon* and by Janauschek, I may be permitted to refer to my *Religious Houses of Medieval England* (London, Sheed and Ward, 1939).

	CISTERCIAN	SAVIGNIAC
1123		Furness[1] (4 July)
1128	Waverley (24 Nov.)	
1130		Neath (25 Oct.)
1131	Tintern (9 May)	Basingwerk (11 July)
1132	Rievaulx (5 March)	Quarr (27 April)
	Fountains (27 Dec.)	
1133	Garendon (28 Oct.)	
		Combermere (3 Nov.)
1135		Calder, Rushen (10 Jan.)
		Swineshead (1 Feb.)
		Stratford Langthorn (25 July)
		Buildwas (8 Aug.)

1 Founded at Tulket; moved to Furness, 1127.

	CISTERCIAN	SAVIGNIAC
1136	Melrose (23 March) [Scotland] from Rievaulx	Buckfast (27 April)
	Ford[1] (3 May)	
	Wardon (8 December)	
1137	Thame (22 July)	
1138	Bordesley (22 Nov.)	Byland[2] (Sept.)
1139	Newminster (5 Jan.)	
	Kirkstead, Louth Park (2 Feb.)	
	Kingswood (7 Sept.)	
1140	Whitland (16 Sept.)	Coggeshall (3 Aug.)
1141	Stoneleigh[3] (?)	

FILIATIONS OUTSIDE ENGLAND

1142		Dundrennan (Scotland) from Rievaulx
	Revesby (9 Aug.)	
1143	Cwmhir (22 July)	
	Pipewell (13 Sept.)	
	Boxley (28 Oct.)	
1145	Woburn (28 May)	
1146	Rufford (13 July)	Lysekloster (Norway) from Fountains
1147	Dore (26 April)	Hovedö (Norway) from Kirkstead (18 May)
	Kirkstall[4] (19 May)	
	Vaudey (23 May)	
	Bittlesden, Bruerne (10 July)	
	Roche (30 July)	
	Sawtry (31 July)	
	Margam (21 Nov.)	
1148	Sawley (6 Jan.)	
	Merevale (10 Oct.)	
1150	Sibton (22 Feb.)	
	Jervaulx[5] (10 March)	
	Combe (10 July)	
	Holm Cultram (30 Dec.)	
1151	Meaux (1 Jan.)	
	Flaxley (30 Sept.)	
	Stanley[6] (?)	
1153	Dieulacres[7] (12 May)	
	Tiltey (22 Sept.)	*Legislation of Chapter of 1152 takes effect*
1164	Strata Florida (1 June)	
1170	Strata Marcella (22 July)	
1172	Bindon (22 or 27 Sept.)	
	Whalley[8] (11 Nov.)	
1176	Croxden[9] (?)	
	Robertsbridge (29 March)	
1179	Caerleon (22 July)	

1 Founded at Brightley; moved to Ford, 1141.
2 Monks from Calder settled at Hood; moved to Old Byland 1143; to Stocking (Cuxwold) 1147; to New Byland 1177.
3 Founded at Radmere; moved to Stoneleigh ? 1154.
4 Founded at Barnoldswick; moved to Kirkstall, 1152.
5 Founded at Fors; moved to Jervaulx 1156.
6 Founded at Lockswell; moved to Stanley 1154.
7 Founded at Pulton; moved to Dieulacres 1 May 1214.
8 Founded at Stanlaw; moved to Whalley 1296.
9 Founded at Chotes; moved to Croxden 28 May 1178 or 9.

CISTERCIAN	FILIATIONS OUTSIDE ENGLAND
1186 Aberconway (24 July)	
1187	Inniscourcy (Ireland) from Furness (1 July)
1193	Gray (Ireland) from Holm Cultram (25 Aug.)
1198 Cleeve (25 June) Cymmer (end of year)	
1200	Cumber (Ireland) from Whitland (25 Jan.) Tintern Parva (Ireland) from Tintern (26 Sept.)
1201 Valle Crucis (28 Jan.) Dunkeswell (? 16 Nov.)	
1204 Beaulieu (13 June)	St Saviour's (Ireland) from Stanley (30 July)
1206	Abbington (Ireland) from Furness (22 March)
1212 Medmenham (18 June)	
1219 Hulton (26 July)	
1220	Saundle (Scotland) from Rushen
1225	Tracton (Ireland) from Whitland (22 Feb.)
1226 Grace Dieu (24 April)	
1239 Netley (25 July)	
1246 Hayles (17 June)	
1247 Newenham (6 Jan.)	
1274 Vale Royal (14 Jan.)	
1280 Buckland (?)	
1281 Rewley (11 Dec.)	
1350 St Mary Graces, London (20 March)	
1437 Oxford, St Bernard's College	

XII. MONASTIC BISHOPS IN ENGLAND AND WALES, 1066–1215

I. BLACK MONKS

Wulfstan (m. and pr. Worcester). WORCESTER, 1062–1095
*Remigius (m. Fécamp). LINCOLN, 1067–1092
*Lanfranc (m. Bec; abb. Caen). CANTERBURY, 1070–1089
*Arnost (m. Bec). ROCHESTER, 1076
*Gundulf (m. Bec). ROCHESTER, 1077–1108
*William of St Carilef (m. St Carilef; abb. St Vincent). DURHAM, 1081–1096
  Herbert Losinga (m. Fécamp; abb. Ramsey). NORWICH, 1091–1119
*Anselm (m. and abb. Bec). CANTERBURY, 1093–1109
*Ralph (m. and abb. Séez). ROCHESTER, 1108–1114; CANTERBURY, 1114–1122
  Ernulf (m. Beauvais; pr. Christ Church). ROCHESTER, 1115–1124
  Seffrid Pelochin (m. Séez; abb. Glastonbury). CHICHESTER, 1125–1145
†Henry of Blois (m. Cluny; abb. Glastonbury). WINCHESTER, 1129–1171
†Robert (m. Lewes). BATH, 1136–1166
*Theobald (m. and abb. Bec). CANTERBURY, 1139–1161
  William de Turbe (m. and pr. Norwich). NORWICH, 1146–1174

* Appointed when living abroad.　　　　　† Cluniac.

†Gilbert Foliot (m. Cluny; abb. Gloucester). HEREFORD, 1148–1163; LONDON, 1163–1187

Walter Durdent (m. and pr. Christ Church). LICHFIELD, 1149–1160

Richard (m. Christ Church; pr. Dover). CANTERBURY, 1174–1184

†Peter de Leia (pr. Wenlock). ST DAVID'S, 1176–1198

†Henry de Sully (pr. Bermondsey; abb. Glastonbury). WORCESTER, 1193–1195

† Cluniac.

II. CISTERCIANS

Henry Murdac (m. Clairvaux; abb. Vauclair; abb. Fountains). YORK, 1147–1153

Baldwin (m. and abb. Ford). WORCESTER, 1180–1185; CANTERBURY, 1185–1190

III. CARTHUSIAN

Hugh of Avalon (m. Grande Chartreuse; pr. Witham). LINCOLN, 1186–1200

IV. AUSTIN CANONS

William of Corbeuil (pr. St Osyth's). CANTERBURY, 1123–1136

Robert de Bethune (pr. Llanthony). HEREFORD, 1131–1148

Adelulf (? c. Huntingdon; pr. Nostell). CARLISLE, 1133–1157

Geoffrey de Henlaw (pr. Llanthony). ST DAVID'S, 1203–1214

The following observations may be made upon the above list:

1. The total number of monks of every kind appointed is only twenty-three out of approximately 150 episcopal appointments made between 1066 and 1215.

2. The number of monks actually holding sees remained strangely constant throughout the period; from three in 1070 it rose to five for a few months in 1090–1, whence it fell to zero for a few months in 1124–5; another maximum of six black monks and one Cistercian was attained 1149–53, whence there was a gradual fall to zero at the death of Hugh of Lincoln in 1200; thence onward till the death of John there was no monk in the episcopate.

3. The number of sees during the reign of William I was fifteen; by the middle of the twelfth century a total of twenty-one was reached.

MONASTIC BISHOPS AFTER THE CONQUEST

It is often stated that a result of the Conquest was an influx of a numerous monastic element into the English episcopate. Such an impression is no doubt given by the high prestige and significance in English history of Lanfranc, Anselm and a few other monastic prelates, but in fact the proportion of bishops of monastic provenance was never so great under William I as it had been under Edgar, Ethelred and Cnut, or even in the last years of the Confessor. In 1062–3 there were at least six monastic bishops; in 1071 only three or at most four; in 1086 five; in 1100 three.[1] Only five of the Conqueror's seventeen odd appointments fell to monks, and two of these were to the unimportant see of Rochester, which was practically in the gift of Lanfranc.

1 [1063] Ealdred (York), Ethelwin (Durham), Leofwin (Lichfield), Siward (suffragan), Ethelric (Selsey), Wulfstan (Worcester).
[1071] Lanfranc, Wulfstan, Remigius (Lincoln) and perhaps Siward.
[1086] Lanfranc, Wulfstan, Remigius, St Carilef (Durham), Gundulf (Rochester).
[1100] Anselm, Gundulf, Herbert Losinga (Thetford-Norwich).

XIII. THE INCREASE IN THE NUMBER OF RELIGIOUS HOUSES IN ENGLAND AND WALES, 1100–1175

These figures are approximate only. Save for the Cistercians, notices of the date of foundation are often wholly wanting; this is particularly so with the houses of Augustinian canons, and above all in the early part of the reign of Henry II, for in the case of numerous foundations the only indication of date is *tempore Henrici II*, and these are not reckoned in the numbers below. The figures for the black canons must therefore be considered as well below the probable minimum. In the case of the black monks, only autonomous houses (or with the Cluniacs fully established priories) are reckoned. To count the numerous cells and "alien" priories would be as misleading as, at the present day, to equate small groups of regulars on parish work with organized *domus formatae*. The aggregate is given in square brackets.

	BLACK MONKS (including) Cluniac)	BLACK CANONS	WHITE MONKS	WHITE CANONS	GILBERT- INES	NUNS
– 1100	*c.* 70	*c.* 5	—	—	—	*c.* 13
– 1136	*c.* 7 [77]	*c.* 55 [60]	17	—	1	*c.* 25 [38]
– 1155	*c.* 7 [84]	*c.* 30 [90]	36 [53]	6	10 [11]	*c.* 25 [63]
– 1176	1 [85]	*c.* 10 [100]	5 [58]	3 [9]	2 [13]	*c.* 12 [75]

GRAND TOTALS

Before 1100:	*c.* 88
At death of Henry I:	*c.* 88 + 105 = 193
At death of Stephen:	*c.* 193 + 114 = 307
In 1175:	*c.* 307 + 33 = 340

For increase after 1175 *v.* Knowles, *Religious Houses of Medieval England*.

XIV. THE DATES OF THE GRANTS OF *INSIGNIA PONTIFICALIA* TO ENGLISH ABBEYS

The privilege granted to abbots of using some, or all, of the episcopal vestments and insignia, rare before *c.* 1050, became increasingly common after that time. Until *c.* 1150 it was a sign that the Curia considered the monastery to be a papal *Eigenkirche*; after that date, it was often merely an isolated favour, granted, e.g. to Glastonbury and (in 1254) to the prior of the cathedral monastery of Winchester. The insignia, seven in number—staff, ring, sandals, gloves, tunicle, dalmatic and mitre—were granted either in batches (as usually before *c.* 1150) or all together. I have noticed the following bestowals upon English houses:

DATE	HOUSE	INSIGNIA	AUTHORITY
1063	St Augustine's	Mitre, sandals	Thorne, 1785; *JL*, 4541
1071	Bury	Staff, ring	Jo. Oxenede, *sub anno*
1161	St Albans	All	*GASA*, I, 132, 158, 182, 199; Harl. Chron. 43 A 24
c. 1170	Evesham	All (save ring already used)	*Chron. Evesh.* 101
– 1174	Westminster	Mitre, ring, gloves	Holtzmann, I, ii, 118, 143; Rad. Dic. I, 404; Flete, 92.
1177	Westminster	Dalmatic, tunicle, sandals	Flete, 96

Date	House	Insignia	Authority
c. 1183	Bury	Mitre, ring	*Jocelini Cronica*, 230
	Bury	Episcopal benediction (first in England)	*Jocelini Cronica*, 261
1192	Glastonbury	All	*Monasticon*, 1, 40; *JL*, 16,823
	Westminster	All	Holtzmann, 1, ii, 300–1

It will be seen that five out of the seven "exempt" houses had some or all of the *pontificalia*. Battle, having as yet no papal privilege, had none, and I have not noted any grant to Malmesbury.

XV. KNIGHT-SERVICE DUE FROM THE MONASTERIES ACCORDING TO THE *CARTAE* OF 1166

The following lists are taken from the data supplied by the *Red Book of the Exchequer*, but there is no difficulty in extracting the figures, and they agree in every respect with those given by Round in *Feudal England*, 225–314. The first list is that of the assessment based on the *cartae* of 1166, the figures in brackets represent what was probably the original assessment; the second and third list represent the regular *dona* for knights from each house and the arbitrary *dona* of 1159 respectively; the sums are in marks.

Monastery	Knights due 1166	Donum for Knights	Arbitrary Donum
Peterborough	60	120	100
Glastonbury	40 [60]	80	—
Bury	40	80	200
Abingdon	30	60	60
Hyde	20	40	150
St Augustine's	15	30	220
Westminster	15?	—	—
Tavistock	15?	—	—
Coventry	10	—	—
*[Shaftesbury]	7 [10]	—	—
St Albans	6	12	100
Evesham	5	10	60
*[Wilton]	5	10	20
Ramsey	4	8	60
Chertsey	3	6	60
St Benet's of Holme	3	6	30
Cerne	2 [3]	6	—
Pershore	2 [3]	—	$7\frac{1}{2}$
Malmesbury	3	—	—
Winchcombe	2	4	$7\frac{1}{2}$
Milton	2	4	—
Sherborne	2	—	10
Muchelney	1	—	—
Abbotsbury	1	2	$7\frac{1}{2}$

* Houses of nuns.

XVI. THE OFFICIALS OF A GREAT MONASTERY

The following is a composite list of the monastic officials in a great abbey towards the end of the twelfth century. It is compiled from the customs of Abingdon, *c.* 1185 (*Chron. Abingd.* II, 297–334), the survey of Abbot Henry de Sully of Glastonbury in 1189 (*Liber Henrici de Soliaco*, ed. J. E. Jackson for Roxburghe Club, 1887, *passim*), the many references to the Bury officials in Jocelin's chronicle and the account of the election of Abbot Hugh (*Mem. St Edmund's*, vols. I and II) covering the years 1180–1215, and the constitutions of Evesham *c.* 1206 (*Chron. Evesh.* 206 *seqq.*).

A = Abingdon, B = Bury, E = Evesham, G = Glastonbury. It does not of course follow that if an official does not occur he did not exist; thus the novice-master appears only on the Bury list.

Prior, B, E, G

Subprior, B, E, G

Third prior, B, E

Novice-master, B

Precentor, A, B, E, G

Succentor, B

Sacrist, A, B, E, G

Subsacrist, B

Cellarer, A, B, E, G (E alone notes two: intern and extern)

Chamberlain, A, B, E, G

Subchamberlain, B, G

Almoner, A, B, E, G

Kitchener, A, B, E

Refectorer, A, B, E, G

Subrefectorer, B

Pittancer, A, B, E

Master of the vestry, B

Master of the book-press, B

Infirmarian, E, G

Kitchener, chamberlain and pittancer of the farmery, A

Master of the works, A, E

Master of the guests, B, E, G

Gardener, A, E, G

Keeper of the granary, G

Hosteler, A

Keeper of the wood, A

Dean (of the Vale), E

Wardens of the shrine, B

XVII. THE NUMBERS OF MONKS IN THE BLACK MONK MONASTERIES

Abingdon, 28 (1100); 78 (1117)[1]

St Albans, 50 (1190)[2]; *c.* 100 (*c.* 1210)[3]

Bath, 40 (1206)[4]

Battle, *c.* 60 (1080)[5]

Bury, *c.* 70–80 (1213)[6]

Canterbury, St Augustine's, 61 (1146)[7]

1 *Chron. Abingd.* II, 49, 148.

2 U.B.= Dom U. Berlière, *Le nombre des moines dans les anciens monastères*, in *RB*, XLI (1929), 231–61; XLII (1930), 31–42. Most of his figures are of dates later than 1200.

3 The figure was fixed as a maximum about this time (*GASA*, I, 234).

4 U.B.

5 The abbey was founded for at least sixty (*Chron. Bell.* 23).

6 The "division list" of the election in 1213 gives sixty-five names, in addition to those of the two candidates; novices and absentees must be added. *V. Mem. S. Edmund's* (Electio Hugonis), II, 75.

7 *Chron. Will. Thorne*, 1807, which there states that the ancient number was regained in that year.

Canterbury, Christ Church, + 60 (*c.* 1080);[1] 100 (1090); ? 140–150 (*c.* 1125);[2] *c.* 80
    (1207)[3]
Colchester, *c.* 25 (1115)[4]
Durham, 23 (1083)[5]
Ely, 50 (1110); ? later *c.* 70[6]
Evesham, 12 (1059); 36 (1077);[7] 67 (*c.* 1095);[8] 30–40 (1206)[9]
Glastonbury, 72 (*c.* 1160);[10] 50 (*c.* 1200)[11]
Gloucester, 11 (1072);[12] 100 (1104)[13]
Norwich, 60 (*c.* 1100)[14]
Peterborough, 60 (1125)[15]
Rochester, 60 (*c.* 1110)[16]
Tewkesbury, 57 (1105)[17]
Westminster, 80 (1085)[18]
Whitby, 36 (1148); 38 (1175, 1176)[19]
Winchester, New Minster, ? *c.* 40 (*c.* 1040)[20]
Worcester, 12 (*c.* 1060); 50 (1088)[21]

XVIII. THE MONASTIC HORARIUM ACCORDING TO THE *REGULARIS CONCORDIA*

(*a*) WINTER—early November

c. 2.30	Rise
	Trina oratio
	Gradual psalms
3.0	NOCTURNS
	Psalms, etc., for Royal House
	Vigils and Lauds of the Dead
	Nocturns of All Saints
5.0	Reading

(*b*) SUMMER

?*c.* 1.30	Rise
	Trina oratio
	Gradual psalms
2.0	NOCTURNS
	Psalms, etc., for Royal House
	Nocturns of All Saints
	(Short interval)
3.30 or 4.0[22]	MATINS

1 Cf. Eadmer, *Ep. ad Glastonienses*, *PL*, CLIX, 805: "Sexagenariam quantitatem ascenderat."
2 There were 100 at Lanfranc's death; he left provision for 150; *c.* 1125 it was the largest house in England. *V.* Gervase, II, 368; Will. Malmesb., *GP*, 71.
3 Sixty-four went into exile in this year (*Ann. Winton., s.a.*).
4 *Monasticon*, IV, 608.
5 Symeon of Durham, I, 122; II, 201–2. Doubtless the numbers soon increased.
6 *Liber Eliensis cont.* ap. Wharton, *Anglia Sacra*, I, 617, where the *numerus debitus* is given as 72.   7 *Chron. Evesh.* 96.
8 *Monasticon*, II, 37. Thirty-two names appear on list of confraternity in *c.* 1075 printed by Thorpe, *Diplom.* 615–17, but novices, etc. must be added.
9 Thirty left in a body in this year; cf. *Chron. Evesh.* 203.
10 Adam of Domerham, II, 417, who states that previously there had been eighty.
11 *Ibid.* II, 385; in *c.* 1200 the commissioners suggested sixty as a fair number to allow for (*ibid.* II, 418).
12 *Monasticon*, I, 543.   13 *Hist. Gloc.* 13.
14 *Monasticon*, IV, 15. The number is suspiciously large for a new foundation.
15 U.B.
16 *Textus Roffensis* (ed. Hearne), 143; cf. Will. Malmesb., *GP*, introd. xxiv, where a chronicle states that the number soon decreased.   17 *Monasticon*, II, 81.
18 U.B.   19 *Cart. Whitb.* (Surtees Soc. LXIX), 9, 10.
20 For New Minster *v.* list of names in *Hyde Register* (ed. Birch), 31 *seqq.*
21 *Monasticon*, I, 599.
22 The length of the Office varied more in the summer than in the winter between ferial and festal days; hence the alternative of sleep that follows.

(a) WINTER

6.0[1] MATINS
Miserere
Psalms, etc., for Royal House
Anthems of Cross, B.V.M., and
    patron saint of church
Matins of All Saints *in porticu*

6.45[2] PRIME
Three psalms and prayers, etc.
Seven penitential psalms
Litany, etc.

7.30 Reading

8.0[3] Change shoes, wash, etc.
Trina oratio
TERCE
MORROW MASS
CHAPTER
Five psalms for dead, etc.

c. 9.45 Work

12.0 SEXT
Psalms, etc., for Royal House
SUNG MASS

c. 1.30 NONE
Psalms, etc., for Royal House

c. 2.0 DINNER

c. 2.45 Work

c. 4.15 VESPERS
Psalms, etc., for Royal House
Anthems, as in morning
Vespers of All Saints
Vespers of Dead

5.30 Change into night shoes
Drink

6.0 Collatio

6.15 COMPLINE
Trina oratio

6.30 Retire

(b) SUMMER

Miserere
Psalms, etc., for Royal House
Anthems of Cross, B.V.M.,
    and patron saint of church
Matins of All Saints *in porticu*
(If day) change and wash, etc.;
    or (if dark) sleep, change
    and wash, etc.

c. 5.0 *Trina oratio*
Reading

6.0 PRIME
Psalms and prayers
MORROW MASS
CHAPTER
Five psalms for dead, etc.

7.30 Work (short period)

8.0 TERCE
SUNG MASS

9.30 Reading

11.30[4] SEXT
Psalms, etc., for Royal House

12.0 DINNER

c. 1.0 Siesta

2.30[5] NONE
Psalms, etc., for Royal House
Drink

c. 3.0 Work

5.30 SUPPER

6.0 VESPERS
Psalms, etc., for Royal House
Anthems, etc., as in morning
Vespers and Matins of All
    Saints
Vespers, Vigils and Lauds of
    the Dead

7.30 Change into night shoes
Collatio

8.0 Compline
Trina oratio

c. 8.15 Retire

1 Matins (i.e. Lauds) were not to be begun till break of day (*usquequo lucescat, Concordia*, ii, 84).

2 Prime was begun when daylight was full (*expectent lucem, ibid*. i, 81).

3 This was to be done *hora secunda* (*ibid*. i, 81).

4 *Mediante hora quinta* (*Concordia*, vi, 90).

5 *Mediante hora octava* (*ibid*. vi, 90).

XIX. THE ALLEGED DIETARY OF ST ETHELWOLD
AT ABINGDON

The evidence brought forward on pp. 458–60 for the abstinence of the English
monks from flesh-meat, agreeing as it does so exactly with all antecedent probability, seems wholly conclusive. A word therefore has to be said regarding
two passages in Abingdon documents, purporting to give the dietary regulations of the founder, St Ethelwold, and asserting that the practice of the house
had been unchanging; in these regulations flesh-meat is expressly.allowed. These
passages were taken without question as fully genuine by O. Cockayne and
Edmund Bishop, as also by myself some years ago (cf. references, *supra*,
p. 458). The passages in question are (i) *Chron. Abingd.* I, 343–7, from the
Historia Monasterii de Abingdon, and (ii) *ibid.* II, 277–9, from the tract *de
Abbatibus Abbendoniae*. The two passages are closely related, the latter having
a *prima facie* appearance of being the rougher and earlier, but the point could
not be decided without careful critical examination. Strong arguments against
their historicity can be drawn from both the character of the manuscripts in
which they occur and the statements which appear in them.

I. The Manuscripts

The History of Abingdon is contained in two manuscripts in the Cottonian
collection at the British Museum, viz. Cott. Claudius C ix [written *c.* 1220] and
Cott. Claudius B vi [written *c.* 1270]. The tract on the abbots is from the same
collection, Cott. Vitellius A xiii [written *c.* 1250]. The editor of the volumes in
the Rolls Series, the Rev. J. Stevenson, adopted as his text the second and later
of the two Claudius manuscripts, which he considered "a revised and improved
copy" of the other (*Chron. Abingd.* I, introd. xv). This was most unfortunate,
since, as has been shown beyond a doubt by Mr (now Professor) F. M. Stenton,
in *The Early History of the abbey of Abingdon* (1913), pp. 1 *seqq.*, the earlier
manuscript contains all that is genuine in the history of the abbey, while the
later one contains many additions that have no claim to acceptance. Moreover,
Stevenson fails to make it clear when he has both manuscripts, and when only
the later one, behind his text. As Mr Stenton justly remarks (*op. cit.* p. 1), "the
whole plan of the edition…is faulty". For our purpose, it is enough to note
that the passage concerning diet in *Chron. Abingd.* I, 343–7, together with another
referring to the same subject (II, 146–9), are not in Cott. Claudius C ix. In
other words, they were presumably written between 1220 and 1270, the very
period when a series of attempts was being made by legates, bishops, visitors
and abbots to reinforce the dietary enactments of the Rule of St Benedict.

II. The Statements made

(*a*) The accounts of St Ethelwold's measures contain references to events in
the first half of the twelfth century; in other words, they are not mere tran-
scripts of an older pre-Conquest document.

(*b*) The passage in the *Chronicle* (I, 343–7) occurs more than two hundred
printed pages after another account of St Ethelwold (I, 121–30). The earlier
account is based on Aelfric's contemporary Life of the saint, the second is not.
The passage in the lives of the abbots is likewise independent of Aelfric's Life

and moreover contradicts it and all that we know from other sources of the revival of 960–70 by stating that Ethelwold found a difficulty in getting recruits and therefore modified the Rule. Thus: "In his diebus corrupta erat tota religio Angliae propter incursionem paganorum [et] propter austeritatem regulae Sancti Benedicti, ita quod vix aliquis susciperet monachatum nisi pauper; et ideo ut divites attraheret instituit [a word is illegible here] et relaxavit quae non sunt in regula Sancti Benedicti. I[nstituit] fercla in refectorio, pellicias, cooptoria et caetera" (*Chron. Abingd., de Abbat. Abben.* II, 279). Contrast Aelfric's account of the number of his disciples, and of Ethelwold's anxiety to follow the best models of the Continent; cf. also the strong words of the *Concordia* (Proem, 79), composed by Ethelwold himself, on this very question of diet, and quoted *supra*, p. 458 note 4.

(c) Both the passage in the History and that in the tract on the abbots are clearly designed to attach the saint's name, and even (1, 347) his solemn anathema, to dietary regulations of the most generous kind, including meat and meat ? pies (*Chron. Abingd.* II, 279: "concessit in refectorio ferclum carne mixtum... et artocreas"), lard all the year save during Lent (*ibid.*), wine, mead, and a vast daily allowance (three *galones*) of beer (*ibid.* and 1, 346).

In brief, it is quite impossible to take these fantastic passages as the legislation of Ethelwold or any early ruler. They would seem rather to represent an extreme and perhaps exaggerated version of thirteenth-century practice or relaxation which an Abingdon monk was endeavouring to father upon the great founder in order to preserve the *status quo* against the attacks of reformers.

XX. THE MEASURES OF MONASTIC BEVERAGES

A note may be permitted on the quantity of beer and wine consumed by the Anglo-Saxons and Anglo-Normans—always something of a wonder to those who study the records of the period. Much depends on the equivalence of the *galo* of the documents to the modern gallon, but so far as I am aware this has always been assumed, and Maitland's calculations based upon it as to the amount of arable required to keep England in beer (*Domesday Book and beyond*, ed. 1897, 439–40) have not been challenged. Bearing in mind that the canons of St Paul's had each an allowance of 30 gallons of beer per week (Maitland, *loc. cit.*) and those of Waltham six bottles a week, each sufficient for ten men at a single meal ("sex bollae cervisiae apte sufficientes in coena una x hominibus", *The Foundation of Waltham Abbey*, ed. Stubbs, 16), the alleged Ethelwoldian allowance at Abingdon of three gallons a day (*Chron. Abingd.* 1, 346–7; II, 278–9) and the *caritas* at Battle of a gallon of wine per monk (*Chron. Bell.* 131: "in mensura vini cuilibet fratrum apponenda nil sit minus galone") seem very moderate. Doubtless we must reckon with the total absence of tea and coffee, of fresh fruit and vegetables during most of the year, and perhaps also of soup, but even so these quantities are on a heroic scale, though we may recollect the prudent reserve of Johnson when questioned as to the thirteen bottles of port alleged to have been drunk at a sitting by Dr Campbell (*Life*, ed. G. F. Hill, 1887, III, 243).

On the other hand the Abingdon regulation (*Chron. Abingd.* 1, 346–7) of a sixth or twelfth of a pint (say, a claret glass and liqueur glass respectively), while comprehensible for mead (*hydromellum*), seems very little for wine, save perhaps of a strong dessert kind.

XXI. CHRONOLOGICAL LIST OF ABBATIAL
DEPOSITIONS, 1070–1215

I append a list, as complete as I can make it, of all abbatial depositions or forced resignations among the black monks from 1070 to 1215; this excludes the Anglo-Saxon abbots deposed by the Conqueror at the beginning of his reign.

1070	Malmesbury	Turold transferred to Peterborough (Will. Malmesb., *GP*, 420)
1083	Glastonbury	Thurstan deposed by William I (*v.s.* pp. 114–15)
1094	Burton	Geoffrey expelled from the abbacy (*Ann. Burton.*, *s.a.* 1094, with no further information)
1102	Abbots of Bury, Milton, Muchelney, Pershore, Peterborough, Ramsey, Tavistock, deposed for "irregular" or "simoniacal" election, or for other reasons, by Anselm at the Council of London	
1132	Peterborough	Henry of Poitou expelled by Henry I (*v.s.* pp. 183–4)
1138	Croyland	Waldef deposed by legate Alberic at Council of Westminster in December (*Chron. Ang. Petrib.*, *s.a.* 1139; Richard of Hexham, 175; cf. *GASA*, I, 69, 120–1; "ad reformationem ordinis, qui in domo Crulandiae emarcuerat", but the accounts of Ordericus Vitalis, II, 267 *seqq.*; IV, 428, and Will. Malmesb., *GP*, 321, suggest that political or racial issues were at work, for the deposed abbot Waldef was a brother of Cospatrick, earl of Dunbar, and a cult of earl Waldef existed at Croyland)
[1143	Ramsey	Intrusion and expulsion of Daniel (*Hist. Rames.* 329)]
c. 1147	Cerne	William the Scot expelled (*v.s.* pp. 653–4)
1148	Whitby	Benedict, who had aroused opposition, impelled to resign by Henry Murdac (*Mem. Whitb.* in *Whitby Chartulary*, ed. J. C. Atkinson, Surtees Society, LXIX, 8–9; Hugo Candidus, 85–6)
c. 1150	Selby	Elias impelled to resign by Henry Murdac (for the whole tory, seen from one angle, *v. Historia Selebeiensis Monasterii* in *Selby Coucher Book* [44–5], and *GASA*, I, 120)
1159	Burton	Robert "deposed and expelled" (*Ann. Burton.*, *s.a.*; he returned 1176 and died 1177)
1160	Westminster	Gervase of Blois removed by Henry II (Flete, *History of Westminster*, 91; cf. [Symeon of Durham], II, 330)
1173–6	St Augustine's	Clarembald, intruded 1163, ejected 1173 or 1176 (Will. Thorne, 1819 *seqq.*; Elmham, 35; Gervase, I, 173, 256)
1175	Peterborough	William deposed by Archbishop Richard at wish of Henry II (Hugo Candidus, 93; Benedict of Peterborough, I, 106; Gervase, I, 256; Rad. Diceto, I, 402)
1175	Shrewsbury	Adam "deposed" (*Ann. Theok.*, *s.a.*, with no further facts)
1191	Muchelney	Robert "ejected" (Richard of Devizes, 420)
1195	Thorney	Robert "deposed" (*Annal. Mon. de Thorney*, Brit. Mus. Cott. MS. Nero C 7, *s.a.*; Gervase, I, 530, records the deposition by Hubert Walter of the abbot: "de dilapidatione rerum monasterii sui accusatus")

1195	York	Robert deposed by Hubert Walter (Roger Hoved., *s.a.*; Rad. Diceto, II, 151, states that the command came from Pope Celestine, together with a further one to imprison the ex-abbot)
1206	Ramsey	Robert resigned or was deposed (cf. *Hist. Rames.* 342; *Chron. Ang. Petrib., s.a.* 1206)
1214	Bardney Evesham Westminster	Deposed by legate Nicholas, *v.s.* pp. 341, 653.

XXII. THE USE OF THE TERM *CLUNIACENSIS* BY GERALD OF WALES

All Gerald's readers will have noticed that he consistently uses the name *Cluniacensis* as synonymous with *niger monachus*; so far as I have noted, he is the first English writer to do so. He was of course well aware that the use was not strictly correct when applied to English houses which had no direct dependence upon Cluny, and at the very beginning of the *Speculum Ecclesiae* states this explicitly, though as the passage occurs on a very mutilated page it can easily escape the reader's notice (IV, 30: "Notandum hic autem quod licet a Cluniaco multa sint tam cellae quam coenobia derivata, multo plura tamen quae nec illi subsunt nec originem ab illo proferunt totum per orbem diffusa sunt" [*cetera desunt*]). Apparently his use of the name was intentionally suggestive of decadence (*ibid.* IV, 30, but the passage is corrupt), for ever since the controversy between Bernard and Peter the Venerable the term Cluniac had come to stand for something that had been challenged and blown upon. But Gerald was not the first to use the name for all black monks; in Italy and France all black monachism was in fact Cluniac or allied in custom; Bernard himself would seem to have regarded *Cluniacensis* and *niger monachus* as interchangeable terms for his own country, and the name is found even in papal documents without any implication of dependence on Cluny. Its use by such a prolific and popular writer as Gerald had, however, unfortunate consequences; when antiquarian studies were resumed in England after the Reformation in the circle of Camden, Selden and Cotton, considerable confusion arose, and it was necessary for the revived Benedictines to demonstrate at some length that English medieval monasticism had been wholly independent of French control; this was one of the *raisons d'être* of Reyner's *Apostolatus Benedictinorum in Anglia*. More recently, owing largely to the unintelligent use of the word by Gerald's editor, J. S. Brewer, in his introductions, no little confusion has been caused to the general and casual reader.

XXIII. *CONVERSI* IN THE ENGLISH MONASTERIES

After the pages dealing with the *conversi* had gone to press, some references to this class of monk have come to my notice which, while not necessarily invalidating the conclusions in the text, make it necessary to warn the reader that the point is still somewhat obscure; *v.* the Durham *Liber Vitae*, ed. 1923,

p. 48 (*c.* 1085), and H. F. Westlake, *Westminster Abbey*, II, 377–9 (later centuries). A Swiss friend informs me that a similar obscurity surrounds the status of the *barbati* of Einsiedeln and other Swiss and German monasteries *c.* 1050–1150 and refers me to the works of Dom Odilo Ringholz and Dom Rudolf Henggeler, O.S.B. Clearly the matter needs further investigation.

I. THE DERIVATION OF THE MONASTERIES OF THE REVIVAL OF THE TENTH CENTURY

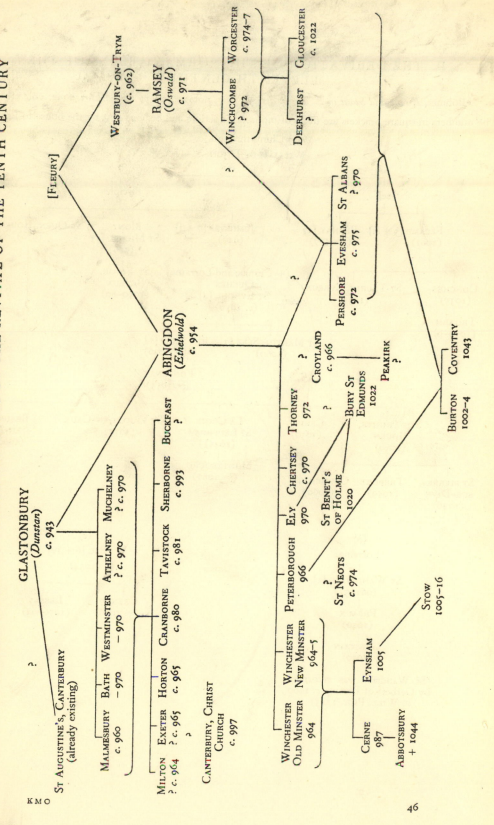

KMO

II. THE DERIVATION OF THE NORMAN ABBEYS OF THE ELEVENTH CENTURY

Böhmer, *Kirche und Staat in E. und in der N.*, p. 7, notes 2 and 3; *Gallia Christiana*, vol. XI.

[The numbers in square brackets are those of monastic superiors and bishops sent by the house to Englan

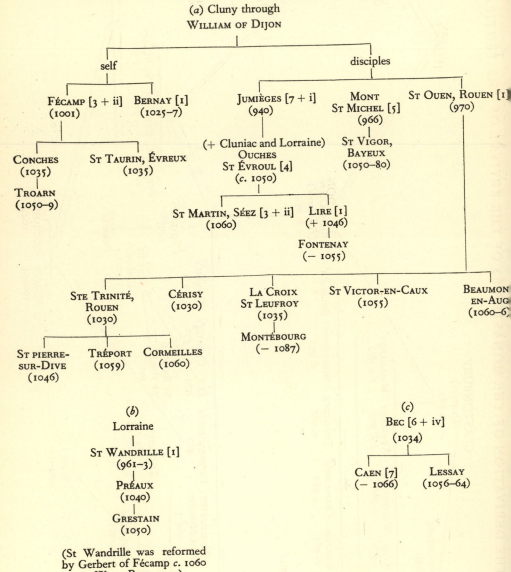

(*a*) Cluny through
WILLIAM OF DIJON

self   disciples

FÉCAMP [3 + ii] BERNAY [1]   JUMIÈGES [7 + i] MONT   ST OUEN, ROUEN [1
(1001)   (1025–7)   (940)   ST MICHEL [5]   (970)
                         (966)

(+ Cluniac and Lorraine)   ST VIGOR,
OUCHES   BAYEUX
CONCHES   ST TAURIN, ÉVREUX   ST ÉVROUL [4]   (1050–80)
(1035)   (1035)   (*c.* 1050)

TROARN
(1050–9)   ST MARTIN, SÉEZ [3 + ii] LIRE [1]
                      (1060)   (+ 1046)

FONTENAY
(– 1055)

STE TRINITÉ,   CÉRISY   LA CROIX   ST VICTOR-EN-CAUX   BEAUMON
ROUEN   (1030)   ST LEUFROY   (1055)   EN-AUG
(1030)   (1035)   (1060–6

MONTÉBOURG
ST PIERRE- TRÉPORT CORMEILLES   (– 1087)
SUR-DIVE   (1059)   (1060)
(1046)

(*b*)
Lorraine

ST WANDRILLE [1]
(961–3)

PRÉAUX
(1040)

GRESTAIN
(1050)

(*c*)
BEC [6 + iv]
(1034)

CAEN [7] LESSAY
(– 1066) (1056–64)

(St Wandrille was reformed
by Gerbert of Fécamp *c.* 1060
v. WILL. PICT. 1243)

III. THE DERIVATION OF THE CLUNIAC HOUSES IN ENGLAND

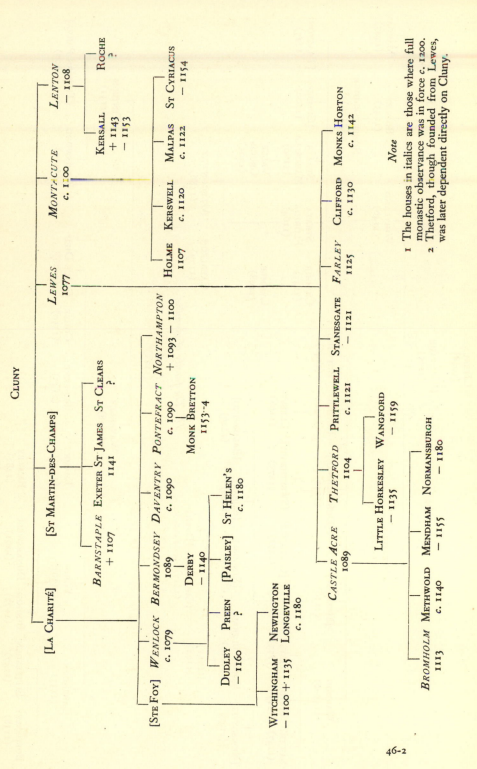

CLUNY

[LA CHARITÉ]

[ST MARTIN-DES-CHAMPS]

BARNSTAPLE EXETER ST JAMES ST CLEARS
+ 1107 1141 ?

[STE FOY] *WENLOCK* *BERMONDSEY* *DAVENTRY* *PONTEFRACT* *NORTHAMPTON*
c. 1079 1089 c. 1090 c. 1090 + 1093 – 1100

DERBY
– 1140

MONK BRETTON
1153–4

DUDLEY PREEN [PAISLEY] ST HELEN'S
– 1160 ? c. 1180

WITCHINGHAM NEWINGTON
– 1100 +'1135 LONGEVILLE
c. 1180

LEWES
1077

HOLME KERSWELL
1107 c. 1120

MONTACUTE
c. 1100

KERSALL
+ 1143
– 1153

MALPAS
c. 1122

LENTON
– 1108

ROCHE
?

ST CYRIACUS
– 1154

CASTLE ACRE *THETFORD* PRITTLEWELL STANESGATE *FARLEY* CLIFFORD MONKS HORTON
1089 1104 c. 1121 – 1121 1125 c. 1130 c. 1142

WANGFORD
– 1159

LITTLE HORKESLEY
– 1135

BROMHOLM METHWOLD MENDHAM NORMANSBURGH
1113 c. 1140 – 1155 – 1180

Note

1 The houses in italics are those where full monastic observance was in force c. 1200.
2 Thetford, though founded from Lewes, was later dependent directly on Cluny.

46-2

IV. THE DERIVATION OF THE ENGLISH AND WELSH CISTERCIAN ABBEYS

I. The family of Clairvaux

II. The family of Aumône

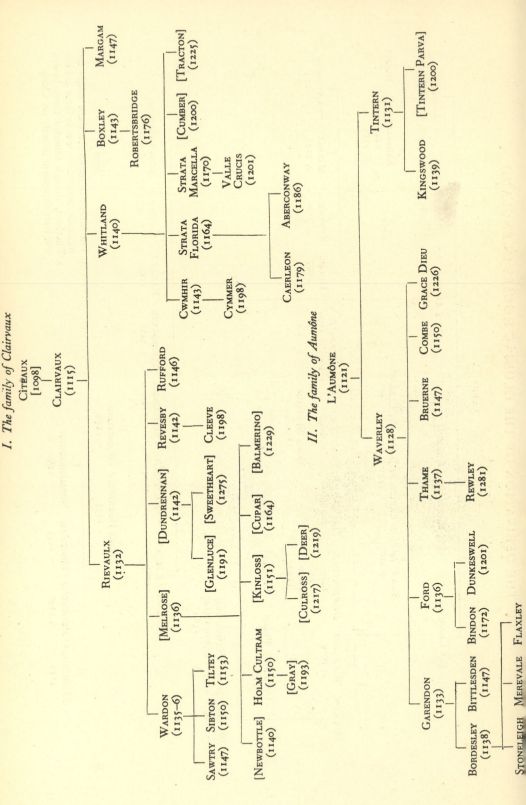

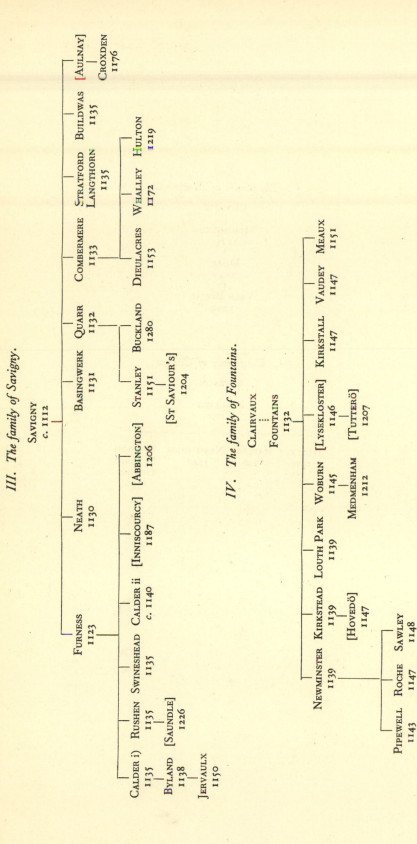

III. The family of Savigny.

SAVIGNY
c. 1112

FURNESS 1123 — NEATH 1130 — BASINGWERK 1131 — QUARR 1132 — COMBERMERE 1133 — STRATFORD LANGTHORN 1135 — BUILDWAS 1135

CALDER i) 1135 — RUSHEN 1135 — SWINESHEAD 1135 — CALDER ii c. 1140 — [INNISCOURCY] 1187 — [ABBINGTON] 1206

STANLEY 1151 — BUCKLAND 1280

[ST SAVIOUR'S] 1204

DIEULACRES 1153 — WHALLEY 1172 — HULTON 1219

[AULNAY] — CROXDEN 1176

BYLAND 1138 — [SAUNDLE] 1226

JERVAULX 1150

IV. The family of Fountains.

CLAIRVAUX
⋮
FOUNTAINS
1132

NEWMINSTER 1139 — KIRKSTEAD 1139 — LOUTH PARK 1139 — WOBURN 1145 — [LYSEKLOSTER] 1146 — KIRKSTALL 1147 — VAUDEY 1147 — MEAUX 1151

[HOVEDÖ] 1147 — MEDMENHAM 1212 — [TUTTERÖ] 1207

PIPEWELL 1143 — ROCHE 1147 — SAWLEY 1148

V. The family of Morimond.

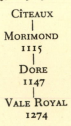

CÎTEAUX
|
MORIMOND
1115
|
DORE
1147
|
VALE ROYAL
1274

VI. The family of Cîteaux.

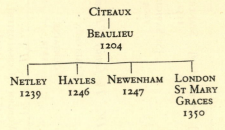

CÎTEAUX
|
BEAULIEU
1204
|

NETLEY	HAYLES	NEWENHAM	LONDON
1239	1246	1247	ST MARY
			GRACES
			1350

BIBLIOGRAPHY

The list which follows is not a bibliography of English monasticism; such a bibliography, for the period concerned, would, at least in regard to contemporary sources, differ little from one of English history in general, for it would not be easy to name a dozen original works or compilations of the eleventh and twelfth centuries which do not contain some information regarding monks or monasteries; the list would, besides, have to include all the cartularies, registers, calendars, etc., printed and unprinted, preserved in the libraries of the country. Nor, on the other hand, is it a complete list of all the works consulted for the purposes of this book. I have examined or read many manuscripts, printed sources, modern works and articles bearing on English monastic life which either contained nothing of value, or at least gave no occasion for quotation or reference. What follows, therefore, is merely a list of all those books and original sources quoted or referred to in the text or notes of this book, and in the case of manuscripts, only those actually quoted are listed here; references to many others will be found in the notes. I may add that when a reference has been given on the authority of another, acknowledgment is made in a footnote, but the book referred to does not as a rule appear in this list.

I. CONTEMPORARY SOURCES

(a) MANUSCRIPTS

Brit. Mus.: Additional MS. 36,985 (Tewkesbury Register). A sixteenth-century transcript of a lost original, containing matter not in *Monasticon*, II, 59.
  Arundel MS. 68, f. 84b (Register of Christ Church, Canterbury, of fourteenth century onwards).
  Cott. Cleop. B i, no. 3, f. 33 (Life, etc., of Gilbert of Sempringham).
  Cott. Domit. XV, no. 2, f. 7 (History of Ely).
  Cott. Nero C 7, no. 13 f. 79 (Thorney Annals).
  Cott. Vespasian B xxiv,,ff. 19–20b (letters concerning Odensee in Evesham Register).
  Cott. Vitellius A xiii, f. 24 (letter of Pope Agatho to Erconwald of London).
Oxford: Bodl. MS. Digby 36 (Life, etc., of Gilbert of Sempringham).
Durham: Chapter MS. B IV 25 (the *de Anima* of Ailred of Rievaulx).

(b) PRINTED SOURCES

Abingdon, Chronicon Monasterii de, ed. J. Stevenson (RS, 2, 2 vols. 1858)
Acta Sanctorum Bollandiana (Brussels and elsewhere, 1643 onwards).
Acta Sanctorum Ordinis S. Benedicti, ed. L. D'Achéry and J. Mabillon (Paris, 1668–1701).
Adalberon of Laon, poems, in *Rerum Gallicarum* (*q.v.*), X, 61–72.
Adami Bremensis Gesta Hannaburgensis Ecclesiae Pontificum, in *MGH, SS,* VII.

Aelfric, Homilies, in *Liber Sermonum Catholicorum*, ed. B. Thorpe (Aelfric Society, 2 vols. London, 1844).
—— Lives of the Saints, ed. W. W. Skeat (EETS, vol. I, 1881; vol. II, 1900).
Aelfric's Colloquy, ed. G. N. Garmonsway (London, 1938).
Aelfrici Colloquium, ed. B. Thorpe, *Analecta Anglo-Saxonica* (ed. 2, London, 1868).
Aethelwold, St, The Benedictional of, ed. G. F. Warner and H. B. Wilson (Roxburghe Club, 1910).
Aethelwoldi, S., *Vita auct. Aelfrico*, in *Chronic. Abingdon.* (*q.v.*), vol. II, Appendix i.
Ailredi, S., *Opera*, in *PL*, CXCV.
—— *De Institutis Inclusarum*, in *Augustini Opera*, ed. Benedictina (reprinted Paris, 1836), I, i; also in *PL*, XXXII, 1451 *seqq.*
—— *De Sanctis Ecclesiae Hagulstadensis*, in *The Priory of Hexham*, ed. J. Raine, SS, XLIV, vol. i (1864), 173–203.
Albani, S., *Chronica Monasterii*, ed. H. T. Riley (RS, 28, 12 vols. 1863–76); vol. IV contains the *Gesta Abbatum S. Albani*.
Alexandri III, Papae, *Litterae et Diplomata*, in *PL*, CC.
Amalarii *de Ordine Antiphonarii*, in *PL*, CV.
Anglo-Saxon Chronicle, The, Two Saxon Chronicles, ed. J. Earle and C. Plummer (2 vols. Oxford, 1892, 1899).
—— The D Text, ed. E. Classen and F. F. Harner (Manchester, 1926).
Anglo-Saxonici Annales, v.s. Liebermann, F., *Ungedruckte...Geschichtsquellen.*
Annales Monastici, ed. H. R. Luard (RS, 36, 5 vols. 1864–9), containing vol. 1: *de Margam, Theokesberia et Burton*; vol. 2: *de Wintonia et Waverleia*; vol. 3: *de Dunstaplia et Bermundeseia*; vol. 4: *de Oseneia et de Wigornia.*
Anselmi, S., *Opera*, in *PL*, CLVIII.
Asser, *de Rebus Gestis Aelfredi*, ed. W. H. Stevenson (Oxford, 1896).
Baedae *Opera Historica*, ed. C. Plummer (2 vols. Oxford, 1896).
Bartholomaei Farnensis Vita, auct. Galfrido Dunelmensi, *v.s.* Durham, Symeon of, *Opera*, I, Appendix II, 295–325.
Beccense, Chronicon, ed. A. A. Porée, for Soc. de l'Histoire de la Normandie, 1883.
Becket, Materials for the History of, ed. J. C. Robertson and J. B. Sheppard (RS, 67, 7 vols. 1875–85).
Bede, Works, ed. J. A. Giles (London, 1843–4).
Bello, Chronicon Monasterii de, ed. J. S. Brewer, Anglia Christiana Society, 1846.
Benedict of Peterborough, Chronicle of the reigns of Henry II and Richard I, ed. W. Stubbs (RS, 49, 2 vols. 1867).
Benigni Divionensis, S., Chronicon, in *PL*, CXLI.
Bermondsey, Annals of, *v.s. Annales Monastici.*
Bernard, A., *v.s.* Cluny.
Bernardi, S., *Opera*, ed. J. Mabillon (reprinted Paris, 1836, and in *PL*, CLXXXII–CLXXXV).
Bernardi Tironensis Vita, auct. Gaufrido Grosso, in *PL*, CLXXII, 1367–1446.
Blesensis, Petri, *Epistolae*, ed. J. A. Giles (4 vols. Oxford, 1846–7); also in *PL*, CCVII.
Bosworth Psalter, The, ed. F. A. Gasquet and E. Bishop (London, 1908).
Brut y Tywysogion, ed. J. Williams ab Ithel (RS, 17, 1860).
Burchardi Decretum, in *PL*, CXL.
Burton, Annals of, *v.s. Annales Monastici.*
Bury, Memorials of the Abbey of St Edmund at, ed. T. Arnold (RS, 96, 3 vols. 1890–6).
Byrhtferth, *Manual*, ed. S. J. Crawford (EETS, 177, 1928).
Cambriae, Annales, ed. J. Williams ab Ithel (RS, 20, 1860).
Cassiani, Joannis, *Opera*, ed. M. Petschenig, in *Corpus SS Eccl. Lat.* (Vienna, 1886–8).
Cassinensis, Chronicon Monasterii, auct. Leone, in *MGH, SS*, VII (1846).
Cassiodori Senatoris Institutiones, ed. R. A. B. Mynors (Oxford, 1937).
Censuum, Liber, ed. P. Fabre et L. Duchesne (Paris, 1889, 1910).

Cisterciensis, Statuta Capitulorum Generalium Ordinis, ed. J. M. Canivez, t. I, 1116–1220 (Louvain, 1933).

Coggeshall, Radulphi de, *Chronicon Anglicanum*, ed. J. Stevenson (RS, 66, 1875).

Coldingham, Geoffrey of, *v.s. Dunelmensis Hist. Scriptores Tres.*

—— Reginald of, ed. *s.n.* [? J. Raine], SS, I (1835).

Colecestrenses, Annales, *v.s.* Liebermann, F., *Ungedruckte Geschichtsquellen.*

Colecestria, Cartularium Monasterii S. Johannis Baptiste de, ed. S. A. Moore (Roxburghe Club, 1897).

Colloquies, Early Scholastic, ed. W. H. Stevenson (*Anecdota Oxoniensia*, Med. and Mod. Series, XV, 1929).

Coventria, Fratris Walteri de, Memoriale, ed. W. Stubbs (RS, 58, 2 vols. 1872–3).

Crawford Charters, The, ed. A. S. Napier and W. H. Stevenson (*Anecdota Oxoniensia*, Med. and Mod. Series, VII, 1895).

Dale Abbey, Chronicle of, ed. W. H. St John Hope in *Journal of the Derbyshire Archaeological Society*, V (1883), 1–30.

Diceto, Radulphi de, *Opera Historica*, ed. W. Stubbs (RS, 68, 2 vols. 1876).

Diurnus, Liber, ed. T. von Sickel (Vienna, 1889–).

Domerham, Adami de, *Historia de rebus gestis Glastoniensibus*, ed. T. Hearne (2 vols. London, 1727).

Domesday Book, The, 4 vols. (London, 1783–1816).

Dunelmensis, Feodarium Prioratus, ed. W. Greenwell (SS, LVIII, 1872).

—— *Historiae Scriptores Tres*, ed. J. Raine (SS, IX, 1839).

—— *Liber Vitae*, ed. J. Stevenson (SS, XIII, 1841).

—— *Liber Vitae*, collotype facsimile, with introd. by A. Hamilton Thompson (SS, CXXXVI, 1923).

Dunstable, Annals of, *v.s. Annales Monastici.*

Dunstan, St, Memorials of, ed. W. Stubbs (RS, 63, 1874).

Durham, The Catalogues of the old monastic Library of, ed. B. Botfield (SS, VII, 1838).

—— Symeon of, *Opera*, ed. T. Arnold (RS, 75, 2 vols. 1882–5).

Eadmeri *Epistola ad Glastonienses*, in *Memorials of St Dunstan, q.v.*

—— *Historia Novorum*, etc., ed. M. Rule (RS, 81, 1884).

—— *Tractatus de conceptione S. Mariae*, ed. H. Thurston and T. Slater, S.J. (Freiburg-im-Breisgau, 1904); also in *PL*, CLIX, 300 *seqq.*

—— *Vita Anselmi*, in *Historia Novorum*, etc., 304–424.

—— *Vita S. Dunstani*, in *Memorials of St Dunstan, q.v.*

Ecgberti, S., *de institutione catholica dialogus*, in *PL*, LXXXIX.

Edward the Confessor, Lives of, ed. H. R. Luard (RS, 3, 1858).

Eliensis, Liber, ed. D. J. Stewart (Anglia Christiana Soc. 1848).

Elmham, Thomas of, *Historia Monasterii S. Augustini Cantuariensis*, ed. C. Hardwick (RS, 8, 1858).

Evesham, Chronicon Monasterii de, ed. W. D. Macray (RS, 29, 1863).

Exchequer, The Red Book of, ed. H. Hall (RS, 99, 3 vols. 1897).

Foliot, G., *Epistolae*, ed. J. A. Giles (2 vols. Oxford, 1845); also in *PL*, CXCIX.

Fountains, Memorials of the Abbey of St Mary of, ed. J. S. Walbran (SS, XLII, vol. I, 1863).

Furness Coucher Book, The, ed. J. C. Atkinson (Chetham Society, IX, 3 vols. Manchester, 1886–).

Gaufridi Saviniacensis, B., Vita, ed. Sauvage in *Analecta Bollandiana*, I (1882), 390–410.

Gervase of Canterbury, *Opera*, ed. W. Stubbs (RS, 73, 2 vols. 1879–80).

Gilberti de Hoiland *Opera*, in *Bernardi Opera*, ed. J. Mabillon, V, 5–395.

Gilbertine Rite, The, ed. R. M. Woolley (HBS, 2 vols. 1921–2).

Giraldi Cambrensis *Opera*, ed. J. S. Brewer, J. F. Dimock and G. F. Warner (RS, 21, 8 vols. 1861–91).

—— *de Invectionibus*, ed. W. S. Davies in *Y Cymmrodor*, XXX, 1920.

Giraldi Cambrensis, The Autobiography of, *v.s.* Butler, H. E.; also *v.s.* Powicke, F. M.

Glaber, Rodulphus, *v.s. Willelmi, S.*

Glamorgancia, *Cartae et alia Munimenta quae ad Dominium de Glamorgancia pertinent* (ed. G. T. Clark, 5 vols. Cardiff, 1910).

Glocestrensis, *Historia et Cartularium Monasterii S. Petri*, ed. W. H. Hart (RS, 31, 3 vols. 1863–7).

Gocelini *Historia translationis S. Augustini*, in *PL*, CLV, 15 *seqq.*

Godrici, S., *Libellus de vita et miraculis*, auct. Reginaldo Dunelmensi, ed. J. Stevenson (SS, XX, 1845).

Gratiani *Decretum*, in *Corpus Juris Canonici*, ed. E. Friedberg (2 vols. Leipzig, 1879–81).

Gregorii Magni, S., *Overa*, in *PL*, LXXV–LXXIX.

—— *Vita*, in *PL*, LXXV.

Guigonis Prioris Cartusiae *Opera*, in *PL*, CLIII.

Gundulfi Vita, in *PL*, CLIX.

Guthlac Roll, The, ed. Sir G. Warner (Roxburghe Club, 1928).

Hemming, *Chartularium, v.s. Wigorniensis.*

Hexham, The Priory of, its Chroniclers, etc., ed. J. Raine (SS, XLIV, 1865).

—— John of, Chronicle, in Symeon of Durham (RS), II, 284–332; also in J. Raine, *The Priory of Hexham* (SS), I, 107–72.

—— Richard of, Chronicle, in *Chronicles of the Reigns of Stephen*, etc. (RS), III, 139–78; also in J. Raine, *The Priory of Hexham* (SS), I, 63–106.

Hoveden, Roger of, *Chronica*, ed. W. Stubbs (RS, 51, 4 vols. 1868–71).

Hugonis, S., Cluniacensis, *Vita*, in *PL*, CLIX.

—— Lincolniensis, *Magna Vita*, ed. J. F. Dimock (RS, 37, 1864).

Hugonis Candidi *Coenobii Burgensis Historia*, in *Historiae Anglicanae Scriptores*, ed. J. Sparke (London, 1723–).

Hugonis Lugdunensis archiepiscopi *Epistolae et Privilegia*, in *PL*, CLVII.

Hugonis Rotomagensis *Opera*, in *PL*, CXCII.

Hyde Abbey, Winchester, The *Liber Vitae* of, ed. W. de G. Birch (Hants. Record Soc. 1892).

———— The Monastic Breviary of, ed. J. B. L. Tolhurst (HBS, vol. I, 1932).

Innocentii III, Papae, *Registrum et Decreta*, in *PL*, CCXIV–CCXVI.

Joannis Diaconi *Opera*, in *PL*, LXXV.

Johannis Glastoniensis *Chronica sive historia de rebus Glastoniensibus*, ed. T. Hearne (Oxford, 1726).

Johannis de Oxenedes *Chronica*, ed. H. Ellis (RS, 13, 1859).

Johannis de Pontissara *Registrum*, ed. C. Deedes (Canterbury and York Soc., London, 1913–15).

Johannis Sarisberiensis *Historia Pontificalis*, ed. R. L. Poole (Oxford, 1927).

—— *Opera*, ed. J. A. Giles (5 vols. Oxford, 1848); also in *PL*, CXCIX.

Juris Canonici, Codex (Rome, 1917).

Kyrkestall, Fundacio Abbathie de, ed. E. K. Clark (Thoresby Soc. IV, Miscellanea, 169–208, Leeds, 1895).

Lanercost, Chronicon de, ed. J. Stevenson (Bannatyne Club, 1839).

Lanfranci *Opera*, ed. J. A. Giles (2 vols. Oxford, 1844).

—— *Vita*, auct. M. Crispin, in *Opera*, ed. Giles.

Leechdoms, Wortcunning and Starcraft of Early England, ed. O. Cockayne (RS, 35, 3 vols. 1864–6).

Lincoln, The *Registrum Antiquissimum* of, ed. C. W. Foster (Lincs. Record Soc. no. 27, vol. I, 1931).

Losinga, Herberti de, primi episcopi Norwicensis, *Epistolae*, ed. R. Anstruther (Brussels, 1846); trans., with additional matter, as Life, Letters and Sermons of Herbert de Losinga, by Goulburn and Symonds (2 vols. Oxford, 1878).

Louth Park, Chronicle of, ed. Venables (Lincs. Record Soc. no. 1, 1891).

Mailros, Chronica de, ed. J. Stevenson (Bannatyne Club, 1835).
Malmesbury, William of, *de Antiquitate ecclesiae Glastoniensis*, ed. Gale, *Historiae Britannicae Scriptores*, XV (Oxford, 1691).
—— *de Gestis Pontificum Anglorum*, ed. N. E. S. A. Hamilton (RS, 52, 1870).
—— *de Gestis Regum Anglorum*, ed. W. Stubbs (RS, 90, 1887–9).
—— *Historiae Novellae*, in *de Gestis Regum.*
—— *Vita Dunstani*, in *Memorials of St Dunstan.*
—— *Vita Wulfstani*, ed. R. R. Darlington (CS, XL, 1928).
Malmesbury Abbey, *Registrum* of, ed. J. S. Brewer (RS, 72, 2 vols. 1879–80).
Manniae, Chronicon Regum, quoted from Stevenson, J., *The Church Historians of England*, vol. V, i.
Map, Walter, Latin Poems attributed to, T. Wright (CS, XVI, 1841).
—— *de Nugis Curialium*, ed. T. Wright (CS, L, 1850).
—— ——ed. M. R. James, in *Anecdota Oxoniensia*, Med. and Mod. Series, part 14 (1914).
Margam, Annals of, *v.s. Annales Monastici*, vol. I.
Melsa (Meaux), *Chronica Monasterii de*, ed. E. A. Bond (RS, 43, 3 vols. 1866–68).
Monumenta Germaniae Historica, ed. G. H. Pertz and others: *Scriptores*, vols. I–XXXII (Hanover, 1826–1913); *Epistolae*, vols. I–VII (Berlin, 1887–1912).
Newburgh, William of, *Historia*, in Stephen... Chronicles of, *q.v.*
Nili, S., Vita, auct. ? Bartholomaeo, in *Acta SS*, Sept. VII, 283 *seqq.*
Orderici Vitalis Ecclesiasticae Historiae, ed. A. Le Prévost and L. Delisle (Société de l'Histoire de France, 5 vols. 1840–55).
Osbert of Clare, The Letters of, ed. E. W. Williamson, with introd. by J. Armitage Robinson (Oxford, 1929).
Oseney, Annals of, *v.s. Annales Monastici*, IV.
Paris, Matthew, *Historia Anglorum*, ed. F. Madden (RS, 44, 3 vols. 1866–9).
—— *Chronica Majora*, ed. H. R. Luard (RS, 57, 7 vols. 1872–84).
Patrologiae cursus completus, series Latina, ed. J. P. Migne (Paris, 1844–64).
Petri Cellensis *Opera*, in *PL*, CCII.
Petri Damiani *Opera*, in *PL*, CXLV.
Petri Venerabilis *Opera*, in *PL*, CLXXXIX.
Petriburgense, Chronicon Angliae, ed. J. A. Giles (Caxton Soc. 1845).
Pipe, Great Roll of the, ed. Pipe Roll Society.
Plymtonienses, Annales, in Liebermann, *Ungedruckte Geschichtsquellen.*
Radingenses, Annales, in Liebermann, *Ungedruckte Geschichtsquellen.*
Rameseia, Cartularium Monasterii de, ed. W. H. Hart and A. P. Lyon (RS, 79, 3 vols. 1884–94).
Ramsey, Abbey, *Chronicon*, ed. W. D. Macray (RS, 83, 1886).
Rerum Gallicarum et Franciscarum Scriptores, ed. M. Bouquet, etc.; re-ed. L. Delisle, vols. I–XIX, 1868–80.
Richard I, Chronicles and Memorials of the Reign of, ed. W. Stubbs (RS, 38, 2 vols. 1864–5).
Richardi S. Victoris *Opera*, in *PL*, CXXVI.
Rievallense, Cartularium, ed. J. C. Atkinson (SS, LXXXIII, 1887).
Robert, Archbishop, The Benedictional of, ed. H. B. Wilson (HBS, XXIV, 1902).
Robert of Jumièges, The Missal of, ed. H. B. Wilson (HBS, XI, 1896).
Roberti (de Arbrissel), *B., Vita*, auct. Baldrico ep. Dolensi, in *Acta SS*, Febr. III, 603–8.
—— *Extrema Conversatio*, auct. Andrea monacho, in *Acta SS*, Febr. III, 608–14.
Roberti, S., of Newminster, *Vita*, ed. P. Grosjean, S.J., in *Analecta Bollandiana*, LVI (1928), 343–60.
Roffensis, Textus, ed. T. Hearne (Oxford, 1720).
Romualdi, S., *Vita*, auct. Petro Damiano, in *PL*, CXLIV, 953 *seqq.*
Salisbury, Charters and Documents of, ed. W. Rich-Jones and W. D. Macray (RS, 97, 1891).

Sarisberiense, Vetus Registrum, ed. W. Rich-Jones (RS, 78, 2 vols. 1883–4).

Satirical Poets and Epigrammatists of the Twelfth Century, Anglo-Latin, ed. T. Wright (RS, 59, 2 vols. 1872).

Scaccarii, Liber Niger, in *Dialogus de scaccario,* ed. A. Hughes and others (Oxford, 1902).

Selebeiensis Monasterii Historia, in Selby Coucher Book, ed. J. T. Fowler (Yorks. Archaeol. Soc., Rec. Ser. 10, 1891).

Soliaco, Henrici de, Liber, ed. J. E. Jackson (Roxburghe Club, 1887).

Somerset, Historia de primordiis episcopatus, ed. J. Hunter (CS, VIII, 1840).

Stephani Grandimontensis, S., *Vita et Regula,* in *PL,* CCIV, 1005–72, 1135–62.

Stephen, Henry II and Richard I, Chronicles of the Reigns of, ed. R. Howlett (RS, 82, 4 vols. 1884–90).

Swapham, Roberti, *continuatio Historiae Hugonis Candidi, v.s.* Hugonis Candidi.

Swithuni, S., *Vita,* auct. Wulfstano, in *Acta SS. OSB,* VII, s. 5.

Tewkesbury, Annals of, *v.s. Annales Monastici,* I.

Thorne, Willelmi, *Chronicon S. Augustini Cantuariensis,* ed. R. Twysden, *Scriptores X* (London, 1652).

Torigni, Robert of, *Chronica,* ed. L. Delisle (Soc. de l'Histoire de Normandie, 2 vols. Rouen, 1872–3); also in *Chronicles of the Reigns of Stephen,* etc.

—— *Tractatus de Immutatione Ordinis Monachorum,* in *PL,* CCII, 1312 *seqq.*

Udalrici Cluniacensis *Consuetudines,* in *PL,* CXLIX.

Vitalis Saviniacensis, B., Vita, auct. Stephano de Fulgeriis, ed. Sauvage (*Analecta Bollandiana,* I, 1882, 355–90).

Waldeni, S., Vita, auct. Jocelino Furnesensi, in *Acta SS,* August, I, 248 *seqq.*

Waltham Abbey, The Foundation of, ed. W. Stubbs (Oxford, 1861).

Waverley, Annals of, *v.s. Annales Monastici,* II.

Wendover, Roger of, *Chronica,* ed. H. G. Hewlett (RS, 84, 3 vols. 1886–9).

Whiteby, Cartularium Abbathiae de, ed. J. C. Atkinson (SS, LXIX, 1879).

Wigorniensis, Chartularium Ecclesiae, of Hemming, ed. T. Hearne (2 vols. Oxford, 1723).

William of Poitiers, ed. Duchesne (Paris, 1619).

Willelmi, S., Vita, auct. Rodulpho Glabro, in *Acta SS. OSB,* I, s. vi, 286; also in *PL,* CXLII, 697 *seqq.*

Willelmi a S. Theodorico *Epistola ad fratres de Monte Dei,* in *Bernardi Opera,* ed. Mabillon, V, 419 *seqq.*

Willibaldi, S., Vita, in *MGH, SS,* XV.

Winchester, Annals of, *v.s. Annales Monastici,* II.

Winchester, St Swithun's, Obedientiary Rolls of, ed. Dean Kitchin (Hants. Rec. Soc. 1892).

Winchester Cathedral Chartulary, ed. A. W. Goodman (Winchester, 1928).

Winchester Troper, The, ed. W. H. Frere (HBS, VIII, 1894).

Wireker, Nigel, in *Satirical Poets, Anglo-Latin,* ed. T. Wright.

Worcester, Antiphonaire Monastique de, in *Paléographie Musicale,* XII (Louvain, 1922).

Worcester, Florence of, Chronicle, ed. B. Thorpe (Eng. Hist. Soc. 2 vols. London, 1848–9).

Worcester, John of, Chronicle, ed. J. H. R. Weaver, in *Anecdota Oxoniensia,* Med. and Mod. Series, 13 (1908).

Worcester Annals, *v.s. Annales Monastici,* IV.

Wulfrici, S., Vita, auct. Johanne Fordensi, ed. Dom M. Bell (Som. Rec. Soc. XLVII, 1933).

Wulfstan, *Sermo Lupi ad Anglos* of, ed. D. Whitelock (London, 1938).

Wykes, Thomae, *Chronica* de, in *Annales Monastici,* IV.

York, Historians of the Church of, ed. J. Raine (RS, 71, 3 vols. 1879–94).

York, St Mary's, Chronicle of, ed. H. H. E. Craster and M. E. Thornton (SS, CXLVIII, 1933).

Yorkshire Charters, Early, 5 vols. 1914–37, ed. W. Farrer (vols. 1–3) and C. T. Clay (vols. 4–5).

II. MODERN WORKS

Albans, St, History of the Abbey of, *v.s.* Williams, L. F. R.

Albers, Dom Bruno, *Consuetudines Monasticae*, 5 vols. (I, Stuttgart and Vienna, 1900; II, III, IV, V, Monte Cassino, 1905, 1907, 1911, 1912).

Ashdown, M., English and Norse Documents (Cambridge, 1930).

Atkins, Sir Ivor, The Church of Worcester from the Eighth to the Twelfth Century, in *The Antiquaries Journal*, XVII, 4 (Oct. 1937), 371–91.

Ault, W. O., Private Jurisdiction in England (*Yale Historical Publications*, Miscellany, vol. 10, New Haven, 1923).

Bale, J., *Index Britanniae Scriptorum*, ed. R. L. Poole and M. Bateson (Oxford, 1902).

Barraclough, G., Mediaeval Germany, 911–1250. Essays by German Historians, translated by G. Barraclough, vol. 2 (Oxford, 1938).
This volume includes:
Essay II. The Proprietary Church as an Element of Medieval Germanic Ecclesiastical Law, by U. Stutz (pp. 35–70). Essay V. The Constitutional History of the Reformed Monasteries during the Investiture Contest, by H. Hirsch (pp. 131–173).

Bateson, M., Aelfric's Letter to the Monks of Eynsham, in *Obedientiary Rolls of St Swithun's*, ed. Kitchin (Hants. Rec. Soc. 1892).

—— Huntingdon Song School, The, in *EHR*, XVIII (1903), 712–13.

—— Rules for Monks and Secular Canons after the revival under King Edgar, in *EHR*, IX (1894), 690–708.

—— Also *v.s.* Bale.

Beddie, J. S., The Ancient Classics in the Medieval Libraries, in *Speculum*, V (1930), 3–20.

Bede: his Life, Times and Writings, ed. A. Hamilton Thompson (Oxford, 1935).

Berlière, Dom Ursmer, Archidiaconés ou Exemptions privilégiées de monastères, Les in *RB*, XL (1928), 116–22.

—— Ascèse bénédictine, L' (Paris and Maredsous, 1927).

—— Cardinal Mathieu d'Albano, Le, in *RB*, XVIII (1901), 113–40, 280–303.

—— Chapitres généraux de l'ordre de S. Benoît, Les, in *RB*, XVIII (1901), 364–98; XIX (1902), 38–75, 268–78, 374–411. Reprinted in *Mélanges* (*v. inf.*), 52–171.

—— Cîteaux, Les origines de, et l'ordre bénédictin du xii siècle, in *Revue d'histoire ecclésiastique*, I (1900), 448–71; II (1901), 253–90.

—— Documents inédits pour servir à l'histoire ecclés. de la Belgique (Maredsous, 1894).

—— Écoles claustrales au Moyen-Âge, Les, in *Bulletin de la Classe des Lettres de l'Académie royale de Belgique* (1921), 550–72.

—— Innocent III et la réorganisation des monastères bénédictins, in *RB*, XXXII (1920), 22–42, 145–59.

—— Mélanges d'histoire bénédictine, sér. 4 (Maredsous, 1902).

—— Nombre des moines dans les anciens monastères, Le, in *RB*, XLI (1929), 231–61; XLII (1930), 31–42.

—— Ordre Monastique, L' (Paris, ed. 1, 1912; ed. 3, 1924).

—— Paroissial, L'Exercice du ministère, par les moines dans le haut Moyen-Âge, in *RB*, XXXIX (1927), 227–50.

Besse, Dom, L'ordre de Cluny et son gouvernement, in *Revue Mabillon*, 1905, 5 *seqq.*, 97 *seq.*, 177 *seqq.*; 1906, 1 *seqq.*

Bilson, J., Architecture of the Cistercians, The, in *Archaeological Journal*, LXVI (1909), 18   280.

—— Beginnings of Gothic Architecture, The, in *Journal of the Royal Institute of British Architects*, ser. 3, VI, 259–89.

Birch, W. de G., *Cartularium Saxonicum* (3 vols. London, 1885–93).

Bishop, E., *v.s.* Bosworth Psalter.

—— Cluniacs and Cistercians, in *DR*, LII (1934), 48–70.

—— Fasting and Abstinence of the Black Monks in England before the Reformation, The Method and Degree of, in *DR*, XLIII (1925), 184–237.

—— *Liturgica Historica* (Oxford, 1918), containing in particular the following:
On the Origins of the Feast of the Conception of the Blessed Virgin Mary, 238–59.
Origins of the Cope as a Church Vestment, 260–75.
Holy Week Rites of Sarum, Hereford and Rouen compared, 276–300.
Gifts of Bishop Henry of Blois, Abbat of Glastonbury, to Winchester Cathedral, 392–401.

Bittermann, H. R., The Organ in the early Middle Ages, in *Speculum*, IV (1929), 390–410.

Blanchard, Dom P., Un monument primitif de la règle cistercienne, in *RB*, XXXI (1914), 35–44.

Bloch, M., La Vie de S. Édouard le Confesseur par Osbert de Clare, in *Analecta Bollandiana*, XLI (1923), 17–44.

Böhmer, H., Eigenkirchentum in England, Das, in *Texte und Forschungen zur Englischen Kulturgeschichte; Festgabe für Felix Liebermann* (Halle, 1921), 301–53.

—— Fälschungen Erzbischof Lanfrancs von Canterbury, Die (Leipzig, 1902).

—— Germanische Christentum, Das, in *Theologische Studien und Kritiken* (Gotha, 1913), 165–280.

—— Kirche und Staat in England und in der Normandie (Leipzig, 1899).

Bolton Priory, History of, *v.s.* Thompson, A. H.

Bras, G. Le (with P. Fournier), Histoire des Collections Canoniques en Occident (2 vols. Paris, 1931–2).

Brechter, Dom Suso, Monte Cassinos erste Zerstörung, in *Studien und Mitteilungen zur Geschichte des Benediktiner-Ordens*, LVI (1938), 109–50.

Brooke, Z. N., The English Church and the Papacy (Cambridge, 1931).

—— Pope Gregory VII's demand for fealty from William the Conqueror, in *EHR*, XXVI (1911), 225–38.

Brown, G. Baldwin, St Cuthbert's Stole and Maniple at Durham, in *Burlington Magazine*, XXIII (April and May 1913).

Bruel, A., *v.s.* Cluny.

Burridge, A. W., L'Immaculée Conception dans la théologie de l'Angleterre médiévale, in *Revue d'histoire ecclésiastique*, XXXII (July 1936), 570–97.

Butler, Dom Cuthbert, Benedict and the Sixth Century, St, in *DR*, XLVIII (1930), 179–97.

—— *Benedicti Regula, S.* (Freiburg-im-Breisgau, 1912, 1927).

—— Benedictine Monachism (London, 1919, 1927).

—— Dunstan's Kyrie, St, in *DR*, V (1885), 49–51.

—— Lausiac History of Palladius, The, in *Texts and Studies* (2 vols. Cambridge, 1898, 1904).

—— Western Mysticism (London, 1922, 1926).

Butler, H. E., The Autobiography of Giraldus Cambrensis (London, 1937).

Calendar of Documents preserved in France, ed. J. H. Round, I, 908–1205 (London, 1899).

Cambridge History of English Literature, vol. I (1907).

Cambridge Medieval History, vols. III (1922) and V (1929).

Chambers, R. W., The Continuity of English Prose from Alfred to More and his School, in Harpsfield's *Life of More*, ed. E. V. Hitchcock (EETS, 1932), xlv–clxxiv; reprinted separately, Oxford, 1933.

Chapman, Dom John, St Benedict and the Sixth Century (London, 1929).

Cheney, C. R., Episcopal Visitation (Manchester, 1931).

—— Papal Legate (John of Ferentino) and English Monasteries in 1206, The, in *EHR*, XLVI (1931), 443–52.

Chew, H. M., Ecclesiastical Tenants-in-chief and Knight-service, The English (Oxford, 1932).

—— Scutage, in *History*, XIV (Oct. 1929), 236 *seqq.*

Christie, A. G. S., English Embroidery (Oxford, 1938).

Clapham, A. W., English Romanesque Architecture before the Conquest (Oxford, 1930).

—— English Romanesque Architecture after the Conquest (Oxford, 1934).

Clark, J. W., The Care of Books (Cambridge, 1901).

Clay, R. M., The Hermits and Anchorites of England (London, 1914).

Cluny, L'Abbaye exempte de, et le Saint-Siège, *v.s.* Letonnelier, G.

—— Millénaire de (2 vols. Mâcon, 1910).

—— Recueil des Chartes de, ed. A. Bernard and A. Bruel (6 vols. 1876–1903).

—— Also *v.s.* Duckett, Evans, Guilloreau and de Valous.

Coulton, G. G., Five Centuries of Religion (Cambridge, vol. 1, 1923; vol. 2, 1927).

—— Monastic Schools in the Middle Ages, reprinted in *Medieval Studies*, no. 10 (London, 1913) from the *Contemporary Review* (June 1913).

Crawford, S. J., Anglo-Saxon influence on Western Christianity, 600–800 (Oxford, 1933).

—— Byrhtferth and the Anonymous Life of Oswald, in *Speculum Religionis: Essays presented to C. G. Montefiore* (Oxford, 1929), 99–111.

Darby, H. C., Historical Geography of England (Cambridge, 1936).

Darlington, R. R., Aethelwig, abbot of Evesham, in *EHR*, XLVIII (1933), 1–22, 177–98.

—— Ecclesiastical Reform in the Late Old English Period, in *EHR*, LI (1936), 385–428.

—— *Vita Wulfstani*, *v.s.* Malmesbury, William of.

Davis, H. W. C., Anarchy of Stephen's Reign, The, in *EHR*, XVIII (1903), 630–41.

—— Battle Abbey, The Chronicle of, in *EHR*, XXIX (1914), 426–34.

—— Liberties of Bury St Edmund's, The, in *EHR*, XXIV (1909), 417–31.

—— *Regesta Regum Anglo-Normannorum* (Oxford, 1913).

Deanesly, M., The *Familia* at Christchurch, Canterbury, 597–832, in *Essays presented to T. F. Tout* (Manchester, 1925), 1–14.

de Ghellinck, Père J., Le Mouvement théologique du xiie siècle (Paris, 1914).

de la Tour, I., Les paroisses rurales du ive au xie siècles (Paris, 1900).

Delatte, Dom P., Commentaire sur la Règle de S. Benoît (Paris, 1913).

Delisle, L., Documents relative to the abbey of Furness, extracted from the archives of Savigny, in *Journal of the Archaeological Association*, VI (1851), 419–24.

—— Ordéric Vital, Notice sur, being introd. to vol. 5 of the edition of Soc. de l'Histoire de France, *q.v. supra.*

—— Rouleaux des Morts (ed. Soc. de l'Histoire de France, Paris, 1866).

Dictionary of National Biography, ed. L. Stephen and S. Lee (London, 1885–).

Dictionnaire d'Archéologie chrétienne et de Liturgie, ed. F. Cabrol and H. Leclercq (Paris, 1903–).

Dictionnaire de Droit Canonique, ed. R. Naz (Paris, 1935–).

Dictionnaire d'Histoire et de Géographie ecclésiastiques, ed. A. Baudrillart, A. de Meyer and E. Van Cauwenbergh (Paris, 1909–).

Dictionnaire de Spiritualité, ed. M. Viller (Paris, 1932–).

Dictionnaire de Théologie Catholique, ed. A. Vacant, E. Mangenot and E. Amann (Paris, 1903–).

Douglas, D. C., Feudal Documents from the Abbey of Bury St Edmunds (Records of the Social and Economic History of England and Wales, VIII, London, 1932).

—— Fragments of an Anglo-Saxon Survey from Bury St Edmunds, in *EHR*, XLIII (1928), 376–83.

—— Odo, Lanfranc and the Domesday survey, in *Essays presented to James Tait* (Manchester, 1933), 47–57.

—— Social Structure of Medieval East Anglia, The (Oxford, 1927).

Duckett, Sir G., Charters and Records of Cluny (Lewes, 1888).

Dudden, F. H., Gregory the Great (2 vols. London, 1905).

Dugdale, W., *v.s.* (*infra*) *Monasticon Anglicanum*.

Emden, A. B., *v.s.* Rashdall, H.

Encyclopaedia Britannica, The, ed. 11 (London, 1910–).

Encyclopedia, The Catholic, ed. 1 (London and New York, 1907–12).

Encyclopedia, The Jewish (London and New York, 1901–25).

Evans, J., Monastic Life at Cluny, 910–1157 (Oxford, 1931).

—— Romanesque Architecture of the Order of Cluny, The (Cambridge, 1938).

Eyton, R. W., The Court, Household and Itinerary of Henry II (London, 1878).

Fabre, P., Étude sur le *Liber Censuum* (Paris, 1892).

Flete, History of Westminster, *v.s.* Robinson, J. A.

Fliche, A., Réforme grégorienne, La, vols. I–III (Louvain, 1924–37).

—— Y a-t-il eu en France et en Angleterre une querelle des investitures? in *RB*, XLVI (1934), 283–95.

Forsey, G. F., Byrhtferth's Preface to Bede's *de Temporibus*, in *Speculum*, III (1928), 505–22.

Fournier, P., *v.s.* Bras, G. Le.

Fox, J. C., Marie de France, in *EHR*, XXV (1910), 303–6.

—— Mary, Abbess of Shaftesbury, in *EHR*, XXVI (1911), 317–26.

Freeman, E. A., The Norman Conquest (Oxford, 1867–79).

Frere, W. H., The Early History of Canons Regular, in *Fasciculus J. W. Clark dicatus* (Cambridge, 1909), 186–216.

—— Also *v.s.* Winchester Troper, The, and *Music, Oxford History of*.

Galbraith, V. H., East Anglian See and the Abbey of Bury St Edmund's, The, in *EHR*, XL (1925), 222–8.

—— Monastic Foundation Charters of the Eleventh and Twelfth Centuries, in the *Cambridge Historical Journal*, IV, 3 (1934), 205–22, 296–8.

Gasquet, Dom A., *v.s.* Bosworth Psalter and *Premonstratensia*.

Gastoué, A., Les Origines du Chant Romain (Paris, 1907).

Glunz, H. H., History of the Vulgate in England (Cambridge, 1933).

Goetting, H., Klösterliche Exemtion in Nord- und Mitteldeutschland vom 8. bis zum 15. Jh., Die, in *Archiv für Urkundenforschung*, 14. i (1935), 105–89.

Gougaud, Dom L., Celtic Christianity (London, 1932).

—— Coutumes claustrales, Anciennes (Ligugé, 1930).

—— Ermites et Reclus (Ligugé, 1928).

—— Essai de bibliographie érémitique, in *RB*, XLV (1933), 281–91.

Graham, R., English Ecclesiastical Studies (London, 1929), containing in particular the following:

    The Relation of Cluny to some other Movements of Monastic Reform, 1–29.

    Life at Cluny in the Eleventh Century, 30–45.

    The Intellectual Influence of English Monasticism between the Tenth and the Twelfth Centuries, 146–87.

    The Monastery of Battle, 188–208.

    The Order of Grandmont and its Houses in England, 209–40.

—— St Gilbert of Sempringham and the Gilbertines (London, 1901).

Guignard, Ph., Monuments primitifs de la règle Cistercienne (Dijon, 1878).

Guilloreau, Dom L., Les Prieurés anglais de l'ordre de Cluny, in *Cluny, Millénaire de*, *q.v.*

Gütschow, E., Innocenz III und England (Munich, 1904).

Haddan, A. W., and Stubbs, W., Councils and Ecclesiastical Documents relating to Great Britain and Ireland, vol. III (Oxford, 1878).

Handschin, J., The Two Winchester Tropers, in *JTS*, XXXVII (1936), 34–49, 156–72.

Hartridge, R. A. R., A History of Vicarages in the Middle Ages (Cambridge, 1930).

Haskins, C. H., Knight-Service in Normandy in the Eleventh Century, in *EHR*, xxii (1907), 636–49.

—— Norman Institutions (Cambridge, Mass., 1918).

—— Renaissance of the Twelfth Century, The (Cambridge, Mass., 1927).

Hermann, H. J., Die Westeuropäischen Handschriften und Inkunabeln (Leipzig, 1926–; in progress).

Hervey, Lord Francis, *Corolla S. Eadmundi* (London, 1907).

Heussi, Carl, Der Ursprung des Mönchtums (Tübingen, 1936).

Hickes, G., *Thesaurus* (3 vols., Oxford, 1703–5).

Hilpisch, Dom S., Geschichte des Benediktinischen Mönchtums (Freiburg-im-Breisgau, 1929).

Hodgkin, R. H., History of the Anglo-Saxons (2 vols. Oxford, 1935).

Hodgkin, T., Political History of England to 1066 (London, 1906).

Hodson, J., The Churches of the Austin Canons, in *Archaeological Journal*, xli, 374, xlii, 96, 215, 331, 440.

Holtzmann, W., Papsturkunden in England (Berlin, i, i–ii, 1932; ii, i–ii, 1936).

Homburger, O., Die Anfänge der Malschule von Winchester im X Jahrhundert (Leipzig, 1912).

Horstman, C., *Nova Legenda Anglie*, vol. ii (Oxford, 1901).

Hückel, G. A., Les poèmes satiriques d'Adalbéron, *v.s.* Adalberon of Laon.

Hüffer, G., Der heilige Bernard von Clairvaux (Münster, 1886).

Hüfner, A., Das Rechtsinstitut der klösterlichen Exemtion in der abendländischen Kirche (Mainz, 1907).

Hunt, R. W., English Learning in the Late Twelfth Century, in *Transactions of the Royal Historical Society*, 4th Series, xix (1936), 19–42.

Jacobs, J., The Jews of Angevin England (London, 1893).

Jaffé, Ph., *Regesta Pontificum Romanorum*, ed. W. Wattenbach, S. Loewenfeld, F. Kaltenbrunner and P. Ewald (2 vols. Leipzig, 1885–8).

James, M. R., Bury, On the Abbey of St Edmund at: I, the Library; II, the Church (Cambridge Archaeological Soc. xxviii, 1895).

—— Bury St Edmunds MSS, in *EHR*, xli (1926), 251–60.

—— Canterbury and Dover, The Ancient Libraries of (Cambridge, 1903).

—— Canterbury Psalter, The (London, 1935).

—— Corpus Christi College, Cambridge, Descriptive Catalogue of the MSS in the Library of (Cambridge, 1909).

—— Jesus College, Cambridge, Descriptive Catalogue of the MSS in the Library of (Cambridge, 1895).

—— Manuscripts, The Homes and Wanderings of (London, 1919).

—— Norwich, The Library of the Cathedral Church, in *Norfolk Archaeol.* xix (1915), 93–116.

—— Peterborough Abbey Library, Lists of MSS formerly in, in *Bibliog. Soc. Trans.* Suppl. 5 (Oxford, 1926).

—— Two Ancient English Scholars, Aldhelm and William of Malmesbury (Glasgow, 1931).

—— Westminster Abbey, The MSS of, with J. A. Robinson (Cambridge, 1908).

—— Also *v.s.* Map, W., and Scholfield, A. F.

Janauschek, P. L., *Originum Cisterciensium . . . Tomus I* (Vienna, 1877).

Keller, W., Die Litterarischen Bestrebungen von Worcester in Angelsächsischer Zeit, in *Quellen und Forschungen*, 1900, 64 (Strassburg, 1900).

—— Zur Litteratur und Sprache von Worcester im x und xi Jahrhundert (Strassburg, 1897).

Kendrick, T. D., Anglo-Saxon Art (London, 1938).

Ker, W. P., English Literature: Medieval (London, 1912).

Knowles, Dom D., Abbatial Elections, in *DR*, XLIX (1931), 252–78.
—— Canterbury, Early Community at Christ Church, The, in *JTS*, XXXIX (1938), 126–31.
—— Canterbury Election of 1205–6, The, in *EHR*, LIII (1938), 211–20.
—— Case of St William of York, The, in *Cambridge Historical Journal*, V, 2 (1936), 162–77, 212–14.
—— Diet of Black Monks, The, in *DR*, LII (1934), 275–90.
—— Growth of Exemption, The, in *DR*, L (1932), 201–31, 396–436.
—— Horarium, The Monastic, in *DR*, LI (1933), 706–25.
—— Norman Plantation, The, in *DR*, XLIX (1931), 441–56.
—— Parish Organization, Monastic, in *DR*, LI (1933), 501–22.
—— Religious Houses of Medieval England, The (London, 1939).
—— Revolt of the Lay Brothers of Sempringham, The, in *EHR*, L (1935), 465–87.
Labbe, P., *Sacrorum Conciliorum nova et amplissima collectio*, ed. J. D. Mansi (Florence and Venice, 1759–98).
Latin Studies, Companion to, ed. Sir J. E. Sandys (ed. 3, Cambridge, 1921).
Leach, A. F., The Schools of Medieval England (London, 1915).
Le Bras, G., *v.s.* Bras, G. Le.
Leclercq, Dom H., L'Ordre bénédictin (Paris, 1930).
Le Couteulx, Dom C., *Annales Ordinis Carthusiensis* (8 vols.: vol. I, Correrie, 1687, continued by modern Carthusians, Montreuil, 1887–91).
Leland, J., The Itinerary of J. Leland, etc., ed. L. T. Smith (5 vols. Oxford, 1906–10).
Lemarignier, J. F., Les privilèges d'exemption et de juridiction ecclésiastique des abbayes normandes (Paris, 1937).
Lesne, Mgr E., Histoire de la propriété ecclésiastique en France (I–IV, Paris, 1910–).
—— Évêché et abbaye, les origines du bénéfice ecclésiastique, in *Revue de l'histoire de l'église de France*, V (1914), 15–50.
Letonnelier, G., L'Abbaye de Cluny et...Exemption, in *Millénaire de Cluny*, *q.v.*
—— L'Abbaye exempte de Cluny et le Saint-Siège (Ligugé, 1923).
Levett, A. E., Courts and Court Rolls of St Albans Abbey, in *Transactions of the Royal Historical Society*, 4th Series, VII (1924).
—— Studies in Manorial History (Oxford, 1938).
Levison, W., Bede the Historian, in *Bede: his Life, ...*, *q.v.*
Liebermann, F., Lanfranc and the Antipope, in *EHR*, XVI (1901), 328–32.
—— Ungedruckte anglo-normannische Geschichtsquellen (Strassburg, 1879).
—— Also *v.s.* Böhmer, H.
Lobel, M. D., The Borough of Bury St Edmunds (Oxford, 1934).
—— The Ecclesiastical Banleuca, in *Oxford Essays in Medieval History presented to H. E. Salter* (Oxford, 1934), 122–40.
Logeman, W. S., text of *Regularis Concordia* in *Anglia*, Neue Folge, I.
Mabillon, Dom J., *Annales Ordinis S. Benedicti* (6 vols. 1703–39).
McCann, Dom Justin, Saint Benedict (London, 1937).
Macdonald, A. J. M., Lanfranc (Oxford, 1926).
—— Eadmer and the Canterbury Privileges, in *JTS*, XXXII (1931), 39–55.
MacLachlan, Dame Laurentia, St Wulstan's Prayer Book, in *JTS*, XXX (1929), 174–7.
McLaughlin, T. P., Le très ancien Droit Monastique de l'Occident (Ligugé, 1935).
Maitland, F. W., Domesday Book and Beyond (Cambridge, 1897).
Mandonnet, P., O.P., Dominique, S., 2nd ed. by H. M. Vicaire (Paris, 1938).
Mansi, J. D., *v.s.* Labbe, P.
Michel, A., Histoire de l'Art (Paris, 1905–29).
Millar, E. G., English Illuminated Manuscripts from the tenth to the thirteenth centuries (Paris and Brussels, 1926).

Mitchell, H. P., Enamels of the School of Godefroid de Claire, Some, in *Burlington Magazine* (five articels), September 1919.

—— English Enamels of the XIIth Century, in *Burlington Magazine*, October 1925.

—— Flotsam of Later Anglo-Saxon Art, I and IV, in *Burlington Magazine*, February and September 1923.

—— Ivory Carvings of the Twelfth Century, Two English, in *Burlington Magazine*, October 1922.

Monasticon Anglicanum, by W. Dugdale; new enlarged edition by J. Caley, H. Ellis and B. Bandinel, 6 vols. in 8 (London, 1817–30).

Montalembert, Cte de, The Monks of the West, an English translation of *Les Moines d'Occident*, with introduction by Dom A. Gasquet (London, 1896).

Morey, Dom A., Bartholomew of Exeter (Cambridge, 1937).

Morin, Dom G., Chant Grégorien, Les véritables Origines du (Maredsous, 1890).

—— L'Idéal Monastique (2nd ed., Paris, 1914).

—— Monastères bénédictins de Rome au Moyen-Age, Les, in *Messager des Fidèles* (later *RB*), IV (1887), 262 *et al.*

—— Ralph de Coggeshall et l'auteur des Distinctiones Monasticae utilisées par dom Pitra, Le cistercien, in *RB*, XLVII (1935), 348–55.

—— Règlements inédits du pape saint Grégoire VII pour les chanoines réguliers, in *RB*, XVIII (1901), 177–83.

Moss, H. St L. B., The Birth of the Middle Ages (Oxford, 1935).

Müller, Dom G., a series of articles on Cistercian origins in *Cistercienser Chronik*, 1898–1916; *v.* list on p. 208. A *résumé* of these and other articles by Dom Müller was issued as a reprint with the title *Vom Cistercienser Orden* (Bregenz, 1927).

Müller, M., Zur Frage nach der Echtheit und Abfassungszeit des "Responsum b. Gregorii ad Augustinum episcopum", in *Theologische Quartalschrift*, CXIII (1932), 94–118.

Music, Grove's Dictionary of, ed. 3, ed. H. C. Colles, vol. v (1928).

Music, Oxford History of, ed. W. H. Hadow; vol. I (1901), The Polyphonic Period, and Introductory volume (1929), ch. vi, by W. H. Frere.

Mynors, R. A. B., Durham Cathedral Manuscripts from the Sixth to the Twelfth Centuries (Oxford, 1939).

Napier, A. S., Sammlung englischer Denkmäler (Berlin, 1880).

Neilson, N., translation of *The Canterbury Domesday Monachorum* in *V.C.H. Kent*, III (1932), 255–69.

Norgate, K., The Angevin Kings (2 vols. London, 1887).

Page, W., Some Remarks on the Churches of the Domesday Survey, in *Archaeologia*, LXVI (1914–15), 61–102.

—— The St Albans School of Painting, in *Archaeologia*, LVIII (1902), part I.

Pantin, W. A., Chapters of the English Black Monks (CS, ser. 3, XLV, i, 1931).

—— General and Provincial Chapters of the English Black Monks, The, in *Transactions of the Royal Historical Soc.*, ser. 4, X (1927), 195–263.

Paré, G., with Prunet, A., and Tremblay, P., La Renaissance du XIIe siècle. Les écoles et l'enseignement (Paris and Ottawa, 1933).

Peerage, The Complete, ed. V. Gibbs (ed. 2, London, 1910–).

Peers, C., Rievaulx Abbey: the Shrine in the Chapter House, in *Archaeological Journal*, LXXXVI (1929), 20 *seqq.*

Pignot, J. H., Histoire de l'Ordre de Cluny (3 vols. Autun and Paris, 1868).

Poole, R. L., Illustrations of the history of mediaeval thought (ed. 1, London, 1884; ed. 2, 1920).

—— Papal Chancery, The (Cambridge, 1915).

—— Robert Pullen and Nicholas Breakspear, in *Essays in Medieval History presented to T. F. Tout* (Manchester, 1925).

Poole, R. L., Also *v.s.* Bale, J., and Johannis Sarisberiensis. . . .

Porée, A. A., Histoire de l'Abbaye du Bec (Évreux, 1901).

Power, E., Medieval English Nunneries (Cambridge, 1922).

Powicke, F. M., Ailred of Rievaulx and his biographer Walter Daniel, in *Bulletin of the John Rylands Library*, VI, nos. 3 and 4 (July 1921 and January 1922); reprinted separately (Manchester, 1922).

—— Dispensator of King David I, The, in *Scottish Historical Review*, XXIII (1925), 34–41.

—— Gerald of Wales, in *Bulletin of the John Rylands Library*, XII (1928), 389–410; reprinted in *The Christian Life in the Middle Ages and other essays* (Oxford, 1935).

—— Maurice of Rievaulx, in *EHR*, XXXVI (1921), 17–25.

—— Stephen Langton (Oxford, 1927).

—— Also *v.s.* Rashdall, H.

Premonstratensia, Collectanea Anglo-, ed. Dom A. Gasquet (CS, ser. 3, VI, 1904).

Pritchard, E. M., The History of St Dogmael's Abbey (London, 1907).

Rand, E. K., The Classics in the Thirteenth Century, in *Speculum*, IV (1929), 249–69.

Rashdall, H., The Universities of Medieval Europe (ed. 2, by F. M. Powicke and A. B. Emden, Oxford, 1936).

Realencyclopädie für protestantische Theologie und Kirche, ed. J. J. Herzog and A. Hauck (1896–1913).

Reyner, Dom C., *Apostolatus Benedictinorum in Anglia* (Douai, 1626).

Robinson, J. Armitage, Byrhtferth and the Life of St Oswald, in *JTS*, XXX (1929), 35–42.

—— Christ Church, Canterbury, The Early Community at, in *JTS*, XXVII (1926), 225–40.

—— Crispin, Gilbert, Abbot of Westminster (Cambridge, 1911).

—— Dunstan, St, The Times of (Oxford, 1923).

—— Lanfranc's Monastic Constitutions, in *JTS*, X (1909), 375–88.

—— Oswald and the Church of Worcester, St, in *British Academy Suppl. Papers*, no. 5 (1919).

—— Somerset Historical Essays (Oxford: for the British Academy, 1921).

—— Wells, The Saxon Bishops of, in *British Academy Suppl. Papers*, no. 4 (1919).

—— Westminster, Flete's History of (Cambridge, 1909).

—— Witham Charterhouse, The Foundation Charter of, in *Proc. of the Somerset Archaeol. Soc.* LXIV (1918), 5 *seqq.*

—— Also *v.s.* Osbert of Clare.

Round, J. H., Burton Abbey Surveys, The, in *EHR*, XX (1905), 275–89.

—— Colchester, The early Charters of St John's Abbey, in *EHR*, XVI (1901), 721–30.

—— Feudal England (London, 1895).

—— Knight-Service into England, The Introduction of, in *EHR*, VI (1891), 417–43, 625–45, and VII (1892), 11–24.

—— Knight-Service of Malmesbury Abbey, The, in *EHR*, XXXII (1917), 249–52.

—— Mandeville, Geoffrey de (London, 1892).

—— Also *v.s.* Calendar of Documents preserved in France.

Rudbourne, *Historia Wintoniensis*, in Wharton, H., *Anglia Sacra, q.v.*

Ryan, J., Irish Monasticism (Dublin, 1931).

Sackur, E., Die Cluniacenser (2 vols. Halle, 1892, 1894).

Salter, H. E., The Cartulary of Eynsham Abbey (Oxford Hist. Soc. XLIX and LI, 1906–7, 1909).

—— Chapters of the Augustinian Canons (Canterbury and York Soc., 1922).

—— Oseney, Cartulary of, vol. VI (Oxford Hist. Soc. CI, 1936).

Sandys, Sir J. E., A History of Classical Scholarship (ed. 3, vol. I, Cambridge, 1921.)

Saunders, O. E., English Art in the Middle Ages (Oxford, 1932).
—— English Illumination (2 vols. Florence and London, 1928).
Savage, E. A., Old English Libraries (London, 1911).
Schmid, Toni, Sveriges Kristnande (Stockholm, 1934).
Schmitz, Dom Philibert, arts. S. Benoît, Bénédictine, (Règle), etc., in *DHG*, *DDC* and *DS*.
Scholfield, A. F., *Elenchus Scriptorum Montacuti Rhodes James* (Cambridge, 1935).
Schreiber, G., Kurie und Kloster im 12 Jahrhundert (2 vols. Stuttgart, 1910).
Schröer, A., Die angelsächsischen Prosabearbeitungen der Benedictinerregel (Cassel, 1885–8).
Schuster, Dom I., *Liber Sacramentorum* (Turin, 1923–); Eng. trans., The Sacramentary, by A. Levelis-Marke (London, 1924–30)
Sisam, K., Aelfric's Catholic Homilies, in *Review of English Studies*, VII (1931), 7–22; VIII (1932), 51–68; IX (1933), 1–12.
Southern, R. W., Ranulf Flambard and early Anglo-Norman Administration, in *Transactions of the Royal Historical Society*, 4th Series, XVI (1933), 95–128.
Spaethen, M., Giraldus Cambrensis und Thomas von Evesham über die von ihnen an der Kurie geführten Prozesse, in *Neues Archiv*, XXXI (1906), 595–649.
Sparke, J., *Historiae Anglicanae Scriptores* (London, 1723).
Steinwerder, A., Rechtsstellung der Kirchen und Klöster nach der Papyri, Die, in *Zeitschrift des Rechtsgeschichte*, Kan. Abt. 1930, 1–50.
Stenton, F. M., Abingdon, The Early History of the Abbey of (Oxford, 1913).
—— *Acta Episcoporum*, in *Cambridge Historical Journal*, III (1929), 1–14.
—— *Benet of Holme, St, and the Norman Conquest*, in *EHR*, XXXVII (1922), 225–35.
—— English Feudalism (Oxford, 1932).
—— Medehamstede and its Colonies, in *Historical Essays in honour of James Tait* (Manchester, 1933).
Stevenson, J., The Church Historians of England, translated (5 vols. London, 1853–8).
Stubbs, W., *Registrum Sacrum Anglicanum* (ed. 2, Oxford, 1897).
—— Select Charters (Oxford, 1874).
—— Seventeen Lectures on Medieval and Modern History (Oxford, 1886).
—— Also *v.s.* Haddan, A. W., and Waltham; the chronicles, etc., edited by Bishop Stubbs appear under their own titles.
Stutz, U., Benefizialwesens von seinen Anfängen bis auf die Zeit Alexanders III, Geschichte des kirchlichen, vol. 1 (Berlin, 1895).
—— Eigenkirche als Element des mittelalterlich-germanischen Kirchenrechts, Die (Berlin, 1895).
—— Eigenkirchentum in England, Das, in *Texte und Forschungen zur Englischen Kulturgeschichte; Festgabe für Felix Liebermann* (Halle, 1921).
—— Gratian und die Eigenkirchen, in *Zeitschrift für Rechtsgeschichte*, XLV (1911), 1 *seqq.*
—— Articles Eigenkirche, Eigenkloster in Hauck's *Realencyclopädie für prot. Theol.*, suppl. vol. XXIII (1913).
Swartwout, R. E., The Monastic Craftsman (Cambridge, 1932).
Sweet, H., An Anglo-Saxon Reader (Oxford, 1908).
Symons, Dom T., Christ Church, Canterbury, The Introduction of Monks at, in *JTS*, XXVII (1926), 409–11.
—— *Regularis Concordia*, The, in *DR*, XL (1922), 15–30.
—— *Regularis Concordia*, The Monastic Observance of the, in *DR*, XLIV (1926), 157–71.
Tait, J., The Medieval English Borough (Manchester, 1936).
Taranger, A., Den Angelsaksiske Kirkes Indflydelse paa den Norske (Christiania, 1890).
Tatlock, J. S. P., Muriel the earliest English poetess, in *Publications of the Mod. Lang. Assoc. of America*, XLVIII (1933), 317–21.

Thomas, P., Le Droit de propriété des laïques sur les églises (Paris, 1906).

Thompson, A. H., *v.s. Bede.*

—— Bolton Priory, History of (Thoresby Society, vol. XXX, Leeds, 1928 for 1924).

—— The Jurisdiction of the Archbishops of York in Gloucestershire, in *Bristol and Gloucestershire Archaeological Society's Transactions*, XLIII, 85–180.

Thompson, M., Carthusian Order in England, The (London, 1930).

—— Fragment of a Witham Chronicle, A, in *Bulletin of the John Rylands Library*, XVI (1932), 482–506.

Thorpe, B., *Analecta Anglo-Saxonica* (London, 1868).

—— *Diplomatarium Anglicum aevi Saxonici* (London, 1865).

—— Also *v.s.* Aelfric and Worcester, Florence of.

Thurston, H., *v.s. Eadmeri Tractatus de conceptione.*

Tillmann, H., Die päpstlichen Legaten in England bis zur Beendigung der Legation Gualas, 1218 (Bonn, 1926).

Tolhurst, J. B. L., Monastic Breviary of Hyde Abbey, Winchester, The (HBS, LXIX, in progress, 1932–).

—— Two Anglo-Saxon Manuscripts of the Winchester School, An Examination of, in *Archaeologia*, LXXXIII (1933), 27 *seqq.*

Tour, Imbart de la, *v.s.* de la Tour.

Trenholme, N. M., The English Monastic Boroughs (*University of Missouri Studies*, Columbia, Miss., 1927).

Tromby, B., Storia critica-cronologica...del ordine Cartusiano (10 vols. Naples, 1773–9).

Turner, C. H., Earliest list of Durham MSS, The, in *JTS*, XIX (1918), 121–32.

—— Early Worcester MSS (Oxford, 1916).

Vacandard, E., Vie de S. Bernard (2 vols.; ed. 1, Paris, 1895–7; references are to ed. 3, 1902).

Valous, G. de, Monachisme clunisien des origines au XVe siècle, Le. Vie intérieure des Monastères et Organisation de l'Ordre (2 vols. Ligugé, 1935).

—— Temporel et la situation financière des établissements de l'Ordre de Cluny du XIIe au XIVe siècle, Le (Ligugé and Paris, 1935).

Van de Vyver, A., Les Œuvres inédites d'Abbon de Fleury, in *RB*, XLVII (1935), 125–69.

Vaughan, H. M., The Benedictine Abbey of St Mary at St Dogmael's, in *Y Cymmrodor*, XXVII (1917), 1–25.

Victoria County Histories, The (London, 1900–in progress: the account of the religious houses, which is usually contained in vol. II, has in most cases appeared).

Vinogradoff, Sir P., English Society in the Eleventh Century (Oxford, 1908).

—— Villainage in England (Oxford, 1892).

Voss, L., Heinrich von Blois (Berlin, 1932).

Wagner, P., Einführung in die Gregorianischen Melodien (ed. 2 and 3, Leipzig, 1910–21); trans. as Introduction to the Gregorian Melodies (Plainsong and Medieval Music Soc., London, 1901).

Wells, Calendar of MSS in the Library of the Dean and Chapter, in *Hist. MSS Commiss. Publications*, vol. LXIII (1906).

Wharton, H., *Anglia Sacra* (2 vols. London, 1691).

Whitelock, D., A Note on the Career of Wulfstan the Homilist, in *EHR*, LII (1937), 460–5.

Whitney, J. P., Peter Damiani, in *Cambridge Historical Journal*, I, 3 (1925), 225–48.

Wilkins, D., *Concilia Magnae Britanniae et Hiberniae* (4 vols. London, 1737).

Williams, L. F. Rushbrook, History of the Abbey of St Albans (London, 1917).

Williams, Watkin, Benedict of Aniane, St, in *DR*, LIV (1936), 357–74.

—— Bernard of Clairvaux, St (Manchester, 1935).

Williams, Watkin, Robert of Molesme, St, in *JTS*, XXXVII (1936), 404–12.

—— William of Dijon, in *DR*, LII (1934), 520–45.

Wilmart, Dom A., Adam Carthusiensis, Magister, in *Mélanges Mandonnet*, II, 145–61 (Paris, 1930–).

—— Aelred abbé de Rievaulx, L'Instigateur du Speculum Charitatis d', in *Revue d'Ascétique et de Mystique*, XIV (1933), 369–94.

—— Ancien monachisme, Une riposte de l', in *RB*, XLVI (1934), 296–344.

—— Anselme, S., La destinataire de la lettre de, sur l'état et les vœux de religion, in *RB*, XXXIX (1926), 331–4.

—— Anselme, Les Homélies attribuées à S., in *Archives d'Histoire doctrinale et littéraire du Moyen-Âge*, II (1927), 5–29.

—— Anselme, S., Une lettre inédite de, à une moniale inconstante, in *RB*, XLI (1928), 319–32.

—— Auteurs spirituels et Textes dévots du Moyen-Âge Latin (Paris, 1932), from which the following are quoted:

L'*Oratio sancti Ambrosii* du Missel Romain, 101–25.

La complainte de Jean de Fécamp sur les fins derniers, 126–37.

Les écrits spirituels des deux Guiges, 217–60.

Les compositions d'Osbert de Clare en l'honneur de sainte Anne, 261–87.

L'Oraison pastorale de l'abbé Aelred, 287–98.

Les méditations d'Étienne de Salley sur les joies de la Vierge Marie, 317–60.

—— Chartreux, La Chronique des Premiers, in *Revue Mabillon*, sér. 2, no. 22 (1926).

—— Cluny, Le couvent et la bibliothèque de, vers le milieu du XIe siècle, in *Revue Mabillon*, XI (1921).

—— Eve et Goscelin, in *RB*, XLVI (1934), 414–38; L (1938), 42–83.

—— Maître Adam chanoine Prémontré devenu chartreux de Witham, in *Analecta Praemonstratensia*, IX (1933), 207–32.

Wilson, H. B., *v.s.* Aethelwold, St, Robert, Archbishop and Robert of Jumièges.

Young, K., The Drama of the Mediaeval Church (2 vols. Oxford, 1933).

INDEX

The following abbreviations are used: A. = Augustinian. abb. = abbess, abbey or abbot. B. = black monk. b. = bishop. C. = Cistercian. c. = canon. Cl. = Cluniac. Gilb. = Gilbertine. m. = monk. Pr. = Premonstratensian. pr. = prior or priory. Sav. = Savigniac.